D1371192

2006

ALTERNATIVE DISPUTE RESOLUTION: THE ADVOCATE'S PERSPECTIVE
Cases and Materials

Third Edition

EDWARD BRUNET

Henry J. Casey Professor of Law
Lewis & Clark Law School

CHARLES B. CRAVER

Freda H. Alverson Professor of Law
George Washingon University Law School

ELLEN E. DEASON

Professor of Law
The Ohio State University
Moritz College of Law

Library of Congress Cataloging-in-Publication Data

Brunet, Edward J.
    Alternative dispute resolution: the advocate's perspective: cases and materials / by Edward Brunet, Charles B. Craver, and Ellen E. Deason. --3rd ed.
        p. cm.
    Includes bibliographical references and index.
    ISBN 0-8205-7025-7 (hard cover)
    1. Dispute resolution (Law)--United States. 2. Mediation--United States. 3. Arbitration and award--United States. I. Craver, Charles B. II. Deason, Ellen E. III. Title.
KF9084.B78 2006
347.73'9--dc22   2006029819

Editorial Offices
744 Broad Street, Newark, NJ 07102 (973) 820-2000
201 Mission St., San Francisco, CA 94105-1831 (415) 908-3200
701 East Water Street, Charlottesville, VA 22902-7587 (434) 972-7600
www.lexis.com

(Pub.3006)

For Katie

—Professor Craver

For June and Michael

—Professor Brunet

For Pat

—Professor Deason

PREFACE

In this Third Edition of this coursebook we have tried to improve and update the basic themes and organization set forth in the earlier editions. Alternative Dispute Resolution has now become institutionalized and has truly come of age. We present the materials with this point in mind. While length and depth of coverage continue to be a challenge, particularly with the popularity of ADR mechanisms, we have tried to keep the materials of similar length to the earlier editions of this book. We continue to stress that most teachers of this course will want to spend time outside the coursebook in order to have their students both negotiate and mediate. We have included a substantial number of simulated mediation and negotiation exercises in the Teacher's Manual.

This casebook is designed for use in a one-semester course that focuses upon the group of alternative dispute resolution processes. Such survey ADR courses are increasingly popular in the law school curriculum and demonstrate that alternative dispute resolution has gained broad acceptance in the American system of resolving disputes.

Four things continue to make this set of materials unique. First, it is our firm belief that the ADR methods cannot be understood without a thorough and initial grounding in negotiation theory and practice. In that spirit, this book contains the most complete treatment of negotiation possible. Only by careful focus on negotiation can the student really comprehend the nuances of mediation and the panoply of court annexed settlement alternatives. Indeed, the reader will find that a theme of this book is that none of the alternatives to litigation can be fully understood without initial rigorous study (including students engaged in simulations) of negotiation. Negotiation is the foundation of alternative dispute resolution. Second, the book stresses the role of the advocate negotiating a settlement, whether the specific alternative is mediation, a court annexed summary jury trial or agency annexed regulatory negotiation. While the book also covers the roles of the neutral, it emphasizes the important task of the attorney and, in particular, the continuing role of negotiation in each of the modes of ADR. Mediation is a form of negotiation in which the advocate should use negotiation skills. Arbitrations often settle before a hearing because of negotiation. Third, the book attempts to present a balanced treatment of ADR and litigation. Most of the prior books in this area are one-sided; they describe ADR techniques with an evangelical fervor and eschew any of the significant criticisms raising questions about various ADR methods. This book integrates the benefits and costs of ADR in an attempt to present a balanced, real-world view of disputing mechanisms. It is only by understanding the potential drawbacks of the various alternatives that the attorney is able to select the optimal mode of disputing. All forms of dispute resolution, including litigation and the modes of ADR described in this text, have costs as well as benefits. Fourth, the book is comprehensive. It offers detailed treatment of negotiation, mediation, arbitration, and government sponsored ADR. Indeed, the book's subparts are detailed enough that the text could be used in a two or three hour law school ADR course in which the teacher chooses to focus on only two or three of the alternatives (for example, a two hour course on negotiation and mediation or a mediation course in which the teacher desired coverage of negotiation prior to treating mediation).

The book's organization follows from the above paragraph. We start with negotiation for two reasons. One, negotiation is and is likely to remain the principle ADR technique. Negotiation is simple, inexpensive and entirely in the hands of the disputants and, for that reason, ought to be the starting mode of dispute resolution. We are confident that readers will find our approach to negotiation both thorough and straightforward. Our thinking is that, while some may be born with innate negotiation skills, virtually anyone can be trained to negotiate competently. Moreover, an initial understanding of negotiation will help the student understand our second subject, assisted negotiation or mediation. Understanding of mediation without prior grounding in negotiation is impossible. Similarly, coverage of court annexed ADR really amounts to learning a variety of settlement techniques, each of which relies upon negotiation. For all these reasons, negotiation probably should come first and be treated rigorously in a survey ADR course.

Each of us views this book as an accompaniment to a set of practice simulations or problems to be done by students. We deem student simulations an essential part of the ADR course. We have placed numerous problems for use in negotiation and mediation simulations in our Teachers Manual. Potential users of this book should consult the Teachers Manual for perusal of these problems. We have tried to draft a wide variety of problems to give the book's users choices as to different types of disputes. We believe strongly that students learn negotiation and mediation by participating in these processes and endorse the idea that a survey course should also involve skills training. Teachers may want to use some of the many videotapes on the individual ADR methods during various points of this course. Individual tapes are recommended in the Teachers Manual. The practical and theoretical reading contained in the negotiation and mediation portions of this book have limited utility if used without integration of real-world simulations and problems. Interjection of problems into the text is needed for any ADR course to reach its potential. We have found that coverage of the text comes alive if fully integrated into post-mortem discussion of simulations.

The organization of the ADR course typically follows this book with negotiation first, followed by mediation and then covering the rest of the alternatives. In contrast, one of us has experimented with starting the ADR course with arbitration. Teachers should give this option some thought. Students find that the unit on arbitration resembles litigation, and, for that reason, is easily digestible at the start of the course. The arbitration sequence of this book involves numerous fascinating cases and the deceptive but critical Federal Arbitration Act. The "familiar" and traditionally demanding feel of the arbitration portion of the course makes it easy to start with at the beginning of a semester. Yet, if arbitration is covered in the second half of a semester, it can be a "reality jolt" for law students who have enjoyed the skills training aspects of negotiation and mediation, usually taught at the start of the ADR course. Teachers who follow the usual path of doing arbitration near the end of a course will need to give thought to helping the students make the transition "back to law school." Tough cases and hard questions are the order of the day for a well-covered arbitration phase of an ADR course. In our experience, law students enjoy greatly participating in the simulations in the negotiation and mediation phases of this course. Because the negotiation and mediation phases of this course involve only minimal doctrine, some students go into a form of withdrawal when they then turn to arbitration, an area in which problems and simulations have little value. Following arbitration, the teacher can adopt the more traditional order of covering negotiation, mediation and other alternatives. Of course, the price of this option is to lose the value of beginning with the least intrusive, most private process, negotiation, and to turn to other varieties of disputing, each of which involves increasingly formal procedures.

We use the typical conventions when editing longer cases and articles excerpts. Where material is omitted within a sentence we have used an ellipse (. . .). We have inserted three asterisks (* * *) to denote longer deletions. While we have retained several case and article citations to provide the students additional authority that may be helpful to electronic use, we do not indicate our many deletions of case authority.

A comprehensive selective ADR Bibliography can be found at the end of the book. This updated Bibliography combines the Negotiation and Mediation citations, which were listed separately in the previous editions. We have used the social science form of citing to books and articles in this Bibliography in the Negotiation (Part One) and Mediation (Part Two) sections of the book. We used the social science citation form in these parts of the book because much of the authority is social science in nature, and we wanted to avoid breaking up the flow of the text with lengthy legal citations. In contrast, we use the standard legal citation system (showing author, title and precise citation) in the parts of the book that are more "legal," arbitration (Part Three) and Government Sponsored ADR (Part Four). There is less text material in these sections and the "legal" citation system meshes well with these more "legal" parts of the book.

ACKNOWLEDGMENTS

We each owe debts of gratitude to those who helped to bring this book to publication. We have benefitted greatly from the writings of scholars cited in the bibliography at the end of the book and thank them for their ideas which have undoubtedly influenced us. We acknowledge the valuable help of student research assistants, James Reidy (Lewis & Clark), Maja Haium (Lewis & Clark), and Becky Hsaio (Emory). We thank our faculty assistants who helped on this project, Lisa Frenz (Lewis & Clark) and Jenny Pursell (Moritz). Finally, we thank those whose financial support aided our research, the Carr Ferguson Summer Research Fund (Lewis & Clark) and the Henry J. Casey Chair in Law (Lewis & Clark).

The authors gratefully acknowledge other authors, publishers, and copyright holders who kindly granted permission to reprint excerpts of their materials. We expressly wish to acknowledge and thank the following firms and individuals for the use of their copyrighted material:

JAI Press, Inc., for Bryant G. Garth, *Privatization and the New Market for Disputes,* 12 Studies in Law, Politics and Society 367 (1992).

The Ohio State Journal on Dispute Resolution, for Judith Resnik, *Alternative Dispute Resolution and Adjudication,* 10 Ohio St. J. on Disp. Res. 211 (1995).

University of Chicago Law Review, for Jethro Lieberman & James F. Henry, *Lessons from the Alternative Dispute Resolution Movement,* 53 U. Chi. L. Rev. 424 (1986).

Yale Law Journal, for Owen Fiss, *Against Settlement,* 93 Yale L.J. 1073 (1984); Trina Grillo, *The Mediation Alternative: Process Dangers for Women,* 100 Yale L.J. 1545 (1991).

Harvard Law Review, for Harry Edwards, *Alternative Dispute Resolution: Panacea or Anathema,* 99 Harv. L. Rev. 668 (1986).

University of Southern California Law Review, for Lon L. Fuller, *Mediation — Its Forms and Functions,* 44 S. Cal. L. Rev. 305 (1971).

The Ohio State Journal on Dispute Resolution, for Jean R. Sternlight, *Lawyers' Representation of Clients in Mediation: Using Economics and Psychology to Structure Advocacy in a Nonadversarial Setting*, 14 Ohio St. J. on Disp. Resol. 269 (1999).

John Wiley & Sons, Inc., for Leonard L. Riskin, *Mediator Orientations, Strategies and Techniques*, 12 Alternatives to High Cost Litig. 111 (1994); Robert A. Baruch Bush & Joseph P. Folger, *The Promise of Mediation* (1994); Tom Arnold, *20 Common Errors in Mediation Advocacy*, 13 Alternatives to High Cost Litig. 69 (1995); Bruce Meyerson, *Lawyers Who Mediate*

Are Not Practicing Law, 14 Alternatives to the High Cost of Litigation 74 (1996).

Gary Friedman, for Gary Friedman & Jack Himmelstein, *Resolving Conflict Together: The Understanding-Based Model of Mediation*, 4 J. Amer. Arb. 225 (2005).

Vermont Law Review & Lawrence Susskind, for Lawrence Susskind, *Environmental Mediation and the Accountability Problem*, 6 Vt. L. Rev. 1 (1981).

Vermont Law Review & Joseph B. Stulberg, for Joseph B. Stulberg, *The Theory and Practice of Mediation: A Reply to Professor Susskind*, 6 Vt. L. Rev. 86 (1981).

The Journal of Dispute Resolution, University of Missouri-Columbia, Center for the Study of Dispute Resolution & Isabelle R. Gunning, for Isabelle R. Gunning, *Diversity Issues in Mediation: Controlling Negative Cultural Myths*, 1995 J. Disp. Resol. 55; Wayne D. Brazil, *Continuing the Conversation about the Current Status and the Future of ADR: A View from the Courts*, 2000 J. Disp. Resol. 11.

Lawrence M. Watson, Jr., for Lawrence M. Watson, Jr., *Effective Legal Representation in Mediation*, in Alternative Dispute Resolution in Florida (1995).

Marquette Law Review, for Ellen E. Deason, *The Quest for Uniformity in Mediation Confidentiality*, 85 Marquette L. Rev. 79, 80-84 (2001).

Michael L. Moffitt, for Michael L. Moffitt, *The Wrong Model, Again: Why the Devil Is Not in the Details of the New Model Standards of Conduct for Mediators*, Dispute Resol. Mag., Spring 2006, at 31.

Joseph B. Stulberg, for Joseph B. Stulberg, *The Model Standards of Conduct: A Reply to Professor Moffitt*, Disp. Resol. Mag., Spring 2006, at 35.

Sarah Rudolph Cole, for Sarah Rudolph Cole, *Mediator Certification Has the Time Come?* Disp. Resol. Mag., Spring 2005, at 7.

The American Bar Association & H. Jay Folberg, for H. Jay Folberg, *Divorce Mediation: A Workable Alternative* (in H. Davidson et al., Alternative Means of Family Dispute Resolution (Howard Davidson et al. eds., (1982)).

American Bar Association, for Edward Brunet & Walter E. Stern, *Drafting the Effective ADR Clause for Natural Resources and Energy Contracts,* 10 Nat. R. & Env. 7 (No. 1, 1996).

Laurie Woods & Sargent Shriver National Center on Poverty Law, for Laurie Woods, *Mediation: A Backlash to Women's Progress on Family Law Issues,* 19 Clearinghouse Rev. 485 (1985).

Emory Law Journal, for Jennifer Gerarda Brown, *The Use of Mediation to Resolve Criminal Cases: A Procedural Critique*, 43 Emory L.J. 1247 (1994).

Louise Phipps Senft & Cynthia A. Savage, for Louise Phipps Senft & Cynthia A. Savage, *ADR in the Courts: Progress, Problems, and Possibilities*, 108 Penn St. L. Rev. 327 (2003).

Florida State University Law Review, for James J. Alfini, *Trashing, Bashing, and Hashing it Out: Is this the End of "Good Mediation"?* 19 Fla. St. U. L. Rev. 47 (1991).

Deborah R. Hensler, for Deborah R. Hensler, *Our Courts, Ourselves: How the Alternative Dispute Resolution Movement Is Re-shaping Our Legal System*, 108 Penn St. L. Rev. 165 (2003).

Harvard Negotiation Law Review, for Nancy A. Welsh, *The Thinning Vision of Self-Determination in Court-Connected Mediation: The Inevitable Price of Institutionalization?* 6 Harv. Negot. L. Rev. 1 (2001).

Willamette Law Review, for Roselle L. Wissler, *The Effects of Mandatory Mediation: Empirical Research on the Experience of Small Claims and Common Pleas Courts*, 33 Willamette L. Rev. 565 (1997).

South Texas Law Review, for Kimberlee K. Kovach, *Good Faith in Mediation — Requested, Recommended, or Required? A New Ethic*, 38 S. Tex. L. Rev. 575 (1997).

John Lande, for John Lande, *Using Dispute System Design Methods to Promote Good-Faith Participation In Court-connected Mediation Programs*, 50 U.C.L.A. L. Rev. 69 (2002).

American Judicature Society & Thomas Lambros & David I. Levine, for Thomas Lambros, *The Summary Jury Trial — An Alternative Method of Resolving Disputes*, 69 Judicature 286 (1986); David I. Levine, *Northern District of California Adopts Early Neutral Evaluation to Expedite Dispute Resolution*, 32 Judicature 235 (1989).

University of Pennsylvania Law Review, for Lisa Bernstein, *Understanding the Limits of Court Connected ADR: A Critique of Federal Court-Annexed Arbitration Programs*, 141 U. Pa. L. Rev. 2169 (1993).

Duke Law Journal, for Anne S. Kim, *Rent-a-Judges and the Cost of Selling Justice*, 44 Duke L.J. 166 (1994).

Georgetown Law Journal, for Philip J. Harter, *Negotiating Regulations: A Cure for Malaise*, 71 Geo. L.J. 66 (1982).

Public Utilities Fortnightly, for Donald I. Marshall, *ADR: Not ABCs of Litigation*, Pub. Util. Fort., Jan. 15, 1993; David C. Bergman, *ADR: Resolution or Complication*, 131 Pub. Util. Fort., Jan. 15, 1993; David S. Cohen, *Mediation: Sanity in the Regulatory Process*, 131 Pub. Util. Fort., Jan. 15, 1993.

SUMMARY TABLE OF CONTENTS

TABLE OF CONTENTS

Page

PART THREE: ARBITRATION

Page

Chapter 1

AN INTRODUCTION TO ALTERNATIVE DISPUTE RESOLUTION

A. THE PANOPLY OF ADR METHODS

This is a book about the increasingly growing number of alternatives to the conventional trial process. Because both legal education and the present dispute resolution system focus heavily on ordinary trial and pre-trial procedures, it is imperative to look closely at other popular means available to process disputes.

A virtual panoply of procedures is presently available to disputants. These materials will closely examine these alternative procedures. We will cover each of the alternatives to litigation thoroughly in the later chapters to this book, but here sketch introductory working definitions.

Traditional Private Alternatives to Trial: These forms of ADR occur pursuant to private contractual interactions. They may occur before the filing of a complaint.

- *Negotiation*: The process of disputants using bargaining techniques to resolve a dispute. Various theories of negotiation exist, ranging from a combative, win-at-all costs style to a more analytical problem-solving approach. These materials will begin by presenting theories of negotiation. They provide an opportunity for students themselves to actually take part in negotiations. A thorough understanding of negotiation is crucial to understanding ADR because almost every type of alternative to trial is based upon a foundation of negotiation. While face-to-face negotiation between disputants is a separate ADR method, it is possible to negotiate within each of the other ADR methods.

- *Mediation*: Mediation adds a third party, the mediator, to the basic negotiation model. The mediator's task is to facilitate the negotiation. Mediation is assisted negotiation. The mediator is not an adjudicator; she does not "decide," but instead helps the parties reach consensus by listening, suggesting and brokering compromise. These materials provide students with the basics on how to mediate as well as how to negotiate when working with a mediator. They also present students with opportunities to act as mediators and as negotiators who use mediation.

- *Arbitration*: The disputing parties go before their chosen private judge, the arbitrator, who is a neutral, unbiased expert on the subject matter of the dispute. After an informal presentation of proof, the arbitrator decides the case in an adjudicatory fashion. The decision need not be legally based and often is a compromise heavily influenced by the facts presented. The decision is binding absent a showing of bias or severe unfairness.

- *Mini-Trial*: A mini-trial involves a private presentation of evidence to a neutral expert who is hired to preside over an abbreviated non-binding "trial" and, if necessary, rule or aid the parties in their settlement discussions. One type of mini-trial is held before the CEOs of disputant companies. In theory, the CEOs will learn by observing the evidence of their opponent and by receiving neutral feedback from the presiding expert. The goal of the mini-trial is settlement; the means is a trial that informs and provides a predictive function.

Court-Annexed Alternatives: These alternatives to trial occur after a case is filed in court and, in many jurisdictions, are mandatory. The alternatives here described are now fully institutionalized and routine.

- *Court-Annexed Mediation*: A court may order mediation, either at the trial or the appellate level. Most programs use volunteer mediators who hold one session without a fee or at a reduced fee. Some newer programs use professional mediators who charge an ordinary fee. Court-annexed mediation is burgeoning in cases involving divorce and family law, and it is being used in all types of cases.

- *Early Neutral Evaluation*: Numerous courts administer early neutral evaluation programs. These programs assign a third-party "neutral," usually a trial attorney, to cases. The neutral studies the case, meets with the parties and makes a pre-trial prediction on the likely outcome that would result from a full trial. The neutral communicates this opinion to counsel in the hope of increasing the quality and quantity of information regarding the dispute. This alternative is predicated on the belief that the parties and their attorneys need the reality check of a third party to more objectively evaluate the strengths and weaknesses of their case and to spur settlement discussions. Disputants need information and early neutral evaluation is a means to provide such information.

- *Judicial Mediation*: Judges sometimes act as mediators in an effort to settle cases. The techniques judges use to mediate usually resemble those of so-called "muscle" mediation. While some judges mediate cases to which they are assigned, other judges try to assign the task of mediation to different judges. The process of judicial mediation, like some other court annexed alternatives, derives from the Rule 16 Pre-trial Conference and has increased with the transition to the judge as "case-manager" rather than mere "case-adjudicator."

- *Summary Jury Trial*: The theory of summary jury trial is to provide the parties with a non-binding sneak preview of a jury verdict in order to promote settlement. Parties are provided a brief time (often three hours for an entire case) to present evidence before a real jury. The evidence is generally submitted in the form of attorney summations. The jury renders a verdict that is non-binding but which, in theory, informs the parties of the probable outcome of the case at a full-blown plenary trial. In order to assure that the jury takes this process seriously, some judges do not fully inform the jury of the non-binding feature of the procedure.

- *Court-Annexed Arbitration*: Mandatory court-annexed arbitration (CAA) exists in many jurisdictions. CAA may apply to all civil cases or to all civil cases under a certain monetary amount (*e.g.*, all civil cases under $100,000 in controversy). The arbitrator hears the evidence and rules based upon the proof. The ruling is non-binding; the parties may obtain a trial *de novo* (or "appeal") by opting for a later conventional trial. In some CAA programs, the party who appeals and does not improve the arbitrated result is penalized by payment of their opponent's attorneys' fees, a percentage of attorneys' fees, or the arbitrator's fee. The CAA arbitrators are usually attorneys who volunteer to sit as arbitrators for reduced rates. Penalties are designed to reduce the number of civil trials.

- *Rent-a-Judge (Private Judging)*: Several states have legislation that permits the parties to hire their own judge who renders a decision. The adjudicator is normally a retired judge. This technique permits the parties to jump the lengthy queue of cases awaiting trial and receive a binding decision from a figure clothed in legitimacy and expertise. In California this system has burgeoned with some private judges charging $500 per hour. Critics lament that private judging creates an expensive, two-track system of justice where the wealthy receive prompt and efficient dispute processing while the less well-off must spend long periods waiting for trial before less popular judges who are not able to enter the more competitive private judging market. Proponents point to happy users.

Administrative Agency-Annexed Alternatives: The volume of agency dispute resolution is huge. These alternatives are used by administrative agencies to resolve disputes pending before them.

- *Regulatory Negotiation*: "Reg-neg," as it is called, involves the joint drafting of an agency regulation by the interested parties. Participants typically include the regulated group or industry, public interest representatives, and agency staff. While it may be possible to negotiate the terms of a regulation without assistance, it is typical to enlist the aid of neutrals in a reg-neg either to mediate or to "convene" the negotiation. Reg-neg developed because of the delay and expense associated with the typical notice and comment rulemaking process.

- *Agency-Annexed Mediation*: Some agencies now are willing to use mediation to resolve disputes before them or in which they are active parties. Agency interest in mediation is high because of the retention of "party control" and the ability to foster early settlements.

- *Agency-Annexed Arbitration*: Some administrative agencies have begun experimenting with arbitration of disputes in which they may be a party. Agency arbitration is controversial because agencies usually find it undesirable to cede decisionmaking control to outside arbitrators. A 1996 change to federal law no longer permits agencies to drop out of arbitration proceedings and revoke earlier agreements to arbitrate.

- *Agency Convening*: The agency supplies a neutral to initiate the dispute resolution process. The neutral "convenes" or starts the procedure of resolving the dispute by consulting with the disputants and exploring their dispute resolution desires. The convener may fade from the scene if the parties choose to negotiate, or may become a mediator or even an arbitrator. Alternatively, the convener may help the parties in their selection of a mediator or arbitrator.

B. COMMON CHARACTERISTICS OF ADR METHODS

Even a brief review of the panoply of ADR methods demonstrates that it would be a mistake to think that Alternative Dispute Resolution methods constitute a monolithic unit. ADR is a generic term that includes widely differing procedures. Each ADR method is individually unique.

Nonetheless, numerous ADR methods share common, overlapping characteristics. For example, ADR methods such as negotiation, mediation and arbitration occur silently and privately. Disputants who strongly desire a lack of publicity are attracted to these methods. Similarly, both negotiation and mediation keep the disputants themselves in control of the controversy. No third party such as a judge, arbitrator, or jury is involved in "deciding" the dispute. Party control is advanced through these devices. Expense is another consideration that is highly relevant. Adjudicatory mechanisms such as trial or arbitration involve more out-of-pocket expenditures than do negotiation and mediation. Arbitration, while informal compared to trial, can still be an expensive option. International arbitrations can be especially expensive. Law or application of legal principles is also a relevant factor. In mediation or negotiation the parties control the result, which can be completely inconsistent with prevailing substantive legal rules. In contrast, a party who prefers that legal rules be applied to the dispute is better off in a conventional trial where courts adhere to existing legal norms. *See* Laura Nader, *Disputing Without the Force of Law*, 88 YALE L.J. 998 (1979).

It is useful to place the ADR mechanisms on a continuum with respect to one another and with respect to litigation. The following graph achieves this result.

CHARACTERISTICS OF DISPUTE RESOLUTION METHODS

Informality	Formality
Less Expensive	Expensive
Fact-Based (No Legal Norms)	Legal Norms
Party Control	Less Party Control
Privacy	Publicity

		Court	Early Neutral		Summary		Court	
Negotiation	Mediation	Annexed Mediation	Evaluation	Mini- Trial	Jury Trial	Arbitration	Annexed Arbitration	Trial

In the above graph, as the mechanisms mentioned move toward the right, certain characteristics increase: formality, expense, application of legal rules, loss of party control, and publicity. In contrast, those mechanisms on the left share the characteristics of informality, lack of expense, fact-based outcomes, party control, and privacy. As the mechanisms approach the right, the relevance of substantive legal norms becomes greater. For example, the neutral in an early neutral evaluation makes a prediction regarding the probable outcome at trial. Summary jury trials and court-annexed arbitrations also rely upon law to offer predicted outcomes. In general, predictability increases as the mechanisms approach the right end of the dispute resolution spectrum.

C.　THE UBIQUITOUS NATURE OF NEGOTIATION

Negotiation skills provide the foundation for successful ADR procedures. Parties use the negotiation process when they try to agree upon the use of ADR techniques to resolve current or future disputes. When disagreements arise, the disputants frequently negotiate about whether they should attempt to resolve their controversy through negotiation, mediation, or arbitration. Disputants who decide to employ mediation assistance are required to negotiate within the mediation process. They negotiate directly with the mediator, through the mediator with opposing parties, and even directly with adversaries with mediator participation. The neutral intervenors are similarly required to use their negotiation skills to convince the disputing parties to prefer the certainty and stability of settlement to the uncertainty and cost of litigation. As a result, observers who only focus on the negotiating discussions between the adversaries themselves ignore the crucial fact that interactions between mediators and disputants really constitute direct negotiations.

Disputants and their attorneys who participate in various court-annexed ADR alternatives routinely employ negotiation skills. For example, parties involved in a summary jury trial often obtain information regarding case strengths and weaknesses that influence subsequent settlement discussions. Similarly, the information supplied by a neutral in an early neutral evaluation

procedure or a mini-trial may ultimately be used by the adversaries to negotiate a resolution of their dispute. Negotiations often play a role in court-annexed
arbitration. Following receipt of an advisory or even binding arbitral award,
the parties frequently negotiate a final resolution of their controversy.

Even when ADR techniques fail to produce final settlement agreements,
negotiation procedures may be used to facilitate required adjudication procedures. The disputants may stipulate the issues to be resolved, the applicable
legal doctrines, and uncontroverted factual matters. They may negotiate
streamlined discovery procedures and an expedited trial process. They may
thus use their negotiation skills to make the necessary adjudication process
more efficient and less financially and emotionally draining for the disputing
parties.

D. ADR, PRIVATE ORDERING AND THE ROLE OF COURTS: SHOULD ADR BE PRIVATE OR PUBLIC?

It is important to place ADR within the overall legal order. Legal philosophy
holds that individual efforts to engage in "private ordering" are likely to work
more successfully than government regulation. *See generally* HENRY M. HART,
JR. & ALBERT M. SACKS, THE LEGAL PROCESS (William N. Eskridge, Jr. &
Philip P. Frickey eds., 1994). This line of reasoning lauds the efforts of private
parties to create their own legal rules or norms and supports laws that
facilitate private ordering. Examples of such laws include the Uniform
Commercial Code, wills and trusts laws, contract doctrine, and property
transactions rules. In each of these areas, private parties structure transactions largely through their own creative efforts. These transactions are
characterized by party intent, efficiency, and a lack of governmental oversight
or intrusion. The parties create their own, private legal order. To the extent
that laws apply in private ordering, they exist to aid private parties and to
facilitate party efforts to custom-craft their own norms.

Private alternatives to trial, such as agreements to arbitrate or mediate,
share many characteristics of private ordering. A contract to mediate or
arbitrate represents a private effort of the individual signatories to create
their own, custom-crafted dispute resolution mechanism. Just as citizens have
a freedom to contract, they possess the freedom to select their own private
manner to resolve disputes. Freedom to contract contemplates freedom to
select a mode of dispute resolution. Providers of arbitration or mediation
services, whether they be not-for-profit organizations such as the American
Arbitration Association or for-profit companies or individuals, represent
nothing more than the assignees of parties who assign their disputes to such
entities for peaceful resolution. Disputants who agree to arbitrate or mediate
manifest their own individual autonomy in selecting a particular form of
disputing.

This is not to suggest that the State has no role in supplying dispute resolution services. Governments have traditionally supplied courts to provide a
peaceful means to resolve disputes. But courts provide a second function in
addition to peacefully terminating disputes. Common-law courts also make
law by carefully interpreting statutes and constitutions. These court-made

laws help to guide and order society. In this way litigation should be seen as a public good. Edward Brunet, *Measuring the Costs of Civil Justice*, 83 MICH. L. REV. 916 (1985). Private disputes are unlikely to produce expository written decisions that society needs as an ordering device. Disputants who select a private ADR method are unlikely to want to pay for a written opinion, and normally want a prompt, private decision that affects only them and has little or no applicability to third parties.[1] ADR providers are likely to follow the demands of their clients, the disputants. Any ADR provider who voluntarily bucks this trend will soon be out of business. Left to the free market, there would be little demand for the written judicial opinion.

Of course, our legal system does not need a written opinion in every case to permit the common law to grow and thrive. Indeed, most decisions of the United States Circuit Courts of Appeals do not result in written, published opinions. Many District Court opinions are similarly not published. People should remember this reality when they consider the public good derived from private ADR procedures.

In some sense private providers of ADR should be perceived as competitors to the entrenched traditional court systems. Each supplies a similar product — dispute termination — and the private ADR providers constantly differentiate their "products" by stressing their speed, privacy, and cost advantages. This state of competition between courts and the private market alternatives[2] has caused courts to change their output. Courts have reacted to the successes of alternatives by innovating and introducing mediation and arbitration into the litigation process. Court-annexed ADR represents a competitive reaction by courts to citizen demand. Litigants can now receive alternatives during conventional cases. Much of this book will focus on mandatory alternatives to trial that are now required when parties prosecute ordinary lawsuits.

The required or mandatory nature of most court-annexed alternatives does not come without controversy. Court-annexed mediation is sometimes made mandatory in the belief that the procedure is valuable in all cases and therefore needs broad application. However, critics respond negatively to mandatory mediation and inquire whether disputants can really be forced to bargain in good faith to a resolution of their dispute. They view the very idea of mandatory mediation as a contradiction in terms and point to the loss of individual autonomy and party control that initially made private mediation successful. To these critics, mandatory mediation is a contradiction in terms.

Judges, presently faced with increasing criminal docket loads (including time-consuming sentencing guideline procedures), have looked to court-annexed ADR as a means to ration their scarce time. Civil trials are increasingly a rarity. In 2004 there were only 5,500 civil trials in federal courts, compared to 14,300 in 1984. The following excerpt suggests that there are many factors that have combined to increased court and private use of ADR.

---

[1] It is true that in some types of arbitration — namely, labor and maritime arbitration — arbitrators write opinions. We will explore these exceptions to the rule in Chapter 8, *infra*.

[2] For recommendation of a "Multi-door Courthouse" that would supply a range of alternatives, see generally Frank Sander, *Varieties of Dispute Processing*, 70 F.R.D. 111, 130-32 (1976).

BRYANT G. GARTH, PRIVATIZATION AND THE NEW MARKET FOR DISPUTES, 12 Studies in Law, Politics, and Society 367, 369–70 (1992) *

The most obvious privatizing reforms in federal and state courts are the various artifices designed to promote settlements. In this category we can count: (1) increased judicial activism to compel parties to reach a settlement; (2) court-annexed arbitration; (3) early neutral evaluation; (4) mini-trials and summary jury trials; (5) economic incentives to compel settlement; and (6) malpractice mediation. These devices are marketed in part as ways to encourage more settlements out of court, based on the agreements of private litigants, but they also have developed an explicit mandate with respect to timing. One aim of these mechanisms is to promote relatively *quick* settlements so that the costs of discovery are limited. This emphasis on new devices and practices . . . confirms the fact that "an adjudicatory model is no longer the sole center of . . . court practice." Courts are now dispensing a variety of disputing products promoted as means to manage their caseloads, and one theme is the encouragement of settlements at the early stages of litigation.

The private market outside the regular courts presents a remarkable array of new and invigorated disputing products. Private judging, arbitration, and mediation have become big business and the objects of considerable attention. The California system of private judging has attracted the most attention and soul-searching, because it provides a clear competitor — or perhaps adjunct — to the regular judges of general courts. California's statutory support of reference to "referees" or a "temporary judge" procedure allows filed cases to go to private judges. It has been reported that 20,000 of the 650,000 cases filed in 1989 went through the private judge system. And while we can refer to the system as outside of the courts, it has been tied into the public system through the use of retired judges and public facilities, and the availability of appeal in the regular courts.

Private judging has helped build the business of the commercial providers, such as the Judicial Arbitration and Mediation Services (JAMS), based in Santa Monica, California, which employs some 160 retired judges to handle about 800 cases a month. Its revenues went from $1 million five years ago to $24 million in the most recent fiscal year. EnDispute reportedly generated $2 million from its offices in Cambridge, Chicago, and Washington, D.C. Judicate, a Philadelphia-based firm with 625 retired judges and powerful ambitions, reportedly grossed $1.4 million in 1989. The United States Arbitration and Mediation (USAM), a franchised service that handled some 4,000 cases in 1988, also should be mentioned. Other apparently important examples outside the courts include the L.A. County Bar Association Mediation for Community and Family and, of course, there are now numerous community mediation centers of one sort or another. More traditional arbitration services, such as those provided by the American Arbitration Association, are also growing in popularity. The domestic private market outside the courts has led to considerable praise and condemnation.

---

* Reprinted from Vol. 12 Studies in Law, Politics and Society, Copyright 1992, pages 369-70, with permission from Elsevier Science.

On the international scene, it should be noted, there has also been a dramatic increase in the number and marketing of centers for international arbitration. The traditional sites of London, Paris, New York, Stockholm, and Geneva, have picked up their activity, and new centers have sprung up in such places as Cairo, Hong Kong, Nigeria, San Francisco, and Vancouver. There are now reportedly at least 30 organizations that administer international arbitrations, such that "international arbitration has become a field of intense competition." Moreover, "the prospect of a unified European market . . . and moves toward market economies in Eastern Europe have led a growing number of countries to put arbitration clauses in international contracts." Private justice in the global setting is becoming increasingly important. The private market has been transformed in the world of commercial transactions.

JUDITH RESNIK, MANY DOORS? CLOSING DOORS? ALTERNATIVE DISPUTE RESOLUTION AND ADJUDICATION, 10 Ohio St. J. on Disp. Res. 211, 212–18 (1995) *

The assumption of many proponents, that ADR will increase the options available to litigants within the publicly financed system, may not be borne out. As the state makes alternative dispute resolution its own, both ADR and adjudication are being reconceptualized. As we proceed into the next century, the commitment to twentieth century style adjudication is waning. In this interaction, we may soon find ourselves with a narrower, not a richer, range of forms of dispute resolution.

As is familiar, neither adjudication nor alternative dispute resolution are inventions of this century, nor are they static concepts. Further, as Professor Ian MacNeil has recently explained, state-based adjudication is the "Johnny-come-lately" to the dispute resolution process. MacNeil has provided a history of the law of arbitration in the United States; his work is helpful to my enterprise. He takes as his task to correct the understanding of the law in the United States about "private" agreements between parties to arbitrate disputes.[4] The description commonly offered is that "the law" has long taken a dim view of the enforcement of such contracts and of arbitration in general. MacNeil brings a different perspective to what he terms this historical picture of "unrelieved judicial or legislative hostility to arbitration."

MacNeil argues that the standard story is wrong; that during the nineteenth century, state legislatures and the common law looked favorably on agreements to arbitrate. He uses, as illustration, legislation such as an Illinois statute of 1873, which permitted parties to refer pending cases to arbitration and to have the help of the court in setting up the arbitration process. With MacNeil's work and other research, contemporary critics of courts can invoke comments from nineteenth century lawyers and judges who, like today's lawyers and judges, complained about adjudication as slow and costly and

---

* Reprinted by permission of the author.

[4] MacNeil describes one of his purposes as correcting the historical record and demonstrating that judicial "hostility" to the enforcement of arbitration is not as longstanding as some have claimed. IAN R. MACNEIL, AMERICAN ARBITRATION LAW: REFORMATION, NATIONALIZATION, INTERNATIONALIZATION, at 17–21 (1992).

argued for arbitration (as well as "mediation and conciliation") as alternative means of resolving disputes.

MacNeil's questions (What came first? Alternative dispute resolution or dispute resolution by the state? What was the state's attitude toward private agreements to arbitrate?) provide a point of departure for my discussion about late twentieth century attitudes and assumptions. Professor MacNeil posits the existence of two systems during both the nineteenth and the twentieth centuries: on the one hand, adjudication as the dispute resolution system of the state, and on the other hand, "private" dispute resolution systems. MacNeil then traces the changing tone of the state's attitudes toward the relationship of the two systems — first encouragement (in the nineteenth century) with some reservations; then hostility and unenforceability of agreements to arbitrate (in the first half of the twentieth century); and most recently, an embrace of such agreements and the federalization of arbitration law in the United States.

My description of more recent history (primarily the last four decades) provides another framing. MacNeil's major assumption — two distinct systems in conversation with each other, with ADR existing apart from the state — is decreasingly reflective of contemporary trends. During the last few decades, ADR has become an integral part of the state's mechanisms for responding to disputes. From one perspective, the two systems are no longer discrete conversants but have begun to be "integrated," "melded," or "collapsed" into each other. From another vantage point, the state's system is increasingly in disarray, and the "private" system is becoming the one of choice, when litigants have the resources and ability to "opt out."[11]

*   *   *

So I turn back less than two decades, to 1976 and the Pound Conference, a meeting of some 250 judges, lawyers, court administrators, law professors, and non-lawyers at which Professor Frank Sander called for a "multi-doored" courthouse. Reviewing his published comments is useful, for what was written not yet twenty years ago seems like it was aimed at a group of people removed from us by many more than two decades.

Professor Sander took as his burden the need to explain the "significant characteristics of various alternative dispute resolution mechanisms." He assumed his readership's familiarity with adjudication; his task was to educate his readers on what else there was and then to persuade his readers of the desirability and utility of those "alternative dispute resolution forms." His purpose was to suggest "promising avenues to explore."

---

[11] See Bryant G. Garth, *Privatization and the New Market for Disputes: A Framework for Analysis and a Preliminary Assessment*, 12B STUD. IN LAW, POL., & SOC'Y 367, 374 (Susan S. Silbey & Austin Sarat eds., 1992) ("Courts will compete for desirable business, and some of the reforms within public courts that have been described as privatization can be seen as part of the competition for an attractive dispute resolution process."); Lauren K. Robel, *Private Justice and the Federal Bench*, 68 IND. L.J. 891, 892 (1993) ("The courts face a burgeoning industry in alternative dispute resolution . . . that threatens to siphon off many civil cases, including those of litigants wealthy enough to afford it.").

Professor Sander's key move was to focus the discussion not on substantive areas (i.e., should tax cases go to a specialized court?) but rather on process. He urged that across a wide variety of disputes, the process should be elaborated, and a mediation, conciliation, or alternative phase be incorporated into it. Professor Sander pointed to some experiments with these processes, labeled "alternative dispute resolution," as evidence of the plausibility of his proposals.

Pause to consider the metaphor that has come to encapsulate his ideas: a "multi-doored courthouse." The image has a good deal of appeal, stemming in part from its implicit reliance on the phrase "access to justice" to posit a structure with several doors of entry. In his reprinted speech, Frank Sander actually described a "lobby" in which a litigant could be "channeled through a screening clerk" to one of six doors, comprising "a diverse panoply of dispute resolution processes." Specifically, one might be sent to "mediation, arbitration, fact finding, malpractice screening panel, superior court," or an ombudsperson.

While "flexible," this model also assumed something presumably stable: the courthouse was a known, readily conjured-up entity. In fact, one of the doors in the Sander lobby was to something called the "superior court." Moreover, one of Professor Sander's goals was to "reserve the courts for those activities for which they are best suited and to avoid swamping and paralyzing them with cases that do not require their unique abilities." Whatever the number of doors, the call was for access to and preservation of the courthouse.

It is fair to say that, within a very short time period (less than two decades), Frank Sander's call has been heard.

* * *

NOTES

1. *Judicial Demand for ADR.* One of the themes of the excerpt from Dean Garth's article is that some of the demand for court-annexed mechanisms comes from judges. Many judges want to offer alternatives to trial in order to encourage settlement. Garth describes this as part of the judicial effort to manage caseloads and seek earlier and quicker settlements. To some extent this represents the idea of judge as case manager and has been described as part of the "case-management movement." *See, e.g.,* Judith Resnik, *Managerial Judges*, 96 HARV. L. REV. 374 (1982); Owen M. Fiss, *The Bureaucratization of the Judiciary*, 92 YALE L.J. 1442 (1983). How should we react to the fact that some of the demand for ADR comes from the "supply side" in the form of judicially mandated procedures? Is such demand the equivalent of private market demand? Isn't judicial demand for ADR less significant than client demand?

2. *Law Entry Barriers.* To date, entry into the business of supplying ADR services is relatively easy. The lawyer who wants to arbitrate merely begins to market herself as an arbitrator. Some provider organizations exist to help clients carefully sort out the large number of potential providers. While entry into the mediation business has been traditionally open, some states have begun to license mediation and to require minimum qualifications for all mediators. The proliferation of new mediation programs has created, in turn, a demand for formal mediator training.

3. *Private-Public Partnering.* Although it is possible to explain the present ADR marketplace as one in which private entities compete with one another and with publicly subsidized courts, substantial cooperation exists between the bench and private providers of ADR. In some jurisdictions judges look to private mediators to supply court-mandated mediation. California legislation permits use of a jury and appeals in privately judged trials. These features require a degree of accommodation between judges and ADR providers. *See, e.g.*, Doris Marie Provine, *Justice A La Carte: On the Privatization of Dispute Resolution*, 12 STUDIES IN LAW, POLITICS, AND SOC'Y 345 (1992).

4. Can the provision of "justice" be a purely private activity? Is there necessarily something "public" about the resolution of disputes? For the view that " 'justice' is an inherently public activity," *see* Geoffrey C. Hazard, Jr. & Paul D. Scott, *The Public Nature of Private Adjudication*, 6 YALE L. & POL'Y. REV. 42, 43 (1988). Hazard and Scott make numerous law and economics arguments to support their position. They argue that courts are public goods and suggest that a free rider problem exists because each "potential user would prefer that someone else pay to keep the system ready for use." *Id.* They contend that the high transaction costs associated with improving the justice system have, together with the free rider problem, prevented meaningful court reform. Hazard and Scott view court-annexed use of private ADR procedures as "streamlined instruments of public justice." *Id.* at 52. In their view, private alternatives borrow procedural and substantive law from the courts and, in so doing, display their true public nature. *Id.* at 54–60. *Accord*, Stephen Ware, *Privatizing Law Through Arbitration*, 83 Minn. L. Rev. 703 (government facilitates privatized law used in arbitration). Public judges operate in open courthouses, hold a degree of public accountability, and write opinions that are freely available to criticize. *See* Judith Resnik, *Failing Faith: Adjudicatory Procedure in Decline*, 53 U. CHI. L. REV. 494, 545-46 (1986) ("[J]udges must work within the reach of the public; some of the processes occur literally in view of the public, and most decisions made in private are reported to the public").

5. Professor Resnik's *Many Doors?* article refers to the concept of the multi-door courthouse. For the classic article that sets forth a call for a full service "Dispute Resolution Center" (sometimes referred to as a "multi-door courthouse"), see Frank E.A. Sander, *Varieties of Dispute Processing*, 70 F.R.D. 111 (1976). Under the vision set forth by Sander, once a case is filed it could be processed in various ways. It could be mediated, litigated or arbitrated, for example.

6. *Freedom in a Democratic State and the Privatization of Justice.* In a democratic society that values personal autonomy, the freedom to select a mode of dispute resolution should normally be respected. "Party autonomy should be the fundamental value that shapes arbitration" and other types of disputing. *See* EDWARD BRUNET, ET AL., AMERICAN ARBITRATION LAW: A CRITICAL APPRAISAL 4 (Cambridge 2005). Professor Richard Reuben stresses the need to connect dispute resolution autonomy with the respect for personal autonomy and freedom inherent in a democracy. *See* Richard C. Reuben, *Democracy and Dispute Resolution: The Problem of Arbitration*, 67 LAW & CONTEMP. PROB. 279, 303 (2004).

E.   THE ADR BANDWAGON AND ITS CRITICS

Much of this book will trace the success and increasing popularity of various alternatives to traditional trial. There is little doubt that ADR is a significant force and that society values alternative modes of dispute processing. The remarkable assimilation of ADR techniques into the courts evidences the present acceptance and respectability of ADR. Note, however, the contrasting views of the following article excerpts. Some ADR critics do not view ADR as a global solution. The following article excerpt represents the optimistic views of those on the ADR Bandwagon.

JETHRO LIEBERMAN & JAMES F. HENRY, LESSONS FROM THE ALTERNATIVE DISPUTE RESOLUTION MOVEMENT, 53 U. Chi. L. Rev. 424, 429–31 (1986) *

A working hypothesis of ADR is that the results of ADR are often superior to court judgments — and even more clearly superior to conventional settlements. Although the hypothesis is difficult to test, it is supported by several considerations.

First, adjudication is characterized by a "winner-take-all" outcome. This cannot be wholly true, for jury damage awards can work compromises, and the parties can shape consent decrees through bargaining. Nevertheless, in many cases, the fundamental issue of liability can be resolved only by holding for the plaintiff or the defendant. ADR, by contrast, is not bound by the zero-sum game of adjudication. While we have defined ADR as concerned with "legal disputes," participants in ADR are free to go beyond the legal definition of the scope of their dispute. They can search for creative solutions to the problem that *gave rise* to the dispute, and those solutions may be far more novel than any remedy a court has the power to provide. In a mini-trial held by Texaco and Borden, for example, the parties resolved a breach-of-contract claim and antitrust counterclaim totaling in the hundreds of millions of dollars by renegotiating the entire contract for the supply of natural gas. Both parties claimed a net gain. No court could have ordered the parties to renegotiate; at best a judge or jury could only have compromised on the amount of damages it awarded the "winner."

Second, in classes of cases involving complex institutions, negotiations conducted by executives are likely to yield results superior to those conducted by the lawyers. The executives are far more familiar than their lawyers with the nuances of their business and can respond more quickly and creatively to proposals raised by their counterparts. We do not mean to diminish the role or responsibilities of lawyers in the negotiations; their legal knowledge will often be crucial to successful settlements and good lawyer-negotiators may be more skillful than poorly trained executive-negotiators. Nevertheless, the business executive may be presumed to be less distracted by the shadow the law casts over the dispute; the executive will look at the complete business picture, unconstrained by the narrow parameters imposed by legal doctrine.

Third, direct involvement by the client can obviate or minimize difficulties arising from the self-interest of lawyers. This point may be particularly instructive for judges. By requiring clients to attend pretrial conferences, judges can be sure that the clients know and approve of the propositions their lawyers will assert in court on their behalf.

Fourth, ADR techniques and processes can be far more systematic than the horsetrading of conventional settlement negotiations. Settlement negotiations are often perceived as consisting of sharp tactics and bluff. "Unprincipled" negotiations occur in large part because the parties lack a means of communicating with each other. ADR processes permit realistic assessments of whether offers and counteroffers are in good faith.

Fifth, properly designed ADR processes make it more likely that settlement decisions will be based on the merits of disputes. As Richard A. Posner has suggested, various factors may contribute to more or less settlement. Delay in the judicial system tends to "increase[] the likelihood of settlement by reducing the stakes in the case," in part because delay diminishes the present value of the ultimate award. Other factors include rules governing prejudgment interest and the availability of pretrial discovery. This analysis could lead the courts to advocate policies that would increase delay (or other costs of litigation) in order to prompt settlement. The resulting settlements would not necessarily be just, however, because they would not have taken account of power disparities. The party with the more meritorious claim might not prevail because he is too poor to amass the requisite evidence through the discovery process. Society may have the *power* to foster higher settlement rates by manipulating the factors that induce people to stay out of court, but many proponents of ADR would not view such policies as consonant with the ADR philosophy. A dispute should not merely be settled; it should be settled justly.

*   *   *

Finally, a sixth reason to think that ADR leads to "better" outcomes is that the use of private neutrals permits the parties to submit their dispute to one with greater expertise in their particular subject than does the luck of the draw in the courtroom. Many complex disputes involve data and concepts that lie beyond the knowledge of generalist judges (and of all juries). The ADR neutral can be selected for a particular expertise, thus saving the parties the cost of educating the fact-finder (and the risk of failing to do so). Moreover, if the parties have personally participated in selecting the neutral, they may be psychologically disposed to accept his statement of the case, whether it is a binding decision (as in arbitration) or an advisory opinion (as in a mini-trial).

Owen Fiss, Against Settlement, 93 Yale L.J. 1073, 1075–90 (1984) *

I do not believe that settlement as a generic practice is preferable to judgment or should be institutionalized on a wholesale and indiscriminate basis. It should be treated instead as a highly problematic technique for streamlining dockets. Settlement is for me the civil analogue of plea bargaining: Consent is often coerced; the bargain may be struck by someone without authority; the absence of a trial and judgment renders subsequent judicial involvement troublesome; and although dockets are trimmed, justice may not be done. Like plea bargaining, settlement is a capitulation to the conditions of mass society and should be neither encouraged nor praised.

* * *

The dispute-resolution story makes settlement appear as a perfect substitute for judgment . . . by trivializing the remedial dimensions of a lawsuit, and also by reducing the social function of the lawsuit to one of resolving private disputes: In that story, settlement appears to achieve exactly the same purpose as judgment — peace between the parties — but at considerably less expense to society. The two quarreling neighbors turn to a court in order to resolve their dispute, and society makes courts available because it wants to aid in the achievement of their private ends or to secure the peace.

In my view, however, the purpose of adjudication should be understood in broader terms. Adjudication uses public resources, and employs not strangers chosen by the parties but public officials chosen by a process in which the public participates. These officials, like members of the legislative and executive branches, possess a power that has been defined and conferred by public law, not by private agreement. Their job is not to maximize the ends of private parties, nor simply to secure the peace, but to explicate and give force to the values embodied in authoritative texts such as the Constitution and statutes: to interpret those values and to bring reality into accord with them. This duty is not discharged when the parties settle.

In our political system, courts are reactive institutions. They do not search out interpretive occasions, but instead wait for others to bring matters to their attention. They also rely for the most part on others to investigate and present the law and facts. A settlement will thereby deprive a court of the occasion, and perhaps even the ability, to render an interpretation. A court cannot proceed (or not proceed very far) in the face of a settlement. To be against settlement is not to urge that parties be "forced" to litigate, since that would interfere with their autonomy and distort the adjudicative process; the parties will be inclined to make the court believe that their bargain is justice. To be against settlement is only to suggest that when the parties settle, society gets less than what appears, and for a price it does not know it is paying. Parties might settle while leaving justice undone. The settlement of a school suit might secure the peace, but not racial equality. Although the parties are prepared to live under the terms they bargained for, and although such

* Reprinted by permission of the Yale Law Journal Company and Fred B. Rothman & Company from the Yale Law Journal, Vol. 93, Pages 1075-90.

peaceful coexistence may be a necessary precondition of justice, and itself a state of affairs to be valued, it is not justice itself. To settle for something means to accept less than some ideal.

I recognize that judges often announce settlements not with a sense of frustration or disappointment, as my account of adjudication might suggest, but with a sigh of relief. But this sigh should be seen for precisely what it is: It is not a recognition that a job is done, nor an acknowledgment that a job need not be done because justice has been secured. It is instead based on another sentiment altogether, namely, that another case has been "moved along," which is true whether or not justice has been done or even needs to be done. Or the sigh might be based on the fact that the agony of judgment has been avoided.

There is, of course, sometimes a value to avoidance, not just to the judge, who is thereby relieved of the need to make or enforce a hard decision, but also to society, which sometimes thrives by masking its basic contradictions. But will settlement result in avoidance when it is most appropriate? Other familiar avoidance devices, such as certiorari, at least promise a devotion to public ends, but settlement is controlled by the litigants, and is subject to their private motivations and all the vagaries of the bargaining process. There are also dangers to avoidance, and these may well outweigh any imagined benefits. Partisans of ADR — Chief Justice Burger, or even President Bok * — may begin with a certain satisfaction with the status quo. But when one sees injustices that cry out for correction — as Congress did when it endorsed the concept of the private attorney general and as the Court of another era did when it sought to enhance access to the courts — the value of avoidance diminishes and the agony of judgment becomes a necessity. Someone has to confront the betrayal of our deepest ideals and be prepared to turn the world upside down to bring those ideals to fruition.

* * *

I . . . see adjudication in more public terms: Civil litigation is an institutional arrangement for using state power to bring a recalcitrant reality closer to our chosen ideals. We turn to the courts because we need to, not because of some quirk in our personalities. We train our students in the tougher arts so that they may help secure all that the law promises, not because we want them to become gladiators or because we take a special pleasure in combat.

To conceive of the civil lawsuit in public terms as America does might be unique. I am willing to assume that no other country . . . has a case like *Brown v. Board of Education* in which the judicial power is used to eradicate the caste structure. I am willing to assume that no other country conceives of law and uses law in quite the way we do. But this should be a source of pride rather than shame. What is unique is not the problem, that we live short of our ideals, but that we alone among the nations of the world seem willing to do something about it. Adjudication American-style is not a reflection of our combativeness but rather a tribute to our inventiveness and perhaps even more to our commitment.

---

* [Editors' Note: Derek Bok, the former President of Harvard University, was an early advocate of ADR.]

Harry Edwards, Alternative Dispute Resolution: Panacea or Anathema, 99 Harv. L. Rev. 668, 676–80 (1986) *

[I]f ADR is extended to resolve difficult issues of constitutional or public law — making use of nonlegal values to resolve important social issues or allowing those the law seeks to regulate to delimit public rights and duties — there is real reason for concern. An oft-forgotten virtue of adjudication is that it ensures the proper resolution and application of public values. In our rush to embrace alternatives to litigation, we must be careful not to endanger what law has accomplished or to destroy this important function of formal adjudication.

* * *

[M]any environmental disputes are now settled by negotiation and mediation instead of adjudication. Indeed, as my colleague Judge Wald recently observed, there is little hope that Superfund legislation can solve our nation's toxic waste problem unless the vast bulk of toxic waste disputes are resolved through negotiation, rather than litigation. Yet, as necessary as environmental negotiation may be, it is still troubling. When Congress or a government agency has enacted strict environmental protection standards, negotiations that compromise these strict standards with weaker standards result in the application of values that are simply inconsistent with the rule of law. Furthermore, environmental mediation and negotiation present the danger that environmental standards will be set by private groups without the democratic checks of governmental institutions. Professor Schoenbrod recently has written of an impressive environmental mediation involving the settlement of disputes concerning the Hudson River. According to Schoenbrod, in that case private parties bypassed federal and state agencies, reached an accommodation on environmental issues, and then presented the settlement to governmental regulators. The alternative to approval of the settlement was continued litigation, which was already in its seventeenth year, with no end in sight.

The resulting agreement may have been laudable in bringing an end to protracted litigation. But surely the mere resolution of a dispute is not proof that the public interest has been served. This is not to say that private settlements can never produce results that are consistent with the public interest; rather, it is to say that private settlements are troubling when we have no assurance that the legislative or agency-mandated standards have been followed, and when we have no satisfactory explanation as to why there may have been a variance from the rule of law.

In the Hudson River example, we should be concerned if private negotiators settled the environmental dispute without any meaningful input or participation from government regulators, or if the private parties negotiated a settlement at variance with the environmental standard that had been established by government agencies. If, however, government agencies promulgated the governing environmental standards pursuant to legislatively

---

* Reprinted by permission of the Harvard Law Review Association and William S. Hein Company from The Harvard Law Review, Vol. 99, pages 668, 676-80.

established rulemaking procedures (which, of course, involve public participation), and if the private parties negotiated a settlement in accordance with these agency standards and subject to agency approval, then the ADR process may be seen to have worked well in conjunction with the rule of law. Indeed, the environmental negotiators may have facilitated the implementation of the rule of law by doing what agency regulators had been unable to achieve for seventeen years.

A subtle variation on this problem of private application of public standards is the acceptance by many ADR advocates of the "broken-telephone" theory of dispute resolution that suggests that disputes are simply "failures to communicate" and will therefore yield to "repair service by the expert 'facilitator.'" This broken-telephone theory was implicitly illustrated in a speech by Rosalynn Carter describing the admittedly important work of the Carter Center at Emory University in Atlanta. The Carter Center recently conducted a seminar that brought together people on both sides of the tobacco controversy. According to Rosalynn Carter, "when those people got together, I won't say they hated each other, but they were enemies. But in the end, they were bringing up ideas about how they could work together."

This result is praiseworthy — mutual understanding and good feeling among disputants obviously facilitates intelligent dispute resolution — but there are some disputes that cannot be resolved simply by mutual agreement and good faith. It is a fact of political life that many disputes reflect sharply contrasting views about fundamental public values that can never be eliminated by techniques that encourage disputants to "understand" each other. Indeed, many disputants understand their opponents all too well. Those who view tobacco as an unacceptable health risk, for example, can never fully reconcile their differences with the tobacco industry, and we should not assume otherwise. One essential function of law is to reflect the public resolution of such irreconcilable differences; lawmakers are forced to choose among these differing visions of the public good. A potential danger of ADR is that disputants who seek only understanding and reconciliation may treat as irrelevant the choices made by our lawmakers and may, as a result, ignore public values reflected in rules of law.

We must also be concerned lest ADR becomes a tool for diminishing the judicial development of legal rights for the disadvantaged. Professor Tony Amsterdam has aptly observed that ADR may result in the reduction of possibilities for legal redress of wrongs suffered by the poor and underprivileged, "in the name of increased access to justice and judicial efficiency." Inexpensive, expeditious, and informal adjudication is not always synonymous with *fair* and *just* adjudication. The decisionmakers may not understand the values at stake and parties to disputes do not always possess equal power and resources. Sometimes because of this inequality and sometimes because of deficiencies in informal processes lacking procedural protections, the use of alternative mechanisms will produce nothing more than inexpensive and ill-informed decisions. And these decisions may merely legitimate decisions made by the existing power structure within society. Additionally, by diverting particular types of cases away from adjudication, we may stifle the development of law in certain disfavored areas of law. Imagine, for example, the impoverished nature of civil rights law that would have resulted had all race discrimination cases in the sixties and seventies been mediated rather than adjudicated. The wholesale diversion of cases involving the legal rights of the poor may result in the definition of these rights by the powerful in our society rather than by the application of fundamental societal values reflected in the rule of law.

Family law offers one example of this concern that ADR will lead to "second-class justice." In the last ten years, women have belatedly gained many new rights, including new laws to protect battered women and new mechanisms to ensure the enforcement of child-support awards. There is a real danger, however, that these new rights will become simply a mirage if all "family law" disputes are blindly pushed into mediation. The issues presented extend beyond questions of unequal bargaining power. For example, battered women often need the batterer ordered out of the home or arrested — goals fundamentally inconsistent with mediation.[36]

Some forms of mediation, however, would protect the public values at stake. Professors Mnookin and Kornhauser suggest, for example, that divorce settlements can be mediated successfully despite disparities in bargaining power by requiring court review of settlements that deviate from a predefined norm. Additionally, some disputes that are not otherwise subject to court review also might be well suited for mediation. Many cases, however, may require nothing less than judicial resolution. At the very least we must carefully evaluate the appropriateness of ADR in the resolution of particular disputes.

*   *   *

NOTES

1. *Point-Counterpoint.* The gulf between the upbeat attitude of Lieberman and Henry and the cautionary concerns set forth by Fiss and Edwards is obviously huge. Our purpose in presenting these views here is to initiate your thinking about the future and appropriate place of ADR. This debate will be revisited in much more detail throughout the course. Note the link between Judge Edwards and Professor Fiss. Each perceives positive attributes of litigation — Judge Edwards sees courts as the appropriate arbiters of issues of public significance and Fiss values the interpretations of law offered only by courts. Are these arguments at all relevant to the contention of Lieberman and Henry that ADR is "superior to court judgments"? Lieberman and Henry

---

[36] As Carol Lefcourt of the National Center on Women and Family Law explains:

> The goals of mediation — communication, reasonable discourse, and joint resolution of adverse interests — work against the most immediate relief the battered woman requires. The goals she seeks are protection from violence, compensation, possession of her home without the batterer, and security for her children. Only the judicial system has the power to remove the batterer from the home, to arrest when necessary, and to enforce the terms of any decree if a new assault occurs. The empirical data now show that the therapeutic model for handling battering is ineffective and that firm law enforcement including imprisonment is required to deter wife abuse.

Lefcourt, *Women, Mediation and Family Law*, 18 CLEARINGHOUSE REV. 266, 268 (1984).

are especially critical of winner-take-all outcomes. Yet, aren't there disputes in which the public interest demands a win-lose result?

2. Mediation advocates have aggressively asserted the numerous benefits of mediation. Consider these comments:

> . . . Mediation is based upon the assumptions that (1) there are a variety of solutions to the issues raised all of which are potentially acceptable to the disputants (neither disputant has to lose, both, in fact, can win); (2) each case is different and any resolution must take into account its unique contextual features; (3) these are private issues and are best decided by norms established by the parties involved, fine-tuned to their particular relationship; (4) these cases must include a process for emotional settlement not simply resolution of the "legal" or "ethical" issues; and (5) the parties will be much more likely to comply with the resolution of the case if they determine the outcome. [Diane Hoffman, *Mediating Life and Death Decisions*, 36 ARIZ. L. REV. 821, 825 (1994).]

For similar contentions about mediation, see ROGER FISHER ET AL., GETTING TO YES (2d ed. 1991); Robert Baruch Bush, *Defining Quality in Dispute Resolution: Taxonomies and Anti-Taxonomies of Quality Arguments*, 66 DENV. U. L. REV. 335 (1989). Are the above assumptions realistic and accurate?

3. Criticisms of ADR range from the philosophical to the practical. Trial lawyers, particularly the plaintiff's bar, are troubled by the impact of mandatory court-annexed arbitration systems upon the right to jury trial. These same critics are concerned with boilerplate arbitration clauses that bind consumers who lack knowledge about the arbitral process and generally fail to point out that a signatory to arbitration loses the right to jury trial. Judge Eisele has argued that the strong right to jury protection of the Seventh Amendment is seriously challenged by the use of mandatory court annexed ADR programs. *See* G. Thomas Eisele, *Differing Visions — Differing Values: A Comment on Judge Parker's Reformation Model for Federal District Courts*, 46 SMU L. REV. 1935 (1993).

4. *A Two-Tier System of Dispute Resolution?* At a more philosophical level, critics of the California Rent-a-Judge phenomenon argue that it is wrong to facilitate an innovation — private judging — that permits the rich to opt into a more efficient and potentially higher quality justice system and leave the less well-off in a lengthy queue of cases awaiting trial. This argument rests somewhat on the notion that litigation is a public good that should be supplied by the state. Critics of rent-a-judge point to a situation in which resource-strapped members of the legislative branch may not want to invest in publicly financed courts because of the success of private judging. *See, e.g.*, Anne Kim, *Rent-a-Judges and the Cost of Selling Justice*, 44 DUKE L.J. 166 (1994); Note, *The California Rent-a-Judge Experiment: Constitutional and Policy Considerations of Pay-As-You-Go Courts*, 94 HARV. L. REV. 1592 (1981). They fear that the publicly financed courts will suffer as the market for public judging grows. Moreover, critics are concerned that development of the published common law would also suffer if private judging expands in the future. Private judges generally do not write opinions which the legal system needs to operate effectively. Are these fears justified?

5. *Power Imbalance?* Another set of concerns regarding ADR has focused upon power imbalances between disputants who participate in ADR. Some feel that protections available in court for less powerful disputants are eliminated in mediation or arbitration. *See, e.g.,* Richard Delgado et al., *Fairness and Formality: Minimizing the Risk of Prejudice in Alternative Dispute Resolution,* 1985 WIS. L. REV. 1359 (questioning fairness of ADR techniques in terms of impact upon certain less powerful disputants and advocating that ADR methods should be used where disputants are of relatively comparable status and power). Other critics worry that resolution of disputes in private could increase the risk of unfair discrimination. Diane Hoffman, *Mediating Life and Death Decisions,* 36 ARIZ. L. REV. 821 (1994) (suggesting that mediation of life and death decisions regarding health care be restricted to disputes between parties of relatively equal bargaining power and pointing out that physicians and hospitals have greater power than the ill and their family members); Randy Kandel, *Power Plays: A Sociolinguistic Study of Inequality in Child Custody Mediation and a Hearsay Analog Solution,* 36 ARIZ. L. REV. 879, 882 (1994) (informal process of child custody mediation "creates a risk of power abuse"); Richard Delgado, *ADR and the Dispossessed: Recent Books About the Deformalization Movement,* 13 LAW & SOC. INQUIRY 145, 152-54 (1988). States have attempted legislative solutions to deal with the problem of power imbalances in mediation. California requires child custody mediators to conduct "negotiations in such a way as to equalize power relationships between the parties." CAL. FAM. CODE § 3162(3) (2000). Is this a realistic or enforceable legislative exhortation?

6. *Avoiding Substantive Law by Using ADR.* Some of the concerns raised about ADR focus on the lack of the application of substantive law in the various ADR alternatives. For example, arbitrators need not apply substantive legal principles, mediators do not "decide" disputes, and negotiating parties may choose to ignore legal doctrine. While the various ADR procedures can use legal rules, ADR is, at its core, lawless. ADR advocates rate the lack of mandatory law application positively. They argue that the inapplicability of law frees the parties to reach more creative, party-crafted solutions. *See* Carrie Menkel-Meadow, *Toward Another View of Legal Negotiation: The Structure of Problem Solving,* 31 U.C.L.A. L. REV. 754, 789-93 (1984). Aren't the arguments of Fiss and Edwards inconsistent with this position? Consider these comments:

> Proponents of compromise solutions that ignore positive law give too little weight to the substantive policies that the positive law promotes. Substantive policies are advanced by "winner-take-all" results and are undercut by solutions to disputes that defy norms. When, for example, a dispute involving federal securities law is resolved through ADR, the parties may be able to avoid the impact of the policies underlying the substantive law. Similarly, a polluter anxious to avoid a stiff penalty for alleged pollution would prefer a less severe mediated sanction resulting from compromise negotiation.

> The "public values" supporting substantive legal norms are result directed. "Public values" support norms designed to reach particular solutions. In contrast, the overriding goal of ADR appears to be to

terminate disputes independent of any specific outcome or result. While dispute termination is itself a worthy policy goal, it represents only one of numerous disputing policies and is by no means paramount. [Edward Brunet, *Questioning the Quality of Alternative Dispute Resolution*, 62 TUL. L. REV. 1, 17 (1987).]

Women's rights advocates have argued that mediation of divorce and property division issues can lull women into a system that lacks enforceable legal rights. These critics point out that women divorcing may achieve better outcomes in court where judges may award women their legal share of their partner's pension than in mediation in which substantive legal rights do not directly apply and may be deemphasized. *See* Laurie Woods, *Mediation: A Backlash to Women's Progress on Family Law Issues*, 19 CLEARINGHOUSE REV. 431 (1985). Women's groups have also criticized using mediation to deal with disputes involving battered women. *See, e.g.*, Lisa G. Lerman, *Mediation of Wife Abuse Cases: The Adverse Impact of Informal Dispute Resolution on Women*, 7 HARV. WOMEN'S L.J. 57 (1984); Tina Grillo, *The Mediation Alternative: Process Dangers for Women*, 100 YALE L.J. 1545 (1991). Similarly, civil rights advocates are troubled by the routine use of mediation or arbitration to resolve employment discrimination disputes. Some employers may be repeat violators of their employees' civil rights, and arbitration or mediation of employee civil rights claims offers these firms the ability to resolve their disputes in secret, far from the public eye. The National Employment Lawyers Association, a group of over 2,300 plaintiffs' lawyers, announced plans to boycott ADR providers that continue to hear employment disputes. Margaret A. Jacobs, *Firms With Policies Requiring Arbitration Are Facing Obstacles*, WALL ST. J., Oct. 16, 1995, at B5. Some ADR providers have responded by adapting special procedures for employment disputes. The EEOC argues that widespread use of arbitration of employment civil rights disputes would dilute the impact of anti-discrimination laws. Mediation of school disputes between students and school administrators also holds similar potential for power imbalances. California deals with this problem by mandating that mediated agreements pertaining to school conflicts be "consistent with the law." CAL. EDUC. CODE § 56500.3(f) (1989 & Supp. 1994).

7. *Culture and ADR.* Some of the growing support for ADR is culturally based. For example, mediation has been the traditional mode of dispute resolution in China for centuries. Not surprisingly, Western business joint ventures with Chinese entities usually call for mediation. China's litigation system understandably mandates pre-trial mediation for all disputes, including those filed in court. The American tradition of respect for an open, public litigation system is not shared throughout the world. Consider these comments from house counsel for Siemens, the second largest company in Germany:

> Siemens' commitment to ADR derives from what is essentially a cultural phenomenon. Its parent company . . . is a large German-based multinational corporation th̃t shares the European preference for resolving disputes privately ŕ ̣d in a non-adversarial manner, as well as a healthy contempt for tᷛe costs and vagaries of the U.S. court and jury system. Thus, our corporate experience, that argues so

strongly for the use of ADR, is supported by our shareholders' cultural approach to dispute resolution. [Walter G. Gans & David Stryker, *ADR: The Siemens' Experience*, DISPUTE RESOLUTION J., Apr.-Sept. 1996, at 40, 41.]

These "cultural" attitudes regarding ADR have spread to American businesses. Hundreds of U.S. firms are signatories to the "pledge" sponsored by the Center for Public Resources (CPR) Institute for Dispute Resolution that requires firms "to explore with that other [disputant] party resolution of the dispute through negotiation or ADR techniques before pursuing full-scale litigation." CPR is seeking a cultural shift in American business thinking about ADR.

8. *Concluding Thoughts for Chaper One.* Each of these issues deserves attention and discussion. As ADR has grown in popularity, its architects and advocates have used innovative techniques to improve or adopt more effective means to resolve disputes. Some of the existing criticisms of ADR will undoubtedly generate future adjustment by ADR users and providers. This book will try to address each of these criticisms and will stress the ability to improve and adopt ADR procedures to our disputing culture.

Part ONE

NEGOTIATION

Chapter 2

BASIC FACTORS AFFECTING THE NEGOTIATION PROCESS

A. INTRODUCTION TO NEGOTIATION

Legal practitioners use their negotiating skills more frequently than their other lawyering talents. They negotiate when they don't even realize they are negotiating. They negotiate with their own partners, associates, legal assistants, secretaries, prospective clients, and current clients — not to mention their regular interactions with attorneys representing other parties (Ryan, 2005, at 235, 263–64). Litigators resolve between 85% and 95% of conflicts through negotiated agreements (Birke & Fox, 1999, at 1; Williams, 1996, at 8–9),[1] and transactional experts use the negotiation process to structure their private and public sector business deals. It is thus apparent that negotiation constitutes the primary form of dispute resolution. When direct negotiations do not produce acceptable results, mediators may be used to assist the bargaining participants with their efforts to achieve mutual accords. Even during these assisted dispute resolution procedures, the advocates continue to negotiate — with the assistance of the neutral facilitators who lack the authority to impose final terms.

Many individuals discount the importance of negotiating skill by naively suggesting that bargaining outcomes are principally determined through the application of objective criteria. They think that nebulous legal doctrines and subjective human needs and interests can be quantified. Unfortunately, when inexact legal concepts are combined with subjective personal judgments, the results are anything but objective (Rachlinski, 2003, at 1165). While it is true that relatively objective factors are used by negotiating parties to calculate their respective bottom lines, a psychological battle of wills is likely to determine the final outcome within the settlement range that lies between those bottom lines. Dr. Chester Karrass, in advertisements for his "Effective Negotiating" course, aptly notes that "In business, you don't get what you deserve, you get what you negotiate." The same truism governs bargaining interactions between lawyers. When groups of law students or practicing attorneys negotiate the identical exercises, it is always amazing how diverse their settlements are. It is only then that they truly appreciate the impact of negotiating ability on the final outcomes of bargaining interactions.

Conscientious attorneys spend many hours each week reading advance sheets pertaining to their respective areas of specialization. When they prepare for bargaining encounters, they spend substantial time on the legal, factual, economic, and political issues, but no more than ten to fifteen minutes formulating their negotiating strategies. In fact, when most attorneys begin

---

[1] To avoid the use of distracting footnotes, abbreviated citations appear in parentheses. Complete citations are provided in the Bibliography at the end of the book.

a negotiation, they have only three things in mind that directly relate to bargaining strategy: (1) their bottom line; (2) their ultimate objectives; and (3) their intended opening offer. After they articulate their opening positions, most "wing it" — viewing bargaining interactions as entirely unstructured. Few take the time to study alternative dispute resolution procedures.

We believe that proficient negotiators generally obtain better results than subject experts who are not well-versed in the art of negotiating. This theory is supported by two empirical studies comparing overall student GPAs and student performance on course bargaining exercises, finding no statistically significant correlation between these two factors (Craver, 2000; Craver, 1986). The explanation for these findings concerns the fact that students with high GPAs tend to have good abstract reasoning skills, while proficient negotiators tend to possess the interpersonal skills (i.e., "emotional intelligence") necessary to interact well with other persons (Goleman, 1995). Professional negotiators always learn enough substantive law to be effective bargainers, while the substantive law experts are unlikely to obtain a corresponding knowledge of interpersonal skills and negotiating techniques. It should thus be apparent that attorneys must continue to update both their substantive knowledge and their dispute resolution skills.

Most Americans are not comfortable negotiators. We have not been raised in a society in which most items are negotiable. We do not regularly barter with merchants over fruits, vegetables, breads, meats, clothing, and other necessities. When we visit supermarkets and department stores, we normally pay the listed prices or forego the items in question. In many other societies, however, people constantly bargain with merchants over these goods, and they view asking prices as merely the beginning of the bargaining process. They feel comfortable with this approach and look forward to negotiating opportunities.

United States lawyers must begin to appreciate the professional and personal enjoyment to be derived from negotiation settings. Each bargaining exchange represents *opportunity*, because it provides the interactants with the chance to improve their respective circumstances. If the parties could not improve their present situations, they would not be communicating with each other. Parties should thus welcome each bargaining interaction as a beneficial and challenging endeavor.

Many individuals dislike the negotiation process because of the ritualistic aspects associated with bargaining interactions. They do not like to waste time at the outset of a negotiation with small talk pertaining to sports, politics, weather, mutual acquaintances, and other seemingly irrelevant considerations. They prefer to begin their transactions with a discussion of the issues of immediate interest. They fail to recognize that these preliminary exchanges put anxious participants at ease and establish a beneficial tone for the more salient talks to come. They also fail to realize that impatient negotiators who hurry the process tend to have longer interactions because the stages break down and must be repeated. In addition, the more quickly individuals seek to conclude their interactions, the less efficiently they structure the final terms due to the lack of effective cooperative bargaining. Lawyers need to understand that patient bargainers who allow the process to develop deliberately tend to have more expeditious and efficient interactions.

The second factor that causes many lawyers to feel uncomfortable during bargaining interactions concerns the deliberate deception associated with most legal negotiations. Side A begins the transaction by stating that it cannot pay more than X when it is perfectly willing to pay 2X, while Side B initially states that it must obtain at least 3X when it would be satisfied with 1½X. The participants are pleased that they have begun the process successfully, even though both have begun with overt misrepresentations! As we shall see in Chapter 5, *infra*, dealing with ethical considerations, misstatements regarding one's settlement intentions and/or values are excluded from the scope of Model Rule 4.1 which proscribes deliberate lawyer misrepresentations. Although it is clear that lawyers may never lie about material fact or material law, it is ethically permissible for negotiators to use deceptive tactics with respect to their actual settlement intentions. Negotiating attorneys must thus learn to distinguish between acceptable "puffing"/"embellishment" and impermissible mendacity.

The legal negotiation process is only indirectly affected by traditional legal concepts. Even though the general parameters of particular transactions are loosely defined by the operative factual circumstances and the pertinent legal principles, the process itself is more directly determined by reference to other disciplines. This is due to the fact that negotiations involve interpersonal, rather than abstract, transactions. As a result, psychological, sociological, communicational, and game theories are the primary phenomena that influence the bargaining process. Lawyers who are unfamiliar with these diverse fields frequently ignore the many psychological, sociological, and communicational factors that govern the negotiation process.

Many legal practitioners are inherently suspicious of social science theories that attempt to evaluate and predict human behavior. These seemingly esoteric concepts do not appear to have discernible foundations. This phenomenon is typified by an example that occurred in one of our first-year Criminal Law classes at the University of Michigan. Dr. Andrew Watson, a psychiatrist on the law faculty, was asked by Professor Yale Kamisar to visit our class. During his discussion of various mens rea doctrines, Dr. Watson interjected his view that most criminals are in prison because they consciously or subconsciously want to be there. Professor Kamisar excitedly challenged this assertion: "Come on, Andy. Three people rob a bank. One is overweight and unable to run as fast as his partners, and he is thus apprehended." The students were generally sympathetic to this perspective, and Dr. Watson did not pursue the matter further. Pandemonium would undoubtedly have reigned had Dr. Watson replied that "the perpetrator in question most likely overate intentionally to become obese and develop diminished mobility so that he would be captured and incarcerated." Most students would have questioned such a Freudian suggestion. Nonetheless, our practice experiences, teaching observations, and review of the pertinent psychological literature over the past thirty years have made us realize that such seemingly farfetched theories should not be rejected too hastily. While the various psychological, sociological, and communicational concepts discussed in Parts I and II of this book should not automatically be accepted as universal truths, they should not be summarily dismissed. They should be mentally indexed for future reference in recognition of the fact they may actually influence the negotiation and mediation processes.

It has recently become fashionable for some academics to suggest that all negotiations should be conducted on a "win-win" basis, with the parties seeking a "fair" result midway between their real positions. It should be obvious that certain negotiations must be undertaken on a "win-win" basis if they are to achieve their desired objectives. On-going negotiations between spouses who are dissolving a marriage but will have future interactions regarding their children, discussions between firms endeavoring to establish future business relationships, and others in symbiotic relationships must be designed to produce results that satisfy the basic needs of both participants if they are to be truly successful for either. Both parties must feel they "won" something from their interaction, or their on-going relationship will be jeopardized. Even in these settings, however, attorneys should not ignore the fact that their clients expect them to obtain better terms than they give up if this can be achieved amicably (Shapiro & Jankowski, 2001, at 5; Mnookin, Peppet & Tulumello, 2000, at 9).

In many legal settings, practitioners encounter highly competitive situations that do not involve continuous dealings. In these circumstances, a few "win-lose" negotiators may only believe they have "won" if they think the other party has "lost." No negotiator should enter a negotiation with the intent to simply defeat or harm the opposing party, because no rational benefit would be derived from this approach. All other factors being equal, negotiators should strive to maximize opponent returns if this does not diminish the value obtained for their own clients. This practice increases the likelihood of agreements and the ultimate honoring of those accords. On the other hand, it must be recognized that in most bargaining transactions, the participants do not possess equal power or equal bargaining skill. One party may be more risk-averse than the other, and the overly anxious participant may be willing to accept less generous terms due to the need to achieve an expeditious and definitive resolution. As a result, one side usually obtains more favorable terms than the other side (Karrass, 1970. at 144). In these settings, we believe that advocates have an ethical obligation to seek the most beneficial agreements they can attain without resorting to unconscionable or unethical behavior (Bastress & Harbaugh, 1990, at 345).

We would be reluctant to suggest that advocates reject offers that seem overly generous to their clients based upon their initial assessments of the underlying circumstances. It is quite possible in these situations that their adversaries possess important information they have not discovered. When opponents evaluate client cases more generously than these attorneys anticipated, we believe that these legal representatives are obliged to defer to the assessments of opposing counsel. These lawyers might otherwise place themselves in the awkward position of having to explain to their clients that they could have obtained better terms had they not concluded that it was more important to ensure a greater degree of success for their opponents.

The art of legal negotiating involves skills rarely taught in traditional law school curricula, even though practicing attorneys frequently encounter bargaining situations. While the negotiation process is clearly applicable to lawsuit settlements, contractual undertakings, real estate and corporate trans-actions, dealings with federal, state, and local regulatory agencies, and so forth, it is easy to ignore its application to other important areas of legal practice. Most clients employ legal counsel either to resolve problems or to prevent their occurrence. They may require professional assistance with respect to established relationships or with the creation of new relationships. In these situations, the retained attorneys can usually advance the interests of their respective clients most effectively through the bargaining process. Lawyers must recognize that two professional practitioners who are inti-mately familiar with the basic needs and interests of their respective clients can generally formulate a more efficient resolution of the underlying client difficulties than can external decision-makers who will rarely possess the same degree of knowledge or understanding.

Both litigators and transactional specialists should also recognize that the negotiation process may provide beneficial results even when no final agree-ments are achieved. Litigation discussions that do not result in case settle-ments may be used to narrow and define the issues to be presented for adjudication, and to generate factual and/or legal stipulations that will expedite trial proceedings. Inter-party talks may also be employed during discovery procedures to enable the participants to agree upon the information to be exchanged. This is why litigators who conclude that no overall settlement agreements are possible should not eschew further case discussions. They must simply shift their focus from final resolutions to interim accords that may streamline the litigation process.

Transactional negotiators should similarly realize the future benefits that may be derived from current interactions that fail to generate immediate deals. These discussions may lay the foundation for future negotiations between the instant parties that will ultimately result in mutual accords. Furthermore, even if the present parties are unlikely to have future dealings once the current talks are terminated, the participating attorneys may themselves engage in future negotiations involving other clients. If these advocates can establish beneficial relationships during the present discus-sions, they greatly enhance the likelihood of success when they have future business encounters.

The negotiation process has little to do with traditional legal doctrines, except those of basic contract law. It is instead governed by the same psychological, sociological, and communicational principles that influence other interpersonal relations. As a result, lawyers who rely primarily on narrow legal frameworks to guide their negotiations are likely to ignore the most relevant factors that affect the negotiation process. They may have a thorough understanding of the applicable legal concepts, but overlook the crucial factors that are likely to determine the outcome of their interactions.

The negotiating ability of people is directly affected by their own personal strengths and weaknesses. The pertinent personal factors vary greatly from individual to individual. Some effective negotiators employ a style that is aggressive and/or somewhat abrasive, while others are equally successful using a calm and even deferential approach. One of us briefly worked with a negotiator who was derisive and occasionally sarcastic. He often treated people with contempt. Although he generated a greater number of nonsettlements than his more personable cohorts, many adversaries gave him what he wanted in an effort to conclude their unpleasant interactions with him.

It is discomforting to negotiate for prolonged periods with nasty individuals. Persons confronted by these adversaries should endeavor either to modify their behavior through "attitudinal bargaining," which will be discussed in Chapter 3 as part of the Preliminary Stage, or to control the interaction in a manner that diminishes the effectiveness of these offensive people. Short sessions conducted on the telephone significantly restrict the capacity of abrasive negotiators to gain momentum and to cause anxiety in their opponents. Whenever the targets of these nasty negotiators feel uncomfortable, they can announce that they have another call or another engagement and terminate the current interaction. By scheduling brief encounters, they can exercise a degree of control that increases their self-esteem and confidence. This enables them to enhance their respective bargaining situations.

At the opposite extreme are seemingly inept characters who evoke such sympathy that they are able to induce their adversaries to concede everything necessary to satisfy the needs of these pathetic souls. A typical example of this type of negotiator was artfully created by actor Peter Falk in his Lieutenant Columbo character. He bumbles along during criminal investigations without any apparent direction or competence, until he adroitly extracts confessions from the guilty parties. Highly skilled "belly-up" negotiators, who will be discussed more fully in Chapter 3, *infra*, are able to use these tactics to fleece unsuspecting opponents. The most amazing characteristic of these interactions concerns the ability of "belly-up" negotiators to induce their cleaned-out adversaries to feel wonderful about the results they achieved! Practitioners must learn to recognize "belly-up" tactics and be careful not to modify their own planned behavior in a manner that favors their manipulative opponents.

Part I of this book does not attempt to define a specific negotiating style that is designed to guarantee optimal results for everyone. Given the diverse personalities possessed by lawyers, no perfect negotiating style exists. Part I instead identifies the important considerations and endeavors to assist individual readers to appreciate their own personal attributes. It is hoped that this approach will enable them to obtain a better understanding of the way in which they react to other people in stressful situations, and, conversely, how others react to them. This will enable them to learn to employ their strengths more effectively in future negotiations, while minimizing the impact of their possible weaknesses.

As the various factors are explored, it is important to recognize that we are concerned with the negotiation *process*. It takes time for the bargaining process to evolve. Certain ritualistic behavior should be anticipated, and identifiable stages have to develop before agreements can be achieved. Less proficient negotiators are often frustrated by the seemingly inordinate time it takes for many opponents to move from an initially adversarial mode to a more conciliatory posture. Impatient participants occasionally attempt to accelerate the process by moving directly to the closing stage in an effort to conclude their transactions expeditiously. They are bewildered when the entire process breaks down. They fail to appreciate the fundamental rule that parties who hasten the negotiation process generally take longer to achieve accords than those who patiently allow the process to develop naturally.

People unfamiliar with the process often suggest that they do not understand the need for seemingly irrelevant "small talk" as bargaining interactions commence, and they dislike the need for participants to discuss ancillary legal and factual topics that do not directly relate to the particular issues in controversy. To demonstrate the difficulty encountered when negotiators are confined to communications restricted to the specific items being exchanged, we occasionally have students engage in a short silent negotiation. They are provided with all of the pertinent information regarding a simple personal injury case — including each side's confidential information and objectives — and are instructed to decide how much money the negligent defendant will pay to the injured plaintiff. They must communicate entirely on paper, and they may only write down monetary sums reflecting offers and demands. They usually feel uncomfortable resolving the problem in this limited manner. By the time they have completed the exercise, they begin to realize that negotiation discussions cannot be confined to the exact issues in dispute. The diverse settlements also demonstrate how differently individuals evaluate the identical transactions.

It is also critical to understand that the negotiation process begins to unfold at the time of first contact between the participants. Following a class exercise, students often describe the commencement of their interaction in the following fashion:

> Our opponents suggested that we meet on Wednesday evening at 8:00, and we agreed. They proposed that we get together at their apartment, and we concurred. After we arrived, they generously provided us with wine and cheese. We discussed the basketball game that had occurred the night before. After approximately thirty minutes of "small talk," the negotiations began.

These students are shocked when we point out how they initially conceded the day, time, and location for their bargaining sessions. They then permitted their opponents to create feelings of obligation, through their offer of food and drink, that might subtly influence the negotiation outcome. They thus placed themselves at a potential disadvantage before they realized that the process had already begun. Although it is possible that these factors might not actually influence the final results of particular exchanges, it is important to acknowledge that they could.

B. THE FACTORS AFFECTING NEGOTIATION

Since all bargaining involves personal interaction, an understanding of the general principles governing human behavior is essential. Advocates must initially determine the personal needs of the direct and indirect (*e.g.,* absent clients) participants to the transaction. They should recognize that participant negotiating styles significantly affect the way in which bargainers interact. The particular type of negotiation involved may similarly affect the techniques that are employed. Once the bargaining interaction commences, participants must focus on the most visible aspect of the negotiation process — verbal and nonverbal communication. When individuals from diverse backgrounds interact, they must be cognizant of the possible impact of their cultural differences.

1. PERSONAL NEEDS OF PARTICIPANTS

Negotiators must recognize that the personal needs of the different participants must be minimally satisfied before successful results can be achieved. Many attorneys make the mistake of focusing their attention exclusively upon the stated needs of their own clients and those which have been expressed on behalf of opposing clients. This practice frequently causes bargainers to ignore other highly relevant information. Lawyers must initially endeavor to ascertain the true underlying needs of their own clients, and then seek to determine the less visible needs of opposing clients and opposing counsel (Riskin, 2002, at 613).

Individuals who seek legal advice often disguise their ulterior motivations when conversing with their own attorneys. They express their apparent objectives in terms that are likely to generate appropriate legal action based upon their stereotyped view of what attorneys do. For example, a defamed individual may express a desire for financial recompense. If the underlying motivations are probed, the attorney may discover that this person would actually prefer an expeditious retraction and a public apology to a delayed monetary judgment. This information would undoubtedly make it easier for the lawyer to achieve an acceptable pretrial resolution.

Clients involved in marital dissolutions may similarly conceal their true feelings. Seemingly objective discussions of alimony, child custody and visitation privileges, and property rights may mask a strong urge for emotional retribution. If this hidden agenda can be adroitly exposed and sympathetically handled, this will enhance the likelihood of a mutual accord. Legal representatives must acknowledge the presence of such disguised feelings in opposing clients and try to understand their nature and strength. The more attorneys appreciate the underlying needs of their respective clients, the more likely they are to negotiate mutually beneficial solutions.

Lawyers frequently expend so much energy concentrating upon the underlying needs of their own clients and of opposing clients that they fail to consider sufficiently their own personal needs and those of their legal adversaries. We have seen skilled practitioners decline simulation exercise settlement offers that would have provided them with results far more favorable than nonsettlements, simply because they feared the possibility of appearing weak or foolish. These situations graphically demonstrate the need negotiators have to gratify their own egos and competitive desires. Since client interests are expected to take precedence over the personal drives of their advocates, such results should never occur — yet they undoubtedly happen on a fairly regular basis.

Opposing counsel have their own personal needs that must be satisfied if settlements are to be obtained. These motivational factors may be manipulated in an effort to precipitate favorably disposed states of mind. The apparent desire of opponents for professional respect may be employed to generate greater concessions through disingenuous appeals to their reputation for reasonableness and fair dealing. The drive most people have to alleviate the internal stress associated with unresolved disputes may also be relied upon to move negotiators inexorably toward beneficial agreements.

Other factors may also influence the willingness of opposing attorneys to accept offers. If their law offices are experiencing temporary cash flow difficulties and if they are operating on contingent fee bases, they may be more inclined to settle cases near the first of each month as their major bills become due. Other litigators may succumb to a different kind of pressure. If they are handling an expansive number of cases, they may not be in a position to devote a substantial amount of time to any one dispute. By noticing all pertinent depositions and filing thorough interrogatories and motions to produce, attorneys can frequently cause these opponents to look more favorably upon settlement proposals to alleviate the inordinate time pressure associated with these particular cases. So long as the information being sought is relevant to the pending action and is being sought in preparation for trial, this practice would not contravene ethical standards.

Some lawyers who are being compensated on an hourly basis feel little incentive to resolve matters on an expeditious basis. When negotiating with attorneys who have apparently been retained on an hourly rate, it may occasionally be necessary to permit the process to develop in a sufficiently deliberate fashion to enable them to generate exalted fees. If reasonable offers are made prematurely, these practitioners will strongly encourage their clients to reject those proposals. While one may question the ethics of attorneys who delay settlement opportunities for the purpose of increasing their fees, advocates who ignore this consideration either have to provide these adversaries with unnecessarily enhanced offers or accept the possibility of avoidable nonsettlements.

2. NEGOTIATING STYLES OF PARTICIPANTS

Most negotiators tend to exhibit either a relatively "*cooperative*" or a relatively "*competitive*" style (Craver, 2003; Schneider, 2002; Shell, 1999, at 9–11; Gifford, 1989, at 8–11; Williams, 1983, at 18–39). "Cooperative" advocates usually employ a "problem-solving" approach (Mnookin, Peppet & Tulumello, 2002; Fisher & Ury, 1981), while "competitive" individuals use a more "adversarial" methodology (Camp, 2002; Dawson, 2001; Ringer, 1973). Certain traits may be employed to distinguish between these two diverse styles.

Cooperative/Problem-Solving	*Competitive/Adversarial*
Move Psychologically *Toward* Opponents	Move Psychologically *Against* Opponents
Try to Maximize *Joint* Return	Try to Maximize *Own* Return
Seek Reasonable Results	Seek Extreme Results
Courteous and Sincere	Adversarial and Disingenuous
Begin with Realistic Opening Positions	Begin with Unrealistic Opening Positions
Rely on Objective Standards Rather Than Neutral Standards	Focus on Own Positions Rather Than Neutral Standards

Cooperative/Problem-Solving	*Competitive/Adversarial*
Rarely Use Threats	Frequently Use Threats
Maximize Information Disclosure	Minimize Information Disclosure
Open and Trusting	Closed and Untrusting
Work to Satisfy Underlying Interests of Opponents	Work to Satisfy Underlying Interests of Own Client
Willing to Make Concessions	Attempt to Make Minimal Concessions
Reason with Opponents	Manipulate Opponents

Cooperative/problem-solving negotiators tend to begin their interactions with realistic positions that are designed to create positive bargaining environments. They work to maintain harmonious relationships through courteous and professional discussions. They readily disclose their critical information, and try to explore the underlying interests of the parties in an effort to expand the overall pie to be divided up. This enables them to seek efficient agreements that maximize the joint gains achieved by the parties. They invoke objective norms to lead the participants toward fair, win-win results. They rarely resort to threats or other disruptive tactics designed to intimidate opponents, preferring cooperative techniques intended to generate reciprocal movement.

Competitive/adversarial negotiators begin with more extreme opening positions that are used to intimidate opponents. They hope to achieve one-sided agreements that favor their own side. They frequently employ threats and other disruptive tactics to keep their opponents on the defensive. They withhold their negative information, and use the disclosure of beneficial information to induce adversaries to think they possess superior strength. They try to induce opponents to bid against themselves by making unreciprocated concessions. When competitive/adversarial bargainers think it will advance their situations, many employ insulting or demeaning behavior.

Many attorneys think that competitive/adversarial negotiators who use aggressive and even abrasive tactics are more likely to achieve beneficial results for their clients than cooperative/problem solving negotiators. This notion was contradicted by an empirical study conducted by Professor Gerald Williams of legal practitioners in Denver and Phoenix in the early 1980s. He found that lawyers considered 65 percent of their colleagues to be "cooperative/problem-solvers," 24 percent to be "competitive/adversarial," and 11 percent to be unclassifiable (Williams, 1983, at 19; Williams, 1992, at 2). Lawyers indicated that the results achieved by effective cooperative/problem-solving negotiators were as beneficial as the results obtained by effective competitive/adversarial bargainers (Williams, 1983, at 41). Nonetheless, while responding attorneys in Professor Williams' study indicated that 59 percent of cooperative/problem-solving negotiators were "effective," they found only 25 percent of competitive/adversarial bargainers "effective" (Williams, 1983, at 19). Furthermore, while a mere 3 percent of cooperative/problem-solving negotiators were considered "ineffective," 33 percent of competitive/adversarial bargainers were.

A more recent study by Professor Andrea Kupfer Schneider of attorneys in Chicago and Milwaukee employed Professor Williams' basic methodology (Schneider, 2000, at 24; Schneider, 2002). Although the percentage of effective cooperative/problem-solving negotiators remained relatively constant, the percentage of effective competitive/adversarial bargainers dropped to 9 percent (Schneider, 2002, at 167). In addition, while the percentage of ineffective cooperative/problem-solvers also remained the same, the percentage of ineffective competitive/adversarials rose to 53 percent. It is also interesting to note that Professor Schneider found competitive/adversarial bargainers in the late 1990s to be less pleasant and more uncivil than the competitive/adversarial negotiators described in Professor Williams' earlier study (Schneider, 2002, at 172). This behavioral change may explain why she found fewer competitive/adversarial negotiators considered effective, and more characterized as ineffective.

Competitive/adversarial negotiators are more likely to employ adversarial bargaining strategies designed to intimidate their opponents than cooperative/problem-solvers. In law suit negotiations, they are more inclined to make "zero offers" (i.e., they offer absolutely nothing) intended to induce less confident plaintiffs either to not file actual law suits or to withdraw the suits they have already filed. Studies of actual law suits, however, indicate that this tactic is likely to *increase* the percentage of cases taken to trial by plaintiffs who are angered by such offensive bargaining behavior and see no possible gain through non-adjudication alternatives (Gross & Syverud, 1991, at 342–45). If defense counsel offer even modest amounts to plaintiffs, they significantly increase the likelihood of settlements, since plaintiffs facing sure gains and the possibility of greater gains or no gains tend to be risk averse and they appreciate the fact that trial costs will decrease the value of judgments obtained through litigation.

In the many years we have practiced and taught legal negotiating, we have not found cooperative/problem solving negotiators less effective than competitive/adversarial bargainers. The notion that one must be uncooperative, selfish, manipulative, and even abrasive to be successful is erroneous. All people have to be able to do to achieve beneficial negotiating results is to possess the capacity to say "no" forcefully and credibly. They can do so courteously and quietly — and be as effective as those who do so more dramatically.

We have only noticed three significant differences with respect to the outcomes achieved by different style negotiators. First, if a truly extreme agreement is reached, the prevailing party is usually a competitive/adversarial negotiator. Since cooperative/problem-solving bargainers tend to be more fair-minded, they generally refuse to take unconscionable advantage of inept or weak opponents. Second, competitive/adversarial advocates generate far more nonsettlements than their cooperative/problem-solving cohorts. The extreme positions taken by competitive/ adversarial bargainers and their frequent use of manipulative and disruptive tactics makes it easy for their opponents to accept the consequences associated with nonsettlements.

The third difference in outcome due to negotiation style concerns the fact that cooperative/problem-solving negotiators tend to achieve more efficient *combined results* than their competitive/adversarial colleagues. Cooperative/problem-solvers are usually open and trusting individuals who seek to enhance the disclosure of information and maximize the overall return to the participants. They are thus more likely to attain higher joint values than are more closed and untrusting competitive/adversarial bargainers who are primarily interested in the maximization of their own side's results (Mnookin & Ross, 1995, at 8–9). Advocates who hope to achieve Pareto efficient agreements that benefit both sides must be willing to cooperate sufficiently to permit the participants to explore areas of possible joint gain. While these people may simultaneously seek to maximize their own client's return, their attempt to enhance opponent interests increases the likelihood of agreement *and* the probability of mutually efficient terms.

When cooperative/problem-solving bargainers interact with other cooperative/ problem-solving individuals, the transaction is usually cooperative (Raiffa, 2002, at 288–91), while interactions between competitive/adversarial negotiators are generally competitive (*Id.* at 298–301). When cooperative/ problem-solving bargainers deal with competitive/adversarial opponents, their transactions tend to be more competitive than cooperative. The cooperative/ problem-solving participants are forced to assume a more competitive posture to avoid the exploitation that would result if they were too open and accommodating with their manipulative and greedy opponents (Tepley, 2005, at 59–60). They have to release their important information in a more strategic fashion to prevent their adversaries from obtaining an information imbalance. These cross-style interactions generate less efficient agreements and increase the likelihood of nonsettlements. This phenomenon would explain why Professor Williams found that a greater percentage of cooperative/problem-solving negotiators are considered effective than competitive/adversarial bargainers.

In his study, Professor Williams found that certain traits are shared by both effective cooperative/problem-solving negotiators and effective competitive/ adversarial bargainers (Williams, 1983, at 20–30). Successful negotiators from both groups are thoroughly prepared, behave in an honest and ethical manner, are perceptive readers of opponent cues, are analytical, realistic, and convincing, and observe the customs and courtesies of the bar. He also found that proficient negotiators from both groups sought to *maximize their own client's return*. Professor Schneider also found this client-maximizing objective among both effective cooperative/problem-solving negotiators and effective competitive/adversarial negotiators (Schneider, 2002, at 188). Since this factor is most associated with competitive/adversarial bargainers, it would suggest that a number of successful negotiators are actually wolves in sheepskin. They exude a cooperative style, but seek competitive objectives.

Most successful negotiators are able to combine the most salient traits associated with the cooperative/problem-solving and the competitive/ adversarial styles (Freund, 1992, at 24–27; Woolf, 1990, at 34–35). They endeavor to maximize client returns, but attempt to accomplish this objective in a congenial and seemingly ingenuous manner. Unlike less proficient negotiators who view bargaining encounters as "fixed pie" endeavors in which one side's gain is the other side's corresponding loss, they realize that in multi-item interactions the parties generally value the various items differently (Mnookin, Peppet & Tulumello, 2000, at 14–15, 174; Thompson, 1998, at 113). They attempt to claim more of the distributive items desired by both sides (Wetlaufer, 1996; Goodpaster, 1996), but look for shared values in recognition of the fact that by maximizing joint returns, they are more likely to obtain the best settlements for their own clients (Shapiro & Jankowski, 2001, at 45–61). Even though they try to manipulate opponent perceptions for their own gain, they rarely resort to truly deceitful tactics. They know that a loss of credibility would undermine their ability to achieve beneficial results. Despite the fact they want as much as possible for themselves, they are not "win-lose" negotiators. They realize that the imposition of poor terms on opponents does not necessarily benefit their own clients. All other factors being equal, they want to maximize opponent satisfaction. So long as it does not require significant concessions on their part, they acknowledge the benefits to be derived from this approach. When they conclude bargaining interactions, they do not compare their results with the terms achieved by their opponents. They instead ask whether they like what they got, realizing that if they attained their objectives they had successful encounters.

Proficient negotiators do not seek to maximize opponent returns for purely altruistic reasons. They understand that this approach most effectively enables them to advance their own interests. First, they have to provide adversaries with sufficiently generous terms to induce them to accept proposed agreements. Second, they want to be sure opponents honor deals agreed upon. If the other side experiences post-agreement "buyer's remorse," they may try to get out of the deal. Finally, they appreciate the fact they are likely to encounter their adversaries in the future. If those people remember them as courteous and professional negotiators, their future bargaining interactions are more likely to be successful.

Effective cooperative/problem-solving and effective competitive/adversarial negotiators realize that people tend to work most diligently to satisfy the needs of opponents they like personally (Lewicki, et al., 1994, at 219-220). Overtly competitive/adversarial bargainers are rarely perceived as likeable. They exude competition and manipulation. Seemingly cooperative bargainers, however, appear to be seeking results that benefit both sides. Since others enjoy interacting with them, these individuals find unsuspecting opponents more willing to lower their guard and make greater concessions. They also generate more positive moods that promote cooperative behavior and the attainment of more efficient joint agreements (Freshman, Hayes & Feldman, 2002; Forgas, 1998).

These eclectic negotiators really employ composite styles. They may be fairly characterized as "competitive/problem-solving" advocates. They seek competitive goals (maximum client returns), but endeavor to accomplish those objectives through "problem-solving" strategies (Allred, 2000; Dawson, 2001, at 128; Kritzer, 1991, at 78–79). This may partially explain why Professor Williams found more effective "cooperative/problem-solving" negotiators than effective "competitive/adversarial" bargainers. It is likely that many effective "competitive" negotiators were so successful in their use of "problem-solving" tactics, that they induced their opponents to characterize them as "cooperative," rather than "competitive."

Professor Kathleen Reardon likes to divide negotiator styles into four slightly different classifications: (1) the "Analyzer," who likes to focus on logic, make rational arguments, and prioritize outcomes; (2) the "Achiever," who likes detailed planning, seeks to control interactions, and focuses on outcomes; (3) the "Motivator," who likes to use creativity to foster collaboration, and encourage innovative thinking in opponents; and (4) the "Mediator," who tries to establish rapport, listens carefully to others, favors consensus, and works to generate mutual gains (Reardon, 2004, at 54–60). Analyzers, Motivators, and Mediators are similar to Cooperative/Problem-Solvers, while Achievers are more like Competitive/Adversarials. When Achievers combine that approach with styles borrowed from Analyzers, Motivators, and/or Mediators, they are analogous to Competitive/Problem-Solvers. As noted above, we believe that such hybrid approaches are optimal for negotiators who hope to advance the interests of their own clients while simultaneously maximizing the returns shared with their opponents.

Over the past several decades, Americans in general and legal practitioners in partitular have become less polite toward one another. We have become more "win-lose" oriented, as more individuals seem to fear an inability to attain their own goals if others get what they want. These changing attitudes are adversely affecting legal practice and negatively influencing bargaining interactions. Lawyers who encounter a lack of civility from opposing negotiators should recognize that such inappropriate behavior is an inadequate substitute for bargaining proficiency. Good negotiators never behave badly. They realize that insulting conduct is unlikely to induce others to give them what they want.

A negotiation approach that emphasizes the problem-solving style is being employed by a number of lawyers in Canada and is beginning to be used by American lawyers — especially family law specialists (see generally Lande, 2003, and authorities cited therein, Cameron, 2004, Gutterman, 2004). Attorneys using the **collaborative law** approach enter into pre-dispute resolution agreements under which the clients and the legal representatives agree to negotiate from the outset employing the problem-solving, interest-based style. They promise to be completely open with each other, minimizing the need for formal discovery procedures, and to work to achieve mutually beneficial accords. To demonstrate their total commitment to the negotiation process, the attorneys include a disqualification clause precluding them from representing their respective clients if the case is not resolved and either party elects to proceed to trial. (See also Peppet, 2005 (suggesting changes in ethical standards that would permit lawyers to negotiate specific standards of candor, openness, and good faith that would apply to their bargaining interactions that would be enforceable through bar disciplinary procedures).)

The general commitment to the problem-solving approach is designed to avoid competitive, value-claiming tactics that might disrupt interest-based bargaining. To the extent these dispute resolution arrangements encourage cooperative interactions, they can be quite beneficial. The most controversial aspect of these undertakings concerns the promise that both lawyers will withdraw if litigation is ultimately initiated (Lande, 2003).

Many litigators, especially in large value cases, find that serious settlement offers are only forthcoming as trial dates approach. When both the plaintiffs and the defendants — especially the defendants in most cases — are convinced that the other side is willing to try the cases if necessary and are fully prepared to do so, they begin to ask whether they want to risk the costs and unpredictability of adjudications.

Whenever litigators begin settlement talks, they should assume they will achieve peaceful resolutions of their claims. Fewer than two percent of federal civil complaints culminate in adjudications today, and similar figures pertain to most state court dockets. It thus behooves lawyers to use nondisruptive, problem-solving techniques that will effectively and efficiently advance client interests. The overwhelming majority of clients want to control their own legal destinies. They rarely wish to have judges, juries, or arbitrators determine their fates. By assuming an interest-based approach, legal representatives further this client objective. On the other hand, if they promise not to represent the clients in the rare instances in which mutual accords cannot be achieved, they may undermine the litigation credibility they need to induce other parties to treat them as seriously as they would opponents who are authorized to litigate if this option becomes necessary.

3. TYPE OF NEGOTIATION

Different kinds of negotiations involve different participants and/or unique considerations that may influence the negotiation process. These factors must be considered when bargaining strategies are being developed. Some transactions are very complex in terms of legal or factual issues, such as complicated antitrust and securities law cases, corporate merger agreements, and international business deals. Other dealings do not raise complex legal or factual issues, such as uncomplicated personal injury disputes and rudimentary contractual arrangements. The more complicated an interaction, the more protracted the negotiation process is likely to be. Parties must obtain a basic understanding of the overall circumstances before mutually acceptable results can be achieved. Efforts to unduly accelerate this process may only serve to create suspicion and prolong the discussions.

Business people often complain about the opportunities they have lost because of excessive legal formalism practiced by many attorneys. While these individuals may underestimate the need for appropriate circumspection with respect to complex legal transactions, there are undoubtedly times when unnecessary emphasis upon legal irrelevancies may preclude beneficial agreements. Negotiators should try to minimize reliance upon pure "legal principle," when this would either prevent agreements or lock the parties into uncompromising positions. Where an arrangement can be structured in alternative ways, flexibility should be permitted to increase the likelihood of success.

In some negotiations, each party is in a position to deal with other persons if an agreement is not reached between the current participants. In other settings, however, the result of a nonsettlement is either an adjudication or no transaction. This factor significantly affects the need of the bargaining parties to achieve mutual accords. When alternative arrangements may be relied upon if the present discussions are not fruitful, the parties have no reason to permit irrational anxiety to generate disadvantageous agreements. On the other hand, when no external options are readily available, bargainers should endeavor to maximize the likelihood of mutual accords. It should be apparent that tactics that may be used in the former situation, due to the relatively minimal risk involved, may be inappropriate in the latter setting.

Some transactions involve one-time interactions between clients, such as tort suits, while others, such as on-going business dealings, marital dissolutions involving child-custody arrangements, and franchisor/franchisee undertakings, entail continuing relationships. When the clients expect to have future dealings, this may influence the tactics used during the current negotiation. Techniques that might adversely affect subsequent interactions should be avoided, to prevent unnecessary future difficulties. Similar considerations apply when an agreement must be satisfied over a period of time, such as a construction contract or a personal performance commitment.

Even when the respective clients are unlikely to have future interactions, there is a good chance their legal representatives will interact again. This will usually preclude any resort to tactics that may produce a short-term gain for the present client at the expense of prospective clients. While one might argue that a lawyer who is obliged to zealously represent the interests of the instant client should not decline to adopt tactics that may be fruitful now because of a fear that this action may have negative future consequences vis-a-vis opposing counsel, we do not agree. If the adoption of such a negotiating strategy would prejudice future dealings with this or other practitioners, the behavior would be beyond the bounds of propriety. No clients should have the right to expect their legal representatives to employ disreputable tactics that would be likely to diminish their ability to represent future clients.

When the immediate clients have complete control over the transaction being conducted, it is generally easy to obtain client consent to negotiated results. On the other hand, when one or both clients have additional constituencies that must ultimately approve any proposed agreement (*e.g.*, negotiating with a governmental entity about a matter that will necessitate the approval of agency officials or participating in a corporate transaction in which any resulting contract must receive board-of-director or shareholder approval), different considerations apply. A complete record should be carefully maintained, so that a detailed explanation can be given to the constituent body regarding the rationale underlying each agreed upon term. This approach will usually facilitate ultimate ratification.

4. VERBAL COMMUNICATION

All bargaining transactions involve communication, whether the interaction is done in person, on the telephone, or through written transmissions. This is accomplished through verbal discourse and through the emission of nonverbal signals. The meaning of different nonverbal signals and nonverbal indications of deception will be explored in Section 5, *infra*.

Direct verbal expressions can convey very different messages, even when they superficially appear to say the same thing. Negotiators must carefully consider the exact words chosen to determine whether speakers actually intend the message they seem to be conveying. If an unambiguous statement is involved, the speaker's assertion is clear. The recipient must decide whether the representation has been made in a credible manner. On the other hand, the inclusion of a "verbal leak" may undermine the seemingly definitive nature of the representation being made and allow the recipient to recognize the equivocal message being conveyed (LePoole, 1991, at 34). Verbal leaks frequently result from our discomfort with overt mendacity. To assuage our consciences, we use modifiers that render out precise statements true, even though the surface message is deliberately misleading. Consider the following examples:

a. "I cannot offer you any more!"

In this statement, the speaker is unequivocally expressing the view that no additional concessions can presently be made. If the nonverbal clues evidence congruent signals (*e.g.*, open, sincere posture with palms extended toward the listener to indicate that nothing is being deceptively hidden), it is likely that the declarant means exactly what is being stated.

b. "I am *not authorized* to offer you any more."

This is a more equivocal communication on its face, because it uses limited client authority as the basis for the representation being made. The reliance upon client authority may be used to provide verisimilitude for a significant misrepresentation. It may alternatively be included for the purpose of indicating that no further concessions will be forthcoming prior to consultations with the absent client.

c. "I am not able to offer you any more *at this time.*"

In this statement, the speaker is indicating that his or her expressed recalcitrance is most likely a temporary condition, as evidenced by the qualifying term "at this time." This type of language is frequently used to convey the message that reciprocal concessions will be made if only the other party will indicate that he or she is amenable to compromise. This supposition can easily be tested through a slight change of position intended to precipitate an appropriate counteroffer.

d. "I *do not believe* that I can offer you any more."

The inclusion of the "do not believe" phrase will probably induce a careful listener to suspect that the statement is disingenuous. A simple, unambiguous declaration, such as Statement **a**, could easily have been used had the speaker intended to convey a definitive message. If this person were subsequently induced to make a seemingly contradictory concession, he or she could try to save face by suggesting that the additional information and/or entreaties of the responding party generated the change of mind.

e. "My client *is not inclined/does not wish* to offer any more."

Phrases like "is not inclined" and "does not wish" constitute classic verbal leaks. Since these speakers do not want to lock themselves into unalterable positions and do not want to make deliberate misrepresentations, they include modifying language that leaves them room for further movement. The critical question is not whether the opponent "is inclined" or "wants" to make additional concessions. It is whether that party will actually do so.

f.   "That's *about as far* as I can go"/"I don't have *much more* room"

Statements like these indicate that the speakers have not reached their true bottom lines. They still have room to move. Patient negotiators can induce them to make additional concessions.

g.   "I *must have* Item 1, I *really want* Item 2, and I *would like to have* Item 3."

This statement includes verbal leaks indicating the degree to which the speaker values the items in question. Item 1 is critical to the deal, because they *must have* it. Item 2 is important, but not a deal-breaker. Item 3 would be nice, but it is not that important to the demanding party. A careful listener should be aware of these semantical distinctions.

Negotiators who discern verbal leaks in opponent statements must be patient. The modifying phrases indicate that further progress is likely, but it may take time for concessions to develop. If the speakers are pushed too quickly, they will feel compelled to preserve their credibility through temporary intransigence. They must be given sufficient time to formulate face-saving explanations for their seemingly inconsistent position changes.

Negotiators must also monitor their own language. During the critical stages of transactions, they should employ more definitive phrases that do not include unintended verbal leaks. This technique makes their representations more effective and forces their opponents to speculate about the veracity of the messages being conveyed. If unequivocal speakers subsequently discover that additional concessions must be made if agreements are to be achieved, they can always take a break "to consult" their clients. They can thereafter modify their previous positions without undermining their own credibility.

h.   Signal Words

"Signal words" may similarly influence the communication process. They may be used by speakers to create disingenuous impressions in the minds of opponents. They may also be employed by listeners to induce speakers to disclose more information than they intended to divulge. Examples of this phenomenon can be observed in the following statements:

(1)   *"To be perfectly candid,* this is the most I can offer you."

Assuming that the declarant has not used phrases such as "to be perfectly candid," "to be honest," etc., throughout the negotiation when making obviously correct assertions, the recipient of this type of message should be suspicious of its veracity. Such a term frequently accompanies a misrepresentation to enhance its credibility. Negotiators should carefully note the manner in which such signal words have been used by the speaker throughout the bargaining session. When they appear in a context suggesting a lack of candor, listeners should be particularly vigilant.

> (2) *"In my humble opinion,* I think that my proposal would satisfy the needs of both of our clients."

Many negotiators effectively use false humility to induce their adversaries to lower their guard in anticipation of an easy interaction. Phrases such as "in my humble opinion," "far be it for me to say," "if I might suggest," and "if you can accept the view of a woman" are often used to soften the competitive nature of the declarants to disguise their hidden desire for bargaining "victories" (Nierenberg & Calero, 1981, at 31). Opponents should recognize the manipulative nature of these phrases.

> (3) *"Do you mind if I suggest . . ."; "How about . . ."; "Have you ever considered . . . ."*

Passive-aggressive negotiators who lack the ability to display their aggression openly often use softening terms such as these to mask their desire to dictate the terms they really want. This approach may subtly undermine negotiations, because they involve "parent" to "child" transactions that fail to accord listeners appropriate "adult" respect (Berne, 1964). More overt examples of such "downers" include "don't be ridiculous" and "don't make me laugh" when rejecting proposals (Nierenberg & Calero, 1981, at 38–39).

> (4) *"You probably lack the authority to accept the generous offer I am proposing."*

Even though this apparently objective statement seems to entail an "adult"-"adult" exchange rationally indicating that the listener is not authorized to make a final commitment to this proposal on behalf of his or her client, it simultaneously involves an *ulterior transaction.* The hidden message is conveyed in a "parent" to "child" form suggesting that the "child" is unable to accept the tendered offer. If the recipient of the message irrationally responds in a child-like manner, he or she may well accept the proposed agreement to spitefully demonstrate his or her capacity to do so (Berne, 1964, at 33).

> (5) *"I understand how you feel"; "I see."*

Good bargainers are active listeners (Ordover & Doneff, 2002, at 18–20). While they do not accept all of the representations being made by their opponents, they interject terms such as these to let speakers know that they are being heard. Patient listening frequently induces less skilled adversaries to disclose more information than they intended because of the supportive environment. It also demonstrates respect for the declarants and helps to create an atmosphere that is conducive to open and collaborative discussions.

i. Body Posture and Speech Pattern Mirroring and Sensory Preference Reflection

When individuals interact with others, they tend to respond more favorably to persons who exhibit body postures and speech patterns similar to their own (Madonik, 2001, at 59, 158–59; Ury, 1991, at 46–47). Negotiators who wish to take advantage of this factor can try to mirror the body postures of those with whom they are interacting. If their opponent leans back in her chair, they lean back in their own chair. If that person decides to cross one leg over the other, they cross the same leg over their other leg to reflect that individual's posture. If their adversary leans forward in her chair, they lean forward in a similar manner. If the other party leans to one side, they adopt a similar position.

They may similarly mirror the speech patterns of their adversary by speaking more slowly when he does so and speaking more rapidly when he picks up the pace. They may similarly work to reflect the other person's speech tone and inflection. If the other party elevates his voice pitch, they may do the same with their voice.

Negotiators mirroring the postures and speech patterns of their opponents must be careful to do so inconspicuously to avoid detection. If they accomplish the desired objective, they will make themselves more likeable to their opponents. On the other hand, if their actions become obvious, their conduct may be perceived as disingenuous and even mocking. Their behavior would have a negative impact and undermine their interaction.

When people think and speak, they tend to employ one of three sensory preferences (Madonik, 2001, at 24–31, 128–29, 160–61; Hogan, 1996, at 144–45). Some individuals have a *visual* orientation. The eyes of such persons either move upward or stare in an unfocused manner. Their words describe visual images of what they are discussing. For example, they may ask if you can *picture* what they are proposing, or they may say that they can *see* what you are requesting. Such visual persons respond most favorably to people who reply in a similar fashion. For example, opponents might describe their position graphically. They might alternatively indicate that they can *see* what is bothering the other side.

Other persons have an *auditory* orientation. When they talk, their eyes tend to move from side to side or move downward and to their left. Their words describe auditory messages. They may ask opponents to *listen to* what they are proposing, or indicate that their proposal has *rung a bell* with them. They might alternatively suggest that adversaries *voice* their opinion about something. These persons are likely to be receptive to opponents who respond with similar auditory references. They might suggest that they *hear* their concerns. Adversaries might indicate that their proposed joint venture would *explode* across the business world or would be received with a *bang* on Wall Street.

The third group of people tend to have a *kinesthetic/feeling* framework. They are individuals who *feel* or *sense* things. When they speak, their eyes tend to move down and to their right. They are likely to say that something *smells bad* or has left a *bad taste* in their mouth. They may rely on a *gut feeling*. To maximize the receptiveness of such persons to opponent communications, others should reflect their kinesthetic/feeling orientation. They might respond that their proposal *feels good*. Adversaries might indicate that they understand why the other side is *not comfortable* with the proposal on the table.

Negotiators who listen carefully for the sensory orientations of opponents should be able to determine whether they are visual, auditory, or kinesthetic/feeling persons. By responding to them in the same framework, they can increase the likelihood their ideas will be favorably received. Such an approach can greatly enhance communication between the bargaining parties.

j.　Framing of Issues

Negotiators should recognize that they can increase the likelihood that opponents will select their preferred choices by the way in which they frame problems. Most people are risk averse when choosing between a *sure gain* and an uncertain alternative that may result in a greater gain or nothing. On the other hand, when one option entails a *definite loss* and the alternative *may* enable them to avoid any loss, most persons become risk takers (Korobkin, 2006, at 308–12; Guthrie, 2003, at 1117–27; Korobkin, 2002, at 14–15; Guthrie, Rachlinski & Wistrich, 2001, at 794–99; Kahneman & Tversky, 1979; Tversky & Kahneman, 1981). For example, assume that you must choose between the following two options:

If you select Option A, you will receive $20,000.

If you select Option B, there is a 20 percent probability that you will receive $100,000 and an 80 percent probability you will receive nothing.

Most individuals would accept the certain $20,000 gain offered by Option A, rather than the risk of receiving nothing associated with Option B — even though Option B provides them with a 20 percent possibility of obtaining $100,000 (Guthrie, 1999, at 54–59; Pratkanis & Aronson, 1991, at 61–63; Bazerman & Neale, 1992, at 33–39).

If the options were framed in the following manner, which would you choose?

If you select Option A, you will lose $20,000.

If you select Option B, there is a 20 percent probability that you will lose $100,000 and an 80 percent probability that you will lose nothing.

When confronted with the second set of alternatives, most individuals choose Option B. They are unwilling to accept the certain loss of $2,000 and prefer the alternative that *may* avoid any loss — despite the fact they have a 20 percent possibility of losing $100,000. This framing phenomenon explains why typical law suit settlement discussions favor defendants. Plaintiffs offered a *sure gain* and the possibility of a greater gain or no gain at trial tend to opt for the certain gain, while defendants facing a *sure loss* and the possibility of a greater loss or no loss at trial tend to sele t the trial option that may provide them with no loss (Guthrie, 2003, at 11. 2–23).

When individuals negotiate, they should present their proposals in a manner that maximizes the likelihood their opponents will accept their preferred choice. They may accomplish this objective by providing opponents with options that appear to provide *certain gain* and force them to choose between these proposals and alternatives that merely involve possible gain. If their opponents are concerned about probable losses, bargainers should propose alternatives that offer a possible avoidance of any loss, because their opponents are more likely to accept these options than alternatives that will result in *definite loss*.

Another factor that can influence the negotiating behavior of parties concerns "regret aversion" (Guthrie, 1999). Most people do not like to make decisions that may be shown by subsequent developments to have been incorrect, because such developments cause them to suffer sincere regret. For example, litigants tend to prefer settlements that avoid the possibility of trials that could culminate in final terms worse than those rejected during settlement discussions. Corporate buyers and sellers similarly prefer current deals that avoid subsequent developments indicating that rejected offers were preferable to the final deals achieved. To effectively use "regret aversion" theory to influence opponent behavior, negotiators should subtly suggest to those individuals that their nonsettlement alternatives may turn out to be worse than what they are presently being offered. To avoid the possibility of discovering that they should not have rejected the sure offers placed before them now, the offerees are likely to accept those terms and get on with their lives.

5. NONVERBAL COMMUNICATION

One of the most important sources of information available to negotiators is frequently overlooked, even though it constitutes a majority of the communication being conveyed (Stark & Flaherty, 2003, at 45; Burgeon, Buller & Woodall, 1996, at 3–4). Although participants concentrate on what is being verbally communicated by their opponents, many fail to focus on the nonverbal signals emanating from those people. Bargainers who ignore nonverbal stimuli are only cognizant of the most controlled communication being sent by opposing parties (Quilliam, 2004, at 9; Ekman & Friesen, 1975, at 135–36). Unless they can train themselves to appreciate the subtle nonverbal signs that significantly influence the negotiation process, they will rarely understand the entire transaction. They may also fail to appreciate the nonverbal messages they are conveying to the other side (Quilliam, 2004, at 11–13).

People with negotiating experience can all recall circumstances in which they sensed that their adversaries were being disingenuous. Numerous "last offers" have been rejected, along with "absolutely final offers" as preludes to more generous proposals that were subsequently accepted. What induced these persons to sense that the allegedly "final" position statements were merely intermediate steps in the overall process? These suppositions are generally based upon the conscious or subconscious reading of nonverbal signals that are not congruent with the verbal messages being conveyed. (Calero 2005, at 89–90.)

True final offers are not casually transmitted from persons who are sitting back in their chair with their arms folded across their chest. The speakers are likely to be leaning slightly forward in the chair with their arms extended and their palms facing outward to demonstrate the openness and sincerity of their positions. It is only when the nonverbal signals are consistent with the words being expressed that the verbal representations become credible.

People should carefully consider the tentative "feelings" they experience during their bargaining interactions (Ryan, 2005, at 275–76). When they sense their opponent is making a misrepresentation or is receptive to their most recent offer despite oral protestations to the contrary, they should attempt to understand the reasons for their suspicions. They may well be based upon their subconscious reception of nonverbal messages that provide an accurate impression of the opponent's actual situation. These interpretive "feelings" should not be rejected until it can be established that they are not premised upon rational considerations.

Most bargainers fail to observe many of the nonverbal signs emanating from their opponents. Some naively believe there is no need to look for these messages, because no competent negotiator would be so careless as to divulge important information in such an inadvertent manner. Anyone who harbors this opinion should consider theatrical performances by well-known actors who can rarely eliminate all involuntary gestures and mannerisms that are really their own instead of those attributable to the characters being portrayed. If these professionals are unable to avoid unintended nonverbal disclosures, surely untrained negotiators will be less successful in this regard.

Many negotiators focus so intently upon the responses they are formulating to counter the oral representations being made by their opponents that they not only fail to hear all of the verbal messages being expressed, but also miss most of the nonverbal stimuli. This problem is compounded by the fact that negotiations involve stressful settings that tend to decrease the cognitive abilities of the participants (Hopmann & Walcott in Drukman, 1977, at 306). Bargainers must force themselves to observe their adversaries more diligently, even while internally planning their own strategies. People who find this bifurcated approach too difficult may wish to have other persons participate on their negotiation teams as observers. These assistants can carefully listen to and observe opposing counsel. They can also determine if any unintended information is being inadvertently disclosed by their own spokespersons.

Some individuals tend to be more adroit readers of nonverbal communication than others. People trained in psychology, counseling, or theatrics are usually more cognizant of nonverbal stimuli. A number of empirical studies have found that women are typically more sensitive to nonverbal messages than their male cohorts (Ford, 1996, at 208–09; Hall, 1984, at 16–17, 27; Mayo & Henley, 1981, at 7; Henley, 1977, at 13–15). Studies have also found that black persons are more attuned to nonverbal signals than are white people (Hall, 1984, at 41–42; Henley, 1977, at 14). These gender and racial differences may reflect the fact that members of groups that have historically had less societal empowerment have learned to be more perceptive with respect to nonverbal clues as a means of offsetting their power imbalance (Henley, 1977, at 14–15).

Persons who are not particularly sensitive to nonverbal stimuli can enhance their ability in this regard. Various books have thoughtfully explored the nonverbal communication area in a manner that is comprehensible to people who have not formally studied this important topic (Dimitrius & Mazzarella,

1998; Morris, 1994; Hall, 1984; Druckman, Rozelle & Baxter, 1982; Henley, 1977; Beir & Valens, 1975; Nierenberg & Calero, 1971; Fast, 1970). By reading several of these books and concentrating more intently on the nonverbal behavior of others in social and business settings, less skilled readers of nonverbal messages can significantly improve their capabilities. They should carefully observe the facial expressions, hand movements, and body postures of those with whom they interact, and they should ask themselves what these movements say about the individuals being watched.

One of the most obvious forms of nonverbal communication involves facial expressions. A derisive smile may be employed to demonstrate disdain for a wholly unacceptable proposal. Conversely, a subtle smile in response to a person's fourth or fifth proposal may indicate that this offer is approaching the other party's area of perceived reasonableness. Such a supposition might be reinforced by the fact that the responding negotiator did not reject this offer with the same alacrity with which the previous submissions were declined. The overture might also have been renounced through the use of a "signal" phrase such as "to be candid" or "to be honest." On the other hand, if a few proposals have been exchanged and a bargainer's effort to make a suggestion believed to be quite reasonable is received with a pained expression (*e.g.*, taut lips and/or the gnashing of teeth evidenced by the visible expansion and contraction of the jaw muscles on both sides of the face), it should be apparent that either or both participants have misperceived the true value of this transaction.

Negotiators should always look for "double messages" that may emanate from clients or adversaries. For example, individuals might verbally suggest how disappointed they are regarding unfortunate developments, while accompanying their sad words with inappropriate signs of pleasure (*e.g.*, smiles). These contradictory facial expressions would strongly suggest that the speakers are not really as disconsolate as their unembellished statements might otherwise indicate. These persons most likely enjoy their current plight and do not want to have their problems alleviated too expeditiously.

Attorneys who negotiate in teams need to establish a specified way to communicate with one another during bargaining sessions that will not inadvertently divulge confidential information. If they fail to resolve this problem beforehand, they may disclose their thoughts through a casual sideways glance or a slight nod toward a partner following a particular offer. They may communicate a similar message when they decide to caucus over an offer following the summary rejection of five prior proposals. It is frequently advantageous when several individuals plan to represent the same party to designate a single speaker who is to make the immediate decisions necessary during the bargaining meetings without the need to consult the other team members first. They can initially announce an intention to caucus every hour or two to discuss developments, to avoid letting their opponents know how interested they are in particular offers.

Negotiators must remember that facial expressions are generally controlled more readily than are less voluntary body movements. Contrived smiles or frowns may be carefully orchestrated to convey deceptive messages, while less voluntary arm, leg, and upper body movements are more likely to communicate true feelings. It is thus imperative for bargaining participants to endeavor to observe as many informative body movements as possible. They should not merely focus upon facial signals. Furthermore, no isolated signal should be given a definitive interpretation. People must look for *changes* in the *usual* behavior of others and predictable *patterns of conduct* (Calero, 2005, at 73; Stark & Flaherty, 2003, at 47).

a. Common Forms of Nonverbal Communication

(1) *Facial Expressions.*

Even though facial expressions are generally the most easily manipulated form of nonverbal communication, subtle clues may frequently be perceived by careful observers. Taut lips may indicate anxiety or frustration. A subtle smile or brief signs of relief around the corners of an opponent's mouth when a new offer is being conveyed may indicate that the offer is approaching or has entered that person's settlement range. This nonverbal signal evidences that individual's belief that a final settlement is likely.

(2) *Flinch — Pained Facial Expression.*

This may be an uncontrolled response to a surprisingly inadequate opening offer. This would sincerely indicate to the offeror the wholly unacceptable nature of his or her initial position. Adroit negotiators may employ a contrived "flinch" to silently challenge opposing party opening offers without having to engage in verbal discourse (Dawson, 1995, at 18–21). Skilled use of the "flinch" may subtly undermine opponent confidence in their position, and it may induce careless adversaries to modify their initial offers before they obtain opening position statements from the flinching party.

(3) *Raising of One Eyebrow.*

The involuntary raising of a single eyebrow generally connotes skepticism or surprise (Morris, 1994, at 51). This signal may sincerely indicate that the actor is suspicious of opponent overtures. It may be disingenuously employed by manipulative negotiators to suggest their disappointment with opponent offers or concessions.

(4) *Raising of Both Eyebrows / Widening of Eyes.*

This is a clear indication of surprise. It is often visible when a negotiator's opening offer or subsequent position change is more generous than the recipient anticipated. It may similarly follow the disclosure of wholly unanticipated information. When negotiators observe such signs, they should suspect potentially serious tactical errors on their part. They should quickly reassess their present situations and try to determine whether they have made inadvertent tactical mistakes.

(5) *Wringing of Hands.*

This is frequently an indication of frustration or tension. Particularly distraught people are likely to twist their hands and fingers into seemingly painful contortions. This message usually emanates from people who are unhappy with substantive developments or anxious about the aggressive tactics being employed by their opponents.

(6) *Tightly Gripping Arm Rests/Drumming on the Table.*

People who are impatient or frustrated often tightly grip the arm rests of the chair they are sitting in or drum their fingers on the table in front of them. Negotiators who are displeased by a perceived lack of progress may engage in this kind of conduct.

(7) *Biting Lower Lip/Biting Fingernails/Running Fingers Through Hair/Rubbing Forehead.*

These signs usually indicate stress or frustration. They tend to emanate from individuals who are disappointed by the lack of negotiation progress or by perceived opponent intransigence.

(8) *Eyes Wandering/Looking at Watch/Crossing & Uncrossing Legs/Doodling.*

These are signs of boredom and/or disinterest (Dimitrius & Mazzarella, 1998, at 62). These signals would indicate that your presentation is not interesting your opponent. You may wish to ask some questions designed to get your adversary more actively involved in the discussions.

(9) *Shifting Back and Forth in Chair/Tilting Head from Side to Side/Opening and Closing Mouth Without Speaking.*

These are indications of indecision (Dimitrius & Mazzarella, 1998, at 67–68). The message sender is not sure how to proceed and is contemplating his or her options. You should patiently and silently wait to give this person the time they need to formulate an opinion they can express.

(10) *Hands Neatly Folded in Lap.*

This often denotes contrite penitence and possibly even submissiveness (Folberg & Taylor, 1984, at 122). This posture tends do be exhibited more by females than by males. If this information appears to be consistent with other signals emanating from the negotiator, the opposing party should encourage this attitude and take advantage of it. It must be recognized, however, that some people who have been carefully raised to be "good little boys and girls" might sit in this fashion merely because of their prior upbringing.

(11) *Sitting on the Edge of One's Chair.*

When this action appears to occur involuntarily following a recent proposal and the posture did not accompany the receipt of previous offers, it may suggest increased interest on the part of the actor. If this interpretation is correct, it may indicate that the offeror is approaching the offeree's zone of expectation. Rarely do persons sit literally on the front of their chair. They only move slightly forward in their seat.

(12) *Hands Touching Face/Playing with Glasses/Looking at Papers or Notes.*

These acts are indications of meditative contemplation. Since people feel awkward sitting perfectly still while they consider proposals and formulate appropriate responses, they frequently resort to these artifices to camouflage their thinking. This conduct may suggest that their opponent's most recent proposal has finally forced them to think seriously about their reply. They plan to reject the new offer, but wish to do so in a more positive manner. They may take twenty or thirty seconds to formulate their more affirmative rejection statement. If they did not employ these diversionary actions before they rejected prior offers, this may demonstrate that they perceive the instant proposal to be quite reasonable.

(13) *Steepling Gesture (Hands Pressed Together with Fingers Uplifted or Hands Together with Interlocked Fingers also Uplifted, with Elbows Out in Expansive Manner).*

This grandiose gesture indicates that the actor feels confident. Negotiators who observe this behavior should be certain they are not conceding more than is necessary, since their opponents appear to be pleased with developments.

(14) *Leaning Back in Chair with Hands on Back of Head.*

This posture is adopted more by males than by females. It is usually an indication of confidence and contentedness. When men who are interacting with women adopt this posture, it is not only a sign of confidence but also an indication of perceived domination. Female negotiators who observe this behavior in male opponents should be especially cautious, because those people may think that things are going their way. This action is also an indication of power and authority, and is frequently employed by superiors when they interact with subordinates.

(15) *Extending Hands Toward Opponent with Fingers Pointed Upward and Palms Facing Out.*

This is common behavior by individuals who are being verbally assaulted by aggressive bargainers. It is a defensive posture used to symbolically (but ineffectively) protect the actors against the oral onslaught emanating from their opponents.

(16) *Rubbing Hands Together in Anticipatory Manner.*

This behavior is often exhibited by anxious negotiators who anticipate beneficial offers from their opponents. This conduct usually suggests an over-eagerness that may be satisfied with a minimal position change.

(17) *Placing Palm of Right Hand over Heart.*

Some people voluntarily or involuntarily place the palm of their right hand over their heart when attempting to appear sincere or credible. If this behavior seems inadvertent, it may be perceived as a sign of true sincerity. If this action appears to be contrived, however, it is likely to be viewed as a disingenuous effort to mislead the opponent.

(18) *Open or Uplifted Hands.*

This technique is generally used to demonstrate openness and sincerity. The open or uplifted hands indicate that the actor has nothing to hide. This is the posture one normally expects to observe when they are being given true final offers. If the gesture appears stilted, it is probably a deliberate attempt to deceive the observer.

(19) *Crossed Arms / Crossed Legs.*

This may constitute a defensive position or an aggressive, adversarial posture, depending on the particular position involved. If the arms are folded high on the chest and the legs are crossed in a "figure-four" position (with the ankle of one leg placed on the knee of the other leg in a typically masculine fashion), this represents a competitive or combative posture. This stance clearly indicates the unresponsiveness of the actor. If the arms are folded low on the chest and one leg is draped across the other, this tends to be a defensive position. The intimidated actor is likely to be leaning back in his or her chair in a subconscious effort to escape the verbal assault emanating from the opponent. Both crossed-arms and crossed legs represent unreceptive postures.

If an opponent begins a negotiation with arms folded and legs crossed, it is beneficial to try to establish sufficient rapport with that person to soften his or her stance prior to the commencement of formal discussions. Serious final offers should never be made when one's arms are folded and one's legs are crossed, because this does not present a credible appearance.

(20) *Standing with Hands on Hips.*

This is a rather aggressive posture that tells others to stay away from the actor (Morris, 1994, at 4). It is often exhibited by angry individuals who do not wish to interact with those around them. People who do not like to negotiate may greet new opponents in this position.

(21) *Gnashing of Teeth.*

This is a frequent indication of anxiety or anger, and is evidenced by the contracting and relaxing of the jaw muscles on both sides of the face. Aggressive negotiators should carefully watch for the gnashing of teeth, the wringing of hands, and other reactions that might suggest the opponent is experiencing substantial stress, because continued combative conduct may precipitate a cessation of the talks.

(22) *Covering and Rubbing One's Eye.*

It is not uncommon for individuals to casually cover and rub one eye when they find it difficult to accept something being communicated to them (Scheflen, 1972, at 79). This is the nonverbal equivalent of the expression "my eye" that may be uttered by someone who doubts the veracity of a speaker's comments. Negotiators who encounter this signal when they are making truthful representations about a crucial fact should recognize the real possibility that their statements are not being given much credibility. They may wish to rephrase their communication in a more believable manner.

(23) *Rubbing Chin in Inquisitive Manner.*

This is another nonverbal sign of disbelief (Morris, 1994, at 31). While the actor may be unwilling to express his or her disbelief verbally, this nonverbal conduct conveys a similar message.

(24) *Picking Imaginary Lint from One's Clothing.*

People who disapprove of or are made particularly uncomfortable by shocking or outrageous statements being made by others may begin to pick imaginary lint from their clothing — especially when they are hesitant to express their disapproval or discomfort directly (Scheflen, 1972, at 109). This behavior is common in response to graphic descriptions of severe injuries or gory medical procedures.

(25) *Casual Touching (e.g., Prolonged Hand Shake; Hand or Arm on Opponent's Shoulder or Forearm).*

This device can be effectively used to indicate one's sincerity and to establish rapport. A warm handshake at the commencement of a bargaining interaction can often reduce the likelihood of interpersonal conflict. Even during negotiation sessions, casual touching of the other participant's hand or forearm can be used as a "personal touch" to maintain harmonious relations. Even though Americans are not as touching as some cultures, we tend to touch each other during interactions more frequently than most of us realize, even when talking with relative strangers. This is true when we communicate with persons of the same or the opposite gender.

On rare occasions, a negotiator may try to place an arm over the shoulder of the opposing party in a condescending fashion to denote a superior-subordinate relationship. This tactic may be used by a larger individual toward a smaller person or by a male toward a female. Since the speculative benefits that might be derived from such patronizing conduct would be minimal and this behavior could easily offend the recipient, use of this approach is definitely not recommended.

(26) *Direct Eye Contact.*

People who make regular eye contact with others are often perceived as being more personable and forthright than those who lack this trait. Negotiators who can maintain nonthreatening eye contact with opponents can frequently create a warmer negotiating environment and enhance their apparent credibility. They are also likely to be more cognizant of the nonverbal messages emanating from their adversaries. On the other hand, intense staring is usually perceived as a highly intimidating and combative act.

(27) *Head Nodding.*

Casual head nodding is generally employed by active listeners to indicate their comprehension of what is being said. Head nodding by listeners is occasionally misinterpreted by speakers as a sign of agreement. Rapid nods, on the other hand, may indicate a lack of interest or be employed by impatient individuals to encourage speakers to get to the point more expeditiously.

(28) *Turning Around in Chair to Look Away from Opponent After Making New Offer.*

This behavior is often engaged in by individuals who hate to compromise. They cannot stand to look at opponents after they make concessions. People interacting with these bargainers should not be personally offended by this seemingly disrespectful conduct, but should expect to see it after many position changes by such opponents.

b. Nonverbal Indications of Deception

The preceding section covered various nonverbal clues that do not pertain specifically to the discovery of deliberate deception. This section explores those inadvertent signals that often indicate the communication of intentional misrepresentations. Readers should not, however, be induced to think that they can discern all or even most of the dishonest statements uttered during their negotiations. Few can hope to be so perceptive.

In his book *Telling Lies*, psychologist Paul Ekman noted that people are surprisingly inept at discovering when they are being deceived (Ekman, 1992, at 86–87; *see also* Ekman, O'Sullivan & Frank, 1999; Frank & Ekman, 1997). This phenomenon may be partially attributable to the fact that mendacity may occur in different forms ranging from mere "puffing" to unabashed prevarication. It must be acknowledged that many of the stereotypically accepted indicia of deceit have little empirical support. This fact was eloquently recognized by an experienced labor arbitrator:

> Anyone driven by the necessity of adjudging credibility, who has listened over a number of years to sworn testimony, knows that as much truth must have been uttered by shifty-eyed, perspiring, lip-licking, nail-biting, guilty-looking, ill at ease, fidgety witnesses as have lies issued from calm, collected, imperturbable, urbane, straight-in-the-eye perjurers [Jones, 1966, at 1286].

Bargainers who rely upon the traditionally cited indicators of deception will undoubtedly reject many generous proposals received from seemingly untrustworthy fidgeters and accept many parsimonious offers made by seemingly reliable Machiavellian negotiators.

Despite the empirically demonstrated unreliability of the conventionally enumerated indicia of dishonesty, there are clues that can meaningfully assist people to evaluate the veracity of opposing negotiators (Lieberman, 1998; Ford, 1996, at 201–03, 213; Ekman, 1992; Ekman, O'Sullivan, Friesen & Scherer, 1991; Druckman, Rozelle & Baxter, 1982). Individuals who plan to make deliberate misrepresentations often emit nonverbal signals that should caution alert observers. Some of these nonverbal messages reflect the stress associated with lying — generated by fear of the truth combined with anxiety regarding the possibility of being caught lying. Other nonverbal behavior is designed to enhance the credibility of the misrepresentations being made. If people are going to engage in mendacious conduct, they want to increase the likelihood they will be believed!

No one signal should be accepted as a definitive indication of deception. Observers must look for *changes* in the speaker's usual behavior and *patterns* of behavior that are consistent with dishonesty. The general anxiety associated with most bargaining encounters may cause someone to exhibit signs of stress, but these should be apparent throughout the critical stages of the interaction. On the other hand, if obvious signs of stress emanated just before the utterance of a questionable statement, the listener should be suspicious. In addition, individuals who are afraid that their truthful representations are not going to be believed may exhibit similar signs of stress (Ekman, 1992, at 94). Verbal leaks, such as the use of "signal words" or repeated or incomplete statements would suggest that these signals are indications of deception.

(1) *Signal Words ("To Be Candid"; "To Be Truthful"; "Frankly").*

When negotiators who have not used these phrases as ordinary figures of speech preface critical comments with such "signal words," their listeners should be especially circumspect. These terms are often employed by deceptive individuals to enhance the credibility of their deliberate deceptions and to induce opponents to listen more intently to the fabrications being uttered (Lieberman, 1998, at 46–47).

(2) *Decrease or Increase in Specificity of Statements.*

When people tell the truth, they fill in the little details as they recall them, adding a substantial amount of incidental information. When individuals fabricate, however, there are no details to remember. As a result, they tend to omit the usual amplifying information, providing the bare details of their lie (Ekman, 1992, at 106). On the other hand, persons who have prepared elaborate lies may provide an excess amount of information in an effort to make their fabrication more credible (Lieberman, 1998, at 31). When they get no response to their misrepresentation, they nervously restate their lie. Specific questions about particular facts can often be helpful to discover whether explicit stories are credible (*see generally* Schweitzer & Croson, 1999).

(3) *Partial Shrug.*

People who shrug their shoulders usually indicate that they are ignorant or indifferent. If they are being deceptive, however, they often exhibit a partial shrug of one shoulder that is only briefly visible (Lieberman, 1998, at 16; Ekman, 1992, at 102–03).

(4) *Increased or Reduced Gross Body Movement.*

When people interact, they move their arms, legs, and torso on a fairly regular basis. Rarely do individuals sit or stand perfectly still. Under stressful circumstances, some persons become more fidgety and move their arms and legs at an increased rate. Other persons, however, behave in a contrary manner when they resort to deceitful tactics. They know that fidgety speakers appear less trustworthy, and they attempt to enhance their credibility by making a discernible effort to decrease their gross body movement. Negotiators should be especially cautious when they evaluate the veracity of statements made by individuals who have obviously increased or decreased their gross body movement.

(5) *Casual Placing of Hand over Mouth.*

Most people have been raised to believe that prevarication is morally wrong. When they engage in deliberate deception, they experience guilty consciences. Psychologists have noticed that liars often place their hand over their mouth when they speak, in a subconscious effort to hold in their morally reprehensible falsehoods (Lieberman, 1998, at 15).

(6) *Unconscious Touching of Nose with Finger Tip or Back of Finger.*

These movements are often considered a subtle equivalent to the "covering of one's mouth" as someone prepares to prevaricate (Hogan, 1996, at 107; Morris, 1994, at 182). While these signals may appear in isolation, it is common for deceivers to initially cover their mouth and then quickly touch the side of their nose.

(7) *Inconsistent Nodding or Shaking of Head.*

When speakers lie, their heads occasionally give them away (Ford, 1996, at 204). For example, people who say that they are unable to do something may casually nod their heads affirmatively, or persons who state that they want to do something may incidentally shake their heads negatively. Their subconscious head movements contradict their misrepresentations and truthfully indicate their actual intentions.

(8) *Eyes Looking Up to Wrong Side.*

When people try to *recall* past events from memory, right handed individuals tend to look up and to the left and left handed persons tend to look up and to the right. On the other hand, when individuals try to *create* an image or fact, right handed persons tend to look up and to the right and left handed people look up and to the left (Quilliam, 2004, at 28–29; Lieberman, 1998, at 162). When a right handed individual looks up and to the right or a left handed person looks up and to the left, it often means they are not trying to recall actual circumstances but rather to create a false story.

(9) *Dilated Pupils and More Frequent Blinking.*

When people experience stress, the pupils of their eyes become dilated and their rate of blinking usually increases (Ekman, 1992, at 114, 142). Even though legal negotiators rarely interact in sufficiently close environments to observe pupil enlargement, increased blinking should be readily discernible.

(10) *Involuntary Raising of Inner Portions of Eyebrows.*

Most individuals are unable to control the muscles that regulate the movement of their inner eyebrows. Under stressful conditions, however, many people experience an involuntary lifting of their *inner* eyebrows or the raising and pulling together of their entire eyebrows (Ekman, 1985, at 134–36). These movements tend to be transient and are frequently overlooked, but they may be noted by discerning observers.

(11) *Narrowing and Tightening of Red Margin of Lips.*

Stress is frequently manifested just before persons speak by the brief narrowing and tightening of the red margin of their lips (Ekman, 1992, at 136). Careful viewers can see the lips of prospective speakers tighten into a narrow line across their lower face prior to their utterance of planned misrepresentations.

(12) *Licking Lips or Running Tongue Over Teeth.*

These are signs of stress and discomfort, and are often associated with deceptive behavior (Dimitrius & Mazzarella, 1998, at 60).

(13) *Higher Pitched Voice.*

People experiencing anxiety often raise their vocal pitch when they speak (Ford, 1996, at 213; Ekman, 1992, at 93). Even though intentional prevaricators attempt to control their voice when they talk, listeners can frequently discern their higher voice pitch.

(14) *More Deliberate or More Rapid Speech.*

Individuals who resort to intentional misrepresentations want to ensure a receptive audience. To accomplish this objective, they often utter their misstatements in a more deliberate manner to be certain their message has been entirely received. On the other hand, people experiencing greater stress may speak more rapidly (Dimitrius & Mazzarella, 1998, at 60; Ekman, 1992, at 93, 122).

(15) *Increased Number of Speech Errors.*

Studies have found that people who are attempting to deceive others tend to have a higher number of speech errors. These may manifest themselves as stuttering, the repeating of phrases, the increased presence of broken phrases, and the inclusion of more nonsubstantive modifiers ("It is clear that. . . ."; "you know") (Ekman, 1992, at 121–22; Gifford, 1989, at 129). It is as if their consciences are disrupting the communication between the brain and the mouth to prevent issuance of their morally wrong prevarications.

(16) *More Frequent Clearing of Throat.*

The tension associated with deceptive behavior often manifests itself in more frequent throat clearing (Gifford, 1989, at 130). As speakers prepare to utter their knowingly false statements, they nervously clear their throats in an obvious manner.

(17) *Change in Frequency of Looking at Listener.*

As some speakers experience the stress associated with their deliberate deception, they become more nervous and look less frequently at their listeners (Lieberman, 1998, at 13). Other deceivers, however, exhibit contrary behavior. They realize that people who look others in the eye are perceived as being more credible. To enhance the likelihood that their misrepresentations will be believed, they make an obvious effort to look more directly at their listeners while they are lying.

(18) *Duping Delight.*

Some individuals enjoy the challenge of successful deception. When they mislead their listeners, they exhibit a smug contempt toward their targets (Ekman, 1992, at 76–79). These deceivers may also exude signs of pleasure (*e.g.* self satisfied smile). These signals are especially likely when these persons are misleading people they think are difficult to fool.

Negotiators should carefully monitor the nonverbal signals emanating from their opponents. They should be especially alert to signs of stress or behavior that appears to be designed to enhance the credibility of questionable representations. While no single sign should be considered conclusive evidence of deception, observable changes in behavior and the presence of suspicious patterns of conduct should cause listeners to become more circumspect.

6. THE IMPACT OF CULTURAL DIFFERENCES

Legal representatives must recognize that negotiations involving participants from diverse cultures frequently develop differently than bargaining interactions involving persons from similar cultures. People tend to negotiate more cooperatively with opponents of the same race, gender, age, and culture than with adversaries of other races, genders, age groups, or cultures — probably due to the fact that similarity induces trust and reduces the need for the interactors to maintain a particular "face" in each other's eyes (Rubin & Brown, 1975, at 163). This may explain why African-Americans tend to perform better when they compete with Caucasian-Americans and when they cooperate with other African-Americans (Fry & Coe, 1980, at 166).

Different meanings may be ascribed to identical speech and behavior by members of different ethnic groups because of their different acculturation experiences (Davidson & Greenhalgh, 1999, at 20–22). Certain cultural groups are more likely to exhibit more cooperative behavior than other groups. For example, while African-Americans tend to speak more forcefully and with greater verbal aggressiveness than Caucasian-Americans (Davidson & Greenhalgh, 1999, at 22), they tend to negotiate more cooperatively than do whites or Mexican-Americans (Rubin & Brown, 1975, at 163). On the other hand, African-Americans tend to make less eye contact while listening to others than do whites, which may erroneously be perceived as an indication of indifference or even disrespect (Harper, Wiens & Matarazzo, 1978, at 188). Female bargainers are also inclined to behave more cooperatively than male negotiators (Rubin & Brown, 1975, at 172). They tend to establish more cooperative seating arrangements and have a closer, more congenial interaction distance (Harper, Wiens & Matarazzo, 1978, at 255, 278).

People from diverse cultural backgrounds bring certain stereotypical baggage to their initial interactions with persons who are different from themselves (Sammataro, 1999, at 555). It is amazing how many common characteristics are attributed by numerous persons to all individuals of a particular race, gender, age, or culture. Professor Rich's study of the perceptions of UCLA undergraduate students in the early 1970's graphically demonstrated how closely Anglos and Chicanos stereotyped African-Americans, Anglos and African-Americans stereotyped Chicanos, and African-Americans and Chicanos stereotyped Anglos (Rich, 1974, at 51–62). Males similarly stereotype females and vice versa (Edwards & White, 1977, at 363–70).

Individuals who commence a negotiation with someone of a different race, gender, age, or culture should understand the need to establish a trusting and cooperative relationship before serious substantive discussions begin. This approach will help to create a cooperative environment that should significantly enhance the likelihood of a mutually beneficial transaction. The preliminary stage of their interaction may be used to generate a modicum of rapport (Davidson & Greenhalgh, 1999, at 19–21). Negotiators must try to minimize the counterproductive stereotypes they may consciously or even subconsciously harbor toward persons of their opponent's race, gender, age, or culture. If they anticipate a difficult interaction as a result of such frequently irrational preconceptions, they are likely to precipitate a self-fulfilling prophecy. They must also endeavor to understand any seemingly illogical reactions their opponent may initially exhibit toward them as a result of that person's stereotypical impressions of them.

Nonminority negotiators who have rarely been the victims of openly discriminatory behavior must also understand that minority group members who have frequently been adversely affected by discriminatory treatment may misinterpret negative bargaining tactics. For example, if two people from the same ethnic background had an unpleasant interaction, it is unlikely that one would suspect the other of discriminatory motives. On the other hand, if a minority group member were treated ungraciously by a nonminority opponent, the former might well interpret this treatment as ethnically-related even when the nonminority participant would have treated a nonminority adversary in a similar manner.

If the first contact negotiators have with opponents indicates that those persons are expecting highly competitive or unpleasant transactions, they should not hesitate to employ "attitudinal bargaining" to disabuse their opponents of this predilection. They should create environments that are physically and psychologically cooperative. They can sit adjacent to, instead of directly across from, opposing counsel. A warm handshake and an open posture can further diminish the combative atmosphere. In a few instances, it may even be necessary to directly broach the subject of negative stereotyping, since this may be the most efficacious manner of defusing the impact of these feelings (Schneider, 1994, at 112-13).

People who participate in bargaining transactions should recognize that the specific circumstances and unique personal traits of the individual negotiators — rather than generalized beliefs regarding ethnic, gender, age, or cultural characteristics — determine the way in which each interaction evolves. Each opponent has to be evaluated and dealt with differently. Is he or she a cooperative/problem-solving, a competitive/adversarial, or a compet-itive/ problem-solving bargainer? Does the other side possess greater, equal, or less bargaining power concerning the issues to be addressed? What negotiating techniques has that individual decided to employ, and what is the most effective way to counter those tactics? As the instant transaction unfolds, strategic changes will have to be made to respond to unanticipated disclosures or changed circumstances.

When negotiators find themselves attributing certain characteristics to their opponents, they must carefully determine whether those attributes are based on specific information pertaining to their particular opponents or to vague generalizations regarding people of their race, gender, age, or culture. If persons only bargained with individuals of the same race, gender, age, and culture, they would quickly realize how different we all are. Some opponents behave cooperatively, while others act in a competitive manner. Some are congenial, while others are unpleasant. Some exhibit win-lose tendencies, while others evidence win-win attitudes. Techniques that would be effective against some opponents would be ineffective against others.

During the years we have taught negotiating skills to law students, we have observed no differences with respect to the results achieved by members of different ethnic groups. Several years ago, one of us reviewed the data from the five years (1977–1982) he had taught culturally-diverse classes at the University of California, Davis. The average results achieved by minority students was compared with the average results attained by nonminority students. African-American, Asian, and Chicano students had to be grouped together, because of the insufficient number of particular ethnic groups to make statistically meaningful comparisons on a more discrete basis. No statistically significant differences between the results achieved by minority and nonminority participants were found with respect to the average results attained or the standard deviations (Craver, 1990, at 17 n.81). A more recent evaluation of nine years of data comparing the negotiation results achieved by Caucasian and African-American students at George Washington University similarly found no statistically significant differences (Craver, 2001). We are thus confident that negotiation skill is truly a reflection of individual capability that is not influenced by one's ethnic characteristics.

a.   Conflicting Inter-Cultural Norms

Verbal and nonverbal signals may have different meanings for people from diverse cultural backgrounds. For instance, punctuality is more important to the average American than it is to people from other cultures (Hall, 1973, at 140-61). It would normally be considered unacceptable for an American to arrive more than five or ten minutes late for a business appointment, while a thirty or forty-five minute delay would not be uncommon in various Latin American countries. Americans often separate business and social discussions, while their counterparts in other areas of the world might feel entirely comfortable conducting business talks during social functions.

Spatial and conversational distances vary greatly among persons from different cultures (Hall, 1973, at 162-85). In North America, it is normally "proper" for interactants who are not close friends to remain at least two feet apart, particularly during formal business conversations. Even though that spatial separation may shrink somewhat in social settings, Americans rarely feel comfortable with the eight-to twelve-inch distances indigenous to some other cultures. This explains why Americans often move backward when people from close-distance cultures "invade" their neutral space. They tend to feel intimidated by such close interactions. This need for more expansive social distance often causes Americans to be viewed by people from other cultures as cold, withdrawn, or disinterested (Harper, Wiens & Matarazzo, 1978, at 249).

Many American negotiators are not afraid to employ overt power techniques to advance their bargaining interests. In other cultures, such as Japan or China, open displays of power are considered crude and unacceptable. Analogous conflicts are encountered with respect to the use of openly aggressive behavior. Since Americans have a reputation for being overly aggressive people, they should attempt to employ less threatening tactics when they interact with persons from less aggressive cultures. They need to remember that one can be forceful without being pushy.

Individuals from disparate socio-economic backgrounds may find it difficult to understand each other's hopes and fears. People from upper-middle class and upper class homes tend to accept the delayed gratification concept without question, based upon the success that has been achieved by their educated ancestors. Persons from lower class families, however, are less likely to postpone current gratification for the nebulous hope of attaining future returns. Negotiators interacting with members of the former group may find it easy to explain the future benefits to be derived from a particular transaction. When dealing with members of the latter group, they may have to emphasize the short-term benefits over the long-term possibilities if they wish to achieve a present agreement.

People from lower socio-economic backgrounds frequently find it traumatic and intimidating when they initially interact with upper class members in the gilded environments typically inhabited by advantaged persons. To counteract this factor, individuals representing lower socio-economic clients may wish to employ a tactic perfected during the 1960's by the late activist Saul Alinsky. He realized that the rich and powerful feel just as uncomfortable in the ghettos occupied by the indigent as the latter group members experience in upper class neighborhoods. He thus invited societal power brokers to negotiate with the economically disadvantaged in the areas inhabited by the latter groups. For the first time, many prominent persons began to understand the tragic plight of the poverty-stricken. They felt great guilt and discomfort in the pathetic residential areas occupied by the poor, and they were adroitly induced to make significant concessions. Negotiators who think they may embarrass their wealthy adversaries by bringing them into the environments inhabited by their disenfranchised clients should not hesitate to use this technique.

b.   Impact of Gender-Related Stereotypes

Gender-based stereotypes continue to cause some lawyers great difficulty when they interact with attorneys of the opposite sex (*see generally* Kolb & Williams, 2000, 2003; Kolb, 2000). Males frequently expect females to behave like "ladies" during their interactions. Overt aggressiveness that would be viewed as vigorous advocacy when employed by men may be characterized as offensive and threatening when used by women (Carli, 2001, at 731–33; Tannen, 1994, at 40–41). This is particularly true when the female in question employs foul language and a loud voice. Male negotiators who would immediately counter these tactics by another man with a quid pro quo response often find it hard to adopt a retaliatory approach against a "lady." When they permit such an irrelevant factor to influence and limit their use of responsive weapons, they provide their female opponents with an inherent bargaining advantage. Men who are similarly unwilling to act as competitively toward female adversaries as they would vis-a-vis male adversaries give further leverage to their female opponents.

Some male negotiators attempt to obtain a psychological advantage against aggressive female bargainers by casting aspersions upon the femininity of those individuals. They hope to embarrass those participants and make them feel self-conscious with respect to the approach they are using. Female negotiators should never allow adversaries to employ this tactic successfully. They have the right to use any technique they think appropriate regardless of the gender-based stereotypes they may contradict. To male attorneys who raise specious objections to their otherwise proper conduct, they may reply that they do not wish to be viewed as "ladies," but merely as legal advocates involved in an interaction in which one's gender is irrelevant.

Female negotiators who find that gender-based beliefs may be negatively affecting their interactions may wish to directly broach the subject of negative stereotyping, since this may be the most effective manner of dealing with the influence of these feelings (Schneider, 1994, at 112-13). They may ask opponents if they find it difficult to negotiate with women. While most male adversaries will quickly deny such beliefs, they are likely to internally reevaluate their treatment of female opponents. Once both sides acknowledge — internally or externally — the possible impact of stereotypical beliefs, they can try to avoid group generalizations and focus on the particular individuals with whom they must currently interact.

Male attorneys occasionally make the mistake of assuming that female opponents do not engage in as many negotiating "games" as male adversaries. Even many women erroneously assume that other females are unlikely to employ the Machiavellian tactics stereotypically attributed to members of the competitive male culture. Men *and* women who expect their female adversaries to behave in a less disingenuous and more cooperative manner often ignore the reality of their interactions and accord a significant bargaining advantage to women who are in fact willing to employ manipulative tactics.

Empirical studies indicate that male and female subjects do not behave identically in competitive settings. Females tend to be initially more trusting and trustworthy than their male cohorts, but they are generally less willing to forgive violations of their trust than are males (Miller & Miller, 2002, at 42–43; Rubin & Brown, 1975, at 171-73). When men prevaricate, it is frequently done on a self-oriented basis intended to enhance their own reputations (braggadocio), while when women dissemble, it is more often done in an other-oriented basis to make other people feel better (*e.g.*, "I love your new outfit"; "you made a great presentation") (DePaulo, et al., 1996, at 986-87; *see also* Feldman, Forrest & Happ, 2002). Persons interacting with female negotiators who exhibit verbal and nonverbal signals consistent with these generalities should realize that they may be able to establish a trusting and cooperative relationship with them — so long as they do not commit unacceptable transgressions.

One observer has suggested that "women are more likely [than men] to avoid competitive situations, less likely to acknowledge competitive wishes, and not likely to do as well in competition." (Stiver, 1983, at 5; *see* Babcock & Laschever, 2003, at 102–03) Many women are apprehensive regarding the negative consequences they associate with competitive achievement, fearing that competitive success will alienate them from others (Gilligan, 1982, at 14-15). Some males candidly admit that they are particularly embarrassed when women opponents obtain extremely beneficial results from them (Miller & Miller, 2002, at 132). Some female students are more critical of women who attain exceptional bargaining results than they are of men who achieve equally advantageous terms (Burton, et al., 1991, at 233).

Males tend to exude more confidence than females in performance-oriented settings (Sax, 2005, at 43). Even when minimally prepared, men think they can "wing it" and get through successfully (Goleman, 1998, at 7). On the other hand, no matter how well prepared women are, they tend to feel unprepared (Evans, 2000, at 84–85, 90–92; McIntosh, 1985). We occasionally observe this distinction with our ADR students who have performed well on negotiation exercises. The successful males think they can achieve beneficial results in any setting, while the successful females continue to express doubts about their own capabilities.

Male confidence may explain why men like to negotiate more than women, and why they tend to seek more beneficial results when they negotiate than their female cohorts (Babcock & Laschever, 2003, at 130–35, 140–41). Men tend to feel more comfortable in risk-taking situations than women (*Id.* at 138). When they bargain, males tend to use more forceful language and exhibit more dominant nonverbal signals (*e.g.*, intense eye contact and louder voices) than females (*Id.* at 105). These gender differences may help to explain why women experience greater anxiety when they have to negotiate than men (*Id.* at 113–14). On the other hand, while men tend to be more win-lose oriented, women tend to be more win-win oriented, making it easier for them to use cooperative bargaining to expand the overall pie and improve the results achieved by both sides (*Id.* at 164–72).

These competitive differences may be attributable to the different acculturation process for boys and girls (Menkel-Meadow, 2000, at 362–64). Many parents continue to be more protective of their daughters than of their sons (Babcock & Laschever, 2003, at 30–31; Marone, 1992, at 42–45). Most boys are exposed to competitive situations at an early age (Tannen, 1990, at 43–47; Gilligan, 1982, at 9). They have been encouraged to participate in little league baseball, basketball, football, soccer, and other competitive athletic endeavors. These activities introduce boys to the "thrill of victory and the agony of defeat" during their formative years (Harragan, 1977, at 75–78, 282). "Traditional girls' games like jump rope and hopscotch are turn-taking games, where competition is indirect since one person's success does not necessarily signify another's failure." (Gilligan, 1982, at 10.) While directly competitive games teach boys how to resolve the disputes that inevitably arise, girls are less likely to have the opportunity to learn those dispute resolution skills (Babcock & Laschever, 2003, at 34–35). By adulthood, men are thus more likely to have become accustomed to the rigors of overt competition. While it is true that little league and interscholastic sports for women have become more competitive in recent years, most continue to be less overtly competitive than corresponding male athletic endeavors (Evans, 2000, at 80). As a result, males are more accepting of the competitive desire of opponents to beat them, and they do not view overtly competitive situations in personal terms. Women, on the other hand, who have not been raised to appreciate ritual battles, tend to view competitive efforts by opponents as personally offensive (Tannen, 1994, at 58–59).

The physical appearance of male and female bargainers may influence the manner in which they are perceived by others (Cash & Janda, 1984, at 46–52). Empirical studies have found that attractive men are likely to be considered more competent than their less attractive male cohorts with respect to their ability to think logically and analytically. Contrary results have been obtained for female subjects, with less attractive women being viewed as more cerebral than their more attractive female colleagues. This stereotypical view of attractive women is frequently based on the theory that good-looking females must not have received the same intellectual capacities as their less attractive cohorts. If this assumption were correct, one would expect attractive males to be similarly disadvantaged with respect to their cerebral capabilities. Women with a "less feminine" appearance ("tailored clothes with a jacket, subtle make-up, and either short hair or hair swept away from the face") are similarly taken more seriously by others and viewed as more assertive, more logical, and less emotional in critical situations — particularly by male respondents — than are women with a "more feminine" appearance (Cash & Janda, 1984, at 46–52).

Other gender-based stereotypes affect the way in which men and women interact in negotiation settings. Males are expected to be more rational and objective, while females are supposed to be more concerned with the preservation of relationships (Pines, Gat & Tal, 2002, at 25, 39; Kray, Thompson & Galinsky, 2001, at 944; Gilligan, 1982). Men tend to define themselves by their achievements, while women tend to define themselves by their relationships (Babcock & Laschever, 2003, at 117). Male negotiators are expected to be dominant and overtly competitive, with women bargainers expected to be passive and accommodating (Babcock & Laschever, 2003, at 62–63, 75; Maccoby & Jacklin, 1974, at 228, 234). In competitive bargaining situations, participants possessing stereotypically male traits might reasonably be expected to outperform participants possessing stereotypically female traits (Kray, Thompson & Galinsky, 2001, at 946). When men and women interact, men tend to speak for longer periods and to interrupt more frequently than women (Deaux, 1976, at 60). If females speak half of the time, they tend to be perceived by the male participants as domineering. This masculine tendency to dominate male-female interactions could provide men with an advantage during negotiations by enabling them to control the discussions.

During interpersonal transactions, men are more likely than women to employ "highly intensive language" to persuade others, and they tend to be more effective using this approach (Burgoon, Dillard & Doran, 1983, at 284, 292). Women, on the other hand, are more inclined to use less intense language during persuasive encounters, and they are usually more effective behaving in that manner. Professor Deborah Tannen has noted that "women are more likely to downplay their certainty [and] men more likely to downplay their doubts," because young girls are taught to temper what they say to avoid the appearance of aggressiveness (Tannen, 1994. at 35–36). For similar reasons, females tend to employ language containing more disclaimers ("I think"; "you know") than their male cohorts (Tannen, 1990, at 227–228; Smeltzer & Watson, 1986, at 78), causing women to be perceived as less forceful. Since women tend to have more acute hearing than men, they often use softer voices than men when interacting with others, and they are more likely than men to view slightly raised voices as aggressive (Sax, 2005, at 18).

Formal education diminishes the presence of gender-based verbal differences. When individuals receive specific training, male-female communication distinctions are largely eliminated (Burrell, Donohue & Allen, 1988, at 453). This factor would explain why male and female lawyers tend to employ similar language when endeavoring to persuade others. Nonetheless, even when women use the identical language as men, they are often perceived as being less influential (Tannen, 1990, at 228; Burrell, Donhoue & Allen, 1988, at 463). This gender-based factor is offset, however, by the fact that women continue to be more sensitive to verbal leaks and nonverbal signals than their male cohorts (Sax, 2005, at 18-19; Miller & Miller, 2002, at 60–61; Hall, 1984, at 15–17; Henley, 1977, at 13–15).

There are indications that males and females differ with respect to their views of appropriate bargaining outcomes. Women tend to believe in "equal" exchanges, while men tend to expect "equitable" distributions (Lewicki, et al., 1994, at 330). These predispositional differences may induce female negotiators to accept equal results despite their possession of greater relative bargaining strength, while male bargainers seek equitable exchanges that reflect power imbalances. Their egalitarian propensity could disadvantage women who hesitate to use favorable power imbalances to obtain more beneficial results for their sides.

Professor Deaux succinctly noted that behavioral predictions based on stereotypical beliefs regarding men and women are likely to be of questionable validity in most settings.

> [D]espite the persistence of stereotypes, the studies of social behavior suggest that there are relatively few characteristics in which men and women consistently differ. Men and women both seem to be capable of being aggressive, helpful, and alternately cooperative and competitive. In other words, there is little evidence that the nature of women and men is so inherently different that we are justified in making stereotyped generalizations. [Deaux, 1976, at 144].

In light of the fact that most law students are relatively competitive persons who have received extensive legal training, one would certainly expect the traditionally found gender-based differences to be of minimal significance.

Several years ago, one of us compared the results achieved over fifteen years by male and female students on Legal Negotiating class exercises. There was not a single year for which the average results achieved by men was statistically different from the results attained by women at the 0.05 level of significance (Craver, 1990, at 12–16 & Table 1). Some people suggested that while the male and female averages might be the same, the individual results might be different with stereotypically competitive males obtaining extremely good or bad results and with stereotypically cooperative females being clustered around the mean. Had the male results been more skewed, the male standard deviations would have been higher than the female standard deviations. The data negated this notion, since the male and female standard deviations were approximately equal throughout the fifteen-year period. In 1999, the similar statistical comparisons were made covering thirteen years of Legal Negotiation course exercises at George Washington University, with no statistically meaningful differences being found with respect to the negotiation results achieved by male and female students (Craver & Barnes, 1999, at 339-44; see also Stuhlmacher & Walters, 1999).

Male negotiators who take female opponents less seriously than they take male adversaries based upon gender-based stereotypes provide their female adversaries with an inherent advantage. Since they do not expect highly competitive or manipulative behavior from women, they are less likely to discern and effectively counter the use of these tactics by female opponents. While women bargainers may understandably be offended by such patronizing attitudes, there is an easy way to get even with these male troglodytes. They should clean them out! We continue to be amazed by the number of proficient female negotiators who accomplish this objective against unsuspecting male opponents.

One other gender-based phenomenon that unfairly affects women should be noted. When men are successful, their performance is usually attributed to intrinsic factors such as intelligence and hard work (Deaux, 1976, at 30–32, 41). When women are successful, however, their achievements are most often attributed to extrinsic variables such as luck or the actions of others. This phenomenon enhances male self-confidence by according them personal credit for their accomplishments, and it undermines female self-confidence by depriving them of personal credit for their achievements. We have personally noticed that even women are inclined to devalue the accomplishments of other females. When teachers and students evaluate the negotiation success of other students, they should be cognizant of this factor and make sure they give females as much credit for their achievements as they grant to equally accomplished males.

Chapter 3

THE NEGOTIATION STAGES

The negotiation process can be logically divided into six distinct stages. These are present in almost all negotiations. Every bargaining interaction begins with the Preparation Stage, as each party attempts to ascertain the pertinent factual, legal, economic, and political information. Each participant establishes a "resistance point" or "bottom line," as well as a more generous "goal." Most of the preparation is carried out by each side alone with minimal interaction with the other prospective participants. Proficient bargainers are always thoroughly prepared, in recognition of the fact that knowledge represents power. Furthermore, individuals who are well-prepared tend to exude an inner confidence in their positions that may induce less diligent opponents to doubt the strength of their own positions.

Once the Preparation Stage is finished, the parties begin direct negotiations — in person, over the telephone, or through the exchange of e-mail messages or written proposals. During the Preliminary Stage, the participants establish their professional identities and the tone for the impending interaction. This is a critical phase, because it creates a positive or a negative atmosphere for the discussions that are to follow. At the conclusion of the Preliminary Stage, the parties enter the Information Stage, as they attempt to obtain as much information as possible regarding each other's strengths and weaknesses. They endeavor to determine the areas of potential overlap and of potential conflict. In short, they want to decide what is available to be divided up and to begin defining the settlement range available to them.

Once the parties think they have discovered the items that may be shared by them and have ascertained the relative values of those items, they enter the Competitive/Distributive Stage. During this portion of the interaction, the participants begin to divide the different items among the interested parties. Throughout the Competitive/Distributive Stage, the negotiators endeavor to claim as many of the available items as possible. This is what renders this portion of the process highly competitive.

Near the end of the Competitive/Distributive Stage, successful negotiators begin to realize that an overall agreement is on the immediate horizon. This is when they enter the most delicate part of the negotiation process — the Closing Stage. Adroit bargainers are careful to keep the interaction moving inexorably toward a mutual accord, but they appreciate the need for continued patience. They recognize that the party that attempts to resolve the remaining issues too quickly is likely to concede more than it should.

By the conclusion of the Closing Stage, most parties have achieved mutual accords. Careless negotiators conclude their discussions at this point and assign drafting of the final terms to an appropriate participant. They forget the fact that in transactions in which money is not the sole item, there is a final stage — the Cooperative or Integrative Stage — that may be used to simultaneously improve the circumstances of both parties. Proficient negotiators realize that the frequent use of disingenuous tactics during competitive interactions may have caused certain items to be assigned to the party that overstated the interest it had in those terms. During the Cooperative Stage, the participants attempt to expand the pie being divided and discern additional exchanges that may concurrently improve their respective levels of satisfaction. It is only through the Cooperative Stage that the parties can guarantee the most efficient distribution of the items available to them.

A. THE PREPARATION STAGE (ESTABLISHING GOALS AND LIMITS)

> If you know the enemy and know yourself, you need not fear the result of a hundred battles. If you know yourself but not the enemy, for every victory gained you will also suffer a defeat. If you know neither the enemy nor yourself, you will succumb in every battle. [Sun Tzu, 1983, at 18.]

People who carefully prepare for a negotiation generally achieve more beneficial results than those who do not (Reardon, 2004, at 32–60; Latz, 2004, at 42). Even though this assertion might seem obvious, it is amazing how many individuals enter negotiations either unprepared or only partially prepared. When the items in dispute are relatively insignificant and the negotiator has already established a firm bottom line — e.g., a nuisance value case where the insurance company representative is willing to offer up to a set amount without going higher — pre-negotiation preparation may not be critical. The person's previous experience with this type of case coupled with his or her establishment of a definite limit will usually provide the needed guidelines. In more complex and more substantial situations, however, there is rarely any substitute for prudent forethought.

The direct correlation between the degree of preparation and negotiation outcome is based upon the fact that knowledge constitutes power in the bargaining context (Young, 1975, at 10–11). Thoroughly prepared negotiators tend to exude greater confidence in their positions than do less prepared advocates. The confidence possessed by more prepared negotiators undermines the self-assurance of their less prepared opponents and causes those individuals to question the certitude of the positions they are asserting. As the under-prepared participants subconsciously defer to the greater certainty exhibited by their more knowledgeable adversaries, they generally make more frequent and more substantial concessions.

1. CLIENT PREPARATION

When it becomes clear that legal representatives must negotiate on behalf of clients, they should take several preliminary steps. They should elicit all of the pertinent factual information possessed by the clients (*see generally* Gifford, 1987). They must also determine what their clients really hope to achieve through legal representation. These individuals frequently do not disclose their true underlying interests and objectives when they are merely asked what they expect to obtain. They only consider options they think attorneys can obtain for them, and they often fail to contemplate alternatives that may actually be available. It is thus necessary to thoroughly probe client objectives, and listen carefully to their responses (Riskin, 2002, at 649–50; Ordover & Doneff, 2002, at 32–33).

Persons who indicate a desire to purchase or lease particular commercial property may suggest that they are only interested in that specific location. When these individuals are asked probing questions regarding their intended use, it often becomes apparent that alternative locations may be equally acceptable. This significantly enhances their bargaining power, by providing them with other options if the immediate negotiations do not progress satisfactorily. Business clients who are contemplating the investment of resources in other firms must be asked about their ultimate objectives. Are they willing to invest their assets in a single venture, or would they prefer to diversify their holdings? Are they willing to risk their principal in an effort to achieve a higher return, or would they prefer a less generous return on an investment that would be likely to retain its overall value?

Clients who preliminarily appear to be interested in obtaining only monetary relief through the legal process may have similarly failed to consider alternative solutions to their underlying difficulties. For example, defamed persons may talk exclusively in terms of monetary objectives, when they would really prefer retractions and public apologies. Individuals contemplating legal action against relatives or neighbors may be happier with apologies and preserved relationships. Permanently injured personal injury clients may concentrate on mere dollar amounts, when they would be equally, or even more, satisfied with structured settlements that would guarantee them lifetime care. A business seller may accept future cash payments, shares of stock in the purchasing firm, or in-kind payments in the form of goods or services provided by the buyer. Attorneys who fail to ascertain the actual underlying interests and needs of their clients may well ignore options that might enhance their bargaining strength (Fisher & Ury, 1981, at 101–11). As a result, they may not fully appreciate the external options available to their clients if no mutual accords are achieved. They may thus fail to represent the interests of their respective clients as effectively as they could if they possessed all of the relevant information.

As lawyers explore client needs and interests, they must attempt to ascertain the degree to which their clients want particular items. Most legal representatives either formally or informally divide client goals into three basic categories: (1) essential; (2) important; and (3) desirable (Cohen, 2003, at 127–28). "Essential" items include objectives the clients must obtain if agreements are to be successfully achieved. "Important" goals concern things the clients would very much like to acquire, but which they would forego if the "essential" terms were resolved in a satisfactory manner. "Desirable" needs involve items of secondary value that the clients would be pleased to obtain, but would be willing to exchange for more important terms.

Attorneys should try to determine how much clients value different levels of attainment for *each* relevant item to be negotiated (Raiffa, 2003, at 129–47). For example, money may be an "essential" issue for a person who has sustained serious injuries in an automobile accident. The client may consider the first $200,000 critical, both to make up for lost earnings and to pay off unpaid medical bills and increased credit card debt. While the client would like to obtain more than $200,000, she may only consider amounts above $200,000 "important," rather than "essential" (Brown, 1997, at 1664, 1669–70). If the client had to choose between a firm offer of $215,000 and a possible loss at trial, she would accept the definitive amount. On the other hand, she would most likely reject an offer of $175,000, since this figure would not satisfy her minimal needs. A firm purchasing land for a new facility may require a minimum of ten acres, but would like to get fifteen or twenty to allow for future expansion. If attorneys representing these parties can appreciate the degree to which each client values different amounts of particular commodities, they can understand how much of the different items they must obtain and the degree to which greater amounts of those items may be traded for other "essential" terms.

Lawyers must also ascertain the relative values of the different items to be negotiated within each broad category. Does the client value Item A twice as much as Item B, or two-thirds as much? How does Item C compare to items A and B? It helps to mentally assign point values for the various items to enable legal representatives to understand how they can maximize overall client satisfaction. Different software programs have been developed to induce parties preparing to negotiate to explore the various issues and to evaluate the degree of personal interest associated with each (Lodder & Zeleznikow, 2005, at 310–12). Advocates must use these relative client preferences to appreciate the items they must try to achieve and the ones that may be traded for other more highly valued terms.

When determining client needs and interests, attorneys should avoid substituting their values for those of their clients (Gifford, 1987, at 819–21). If clients are more or less risk-averse than their lawyers, the client preferences should be respected. Legal representatives should be hesitant to tell clients they are wrong when they articulate preferences their attorneys find strange. While it is entirely appropriate for lawyers to probe client objectives to be certain the clients comprehend the alternatives and truly desire what they have requested, it is inappropriate for practitioners to disregard client interests they do not agree with.

Once attorneys obtain a basic understanding of particular client problems, they should educate those clients concerning the manner in which the representational process is likely to unfold. Clients should be told what their legal advocates hope to achieve. This should be done with appropriate circumspection, because all of the operative factual circumstances may not yet be known and it is counterproductive to elevate client expectations unnecessarily. When negotiators raise client expectations unduly during the preliminary portion of the bargaining process, the clients may be dissatisfied with ultimate agreements they would have initially been pleased to achieve.

Clients should be acquainted with the procedural phases that are likely to develop. Even when clients appear to desire litigation to vindicate their rights, their legal advocates should at least briefly mention the likelihood of settlement discussions. While angry clients may initially reject the possibility of compromise, it is beneficial to plant this idea in their heads at an early date. As they begin to appreciate the financial and emotional costs of litigation, they are likely to become more receptive to negotiated solutions.

The negotiation process should be briefly explained, so that the clients will understand the anticipated time-frame and the usual need for numerous preliminary and substantive contacts with opposing counsel before the consummation of final accords. As the process evolves, clients should be regularly informed of bargaining developments, even if they are not immediately significant, to apprise them of the fact their lawyers are continuing to be concerned with their circumstances. This practice makes it easier for clients to understand and appreciate the legal services being provided, and it enhances the likelihood that they will appreciate the value of ultimately recommended agreements.

Some clients express a desire to participate personally in the negotiations affecting their interests. It is generally advisable to preclude their participatory role. During preliminary discussions with the opposing party, it may be cathartic for that party to cast some aspersions upon the other lawyer's client regarding the unfortunate circumstances that have precipitated the need for the current settlement talks. This is especially likely with respect to conflicts of an emotional nature — e.g., marital or partnership dissolutions, neighborhood disputes, or wrongful termination claims. So long as the comments being expressed are not intemperate, it may be beneficial to permit the other party to use this technique to vent pent-up animosity that might otherwise disrupt subsequent negotiations. If clients were present during these emotional disclosures, either they would react adversely or their counsel would feel compelled to intervene before the cathartic process had been completed.

Clients who are present during negotiating sessions frequently divulge — either verbally or through nonverbal signals — information their counsel did not intend to disclose. Their presence may also preclude the use of negotiating techniques that their counsel may wish to employ (Ilich, 1973, at 26–27). For example, it is easy to rely upon one side's "limited authority" when the client is absent. It is even possible to use a "Mutt and Jeff" reasonable attorney/ unreasonable client approach, by casting the missing client in the role of the unyielding party who requires more concessions if a mutual accord is to be achieved. It should also be recognized that some attorneys may find it difficult or even embarrassing to use these or other effective negotiating tactics if they were forced to do so in front of their respective clients (Rubin & Brown, 1975, at 127-28).

2. LAWYER PREPARATION

Once lawyers have ascertained the pertinent factual circumstances and underlying client interests, they must become thoroughly acquainted with the applicable legal doctrines. They must develop cogent theories that support their positions and anticipate the counter-arguments that are likely to be made by opposing counsel. This latter exercise is especially important, because negotiators who are confronted by anticipated contentions are unlikely to have their confidence undermined by those claims. On the other hand, if unexpected concepts are advanced, these may cause unprepared negotiators to lose confidence in their positions and induce them to make unintended concessions.

Once attorneys have become familiar with the relevant factual and legal matters affecting their own side, they must determine what Fisher and Ury call their BATNA — Best Alternative to a Negotiated Agreement (Fisher & Ury, 1981, at 101-11). This establishes their *bottom line*. Lawyers should not enter into agreements that are worse than what would happen if no accords were achieved. Such agreements are worse than nonsettlements (Korobkin, 2000, at 1797; LePoole, 1991, at 60–61).

a. Determining Expected Value of Interaction

Negotiators who do not initially understand the consequences of nonsettlements must take the time to develop their nonsettlement options. They need to be imaginative and bold. For example, when they believe that only one specific commercial property would satisfy client needs, they must reassess the situation. They have to probe underlying client needs and interests to determine what is really required. They must next endeavor to locate other properties that might provide the client with what is needed. During this process, they might even discover a better property or a reasonably acceptable location that can be acquired or leased for less money. Even if no equivalent alternatives are discerned, the information gathered through this process directly defines the parameters for the primary negotiation. Through the judicious disclosure of information concerning their external options to opposing counsel, these bargainers can more effectively strive to obtain optimal terms for their client.

When the alternative to a negotiated resolution is an administrative or judicial proceeding, lawyers must carefully assess the likely outcome of the adjudication process. Not only must they review the pertinent factual circumstances and legal doctrines, they must also evaluate such subjective factors as witness credibility and the tribunal sympathy that may be accorded the different parties involved. Even when it appears that their client should theoretically prevail, if the adjudicator provides their sympathetic opponent with something, they must consider this possibility. When they attempt to assess the likely trial result, they must not only predict which party is likely to prevail with what degree of probability (e.g., 60% or 70% likelihood), but also the expected result of such a judgment. Thus if they were to conclude that their opponent would probably win 60% of the time with an expected award of $100,000, the anticipated adjudicated value of the case would be $60,000 ($100,000 $\times$ 0.6).

The monetary and nonmonetary transactional costs associated with settlement and nonsettlement must be similarly considered. It is obvious that a negotiated agreement avoids many of the costs of trial. It must be remembered that such a result also avoids the psychological trauma associated with litigation and provides a definitive result at a specific time. These factors are particularly important to risk-averse clients. Negotiators must also recognize that these factors affect their opponents. They must not ignore these considerations when they estimate the nonsettlement alternatives available to the other side.

Litigants must also appreciate the fact that projected transaction costs should be *subtracted from* the anticipated plaintiff's trial result, since these costs will diminish the value of any plaintiff verdict, and be *added to* the defendant's expected result, since the defendant will incur these expenses no matter who prevails at trial. This seemingly contradictory impact of transaction costs greatly encourages both sides to settle disputes. Once the plaintiff realizes the degree to which transaction costs will decrease any award obtained and the defendant recognizes how much the transaction costs will enlarge its ultimate liability, the distance between their overall positions narrows substantially.

Attorneys must employ formal and informal discovery techniques to obtain the relevant information possessed by opposing parties. They must endeavor to understand the underlying needs and interests of their adversaries, since this will enable them to explore proposals that may prove beneficial to both sides. They must also attempt to determine the options available to *opposing clients* if no mutual accords are achieved through the present negotiations (Korobkin, 2000, at 1797–99). What is their BATNA? These opponent alternatives directly affect the power balance between the parties and the likelihood of an agreement. If the other side's nonsettlement alternatives are worse than this party's external options, this side possesses greater bargaining power. The cost of disagreement to this side is less onerous than the cost of nonconcurrence to the other participant. In addition, if legal representatives do not ultimately offer adversaries terms that are preferable to those parties' nonsettlement options, these negotiators will be unlikely to produce mutually beneficial results.

Negotiators must similarly attempt to understand the strengths and weaknesses possessed by their own clients and by their adversaries. During this crucial process, they must try to avoid the tendency of advocates to overestimate their own weaknesses and to underestimate the weaknesses of their opponents. Since lawyers are intimately familiar with their own client situations, they tend to recognize and amplify their areas of vulnerability. They simultaneously assume — usually incorrectly — that opposing counsel possess the same information as they do regarding these matters. They ignore the fact that they have successfully concealed many of their weaknesses from their opponents. They must ask themselves what their adversaries are likely to know about their particular circumstances.

Negotiators must then review the limited information they have elicited from their opponents. Most are unaware of or overlook the negative factors affecting their adversaries, because those pieces of information have been carefully camouflaged. They thus assume the presence of unwarranted adversarial strength. To counter this tendency, negotiators must ask themselves what negative factors may influence their opponents that have not been disclosed during bargaining discussions.

Negotiators frequently make assumptions regarding opposing value systems that do not bear any resemblance to reality but do affect their assessment of opponent resolve. For example, counsel for large law firms often fear opponents represented by legal aid attorneys, since those clients do not have to pay for the legal services they receive. On the other hand, legal aid lawyers may be afraid of large law firms, because those entities are presumed to possess greater financial resources and lower per-attorney workloads. If the large firm lawyers or the legal aid attorneys were to understand the actual strengths they possess and recognize the trepidations affecting their opponents, they could significantly enhance their bargaining power!

Lawyers who represent wealthy corporate clients may be apprehensive with respect to opponents on the verge of bankruptcy, thinking that such parties would have nothing to lose by not resolving ongoing conflicts. When such lawyers are asked what would happen to the owners of the financially moribund firms if they actually went out of business, these initially fearful attorneys begin to recognize that their opponents' fear of failure and concomitant loss of employment would indeed exert pressure on those individuals. Counsel representing parties on the verge of bankruptcy must similarly change their focus from the seemingly powerful economic position of their corporate adversaries to the advantage that may be derived from even casual reference to their client's possible resort to bankruptcy.

Before negotiators accord their opponents more respect than they deserve, they should carefully reassess their own strengths and reconsider the actual pressures affecting their adversaries. They should also recognize that even the most professional bargainers find it difficult to place themselves truly in the shoes of opponents when they endeavor to comprehend their adversaries' circumstances. It is simply impossible for them to disregard their own value systems and to substitute those of their opponents. This phenomenon is obvious when plaintiff attorneys try to understand the view of defense lawyers, and when defense specialists attempt to appreciate the perspective of plaintiff representatives. In the corporate world, takeover advisors often find it difficult to comprehend the viewpoint of target firms, and vice versa.

b. Establishing High Aspiration Levels

It is vital for people preparing for bargaining transactions to understand that negotiators obtain higher and more satisfactory outcomes when they begin their interactions with substantial rather than moderate goals (Orr & Guthrie, 2006, at 624–25; Korobkin, 2002, at 4, 20–30; Dawson, 1995, at 3–10; Bazerman & Neale, 1992, at 28; Rubin & Brown, 1975, at 267). These objectives should always be more beneficial than their bottom lines if the negotiators hope to obtain optimal results (LePoole, 1991, at 62–63). When people initially request considerable terms, their opponents are frequently relieved by the seemingly "reasonable" compromise that is ultimately achieved, despite the fact the settlement provisions objectively favor the person who began with the excessive position (Pratkanis & Aronson, 1991, at 182). We have seen this postulate confirmed many times by our more proficient negotiating students who initially take the time to establish elevated aspiration levels before they commence negotiations with their opponents (Kramer, 2001, at 37; Shell, 1999, at 31-33; Brown, 1997; White & Neale, 1994, at 305-07; Karrass, 1970, at 17-18). If they are involved in multi-item exchanges, they carefully establish goals for *each* term, recognizing that if they fail to do so for every issue, they may readily forfeit the items for which they have no set aspirations (LePoole, 1991, at 59). They ascertain the pertinent factual circumstances and applicable legal principles. They also review their estimate of *opponent* nonsettlement options and try to visualize final offers that reasonably risk averse opponents would be unlikely to reject when facing the possibility of bargaining stalemates (Brown, 1997, at 1668–69). They then determine what would be the most generous results they could reasonably hope to obtain. They then *increase* their goals and formulate arguments that make their seemingly excessive objectives appear reasonable! They do not begin to interact with their adversaries until they have established specific goals for the issues to be negotiated and feel entirely comfortable with the beneficial positions they have developed. Less certain adversaries tend to defer to the definitive expectations of these more prepared participants (Brown, 1997, at 1675).

Proficient bargainers use their *aspiration levels* as their goals when they negotiate, and they work diligently to achieve those elevated objectives. They only focus on their bottom lines when they have to decide whether to continue interactions that appear to be going nowhere. On the other hand, less skilled negotiators tend to focus excessively on their *bottom lines* from the beginning of their interactions. Once they attain these minimal objectives, they relax, knowing that some agreement will be achieved and they no longer work as hard to surpass their bottom-line goals. Observant opponents can discern their relaxed states and become less generous with respect to substantive concessions. These bottom-line oriented negotiators thus settle for less generous final terms than their cohorts who continue to focus on their aspiration levels throughout their bargaining encounters (Shell, 1999, at 24–32).

When the previous opponents of successful negotiators are asked why they ultimately acquiesced to the substantial demands of those persons, the most common response indicates that they were persuaded by the overt confidence exhibited by those bargainers. The carefully prepared individuals seemed so certain that their positions were appropriate that their less successful adversaries decided they had to reevaluate their own circumstances. Since it is difficult to quantify the objective reasonableness of the positions being taken in most isolated negotiations and one's exuded confidence level can significantly influence the final outcome of these subjective interpersonal transactions, negotiators who can bolster their confidence through diligent aspiration-level preparation usually prevail over their less prepared adversaries (Kahneman & Tversky, 1995, at 49).

When individuals prepare for bargaining encounters, they must establish generous — but realistically attainable — objectives. If their goals are entirely unreasonable, they may discourage their opponents and induce those persons to think that mutually acceptable agreements are not achievable. Their effective narrowing of the settlement range available to the bargaining parties may thus increase the probability of nonsettlements (Korobkin, 2002, at 62–63). People who begin discussions with unduly elevated goals may encounter an additional problem. Once they get into the negotiations and realize that their objectives are unattainable, they lose this important touchstone and may move quickly toward their bottom lines. When bargainers realize that their preliminary aspirations are unrealistic, they need to take a short break to establish new goals they believe may be achieved. This gives them another benchmark well above their reservation points.

We occasionally have students or attorneys tell us that they must be effective bargainers since they always get what they want when they negotiate. These individuals are usually less effective negotiators. There is only one way to repeatedly obtain everything one wants when one negotiates — don't want anything! Such persons regularly get when they want and are the happiest of bargainers, until they work on identical exercises with other groups of negotiators and discover how modest their own returns are compared to other individuals representing the same side. Individuals with appropriately elevated bargaining objectives frequently come up short. They are disappointed by their inability to achieve everything they sought and think they did poorly. Effective negotiators must recognize the fact that they will often fail to achieve all of their lofty targets. This indicates that they began with beneficial aspirations. On the other hand, persons who always attain their modest goals must *raise their objectives*. They need to do so in ten to fifteen percent increments, because if they try to double or triple their goals, they will fail and return to their old habits. If they continue to attain their elevated goals, they should raise them again by ten to fifteen percent. They should continue this incremental process until they begin to come up short. Only then can the be confident that they are setting appropriately elevated objectives.

Many individuals are hesitant to formulate excessive opening offers for fear of offending their opponents. Proficient negotiators generally devise the most extreme positions they can rationally defend (Orr & Guthrie, 2006, at 624–25; Shell, 1999, at 160-61; Schoonmaker, 1989, at 141–42). They recognize that if their initial demands are truly excessive, they will feel embarrassed when they attempt to justify their positions and undermine their credibility. On the other hand, if they begin with inappropriately deflated demands, they immediately place themselves at a distinct disadvantage. When in doubt, negotiators should select more, rather than less, beneficial opening offers (Dawson, 2001, at 13–18; Korobkin & Guthrie, 1994; Kritzer, 1991, at 54–55). It is far easier to retreat from excessive positions than it is to counteract the negative impact of unrealistically low demands, and the offeror's subsequent concessions are likely to induce opponents to think they are getting better deals even when they are actually receiving less generous final terms (Cialdini, 1993, at 49–50).

Some individuals prefer to commence bargaining interactions with modest proposals they hope will generate reciprocal behavior by their opponents. Opening offers that are overly generous to adversaries are likely to have the opposite effect due to "anchoring" (Orr & Guthrie, 2006, at 599–611; Korobkin, 2002, at 30–36; Shell, 1999, at 161-62; Birke & Fox, 1999, at 40–41; Korobkin & Guthrie, 1994, at 138-42; Lewicki, et al., 1994, at 63). When people receive better offers than they anticipated, they question their own preliminary assessments and *increase their aspiration levels*. This anchoring effect disadvantages advocates who make unduly generous opening offers. On the other hand, bargainers who begin with parsimonious preliminary offers have the opposite anchoring impact. They cause a reduction in opponent expectations. By inducing adversaries to decrease their expectations, they enhance the likelihood they will obtain final terms that are beneficial to their own clients.

We have noticed a seemingly contradictory phenomenon that should be mentioned. The most successful negotiators frequently obtain terms that are less beneficial than they hoped to achieve — even though they are objectively good for their clients — and they are disappointed with their seemingly substandard performances. Less proficient bargainers, however, rarely experience these feelings of self-doubt. They generally attain their modest objectives, and are pleased with their results. It is only when they engage in exercises with other negotiators working on identical problems that they discover that their settlements are not as good as they thought. They do not obtain optimal terms for their clients, because they do not seek very much. These individuals finally appreciate the fact that bargainers can only achieve their initial goals in all transactions if they begin with deflated expectations. Practitioners who always attain their modest goals must raise their expectation levels. They should start by elevating their future objectives by 10 to 15 percent — if they try to double or triple their planned goals, they will fail and return to their former habits. They should continue this practice until they begin to periodically fall short of their targets. At that point, they can be confident they have learned to establish appropriate aspiration levels.

Skilled bargainers recognize the importance of opening offers, and they carefully formulate their initial proposals (Bartos in Zartman, 1978, at 20). After they establish appropriately elevated aspiration levels, they try to plan negotiating sequences likely to culminate in optimal results. To accomplish this task, they must necessarily make some predictions regarding the expected behavior of their opponents. They endeavor to place themselves in the shoes of their adversaries to determine what their opening positions and target areas are likely to be. Since bargainers tend to move inexorably toward the mid-point between their respective opening positions, proficient negotiators attempt to establish initial offers that, when averaged with the anticipated opening offer of their opponents, approximate their desired objectives (Dawson, 2001, at 18–20). This phenomenon explains why most negotiators prefer to have opposing counsel articulate their opening positions first. Once their adversaries have taken their firm positions, these individuals carefully adjust their initial proposals to keep their target points near the center of the opening offers.

On some occasions, preliminary opponent offers are more favorable than was anticipated. When this occurs, adroit negotiators should immediately reassess their initial positions *and* target areas in recognition of the fact that opposing counsel may be cognizant of circumstances of which they are not aware. Bargainers who fail to modify their behavior *and* goals in response to unexpectedly generous opponent offers may inappropriately deprive their clients of beneficial terms their adversaries apparently believe they deserve.

c. Articulating Principled Opening Offers

When negotiators formulate initial offers, they should simultaneously develop principled rationales they can employ to explain the exact manner in which they arrived at their positions (Ilich, 1992, at 112; Freund, 1992, at 122–23). For example, if attorneys representing a plaintiff in a personal injury case wish to initially demand $500,000, they should carefully substantiate, both factually and legally, the liability of the defendant. They must next calculate the medical expenses, likely future rehabilitation costs, prior and anticipated lost earnings, property loss, etc. and add an appropriate amount for pain and suffering. They should not merely request a lump sum (e.g., $350,000) for the pain and suffering, because such a general figure can be easily discounted. They should instead calculate the overall number of months or years for which pain and suffering relief would be appropriate, compute the number of days or even hours involved, and determine the amount per day or hour required to attain their target figure. The development of a specific figure supported by logical assertions demonstrates a reasoned commitment to that position (Krieger, et al., 1999, at 282-83).

Plaintiff lawyers should try to induce defendant attorneys to view the case from the plaintiff's perspective. They should develop a presentation that effectively asks their opponents how much *they* would expect if *they* were afflicted with injuries as extensive as those experienced by the plaintiff. To demonstrate the potential impact of this technique, we frequently ask students how much they would demand in exchange for our right to tear off their right arm. This question is usually greeted with incredulity. After giving them a brief period to contemplate monetary sums, we inform the students that they are members of a jury that must decide the amount to be awarded to our client — a person whose right arm was severed because of the clear negligence of the defendant. This inquiry is treated with complete respect, and the monetary figures they envision in response to this query are substantially lower than the figures they contemplated in response to our initial question.

When plaintiff advocates present their detailed computations to opposing counsel, their comprehensive approach allows them to accomplish several objectives. It provides a highly principled rationale that carefully documents the various elements of their overall figure, and it gives their position the aura of objective legitimacy. If their adversary asks how they could expect such a large amount, they can reiterate the detailed foundation for their demand. If they are fortunate, the opposing party may merely suggest that their estimates for future rehabilitation and/or pain and suffering are excessive. The other side is implicitly conceding liability and the need to compensate the plaintiff for the property loss, medical expenses, and lost earnings. It is also acknowledging the need to provide monetary relief for both of the controverted items. The disagreement merely involves the amount the defendant must pay for these components. This approach effectively allows plaintiff-attorneys to seize control of the negotiation agenda and to dictate the way in which the discussions proceed.

The lawyers representing the defendants in this scenario should be prepared to respond to the initial plaintiff demand in a similarly "principled" manner. Instead of succumbing to the blandishments of plaintiff attorneys, they should begin their own presentations with their own analysis of the liability issue. They need to indicate why their client has limited or nonexistent exposure. When they address the damage question, they must do so from a more realistic perspective reflecting their client's situation. They should not permit their feelings of sympathy for the plaintiff to distort their judgment (Birke & Fox, 1999, at 11). They must point out the typical awards for cases of this nature reported in recent issues of *Jury Verdict Reports* pertaining to their jurisdiction. They need to change the focus of discussion from the amount they would accept for the plaintiff's injuries to the amount representative jurors would be likely to award if the case were tried. They should then discount this figure to take account of the monetary and psychological costs of trial and to reflect the limited nature of defendant liability.

Plaintiff and defendant advocates should plan their respective negotiation strategies as if they were choreographing a ballet. They should create a visual image of a successful bargaining interaction in their mind (Hogan, 1996, at 31). How do they plan to move from their opening position to their ultimate goal? (Latz, 2004, at 146–48; Schoonmaker, 1989, at 43–48). Since they do not know the exact manner in which opposing counsel will respond to their initial entreaties, they must, of course, retain substantial flexibility. They should formulate primary and alternate plans that will enable them to effectively counter unexpected opponent gambits. As will be discussed more thoroughly in Section D, *infra*, they must devise anticipated concession patterns, with principled reasons being prepared to indicate why each particular concession is being made. They must be ready to modify their behavior and objectives as they receive new information from their opponents (Gulliver, 1979, at 100). They must be prepared to make "final offers" that will be sufficiently tempting to their opponents vis-a-vis the external options available to those parties, that they will hesitate to accept the risks associated with the nonsettlements alternatives.

Similar strategic planning must be undertaken by attorneys participating in transactional negotiations. For example, the offeror and the offeree in a corporate buyout should evaluate each component of the target firm's assets as they prepare their principled opening offers from the perspective of their respective clients. They must value the real property, the building and equipment, the inventory, the accounts receivable, patents and copyrights, good will, and other pertinent factors. The prospective buyer devalues these items as much as realistically defensible, with the seller doing the same in the opposite direction. This approach enables buyer and seller representatives to begin with specific opening offers that are rationally supportable and more persuasive than the use of round numbers. Individuals who commence bargaining interactions with such principled positions will find that their opponents treat their initial offers more seriously than they do unexplained opening proposals.

Table 1 sets forth a Negotiation Preparation Form that may be used by individuals getting ready for a negotiation. It asks advocates to consider the issues that will determine the value of their impending transaction and the bargaining leverage possessed by the respective participants. It is applicable to both litigation settings and transactional encounters.

TABLE 1

Negotiation Preparation Form

1. Your *"resistance point"* — minimum terms you would accept given your Best Alternative to a Negotiated Agreement (BATNA) — Do not forget to include your monetary and nonmonetary transaction costs:

2. Your *"target point"* (best result you hope to achieve) — Be certain that your target point is sufficiently high. Never commence a negotiation until you have mentally solidified your ultimate objective:

3. Your educated estimate of *opponent's "resistance point"* — Be certain to include monetary and nonmonetary transaction costs when estimating the nonsettlement options that appear to be available to your opponent:

4. Your estimate of *opponent's "target point"* — Try to use your opponent's value system when estimating his/her target point:

5. *Your factual and legal leverage* with respect to each issue (strengths and weaknesses) — Prepare logical explanations supporting each strength and articulate the ways in which you might minimize your weaknesses. What is the best alternative result you could achieve through other channels if no agreement can be attained through the negotiation process? What are the monetary, psychological, tax-related, temporal, etc., costs associated with settlement and nonsettlement?

6. Your *opponent's factual and legal leverage* with respect to each issue — What counter-arguments can you devise to challenge the assertions you expect your opponent to make?

7. Your *planned opening position* — Try to begin the process with an offer as far from your target point as you can rationally defend. Prepare logical explanations to support each component of your "principled" opening offer:

8. What *information* do you *plan to elicit* during the Information Phase to determine the opponent's underlying needs, interests, and objectives? What questions do you anticipate using?

9. What *information* are *you willing to disclose* and how do you plan to divulge it? How do you plan to prevent the disclosure of sensitive information (*"blocking techniques"*)?

10. Your *negotiation strategy* (agenda and tactics) — How do you envision moving from your opening position to where you wish to end up? Plan your anticipated concession pattern carefully to disclose only the information you intend to divulge and prepare "principled" explanations to support each planned concession:

11. Your prediction of *opponent's negotiation strategy* and your planned countermeasures — How might you neutralize your opponent's strengths and exploit his or her weaknesses:

Neophyte litigators should recognize that they can greatly enhance their on-going bargaining power if they initially establish reputations as outstanding trial lawyers and individuals who are not afraid to employ the adjudication option if beneficial settlements cannot be negotiated. Attorneys who are not respected litigators are not accorded the same deference at the bargaining table as those who have demonstrated their litigation skills. This is based on the fact that other lawyers assume less onerous nonsettlement options for less proficient litigation opponents than they do for highly skilled adversaries. Furthermore, even talented litigators are not granted as much respect during negotiations as they might otherwise deserve, when they exude a reluctance to go to trial. Once young attorneys establish reputations as outstanding litigators who enjoy the trial process, they can expect to settle far more cases and achieve better results than they ever contemplated.

Attorneys involved in multi-party litigation or large corporate or governmental transactions may occasionally be required to participate in negotiations that include a large number of persons. If the interaction is to be successfully concluded, it is imperative that the individuals on the same side develop unified goals and a coordinated strategy. Each interest group must meet and decide on their basic objectives and the appropriate means of achieving those goals. If the inter-group discussions begin before a common team plan has been formulated, proficient opponents will discern and exploit intra-group weaknesses. Substantive disagreements will undermine bargaining effectiveness, and strategic conflicts will preclude the presentation of a united front.

When expansive bargaining teams are involved, they must decide which persons will speak during inter-party discussions. It is unwise and risky to allow more than three or four representatives to participate actively, since opponents will attempt to benefit from internal group discord. Passive team members must be careful to avoid the unintended disclosure of information through inadvertent nonverbal signals. The individuals who are to do the major speaking must ensure that they work together in a unified manner. When the expertise of other team members is required, designated representatives can elicit the requisite facts in an appropriate fashion.

One final issue that is often ignored by negotiators should be briefly mentioned. Most people preparing for a negotiation are so concerned with the substantive and procedural aspects of the process that they fail to consider the importance of the location and the setting for the bargaining discussions — the "contextual" factors (Schoonmaker, 1989, at 48–49). Most individuals feel more comfortable in familiar surroundings; thus they prefer, if possible, to negotiate in their own environment. Of course, those persons who like to storm out of bargaining sessions to demonstrate how determined they are may wish to negotiate at opponent offices, since it is embarrassing to walk out of one's own office!

When negotiations are scheduled for an attorney's own office, he or she should decide ahead of time upon the manner in which he or she wants to control the basic environment. Combative negotiators frequently establish adversarial settings in which the participants directly face each other across square or rectangular bargaining tables (see Figure 1). They may provide themselves with chairs that are higher and more comfortable than those given to their adversaries. A few negotiators may even cut off a small piece from each of the front legs of the chairs to be used by their opponents to make those people feel uncomfortable during the bargaining interactions. Bargainers may also place their own seats near the middle of the room and locate those to be used by their adversaries with their backs near or against the office wall. This type of seating arrangement tends to make those participants with their chairs near or against the wall behave in a defensive manner. A few individuals may even arrange their offices so that their opponents have bright sunlight in their eyes, making it more difficult for them to observe nonverbal signals. While these tactics may seem absurd to many, it must be remembered that if such tactics give the users a psychological advantage, they may actually influence the ultimate outcome of bargaining interactions.

When lawyers enter the office of an opposing party and feel uncomfortable, they should immediately survey their surroundings to determine if manipulative techniques are being employed. If they discover the existence of bargaining artifices, they should suspect that other similarly opprobrious tactics may be used against them (Ilich, 1973, at 31). To counter such techniques as lowered chairs or poorly positioned seats, negotiators may elect to remain standing during the discussions so that they can look down at their adversaries. They may rearrange the furniture in a more cooperative configuration or look for another more neutral setting in the office and suggest that the discussions occur in that area. They may alternatively wait until their opponents leave the room, to get coffee or to caucus, and exchange places with them! As soon as their adversaries return to the room, they will realize that their unbalanced environment has been discovered. Their resulting embarrassment may soften their subsequent behavior.

Individuals who wish to encourage cooperative "win-win" bargaining sessions should use a round table where the seats are not located directly opposite each other, or have the negotiators sit next to each other in an L-shaped configuration (see Figure 1). They should similarly ensure the development of a hospitable, nonthreatening environment. (Excellent descriptions of these setting-related phenomena may be found in Korda, 1975.)

FIGURE 1

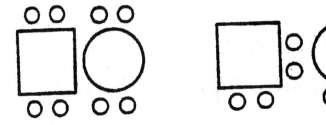

Adversarial Settings   Cooperative Settings

B. THE PRELIMINARY STAGE (ESTABLISHING IDENTITIES AND TONE)

Individuals who have previously opposed one another at the bargaining table are usually familiar with each other's basic negotiating style. They are generally able to commence new negotiations without the need for the formal creation of preliminary ground rules. Nonetheless, they should still take some time to initially reestablish cordial environments that will contribute positively to their impending substantive discussions. Individuals who have not had extensive prior dealings with one another should normally expect to spend the initial period of their interaction establishing their personal and professional identities and the tone for their substantive negotiations. Both formal and informal guidelines must usually be developed (Schoonmaker, 1989, at 52–62).

1.   ESTABLISHMENT OF NEGOTIATOR IDENTITIES

Attorneys who are unfamiliar with the negotiating philosophy and approach of opposing counsel should initially endeavor to obtain pre-negotiation information about their adversaries from people in their own firm and from other lawyers they know. It is particularly important to ascertain whether they can expect candor or dissembling — cooperation or open competition. Are their opponents likely to begin the process with realistic offers or extreme positions? It is generally beneficial to try to establish an atmosphere that is conducive to cooperative, "win-win" interactions. Individuals who encounter seemingly cooperative opponents should expeditiously seek to determine whether those people's apparent predisposition toward a cooperative transaction is consistent with their actual behavior. Until they verify this fact, they should not disclose excessive amounts of critical information regarding their strengths and weaknesses without obtaining reciprocal responses from their opponents. They might otherwise permit Machiavellian adversaries to create false impressions of cooperation so they can take unfair advantage of the situation (Lowenthal, 1982, at 82).

Attorneys who meet professionally for the first time frequently engage in games of one-upmanship. Individuals from prestigious firms hand opposing counsel gilded business cards indicating that they are with "Sullivan, Weiss, Wasp & Wealth" or similarly impressive entities. Persons with prominent government agencies (e.g., U.S. Justice Department or State Attorney General's Office) make equally grand gestures. Some lawyers even ask prospective adversaries where they went to law school, whether they were on the law review, and where they finished academically in their respective graduating classes. If the persons being questioned in this a manner have distinguished academic backgrounds, they may gain a psychological advantage through their disclosures. Others may prefer to ignore these inquiries. Individuals who do not have distinguished academic backgrounds should remember that there is no statistically significant correlation between negotiation exercise results achieved by law students and their overall law school grade point averages (Craver, 2000; Craver, 1986). They should also realize that persons who resort to such gamesmanship tend to be insecure negotiators who are concerned about their own competence!

2.   ESTABLISHMENT OF NEGOTIATION TONE — ATTITUDINAL BARGAINING

Empirical studies indicate that competitive individuals generally behave competitively regardless of the behavior of their opponents, while cooperative persons tend to behave like those with whom they interact — cooperatively with cooperative opponents and competitively with competitive adversaries (Rubin & Brown, 1975, at 185). This phenomenon is based on the fact that cooperative persons see the world as being composed of both cooperative and competitive individuals, while competitive people believe that others behave in a uniformly competitive manner (Rubin & Brown, 1975, at 185; Zartman & Berman, 1982, at 25). Cooperative negotiators feel more comfortable interacting with other cooperative persons, because this permits them to employ the cooperative style they prefer to use. Nonetheless, when they encounter competitive opponents, they appropriately recognize the need to behave more competitively to prevent exploitation by their adversarial opponents. Since competitive negotiators consider all opponents adversarial, they think that an adversarial approach is required to best advance the interests of their own clients.

Some people exhibit overtly competitive tendencies at the outset of negotiations. They deliberately create competitive office environments. When they negotiate in the offices of other people, they select seats directly across from — instead of adjacent to — their opponents. They are likely to sit initially with their arms folded across their chest and with their legs crossed. They exude little personal warmth. Some continue to address opposing counsel as "Mr. or Ms. _____ " instead of by their first names, even when they are themselves being addressed on a first-name basis. This permits them to depersonalize their interaction with persons they view as the enemy. This device also allows them to employ tactics they would not be likely to use against someone they knew more personally.

The initial part of a negotiation is crucial, because the participants generally create an atmosphere that affects their entire transaction. If the interaction begins on an unpleasant or distrusting note, subsequent discussions are likely to be less open and more adversarial than if the process had begun in a congenial and cooperative manner (Woolf, 1990, at 34–35; Scott, 1981, at 6–10). Even inherently competitive legal negotiations do not have to be conducted in a hostile fashion. In fact, advocates who can induce their opponents to like them are usually able to obtain better results than bargainers who do not generate sympathetic feelings (Birke & Fox, 1999, at 54).

Studies have found that persons who commence bargaining interactions in positive moods negotiate more cooperatively and are more likely to employ problem-solving efforts designed to maximize the joint returns achieved by the parties (Ryan, 2005, at 269–70; Freshman, Hayes & Feldman, 2002, at 15, 19; Riskin, 2002, at 657–58; Thompson, Nadler & Kim, 1999, at 142–44; Forgas, 1998, at 566–74). On the other hand, people who begin their encounters in negative moods negotiate more adversarially and tend to generate less efficient overall results. In addition, negative mood participants are more likely to resort to deceptive tactics than others, while positive mood actors are more likely to honor the agreements reached than their negative mood cohorts (Freshman, Hayes & Feldman, 2002, at 22–24; Thompson, Nadler & Kim, 1999, at 143). It is thus beneficial for individuals beginning bargaining encounters to take a few minutes to create supportive environments designed to generate positive moods that should make their interactions more pleasant and enhance the probability they will maximize the joint returns achieved. (Fisher & Shapiro, 2005, at 7–9.)

As lawyers begin the negotiation process, they should take the time to develop positive rapport with opposing counsel. Through warm eye contact and a pleasant demeanor, they can establish a mutually supportive environment. This will enhance future communication, and reduce the unproductive anxiety and anger created by overtly adversarial conduct (Nadler, 2004, at 237–47). Each person must acknowledge that the other participants are not evil opponents — they are merely attempting to obtain beneficial terms for their clients. Negotiators must recognize that they can be forceful advocates without resorting to disagreeable tactics (Woolf, 1990, at 34–35). Those individuals who equate offensive behavior with effective negotiating strategy are likely to be doubly disappointed — their professional interactions will be increasingly unpleasant and they will find it more difficult to obtain optimal results for their clients.

Attorneys who encounter openly competitive "win-lose" opponents should recognize that while they may not be able to convert these individuals into cooperative "win-win" negotiators, they may be able to diminish the competitive aspects of their forthcoming interaction. A friendly introduction, a sincere smile, and a warm, prolonged handshake may be used to establish a more personal relationship. They should emit nonthreatening nonverbal signals and attempt to sit in a cooperative position. They might ask about their opponent's family and colleagues, while making similar disclosures about themselves. They may thus be able to establish a first-name relationship that accentuates the personal nature of their transaction. Even when conciliatory efforts do not substantially diminish the competitiveness exuded by opposing counsel, lawyers must remember that client legal problems — not opponent behavior — constitute the real "enemy" that must be overcome (Zartman & Berman, 1982, at 144).

It is beneficial to depersonalize the conflict, but personalize the interaction. Lawyers should try to separate the people from the problem to be negotiated, to minimize the impact of negative emotional feelings. On the other hand, they should endeavor to personalize the bargaining encounter by establishing rapport with the other side. No matter how large the clients being represented by the two advocates, it is John and Mary interacting — not the XYZ Corporation and the U.S. Department of Justice.

When opposing negotiators exhibit overtly competitive or even abrasive behavior at the commencement of the negotiation process, their adversaries should recognize their right to initiate "*attitudinal bargaining.*" They may appropriately indicate their unwillingness to view the bargaining process as a combative exercise, and suggest their desire to establish some preliminary ground rules (Kramer, 2001, at 264–65; Steinberg, 1998, at 144-49). Litigators may suggest that if the other side prefers open hostility, a trial setting would be the appropriate forum due to the presence of a presiding official. Transactional negotiators may indicate that their clients are seeking mutually beneficial on-going relationships that cannot be created through unnecessarily adversarial behavior. "Attitudinal bargaining" may often be used to induce opponents to tone down their inappropriate conduct and enable the participants to develop more hospitable negotiating environments.

When attitudinal bargaining fails to generate appropriate behavior, individuals who know they must interact with nasty opponents should try to control their encounters in ways that diminish the ability of their adversaries to affect them. For example, against sarcastic or belittling opponents, they could use the telephone to conduct their talks. When the offensive conduct of adversaries begins to bother them, they can indicate that they have another call or another matter to take care of and break off discussions. They can call back the other side after they have calmed down. If particularly aggressive opponents try to intimidate them by invading their space during in-person encounters, they could meet in a conference room containing a large table and place their adversaries on the opposite side. This would make it difficult for their adversaries to invade their space, because such behavior would be pathetically obvious.

Negotiators who have learned, either from previous personal experience or from other reliable sources, that particular adversaries approach negotiations in a competitive manner should initially attempt to demonstrate their willingness to engage in mutually cooperative behavior. Although they should be careful not to disclose too much significant information without receiving some reciprocal cooperation, evidence suggests that cooperative conduct promotes the development of trust and contributes to the establishment of mutually supportive relationships (Ury, 1991; Rubin & Brown, 1975, at 263). If these tactics do not produce the desired behavioral results, the unsuccessful initiators of cooperative conduct can still adopt a more circumspect approach. On the other hand, if they initially respond to the competitive overtures of opposing counsel with competitive conduct of their own, it is likely that an unpleasant, combative negotiation will result.

Attorneys who encounter opponents who initially exhibit cooperative tendencies should be careful to reinforce that behavior. It will make their professional interactions more harmonious, and minimize the likelihood that opposing counsel will resort to inappropriate tactics. Manipulative negotiators may even wish to encourage a cooperative attitude, so they can themselves employ disguised competitive techniques to advance their own objectives. If they are adroit negotiators, they may be able to maintain a pleasant bargaining environment, while they disingenuously seek to obtain more favorable results for their own clients. Sincerely cooperative bargainers should always be aware of the possibility of such opponent stratagems, to protect themselves from their own cooperative nature.

Lawyers should appreciate the benefits that may be derived at the beginning of a conflict-resolution interaction from an acknowledgment of the other party's plight and the issuance of an apology (Folberg & Golann, 2006. at 171–77; Brown, 2004b; Fuchs-Burnett, 2002; O'Hara & Yarn, 2002). Most individuals only resort to litigation after all other efforts to achieve mutual resolutions of the underlying controversies have failed. The aggrieved persons are frustrated and angry regarding the perceived unwillingness of the responsible parties to acknowledge their contribution to the problem. If the seemingly responsible individuals would simply indicate an understanding of the injured party's plight and state that they are sorry for what had happened to those persons — without necessarily admitting any legal responsibility — the aggrieved persons might accept their expressions of sympathy and either endure their fate alone or work constructively to generate mutually acceptable resolutions.

Some might suggest that an effective apology must include a clear admission of responsibility for the injuries sustained (Pavlick, 2003, at 835–36), but we have not found this to be true. If someone sincerely sympathizes with the loss suffered by the other side or acknowledges the basis for that side's negative feelings, this can significantly diminish the impact of those negative emotions, even if the sympathizing party does not admit personal liability. Negotiators should remember that many highly controverted legal disputes are quickly settled following the expression of appropriate contrition by the responsible parties.

Should evidence of apologies be admissible in subsequent trials to bolster plaintiff claims of defendant liability or to reduce the amount of damages to be awarded to prevent opportunistic behavior by insincere apologists who use their seeming contrition to obtain strategic benefits during case settlement discussions? (O'Hara & Yarn, 2002). If apologies are admitted solely for the purpose of establishing liability against the apologists, this would discourage contrite conduct by rational actors and encourage opportunistic behavior by claimants. On the other hand, if apologies are admissible by defendants to demonstrate — sincerely or insincerely — their contrition, this would tend to reduce damage awards against the apologists. To counteract these phenomena, Professors O'Hara and Yarn suggest that apologies either be admissible both to establish liability and to mitigate damages or for neither purpose. This approach would decrease the risk to sincere apologists, and diminish opportunistic behavior by claimants who only wish to elicit apologies they can use to establish defendant liability at trial (O'Hara & Yarn, 2002, at 1191).

C. THE INFORMATION STAGE (VALUE CREATION)

Following the preliminary establishment of negotiator identities and the possible use of "attitudinal bargaining" to create a mutually acceptable atmosphere for the impending interaction, the first truly formal stage of the negotiation process begins. Individuals can usually recognize the commencement of the "Information Stage," because this point coincides with a shift from innocuous "small talk" to questions regarding each party's respective needs and objectives. During this part of the process, the participants try to determine what items are available for joint distribution. They should also look for ways in which they might expand the areas of mutual interest — i.e., engage in "value creation." The more effectively they can accomplish these objectives, the more efficiently they should be able to conclude their interaction successfully (Mnookin, Peppet & Tulumello, 2000, at 11–43). The most effective way to elicit information from opponents is to *ask questions* (Salacuse, 2003, at 48–52; Stone, Patton & Heen, 1999, at 172-73; Thompson, 1998, at 60–61; Barkai, 1996, at 735-36). People who continue to use declarative sentences give up information — they do not obtain it.

1. FOCUS ON WHAT EACH SIDE WANTS AND KNOWS

The focus of the Information Stage is always on the knowledge and desires of the *opposing party*. Each participant asks the other side what items it wants and why it wants to obtain them. Each side wants to obtain as much information about the opponent as possible, without disclosing too much of their own confidential information. Advocates may initially attempt to ascertain the expertise of opposing counsel with respect to the type of legal transaction involved, and they may ask about the resources available to the other side. Is the opposing client represented by a large law firm with many experienced specialists and with substantial resources, or by a relatively small firm with limited financial capability? What resources are available to the client involved?

During the preliminary stages of the Information Stage, many parties make the mistake of asking narrow, highly-focused questions that can be answered with brief responses. As a result, they merely confirm what they already suspect. It is far more effective to ask broad, open-ended information-seeking questions (Volkama, 2006, 46–47; Korobkin, 2002, at 12; Ordover & Doneff, 2002, at 20–22; Ilich, 1992, at 68; Stone, Patton & Heen, 1999, at 174-75; Goldman, 1991, at 134; Bastress & Harbaugh, 1990, at 413; Gifford, 1989, at 124-25). Negotiators want to induce their opponents to talk. The more people speak, the more information they directly and indirectly disclose (Cohen, 2003, at 226–29). If participants suspect something about a particular issue, they should formulate an expansive inquiry covering that area. The persons being interrogated have no way of knowing what their questioners already comprehend. They often erroneously assume the questioners know more about their situations than those opponents actually know (Van Boven, Gilovich & Medvec, 2003, at 118–24). When they respond to the broad inquiry, they tend to divulge new leads and additional pieces of information. No matter how carefully they plan their responses, they are likely to include informative verbal leaks.

When opponents appear to have answered particular questions, additional information can often be elicited through silence (Miller & Miller, 2002, at 70). The persons who asked the inquiries simply say nothing for ten or twenty seconds after the other parties have responded. Such silent pauses may induce careless negotiators to fill the void with further comments. As they do so, they usually provide new pieces of information and new leads that can be explored through different questions. On the other hand, once negotiators have given intended answers, they should become quiet and patiently await new questions or statements from their opponents. They should not allow questioner silence to induce them to say more.

Once questioners think they have elicited a sufficient amount of general information, they may wish to use more specific queries to confirm their understandings. Opponents may attempt to avoid direct responses to these inquiries in an effort to prevent the disclosure of particular information. They may ignore the questions or provide ambiguous answers. When this occurs, the questioners should rephrase their inquiries in a manner that will compel the respondents to provide more definitive replies (Gifford, 1989, at 123). They should not permit opponents to employ evasive tactics to avoid the disclosure of pertinent information.

The questioning process not only enables interrogators to elicit beneficial responses, but may also permit them to seize control of the preliminary stages of the interaction (Ilich, 1973, at 142). Effective questioners can steer the discussions in the direction they wish to proceed, and they may be able to avoid the exploration of issues they prefer to ignore. This permits them to obtain more crucial knowledge than their opponents during the early part of their interaction, and they may use their cognitive advantage to enhance their confidence and their bargaining potential.

Negotiators must listen intently and observe carefully during the Information Stage (Ordover & Doneff, 2002, at 23–26; Shapiro & Jankowski, 2001, at 76–77; Goleman, 1998, at 178-80; Steinberg, 1998, at 166-68; Barkai, 1996, at 728, 737-42). They should try to maintain supportive eye contact to encourage further opponent disclosures and to allow them to discern verbal leaks and nonverbal signals. Smiles and occasional head nods are likely to generate more open responses from people who feel they are being heard (Cohen, 2003, at 226–27). Questioners should take minimal notes. When people write, they miss much of what is being said, and they are oblivious to most of the nonverbal cues emanating from the respondents. Active listeners who concentrate on the answers being elicited by their own queries are often surprised by how much they remember about the replies they receive. They usually recall far more than others who asked the same questions but who attempted to write down as much as they could during the exchanges. Negotiators must not only listen carefully to what is being said, bt also to what is not being covered, since omitted areas may suggest weaknesses adversaries do not wish to address (Kramer, 2001, at 234).

It is amazing how much verbal and nonverbal communication is missed by participants during bargaining interactions. When we videotape students and replay the tapes, the participants are shocked at two things: (1) how much their opponents said that they never heard and (2) how much they said that they do not recall having stated. They are so busy thinking about what was just said and what they plan to say next and what negotiating techniques are being employed by their adversaries and which tactics they plan to use next, that they fail to perceive many obvious verbal and nonverbal signals.

Participants must proceed slowly during the Information Stage. Patience is generally rewarded with the attainment of greater knowledge. Too many negotiators are anxious to solidify the deal they hope to consummate, and they rush through the Information Stage. They can hardly wait to begin and conclude the substantive discussions (McCormack, 1984, at 152). This conduct is frequently counterproductive. When advocate anxiety generates an abbreviated Information Stage, the impatient negotiators may easily ignore crucial verbal and nonverbal signals emanating from their opponents. Important pieces of information may not be ascertained and considered. The shortened interaction may thus culminate in a final agreement that is not as beneficial as the accord that could have been obtained had the questioning process been permitted to unfold more deliberately. When negotiators sense that participant anxiety is causing the process to evolve in an accelerated manner, they should adopt a more deliberate approach. They can ask more detailed questions or provide more leisurely answers and comments. They should be careful, however, not to let the situation cause them to disclose more of their confidential information than they intended.

2. CRITICAL NATURE OF INFORMATION RETRIEVAL

Since negotiators cannot unilaterally impose their expectations on opposing parties, they cannot hope to achieve mutual accords until they have become aware of the needs and interests of their adversaries, and have sought to at least partially satisfy the underlying goals of those participants. Negotiators on one side cannot obtain the requisite insights into these factors in isolation but must endeavor to learn as much as possible about opponent potential and actual choices, their preferences and their intensity, their planned strategy, and their operative strengths and weaknesses (Gulliver, 1979, at 107). Bargainers must always be cognizant of the fact that opponent perceptions of particular situations may be more favorable to their own positions than they ever anticipated. Only through careful and patient probing may they successfully discern such beneficial circumstances.

Negotiating parties must initially identify the issues to be resolved (Schoonmaker, 1989, at 14–15). Since bargaining is a problem-solving process, fruitful results can only be achieved when all of the participants understand the underlying matters that must be mutually resolved. It is only at this point that the negotiators can begin to recognize and explore the relevant options and their consequences. Advocates who ignore this consideration are likely to obtain inefficient accords.

Once the negotiators have identified the different issues to be exchanged, they should begin to determine the relative value of each of those items to the opposing side. They should ask whether Item 1 is more or less important than Item 2 or Item 3. How much more does the other side value Item 1 versus Item 2 — twice as much or only fifty percent more? How do Items 1 and 2 compare to Item 3? Questioners should listen carefully for verbal leaks that may disclose the relative interests of the opponents. Which items do they *have* to obtain (i.e., "essential" terms); do they *really want* to get (i.e., "important" terms); and would they *like* to get (i.e., "desirable" terms). Rational opponents should be willing to trade "important" terms for "essential" items or other "important" terms, and they should be willing to trade "desirable" items for "essential" or "important" terms.

Questioners should also compare their own rankings of the different issues with those of the other side. This enables them to begin to look for possible exchanges that will allow the bargaining parties to expand the overall pie to be divided and enable them to maximize the joint returns generated. Each side should be willing to trade items they value less for terms they prefer more. When both sides value the items equally, they will compete for those terms. On the other hand, when they value items differently, they should look for trades that will simultaneously enhance their respective positions.

Negotiators frequently wonder whether they should state their positions first or attempt to induce their opponents to do so. Since there is no statistical correlation between who makes the initial offer and the outcome of an interaction (Thompson, 1998, at 31; Bastress & Harbaugh, 1990, at 493), many people believe that this factor is irrelevant. Some bargaining experts even prefer to go first, because they think this tactic enables them to define the basic negotiation range and discourage wholly unrealistic opponent offers (Freund, 1992, at 114-15). Even individuals who frequently employ this technique, however, recognize the need to be cautious in some circumstances. "Don't go first unless you know value (or are well advised on that score) and have formulated a realistic expectation to guide your negotiating strategy." (Freund, 1992, at 115.)

Individuals who announce firm, beneficial opening offers can gain a significant advantage over less prepared opponents who are not sure where to begin (Thompson, 2005, at 49). Such offers can anchor the talks and induce less confident adversaries to begin closer to where the opening persons hope to end up. Against thoroughly prepared people who have established their own firm aspiration levels and set opening offers, however, preemptive opening offers are unlikely to have such a beneficial anchoring impact.

The use of preemptive first offers can be an especially effective bargaining technique when both sides have a realistic understanding of the actual value of the items to be discussed. In situations in which no common value system can be relied upon to guide the participants, many negotiators prefer to have opponents make the initial offers (Shapiro & Jankowski, 2001, at 148). There are three reasons for this view.

First, if one or both sides have miscalculated the value of the transaction, the individuals who go first will disclose the misunderstanding and place themselves at a disadvantage. For example, plaintiff attorneys may hope to obtain $75,000 for their client. Even though skilled negotiators are frequently able to accurately predict the opening positions that are likely to be articulated by their opponents, they can never be certain that their preliminary prognostications are correct. The opponents may know more about their own weaknesses than was unilaterally surmised, or they may have overestimated the strength possessed by the plaintiff. If defense counsel initially offer more than plaintiff lawyers anticipated — e.g., $50,000, $75,000, or more — the plaintiff representatives can immediately reassess their circumstances and adjust their opening demand upward to provide them with the flexibility they need to test their increased value hypothesis. Instead of beginning in the $150,000 to $200,000 range, they might start with a demand of $400,000 or $500,000. This approach may enable them to achieve settlements in the $200,000 to $250,000 range, despite the fact they never comprehend why the other side is willing to provide such generous terms.

A second factor involves a phenomenon known as "bracketing." If negotiators induce their opponents to make the initial offers, they can adjust their own first offers to place their real goal midway between their opening positions ["bracketing"] (Birke & Fox, 1999, at 41; Dawson, 2001, at 18–20). For example, if people hope to get $300,000 and opposing counsel initially offer $100,000, they can begin with a demand in the $500,000 range to keep their $300,000 target in the middle. Since parties tend to move inexorably toward the center of their opening positions, due to the generally accepted obligation of bargaining parties to make reciprocal concessions, the person who goes second can easily manipulate the central point and place his or her adversary at a psychological disadvantage.

The third reason for inducing opponents to make the first offers concerns the fact that while opening *offers* do not statistically influence negotiation outcomes, initial *concessions* do. There is a slight, but statistically significant, inverse correlation between opening concessions and final results, with persons who make the initial concessions tending to do less well than their opponents (Kritzer, 1991, at 68; Bastress & Harbaugh, 1990, at 493). People who make the first concessions tend to be anxious negotiators who make more and larger concessions than their opponents (Schoonmaker, 1989, at 101). Individuals who can induce their opponents to issue the first offers have a good chance of persuading them to make the initial concessions. After their opponents make the first offer, this side's opening position looks like a counteroffer. It is thus easy for this side to look to their opponents for the next position statement — e.g., the first concession.

It is not easy to persuade all opponents to make the initial offers. In some negotiations, the circumstances dictate the persons who are expected to go first. This obligation often falls upon the ones who initiate the discussions. Nonetheless, adroit bargainers may be able to avoid having to make the first real offer even when they originate the interaction. For example, individuals who have indicated a desire to sell certain property may respond to inquiries regarding the amount they want to obtain by asking the prospective purchasers how much they are willing to pay (Ilich, 1973, at 169). This approach may induce defendants to make the first definitive offers. If the respondents are careless, they may be induced to disclose important information through initial offers that should not have been made first. The seller may alternatively announce a wholly unreasonable asking price, hoping to impel prospective buyers to articulate the first real offers. Plaintiff lawyers may write demand letters that detail the injuries sustained by their clients, but omit specific dollar amounts for the items listed.

There are occasions when both parties are being so coy that neither is willing to initiate the substantive discussions. The participants continue to ask each other questions and talk around the actual issues to be addressed, but neither side is willing to place a firm offer on the table. If this situation continues, the negotiators may give up or simply reach an impasse. If someone has sought to induce the other party to articulate the first offer by asking what they hope to achieve and they have received no substantive response, they may have to begin the real discussions with an offer of their own. They should be careful to leave themselves sufficient bargaining room. Although they should not start with a wholly unrealistic position that could undermine the interaction, they should begin with a position that allows them flexibility once the other side states its position.

What should a party do if they finally place their position on the table and receive no meaningful response from the other side? They must be especially careful not to bid against themselves by making consecutive and unreciprocated opening offers. They should be patient and use silence to induce the other side to respond in a substantive way. If no counteroffer is forthcoming, they should expressly ask the other party to indicate what it hopes to achieve. If this approach fails to generate a meaningful response, they should indicate their willingness to terminate the present discussions to give the other side the time they need to formulate its opening position. If a recess in talks becomes necessary, it can be beneficial to agree upon a future meeting time to avoid the possibility that neither negotiator will feel comfortable assuming the responsibility to initiate the subsequent talks.

It is important to recognize that the opponents-go-first technique is only of assistance when it generates the first *real offer*. For example, plaintiff lawyers who hope to achieve a $100,000 settlement may have been contemplating a $250,000 initial demand. If they instead decide to open the negotiation process with an unprincipled $1,000,000 figure, it should be apparent that no *real* offer has yet been made. Defendant attorneys who planned not to disclose their own opening position until after they received the first demand from their adversaries should not be induced to divulge their own figure in response to this outrageous initiating statement. They must acknowledge the disingenuous nature of the $1,000,000 demand and patiently continue the preliminary discussions. Lawyers must not focus so intently on the first offer issue that they fail to understand how easily they can be deceived by false opening offers.

Negotiators who are presented with wholly unreasonable opening offers must not react to those terms in a nonchalant manner. If they casually reject these offers, they may lead opponents to believe that their positions are not truly extreme. It will become increasingly difficult to disabuse them of this erroneous notion, and the likelihood of nonsettlements increases. It is incumbent upon individuals who receive obviously unrealistic offers to reject them swiftly and unambiguously (Freund, 1992, at 125–26). They must immediately convey their belief in the absurd nature of the terms being stated. This action would probably preclude subsequent misunderstandings that could adversely affect future negotiation progress.

Parties to a negotiation normally begin the process with the establishment of "*target points*" they hope to achieve (i.e., their aspiration level) and "*resistance points*" they do not plan to go above or below, preferring to accept the consequences of nonsettlements if terms at least as favorable as these bottom lines cannot be achieved (Menkel-Meadow, 1984, at 769; Bellow & Moulton, 1981, at 58-63). This phenomenon is graphically depicted in Figure 2.

FIGURE 2

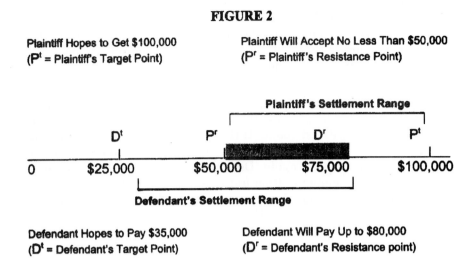

Plaintiff Hopes to Get $100,000
(P^t = Plaintiff's Target Point)

Plaintiff Will Accept No Less Than $50,000
(P^r = Plaintiff's Resistance Point)

Defendant Hopes to Pay $35,000
(D^t = Defendant's Target Point)

Defendant Will Pay Up to $80,000
(D^r = Defendant's Resistance point)

The **HIGHLIGHTED AREA** in Figure 2 between P^r ($50,000) and D^r ($80,000) represents the parties' "Zone of Agreement." The plaintiff will accept the trial alternative, rather than agree to less than $50,000, while the defendant would choose to litigate if more than $80,000 continues to be demanded. The negotiation process will determine whether a final agreement will be closer to the $50,000 or the $80,000 figure (Korobkin, 2000).

In some situations, the parties initially establish settlement ranges that do not overlap or that coincide only minimally. In the former setting, no negotiated settlement can be achieved, unless one or both parties realize the need to reassess their original positions. In the latter situation, it will be difficult for adversaries to locate the narrow zone of agreement. Nonetheless, when proficient negotiators begin to recognize the existence of minimal or nonexistent zones of agreement, they are often able to convince each other during the Information Stage of their need to reassess their preconceived settlement ranges. They are thus able to create or expand their zones of agreement and enhance the likelihood of mutual accords. When ample zones of agreement initially exist, negotiators should have little difficulty reaching mutually acceptable agreements. The only issue to be resolved concerns the party that is to achieve the more favorable results (i.e., a final settlement on its side of the zone-of-agreement midpoint).

3. CATEGORIES OF INFORMATION REGARDING OPPONENT'S SITUATION

Professional negotiators always endeavor to learn as much as possible about the personal skill and experience of their adversaries. During the pre-negotiation stage, they gather pertinent input from other lawyers who have previously confronted opposing counsel. They try to ascertain what tactics their adversaries prefer to use and how they normally respond to various techniques. Are opposing counsel "true believers" who are blind to the merits of the positions espoused by others, or are they pragmatists who recognize that negotiators are merely advocates for the positions of their respective clients? Once the actual negotiation commences, adroit bargainers attempt to verify the information they have amassed about their adversaries. When they discern reactions that differ from what they initially expected, they are prepared to make new judgments that acknowledge that individuals react differently in diverse circumstances. They then adjust their planned strategy accordingly.

The manner in which adversaries present their preliminary demands is frequently revealing with respect to multiple item transactions. While bargainers may initially list the different terms to be discussed during the current interaction, they normally focus on finite groups of topics once serious negotiations commence. Anxious negotiators frequently begin the substantive talks with several of their most important topics in an effort to produce an expeditious, albeit tentative, resolution of those issues. They are nervous, risk-averse advocates who wish to diminish the tension associated with the uncertainty that is inherent in the bargaining process. They believe they can significantly decrease their fear of a nonsettlement by achieving accelerated progress on their primary topics. They unfortunately fail to realize that this approach may actually enhance the probability of a counterproductive stalemate. If their principal objectives correspond with the primary goals of their adversaries, this presentation sequence is likely to cause an immediate clash of wills. Opposing counsel may rapidly decide that irreconcilable differences exist, and they may conclude that little progress is presently attainable. This result can only exacerbate the anxiety being experienced by the party endeavoring to achieve an expeditious resolution.

Other negotiators prefer to begin the bargaining process with their less significant subjects, hoping to make rapid progress on these less disputed items. This approach is likely to develop a cooperative atmosphere that will facilitate compromise when the more controverted subjects are subsequently explored (Cohen, 2003, at 132–33; Watkins & Rosegrant, 2001, at 21–22; Rubin & Brown, 1975, at 148). The advantage of this approach is that it develops in both parties a psychological commitment to the negotiation process. If there are fifteen basic items in dispute and the parties are able to achieve tentative agreement on ten or eleven with minimal difficulty, the participants begin to sense a successful interaction. They do not wish to negate this progress with an impasse on the remaining issues. They are thus more likely to work diligently to avoid unproductive stalemates with respect to the last four or five topics (Karrass, 1970, at 72–73).

On rare occasions, a particular issue must be resolved in a definite manner if any satisfactory deal is to be achieved. When this is true, many negotiators prefer to raise this issue at the outset and directly indicate how it must be handled (Schoonmaker, 1989, at 66). The other side may agree to this approach, so long as a critical topic for them is resolved in a manner they find acceptable. Once these key terms have been exchanged, the negotiators return to the less significant issues and work their way up toward the other important terms. If the parties are unwilling to agree preliminarily upon a mutually acceptable resolution of these essential items, they usually terminate the interaction, since they do not believe that further discussions would be beneficial.

Individuals who decide to present their less significant items first can employ either of two approaches to enhance their probability of prevailing when the more important issues are subsequently discussed. Some believe that it is appropriate to make tentative, but seemingly magnanimous, concessions on the early subjects, to create feelings of guilt and obligation in their opponents. They hope that this pattern will induce reciprocal concessions from their adversaries when the primary topics are being resolved. If this technique does not produce the desired results, they can always reopen talks pertaining to the preliminarily settled matters. Other negotiators think that they should strive to obtain favorable concessions on the early items, to establish concessionary mind-sets in their opponents. If they can generate favorable bargaining momentum, they may be able to induce opposing counsel to continue their concession-oriented disposition with respect to the primary topics. If they are successful in this regard, they may end up with everything they want!

Discerning negotiators can often obtain crucial information from the groups of items initially emphasized by opponents when serious discussions commence. Most bargainers begin with a cluster of their most important or their least important topics. They rarely mix significant and insignificant items. If opponents initiate the auction process with a group of five items, four of which are insignificant to the offeree and one of which is relatively important, it is likely that all five topics are unimportant to the offeror. An adroit offeree can casually claim the beneficial term during the early discussions and obtain a significant benefit in exchange for almost nothing. The opponent may conversely begin with five items, four of which are critical to the offeree and one of which is relatively unimportant. It is likely that all five terms are significant to the offeror. This knowledge permits the offeree to use this topic as a bargaining chip that may be exchanged for a more substantial item.

4. CONTROLLING DISCLOSURE OF OWN SIDE'S INFORMATION

As individuals prepare for a negotiation, they must decide several things regarding their own side's information. What information are they willing to disclose, and how do they plan to divulge it? What sensitive information do they wish to withhold, and how do they plan to avoid the disclosure of those facts? People who resolve these critical issues *before* they begin to interact with their opponents tend to have more successful Information Stages than those who do not think about them until forced to do so in the midst of the actual negotiation.

If the negotiation process is to develop in an efficacious manner, both sides have to exchange some information. A number of participants consider this a straightforward part of the transaction, and they see no reason to employ manipulative disclosure techniques. They abhor the disingenuous tactics used by many bargainers to advance their interests, and they prefer the direct approach. Once the Information Stage begins, they simply tell their opponents what they wish to obtain and why they believe they deserve the terms they are seeking (Kritzer, 1991, at 48). They naively think that their voluntary disclosures will be well received by their opponents. In most legal transactions, however, they are incorrect, because competitive adversaries can take advantage of their candor to obtain more favorable terms (Kritzer, 1991, at 78–79).

Sincerely open negotiators may encounter additional problems. As straightforward representatives honestly disclose their fundamental information, their opponents tend to become suspicious. Bargainers are not used to such a candid approach, and they begin to think that they are being manipulated. They suspect that pertinent facts are being withheld, and that the knowledge being shared is being embellished in a disingenuous fashion. Because of these suppositions, they do not listen as carefully as they should to what the speaker is telling them. Furthermore, they discount much of what they do hear as self-serving disclosures (Mnookin, Peppet & Tulumello, 2000, at 165; Mnookin & Ross, 1995, at 22–23). They thus miss important revelations and give diminished credence to the facts they do comprehend.

Negotiators should not readily volunteer their most significant information. They should instead make their opponents work to extract it. The most pertinent facts should be slowly divulged in response to opponent inquiries. When adversaries ask questions, they generally listen intently to the replies they elicit. After all, they want to hear the answers to their own inquiries. They thus perceive more of what the responder is saying. Furthermore, since they attribute the speaker's revelations to their own questioning skills, they accord them more credibility than they would if the same facts were voluntarily divulged.

When negotiators disclose their critical information, they should frame their presentations in a manner that enables them to simultaneously advance their underlying interests. They can accomplish this objective by formulating "principled" positions that are accompanied by succinct rationales explaining the reasons they deserve those terms. This approach forces opponents to treat their position statements seriously, and it makes it more difficult for their adversaries to summarily reject their offers (Freund, 1992, at 122-23). This is based on the fact that most people find it easier to decline unexplained requests than to rebuff substantiated entreaties (Pratkanis & Aronson, 1991, at 26–27).

Bargainers should also endeavor to present opponents with options that subtly favor the positions the offerors would like to obtain. People offered a certain gain and the possibility of a greater benefit tend to accept the sure gain, while individuals who must choose between a certain loss and the possibility of no loss tend to opt for the chance to experience no loss (Bazerman & Neale, 1992, at 33–39; Pratkanis & Aronson, 1991, at 61–63). Whenever possible, negotiators should frame their offers in terms that would provide their opponents with certain benefits. If those persons are forced to choose between the definitive gains being offered and the possibility of more advantageous external alternatives, most will select the certainty associated with the negotiated gain. On the other hand, if opponents are compelled to choose between the sure loss associated with a bargained agreement and the possibility of avoiding any loss through an external option, they will more readily accept the nonsettlement alternative.

Negotiators are frequently concerned about sensitive information they do not wish to share with their opponents. They are hesitant to directly inform their adversaries of their reluctance to discuss these areas, because this approach is likely to generate distrust and enhance opponent interest in these issues. When they are specifically asked about these areas, they become embarrassed and disconcerted. Even though they had planned to avoid the disclosure of this information, they find themselves divulging their secret thoughts.

It is much easier to avoid the unintended disclosure of critical information if the opponents are unaware of the fact that knowledge is being withheld. The most effective way to accomplish this objective is through the use of "blocking techniques" (Teply, 2005, at 195–98; Latz, 2004, at 64–66; Bastress & Harbaugh, 1990, at 422–28; Freund, 1992, at 64–65). These tactics enable adroit negotiators to protect their crucial information without arousing the opponents' suspicions. Individuals who want to perfect these avoidance skills should watch politicians being interviewed on talk shows. If they listen carefully, they will be amazed at the number of probing questions that go unanswered.

a. Ignore the Intrusive Question

People who do not like inquiries posed by their opponents should simply ignore them. They should continue the current conversation or change the focus to other topics they prefer to explore. If they are effective, their opponents will not even realize that their queries have not been addressed, and they will direct their attention to the areas being discussed.

b. Answer the Beneficial Part of Compound Questions

Persons frequently ask complex questions that contain several parts. For example, a reporter may ask political candidates whether they would be willing to raise taxes to lower the deficit. Cautious politicians are hesitant to discuss the possibility of tax increases, so they focus entirely on the deficit reduction aspect of the query. Negotiators can use the same approach when opponents formulate compound questions. They can answer the part(s) they like and ignore the other portion(s).

c. Over- or Under-Answer the Question

When negotiators are asked specific questions regarding delicate areas, they can often prevent meaningful disclosures through the use of general responses. When they are asked expansive inquiries, they can respond with narrow answers. By over-answering narrow questions and under-answering broad inquiries, they can usually protect their sensitive information.

d. Misconstrue the Question and Answer the Reframed Inquiry

Politicians are regularly asked whether they would be willing to increase taxes. Even though these specific inquiries do not seem easy to ignore, proficient candidates are able to redirect the focus of what is being asked. "I can tell by your question that you are concerned about the deficit, and let me address that important topic. . . ." Negotiators can use the same technique. They can reframe and redirect touchy questions and then answer the queries they have reformulated.

e. Answer Opponent's Question With Own Question

Negotiators can often avoid the need to answer delicate inquiries by responding with questions of their own. If they do this adroitly, they can change the focus from themselves back to the original interrogators.

> <u>Opponent</u>: Is your client willing to compensate my client for the loss of consortium caused by the injuries inflicted by his/her negligence?

> <u>You</u>: Isn't it true that your client's marriage was in disarray prior to the accident?

> <u>Opponent</u>: I agree that they did not have a perfect relationship, but don't you think they deserve compensation for the fact that the serious injuries did have an impact?

> <u>You</u>: What kind of difficulties were they experiencing?

Individuals may respond in a similar manner when they are asked about their bargaining authority. For example, if an opponent asks if they are authorized to pay or accept $100,000, they can refocus the discussion by asking their opponent if he or she is authorized to accept that amount. They may alternatively treat this type of question as a new offer, praise the other party for its movement, but indicate why the new $100,000 figure is unacceptable. Opponents who did not intend their inquiry to constitute a new offer will retreat quickly in an effort to avoid further embarrassment.

f. Rule the Question Out of Bounds

Negotiators who are asked about such matters as their authorized limits or special research they have conducted should not hesitate to indicate that they do not respond to inquiries that seek confidential information protected by the attorney-client privilege or nondiscoverable matters covered by the work-product doctrine. They should be careful to be sufficiently consistent with respect to this approach that they do not disclose critical information inadvertently. For example, if they respond that they are not authorized to agree to particular terms when they actually lack that prerogative, they should not rule questions regarding their authorized limits out of bounds when they do possess the requisite authority. People who deal with them regularly will quickly discern the different treatment being given to these inquiries, and will realize that they only refuse to respond to these queries when they are actually authorized to agree to what is being asked.

Negotiators must plan their blocking techniques in advance and vary them during their discussions. They might ignore one question, under-answer another, and respond to a third with an inquiry of their own. If they are proficient, they will be able to evade a number of questions without their opponents recognizing the degree to which they are withholding information.

5. NONADVERSARIAL PROBING OF UNDERLYING INTERESTS AND OBJECTIVES

Although most legal practitioners understandably view the negotiation process as an adversarial interaction, they should recognize the benefits that may be derived during the Information Stage through the use of relatively nonadversarial questioning techniques. Advocates who approach bargaining sessions in a combative, trial-like manner are usually unable to obtain all of the information they need to possess before they can achieve optimal results. Their opponents generally sense their "win-lose" style and endeavor to protect themselves through the judicious release of pertinent information. They withhold important information that might otherwise be openly divulged, and they may even be induced by such competitive tactics to respond in kind. Adversarial negotiators tend to lock themselves into set positions they defend with strident arguments. They seem to believe they can intimidate opposing counsel into submission. They frequently ignore or fail to comprehend protestations regarding their interpretation of the applicable facts and legal doctrines. They thus fail to acknowledge new information that might induce them to consider alternative proposals that might prove to be mutually advantageous.

When a wide zone of agreement (see Figure 2, *supra*) exists with respect to a particular negotiation, the parties should encounter minimal difficulty achieving agreement. Their resulting accord will probably not, however, be a Pareto superior solution — where neither party could enhance its position without simultaneously worsening the condition of the other side. If the participants had developed a more open information exchange, they would likely have discovered a more efficient overall result. In many other bargaining situations, the zone of agreement tentatively ascertained by the parties during their preliminary information phase may be limited or nonexistent. If they were to accept this apparent situation at face value, they might well conclude — usually erroneously — that no mutual resolution is possible. Such a predicament may often be avoided through a more expansive exploration of the parties' respective underlying needs and interests (*see generally* Mnookin, Peppet & Tulumello, 2000; Fisher & Ury, 1981).

When advocates reach a tentative impasse during an important negotiation, they often ask a respected neutral to intervene. It is hoped that this mediator will be able to reopen communication channels and induce the disputants to consider alternatives they might not have contemplated during their own increasingly combative discussions (see Part II, *infra*). Adroit negotiators do not always have to employ an outside person to perform this function. If they can decrease their adversarial behavior and effectively activate their own mediative capabilities, they can enhance the likelihood of achieving optimal results.

Negotiators who want to create a more mediative/cooperative atmosphere need to replace leading questions that are intended implicitly or overtly to challenge the positions being taken by opposing counsel with less threatening, seemingly neutral inquiries. Both parties must develop sufficient trust to enable them to explore their respective underlying assumptions, values, and goals in a relatively candid manner. Objective questions can be used to carefully review each side's understanding of the relevant factual circumstances and applicable legal doctrines. If both sides can agree upon these basic factors in a noncompetitive fashion, the probability that they will achieve mutually beneficial results can be significantly increased (Fisher & Ury, 1981, at 41–57).

Each side needs to comprehend the external and internal pressures influencing the other party, since such factors directly affect that party's assessment of the situation. Do they have a constituency that has established some irrational constraints? Are they using an unanticipated value system to assess their perception of bargaining proposals? Have their previously articulated positions truly reflected their underlying needs and interests? Have they restricted their offers to legalistic options, when they would really prefer some nonlegal alternative? Too many negotiators limit their discussions to those items that could be achieved through formal legal channels, without recognizing that bargainers generally possess the capacity to formulate other resolutions of their differences. While administrative and judicial tribunals are constrained by conventional remedial doctrines, it is important for negotiators to remember that they may normally agree to any mutually advantageous terms that do not contravene applicable legal prohibitions.

The key to finding solutions to difficult negotiations does not merely involve compromise, but also the ability of the participants to expand the available resources that may be distributed (Raiffa, 2003, at 198–201; Mnookin, Peppet & Tulumello, 2000; Menkel-Meadow, 1984, at 813). Too many negotiators make the mistake of assuming that both sides have similar value systems and analogous utility functions generating a "fixed pie" to be divided (Birke & Fox, 1999, at 30–31; Gillespie, et al., 1999, at 367). They thus believe that their opponents want the same terms they desire. This erroneous assumption causes them to view their interactions as entirely distributive, zero-sum transactions in which one side cannot gain without the other experiencing an equal loss. Extremely competitive/adversarial bargainers tend to think in this fashion. As a result, they frequently achieve inefficient settlement terms or end up with needless nonsettlements. These people fail to realize that in multiple item negotiations, parties tend to value the various items in dispute quite differently (Dawson, 1995, at 287). This allows them to look for trade-offs that can simultaneously benefit both sides. Through the use of brainstorming techniques, negotiators can frequently discover new options that can effectively enlarge the overall pie being divided (Watkins, 2001, at 124; Shapiro & Jankowski, 2001, at 201–03; Lewicki, Saunders & Minton, 1999, at 343). For example, parties involved in a marital dissolution may both be fighting for sole custody of the children, when only one spouse really wants this responsibility. If the spouse who does not strongly desire sole custody is provided with adequate visitation rights, and perhaps other terms that would not be very onerous from the other spouse's perspective, an amicable arrangement may be achievable. It might alternatively be possible to work out some joint custody agreement that would be acceptable to the two disputants — and good for the children involved.

If negotiators hope to expand the overall pie and look for mutually beneficial exchanges, they must initially classify the goals sought by their respective sides as "essential," "important," or "desirable." They must then endeavor to determine the degree to which their own side's aims conflict with the goals of their adversary (Raiffa, 2003, at 199–201; Menkel-Meadow, 2001, at 109–11; Watkins & Rosegrant, 2001, at 22–23; Goldman, 1991, at 8–11; Young, 1975, at 10–12). In some instances, both parties may actually desire the identical result. In others, each may wish to attain independent objectives that do not conflict with the interests of their opponent. In only some areas will both parties want to obtain the same terms. The ramifications of this phenomenon are graphically represented in Table 2 (taken from Bastress & Harbaugh, 1990, at 483).

TABLE 2

	Shared Needs	Independent Needs		Conflicting Needs	
		SIDE A	SIDE B	SIDE A	SIDE B
Essential Needs					
Important Needs					
Desirable Needs					

Proficient negotiators are able to ascertain the areas of shared needs and independent needs and ensure the appropriate distribution of these non-conflicting items. To the extent they accomplish this goal, they can effectively expand the pie to be divided and significantly enhance the likelihood of an overall accord. As both sides recognize the mutual gains that may be achieved, the areas of conflict seem less significant. Since they realize that many of their other objectives can be attained, they are more willing to consider realistic compromises with respect to the controverted issues.

When negotiators attempt to resolve disputes over the conflicting terms, they must remember the degree of interest their respective clients have expressed regarding these items. If one side considers a disputed matter "essential" while the other side views it as "important" or "desirable," the participants should be able to generate a mutual accommodation by assigning that item to the side that values it more in exchange for something the other side considers important.

Competitive/adversarial bargainers, particularly those with win-lose mentalities, may be hesitant to accept this approach. They think that their aggressive tactics should enable them to seize the "essential" and "important" items for their own side, regardless of the other side's value system. While they may occasionally be able to achieve this type of skewed result against inept or careless opponents, they can rarely hope to do so against skilled adversaries. It thus behooves them to explore the areas that may generate joint gains. To the extent they can satisfy opponent interests at little or no cost to their own client, they greatly increase the likelihood of a beneficial agreement from their own side's perspective (Kramer, 2001, at 126). So long as they are able to obtain what their own client desires, they should not be displeased by the fact that their opponent's interests have also been satisfied.

On some occasions, negotiators do not achieve optimal agreements due to their failure to consider unstated alternatives. They focus entirely on the positions that have been enunciated by the participants and ignore the possibility that other formulations may more effectively satisfy the underlying interests of the parties. Brainstorming negotiators who can explore their respective interests and objectives in a nonthreatening and neutral manner can usually discover options not previously contemplated by them or their clients. This is particularly true when they are not afraid to be innovative. Each party can then indicate candidly which of the newly discovered alternatives are better or worse for them compared to their previously articulated position statements. Their areas of mutual gain should be emphasized, with their areas of direct conflict being minimized.

As more beneficial alternatives are ascertained and divided, areas that previously appeared to create insurmountable barriers may no longer seem so important. This is why negotiators should not focus merely on their stated positions, but should instead explore the underlying motivational factors of their respective clients. They should not permit themselves to become locked into unyielding positions, because this situation usually precipitates counterproductive results (Fisher & Ury, 1981, at 5). Even though the parties might not ultimately receive what they initially demanded, if both can finally obtain terms that satisfy their true needs, the negotiation process will have functioned effectively. Such a result would generally be impossible, however, without a carefully developed and thoroughly explored Information Stage. Those individuals who ignore this reality and try to curtail the Information Stage to permit more rapid movement into the Competitive/Distributive Stage normally pay dearly for their tactical oversight.

D.   THE COMPETITIVE/DISTRIBUTIVE STAGE (VALUE CLAIMING)

During the Information Phase, negotiators focus primarily upon the needs, interests, and objectives of their *opponents*. They attempt to determine the different alternatives that may satisfy the underlying goals of both parties. Through this process, effective participants are able to determine most, if not all, of the basic economic and noneconomic items that may be divided between them. Once this informational objective is achieved, the focus of the discussions changes from what the opposing parties hope to achieve to what the negotiators want to obtain for their *own clients*. The demarcation between the Information Stage and the Competitive/Distributive Stage may be readily discerned. The bargainers are no longer asking questions regarding each other's circumstances. They are instead articulating their own side's specific demands. Interrogatory sentences are replaced by declaratory statements, as may be seen in the following examples:

INFORMATION STAGE EXCHANGES

(1) What does your client want to obtain from this transaction?

(2) Why does your client hope to achieve those objectives?

(3) What other items might alternatively satisfy the underlying needs and interests of your client?

(4) Do you think that ——————— might provide your client with what he/she really has to have?

(5) What does your client plan to do if he/she is unable to reach a deal with us?

COMPETITIVE/DISTRIBUTIVE STAGE EXCHANGES

(1) If these discussions are going to be mutually beneficial, my client must obtain at least ——————— .

(2) If your client is not willing to provide us with at least ——————— , we are not going to be able to reach an agreement.

(3) If your client plans to demand more than ——————— , no settlement can possibly be achieved.

(4) I am not in a position to offer you more than ——————— .

(5) As I understand this case, your client is not entitled to more than

——————— .

Although the Information Stage is an important part of the negotiation process, it is the Competitive/Distributive Stage that determines what each party ultimately receives. Some people prefer to regard this part of the bargaining process as the "Distributive" Stage, because it is during this portion of their interaction that the participants actually divide between them the items they think are available for distribution. Others prefer the term "Competitive" Stage, to emphasize the inherent competition indigenous to this "*value claiming*" part of the transaction. The negotiators should diligently seek to advance the interests of their own clients, preferring to obtain as much as possible within the bounds of propriety.

The parties are not merely endeavoring to divide up the available bargaining items in a wholly equitable manner, because there are seldom objective standards that can be employed to determine what each side "deserves" to receive. Negotiators rarely possess equal bargaining power and identical proficiency, and the participants with greater strength and skill should be able to obtain more beneficial results than their weaker opponents. Furthermore, the parties generally value the various items quite differently, thus preventing any truly detached comparison of the terms received by each (Karrass, 1970, at 144–145). The critical question at the conclusion of a negotiation is not whether a party obtained all of what it initially wanted or whether it did better or worse than the other side, but whether, given its situation, the party is pleased with what it received.

If one negotiator truly believes — correctly or erroneously — that his or her client deserves more than opposing counsel tentatively thinks should be granted, the bargainer with the firmer belief will generally be more successful than their uncertain adversary. The negotiation process is a psychological interaction in which reality is defined more by the perceptions of the participants than by external criteria. Negotiators who ignore this fact and attempt to obtain only "fair" results for their clients tend to achieve less beneficial agreements than they might otherwise have attained. If they fail to recognize the competitive aspect of their exchange, they may not exercise the degree of circumspection warranted in such adversarial circumstances.

Although negotiators should never try to injure their opponents because of an irrational "win-lose" mentality, they should realize that their own preliminary assessments may have either overemphasized their own weaknesses or overestimated the strengths of their adversary. It is only through a rigorous Competitive/Distributive Stage that they can test their tentative, pre-negotiation evaluations. If their opponent has concluded that they should receive more than they anticipated, it would normally be improper for them to ignore that side's generosity. Their opponent is probably aware of circumstances unknown to them, and it would be appropriate in such circumstances for them to defer to the perspective of opposing counsel.

1. POWER BARGAINING AND CONCESSION STRATEGY

The Competitive/Distributive Stage generally involves some power bargaining, as the advocates try to obtain optimal results for their respective clients with respect to the items both sides hope to obtain (Wetlaufer, 1996). The purpose of power bargaining is to influence opponent conceptions pertaining to the interaction. This may be accomplished by inducing those persons to reassess their own situations. Have operative weaknesses been ignored or inappropriately minimized? Have strengths been overestimated? Subtle questions and disclosures may be used to undermine the confidence opposing parties have in their own positions. For example, a party trying to lease commercial space to a business firm may know that the firm is considering alternative locations. By emphasizing the parking and public transportation associated with their building that are not available at the other locations, lessor representatives can weaken opponent beliefs regarding the equivalency of the other sites.

Adroit negotiators may similarly expand their own bargaining power by convincing opponents that they possess greater strength or less vulnerability than their adversaries initially anticipated (Bacharach & Lawler, 1981, at 60–63). They may do this by mentioning the fact that other parties have approached them regarding the space in question. If they suspect that the other side thinks they desperately need immediate cash to pay off a balloon note that is coming due, they can casually indicate that they recently refinanced the building and entered into a long-term financial arrangement.

Self-assurance is an important attribute possessed by most successful negotiators. They exude an inner confidence in their positions, and always appear to be in control of themselves and their bargaining interactions. They do not seem to fear the possibility of nonsettlements, suggesting to opponents that they have developed alternative options that will protect client interests should the negotiation process be unproductive. This confidence frequently causes adversaries to accord these individuals more power and respect than they objectively deserve.

Since there is no such thing as actual bargaining power, but merely the parties' perceptions of it, confident participants often obtain negotiated results far beyond what others might have achieved in the identical circumstances. Their adversaries begin to assume that these seemingly invulnerable individuals can attain beneficial outcomes through external channels if the present negotiation is unsuccessful, and they begin to ignore the external options that might be available to their own side. As a result, their opponents tend to exaggerate their own perceived need to settle. They feel that everything will be lost if they are unable to achieve mutually acceptable terms. As their perceived cost of nonsettlement increases and their perception of the opponent's cost of nonsettlement decreases, the bargaining authority they accord to their adversaries expands dramatically. Negotiation participants should always remember this phenomenon, and regularly review their actual circumstances to determine if they have irrationally overestimated the strength of their opponent or unreasonably undervalued their own side's situation. No matter how invulnerable their opponent's position may seem, they must go behind that side's facade and ask themselves what weaknesses they would have if they were in that party's shoes.

Proficient negotiators commence bargaining interactions with appropriately elevated aspiration levels. Less successful advocates begin with deflated objectives, fearing that their initial demands may engender hostility if they are not modest and reasonable. While this may be true, it is apparent that those who commence negotiations with unpretentious objectives invariably achieve moderate results (Karrass, 1970, at 17–18). Once negotiators accept this reality and begin bargaining talks with appropriately raised aspirations, they find that opponents are more likely to defer to their judgements and grant them greater concessions.

Persuasive bargainers begin the Competitive/Distributive Stage with "principled" positions that rationally explain their underlying bases. This bolsters the confidence these negotiators have in their own positions. They also start with carefully developed concession patterns (Freund, 1992, at 130-41). They know how they plan to move from their opening offers toward their final objectives. They may intend to make several deliberate, but expansive, concessions, or prefer to employ a series of incremental position changes. Negotiators know that this aspect of their strategy must be thoughtfully choreographed to maximize their bargaining effectiveness. They recognize the need to make "principled" concessions that may be rationally explained to opponents. This lets others know why the precise position change is occurring, and it indicates why a greater modification is not presently warranted. This approach also helps keep them at their new position until they obtain a reciprocal concession from the other side. Their concession strategy should be based upon their pre-negotiation planning and the new insights developed during the Information Stage.

The anticipated timing of concessions is critical. Many risk-averse individuals find it difficult to cope with the uncertainty associated with the negotiation process. They often make rapid concessions in a desperate effort to precipitate mutual accords. They ignore the fact that approximately 80 percent of position changes tend to occur during the last 20 percent of the interaction (Dawson, 2001, at 171). Those who attempt to expedite the transaction in an artificial manner usually pay a high price for their impatience (LePoole, 1991, at 72). Proficient opponents have little difficulty inducing these persons to close most of the distance between their opening offers. In addition, people who generate position changes easily tend to devalue them, while individuals who have to work diligently to obtain concessions tend to appreciate them (Cohen, 2003, at 150–51). Negotiators should thus take their time when making concessions, to induce opponents to invest sufficient time in the process to value the new offers they receive.

Concessions must be carefully formulated and strategically made. If properly used, a concession can signal both a cooperative attitude and a sufficient firmness to indicate the need for a counteroffer if the opponent desires to continue the negotiation process. If carelessly issued, however, a concession can conversely signal anxiety and a loss of control. This type of crisis may arise, for example, when a concession is made in a tentative and unprincipled manner by an individual who continues to talk nervously and defensively after the concession has been communicated. Such a transaction indicates that the speaker does not expect immediate reciprocity from opposing counsel. When adroit bargainers encounter these individuals, they should subtly encourage them to keep talking, because this approach frequently precipitates additional, unanswered concessions (Harsany, 1975, at 80–81). To avoid this problem, skilled negotiators make their concessions with appropriate explanations (i.e., "principled" concessions), and they then shift the focus to their opponents. They accomplish this shift with appropriate silence and patience following their concession, indicating that some reciprocal behavior must be forthcoming if the interaction is to continue.

Hartje has insightfully recognized that a concession should emerge in four parts:

> (1) A well reasoned, carefully justified relinquishment of a previous position.

> (2) The arrival at a new bargaining point to which the negotiator is committed for reasons of principle, fairness, cost, precedent, logic, client direction, lack of authority, and so forth.

> (3) An extraction, on the basis of the spirit of compromise and good faith bargaining, of a counter concession with a willingness to entertain further discussion.

> (4) Any concession and a new commitment point should be articulated in the language of the parties' needs or interests rather than some mechanical position or posture. [Hartje, 1984, at 167.]

The amount and timing of each position change are crucial. Each successive concession should be smaller than the preceding one, and each should normally be made in response to an appropriate counteroffer from the opponent. Consider, for example, a plaintiff personal injury lawyer who hopes to achieve a settlement in the $40,000 to $50,000 range for an automobile accident victim who suffered a severe whiplash injury, including cracked vertebrae, that necessitated painful treatment and the wearing of a cervical collar for the past eight months. The plaintiff continues to experience less severe pain that is expected to abate within the next four months. Plaintiff attorney might employ the following approach:

Plaintiff: I'm willing to start the bargaining process with a demand for $97,000. The plaintiff has had $10,000 in medical bills, lost a $5,000 automobile, and lost $8,000 in earnings. He/she will require some additional rehabilitative treatment that should cost about $2,000. He/she experienced excruciating pain for the past eight months and is expected to have less severe discomfort over the next four months. An appropriate amount for the first eight months of extreme pain might reasonably be calculated at $10 per hour for 5760 hours (8 mos. × 30 days per mo. × 24 hrs. per day) or $57,600. For the next four months of pain, a rate of $5 per hour covering 2880 hours (4 mos. × 30 days per mo. × 24 hrs. per day) would properly amount to $14,400.

Defendant: [Responds with an opening offer of $15,000 covering the medical expenses and the cost of the destroyed automobile. Defendant suggests that it is not clear that the defendant was at fault.]

Plaintiff: I'm glad that you have at least indicated a willingness to approach this matter seriously, instead of with an unreasonably low offer. But, you have clearly failed to consider lost earnings, the expected cost of future rehabilitative treatment, and plaintiff's substantial pain and suffering. On the other hand, it is possible that a jury might find that the defendant was not negligent. My review of the facts, however, suggests that this is not very likely. We have found an independent witness who will testify that the defendant was driving carelessly. Nonetheless, recognizing the 20% possibility of a verdict for the defendant, I would be willing to reduce our demand to $77,600 (80% of $97,000).

Defendant: [Responds with an offer of $25,000 covering all of the expenses except those pertaining to pain and suffering. Suggests that plaintiff was probably partially responsible for the accident in dispute, which is relevant in our presumably comparative negligence jurisdiction.]

Plaintiff: I'm glad to see that we're making some real progress. But once you acknowledge that the plaintiff is entitled to something, you have to recognize his/her right to relief for his/her severe pain and suffering. I realize that the plaintiff may have contributed somewhat to the accident, and if we assume for the sake of argument that he/she was 15% responsible, we would be willing to accept $65,960 (85% of prior demand of $77,600).

Defendant: [Counters with an offer of $34,000, admitting that plaintiff is entitled to some compensation for his/her pain and suffering, but suggests that plaintiff's demand regarding this item is excessive.]

Plaintiff: I appreciate your good faith and am confident that we can resolve this matter amicably. However, your suggested award of $9,000 for plaintiff's pain and suffering is wholly inadequate. Even if we reduced the amount for the first eight months of extreme pain to $8 per hour and that for the next four months to $4 per hour, he/she would still be entitled to $57,600

(8 mos. × 30 days per mo. × 24 hrs. per day × $8 per hr. = $46,080, plus 4 mos. × 30 days per mo. × 24 hrs. per day × $4 per hr. = $11,520). When this is reduced by the 20% possibility of a verdict for the defendant and by a possible 15% degree of plaintiff's own negligence, the total for pain and suffering becomes $39,168. When this is added to the $17,000 in other expenses ($25,000 reduced by 20% and by 15%), the total due becomes $56,168.

Defendant: [Admits the partial forcefulness of plaintiff's arguments, but still claims that the amount being sought for pain and suffering is somewhat elevated, particularly with respect to that pertaining to the next four months. Counters with an offer of $42,000.]

Plaintiff: I'll admit that the plaintiff's discomfort is much less now than it was during the past eight months, but he/she still continues to experience some real pain. If we were to utilize a $2 per hour figure for the pain and suffering over the next four months, instead of the $4 figure, we could reduce our demand by $3,917 (4 mos. × 30 days per mo. × 24 hrs. per day × $2 per hr. = $5,760, which must be reduced by the 20% and 15% factors previously cited to equal $3,917). We would thus be willing to accept $52,251.

Defendant: [Admits that the plaintiff is entitled to some monetary relief for the remaining four months of pain and suffering and offers $45,600.]

[From these positions, the plaintiff attorney should use similarly principled explanations to reduce his/her demand to the $50,000–$51,000 range, while the defendant lawyer increases his/her offer to the $48,000–$49,000 range. The parties would be likely to arrive at a final settlement figure near the midpoint of these last offers. The plaintiff attorney should thus achieve a result near the upper end of his/her initial target range.]

It is important to emphasize the highly "principled" rationale given by the plaintiff lawyer to explain each particular position modification. Following each new demand, he/she immediately shifted the focus to defendant counsel to precipitate an appropriate counter offer from that party. It should also be noted how each party's successive concessions diminished in size, as would generally be expected during a negotiation. Successful negotiators tend to make both fewer and smaller concessions than their less successful adversaries (Karrass, 1970, at 18–19).

As is graphically demonstrated by the above exchange, it is crucial for negotiators to plan their anticipated concession pattern prior to the commencement of the Competitive/Distributive Stage. Nevertheless, they must recognize that opponents will not always react as they initially expected. They must thus be prepared to alter their planned behavior as new information regarding adversary strengths, weaknesses, and preferences is ascertained (Gulliver, 1979, at 100). Not only should they be prepared to adjust their aspiration level when appropriate, they must also be ready to change their concession strategy accordingly — based upon mutually acknowledged objective criteria (Fisher & Ury, 1981, at 88–89). They must be patient, realizing that a particular transaction may take more time to complete than they originally anticipated. When concessions are small and the issues are numerous and/or complex, negotiators must permit the process to unfold deliberately. If they attempt to unduly accelerate the transaction, they may place themselves at a tactical disadvantage (Rubin & Brown, 1975, at 145). They would exude a fear of nonsettlement that could be exploited by an alert opponent.

Bargainers who do not carefully monitor their concession patterns frequently encounter unexpected difficulty. Some find themselves making unintended consecutive concessions that are not matched by reciprocal counter offers. Through this practice, they give up more than they planned to concede. They should rely upon the generally recognized "norm of reciprocity" (Pratkanis & Aronson, 1991, at 180-81) to extract corresponding position changes from recalcitrant adversaries. Irrational concession patterns cause similar problems. For example, if a negotiator's first concession is $10,000, the second concession is $8,000, and the third concession is $6,000, it would normally make no sense to make a fourth concession of $9,000. Such a pattern would probably indicate that the bargainer does not know what he or she is doing or that he or she unsuccessfully attempted to establish a false position that could not be sustained after the first three concessions had been made. Either circumstance would be likely to confuse opponents and undermine the negotiation process (Hartje, 1984, at 166; Hamner & Yukl in Drukman, 1977, at 139). If the person fruitlessly sought to establish a false resistance point, he or she should not disclose this failure during the present discussions. It would be preferable for the individual to suspend the talks to enable him or her to confer with the absent client. This procedure would enable the bargainer to restart the interaction at a later date with an appropriately modified concession pattern.

One additional consideration regarding concession strategy should be noted. When negotiators establish their anticipated opening positions and target areas, they must recognize the need to ultimately reach a settlement range that is sufficiently generous to induce opposing counsel to view agreement as a viable alternative to a nonsettlement. If their planned bottom line is too one-sided, this may encourage the opponent to reject it in favor of the consequences of no accord. Only when bargainers make final offers that truly tempt their adversaries vis-a-vis the results of nonsettlement can they reasonably expect their final offers to be seriously considered. The actual range varies in each situation, depending upon the applicable circumstances and the personal traits of the participants. While some negotiators and their clients may be readily willing to accept the possibility of nonsettlements, more risk-averse individuals are not. People dealing with risk-averse parties should be careful not to be needlessly generous, recognizing that even less beneficial final offers may be viewed by these persons as preferable to the risks associated with bargaining stalemates. This might be particularly true, for instance, for plaintiff demands that are just within the limits of defendant insurance policies, in states where "bad faith" rejections of such demands could subject defendant insurance carriers to liability for the entire amount of subsequently obtained verdicts in excess of actual policy limits.

Negotiators must always remember their nonsettlement options and their preliminarily established resistance points as they near their bottom lines during bargaining interactions. They must recognize that it would be irrational to accept proposed terms that are less beneficial than their external alternatives. As the Competitive/Distributive Stage evolves and they approach their resistance points, many advocates feel greater settlement pressure than is warranted. When the terms being offered by opponents are not meaningfully better than their nonsettlement options, participants approaching their bottom lines possess more — not less — bargaining power than the offerors. They have little to lose if no mutual accords are achieved, and they should not be afraid to reject the disadvantageous proposals that are on the table. Instead of exuding weakness, as so many negotiators do in these circumstances, they should project strength. Since their opponents are likely to lose more than they lose from nonsettlements, they can confidently demand further concessions as a prerequisite to any final agreement.

As the Competitive/Distributive Stage evolves, the parties usually encounter temporary impasses. The participants are presumably endeavoring to obtain optimal terms for their respective clients, and each is hoping to induce the other to make the next position change. Individuals who have viable external options should not hesitate to disclose — at least minimally — this critical fact. The more their adversaries know about these matters, the more likely they are to acknowledge the need for more accommodating behavior. It is usually preferable to convey this information in a calm and non-confrontational fashion (Freund, 1992, at 47). Advocates who refuse to divulge the parameters of their nonsettlement alternatives at critical stages frequently fail to achieve accords they might have attained had their opponents been fully aware of their actual circumstances.

A cooperative/problem-solving approach is more likely to produce beneficial results than a competitive/adversarial strategy. The former permits the participants to explore the opportunity for mutual gain in a relatively objective and detached manner (Gifford, 1989, at 16-18), while the latter style is more likely to generate mistrust and an unwillingness to share sensitive information. Furthermore, cooperative/problem-solving overtures minimize inter-party conflict and help to create a positive bargaining atmosphere.

On some occasions, negotiators encounter stereotypical compet-itive/adversarial opponents who hope to achieve win-lose results. As these adversaries resort to offensive and disruptive tactics, it is easy to contemplate a quid pro quo response. When this takes place, however, the entire process tends to break down. Patient and calm participants can frequently use different techniques to disarm nasty and abrasive adversaries. In response to loud diatribes, they can tranquilly explore the relevant circumstances in a wholly professional manner (Freund, 1992, at 87). They should attempt to ascertain and emphasize the areas of positional overlap, and minimize the focus on the highly controverted items (Lewicki, et al., 1994, at 152-53; Ury, 1991, at 106-07).

When specific offers are met with harsh, unreceptive replies, negotiators can employ their questioning skills to direct the attention of their opponents to appropriate areas. This may enable them to elicit information from their adversaries regarding their underlying needs and interests (Bazerman & Neale, 1992, at 90–95). As they obtain helpful insights regarding the other side's value system, they should divulge facts concerning their own side's objectives. This may permit them to generate a minimal degree of trust and allow them to encourage a mutual, problem-solving effort (Lewicki, et al., 1994, at 143-59).

Opponents who are summarily rejecting everything being proposed by the other side need to have their negative mind-set altered. Adroit negotiators may often accomplish this objective through a series of questions that are designed to elicit affirmative responses from the uncooperative participants (Gray, 2003, at 308).

Cooperative Party: I gather you are dissatisfied with our proposal?

Adversarial Party: You're damn right I am!

Cooperative Party: I understand you are most concerned about the fact that our offer doesn't help you with respect to _____ ?

Adversarial Party: That is correct. If there is going to be any agreement, you are going to have to satisfy our needs regarding _____ .

Cooperative Party: I assume that if you cannot obtain _____ (the exact term being demanded), you might be able to live with an alternative such as _____ ?

Adversarial Party: That is something we might seriously consider.

Cooperative Party: I think that we can alter our position to accommodate your concerns. If we were to provide _____ , I gather that this would begin to satisfy your side's basic needs?

Adversarial Party: Yes. That would be a vast improvement over where we began this exchange. Is there some way you might be able to address our needs pertaining to _____ ?

Through such inquiries, cooperative parties can induce adversarial opponents to replace their unreceptive attitudes with problem-solving mind-sets. These kinds of transformations significantly enhance the probability of mutual accords.

2.   COMMON POWER BARGAINING TECHNIQUES

During the Competitive/Distributive Stage of negotiations, the participants employ various techniques to advance their respective interests. Different tactics may be used in isolation or in combination with one or more other power bargaining ploys. Negotiators should learn to vary their approach to keep opponents off balance. If bargainers become too predictable, their tactics lose their effectiveness. During bargaining interactions, participants must remember the sequence of their presentations and carefully monitor the verbal and nonverbal responses emanating from their opponents to determine which techniques appear to be functioning most effectively. They must simultaneously endeavor to ascertain the techniques being employed by their opponents, to enable them to counter those tactics.

Problems and misunderstandings frequently arise during the Compet-itive/Distributive Stage of negotiations, when one or both participants fail to listen sufficiently to the communications coming from the other parties. As people negotiate, they tend to concentrate on what they are saying and what they are planning to say. As a result, they fail to discern many of the verbal leaks and nonverbal signals emanating from the other participants. They instead attribute to their opponents what they expect them to be saying. In many instances, parties do not realize that their adversaries are discreetly or even openly indicating accommodating attitudes, because they have already assumed unreceptive responses. Furthermore, if negotiators think that the failure of opponents to "hear" all of their signals is undermining the bargaining process, they should wait until they can regain the full attention of their adversaries and clarify the issues in question.

a. Argument

The power bargaining tactic employed most frequently by lawyers involves legal and nonlegal argument (Williams, 1983, at 79–81). When the facts support their positions, they emphasize the factual aspects of the transaction. When applicable legal doctrines favor their claim, they cite appropriate statutes, decisions, and/or scholarly authorities. Public policy considerations are invoked when they advance client interests. When large business transactions are being discussed, the participants often include economic and even political considerations.

Competitive negotiators may adopt rhetorical and psychological maneuvers that are designed, subtly or overtly, to induce opponent acquiescence, without regard to the substantive merits. Their primary objective is to prevail, not to elucidate or to promote understanding (Condlin, 1985, at 73). These individuals hope to persuade adversaries through the use of seemingly objective contentions that do not appear to be unduly slanted in the direction of their own clients.

Adroit negotiators should be able to combine competitive and cooperative forms of argument. When they believe they can effectively advance client interests through the use of one-sided assertions that do not disclose adverse information that opposing counsel may not have discovered, they may decide to make representations skewed toward their positions. On the other hand, when weaknesses have already been disclosed, such a biased approach would be unlikely to have the intended impact. In these circumstances, it would be preferable to use a more even-handed technique. They could explore the pertinent considerations in a relatively neutral fashion, hoping to induce their adversaries to agree with their assessments.

Even when negotiators employ cooperative arguments, it should be recognized that they are endeavoring to generate conclusions favorable to their positions. While they may eschew obviously competitive tactics for strategic reasons, they are still attempting to articulate their thoughts in a manner that should precipitate beneficial results. Individuals who ignore this fact and are seduced by seemingly candid discussions to disclose everything regarding their own aspirations and concerns frequently find themselves at a disadvantage (Lowenthal, 1982, at 85). Very few successful bargainers are willing to divulge everything that adversely affects their case, even when they claim to be engaged in completely open evaluations of their situations.

Persuasive argument cannot be presented in an obviously one-sided manner. Strident assertions that do not seem to have rational foundations are unlikely to influence respondents. If competitive or cooperative contentions are to have any meaningful impact, they must appear to be even-handed and relatively objective (Bastress & Harbaugh, 1990, at 437–38; Zartman & Berman, 1982, at 115). They must be presented in a logical and orderly sequence that will have a cumulative effect upon the recipients. Negotiations usually involve repetitive communications, as each party seeks to alter the other's assessment of the operative circumstances. Cogent arguments should not be restated in a verbatim fashion. They should instead be expressed in different formulations to enhance their persuasiveness.

Effective arguments are presented in a comprehensive, rather than a conclusionary manner (Bastress & Harbaugh, 1990, at 435–37). Applicable factual and legal information is disclosed with appropriate detail. For example, a plaintiff lawyer who merely claims that a broken leg is worth $5,000 would not be as likely to persuade an adversary as would an attorney who carefully describes the exact injury suffered and compares it with comparable situations cited in *Jury Verdict Reports* for the relevant geographical area indicating that a $5,000 figure is reasonable with respect to such an injury. Negotiators who ignore this consideration may frequently be challenged by effective counter arguments demonstrating that underlying factual and/or legal assumptions inherent in their initial conclusionary representations are distinguishable from the present circumstances.

Persuasive arguments are insightful and carefully articulated. If their content is not fully comprehended and their underlying logic is not understood, their degree of influence is appreciably diminished. Efficacious assertions go beyond what is expected by opponents. Contentions that do not surprise the receiving parties rarely undermine the confidence those people have in their preconceived positions. However, assertions that raise issues not previously contemplated by the recipients are likely to induce those individuals to recognize the need for reassessment of their current perceptions.

Negotiators should not ignore the potential persuasiveness of emotional contentions (Bastress & Harbaugh, 1990, at 439-40). Attorneys are generally intelligent people. They are able to deflect cerebral arguments that are based entirely on logical analysis. On the other hand, many perspicacious individuals have a difficult time countering emotional claims that generate feelings of guilt or compassion and interfere with their ability to analyze situations in an objective manner. Advocates should not hesitate to formulate arguments that are designed to elicit emotional responses, because these frequently produce beneficial results.

Successful negotiators are generally persons who can develop innovative and unanticipated arguments that effectively contradict preconceived assumptions. Once opponents are impelled to internally question the rationales they previously developed to support their perceptions of the transaction, they tend to suffer a significant loss of bargaining confidence. The removal of their underlying positional foundations normally induces them to consider more seriously the legal and factual interpretations being offered by their opponents. It is this very process that causes them to move inexorably toward the entreaties of their adversaries.

When complex legal and/or factual issues are involved, they should be broken down into manageable subparts. This permits adroit negotiators to achieve agreement on various uncontroverted subissues, which enhances the likelihood of an overall accord (Hartje, 1984, at 156). This technique creates an atmosphere of cooperation and generates bargaining momentum toward a final settlement (Ilich, 1973, at 147). It frequently permits disputants to minimize the direct conflict indigenous to the larger issues, and allows them to make progress in a less adversarial environment.

Former Supreme Court Justice and former United Nations Ambassador Arthur J. Goldberg succinctly noted the attributes of successful bargainers:

> The best negotiator is not an advocate. The best negotiator is a man who could perform the role of mediator in the negotiations if he were called upon to perform that role. In other words, while he may have to engage in advocacy to reach a common ground, he should never be overly persuaded by his own advocacy. Advocacy should be a tactic and not an end in the negotiations. [Zartman & Berman, 1982, at 115.]

Negotiators must always recognize the need to retain their detached objectivity, even when they seem to be making forceful arguments. They should never become so enamored with their own assertions that they either fail to remember the overstated nature of their claims or ignore valid considerations being articulated by their opponents. Those individuals who permit the exuberance generated by their own arguments to cloud their judgment often find that they have failed to achieve beneficial agreements that were otherwise attainable. These people are also unable to provide their clients with the professional objectivity that clients need and have the right to expect from legal counsel.

b. Threats, Warnings, and Promises

It is rare for negotiations to occur without the presence of overt or implicit threats. The stereotypical threat consists of "a communication from one party to a second indicating that, if the second party does not settle according to terms acceptable to the first party, the first party will take action unpleasant or detrimental to the second party." (Lowenthal, 1982, at 86.) Threats are employed to indicate to recalcitrant parties that the cost of disagreeing with proposed offers transcends the cost of acquiescence (Schelling, 1975, at 329-34). Some negotiators eschew the use of formal "threats," preferring to resort to less confrontational "warnings." They merely caution opponents about the consequences that will naturally result from their failure to accept mutual resolutions of the underlying disputes (Freund, 1992, at 212-13; Ikle, 1964, at 62–63). These "warnings" are not premised upon action the declarants plan to take against the opposing parties, but rather the events that will independently evolve if no settlements are achieved.

When adverse consequences are likely to result if agreements are not achieved, it is frequently beneficial to articulate the negative possibilities as "warnings" rather than "threats" (Elster, 1995, at 252–53). For example, instead of litigators suggesting that they will initiate a lawsuit if no settlement is reached, they may alternatively indicate that their client will do so — as if their client were a wholly independent and uncontrollable actor. Labor union negotiators may similarly state that bargaining unit workers will go on strike if a new collective contract is not attained, instead of suggesting that they will request a walk out. The use of the warning device softens the statement being made. Since the resulting consequences are not based directly on what the speakers will do themselves, it makes it more palatable to the listeners (Mayer, 1996, at 64–65). In addition, the warning technique enhances the credibility of the negative alternatives being discussed, because the speakers are suggesting that the adverse consequences will result from the actions of third parties over whom they exert minimal or no control.

Psychologists and game theorists carefully distinguish between negative "*threats*" and affirmative "*promises*" (Pruitt & Rubin, 1986, at 51–55; Schelling, 1975, at 335-37). A promise does not involve the suggestion of negative consequences, but instead consists of "an expressed intention to behave in a way that appears beneficial to the interests of another." (Rubin & Brown, 1975, at 278.) For example, a bargainer might promise to respond with beneficence if the opponent takes certain action. It is hoped that this affirmative promise will induce the desired response without the need for resort to a negative threat. Furthermore, a promise is a face-saving technique, because the opponent is told that the suggested position change will be reciprocated. On the other hand, a party that is threatened with negative consequences if specified action is not taken is never certain that any benefit will result if it agrees to do what the threatening party is demanding.

Implicit in any promise is the threat to refrain from acting positively if the other party fails to behave appropriately. In this sense, even promises may be considered subtle "threats." The one significant distinction between affirmative promises and negative threats concerns the fact that use of the former tactic tends to elicit a general liking of the transmitter, while use of the latter technique tends to generate hostility (Rubin & Brown, 1975, at 285). It is thus easy to understand why affirmative promises are more likely to contribute to an atmosphere of cooperation than negative threats which create a more competitive environment.

Almost all negotiators frequently use the classic promise technique. After extensive discussions, the parties are only $5,000 apart. One of the participants reasonably suggests that they close the remaining gap by "splitting the difference." It is more productive to propose that each party simultaneously move $2,500, than to threaten dire consequences if the other side does not unilaterally concede $2,500. Bargainers should not hesitate to employ promises earlier in their interactions to break temporary impasses. When it appears that each side is afraid to modify its position without some indication that this action will be reciprocated, one participant can propose that they agree to prepare new position statements that will be disclosed concurrently. This permits both sides to move together without fear that their movement will be ignored by the other party.

Promises, threats, and warnings convey significant information regarding the transmitter's perception of the other party's circumstances. Positive promises clearly indicate what the promisor believes the recipient wants to obtain, while negative threats disclose what the threatener thinks the listener fears. Recipients of this information may be able to use it to their advantage. If, for example, the opponent appears to believe that they wish to obtain a particular item that is not highly valued by their client, they may endeavor to extract some other meaningful term in exchange for this issue. Conversely, if their adversary suggests through a threat that he or she thinks that they would lose more from a nonsettlement than they actually would, it would normally be productive to disabuse the opponent of this misconception so that he or she will not assume that they have a greater need to reach agreement than they do.

It is interesting to note that negotiators tend to transmit affirmative promises more frequently than they do negative threats (Rubin & Brown, 1975, at 282). This fact frequently surprises bargainers, because most people remember more of the threats made than the promises issued during bargaining discussions. It is also important to understand that "the use of [affirmative] promises tends to increase the likelihood of bargainers reaching a mutually favorable agreement, while the use of [negative] threats tends to reduce this likelihood." (Rubin & Brown, 1975, at 286.) This demonstrates that negotiators can usually obtain consistently better results through the use of affirmative tactics that contribute to a cooperative atmosphere, than they are likely to achieve through negative techniques that detract from the bargaining process.

Bargainers who plan to employ express or implicit threats need to understand the characteristics of effective threats. They must be certain that their threats are comprehended by their opponents. Some individuals transmit such vague threats that they often go unnoticed. Threats can only be influential when the other party is cognizant of their issuance. It is similarly important to formulate threats that are credible to opponents. A credible threat is one that is reasonably proportionate to the action the declarant intends to deter — insignificant threats are usually ignored, while truly excessive threats tend to be dismissed as irrational (Lebow, 1996, at 92–93; Lowenthal, 1982, at 86). The believability of threats may be further bolstered by corroborative behavior. For example, a party threatening to take certain action detrimental to the opposing side if no agreement is reached is more convincing if the threatening party openly prepares for its effectuation.

Parties contemplating the use of affirmative promises or negative threats to advance their bargaining interests should carefully evaluate the possible risks and benefits that may be associated with such action before they act. They need to consider the manner in which their proposed challenge is likely to be perceived. They should especially remember that negative threats tend to increase the competitiveness of the individual being threatened, thereby heightening the risk of retaliation and/or intransigence (Lowenthal, 1982, at 88). It should finally be recognized that parties should never issue ultimatums they are not prepared and able to carry out, because their failure to effectuate promised action when their bluff is called substantially undermines their negotiating credibility (Mayer, 1996, at 64).

Negotiators should always remember that a threat or warning is most influential while it is outstanding — i.e., articulated but not yet effectuated. The party facing the negative consequences must decide whether it is better off acceding to the threatening side's demands or accepting the results of noncompliance. Once the threatened party decides to accept the negative consequences associated with noncompliance, the impact of the threat or warning is dissipated. It is no longer likely to influence the behavior of the party that has decided to accept the impact of its recalcitrance.

Negotiators who are threatened with negative consequences if they do not modify their current positions must always consider a crucial factor. What is the likely result if no agreement is reached with the instant opponent? If their external options are more beneficial than would be the result if they acceded to their opponent's threat, they should not be afraid to retain their present positions. If they wish to preserve a positive bargaining atmosphere, hoping that the other side will reassess its circumstances, they can simply ignore the threat (Cohen, 2003, at 273–75; Bastress & Harbaugh, 1990, at 461–62). If they behave as if no ultimatum has been issued, their adversary may be able to withdraw the threat without suffering a loss of face.

c. Rational and Emotional Appeals

Negotiators who are presented with objective arguments that undercut their positions frequently counter these assertions with rational or emotional appeals. Through the use of rational appeals, they endeavor to logically challenge the foundations underlying the contentions being advanced. They attempt to demonstrate the lack of any legal or factual basis for the arguments being articulated. If they are successful, they may be able to induce their opponent to reconsider the substantiality of the claims being conveyed.

Even when bargainers are unable to rationally undermine arguments being made, they may formulate emotional appeals that may diminish the effectiveness of those claims. This tactic is particularly potent when used against emotional opponents. While wholly cerebral challenges would be unlikely to undercut the confidence of intelligent individuals who have articulated objectively cogent contentions, emotional pleas may cause those persons to question the forcefulness of their assertions. The use of emotional appeals to highly intelligent but emotional people frequently diminishes the ability of those bargainers to rely entirely upon rational and objective factors. If it can be demonstrated that their logical arguments would inflict a seemingly unconscionable impact upon other parties, it may be possible to convince them to resort to a more conciliatory approach.

d. Ridicule and Humor

Ridicule and humor are frequently used by negotiators to indicate their scorn for unreasonable positions being taken by opponents. For example, in response to extremely one-sided initial offers, many bargainers openly smile or sarcastically laugh. This can be done in a humorous manner or in a disdainful fashion. If this technique achieves its intended objective, it will embarrass adversaries who have articulated knowingly ridiculous demands and induce them to formulate new positions that are more reasonable than their originally disclosed offers.

Some negotiators use more than a mere smile or laugh to signal their displeasure with absurd demands. They respond directly with a sarcastic retort. When confronted with obviously excessive claims, they might ask whether opposing counsel would also like to obtain the client's firstborn child and/or a quit claim deed to the light side of the moon! Through this device, recipients of outrageous demands can clearly indicate their dissatisfaction without having to discuss the merits involved. Many individuals prefer this approach, fearing that substantive challenges might mislead unrealistic opponents into believing that their initial offers are not truly unacceptable.

Humor may be employed to soften the impact of negative statements. When negotiators want to indicate their displeasure with particular proposals or with certain opponent conduct, they can do so with smiles on their faces and twinkles in their eyes. The recipients of these statements will not be sure if the speakers actually intended their devastating pronouncements. If the speakers are asked if they really intended what was communicated, they can always suggest they were only kidding! Nonetheless, their points have been made and have been comprehended by their listeners. Individuals who do not feel comfortable using humor in this manner should refrain from doing so, because they are likely to be taken seriously and be unable to defuse the anxious situation with jocularity.

Humor can be employed to accomplish other bargaining objectives. Studies indicate that the use of appropriate humor tends to increase the likability of the communicator (O'Quin & Aronoff, 1981). People should not be afraid to use humor, particularly during the preliminary stages of negotiations, to develop more open and trusting relationships with opponents. Many individuals may even use humor as a means of precipitating concessions, because evidence suggests that subjects who receive demands accompanied by humor are more likely to acquiesce than those who receive unembellished demands (O'Quin & Aronoff, 1981, at 354). Humor may be used during tense negotiations to relieve anxiety and reopen blocked communication channels (Ilich, 1973, at 186–87). A joking comment can remind the participants not to take the bargaining process personally.

e. Control of Agenda

Many individuals attempt to advance their negotiating objectives through control of the agenda. They try to limit talks to those topics that are of interest to their own clients. Proficient negotiators may accomplish this objective by beginning serious discussions with "principled" opening offers that list and value the components of the deal they want to achieve. They hope to resolve these matters favorably, before being forced to tackle other items their opponents wish to raise. If they are fortunate, their control of the agenda my even induce careless adversaries to overlook subjects that should have been discussed before consummation of an overall agreement.

Even when negotiators cannot control the specific topics to be considered, they may be able to influence the order in which they are taken up. They may thus be able to resolve certain items important to their clients before other less significant subjects are encountered. When bargainers do not like the order in which opponents are endeavoring to present topics, they should not hesitate to indicate their dissatisfaction and attempt to negotiate the manner in which the parties should proceed. This form of "attitudinal bargaining" may permit them to seize control of the agenda. Even when they are unable to obtain complete control, they should at least be able to counteract an ordering scheme that negatively affects their bargaining interests.

f. Intransigence

Successful negotiators tend to be individuals who have the ability at critical points during their interactions to convince opponents that those people must make appropriate concessions if the discussions are to continue. This may be accomplished through sheer intransigence. People exude an uncompromising attitude that is intended to make opponents believe that no further progress can be achieved if those adversaries do not modify their current positions. Such an unyielding strategy works most effectively against risk-averse individuals who fear the real or imagined consequences of nonsettlements. When opponents have options available to them outside the present negotiation arena and they appear to be willing to avail themselves of those alternatives if necessary, the use of an obstinate approach is unlikely to be productive.

g. Straightforwardness

Most people expect opponents to be circumspect during bargaining discussions. In some situations, this preconception can be used to one's advantage. If negotiators can surprise adversaries with what appears to be complete candor, they may be able to generate feelings of guilt and/or embarrassment in those persons due to their own continued use of disingenuous bargaining tactics. People who experience guilt or embarrassment often attempt to regain social acceptance by doing something to please those around them. When guilt or embarrassment is created at the bargaining table, it may well induce concessionary behavior that is intended to alleviate the anxiety being felt. Even if a straightforward approach does not immediately precipitate a concession, it may alternatively induce reciprocal candor that should enhance the overall negotiating environment. However, bargainers should not allow these tactics to cause them to respond with so much openness that they place themselves at a disadvantage vis-a-vis someone who is not being as candid.

h. Flattery

Real or feigned respect for opponents may cause them to become more accommodating at the bargaining table. The recipients of complimentary treatment may be induced to feel sympathetic toward their seemingly less talented adversaries, and this may cause them to become less aggressive negotiators. If advocates are made to feel good about themselves because of the respect being accorded them by bargaining opponents, they may not feel the same need to demonstrate their negotiating skill as they would against other less respectful opponents. They may thus be persuaded to lower their guard and to behave in a more conciliatory manner. Even if flattery does not accomplish this Machiavellian objective, it is likely to create a more pleasant atmosphere and make the negotiations progress more smoothly.

i. Manipulation of Contextual Factors

Some individuals attempt to gain a psychological advantage at the bargaining table through their manipulation of contextual factors — the day, time, location, and environment for the negotiations. When they are able to obtain concessions pertaining to these factors, this bolsters their confidence with respect to their subsequent handling of the substantive issues. This approach also permits them to establish a concessionary mentality in prospective opponents. People who begin a negotiation by conceding the date, time, and location for the impending interaction may well continue this pattern when the substantive items are discussed.

The concessionary predisposition of opponents may be further heightened through the feelings of obligation that may be created when persons are provided with complimentary food and drink at the outset of their interaction. While some people may question whether insignificant gratuities could possibly influence a person's bargaining behavior, many negotiators prefer to be the provider of such generosity rather than the recipient. Those who doubt the impact of pre-negotiation offerings should take the time to observe the behavior of the adroit religious solicitors who operate in airport lobbies. They initiate their interactions with small flowers or other relatively insignificant gifts. They then attempt to establish some degree of rapport through casual touching and seemingly sincere eye contact. It is amazing to see how quickly persons who decline to make contributions try to return the flower or gift they have received!

j. Silence

Silence is one of the most potent, yet frequently overlooked, power bargaining techniques (Steinberg, 1998, at 171).

> Only the amateur fears to be silent for a moment lest interest lag. He depends solely on words to capture attention. The artful performer knows that rhythm patterns require silence too, and nothing is more dramatic and effective than a long motionless pause after a statement. It permits absorption of the thought. It permits reflection. But more important, it compels attention to what has been said as if an italicized finger had been pointed at it. [L. Nizer, THINKING ON YOUR FEET (1963), at 26].

Many less competent negotiators fear silence. They are afraid they will lose control of the interaction if they stop talking, and they remember the awkwardness they have experienced in social settings during prolonged pauses. They thus feel compelled to speak. When they do, they tend to disclose, both verbally and nonverbally, information they did not intend to divulge (McCormack, 1984, at 108–11). They often find themselves making unintended concessions. When they are confronted by further silence from their opponents, they frequently continue their verbal leakage and concomitant loss of control.

When negotiators have something important to say, they should simply convey their intended message and become quiet. There is no need to emphasize the point with unnecessary reiteration. A clear, succinct expression accentuates the crucial nature of their communication and provides their adversary with the opportunity to absorb what has been said (Mayer, 1996, at 30). This rule is particularly critical when concessions or offers are being disclosed. Bargainers should unequivocally articulate their new positions and then quietly and patiently await responses from the receiving parties. If silence makes them feel uncomfortable, they should review their papers or otherwise look busy. They may alternatively play with their glasses or stroke their cheek. This signals to opponents that they expect those persons to reply before they say anything further.

People who discern in opponents an inability or a reluctance to remain silent should use pregnant pauses to their own advantage. After loquacious adversaries explain their positions or make offers, they may become disconcerted if no response is immediately forthcoming. As their bargaining anxiety increases, periods of silence become more unbearable. If their representations are met with cold silence, they may be induced to say more. As they fill the silent void, they frequently disclose more information, and occasionally make further unanswered concessions.

Individuals who are confronted by taciturn opponents should not assume sole responsibility to keep the discussions moving. They may decide to sit quietly until their opponents respond. If they feel too uncomfortable with this approach, they may alternatively use questions to force their adversaries to participate in the interaction. They should formulate inquiries that cannot be answered with a mere "yes" or "no," but that require some elaboration.

k. Patience

People involved in legal transactions must recognize that the negotiation process takes time to unfold. Participants who endeavor to accelerate developments in a precipitous fashion usually obtain less beneficial results than they would have attained with greater patience. Offers that would be entirely acceptable if conveyed during the latter stages of a negotiation may not be attractive if broached prematurely. The participants have to be given sufficient time to recognize that a negotiated result is preferable to their external options.

Both sides of a negotiation experience anxiety associated with the uncertainty that is inherent in these interactions. Those participants who can effectively control the tension they feel and exude a quiet confidence are generally able to achieve more favorable agreements. They have the mental and physical stamina needed to withstand prolonged discussions. They lead opponents to believe that they are willing to take as much time as is required for them to attain their bargaining objectives. It is amazing to note the number of negotiators who indicate that they finally acceded to opponent demands merely because they were unwilling to continue the process further. They had become fatigued and wanted to conclude the transaction. They failed to appreciate the effective tactic that had been used against them. They usually attributed their opponent's success to pure fortuity!

Those negotiators who like to use patience to wear down opponents should try to develop styles that are sufficiently pleasant to keep the process going when little progress is being made. When undue tension builds up, they should carefully strive to dissipate it. When silence threatens to disrupt the talks, they need to know how to reopen communication without making unintended disclosures or concessions. They must master the art of dissembling. As soon as the negotiation process has been rejuvenated sufficiently to guarantee its continuation, they can again shift the focus to their adversaries.

l. Creation of Guilt, Embarrassment, or Indebtedness

Studies indicate that parties who experience guilt, embarrassment, or indebtedness are particularly susceptible to requests for concessions. They try to relieve their social discomfort by satisfying the needs of those around them. During bargaining interactions, these factors often induce disconcerted participants to make magnanimous concessions. Some negotiators attempt to establish feelings of guilt or embarrassment by suggesting that their opponent was late for a scheduled meeting or was otherwise inconsiderate. They may alternatively blame their adversary's client for their current predicament. If they are successful in this regard, they may obtain a bargaining advantage. A simple apology can usually defuse this tactic.

Feelings of indebtedness may similarly precipitate concessions. If food and drink are to be consumed, it is preferable to be the one providing them, rather than the one accepting the hospitality. Even though some people may not permit gratuities to influence their bargaining behavior, others may unconsciously alter their conduct to their host's advantage. If important negotiations are involved, the cost of gracious hospitality toward opponents is frequently recouped in the final settlements achieved.

m. Constructive Ambiguity

During complex, multifaceted transactions, negotiators occasionally permit disagreement over an inconsequential item to preclude consensus regarding the more significant topics. Were they to assess the actual circumstances in a detached manner, they would probably realize that the tangential area in dispute is not likely to become relevant during the life of their proposed agreement. When neither party is willing — or politically able — to ignore the controverted subject, they may contemplate the drafting of a provision that appears to cover the offending topic, but that does not actually resolve the matter. The use of such "constructive ambiguity" may enable parties to achieve an agreement that would otherwise have been impossible (Zartman & Berman, 1982, at 123; Ikle, 1964, at 15). If, as is often the case, that particular provision is never questioned, the parties will have accomplished their overall objective. However, even when that contractual term subsequently does become the focus of debate, the parties can resolve their previously planned ambiguity either through further negotiations, in a less contentious environment, or by way of an arbitral or judicial determination. Even the party that ultimately loses that proceeding would end up in a better position than would have been attained had the bargainers initially allowed their discord with respect to this particular term to defeat their entire accord.

When deciding whether to adopt "constructive ambiguity" pertaining to a presently irreconcilable term, parties must consider several basic factors. How important is the disputed subject? How likely is it that the parties will be affected by this provision during the life of their agreement? What would be the consequences of a nonsettlement caused by the lack of accord with respect to this issue? If the overall costs of nonsettlement would clearly transcend both the costs of agreement *and* the risk associated with the adoption of the ambiguous contract term, the parties should seriously consider the use of this technique to produce an agreement. By providing an expeditious and relatively inexpensive arbitration procedure to resolve disputes arising under their agreement, parties can further minimize the transaction costs that would be involved if the matter ultimately had to be adjudicated.

3.   ALWAYS REMEMBER CURRENT NONSETTLEMENT ALTERNATIVES

Throughout the Distributive Stage, negotiators should always remember their *current* nonsettlement alternatives. It is no longer relevant what they were six months or a year ago, when these individuals began to prepare for the present interaction. The passage of time has generally affected the options that were available then. The discovery process many have strengthened or weakened the case of litigators, while changes in the business market may have influenced the value of the firm being purchased or sold or the technology being licensed. Has the market improved the situation of the firm being purchased or sold? Are the technology rights being licensed worth more or less than they were a year ago?

If bargainers fail to appreciate changes in the value of their immediate interaction, they may enter into an arrangement that is not better than what they would have with no agreement. They must always remember that a bad deal is worse than no deal. When nonsettlement alternatives are presently more beneficial than the terms being offered at the bargaining table, they should not hesitate to walk away from the current discussions. They should do this as pleasantly as possible for two reasons. First, when their opponents realize that they are really willing to end the interaction, their adversaries may reconsider their position and offer them more beneficial terms. Second, even if the present negotiations fail to regenerate and no accord is achieved, the parties may see each other in the future. If the other side remembers these talks favorably, even if no agreement was achieved, future negotiations are likely to progress more smoothly than if these talks ended on an unpleasant note.

4.   PSYCHOLOGICAL ENTRAPMENT

When we teach legal negotiating, we occasionally auction off a $1 bill. Our approach is different from traditional auctions. We announce that the $1 bill will be given to the highest bidder in exchange for his or her bid. We then emphasize the unusual fact that the second highest bidder will be required to provide us with the amount of his or her losing bid, even though that person will not get the $1 bill. The opening bid cannot exceed $0.50, and all subsequent offers must be divisible by $0.05 to avoid penny increments.

The bidding opens immediately at $0.50. Thereafter, offers of $0.60, $0.70, and $0.80 tend to be made in rapid succession. By this point, we casually indicate that we are already guaranteed a profit from the transaction. The audience becomes suspicious. The bidding continues to the $0.85 or $0.90 level. A participant will almost always offer $0.95. That person apparently assumes that no one would offer more, because they could not possibly receive any financial gain from a higher bid. What this bidder forgets is the fact that the second highest bidder is required to pay us his or her bid even though he or she does not get the $1 bill. As a result, when the second highest bidder is confronted with a bid of $0.95, he or she will quickly offer $1 in an effort to break even. Individuals who recognize the unusual nature of our auction before any $0.90 or $0.95 bid has been entered omit the $0.95 offer and move directly to the $1 figure, hoping to end the auction with no loss to themselves.

Once a $1 bid has been received, the process comes to a temporary halt. Both the participants and the observers are shocked by the developments that have occurred. We then remind the second highest bidder, who has bid $0.90 or $0.95, that he or she can reduce his or her overall loss by offering $1.05. Even though this act would force that person to pay more than $1.00, it will permit him or her to limit the loss to a mere $0.05. We are always able to generate a $1.05 bid. The person who had offered $1.00 must now reassess his or her situation. That individual felt confident about the prospect of breaking even, until the upstart bidder made the seemingly irrational offer of $1.05. The only way to outsmart that devious character is to suggest a figure of $1.10 or $1.15, which is expeditiously offered. After the $1.00 barrier is broken, the bidding frequently continues to the $1.75 or $2.00 level, before one of the two remaining participants decides to terminate the auction. On several occasions, we have received final bids in the $2.50 to $3.00 range.

The purpose of this seemingly frivolous exercise is to demonstrate graphically the ease with which auction participants may become psychologically entrapped by the process itself (Cohen, 2003, at 250–52; Brockner & Rubin, 1985). They initially believe they will make a profit from the transaction. They quickly discover, however, that they will be forced to accept a loss. The only question concerns the amount of their ultimate deficit. Perspicacious participants tend to minimize their exposure by terminating the auction process early, while less discerning and more competitive bidders continue for a longer period of time. One of us once sold our $1 bill for $20 to a student who actually thought he had won!

The dollar auction provides a perfect example of a phenomenon known as "winner's curse" (Bazerman & Neale, 1992, at 152-55; Murnighan, 1992, at 186-87). Auction participants who initially hoped to make a profit ultimately want to at least "beat" the remaining bidder. The individual who finally prevails only does so when no one else thinks that further bidding would be rational. The highest bidder then "wins" what others no longer value at the price level involved — experiencing the dreaded "winner's curse."

Practitioners must never permit themselves to become so caught up in the negotiation "game" that they find themselves compelled to achieve final settlements no matter the cost. They must learn to recognize when they have become involved in losing endeavors and to know how to minimize their losses. Those persons who become psychologically entrapped by the process itself usually pay a high price for their continued participation. Except in rare circumstances, bargainers always have alternatives to nonsettlements that they can fall back on. Those individuals who ignore this crucial fact should take the time to ascertain the results of non-agreement before they become overly enmeshed in the bargaining process. Once it becomes apparent that their nonsettlement options are less onerous than the concessions that would be required to achieve final accords, these advocates should readily accept the fact that their non-negotiated solutions constitute the preferable choice.

Participants should never continue negotiations merely because they have become psychologically entrapped by the substantial amount of time and resources they may have already expended in an unsuccessful effort to obtain beneficial terms. This is particularly true when they are tempted to extend present interactions for the purpose of punishing or defeating their recalcitrant opponents. Although they may understandably feel frustrated by their inability to achieve final resolutions through the bargaining process, it does no good to sustain additional losses in a misguided effort to retaliate against their uncooperative adversaries. Even if they were able to generate accords through stubborn persistence, the overall cost to them and their clients would exceed the cost of the nonsettlement alternatives they could have relied upon.

Individuals often become entrapped by the bargaining process because of the time and effort they have expended in an effort to achieve agreement. They feel that these endeavors will be wasted if they do not obtain mutual accords. They must recognize that their efforts have not been for naught. They had to expend this energy to determine whether they could obtain better results through the bargaining process than through their external options. They have gathered critical information regarding the benefits that are presently available through negotiation procedures. Had they not employed their negotiation skills, they would never have confirmed the preferable nature of their non-agreement alternatives.

Some negotiators regularly exhibit behavior suggesting to opponents that they fear the consequences of nonsettlements. Some casually note that they do not wish to expose their clients to the psychological trauma and monetary costs associated with adjudications. They mention their concern regarding adverse publicity in typical cases that would be unlikely to generate meaningful community notice. It must be remembered that very few lawsuits involve sufficient notoriety to engender any degree of public attention. Those participants who exude a fear of nonsettlement generally attain less beneficial results than those people who evidence a willingness to accept the consequences of non-negotiated results when the latter course would produce preferable outcomes.

Negotiators should recognize how easy it is to become psychologically entrapped by the bargaining process. Before individuals commence negotiations, they should establish appropriate bargaining limits. They must consider the consequences of nonsettlement and recognize when mutual accords would be more onerous than non-negotiated results. Unless they obtain information that objectively induces them to alter their preliminary assessments, they should be prepared to terminate their participation in the negotiation process once it becomes apparent that they cannot obtain beneficial solutions through that means. They should do so courteously and inform their opponents that the terms currently being offered are simply unacceptable. This conduct may induce the other side to reconsider its situation and generate further discussions. If it does not, these participants should take advantage of their external options. If they instead continue to negotiate in a desperate effort to achieve any agreement, they are likely to experience "winner's curse."

When negotiators understand the degree to which their own investment of time and effort may make it difficult for them to walk away from protracted bargaining interactions without agreements, they should appreciate the degree to which this same phenomenon influences their opponents (Cohen, 2003, at 250–54, 291). Results achieved easily are usually not as highly valued as results people have to work to attain. Negotiators should thus strive to entrap careless adversaries by making those persons work diligently for the results they obtain. Instead of meeting only once or twice, it may be beneficial to schedule three, four, or even five separate bargaining sessions. Concessions should not be made quickly, but should be granted begrudgingly after lengthy discussions. The more opponents have to work to move the other side in their direction, the more they want to achieve final accords — even if the terms are not as beneficial as those they initially hoped to get. In fact, if they become entirely entrapped by their investment of time and effort in the bargaining process, they may forget their own nonsettlement options and agree to terms that are worse than what they would have achieved with no agreement.

E.   THE CLOSING STAGE (VALUE SOLIDIFYING)

Near the end of the Competitive/Distributive Stage, one or both participants begin to realize that a mutual accord is likely. The negotiators feel a sense of relief, as the anxiety associated with the uncertainty indigenous to the negotiation process is alleviated by the seemingly imminent attainment of an agreement. Careful observers can often see slight signs of relief around the mouths of individuals who reach this state. The participants may also exhibit a more relaxed body posture. As these bargainers become psychologically committed to settlement, they want to move expeditiously toward the conclusion of the transaction. They should avoid this temptation.

The Closing Stage is a critical part of bargaining interactions. The majority of concessions tend to be made during the concluding portion of negotiations (Dawson, 2001, at 171), and overly anxious participants may forfeit much of what they obtained during the Competitive/Distributive Stage if they are not vigilant. They must remain patient and permit the final part of the process to develop in a deliberate fashion.

As the Closing Stage begins, too many bargainers see the end in sight and are overly eager to conclude the transaction. Instead of being a time for swift action, this is a time for patient perseverance. Negotiators must continue to employ the techniques that got them to this point. They should be especially cognizant of their overall and their immediate concession patterns. They should remember their prior position changes, and attempt to make smaller and, if possible, less frequent concessions than their opponents. If they fail to follow this admonition and try to reach common ground too quickly, they are likely to close most of the distance still separating the parties.

Less successful negotiators tend to make excessive and unreciprocated concessions during the Closing Stage in an effort to guarantee a final agreement. When they are later asked about this behavior, they usually indicate that they did not wish to risk the possibility of a nonsettlement at this stage of the transaction. They emphasize their belief that the accord achieved is better for their client than no pact. When they are asked how much their opponents desired a final accord, they are dumbfounded. They have completely ignored this crucial consideration.

By the end of the Competitive/Distributive Stage, *both* sides have become psychologically committed to a joint resolution. Neither wants their previous bargaining efforts to culminate in failure. Less proficient negotiators tend to focus entirely on their own side's craving for an agreement, and they disregard the settlement pressure influencing their opponents. This phenomenon causes them to increase the pressure on themselves and to discount the anxiety being experienced by their adversaries. They thus assume that they must close more of the remaining gap than their opponents if they are going to ensure a final accord.

As the closing phase begins, *both* parties want an agreement. They would not have expended the time and effort needed to get to this point if this were not true. It is thus appropriate for each side to expect the other to move with it toward the final accord. Negotiators should be certain that they do not make unreciprocated concessions. They should also avoid excessive position changes that are not matched by the other side. Bargainers should only contemplate the making of greater concessions than their adversaries when their opponents have been more accommodating during the earlier stages of the transaction and the verbal and nonverbal messages emanating from those participants clearly indicate that they are approaching their resistance point.

When participants enter the Closing Stage, they must acknowledge that the time is propitious for settlement. It is imperative that they keep the process moving inexorably toward a satisfactory conclusion. They should normally eschew disruptive tactics that may impede continued progress. If someone breaks off discussions at this point, it may take days or even weeks to again achieve such auspicious circumstances. Instead of employing negative threats, they should resort to affirmative promises that permit their opponents to move in a face-saving way. Temporary impasses may be effectively overcome through the promise of concurrent position changes. If they fear that a bargaining hiatus might provide their opponents with the opportunity to reassess the existing circumstances in a manner that might jeopardize a mutual accord, they should subtly work to encourage a final resolution by the conclusion of the instant session.

Patience and silence are two of the most efficacious techniques during the Closing Stage. Negotiators should rely on "principled" concessions to clarify the extent of each position change. Following the succinct explanation for each concession being made, speakers must become quiet and patiently await the other side's response. They must refrain from reiterations that serve to highlight their anxiety, and they should not contemplate further movement without appropriate reciprocity from the other party. Guilt can also be an effective factor. By reminding opponents of the numerous position changes they made during the earlier stages of the process, proficient bargainers can often generate opponent guilt and convince those participants that they are obliged to provide more generous concessions during the Closing Stage.

If adversaries have previously locked themselves into seemingly uncompromising positions by relying on their limited authority, they should be given a face-saving way out. For example, they might be told that the suggested agreement is fair and be encouraged to telephone their client to obtain approval of this new position. It is irrelevant whether they call their client or order a pizza, so long as they are able to return to the bargaining table with the necessary authorization.

Proficient negotiators are frequently able to obtain a significant advantage during the concluding portions of interactions. As they sense heightened opponent excitement, they project an insouciant attitude. They want their adversaries to think they are wholly unconcerned about the seemingly impending accord. The more they are able to accomplish this objective, the more they can induce opponents to feel a greater need to close the remaining gap (Dawson, 2001, at 173–76). As those participants make more expansive and more frequent concessions in an effort to conclude the interaction, they significantly enhance the final terms attained by the persevering side. When opponents make beneficent concessions, they should be praised for their reasonableness and encouraged to continue their admirable movement.

Overly anxious adversaries occasionally attempt to end the bargaining process by prematurely offering to split the remaining distance between the parties. Adroit bargainers may take advantage of this proposal by pointing out their previous concessions and suggesting that the parties split the *distance remaining after* the opponents offered to split the difference. If this technique is successful, it induces the opponents to close 75 percent of the remaining gap while requiring this party to close only 25 percent.

The Closing Stage is highly competitive part of a negotiation. It frequently involves a significant number of position changes and a substantial amount of participant movement. As noted earlier, a majority of concessions tend to be made during the last portion of bargaining interactions. Negotiators who think that this portion of the transaction consists primarily of cooperative behavior are likely to obtain less beneficial results than manipulative opponents who recognize the competitive aspect of this phase and who are able to induce naive participants to close most of the outstanding distance between the two sides. As they formulate their closing strategies, individuals must always remember how intently their adversaries want to achieve a mutual accord. Their opponents may even wish to do so more earnestly than they do. Individuals should not hesitate to take advantage of this fact. If they can project a nonchalant attitude, their anxious opponents may decide that they are the ones who must give in if a final deal is to be consummated.

F.   THE COOPERATIVE/INTEGRATIVE STAGE (VALUE MAXIMIZING)

Once the Competitive/Distributive and Closing Stages of a negotiation have been successfully completed through the attainment of a mutually acceptable agreement, many parties consider the bargaining process finished. While this conclusion may be warranted with respect to zero-or constant-sum problems — where neither party could obtain more favorable results without a corresponding loss being imposed on the other party — it is certainly not correct regarding multi-issue, non-constant-sum disputes. It is not always true even for seemingly zero-or constant-sum transactions.

In a personal injury case involving a permanently-injured plaintiff who will require substantial future care, the parties may initially discuss only monetary demands and offers that are to be satisfied immediately. The plaintiff attorney wants to obtain a sufficiently large settlement to provide lifetime care for the plaintiff, but the defendant insurance carrier does not wish to give such a substantial sum to the plaintiff at the present time. It may be possible to simultaneously satisfy the underlying needs and interests of both parties through a structured settlement plan that guarantees the plaintiff continued treatment and that does not require the defendant insurance company to make an enormous payout now. Through the development of this innovative alternative, the negotiating parties are able to convert a seemingly zero-sum interaction into a non-zero-sum transaction.

When people are involved in negotiations pertaining to various issues, they tend to assume a "fixed pie" that cannot be expanded (Birke & Fox, 1999, at 30–31). This is rarely correct. Negotiators should instead assume the presence of a non-constant-sum interaction. It would be unlikely that both parties would value each and every item identically and oppositely (Mnookin, Peppet & Tulumello, 2000, at 14–16). As a result, it is usually possible for the participants to formulate proposals that may concurrently advance the interests of everyone involved. They may best accomplish this objective through an efficacious Cooperative/Integrative Stage.

1.   THE SEARCH FOR UNDISCOVERED ALTERNATIVES

During the Information Stage, the parties over-or under-state the value of various items for strategic purposes. During the Competitive/Distributive and Closing Stages of a negotiation, the participants tend to be cautious and manipulative. Complete disclosure of underlying interests and objectives rarely occurs. Both sides try to employ power bargaining techniques aimed at the achievement of results favorable to their own respective circumstances. Because of the tension created by these power bargaining tactics, Pareto superior arrangements — where neither party may improve its position without worsening the other side's situation — are generally not attained due to the lack of candid disclosure of party goals and settlement intentions. The participants are more likely to only achieve "acceptable" terms. If they were to conclude their negotiation at this point, they may leave a substantial amount of potential, yet untapped, joint satisfaction on the bargaining table.

Once a tentative accord has been achieved through the competitive process, it is generally advantageous for the negotiators to explore alternative trade-offs that may concurrently enhance the interests of both sides. The participants may be mentally, and even physically, exhausted due to the anxiety associated with the Competitive/Distributive and Closing Stages, and they may understandably wish to memorialize their agreement and terminate their interaction. They should, however, at least briefly endeavor to explore alternative formulations that may prove to be mutually advantageous and that were ignored due to the pressure indigenous to their competitive bargaining.

In simulation exercises, it is easy to determine the extent to which the negotiators have successfully employed the Cooperative/Integrative Stage. By comparing the aggregate point totals achieved by each pair of opponents, one may assess the degree to which the participants were able to maximize their joint results. This does not mean that neither side is expected to have obtained more favorable results than its adversary. It merely evaluates the degree to which the participants were able to ascertain and distribute the total available points — regardless of which side attained more or less of them. For example, where two opponents may potentially divide a total of approximately 1000 points, teams with extraordinary cooperative skills may reach an agreement giving them a combined total of 950–1000 points. Less cooperative groups, on the other hand, may only end up with a joint total of 700–750 points. These results graphically demonstrate to the participants the benefits to be derived from cooperative bargaining. Had the latter negotiators been more cooperative, they would have been able to share an additional 250–300 points. Such an effort would certainly have enhanced the interests of both sides, with each being able to increase their final level of satisfaction.

If the Cooperative/Integrative Stage is to be employed successfully, several prerequisites must be established. The parties must initially achieve a tentative accord. This would usually be precipitated through the use of at least some competitive bargaining tactics. Negotiators who do not discern any Information or Competitive/Distributive Stage should be concerned about the real possibility that they have been preempted. Parties must generally ascertain the topics that are available for distribution and decide how those items are to be divided between them. If one party is able to convince the opponent that there is no need for the employment of competitive behavior and suggests that the participants exclusively resort to cooperative techniques, it is likely that the moving participant has already won the Competitive/Distributive Stage by default. He or she has unilaterally dictated the fundamental division of the available topics, and now wishes to determine whether it may use the Cooperative/Integrative Stage to obtain a further advantage. It is for this reason that negotiators should be careful to ensure the presence of a minimal Competitive/Distributive Stage and usually a Closing Stage *before* they permit transition to the Cooperative/Integrative Stage.

Once the Competitive/Distributive Stage and the Closing Stage have been tentatively concluded, one party should suggest passage into the Cooperative/Integrative Stage. If they fear that their opponent may be reluctant to progress in this direction until a provisional accord has been solidified, it may be beneficial to have the parties execute the settlement they have already negotiated. A participant should then propose that the parties explore alternative formulations to be certain they have not — in the heat of battle — overlooked mutually advantageous options.

It is imperative that both parties recognize their movement from the Competitive/Distributive Stage through the Closing Stage into the Cooperative/Integrative Stage. If one side attempts to move into the Cooperative/Integrative Stage without the understanding of the other participant, problems are likely to arise. As the cooperative bargainer begins to suggest alternative proposals, they may be less advantageous to the other participant than previously articulated offers. If the recipient of these new proposals does not view them as incipient cooperative overtures, he or she may suspect disingenuous competitive tactics. Why else would an opponent suggest less beneficial terms during the competitive portion of the interaction? Allegations of bad faith and improper dealing would probably be made, and the bargaining process may be completely disrupted. It is for this reason that a party contemplating movement toward cooperative efforts should ensure that the opponent understands the intended transition. If the circumstances do not themselves suggest the achievement of a tentative agreement and the obvious commencement of cooperative techniques, this fact should be expressly communicated.

Once parties enter the Cooperative/Integrative Stage, they should endeavor to ascertain the presence of previously unnoticed alternatives that might be mutually beneficial. They must attempt to expand the overall economic and noneconomic pie to be divided between them (Mnookin, Peppet & Tulumello, 2000, at 11–43; Fisher & Ury, 1981, at 58–83). Perhaps they have failed to consider options that would equally or even more effectively satisfy the underlying needs and interests of one side with less cost to the other party (Karrass, 1970, at 145). To accomplish this objective, the negotiators must be willing to candidly disclose the underlying interests and objectives of their respective clients. Although they have presumably explored many of these factors during the Competitive/Distributive Stage and the Closing Stage, it must be recognized that normal circumspection and the use of some disingenuous bargaining techniques probably precluded complete disclosure during the competitive discussions. Once a tentative agreement has been reached, the parties should no longer be afraid of more open deliberations. Even if they are unable to achieve a more mutually advantageous arrangement, they can be certain of at least a final resolution on their initially specified terms. It thus behooves them to be direct and unreserved.

Both sides must exhibit substantial candor during this process if it is to function optimally. Through the use of objective and relatively neutral inquiries, the participants should explore their respective needs and goals. They should use brainstorming techniques to develop options that were not previously considered. When one side asks the other if another resolution would be as good or better for it than what has already been agreed upon, the responding participant must be forthright. If the proposed term would not be as preferable, the parties should contemplate other options. It is only when they have effectively explored all of the possible formulations that they can truly determine whether their initial agreement has optimally satisfied their joint needs.

An inherent aspect of the Cooperative/Integrative Stage concerns the fact that certain trade-offs made during the highly contested Competitive/Distributive and Closing Stages may not have been achieved with exemplary communication. Participants have usually over-and under-stated the value of items for strategic reasons. As a result, one party may have ended up with an item it did not value as highly as the opponent, while the other side may have obtained some term it did not want as much as the first party. If the negotiators can identify these topics during their cooperative discussions, they would clearly benefit from an appropriate rearrangement of their previously ordered settlement. These two terms should certainly be exchanged, with each party receiving more satisfaction than it had previously attained.

As the participants enter the Cooperative/Integrative Stage, they must be careful to preserve their basic credibility. They may have deceived their opponents during the Information, the Competitive/Distributive, and the Closing Stages regarding client values or settlement intentions. In the Cooperative/ Integrative Stage, they hope to correct the inefficiencies that may have been generated by their deceptive tactics. If they are too candid about their previous prevarication, however, their opponents may begin to question the truthfulness of many of their prior representations and seek to renegotiate the entire agreement (Condlin, 1992, at 44-5). This would be a disaster. It is thus imperative that bargainers not overtly undermine their credibility while they are attempting to improve their respective positions during the Cooperative/Integrative Stage.

2. THE COMPETITIVE ASPECT OF COOPERATIVE BARGAINING

It is important for individuals participating in cooperative bargaining to understand the competitive undercurrent that is present even during these discussions. While participants are using cooperative techniques to expand the overall pie and improve the results achieved by both sides, some may simultaneously employ competitive tactics to enable them to claim more than their share of the newly discovered areas for mutual gain. For example, consider the situation in which the parties were unable during the Competitive/Distributive and Closing Stages of their interaction to discover the existence of an additional "200 points" of possible joint satisfaction. If one participant can adroitly ascertain this deficiency, he or she may take advantage of that finding. This individual could draft a new proposal providing an extra ten to twenty "points" for the opponent while giving the remaining 180 to 190 "points" to his or her own client. The devious participant may even attempt to enhance his or her credibility by suggesting that the proposed modification would only "slightly improve" his or her client's circumstances. Since the other party would be better off under this suggested arrangement than under their initial agreement, it might readily assent to this proposal without recognizing the deliberate imbalance involved.

Bargainers should attempt to protect client interests during the Cooperative/Integrative Stage by insisting on full disclosure before they merely accept a more beneficial arrangement. If they have any doubts, they should suggest several alternative formulations of their own to determine whether or not they may be able to obtain more of the newly discovered "points." It is only when they reasonably conclude that an equitable distribution of the excess "points" is being achieved that they should accept a final agreement. By employing some of the techniques usually associated with low-key competitive interactions, negotiators can ensure that client interests are not unfairly and unnecessarily sacrificed during the Cooperative/Integrative Stage.

As the overall terms are being finalized, negotiators should remember how important it is to leave their opponents with the feeling they got a good deal.

If their adversaries are left with a good impression, they will be more likely to honor the accord and more likely to behave cooperatively when the parties interact in the future. Some advocates attempt to accomplish this objective by making the final concession on a matter they do not highly value (Dawson, 2001, at 102–03). Even a minimal position change at this point is likely to be appreciated by the other side (Steinberg, 1998, at 215). Others try to do it by congratulating their opponents on the mutually beneficial agreement achieved (Dawson, 2001, at 143–44). Individuals must be careful, however, not to be too effusive. When negotiators lavish praise on their opponents at the conclusion of bargaining interactions, those individuals tend to become suspicious and think they got a poor deal.

When the bargaining process has concluded with the achievement of an overall agreement, the participants should take the time to *review* the specific *terms agreed upon* before they adjourn their discussions. Negotiators may think they have covered everything and be surprised to learn that certain items were never fully resolved. They may alternatively discover that their opponent believes that a particular term has been resolved in a manner that is inconsistent with their own understanding. If the negotiators take a few minutes to jointly summarize their accord, they may be able to avoid subsequent difficulties. If they discover a problem, they may find it easier to resolve while they are psychologically committed to settlement than at a later date when they may not be in such an accommodating frame of mind. Whenever possible, it is beneficial to reduce the basic terms to writing and to have both sides initial each of the terms agreed upon. This practice usually prevents the development of misunderstandings during the final drafting process.

3. ALWAYS ENDEAVOR TO DRAFT THE FINAL AGREEMENT

Once the Competitive/Distributive, Closing, and Cooperative/Integrative Stages have been completed and a final accord has been achieved, many negotiators are readily willing to permit opposing counsel to prepare the settlement agreement. While this may save them time and effort, it is a risky practice. It is unlikely that they and their opponent would employ identical language to memorialize the specific terms agreed upon. Each would use slightly different terminology to represent his or her own perceptions. To ensure that their client's particular interests are optimally protected, bargainers should always try to be the one to draft the operative document (Dawson, 2001, at 130–31; Karrass, 1985, at 181–82).

No competent attorney should ever contemplate the omission of terms actually agreed upon or the inclusion of items not covered by the parties' oral understanding. Either practice would be wholly unethical and would constitute fraud. Such disreputable behavior could subject the responsible practitioner and his or her client to substantial liability and untoward legal problems. Why then should lawyers insist upon the right to prepare the final accord? It is simply to allow them to draft a document that unambiguously reflects their perception of the overall agreement achieved by the parties.

Each provision should be carefully prepared to state precisely what the drafting party thinks was agreed upon. When the resulting contract is presented to the other party for execution, that party is frequently reluctant to propose alternative language, unless serious questions regarding the content of particular clauses are raised. Doubts tend to be resolved in favor of the proffered terminology. This approach best ensures that the final contract most effectively reflects the interests of the party who drafted it.

If negotiators are unable to prepare the ultimate agreement, they should carefully compare the terms of the document drafted by the other side with their notes and recollections of the interaction, to be positive that their understanding of the bargaining results is accurately represented. Draft reviewers must go through a three-step process. First, is there any language in the draft they do not like? If so, they should mark up the draft and be prepared to discuss their proposed changes with the drafting party. Second, has anything been included in the draft that was not expressly agreed upon? Nothing is "boilerplate" until both sides accept it. For example, the drafter may have specified the applicability of the laws of a particular state if disagreements arise over the interpretation of their agreement, when the other party would prefer reliance upon the laws of another jurisdiction. The drafting party may have included a dispute resolution mechanism that is not favored by the other side. Finally, has anything been omitted that was agreed upon? Draft reviewers usually look carefully at the language before them, instead of contemplating terms that may have been left out. When lawyers review draft provisions, they should check off the areas of their notes covered by each provision. When they are finished, they should see if any areas of their notes remain unchecked.

Agreement reviewers should not hesitate to question seemingly equivocal language that may cause future interpretive difficulties or challenge phrases that do not appear to describe precisely what they think was intended by the contracting parties. Since practitioners now use word processors to draft contractual documents, it is easy to accommodate additions, deletions, or modifications. Bargainers should never permit opponents to make them feel guilty about changes they think should be made in prepared agreements. It is always appropriate for non-drafting parties to be certain that the final language truly reflects what has been achieved through the negotiation process. If the other side repeatedly objects to proposed modifications because of the additional work involved, the party suggesting the necessary alterations can effectively silence those protestations by offering to accept responsibility for the final stages of the drafting process.

In recent years, a few unscrupulous practitioners in the corporate area have decided to take advantage of the drafting stage of extensive business documents to obtain benefits not attained during the negotiation process. They include provisions that were never agreed upon, or modify or omit terms that were jointly accepted. They attempt to accomplish their deceitful objective by providing their opponents with copies of the written agreement at the eleventh hour, hoping that time pressure will induce their unsuspecting adversaries to review the final draft in a cursory manner. Lawyers who encounter this tactic should examine each clause of the draft agreement with care to be certain it represents the actual accord achieved. They should not hesitate to redraft improper provisions. If their proposed terms are rejected by opposing counsel, they should insist upon a session with the clients present to determine which draft represents the true intentions of the parties. When this type of meeting is proposed, deceptive drafters are likely to "correct" the "inadvertent misunderstandings" before the clients ever get together. If a client session were to occur and the other side enthusiastically supported the dishonest drafting practices of their attorneys, it would be appropriate for the misled lawyers to recommend that their client do business with another party.

When negotiators reviewing draft agreements discover apparent discrepancies, they should contact their opponents and politely question the pertinent language. They should not initially assume deliberate opponent deception. It is always possible that the persons challenging the prepared terminology are mistaken and that the proposed terms actually reflect what was agreed upon. The reviewers may have forgotten modifications quickly adopted near the conclusion of the negotiation process. It is also possible that the drafting parties made honest mistakes that they will happily correct once they have examined their notes of the bargaining interaction. Even when document reviewers suspect intentional deception by drafting parties, they should still provide their opponents with a face-saving way out of the predicament. The best way to accomplish the desired result is to assume an honest mistake and give the drafters the opportunity to "correct" the erroneous provisions. If the reviewers directly challenge opponent integrity, the dispute is likely to escalate, endangering the entire accord.

4. USING THE TIT-FOR-TAT APPROACH TO ENCOURAGE COOPERATIVE BEHAVIOR

Individuals who recognize that competitive/adversarial conduct tends to produce less efficient agreements than cooperative/problem-solving behavior may follow the "tit-for-tat" approach devised by Professor Anatol Rapoport to encourage cooperative, rather than competitive, interactions (Axelrod, 1984). He realized that people who demonstrate a willingness to conduct win-win interactions are more likely to generate win-win responses from opponents than persons who exhibit a propensity for win-lose transactions. To accomplish the desired objective, Professor Rapoport developed some fundamental principles that should be followed by bargainers who wish to encourage cooperative exchanges (Axelrod, 1984, at 109-24).

a. Don't Be Envious of Your Opponent's Results

Negotiators should not judge their own success by how well they think their opponents have done, because they are comparing dissimilar commodities. Rarely do participants on both sides possess equal power and equal skill. Parties with greater strength and ability should be able to obtain more favorable results than their weaker adversaries. Nonetheless, if advocates who possess less power get beneficial results for their clients, they should be pleased with their accords. Their terms are not diminished by the fact their opponents are pleased with what they obtained, nor are they enhanced by the fact their adversaries have done poorly (Murnighan, 1992, at 22–23). If both sides do well, they both win; if both do poorly, they both lose.

b. Be Nice When the Interaction Begins

People who want to promote cooperative conduct should make it clear at the outset of an interaction that they do not plan to resort to competitive/adversarial tactics unless they are forced to do so to counteract the competitive/adversarial behavior of their opponents. Since cooperative/problem-solving people tend to bargain in a cooperative fashion with other cooperative/problem-solving participants, this approach will usually induce cooperative/problem-solving opponents to respond in kind. Even marginally competitive/adversarial negotiators may be persuaded to reciprocate cooperative initiatives if they know that competitive/ adversarial techniques will be challenged.

c. Be Provocable When Confronted with Uncooperative Conduct

Some cooperative/problem-solving negotiators do not know how to respond to competitive/adversarial styles. They continue to be open and accommodating, and place themselves at a disadvantage. Proficient cooperative/problem-solving individuals, however, realize that overtly competitive behavior must be confronted and dealt with when it occurs. For example, after a "final" agreement has been reached, manipulative opponents may use the "nibble" technique (*see* Chapter 4, *infra*) to steal an item. They may indicate that their client is dissatisfied with a particular term and insist upon a "slight modification" of the accord. Naive persons might be afraid to let the entire deal unravel, and concede the requested item. Provocable negotiators would realize that both sides want the final accord and that the other party is not entitled to a unilateral concession at this stage of the interaction. They would thus insist upon a reciprocal concession as a prerequisite to any movement on their part. If the opponents are sincere bargainers, they will acknowledge the propriety of this approach and discuss an appropriate exchange. Disingenuous competitive advocates will realize that they are not going to obtain a modification for nothing, and they will normally insist upon the terms previously agreed upon.

d. Be a Forgiving Participant

When negotiators encounter improper behavior, they often hold grudges that adversely affect future interactions with the offending persons. Professional bargainers know that these challenges should not be taken personally. They merely respond to inappropriate tactics in a provocable manner, to discourage future repetition, and then return to a cooperative mode. So long as their opponents exhibit cooperative behavior thereafter, they are perfectly willing to forgive the previous transgressions.

Proficient negotiators do not personalize opponent efforts to employ manipulative tactics. They recognize that these adversaries are merely attempting to advance their client's interests. They realize that the opportunistic behavior of these opponents is not based on any personal animosity toward them. Individuals who tend to personalize such conduct by other negotiators must acknowledge their professional indebtedness to their adversaries. If they had no one to interact with, they would be unable to earn a living!

e. Be Transparent and Establish an Appropriate Reputation

Cooperative negotiators who wish to encourage similar behavior in others should try to project a cooperative image. They should also make it clear that they will not yield to inappropriate tactics. They realize that if opponents know they are cooperative, but provocable participants, those individuals will be less likely to resort to inappropriately adversarial conduct. Their opponents will understand that if they employ adversarial techniques, these persons will take retaliatory action. Their adversaries will also realize that if they behave in a cooperative manner, their problem-solving approach will be reciprocated.

G. POST-NEGOTIATION ASSESSMENT

Each time individuals successfully or unsuccessfully complete a significant negotiation, they should briefly review the manner in which that interaction developed. If lawyers want to improve their negotiating skills, they have to learn from their prior encounters. Those people who merely forget about the transaction and move on to other bargaining situations rarely learn from their previous experiences. It is only through objective post-mortems that individuals can continuously enhance their negotiating capabilities.

The first analysis should focus upon the Preparation Stage. Was their pre-interaction planning sufficiently thorough? Did they carefully evaluate their nonsettlement options (i.e., their bottom line) and the nonsettlement alternatives available to their opponents? Did they establish an appropriate aspiration level for *each* issue to be addressed? Did they plan a beneficial and principled opening offer? Did their pre-bargaining prognostications prove to be accurate? If not, what might have been done to provide a better preliminary assessment? Which party dictated the contextual factors such as time and location? Might these seemingly ancillary considerations have influenced the substantive aspects of the transaction?

Did they have a good Preliminary Stage? Did they take the time to establish rapport with their opponent? Did they try to personalize their relationship and create a positive bargaining environment? If they did not like the way their adversary began the interaction, did they employ "attitudinal bargaining" to modify that person's behavior?

The Information Stage must be similarly explored. How thoroughly was the information phase developed? Did they ask their opponent open-ended, information-seeking questions? Were both parties relatively candid or were they unusually circumspect? Was the unreciprocated candor of one side detrimental to its cause during the subsequent discussions? Were unintended disclosures inadvertently made through either verbal leaks or nonverbal signs? If so, how might they have been prevented? Were the participants able to ascertain the knowledge they needed to foster an efficient and productive Compet-itive/Distributive Stage? What other pertinent information should have been divulged, and when and how should it have been revealed?

The Competitive/Distributive Stage should next be examined. Which party made the first offer? The first *"real"* offer? Was an appropriate explanation used to support the precise proposal articulated — i.e., was a "principled" opening position stated? Could a different rationale have been employed more persuasively? How did the opponents react to the preliminary offer and its accompanying elucidation? Did they appear to be genuinely surprised, or did the proffered terms seem to be close to what they had apparently anticipated? Did the participants who made the initial offer make another proposal prior to the receipt of any definitive offer from the other side? If so, what precipitated this conduct?

What specific bargaining techniques were employed by the opponents? How were they countered? Could they have been more effectively neutralized? What particular tactics were employed by you to enhance your position? Did the opponents appear to recognize them? What countermeasures did the opponents adopt to undermine your maneuvers? What different approaches might have been employed by you to advance your position more forcefully? What other tactics might your opponents have used more effectively against you? How could you have minimized the impact of those measures? Did either side resort to deceitful tactics or deliberate misrepresentations to advance its position? If so, how were these devices discovered and how were they countered? What impact would these tactics have on future interactions involving the same participants?

It is informative to explore the concession patterns of the two sides. Which party made the first concession and how was it generated? Were subsequent concessions by each side matched by reciprocal movement from the other party, or were either excessive or consecutive concessions made by one side? Was each concession accompanied by an appropriate explanation — i.e., were "principled" concessions articulated? What was the exact size of each concession? Did successive position modifications involve consistently decreasing increments? If not, did one party unsuccessfully attempt to establish a false resistance point that could not be sustained? How close to the midpoint between the opening offers was the final settlement?

How did the Closing Stage evolve? Did it develop deliberately, with the parties moving together toward the final agreement or did one participant close an excessive amount of the distance dividing the parties? Did the bargainers continue to use the techniques that got them to this stage of the interaction, or did they resort to less effective tactics? Did you exude sufficient patience to induce overanxious opponents to move more quickly toward closure than you? What ultimately caused you to accept the terms agreed upon or to reject the final offer that was made before the discussions were terminated?

Did the parties attempt to employ the Cooperative/Integrative Stage to maximize their joint gains? Had a tentative accord been achieved before the initiation of cooperative bargaining? Did the Cooperative/Integrative Stage significantly enhance the return to each party? Were the Cooperative-Integrative Stage participants relatively candid about their respective needs and interests, or did a counterproductive competitive atmosphere permeate this portion of the interaction? How might the cooperative experience have been improved?

How did time pressures influence the negotiation process? Did one party appear to be operating under greater time constraints than the other? Was the party with less time pressure able to take advantage of this situation?

Did the time factor generate a greater number of concessions or more sizable position changes as the impending deadline approached?

Negotiators should always ask whether one side appeared to obtain more beneficial results than the other party. They should not merely ask whether their own side was satisfied with the final accord, because winning and losing participants tend to express equal satisfaction with the settlement achieved (Karrass, 1970, at 24). If one side seemed to fare better than the other, what did it do to generate this outcome? What might the less successful bargainer have done differently? Did client constraints contribute to an unequal result? If so, what might have been done to minimize the impact of this factor? If no settlement was ultimately attained, was client recalcitrance the primary factor? If the client rejected a final proposal you thought should have been accepted or accepted final terms you thought should have been rejected, how might you have more effectively educated the client regarding the negotiation process and the substantive merits of his or her situation?

Bargainers should ask two final questions. What did they do that they wish they had not done? This inquiry relates to a mistake they may have made. If it was a mere tactical error, they should realize that their opponents were probably unaware of their mistake. If a true mistake was made — such as a mathematical error — the best way to deal with it is directly. Confess the mistake, apologize, and make the necessary modification(s) in the originally stated position.

Advocates should similarly ask themselves what they did not do that they wish they had done. This question usually relates to a new tactic they encountered that they did not think they handled well. They should ask their colleagues if they have ever encountered this approach. If so, how did they deal with it? If not, how would they try to counter such behavior? The more negotiators plan effective responses to opponent tactics they may encounter during future interactions, the more effectively they should deal with those techniques when they next experience them.

Through the use of the brief checklist set forth in Table 3, negotiators may readily review almost any bargaining interaction. While it is certainly true that experience may be an excellent teacher, it must be remembered that experience without the benefit of meaningful post-transaction evaluation is of limited value. The time expended during the appraisal process should be amply recouped through improved future performance.

TABLE 3

Post Negotiation Evaluation Checklist

1.　Was your *pre-negotiation preparation* sufficiently thorough? Were you completely familiar with the operative facts and law? Did you fully understand your client's value system and nonsettlement alternatives? Did you carefully estimate your opponent's nonsettlement options?

2.　Was your *initial aspiration level* high enough? Did you establish a firm goal for *each issue* to be addressed? If you obtained everything you sought, was this due to the fact you did not establish sufficiently elevated objectives? Did you prepare a beneficial and principled opening offer?

3.   Did your *pre-bargaining prognostications* prove to be accurate? Did your opponent begin near where you thought he/she would begin? If not, what caused your miscalculations?

4.   Which party dictated the *contextual factors* such as time and location? Did this factor influence the negotiations?

5.   Did you have a good *Preliminary Stage*? Did you establish a beneficial relationship with your opponent and create a positive negotiating environment? If you encountered offensive behavior, did you employ "attitudinal bargaining" to modify that conduct?

6.   Did the *Information Stage* develop sufficiently to provide the participants with the knowledge they needed to understand their respective needs and interests and to enable them to consummate an optimal agreement?

7.   Were any unintended *verbal leaks* or *nonverbal disclosures* made? What precipitated these revelations? Were you able to employ *Blocking Techniques* to prevent the disclosure of sensitive information?

8.   Who made the *first offer*? The first "*real*" offer? Was a "principled" initial offer articulated by you? By your opponent?

9.   How did your *opponent react* to your initial proposal? How did you react to your opponent's opening offer?

10. Were *consecutive opening offers* made by one party before the other side disclosed its initial position? What induced that party to engage in this conduct?

11. What specific *bargaining techniques* were employed by your opponent and how were these tactics countered by you? What else might you have done to counter these tactics more effectively?

12. What particular *negotiation devices* were employed by you to advance your position? Did the opponent appear to recognize the various techniques you used, and, if so, how did he/she endeavor to minimize their impact? What other tactics might you have used to advance your position more forcefully?

13. Which party made the *first concession* and how was it precipitated? Were subsequent concessions made on an alternating basis? (You should keep a record of each concession made by you and by your opponent throughout the interaction.)

14. Were "*principled*" *concessions* articulated by you? By your opponent? Did successive position changes involve decreasing increments and were those increments relatively reciprocal to the other side's concomitant movement?

15. How did the parties *close the deal* once they realized that they had overlapping needs and interests? Did either side appear to make greater concessions during the Closing Stage?

16. Did the parties resort to *cooperative/integrative bargaining* to maximize their aggregate return?

17. How close to the midpoint between the initial *real* offers was the final settlement?

18. How did time pressures influence the parties and their respective concession patterns? Try not to ignore the time pressures that affected your opponent.

19. Did either party resort to *deceitful tactics* or deliberate misrepresentations to enhance its situation? Did these pertain to material law or fact, or only to the speaker's value system or settlement intentions?

20. What finally induced you to accept the terms agreed upon or to reject the final offer made by the other party?

21. Did either party appear to obtain more favorable terms than the other side, and, if so, how was this result accomplished? What could the less successful participant have done differently to improve its situation?

22. If no settlement was achieved, what might have been done differently with respect to client preparation and/or bargaining developments to produce a different result?

23. What did you do that you wish you had not done? Do you think your opponent was aware of your error? How could you avoid such a mistake in the future?

24. What did you not do that you wish you had done to counteract unexpected opponent behavior? How could you most effectively counter this approach in the future?

Chapter 4

NEGOTIATING GAMES/TECHNIQUES

A. INTRODUCTION

People who participate in the negotiation process employ various games and techniques to advance their interests. Some of these tactics are natural extensions of the individuals using them. For example, persons with aggressive personalities may intuitively adopt an aggressive negotiating style, while calm bargainers may use a laid-back approach. Whether negotiators embrace a cooperative/problem-solving, a competitive/adversarial, or a competitive/problem-solving style, they must employ different devices that are designed to advance their positions.

Seemingly ingenuous comments that disguise ulterior motives are common to almost all negotiations. For instance, advocates may attempt to convince opponents that they possess more beneficial alternatives to nonsettlement than they actually do. If their representations in this regard are believed, their bargaining power will be meaningfully enhanced by the fact that their adversaries think they are not under great pressure to reach an immediate accord. Other advocates may resort to false flattery to soften strong opponents or use feigned weakness or apparent ineptitude to evoke sympathy from those adversaries.

Some communications contain dual messages — one seemingly objective and forthright and the other subtle and ulterior. For example, a real estate seller might candidly suggest to someone who would apparently like to purchase property that he or she can barely afford, "you probably can't afford this house." Although this overtly "adult"-to-"adult" statement may be objectively correct, the seller does not wish to convince the prospective purchaser of this fact, because that would preclude any sale. The ulterior message is surreptitiously conveyed on a "parent"-to-"child" level, with the "parent"-seller telling the "child"-prospective buyer that he or she cannot do something. If the desired response is generated, the prospective purchaser will respond with a "child"-like "Yes, I can!" (Berne, 1964, at 33–34.) If this device functions properly, the salesperson will be able to sell a house to someone who was not planning to select such an expensive property.

Negotiators should normally be suspicious of statements suggesting that a contemplated transaction cannot or should not be consummated. If the communicators of these messages truly believed this fact, they would not have any reason to participate in the bargaining process. If, despite such communications, the speakers exhibit a desire to engage in further discussions, it is likely that they are attempting to subconsciously entrap the unsuspecting respondents into accepting what are probably disadvantageous arrangements.

There are a relatively finite number of styles or approaches that may be adopted by bargainers. It is thus possible to categorize and explore the various techniques negotiators would be likely to encounter (*see generally* Levinson, Smith & Wilson, 1999). If advocates acquaint themselves with the commonly used approaches, they can more readily identify the bargaining tactics being used against them and understand the strengths and weaknesses associated with those maneuvers. This facilitates their ability to counteract them. It additionally enhances their bargaining confidence and thus improves their chances of achieving beneficial results. Negotiators must also appreciate the different techniques, so they can determine which tactics they should employ to advance their own interests.

It is fairly easy to keep track of the tactics used by negotiators who either employ one approach most of the time or use different techniques one at a time in sequence. It is more difficult to identify the devices being used by negotiators who employ various maneuvers simultaneously (*e.g.*, "Mutt and Jeff," "Anger," and "Limited Authority"). Participants adopt such a diverse approach to keep their opponents off balance. Their adversaries should carefully monitor and respond to the particular tactics being employed during the various portions of their interaction, so they can effectively counter those bargaining games.

B. COMMON NEGOTIATION TECHNIQUES

1. NUMERICALLY SUPERIOR BARGAINING TEAM

Most legal negotiations are conducted on a one-on-one basis, with a single attorney interacting with a single opponent. In some instances, however, parties attempt to obtain a tactical and psychological advantage by including extra people on their bargaining team. They hope that the additional participants will intimidate their lone adversary and be more likely to discern the verbal leaks and nonverbal messages being emitted by that individual (Hodgson, Sano & Graham, 2000, at 25). These extra participants may similarly monitor the verbal and nonverbal signals communicated by their opponent while one of their partners is talking and by the other members of their own bargaining team. Parties with expanded negotiating teams also think the excessive verbal and nonverbal stimuli emanating from the different participators will confuse someone who has to observe, listen, plan, and speak simultaneously. Furthermore, the additional participants provide the primary representative with someone to consult during separate caucuses.

The addition of even a single negotiating partner can significantly diminish the advantage that opponents may derive from an expansive bargaining team. Even if the extra person does not speak, he or she can carefully monitor the nonverbal clues and verbal messages emanating from both sides, while his or her co-counsel is actively interacting with the opponents. When adversaries attempt to overload their bargaining teams in an unconscionable fashion, it would not be inappropriate for someone to refuse to meet with that group until it is reduced to a more manageable size. If such a reduction could not be achieved, due to the various constituencies that must be represented on the opposing team, it might be necessary to bring additional people to the sessions to counterbalance the sheer size of that group. It might also be possible to counteract this technique by conducting telephone interactions that decrease the impact of multiple opponents.

In rare instances, institutional considerations require opposing bargaining teams to include a number of representatives from diverse constituencies. This is typical of labor union negotiating groups and governmental negotiations involving different departments. During these interactions, one side may have only two or three representatives, while the opposing team consists of ten or fifteen participants. On these occasions, the smaller group may actually have an advantage. Unless the more expansive opposing teams have carefully coordinated their goals and planned their approach during the Preparation Stage, the members of that group may emit mixed signals that will undermine group solidarity (Brodt & Thompson, 2001, at 212; LePoole, 1991, at 98–101). Some may even nod their heads affirmatively, while others verbally reject the proposals being discussed. Individuals dealing with enlarged bargaining groups should not hesitate to employ tactics that are designed to divide and conquer their disorganized opponents.

Organizations that must conduct negotiations through expanded group participation may be disadvantaged by a lack of intragroup preparation, and the resulting lack of group cohesiveness. If they lack common objectives and a unified strategy, proficient opponents may exploit their weaknesses. On the other hand, well prepared groups may actually outperform smaller teams if they can take advantage of their capacity to look more carefully for verbal leaks and nonverbal cues emanating from the other side (Brodt & Thompson, 2001, at 211–12). Well coordinated groups can reinforce their common beliefs and their jointly developed objectives.

Larger negotiation groups often behave more competitively, and they are less likely to employ cooperative strategies due to pressure to achieve beneficial group returns (Brodt & Thompson, 2001, at 213). This approach may generate optimal results with respect to distributive interactions that involve such issues as money, but it can create problems when integrative issues are involved. If group dynamics inhibit cooperative bargaining designed to expand the overall pie and enhance joint returns, both sides may suffer from an inability to generate efficient resolutions that may have been achieved through more integrative discussions.

2. USE OF ASYMMETRICAL TIME PRESSURE

During the preliminary stages of an interaction, negotiators occasionally discover the existence of time constraints that affect the other party more than they influence their own side. Japanese bargainers frequently employ this factor to their advantage when they are visited by foreign corporate representatives. They initially ask about the return flight schedule of their guests — ostensibly to allow them to reconfirm those flights. They then use generous hospitality to preclude the commencement of substantive discussions until a few days before their visitors are planning to return home. The Japanese negotiators recognize that their foreign agents do not want to return home without an agreement. This forces those visitors to consider extra, last-minute concessions in an effort to achieve a final accord while they are still in Japan.

Similar tactics are often employed by insurance company representatives who determine that plaintiffs are overly eager to settle their cases to avoid the two or three year wait for trial dates. By exuding unlimited patience, these insurance lawyers are often able to convince plaintiff-attorneys that they have to make greater concessions if accords are to be achieved within the time-frames that have been artificially established by the plaintiffs (LePoole, 1991, at 104–05).

Whenever possible, negotiators should try to withhold information that might suggest the existence of an asymmetrical time constraint (Dawson, 2001, at 174). For example, individuals traveling to another country to discuss a possible business venture should refrain from booking a definite return flight. When their hosts ask them when they plan to return home, they should reply that they are prepared to remain as long as it takes to fully explore the possibility of a mutually beneficial relationship. If they can exhibit a patient demeanor, they can increase the likelihood of achieving an expeditious and beneficial agreement. Attorneys whose clients have established artificially abbreviated time-frames should similarly try to keep that information confidential. They should also inform their clients how much bargaining leverage they will lose if they are unwilling to wait until an impending trial date induces parsimonious opponents to increase their offers. If they can convince their opponents that they are not being influenced by the time factor, they can substantially enhance their bargaining posture.

When transactional bargainers have certain deadlines that must be met and their opponents are not operating under a similar constraint, they may take preemptive action to neutralize the time factor. They can announce at the beginning of discussions that everything must be concluded by their deadline if a mutual accord is to be achieved (Freund, 1992, at 148-49). Through this approach, they can impose their time constraint on their adversaries and deprive them of the opportunity to use this factor to their advantage. Negotiators should only make statements of this kind when they truly have deadlines that must be satisfied if agreements are to be attained.

3. EXTREME INITIAL DEMANDS/OFFERS

Empirical studies have demonstrated that people who enter negotiations with high aspiration levels generally obtain more beneficial results than those who begin with less generous expectations. It thus behooves bargainers to commence their interactions with high demands or low offers (Dawson, 2001, at 13–18). Bargainers who can rationally defend their seemingly unreasonable initial offers may be able to induce careless adversaries to reconsider their own preliminary assessments. Once those individuals begin to doubt the propriety of their own positions, they are in trouble. They may even lose touch with reality and accept the skewed representations being advanced by their opponents.

Individuals who are formulating initial demands/offers should not make them so obviously unrealistic that they cannot be rationally defended. Clearly absurd opening demands/offers will suffer from a lack of legitimacy, and may create unintended difficulties. If the recipients of outlandish proposals conclude that the matters in dispute cannot reasonably be resolved through the negotiation process, they may terminate the present discussions. Even when interactions are not discontinued, participants who have articulated extreme positions may find it impossible to make the necessary concessions in an orderly manner. They may thus be forced to make large, irrational position changes, causing a concomitant loss of control.

Persons confronted by truly unreasonable initial demands/offers should not casually indicate their displeasure with those positions, because this response may lead their opponents to think that their demands/offers are not wholly unrealistic. This would be likely to induce those people to raise their aspiration level in a way that would probably generate nonsettlements. Recipients of outrageous opening demands/offers should immediately and directly express their displeasure with such positions, to disabuse the offerors of any thought their entreaties are not absurd.

Individuals who begin with extreme positions are often unsure of their situations. To protect themselves, they start with what they suspect are unreasonable proposals. They expect their opponents to react with disapproval and actually feel better when their adversaries do so. This confirms their initial view that their starting positions were excessive, and they place greater faith in their preliminary assessments.

Once the recipients of extreme offers have indicated how unrealistic those positions are, they may respond in one of three ways. They may indicate that they do not plan to articulate their own initial offer until the other side sets forth a reasonable position. The primary difficulty with this approach is the fact it requires the unreasonable participants to "bid against themselves" — i.e., to make consecutive concessions. Proficient negotiators are loathe to make unreciprocated position changes. Some individuals may counter extreme demands/offers with outlandish positions of their own. When challenged by their opponents, they indicate that their initial offer is no more unreasonable than that of the other side. They can then suggest their willingness to provide a realistic offer, if their opponent will agree to do the same. Such "attitudinal" bargaining is always appropriate in these circumstances.

A few negotiators try to ignore unrealistic opening offers made by opponents and articulate realistic offers of their own, hoping to embarrass their adversaries. This approach may create unanticipated problems. After several concessions have been made by both sides, the party that started with the extreme position is likely to emphasize how far it has moved compared to the side that began with a reasonable figure. In many cases, the persons who started with the realistic positions are likely to pay more or accept less than they should, because of the guilt they encounter when attempting to induce their unreasonable opponents to make concessions on a ten-to-one basis throughout the entire interaction.

4. USE OF PROBING QUESTIONS

Negotiators confronted by uncompromising positions taken by opponents may generate a more flexible atmosphere through the use of probing questions (Mayer, 1996, at 68). Instead of directly challenging those positions — a tactic that would likely cause the other side to become more resolute — they can separate the different items and propound a series of questions that are designed to force the opponents to explain each aspect of their offer. For example, if participants in a corporate buyout were to make a wholly unrealistic offer or demand, the recipient could ask those persons how much they have allotted for the real property. If the questioner receives a realistic response, he or she writes it down. If the figure mentioned is unreasonably high or low, the questioner may cite a recent appraisal and ask how the respondents calculated their figure. Once a realistic amount is obtained for this item, the questioner can move on to the proposed figure for the building and equipment, the inventory, the accounts receivable, the patent, trade, or copy rights, the corporate good will, and other relevant considerations.

If these inquiries are carefully formulated in a relatively neutral and nonjudgmental manner, they may induce the other side to examine the partisan bases underlying their position statement. As each component is addressed, the opponents must either articulate rational explanations or begin to recognize the lack of any sound foundation for that aspect of their offer. When adversaries do not respond thoughtfully to queries that are posed, they should be reframed and asked again. When this process is finished and the different amounts are totaled, the sum is usually four or five times what was originally offered or one-fourth or one-fifth of what was initially demanded. This is due to the fact that negotiators who begin with truly unrealistic offers have made them up and have no idea how to defend them on a component-by-component basis.

5. BOULWAREISM

This technique derives its name from Lemuel Boulware, a former Vice President for Labor Relations at General Electric. Mr. Boulware was not enamored of traditional "auction" bargaining that consisted of extreme initial positions, the making of time-consuming concessions, and the achievement of final collective bargaining agreements similar to those the parties initially knew they would reach. He thus decided to determine ahead of time what the company was willing to commit to wage and benefit increases. He surveyed the employees to ascertain their interests, and formulated a complete "best-offer-first" package. This offer was then presented to union negotiators on a "take-it-or-leave-it" basis. This approach precipitated a work stoppage and resulted in protracted unfair labor practice litigation.

The term "Boulwareism" is now associated with best-offer-first (offeror's perspective) or take-it-or-leave-it (offeree's perspective) bargaining. Many insurance company representatives endeavor to establish reputations as people who make one firm, fair offer. If that proposal is not accepted by plaintiff-counsel, they plan to go to trial. A few individuals are able to employ this technique effectively. They make reasonable offers in a relatively non-threatening manner, and many of their firm offers are accepted. On the other hand, individuals using Boulwareism must recognize that this approach may actually cost their insurance clients money. Had they been willing to engage in conventional auction bargaining, they may have been able to settle many cases for less than they were initially willing to pay. In addition, they may have avoided the rejection of what might otherwise have been acceptable terms, but were rejected because of the patronizing way in which they were presented.

Rarely can the representatives on one side definitively determine the true value of an impending bargaining transaction before they meet with their opponents. No matter how thoroughly they review the information preliminarily available to them, they must remember that it is impossible to ascertain the real value of a prospective deal prior to discussions with the people representing the other side. Only through these inter-party exchanges can they learn how much their adversaries desire an agreement. They must assess how risk-averse their opponents are, and the degree to which time pressure may be influencing those persons. Without such critical information, it is not possible to calculate accurately what is truly required to satisfy opponent needs and interests.

Negotiators should also hesitate to adopt a Boulwareistic approach because of the impact of this tactic on opponents. It exudes a paternalistic arrogance, with offerors effectively informing offerees, in a "parent"-to-"child" interaction, that they know what is best for both sides. Few lawyers are willing to defer so readily to the superior knowledge of opposing counsel. This technique also deprives opponents of the opportunity to participate meaningfully in the bargaining process. Even if plaintiff-attorneys would initially have been pleased to resolve their case for $50,000, they may not be satisfied with a take-it-or-leave-it first offer of $50,000. Plaintiff-counsel want to explore the case through the Information Stage and to exhibit their negotiating skill through the Competitive/ Distributive and Closing Stages. When the process is completed, they want to think that their own personal ability influenced the outcome. This permits them to explain to their client how the insurance carrier opened with an unacceptably low offer, but they were able to achieve a more generous final result.

If insurance company attorneys willing to pay $50,000 begin the negotiation process with an offer of $20,000 and become difficult once they get to the $40,000 to $45,000 range, they may resolve the claim for $42,000 or $43,000 — saving their client $7,000 or $8,000! Moreover, the plaintiff-representatives would probably be more satisfied with the $42,000 or $43,000 obtained through the auction process than with the $50,000 offered in a Boulwareistic fashion.

People contemplating the use of Boulwareism must realize that this approach may only be employed effectively by negotiators who possess significant power. If weak participants attempt to use this technique, their take-it-or-leave-it demands are likely to be unceremoniously rejected. When bargainers enjoy a clear strength advantage, there is no reason to use this approach — except to avoid the need to engage in any real give-and-take negotiating. The more power negotiators have, the more generous they should be with *process*. They should permit opponents to participate meaningfully in the interaction and let them think they influenced the outcome. The use of more traditional auction bargaining techniques increases the likelihood the parties will reach mutual accords. It simultaneously provides advocates employing conventional tactics with the opportunity to achieve final terms that are better from their side's perspective than they were initially willing to offer.

Very few people can evaluate unabashed take-it-or-leave-it initial offers on the merits alone. This approach is an affront to their right to participate in the process on an "adult"-to-"adult" basis and to influence the outcome. Lawyers frequently reject Boulwareistic offers merely to demonstrate to offensive opponents that they cannot be treated in such an arrogant fashion. Nonetheless, recipients of Boulwareistic offers should attempt to evaluate the propriety of those proposals in a detached fashion that is unaffected by the offensive manner in which they have been presented. If the offers constitute truly reasonable proposals and they are certain they are not going to obtain more beneficial proposals, they should recommend them to their clients.

6. SETTLEMENT BROCHURE

Some legal advocates, particularly in the personal injury field, attempt to enhance their bargaining posture through the preparation of pre-negotiation settlement brochures. These consist of written documents that specifically articulate the factual and legal bases for the claims being asserted, and describe the full extent of plaintiff injuries. Each item for which monetary relief is being sought is separately listed and explained in an attempt to establish highly "principled" opening demands (Steinberg, 1998, at 70–71). When available, photographs depicting the accident scene and/or the injuries sustained by plaintiffs are included in an effort to evoke guilt and sympathy. Video replays may be employed to recreate the relevant events or to demonstrate pre-and post-accident plaintiff capabilities.

Settlement brochures may subconsciously be accorded greater respect than would verbal recitations, due to the aura of legitimacy associated with printed documents. The use of this technique may bolster the confidence of plaintiff-attorneys, and may enable them to seize control of the negotiating agenda at the outset of the bargaining process. Although some lawyers do not provide opponents with copies of settlement brochures until their first formal meeting, others have them delivered several days in advance of initial sessions to enable their opponent to review these documents before they meet.

Individuals who are presented with settlement brochures should be careful not to accord them greater respect than they deserve. The recipients should treat the factual and legal representations set forth in those documents as they would identical verbal statements. While few attorneys would think of making deliberate factual or legal misrepresentations in writing, most would not hesitate to engage in "puffing" or "embellishment." If recipients are provided with these instruments before the first bargaining session, they should thoroughly review the assertions made by their opponents and prepare effective counter arguments. They should be cautious not to allow their adversaries to use their settlement brochures to control the agenda of their interaction.

Advocates who prepare settlement brochures frequently use charts, tables, or graphs to depict likely *future* consequences for which compensation is being sought. These may include lost earnings, future medical expenses, and/or continuing pain and suffering. Individuals presented with these claims should carefully review the assumptions underlying those projections. Has plaintiff-counsel assumed that an eighth-grade dropout working part-time at a fast-food restaurant for $7.00/hr. was planning to return to school and become a brain surgeon with future annual earnings of $500,000? Have they assumed annual pay raises of 10% when recent annual increases have been in the 3–4% range? Have they assumed an excessive inflation rate with respect to future medical expenses? Once these underlying assumptions are accepted, the brochure projections logically follow. This is why the basic assumptions must be perused.

Some defense counsel counter plaintiff settlement brochures with brochures of their own. After they receive opponent position statements, they prepare their own counter arguments explaining why liability is nonexistent or limited and describing the limited damages involved. They are thus able to counteract the impact of plaintiff brochures with their own equally forceful written position statements. If they are persuasive, they may even be able to induce plaintiff-lawyers to approach the verbal discussions from the perspective of their agenda.

7. MULTIPLE/EQUAL VALUE OFFERS

When multiple issue negotiations are involved, some participants attempt to disclose their own relative item values and elicit similar information regarding their opponents through the use of multiple/equal value offers (Dietmeyer & Kaplan, 2004, at 131–41). They formulate several different offers that vary what they are seeking and what they are willing to give the other side. These diverse offers have a common theme. Each one provides the offeror with a relatively equal level of satisfaction. People who use this technique hope to let the other side understand the different amounts of the various items they must obtain to create equal client satisfaction.

Multiple/equal value offerors hope to induce their opponents to let them know which of these diverse offers is preferable from their perspective. They want their adversaries to indicate in their counter-offers the terms they prefer to obtain and the issues they are willing to concede to the initial offerors. The parties can then work to generate efficient agreements that maximize the joint returns achieved by the bargaining parties.

When employed carefully with trustworthy opponents, this approach allows the offerors to let the opposing side know which term combinations they value equally. The offerors thus disclose the relative priorities associated with their underlying needs and interests. They hope their adversaries will share their underlying priorities through their critiques of the initial offers and their own counter-offers.

As the parties explore their respective bundled offers and counter-offers, they can discard less efficient formulations, and focus on the mutually beneficial packages. If the use of multiple/equal value offers is to function effectively, the negotiating participants must indicate, with some degree of candor, which items are essential, important, and desirable, and how much of each they hope to obtain. This allows each side to appreciate the other's basic interests and encourages the development of mutually beneficial accords.

Parties initiating the use of multiple/equal value offers are counting on reciprocal candor from the other side. The offerors have to a significant degree disclosed their relative values. If the other side counters with manipulative and disingenuous offers designed to exploit the original offerors' openness, it may be able to claim an excessive share of the joint value created.

A second risk concerns the articulation of an excessive number of package offers. Individuals who are presented with two, three, or even four options usually do a good job of determining which alternative is preferable. On the other hand, persons presented with a greater number of options often become confused. They fail to evaluate all of the options together, but instead make comparisons among finite groups (*see generally* Schwartz, 2004). As a result, even though Package 2 may be optimal, one side may only compare Packages 3, 4, and 5 and select the preferable one of these. They fail to compare the one picked with Package 2 and end up with an inferior choice. It thus behooves negotiators using multiple/equal value offers to limit the number articulated at one time to a manageable number the recipients can assess together. This is especially important when many items are involved and offer recipients must compare expansive packages with one another. Offerors who suspect that the "paradox of choice" may be affecting the assessments of offer recipients may minimize this phenomenon by asking those parties if they have compared the offer they said they preferred with all of the other packages which have been tendered.

8. LIMITED CLIENT AUTHORITY

Many advocates indicate during the preliminary stages of a negotiation that they do not possess final authority from their client regarding the matter in dispute. Some people who possess real authority employ this technique to reserve the right to check with their absent clients and reassess the terms agreed upon before tentative agreement can formally bind their side. Other negotiators really do have external constituencies that must ultimately approve preliminary accords before they can become operative. For example, labor organizations must generally have collective contracts ratified by members, and representatives of municipal, state, and federal government entities must usually obtain legislative or departmental approval before their agreements become effective.

The advantage of a limited authority approach — whether fanciful or real — is that it permits participants using this device to obtain definitive commitments from opponents who are authorized to make binding commitments on behalf of their clients. The unbound bargainers can thereafter seek beneficial modifications of their negotiated contracts based upon "unexpected" client demands. Once opponents become familiar with this tactic, they begin to hold back some of the items they are initially prepared to commit. This allows them to increase their final offers after the first contracts are rejected. As it becomes apparent to individuals who use limited authority to obtain additional concessions at the end of transactions that adversaries are effectively counteracting this approach, they begin to recognize the futility of this technique.

Bargainers who encounter opponents who initially indicate that they lack the authority to bind their clients may frequently find it advantageous to state that they similarly lack final client authority over the issues being discussed. This permits them to "check" with their own absent principals before they make any final commitments. If they are unable to claim limited authority of their own, they may alternatively refuse to bargain with agents who do not possess a meaningful degree of final control.

An opponent's alleged lack of client authority may occasionally be an impediment to a final agreement. That person may have indicated that he or she is not empowered to accept a certain offer that is really within the scope of his or her authorized limits. It is rarely helpful to challenge that person directly with respect to this issue, because he or she is unlikely to admit overt prevarication. It is far more productive to provide that individual with a face-saving escape. By suggesting that he or she privately contact the client to request permission to agree to the offer on the table, a final accord may be achieved without the need for unnecessary accusations or recriminations. This approach best serves client interests by maximizing the likelihood of an ultimate settlement.

9. LACK OF CLIENT AUTHORITY

Negotiators occasionally receive telephone calls from opponent agents who indicate a desire to ascertain the thoughts of the unsuspecting call recipients. The people being called are asked what they hope to achieve from the impending interaction. When these targets openly disclose their initial positions, they are told that the suggested terms are outrageous and wholly unacceptable. The callers even indicate that they could not possibly convey those proposals to their superiors. This device is designed to make naive respondents feel guilty about their allegedly extreme demands and to induce them to unilaterally modify their opening offers to the benefit of their adversaries.

It is impossible to bargain meaningfully with people who lack the authority to speak for their own clients. The participants who possess real client authority can only bid against themselves by articulating consecutive opening offers. When unauthorized opponents telephone, it is apparent that they do not plan to conduct serious negotiations. They hope to obtain several concessions as a prerequisite to participation by the people on their side. Negotiators should not succumb to this approach. If they are willing to do so, they should disclose their initial offers. When the unauthorized callers criticize their position statements, they should ask the callers to state their own demands. When the callers indicate a lack of capacity to do so, the call recipients should ask the callers to state their own positions. If they indicate that they lack the authority to do so, they should be told to get some authority and to state their own positions to enable the participants to discuss their respective positions. If they are unable to get such authority, they should be instructed to have someone with actual authority contact them. Only when the representatives of both sides possess the authority to articulate meaningful offers can real bargaining take place.

10. "Nibble" Technique

Some negotiators "agree" to final accords with apparent authority. Several days later, they approach their opponents with seeming embarrassment and explain that they did not really possess the authority to bind their clients. They sheepishly indicate that their principals are dissatisfied with what was negotiated and require several additional concessions before they will accept the other terms of the agreements. Since the unsuspecting opponents and their clients are now psychologically committed to final settlements and do not want to permit these items to negate their previous efforts, they normally agree to the requested modifications. The "nibble" technique is frequently employed by car salespeople who induce prospective buyers to agree to pay a certain amount for a particular automobile. The salesperson thereafter checks with the "sales manager" — who may not even exist — and contritely informs the psychologically committed customers that several hundred additional dollars are required to consummate the sales transaction. It is amazing how frequently this tactic is successfully employed (G. Karrass, 1985, at 109–110).

Individuals confronted by "nibblers" often make the mistake of focusing entirely on the desire of their own clients to preserve the accords previously reached. They fail to direct their attention to the *opposing parties* and to acknowledge the fact that those people also want to retain the terms already agreed upon. If they did not have that similar objective, they would not have participated in the antecedent negotiations. Persons who are asked for one or two additional concessions to cement deals must not be afraid to say "no" or to demand reciprocity for the requested position changes.

When negotiators suspect that they are interacting with opponents who may try to use disingenuous client disgruntlement to obtain post-agreement concessions, they should mentally select the particular terms they would like to have modified in their favor. When their adversaries request the anticipated changes, they can indicate how relieved they are to address this matter, because of the dissatisfaction of their own clients regarding the current agreement. If their opponents are acting in good faith, they will acknowledge the need for reciprocity and address the proposed exchanges. On the other hand, individuals who are insincerely using the "nibble" technique to "steal" items will be reluctant to do so. They will usually reject further discussions and insist upon the terms that were initially agreed upon! When the "nibbler" puts his or her hand in your pocket in an effort to pick it, you should remember to reach into that person's pocket to extract a reciprocal benefit.

11. Use of Decreasing Offers/Increasing Demands and Limited Time Offers

During the preliminary stages of some law suits — particularly those of relatively modest value — a few attorneys make fairly realistic offers or demands that they say must be accepted by specified dates. They make it clear that if their proposed terms are not accepted in a timely manner, they may withdraw those offers entirely, begin to reduce the amounts being offered, or increase the amounts being demanded (Freund, 1992, at 79–81). This technique is usually based on the fact that proposers will have to expend time and money preparing for trial if their initial terms are not accepted. They thus plan to revoke their earlier offers and get ready for trial — or to decrease their subsequent offers or increase their subsequent demands in proportion to their increased litigation expenses.

Negotiators who employ this approach should establish reputations as people who carry out their stated intentions and carefully apprise opponents of their exact intentions in this regard. This maximizes the likelihood that their initial proposals will be accepted, and it minimizes the possibility of confusion. It is generally assumed — absent unexpected intervening circumstances — that extended offers will remain on the table and that subsequent offers will not be less generous than earlier offers. If bargainers inexplicably withdraw or reduce outstanding offers without previously informing opponents of this possibility or providing valid explanations based on new information, their action is likely to provoke hostility and claims of unethical conduct. It will also generate nonsettlements in situations in which agreements might otherwise have been achieved.

12. REAL OR FEIGNED ANGER

Resort to real or feigned anger during the critical stages of a negotiation may effectively convince opponents of the seriousness of one's position. It may also intimidate adversaries and convince them of the need to make concessions if the bargaining process is to continue. Although controlled anger is normally employed by proficient negotiators to accomplish these objectives, there are occasions when true anger is displayed.

The use of real anger can be dangerous, because people who permit bargaining frustration to precipitate unplanned diatribes frequently disclose more information during their outbursts than they intended. For example, a defendant-lawyer who has offered $75,000 to a plaintiff-attorney who is steadfastly demanding $150,000 might finally explode with a statement indicating that "this case cannot be resolved for more $100,000!" This exclamation would strongly suggest to plaintiff-counsel that the defendant insurance company is presently willing to pay $100,000, but little above that figure. This is critical information, because it provides the plaintiff-lawyer with a good approximation of the defendant's resistance point. If the plaintiff-attorney was hoping to achieve a result in excess of $100,000, he or she should realize that this result is unlikely during the current negotiations. It may thus be necessary to plan subsequent discussions, with the expectation that greater time pressure may ultimately induce the defendant insurer to reconsider its current upper limit.

Individuals who wish to employ feigned anger to advance their position should plan their tactic with care. They should decide which words would be most likely to influence their opponent's assessment of the transaction, and try to limit their apparent outburst to those comments. They should simultaneously watch for signs of increased frustration and anxiety on the part of their adversary (e.g., clenched teeth, wringing of hands, or placing of open hands in front of self as defensive measure against the verbal onslaught), to be certain not to precipitate an unintended reaction such as the cessation of talks.

People who find themselves berated by an angry opponent may be tempted to respond with their own retaliatory diatribe to convince their opponent that they cannot be intimidated by such irrational tactics. This quid pro quo approach would involve obvious risks. At a minimum, the vituperative exchange would probably have a deleterious impact on the bargaining atmosphere. It may even precipitate a cessation of meaningful discussions and force the participants to resort to their nonsettlement alternatives. While this response might be appropriate to counteract the conduct of a truly angry opponent or an aggressive bully, there is a more productive way to react to contrived opponent anger. The targets of these outbursts should listen intently for inadvertent verbal leaks and watch for informative nonverbal signals. Their quiet styles may disconcert loud and abusive opponents (Shapiro & Jankowski, 2001, at 178).

Negotiators with sincere demeanors may effectively counter angry eruptions by indicating that they have been personally offended by the ad hominem attack. They should indicate that they cannot understand how their reasonable and fair approach can be subject to such an intemperate challenge. They might even recite several of their recent position changes to demonstrate their sincere efforts to accommodate opponent needs. If they are successful in this regard, they may create feelings of guilt and embarrassment in the attacking party. This technique may even shame that person into a conciliatory concession.

13. AGGRESSIVE BEHAVIOR

Aggressive behavior is usually intended to have an impact similar to that associated with real or feigned anger. It is supposed to convince opponents of the seriousness of one's position. It is also used by anxious individuals to maintain control of the bargaining agenda. By being overly assertive, aggressive negotiators may be able to dominate the interaction. This technique is most effectively employed by naturally aggressive individuals. Less assertive persons who try to adopt an uncharacteristically aggressive approach do not feel comfortable with this style, and they are often unable to project a credible image.

Some highly combative negotiators attempt to augment their aggressive style with gratuitous sarcasm. Their goal is to make their opponents feel so uncomfortable they will be induced to make excessive concessions in an effort to end their unpleasant interaction. Individuals who use this approach judiciously may obtain beneficial agreements on some occasions, but they risk needless nonsettlements from opponents who refuse to tolerate their offensive behavior. They also tend to generate accords that are not as efficient as they might have achieved if the parties had developed more cordial and trusting relationships.

Well-mannered negotiators who attempt to counter offensively aggressive bargainers with quid pro quo attacks are likely to fail, because of the capacity of those individuals to out-insult almost anyone. People who encounter these adversaries should diminish the aggregate impact of their demeaning techniques through the use of short, carefully controlled interactions. Telephone discussions may be used to limit each exchange. When discussions become tense, the targets of aggressive opponents can indicate that they have to take care of other business and terminate their immediate interactions. They can thereafter re-call their opponents when they are more inclined to tolerate their behavior. Personal meetings should, if possible, be restricted to sessions of less than one hour in duration. These abbreviated discussions can prevent abrasive advocates from generating sarcasm momentum. It also makes it easier for the objects of such insults to retain control over their own emotions.

Aggressive negotiators, particularly those who use abrasive tactics, should carefully monitor their opponents for nonverbal indications of excessive frustration and stress. They should look for clenched teeth, crossed arms and legs, increased gross body movement, and similar signals. If they are unaware of these signs, their conduct may generate unintended interactional breaks.

14. WALKING OUT/HANGING UP TELEPHONE

This technique is frequently employed by demonstrative negotiators who want to convince their opponents that they are unwilling to make additional concessions. Once the parties have narrowed the distance between their respective positions, these individuals walk out or slam down the receiver in an effort to induce risk-averse adversaries to close all or most or the remaining gap. This approach may induce overly anxious opponents to cave in.

Bargainers should not permit this type of bullying conduct to intimidate them into unwarranted and unreciprocated concessions. Targets of such behavior should not run after their departing opponents or re-telephone people who have deliberately terminated their present interaction. This would be viewed as a sign of weakness that may be exploited. They should instead give their demonstrative opponent time to calm down and reflect on the current positions on the table. They should also reevaluate their nonsettlement options to be sure they will not succumb to unreasonable opponent demands. If targets of this intimidating conduct are able to maintain their resolve, their bullying adversaries are likely to resume negotiations and make new counter offers.

15. IRRATIONAL BEHAVIOR

A few negotiators attempt to gain a bargaining advantage through seemingly irrational conduct. Some of these advocates attribute the irrationality to their absent clients (see "Mutt and Jeff" approach discussed below), while others exhibit their own bizarre behavior. These individuals hope to convince opponents that they cannot be dealt with logically. Adversaries must either accept their one-sided demands or face the consequences associated with an ongoing dispute with an unstable party.

People who encounter aberrant opponents tend to become frightened. They fear that these irrational bargainers will destroy both sides. To avoid these dire consequences, they frequently accept the dictates of these seemingly illogical adversaries. As a result, they end up with agreements that are worse than their nonsettlement options.

Few legal advocates or their corporate clients are truly irrational. If they were, they would be unable to achieve successful results on a consistent basis. In most instances in which bizarre behavior is encountered, the actors are crazy like a fox — using feigned irrationality to advance their bargaining objectives. The most effective way to counter contrived preposterousness is to ignore it and respond in a wholly rational manner. As soon as these manipulative opponents caucus to consider proposed terms, they cease their illogical conduct and rationally evaluate the proposals on the table. Once they realize that their strange behavior is not having its expected impact, they are likely to forego this approach.

On rare occasions, truly irrational opponents are encountered. While these individuals may be the legal advocates themselves, they are more frequently the individual clients involved. When such people participate in negotiations, it is impossible to deal with them logically. They are incapable of evaluating bargaining proposals and nonsettlement options in a realistic manner. They continue to reiterate their unsound proposals in an unthinking fashion no matter the risks involved. Opponents must either give in to their positions or accept their nonsettlement alternatives.

When negotiators are forced to interact with truly bizarre adversaries, they must carefully reevaluate their own nonsettlement alternatives. They should avoid agreements that are less beneficial than their external options. They should only accept the dictates of unstable opponents when those terms are preferable to continued disagreement. Even when agreements are consummated with illogical adversaries, bargainers must recognize the subsequent difficulties that may be encountered during the performance stages of their relationship. To protect client interests, advocates who enter into contracts with such opponents should try to minimize the risks associated with non-or partial performance.

16. FALSE DEMANDS

Alert negotiators occasionally discover during the Information Stage that their opponents want some item that is not valued by their own client. When this knowledge is obtained, many bargainers endeavor to take advantage of the situation. They try to avoid providing the other side with this topic in exchange for an insignificant term. They instead attempt to extract a more substantial concession. To accomplish this objective, they mention how important that subject is to their client, and they include it with their initial demands. If they are able to convince their opponents that this issue is of major value to their side, they may be able to enhance their client's position with what is actually a meaningless concession on their part.

A serious risk is associated with false demands. If individuals employing this technique are too persuasive, they may find themselves the tragic beneficiaries of an unwanted bargaining chip. It would be inadvisable for them to attempt to rectify this tactical error with a straightforward admission of deception, because this would probably impede further negotiation progress. They should tentatively accept the item in question. As the interaction evolves, they should exchange this term for another more useful topic. Even if their opponents recognize their predicament, those participants should generally permit them to employ this face-saving escape route. Little would be gained by an overt challenge to the deceptive actor's personal integrity, and the risk to the bargaining process would be substantial.

17.   If It Weren't For You (Or Your Client)

Some parties attempt to make their adversaries feel guilty by suggesting during a negotiation that they would not be involved in this predicament if it were not for the improper actions of the opposing clients.

> (1) "If only your client had not driven while intoxicated . . . ."

> (2) "If only your client had completely satisfied his/her contractual obligations . . . ."

> (3) "If only you had been willing to make a more reasonable offer at the outset of these negotiations . . . ."

> (4) "If only you had arrived at the appointed hour for our discussions, . . ."

Lawyers should recognize that these tactics are designed to generate inappropriate guilt or embarrassment. They should not permit this type of conduct to influence their bargaining behavior (Shapiro & Jankowski, 2001, at 179–80). It is obvious that if the clients of both participants had behaved properly, there would be no need for lawsuit settlement discussions. If both parties had disclosed all of the pertinent information at the outset of their interaction and had established objectives considered reasonable and appropriate by both sides, their legal advocates would probably not be currently involved in dispute resolution talks. These considerations are indigenous to almost all bargaining transactions. If it weren't for such circumstances, most attorneys would be superfluous!

Manipulative opponents may endeavor to create feelings of guilt or embarrassment by focusing on insignificant personal transgressions. When advocates are unavoidably late for scheduled meetings or forget to bring certain documents, they should merely apologize for their oversight and thereafter ignore these matters. If their adversaries continue to refer to these petty issues, they may turn the tables by asking their accusers why they are using such trivial misdeeds to impede the substantive talks.

18.   Alleged Expertise/Snow Job

A few individuals attempt to overwhelm bargaining opponents with factual and/or legal details that are really not relevant to the basic interaction. They cite factual matters and legal doctrines that are of no meaningful concern to the negotiating parties. They hope to bolster their own bargaining confidence through demonstrations of their thorough knowledge, and they want to intimidate adversaries who have not developed such expertise.

People should not permit opponents to overwhelm them with factual or legal minutiae. When someone tries to focus upon marginally relevant details, they should be praised for their thorough preparation and be asked to concentrate upon the more salient items. If necessary, they should be asked to summarize their positions without the need for repeated reference to superfluous data. Skilled opponents may even be able to make these "experts" appear silly, and induce them to become more cooperative in an effort to overcome their resulting embarrassment.

19. BRACKETING

Some negotiators, especially in transactions pertaining primarily to money, use a technique designed to lead opponents to the figure they hope to achieve. They work to elicit opening offers from the other side, then begin with an offer or demand that is as far away from their goal as is the other side's initial offer. For example, if the defendant begins with an offer of $100,000 and the plaintiff hopes to settle for $300,000, the plaintiff attorney counters with a demand of $500,000. If the defendant moves to $150,000, the plaintiff reduces her demand to $450,000, carefully keeping her $300,000 objective between the two sides' current positions. When the defendant goes up to $200,000, the plaintiff comes down to $400,000. As the participants move toward the center of their positions, the plaintiff counsel can steer the defense attorney toward her $300,000 goal.

When one party appears to be employing Bracketing, the other may occasionally respond with *"Double Bracketing"* (Halpern, 2003). When the plaintiff counsel reduces her demand to $400,000 in response to a defendant offer of $200,000, the defense attorney indicates that he is unable to go as high as the $300,000 midpoint between their current positions. He then suggests a settlement at $250,000 — half way between the plaintiff's apparent objective of $300,000 and the defendant's current $200,000 offer. If the defense counsel can induce the plaintiff lawyer to succumb to this entreaty, the parties will settle at $50,000 below the plaintiff's preliminary goal.

20. DISINGENUOUS CONSECUTIVE CONCESSIONS

Whenever bargainers lose track of the offers and counteroffers being made and inadvertently make consecutive concessions, they place themselves at a disadvantage. They have probably become confused due to negotiating anxiety and pressure, and are moving aimlessly toward the positions being articulated by their opponents. They normally do not realize that they are making unreciprocated position changes. Opponents of these individuals should encourage further concessions by challenging the sufficiency of their position changes or through patience and prolonged silence following each concession.

Other negotiators attempt to use seemingly consecutive concessions to create feelings of guilt and obligation in their adversaries. For example, they might be contemplating a move from their current demand of $500,000 to a new demand of $400,000. Instead of making a "principled" $100,000 concession, they adopt a different approach. They first move to $450,000, with an appropriate explanation for their action. After a reasonable amount of discussion, they then mention a figure of $420,000, which is accompanied by a suitable rationale. They finally move majestically to $400,000. At this point, they indicate that they have made three unanswered concessions. They hope to induce their unsuspecting opponents to respond with a greater counteroffer than would likely have been produced by a direct move from $500,000 to $400,000. They not only plan to accomplish this result through guilt and obligation, but also from the fact that their successive $50,000, $30,000, and $20,000 position changes suggest that they are approaching their bottom line.

Recipients of consecutive concessions should become suspicious when they are specifically apprised of such position changes by participants who have made them. Sincerely confused concession-makers are unaware of the fact they have made consecutive concessions. If they are clearly cognizant of their behavior, the recipients of their apparent largesse should realize that this technique is probably being deliberately used as a bargaining strategy. They should not be overly impressed by the consecutive nature of the concessions, but should instead focus upon the aggregate movement involved. They should then respond as they would have if they had been given a direct $100,000 position change.

21. UPROAR

Negotiation participants occasionally threaten dire consequences if mutual accords are not achieved. They then indicate that the predicted havoc can be avoided if the other side agrees to the terms they are offering. Careless bargainers may be influenced by this devious technique, if they merely focus upon the damage they will suffer if the dreaded consequences occur. For example, a school district may attempt to enhance its bargaining power by threatening to lay off all of the untenured teachers if their representative labor organization does not moderate its demands. The pink-slipped teachers and their tenured colleagues may panic and immediately reduce their requests. When they behave in this manner, they wholly ignore the fact that the threatened layoffs would eliminate most of the English department or create such understaffing that the local school district would no longer be eligible for state education funding.

When extreme consequences are threatened, the affected party should ask two fundamental questions. First, what is the probability that the promised havoc would occur if no accord were attained? In many instances, they would realize that no devastation is likely to result from their refusal to give in to opponent demands. Second, if it is possible that the promised cataclysm may take place, how would that event affect the *other side*? A detached assessment may indicate that the negative consequences would be far greater for the threatening party than for the party being threatened. If this were true, the threatening party would have more to lose if no agreement were achieved, and it would actually be under greater pressure to avoid a nonsettlement. If the threatened participants can be patient, they should be able to benefit from this favorable power imbalance.

22. BR'ER RABBIT

In *Uncle Remus, His Songs and His Sayings* (1880), Joel Chandler Harris created an unforgettable character named Br'er Rabbit. The story involves a rabbit who is captured by the fox. The rabbit employs reverse psychology to effectuate his escape. While the fox is contemplating his fate, Br'er Rabbit says:

> I don't care what you do with me, so long as you don't fling me in that brier-patch. Roast me, but don't fling me in that brier-patch. . . . Drown me just as deep as you please, but don't fling me in that brier-patch. . . . Skin me, snatch out my eyeballs, tear out my ears by the roots, and cut off my legs, but don't fling me in that brier-patch.

Since the fox wanted to punish Br'er Rabbit, he chose the one alternative the rabbit appeared to fear most. He flung him in the brier-patch, and Br'er Rabbit escaped!

Adroit negotiators frequently employ the "Br'er Rabbit" approach to obtain beneficial terms from retributive, win-lose opponents who judge their own success not by how well they have done, but by how poorly they think their adversaries have done. Br'er Rabbit bargainers subtly suggest to such opponents that they or their clients would suffer greatly if certain action were either taken or withheld, when they actually hope to obtain the very results being eschewed. They then ask for other items they do not really hope to obtain. Their adversaries are so intent on ensuring their complete defeat that they insist upon the circumstances the Br'er Rabbit negotiators appear to want least.

The Br'er Rabbit technique may be successfully used to obtain favorable results from win-lose opponents. Nonetheless, this approach involves serious risks. If it is employed against win-win opponents, they may be induced to agree to terms that the manipulative participants may not really desire. When their opponents grant them their verbally preferred choices, they may be forced to accept the less beneficial terms they receive.

23. So What

When negotiators make concessions, they want to be certain that opponents acknowledge their generosity. This enhances the likelihood their own movement will generate appropriate counteroffers. A few individuals attempt to avoid their obligation to take reciprocal action by downplaying the significance of concessions given to them. They act as if the items that have been granted are of little or no value to their side. Bargainers should never permit opponents to discount the value of sincere concessions. If something they have just given up is really not regarded highly by their adversaries, those participants would not mind if they took it back! It is amazing how quickly disingenuous opponents protest when advocates endeavor to regain concessions that have been characterized as meaningless.

24. Feigned Boredom or Disinterest

A few negotiators try to appear completely disinterested or inattentive when their opponents are making their most salient arguments. This technique is intended to undermine the significance of the statements being made and the confidence of the speakers. It can be frustrating to encounter such adversaries. Some people make the mistake of countering these tactics with more forceful and frequently louder assertions. These contentions are likely to be received with equal disdain. It is usually more efficacious to force these opponents to participate in the interaction. They should be asked questions that cannot be answered with a mere "yes" or "no." These persons should be required to expose the specific weaknesses they perceive in the representations they do not seem to respect. If they can be induced to participate more directly in the discussions, their previously displayed disinterest usually disappears.

25. MUTT AND JEFF (GOOD COP/BAD COP)

The Mutt and Jeff routine constitutes one of the most common bargaining techniques. One seemingly reasonable negotiator softens opponent resistance by professing sympathy toward the "generous" concessions being made by the other side. When the opponents begin to think a final accord is on the horizon, the reasonable person's partner summarily rejects the new offer as entirely inadequate. The unreasonable participant castigates the opponents for their parsimonious concessions and insincere desire to achieve a fair accord. Just as the opponents are preparing to explode at the unreasonable participant, the reasonable partner assuages their feelings and suggests that if some additional concessions are made, he or she could probably induce his or her seemingly irrational partner to accept the new terms. It is amazing how diligently most people interacting with Mutt and Jeff bargainers strive to formulate proposals that will satisfy the openly critical participant.

Devious negotiators occasionally employ the Mutt and Jeff approach with the truly unreasonable person assuming the role of the "reasonable" party. That individual instructs his or her partner to reject every new opponent offer in an outraged manner. The "unreasonable" participant then suggests that no settlement is possible, so long as the opponents continue to evidence such an unyielding attitude. The "unreasonable" partner is occasionally expected to get up and head toward the exit — only to be prevailed upon to return reluctantly to the bargaining table through the valiant efforts of his or her "conciliatory" partner.

Mutt and Jeff tactics may even be used by single negotiators. They can claim that their absent client suffers from delusions of grandeur that must be satisfied if any agreement is to be reached. These manipulative bargainers repeatedly praise their opponents for the munificent concessions being made, but insist that greater movement is necessary to satisfy the excessive aspirations of their irrational client. It is ironic to note that their absent client may actually be receptive to any fair resolution. Since the opponents have no way of knowing this, they usually accept the representations regarding extravagant client intransigence at face value. The adversaries then endeavor to satisfy the allegedly unrealistic needs of the missing client.

Negotiators who encounter Mutt and Jeff tactics should not directly challenge the apparently devious scheme being used against them. It is possible that their opponents are not really engaged in a disingenuous exercise. One opponent may actually disagree with his or her partner's assessment of the situation. Allegations regarding the apparently manipulative tactics being used by those individuals would probably create a tense and unproductive bargaining environment — particularly when the opponents have not deliberately adopted a Mutt and Jeff style. Such accusations might also induce truly Machiavellian adversaries to embrace some other manipulative approach. Since it is generally easier to counter techniques that have already been identified, there is no reason to provide deceptive opponents with the opportunity to switch to other practices that might not be so easily recognized and neutralized.

Individuals who encounter Mutt and Jeff bargainers tend to make the mistake of allowing the seemingly unreasonable participants to control the entire interaction. They direct their arguments and offers to those persons in an effort to obtain their reluctant approval. It is beneficial to include the reasonable participants in the discussions in an effort to obtain their acquiescence before attempting to satisfy their irrational partners. In a few instances, the more conciliatory opponents may actually indicate a willingness to accept particular proposals that will be characterized as unacceptable by their associates. If the unified position of the opponents can be shattered in this fashion, it may be possible to whipsaw the reasonable individuals against their unreasonable partners.

If the persons representing the other side are truly employing a Mutt and Jeff approach, the reasonable participants will never suggest their willingness to assent to the particular terms being offered. Those individuals will instead reiterate their desire to obtain the acquiescence of their unreasonable partners. When this occurs, the reasonable participants should again be asked — not if their partners would be likely to accept the terms being proposed — but whether *they* would be willing to accept those conditions. Proficient "reasonable" participants will never indicate their acceptance of the proffered terms, without the acquiescence of their partners, and it will become clear that the opponents are using disingenuous tactics.

26. BELLY-UP ("YES. . . , BUT. . . .")

Some individuals use a bargaining style that is particularly difficult for opponents to counter. They act like wolves in sheepskin. They wear bedraggled outfits to the offices of their adversaries and indicate how bounteous those environments are. They then profess their lack of negotiating ability and legal perspicuity in an effort to evoke sympathy and to lure unsuspecting adversaries into a false sense of security. They readily acknowledge the superior competence of those with whom they interact, and shamelessly exhibit a complete lack of ability. They ask their adversaries what those people think would be fair.

The epitome of the Belly-Up person was effectively created by actor Peter Falk in his Lt. Columbo detective character. That inspector seemed to bumble along during criminal investigations with no apparent plan. When he interviewed suspects, he did so in a wholly disorganized manner. By the time the suspects realized that Lt. Columbo really understood what was happening, they had already confessed and were in police custody! Another example of this type of person was provided by the late Senator Sam Ervin of North Carolina. During the Senate Watergate Hearings, the general public became well acquainted with his masterful, down-home style. This casual "country lawyer" quoted Biblical parables and recited southern homilies while adroitly obtaining confessions to High Crimes and Misdemeanors from intelligent administration witnesses who thought they could easily outsmart this innocuous old man. One should be especially suspicious of any self-proclaimed "country lawyer" who graduated from the Harvard Law School!

Especially devious Belly-Up negotiators may resort to more outrageous conduct. When opponents take tough positions, they place their hand over their heart and display pained facial expressions. If their adversaries continue to push for beneficial terms, these participants may reach into their desk drawer and extract nitroglycerin tablets! We have met several attorneys who have bragged about the effectiveness of this tactic. If you are certain these opponents do not suffer from chest pains, you can continue your aggressive approach. If, however, you were to suspect real heart problems, you should recess your discussions and contact a senior partner in the opposing law firm. Explain to that person that you are engaged in a difficult interaction with X, and indicate that you are concerned about that individual's physical or emotional capacity to participate. If the partner downplays that person's condition, you can assume that he or she is using a Belly-Up style to take advantage of you. On the other hand, if the partner suggests the participation of another attorney, you should be pleased to interact with that person. Never continue negotiations with someone you think may suffer serious health consequences as a result of your legal interactions.

Belly-Up bargainers are difficult people to deal with, because they effectively refuse to participate in the negotiation process. They ask their opponents to permit them to forego traditional auction bargaining due to their professed inability to negotiate competently. They merely want their respected and honorable adversaries to formulate fair and reasonable arrangements that will not unfairly disadvantage the unfortunate clients who have chosen such pathetic legal representatives. Even though their thoroughly prepared opponents have established high aspiration levels and "principled" opening positions, the Belly-Up negotiators are able to induce them to significantly modify their planned approach.

Belly-Up: I've never had any real experience with cases as complicated as this one, so I'm glad to be dealing with someone who is an acknowledged expert and a most respected member of the legal community. I don't know what my client actually deserves, so I'll have to rely upon your experience and judgment. What do you think would be appropriate in a situation like this?

Opponent: [Although the opposing counsel had planned to articulate a tough opening position, he/she decides that it would be unconscionable to take advantage of such an inept practitioner and his/her poor, unsuspecting client. The opponent thus formulates an eminently reasonable proposal.]

Belly-Up: *Yes,* that's an extremely generous offer. I can readily understand why you have such an outstanding reputation among the judges and lawyers in our community. *But,* it doesn't really satisfy the needs of my client who was hoping to obtain more in the areas of _____ and _____ . I was anticipating that you would be able to recognize my client's requirements with respect to these matters.

Opponent: [Instead of asking the Belly-Up negotiator to suggest a definitive counteroffer that would directly reflect his/her client's underlying needs and interests and be subject to objective exploration, the acknowledged expert decides to modify his/her initial offer in an effort to demonstrate that he/she really does understand what the other party's client has to obtain.]

Belly-Up: *Yes,* that's a vast improvement over your first proposal. I'm so relieved that you are not trying to take unfair advantage of your superior position. Thank you for so wisely recognizing the needs of my client with respect to [the areas enhanced by the new offer], *but* your proposal still doesn't seem to go far enough. I would be embarrassed if I had to recommend that proposal to my client, because he/she was certain that you would be able to suggest more advantageous terms with respect to _____ and _____ .

Opponent: [Feels pleased that his/her second proposal was more suited to the needs and interests of the other lawyer's client. The parties seem near to a final solution, and the opponent eagerly suggests an even better package.]

Belly-Up: Oh *yes,* that's much better. Those modifications certainly take care of my client's concerns regarding _____ and _____ , *but* your new proposal doesn't adequately protect his/her interests with respect to _____ . I wonder if there might be some way to make a slight change in this regard?

Opponent: [Feels gratified and continues his/her valiant effort to demonstrate the ability to formulate a fair arrangement that will adequately satisfy the basic needs of the other negotiator's client.]

By the conclusion of their interaction, the Belly-Up bargainer has usually achieved a magnificent accord for his or her client, while the opposing counsel has been left figuratively naked. The extraordinary aspect of this transaction is that the opposing negotiator feels truly gratified that he or she has been able to satisfy the underlying needs of the other lawyer's poor client! It requires unbelievable skill to fleece an opponent and leave that person with a feeling of accomplishment and exhilaration!

Negotiators should never permit seemingly inept opponents to evoke such sympathy that they concede everything in an effort to formulate solutions that are acceptable to those pathetic souls. It is not fair for those devious individuals to force their adversaries to do all of the work. Instead of allowing Belly-Up bargainers to alter their initially planned approach, negotiators should begin with their originally formulated "principled" offers and require those people to participate actively in the process. When the Belly-Up participants challenge these opening proposals, they should be forced to articulate their own positions, so they can be evaluated and attacked. It is generally painful for Belly-Up bargainers to interact in such a conventional manner. They are not used to formulating and defending their own proposals. They are much more comfortable trying to evoke sympathy by criticizing the offers being made to them. Once these individuals are induced to participate in the usual give-and-take, they tend to lose much of their bargaining effectiveness.

27. PASSIVE-AGGRESSIVE

Passive-Aggressive negotiators are frequently as difficult to deal with as Belly-Up bargainers. Instead of directly challenging the tactics and proposals of their opponents, they employ oblique, but aggressive, forms of passive resistance. They tend to pout when they are unable to obtain favorable offers, and they resort to obstructionism and procrastination to achieve their objectives. For example, they may show up late for scheduled bargaining sessions or appear with incorrect files or documents. They may similarly exhibit inefficiency or ineptitude in an effort to frustrate the negotiation progress and to precipitate concessions from impatient opponents. They may even "lose" unsatisfactory proposals that were sent to them and act as if they never arrived. When they are expected to draft final accords, they often take an inordinate amount of time to accomplish their task and may even fail to prepare any written document.

It is particularly frustrating to interact with Passive-Aggressive individuals, because they tend to react to problems and confrontations in an indirect manner. Instead of expressing their actual thoughts in a direct fashion, they employ passive techniques to evidence their displeasure. People who deal with them must recognize the hostility represented by their Passive-Aggressive behavior. They are usually individuals who are uncomfortable with and/or frustrated by the negotiation process. They may not feel comfortable engaging in the conventional give-and-take, they may dislike their immediate circumstances, or they may be displeased with their current opponents. Since these factors can rarely be altered, it is more productive to take steps that will beneficially modify the actual behavior of these Passive-Aggressive participants.

Copies of important papers should be obtained through other avenues in case Passive-Aggressive opponents claim an inability to locate their own copies. Since Passive-Aggressive individuals do not say "no" easily — an overtly aggressive act — it is beneficial to present them with seemingly realistic offers they cannot reject. When given these proposals, they tend to acquiesce in a passive manner. Once agreements are reached, the moving parties should always offer to prepare the necessary documents. Even if the Passive-Aggressive participants insist upon the opportunity to draft the terms, their opponents should prepare their own draft agreements in case they fail to do so. Once Passive-Aggressive negotiators are presented with such a fait accompli, they usually accept their fate and execute the proffered agreements. In those infrequent cases in which Passive-Aggressive opponents do not respond, it may be necessary to have messengers personally deliver the final documents to them and wait for those papers to be duly executed.

28. WEAKENING AN OPPONENT'S POSITION OF STRENGTH

Negotiators must remember that bargaining power is rarely defined by objective factors. The strength of each party tends to be determined by the opponent's *perception* of the interaction, rather than by the actual circumstances (Cohen, 2003, at 167, 239; Shell, 1999, at 111; Lewicki, et al., 1994, at 296-97). If adroit negotiators can convince seemingly stronger opponents that they are unaware of that party's superior strength, this may effectively weaken that side's position and cause opposing counsel to suffer a concomitant loss of negotiating confidence.

This phenomenon explains why young children become intuitively gifted negotiators despite their obvious lack of objective power. When they interact with seemingly omnipotent parents, they disarm their adversaries by ignoring the power imbalance. They also recognize their ability to threaten irrational, self-destructive behavior if they do not achieve their ultimate objectives, because parents are obliged to prevent such "child-like" conduct. Once parents begin to doubt their actual power, they lose confidence and are easy targets for their manipulative offspring!

A factor that significantly influences a party's assessment of the power it objectively possesses concerns the alternatives that side thinks are available to it should no settlement be achieved during the present negotiations. If several options appear to constitute viable substitutes for bargained results, that party should understand the enhanced strength it enjoys. If an opponent can convince that party that it really does not have as many nonsettlement alternatives as believed or that those options are not as advantageous as it thinks, the power balance can be effectively shifted in favor of the manipulative actor (Shell, 1999, at 149-53).

Bargainers who are able to use verbal and nonverbal messages to indicate that they do not accord any credence to the actual power possessed by their adversaries can meaningfully undermine opponent authority. If this strength-diffusing objective is accomplished, the ability of their adversaries to use their objectively superior circumstances to influence the negotiation outcome will be greatly diminished. Opposing negotiators may be so demoralized by this tactic that they readily accept less beneficial terms than they could otherwise have obtained.

29. ENHANCEMENT OF WEAK BARGAINING POSITION

Representatives who find themselves with apparently anemic bargaining positions should not automatically concede everything. Even when they are unable to ignore the superior power possessed by their opponents, they may be able to take action that will permit them to artificially enhance their own situations. If they can effectively convince their adversaries that they have adopted an inflexible posture that they cannot reasonably modify, they may be able to force their stronger opponents to moderate their demands (Schelling, 1956, at 283).

Some negotiators circumscribe their bargaining freedom through reliance upon limited client authority. They have their principals provide them with narrowly prescribed discretion, and they openly convey these client constraints to their opponents. Devious bargainers may combine this limited-authority practice with the Mutt and Jeff approach, using their absent clients as the unreasonable parties who must be satisfied before final agreements can be achieved. If they can induce their adversaries to accept the contrived limits under which they appear to be operating, they may persuade those persons to reconsider their own positions. If the other participants seriously want to achieve mutual accords, they may be compelled to recognize the need to reduce their demands below what might otherwise be warranted in light of the strength they actually possess.

Powerful opponents who are confronted by limited authority claims may attempt to neutralize the artificially curtailed parameters by suggesting — perhaps with opposing clients in attendance — that the prescribed client limits are unreasonably narrow. If the recalcitrant clients can be induced to modify their previous instructions, the use of this ploy by their agents to enhance their negotiating posture will be seriously undermined. It is difficult to employ this technique to precipitate an expansion of bargaining agent discretion when those representatives have already taken the time to convince their principals that anything less than the previously formulated and expressed minimum settlement terms should be unacceptable. However, before negotiators decide to lock their clients into uncompromising positions in a desperate effort to enlarge their bargaining power, they should understand the significant risk associated with such client indoctrination. If it turns out that legal counsel's preliminary evaluation of the interaction was incorrect, this approach may preclude agreement. Their clients would be unlikely to move beyond the prescribed positions, and the opponents may conclude that they would be better off accepting the consequences of nonsettlements.

Negotiators who find themselves discussing an important item over which they possess minimal bargaining leverage may alternatively counteract this deficiency by postponing any final decision on that issue until other matters are explored. They may thus delay final resolution of the matter until other terms are mentioned that the opponent seriously wants to obtain. They may then be in a position to use their stronger posture with respect to the other items to enhance their less potent situation vis-a-vis the former topic.

If a continuing, symbiotic relationship is involved (*e.g.*, franchisor-franchisee; labor-management), a party that temporarily finds itself in disadvantageous circumstances may be able to offset the ephemeral advantage enjoyed by the other party by indicating that any short-term "win" attained by the presently stronger side may result in a mutually destructive Pyrrhic victory. This technique may effectively remind the party with the instant superiority that appropriately moderated demands are necessary to guarantee continued harmonious dealings. A party involved in a continuous relationship may similarly avoid the consequences of a currently weakened position by postponing negotiations until a more propitious time when the balance of power has shifted more toward equilibrium.

30. CONFRONTING OPPONENT INFLEXIBILITY

It can be a frustrating experience to be involved in a negotiation with parties who are unalterably committed to unacceptable positions. It is tempting to challenge their uncompromising stands directly. This approach entails a serious risk that the bargaining process will be irreversibly disrupted by the unwill-ingness of opponents to acknowledge openly the unreasonableness of their existing proposals. It is generally more productive to employ less confrontational techniques that will provide the other participants with a face-saving means of modifying their obstinate dispositions (Ury, 1991, at 90–109).

Negotiators should attempt to induce seemingly inflexible opponents to focus objectively upon the underlying needs and interests of their clients. It is usually easier to precipitate position reappraisals through needs and interests analyses than through discussions focusing exclusively on adamantly articulated positions. Once the underlying objectives have been discerned and explored, it may be possible to formulate alternative solutions that may prove to be mutually beneficial.

During interactions with intransigent opponents, it is helpful to emphasize the areas of common interest, rather than the zone of disagreement. If they can be induced to realize the advantageous results their own side can achieve through agreement on the less controverted items, there is a substantial likelihood they will become more conciliatory with respect to the remaining issues in dispute. As they become psychologically committed to the opportunity to attain a mutually beneficial accord, they are increasingly hesitant to allow a few unresolved topics to preclude an overall agreement.

31. SPLITTING THE DIFFERENCE

One of the most common techniques used to achieve final agreements following detailed auction bargaining that has brought the parties close together involves splitting the difference that remains between their most recent offers. Instead of threatening opponents with dire nonsettlement consequences if final terms are not achieved, the moving parties use the face-saving "promise" technique to generate simultaneous movement. For instance, parties may have commenced their interaction with a plaintiff demand for $100,000 and a defendant offer of $20,000. After various offers and counter offers have been exchanged, the plaintiff is requesting $60,000, and the defendant is offering $50,000. One of the two participants may suggest that they "split the difference" and agree to $55,000. This is an expeditious method of reaching the point these negotiators would probably have attained had they continued to rely upon other traditional bargaining techniques.

People who are asked to split the outstanding difference to achieve final accords should consider the previous bargaining sequence before they too readily assent to this proposal (Freund, 1992, at 158-59). They must first decide whether their opponents unfairly skewed the apparent settlement range in their favor through a biased opening offer. For example, plaintiffs in personal injury cases can begin with almost any initial demands, while defendant insurance carriers are more constrained. They cannot realistically ask a plaintiff to compensate their client for the psychological trauma he or she suffered when he or she drove through a red light at an excessive rate of speed while under the influence of alcohol and struck the disabled plaintiff in a crosswalk! If an unreasonably skewed initial offer has been made, it is important to be certain that the negotiation process has effectively negated the unfair advantage associated with that proposal *before* the parties contemplate splitting the remaining difference to achieve a final settlement.

People who are contemplating use of the split-the-difference technique to close the remaining gap between them should similarly review the prior concessions that have been made by both parties. If one has already made six concessions while the other has only made five, it would normally be inappropriate to split the remaining difference until the second party has made one more reciprocal concession. The final result would otherwise be biased in favor of that person's client.

Some experts believe it is beneficial to let opponents offer to split-the-difference first (Dawson, 2001, at 63–64). This provides the recipient of this offer with the opportunity to decide whether it is tactically advantageous to accede to this request. It also gives the recipient the chance to obtain one last bargaining edge. Once the opponent offers to split the distance remaining between the parties, the offeree can treat the midpoint between the parties' existing positions as a new opponent offer and suggest that they split the distance that *remains* between that new opponent position and this side's most recent proposal. For example, once the plaintiff in the above hypothetical suggests an agreement at $55,000, the defendant may indicate a willingness to conclude the transaction at $52,500 — half way between $55,000 and $50,000. An overly anxious plaintiff may succumb to this blandishment in an effort to end the interaction. A more careful participant would reiterate the $55,000 figure and state that no further concessions will be made. In most cases, the manipulative defendant attorneys will realize that their effort to obtain an unfair advantage is not going to succeed, and they will accept the originally proffered amount.

32.   "Final Offer" Checks Tendered by Defense Lawyers

When protracted negotiations have failed to bring plaintiffs and defendants together, defense attorneys occasionally send checks to plaintiffs through their legal representatives containing amounts somewhere between the last positions of the two sides. The defense lawyers explicitly indicate that the cashing of these checks will constitute full settlement of the underlying claims. In large value cases, defense attorneys usually include formal releases that must be signed before plaintiffs may cash the accompanying checks. In many cases, the plaintiffs accept these checks — reflecting the impact of gain-loss framing which demonstrates that individuals offered sure gains and the possibility of greater gains or no gains tend to be risk averse and accept the certain gains. This technique is especially effective where plaintiffs recognize that liability is uncertain and they may obtain nothing at trial. Attorneys making such "final offers" must be prepared to try the cases if their offers are rejected, or they would suffer substantial credibility losses.

Defense lawyers who contemplate resort to "final offer" checks should only take such action after extended bargaining exchanges. If they make such offers prematurely, their entreaties lack credibility. Such untimely proposals would also be likely to induce plaintiffs who are not yet ready to contemplate final settlements to opt for litigation.

Plaintiff attorneys receiving "final offer" checks may — with client concurrence — try to keep the negotiation process going by ignoring the finality of the offers they have received. They can make their own counteroffers somewhere between their own former positions and the amounts specified in the defendant checks. This approach may allow "final offer" defense attorneys to continue to negotiate without suffering credibility losses. They could respond with new offers of their own and continue the bargaining process. If such plaintiff responses fail to generate further offers from defendants, the plaintiffs have to decide whether to accept the defendant checks or to move toward trial.

33. TELEPHONE NEGOTIATIONS

The vast majority of settlement negotiations are conducted wholly or at least partially on the telephone, because complete reliance on personal meetings is unduly expensive and time-consuming. Telephone negotiations involve the same stages and conventional bargaining techniques as personal interactions. They usually consist of a series of shorter exchanges than personal transactions, and they preclude visual contact except where video telephones are available. Advocates who make the mistake of treating these electronic exchanges less seriously than they would face-to-face interactions place themselves at a disadvantage.

Attorneys should realize that telephone exchanges are less personal than face-to-face interactions. This factor makes it easier for participants to employ overtly competitive or even deliberately deceptive tactics. It also makes it easier for parties to reject proposals being suggested by their opponents (Cohen, 1980, at 210-11). Negotiators should recognize that since telephone discussions tend to be more abbreviated than personal encounters, it is more difficult to create a psychological commitment to settlement through only one or two telephone exchanges.

Many lawyers think that telephone conversations are less revealing than personal talks, because they do not involve visual interactions. They act as if opposing counsel cannot perceive nonverbal signals during these transactions. This presumption is incorrect. Some psychologists have suggested that many individuals are more adept at reading nonverbal messages during telephone exchanges than they are during personal interactions. This phenomenon is attributable to the fact that personal interactions involve a myriad of simultaneous nonverbal stimuli that are often too numerous to be proficiently discerned and interpreted. When people speak on the telephone, however, they are not as likely to be overwhelmed by the various nonverbal clues emanating from the other party. They only have to concentrate upon the aural messages being received to hear the verbal leaks and the nonverbal messages being communicated.

A substantial number of nonverbal clues are discernible during telephone interactions. Careful listeners can hear changes in the pitch, pace, tone, and volume of the speakers. A pregnant pause may indicate that a particular offer is being seriously considered by a recipient who did not hesitate before rejecting previous proposals. When the most recent suggestion is being verbally renounced, the initial pause would suggest that the proposal has approached or entered the other party's zone of reasonableness. A sigh in response to a new proposal may similarly indicate that the recipient is now confident that some settlement will be achieved.

Voice inflection may be equally informative. People who respond to communicated offers with perceptibly increased levels of excitement may nonverbally suggest that they are more pleased with those proposals than their verbal responses might otherwise indicate. The topic sequence presented by parties might inadvertently reveal the items they value most, because most negotiators tend to begin the discussions with either their most important or their least important subjects.

Professor Ekman's seminal book on deception noted that individuals who engage in prevarication tend to speak more deliberately and with higher pitched voices (Ekman, 1992, at 92–94). Attentive listeners could easily perceive these phenomena. They could additionally note the use of signal words such as "to be candid" or "to be truthful" that many persons use to preface misrepresentations they hope will be unquestioningly accepted.

Advocates engaged in telephone negotiations should listen intently for verbal leaks and nonverbal signals being emitted by their opponents. They must simultaneously recognize the ability of their adversaries to discern the various verbal leaks and nonverbal messages emanating from themselves. They should thus be as careful to control their verbal leaks and their nonverbal signals during telephone exchanges as they would during personal encounters. Participants who ignore this consideration and treat telephone discussions casually may place themselves at a disadvantage. Following each telephonic exchange, a record of the negotiation developments should always be entered in the case file for future reference.

It is usually more advantageous to be the caller rather than the recipient of the call, because the caller has the opportunity to prepare for the exchange. Negotiators who plan to phone opponents to discuss particular cases should prepare as diligently for these interactions as they would for face-to-face exchanges. This preliminary effort is usually rewarded. Since they have the opportunity to surprise unsuspecting adversaries, they may subtly gain the upper hand (Woolf, 1990, at 161). The other participants are unlikely to anticipate their call and are not prepared for the conversation that is about to occur. This permits phoning parties to advance more persuasive arguments and to elicit less planned counteroffers than would have been possible during a formally scheduled interaction.

Individuals who receive unexpected telephone calls from opponents should internally assess their degree of preparedness. If they are not fully conversant regarding the pertinent factual circumstances, legal doctrines, and prior settlement discussions, they should not make the mistake of plunging ignorantly into uncharted waters. They should not hesitate to suggest that they are presently occupied and unable to talk. They can thereafter peruse the file and telephone the other party when they are completely prepared. When they reach the initial caller, they can merely say they are returning that person's call. Their subsequent silence can adroitly return the focus to the other party.

Many negotiators prefer personal interactions to telephone discussions. They like the psychological atmosphere they can personally establish, and they believe they are more proficient readers of nonverbal signals during face-to-face encounters than during telephone talks. They also prefer several longer personal interactions to numerous brief telephone exchanges. These people should not hesitate to insist upon personal sessions when serious transactions are involved, and they think this will provide them with a bargaining advantage.

34. NEGOTIATING BY MAIL, E-MAIL, OR THROUGH FAX TRANSMISSIONS

A surprising number of individuals like to conduct their negotiations primarily or entirely through mail, e-mail, or fax transmissions. They do not merely transmit written versions of terms orally discussed during earlier interactions. They limit most, if not all, of their interactions to written communications. Most people who endeavor to restrict their bargaining communications to mail, e-mail, or fax exchanges are not comfortable with the traditional negotiation process. They do not like the seemingly amorphous nature of that process, and they do not relish the split-second tactical decisions that must be made during personal interactions. They forget that negotiations involve uniquely personal transactions that are not easily conducted entirely through written communications (Thompson & Nadler, 2002; Nadler, 2001; Nadler, Kurtzberg & Thompson, 2002).

People contemplating bargaining interactions that will be primarily conducted through the exchange of letters, e-mail, or fax transmissions should appreciate how difficult it is to establish rapport with opponents through those written mediums. It would thus be beneficial to initially telephone their adversaries to exchange some personal information and to establish minimal relationships (Thompson & Nadler, 2002; Nadler, 2001). Individuals who first create mutual relations through such oral exchanges are likely to find their subsequent negotiations more pleasant and more efficient (Thompson & Nadler, 2002, at 115; Nadler, 2001, at 341; Morris, Nadler, Kurtzberg & Thompson, 2002, at 97).

The use of mail, e-mail, or fax transmissions to conduct basic negotiations is generally a cumbersome and inefficient process (Thompson & Nadler, 2002, at 112). Every communication has to be drafted and thoroughly edited before being sent to the other side. The opponents must then read and digest all of the written passages, and formulate their own replies. Written positions seem to be more intractable than those expressed orally over the telephone or in person, because of the definitive nature of written documents. When people present their proposals orally, their voice inflections and nonverbal signals may indicate a willingness to be flexible with respect to certain items. Written communications rarely convey this critical information. In addition, written encounters tend to produce less efficient outcomes, because of the lack of effective cooperative bargaining (Thompson, 1998, at 281).

Written exchanges are often misinterpreted. As the recipients review and evaluate the positions transmitted by their opponents, they may read more or less into the stated terms than was actually intended. They may interpret seemingly innocuous language as deliberately inflammatory. As they reread the pertinent passages, they tend to reinforce their preliminary impressions. Their misinter-pretations may be compounded by their escalated written responses to the devious terms they think their opponents intended to convey. When the original senders receive written counter offers, they may not comprehend their uncompromising or negative tone. They may further exacerbate the situation with antagonistic responses of their own (Thompson & Nadler, 2002, at 119; Nadler, 2001, at 337–38).

When individuals negotiate in person or on the telephone, they can immediately hear the way in which their opponents perceive their articulated positions. Their adversaries can quickly ask questions to clarify seemingly ambiguous proposals. If speakers realize that their true intentions are being misunderstood, they can expeditiously correct the misperceptions. The participants can also indicate through verbal leaks or nonverbal signals their willingness to modify stated proposals, and this flexibility can keep the process moving toward a successful conclusion.

Some complex transactions involve numerous terms that must be carefully formulated to protect client interests. In these cases, it is entirely appropriate for the negotiators to exchange draft proposals through the mail, e-mail, or via fax transmissions. To avoid communication difficulties, however, each mail, e-mail, or fax transmission should be followed by a telephone call. This enables the sending party to ascertain the manner in which the written communication has been received. If it appears that the recipient has read something into the written proposals that was not intended, the misinterpretation can be quickly corrected.

35. NEGOTIATING WITH GOVERNMENT AGENCIES

When private-sector parties interact with government agencies, they frequently experience cross-cultural difficulties, due to the different value systems involved. When private sector lawyers evaluate prospective client transactions, they almost always engage in cost-benefit analyses based upon the projected legal costs, the financial benefits to be derived from the transactions in question, and the value of their external alternatives. With the possible exception of tax-collecting agencies, most government representatives are not concerned about these factors. They assume a better than average likelihood of prevailing in any resulting litigation, because of the judicial deference they think is accorded to statutes, regulations, and administrative determinations. In addition, government officials tend to ignore the costs associated with litigation, since they are not charged for the legal services involved.

Government bureaucrats recognize the power advantage they enjoy over most private sector parties. They know that most companies do not want to become embroiled in protracted battles with federal or state departments that seem to have unlimited resources. They know they can frighten corporate officials through extensive pre-trial litigation or negotiations that will generate substantial legal fees. They do not hesitate to remind private sector firms that they receive cost-free representation by Justice Department or Attorney General lawyers. If they sense that private companies are afraid of possible litigation, they are usually willing to take advantage of this weakness. It is thus necessary for firms to give serious thought to litigation when that course becomes necessary. When government officials realize that they may be forced to defend their actions before judicial tribunals, they often exhibit more accommodating behavior.

Private sector attorneys often find it frustrating to deal with government lawyers, because those persons rarely possess significant authority. Agency officials who must assume responsibility for departmental determinations are hesitant to provide their own lawyers with the power these advocates require to conclude most interactions. Their attorneys can merely elicit offers from private parties that must be communicated to administrative decision-makers. Government legal practitioners find this as frustrating as their opponents. They would like to be able to resolve matters directly, but must usually function as intermediaries between outside parties and relevant agency officials. Although experienced government lawyers frequently have a good idea what they can sell to their superiors, many junior attorneys do not possess this knowledge. Since they do not want to be criticized for overstepping their authority, they tend to be cautious. They feel the need to clear even minor issues with agency officials before they suggest possible solutions to their opponents.

Agency officials normally consider applicable statutes and regulations sacrosanct. People who contemplate challenges to the propriety of these rules are likely to encounter stiff resistance. Most agency representatives are prepared to litigate statutory or regulation challenges to the Supreme Court. It is thus more productive to formulate positions that do not directly attack the legality of agency rules. Company attorneys should look for ways to interpret applicable statutes or regulations in a manner that will produce the desired results. Even strained statutory constructions may be beneficial, because they permit agency decision-makers to accede to their demands in a face-saving fashion.

Another frustration experienced by people dealing with government bureaucracies concerns the seeming unwillingness of many officials to make definitive decisions. This reluctance is based upon the fact that with hundreds or thousands of government personnel, employees rarely stand out for making exemplary determinations. They are more likely to be noticed when they make questionable decisions. To avoid possible criticism, many government bureaucrats have modified the plaque that stood on President Truman's desk — "The Buck Stops Here" — to read "Keep the Buck Moving." They recognize that they are unlikely to be chastised for decisions they did not make!

When private sector attorneys encounter government representatives who are afraid to make decisions, they should use two approaches. They should first try to convince their immediate opponents that it is in their interest to make the requested decision. They must not hesitate to give the government attorneys with whom they are interacting the information they need to persuade their agency superiors. When the immediate agency representatives are unwilling to accept proposed solutions, it may be beneficial to approach higher officials who may have the courage to make the necessary decisions. Private firm lawyers should determine who has the power to grant the results they desire and figure out how to reach those individuals.

Chapter 5

NEGOTIATION ETHICS

It is easy to exhort lawyers to behave in an exemplary manner when they participate in the negotiation process:

> [T]he lawyer is not free to do anything his client might do in the same circumstances. . . . [T]he lawyer must be at least as candid and honest as his client would be required to be. . . . Beyond that, the profession should embrace an affirmative ethical standard for attorneys' professional relationships with courts, other lawyers and the public: *The lawyer must act honestly and in good faith.* Another lawyer . . . should not need to exercise the same degree of caution that he would if trading for reputedly antique copper jugs in an oriental bazaar. . . . [S]urely the professional standards must ultimately impose upon him a duty not to accept an unconscionable deal. While some difficulty in line-drawing is inevitable when such a distinction is sought to be made, there must be a point at which the lawyer cannot ethically accept an arrangement that is completely unfair to the other side. . . . [Rubin, 1975, at 589, 591 (emphasis in original)].

Despite the nobility of such pronouncements, others maintain that "Pious and generalized assertions that the negotiator must be 'honest' or that the lawyer must use 'candor' are not helpful" (White, 1980, at 929). They believe that negotiation transactions involve an inherently deceptive process in which a certain amount of "puffing" and "embellishment" is expected.

A. APPROPRIATE AND INAPPROPRIATE MISREPRESENTATIONS

Experienced practitioners occasionally indicate that they have rarely participated in legal negotiations in which both participants did not lie, yet they maintain that they have encountered few dishonest attorneys. These lawyers note that the fundamental question is not whether negotiators may "lie," but when and about what they may permissibly dissemble. Students initially find it difficult to accept the notion that disingenuous "puffing" and deliberate mendacity do not always constitute reprehensible conduct.

It is ironic to note that deceptive tactics are usually employed at the outset of a bargaining interaction. Side A, which is willing to pay 2X informs Side B that it cannot pay more than X. Side B, which is willing to accept 1½ X, states that it must obtain at least 2½ X if a deal is to be achieved. Both participants are pleased that their transaction has begun successfully, even though both have begun with intentionally misleading statements. Some lawyers attempt to circumvent this moral dilemma by formulating opening positions that do not directly misstate their actual intentions. For example, Side A may indicate that it "doesn't *wish to* pay more than X," or Side B may say that it "would not be *inclined to* accept less than 2½ X." While these initial statements might be technically true, the italicized verbal leaks ("wish to"/ "inclined to") would inform attentive opponents that these speakers do not really mean what they appear to be communicating.

When students or practicing attorneys are asked whether they expect opposing counsel to candidly disclose their authorized limits or their actual bottom lines at the beginning of interactions, most exhibit discernible discomfort. They recall the numerous times they have commenced bargaining discussions with exaggerated position statements they did not expect their adversaries to take literally. This is when they begin to appreciate the ethical dilemma confronted regularly by all legal negotiators.

> On the one hand the negotiator must be fair and truthful; on the other he must mislead his opponent. Like the poker player, a negotiator hopes that his opponent will overestimate the value of his hand. Like the poker player, in a variety of ways he must facilitate his opponent's inaccurate assessment. The critical difference between those who are successful negotiators and those who are not lies in this capacity both to mislead and not to be misled. . . . [A] careful examination of the behavior of even the most forthright, honest, and trustworthy negotiators will show them actively engaged in misleading their opponents about their true position. . . . To conceal one's true position, to mislead an opponent about one's true settling point is the essence of negotiation. [White, 1980, at 927–28].

Some writers criticize the use of deceptive negotiating tactics to further client interests (Alfini, 1999). They maintain that these devices diminish the likelihood of Pareto optimal results, because "deception tends to shift wealth from the risk-averse to the risk-tolerant" (Peters, 1987, at 7). Although this observation is undoubtedly true, it is unlikely to discourage the pervasive use of ethically permissible tactics that are designed to deceive risk-averse opponents into believing they must accept less beneficial terms than they need actually accept. It is thus unproductive to discuss a utopian negotiation world in which complete disclosure is the norm. The real question concerns the types of deceptive tactics that may ethically be employed to enhance bargaining interests (Norton, 1989). Attorneys who believe that no prevarication is ever proper during bargaining encounters place themselves and their clients at a disadvantage, since they permit their less candid opponents to obtain settlements that transcend the terms to which they are objectively entitled (Wetlaufer, 1990, at 1230).

The rather schizophrenic nature of the ethical dilemma encountered by legal negotiators is apparent in the ABA Model Rules of Professional Conduct, which were adopted by the House of Delegates in August of 1983. Rule 4.1(a), which corresponds to EC 7-102(A)(5) under the ABA Code of Professional Responsibility, states that "a lawyer shall not knowingly make a false statement of material fact or law to a third person" (Morgan & Rotunda, 2004, at 92). This seemingly unequivocal principle is intended to apply to both litigation and negotiation settings (Rotunda, 1995, at 167). An explanatory Comment under this Rule reiterates the fact that "A Lawyer is required to be truthful when dealing with others on a client's behalf. . . ." Nonetheless, a subsequent Comment acknowledges the difficulty of defining "truthfulness" in the unique context of the negotiation process:

> Whether a particular statement should be regarded as one of fact can depend on the circumstances. Under generally accepted conventions in negotiation, certain types of statements ordinarily are not taken as statements of material fact. Estimates of price or value placed on the subject of a transaction and a party's intentions as to an acceptable settlement of a claim are in this category. . . .

Even state bars that have not appended this Comment to their version of Rule 4.1 have recognized the ethical distinctions set forth in that Comment.

Although the ABA Model Rules unambiguously proscribe all lawyer prevarication, they reasonably, but confusingly, exclude mere "puffing" and dissembling regarding one's true minimum objectives (Rotunda, 1995, at 167–68; Lowenthal, 1982, at 101). These important exceptions appropriately recognize that disingenuous behavior is indigenous to most legal negotiations and could not realistically be prevented due to the nonpublic nature of most bargaining interactions.

> If one negotiator lies to another, only by happenstance will the other discover the lie. If the settlement is concluded by negotiation, there will be no trial, no public testimony by conflicting witnesses, and thus no opportunity to examine the truthfulness of assertions made during the negotiation. Consequently, in negotiation, more than in other contexts, ethical norms can probably be violated with greater confidence that there will be no discovery and punishment. [White, 1980, at 926. it;But cf. *Monroe v. State Bar*, 10 Cal. Rptr. 257, 261, 358 P.2d 529, 533 (1961) (sustaining a nine-month suspension of a practitioner, since "Intentionally deceiving opposing counsel is ground for disciplinary action.")].

One of the inherent conflicts associated with this area concerns the fact that what people label acceptable "puffing" when they make value-based representations during legal negotiations may be considered improper mendacity when uttered by opposing counsel.

Even though advocate prevarication during legal negotiations rarely results in bar disciplinary action, lawyers must recognize that other risks are created by dishonest bargaining behavior. Attorneys who deliberately deceive opponents or who withhold information they are legally obliged to disclose may be guilty of fraud. Contracts procured through fraudulent acts of commission or omission are voidable, and the responsible advocates and their clients may be held liable for monetary damages (Perschbacher, 1985, at 86–94, 126-30; Rubin, 1975, at 587). It would be particularly embarrassing for lawyers to make misrepresentations that could cause their clients additional legal problems transcending those the attorneys were endeavoring to resolve. Since the adversely affected clients might thereafter sue their culpable former counsel for legal malpractice, the ultimate injury to the reputations and practices of the deceptive attorneys could be momentous (Perschbacher, 1985, at 81–86, 107-12). Legal representatives who employ clearly improper bargaining tactics may even subject themselves to judicial sanctions (e.g., *Eash v. Riggins Trucking, Inc.*, 757 F.2d 557 (3d Cir. 1985)).

Most legal representatives conduct their negotiations with appropriate candor, because they are moral individuals and/or they recognize that such professional behavior is mandated by the applicable ethical standards. A few others, however, do not feel so constrained. These persons should consider the practical risks associated with disreputable bargaining conduct. Even if their deceitful action is not reported to the state bar and never results in personal liability for fraud or legal malpractice, their aberrational behavior is likely to be discovered eventually by their fellow practitioners. As other attorneys learn that particular lawyers are not trustworthy, future interactions become more difficult for those persons (Herman, Cary & Kennedy, 2001, at 175–76; Murnighan, 1992, at 230-31). Oral representations on the telephone and handshake arrangements are no longer acceptable. Executed written documents are required for even rudimentary transactions. Factual and legal assertions are no longer accepted without time-consuming and expensive verification. Attorneys who contemplate the employment of unacceptable deception to further present client interests should be cognizant of the fact that such conduct may seriously jeopardize their future effectiveness. No short-term gain achieved through deviant behavior should ever be permitted to outweigh the probable long-term consequences of those improper actions.

When lawyers negotiate, they must constantly decide whether they are going to divulge relevant legal and factual information to opposing counsel. If they decide to disclose some pertinent information, may they do so partially or is complete disclosure required? They must also determine the areas they may permissibly misrepresent and the areas they may not distort.

1. NONDISCLOSURE OF INFORMATION

Even though Model Rule 4.1(a) states that attorneys must be truthful when they make statements concerning material law or fact, Comment 1 expressly indicates that lawyers have "no affirmative duty to inform an opposing party of relevant facts." (Morgan & Rotunda, 2004, at 93.) In the absence of special relationships or express contractual or statutory duties, practitioners are normally not obliged to divulge relevant legal or factual information to their adversaries (McKay, 1990, at 19). This doctrine is premised upon the duty of representatives to conduct their own legal research and factual investigations. Under our adversary system, attorneys do not have the right to expect their opponents to assist them in this regard. It is only when cases reach tribunals that Model Rule 3.3(a)(2) imposes an obligation on advocates "to disclose to the tribunal legal authority in the controlling jurisdiction known to the lawyer to be directly adverse to the position of the client and not disclosed by opposing counsel." (Morgan & Rotunda, 2004, at 79.) No such duty is imposed, however, with respect to pertinent factual circumstances that are not discovered by opposing counsel.

Stare v. Tate, 21 Cal. App. 3d 432, 98 Cal. Rptr. 264 (1971), involved divorce negotiations endeavoring to divide the spouses' community property on an equal basis. When valuing certain property, Ms. Stare's attorney made a mathematical error that understated the actual value by $100,000. Although Mr. Tate and his lawyer were aware of this miscalculation, they agreed to settlement terms that deprived Ms. Stare of $50,000. Since Mr. Tate and his lawyer were fully aware of Ms. Stare's mistake and sought to take unfair advantage of it, the court reformed the property settlement to provide Ms. Stare with the extra $50,000 she deserved.

Brown v. County of Genesee, 872 F.2d 169 (6th Cir. 1989), concerned a county attorney who was negotiating the settlement of a Rehabilitation Act claim with the lawyer representing a diabetic employee. The claimant's attorney made a proposal to place the employee at a certain salary level which they believed to be the highest she could attain, when she could actually have been placed at a higher level. The court found that the county attorney had no legal or ethical duty to correct their erroneous belief in this regard, since the mistake by the claimant and her counsel was due to their failure to examine or to understand the public records available to everyone, and her counsel could have requested this information. The court thus refused to modify the claimant's settlement agreement to allow her to receive the higher salary, because the mistaken belief was unilateral, rather than mutual. Should the county attorney, as a public officer, have been under an affirmative duty to correct the claimant's obvious misunderstanding?

Suppose the attorneys representing a severely injured plaintiff learn, during the critical stages of settlement talks, that their client has died due to unrelated factors. Would they be under any ethical duty to disclose this fact to defense counsel who are clearly assuming continuing pain and medical care for the plaintiff? Although one court has held that "plaintiff's attorney clearly had a duty to disclose the death of his client both to the Court and to opposing counsel prior to negotiating a settlement agreement" (*Virzi v. Grand Trunk Warehouse & Cold Storage Co.*, 571 F. Supp. 507, 512 (E.D. Mich. 1983)), this conclusion is not required by the Comment to Rule 4.1 pertaining to negotiation discussions. Nonetheless, since the death of the plaintiff would necessitate the substitution of plaintiff's estate executor, plaintiff counsel might well be under a duty to notify defense attorneys of this development before concluding any agreement that would affect the estate. (*See also Kentucky Bar Assn. v. Geisler*, 938 S.W.2d 578 (Ky. Sup. Ct. 1997) (sustaining public reprimand for plaintiff attorney who failed to notify defense counsel that plaintiff had died during their civil case negotiations).)

A similar issue would arise if plaintiff lawyers learned that their client had miraculously recovered from the serious condition that provides the basis for the current law suit. If plaintiff attorneys had previously answered defendant interrogatories concerning the health of the plaintiff, they would probably be obligated under Fed. R. Civ. P. 26(e)(2) to supplement their previous responses.

> A party is under a duty seasonably to amend a prior response to an interrogatory, request for production, or request for admission if the party learns that the response is in some material respect incomplete or incorrect and if the additional or corrective information has not otherwise been made known to the other parties during the discovery process or in writing.

Suppose the party possessing the relevant information regarding the plaintiff is not the plaintiff's attorney, but rather defense counsel? This issue was confronted by the Minnesota Supreme Court in *Spaulding v. Zimmerman*, 263 Minn. 346, 116 N.W.2d 704 (1962). Plaintiff Spaulding was injured in an automobile accident when Defendant Ledermann's car, in which plaintiff was riding, collided with Defendant Zimmerman's vehicle. He suffered multiple rib fractures, bilateral fractures of the clavicles, and a severe cerebral concussion. Several doctors who treated the plaintiff concluded that his injuries had healed. As the trial date approached, the defense attorneys had Spaulding examined by a neurologist who was expected to provide expert testimony for the defense. That physician agreed that the ribs and clavicles had healed, but discovered a life-threatening aneurysm on Spaulding's aorta. Defense counsel were never asked by plaintiff counsel about the results of this examination, and they did not volunteer information about it.

A settlement agreement was achieved, which had to be approved by the trial court since Spaulding was a minor. After the case was settled, Spaulding discovered the aneurysm (which was surgically repaired) and sued to set aside the prior settlement. The trial court vacated the settlement, and this decision was sustained by the Minnesota Supreme Court. Despite the fact that most people would undoubtedly regard an affirmative duty to disclose the crucial information as the morally correct approach, the Minnesota Supreme Court appropriately determined that the defense attorneys were under no ethical duty to volunteer the new medical information to plaintiff counsel. In fact, without client consent, the confidentiality preservation obligation then imposed by Model Rule 1.6 precluded volitional disclosure by defense counsel under these circumstances (Morgan & Rotunda, 2004, at 179–80). Comment 5 explicitly indicated that "[t]he confidentiality rule applies not merely to matters communicated in confidence by the client but also to all information relating to the representation, whatever its source." (Morgan & Rotunda, 2004, at 180–81.)

The *Spaulding* Court circumvented the Rule 1.6 prohibition by holding that as officers of the court defense counsel had an affirmative duty to disclose the newly discovered medical information to the trial court prior to its approval of the settlement agreement. Had Spaulding not been a minor, the Court may have had to enforce the original accord, because of the absence of any trial court involvement in the settlement process. If courts are unwilling to impose affirmative disclosure obligations on advocates who possess such critical information regarding opposing clients, they should sustain the resulting settlement agreements despite the lack of disclosure. This would at least permit defense lawyers to release the negative information as soon as the settlement terms have been satisfied. By voiding such agreements after plaintiffs learn of the withheld information, courts effectively require defense attorneys to remain silent even after the law suits have been fully resolved.

The Restatement (3rd) of the Law Governing Lawyers attempts to protect defense attorneys who decide to divulge medical information in *Spaulding* situations. Section 66 states that lawyers who voluntarily disclose information concerning conditions posing a risk of death or serious bodily injury to their opponents shall not be found in violation of Rule 1.6 nor be subject to legal malpractice liability to their own clients. In 2002, the ABA House of Delegates amended Model Rule 1.6 to comport with Section 66 of the Restatement. Amended Rule 1.6(b)(1) permits — but does not require — attorneys to disclose otherwise confidential information when necessary "to prevent reasonably certain death or substantial bodily harm." (Morgan & Rotunda, 2004, at 22). States with Model Rules will most likely accept this ABA amendment or reinterpret traditional Rule 1.6 to allow such disclosures.

In 2003, the ABA House of Delegates further amended Model Rule 1.6 to permit — but not require — a lawyer to reveal confidential client information "to prevent the client from committing a crime or fraud that is reasonably certain to result in substantial injury to the financial interests or property of another and in furtherance of which the client has used or is using the lawyer's services." (Rule 1.6(b)(2), Morgan & Rotunda, 2004, at 22). New Rule 1.6(b)(3) similarly permits a lawyer to disclose confidential client information to prevent or mitigate substantial injury to the financial interests or property of another that has or is reasonably certain to result from client criminal action or fraud in furtherance of which the client has used the lawyers services (Morgan & Rotunda, 2004, at 22–23). This exception does not apply where an attorney has been retained to represent the client with respect to the criminal or fraudulent acts in question (Comment 8 to Rule 1.6, Morgan & Rotunda, 2004, at 25). Attorneys can easily avoid these disclosure problems by remembering to ask appropriate questions concerning uncertain areas before they enter into settlement agreements. Defense lawyers can directly ask if the plaintiff's condition has changed in any way. Plaintiff representatives could not ethically lie about the condition of their client. If they were to use blocking techniques to avoid direct responses,defense lawyers should restate their inquiries and demand specific answers. If plaintiff attorneys know that defense counsel have had the plaintiff examined by a medical expert, they should always ask about the results of that examination. While defense counsel may merely confirm what plaintiff lawyers already know, it is possible plaintiff attorneys will obtain new information that will affect settlement discussions.

Suppose plaintiff or defense lawyers are on the verge of a law suit settlement based upon a line of State Supreme Court cases favoring their client. The morning of the day they are likely to conclude their transaction, the State Supreme Court issues an opinion overturning these beneficial decisions and indicating that the new rule applies to all pending cases. Would knowledgeable attorneys be obligated to inform their unsuspecting opponents about this critical legal development? Almost all practitioners asked this question respond in the negative, based upon their belief that opposing counsel are obliged to conduct their own legal research. Sagacious lawyers would recognize, however, that they could no longer rely upon the overturned decisions to support their contentions, because those legal misrepresentations would contravene Rule 4.1. On the other hand, they could probably ask their unsuspecting adversaries if they could cite a single case supporting their position!

2. PARTIAL DISCLOSURE OF INFORMATION

Negotiators regularly use selective disclosures to advance their positions. They emphasize the legal doctrines and factual information beneficial to their claims and withhold the circumstances that are not helpful. In most instances, these selective disclosures are expected by opponents and are considered an inherent part of bargaining interactions. When attorneys focus on their strengths, opposing counsel must attempt to ascertain their hidden weaknesses. They should carefully listen for verbal leaks that may indicate the existence of possible problems. Probing questions may be used to elicit negative information, and external research may be employed to gather other relevant data. These efforts are particularly important when opponents limit their disclosures to those circumstances favoring their clients, since their partial disclosures may cause listeners to make erroneous assumptions.

When we discuss negotiating ethics with legal practitioners, we often ask if lawyers are under a duty to disclose information to correct erroneous factual or legal assumptions being made by opposing counsel. Most respondents perceive no obligation to correct legal or factual misunderstandings generated solely by the carelessness of opposing attorneys. Respondents only hesitate when opponent misperceptions may have resulted from misinterpretations of seemingly honest statements made by them. For example, when a plaintiff attorney embellishes the pain being experienced by a client with a severely sprained ankle, the defense lawyer may indicate how painful *broken* ankles can be. If the plaintiff representative has said nothing to create this false impression, should he or she be obliged to correct the obvious defense counsel error? Although some respondents believe that an affirmative duty to correct the misperception may exist here — due to the fact plaintiff embellishments may have inadvertently contributed to the misunderstanding — most respondents feel no such obligation. So long as they have not directly precipitated the erroneous belief, they see no duty to correct it.

When opponent misperceptions concern legal doctrines, almost no respondents perceive a duty to correct those misconceptions. They indicate that each side is obliged to conduct its own legal research. If opposing counsel make incorrect assumptions or carelessly fail to locate applicable statutes or cases, those advocates do not have the right to expect their adversaries to provide them with legal assistance.

Under some circumstances, partial answers may mislead opposing counsel as effectively as direct misrepresentations. For example, the plaintiff in *Spaulding v. Zimmerman*, 263 Minn. 346, 116 N.W.2d 704 (1962), discussed in Section 1, sustained cracked ribs and fractured clavicles in an automobile accident. After the ribs and clavicles had healed, the defense lawyers had the plaintiff examined by their medical expert who detected an aortic aneurysm that plaintiff lawyers did not know about. As noted earlier, the defense counsel were probably under no ethical obligation to voluntarily disclose the existence of the aneurysm, and they could use blocking techniques to avoid the need to answer those inquiries.

Could defense attorneys respond to plaintiff counsel questions regarding the findings of their medical expert by indicating that "the ribs and clavicles have healed nicely"? Would this partial disclosure constitute a deliberate misrepresentation of material fact, because the defendant lawyers must realize that plaintiff counsel are interpreting this statement in a more expansive manner? Most practitioners have indicated that they would refuse to provide partial responses that would mislead plaintiff counsel into believing the plaintiff had completely recovered (*see* Herman, Cary & Kennedy, 2001, at 176–77). Recipients of answers limited to such specific conditions should become suspicious and ask follow-up inquiries about other problems that may have been discovered.

3.   Overt Misrepresentation of Information

When lawyers are asked if negotiators may overtly misrepresent legal or factual matters, most provide immediate negative replies. Many cite Model Rule 4.1 and suggest that this prohibition covers all intentional misrepresentations. While they are correct with respect to deliberate misstatements concerning material legal doctrines, they are not entirely correct with respect to factual issues. Almost all negotiators expect opponents to engage in "puffing" and "embellishment." Advocates who hope to obtain $50,000 settlements may initially indicate that it will take $150,000 or even $250,000 to resolve this dispute. They may also embellish the pain experienced by their client, so long as their exaggerations do not transcend the bounds of expected propriety. Individuals involved in a corporate buyout may initially over or under value the real property, the building and equipment, the inventory, the accounts receivable, the patent rights and trademarks, and the good will.

It is clear that lawyers may not intentionally misrepresent *material* facts, but it is not always apparent what facts are *"material."* The previously noted Comment to Rule 4.1 acknowledges that "estimates of price or value placed on the subject of a transaction and a party's intentions as to an acceptable settlement of a claim" do not constitute *"material"* facts under that provision. It is thus ethical for legal negotiators to misrepresent the value their client places on particular items. For example, attorneys representing a spouse involved in a marital dissolution may indicate that their client wants joint custody of the children, when he or she does not. Lawyers representing a party attempting to purchase a particular company may understate their side's belief regarding the value of the good will associated with the target firm. So long as the statement conveys their side's belief — and does not falsely indicate the view of an outside expert, such as an accountant — no Rule 4.1 violation would occur.

Negotiators may also misrepresent client settlement intentions. They may ethically suggest to opposing counsel that an outstanding offer is unacceptable, even though they know the proposed terms would be accepted if no additional concessions could be generated. It is critical, however, to distinguish between mere "puffing" and the overt misrepresentation of material fact. Although an attorney representing a property seller may ethically indicate that the owner will not part with the property for less than $1,000,000, when he or she thinks — or even knows — that the client would consider lower offers if necessary, the lawyer could not state that the owner has been offered $1,000,000 by someone else, when no such offer has been received. The first statement would be regarded by most people as acceptable "puffing," while the latter statement would be a clear misrepresentation of material fact (Mnookin, Peppet & Tulumello, 2000, at 278). We even think it would be unethical to inform this prospective purchaser that the client has received another offer — without mentioning any amount — when no such offer has been received. On the other hand, the attorney could ethically indicate that other persons are interested in the property and suggest that the owner will not accept less than $1,000,000. What if the seller has received an offer from another person, but it is well below $1,000,000? Clearly the seller's attorney could not misrepresent the exact offer received. The lawyer might, however, note that another offer has been received and suggest that the prospective purchaser will have to offer at least $1,000,000 if he or she hopes to obtain the property. If this bidder were to ask what the exact offer is, the seller's representative could simply say that the owner will not accept less than $1,000,000.

It is important to emphasize that this Rule 4.1 exception does not excuse all misstatements regarding client settlement intentions. During the early stages of interactions, most practitioners do not expect opponents to disclose exact client desires. Nonetheless, as bargainers approach final agreements, they anticipate a greater degree of candor. If negotiators were to deliberately deceive adversaries about this issue during the Closing Stage or the Cooperative Stage, most attorneys would consider them dishonest, even though Rule 4.1 would remain inapplicable.

The relevant Comment to Rule 4.1 is explicitly restricted to *negotiations* with *opposing counsel*. Outside that narrow setting, statements pertaining to client settlement objectives may well constitute "material" fact. *ABA Formal Opinion 93–370* (1993), indicated that a knowing misrepresentation regarding client settlement intentions to a judge during pretrial meetings would be impermissible, since the misstatement would not be confined to adversarial bargaining interactions (Rotunda, 1995, at 168). (*See also* Kovach, 2001; Alfini, 1999; Meyerson, 1997 (arguing for greater degree of candor when advocates are communicating with mediators).)

When material facts are involved, attorneys may not deliberately misrepresent the actual circumstances. They may employ blocking techniques to avoid answering opponent questions, but they may not provide false or misleading answers. If they decide to respond to inquiries pertaining to material facts, they must do so honestly. They must also be careful not to issue partially correct statements they know will be misinterpreted by their opponents.

A critical distinction is drawn between statements of lawyer opinion and statements of material fact. When attorneys merely express their opinions — e.g., "I think the defendant had consumed too much alcohol"; "I believe the plaintiff will encounter future medical difficulties" — they are not constrained by Rule 4.1 even though some speculation is involved. Opposing counsel know that these recitations only concern the personal views of the speakers. These statements are critically different from lawyer statements indicating that they have witnesses who can testify to these matters. If representations regarding witness information were false, the misstatements would clearly contravene Rule 4.1.

A frequently debated area concerns representations about one's authorized limits. Many attorneys refuse to answer "unfair" questions concerning their authorized limits, because these inquiries pertain to confidential attorney-client communications. If negotiators decide to respond to these queries, must they do so honestly? Some lawyers believe that truthful responses are required, since they concern material facts. Other practitioners assert that responses about client authorizations merely reflect client values and settlement intentions and are thus excluded from the scope of Rule 4.1 by the drafter's Comment. As a result, they think that attorneys may lie about these matters (Rubin, 1995, at 453–54).

Negotiators who know they cannot avoid the impact of questions concerning their authorized limits by labeling them "unfair" and who find it difficult to provide false responses can employ an alternative approach. If plaintiff counsel who is demanding $125,000 asks the defense attorney who is presently offering $75,000 whether he or she is authorized to provide $100,000, the recipient may treat the $100,000 figure as a new plaintiff proposal. That individual can indicate that the $100,000 sum suggested by plaintiff counsel is still excessive. The plaintiff attorney is likely to become preoccupied with the need to clarify the fact that he or she did not mean to suggest any reduction in his or her recent $125,000 demand. That person would probably forego further attempts to ascertain the authorized limits possessed by the defendant attorney!

B.   UNCONSCIONABLE TACTICS AND AGREEMENTS

In recent years, a number of legal representatives — especially in large urban areas — have decided to employ highly offensive tactics to advance client interests. They may be rude, sarcastic, or nasty. These individuals erroneously equate discourteous actions with effective advocacy. They use these techniques as a substitute for lawyering skill. Proficient practitioners recognize that impolite behavior is the antithesis of competent representation.

Legal representatives should eschew tactics that are merely designed to humiliate or harass opponents. ABA Model Rule 4.4 expressly states that "a lawyer shall not use means that have no substantial purpose other than to embarrass, delay, or burden a third person . . . ." (Morgan & Rotunda, 2004, at 96; Herman, Cary & Kennedy, 2001, at 178; Lowenthal, 1982, at 102.) Demented win-lose negotiators may endeavor to achieve total annihilation of adversaries through the cruel and unnecessary degradation of opposing counsel. Not only is such behavior morally reprehensible, but it needlessly exposes the perpetrators to future recriminations that could be avoided through common courtesy. In litigation situations, it may expose the inappropriate actors to judicial sanctions. (*See, e.g., Lee v. American Eagle Airlines*, 2000 U.S. Dist. LEXIS 4198 (S.D. Fla. 2000) (unruly behavior by plaintiff lawyers warranted significant reduction in attorney fees they earned on behalf of prevailing plaintiff).) This approach also guarantees the offensive actors far more nonsettltments than are experienced by their more cooperative cohorts.

Lawyers negotiate regularly on the telephone. In the near future, most people will use video phones via Internet connections. Since most people do not hear many words communicated during these discussions — and would undoubtedly miss many nonverbal signals being emitted during video phone exchanges — they may be tempted to secretly tape their bargaining conversations to enable them to review these interactions carefully once they have been concluded. Would such conduct be unethical? Although federal law does not prohibit the secret taping of telephone calls by one of the participants without the other party's knowledge, some states make such conduct illegal. In those jurisdictions, it would obviously be improper for lawyers to contravene these statutory prohibitions. What if such secret taping is not illegal? Some State Bar Associations have indicated that where secret taping is not proscribed by law, attorneys do not behave unethically when they engage in such behavior (Pitulla, 1994, at 102). Other State Bar Associations, however, have reached the opposite conclusion, believing that attorneys conducting telephone conversations with other lawyers have the right to expect those discussions to remain untaped without the knowledge and consent of both parties.

Rule 4.3 of the 1980 Discussion Draft of the ABA Model Rules would have instructed attorneys not to conclude any agreement "the lawyer knows or reasonably should know . . . would be held to be unconscionable as a matter of law." (Lowenthal, 1982, at 103). This provision would have substantially codified the admonition of Judge Rubin against the negotiation of "unconscionable deals" (Rubin, 1975, at 591). Nonetheless, this proposal was omitted from the final draft, most likely because of its superfluous nature. If negotiated contracts are "unconscionable as a matter of law," they are subject to legal challenges that may vitiate the entire deals. It thus behooves legal advocates to avoid the consummation of truly unconscionable transactions.

What about seemingly one-sided arrangements that have not been procured through improper means and do not constitute legally unconscionable agreements? Should it be considered unethical or morally reprehensible for attorneys to negotiate such contracts? This concept would place the responsible advocates in a tenuous position. If courts would be unlikely to find the proposed agreements unlawful and the opposing parties were perfectly willing to consummate the apparently skewed transactions, should the prevailing legal representatives refuse to conclude the deals merely because they believe the transactions might unreasonably disadvantage their opponents? Why should the subjective personal judgment of these lawyers take precedence over the willingness of their opponents and their attorneys to conclude the proposed exchanges? These individuals may not know and may never know why their opponents considered these deals "fair." Their adversaries may have been aware of factual or legal circumstances that either undermined their own positions or bolstered those of the other side.

Some lawyers might understandably feel compelled to mention the apparently one-sided aspect of proposed transactions to their own clients. A few might even feel the need to explore this concern at least obliquely with opposing counsel. Would it be appropriate for them to refuse to consummate the agreements even when the other participants still favor their execution? If they continued to sanctimoniously oppose the proposed deals, should they be subject to bar discipline for failing to represent their clients with appropriate zeal or to liability for legal malpractice? Attorneys who are positioned to conclude arrangements that would substantially benefit their clients should be hesitant to vitiate those transactions based solely upon their own personal conviction that the proffered terms are "unfair" to their opponents even though they appear to be entirely lawful.

Once settlement agreements are achieved, attorneys are obliged to prepare documents that reflect the actual intentions of the negotiating parties. If a lawyer were to deliberately change a term or delete something that was agreed upon, the client may be held liable for fraud and the attorney would be subject to discipline (*see, e.g., Crane v. State Bar*, 30 Cal. 3d 117, 635 P.2d 163 (1981)). If one side has prepared the settlement agreement and the other side realizes that the drafter has inadvertently omitted an important provision, while no specific Model Rule directly addresses this situation, *ABA Formal Opin. 86–1518* (1986) indicates that the party aware of the omission should contact the drafting attorney to correct the error.

Suppose the lawyer for one party receives documents from opposing counsel that contain confidential client information and were clearly not intended to be sent to the receiving party? May the recipient examine the confidential material to gain a bargaining advantage over the sender? *ABA Formal Opins. 94-382* (1994) and *92-368* (1992) provide that the recipient of such unintended confidential information shall refrain from reviewing them, notify the sending party, and abide by the sender's instructions with respect to the appropriate way to rectify the sender's inadvertent error.

Practitioners and law students occasionally ask whether lawyers who represent clients in civil actions arising out of arguably criminal conduct may suggest the possibility of criminal prosecution if the civil suit negotiations are not completed successfully. DR 7-105(A), of the ABA Code of Professional Responsibility, that is still followed by some jurisdictions, states that lawyers shall not "threaten to present criminal charges solely to obtain an advantage in a civil matter" (Morgan & Rotunda, 2004, at 326). This provision might be read to preclude the mention of possible criminal action to advance civil suit discussions. Courts have appropriately acknowledged, however, that neither DR 7-105(A), nor extortion or compounding of felony prohibitions should be interpreted to prevent civil litigants from mentioning the availability of criminal action if related civil claims are not resolved or to preclude clients from agreeing to forego the filing of criminal charges in exchange for money paid to resolve their civil suits (*e.g., Committee on Legal Ethics v. Printz*, 416 S.E.2d 720 (W. Va. Sup. Ct. 1992)). Nonetheless, legal representatives must be careful not to use the threat of criminal prosecution to obtain *more* than is actually owed or have their clients agree not to testify at future criminal trials. "Seeking payment beyond restitution in exchange for foregoing criminal prosecution or seeking any payments in exchange for not testifying at a criminal trial . . . are still clearly prohibited." (416 S.E.2d at 727.) (*See also In re Charles*, 290 Or. 127, 618 P.2d 1281 (1980) (unethical for attorney to threaten possibility of criminal charges *solely* to obtain advantage regarding negotiations pertaining to related civil matter).) A threat to invoke criminal proceedings to enhance one's bargaining position in an unrelated civil dispute would almost certainly be improper, because of the extortionate nature of the such conduct (*Bluestein v. State Bar*, 13 Cal. 3d 162, 529 P.2d 599 (1974)).

The Model Rules do not contain any provision analogous to DR 7-105(A), and it is clear that the drafters deliberately chose not to prohibit the threat of criminal action to advance civil suit settlement talks pertaining to the same operative circumstances (Pitulla, 1992, at 106). As a result, the ABA Standing Committee on Ethics and Professional Responsibility indicated in *Formal Opinion 92-363* (1992), that it is not unethical under the Model Rules for attorneys to mention the possibility of criminal charges during civil suit negotiations, so long as they do "not attempt to exert or suggest improper influence over the criminal process." (Pitulla, 1992, at 106.) Nevertheless, legal representatives must still not demand excessive compensation that may contravene applicable extortion provisions or promise that their clients will not testify at future criminal trials, since such a commitment would contravene public policy.

C. POTENTIAL ATTORNEY-CLIENT CONFLICTS OF INTEREST

Clients obtain the services of attorneys to benefit from the legal expertise provided by such specialists and to obtain the advice of detached professionals. In most cases, attorneys provide clients with unbiased advice and work diligently to further client interests. In some instances, however, the interests of the clients and their lawyers may diverge (Korobkin, 2002, at 310–12). For example, individuals who claim to have been wrongfully discharged from employment may prefer reinstatement to their former positions over generous back pay agreements. Their attorneys, who are probably being compensated on a contingent fee basis, cannot get one-third or forty percent of their reinstatement. As a result, their legal representatives may encourage them to forego reinstatement in favor of greater monetary relief. A victim of sexual or racial harassment may prefer an apology to monetary compensation. Their contingent fee counsel may prefer more tangible relief, and fail to seek the relief the client really wants to obtain.

Lawyers must always recognize the unfailing duty they owe to their clients. Under Model Rule 1.2(a), attorneys "shall abide by a client's decisions concerning the objectives of representation" and "shall abide by a client's decision whether to settle a matter." (Morgan & Rotunda, 2004, at 12.) While attorneys may attempt to influence the objectives they think clients should seek, once clients have decided what they want to obtain from the legal representation, their lawyers must work diligently to satisfy those client objectives. Even when attorneys do not like offers made by opposing parties, they must acknowledge their ethical obligation under Model Rule 1.4(a) to keep their clients reasonably informed about the status of matters (Morgan & Rotunda, 2004, at 16). Lawyers may only reject offers of settlement without client consultation where the clients have already made it clear that such proposals would be unacceptable. (*See* Comment 2 to Model Rule 1.4 in Morgan & Rotunda, 2004, at 17.)

D. CONCLUDING ADMONITIONS

It is not particularly useful to engage in a pious and hypocritical discussion of negotiation ethics. If we were to suggest that all mendacity should be proscribed, even generally accepted "puffing" and "embellishment" would be precluded. Questions about authorized limits or minimum settlement objectives could no longer be answered with the frequent dissembling or outright prevarication. Most professional bargainers who have been asked about these ethical issues have indicated that deceptive replies are not inappropriate in these circumstances. They believe that advocates who ask these questions have no right to expect forthright replies. The inquiries pertain to confidential lawyer-client issues that concern excluded client values or settlement intentions. As a result, most attorneys suggest that questions related to these areas need not be candidly disclosed during the negotiation process.

Despite the contrary view of some members of the public, we have generally found attorneys to be conscientious and honorable people. We have encountered few instances of questionable behavior. We would thus like to conclude with several admonitions. Lawyers must remember that they have to live with their own consciences, and not those of their clients or their partners. They must employ tactics they feel comfortable using, even in those situations in which other people encourage them to employ less reputable behavior. If they adopt techniques they do not consider acceptable, not only will they experience personal discomfort but they will also fail to achieve their intended objective due to the fact they will not appear credible when using those tactics. Attorneys must also acknowledge that they are members of a special profession and owe certain duties to the public that transcend those owed by people engaged in other businesses (Condlin, 1992, at 77).

Lawyers are not guarantors — they are only legal advocates. They are not supposed to guarantee client victory no matter how disreputably they must act to do so. They should never countenance witness perjury or the withholding of subpoenaed documents. While they should zealously endeavor to advance client interests, they should recognize their moral obligation to follow the ethical rules applicable to all attorneys.

Legal representatives should never be willing to jeopardize long-term professional relationships for the narrow interests of particular clients. Zealous representation should never be thought to require the employment of personally compromising techniques. Legal advocates must recognize the numerous times they interact with other lawyers every day. They may request or be asked about relevant information. They or their opponents may ask for brief continuances or other professional courtesies. Individuals who do not have reputations for basic integrity and professional decency will find it difficult to interact with their peers.

Untrustworthy advocates encounter substantial difficulty when they negotiate with others. Their oral representations have to be verified and reduced to writing, and their opponents distrust their written documents. Negotiations are especially problematic and cumbersome. If nothing else moves lawyers to behave in an ethical and dignified manner, their hope for long and successful legal careers should induce them to avoid conduct that might undermine their future effectiveness.

Attorneys should diligently strive to advance client objectives while simultaneously maintaining their personal integrity. This philosophy will enable them to optimally serve the interests of both their clients and society. Legal practitioners who are asked about their insistence on ethical behavior may take refuge in an aphorism of Mark Twain: "Always do right. This will gratify some people, and astonish the rest!"

Part TWO

MEDIATION

Chapter 6

THE NATURE OF MEDIATION

A. THE ESSENTIAL CHARACTERISTICS OF MEDIATION

In recent years, legal practitioners and their clients have begun to recognize that mediation efforts constitute an important part of the dispute resolution process. Attorneys have also begun to acknowledge the need to inform new clients of the availability of alternative dispute resolution procedures such as mediation at the beginning of their professional relationships (Kovach, 1994, at 65). This practice increases client receptivity to ADR assistance when the time is propitious, and it enhances the probability of successful neutral intervention.

Experts have articulated the benefits that *advocates* may derive from their own use of mediative problem-solving techniques during bargaining interactions (Menkel-Meadow, 1984; Fisher & Ury, 1981). Negotiators who are familiar with mediative approaches can often employ similar problem-solving tactics during their own bargaining transactions to further client interests and enhance the likelihood of efficient agreements (Slaikeu, 1996). Attorneys regularly use conciliative skills to convince recalcitrant clients of the reasonableness of offers being advanced by opposing parties.

Advocates should also understand the role of mediators, so they can properly prepare themselves and their clients for mediation sessions and maximize the benefits that may be derived from third-party intervention. Practitioners who occasionally or regularly act as mediators must also familiarize themselves with the techniques employed by successful mediators. Their experiences as neutral intervenors should also increase their knowledge of the negotiation process and enhance their ability to function as effective negotiators when they represent future clients.

While different types of mediation exist for different types of disputes, there are numerous characteristics common to most forms of mediation. A review of these common traits is useful to understanding the mediation process.

1. FACILITATED NEGOTIATION

Mediation is, at its core, an assisted negotiation. Mediation represents negotiation of a dispute with the adversaries using a third party, the mediator, to aid the process. The mediator brings "value added" to the dispute by introducing techniques that enable the negotiators to settle their differences more readily. The mediator is an agent of the parties, retained to aid them in resolving the dispute.

2. PARTY CONTROL AND SELF-DETERMINATION

In mediation the parties control the proceedings. Results are not decided or imposed by the mediator. The adversaries control their own destiny. They decide to make peace or to continue in their dispute. The critical aspect of mediation is *party autonomy and self-determination*. While some mediators may suggest avenues for possible dispute resolution or point out common interests between the adversaries, the parties themselves, not the mediator, make the important decisional choices. Mediation is built on a foundation of party control and their reluctance to cede or transfer this control to third parties. During mediation "even when attending with counsel, the parties usually present their own viewpoints . . . encouraged by a mediator who asks them what brought them to this point in the conflict." (Rogers & McEwen, 1994, § 1.01, at 1).

3. NEUTRALITY OF THE MEDIATOR

The mediator is a *neutral* third party. The mediator is expected to be impartial as between the parties to the dispute and not favor either one in conducting the process (although there are exceptions to that principle in the context of international disputes between nations). Many theorists maintain that a mediator must also be impartial in a second way — in terms of the outcome of the process. This neutrality should extend to the content of any resolution reached by the parties and also to whether or not they reach a resolution at all. Some would draw a line at content-neutrality, however, when the result would be unfair to one of the parties or have detrimental effects on individuals with interests that are not represented at the table.

4. PRIVACY

Mediations involve private dispute resolution efforts. They occur in private far from the public eye. The private forums where mediations occur include law offices, hotel conference facilities, rented office space, business premises, and even personal homes.

Confidentiality is a hallmark of mediation. As a general rule, party communications to a mediator are intended by the party to be confidential and are treated as such by the mediator. Numerous states have legislation mandating that communications made during mediation sessions be confidential. Legislation establishing mediation confidentiality advances the mediation process and thereby helps to reduce the number of disputes that require conventional litigation. Mediators have generally opposed efforts to force them to reveal facts learned during mediation. Privacy is important in mediation in two separate ways. First, the substance of statements made by adversaries in mediation involves essentially settlement discussion. Settlement is promoted by keeping statements made during settlement negotiations confidential. Second, statements made by an adversary to a mediator are often made in separate and private "caucus" meetings and are intended to be kept confidential from the other party.

5. LEGAL SUBSERVIENCE

Legal norms are not specifically applied in mediation. Because the mediator is not a judge, the non-adjudicatory role of the mediator means that conventional legal rules are not directly applicable to mediation. It would be wrong, however, to suggest that law has no role in mediation. Law occupies an important place in mediation but a necessarily subservient or secondary one. Because mediation is a form of facilitated negotiation, the role of law in mediation is similar to its position in negotiation. Mediated bargaining, like negotiated bargaining, occurs with the parties being "influenced" by legal rules. The adversaries bargain "in the shadow of the law." (*See* Mnookin & Kornhauser, 1979). In mediation the parties may choose to ignore potentially relevant law or, alternatively, negotiate with the thought that if they go to court, relevant law will be in their favor. The mediator's main task is to assist the parties to reach agreement and, for that reason, mediators may deemphasize or diminish the role of law in their own efforts to guide the parties to settlement. Consequently, it is good mediation practice for a mediator to counsel unrepresented parties to have a lawyer review any settlements reached in mediation.

6. Consensual Mediation as Contract

In some respects mediation operates as a contract. Aside from mandatory mediation in court-annexed programs, the choice to use mediation is a consensual one and often is embodied in a contract. The parties may select the mediation option as part of a pre-dispute contract signed well before any dispute exists. Alternatively, the parties may sign a written agreement to mediate after their dispute has arisen or may just agree to mediate without a formal, written contract. In either case the decision to mediate was made pursuant to the norms of agreement that we term "contract."

In addition to consent arising at the very beginning of mediation, contracts have a definite place at the end of the mediation process. If the parties are successful in reaching settlement of their dispute they typically terminate a mediation by signing a contract. This document is a settlement agreement and may merely settle the existing claims. It may, however, go beyond the settlement of the instant mediated dispute and additionally delineate elements of the parties' relationship in a full contractual sense. Many parties to mediation already have a preexisting relationship (e.g., divorced parents, franchisee-franchisor). This relationship may merit a contract defining the precise terms of its existence.

7. Common Ground and Common Interests

Although some observers have suggested that compromise is the essence of mediation, this platitude is overly simplistic. The distinguishing feature of mediation is the ability of the mediator to help the parties resolve their dispute by assisting them to identify shared interests and common ground for agreement. While this process of identifying shared goals and common areas of interest may seem like compromise, it should be recognized that each adversary has a selfish, purposeful motive to end the dispute with terms beneficial to its side.

8. Empowerment and Recognition

During the mediation process, some parties may become "empowered" and achieve "recognition" by their opponents.

Empowerment involves the mediation adversary gaining improved negotiating ability and a general sense of self-worth and confidence. These improvements in empowerment allow the party to more clearly perceive both their goals and necessary strategies. Recognition, appreciation of and respect toward the adversary, facilitates meaningful negotiation and aids empowerment. When both empowerment and recognition are achieved, mediation is said to be "transformative" and will result in "success" even if no agreement is achieved. The full theory of "transformative mediation" is set out in ROBERT BARUCH BUSH & JOSEPH FOLGER, TRANSFORMATIVE MEDIATION (1994).

The following two excerpts explore some of the benefits of mediation. The first, a classic explanation of the process, explains the creative potential of mediation. The second takes the common viewpoint that mediation is assisted negotiation. It examines the value that mediation can add in terms of helping to overcome common barriers to a negotiated agreement.

LON L. FULLER, MEDIATION — ITS FORMS AND FUNCTIONS, 44 S. Cal. L. Rev. 305, 308–09, 318, 325–26 (1971) *

[M]ediation is commonly directed, not toward achieving conformity to norms, but toward the creation of the relevant norms themselves. This is true, for example, in the very common case where the mediator assists the parties in working out the terms of a contract defining their rights and duties toward one another. In such a case there is no pre-existing structure that can guide mediation; it is the mediational process that produces the structure.

It may be suggested that mediation is always, in any event, directed toward bringing about a more harmonious relationship between the parties, whether this be achieved through explicit agreement, through a reciprocal acceptance of the "social norms" relevant to their relationship, or simply because the parties have been helped to a new and more perceptive understanding of one another's problems. The fact that in ordinary usage the terms "mediation" and "conciliation" are largely interchangeable tends to reinforce this view of the matter.

But at this point we encounter the inconvenient fact that mediation can be directed, not toward cementing a relationship, but toward terminating it. In a form of mediation that is coming to be called "marriage therapy" mediative efforts between husband and wife may be undertaken by a psychoanalyst, a psychiatrist, a social worker, a marriage counsellor, or even a friendly neighbor. In this situation it will not infrequently turn out that the most effective use of mediation will be in assisting the parties to accept the inevitability of divorce. In a radically different context one of the most dramatically successful uses of mediation I ever witnessed involved a case in which an astute mediator helped the parties rescind a business contract. Two

---

corporations were entrapped by a long-term supply contract that had become burdensome and disadvantageous to both. Cancelling it, however, was a complicated matter, requiring a period of "phasing out" and various financial adjustments back and forth. For some time the parties had been chiefly engaged in reciprocal threats of a law suit. On the advice of an attorney for one of the parties, a mediator (whose previous experience had been almost entirely in the field of labor relations) was brought in. Within no time at all a severance of relations was accomplished and the two firms parted company happily.

Thus we find that mediation may be directed toward, and result in discrepant and even diametrically opposed results. This circumstance argues against our being able to derive any general structure of the mediational process from some identifiable goal shared by all mediational efforts. We may, of course, indulge in observations to the effect that the mere presence of a third person tends to put the parties on their good behavior, that the mediator can direct their verbal exchanges away from recrimination and toward the issues that need to be faced, that by receiving separate and confidential communications from the parties he can gradually bring into the open issues so deep-cutting that the parties themselves had shared a tacit taboo against any discussion of them and that, finally, he can by his management of the interchange demonstrate to the parties that it is possible to discuss divisive issues without either rancor or evasion.

*   *   *

[The negotiation process] can often be greatly facilitated through the services of a skillful mediator. His assistance can speed the negotiations, reduce the likelihood of miscalculation, and generally help the parties to reach a sounder agreement, an adjustment of their divergent valuations that will produce something like an optimum yield of the gains of reciprocity. These things the mediator can accomplish by holding separate confidential meetings with the parties, where each party gives the mediator a relatively full and candid account of the internal posture of his own interests. Armed with this information, but without making a premature disclosure of its details, the mediator can then help to shape the negotiations in such a way that they will proceed most directly to their goal, with a minimum of waste and friction.

*   *   *

* * * [T]he central quality of mediation * * * [is] its capacity to reorient the parties toward each other, not by imposing rules on them, but by helping them to achieve a new and shared perception of their relationship, a perception that will redirect their attitudes and dispositions toward one another.

*   *   *

This quality of mediation becomes most visible when the proper function of the mediator turns out to be, not that of inducing the parties to accept formal rules for the governance of their future relations, but that of helping them to free themselves from the encumbrance of rules and of accepting, instead, a relationship of mutual respect, trust and understanding that will enable them to meet shared contingencies without the aid of formal prescriptions laid down in advance. * * *

* * * [I]t should be remembered that the primary function of the mediator in the collective bargaining situation is not to propose rules to the parties and to secure their acceptance of them, but to induce the mutual trust and understanding that will enable the parties to work out their own rules. The creation of rules is a process that cannot itself be rule-bound; it must be guided by a sense of shared responsibility and a realization that the adversary aspects of the operation are part of a larger collaborative undertaking. The primary task of the [mediator] is to induce this attitude of mind and spirit, though to be sure, he does this primarily by helping the parties to perceive the concrete ways in which this shared attitude can redound to their mutual benefit.

JEAN R. STERNLIGHT, LAWYERS' REPRESENTATION OF CLIENTS IN MEDIATION: USING ECONOMICS AND PSYCHOLOGY TO STRUCTURE ADVOCACY IN A NONADVERSARIAL SETTING, 14 Ohio St. J. on Disp. Resol. 269, 332–44 (1999) *

Many praise mediation as a valuable dispute resolution technique because it can aid parties in achieving mutually acceptable settlements that they would not have reached through nonfacilitated negotiation. Two features are key. First, as compared to nonfacilitated negotiations, mediation possesses the additional feature of a mediator — a third-party neutral whose role is to help the participants discuss their dispute and potentially work out a solution. Second, mediation potentially allows represented parties to play a direct role in the negotiation.

* * *

[B]oth of these distinguishing features of mediation potentially allow parties to surmount economic, psychological, and principal-agent barriers to successful negotiation. * * *

A. Using Mediation to Surmount Economic Barriers to Settlement

Mediation can effectively help overcome both barriers to successful negotiation that were identified by the traditional economic model — lack of information and blustering positional bargaining techniques.

1. *Conveying Information.* The mediation process can be extremely effective in helping both sides exchange information and thereby learn more about each other's litigation strengths and weaknesses, each other's interests, and even their own interests. [P]arties and their attorneys are brought face-to-face with their opponents in an environment where they can have a direct discussion. Attorneys can speak directly to opposing clients without having their comments filtered by an opposing attorney. As well, the exchange of information can proceed much more rapidly and efficiently than if the attorneys in a

negotiation had to repeatedly defer and state that they would raise various points or obtain certain information from their own clients.

*   *   *

In addition, the trained mediator can ask questions that parties may not have thought to ask, can offer creative suggestions, and can help parties to better understand their own and each other's interests. By creating an atmosphere of trust, or by at least earning the trust of the opposing parties, the mediator can encourage participants to disclose information they would not have revealed in an unfacilitated setting.

2. *Avoiding Problems of Positional Bargaining.* Mediation can help avoid the pitfalls of positional bargaining in several ways. First, because parties and their attorneys have an opportunity to speak with one another directly, and to question each others' motives and interests, it is easier to use interest-based techniques. Lawyers often find it natural to fall into positional bargaining. Clients, by contrast, may more easily see that no one's interest will be served if the negotiations founder and the dispute has to be litigated. They may therefore be more receptive to creative problem-solving approaches.

*   *   *

Second, the mediator can help defuse competitive bargaining problems in a variety of ways. She can directly question not only the attorneys but also their clients as to their background interests and motivations. Also, she can facilitate the flow of information. Whereas positional pressures might make negotiators reluctant to share information for fear of losing face or momentum, mediators can serve as conduits for such information. Finally, the mediator can help blunt the conflict escalation that may both result from and cause positional bargaining by evincing sympathy, building trust, and using such techniques as separating hostile parties.

B. Using Mediation to Surmount Psychological Barriers to Settlement

Mediation can help to surmount psychological barriers to settlement by allowing parties to deal with one another directly. Also, the mediator can both improve the character and quality of the participants' communications with one another and help parties to better understand their own goals and positions. * * *

1. *Over-Optimism.* Mediation employs several devices to defeat the over-optimism that may stand in the way of a reasonable and fair settlement. First, it allows not only the lawyers but also the parties to take a close look at their opponent and to hear the opposing side's arguments. Absent mediation, most parties would not have the opportunity to hear the other side's point of view until the trial itself. While a party's lawyer presumably does her best to describe the strengths of the opponent's position, even the lawyer may not have full knowledge of the opponent's case. Moreover, diverging incentives may sometimes cause lawyers to exaggerate the strength of their own clients' positions, even in private conversations with their clients. Therefore, where no mediation has occurred many clients are shocked and alarmed to hear at trial how strong the other side's case is. By then, however, it may be too late

to reach a mutually beneficial settlement. Mediation allows parties to hear the opposing party's story, to view the credibility of the opposing side's witnesses, and to hear a summary of the opposing side's experts' opinions, if not the opinions themselves.

Second, mediation can show a party that her own position is not as strong as she may have thought or as her lawyer may have led her to believe. The opposing attorney or party can point out weaknesses in the case using charts, diagrams, videos, or occasionally even cross-examination type techniques. Practitioner-oriented materials guide attorneys in effectively deflating the expectations of the opposing party in mediation.

Third, the mediator helps deflate expectations by serving as a "reality check." While mediators may perform this role in different ways, some merely by asking questions and others by offering evaluations, it is well recognized that an important part of mediators' function is to bring the participants' views of the dispute closer to reality. In fact, some attorneys explicitly ask mediators, in private, to help bring their clients' views of the case back to reality.

Fourth, as noted above, attorneys may also be over-optimistic about their chances of success. The techniques noted above can be important to help attorneys as well as clients see the dispute more realistically.

2. *Anchoring*. Mediation can help defeat irrational anchoring tendencies by allowing participants and the mediator to question the basis of a party's position. Much as was described above, in connection with over-optimism, mediation allows parties to interact directly with each other, the opposing attorney, and the mediator. These interactions can be used to attempt to convince parties that their "anchored" view of the world is not rational and does not serve their best interest. For example, a mediator might help a party to recognize that the settlement offered is far preferable to the costs and risks of going to trial, even though the offer would not make the party completely whole.

3. *Risk Aversion, Risk Preference, and Framing*. [P]ersons' reactions to a particular settlement proposal may vary substantially depending on how that proposal is framed. Specifically, a party will be more receptive to a proposal that is framed as a gain relative to the status quo than as a loss. While a party's own attorney can attempt to do this reframing, often the mediator or even the opposing party or her attorney can be more successful at this task. * * *

4. *Reactive Devaluation*. The mediation process can be very useful in eliminating or at least reducing reactive devaluation. Here, the role of the mediator is crucial. As Robert Mnookin and Lee Ross explain, "the settlement proposal in question can be made to come, or seem to come, from the third party or some collaborative effort rather than one of the principals acting unilaterally." That is, the mediator can take an idea obtained from one of the parties and offer it as her own. Also, the mediator can help explain why a particular offer is being made and why it is being made at a particular time, thereby reducing the seeming significance of the authorship of the offer.

C. Using Mediation to Surmount Principal-Agent Barriers to Appropriate Settlement

One of the greatest and yet unsung benefits of mediation is that it helps parties overcome problems that are created when they are represented by attorneys or agents in settlement negotiations. These benefits stem primarily from the fact that parties, participating directly in the mediation process, can learn about various aspects of the dispute on their own rather than through their lawyer's filter. As well, the parties can express themselves directly instead of relying on their lawyers to be their voice. By participating directly in the process, parties can avoid some of the problems created by the divergence of incentives between lawyer and client. * * *

1. *Dealing with Diverging Monetary Incentives.* Where parties participate directly in mediation, they limit the attorneys' ability to influence the parties' decisions on whether or not to settle the case and on what terms. In the extreme, where an attorney who is being paid by the hour has deliberately attempted to convince the client that settlement would be a bad idea so that the attorney can run up her own fees, mediation may prove quite an eye-opener. The client may learn that the other side has some good explanations for her conduct, has lots of favorable legal precedent, and has some evidence that she will use to undercut the client's own position. Also, the client may learn that she and her opponent have more in common than she thought and that it may be possible to work out a mutually acceptable agreement, perhaps involving a future business relationship. Most blatantly, a mediator or opposing attorney or party may even use a question or statement to educate a party as to her own attorney's financial stake in the case.

Parties' participation in mediation may also encourage their attorneys to prepare more thoroughly than they might have done for a negotiation. Attorneys, like many people, focus on the most pressing crisis in the office. Their financial incentives may be such that a negotiation in a case not scheduled to go to trial for a year or so has relatively low priority. However, where an attorney knows she will be on display before her client, as well as appearing live before the opposing client and mediator, she will have added reason to review the case carefully and assemble her best arguments. That is, the performance requirement may counter the attorney's tendency to prepare inadequately, and more adequate preparation may make a settlement possible.

Mediation also helps deal with the phenomenon of the attorney who is afraid to give her own client bad news about the case, wary that conveying such news will jeopardize the attorney-client relationship. Attorneys are actually conscious of this tendency and are not necessarily deliberately seeking to mislead their own clients. Rather, through unpleasant experience, they have learned that it often does not work well for them to be the bearer of bad tidings. Thus, attorneys will frequently welcome and sometimes even privately desire that the opposing attorney or the mediator bring their own client back to earth. Again, where the client participates directly in the mediation such communications are possible.

* * *

2. *Dealing with Diverging Nonmonetary Incentives.* Mediation offers parties an opportunity to voice their requests for nonmonetary relief that their

attorneys may not have emphasized. * * * [A]lthough clients are not exclusively interested in money, attorneys tend to emphasize the monetary aspects of settlement. In a mediation, the client, in an opening statement or in the course of subsequent discussion, can make it clear that she also cares about nonmonetary relief such as an apology, reinstatement, or establishing a new business relationship. Particularly where the opposing client is also present and hears the expression of these needs, it may turn out that the parties are able to reach a mutually acceptable settlement that might not have been envisioned by the attorneys. That is, a negotiation that might have foundered as a purely dollar-based positional bargaining attempt may succeed once the nonmonetary goals are introduced. Focusing on nonmonetary side issues may also speed up a monetary settlement. At times seemingly minor items such as an honorary plaque may be worth more to a client than an attorney might imagine. Once agreement is reached on the emotional points, the dollar aspects of the agreement may fall into place.

Mediation can also help deal with the fact that an attorney's nonmonetary needs may be leading the attorney to advise against settlement. In the course of the mediation discussions, the client may come to realize that her own interests would be well served by the proposed settlement and that it is her attorney's nonmonetary need, such as her drive to try her first case, that is the road block. If the client sees this problem she can, of course, insist on settling the case.

Also, mediation can meet clients' desires for expression and communication. [I]t is a mistake to view mediation exclusively as a tool to obtain better outcomes. Rather, the process of mediation itself is important to many clients. Mediation may meet clients' nonmonetary desires for control, expression, communication, justice, or perhaps even vengeance, by allowing them to express themselves and also to learn more about their opponents' perspectives.

Mediation can also help a client come to terms with the fact that given her nonmonetary aspirations, the proposed settlement may not be desirable. Whereas the client's attorney, who is typically focused primarily on monetary relief, may be encouraging the client to accept the settlement, the client may realize at mediation that she would rather take her chances in court in order to secure such possible advantages as publicity, precedent, or vindication. As noted earlier, by participating directly in the mediation the client may become better apprised of her own goals and aspirations as well as of her alternatives and thus better able to make an informed choice rather than simply depend on the advice of her attorney.

3. *Dealing with Diverging Psychologies.* Mediation allows participating clients to see with their own eyes, speak with their own voices, and use their own creative talents. By participating directly in the mediation, the client has the opportunity to view the opponent, the opponent's attorney, and any witnesses directly rather than through the filter of her attorney. A good mediator can facilitate these opportunities. For example, whereas the attorney may have responded cynically to the opponent's apology, it may be meaningful for the client. Where the attorney may have regarded the opponent's story as hogwash, the client may see it as compelling. That is, the client's view is not restricted by the lawyer's cold, rational, and perhaps even cynical lens.

In addition, the client may come to realize that her own attitude toward risk differs from that of her attorney and that she is not willing to take certain risks that might interest the attorney. For these reasons, the client may come to favor a settlement that she previously opposed.

The client can also increase the likelihood of settlement by bringing more emotion to the proceeding than the attorney would likely use. Whereas the client may feel a need to get certain issues off her chest and feel that she has been fully heard, the lawyer's instinct may well be to avoid emotion and upset and keep the discussion on an even and rational keel. Yet, the client may not feel able to settle the matter and put the dispute behind her until she has discharged her emotional feelings. Mediation can provide the client with an opportunity to vent. If the client gives at least a portion of the opening statement, she can immediately explain her perspective to the opposing party. Later in the mediation, as well, the client can further spell out her views and feelings in response to specific questions. Moreover, she can gain some satisfaction by expressing her views directly to the other party in a face-to-face encounter.

Finally, * * * mediation can increase the likelihood of settlement by providing a venue for the clients to be creative and to approach the negotiation from a problem-solving orientation. By nature or by culture, attorneys seem to fall into the pattern of positional bargaining. Clients, however, may be able to break free of this constraint to search for a settlement that is mutually beneficial. Particularly with the assistance of a mediator, clients will be able to introduce new interests and objectives into the discussion, thereby increasing the likelihood of a settlement.

NOTES

1. What does Professor Fuller think is the essential quality of mediation? Is reaching a resolution the most important benefit?

2. Professor Fuller refers to mediation having the ability to create norms. What is the nature of these norms? Will the norms be legal principles? Where do the norms come from? Is norm-creation necessarily part of mediation?

3. Fuller also refers to mediation's ability to terminate a relationship. It is easier to see how creating norms might be involved at the initiation of a relationship. In what ways might termination be "creative"? Is a termination of a relationship achieved through mediation a "success"?

4. With the growth of mediation, the process is used in situations that are not characterized by prior or ongoing relationships. It is not uncommon to see mediation of tort issues, for example. Do the theories regarding mediation set forth by Fuller support use of mediation beyond long-term relationships?

5. *Party attendance.*Professor Sternlight emphasizes the importance of the parties' attendance at the mediation session. Do you agree with her? What are some of the problems that could result from a client's participation in the process? Do you think the benefits outweigh the problems? Should that determination be made for each individual mediation?

6. *Procedural Justice.* Some maintain that one of the important benefits mediation offers is a sense of procedural justice for those who participate in the process. Procedural justice concerns the fairness of a process, as distinct from the fairness of the outcomes that are reached in a process. Disputants are inclined to see a process as fair if three primary criteria are met: disputants have an opportunity to express their version of events; disputants are confident that their version of events is considered in a neutral setting; and they feel they are treated with respect and dignity. These factors are thought to reflect individuals' need to express their story (often referred to as "voice") and their need to be treated as valued members of society. An individual who believes that just procedures are used to resolve a dispute is more likely to view the distributive outcome as just, even if it does not favor him. (*See* Nancy Welsh, *Making Deals in Court-Connected Mediation: What's Justice Got to Do With It?* 79 WASH. U. L.Q. 787 (2001).)

How is a party's "voice" different in mediation than in adjudication? Who is actually speaking and what is the permitted content of that speech? What attributes must a mediator display in order for a party to feel that a mediation satisfied her needs for procedural justice?

7. *Social Justice.* In addition, some contend that mediation promotes and builds social justice. (*See, e.g.,* Shonholtz, 1987.) According to this view, mediation in a neighborhood justice setting helps adversaries and their peers to unite because of mediation's focus on common interests. Mediation also supports social justice because the processes of mediation build confidence and awareness of self-help possibilities. Adherents to this social justice vision of mediation point to how neighborhood mediation has led to the formation of tenants' associations and collective action against local governments, developers, and landlords — all entities that were much more powerful than private individuals who had not united through common interests that were first identified in mediation.

B. APPROACHES TO THE MEDIATION PROCESS

Proficient mediators tend to possess common characteristics no matter what styles they employ (Slaikeu, 1996, at 17–18). They are objective individuals who are cognizant of their own biases. They have excellent communication skills — i.e., they are both good, empathetic listeners and assertive speakers. They are adept readers of nonverbal signals. They have good interpersonal skills that enable them to interact well with people with diverse backgrounds and different personalities. They understand the negotiation process and the way in which conciliators can enhance that process. They are flexible and can modify their usual styles when particular dispute circumstances suggest the need for a different approach (Golann, 2000).

Yet mediation can vary greatly depending on such factors as the type of dispute, the culture of the participants, the strategies of the mediator, and the goals of the parties. The flexibility that is the hallmark of mediation also makes the process hard to characterize. The following section explores the fundamental attributes of mediation through analyses of what persons who call themselves mediators actually do and theorists' conceptualizations of mediation. There is a great deal of variation in what mediators do and how it is characterized. This variation raises some important questions: How many processes can be included under the umbrella of "mediation"? Is there any advantage to differentiating some approaches and labeling them as processes distinct from "mediation"?

1. Two Continua: Narrow-Broad Problem Definitions And Evaluative-Facilitative Mediator Roles

The following article by law professor and mediator Leonard Riskin provides a vocabulary that is commonly used to distinguish the approaches of mediators working in a Western mediation tradition. It sparked a debate over what should be considered "mediation." As you read the excerpt, consider whether or not evaluation is an appropriate function for mediators.

Leonard L. Riskin, Mediator Orientations, Strategies and Techniques, 12 Alternatives to High Cost Litig. 111, 111–14 (1994) *

Almost every conversation about "mediation" suffers from ambiguity. People have disparate visions of what mediation is or should be. Yet we lack a comprehensive system for describing these visions. This causes confusion when people try to choose between mediation and another process or grapple with how to train, evaluate, regulate, or select mediators.

I propose a system for classifying mediator orientations. Such a system can help parties select a mediator and deal with the thorny issue of whether the mediator should have subject-matter expertise. The classification system starts with two principal questions: 1. Does the mediator tend to define problems *narrowly* or *broadly*? 2. Does the mediator think she should *evaluate* — make assessments or predictions or proposals for agreements — or *facilitate* the parties' negotiation without evaluating?

The answers reflect the mediator's beliefs about the nature and scope of mediation and her assumptions about the parties' expectations.

Problem Definition

Mediators with a *narrow* focus assume that the parties have come to them for help in solving a technical problem. The parties have defined this problem in advance through the *positions* they have asserted in negotiations or pleadings. Often it involves a question such as, "Who pays how much to whom?" or "Who can use such-and-such property?" As framed, these questions rest on "win-lose" (or "distributive") assumptions. In other words, the participants must divide a limited resource; whatever one gains, the other must lose.

The likely court outcome — along with uncertainty, delay and expense — drives much of the mediation process. Parties, seeking a compromise, will bargain adversarially, emphasizing positions over interests.

A mediator who starts with a *broad* orientation, on the other hand, assumes that the parties can benefit if the mediation goes beyond the narrow issues

---

that normally define legal disputes. Important interests often lie beneath the positions that the participants assert. Accordingly, the mediator should help the participants understand and fulfill those interests — at least if they wish to do so.

The Mediator's Role

The *evaluative* mediator assumes that the participants want and need the mediator to provide some direction as to the appropriate grounds for settlement — based on law, industry practice or technology. She also assumes that the mediator is qualified to give such direction by virtue of her experience, training and objectivity.

The *facilitative* mediator assumes the parties are intelligent, able to work with their counterparts, and capable of understanding their situations better than either their lawyers or the mediator. So the parties may develop better solutions than any that the mediator might create. For these reasons, the facilitative mediator assumes that his principal mission is to enhance and clarify communications between the parties in order to help them decide what to do.

The facilitative mediator believes it is inappropriate for the mediator to give his opinion, for at least two reasons. First, such opinions might impair the appearance of impartiality and thereby interfere with the mediator's ability to function. Second, the mediator might not know enough — about the details of the case or the relevant law, practices or technology — to give an informed opinion.

Each of the two principal questions — Does the mediator tend toward a narrow or broad focus? and Does the mediator favor an evaluative or facilitative role? — yield responses that fall along a continuum. Thus, a mediator's orientation will be more or less broad and more or less evaluative.

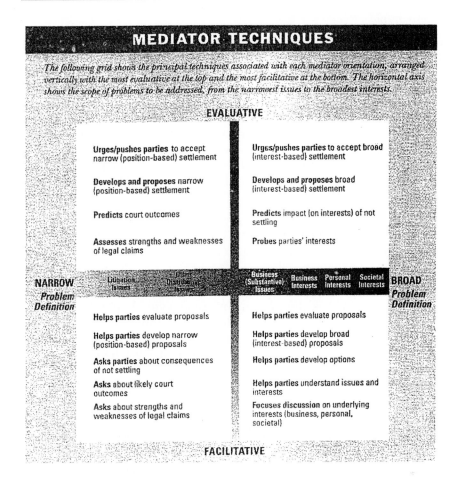

MEDIATOR TECHNIQUES

The following grid shows the principal techniques associated with each mediator orientation, arranged vertically with the most evaluative at the top and the most facilitative at the bottom. The horizontal axis shows the scope of problems to be addressed, from the narrowest issues to the broadest interests.

EVALUATIVE

Urges/pushes parties to accept narrow (position-based) settlement

Develops and proposes narrow (position-based) settlement

Predicts court outcomes

Assesses strengths and weaknesses of legal claims

Urges/pushes parties to accept broad (interest-based) settlement

Develops and proposes broad (interest-based) settlement

Predicts impact (on interests) of not settling

Probes parties' interests

NARROW Problem Definition

Litigation Issues | Other Distributive Issues | Business (Substantive) Issues | Business Interests | Personal Interests | Societal Interests

BROAD Problem Definition

Helps parties evaluate proposals

Helps parties develop narrow (position-based) proposals

Asks parties about consequences of not settling

Asks about likely court outcomes

Asks about strengths and weaknesses of legal claims

Helps parties evaluate proposals

Helps parties develop broad (interest-based) proposals

Helps parties develop options

Helps parties understand issues and interests

Focuses discussion on underlying interests (business, personal, societal)

FACILITATIVE

Strategies and Techniques of Each Orientation

Each *orientation* derives from assumptions or beliefs about the mediator's role and about the appropriate focus of a mediation. A mediator employs *strategies* — plans — to conduct the mediation. And he uses *techniques* — particular moves or behaviors — to effectuate those strategies. Here are selected strategies and techniques that typify each mediation orientation.

Evaluative-Narrow

The principal strategy of the evaluative-narrow mediator is to help the parties understand the strengths and weaknesses of their positions and the likely outcome at trial. To accomplish this, the evaluative-narrow mediator typically will first carefully study relevant documents, such as pleadings, depositions, reports and mediation briefs. Then, in the mediation, she employs evaluative techniques, * * * which are listed [on the grid] from most to least evaluative.

* * *

Facilitative-Narrow

Like the evaluative-narrow, the facilitative-narrow mediator plans to help the participants become "realistic" about their litigation situations. But he employs different techniques. He does not use his own assessments, predictions or proposals. Nor does he apply pressure. Moreover, he probably will not request or study relevant documents, such as pleadings, depositions, reports, or mediation briefs. Instead, because he believes that the burden of decision should rest with the parties, the facilitative-narrow mediator might ask questions — generally in private caucuses — to help the participants understand both sides' legal positions and the consequences of non-settlement. Also in private caucuses, he helps each side assess proposals in light of the alternatives.

* * *

Evaluative-Broad

The evaluative-broad mediator also helps the parties understand their circumstances and options. However, she has a different notion of what this requires. So she emphasizes the parties' interests over their positions and proposes solutions designed to accommodate these interests. In addition, because the evaluative-broad mediator constructs the agreement, she emphasizes her own understanding of the circumstances at least as much as the parties'.

* * *

The evaluative-broad mediator also provides predictions, assessments and recommendations. But she emphasizes options that address underlying interests, rather than those that propose only compromise on narrow issues. In the mediation of a contract dispute between two corporations, for instance, while the facilitative-narrow mediator might propose a strictly monetary settlement, the evaluative-broad mediator might suggest new ways for the firms to collaborate (perhaps in addition to a monetary settlement).

Facilitative-Broad

The facilitative-broad mediator seeks to help the parties define, understand and resolve the problems they wish to address. She encourages them to consider underlying interests rather than positions and helps them generate and assess proposals designed to accommodate those interests. * * *

The facilitative-broad mediator does not provide assessments, predictions or proposals. However, to help the participants better understand their legal situations, she will likely allow the parties to present and discuss their legal arguments. In addition, she might ask questions and * * * focus discussion on underlying interests.

In a broad mediation, however, legal argument generally occupies a lesser position than it does in a narrow one. And because he emphasizes the participants' role in defining the problems and in developing and evaluating proposals, the facilitative-broad mediator does not need to fully understand the legal posture of the case. Accordingly, he is less likely to request or study litigation documents, technical reports or mediation briefs.

However, the facilitative-broad mediator must be able to quickly grasp the legal and substantive issues and to respond to the dynamics of the situation. He needs to help the parties realistically evaluate proposals to determine whether they address the parties' underlying interests.

Mediator Techniques

Mediators usually have a predominant orientation, whether they know it or not, that is based on a combination of their personalities, experiences, education, and training. Thus, many retired judges, when they mediate, tend toward an evaluative-narrow orientation.

Yet mediators do not always behave consistently with the predominant orientations they express. Some mediators lack a clear grasp of the essence of their own expressed orientation. It is also common for mediators to employ a strategy generally associated with an orientation other than their own. This might help them carry out a strategy associated with their predominant orientation. For example, a prominent facilitative-broad mediator who often conducts sessions with parties only — not their lawyers — routinely predicts judicial outcomes. But he also emphasizes the principles underlying the relevant rules of law. He then encourages the parties to develop a resolution that makes sense for them and meets their own sense of fairness; in essence, he evaluates in order to free the parties from the potentially narrowing effects of law.

In addition, many mediators will depart from their orientations to respond to the dynamics of the situation. A prominent evaluative-broad mediator, for instance, typically learns as much as he can about the case and the parties' circumstances and then develops a proposal, which he tries to persuade the parties to accept. If they do not accept the proposal, he becomes more facilitative.

Another example: an evaluative-narrow mediator may explore underlying interests (a technique normally associated with the broad orientations) after her accustomed narrow focus results in a deadlock. And a facilitative-broad mediator might use a mildly evaluative tactic as a last resort. For instance, he might toss out a figure that he thinks the parties might be willing to agree upon, while stating that the figure does not represent his prediction of what would happen in court.

*   *   *

Subject-Matter Expertise

In selecting a mediator, what is the relevance of "subject-matter expertise?" The term could mean substantial understanding of either the law, customary practices, or technology associated with the dispute. In a patent infringement lawsuit, for instance, a mediator with subject-matter expertise could be familiar with the patent law or litigation, practices in the industry, or the relevant technology — or with all three of these areas.

The need for subject-matter expertise typically increases to the extent that the parties seek evaluations — assessments, predictions or proposals — from the mediator. The kind of subject-matter expertise needed depends on the kind of evaluation or direction the parties seek. If they want a prediction about what would happen in court, they need a mediator with a strong background in related litigation. If they want suggestions about how to structure future business relations, perhaps the mediator should understand the relevant industries. If they want to propose new government regulations (as in a regulatory negotiation), they might wish to retain a mediator who understands administrative law and procedure.

In contrast, to the extent that the parties feel capable of understanding their circumstances and developing potential solutions — singly, jointly or with assistance from outside experts — they might prefer a mediator with great skill in the mediation process, even if she lacks subject-matter expertise. In such circumstances, the mediator need only have a rough understanding of the relevant law, customs and technology. In fact, too much subject-matter expertise could incline some mediators toward a more evaluative role, and could thereby interfere with developing creative solutions.

NOTES

1. Does the grid have implications for the roles of lawyers and their clients in mediation? According to one commentator:

> [t]o be effective, a lawyer must constantly remember that the dispute belongs to the client. During mediation the client makes decisions about the case. Sometimes these decisions are at variance with legal advice, and sometimes they are made while both the lawyer and a third party are present. This apparent loss of control makes some lawyers uncomfortable. * * * [Norman Brand, *Learning to Use the Mediation Process — A Guide for Lawyers*, 47 ARB. J. 6, 12 (Dec. 1992).]

Might lawyers feel more comfortable in one quadrant of the grid than others? Which quadrant do you think would give lawyers the greatest sense of control? Which is most similar to the settlement conferences lawyers experience in court?

2. Many mediators regard Riskin's "facilitative" mediation as the classic style of mediation, and training programs tend to be based on a facilitative approach. Nonetheless, evaluative approaches are common, especially in court-annexed mediation and in mediations with parties represented by lawyers. (Court-annexed mediation is discussed in Chapter 14.)

Some mediation scholars argue that evaluation is not an appropriate role for a mediator and that evaluative processes should not be called "mediation." They argue that the roles of evaluating and facilitating are at odds and that evaluation triggers an emphasis on positions, which is not helpful in mediation. *See, e.g.,* Lela P. Love, *The Top Ten Reasons Why Mediators Should Not Evaluate*, 24 FLA. ST. L. REV. 937 (1997). There are proposals to call a mixed process "mediation plus evaluation" in order to help parties and their attorneys identify their choices. *See* Lela P. Love & Kimberly K. Kovach, *ADR: An Eclectic Array of Processes, Rather than One Eclectic Process*, 2000 J. DISP. RESOL. 295.

Others respond that sophisticated parties should be able to choose the process that best meets their needs and that a "frank assessment of the risk" can be important in reducing a client's expectations. *See* John Bickerman, *Evaluative Mediator Responds*, 14 ALTERNATIVES TO THE HIGH COST OF LITIG. 70 (1996). They object to "ironclad formulas" and contend that if a recalcitrant party is making unreasonable demands, an evaluation can give the party "some insight into the default legal rules that govern the topic." Mediators should therefore remain "free to provide necessary guidance as to the outcomes that might obtain in the legal regime." Jeffrey W. Stempel, *The Inevitability of the Eclectic: Liberating ADR from Ideology*, 2000 J. DISP. RESOL. 247, 248.

Do you think that facilitating and evaluating are incompatible roles? How might a party who has received an unfavorable evaluation view the mediator's impartiality? If a central value of mediation is party self-determination, why should a mediator refuse to evaluate when a party requests it? Is a party who knows nothing about the applicable law or what the outcome might be in an adjudication effectively able to exercise self-determination? If a party is uninformed, what might be the consequences for the fairness of the outcome?

3. Are there guiding principles for an attorney selecting a mediator? Riskin provides the following advice:

> Often the litigation process encourages a narrow perspective on the dispute. If litigation-oriented lawyers are selecting the mediator, they may be inclined toward a litigation-like outcome, which is best provided by an evaluative-narrow mediator (a category in which retired-judge mediators are heavily represented). Unless the lawyers are sophisticated about mediation, however, they might see only the virtues of this approach — its simplicity and efficiency — and not its potential drawbacks.
>
> Such drawbacks include the risk that the evaluative-narrow approach could foreclose a creative, interest-based agreement. Similarly, a party originally inclined toward dealing collaboratively with underlying interests may learn during the mediation that the other side insists on a narrow approach and needs guidance from the mediator in order to reach resolution. For all these reasons, it may be wise to select a mediator whose background and experience make her versatile. [Riskin, 1994, at 114.]

4. From a client's perspective, are there disputes that are more appropriate for either broad or narrow approaches? Facilitative or evaluative? Are there issues for which the background legal regime is more (or less) relevant? Professor Stempel comments:

> [I]t may be that the mixture of facilitation and evaluation in mediation varies with the type of case under consideration as well as with the particular disputants and mediator involved. * * * [O]ne appropriately finds more facilitative mediation in certain types of cases and more evaluative mediation in other types of cases. For example, family law matters, particularly issues of child custody and visitation, appear to more closely track the facilitative model. Commercial matters such as contract damage claims are likely to see more evaluation. [Stempel, 200, at 250.]

If unreasonable demands, recalcitrant parties, and reliance on the "shadow of the law" make evaluation appropriate, are those characteristics more likely to be associated with certain types of cases? What about a personal injury case defended by an insurance company stemming from an accident between strangers? Dissolution of a partnership? A workplace dispute among co-workers? Some scholars argue that it is not possible to determine the appropriateness of an evaluative approach from the type of case. (*See* Love & Kovach, 2000.)

5. In a recent article, Professor Riskin revised the terminology of his grid to clarify that the "essence" of mediation is facilitation. He replaced "facilitative" with "elicitive" and "evaluative" with "directive." Leonard L. Riskin, *Decisionmaking in Mediation: The New Old Grid and the New New Grid System*, 79 NOTRE DAME L. REV. 1 (2003). The problem with the term "evaluation" is that it describes a range of activities, which "could range from behavior that is principally informative (e.g., "Your case is weak on x.") to directive (e.g., "You should pay $ y."), which I considered an extreme form of evaluation." *Id.* at 13. Riskin's real concern was not with evaluation per se, but with directive threats to party self-determination. Riskin explains:

> I failed to emphasize that evaluation by the mediator — depending on the exact circumstances and the kind of evaluation presented — can either foster or impair self-determination, or both foster and impair it. * * * [O]ften mediators give evaluations without intending to direct the parties toward a particular solution. In addition, when evaluation by the mediator offers the only realistic opportunity for a party to understand the likely alternative outcome — say, in a court or administrative proceeding — it might support self-determination for that party by fostering informed consent; but it also might impair self-determination by limiting either party's imagination or precluding their efforts to address underlying interests. In such situations — which can arise when a mediation participant does not have ready access to a lawyer (for example, in some mediations connected with small claims or divorce proceedings) or has a lawyer who is unfamiliar with the relevant law or litigation practices — evaluation (in the sense of a prediction about what would happen in a court or administrative proceeding) also may promote other values, such as fairness, and social policies associated with the relevant law.

> And there is a still more fundamental problem. The greatest threat to self-determination is caused by behavior that I placed at the extreme north end of the evaluative continuum, behavior "intended to direct some or all of the outcomes of a mediation." I refer to a mediator who "urges/pushes parties to accept . . . settlement." Such interventions, however, do not rightly belong on the same continuum as most other evaluations, because, as I maintained above, evaluations are not necessarily intended to direct an outcome and do not always have that effect. In retrospect, I should have labeled them "directive" and distinguished them from "evaluative" interventions which, as explained above, can be either directive or non-directive, or both. [*Id.* at 19–20.]

6. Riskin's revision suggests that part of the disagreement about evaluation might be due to terminology. How would you categorize the following alternative mediator statements?

[M]ediator to defendant in a personal injury case[:]

"You understand that I am not a judge or an arbiter, and, in fact, no one can accurately predict what a particular judge or jury would do in a given case, but I'd like to review with you what the plaintiff's attorney just said about the question of liability. As you listen to me restate the point, please consider how a judge or jury might react."

* * *

"This case is worth something between $25,000 and $35,000. Your demand for $100,000 is out of the ballpark."

* * *

[M]ediator to father in a custody and visitation case[:]

"Your proposal is that your child spends three days with you a week, including those weeks when school is in session. That will involve a bus commute for Danny to and from school, an hour and a half each way, when he is staying with you. Have you considered how spending three hours on a bus on school days will impact your son?"

* * *

"It would be psychologically damaging for a seven year-old child to spend three hours on a school bus he uses only once or twice a week." [Love & Kovach, 2000, at 304–05.]

They are all in some sense "evaluative," aren't they? But who is conducting the evaluation? What is the form of each statement? Professors Love and Kovach consider the first statement in each pair to be facilitative "reality testing" and the second to be "neutral evaluation." Is using a question enough to avoid being directive? Consider the following analysis:

The language of the mediator is important. The range of appropriateness is wide, making determination of whether a statement is an imperative less clear as the mediator moves across the range. That is, it would probably be clear that (1) "you should sell the house" is an imperative, and therefore inappropriate. But are the following imperatives? (2) "Have you considered selling the house?" (3) "You may want to consider selling the house." (4) "Do you want to consider selling the house as one of your options?" If these are not imperatives, what is the distinction between them?

* * *

Statement 1 is a clear command to act. Question 2 allows the party to consider or not consider the act. However, question 2 could also be an embedded suggestion if the client hears it as a suggestion to act;

in that situation it becomes an imperative. Statement 3 is an offering to the client that places the right of selection on the client. As in 2, this may be received by the client as a suggestion/imperative. Statement 4, on the other hand, places the offer in the context of a range of options explicitly making the right of selection the clients. [John M. Haynes, *Mediation and Therapy: An Alternative View*, 10 MEDIATION Q. 21, 26–27 (1992).]

2. PROBLEM-SOLVING THROUGH UNDERSTANDING

Riskin's facilitative mediation is generally regarded as the prototypical problem-solving approach. The following article describes an approach to mediation that is set in the framework of problem-solving, but adds an emphasis on the parties working together with an understanding of the law and the conflict.

GARY FRIEDMAN & JACK HIMMELSTEIN, RESOLVING CONFLICT TOGETHER: THE UNDERSTANDING-BASED MODEL OF MEDIATION, 4 J. Amer. Arb. 225, 226–30 (2005)[*]

A. Four Interacting Principles Guide This Work

1. *Developing Understanding:* The overarching goal of this approach to mediation is to resolve conflict through understanding. Deeper understanding by the parties of their own and each other's perspectives, priorities, and concerns enables them to work through their conflict together. With an enhanced understanding of the whole situation, the parties are able to shape creative and mutually rewarding solutions that reflect their personal, business, and economic interests.

We, therefore, rely heavily on *the power of understanding* rather than the power of coercion or persuasion to drive the mediation process. We want *everything* to be understood, from how we will work together, to the true nature of the conflict in which the parties are enmeshed, where it came from, how it grew, and how they might free themselves from it. We believe the parties should understand the legal implications of their case, but that the law should not usurp or direct our mediation. We put as much weight on the personal, practical, or business related aspects of any conflict as on the legal aspect. In finding a resolution, we want the parties to recognize what is important to themselves in the dispute, and to understand what is important to the other side. We strive for a resolution to satisfy both.

2. *Going Underneath the Problem:* Experience has shown us that *conflicts are best resolved by uncovering what lies underneath* them. Conflict is rarely just about money, or who did what to whom. It also has subjective dimensions, the beliefs, and assumptions of the individuals caught in its grasp, their feelings, such as anger and fear, the need to assign blame, the desire for self-justification. There are also assumptions about the nature of conflict itself, which support the conflict and keep it going-like the theory of the exclusivity of right and wrong. And there are ideas about how conflicts must be

resolved-such as the belief that the other person must change his position or that an authoritative third party must decide the outcome.

We need breadth and depth of understanding to hope to break out of such a complex and multilayered situation, what we call a "conflict trap." Repeatedly, we find that the basis for resolution comes from discovering together with the parties what lies at the very heart of their dispute, which is often a surprise to the parties, and which often has a profound [e]ffect on their work together.

3. *Party Responsibility:* This approach is also grounded in the simple premise that the person in the best position to determine the wisest solution to a dispute is not a third party, whether court, judge, or mediator, but the individuals who created and are living the problem. Therefore, *we ask disputants to assume the primary responsibility for working things through, and we ask that they work things through together.* As we like to think about it: Let the parties own their conflict.

4. *Working Together:* When we promote *working together,* we mean that all meetings with the mediator occur with all parties present (including lawyers if they have a role). There is "no caucusing," no shuttling back and forth; no secrets to keep from one party or the other; no private meetings, except for those between the parties and their counsel. Instead of being responsible for fashioning an acceptable solution, the mediator's job is to enable the parties to reach a mutually agreeable solution together.

We believe the impulse to work through conflict together is a natural part of the human condition, though it may be nascent, buried, or blocked. It is hardly recognized in the legal community, but we have seen it, waiting to be tapped and given room for expression. And we have seen it succeed for many thousands of individuals and organizations. * * *

The [Understanding-Based] model shares much in common with a number of other approaches to mediation. For example, we stress the importance of articulating interests that underlie the parties conflicting positions and developing solutions that will serve those interests. There is also much that distinguishes this approach.

B. Parties Responsibility and Non-Caucus Approach

In the Understanding-Based Model, the emphasis is on the parties' responsibility for the decisions they will make. In this approach, the assumption is that it is the parties, not the professionals, who have the best understanding of what underlies the dispute and are in the best position to find the solution. It is *their* conflict, and *they* hold the key t , reaching a solution that best serves them both. Meeting together with the p .rties (and counsel) follows from these assumptions about parties' responsibility.

Many other approaches to mediation recommend that the mediator shuttle back and forth between the parties (caucusing), gaining information that he or she holds confidential. Our central problem with caucusing is that the mediator ends up with the fullest picture of the problem and is, therefore, in the best position to solve it. The mediator, armed with that fuller view, can readily urge or manipulate the parties to the end he or she shapes. The emphasis here, in contrast, is on understanding and voluntariness as the basis for resolving the conflict rather than persuasion or coercion.

We view the mediator's role in the Understanding-based approach as assisting the parties to gain sufficient understanding of their own and each other's perspective so as to be able to decide together how to resolve their dispute. The parties not only know first hand everything that transpires; they have control over fashioning an outcome that will work for both. And they also participate with the mediator (and counsel) in designing a process by which they can honor what they each value and help them reach a result that reflects what is important to both of them. As mediators, our goal is to support the parties in working through their conflict together — in ways that respect their differing perspectives, needs, and interests as well as their common goals.

To work in this way is challenging for both the mediator and the parties. The parties' motivation and willingness to work together is critical to the success of this approach. Mediators often assume that the parties (and their counsel) simply do not want to work together, and therefore keep the parties apart. In our experience, many parties (and counsel) simply accept that they will not work together and that the mediator will be responsible for crafting the solution. But once educated how staying in the same room might be valuable, many are motivated to do so. If the parties (and the mediator) are willing, working together throughout can be as rewarding as it is demanding.

C. Role of Law and Lawyers

Mediators tend to be divided in how they approach the role of law in mediation. Some rely heavily on what a court would decide if the case were to go to trial, authoritatively suggesting or implying that law should be the controlling standard used to end the conflict. Other mediators, concerned that the parties might simply defer too readily to the law and miss the opportunity to find more creative decisions, try to keep the law out of mediation altogether.

In this model, we welcome lawyers' participation and we include the law. But we do not assume that the parties will or should rely solely or primarily on the law. Rather, the importance the parties give to the law is up to them. Our goals are (1) to educate the parties about the law and possible legal outcomes and (2) to support their freedom to fashion their own creative solutions that may differ from what a court might decide. In this way, the parties learn that they can together reach agreements that respond to both their individual interests and their common goals while also being well informed about their legal rights and the judicial alternatives to a mediated settlement.

This approach to the law's place in mediation draws upon lawyers' knowledge and skills in ways both similar to and different from their traditional roles. To participate in this problem-solving approach to mediation requires many lawyers to shift from reliance on a stance of adversary advocacy to one of collaborative support. For some lawyers, this can be a challenge, but a rewarding one.

As we view the lawyers' role in mediation, they are there to protect their clients and to inform them about the legal alternative, both of which are quite comfortable for most lawyers. At the same time, they are also called upon to support their clients' active participation and open dialogue, which may be a stretch for many lawyers. The lawyers also participate by helping their clients design the mediation process and supporting their clients as the parties create the solutions to their conflict that may be quite different from what a court might do but which better serve what they really care about.

NOTES

1. What do Friedman and Himmelstein mean when they state that lawyers need to move from "a stance of adversary advocacy to one of collaborative support?" Do they mean collaborative support for the other side or for the lawyer's client? Are lawyers well trained in law school to "support their clients' active participation and open dialogue?" What type of relationship would the lawyer need with the client?

2. In contrast to the understanding-based model of mediation, an economic analysis emphasizes caucusing in analyzing the value a mediator brings to a negotiation by controlling the flow of information. Hidden information can be a major impediment to settlement. "By shuttling back and forth between meetings with individual disputants, mediators can collect and distribute private information." (Brown & Ayres, 1994 at 326.) Brown and Ayres contend that mediators do this by sending "noisy translations of information disclosed during private caucuses." (*Id.* at 328.) For example, a mediator might determine based on caucuses that there is a zone of agreement between the parties or that a set of trade-offs might bring the parties closer to agreement. "Revealing that there are gains from trade or that a particular set of trades might be acceptable to the other side has the effect of indirectly disclosing to each party some of the mediator's private discussions with the other side." (*Id.* at 327.)

This economic theory helps to explain an important aspect of mediation practice: While mediators need to keep certain information confidential, they also need to transfer new, valuable information to disputants. Some of the information transferred will not be in the same form as it was when the mediator gained access to it. As transferred to a disputant, selected information may be "noisy." The mediator may take X, a piece of information learned in confidence from disputant A, and later ask disputant B "how would you react if your disputant A had decided to do X?" This process of filtering and conveying ideas to get negotiation movement and new information from a disputant lies at the heart of the mediation process.

How do you think Friedman and Himmelstein might respond? If the understanding-based model of mediation does not rely on caucuses, what is the special contribution of the mediator? Are there alternatives to "noisy translation" by the mediator that can foster the flow of information in a joint session? Friedman and Himmelstein stress the need for the parties to take responsibility for the process. Is direct information exchange risky? Does it require a different level of commitment from the parties?

3. Transformative Mediation

Many successful mediators focus on the larger issues between the parties that transcend settlement. Their vision is said to be "transformative," because they assist the parties to create new relationships. (*See* Kolb, 1994, at 466–68.) In a thoughtful book, Robert A. Baruch Bush and Joseph Folger use this term to identify a novel approach to mediation. (Bush & Folger, 1994; *see also* Della Noce, 1999.) They reject intervention designed to settle a dispute through problem-solving in favor of a relationship-oriented approach that is designed to transform disputants into relatively self-sufficient problem solvers. Bush and Folger believe that the mere goal of resolving the dispute tends to overstate the problem-solving or settlement nature of mediation and stress too strongly the idea that the mediator's goal is to create adversary satisfaction by terminating the dispute. Instead, they contend that a mediator should seek to help disputants attain *empowerment* — an improved sense of the disputant's own problem-solving capabilities — and *recognition* — a better appreciation and awareness of the adversary's situation.

Robert A. Baruch Bush & Joseph P. Folger, The Promise of Mediation 81–85 (1994) *

To construct a different approach to mediation practice, we have to begin with the underlying basis on which practice rests and reexamine our views of both what conflict is and what the ideal response to conflict should be. Rethinking the problem-solving orientation starts by questioning the premise that conflicts need to be viewed as problems in the first place. A different premise would suggest that disputes can be viewed *not* as problems at all but as opportunities for moral growth and transformation. This different view is the *transformative orientation* to conflict.

In this transformative orientation, a conflict is first and foremost a potential occasion for growth in two critical and interrelated dimensions of human morality. The first dimension involves strengthening the self. This occurs through realizing and strengthening one's inherent human capacity for dealing with difficulties of all kinds by engaging in conscious and deliberate reflection, choice, and action. The second dimension involves reaching beyond the self to relate to others. This occurs through realizing and strengthening one's inherent human capacity for experiencing and expressing concern and consideration for others, especially others whose situation is "different" from one's own. Moral thinkers * * * suggest that full moral development involves an *integration* of individual autonomy and concern for others, of strength and compassion. Therefore, bringing out both of these inherent capacities *together* is the essence of human moral maturity. In the transformative view, conflicts are seen as opportunities for developing and exercising both of these capacities, and thus moving toward full moral development.

A conflict confronts each party with a challenge, a difficulty or adversity to be grappled with. This challenge presents parties with the opportunity to clarify for themselves their needs and values, what causes them dissatisfaction and satisfaction. It also gives them the chance to discover and strengthen

---

their own resources for addressing both substantive concerns and relational issues. In short, conflict affords people the opportunity to develop and exercise both self-determination and self-reliance. Moreover, the emergence of conflict confronts each party with a differently situated other who holds a contrary viewpoint. This encounter presents each party with an opportunity for acknowledging the perspectives of others. It gives the individual the chance to feel and express some degree of understanding and concern for another, despite diversity and disagreement. Conflict thus gives people the occasion to develop and exercise respect and consideration for others. In sum, conflicts embody valuable opportunities for both dimensions of moral growth, perhaps to a greater degree than most other human experiences. This may be why the Chinese have a tradition of using identical characters to depict crisis and opportunity.

In the transformative orientation, the ideal response to a conflict is not to solve "the problem." Instead, it is to *help transform* the individuals involved, in both dimensions of moral growth. Responding to conflicts productively means utilizing the opportunities they present to change and transform the parties as human beings. It means encouraging and helping the parties to use the conflict to realize and actualize their inherent capacities both for strength of self and for relating to others. It means bringing out the intrinsic goodness that lies within the parties as human beings. If this is done, then the response to conflict itself helps transform individuals from fearful, defensive, or self-centered beings into confident, responsive, and caring ones, ultimately transforming society as well. * * *

* * *

Success has different meanings in the problem-solving and transformative approaches to mediation. In problem-solving mediation, success is achieved when an agreement is reached that solves the problem and satisfies all sides. At the simplest level, problem-solving mediation defines the objective as improving the parties' *situation* from what it was before. The transformative approach instead defines the objective as improving *the parties themselves* from what they were before. In transformative mediation, success is achieved when the parties as persons are changed for the better, to some degree, by what has occurred in the mediation process. More specifically, transformative mediation is successful when the parties experience growth in both dimensions of moral development mentioned earlier — developing both the capacity for strength of self and the capacity for relating to others. These are the objectives of *empowerment* and *recognition*.

In a transformative approach, empowerment and recognition are the two most important effects that mediation can produce, and achieving them is its most important objective. * * * In the most general terms, empowerment is achieved when disputing parties experience a strengthened awareness of their own self-worth and their own ability to deal with whatever difficulties they face, regardless of external constraints. Recognition is achieved when, given some degree of empowerment, disputing parties experience an expanded willingness to acknowledge and be responsive to other parties' situations and common human qualities.

NOTES

1. Bush and Folger contend that empowered participants who truly appreciate the interests and viewpoints of their opponents can optimally work to achieve their own mutually acceptable solutions. Even when immediate agreements are not attained during relationship-oriented mediation, Bush and Folger maintain that empowered parties will be better able to handle future bargaining interactions due to their new found problem-solving skills (Bush & Folger, 1994, at 200–01).

2. The Bush-Folger theory that mediators should strive to attain disputant empowerment and recognition is not shared by all mediators. Some mediators have a very simple goal, namely, settlement of a case. For a critique of "transformative mediation" that finds a lack of evidence that such mediation really works, see Neal Milner, *Mediation and Political Theory: A Critique of Bush and Folger*, 21 Law & Soc. Inquiry 737 (1996).

3. The transformative mediation model was adopted by the U.S. Postal Service for its REDRESS program for disputes that involve allegations of discrimination by its workers. Disputes between employees and supervisors are mediated during working hours by outside contractors trained in transformative techniques. The program uses participation rate rather than settlement rate as a measure of its success. Since the program began in 1994, Professor Lisa Bingham has studied its implementation. She reports high levels of participant satisfaction with the mediation process (91–92%), the mediators (96–97%), and the outcomes (ranging from 64% for complainants to 69% for supervisors). She documented a significant drop in formal discrimination complaints and positive changes in communication patterns during mediation. There is also evidence that communication skills were taken back to the workplace; the rate at which disputes were resolved before they reached mediation increased over five years from 2% to 14%. (*See* Lisa B. Bingham, *Mediation at Work: Transforming Workplace Conflict at the United States Postal Service*, IBM Center for the Business of Government (2003), available at http://www.businessofgovernment.org/pdfs/Bingham_Report.pdf.)

4. As you read, Bush and Folger distinguish transformative mediation from problem-solving. Is there a relationship between Bush's and Folger's "recognition" in transformative mediation and "understanding" in Friedman's and Himmelstein's model? Even if the goals of problem-solving and transformative mediation are different, do you think mediator strategies and techniques are entirely different in these approaches? Would empowerment and recognition help parties in a problem-solving mediation?

4. OTHER MODELS OF MEDIATION

There are additional approaches to categorizing mediator styles. For example, based on a study of labor mediators, Professor Kolb distinguished "dealmakers" who decide what is best for the parties and control the process to get them to accept it, from "orchestrators," who concentrate on opening communication channels and getting the parties to acknowledge unrealistic expectations. (*See* Kolb, 1983 (describing state and federal labor mediator styles).)

Anthropology and sociology Professors Silbey and Merry observed a "bargaining" style of mediation and a contrasting "therapeutic" style of mediation. In bargaining mode, the purpose is to reach a settlement, while the therapeutic approach concentrates on communication with the purpose of "help[ing] people reach mutual understanding through collective agreements." (Susan S. Silbey & Sally E. Merry, *Mediator Settlement Strategies*, 8 L. & POL'Y Q. 7, 19 (1986)). In the bargaining style, mediators rely more heavily on caucuses and seem to view disputes as a result of differing interests that can be resolved through trade-offs. In the therapeutic style, parties are encouraged to express emotions and mediators maximize direct contact between the parties.

Another taxonomy of mediation emphasizes the role of norms in the process. Professor Waldman maintains that mediation comprises three distinct models: norm-generating, norm-educating, and norm-advocating forms of mediation. (Ellen A. Waldman, *Identifying the Role of Social Norms in Mediation: A Multiple Model Approach*, 48 HASTINGS L. REV. 703, (1997).) The norm-generating model follows Lon Fuller's traditional conception of mediation, with its focus on creating norms. Parties are encouraged to consider innovative options without the constraint of social norms. Under the norm-educating model of mediation,

> the parties should be educated about their legal rights. However, if one or both of the parties decides to waive those rights, the mediator does not object. The norm-educating mediator views the parties, not society, as rightful possessor of the dispute. Consequently, the parties may, if they choose, reach a resolution that does not correspond entirely with societal norms. [*Id.* at 741.]

Waldman maintains that the norm-educating model is often used in divorce mediation and in other disputes where legal and social norms are an important backdrop. The mediator in the norm-advocating model goes one step further. Waldman characterizes an example as follows:

> [T]he mediator not only educated the parties about the relevant legal and ethical norms, but also insisted on their incorporation into the agreement. In this sense, her role extended beyond that of an educator; she became, to some degree, a safeguarder of social norms and values. She apprised the parties of relevant social norms, not simply to facilitate the parties' informed decisionmaking and provide a beginning framework for discussion; she provided information about legal and ethical norms to secure their implementation. [*Id.* at 745.]

This approach is not common, but Waldman finds it appropriate for disputes in which there are important societal interests not represented by the parties, such as environmental disputes, and certain bioethical disputes.

NOTES

1. This discussion of characterizations of mediators' approaches is not exhaustive. How can an individual with a dispute be expected to distinguish among the various approaches to mediation when many lawyers do not even know the difference between mediation and arbitration? How will you, as a lawyer, approach this problem?

2. Riskin's grid seems to fall primarily within Silbey's and Merry's "bargaining" characterization. Have you seen elements of a "therapeutic" approach in any of the other mediation models described above?

3. Is norm-education related to any of the ways in which a mediator might use some types of evaluative techniques? What is its relationship to the understanding-based model of mediation? Is it preferable for the mediator or for attorneys to take responsibility for norm education? What are the risks associated with the mediator taking on this role?

4. Do you think "norm-advocating" should be included as part of the category of dispute resolution we call "mediation"? What about "dealmakers" in the labor context? Are either of these mediator approaches at odds with any of the essential characteristics of mediation? Are there reasons to argue that "secur[ing]" the "implementation" of norms should be limited to adjudicatory settings? Does it make a difference if the parties agree with the norms the mediator advocates?

5. Do the various mediator roles have implications for how a lawyer and client should select a mediator? Should a mediator who is not a lawyer use evaluative techniques or a norm-educating or a norm-advocating model in a dispute with significant legal issues? What about a lawyer who is a mediation expert but does not practice in the area of law at issue? Are lawyer-mediators qualified to undertake a therapeutic approach? A transformative approach?

C. THE STAGES OF MEDIATION

1. THE PRELIMINARY STAGE

a. Mediator Selection

If the parties are not assigned a mediator in a court-annexed mediation program, they must select one before the introductory joint session. This process need not, but can be, contentious. ADR sponsors are helpful in supplying lists of approved mediators.

When negotiating parties seek the assistance of neutral intervenors, they should carefully evaluate the type of mediation assistance they desire. Do they want the help of a mediator who is willing to evaluate? This may depend on the nature of the barriers the parties have faced in unassisted negotiation. For example, if one party has an unrealistic view of the value of the case, an evaluation may be helpful to break an impasse should one occur in mediation. Do they want the help of a transformative mediator? Parties in an ongoing relationship may be particularly interested in this approach. Do they want a focus on reaching a settlement of the current dispute? Then perhaps another style would be more appropriate. Are they comfortable with a process that will be conducted in joint session? Then the understanding model might be appropriate.

Once parties determine the type of mediation assistance they prefer, they must decide how many mediators they need. In the vast majority of negotiation situations, one proficient neutral should be sufficient. So long as that individual has the respect of both parties, he or she should be capable of providing the requisite help. In some cases, however, multiple mediators may be beneficial. If unusually technical negotiation issues are involved, the parties may want neutral intervenors who are both substantive experts and process experts. Since they may not be able to find both qualities in the same person, they may wish to use two or three neutrals who may each provide different expertise.

When family disputes are involved, pairs of mediators are often employed. One is usually familiar with the legal issues and the negotiation process, while the other is a social worker or a counselor. The former tries to enhance the bargaining interaction, while the latter works to diminish the psychological trauma affecting the disputants and their children.

Multiple neutrals may also be required in cases in which mutual distrust or significant cultural differences would preclude the selection of a single mediator. In these instances, the parties may each name a preferred neutral and have those two individuals select a third person who would be relatively acceptable to both sides. For example, international business controversies may concern firms from diverse areas of the world that do not trust neutrals from the opposing company's culture. Each firm could select a neutral from its own culture and authorize those two to select the third from a neutral nation.

In some cases, parties can readily agree upon the designation of a mutually respected mediator. In many cases, however, the lack of inter-party trust and conflict-related animosity may preclude joint agreement on this vital issue. Parties unable to agree upon a single neutral may request assistance from private or public conciliation services. Private entities such as the American Arbitration Association, the International Chamber of Commerce, the Lawyers Mediation Service, or J.A.M.S. may provide lists of qualified mediators. In some instances, local courts or government agencies may provide the names of potential intervenors. If particular expertise would be helpful, the parties may request the names of individuals who possess the requisite knowledge. After the parties receive a list of qualified neutrals, they should evaluate the backgrounds of those people to ensure their impartiality and acceptability. If they have previously acted as advocates, which sides did they represent? If prior mediation clients are listed, the parties may wish to telephone those persons to determine their views of the mediators. Some parties even telephone the candidates themselves to ascertain their levels of professional experience, their mediation philosophies, and their fee schedules.

Once the parties have reviewed the list of qualified neutrals, they can select the most acceptable candidate. If they are unable to agree upon a single person, they may agree to strike names alternately until one remains. That individual then becomes their intervenor. In rare instances in which the parties are not satisfied with any of the names on the provided list, they may request an additional list of candidates. Since party confidence in the designated neutral is critical to that individual's capacity to provide effective mediation assistance, the disputants should take the time to select someone with whom they are likely to feel comfortable.

b.   Timing of Initial Mediation Intervention

The timing of initial mediation efforts can be crucial with respect to both litigation settlement discussions and transactional talks. If neutral intervention occurs prematurely, the parties may be unreceptive. On the other hand, if conciliatory attempts begin in a belated manner, the parties may already be locked into unyielding positions that will be difficult to alter.

On many occasions, plaintiffs are not receptive to settlement discussions at the outset of litigation. They are angry and want to obtain retribution for the wrongs committed against them. At this point, they view their legal representatives as gladiators who have been retained to vanquish their evil adversaries. Defendants feel wrongly accused and demand complete vindication. When parties have this mind-set, negotiations — even when mediator assisted — are unlikely to produce beneficial results. Legal advocates and prospective conciliators must wait until these persons have begun to recognize the monetary and psychological costs associated with continued warfare before they can effectively encourage transition from the gladiator mode to a conciliatory state. Premature neutral intervention is unlikely to be fruitful.

Once plaintiff and defendant attorneys have become knowledgeable regarding the factual and legal issues involved and have apprised their respective clients of the costs and risks associated with contemporary litigation, the time is ripe for settlement discussions. During the early stages of the litigation process, the parties often contemplate settlement possibilities with relatively open minds. They have not yet convinced themselves of the seeming invincibility of their respective positions. At this point, gentle but persistent encouragement by neutral intervenors should be sufficient to ensure continued settlement discussions.

In some cases, litigants are unable to commence settlement talks on their own — usually because the parties naively believe that whoever initiates settlement efforts will exude a weakness that may be exploited by their opponent. Trial judges who encounter such circumstances can permit the parties to save face by initiating the negotiation process for them (Rubin & Brown, 1975, at 47, 58). Even in the absence of a court-annexed mediation program, judges may broach the topic of settlement and encourage the litigants to explore the operative circumstances by themselves. They may suggest that a judicial officer is available to participate more actively at any time either or both parties request assistance. They should also advise the parties of the benefits they may derive from outside mediative intervention.

It is the immediacy of impending trial dates that induces most attorneys and their clients to acknowledge that increasing financial and emotional pressures militate in favor of non-adjudicated resolutions. Settlement pressure is effectively enhanced by judges who work diligently during the pretrial stages to keep cases moving inexorably toward trial. Unnecessary delays should be avoided whenever possible.

Shortly before scheduled trial dates, the litigants are more anxious to avoid the need for the high cost and imposed solutions of formal adjudications. The parties are psychologically exhausted. At this moment, the litigants are most amenable to conciliative assistance. Either or both parties may indicate a receptiveness to mediator intervention. If they fail to do so, judges should encourage neutral involvement by a judicial official or an outside individual.

Judges and mediators should conversely understand that once trials have commenced, the parties tend to become temporarily disinterested in on-going settlement discussions. By this point, the economies associated with mutual resolutions have significantly diminished, the parties are wholly prepared for adjudication, and each side is psychologically convinced that it will achieve beneficial results (Kahneman & Tversky, 1995, at 46–50). As the adjudication process unfolds, however, unanticipated developments may induce one or both parties to reconsider the benefits that may be derived from further settlement discussions. Mediators who felt ineffective at the outset of the trial may now encounter greater party receptivity.

The timing of initial intervention is also likely to be critical with respect to transactional negotiations. Business parties must initially assess the economic benefits that may be derived from contemplated transactions and plan their opening positions. Unlike many litigants, business parties usually have no difficulty initiating discussions. If talks are progressing well, there may be no need for mediative assistance. Nonetheless, if problems are encountered, the parties should acknowledge the benefits that may be derived from neutral intervention. Too often, business firms that are unable to achieve mutual accords on their own give up and walk away. If they continue to believe that mutually beneficial deals could be structured, they should not hesitate to request mediative assistance.

When transactional discussions are not fruitful, the parties should not wait until a complete cessation of talks before they ask for neutral intervention. Once unyielding final positions are reached, the parties are likely to give up on the current negotiations and begin to contemplate other business partners. It thus behooves business negotiators to seek mediative help *before* they become wholly unreceptive to further discussions.

c. Party and Mediator Preparation

Parties frequently fail to appreciate the fact that mediation is *assisted negotiation*. As a result, they go to scheduled mediation sessions unprepared. This lack of planning causes many advocates to be less forceful than they could have been. It also undermines the capacity of the neutral intervenors to perform their functions effectively.

Parties and their attorneys should prepare for scheduled mediation as they would for any negotiation (Kovach, 1994, at 77–79). They must be thoroughly familiar with the operative facts and relevant legal doctrines. They should also review the previous bargaining sessions with their opponents, to comprehend how their transaction has developed and why they may have been unable to achieve mutually acceptable terms on their own. They must appreciate the underlying needs and interests of their own client and those of the other side. They must remember the negotiating styles of their opponents.

Advocates must realize the need to be prepared *to negotiate* during the impending mediation sessions — with the neutral intervenor and directly or indirectly with their opponents. They should thus formulate principled opening positions that can be divided into components and be rationally defended on a component-by-component basis. They must reconsider their initially established goals in light of their previous negotiations with their adversaries. They should either reconfirm the propriety of their prior bargaining objectives or develop rationales to support their modified goals. They must finally review their nonsettlement alternatives to ensure they do not make the mistake of accepting mediator-generated terms that are actually worse than what would happen if no agreement were achieved. This error occasionally happens when parties try to please the neutral participants and forget about their own needs and interests. Parties must always remember that no agreement is preferable to one that is less beneficial than their best nonsettlement option.

They should attempt to become familiar with the mediation style of the designated conciliator. If they have not dealt with this person before, advocates should not hesitate to ask other attorneys about the mediation style of the neutral participant.

The attorney and client should discuss division of responsibilities for their presentation of the problem in the initial joint session and who will take the lead in negotiation. The assignment of responsibilities will depend on the client, the dispute, and the barriers to resolution, topics discussed further in section E. Clients should be cautioned about nonverbal signals, to minimize the likelihood they will inadvertently disclose confidential information to their opponents.

Is the mediator someone who likes to interact directly with the clients themselves? If yes, each client must be prepared for this possibility. In some instances, it may be beneficial to give the client a mini-course on negotiating to enable that person to forcefully advance his own interests when asked to do so. This type of preparation is particularly important with respect to mediators who ask the legal representatives to leave the room so that she may discuss the transaction with the clients alone. If an attorney thinks that his client would be at an unfair disadvantage if she had to negotiate without the assistance of counsel, the lawyer should refuse to leave the client alone.

Designated mediators should also prepare for scheduled sessions to the extent possible (Kovach, 1994, at 70–76). They should review any written materials given to them by the parties to familiarize themselves with the basic issues, the current party positions, and apparent party interests. Mediators involved with litigation disputes generally receive copies of the complaint, answer, and relevant motions. These documents can provide them with important information. Even neutrals dealing with transactional controversies may be given copies of prior proposals and supporting position statements. These can be quite informative.

It can be beneficial for mediators to become familiar with advocate negotiating styles prior to scheduled meetings. They may ask other mediators or even other advocates they know about the individuals with whom they must interact. For example, when former President Carter was preparing for his Camp David meetings with Egypt's Anwar Sadat and Israel's Menachem Begin, he reviewed detailed psychological profiles on each that had been prepared for him by United States intelligence experts (Kolb, 1994, at 377). He believed that this information was particularly helpful when he was attempting to determine the appeals that would be likely to persuade the foreign leaders involved and the topics he should avoid discussing.

d. Preliminary Mediator-Party Contact

When parties first select a mediator or a neutral, the parties either contact that individual or that person contacts the parties. It is imperative that these contacts be handled in a manner that avoids any appearance of partiality (Moore, 1996, at 81–97). One party frequently telephones the mediator to inform that person of his/her appointment and to schedule the first meeting. While it is entirely appropriate for the contacting party to describe the general controversy, many mediators are hesitant to have the caller describe their own side's position. They fear that such one-sided communication may cause the other side to suspect possible mediator bias. Similar procedures are generally followed if the mediator contacts each party separately.

To avoid possible misunderstandings, parties often arrange conference calls that permit them to speak to the neutral intervenor together. Mediators who must initially telephone the parties frequently use this same technique to communicate with both sides simultaneously. Nonetheless, other neutrals consider these precautions unnecessary. They do not hesitate to call the parties separately or to accept ex parte communications and to discuss particular party positions during these exchanges. They assume that both sides will recognize that they are doing this and will not allow these contacts to compromise their impartiality.

During their preliminary communications with the parties, mediators generally provide a brief summary of their view of the mediation process (Kovach, 2000, at 106–09). They emphasize their impartial function and the fact they do not plan to support the positions of either side. They remind the participants that they lack the authority to impose any terms the parties do not find mutually acceptable. Most note that all mediation discussions will remain confidential and may not be used in subsequent judicial or arbitral proceedings. If voluntary mediation is involved, mediators should be certain the parties have knowingly agreed to participate in the conciliation process. This is especially important when parties are not represented by legal counsel (Nolan-Haley, 1999, at 832–33).

2. THE INITIAL SESSION

Most mediators prefer to conduct the initial meeting at a neutral location — the mediator's office or another non-party site (Slaikeu, 1996, at 65–66). They reasonably fear that if they meet at the offices of one of the parties, the other side will feel intimidated or disrespected. Nonetheless, when the parties themselves express a desire to meet at one side's place of business, neutrals normally honor that request.

An ideal meeting room has enough space to accommodate all of the participants, it is sufficiently private to preclude unwanted interruptions, and it has external space that may be used for separate caucus sessions by the parties alone or with mediator involvement. The furniture should be arranged in a nonconfrontational configuration. When bargaining adversaries who have been unable to achieve mutual accords interact, they tend to sit directly across from one another in highly combative positions. They often sit with their arms folded across their chests and with their legs crossed — highly unreceptive postures. Neutral intervenors should try to create a more conciliatory atmosphere (Kagel & Kelly, 1989, at 109).

Whenever possible, the participants should be encouraged to address each other on a first name basis to reinforce the informal and personal nature of the interaction. It is generally easier for people to disagree with impersonal opponents than personalized adversaries.

Mediators should assume control over the sessions (Slaikeu, 1996, at 75–76). Someone must determine how the discussions are going to proceed, and the neutral participants are in the best position to do this. If they fail to assume a leadership role, the negotiations may deteriorate into unproductive adversarial exchanges. The establishment of mediator control also enhances the ultimate capacity of the neutral intervenors to generate discussions that are most likely to produce beneficial results.

a. Mediator's Opening Statement

As soon as the parties are comfortable, the mediator should explain the mediation process (Slaikeu, 1996, at 77–80; Kovach, 1994, at 82–85). This is especially important when inexperienced advocates or clients are present. The neutral intervenors should emphasize the fact they lack the authority to impose settlement terms and that the process belongs to the parties themselves. Mediation is not a win-lose adjudication, but potentially a win-win form of assisted negotiation. The mediators are merely present to encourage interparty bargaining and facilitate the consideration of alternative proposals. The parties will have the final say with respect to any terms that may be agreed upon.

Confidentiality is a crucial aspect of the mediation process. This factor encourages the participants to speak openly about their interests, concerns, and desires. If they thought that their candid disclosures could be used against them in subsequent proceedings, few participants would be forthcoming and little progress could be made. Most mediators specifically remind litigants that evidentiary rules generally preclude the admission of settlement discussions in subsequent arbitral or judicial proceedings (Fed. R. Evid. 408; Kovach, 1994, at 144; Kirtley, 1995).

Confidentiality is especially important with respect to disclosures made during separate caucus sessions conducted by the mediator with each side. Neutral intervenors must emphasize the fact that all information disclosed during separate caucuses will remain confidential — unless the interested party authorizes the mediator to convey that knowledge to the other side or disclosure is required under a special statute pertaining to the particular circumstances involved (Slaikeu, 1996, at 76). Mediators frequently remind the participants that they may not be compelled by either party to divulge mediation disclosures in any other forum. Some mediators even express these ground rules in separate confidentiality contracts to be signed by the parties and give copies to the participants. Others choose to rely upon their oral representations.

b. Parties' Initial Presentations

Once the fundamental guidelines have been established, mediators generally ask the parties to summarize their respective positions. Each side is given the opportunity to accomplish this objective free from opponent interruptions (Gulliver, 1979, at 221–25). Whenever one side objects to something contained in the other side's presentation, it is gently but firmly told it will have the chance to express its views once this party is finished speaking. During these summaries, mediators usually take brief notes, and they occasionally ask questions to clarify uncertain points. They want to be certain they fully comprehend the underlying issues and interests. They also want to be certain each side has heard the other's perspective. Mediators should carefully listen for allusions to hidden agendas that are not being openly discussed by the disputants, but will have to be addressed before mutual accords can be achieved (Folberg & Taylor, 1984, at 42).

Full party disclosure may be enhanced through "active listening." Nonjudgmental but empathetic interjections such as "I understand," "I see," "I understand how you feel," "um hum," etc. can be used to encourage participant openness (Slaikeu, 1996, at 227–29; Kovach, 1994, at 33). Warm eye contact and an open face can also be beneficial. This approach encourages both sides to thoroughly express their underlying feelings and beliefs in a relatively sympathetic atmosphere (Della Noce, 1999, at 283–86). The mediator is actively listening to their circumstances, and each party feels that the opposing side is finally being forced to appreciate its side of the controversy. After the parties have summarized their respective positions, it is generally beneficial for the neutral to restate those positions to demonstrate a basic comprehension of the relevant information and to reflect the apparent feelings of the parties (Folberg & Taylor, 1984, at 112–15). This lets the participants know that they have been heard and their feelings have been validated.

When emotionally-charged controversies and relationships are involved, cathartic "venting" may permit the dissipation of strong feelings that might preclude the realistic consideration of possible solutions. The mediator should allow the requisite venting in an environment that is likely to minimize the creation of unproductive animosity (Kovach, 1994, at 25). While candid feelings may be expressed, intemperate personal attacks must not be tolerated. Extreme statements can be adroitly reframed to make them more palatable to the other side (Slaikeu, 1996, at 231–33). For example, "I don't think that referring to X as a 'total jerk' or an 'asshole' is likely to induce X to consider your position with an open mind. Let's focus instead on the specific issues that are bothering you." Once both sides have been allowed to participate fully in the cathartic process, they may be able to put their emotional baggage behind them and get on with more productive discussions.

c. Guided Discussion and Negotiation

During their frequently protracted one-on-one negotiations, parties that have been unable to achieve mutual accommodations of their competing interests often lock themselves into unalterable "principled" positions. They reach the point at which they are merely reiterating their respective positions in a nonconciliatory manner. They are so intent on the advancement of their own interests that they fail to listen meaningfully to the representations and suggestions being articulated by their opponents (Matz, 1999).

When mediators become involved in the negotiation process, they must initially endeavor to reestablish meaningful communication between the parties (Moore, 1996, at 182–85). If efforts are to have a beneficial impact, the participants must be induced to listen carefully to one another and to the neutral facilitator. They must be persuaded to appreciate the underlying interests and fundamental objectives of each other. During the initial joint session, the mediator must assist the parties to reopen blocked communication channels. If the parties cannot agree upon the precise issues to be resolved, with each preferring its own formulations, the neutral should reframe the underlying problems in a way that will be acceptable to both sides (Moore, 1996, at 217–22; Kovach, 1994, at 108–09). This neutral reformation of the underlying issues can induce the participants to begin to view the disputed items in a more dispassionate manner.

The presence of individual clients or corporate officers with decision-making authority is normally required at the mediation conference. It is beneficial to have both parties articulate their respective positions in environments in which each is compelled to listen to the underlying reasoning and objectives of the other. This procedure may induce previously recalcitrant opponents to acquire a greater appreciation for rationales that have been summarily rejected in a pro forma manner during prior discussions. This technique also allows the neutral to obtain and demonstrate an unbiased familiarity with the operative facts and applicable legal doctrines. This enhances the neutral's credibility and the acceptability of settlement proposals he or she subsequently suggests.

When it appears that one or both advocates are not seriously listening to the positions being articulated by opposing counsel, it may be beneficial to employ a different approach. Each participant may be asked to summarize the views of the other side until it is apparent that he actually understands the other party's situation. This role-reversal technique generally enhances each party's respect for the other side's interests and positions.

The mediator must recognize the factors that are likely to impede an objective exploration of the pertinent factual and legal issues by the parties during initial settlement conferences. The frustrations that have been generated during the previous unsuccessful negotiations may have made it difficult for the disputants to evaluate the relevant circumstances in an objective manner. Their myopic focus on their unyielding positions may have precluded their realistic consideration of alternative formulations that may beneficially accommodate their competing interests. Proficient mediators can effectively reopen blocked communication channels and induce recalcitrant participants to interact on a more open and professional basis.

Communication problems occasionally arise from unrealistic client expectations. Mediators should be cognizant of direct or indirect indications that lawyers are having difficulty moderating excessive client aspirations. Legal practitioners might, for example, acknowledge the reasonableness of positions being articulated by opposing counsel, but suggest that their client is unwilling to consider those terms. Other lawyers may merely express client opposition to settlement proposals without providing any support for the client intransigence. When it becomes apparent that clients do not appreciate the legal and/or economic realities involved, the mediator should attempt to enlighten those people in a fashion that does not embarrass them or their legal representatives. An objective but candid discussion of the way in which similar cases or transactions have recently been adjudicated or settled can be particularly persuasive.

Mediators must appreciate the fact that some clients do not entirely trust their own legal counsel. This is especially true with respect to plaintiffs who are being represented on a contingent fee basis. These claimants fear that their attorneys are more interested in expeditious settlements to enable them to obtain their legal fees quickly than in protracted adjudications that may ultimately provide more generous results. When such client suspicions are detected and it appears that counsel are actually providing accurate legal advice, mediators should not hesitate to indicate how proficiently their attorneys are advancing their interests.

During some introductory mediation sessions, the parties begin to negotiate meaningfully with one another. If they appear to be making actual progress, it is a propitious moment for the neutral participant to engage in passive mediation. The intervenor should smile benignly at the person speaking, until he is finished. If the mediator then turns toward the other party for a response, she is likely to generate further discussion. So long as the parties continue to exchange information and ideas, the mediator should maintain a low profile and permit the advocates to conduct their own talks. When inter-party communication begins to lag, the conciliator may interject questions designed to stimulate further negotiation progress or suggest alternatives the participants may not have contemplated.

d. Exploring Settlement Options

Advocates who have reached an impasse during their own negotiations frequently focus exclusively on their own stated positions, causing them to ignore other possible options. Neither is willing to suggest new alternatives, lest they be perceived as weak. The mediator can significantly enhance the bargaining process and facilitate creative options by encouraging the parties to explore other formulations in a non-threatening manner under circumstances that do not require either advocate to make overt concessions (Moore, 1996, at 244–61; Folberg & Taylor, 1984, at 49–53). If the way in which particular issues are phrased appears to impede open discussions, the mediator can either reframe them in a manner both parties find palatable or divide those issues into manageable subparts (Moore, 1996, at 219–23; Kovach, 1994, at 128–29).

A special meeting may be scheduled for the express purpose of permitting the exploration of alternative settlement options (Moore, 1996, at 244–49; Fisher & Ury, 1991, at 56–80). The mediator should encourage the parties to explain their needs, interests, and objectives (Matz, 1999). The advocates should be prompted by careful, gentle probing to discuss these critical issues. What does each side really hope to achieve? What do the parties fear might occur if they do not attain their goals or if they accede to certain proposals being suggested by their opponent? If the participants can be induced to express themselves in a candid fashion, this substantially enhances the likelihood of negotiated resolutions (Fisher & Ury, 1991, at 40–55). Whenever possible, the mediator should encourage the parties to agree on objective standards they can use to guide their evaluations and exchanges (Folberg & Taylor, 1984, at 57).

An effective needs and interests analysis stimulates the disclosure of information not previously divulged (Kagel & Kelly, 1989, at 123–24). Communication channels are usually reopened, and stalled negotiations are revitalized in a way that does not cause either party to suffer a loss of face (Folberg & Taylor, 1984, at 53–57). Mediator patience is crucial during this phase, because it takes time for the advocates to move from the adversarial mode to the cooperative mode. If the neutral facilitator attempts to rush things, the problem-solving process is likely to break down. Once relatively cooperative communication has been reestablished, conciliator silence, accompanied by supportive smiles and gestures, may be sufficient to encourage the parties to engage in meaningful bargaining. When necessary, the interjection of non-threatening inquiries and suggested options may be employed to maintain a positive negotiating environment.

The parties must be encouraged to explore bargaining alternatives that have not been previously considered due to the competitive nature of their interaction. Lawsuit disputants must recognize their capacity to formulate solutions that could not be achieved through the adjudication process. For example, an individual suing a neighbor who cut down a beautiful tree on the complaining party's side of their property line may prefer a sincere apology and a replacement tree to protracted litigation and a permanently strained relationship. A plaintiff involved in a defamation action may prefer an immediate public retraction to the possibility of future monetary relief. Divorcing spouses might consider special child-care arrangements that a judge would be reluctant to order. A severely injured plaintiff may prefer a structured settlement that will guarantee lifetime care to a substantial present verdict that may be exhausted prematurely.

Even transactional negotiators should be encouraged to examine unarticulated alternatives. If parties discussing an international business arrangement cannot agree whether to specify contractual payment in the currency of the seller or the purchaser, they might consider the use of a market-basket currency such as that of the European Union. Parties disagreeing on the official language to govern their relationship may agree upon a dual language approach or the use of a neutral third language. Parties negotiating the sale of business assets may disagree about the one to assume the risk of unknown liability. The buyer typically wants to exclude responsibility for unknown liabilities, while the seller wants the buyer to assume all liabilities. These firms can resolve their controversy by establishing an escrow account funded by the buyer to cover unknown liabilities for a specified period of time, with excess escrow funds being returned to the buyer at the expiration of that time period.

Reasonable substitutes for articulated demands should be sought during these brainstorming sessions. The participants should be encouraged to think of options that would beneficially satisfy the underlying needs and interests of both sides (Folberg & Taylor, 1984, at 49–53). They need to engage in cooperative problem-solving that is designed to generate "win-win" results (Hartje, 1984, at 173–74). Significant issues must be distinguished from less important matters, and the parties must be induced to focus primarily on those topics that have to be resolved if a final accord is to be achieved. How might the critical needs of each client be satisfied or protected by different options? Which alternatives acceptable to one side would least trammel the interests of the other party?

It is occasionally helpful to have the advocates engage in role reversal. Once the underlying needs and interests of the parties have been discerned, each legal representative can be asked to indicate the ways in which his/her opponent's rights may be optimally protected (Hartje, 1984, at 161). This technique may generate options that have been previously ignored. It should simultaneously induce each side to develop a greater appreciation for the needs of the other side.

Mediators should always try not to place disputants in positions in which they would be required to make overt capitulations. A face-saving means of compromise should be provided whenever possible. For example, a truly significant concession may be counterbalanced by a seemingly reciprocal relinquishment to preserve the aura of mutuality. Lawyers should be provided with rationales they can use to convince their clients of the reasonableness of settlement proposals their principals might otherwise be reluctant to accept.

Litigators who exhibit "true-believer," win-lose personality traits (Hoffer, 1951), may challenge the patience of the most professional mediators. They often lack the capacity to tolerate the uncertainty associated with close cases, and they minimize their internal dissonance by convincing themselves of the unassailable virtue of their positions (Kahneman & Tversky, 1995, at 46–49). By the time they have completed their pretrial preparations, they have become certain of total victory. It is particularly difficult for conciliators to deal with these persons, because they fear that their acknowledgement of weakness will undermine their ability to aggressively litigate the matter if that becomes necessary. Transactional negotiators occasionally exhibit true-believer styles, as they convince themselves of their entitlement to everything they have requested from their opponents.

Adroit mediators may induce true-believer individuals to explore the relevant issues in an abstract, hypothetical fashion that permits them to detach the conciliation evaluations from the circumstances of the actual interaction. For example: "If, for the sake of discussion, we were to assume. . . , how might this hypothetical issue be appropriately analyzed and resolved?" It is almost never productive for mediators to directly challenge the personally held beliefs of true-believer negotiators, because they are normally able to reject these overtures in a manner that allows them to preserve their false inner confidence and prevent meaningful exploration of the underlying issues.

Joint mediation sessions do not always move inexorably toward mutual accords. Mediators must be cognizant of those verbal and nonverbal signals that indicate that joint meetings are approaching an irreconcilable impasse. The parties are continuing to place exaggerated emphasis on unyielding, legalistic positions that are designed more to impress their respective clients than to influence their opponents. The participants may be wringing their hands and/or gnashing their teeth in utter frustration regarding the lack of progress, or they have crossed their arms and legs in a wholly unreceptive manner. When these negative signs are perceived, it may be time to suggest separate mediation sessions.

3. THE CAUCUS: CONDUCTING SEPARATE MEDIATION SESSIONS

When joint meetings do not achieve fruitful results, it is frequently benefi-cial to propose separate caucuses, meetings between one party and the mediator. Since separate encounters can only be effective when undertaken with the cooperation and confidence of the parties, it is advantageous to ask the participants if they would be amenable to a bifurcated approach. If one side is really opposed to this technique, it would be unlikely that separate sessions would be productive. In most instances, the parties readily consent to separate caucuses, and their commitment to this process enhances the likelihood of success.

What happens at each caucus is, of course, largely dictated by the strategy of the mediator and the desires of the parties. The term "shuttle mediation" implies that the mediator keeps shuttling between the two disputing camps trying to broker a settlement. This may entail the mediator seeking to end each caucus by obtaining authority to convey a settlement offer to the other side.

Mediators who are considering the use of segregated discussions should explain at a joint session that they would like to explore the matter with each side individually. The mediators should emphasize the fact that they do not intend to support either side as such. They merely wish to explore each party's underlying needs, interests, and objectives in an environment that may be more conducive to candor than a joint meeting. They must expressly promise to maintain the confidences shared by the participants during private discus-sions — except where they are specifically authorized to divulge the informa-tion in question. Once these basic guidelines are established, the disputants are ready for separate mediation sessions.

During the separate meetings, mediators must endeavor, in a non-judgmental manner, to ascertain the true underlying interests and beliefs of the respective participants (Slaikeu, 1996, at 91–109). Most mediators also begin to deter-mine the minimal goals each side hopes to achieve. When they first meet with each participant, they should reaffirm the fact that all discussions will remain confidential unless they are expressly given permission to convey certain information to the other side. They should note, however, that they do plan to convey general principles that are divulged without disclosing particular details. For example, if a plaintiff in a wrongful termination case indicates a willingness to forego reinstatement in favor of an appropriate monetary arrangement, the neutral intervenor may have to indirectly disclose this objective when exploring possible resolutions with the defendant-employer. This would be accomplished without the disclosure of the monetary range being contemplated by the plaintiff.

When separate caucus meetings commence, it is often advantageous for the neutral intervenors to ask each participant what they — as mediators — should know that they were unable to learn during the joint discussions. This inquiry acknowledges the fact that disputing parties are frequently willing to divulge information to mediators in confidence that they would be unwilling to disclose in the presence of their adversaries. This question must be propounded in an open and wholly non-threatening manner to encourage the desired candor. At this stage, mediators should try not to put participants on the defensive by asking them to explain their behavior. Individuals who are asked *why* they have or have not done something are likely to withdraw from the process. It is more productive to ask them about their aspirations and their concerns.

Mediators should be aware of the fact that particular disputants may not understand the negotiation process (Slaikeu, 1996, at 48). When necessary, conciliators should not hesitate to provide one or both sides with a mini-course on bargaining procedures. A brief discussion of the negotiation stages and the problem-solving approach may be helpful with respect to the uninitiated. Since personal embarrassment may result if this educational function were performed during joint sessions, it is preferable to cover this topic during separate meetings.

During the early portion of separate sessions, it is often instructive to ask the participants to explain any concerns they may have regarding the ramifications they associate with specific settlement terms that are being considered. One or both parties may think that a negotiated agreement on the current issues may prejudice another matter involving the same participants or adversely affect some other relationship. If these concerns are well founded, they will have to be addressed before any resolution of the immediate controversy can be amicably obtained. For example, a defendant might fear that a settlement of the present case might generate law suits by other similarly situated individuals. A business firm may fear that an agreement with respect to the instant matter may affect other contracts that contain "most favored nation" (MFN) clauses requiring it to give equally advantageous terms to other contractual partners. A confidentiality clause may assuage the concerns of the defendant that fears additional law suits, while a rearrangement of the relevant terms may take care of the concerns of the corporation with MFN clauses in other contracts by avoiding the inclusion of provisions that would be affected by those MFN obligations.

It is not unusual for mediators to conclude that the fears expressed in private by negotiating parties appear to be unfounded. A thoughtful and empathetic assessment of the real consequences of bargained results may help to alleviate the anxiety that is preventing a mutual resolution of the current problems. This must be done with sensitivity to the feelings of the concerned participants and in a manner designed to induce those parties to recognize the fact that their fears are unreasonable. The following example may be instructive:

Side A Negotiator: If we enter into a ten year lease with Side B, we may lose out on a better deal that may arise in the coming years. Yet Side B is unwilling to enter into a lease of shorter duration, and this is the building we would really like to lease.

Mediator: Haven't you been looking for new space for several years now?

Side A Negotiator: Yes, we have.

Mediator: Have you noticed a lowering of rents over that period of time?

Side A Negotiator: As a matter of fact, we haven't. Rents have actually been rising at the rate of two to three percent per year.

Mediator: Do you really think Side B will be giving other parties lower rents in the next several years?

Side A Negotiator: Now that you mention it, I doubt that will happen.

If the concerns expressed by Side A regarding possible future rent reductions were valid, then the mediator would have to explore options that might assuage those fears:

Mediator: I can understand why you would not like to lock your firm into a ten year rent commitment. Would you be willing to do so if Side B agreed to include a clause promising to give your firm the benefit of any future rent reductions given to other companies? What if Side B agreed to a clause providing for the reopening of the rent issue after the first five years of the lease?

While meeting separately with the participants, mediators should look for possible intra-group difficulties that may impede settlement talks (Slaikeu, 1996, at 24–25, 56–57). What constituencies must be satisfied before any accord can be approved? What are their underlying interests and how may they be addressed? Are all interested constituencies currently represented at the negotiation table? If not, how might that objective be accomplished? Advocates who are ignoring constituent conflicts must be convinced of the need for full intra-group participation if the assisted discussions are to be successful.

During some separate sessions, parties continue to assert wholly unrealistic positions. If mediators were to directly challenge those views, the parties would probably become defensive and more intransigent. It is more productive to explore these positions in a nonthreatening manner. This can be accomplished through the use of probing questions. The conciliator takes out a writing pad and explains how helpful it would be for him/her to fully comprehend the way in which that particular party has calculated its current position. The mediator wants to induce that side to break its overall demand/offer into components that must be valued on an individualized basis.

The probing questions initially pertain to the more finite aspects of the party's position to leave minimal room for puffing. How has that side valued the real property or the destroyed automobile? If the response is realistic, the neutral intervenor merely writes it down and goes on to the value of the building and equipment or the lost earnings. If it is unreasonable, the conciliator may cite a recent property appraisal or blue book car valuation that is substantially different from the one being offered, followed by a seemingly innocent question regarding the way in which the participant determined its valuation. In most cases, the party will feel embarrassed and be induced to provide a more realistic figure.

Most advocates advancing unreasonable positions are unprepared for component-by-component valuations. When they are forced to provide appraisals for each aspect of their overall positions, they tend to give more defensible numbers. Once this questioning process is finished, the final figure is often one-fourth of what was being demanded or four times what was being offered. This technique can greatly narrow the distance between the disputants.

When negotiators reach impasses, they are usually focusing almost entirely on their areas of disagreement. As a result, they frequently fail to consider other areas where their interests may overlap. Mediators must be especially attuned to the issues in which the interests of the parties are not diametrically opposed. These items should be highlighted, because they may provide the basis for cooperative solutions that may simultaneously enhance the needs of both sides. Points of immediate confrontation can be minimized through the development of alternative formulations that emphasize the areas of common interest and downplay the areas of direct conflict. Mediators are also attuned to the priorities of the parties. Trade-offs may be possible if one party values an item highly that the other party does not feel strongly about.

As the parties tentatively resolve the less controverted issues, they become psychologically committed to an overall settlement. Their focus on the mutually agreeable terms begins to convince them that the conflicted items are not as important as they initially thought. They do not want to permit their substantial progress on the cooperative issues to be negated through impasses on the few remaining terms. As a result, both sides become more amenable to settlement, making the mediator's job easier.

Once the underlying needs and interests have been determined and possibly acceptable alternatives have been explored with the individual parties, mediators generally attempt to formulate comprehensive proposals they hope will lead to final agreements. They may first review the strengths and weaknesses of the terms being proposed by each side to demonstrate the significant risks associated with nonsettlement (Slaikeu, 1996, at 104–05). Financial and emotional transaction costs may also be noted.

When a number of different issues are involved, some mediators employ the *single-text* approach. When the time is ripe, the neutral intervenors may draft a single document that reflects the areas of discerned commonality and appears to entail reciprocal concessions by both sides (Slaikeu, 1996, at 123–29). After the single text is prepared, the mediator shares that document with each party during separate sessions. The neutral listens carefully to each side's criticisms and suggestions, and then redrafts the appropriate provisions. Even when advocates submit their own proposed terms, the mediator may choose to incorporate those suggestions into one single text. In this manner, the mediator retains control over the drafting process, and she is only required to work with a single official document. This avoids the problems that are often created when each participant attempts to work from its own written submission.

The single-text device also enables the mediator to negate two frequent impediments to final agreements. Advocates tend to be suspicious of proposals suggested by their adversaries. They assume that opponents are attempting to obtain provisions that satisfy their own interests. (Regarding this "reactive devaluation" tendency, *see* Ross, 1995, at 26 ff.) The single-text format generates an overall draft formulated by the neutral intervenor who has no reason to favor one party over the other. The participants are thus more receptive to terms coming from the unbiased mediator.

The single-text device also enables the neutral intervenor to formulate proposals that appear to provide *gains,* rather than *losses,* for both sides. Since people tend to accept a *sure gain* over a possibly greater gain but reject a *certain loss* they might possibly avoid, final proposals that seem to guarantee *sure gains* for both sides are more likely to be found acceptable by the disputants (Korobkin & Guthrie, 1994, at 129–38). Even in the litigation context, the conciliator should emphasize the gain each side will receive from the final resolution of their controversy. The plaintiff will receive the sure benefit of the settlement, while the defendant will get the certain gain of the transaction costs it will not have to expend as a result of the joint agreement.

Some mediators disapprove of a single text approach on the grounds that mediators should not write the settlement agreement. They may refuse to draft any writing purporting to settle the dispute. There are several reasons for this attitude. The mediator may feel that, as a neutral, drafting even a single text compromises neutrality. Some mediators also think that the drafting of a single text may discourage parties from seeking their own legal representation.

When mediation efforts are not moving expeditiously toward settlement, neutral intervenors must be patient. If they attempt to rush the parties, unproductive intransigence is likely to result. It takes time for combatants to reconsider the merits of established positions, and to reevaluate their real nonsettlement alternatives. It is unlikely that meaningful settlement discussions can occur again until the participants have had the chance to reassess their respective situations.

Mediators should never give parties legal advice, because this would be inconsistent with their neutral facilitation role. If unrepresented persons ask for such advice, they should be encouraged to contact attorneys who can provide them with the requisite advice. What should mediators do if one or both parties ask them to evaluate the issues being discussed? Some neutrals steadfastly refuse to express their opinions regarding the merits of disputes, fearing this may compromise their impartiality (*see, e.g.,* Love, 1997). Other mediators, however, are willing to engage in evaluative discourses (*see, e.g.,* Stempel, 1997). They usually try to avoid definitive opinions, preferring to talk in generalities that focus on the strengths and weaknesses of the positions of both sides. This approach can be especially effective when used to question unrealistic party positions.

4. THE CLOSING STAGE

Once the parties have agreed upon the terms contained in the mediator's text, the neutral drafter should carefully review the items agreed upon to be sure that there are no misunderstandings. She should also be certain that the specified terms satisfy the critical underlying interests of both sides (Slaikeu, 1996, at 165–68). If the mediator is concerned that a party may subsequently attempt to modify or reject some of the pertinent provisions, she can ask the participants to indicate their assent to everything by initialing each term.

The mediator may also avoid future difficulties by agreeing to prepare the final settlement agreement for the parties (Folberg & Taylor, 1984, at 60–61). This function should not entail much additional work, because the accord would be based on the final text approved by the disputants. The neutral participant would merely have to clarify ambiguous language and clean up unartfully drafted provisions. Some mediators refuse to draft agreements on the theory that the final agreement belongs to the parties.

There are mediations that close without agreement of the parties. Impasse is always a possibility, and, in the opinion of relationship-oriented mediators, not necessarily a failure if empowerment or recognition has taken place. When it is apparent to all the participants that no agreement can be reached, the mediation should end. Prior to discharging the disputants, it is common for the mediator to acknowledge any progress that has been made since the beginning of the mediation and to identify possible exploratory grounds for a future agreement. Mediators do their best to close a session that does not result in agreement on a positive note, leaving the parties to consider their potential non-settlement options.

D. LAW, NEUTRALITY, AND FAIRNESS IN MEDIATION

To what extent should a mediator bear some responsibility for the outcome, as distinct from the process, of a mediation? Under the principles of party autonomy and self-determination, one can argue that in mediation all outcome-determining norms must be generated by the parties. The mediator is not a judge applying legal and social conceptions of justice embodied in statutes or the common law. Instead, the dominant view holds, the mediator must stay neutral as to the content of the parties' agreement, which must derive its authority from the mutual assent of the parties. But are there limits to this principle? Can strict mediator neutrality lead to injustice?

The three excerpts in this section explore these questions. The first two, by Professors Susskind and Stulberg, are classic analyses of the importance of ensuring a fair outcome in environmental disputes and of neutrality in mediation. The third, by Professor Gunning, considers the issues in the context of disputes involving parties who bring negative cultural myths to mediation.

LAWRENCE SUSSKIND, ENVIRONMENTAL MEDIATION AND THE ACCOUNTABILITY PROBLEM, 6 Vt. L. Rev. 1, 6–8, 15–16, 18, 46–47 (1981) *

* * * The success of most mediation efforts tends to be measured in rather narrow terms. If the parties to a labor dispute are pleased with the agreement they have reached voluntarily, and the bargain holds, the mediator is presumed to have done a good job. In the environmental field, there are reasons that a broader definition of success is needed — one that is more attentive to the interests of all segments of society.

If the parties involved in environmental mediation reach an agreement, but fail to maximize the joint gains possible, environmental quality and natural resources will actually be lost. If the key parties involved in an environmental dispute reach an agreement with which they are pleased, but fail to take account of all impacts on those interests not represented directly in the negotiations, the public health and safety could be seriously jeopardized. If the key parties to a dispute reach an agreement, but selfishly ignore the interests of future generations, short term agreements could set off environmental time bombs that cannot be defused. Although the key stakeholders in an environmental dispute may pay only a small price for failing to reach an agreement, their failure could impose substantial costs on many groups, who may be affected indefinitely. Finally, the parties to environmental disputes must be sensitive to the ways in which their agreements set precedents; even informal settlements have a way of becoming binding on others who find themselves in similar situations.

* * *

The classic model of labor mediation places little emphasis on the mediator's role as a representative of diffuse, inarticulate, or hard-to-organize interests. All the appropriate parties to a labor management dispute are presumed to be present at the bargaining table. Thus, the problems of protecting unrepresented segments of the society or reducing impacts on the community-at-large receive little, if any, attention. Joint net gains are presumed to be maximized through the interaction of the parties and their ability to know for themselves how best to achieve their objectives. No effort is made to bolster the claims or abilities of the weaker stakeholders. Precedent is not a concern; indeed, one of the presumed strengths of labor mediation is that parties are free to devise agreements of their own design. Finally, spillovers, externalities, and long-term impacts are, for the most part, ignored since the time frame for implementing most labor-management agreements is relatively short. The parties will usually face the same adversaries again in a few years which makes it easier for them to hold each other to their agreements.

Although procedural fairness and ethical behavior on the part of labor mediators and self-interest maximizing behavior on the part of the participants in labor-management negotiations are presumed to be sufficient to ensure just and stable agreements, these assumptions are inappropriate in the environmental field. Just and stable agreements in the environmental

---

field require much closer attention to the interests of those unable to represent themselves. Joint net gains can be achieved only if the parties attempt to understand the complex ecological systems involved and to generate appropriate compromises that go beyond their self-interests. In short, self-interested negotiation must be replaced by "principled negotiation."

*   *   *

* * * [E]nvironmental mediators ought to accept responsibility for ensuring (1) that the interests of parties not directly involved in negotiations, but with a stake in the outcome, are adequately represented and protected; (2) that agreements are as fair and stable as possible, and (3) that agreements reached are interpreted as intended by the community-at-large and set constructive precedents.

*   *   *

Environmental mediators ought to be concerned about (1) the impacts of negotiated agreements on underrepresented or unrepresentable groups in the community; (2) the possibility that joint net gains have not been maximized; (3) the long-term or spillover effects of the settlements they help to reach; and (4) the precedents that they set and the precedents upon which agreements are based. To be effective an environmental mediator will need to be knowledgeable about the substance of disputes and the intricacies of the regulatory context within which decisions are embedded. An environmental mediator should be committed to procedural fairness — all parties should have an opportunity to be represented by individuals with the technical sophistication to bargain effectively on their behalf. Environmental mediators should also be concerned that the agreements they help to reach are just and stable. To fulfill these responsibilities, environmental mediators will have to intervene more often and more forcefully than their counterparts in the labor-management field. Although such intervention may make it difficult to retain the appearance of neutrality and the trust of the active parties, environmental mediators cannot fulfill their responsibilities to the community-at-large if they remain passive.

JOSEPH B. STULBERG, THE THEORY AND PRACTICE OF MEDIATION: A REPLY TO PROFESSOR SUSSKIND, 6 Vt. L. Rev. 86–88, 96–97, 108–09, 112–14, 117 (1981) *

* * * Susskind's argument is novel in that he asserts that the mediator of environmental disputes, unlike his counterpart in labor management, community, or international disputes, should not be neutral and should be held accountable for the mediated outcome. Since most mediators believe that a commitment to impartiality and neutrality is the defining principle of their role, Susskind's argument carries significant consequences for mediation.

The basis of this article is that Susskind's demand for a non-neutral intervenor is conceptually and pragmatically incompatible with the goals and

---

* Copyright © 1981. Reprinted with permission of the author and the *Vermont Law Review.*

purposes of mediation. The intervenor posture that Susskind advocates is not anchored by any principles or obligations of office. The intervenor's conduct, strategies or contribution to the dispute settlement process is, therefore, neither predictable nor consistent. It is precisely a mediator's commitment to neutrality which ensures responsible actions on the part of the mediator and permits mediation to be an effective, principled dispute settlement procedure.

* * *

At a substantive level, Susskind argues that the mediator must ensure that the negotiated agreements are fair. The most dramatic example of the difference between the traditional neutral mediator and Susskind's environmental mediator is the person Susskind describes and endorses as a mediator with "clout." For Susskind, the term "clout" applies to a mediator publicly committed to a particular substantive outcome with the power to move the contesting parties toward an agreement. In contrast, the traditional mediator would view that public commitment as the signal reason for disqualifying himself from service.

It is more than a mere terminological quibble to analyze whether a mediator must be someone who is committed to a posture of neutrality. Such a commitment enables both the mediation process and the mediator to operate effectively. A commitment of neutrality provides the mediator with a principled rather than opportunistic basis for service. As a result, the parties will use his services in ways that would be foreclosed to the "mediator with clout." * * *

* * *

* * * [A] mediator must be neutral with regard to outcome. Parties negotiate because they lack the power to achieve their objectives unilaterally. They negotiate with those persons or representatives of groups whose cooperation they need to achieve their objective. If the mediator is neutral and remains so, then he and his office invite a bond of trust to develop between him and the parties. If the mediator's job is to assist the parties to reach a resolution, and his commitment to neutrality ensures confidentiality, then, in an important sense, the parties have nothing to lose and everything to gain by the mediator's intervention. In these two bases of assistance and neutrality there is no way the mediator could jeopardize or abridge the substantive interests of the respective parties.

* * *

There is a variety of information that parties will entrust to a neutral mediator, including a statement of their priorities, acceptable trade-offs, and their desired timing for demonstrating movement and flexibility. All of these postures are aimed to achieve a resolution without fear that such information will be carelessly shared or that it will surface in public forums in a manner calculated to embarass or exploit the parties into undesired movement. This type of trust is secured and reinforced only if the mediator is neutral, has no power to insist upon a particular outcome, and honors the confidences placed in him. If any of these characteristics is absent, then the parties must calculate what information they will share with the mediator, just as they do in communicating with any of the parties to the controversy.

* * *

* * * At issue is an understanding of, and respect for, what the parties to the mediation session are entitled to expect from the intervenor. Will confidences be honored? Who sets the agenda in terms of issues to be discussed?

Will the order in which the issues are discussed be skewed so as to insure the mediator's desired outcome? Will meeting times be scheduled for the convenience of the parties or might they be arranged by the intervenor in order to make it difficult for some (i.e. "obstreperous") parties to attend and voice objections to the intervenor's preferred position? Will the mediator refuse to schedule meetings if the one party whose position the mediator supports demands that future meetings be conditional upon the other parties having made particular concessions?

One can certainly offer answers to these various problems, but Susskind's burden is more substantial. First, he should demonstrate how a mediator committed to neutrality cannot render effective service in an environmental dispute. Second, he should explain the obligations of office that the "mediator with clout" assumes when he renders his services. Is it appropriate, for example, for the "mediator with clout" to threaten a recalcitrant party with political retaliation? If not, why not? Third, Susskind should illustrate the value derived, if any, by labeling such intervention "mediation," since it differs in so many striking ways from mediation in labor-management collective bargaining, community dispute negotiations, court-diversion programs, and countless other private dispute settlement systems. Clarification is necessary to insure a degree of consistency in program posture and purpose among those encouraged to experiment with "mediation" programs as an alternative dispute settlement procedure.

* * *

* * * [I]f mediation as a dispute settlement procedure is defective in insuring that "the public interest" is secured, then the appropriate response is to employ a different dispute settlement procedure which more closely insures it. To suggest that an environmental mediator assume the responsibility of protecting the public's interest within the mediation context is comparable to suggesting that the way to avoid impasses in mediation is to authorize the mediator to impose dispositive, enforceable decisions on the parties.

[Susskind's] proposal is not simply adding a different twist to the mediation process; it is converting it from mediation to arbitration in the interest of promoting finality. Susskind has yet to meet the burden of justifying how the environmental mediator can assume this particular responsibility to the "public" without simultaneously converting the dispute settlement procedure into something other than mediation.

* * * Susskind suggests that "[e]nvironmental mediators ought to be concerned. . . about . . . the possibility that joint net gains have not been maximized [and about] . . . the long-term or spillover effects of the settlements they help to reach." Susskind proposes that it is the mediator's responsibility as an objective observer to insure that the final solution secures the greatest overall net benefits for each party, without leaving any party worse off than it was in its original configuration (the Pareto-optimal principle). He further suggests that the solution agreed upon should have the least possible adverse impact on other aspects of present or future community life. Simply stating the proposed responsibility for the mediator in this way reveals how awesome the task is that Susskind is proposing for the environmental mediator. To insure that the Pareto principle is met, the environmental mediator must be able to generate, or at least guarantee, consideration of every possible technical solution to the environmental problem. He must secure demographic information on all persons affected by the dispute and factor their interests, desires, aspirations, preferences and values into the solution. He must project alternative development plans for jobs, tax bases, population trends, aesthetic values, school development and recreational needs for each possible solution. He must calculate the advantages and disadvantages of each solution against retaining the status quo, including the costs involved in using alternative dispute settlement procedures. And the list goes on.

Although these tasks might constitute a city planner's dream, they involve a host of analytical problems concerning logical theories of probability, measurement, interpersonal comparisons, and contrary-to-fact conditionals. These problems catapult the mediator's task into an intellectual war-zone which raises the serious possibility that Pareto-optimal outcomes in the context of an environmental dispute are not, in principle, possible. * * *

A more troublesome question arises, however, regarding the justification for a mediator to block an agreement that fails to meet the requirements of the Pareto principle. Who authorized the mediator to design or insure the attainment of the "optimal" outcome as so conceived? Clearly, it is preferable for persons to act as rational agents and do the "right" thing. Even conceding, however, the dubious proposition that the mediator could identify the "right" course of action as defined by the Pareto principle, on what basis does the mediator assume as an obligation of office that he help parties do only what is "right" and not necessarily that which is possible?

Susskind apparently contends that such a responsibility emanates from the nature of environmental disputes, particularly because the spillover effect of particular agreements could irrevocably preclude certain options from again being entertained. That position, however, simply reveals Susskind's bias in the environmental versus pro-development dispute and his attempt to incorporate it as a principle of the mediation process; it is not an independent justification for conferring such authority to a mediator.

It is not unique to environmental disputes that decisions made today foreclose certain options for tomorrow. Life is replete with such instances. In the labor-management sector, for example, agreement on a particular wage settlement might retard the development of mass transportation and thereby irrevocably increase the level of air pollution resulting from the use of automobiles. Why should that fact, however, allow the labor mediator the authority in collective bargaining negotiations to insist upon, and indeed impose, Pareto-optimal outcomes in collective bargaining negotiations? Susskind's argument confuses a desired state of affairs with the justification for conduct within an institutional role.

If we were to accept the obligations of office that Susskind ascribes to the environmental mediator with regard to insuring Pareto-optimal outcomes, then the environmental mediator is simply a person who uses his entry into the dispute to become a social conscience, environmental policeman, or social critic and who carries no other obligations to the process or the participants beyond assuring Pareto-optimality. It is, in its most benign form, an invitation to permit philosopher-kings to participate in the affairs of the citizenry.

*   *   *

* * * The way to insure the continued integrity and usefulness of mediation as a dispute settlement procedure * * * is to be certain that we do not demand that it perform functions beyond the scope of its institutional and conceptual capacity.

* * * Contrary to Susskind's suggestion, the mediator actually gains his strength — his "clout" — precisely because of his basic commitment to a posture of neutrality.

NOTES

1. Professor Susskind illustrates his thesis with descriptions of several major environmental mediations. Excerpts are located in Chapter 8.

2. If mediation is assisted negotiation, is it necessarily tied to interest-based negotiation? If so, is there room for the "principled negotiation" Susskind sees as necessary to resolve environmental disputes fairly? Do we have a tradition of "principled negotiation" in the United States? Should we?

3. Do you think that the goals Susskind sets for the resolution of environmental disputes are uniquely important for environmental disputes? Are there other types of disputes that should take the interests of future generations and weaker parties into account? When Susskind asserts that joint net gains need to be maximized, is that any different from saying that the agreement should be the best that is possible for all concerned? Is there any reason that meeting this Paerto-optimal standard is more a concern for the resolution of environmental disputes than for other types of disputes? Is Susskind essentially saying that environmental resolutions are important? Are resolutions of environmental disputes alone in creating concerns about spill-over effects or precedents? If these factors are important for disputes in other contexts, can Susskind make the claim that environmental mediation is special in its need for mediators to ensure the fairness and stability of the outcome? Is that the claim he is necessarily making?

4. What are the implications of Susskind's proposal for the desirable skill set of an environmental mediator? Is it realistic to expect mediators to be experts in ecology and all the other relevant disciplines? Are there ways a mediator could work with experts to overcome insufficient substantive knowledge?

5. Professor Susskind refers to mediators' "responsibility to the community-at-large." Do you agree that mediators have this responsibility? If so, what is that responsibility in your view? How would Professor Stulberg define mediators' responsibility?

6. One of Professor Stulberg's objections to Professor Susskind's views is that the actions a mediator would take to ensure a mediated outcome is just and fair would interfere with maintaining her neutrality. Why does he believe that neutrality is crucial to the mediation process? If neutrality is tied up with the importance of trust in the mediator, is it possible that confidentiality provisions can serve the same function by encouraging candid disclosures?

7. Is it even possible for a mediator to be neutral? Consider Stulberg's comments on this question:

> It is certainly the case that each of us is not neutral with regard to everything. Each of us has preferences, interests, commitments to certain moral principles and to an evolving philosophy of life which, when challenged or transgressed, will prompt us into advocating and acting in a manner that is faithful to these dictates. There is clearly no reason to be apologetic or hesitant about defending or advocating such considered judgments. * * * What is important is that one keep distinct his personal posture of judgment from the rule-defined practice of the mediator and act accordingly. [6 Vt. L. Rev. at 116.]

Do you think that most individuals are aware of all the subjects on which they hold views that reflect judgments? If not, how can an individual keep those judgments separate from his intervention as a mediator?

8. If a mediator has no obligation to ensure a fair resolution, does a mediator have to go along with a resolution that satisfies the parties but that the mediator finds morally objectionable? Stulberg proposes that a mediator can withdraw if "he does not want to lend his personal presence and reputation, or the prestige of the mediation process, to that agreement. (*Id.*) Is that a sufficient response in your view?

9. Does Stulberg object to the process Susskind advocates, or does he merely object to Susskind classifying it as mediation? Stulberg maintains that he is not claiming that Susskind's "mediator with clout" is not an effective intervenor.

> There are many types of "intervenors with clout," a police officer, parent, government regulatory agency, psychologist, marriage counselor, meeting facilitator, corporate executive, and school principal. For certain kinds of dispute settings, those persons intervene with clout in much the same way that Susskind proposes for his environmental dispute mediator. Such a description does not make these persons mediators nor does it make their intervention ineffective or less effective than service rendered by a mediator. It simply constitutes a different kind of intervention posture from that of a mediator. [*Id.* at 87–88.]

Why does Stulberg think it is important to distinguish mediation from an intervention by a person with clout who can affect the outcome of a dispute?

ISABELLE R. GUNNING, DIVERSITY ISSUES IN MEDIATION: CONTROLLING NEGATIVE CULTURAL MYTHS, 1995 J. Disp. Resol. 55, 79–84, 86 *

In the mediation process, parties will always identify relevant identity and organizational categories and draw upon the cultural myths which relate to those categories which most help to legitimate their narratives. When minority or disadvantaged group members participate in mediation, the cultural myths that will be accessed are largely negative and often wholly reliant, not upon personal experience or truth, but upon taboos inculcated during childhood and reaffirmed through the media and other cultural mediums. For these taboos to be reflected upon and diminished, they must be confronted and contrasted with American Creed values and beliefs [that support the ideals of liberty and equality and are thus antithetical to the legacy of racism and prejudice]. But, unlike * * * the courtroom context where procedural mechanisms provide a method and forum for some kind of confrontation and reflection, the mediation context lacks those procedures. The classic and apparently neutral language that mediators are admonished to use — "How would you like to see this resolved" or "What did the other party say" — can unintentionally contribute to the repetition of whatever is the primary narrative and its interpretive framework. For a primary narrative, the one which nests most comfortably within the larger cultural myths, to be transformed, the context and moral codes must be changed. Different and perhaps new cultural myths must be accessed, created and injected into the narrative interaction process. The mediator not only has to recognize that some of the cultural myths at work in the mediation process are drawn from negative taboos relating to disadvantaged groups but she may also need to flag for the parties that that is what is occurring. She may need particular training to accomplish the first and she may need permission to intervene to accomplish the second. This last may be the most difficult. The American model of mediation emphasizes "neutrality" in a mediator and generally defines neutrality as requiring non-intervention on the part of the mediator.

Given the problem of the influence of negative cultural myths in the mediation process, some intervention during the mediation is appropriate under certain circumstances. Intervention would be designed to act in much the way that procedural mechanisms function in the litigation context, i.e., to provide a method for confronting the participants with the tension between American Creed values and prejudicial attitudes. * * *

* * *

[A] major criticism of the use of intervention techniques in mediation involve[s] undermining the neutrality of the mediator. The mediator needs to be neutral so that the parties can arrive at their own agreement; their self-determination must be preserved.

Robert A. Baruch Bush has surveyed the problem of introducing values in various kinds of mediations in studying a variety of ethical dilemmas facing mediators in Florida. He explores a range of situations including those where a mediator might be inclined to intervene or terminate a mediation because of an unfair solution, or to interject specialized information or to persuade one party from employing deception. For example, he recounts divorce mediations where the husband believes that the family home counts as his legal property and is bullying his wife into accepting his interpretation even though under the law of the state he is incorrect and even though this clearly disadvantages the wife, or where a housewife is succumbing to her husband's superior business acumen into accepting a financially disadvantageous settlement. Although he recognizes the power imbalance and the injustice of the proposed result, Bush argues that to go beyond "the normal steps of questioning the parties regarding their understanding of the terms and consequences of the settlement" risks compromising the mediator's neutrality or impartiality and infringing on both parties' self-determination. Similarly, in situations where there are no power imbalances, but the mediator believes that the outcome is unfair, for example, when a mediator sees a landlord agreeing to subject herself to a Child Protective Services investigation in a last ditch effort to get her tenant to stop harassing her, even to suggest that the parties take some time to think or "cool off" or see a lawyer is seen as "deny(ing) self-determination, impos(ing) the mediator's values on the parties, compromising impartiality."

Even providing information is not neutral and unproblematic. In an example, again a divorce, where a wife believes that her husband has a dangerous mental condition and the mediator knows that family therapy literature identifies the husband's condition as a normal "post-divorce trauma", Bush is concerned that providing the information is "inherently directive or controlling." Again self-determination is undermined and the mediator's neutrality or impartiality may also be compromised as the information is likely to help one side only. Even when a mediator knows that one party is concealing relevant information or lying, Bush believes that for the mediator to in anyway police this abuse intrudes on "decision-making autonomy and . . . self-determination" in part because it is his view that "even if there is a nondisclosure, all parties know that this is a risk of negotiation."

While Bush raises some important points, he seems to go too far. In focusing on the preservation of that aspect of self-determination which involves the parties' self-reliance in their decision-making, he violates other aspects of self-determination. It is difficult to imagine an authentic type of self-determination without informed decision-making or consent. Yet when the wife is not told of property law or business law, the landlord not informed of the reach of Protective Services, the husband and wife are not told of his syndrome and the open and honest party is not told of the nondisclosure or lie, the parties cannot make an informed decision. Similarly, informed consent involves making volitional decisions, but if a wife is being bullied then a serious question about the voluntariness of her agreement is raised.

Moreover, the "normal steps of questioning the parties" about their understanding of the terms and consequences is not neutral. In the narrative struggle over social definitions and relations, the party with the primary narrative and the party with the greater number of positive historical and cultural myths within which to nest his story will be advantaged by "neutral" questioning. He will, in essence, be encouraged to reconstitute his interpretive framework and the weaker party will too often be left doing the same reconstituting or repeating and strengthening that interpretive framework.

*   *   *

More problematic than Bush's concerns are those expressed by Trina Grillo. Grillo, like Bush, is concerned with taking the process away from the parties. But Grillo is not as indifferent to the issue of "fairness" in an agreement or to the problem of power imbalances working against disadvantaged groups. She has two concerns: 1) while the mediator may be filled with good intentions, he may lack the skill and knowledge in psychological issues or even sufficient time to achieve his ultimate goal; and 2) the mediator may be just as likely to share historical myths and assumptions about the role of women and men and thus intentionally maintain the power differential between husband and wife.

In part, Grillo's concerns involve the issue of the kind of training mediators ought to have in order to combat negative interpretive frameworks which disadvantage some parties. In part, her concern raises the issue of the mediator imposing her values upon the parties. As other scholars have noted, no decision-maker or authority figure is ever truly neutral; she or he will always carry pre-existing stories and interpretive frameworks on how reality usually functions. If the mediator is allowed to intervene actively, the likelihood is that he will intrude his own interpretive framework and thus benefit whichever narrative is in accordance with his own interpretive framework. However, if the mediator does nothing and the parties enter the mediation with societal power imbalances, with uneven collections of cultural myths from which to use in their narrative struggle, the mediator's "neutrality" or silence will benefit the more powerful party. The thorny issue of whether a mediator prefers one side over another is not resolved by the notion of neutrality. Rather, it raises the questions of whether there are shared values in the American community or if such shared values can be created such that all parties, including the mediator, could agree upon them as the standard to use in a mediation.

Mediation, as a method of resolving disputes, has a long tradition that is not exclusively American. The American emphasis on non-intervention as the mark of neutrality is a product of the culture. Other cultures have made different choices on the "activism" of mediators. For example in both the Navajo Peacemaker Court and the Filipino Katarungang Pambarangay system, traditional methods of non-adversarial dispute resolution are kept alive which involve "mediators," called peacemakers or barangay captains, who intervene much more actively than their American counterparts even though they too are not decision-makers for the parties. In both these kinds of mediations, the mediators have confidence in their own knowledge of the community values which all participants are assumed to share. Two aspects of these mediations mark them especially: 1) the mediators openly inject concerns larger than the participants themselves; for example, community harmony and even spiritual guidance which they understand the parties share; and 2) the mediators are rarely ever strangers or unknown volunteers or professionals even though they are not to be biased towards one side or the other.

* * *

Equality as a core American Creed value dates back to the birth of the United States as a separate nation. We really can all agree that equality is a shared American value. But the concern that the mediator will just impose her values upon the parties still arises as we struggle with the questions of what "equality" means under any particular set of circumstances. The history of the notion of equality in American culture shows that it is a concept that has expanded over time. For example, "All men are created equal" moved from meaning only propertied white men to adult human beings, both male and female and of all races. But while the fluidity of the definition of equality historically can show how difficult it is to define, it also reveals that defining and redefining core values is an essential aspect of American political and legal life. Constitutional law, in particular, reveals through appellate cases the history of the adversarial legal system in defining and redefining core concepts like equality as various "out" groups — racial minorities, religious minorities, women and gays and lesbians — raise challenges to old definitions and become the catalysts for the entire society to craft new definitions.

While the identification of shared values in a homogeneous society can be daunting enough, it perhaps seems impossible to do so in a heterogeneous society like the United States. While the political and legal history of the United States reveals that it is difficult to define and redefine shared values, it also shows that it can and must be done. Some array of articulated or unarticulated shared values will be applied in social life. Without the conflict of definition and redefinition one is only assured that the status quo, the values of the most economically powerful minority will be imposed not that shared values will result.

In order to structure mediation so that it can work most of the time in favor of everybody, the value of equality must be introduced, injected when necessary. Mediation, then, becomes another locus in American political, social and legal life where ideas about equality are defined and redefined. When parties' conflicts are stymied by the presence of negative cultural myths and interpretive frameworks about disadvantaged identity groups, then the injection of equality values is appropriate so that the parties can try to either identify shared positive cultural myths and interpretive frameworks or to create them.

NOTES

1. What type of "cultural myths" does Professor Gunning have in mind? In an earlier part of her article, Gunning describes a mediation between a Korean-American and an African-American in which the African-American aligned the Korean-American with the white majority based on cultural myths of Asian-Americans as the "model minority." She also describes the tendency to merge distinct Asian cultures as indistinguishable. In another mediation, she encountered cultural myths about the criminal character of "illegals," a term usually associated with Latino immigrants. Can you identify cultural myths that you tend to accept?

2. Gunning maintains that when parties come to mediation with societal power imbalances, the mediator's silence is not neutral, but rather reinforces the more powerful, usually majority, set of interpretive frameworks. Is an intervention by the mediator the only way in which cultural myths can be challenged in mediation? If the party that is the object of the myths is left to challenge them, what is likely to be the effect of the power imbalance those myths create? Isn't part of the problem that individuals operate on the basis of myths without recognizing that is what they are doing?

3. Are fairness and justice issues limited to mediations on environmental issues or mediations involving different cultural groups? Gunning notes that intervention or "activist mediation" has also been called for in other contexts:

> Feminist mediators have grappled with the introduction of values in order to identify and equalize power imbalances and negative interpretive framework issues in the family mediation context. Other mediation experts have advocated that activism be employed in community mediations where public policy issues are implicated, for example, where different groups of people such as homeowners and homeless activists or minority group members and their local police have conflicts. Several professional standards for mediators include a duty to ensure the "fairness" of an agreement. Here too the concerns which lead to such proposals reflect concerns for power imbalances among the participants which are supported by the interpretive frameworks which accord certain groups fewer legitimating cultural myths than others. [Gunning, 1996, at 80–81.]

4. Even if one is in agreement that mediators should introduce an "equality principle" into a mediation when necessary, how should this be accomplished? What is to prevent the mediator from imposing her own values on the parties? As Gunning acknowledges, "we struggle with the questions of what 'equality' means under any particular set of circumstances." (Gunning, 1996, at 86.)

5. The examples Gunning raises of mediators who bring community values to mediation are drawn from cultures with a more collectivist orientation than the individualistic American culture. Would American disputants accept the type of intervention she envisions? To what extent do Americans embrace the importance of connectedness and community?

6. Gunning advocates training mediators to recognize the power imbalances that result from negative cultural myths and interpretive frameworks. She suggests that mediator training include hypotheticals that involve racial tension as a way to increase mediator sensitivity. She proposes using co-mediators rather than a single mediator whose background matches one of the disputants. She also points out that not all disputes are necessarily suitable for mediation; the presence of negative cultural myths can signal a larger political power struggle that may need to be resolved in the larger community.

E. THE ADVOCATE'S ROLE IN MEDIATION

This section focuses on a topic that has been woven through the previous materials on mediation — the role of an attorney representing a client in mediation. Many attorneys fail to consider how their advocacy role might differ in mediation from the familiar patterns of unassisted negotiation. Many attorneys also assume that, as the advocate, they should take the lead. They see client participation as high risk and, while they may concede that the client should be present, some attorneys maintain that the client should say as little as possible. The following excerpt takes issue with that view and argues that a problem-solving approach to mediation entails a case-by-case analysis of the appropriate division of responsibility between lawyer and client.

JEAN R. STERNLIGHT, LAWYERS' REPRESENTATION OF CLIENTS IN MEDIATION: USING ECONOMICS AND PSYCHOLOGY TO STRUCTURE ADVOCACY IN A NONADVERSARIAL SETTING, 14 Ohio St. J. on Disp. Resol. 269, 269–270, 274, 291–92, 295–96, 348–49, 354–58, 362, 365 (1999) [*]

Many believe that lawyers' adversarial methods and mindsets are inherently inconsistent with mediation. Lawyers' emphasis on advocacy and winning is seen as ill-suited to mediation's nonadversarial, problem-solving approach to dispute resolution. Yet, as mediation grows increasingly common, lawyers are frequently accompanying their clients to mediation and often play a critical and direct part in the process. Particularly where disputes are complex or involve relatively large sums of money, it is likely that one or both disputants will be represented by an attorney at the mediation.

* * *

[L]awyers need to be particularly vigilant in guarding against their own tendencies to behave in mediation exactly as they would in litigation. Instead, to serve their clients' interests, and in light of the conflicts of interest and perception between lawyers and their own clients, attorneys should often encourage their clients to play an active role in the mediation, allow the discussion to focus on emotional as well as legal concerns, and work toward mutually beneficial rather than win-or-lose solutions. Those lawyers who, seeking to advocate strongly on behalf of their clients, take steps to dominate the mediation, focus exclusively on legal issues, and minimize their clients' direct participation, will often ill serve their clients' true needs and interests. Such overly zealous advocates are frequently poor advocates.

If advocacy is defined broadly as supporting or pleading the cause of another, there is no inconsistency between advocacy and mediation. Permitting an attorney to act as an advocate for her client simply allows that attorney to speak and make arguments on her client's behalf and to help her client achieve her goals. * * * While some parties may be comfortable participating pro se, others may prefer to be aided by an attorney. If a party can advocate for her own interests, this Author sees no reason why her representative should not also be permitted to "advocate" on her behalf.

Nor is it clear why "adversarial" behavior, at least broadly defined, is necessarily inconsistent with mediation. To the extent that acting adversarially means advocating only on behalf of one's own client and not on behalf of any other party or on behalf of the process or system, the conduct is easy to reconcile with mediation. The problem-solving that works well in mediation does not require sacrifice of one's self-interest, but rather allows parties to search for solutions that are mutually beneficial.

* * *

Yet, while attorneys may appropriately advocate for their clients in mediation, it is certainly true that those attorneys who attempt to employ traditional "zealous" litigation tools when representing their clients in mediation may frequently (but not always) fail either to fulfill their clients' wishes or to serve their clients' interests. Those who would hoard information, rely solely on legal rather than emotional arguments, or refuse to let their clients speak freely will often have little success in mediation. This is not because attorneys ought not to advocate for their clients, but rather because attorneys ought not to advocate poorly on behalf of their clients. * * *

* * *

* * * Too many lawyers and clients have never thought seriously about how the lawyer-client relationship should work in the context of a mediation. Many lawyers, particularly those with extensive deposition or trial experience, have simply transferred their assumptions and behavior from those areas to the mediation forum without thinking through the differences between a trial or a deposition and a mediation. Such lawyers often instinctively try to do all the talking for the client, tell the client not to volunteer anything, try to stifle emotional outbursts, and focus primarily on establishing the superiority of their clients' legal positions rather than on a problem-solving approach. While this dominating approach may be appropriate in certain mediations, adopting it as a general rule will prevent the use of mediation to overcome the various barriers to negotiation.

Equally inappropriately, some lawyers, like some mediators, assume that mediation is exclusively the clients' process and either fail to attend altogether or do attend but act as the much discussed "potted plant." Such a lawyer may figure that because comments made in mediation are protected by confidentiality, and because no settlement can be reached without her client's agreement, the lawyer need not worry much, if at all, about protecting her client's interests. Again, while this approach may sometimes be appropriate, adopting it unthinkingly in every case is a mistake which may subject certain clients to coercion and abuse and ultimately cause them to accept a settlement which is unfair.

Instead of exclusively taking one approach or the other, lawyers and their clients should divide their responsibilities on a case-by-case basis after taking into account such factors as the nature of the clients and their attorneys, the respective goals of these participants, and the nature of the dispute. * * *

Proposed Guidelines for Determining the Respective Roles of Lawyer and Client

While a lawyer should consult with her client in determining how best to divide mediation responsibilities, the lawyer should still play a key role in helping the client to make this decision. As the lawyer does in other contexts, she should facilitate the client's choice by helping to lay out the advantages and disadvantages of various options. The lawyer should also be prepared to recommend particular divisions of responsibility given the client's expressed needs and desires. * * * [A]ttorneys [should] ask themselves the following two interrelated questions to help determine how to divide mediation responsibilities: (1) who is this particular client and (2) what barriers seem to be preventing the case from settling.

1. Who Is this Client?

* * *

a. Is This a Client Who Would Benefit from Playing an Active Role in the Mediation?

An attorney preparing to represent a client in a mediation should consider not only how the client's participation is likely to affect the value of the case, but also what benefits the mediation might potentially provide to the client. In doing so, attorneys will find it useful to think in terms of the possible economic and psychological barriers to negotiation and also to consider the many potential conflicts of interest between attorneys and their clients.

Although attorneys often think about cases primarily in terms of likelihood of success on the merits and consequential dollar value, either in court or in a settlement, they should recognize that clients' interests are not necessarily so narrow. Sometimes the client's interests are such that she would benefit from playing an active role in the mediation, even assuming for the sake of argument that such participation might lower the dollar value of the case. For example, the client may have nonmonetary interests or psychological needs such that she seeks an opportunity to voice her concerns or sense of injury to the opposing attorney. Or, the client may feel a strong need to apologize to the opposing party. Alternatively, the client may seek to preserve her relationship with the opposing party. In these and many other situations, it may be beneficial for the client to be provided with extensive opportunities to speak and listen in the mediation, even when such behavior might not be desirable from a purely financial perspective.

b. Is This a Client Who Requires Protection by the Attorney?

The attorney should also attempt to determine whether, in the particular context of the mediation, the client would best be served by having the lawyer play a dominant role. Attorneys can potentially protect clients in a mediation both by speaking on their behalf and also, in terms of perception, by effectively standing between the client and the opposing party or attorney.

The attorney should ask herself whether this particular client would benefit by having the attorney speak for her. Is the client inarticulate? Shy? Prone to anger quickly in a context when such anger would be detrimental to the client's interests or wishes? Alternatively, is the client incapable of providing the analysis that is required? Is she likely to say things she later regrets or that jeopardize her case? Some clients may have some of these characteristics. Certainly, they are not shared by all clients.

As well, the attorney should ask herself whether the client would benefit by having the attorney protect her from the opposing party. Although, ideally, mediation should be an opportunity for clients to communicate directly with one another, sometimes such direct communication by clients or their attorneys may be undesirable. At one extreme, if the client has been subjected to domestic abuse by the opposing party, it may be not only emotionally distressing but also coercive and even unsafe for the victim to converse directly with her abuser. A victim of sexual harassment may similarly be unable to bargain as an equal with her harasser. Even in personal injury or commercial disputes, certain clients may be subject to browbeating or coercion by the opposing party or attorney. Where a client's attorney fears that direct confrontations would have such an impact, she should at least recommend setting up the mediation so as to minimize such problems. For example, the attorney might request that the parties break into caucus immediately, or the attorney might attempt to interrupt the opposing party's presentation or to prevent certain presentations from being made.

In answering these questions, the attorney should be sure to approach them separately. A client who is not good at speaking up for herself might well be perfectly capable of hearing directly from the opposing party or vice versa.

2. What Are the Barriers to Negotiation?

Once having considered who the client is, an attorney can best analyze how to divide mediation responsibilities with her client by attempting to determine what, if any, barriers are preventing the case from settling in a way that would serve the client's interests. If a case goes to mediation, it is because the parties and their attorneys have not yet reached a mutually acceptable agreement. Why have they not? What has stopped them from predicting how a court would resolve the dispute and reaching the same solution on their own? Or, what has prevented them from reaching an even better solution than the one the court might impose? By focusing on the dispute in this fashion, clients and their attorneys will begin to see how they ought to divide their responsibilities so as to best overcome the barriers to a negotiated agreement. [The following excerpts are selected from Sternlight's discussion of potential barriers to settlement. She] uses the following nomenclature: the primary client is labeled "A," her lawyer "AL," her opponent "B," and her opponent's lawyer "BL." * * *

* * *

B Has Unrealistic Expectations Based on Lack of Information. If B is blocking a fair settlement because she has unrealistically high expectations regarding her likelihood of success at trial, AL and A should attempt to convince B that B's expectations are overblown. Each may have a role to play, depending on the nature of the misinformation. For example, sometimes a party may refuse to settle because she believes the opposing party will be a terrible witness who will therefore lose big at trial. In this situation, it may be desirable to allow that supposedly terrible witness, A, to play a very active role in the mediation to disprove B's false belief. Alternatively, if B thinks she has a sure winner in terms of the law, it may be important to have AL make a lengthy legal presentation to convince B that she is being overoptimistic. Usually AL will be better suited than A to convince B that her case is problematic in terms of the law.

* * *

A Has Unrealistic Expectations Based on Lack of Information. A may be unrealistically optimistic about her own chances of success because AL has failed to provide her client with complete information as to the negative aspects of her claim. As has been discussed, AL may fear that if she provides A with an accurate assessment of her chances A might become dissatisfied with AL's work as her attorney. Also, even where AL attempts to be completely honest with her client she may find that her client still sees the case in an over-optimistic light. AL can effectively deal with this phenomenon by letting A play an active part in the mediation. In this way, the mediator, the opposing attorney, and even the opposing client can all educate A as to the problems with her claim and the strengths of B's position. AL will not have to perform this educational function on her own.

A Is Engaging in Strategic Behavior. AL may realize that her own client A is not approaching the dispute from a problem-solving standpoint but rather is hoarding information and otherwise engaging in competitive behavior that may make it difficult to settle the dispute. AL may attempt to counter this tendency by encouraging A to participate actively in the mediation. If A begins to speak directly to the opposing party and to the mediator, A may start to see the benefits of working together toward a positive solution. By contrast, if A sits silently as AL serves as her gladiator, A may well become further rooted in her win-lose mentality.

A Has Unmet Nonmonetary Goals. A may feel unable or unwilling to settle until she has expressed her feelings toward B, has received an apology from B, has apologized to B, has had her honor restored, or has achieved justice. In these circumstances, it may well be desirable to let A play an important and direct role in the mediation. By presenting at least a significant portion of the opening statement, A may, for example, vent her anger or make or demand an apology. By participating actively in the joint session, A can also work toward a problem-solving solution that can help meet her nonmonetary needs.

* * *

Anyone who says they have a simple answer to the question of how lawyers and clients should divide their responsibilities in a mediation must be wrong. Either their answer is not simple or their answer is not right. The answer is complicated because the division of responsibilities should vary substantially depending upon who the client is, who the lawyer is, and what factors appear to be blocking a reasonable and fair settlement of the dispute. Allowing clients to participate actively and directly in a mediation can be critically important in overcoming barriers to settlement. * * * Yet, at the same time, attorneys must sometimes play a more dominant protective role to ensure that their clients are not duped, harmed, coerced, or otherwise taken advantage of in the course of mediation.

NOTES

1. From the perspective of effective representation, do some of the advantages Professor Sternlight suggests for client participation, such as the opportunity to vent, worry you? Is she giving undue weight to clients' nonmonetary concerns? Can you generalize about the weight clients place on nonmonetary vs. monetary goals in resolving a dispute?

2. Not all attorneys agree that clients should attend mediation sessions. They argue that, as professionals, lawyers have a better understanding of the mediation process. If lawyers can be convinced that a proposal is reasonable, they can be counted on to recommend it to the client. Furthermore, when clients are not present, attorneys often feel less need to posture and openly support the client's position. They can be more forthright about the strengths and weaknesses of the case. Finally, if the client is not present, he cannot hurt his case with an inadvertent remark. Do these arguments convince you?

3. If a client is to attend and take an active role in mediation, what type of preparation is appropriate?

The following two excerpts were written by lawyers with experience both as litigators and as mediators. The first examines advocacy in the party's initial statement. This is one element of a mediation session that can be planned in detail in advance. A common division of labor is that the attorney presents the legal claim and supporting arguments while the client discusses the business or personal effects of the situation and how she would like to resolve it. The second offers advice on the mediation process overall by identifying common attorney errors in mediation advocacy.

LAWRENCE M. WATSON, JR., EFFECTIVE LEGAL REPRESENTATION IN MEDIATION, *in* **ALTERNATIVE DISPUTE RESOLUTION IN FLORIDA 2-1, 2-14 to 2-26 (1995)** *

Making Opening Presentations

a. *Purpose and Significance.* Opening presentations are one of the most important parts of the mediation process. The obvious purpose of the opening presentation is to describe the dispute to the mediator and define the issues to be adjudicated should the matter go to trial or arbitration. A number of other messages are sent in opening presentations, however, and a number of other critical objectives can be achieved. Careful and thoughtful preparation by counsel for this phase of the proceedings is essential. Opening presentations provide an opportunity for the lawyer to do far more than merely describe the case as a legally recognized claim; the attorney also has the opportunity to plead the client's entire cause.

b. *Presenting a Claim.* Presenting a legally recognizable claim is a critical goal in opening presentations. The attorney must try to convincingly present the client's legal position to both the mediator (to ensure that he or she understands the points in dispute and thus appropriately directs the focus of following discussions) and the opposing party (to ensure that he or she gains a clear understanding of the totality of the dispute). In presenting the claim, the advocate also should firmly and persuasively raise the plausibility of an unfavorable outcome for the opposition should the matter be adjudicated on the merits of the parties' positions. The objective is to diminish the value of the opposing party's alternatives to a negotiated settlement.

c. *Presenting Parties' Interests.* Quite beyond presenting legal positions, opening presentations afford the attorney an opportunity to address the interests of the parties in reaching a fair settlement of the dispute. Matters that would never come into play in a courtroom, such as business trade-offs, confidentiality, future relationships, precedents, reputation, and costs, can be advanced to influence a favorable outcome. In fact, in mediation the parties are free to, and should, address any facts or circumstances having a direct and real bearing on settlement of a claim.

In opening presentations, the lawyer may deal with emotional issues, hearsay, impressions, rumors, and real and perceived damages — a host of factors that directly bear on the dispute in the minds of the parties but that may not be entirely relevant or appropriate for consideration in court.

d. *Expressing Emotions.* Opening presentations can also provide an important opportunity for the client to "vent"; that is, for the client to present (and, it is hoped, exhaust) his or her emotional position regarding the dispute. A short, direct statement by the client expressing this aspect of the dispute will clear the client's emotional agenda of items that, if not stated, may block fair consideration of settlement alternatives. After expressing feelings to someone in authority (getting their "day in court"), clients may more readily turn to pragmatic negotiations.

---

e. *Evaluating Total Dispute*. Finally, opening presentations provide an opportunity for the attorney and client to listen and learn; to develop an appreciation for both sides of the dispute. Although it is not expected that anyone will be won over or induced to change their minds on hearing an opening presentation, the parties are nonetheless given a chance to form a realistic appreciation for the other side's position and to hear it contrasted with their own. In this respect, opening presentations offer a view of the opposition's case that traditional discovery cannot reveal. The attorney and the client will see the other side of the argument formally advanced in a comprehensive, inclusive fashion that generally isn't available until trial.

f. *Devising Form Of Opening Presentation*. Opening presentations made in mediation are roughly in the form of opening statements at trial. More accurately, perhaps, opening presentations should take the form of an explanatory and informative speech that seeks to instruct more than persuade. The challenge of the opening presentation in a mediation is to communicate.

The opening presentation affords an excellent opportunity to use creative visual aids to make the client's position more understandable and compelling. Examples include the following:

1. Enlarged time line charts illustrating the chronological sequence of events in complex cases.

2. Organizational charts describing relationships between the parties, controlling agreements, or business transactions.

3. Blown-up diagrams or photographs of the scene.

4. Schematics or illustrations of products involved.

5. Construction drawings with annotations.

6. Damage summaries and calculations.

Perhaps the biggest adjustment a trial lawyer must make in developing and delivering a mediation presentation is in the overall tone and in the treatment of the opposition. Both should be firm and factual, but neither should be overly zealous or excitable. The attorney must remember that mediation is a consensual process aimed at creating a logical basis for re-evaluating legal positions, recognizing individual interests, and moving to an agreement that accommodates and compromises. To convince a party to change a position, the attorney must deal with what underlies that position in a manner that does not directly attack its moral legitimacy or legal correctness.

In the following actual cases, an imaginative and relevant opening presentation went directly to the real issues (not necessarily the legal elements of the case) impacting settlement:

CASE 1: Jones, a mechanic, was severely injured while working with a product manufactured by Acme. There is a nationwide history of the Acme product becoming susceptible to an injury-causing explosion when operated improperly. Despite warnings on the product and published literature, users tend to follow traditional methods of operation that often lead to disastrous results. Jones was no exception. His claim questioned the sufficiency of the product design and the warnings. Acme's defense raised comparative negligence as a primary issue.

In addition to carefully preparing his case in a conventional manner, Mr. Jones's attorney obtained statistics from consumer groups describing the outcome of previous lawsuits against Acme and other manufacturers. His demand, developed in consultation with Jones and his family, was heavily influenced by a personal interest in getting "what these cases are getting nationwide" and "what Acme paid elsewhere."

During the course of the mediation, the defense attorneys directly addressed the desire expressed by Jones's attorney to obtain a settlement comparable to those in other cases. They did so by presenting an enlarged chart showing every other case in the country that involved an explosion of the Acme product, listing all distinguishing facts, and reporting their actual present status or outcome after settlement, trial, or appeal. This data was used to illustrate that the statistical information received by the plaintiff was neither entirely complete nor current, and that a substantial number of the Acme cases were victories for the defense.

After thus dealing with Jones's expressed interest to be treated comparably with other claimants, the defense attorneys addressed the technical issues involved in the parties' respective legal positions. They produced an enlarged reprint of the applicable jury instructions on comparative negligence. After the instructions were carefully discussed, another chart was presented bearing the title, "Plaintiff's Acts of Comparative Negligence." On it, each act by Jones that arguably contributed to his own injury was listed beneath a peel-off cover. One by one, the covers were removed, each act thoroughly discussed, and the evidence of each act outlined. As each act was discussed, an estimate of the percentage of fault the jury might apply to that act was made. Several acts of comparative negligence were thus described, and each was given its own percentage contribution to the injury. Not surprisingly, when the chart stood fully explained and the percentages for each act of negligence by Jones had been added, the chart revealed the result a far greater percentage of fault attributable to the plaintiff than to the defendant.

The defense attorneys, in non-argumentative, non-confrontational tones, thus dealt with the impressions directly influencing the plaintiff's thinking on the value of his case and underscored the potential legal impact of their comparative negligence defense. The claimant's position changed and the case settled with an agreement satisfactory to both sides.

CASE 2: A complex mortgage foreclosure on a shopping center was filed that drew a counterclaim on the note and raised a major issue as to the existence and amount of any deficiency after the foreclosure sale. The defendant debtor was the developer of the shopping center and currently served as landlord to retail tenants struggling to stay alive. It was anticipated that the foreclosure action would drive off the few remaining tenants and doom the shopping center.

The entire opening presentation in mediation dealt with the business interests of both parties that arguably called for a deal rather than a trial. A "position paper" prepared by the defendant developer was distributed. It was entitled, "Why (Lender) Should Settle." The position paper explored the probable cost and consequences of every possible variation of what could occur if the litigation proceeded; i.e., winning the foreclosure, the counterclaim, and the deficiency, then suffering the costs and time consumed with an appeal; winning the foreclosure, losing the counterclaim, losing the deficiency issue and owing money; losing the foreclosure, losing the counterclaim, and facing fee and expense assessments.

Another chart was prepared graphically showing the status of every lease, the income each one generated, and a brief statement of the attitude toward the lawsuit expressed by some of the key tenants. The illustration provided an excellent description of the critical economic balance being maintained at the center. The result was a very compelling argument that a settlement was essential to every party to the dispute.

The presentation then concluded with an enlarged chart depicting the benefits of settlement, including everything from the future business dealings of the specific parties to the overall economic welfare of the community.

*   *   *

In other situations, imaginative attorneys have used blow-ups of key provisions in case opinions to illustrate the probable outcome of pending motions or preliminary rulings; overhead views to contrast conflicting or inconsistent construction specifications with blueprints and contract terms; and videotapes to illustrate everything from manufacturing techniques to construction methodology. In short, the attorneys used whatever was needed to meet the objectives of opening presentations in mediation — informing the mediator, telling the client's story, and giving the opposition a taste of the other side of the argument — everything necessary to "plead the cause."

g. *Involving the Client.* One final but very important note on opening presentations is that the attorney must not forget the client. Although the lawyer must exercise professional judgment to control presentation of data at trial, the mediation process belongs more to the client than to the attorney. The attorney should not automatically exclude the client from presenting information directly to the mediator and opposing party. In court, attorneys must control the flow of data to the judge and jury in order to comply with the laws of evidence, procedure, and precedent. In mediation, there are no such rules to restrict the parties from saying whatever they want, whenever they want. As noted. . ., one objective of opening presentations is to vent the client's frustration, dismay, anger, or emotional turmoil associated with the dispute. More often than not, the client is the best person to express these feelings and to make them understood.

If the client's emotions are not aired in opening presentations, it is absolutely essential that they be cleared in the private caucuses to follow.

TOM ARNOLD, 20 COMMON ERRORS IN MEDIATION ADVOCACY, 13 Alternatives to High Cost Litig. 69–71 (1995) *

Trial lawyers who are unaccustomed to being mediation advocates often miss important arguments. Here are 20 common errors, and ways to correct them.

Problem 1: Wrong client in the room. CEOs settle more cases than vice presidents, house counsel or other agents. Why? For one thing, they don't need to worry about criticism back at the office. Any lesser agent, even with explicit "authority," typically must please a constituency which was not a participant in the give and take of the mediation. That makes it hard to settle cases.

A client's personality also can be a factor. A "Rambo," who is aggressive, critical, unforgiving, or self-righteous doesn't tend to be conciliatory. The best peace-makers show creativity, and tolerance for the mistakes of others. Of course, it also helps to know the subject.

Problem 2: Wrong lawyer in the room. Many capable trial lawyers are so confident that they can persuade a jury of anything (after all, they've done it before), that they discount the importance of preserving relationships, as well as the exorbitant costs and emotional drain of litigation. They can smell a "win" in the court room, and so approach mediation with a measure of ambivalence.

Transaction lawyers, in contrast, tend to be better mediation counsel. At a minimum, parties should look for sensitive, flexible, understanding people who will do their homework, no matter their job experience. Good preparation makes for more and better settlements. A lawyer who won't prepare is the wrong lawyer.

Problem 3: Wrong mediator in the room. Some mediators are generous about lending their conference rooms but bring nothing to the table. Some of them determine their view of the case and urge the parties to accept that view without exploring likely win-win alternatives.

The best mediators can work within a range of styles that * * * fall along a continuum, from being totally facilitative, to offering an evaluation of the case. Ideally, mediators should fit the mediation style to the case and the parties before them, often moving from style to style as a mediation progresses.

Masters of the process can render valuable services whether or not they have substantive expertise. When do the parties need an expert? When they want an evaluative mediator, or someone who can cast meaningful lights and shadows on the merits of the case and alternative settlements.

It may not always be possible to know and evaluate a mediator and fit the choice of mediator to your case. But the wrong mediator may fail to get a settlement another mediator might have finessed.

Problem 4: Wrong case. Almost every type of case, from antitrust or patent infringement to unfair competition and employment disputes, is a likely candidate for mediation. Occasionally, cases don't fit the mold, not because of the substance of the dispute, but because one or both parties want to set a precedent.

For example, a franchisor that needs a legal precedent construing a key clause that is found in 3,000 franchise agreements might not want to submit the case to mediation. Likewise, an infringement suit early in the life of an uncertain patent might be better resolved in court; getting the Federal Circuit stamp of validity could generate industry respect not obtainable from ADR.

Problem 5: Omitting client preparation. Lawyers should educate their clients about the process. Clients need to know the answers to the types of questions the mediator is likely to ask. At the same time, they need to understand that the other party (rather than the mediator) should be the focus of each side's presentation.

In addition, lawyers should interview clients about the client's and the adversary's "best alternative to negotiated agreement," and "worst alternative to negotiated agreement." * * * A party should accept any offer better than his perceived BATNA and reject any offer seen as worse than his perceived WATNA. So the BATNAs and WATNAs are critical frames of reference for accepting offers and for determining what offers to propose to the other parties. A weak or false understanding of either party's BATNA or WATNA obstructs settlements and begets bad settlements.

Other topics to cover with the client:

— the difference between their interests and their legal positions;

— the variety of options that might settle the case;

— the strengths and weaknesses of their case;

— objective independent standards of evaluation;

— the importance of apology and empathy.

Problem 6: Not letting a client open for herself. At least as often as not, letting the properly coached client do most, or even all, of the opening and tell the story in her own words works much better than lengthy openings by the lawyer.

Problem 7: Addressing the mediator instead of the other side. Most lawyers open the mediation with a statement directed at the mediator, comparable to opening statements to a judge or jury. Highly adversarial in tone, it overlooks the interests of the other side that gave rise to the dispute.

Why is this strategy a mistake? The "judge or jury" you should be trying to persuade in a mediation is not the mediator, but the adversary. If you want to make the other party sympathetic to your cause, don't hurt him. For the same reason, plenary sessions should demonstrate your client's humanity, respect, warmth, apologies and sympathy. Stay away from inflammatory issues, which are better addressed by the mediator in private caucuses with the other side.

Problem 8: Making the lawyer the center of the process. Unless the client is highly unappealing or inarticulate, the client should be the center of the process. The company representative for the other side may not have attended depositions, so is unaware of the impact your client could have on a judge or jury if the mediation fails. People pay more attention to appealing plaintiffs, so show them off. Prepare the client to speak and be spoken to by the mediator and the adversary. He should be able to explain why he feels the way he does, why he is or is not responsible, and why any damages he caused are great or only peanuts. But he should also extend empathy to the other party.

Problem 9: Failure to use advocacy tools effectively. You'll want to prepare your materials for maximum persuasive impact. Exhibits, charts, and copies of relevant cases or contracts with key phrases highlighted can be valuable visual aids. A 90-second video showing key witnesses in depositions making important admissions, followed by a readable size copy of an important document with some relevant language underlined, can pack a punch.

Problem 10: Timing mistakes. Get and give critical discovery, but don't spend exorbitant time or sums in discovery and trial prep before seeking mediation.

Mediation can identify what's truly necessary discovery and avoid unnecessary discovery. One of my own war stories: With a mediation under way and both parties relying on their perception of the views of a certain vice president, I leaned over, picked up the phone, called the vice president, introduced myself as the mediator, and asked whether he could give us a deposition the following morning. "No," said he, "I've got a Board meeting at 10:00." "How about 7:30 a.m., with a one-hour limit?" I asked. "It really is pretty important that this decision not be delayed." The parties took the deposition and settled the case before the 10:00 board meeting.

Problem 11: Failure to listen to the other side. Many lawyers and clients seem incapable of giving open-minded attention to what the other side is saying. That could cost a settlement.

Problem 12: Failure to identify perceptions and motivations. Seek first to understand, only then to be understood. [It is useful to] brainstorm to determine the other party's motivations and perceptions. Prepare a chart summarizing how your adversary sees the issues. * * *

Problem 13: Hurting, humiliating, threatening, or commanding. Don't poison the well from which you must drink to get a settlement. That means you don't hurt, humiliate or ridicule the other folks. Avoid pejoratives like "malingerer," "fraud," "cheat," "crook," or "liar." You can be strong on what your evidence will be and still be a decent human being. All settlements are based upon trust to some degree. If you anger the other side, they won't trust you. This inhibits settlement. The same can be said for threats, like a threat to get the other lawyer's license revoked for pursuing such a frivolous cause, or for his grossly inaccurate pleadings. Ultimatums destroy the process, and destroy credibility. Yes, there is a time in mediation to walk out — whether or not you plan to return. But a series of ultimatums, or even one ultimatum, most often is very counterproductive.

Problem 14: The backwards step. A party who offered to pay $300,000 before the mediation, and comes to the mediation table willing to offer only $200,000, injures its own credibility and engenders bad feelings from the other side. Without some clear and dramatic reasons for the reduction in the offer, it can be hard to overcome the damage done. * * *

Problem 15: Too many people. Advisors — people to whom the decision-maker must display respect and courtesy, people who feel that since they are there they must put in their two bits worth — all delay a mediation immeasurably. A caucus that with only one lawyer and vice president would take 20 minutes, with five people could take an hour and 20 minutes. What could have been a one-day mediation stretches to two or three.

This is one context in which I use the "one martini lunch." Once I think that everyone present understands all the issues, I will send principals who have been respectful out to negotiate alone. Most come back with an expression of oral settlement within three hours. Of course, the next step is to brush up on details they overlooked, draw up a written agreement and get it signed. But usually those finishing touches don't ruin the deal.

Problem 16: Closing too fast. A party who opens at $1 million, and moves immediately to $500,000, gives the impression of having more to give. Rightly or wrongly, the other side probably will not accept the $500,000 offer because they expect more give. By contrast, moving from $1 million to $750,000, $600,000, $575,000, $560,000, $550,000, sends no message of yield below $500,000, and may induce a $500,000 proposal that can be accepted. The "dance" is part of communication. Skip the dance, lose the communication, and risk losing settlement at your own figure.

Problem 17: Failure to truly close. Unless parties have strong reasons to "sleep on" their agreement, to further evaluate the deal, or to check on possibly forgotten details, it is better to get some sort of enforceable contract written and signed before the parties separate. Too often, when left to think overnight and draft tomorrow, the parties think of new ideas that delay or prevent closing.

Problem 18: Breaching a confidentiality. Sometimes parties to a mediation unthinkingly, or irresponsibly, disclose in open court information revealed confidentially in a mediation. When information is highly sensitive, consider keeping it confidential with the mediator. Or if revealed to the adversary in a mediation where the case did not settle, consider moving before the trial begins for an order in limine to bind both sides to the confidentiality agreement.

Problem 19: Lack of patience and perseverance. The mediation "dance" takes time. Good mediation advocates have patience and perseverance.

Problem 20: Misunderstanding conflict. A dispute is a problem to be solved together, not a combat to be won. To prepare for mediation, rehearse answers to the following questions, which the mediator is likely to ask:

— How do you feel about this dispute? Or about the other party?

— What do you really want in the resolution of this dispute?

— What are your expectations from a trial? Are they realistic?

— What are the weaknesses in your case?

— What law or fact in your case would you like to change?

— What scares you most?

— What would it feel like to be in your adversary's shoes?

— What specific evidence do you have to support each element of your case?

— What will the jury charge and interrogatories probably be?

— What is the probability of a verdict your way on liability?

— What is the range of damages you think a jury would return in his case if it found liability?

— What are the likely settlement structures, from among the following possibilities: Terms, dollars, injunction, services, performance, product, recision, apology, costs, attorney fees, releases.

— What constituency pressures burden the other party? Which ones burden you?

NOTES

1. How would you characterize the tone of an effective opening statement in mediation? How is it different from the type of advocacy that would be appropriate in court? Do you think it is any less challenging?

2. One effective technique for presenting a strong case in mediation in a dispassionate way that avoids angering the other side is to frame the argument in terms of what one *would* do in front of a jury: "I would explain that the materials my client received were defective. . .." rather than "The materials my client received were defective. . .." Can you think of other techniques that would be conducive to setting a problem-solving atmosphere?

3. Are there advantages to having an opportunity to make a presentation without being interrupted by objections and without the need to elicit points through questions? In terms of the client's sense of procedural justice, do you think mediation or adjudication provides a more satisfying way for a client to express herself?

4. Problem number 21 on Arnold's list could be failing to memorialize the agreement before ending the mediation session. Some observers might even list it as problem number 1. At the end of a lengthy mediation everyone is tired and ready to leave. The temptation is to shake hands and leave the drafting for the next day. This is a risky choice because sometimes the agreement is not ironed out as well as the participants believe. Many of the litigated cases in which a party is trying to enforce an oral agreement reached in mediation stem from a mediation session in which the parties reached an agreement in principle but left the details to the attorneys to draft. (*See* Coben & Thompson, 2006, at 79, 142–43.) Drafting an agreement on the spot can reveal misperceptions and miscommunications that could otherwise surface later. Complex agreements, however, may require extensive drafting that is not practical at a mediation session. In this situation, however, an attorney should consider using a memorandum of understanding, signed by both parties, to record the key terms of the agreement. Another technique is to come to the mediation armed with drafts of releases and other documents that can be modified and signed. If disagreements about the settlement do arise during delayed drafting, what would be one sensible course for the parties and their attorneys?

Chapter 7

LEGAL AND PUBLIC POLICY ISSUES IN MEDIATION

A. CONFIDENTIALITY

The assurance of confidentiality is crucial to the mediation process. From the parties' perspective, in order to be willing to discuss their situation candidly in mediation they need to be confident that what they say will not be disclosed against their wishes on two levels: within the process and outside the process. Within the mediation process, a party needs to be able to trust that the mediator will not convey sensitive information disclosed in caucus to the adverse party without permission. Outside the process, parties may need protection from disclosures in court proceedings or they may seek privacy from the press or public. Without legal protections, adverse disclosures could either be initiated by someone who participated in the mediation or sought by someone who did not. In addition to the parties' interest in preventing disclosures, the mediator also has a professional interest in maintaining confidentiality. Furthermore, for court-connected mediation programs, courts have separate concerns linked to the integrity of their processes. The following except discusses these multiple perspectives on the rationales for confidentiality in the complex setting of mediation.

ELLEN E. DEASON, THE QUEST FOR UNIFORMITY IN MEDIATION CONFIDENTIALITY, 85 Marquette L. Rev. 79, 80–84 (2001) *

A fundamental part of the difficulty in communicating with an adversary is the threat of disclosure to one's disadvantage. This threat has more facets in mediation than in other protected settings. In an attorney-client consultation, for example, disclosures typically do not originate from either of the pair who exchanges information. Instead, the privilege functions to prevent an outside adversary from compelling the attorney or client to reveal their communications. In mediation, however, the adversary with whom the exchange needs to take place is also a major source of potential disclosures. If a lawsuit is a possibility, or especially if one is already underway, much that might be said in a good faith attempt to reach settlement during a mediation could become an admission against interest in the courtroom in the absence of confidentiality protections. It would be unrealistic to trust that the opposing party would refrain from using these communications to its litigation advantage. Even without a lawsuit, by the time disputing parties reach mediation, their relationship often has degenerated into animosity and distrust. Therefore, in many mediations, confidentiality does far more than merely enhance the candid nature of the discussion; between some adversaries, confidentiality may be akin to a precondition for any discussion.

Because mediation involves communications with an adversary, the legal structures that promote confidentiality must do more than function as a restraint on outside parties who seek disclosure; they must also provide a substitute for trust between those who are communicating. This is accomplished by limiting the adverse party's ability to disclose or make use of mediation communications. In this respect, assurances of confidentiality reduce the chilling potential of disclosures, whether initiated from inside or outside the group of mediation participants. Parties are then free to explore possibilities for a resolution to their dispute without worrying about the consequences in the courtroom if their exploration does not succeed.

Second, confidentiality is important for maintaining the neutrality of the mediator. * * * [A] mediator who testifies will inevitably be seen as acting contrary to the interests of one of the parties, which necessarily destroys her neutrality. It is true that this departure from neutrality is not personal or intentional when a mediator is compelled to testify under subpoena. Nonetheless, if a mediator can be converted into the opposing party's weapon in court, then her neutrality is only temporary and illusory.

* * *

Third, when a dispute in mediation is also the subject of a lawsuit, confidentiality provisions perform an important role by keeping the judging function separate from the mediation function. This separation is especially important for court-annexed mediation programs or referrals from other decision-making bodies, because the referral links these functions more closely than when a privately mediated dispute is later litigated. Without assurances of confidentiality between court mediators and judges or arbitrators, parties may fear that their conversations with the mediator could be conveyed informally to the decision-maker. This fear of backdoor disclosures could be quite chilling for mediation, notwithstanding limitations on introducing mediation information as evidence in a lawsuit. The problem is especially great if the parties face the prospect of a bench trial in the event that they fail to settle the case.

Moreover, confidentiality between mediators and judges helps protect the integrity of both processes. As with other *ex parte* communications, communications between a mediator and the assigned judge cast doubt on the judge's decision-making neutrality. Such communications can also raise questions about the independence of the mediator from judicial influences. When courts provide mediation, and especially when they mandate mediation, they need to carefully prevent improper cross-communication if they are to avoid the appearance of bias on the part of the judge or mediator.

In sum, the challenge of communicating with an adversary, the presence of a neutral intermediary, and the potential for information informally reaching a judge all make confidentiality especially important for mediation. Each of these aspects of mediation also carries its own implications for how confidentiality protections need to be structured.

1. LEGAL METHODS FOR PROTECTING CONFIDENTIALITY

Confidentiality within the mediation process is not controlled by law, but is an obligation of the mediator as a matter of professional responsibility. The Model Standards of Conduct for Mediators, adopted in 2005 by the American Arbitration Association, the American Bar Association and the Association for Conflict Resolution, provide in Standard V(B):

> A mediator who meets with any persons in private session during a mediation shall not convey directly or indirectly to any other person, any information that was obtained during that private session without the consent of the disclosing person.

Outside the mediation process, several legal mechanisms provide varying degrees of protection against disclosures of communications made during mediation. The primary mechanisms are evidentiary exclusionary rules, agreements by the parties, privileges, and court rules.

a. Evidentiary Exclusionary Rules

To encourage parties to settle their disputes, Rule 408 of the Federal Rules of Evidence provides confidentiality protection for settlement discussions. Most states have an identical provision in their evidentiary codes. When mediations serve as settlement discussions, Rule 408 protects the confidentiality of mediation communications. Rule 408 provides:

> Rule 408. Compromise and Offers to Compromise. Evidence of (1) furnishing or offering or promising to furnish, or (2) accepting or offering or promising to accept, a valuable consideration in compromising or attempting to compromise a claim which was disputed as to either validity or amount, is not admissible to prove liability for or invalidity of the claim or its amount. Evidence of conduct or statements made in compromise negotiations is likewise not admissible. This rule does not require the exclusion of any evidence otherwise discoverable merely because it is presented in the course of compromise negotiations. This rule also does not require exclusion when the evidence is offered for another purpose, such as proving bias or prejudice of a witness, negativing a contention of undue delay, or proving an effort to obstruct a criminal investigation or prosecution.

Although some legal experts argue that the protections of Rule 408 are sufficient for mediation, it does not cover a number of situations in which communications are commonly sought or disclosed.

NOTES

1. The Big State University fired the coach of the women's basketball team amid rumors of sexual misconduct on his part. The coach, now employed at Little State U, has sued Big State U, alleging that his termination was motivated by racial discrimination. He seeks back pay for the period he was unemployed. The coach and the director of athletics participated in a mediation but were unable to settle the case. How would Rule 408 apply in the following circumstances?

a. The coach notices a deposition of the mediator. Big State U and the mediator object.

b. At trial, the coach seeks to testify about certain statements the athletic director made during the mediation as evidence of Big State U's liability.

c. At trial, the coach seeks to introduce an offer of reinstatement made by the athletic director during the mediation as evidence of Big State U's liability.

d. At trial, the athletic director claims that the coach was fired for misconduct. The coach seeks to introduce evidence of the offer of reinstatement to impeach this testimony.

e. The coach and Big State U stipulate that each party should be able to testify about a discussion that occurred during the mediation concerning the retirement terms for prior coaches. The coach thinks this evidence will help him prove liability; the university thinks it will help it defend against the coach's claim.

f. The coach writes a letter to the local newspaper in which he describes the mediation and everything the athletic director said during the process.

g. One of the players on the basketball team files suit against Big State U claiming that it failed to adequately supervise the coach, and that he had engaged in sexual harassment. Big State U denies these allegations. At trial, the player seeks to introduce evidence of the athletic director's statements to the coach during the mediation.

h. The local newspaper files a Freedom of Information Act suit under applicable state law seeking notes the mediator took during the mediation. Notes taken at meetings of state employees or officials are typically treated as public records for purposes of the state Freedom of Information Act.

b. Confidentiality Agreements

Parties often sign agreements to keep the content of a mediation confidential either as part of an agreement to mediate or at the start of the mediation session. Such agreements are enforceable contracts that, if breached, could give rise to a cause of action for money damages. In a subsequent court proceeding, a judge *may* enforce a confidentiality agreement by excluding evidence of what took place during a mediation. The following case discusses the factors that a court should consider in deciding whether to enforce a confidentiality agreement for settlement discussions.

TOWER ACTON HOLDINGS, LLC v. LOS ANGELES COUNTY WATERWORKS DISTRICT NO. 37
129 Cal. Rptr. 2d 640, 641–42, 647–49 (Cal. Ct. App. 2002), *as modified on denial of reh'g* (2003)

CROSKEY, J.

[Developers brought breach of contract and breach of the covenant of good faith and fair dealing claims against the Los Angeles County Waterworks District No. 37 (District). The contract was a Master Service Agreement (M.S.A.) for the creation of a water system. The construction of the infrastructure necessary to deliver water to their housing development was to be financed by a community facilities district formed by the developers. The developers sued the District for reimbursement for creating surplus water capacity.] The specific contractual provision allegedly breached by District was one that required District to ensure that "future development" would pay its "fair share" for the cost of building the Acton III Water Improvements.

*   *   *

Plaintiffs negotiated with District for a "reimbursement agreement" that would have increased the number of users subject to paying for the improvements and increased the total repayment owed to the bondholders. When District refused to agree to the terms Plaintiffs wanted, they sued, contending that District had breached the M.S.A. and the covenant of good faith and fair dealing implied therein by failing to ensure that "future development" would pay its "fair share" for the Acton III Water Improvements. Specifically, they alleged that District had acted in bad faith by unreasonably taking the position that (1) it could not agree to Plaintiffs' proposed interest rate and term because it was constrained by the Public Contract Code, and (2) certain properties should not be subject to paying for the Acton III Water Improvements, because they were not *directly* benefited by the Acton III Water Improvements. * * *

The jury returned a nine-to-three verdict in favor of Plaintiffs and against District. District appeals from the resulting $10 million judgment and a post-judgment award of attorney fees entered in favor of Plaintiffs. After a careful review of the extensive record, we conclude that the trial court committed reversible error when it instructed the jury that the Public Contract Code was not applicable, and admitted over objection evidence of the parties' settlement negotiations.

*   *   *

It Was Error to Admit Evidence of Settlement Negotiations

District contends that the trial court erred by admitting, over its objections, evidence related to the parties' attempts to reach a reimbursement agreement. It relies on a stipulation between Plaintiffs and District that it asserts prevented the use of any such materials at trial. We agree with District that such evidence was inadmissible.

The parties had entered into an agreement in March 1997, before Plaintiffs filed their claim or complaint against District, that no materials or discussions from their negotiations could be used in subsequent litigation. The agreement provided that it would be effective "until such agreement is terminated by either party in writing." In May, before filing their claim, Plaintiffs wrote to District, stating that they intended to file a claim to protect their interests, but that they continued to wish to work with District to try to resolve the parties' disputes without litigation. In fact, even after Plaintiffs filed their complaint, they and District continued for several years to attempt to resolve the reimbursement issue, and exchanged various letters and drafts of possible agreements.

The trial court concluded that the agreement that these materials could not be used at trial terminated when Plaintiffs filed their complaint, and that evidence of discussions after that date were admissible. This was error. The agreement provided that it would be effective "until such agreement is terminated by either party in writing," and there was no writing that terminated the agreement. Plaintiffs' complaint, although a "writing," did not state that it terminated the agreement, and there is no reason to treat the filing of the complaint as having such an effect, particularly as the parties continued to negotiate a resolution of their differences long after the complaint was filed.

Plaintiffs contend that evidence of these negotiations was admissible, regardless of the agreement to the contrary, * * * because such evidence was offered to prove District's bad faith, not its liability. However, the parties' agreement was not worded so as to apply only to exclude evidence used to prove liability. Thus, as we now discuss, if such agreement was not contrary to public policy, it was enforceable as written. This means that evidence of the parties' negotiations should have been excluded no matter for what reason it was offered.

There is little case law on the enforceability of contracts to protect the confidentiality of settlement communications. (See Brazil, *Protecting The Confidentiality of Settlement Negotiations* (1988) 39 Hastings L.J. 955, 1026–1039 (1988).) According to one commentator, the enforceability of such contracts is not always clear, because it is possible that a judge might refuse to enforce such an agreement on the ground that it provides a method of excluding evidence not specifically adopted by the Legislature, or because a judge might view it as invading a judicial prerogative, such as restricting the court's power to make sure the jury receives all evidence that will help it ascertain the truth, particularly if the evidence, although contractually-excluded, is relevant to prove that the parties engaged in illegal conduct or set up a relationship that violated public policy.

The same commentator opined, however, that confidentiality contracts that threaten none of these more compelling public policies may be as enforceable as any other contract, if the contracting parties are competent and represented by counsel, and there are not dangerous differences in bargaining power between them. Thus, a confidentiality contract that is not otherwise objection-able, and that supports some public policy, will be enforced. (See, e.g., *Simrin v. Simrin* (1965) 233 Cal.App.2d 90, 94–95, 43 Cal.Rptr. 376 [enforcing agreement by husband and wife that statements made to rabbi acting as a marriage counselor would be confidential; although clergyman-penitent privi-lege did not apply because the rabbi was not acting as a spiritual advisor, the agreement did not violate public policy favoring attempts to preserve marital unit].)

As already suggested, however, courts will not enforce such agreements if their purpose or effect violates public policy. This is because a law established for a public reason cannot be waived or circumvented by a private act or agreement, nor will a court enforce a contract made in violation of established public policy.

Regardless of the particular facts of a case, these same principles could be applied to honor, or refuse to honor, a contract that the parties would not disclose or admit at trial communications occurring during settlement negotiations. So, too, courts could apply precedents related to the enforceability of stipulations to relieve a party of an apparent contractual commitment limiting the admissibility of communications made or acts committed during the course of settlement discussions, for example, because of fraud, misrepresentation, mistake of fact, or excusable neglect, or because there has been such a substantial change in circumstances that binding the party to the stipulation would be unfair.

In this case, there is no reason that the exclusion agreement between Plaintiffs and District should not be enforced. There is no evidence that the agreement was obtained by fraud, misrepresentation, mistake of fact, or excusable neglect, or that there was a substantial change in circumstances that would make enforcing the agreement unfair to Plaintiffs, particularly as Plaintiffs could have unilaterally terminated the agreement at any time. Nor does public policy militate against enforcing the agreement. California's public policy is to encourage settlement. Settlement is encouraged by allowing the parties to communicate freely, without fear that their communications may be used against them if settlement negotiations are not successful.

The admission of such evidence was prejudicial in light of the erroneous instruction that the Public Contract Code did not apply and for the same reasons. Here, given the absence of any other evidence of bad faith, it is reasonably probable that a different verdict would have resulted absent the improperly admitted evidence combined with the legally-incorrect jury instruction that the Public Contract Code did not apply and counsel's argument that District's insistence that its determination of an interest rate and timeframe was controlled by the Public Contract Code constituted bad faith.

NOTES

1. If one of the parties had terminated the confidentiality agreement, what evidentiary ruling would the court have made if it applied a state version of Federal Rule of Evidence 408?

2. The *Simrin* case, mentioned by the court in *Tower Acton Holdings*, concerned an action by a divorced mother to alter the child custody provisions of the divorce decree. The former wife sought testimony from the rabbi who had counseled the couple before their divorce. Prior to the counseling, they had signed an agreement that their communications with him would be confidential and that neither would call him as a witness in a divorce action. The court held the parties to their agreement and refused to compel the rabbi's testimony. It weighed the public policies implicated in its decision as follows:

> [The wife] argues that to hold her to her bargain with the rabbi and with her husband is to sanction a contract to suppress evidence contrary to public policy. However, public policy also strongly favors procedures designed to preserve marriages, and counseling has become a promising means to that end. The two policies are here in conflict and we resolve the conflict by holding the parties to their

agreement. If a husband or wife must speak guardedly for fear of making an admission that might be used in court, the purpose of counseling is frustrated. One should not be permitted, under cover of suppression of evidence, to repudiate an agreement so deeply affecting the marriage relationship. For the unwary spouse who speaks freely, repudiation would prove a trap; for the wily, a vehicle for making self-serving declarations. [*Simrin v. Simrin*, 43 Cal. Rptr. 376, 379 (Cal. Ct. App. 1965).]

3. In other settings, courts have invoked public policy in refusing to enforce confidentiality agreements for settlement related activities. For example, in *Grumman Aerospace Corp. v. Titanium Metals Corp. of America*, 91 F.R.D. 84 (E.D.N.Y. 1984), a consultant had prepared a economic analysis of price fixing in the titanium industry for the U.S. Department of Defense as part of a settlement process. The report contained confidential business information that the companies had agreed to provide only under a confidentiality agreement. When Grumman, who was not a party to the agreement, sought the report in subsequent litigation the court held that the parties to the agreement could not foreclose others from obtaining relevant documents in discovery by contracting privately for confidentiality. Other courts have, however, enforced confidentiality agreements against third parties when they have been entered as stipulated protective orders under Federal Rule of Civil Procedure 26(c). (*See, e.g., Martindale v. International Telephone & Telegraph Corp.*, 594 F.2d 291 (2d Cir. 1979).)

4. Public records statutes may also trump confidentiality agreements for settlement documents. (*Cf. Tribune-Review Publishing Co. v. Westmoreland County Housing Auth.*, 833 A.2d 112 (Pa. 2003) (settlement agreement is a public document under state "Right to Know" statute and confidentiality clause is void as against public policy). (*But see Pierce v. St. Vrain Valley School Dist.*, 981 P.2d 600 (Colo. 1999) (state Open Records Act did not cover settlement agreement with former employee).)

5. Reconsider the hypothetical about the fired basketball coach. How would your answers be different if the coach and athletic director had signed a confidentiality agreement prior to their mediation?

c. **Mediation Privileges**

A privilege is an evidentiary mechanism that allows the holder of the privilege to refuse to disclose, and to block others from disclosing, privileged communications. Privileges operate at evidentiary hearings and also in discovery under the terms of Federal Rule of Civil Procedure 26(b), which authorizes discovery "regarding any matter, not privileged, that is relevant to the claim or defense of any party. . . ." A privilege is more flexible than an evidentiary exclusion in that it places the decision to disclose in the hands of the holder, who may waive his privilege. Privileges may be created by statute or by court decisions. The following case created a common law mediation privilege that is applicable in federal courts in the Ninth Circuit.

FOLB v. MOTION PICTURE INDUSTRY PENSION & HEALTH PLANS

16 F. Supp. 2d 1164, 1166–67, 1170–81 (C.D. Cal. 1998), aff'd, 216 F.3d 1082 (9th Cir. 2000)

Paez, District Judge.

I.
Introduction and Factual Background

Plaintiff Scott Folb contends that defendants discriminated against him on the basis of gender and retaliated against him because he objected when Directors of the Motion Picture Industry Pension & Health Plans (the "Plans") violated fiduciary duties under the Employee Retirement Income Security Act of 1974 ("ERISA"). Defendants allegedly relied on a complaint that Folb had sexually harassed another employee, Vivian Vasquez, as a pretext to discharge him for his whistle-blowing activities.

* * *

In approximately February 1997, Vasquez and the Plans attended a formal mediation with a neutral in an attempt to settle Vasquez' potential claims against defendants arising out of the alleged sexual harassment. Vasquez and the Plans signed a contract agreeing to maintain the confidentiality of the mediation and all statements made in it. * * * The parties apparently did not reach an agreement during the mediation. After the mediation, counsel presumably engaged in further settlement negotiations and the parties ultimately settled Vasquez' potential claims against the Plans. * * *

* * * Folb sought to compel production of (1) Vasquez' mediation brief; (2) correspondence between Vasquez' counsel and counsel for the Plans regarding mediation or other settlement discussions; and (3) notes to the file prepared by Vasquez' counsel regarding settlement communications. Folb argues that the Plans are trying to take a position in this litigation that is inconsistent with the position he believes they took in settlement negotiations with Vasquez. Folb suggests that the Plans will argue that he was properly terminated for sexually harassing Vasquez, despite the fact that they may have argued in mediation or settlement negotiations with Vasquez that she was never sexually harassed at all. * * *

II.
Discussion

* * *

3. Federal Mediation Privilege

The federal courts are authorized to define new privileges based on interpretation of "common law principles . . . in the light of reason and experience." *Jaffee* [*v. Redmond*], 518 U.S. [1, 8 (1996)]. * * * Nonetheless, that authority must be exercised with caution because the creation of a new privilege is based upon considerations of public policy. In general, the appropriate question is not whether a federal mediation privilege should exist in the abstract, but whether "(1) the need for that privilege is so clear, and (2) the desirable contours of that privilege are so evident, that it is appropriate for this [c]ourt to craft it in common law fashion, under Rule 501."

The general rule is that the public is entitled to every person's evidence and that testimonial privileges are disfavored. Consequently,

> we start with the primary assumption that there is a general duty to give what testimony one is capable of giving. . . . Exceptions from the general rule disfavoring testimonial privileges may be justified, however, by a "public good transcending the normally predominant principle of utilizing all rational means for ascertaining the truth."

Jaffee, 518 U.S. at 9. To determine whether an asserted privilege constitutes such a public good, in light of reason and experience, the Court must consider (1) whether the asserted privilege is "rooted in the imperative need for confidence and trust[;]" (2) whether the privilege would serve public ends; (3) whether the evidentiary detriment caused by exercise of the privilege is modest; and (4) whether denial of the federal privilege would frustrate a parallel privilege adopted by the states. *Id.* at 9–13.

a. Need for Confidence and Trust

[S]everal courts have looked to Fed. R. Evid. 408 for protection of settlement negotiations, whether conducted with the assistance of a mediator or in private. * * *

Rule 408 provides that "[e]vidence of conduct of statements made in compromise negotiations is [ ] not admissible." Viewed in combination with Fed. R. Civ. P. 26(b), Rule 408 only protects disputants from disclosure of information to the trier of fact, not from discovery by a third party. Consequently, without a federal mediation privilege under Rule 501, information exchanged in a confidential mediation, like any other information, is subject to the liberal discovery rules of the Federal Rules of Civil Procedure * * * .

To determine whether there is a need for confidentiality in mediation proceedings, the Court looks first to judicial and Congressional pronouncements on the issue. No federal court has definitively adopted a mediation privilege as federal common law under Rule 501. In one of the leading cases on the treatment of confidential communications in mediation, however, the Ninth Circuit approved revocation of a subpoena that would have required a Federal Mediation and Conciliation Service ("FMCS") mediator to testify in a National Labor Relations Board ("NLRB") enforcement proceeding. *National Labor Relations Board v. Joseph Macaluso, Inc.*, 618 F.2d 51, 52 (9th Cir. 1980). Relying on United States policy favoring resolution of labor disputes through collective bargaining and on Congress' creation of government facilities for mediation, the Ninth Circuit in *Macaluso* concluded that "the public interest in maintaining the perceived and actual impartiality of federal mediators does outweigh the benefits derivable from [the mediator's] testimony." *Id.* at 54 (citing 29 U.S.C. § 171(a)(b)).

The Ninth Circuit's conclusion that requiring a federal mediator to disclose information about the mediation proceedings would inevitably impair or destroy the usefulness of the FMCS in future proceedings is equally applicable in the context of private mediation. Admittedly, the express federal interest in preserving a labor mediation system establishes a stronger basis for a mediator privilege in the context of NLRB proceedings. Nonetheless, mediation in other contexts has clearly become a critical alternative to full-blown litigation, providing the parties a more cost-effective method of resolving disputes and allowing the courts to keep up with ever more unmanageable dockets.

Focusing on the role of the mediator, the *Macaluso* court emphasized that "the purpose of excluding mediator testimony . . . is to avoid a breach of impartiality, not a breach of confidentiality." *Macaluso*, 618 F.2d at 56 n.3. Nevertheless, rules protecting the confidentiality of mediation proceedings and rules protecting the actual or perceived impartiality of mediators serve the same ultimate purpose: encouraging parties to attend mediation and communicate openly and honestly in order to facilitate successful alternative dispute resolution.

> [C]onciliators must maintain a reputation for impartiality, and the parties to conciliation conferences must feel free to talk without any fear that the conciliator may subsequently make disclosures as a witness in some other proceeding, to the possible disadvantage of a party to the conference. If conciliators were permitted or required to testify about their activities, or if the production of notes or reports of their activities could be required, not even the strictest adherence to purely factual matters would prevent the evidence from favoring or seeming to favor one side.

Id. at 55. Whether information divulged in mediation proceedings is disclosed through the compelled testimony of a mediator or the compelled disclosure of documents conveyed to or prepared by the mediator, the side most forthcoming in the mediation process is penalized when third parties can discover confidential communications with the mediator. Refusing to establish a privilege to protect confidential communications in mediation proceedings creates an incentive for participants to withhold sensitive information in mediation or refuse to participate at all.

Today, the Court is faced with a somewhat more attenuated concern: whether the "imperative need for confidence and trust" that would support creation of a privilege protecting confidential communications with a mediator should extend so far as to protect all oral and written communications between the parties to a mediation. Before delving into the heart of the matter, we must also clarify what constitutes "mediation" for purposes of the Court's analysis today. Given the facts presented by the parties before the Court, we need only consider whether communications between parties who agreed in writing to participate in a confidential mediation with a neutral third party should be privileged and whether that privilege should extend to communications between the parties after they have concluded their formal mediation with the neutral.

Several commentators have suggested that successful mediation requires open communication between parties to a dispute. *See, e.g.,* Alan Kirtley, "The Mediation Privilege's Transition from Theory to Implementation: Designing a Mediation Privilege Standard to Protect Mediation Participants, the Process and the Public Interest," 1995 J. DISP. RESOL. 1, 8, 16 (collecting sources indicating weight of scholarly authority suggests confidentiality is essential to mediation). Kirtley argues that

> [w]ithout adequate legal protection, a party's candor in mediation might well be "rewarded" by a discovery request or the revelation of mediation information at trial. A principal purpose of the mediation privilege is to provide mediation parties protection against these downside risks of a failed mediation.

Id. at 9–10. In general, however, the academic literature provides little analysis of whether communications disclosed to the opposing party in the course of mediation proceedings should be accorded the same level of protection as private communications between one party and the mediator.

One self-described "heretical" commentator has expressed doubt over the need for a mediation privilege to protect confidentiality in mediation.

> Although most mediators assert that confidentiality is essential to the process, there is no data of which I am aware that supports this claim, and I am dubious that such data could be collected. Moreover, mediation has flourished without recognition of a privilege, most likely on assurance given by the parties and the mediator that they agree to keep mediation matters confidential, their awareness that attempts to use the fruits of mediation for litigation purposes are rare, and that courts, in appropriate instances, will accord mediation evidence Rule 408 and public policy-based protection.

Eric D. Green, *A Heretical View of the Mediation Privilege*, 2 OHIO ST. J. ON DISP. RESOL. 1, 32 (1986) (arguing campaign to obtain blanket mediation privilege rests on "faulty logic, inadequate data, and short-sighted professional self-interest").

* * *

Legal authority on the necessity of protecting confidential communications between the parties to a mediation is sparse. In an early decision by the Second Circuit, the court stated:

> [i]f participants cannot rely on the confidential treatment of everything that transpires during [mediation] sessions then counsel of necessity will feel constrained to conduct themselves in a cautious, tight-lipped, noncommital manner more suitable to poker players in a high-stakes game than adversaries attempting to arrive at a just solution of a civil dispute. This atmosphere if allowed to exist would surely destroy the effectiveness of a program which has led to settlements and withdrawals of some appeals and to the simplification of issues in other appeals, thereby expediting cases at a time when the judicial resources of this Court are sorely taxed.

Lake Utopia Paper Ltd. v. Connelly Containers, Inc., 608 F.2d 928 (2d Cir. 1979).

At least one district court has concluded that confidential information disclosed in alternative dispute resolution ("ADR") proceedings is privileged. *See United States v. Gullo,* 672 F. Supp. 99, 104 (W.D.N.Y.1987). In *Gullo,* the court found that the confidentiality provision in New York's Community Dispute Resolution Centers Program served to ensure the effectiveness and continued existence of the program. Looking to Rule 501, the court concluded, on balance, that the privilege afforded under New York law should be recognized by the federal court. Having concluded that the information was protected, the *Gullo* court suppressed evidence in a criminal proceeding of all statements made during the dispute resolution process, as well as the terms and conditions of the settlement.

*   *   *

[T]he majority of courts to consider the issue appear to have concluded that the need for confidentiality and trust between participants in a mediation proceeding is sufficiently imperative to necessitate the creation of some form of privilege. This conclusion takes on added significance when considered in conjunction with the fact that many federal district courts rely on the success of ADR proceedings to minimize the size of their dockets.

*   *   *

b. Public Ends

A new privilege must serve a public good sufficiently important to justify creating an exception to the "general rule disfavoring testimonial privileges." *Jaffee,* 518 U.S. at 9. * * *

*   *   *

[A] mediation privilege would serve important public ends by promoting conciliatory relationships among parties to a dispute, by reducing litigation costs and by decreasing the size of state and federal court dockets, thereby increasing the quality of justice in those cases that do not settle voluntarily.

c. Evidentiary Detriment

In assessing the necessity of adopting a new privilege, the courts must consider whether "the likely evidentiary benefit that would result from the denial of the privilege is modest." *Jaffee,* 518 U.S. at 11–12. * * *

Where, as here, an employer is sued by one employee claiming wrongful termination based on false allegations of sexual harassment and by another employee asserting a claim for sexual harassment perpetrated by the other employee, a blanket mediation privilege might permit an unscrupulous employer to garner the benefit of the two employees' opposing positions. In open mediation proceedings, the employer would be forced to strike a balance between the two parties positions rather than taking one employee's side in the first case and then shifting to the other side when defending against charges by the second employee. Despite the potential moral implications of fostering such duplicity, however, there is very little *evidentiary* benefit to be gained by refusing to recognize a mediation privilege.

First, evidence disclosed in mediation may be obtained directly from the parties to the mediation by using normal discovery channels. For example, a person's admission in mediation proceedings may, at least theoretically, be elicited in response to a request for admission or to questions in a deposition or in written interrogatories. In addition, to the extent a party takes advantage of the opportunity to use the cloak of confidentiality to take inconsistent positions in related litigation, evidence of that inconsistent position only comes into being as a result of the party's willingness to attend mediation. Absent a privilege protecting the confidentiality of mediation, the inconsistent position would presumably never come to light.

* * *

d. Mediation Privilege in the 50 States

In assessing a proposed privilege, a federal court should look to a consistent body of state legislative and judicial decisions adopting such a privilege as an important indicator of both reason and experience. *Jaffee,* 518 U.S. at 12–13. Put simply, "the policy decisions of the States bear on the question whether federal courts should recognize a new privilege or amend the coverage of an existing one." Practically speaking, the confidential status accorded to mediation proceedings by the states will be of limited value if the federal courts decline to adopt a federal mediation privilege.

* * *

At the forefront of the inquiry * * * is the fact that every state in the Union, with the exception of Delaware, has adopted a mediation privilege of one type or another. * * * While some states provide only limited protection, a majority of the states go beyond protecting communications in private sessions with the mediator, requiring that the entire process be confidential. A number of states provide explicitly that information disclosed in mediation proceedings is not subject to discovery.

The fact that the states have not settled on the scope of protection to provide should not prevent the federal courts from determining that in light of reason and experience we should adopt a federal mediation privilege. While the contours of such a federal privilege need to be fleshed out over time, state legislatures and state courts have overwhelmingly chosen to protect confidential communications in mediation proceedings in order to facilitate settlement of disputes through alternative dispute resolution. "Denial of the federal privilege . . . would frustrate the purposes of the state legislation that was enacted to foster these confidential communications." Accordingly, this Court finds it is appropriate, in light of reason and experience, to adopt a federal mediation privilege applicable to all communications made in conjunction with a formal mediation.

e. Contours of the Privilege

* * *

On the facts presented here, the Court concludes that communications to the mediator and communications between parties during the mediation are protected. In addition, communications in preparation for and during the course of a mediation with a neutral must be protected. Subsequent negotiations between the parties, however, are not protected even if they include information initially disclosed in the mediation. To protect additional communications, the parties are required to return to mediation. A contrary rule would permit a party to claim the privilege with respect to any settlement negotiations so long as the communications took place following an attempt to mediate the dispute.

III.
Conclusion

* * *

In short, the Court concludes that encouraging mediation by adopting a federal mediation privilege under Fed. R. Evid. 501 will provide "a public good transcending the normally predominant principle of utilizing all rational means for ascertaining the truth." *Jaffee,* 518 U.S. at 9.

NOTES

1. A privilege has a "holder," who is entitled to waive the privilege if she does not object to disclosing the communication at issue. Can you tell who holds the mediation privilege established in *Folb*? Who do you think should be a holder? Each party? The mediator? Both? What mediation values and rationales for protecting mediation communications are advanced by making the parties holders? The mediator?

2. In the hypothetical on the fired coach, which disclosures of mediation communications could be blocked if the parties held a mediation privilege? What difference might it make if the mediator held one?

3. The privilege created in *Folb* is limited in that it extends only to "communications disclosed in conjunction with mediation conducted with a neutral." (16 F. Supp. 2d at 1180.) The court explicitly excluded post-mediation communications from the privilege based on the following reasoning:

> Any interpretation of Rule 501 must be consistent with Rule 408. To protect settlement communications not related to mediation would invade Rule 408's domain; only Congress is authorized to amend the scope of protection afforded by Rule 408. Consequently, any post-mediation communications are protected only by Rule 408's limitations on admissibility. [*Id.*]

Do you agree with the court? What defines the end of a mediation? When the parties leave the presence of the mediator? What if they meet again the next day without the mediator and reach a settlement based on proposals discussed in mediation? Does a mediation continue until the parties declare it at an end?

4. Other federal courts have also created privileges applicable to mediation. *Sheldone v. Pennsylvania Turnpike Comm'n*, 104 F. Supp. 511, 517 (W.D. Pa. 2000), established a privilege for communications "made in connection with or during" a mediation. To the extent this privilege might cover communications following the close of a mediation session, it is potentially broader in scope than the *Folb* privilege. In *Goodyear Tire & Rubber Co. v. Chiles Power Supply, Inc.*, 332 F.3d 976, 982 (6th Cir. 2003), the Sixth Circuit approved a privilege that is not limited to mediation, but protects "any communications made in furtherance of settlement." What are the advantages and disadvantages of adopting privileges through the common law process versus statutory enactment?

5. While there is no statutory mediation privilege that applies in general in the federal courts, the Administrative Dispute Resolution Act contains confidentiality provisions for federal agency mediation programs that function like a privilege (*see* 5 U.S.C. § 574). The Act's protections are more limited than the privilege adopted in *Folb*, however, in they do not cover communications made by a party in joint session with the other party. (5 U.S.C. § 574 (b)(7).)

All the states provide some form of statutory protection against disclosure of mediation communications in court proceedings. About half have general statutes that cover all mediations. Others have more limited enactments that govern specific mediation programs. The type and extent of protection provided by state statute varies immensely. Privilege is the most common legal mechanism, but some statutes rely on evidentiary exclusions, provisions restricting mediator testimony, or provisions that are not easily classified. In response to this variation, and to needs created by the growth of mediation, the National Conference of Commissioners on Uniform State Law and the American Bar Association developed the Uniform Mediation Act (UMA), which is reprinted in Appendix E. The UMA has been enacted in nine jurisdictions and is under consideration in others. It contains the following three mediation privileges:

Uniform Mediation Act (as amended 2003)

Section 4. Privilege Against Disclosure; Admissibility; Discovery.

(a) Except as otherwise provided in Section 6, a mediation communication is privileged as provided in subsection (b) and is not subject to discovery or admissible in evidence in a proceeding unless waived or precluded as provided by Section 5.

(b) In a proceeding, the following privileges apply:

(1) A mediation party may refuse to disclose, and may prevent any other person from disclosing, a mediation communication.

(2) A mediator may refuse to disclose a mediation communication, and may prevent any other person from disclosing a mediation communication of the mediator.

(3) A nonparty participant may refuse to disclose, and may prevent any other person from disclosing, a mediation communication of the nonparty participant.

(c) Evidence or information that is otherwise admissible or subject to discovery does not become inadmissible or protected from discovery solely by reason of its disclosure or use in a mediation.

NOTES

1. Under the UMA privileges what is the scope of each holder's ability to refuse to disclose and of his ability to block another from disclosing mediation communications? What policy considerations support this variation?

2. The UMA privileges apply to disclosures of mediation communications in court proceedings, arbitral proceedings, other adjudicative processes, and legislative hearings. The statute does not establish a more general obligation of confidentiality that would apply outside the context of legal proceedings. Instead, it provides that "mediation communications are confidential to the extent agreed by the parties or provided by other law or rule of this State." (UMA § 8.) This is a controversial section. The comments to the provision describe "the tension * * * between contradictory sets of party expectations" and explain the drafters' reasoning as follows:

> Party expectations regarding such disclosures outside of proceedings are complex. On the one hand, parties may reasonably expect in many situations that their mediation communications will not be disclosed to others, that the statements they make in mediation "will stay in the room." * * * Indeed, parties may choose to resolve their disputes through mediation in order to assure this kind of privacy concerning their dispute and related communications. On the other hand, those same parties may also reasonably expect that they can discuss their mediations with spouses, family members and others without the risk of civil liability that might accompany an affirmative statutory duty prohibiting such disclosures. Such disclosures often have salutary effects-such as bringing closure on issues of conflict and educating others about the benefits of mediation or the underlying causes of a dispute.

* * *

> [U]niformity is not necessary or even appropriate with regard to the disclosure of mediation communications outside of proceedings. In some situations, parties may prefer absolute non-disclosure to any third party, in other situations, parties may wish to permit, even encourage, disclosures to family members, business associates, even the media. These decisions are best left to the good judgment of the parties, to decide what is appropriate under the unique facts and

circumstances of their disputes, a policy that furthers the Act's fundamental principle of party self-determination. Such confidentiality agreements are common in law, and are enforceable in courts. [UMA § 8 reporter's notes.]

Do you agree with the drafters' choice? What would be the dangers of establishing a rule of general confidentiality and then allowing the parties to make exceptions by agreement? What implications does the UMA's provision have for attorneys representing parties in mediation?

d. Court Rules for Mediation Programs

A fourth source of protection against disclosure of mediation communications is often available if the mediation was conducted as part of a state or federal court-connected mediation program. In the federal courts, the Alternative Dispute Resolution Act of 1998 requires federal district courts to protect confidentiality in their ADR programs by local rule. *See* 28 U.S.C. § 652(d). The federal courts of appeals, which offer mediation pursuant to Federal Rule of Appellate Procedure 33, also provide for confidentiality by rule. The U.S. Court of Appeals for the Fourth Circuit interpreted its rule in the following case.

In re ANONYMOUS
283 F.3d 627 (4th Cir. 2002)

Before WILLIAMS, TRAXLER, and KING, Circuit Judges.

PER CURIAM:

This attorney discipline action arises out of a dispute over litigation expenses between an attorney (Local Counsel) and his client (Client), which developed following a successful mediation (the mediation) conducted by the Office of the Circuit Mediator for this Court (the OCM). Local Counsel and Client agreed to resolve their "expense dispute" before an arbitral panel sponsored by the Virginia State Bar (the VSB arbitration). In their submissions to the VSB arbitration, Client, Local Counsel, and a third party[3] (Current Counsel) (collectively, the participants), disclosed information about or relating to the mediation and also sought responses to interrogatories from the Circuit Mediator. Upon being informed of these disclosures and the discovery effort, the Standing Panel on Attorney Discipline ordered each participant to submit briefs and present argument regarding the propriety of their disclosures in light of the confidentiality provisions of our Local Rule 33. * * *

I.

On March 21, 1997, Client retained the services of an attorney to initiate a Title VII claim for retaliatory firing. In the fee agreement signed by Client, she agreed to pay attorney's fees in the amount of 40% of the total recovery

---

[3] This third party attended the mediation conference as a "friend" of Client, by consent of the parties and the mediator, and currently serves as Client's counsel in the expense dispute. He was not acting in a representative capacity during the mediation conference.

if the matter were resolved after trial and 33 1/3% if the matter settled. "In addition to" the attorney's fees, Client agreed to pay all expenses of litigation, out-of-pocket expenses, and court costs.

In March 1998, the retained attorney hired Local Counsel to aid in preparation of Client's trial. The retained attorney advised Local Counsel that she had obtained a signed fee agreement from Client, but Client did not execute a separate fee agreement with Local Counsel. Local Counsel thereafter advanced the majority of Client's litigation expenses and costs. On March 28, 2000, the Title VII case was tried before a jury. After a three-day trial, the jury returned a substantial verdict in favor of Client, which the district court reduced to comport with Title VII's statutory damages cap. Both Client and the defendant appealed to this Court.

After filing their notices of appeal, a mediation conference was conducted before the OCM in December 2000. In attendance at the mediation conference were Client, Local Counsel, Current Counsel, the defendant, the defendant's two attorneys, and the Circuit Mediator. All those in attendance agreed to the confidentiality provision of Rule 33. The mediation conference culminated in a settlement agreement, and this Court entered an order dismissing the appeals.

Subsequent to the mediation conference but prior to the order of dismissal, the expense dispute underlying the current proceeding came to light. Client and Local Counsel agreed to resolve the expense dispute using the VSB arbitration, and Client retained Current Counsel to represent her in the VSB arbitration. On March 1, 2001, acting in his capacity as Client's lawyer, Current Counsel submitted several documents to the VSB arbitration on Client's behalf, including a copy of the settlement points of agreement from the mediation conference, a copy of the typed settlement agreement, and a statement in which Client described conversations that took place during and after the mediation conference. Acting in his capacity as a witness at the mediation conference, Current Counsel submitted his own statement detailing his recollection of certain discussions that took place during and after the mediation conference.

On March 21, 2001, Local Counsel requested the consent of defendant to the disclosure of statements made during the mediation conference. Defendant, through its counsel, granted consent to the disclosure "solely for the purpose of the Bar mediation." On the same day, Local Counsel telephoned the Circuit Mediator, informed her of the dispute concerning the reimbursement of expenses and costs, and requested her consent to the disclosure of statements made during the mediation conference. The Circuit Mediator responded that she was unable to give consent without instruction from this Court, and the mediator requested Local Counsel to submit a written, specific request detailing what he proposed to disclose. On March 22, 2001, prior to gaining consent from this Court, and without presenting any further request in support of such consent, Local Counsel submitted several documents to the VSB arbitration, including a statement wherein he described discussions that he had with Client at the mediation conference.

On March 27, 2001, Local Counsel wrote the Circuit Mediator, reiterating his request for her consent to disclose matters discussed during the mediation conference and to disclose notes Local Counsel prepared during the mediation conference. Local Counsel informed the Circuit Mediator that Client and Current Counsel already had breached the mediation's confidentiality, and he asked her to respond in writing to three informal interrogatories. With respect to the interrogatories, Local Counsel noted that he would supply the answers to the VSB arbitration panel, and he would not require the Circuit Mediator to appear at the arbitration.[6]

* * *

II.

* * * Rule 33 currently provides in pertinent part as follows:

> Information disclosed in the mediation process shall be kept confidential and shall not be disclosed to the judges deciding the appeal or to any other person outside the mediation program participants. Confidentiality is required of all participants in the mediation proceedings. All statements, documents, and discussions in such proceedings shall be kept confidential. The mediator, attorneys, and other participants in the mediation shall not disclose such statements, documents, or discussions without prior approval of the Standing Panel on Attorney Discipline.

4th Cir. R. 33.[7] The participants do not deny that they each submitted statements to the VSB arbitration revealing information disclosed during the mediation conference. Further, Current Counsel and Client concede that they submitted the settlement agreement itself, as well as notes regarding the settlement agreement, to the VSB arbitration. Despite the apparent violations of the plain language of the Rule, the participants maintain, for a variety of reasons, that their disclosures did not violate the confidentiality required by Rule 33.

---

[6] The informal interrogatories posed to the Circuit Mediator by Local Counsel on March 27, 2001, were the following:

1. Did you hear [Local Counsel] discuss with [Client] that her litigation expense obligation was to be taken out of [Client's] portion of the recovery, at the mediation in this matter held in Durham, North Carolina [i]n December [ ] 2000?

2. Did you hear [Local Counsel] waive his or her firm's entitlement to expense reimbursement or advise [Client] that the case expenses would be taken out of [Local Counsel's] contingent fee portion of the settlement?

3. Did you hear [Local Counsel] estimate [Client's] litigation and appellate expenses at or about $20,000 (or any other number) at the mediation . . . in this matter held in Durham, North Carolina [i]n December [ ] 2000?

[7] Rule 33 was amended on December 11, 2001, following notice and public comment. The prior relevant text of Rule 33 provided: "Information disclosed in the mediation process shall be kept confidential and shall not be disclosed by a circuit mediator, counsel, or parties to the judges deciding the appeal or to any other person outside the mediation program participants." Because the added language merely clarifies the previous rule, we find it helpful in resolving the current action. To the extent that the amendment eliminated ambiguity that existed at the time of the participants' disclosures, this ambiguity will be taken into account when determining whether or to what extent sanctions are warranted.

A.

The participants first argue that their disclosures were not prohibited by Rule 33 because the disclosures did not involve matters central to the mediated dispute. The unambiguous text of Rule 33, however, does not draw the suggested distinction; instead, it prohibits the disclosure of "*[a]ll* statements, documents, and discussions." 4th Cir. R. 33 (emphasis added).[8] Moreover, because the confidentiality provision as written provides clear guidance in the form of a bright line rule, we decline to adopt an exception allowing for the disclosure of matters collaterally related to the mediation.

B.

The participants next argue that because their submissions were made to a confidential forum, the submissions should not be construed as violating Rule 33. Again, the unambiguous text of Rule 33 does not provide an exception for disclosures made to a confidential forum. Rather, it has at all relevant times restricted disclosures "to any other person outside the mediation program participants." The participants concede, as they must, that the members of the VSB arbitration are "person[s] outside the mediation program participants." Thus, the submissions made to the VSB arbitration panel by the participants breached the unambiguous text of Rule 33.

C.

Current Counsel also asserts that, because he was not acting as counsel during the mediation conference and because he was not a party to the mediated dispute when he attended the mediation conference, his disclosures did not fall within the scope of Rule 33. At the time of Current Counsel's submissions, Rule 33 provided, "Information disclosed in the mediation process shall be kept confidential and shall not be disclosed *by a circuit mediator, counsel, or parties* to the judges deciding the appeal or to any other person outside the mediation program participants." Rule 33 (emphasis added). As is made clear by our recent amendment to Rule 33, the term "parties," as used in the earlier version of Rule 33, is not limited to the formal parties of the mediated dispute, as Current Counsel asserts, but instead applies to all participants in the mediation, including attendants at the mediation conference. Moreover, it is significant to us that Current Counsel is a lawyer, who was made aware of Rule 33's confidentiality provision prior to his participation in the mediation conference, and who explicitly agreed to abide thereby. Thus, we reject Current Counsel's contention that his disclosures did not fall within the scope of Rule 33.

D.

The participants also argue that due process requires us to conclude that their submissions did not violate Rule 33, in that a contrary conclusion would

---

[8] Indeed, this language, added in the 2001 amendments to Rule 33, merely clarified the prior Rule's equally broad protection of "information disclosed in the mediation process."

deny Client and Local Counsel the right to resolve their expense dispute. We disagree. Rule 33, in both its current and previous form, does not deprive participants of a forum for resolution of disputes; rather; it limits the availability and use of information gleaned during the mediation in subsequent proceedings. Courts routinely have recognized the substantial interest of preserving confidentiality in mediation proceedings as justifying restrictions on the use of information obtained during the mediation. Further, Rule 33 does not and has never precluded requests for consent to disclosures * * * . Accordingly, we reject the participants' claim that due process renders the confidentiality provision of Rule 33 unenforceable.

* * *

Thus, despite their various protestations to the contrary, we conclude that Client, Local Counsel, and Current Counsel each breached Rule 33's confidentiality provision by disclosing information obtained during the mediation to persons other than the mediation program participants.

III.

We next turn to the question of whether the violations of Rule 33 committed by Client, Legal Counsel, and Current Counsel warrant the imposition of sanctions by the Standing Panel. In assessing the sanctions issue, we review the totality of the circumstances, and determine, first, whether sanctions are warranted, and if warranted, the severity of any such sanctions. In so doing, we analyze and weigh the following and other relevant factors: (1) whether the mediator explained the extent of the confidentiality rules, and the clarity of such explanation; (2) whether the parties executed a confidentiality agreement; (3) the extent of willfulness or bad faith involved in the breach of confidentiality Rule; (4) the severity or adverse impact of the disclosure on the parties or the case; and (5) the severity or adverse impact of the disclosure on the mediation program.

Applying these factors, we note that the participants agree that the mediator clearly explained the confidentiality provision prior to commencement of the mediation conference and that they each agreed to abide by it. Although no one executed a confidentiality agreement at that time, the settlement agreement, which Client and Local Counsel both signed, contained a confidentiality provision that provides for confidentiality as to all of the "terms of the agreement." On the other hand, at the time of these disclosures, we had not previously interpreted the scope of Rule 33, and Current Counsel, as a participant but not a formal party to the mediated dispute, had some basis, however modest, for asserting that his disclosures did not fall within the literal scope of the former Rule's prohibition. Additionally, Local Counsel had some basis to believe that his disclosures did not breach confidentiality, in that the Model Rules of Professional Conduct provide an exception to confidentiality for disclosures of confidential client information where the disclosures are for the purpose of establishing an attorney's entitlement to compensation. Model Rules of Prof'l Conduct R. 1.6(b)(2) & cmt. 18; Restatement (Third) of Law Governing Lawyers § 65 (1998).

Weighing these factors and considering the participants' statements and submissions before the Standing Panel, we are convinced that none of the participants intended to violate Rule 33, and we are unable to conclude that the disclosures were made in bad faith or with malice. Moreover, the disclosures have not had an adverse impact on the mediated dispute, and because the disclosures were made to a non-public, confidential forum, any adverse impact on the mediation program has been slight. Accordingly, considering the totality of the circumstances, we conclude that the violations of Rule 33 are not sufficient to warrant sanctions in this case.

IV.

The participants next contend that, pursuant to Rule 33's provision allowing participants to seek the Standing Panel's approval for future disclosures of confidential information, we should grant a limited waiver of confidentiality to permit the VSB arbitration to consider their previously-submitted disclosures in resolving the expense dispute. Local Counsel also argues that we should grant consent for the Circuit Mediator to submit written answers to the informal interrogatories posed in his letter dated March 27, 2001. We address each argument in turn, setting forth the standard by which we will determine whether waiver is appropriate in each context.

A.

To determine when the Standing Panel should grant a waiver of confidentiality to the participants, it is necessary to examine the relevant interests protected by non-disclosure. The assurance of confidentiality is essential to the integrity and success of the Court's mediation program, in that confidentiality encourages candor between the parties and on the part of the mediator, and confidentiality serves to protect the mediation program from being used as a discovery tool for creative attorneys. * * * In a program like ours, where participation is mandatory and the mediation is directed and sanctioned by the Court, "the argument for protecting confidential communications may be even stronger because participants are often assured that all discussions and documents related to the proceeding will be protected from forced disclosure." *Folb v. Motion Picture Indus. Pension & Health Plans*, 16 F. Supp. 2d 1164, 1176 n. 9 (C.D. Cal. 1998), *aff'd* 216 F.3d 1082 (9th Cir.2000).

On the other hand, we must recognize that under certain circumstances, non-disclosure may result in an untenable "loss of information to the public and the justice system." Thus, in determining whether waiver is appropriate, we must balance the public interest in protecting the confidentiality of the settlement process and countervailing interests, such as the right to every person's evidence.

We believe that the balance between these interests is best resolved by disallowing disclosure unless the party seeking such disclosure can demonstrate that "manifest injustice" will result from non-disclosure. *Cf.* Administrative Dispute Resolution Act of 1996, 5 U.S.C. § 574(a)(4)(A) (1998) (providing that disclosures of dispute resolution communications are prohibited unless, inter alia, a court determines that disclosure is necessary to prevent "manifest injustice"). Application of the manifest injustice standard requires the party seeking disclosure to demonstrate that the harm caused by non-disclosure will be manifestly greater than the harm caused by disclosure.

* * *

With these general principles in mind, we turn to our application of the manifest injustice standard to Local Counsel's and Client's submissions. Local Counsel and Client agree that disclosure of information related to the mediation proceedings is critical to resolution of their expense dispute. As Local Counsel and Client note, the expense dispute arose during the mediation conference, and resolution of the dispute requires disclosures relating to the context of the dispute's origination. Additionally, portions of information disclosed during the mediation may shed light on their understanding of the expense obligation at that time. Specifically, Client contends that the disbursement of the settlement proceeds between herself and Local Counsel, which is set forth in the settlement agreement, is evidence that her obligation to reimburse legal expenses was incorporated into Local Counsel's share of the settlement proceeds. In response, Local Counsel argues that conversations that took place during the mediation conference are evidence that Client understood that the settlement agreement did not affect Client's obligation to reimburse the litigation expenses in any manner, and he contends that his notes regarding the settlement conference corroborate his assertion that these conversations took place. Insofar as the mediation conference was the genesis of the expense dispute and information divulged during the conference is critical to resolution of the expense dispute, the harm resulting from non disclosure might, in the context of the expense dispute, be substantial.

Further, any harm resulting from disclosure would be slight, in that the contemplated disclosures will be made to a non-public, confidential forum, and all of the attendants of the mediation, excluding the Circuit Mediator, have consented to a limited waiver of confidentiality for disclosures relating to the expense dispute. *Cf.* 5 U.S.C. § 574(a)(1) (allowing for disclosure of confidential settlement information where all parties consent to disclosure). Additionally, it is significant that little mention needs to be made regarding the mediation of the substantive merits of the appeal. In light of these considerations, we conclude that Local Counsel and Client have demonstrated that non-disclosure of limited and relevant information related to the mediation would cause manifestly greater harm than the disclosure of such information. Accordingly, we grant conditional consent for Local Counsel and Client to disclose the following limited material: (1) conversations that took place during the mediation regarding the expense dispute and their notes, or portions thereof, regarding the settlement negotiations corroborating these conversations; and (2) the settlement agreement and notes regarding the settlement agreement, but only to the extent that these materials explain or relate to the disbursement of the settlement funds. Our consent is conditioned upon Local Counsel and Client securing from the VSB arbitral panel its written agreement to abide by Rule 33's confidentiality provision. We caution Local Counsel and Client to adhere strictly to the parameters of this limited waiver, and we direct that all previous submissions outside the confines of this waiver be withdrawn from the VSB arbitration.

* * *

B.

Turning to the question of whether to consent for the Circuit Mediator to divulge information related to the mediation, we observe that allowing disclosures by the mediator in subsequent proceedings implicates concerns well beyond those implicated by disclosures of other participants to a mediation. For example, our granting of consent for the mediator to participate in any manner in a subsequent proceeding would encourage perceptions of bias in future mediation sessions involving comparable parties and issues, and it might encourage creative attorneys to attempt to use our court officers and mediation program as a discovery tool. * * * In light of these heightened concerns unique to disclosures by the Circuit Mediator, the threshold for granting of consent to disclosures by the mediator is substantially higher than that for disclosures by other participants. Thus, we will consent for the Circuit Mediator to disclose confidential information only where such disclosure is mandated by manifest injustice, is indispensable to resolution of an important subsequent dispute, and is not going to damage our mediation program.

In this situation, Local Counsel has failed to establish that the expense dispute is incapable of resolution absent the Circuit Mediator's involvement. Further, Client objects to the Circuit Mediator's involvement, contending that she will be biased in her responses to Local Counsel's inquiries. And the mediation program may be damaged when a party who has been assured of confidentiality subsequently faces a disclosure of confidential material by a mediator who is perceived, rightly or wrongly, as biased. This perception of bias is the type of damage against which our confidentiality rule, as applied to the Circuit Mediator, is attempting to protect. Accordingly, we decline to consent for the Circuit Mediator to respond to the informal interrogatories posed by Local Counsel or to otherwise disclose confidential information in the expense dispute.

NOTES

1. Do you think the Fourth Circuit's confidentiality rule is clear? What legal mechanism does it use to protect mediation communications? Does the rule's prohibition on disclosure extend to a client's description of mediation events to her non-participating spouse?

2. The Fourth Circuit's Office of the Circuit Mediator requested that the court use this case to adopt a federal mediation privilege. The court declined, saying "[b]ecause we are able to interpret and apply Rule 33 without the adoption and application of a federal mediation privilege, we will reserve this issue for another day." (283 F.3d 627, 639 n.16.) As a litigant, would you prefer the protections of a privilege or this local rule? For comparison, consider how parties go about waiving their privilege under the UMA: "A privilege * * * may be waived in a [writing or electronic] record or orally during a proceeding if it is expressly waived by all parties to the mediation. . . ." (UMA § 5(a).)

3. In the federal district courts, the Alternative Dispute Resolution Act of 1998 requires courts to adopt local rules that "provide for confidentiality" of

ADR processes and "prohibit disclosure of confidential dispute resolution communications." (28 U.S.C. § 652(d).) Courts have held that this language does not establish a privilege for mediation communications, but rather "provide[s] only a general mandate to establish the confidentiality of court-ordered mediation proceedings." (*Folb v. Motion Picture Indus. Pension & Health Plans*, 16 F. Supp. 2d 1164, 1176 (C.D. Cal. 1998), *aff'd mem.* 216 F.3d 1082 (9th Cir. 2000). *See also FDIC v. White*, 76 F. Supp. 736, 738 (N.D. Tex. 1999).)

4. Similarly, some courts have distinguished broad "confidentiality" language in a local mediation rule from an evidentiary privilege. Consider a rule that promises "[a]ll communications made during ADR procedures are confidential and protected from disclosure." In a case in which a party to a mediated settlement claimed coercion through threats of criminal prosecution, the court held that this rule did not establish an evidentiary privilege and admitted testimony detailing mediation communications in order to resolve the allegations. (*FDIC v. White*, 76 F. Supp. 2d 736 (N.D. Tex. 1999).)

5. Because local confidentiality rules have been adopted circuit by circuit and district by district, they vary greatly in scope and clarity. Some local rules use the language of privilege, but many simply protect "confidentiality" without specifying a legal mechanism for that protection. Other rules appear to limit disclosures in the mediated case itself, but are silent or ambiguous on disclosures about the mediation in future cases or to other courts. (Ellen E. Deason, *Predictable Mediation Confidentiality in the U.S. Federal System*, 17 OHIO ST. J. ON DISP. RESOL. 239, 311–12 (2002).) For a review of local confidentiality rules see Comment, *No Confidence: The Problem of Confidentiality by Local Rule in the ADR Act of 1998*, 78 TEX. L. REV. 1015 (2000).

6. In addition to its privilege against disclosures in legal proceedings, the UMA addresses the need to keep mediation communications separate from formal court proceedings by prohibiting communications between the mediator and a judge who might rule on the matter, with only narrowly defined exceptions. The information a mediator may disclose includes "whether the mediation occurred or has terminated, whether a settlement was reached, and attendance." (UMA § 7(b)(1).)

2. EXCEPTIONS TO CONFIDENTIALITY FOR MEDIATION COMMUNICATIONS

There can be negative consequences to prohibiting disclosures of mediation communications. In general terms, maintaining confidentiality runs counter to the principle that, in Wigmore's terms, the courts are entitle to "every man's evidence." More specifically, while encouraging candid participation in mediation is an important value, there are other competing values that weigh in favor of disclosure. Thus when a legislature adopts a privilege, it often establishes exceptions for circumstances in which it determines, as a matter of public policy, that the benefits of disclosing the information outweigh the benefits of confidentiality. It may also (or instead) authorize courts to make exceptions on a case-by-case basis. The following case illustrates a court using a balancing analysis to determine if disclosure is appropriate in the context of a specific criminal proceeding.

NEW JERSEY v. WILLIAMS
184 N.J. 432, 877 A.2d 1258 (2005)

Justice ZAZZALI delivered the opinion of the Court.

In this appeal, we must decide whether a mediator appointed by a court under Rule 1:40 may testify in a subsequent criminal proceeding regarding a participant's statements made during mediation.

Defendant's brother-in-law [Bocoum] phoned defendant and left several taunting messages, leading to a face-to-face argument that quickly escalated into a physical fight. Defendant claims that his brother-in-law hit him in the shoulder with a large construction shovel. The brother-in-law counters that defendant retrieved a machete from the trunk of his car and cut the brother-in-law's wrist and foot. Police later apprehended defendant in his apartment where they found a machete.

* * *

While in police custody, an officer advised defendant that he could file a municipal court complaint against Bocoum and Renee [his wife] for making harassing phone calls. After defendant filed the complaint, the municipal court, pursuant to Rule 1:40, appointed Pastor Josiah Hall to mediate the dispute. The parties were unable to resolve their dispute through mediation, and Hall referred the matter back to the municipal court.

A grand jury indicted defendant for third-degree aggravated assault, third-degree possession of a weapon for an unlawful purpose, and fourth-degree unlawful possession of a weapon. At trial, Renee Oliver, who was testifying for the State, pointed out Hall, the mediator, who was seated in the audience section of the courtroom. At a recess, defense counsel spoke with Hall and then requested permission to call him as a defense witness. With the jury excused, the court interviewed Hall, who confirmed that he was the mediator who conducted the mediation between defendant and Bocoum more than a year earlier. He said that he attended the trial because defendant had stopped by his house and told him that the trial was scheduled to start. Although Hall denied being a "friend" of defendant, he indicated that he lived near defendant's mother, and, as a pastor, he was obligated "to be friendly with everybody."

Hall described defendant and Bocoum's exchange during the mediation:

> They were talking about the fight that they has. [Defendant] says that they went into a fight and they come together and he picked up the next gentleman and he threw him and they fell into a garbage bin, okay? . . . I ask [defendant] did you use a weapon and he says no.

> The other fellow says that it was a fight and there was a shovel at the door and he picked up the shovel and — but he didn't make any hit with it.

Hall said that the mediation session quickly became chaotic, with both defendant and Bocoum "talking at the same time." According to Hall, Bocoum

"said he's the one that picked up the shovel. It seemed like he picked up —
to my understanding, the little knowledge I have — he picked up the shovel,
but he didn't say he hit [defendant] with it or nothing." Hall also recalled that
he "didn't hear nothing about a machete."

After interviewing Hall, the court rejected defendant's proffer of Hall's
testimony. * * *

The jury convicted defendant of third-degree aggravated assault and fourth-
degree possession of a weapon. Defendant was acquitted of a third-degree
weapons charge. The trial court sentenced defendant to three years probation,
imposed $1,162 in fines and court costs, and required defendant to complete
anger management counseling and community service.

* * *

II.

Defendant contends that the mediator's testimony may serve to exculpate
him and that the trial court's refusal to allow the mediator to testify deprived
him of his right to fully present a defense. Defendant explains that his defense
depends on whether he can establish that he acted in self-defense. He
maintains that "[t]he relevance and probative value of Pastor Hall's proffered
testimony was clear and substantial, as it would have established, from an
unbiased witness, that Bocoum indeed wielded a shovel during the fight."
Defendant insists that his right to compulsory process was violated when he
was unable to proffer the mediator's testimony as substantive evidence that
Bocoum had the shovel and to boost defendant's own credibility as a prior
consistent statement. Defendant further argues that the trial court's ruling
interfered with his ability to impeach the credibility of the State's witnesses
regarding their testimony that Bocoum did not charge at defendant with the
shovel. Accordingly, defendant urges this Court to relax Rule 1:40-4(c) to allow
the mediator to testify on remand.

* * *

III.

Before addressing the central issue in this appeal — whether, and under
what circumstances, a mediator's testimony may be excluded from a criminal
trial — we first set forth the background of the mediator's privilege and the
rights that defendant claims are impaired by that privilege.

A.

Bocoum made statements, which defendant alleges are exculpatory, during
a mediation session that the municipal court ordered as part of the Complementary Dispute Resolution Programs (CDR), Rule 1:40. CDR features
procedures that either encourage settlement, narrow issues for adjudication,
or both. Rule 1:40-1 describes those procedures as "an integral part of the
judicial process, intended to enhance its quality and efficacy." Among the

various CDR alternatives, a court may order the parties to participate in mediation, during which a neutral person "facilitates communication between parties in an effort to promote settlement without imposition of the mediator's own judgment regarding the issues in dispute."

Rule 1:40-4(c) governs the confidentiality of statements made during mediation:

> [N]o disclosure made by a party during mediation shall be admitted as evidence against that party in any civil, criminal, or quasi-criminal proceeding. . . . *No mediator may participate in any subsequent hearing or trial of the mediated matter or appear as witness or counsel for any person in the same or any related matter.* (Emphasis added.)

In this matter, the mediator's act of testifying constitutes an "appear[ance] as [a] witness." And, although defendant's municipal court proceeding dealt primarily with the allegedly harassing phone messages from Bocoum that precipitated the fight, the municipal action also is a "matter" that is "related" to defendant's "subsequent . . . trial" for assault and weapons charges. Therefore, under a plain reading of Rule 1:40-4(c), the trial court correctly prevented the jury from hearing the mediator's testimony.

Defendant asks this Court to relax the Rule 1:40-4(c) prohibition of mediator testimony under Rule 1:1-2, which provides that court rules "shall be construed to secure a just determination . . . [and] fairness in administration." . . . The CDR rules allow relaxation or modification if an "injustice or inequity would otherwise result." R. 1:40-10.

* * *

B.

Determining whether relaxation is appropriate in this appeal requires an examination and balancing of the interests that are at stake. The Fourteenth Amendment guarantees every criminal defendant the right to a fair trial. At its core, that guarantee requires a "fair opportunity to defend against the State's accusations." *Chambers v. Mississippi*, 410 U.S. 284, 294 (1973). The Supreme Court has explained that this right is effectuated "largely through the several provisions of the Sixth Amendment," which entitles a defendant "to be confronted with the witnesses against him" and "to have compulsory process" to secure testimonial and other evidence. Our State Constitution, containing identical wording, affords those same rights.

The confrontation right assures a defendant the opportunity to cross-examine and impeach the State's witnesses. *See Davis v. Alaska*, 415 U.S. 308, 315–16 (1974). "The right to confront and cross-examine accusing witnesses is among the minimum essentials of a fair trial." The right to compulsory process is grounded in similar sentiments: "Few rights are more fundamental than that of an accused to present witnesses in his own defense." Together, the rights of confrontation and compulsory process guarantee "a meaningful opportunity to present a complete defense." "That opportunity would be an empty one if the State were permitted to exclude competent, reliable evidence bearing on . . . credibility . . . when such evidence is central to the defendant's claim of innocence."

But the rights to confront State witnesses and to present favorable witnesses are "not absolute, and may, in appropriate circumstances, bow to competing interests." * * *

IV.

With that law as a backdrop, we now must determine whether the trial court's exclusion of the mediator's testimony under Rule 1:40-4(c) was constitutionally permissible.

The recently enacted Uniform Mediation Act (UMA), N.J.S.A. 2A:23C-1 to -13, was not in effect when the trial court excluded mediator testimony in this matter. . . . [However,] the UMA principles, in general, are an appropriate analytical framework for the determination whether defendant can overcome the mediator's privilege not to testify.

The UMA protects mediation confidentiality by empowering disputants, mediators, and nonparty participants to "refuse to disclose, and [to] prevent any other person from disclosing, a mediation communication." The privilege yields, however, if a court determines "that the mediation communication is sought or offered in" a criminal proceeding, "that there is a need for the evidence that substantially outweighs the interest in protecting confidentiality," and "that the proponent of the evidence has shown that the evidence is not otherwise available." The burden is on defendant to satisfy these requirements, and he can only prevail if he meets each condition.

As noted, the UMA states that the privilege gives way if the need for the evidence "substantially outweighs" the interest in protecting confidentiality. Defendant asserts, and the State disagrees, that the qualifier "substantially" represents an unconstitutional evidentiary restriction. Defendant adds that the Court should consider only whether the need "outweighs" the confidentiality interests, a standard that is less burdensome for defendant.

We do not determine the constitutionality of the UMA standard in this appeal for three reasons. First, as noted above, the UMA was not in effect when the events at issue in this trial occurred. Second, the parties raised the issue for the first time after oral argument before the Court in this matter. It is appropriate that we defer consideration until litigants can fully argue and brief the subject in a proper case. Third, we need not address that question now because its resolution is not necessary to our disposition. That is so because even when we apply defendant's standard, the mediator's testimony does not outweigh — let alone substantially outweigh — the interest in protecting confidentiality.

The first requirement is clearly satisfied because defendant is on trial for assault and weapons charges and seeks to introduce evidence of mediation statements into that trial. Therefore, we must assess whether the interest in maintaining mediation confidentiality is outweighed by the defendant's need for the mediator's testimony. Finally, we consider whether the substance of the testimony is available from other sources. Ultimately, we conclude that defendant has not met those requirements and, therefore, cannot defeat the privilege against mediator testimony.

A.

We begin by considering the "interest in protecting confidentiality" and examining the social and legal significance of mediation. An integral part of the increasingly prevalent practice of alternative dispute resolution (ADR), mediation is designed to encourage parties to reach compromise and settlement. Courts have long-recognized that public policy favors settlement of legal disputes and that confidentiality is a "fundamental ingredient of the settlement process." The rationale is simple: "If settlement offers were to be treated as admissions of liability, many of them might never be made."

Successful mediation, with its emphasis on conciliation, depends on confidentiality perhaps more than any other form of ADR. Confidentiality allows "the parties participating [to] feel that they may be open and honest among themselves. . . . Without such assurances, disputants may be unwilling to reveal relevant information and may be hesitant to disclose potential accommodations that might appear to compromise the positions they have taken." Indeed, mediation stands in stark contrast to formal adjudication, and even arbitration, in which the avowed goal is to uncover and present evidence of claims and defenses in an adversarial setting. Mediation sessions, on the other hand, "are not conducted under oath, do not follow traditional rules of evidence, and are not limited to developing the facts." Mediation communications, which "would not [even] exist but for the settlement attempt," are made by parties "without the expectation that they will later be bound by them." Ultimately, allowing participants to treat mediation as a fact-finding expedition would sabotage its effectiveness.

If mediation confidentiality is important, the appearance of mediator impartiality is imperative. A mediator, although neutral, often takes an active role in promoting candid dialogue "by identifying issues [and] encouraging parties to accommodate each others' interests." To perform that function, a mediator must be able "to instill the trust and confidence of the participants in the mediation process. That confidence is insured if the participants trust that information conveyed to the mediator will remain in confidence. Neutrality is the essence of the mediation process." Thus, courts should be especially wary of mediator testimony because "no matter how carefully presented, [it] *will inevitably be characterized so as to favor one side or the other.*"

* * *

Defendant argues that the admission of the mediator's testimony would not "obliterate the whole dispute resolution process" because "[t]he only prejudice posed by Pastor Hall's testimony . . . was inconvenience to the mediator and the municipal court. Such inconvenience was relatively insignificant." According to defendant, mediation participants cannot reasonably expect their assertions to be confidential because Rule 1:40-4(c) allows the admission of statements of a mediation participant if that participant is not a party to the later proceeding where admission is sought. Defendant contends that, as a non-party to this matter, Bocoum has no interest in defendant's prosecution and, therefore, no reason to complain about the manner in which his statements are used.

Defendant's position trivializes the harm that will result if parties are routinely able to obtain compulsory process over mediators. Simply because the mediator does not actually testify *against* the victim (who is, by definition, a non-party to a State criminal prosecution) does not mean that the victim is unaffected by the prospect that his statements, made with assurances of confidentiality, will be used to exculpate the person who victimized him. In such circumstances, the victim could hardly be expected to trust that the mediator was impartial.

* * *

B.

Because there is a substantial interest in protecting mediation confidentiality, we must consider defendant's need for the mediator's testimony. To ascertain whether that testimony is "necessary to prove" self-defense, we assess its "nature and quality."

The mediator's testimony in this matter does not exhibit the indicia of reliability and trustworthiness demanded of competent evidence. Indeed, the mediator's description of the session gives the overall impression of bedlam, making it difficult to accurately attribute specific statements to individual speakers. For instance, the mediator explained that the mediation participants "started to raise their voices," and all the parties were "talking at the same time." The mediator was forced to tell the participants to speak "only one person at a time," but once a question was asked, "both of them start [ed]." During this exchange, the mediator recalled, "[o]ne is saying I picked you up and I threw you; the other one said there was a shovel, I picked up the shovel." When pressed by the trial court, the mediator identified Bocoum as the one who said he had the shovel, at least "to [his] understanding, the little knowledge" he had. Moreover, all of these statements were made after the mediator explicitly informed the parties that "[t]he mediation room is confidential," and no transcript or recording was made.

There are other indications that suggest that the mediator's testimony is not trustworthy. For example, although the mediator insisted that he and defendant were not "friend[s]," the mediator's appearance in the courtroom raises questions concerning his neutrality. The mediator, who lives on the same street as defendant's mother, attended the trial after defendant stopped by his house and informed him that the trial was about to begin. Then, defense counsel conferred with the mediator outside the courtroom, elicited his recollection of the mediation, and asked him to testify.

Furthermore, the mediator's testimony does not corroborate defendant's version of what transpired during the fight. Defendant testified that Bocoum hit him in the shoulder with the shovel, entitling defendant to defend himself. The mediator, however, testified that Bocoum said he "picked up the shovel . . . but he didn't make any hit with it." Thus, even on the basic point of whether Bocoum hit defendant, the probative value of the mediator's testimony is diminished because it does not substantiate defendant's contention.

Finally, by asking the mediator to divulge the disputants' statements made during mediation, the defense induced the mediator's breach of confidentiality without first seeking the court's permission. Defendant now seeks to benefit from that breach. Condoning such behavior would encourage all similarly situated defendants to do likewise. As the trial court explained: "[B]ecause someone else has already violated the rule [(i.e., defense counsel)], that doesn't mean the court should now disregard the rule. That would be solicitation for rules not to be followed." * * *

In sum, the mediator's testimony was not sufficiently probative to strengthen defendant's assertion of self-defense. In light of the importance of preserving the role of mediation as a forum for dispute resolution, we conclude that defendant's need for the mediator's testimony does not outweigh the interest in protecting mediation confidentiality.

C.

Apart from whether the need for the mediator's testimony outweighed the interest in confidentiality, we also consider whether defendant failed to demonstrate that evidence of Bocoum's use of the shovel was "not otherwise available."

Both parties had access to, and presented at trial, substantial evidence from other sources bearing on the issue of self-defense. Although three state eyewitnesses testified that Bocoum did not have the shovel, defense counsel thoroughly cross-examined them in an effort to discredit that testimony. Further, Kia Williams, defendant's wife, testified that her brother Robert confessed to her that he had lied during his testimony and that Bocoum had, in fact, wielded the shovel. Finally, testifying on his own behalf, defendant related his version of the fight and accused Bocoum of attacking him with a "long construction shovel": "[H]e take up the shovel . . . and he hit me on the shoulder." At that point, according to defendant, he and Bocoum began wrestling, causing Bocoum to drop the shovel. As defendant was preparing to leave, "Bocoum grabbed the shovel from [Robert] and run . . . across the street. . . . [H]e come towards to hit my car." The jury also was presented with excerpts from defendant's written statement to the police, in which he claimed that Bocoum "came out with a big, long shovel in his hand . . . and he swing at me with the shovel." Accordingly, we conclude that defendant failed to demonstrate that evidence concerning Bocoum's use of the shovel was otherwise unavailable.

We note that defendant's own trial testimony recounted Bocoum's mediation statements about the shovel. Under the UMA, there is a serious question, however, whether defendant should have been allowed to testify at all regarding Bocoum's mediation communications. The UMA's confidentiality provision applies with equal force to a mediation participant, such as defendant, as it does to the mediator. Nonetheless, the parties have not raised that issue before us, and we decline to address it further.

That said, in an exchange with defense counsel at trial, defendant testified as follows:

Q. Okay. I asked you what did Brahima Bocoum say [at the mediation]. . . . What did Brahima Bocoum say happened?

A. Yeah. I told him he have a shovel. He said yes, he have the shovel.

Q. You heard Brahima Bocoum say he had a shovel?

A. Yeah.

Therefore, in this matter, the jury heard evidence of Bocoum's purported inconsistent statement.

D.

Defendant had the opportunity to present substantial evidence, including his own testimony regarding mediation communications, to support his assertion of self-defense and to cross-examine Bocoum. Thus, defendant received that which the Confrontation Clause guarantees: "an opportunity for effective cross-examination, not cross-examination that is effective in whatever way, and to whatever extent, the defense might wish."

V.

Ultimately, the trial court's rejection of defendant's proffer of the mediator's testimony rested upon the sound policy justifications underlying mediation confidentiality. Accordingly, we affirm the Appellate Division because defendant has not made the requisite showings to overcome the mediation privilege in this matter. Defendant's need for the mediator's testimony does not outweigh the interest in mediation confidentiality, and defendant has failed to show that the evidence was not otherwise available.

LONG, J., Dissenting.

* * *

I disagree with the Court's conclusions regarding the "need" for the mediator's testimony and whether it was "otherwise available" * * * . Obviously, those are fact-sensitive conclusions. However, the facts in this case do not support them. This case was a pitched credibility battle over whether defendant acted in self-defense when confronted by Bocoum, wielding a shovel against him. Defendant testified that Bocoum had a shovel. Bocoum testified that he did not. All of the other witnesses were partisans of defendant or Bocoum, related by blood or marriage. Renee Oliver, Bocoum's wife, and her brother, Robert Eckford, supported Bocoum's position that he never picked up or swung a shovel at defendant. Kia Williams, defendant's wife and the sister of Renee and Robert, testified that Robert admitted to her on more than one occasion that Bocoum did wield a shovel and that he had lied in his testimony.

Defendant, the most interested of all witnesses, testified that Bocoum admitted during mediation that he had a shovel. If Bocoum made that admission, it was in direct conflict with his trial testimony and dramatically undercut his credibility on the fundamental issue in the case: self-defense. I disagree with the majority's conclusion that defense evidence on the subject obviated the need for the mediator's testimony.

The mediator's position as the only objective witness placed him in an entirely distinct role from the other witnesses in the case. The evidence that the mediator could have given was therefore different in kind from that of defendant. Because the mediator was the only witness without a proverbial "ax to grind", his testimony was not "otherwise available", nor was it cumulative. Indeed, it could have turned the tide in this very close case. Therefore, it was essential both to the defense of the criminal charges against defendant and to the very fairness of the trial. That was a sufficient basis on which to breach the mediator's privilege.

Finally, I believe that this Court overstepped its bounds in declaring that the mediator's testimony "does not exhibit the indicia of reliability and trustworthiness demanded of competent evidence." In support of its conclusion, the majority has excerpted portions of the mediator's testimony that, to me, do not fully reflect the entire colloquy. The complete transcript of the mediator's testimony leaves a different impression than those excerpts:

> Mediator: They were talking about the fight that they has. Carl [Williams] says that they went into a fight and they come together and he picked up the next gentleman and he threw him and they fell into a garbage bin, okay? He says — and I ask him did you use a weapon and he says no.
>
> *The other fellow says that it was a fight and there was a shovel at the door and he picked up the shovel and — but he didn't make any hit with it.* The wife says that she threw her shoes at Carl.
>
> They started to raise their voices. I says you know what? My part of this court is, if I started to ask questions, only one person at a time. And both of them start. I says okay, listen, let me — case closed. And I send it back to the judge.
>
> Trial Judge: So you weren't able to get an account given by any one of them sitting down talking without other people talking at the same time?
>
> Mediator: Both of them was talking at the same time. One is saying I picked you up and threw you; *the other one said there was a shovel, I picked up the shovel.* And they were talking, going on. I says let the case close, send it back for trial. Because I'm only there to settle the cases.
>
> If I get settled, then I wrote it up, wrote a statement up, and I signed it; then both parties sign it and the judge signs it. They both get a copy and they go home, settled. If I doesn't settle it, then I send it back.
>
> Trial Judge: Did you have any contact with any of them between the time you mediated it and last Friday?
>
> Mediator: No. I don't even know the people here, if I saw them right now, the people might come in, I wouldn't even know them, 'cause I only — Carl, I met him the first time in court.

Trial Judge: Then you didn't see him again until last Friday?

Mediator: To be frank, I saw him before Friday, but we didn't have no contact with nothing like this case.

Trial Judge: *Oh. Well, are you able to remember today who said that the one fellow had a shovel, whether Carl said he had a shovel or the guy said —*

Mediator: *The guy says he has a shovel; he picked up the shovel; it was some place at the door.*

Trial Judge: *It wasn't Carl that said the guy picked up the shovel?*

Mediator: *No. The next guy — I don't know his name; I don't remember his name — he said he's the one that picked up the shovel. It seemed like he picked up — to my understanding, the little knowledge that I have — he picked up the shovel, but he didn't say he hit Carl with it or nothing. And they both started to wrestle.* (Emphasis added.)

There is nothing unclear about that testimony. Plainly, Bocoum admitted, in the mediator's presence, to wielding a shovel. That, in turn, rendered the mediator's testimony "relevant and necessary" to the defense. Any further concerns over the mediator's quality as a witness (e.g., ability to recollect or bias) went to the weight to be accorded to his testimony by the jury, not its admissibility. For all those reasons, I dissent.

Justice ALBIN joins in this opinion.

NOTES

1. Other courts have reached a different outcome in criminal cases. For example, in *State v. Castellano*, 460 So. 2d 480 (Fla. 1984), a defendant charged with first degree murder claimed self-defense. The court decided that he could subpoena the community mediator who had mediated a dispute between the defendant and his victim. The defendant argued that the mediator's testimony would support his claim of self-defense because the mediator had witnessed the victim making death threats to the defendant during the mediation.

2. In criminal proceedings and actions to enforce agreements reached in mediation, the UMA sets a balancing standard for a judge to apply in determining whether to admit evidence of mediation communications. (UMA § 6(b).) But the UMA and other statutes also establish exceptions that do not require case-by-case consideration; instead, the legislature has decided to permit disclosures in defined circumstances as a matter of public policy. (*See, e.g.,* UMA § 6(a).) For mediation participants who must decide what information they are willing to share, wouldn't bright line statutory rules provide clearer guidance? If you favor bright line rules, how would you craft one for criminal cases — would you make an exception to the mediation privilege and permit disclosures in all criminal cases or allow mediation participants to prevent disclosures in all cases? Would you use the same rule for felony and misdemeanor proceedings? Should it make any difference whether the defense or the prosecution seek to introduce evidence from a mediation? Do the constitutional protections for criminal defendants influence your views?

3. If you were a judge, would you decide in favor of disclosure or mediation confidentiality in the following situations? Should a legislature considering a mediation privilege adopt an exception that would cover these circumstances?

a. No agreement was reached in a mediation between a priest and the parents of a child who claims that the priest fondled her. The parents want to make the allegations public and report the priest to the state child abuse agency. But they signed a confidentiality agreement and a state statute establishes an exclusionary rule for mediation communications. The priest's diocese seeks an injunction to prevent the breach of confidentiality by the parents. Should the confidentiality agreement and privilege be overcome by public policy against such behavior? Some states have a requirement that certain professionals, such as social workers, teachers, and lawyers, must report child abuse. Should that reporting requirement affect the decision? (*See CR & SR v. E*, 573 So. 2d 1088 (Fla. Dist Ct. App. 1991); UMA §§ 6(a)(7); 7(b)(3).)

b. During a mediation in a state with a mediation privilege, the parties to a lawsuit reached a settlement agreement. One party did not live up to the terms of the signed, written agreement and the other went to court to enforce it. The proffered defense is as follows: "I have a history of heart problems. The mediation went on all day. I started having chest pains and asked the mediator to end the session so I could go to the emergency room. He refused. I signed the agreement under duress and great pain." Should there be an exception to the privilege to allow the party to testify as to what the mediator said in order to establish a contract defense of duress? Should either party be able to call the mediator as a witness? (*See Randle v. Mid Gulf*, 1996 Tex. App. LEXIS 3451; UMA §§ 6(a)(5); 6(b)(2).)

c. In a mediation between rival gang members, one of the gang leaders describes a plan to rob a grocery store in the middle of the night when it is closed. What, if anything, should the mediator be able to do? What if the plan is instead to set fire to an occupied building? (*See* UMA §§ 6(a)(3); 7(b)(2).)

d. During a mediation, it becomes apparent that a crucial defendant was not named in the suit. It also becomes apparent that the missing defendant is a client of the plaintiff's lawyer. What, if anything, should the defendant's lawyer or the mediator be able to do about this situation? (*See In re Waller*, 573 A.2d 780 (D.C. 1990); UMA §§ 6(a)(6), 6(c).)

4. California is an example of a state that has taken a very strict approach toward disclosures of mediation communications. Section 1119 of the California Evidence Code makes oral and written communications made in the course of a mediation or mediation consultation inadmissible in court and requires that they remain confidential. There are opportunities for mediation parties to waive confidentiality under some circumstances (*see, e.g.,* §§ 1121, 1122), but the statute does not contain public policy exceptions to confidentiality. Courts in California have repeatedly crafted exceptions to permit disclosures, but have been reversed by the California Supreme Court, which has declared "[t]o carry out the purpose of encouraging mediation ensuring confidentiality, the statutory scheme * * * unqualifiedly bars disclosure of communications made during mediation absent an express statutory exception." (*Foxgate*

Homeowner's Association, Inc. v. Bramalea California, Inc., 25 P.3d 1117, 1126 (Cal. 2001) (rejecting an exception to confidentiality to permit mediator to disclose to the court sanctionable conduct [by an attorney] in mediation).) Do you favor this absolute approach to preventing disclosure of mediation communications? What might be the consequences?

3. ENFORCING CONFIDENTIALITY RULES

LAWSON v. BROWN'S HOME DAY CARE CENTER, INC.
172 Vt. 574, 776 A.2d 390 (2001)

Duncan Kilmartin, a counsel for defendants in this case, appeals the Caledonia Superior Court's order imposing a $2,000 sanction on him for filing unsealed information from a confidential mediation session with the court. He claims the court did not afford him procedural due process and erred because his professional responsibilities required him to make the disclosure. We reverse and remand for a determination on the issue of Kilmartin's motivation in making the disclosure.

In September 1997, plaintiffs Katherine and Bradley Lawson, represented by attorney Gareth Caldbeck, filed the underlying civil action to recover damages for injuries to their daughter Jordan Lawson, who choked on a rattle while at Brown's Day Care Center. The Cooperative Insurance Company retained Kilmartin to represent defendants. Defendants also retained separate counsel due to the prospect of an award in excess of their insurance coverage. After the case settled, the superior court sanctioned Kilmartin $2,000 and Caldbeck $1,000. Kilmartin appeals; Caldbeck does not appeal the sanction.

This case proceeded in an atmosphere of unbecoming hostility between Kilmartin and Caldbeck, expressed in numerous filings with the court. The wrangling escalated to the point where, in April 1998, the court commanded, "in filings with the court, the attorneys shall refrain from the use of rhetoric containing personal criticism." Nevertheless, as the court later noted, "Unfortunately, the filings of such documents did not stop." For example, on June 18, 1998, Kilmartin filed an "emergency" motion to disqualify Caldbeck on the basis of obstruction of justice, subornation of perjury, and presentation of false evidence. Kilmartin based the motion on the belief that Caldbeck had submitted false affidavits in the case. The court denied the June 18 motion, stating that the "factual discrepancies described in the [m]otion are not unusual ones to occur in discovery, and the court will not rule on an *ex parte* basis that they constitute a reason to halt a planned discovery process or an early neutral evaluation of the case."

Under a pretrial scheduling order, the court instructed the parties to engage in mediation with attorney Peter Joslin. The parties and their respective counsel met with Joslin on June 22, 1998, at which time the parties agreed that all mediation proceedings were to remain confidential.

On June 26, 1998, Kilmartin filed with the court an unsealed document entitled "Confidential Disclosure under DR 1-103(A)," disclosing discussions that took place during the mediation session and attaching a copy of a proposed settlement agreement. Disciplinary Rule 1-103(A) of Vermont's Code of Professional Responsibility, applicable when Kilmartin made the disclosures, states: "A lawyer possessing unprivileged knowledge of a violation of DR 1-102 shall report such knowledge to a tribunal or other authority. . . ." DR 1-102 prohibits a lawyer from engaging in "illegal conduct involving moral turpitude," *id.* 1-102(A)(3); engaging in conduct involving "dishonesty, fraud, deceit, or misrepresentation," *id.* 1-102(A)(4); or engaging in conduct that is "prejudicial to the administration of justice," *id.* 1-102(A)(5).

Kilmartin asserted that Caldbeck had committed (1) a violation of 13 V.S.A. § 8 when, during the mediation, he proposed settlement terms under which defendants would refrain from making or authorizing "any claims, complaints or allegations, civil or criminal, against any parties or other persons" arising out of the lawsuit, and (2) a violation of DR 1-102 based on Caldbeck's negotiating demand that Kilmartin forego any criminal or disciplinary complaint against him. Accordingly, he disclosed this perceived transgression, citing DR 1-103(A) which requires attorneys in this state to report misconduct by other attorneys unless the information is privileged.[2] After reading the cover and title pages accompanying the disclosure, the court returned the disclosure (unread) to Kilmartin, explaining in a notation written on the cover page that it would "not participate in ex parte communications concerning the case."

On July 2, Kilmartin filed a motion seeking permission to appeal the denial of his June 18 motion or, in the alternative to, to disqualify Caldbeck. This motion included the June 26 mediation disclosure. Caldbeck's response, filed on July 6, also described statements made during mediation, but requested that the court seal Kilmartin's motion. Thus began an exchange of several filings between the parties that disclosed more information pertaining to the confidential mediation. The court ordered the temporary seal of certain pages of these documents on three separate occasions, making clear that its reason for doing so was to protect the confidentiality of the parties' mediation and settlement discussions. On August 24, the court released the record from temporary seal, except for a portion of the draft settlement proposal regarding the settlement amount that is now permanently sealed. The court then ordered Kilmartin and Caldbeck to "appear and show cause why the court should not impose sanctions for violating the confidentiality of the mediation session by filing documents with the court containing descriptions of discussions at the mediation session and related negotiations and proposed terms of settlement."

---

[2] The information at issue here was not protected by an attorney-client privilege. See *In re Himmel,* 125 Ill.2d 531, 127 Ill. 708, 533 N.E.2d 790, 794 (1988) (information disclosed to attorney by client in presence of third parties not protected by attorney-client privilege). Moreover, our evidence rules make information disclosed in mediation inadmissible, but not privileged. See V.R.E. 408. The parties could not create an evidentiary privilege by agreement. Even if they could, it would be a large stretch to interpret an informal oral agreement as creating an evidentiary privilege that insulates a party to a mediation from the consequences of criminal or ethical misconduct. The duty of disclosure is even broader under the Rules of Professional Conduct. Rule 8.3(c) requires disclosure unless the information is covered by the lawyer confidentiality rule, Rule 1.6. There is no exception for mediation proceedings even where mediation is covered by an evidentiary privilege.

The superior court sanction decision, delivered orally on the record shortly after the close of the September 2 hearing, shows that the court imposed the sanction for the following reasons:

1. The lawyers entered into a "verbal agreement that what took place at the mediation session was confidential."

2. The session took place pursuant to an order of the court so the attorneys made their promise "in connection with court business" and their "obligations ran not just to the parties themselves, but to the court and the court processes."

3. The attorneys had no reasonable expectation that they could file documents with the court and have them sealed.

4. Although there may be exceptions to confidentiality, the material disclosed "is precisely the kind of material" subject to confidentiality.

The trial court reasoned that the agreement of confidentiality, entered into by all parties, coupled with the fact that mediation occurred under a court order justified the sanctions. The court stated that it was "dealing with a situation where this was a session required by the court, conducted by a person appointed by the court who did obtain the agreement for confidentiality by all present, including the attorneys."

Nevertheless, it is important to recognize what is not part of the court's decision. There is no finding that Kilmartin made the filings for an improper purpose or in bad faith. Indeed, there is no finding that Kilmartin did not make the filing for exactly the purpose he stated: to disclose unethical conduct and/or potentially criminal conduct and to disqualify the opposing lawyer.

Although the decision does talk of expectations as to sealing, there is no indication that it would not be equally applicable to a complaint to the Professional Conduct Board or a complaint to the state's attorney. The rationale clearly covers disclosure to anyone not part of the mediation. The unstated assumption behind the decision of the court is that an attorney in Kilmartin's position could never disclose anything that occurred in the mediation for any reason. The court's order is broad enough to make a person who commits professional misconduct, even criminal misconduct, during a mediation immune from disciplinary sanction or prosecution because no one can lawfully disclose the misconduct.

Although we have held that a court may sanction attorneys for misconduct through its inherent powers, here the court found no exceptional circumstances and did not find that Kilmartin acted in bad faith. A finding of bad faith is essential to the court's power to impose the sanction it did. Kilmartin is entitled to some explanation why the reasons for the disclosure were not only wrong, but so wrong that they were advanced in bad faith. The United States Supreme Court has observed that "[b]ecause inherent powers are shielded from direct democratic controls, they must be exercised with restraint and discretion." * * *

Even if we could accept the court's broad rationale for the sanctions it imposed, we are still faced with Kilmartin's argument that he is entitled to notice that his conduct was improper. Although we recognize that Kilmartin had notice of the hearing and an opportunity to be heard, our concern is whether he had notice that the conduct he engaged in could subject him to sanction. Although the superior court indicated that it would not disqualify Caldbeck as sought by Kilmartin, it never stated his conduct in seeking Caldbeck's disqualification was improper until its decision imposing sanctions. Thus, the rationale for the sanctions depends upon the court's conclusion that Kilmartin knew he was violating his obligation of confidentiality, even in the face of Kilmartin's assertion that the Code imposed upon him an obligation of disclosure. We find it difficult to conclude that Kilmartin had fair warning of the obligation he is charged with violating, when he consistently asserted that he had the opposite obligation and the court never addressed his position. As recent commentators on the ethical obligations of lawyers in mediation observed, "[p]eople understand confidentiality to mean different things, from totally secret and never to be mentioned anywhere or to anyone, to a protection only from future court actions, that allows disclosure in other circumstances." F. Furlan, et al., *Ethical Guidelines for Attorney-Mediators; Are Attorneys Bound by Ethical Codes for Lawyers When Acting as Mediators?*, 14 J. AM. ACAD. MATRIM. L. 267, 305 (1997).

In this regard, it is important to note that the sanction imposed upon Kilmartin is essentially punitive-it will go to the State of Vermont and not to a litigant. Indeed, the superior court called the sanction a "fine." In the recent case of *Bigelow v. Bigelow*, 171 Vt. 100, — — , 759 A.2d 67, 72–73 (2000), we found that special due process concerns are raised when the court orders a monetary penalty payable to the court. Thus, the attorney to be sanctioned is entitled to "specific notice of the possibility of nonremedial sanctions, the opportunity to respond to such fines, and other procedural safeguards." [We have] held that a substantial fine could be imposed only through the procedures applicable to a criminal proceeding because the adjudication was fundamentally indistinguishable from criminal contempt. Moreover, we reversed in *Bigelow* because the attorney was not informed that he could be subject to a punitive sanction. The identical circumstances are present here and only heighten concerns that Kilmartin did not have fair warning of the possible consequences of his actions. We conclude, however, that the lack of fair warning would have been addressed by a finding of bad faith. If the court found that Kilmartin acted in bad faith in making the disclosures, there would be no violation of his due process rights because attorneys in this state are on notice that negotiating in bad faith during settlement negotiations can result in sanctions.

Although Caldbeck claimed that Kilmartin filed the mediation material primarily to try the underlying action in the press, we express no opinion on whether Kilmartin acted from improper motives; we leave that to the trial court on remand. We decide only that it was error for the court to have imposed sanctions without finding any improper motives or bad faith and ignoring Kilmartin's justification for making the filing, a justification that is valid on its face. On remand, if the court finds that Kilmartin revealed the mediation materials in bad faith, then a sanction would be an appropriate exercise of the court's inherent powers.

Reversed and remanded.

NOTES

1. Is there any doubt that both attorneys violated the confidentiality agreement that governed the mediation? Were these violations negligent or intentional breaches of confidentiality? If one attorney has disclosed mediation communications, should that open the door for the opposing attorney to do the same? Should the trial court have sanctioned Attorney Kilmartin for attempting to report attorney misconduct? Which value is more important, confidentiality for mediation communications or maintaining ethical standards in the legal profession? What do you think motivated the judge to impose the sanction?

2. The UMA provides an exception to the mediation privilege for mediation communications that are "sought or offered to prove or disprove a claim or complaint of professional misconduct or malpractice filed against a mediation party, nonparty participant, or representative of a party based on conduct occurring during a mediation." (UMA § 6(a)(6).) A mediator may not be compelled to provide evidence, however. (UMA § 6(c).) If this provision had been in effect in Vermont, would it have permitted defense counsel's disclosures?

3. Would bad faith be a necessary finding for a sanction if Vermont had a statute creating a mediation privilege or if the trial court had a confidentiality rule governing mediations? Would a statute or rule that doesn't explicitly authorize sanctions provide the notice the court decided was required absent a finding of bad faith? Do you think any sanctions should ever be imposed without a finding that the disclosure was made in bad faith?

4. *In re Anonymous*, 283 F.3d 627 (2002), which you read in Part 1(d), illustrates some of the factors that may enter into a determination that sanctions are not appropriate even when the court determines that confidentiality provisions were violated. Although the court did not address the topic specifically, lack of notice appears to underlie the court's decision not to sanction. Given that the local rule that provided the relevant confidentiality protections was somewhat ambiguous and, although the court quickly amended it to expand its scope, this "interpretation" occurred after the violations, would you be comfortable if the court had imposed sanctions? On the other hand, how strong is the court's conclusion that any harm from the disclosures was minimal because they were made in arbitration, another confidential proceeding? Does this reasoning make sense given the rationales for maintaining confidentiality and the purpose for the disclosures in the arbitration?

LAWSON v. BROWN'S HOME DAY CARE CENTER, INC.
177 Vt. 528, 861 A.2d 1048, 1049–51 (2004)

Duncan Kilmartin appeals from the trial court's order, on remand, upholding its imposition of $2000 in sanctions. The court found that Kilmartin acted in bad faith in filing unsealed materials from a confidential session with the court. * * *

* * *

¶ 7. On remand, and after a hearing, the trial court issued a lengthy order upholding its imposition of sanctions after finding that Kilmartin acted in bad faith. In reaching its conclusion, the court considered Kilmartin's justification for his behavior, i.e., "to disclose unethical conduct and/or potentially criminal conduct and to disqualify the opposing lawyer," in light of all the facts and circumstances. The court found Kilmartin's explanation inconsistent with his conduct, and, based on numerous findings, it concluded that Kilmartin had acted in bad faith in filing confidential materials with the court.

¶ 8. To place Kilmartin's behavior in context, the court first recounted in detail the "unnecessary, unprofessional, and distracting" behavior exhibited by counsel in the underlying proceedings. The court turned next to the specific acts that formed the basis of its sanction order: Kilmartin's repeated filing of documents protected by the confidentiality of the mediation process. As the court explained, on July 2, 1998, Kilmartin filed a complicated motion seeking permission to appeal the court's denial of his emergency motion to Caldbeck, or alternatively, to suspend and disqualify Caldbeck. In his motion, Kilmartin accused Caldbeck of misconduct in preparation of the settlement agreement, and he repeated his earlier charge that Caldbeck had prepared false affidavits. Kilmartin described specific discussions that took place during the June 22 mediation session, and attached a draft settlement agreement as an exhibit. Kilmartin did not request that any portion of the motion be sealed, and it became a matter of public record upon filing, even though the settlement process was ongoing. Kilmartin filed two additional motions that included discussions of events that had occurred during mediation, as well as an affidavit from a mediation participant.

¶ 9. The court compared this behavior with the justification proffered by Kilmartin, and found that, although his claimed purposes appeared facially valid, they did not justify his actions. The court explained that if Kilmartin's purpose was to disclose unethical conduct, the filing of confidential material from the mediation session with the trial court three times between July 2 and July 10 in the context of the filing of civil motions was not the way to do it. Similarly, the court found that if Kilmartin's purpose was to disclose potentially criminal conduct, the filing of the confidential material in motions with the trial court was ineffectual. If his intent was to disqualify Caldbeck, the court found no reason why this required him to place confidential mediation information into the public record when reasonable alternatives existed. Moreover, the court found that this asserted purpose did not justify the filing of confidential material not only once, but repeatedly, including after the court had ordered that it would temporarily seal such material. Thus, because Kilmartin's stated objectives were inconsistent with his conduct, the court found that this raised serious questions about his motivation.

¶ 10. The court placed significant importance on the context in which the filings had occurred. As the court found, at the time of Kilmartin's actions: there was a high degree of animosity between the parties; Kilmartin had engaged in a pattern of "baiting" Caldbeck; Kilmartin had been sanctioned twice for discovery violations that involved wilful, knowing refusals to provide information to Caldbeck; Kilmartin had already tried twice unsuccessfully to disqualify Caldbeck, and his behavior occurred in the context of a third attempt; Kilmartin acted swiftly to seek Caldbeck's disqualification without the support of defendants' other attorneys at a time when the case was already substantially settled; the disqualification of Caldbeck would have deprived plaintiffs of the one attorney familiar with their case at a time when they were near settlement, and it would have foiled Caldbeck's attempt to settle the claim in a timely manner; and most importantly, none of Kilmartin's stated purposes were advanced by the public filing of confidential material from the mediation process.

¶ 11. Based on its findings, the court found the presence of five elements that, collectively, compelled a finding of bad faith. These included: (1) the conduct was in violation of a duty to the court; (2) the conduct was not the result of an inadvertent mistake but consisted of conscious acts; (3) the proffered justification, though valid on its face, was not supported by the actual conduct; (4) the conduct was prompted by an improper purpose; and (5) it involved ill will. After analyzing Kilmartin's behavior with respect to each of these factors, the court upheld its imposition of sanctions.

* * *

Affirmed.

NOTES

1. What is your opinion now about whether sanctioning Attorney Kilmartin was justified in the *Brown's Home Day Care* case? Was a fine paid to the court the most effective sanction in this situation? Are there alternatives?

2. Despite the emphasis on confidentiality in the law of mediation, it appears that violations often go unnoticed or unpunished. In a database of 1123 state and federal cases decided from 1999 to 2003 that involved a significant mediation issue, Professors Coben and Thompson found more than 350 cases (exceeding one-third of the database) in which courts considered mediation evidence without any indication that either party raised confidentiality issues. These included cases in which mediators testified, participants provided evidence of mediators' actions or statements, or parties or lawyers provided evidence about a mediation in which they had participated. (James R. Coben & Peter N. Thompson, *Disputing Irony: A Systematic Look at Litigation About Mediation*, HARV. NEG. L. REV. 43, 50, 59 (2006).)

Even when a party raised an objection to a breach of confidentiality, sanctions were rarely imposed in the cases in the database. Coben and Thompson conclude: "It appears that courts are reluctant to impose sanctions for violating mediation confidentiality requirements. Warning about future sanctions or admonishment for improper behavior seem to be the extent of the courts' willingness to impose sanctions absent some finding of bad faith." (*Id.* at 123.)

3. Cases in which courts do recognize misuse of confidential mediation communications tend to follow one of three patterns. First, courts often simply strike the offending material or state that they will disregard it. Second, courts often warn the attorney or party not to repeat the violation. And third, there are a few cases in which courts impose monetary sanctions. (*See* Sarah Rudolph Cole, *Protecting Confidentiality in Mediation: A Promise Unfulfilled?*, 54 KAN. L. REV. __ (2006).)

4. There are exceptional cases in which significant sanctions have been imposed for confidentiality violations. In *Paranzino v. Barnett Bank of South Florida*, 690 So. 2d 725 (Fla. Ct. App. 1997), the parties attended a court-ordered mediation in a breach of contract action filed by a customer against a bank. The agreement to mediate, which was signed by the parties, called for the mediation to be confidential. After impasse, the *Miami Herald* newspaper published a story in which the plaintiff and her attorney disclosed a settlement offer made by the bank during the mediation. The trial court struck the plaintiff's pleadings and dismissed the suit. The court of appeals affirmed the trial court's sanction, finding no abuse of discretion and that the disclosure was flagrant and willful.

B.   ENFORCEMENT OF AGREEMENTS TO MEDIATE AND MEDIATED SETTLEMENT AGREEMENTS

1.   AGREEMENTS TO MEDIATE

Private mediations are conducted pursuant to agreements to mediate between the parties. These agreements typically set forth arrangements for the mediation and either specify a mutually-acceptable mediator or a method for selecting one. They usually contain confidentiality provisions as discussed in Part A.

Agreements are also used in some court-connected mediation programs. In that context the terms may merely reiterate court rules governing the program, but even so they serve a notice function and help ensure that the parties understand those rules. Signing an agreement in a court-connected mediation also provides a vehicle for the parties to commit to the process and to the confidentiality of the proceedings.

There are few cases concerning agreements to mediate because they have mostly been entered into voluntarily by parties who are willing to use mediation to resolve a specific, existing dispute. With the advent of pre-dispute mediation agreements, however, conflicts about obligations to mediate are more likely to arise. The following case evaluates the enforcement of a pre-dispute mediation agreement as a question of contract law.

GARRETT v. HOOTERS-TOLEDO
295 F. Supp. 2d 774 (N.D. Ohio 2003)

CARR, District Judge.

This is a gender discrimination case in which the plaintiff, Rachel Garrett, alleges that her former employer, a Hooters restaurant in Toledo, Ohio, wrongfully discharged her after she disclosed to her manager that she was pregnant. * * *

BACKGROUND

A. Alternative Dispute Resolution Agreement

Plaintiff began working at Hooters restaurant in April, 1999. The restaurant did not require plaintiff to sign an arbitration agreement at that time. A couple of months thereafter Hooters adopted a policy that required any employee who wished to be considered for any job change, bonus, promotion, or transfer to accept the terms and conditions of Hooter's "Agreement to Mediate and Arbitrate Employment-Related Disputes" ("ADR Agreement").

On June 27, 1999, defendant Chris Reil, plaintiff's manager at Hooters, gave plaintiff a copy of the ADR Agreement and a binder entitled "Rules and Procedures for Alternative Resolution of Employment-Related Disputes." Plaintiff claims that she did not understand the materials, but carried them around with her in her bag for several weeks. Defendants claim that Reil offered to answer employees' questions about the agreement, but neither plaintiff nor any other employee asked any questions of him.

Plaintiff alleges that when she arrived at work on August 9, 1999, she was told that she had to sign the agreement, or she could not work another shift at Hooters. She signed the agreement. Defendants' motion seeks to enforce the agreement's mediation and arbitration provisions.

Those provisions require an employee first to file a request for mediation to resolve a claim or dispute against Hooters. Once mediation has been requested, the employee can then "initiate a resolution," which triggers the agreement's arbitration provisions. The mediation procedure, while mandatory, is not binding. The outcome of arbitration is binding.

B. Plaintiff's Pregnancy and Termination

Plaintiff worked at Hooters for over three years, until she was terminated on July 17, 2002. Plaintiff alleges that she was terminated by defendants because she became pregnant in June, 2002.

Plaintiff told defendant Reil that she was pregnant on June 18, 2002. She alleges that Reil did not speak to her for several days after this disclosure, and he reduced the number of shifts to which she was assigned to work.

Plaintiff also alleges that she requested permission to wear a modified maternity uniform, but Reil denied her request. She claims that when she complained that other employees' similar requests had been granted, Reil responded "Not while I have been here" and ordered her to go home early. Plaintiff alleges that Reil had harassed other employees who asked to wear pants during their pregnancies.

Additionally, plaintiff claims that Reil permitted plaintiff's co-workers to "harass plaintiff and make crude comments about her pregnancy." Plaintiff claims that she received a phone call from Hooters management on July 16, 2002, asking her to come to a meeting the next morning. At this meeting, plaintiff was terminated. She alleges that her position was filled by a non-pregnant person.

Defendants deny plaintiff's allegations and claim that she was assigned to the same number of shifts she had been before she disclosed her pregnancy. Defendants also assert that plaintiff did not ask for permission to wear the approved Hooters maternity uniform, but instead requested to wear sweatpants. Defendants assert that Reil told her she could not wear sweatpants without a doctor's note and deny that Reil made any harassing comments to plaintiff. Defendants claim that all pregnant servers are allowed to wear the maternity uniform, but that plaintiff never asked to do so. Defendants admit that plaintiff was asked to go home after Reil denied her request to wear a modified uniform, but allege that she was asked to leave because "she threw a tantrum over being denied the right to wear sweatpants."

Defendants assert that other Hooters employees have become pregnant, worked throughout their pregnancies, and returned to work at Hooters after giving birth.

*   *   *

DISCUSSION

Plaintiff argues that the ADR Agreement is "revocable because it is unconscionable" according to Ohio common law.

Under Ohio law, a contract is unconscionable where one party has been misled as to its meaning, where a severe imbalance of bargaining power exists, or where the specific contractual clause is outrageous. Unconscionability is generally recognized to include an absence of meaningful choice on the part of one of the parties to a contract, combined with contract terms that are unreasonably favorable to the other party.

The unconscionability doctrine embodies two separate components: "(1) substantive unconscionability, *i.e.,* unfair and unreasonable contract terms, and (2) procedural unconscionability, *i.e.,* individualized circumstances surrounding each of the parties to a contract such that no voluntary meeting of the minds was possible." A certain "quantum" of both substantive and procedural unconscionability must be present to find a contract unconscionable.

A. Substantive Unconscionability

"Substantive unconscionability involves those factors which relate to the *contract terms themselves* and whether *they* are commercially reasonable. Because the determination of commercial reasonableness varies with the content of the contract terms at issue in any given case, no generally accepted list of factors has been developed for this category of unconscionability."

1. Cost Splitting Provision of ADR Agreement

[The court discussed Plaintiff's claim that the cost splitting provision of the ADR Agreement prevented plaintiff and other potential claimants from vindicating their statutory rights. It concluded that although plaintiff's arguments were generally persuasive, the record was insufficient to establish a factual basis for substantive unconscionability of the cost splitting provision.]

2. Time Limit for Filing a Claim

The ADR Agreement states that all claims against Hooters should be filed within ten days from the last day on which the claim arose. Claimants are required first to file a request for mediation, which is non-binding and from which lawyers are excluded from participating. Once mediation is initiated, the claimant must "initiate a resolution" (request arbitration) within 180 days from the last day on which the claim arose, or within the time limit set forth by the appropriate government agency if the claimant has a right to file with such agency. Even if the parties are still mediating the dispute under that provision of the agreement, the claim for resolution must be filed within the arbitration time limit or it is forfeited.

*   *   *

The ten day time limit for bringing a claim is unreasonable and unfair. Few, if any potential claimants would be able to assess their situation, with or without consulting an attorney, within such time period. As a practical matter, this ten day period would be too short to enable a terminated worker to locate and meet with an attorney. This extreme limitation has no apparent justification, and, even if defendants tried to justify this draconian term, the severely adverse impact on a claimant's ability meaningfully to assess and assert her rights would greatly outweigh such justification. The sole purpose — and, in any event, the clear effect — of this limitation is to eliminate the likelihood that discharged employees will challenge their terminations, even if the ADR Agreement otherwise is reasonable and fair.

Support for this conclusion is found in the Third Circuit's recent decision in *Alexander v. Anthony Int'l, L.P.*, 341 F.3d 256, 266 (3d Cir.2003), in which the court held that a *thirty* day time limit in an arbitration agreement was substantively unconscionable because it was "clearly unreasonable and unduly favorable to [the employer]." In the instant case, the time limit is only *ten* days, twenty days shorter than the limit in *Alexander*, and is even more substantively unconscionable than the limitations period in that case.

3. Mediation Requirement

Even aside from the ten day limitation, the mediation requirement has other substantively unconscionable aspects. Plaintiff alleges that she was presented with a "take it or leave it" demand to sign the agreement. At the very least, this combination of coerciveness coupled with the fundamental inequality of bargaining power that exists between a lone former employee and a large, sophisticated, nation-wide employer gives rise to a need to scrutinize the ADR Agreement with particular care to ensure that the mediation requirement is not an effective barrier to redress.

A claimant's inability to be represented by counsel unfairly disadvantages her and favors the defendants. The agreement simply refers, moreover, to mediation between "the parties": there is no indication of the extent to which the parties can call witnesses, or who their representatives may be. Though defendants likewise forego representation, an imbalance may arise if the participants include company representatives, such as human relations personnel, who have experience in dealing with claims of unfair or improper treatment.

Mediation is to be conducted in Jefferson County, Kentucky, before two mediators, one of whom is to be selected by the plaintiff and the other by the defendants from a list of purportedly neutral mediators provided by the company. The likelihood that a claimant would have any basis on which to choose a mediator who might be open to her contentions is slight, if nonexistent. She would probably be as well off throwing a dart at the company's list as she would be to attempt any other method of choosing a mediator. This "trust us" aspect of the method by which mediators are selected supports the finding of unconscionability of the mediation process.

Forum selection clauses generally are presumed to be *prima facie* valid, but "a forum selection clause may be unconscionable if the place or manner in which arbitration is to occur is unreasonable taking into account the respective circumstances of the parties." In the instant case, there appears to be little justification for the requirement that mediation and arbitration be conducted in Jefferson County (i.e. Louisville), Kentucky. If the term "the parties" were to be given a limited meaning, and include only the plaintiff and the defendants, no reason appears not to have the mediation conducted in Toledo.

The obligation to travel to Kentucky becomes more onerous if plaintiff were to desire to have witnesses appear on her behalf. Whether she or the company could do so is not clear from the ADR Agreement, which simply provides that the mediators would determine the format. If the parties could call witnesses, it is likely that, as a practical matter, only the company would be in a position to do so at a mediation held in Kentucky.There can be no doubt that the mediation requirement and the ADR Agreement as a whole are written to discourage potential claimants from pursuing their claims; the agreement's rules impose burdens and barriers that would routinely deter former employees from vindicating their rights. Even if a former employee were able successfully to overcome these barriers, it appears to be very unlikely that she could prevail.

On balance, the agreement is unreasonable and unfair because it require claimants to participate in a process designed to be, and which is, excessively and unjustifiably favorable to Hooters. The requirement to mediate, which must be undertaken before arbitration can be sought, is substantively unconscionable. The unconscionability of this precondition to arbitration renders the balance of the ADR Agreement unconscionable and unenforceable.

B. Procedural Unconscionability

In determining procedural unconscionability, Ohio courts look to "factors bearing on the relative bargaining position of the contracting parties, including their age, education, intelligence, business acumen and experience, relative bargaining power, who drafted the contract, whether the terms were explained to the weaker party, and whether alterations in the printed terms were possible." "The crucial question is whether 'each party to the contract, considering his obvious education or lack of it, [had] a reasonable opportunity to understand the terms of the contract, or were the important terms hidden in a maze of fine print . . . ?' "

The ADR Agreement signed by plaintiff in this case is procedurally, as well as substantively, unconscionable. Defendants wrote the ADR Agreement, which I have already decided is unreasonable and unfair, and presented it to plaintiff after she had been working for defendants for approximately three months. Plaintiff claims that she earned more money working for defendants than she had at any previous job she had held, and that she would have done anything to keep her position. Defendants told plaintiff that she must sign and accept the agreement in order to be eligible for any job change, including promotions, bonuses, or job transfers. Defendants did not explain the agreement and its implications to employees, including plaintiff, but merely suggested that they read it and ask questions if they did not understand. Plaintiff claims that she tried to read it, but did not understand either its terms or its future ramifications. Later, after plaintiff had possession of the agreement for about a month, defendants, according to the plaintiff, told her that she had to sign it or she could not work another shift. Plaintiff, accordingly, signed and accepted the agreement, though she states that she still did not understand what it meant.

Plaintiff had no opportunity to negotiate the terms of the ADR Agreement. Surely, had she been able to understand the impact of the rights she was giving up and the limitations to which she was acquiescing, plaintiff and any other person in her position would have objected to many of the provisions of the agreement. Even if she had done so, however, it is clear that plaintiff would not have been able to continue working at Hooters for very long if she had declined to accept the ADR Agreement as written and presented to her. Even if defendants had allowed her to continue working shifts as a waitress, she would have been ineligible for any raise, promotion, or transfer.

Therefore, my conclusion that the ADR Agreement is procedurally unconscionable is not reliant, as defendants claim, on whether plaintiff would certainly have lost her job had she not accepted the agreement. The unequal bargaining power between the parties, coupled with plaintiff's lack of sophistication and the clearly demonstrated pressures on her to accept the agreement, no matter what it said, make defendants' motion and its supplemental memorandum in support of its motion unpersuasive. Plaintiff's acceptance of the agreement was not freely given, and the agreement is procedurally unconscionable.

CONCLUSION

Because it is both substantively and procedurally unconscionable, the ADR Agreement violates Ohio common law and is unenforceable.

NOTES

1. The agreement in *Garrett v. Hooters-Toledo* moves the parties in a stepwise fashion to subsequent methods of dispute resolution if the first method is unsuccessful. Why would an employer be interested in a dispute resolution program that relies on mediation first, followed, if necessary, by arbitration? Why do you think the fired employee did not take advantage of the opportunity to mediate when she would not have been bound by the outcome?

2. Unconscionability is more typically claimed in an attempt to avoid pre-dispute arbitration agreements, which are frequently used in employment and consumer contexts. Do you agree with the court's conclusion in *Garrett v. Hooters-Toledo* that the ADR agreement should not be enforced? Do you think that the court would have reached the same conclusion about the unconscionability of the mediation provision if it had not been coupled with a commitment to arbitrate?

3. One could argue on policy grounds that employees should not be required to "agree" as a condition of employment to a process that is supposed to be consensual. But is the arguable coercion here distinguishable from a court order requiring litigants to mediate a case?

2.   MEDIATED AGREEMENTS

Mediation may end without the parties coming to a resolution of their dispute, but when they do reach a resolution, it typically takes the form of an agreement. Enforcement of mediated settlement agreements is the most frequently issue in litigation concerning mediation. (Coben & Thompson, 2006). These cases implicate one of the core values of mediation — that parties guide the process through their exercise of self-determination. Enforcing an agreement imposed on one of the parties is inconsistent with this principle.

Disputes arise about mediated agreements for a number of reasons. In one category of cases, a party contends that no agreement was reached. These cases often involve oral agreements or, as in the following case, written agreements that were not signed by all the parties. Alternatively, a party may argue that no agreement was reached because she signed only an informal written document or a memorandum of understanding, not a final agreement. In that case, the question for the court is whether the memorandum was meant as a final agreement, with only the formalities of memorialization to follow, or as a more tentative "agreement to agree," made with the anticipation that the parties would work out the details later.

KAISER FOUNDATION HEALTH PLAN v. DOE
136 Or. App. 566, 903 P.2d 375 (Or. Ct. App. 1995), *modified on other grounds,* 908 P.2d 850 (1996)

EDMONDS, J.

Plaintiff appeals a judgment for defendant on a claim that sought a declaration that the parties had entered into an enforceable oral settlement agreement and specific enforcement of the same. Plaintiff argues that the court erred in holding that the agreement was not binding. We review *de novo* and reverse.

Defendant is a nurse who was employed with plaintiff for several years. In 1993, she notified Myrna Baker, the Director of Human Resources for plaintiff, that she had been sexually harassed by one of plaintiffs doctors, "Smith."[1] Defendant thereafter filed a grievance with her union and a complaint with the Bureau of Labor and Industries (BOLl) against Smith, plaintiff, and plaintiff's local affiliate.

One of plaintiffs attorneys, Eileen Drake, contacted defendant's attorney, Henry Kaplan, regarding the allegations and the possibility of settlement. Ultimately, defendant agreed to mediate her complaints with a private mediator. On the morning of August 18, 1993, the parties began a mediation conference that included the mediator, Baker, plaintiffs attorneys, defendant and her husband, Kaplan, and Smith's attorney. The mediator placed the parties in separate rooms and contacted each party separately during the mediation process. During that time, defendant and her husband had no contact with anyone except the mediator and Kaplan. At midday, the parties' attorneys met with the mediator for lunch to discuss the case. Plaintiffs attorneys apprised Kaplan of some evidence that they had discovered regarding defendant's conduct at work and explained that defendant would possibly be subject to disciplinary procedures, should she continue to work for plaintiff. After lunch, Kaplan shared this information with defendant. Late in the day, the attorneys, after meeting with the mediator, arrived at a proposed agreement, which Kaplan urged defendant to accept. The terms of the proposal included a cash payment from plaintiff in exchange for defendant's agreement to resign voluntarily from plaintiffs employment. Defendant wanted a few days to think about the proposal, because she had anticipated a settlement that would permit her to retain her job. However, plaintiffs attorneys said that the offer would be withdrawn if it was not accepted on that day. Thereafter, defendant authorized Kaplan to accept the terms of the offer, but instructed him to wait a few hours before notifying plaintiff of the acceptance.

Thereupon, defendant and her husband left for dinner, and Kaplan returned to the mediation site where all the attorneys signed a document to confirm the terms they had agreed constituted the offer. The document read:

"Essential Terms of Agreement

"[Plaintiff], [plaintiffs local affiliate], and [Smith] will pay [defendant] the sum of $65,000

"[Defendant] will voluntarily resign effective immediately

"[Defendant] will not reapply to [plaintiff] or [plaintiffs local affiliate] for employment in the future

"The settlement agreement will include a mutual confidentiality clause

---

[1] Plaintiff has chosen not to use the real names of some of the parties involved in order to maintain confidentiality.

"[Defendant] may say 'the parties have resolved their differences,' 'I have reached a mutually acceptable basis for voluntarily quitting,' 'I've decided to move to another position'

"The settlement agreement will include an arbitration provision

"[Plaintiff] will not challenge any rights [defendant] may have to unemployment benefits

"[Defendant] will receive the value of any accrued vacation

"[Defendant's] pension rights will not be affected

"[Defendant] will prepare and file any documents necessary to dismiss the BOLI claim, her workers' [compensation] claim and union grievance (all with prejudice)

"The settlement agreement will include a complete and full mutual release

"[Defendant] will be provided assistance with resume preparation and interview skills through Career Makers"

After the attorneys signed the document, Kaplan told plaintiffs attorneys that he would contact them within a few hours with either defendant's acceptance or rejection of the proposed agreement. The attorneys agreed that if defendant accepted the terms, Christine Kitchel, one of plaintiffs attorneys, would draft a formal settlement agreement for all the parties to sign.

Later that evening, Kaplan contacted Kitchel to clarify the breadth of the confidentiality provision in the agreement. He testified at trial that he was concerned that the way they "had worded and discussed the confidentiality provision, [defendant] couldn't even talk about [the sexual harassment] to her psychotherapist. * * * Kitchel and Kaplan then agreed that the confidentiality provision would not prohibit defendant from discussing the case with her psychotherapist. Kaplan called Kitchel a second time to make certain that the money received in the settlement would be characterized by plaintiff for tax purposes as compensation for pain and suffering. After receiving a satisfactory answer from Kitchel, Kaplan told Kitchel that defendant had accepted the terms. He then notified the mediator that they had "settled the case." He also notified defendant either before or after his second call to Kitchel that he was about to accept, or had just accepted, the settlement terms on defendant's behalf.

Two days later, defendant notified Kaplan that she declined to settle her claims. On August 26, she sent a letter to Kaplan which stated:

"As of August 20, 1993, I rescinded on a verbal agreement with Kaiser which I made under extreme duress."

Meanwhile, on August 25, Kitchel had delivered to Kaplan a draft of a proposed written settlement. Kaplan notified Drake on August 30 that defendant did "not wish to enter into a settlement agreement along the lines we discussed at the mediation session on August 18." This lawsuit resulted.

Plaintiffs complaint alleges that the parties reached a valid and enforceable oral settlement agreement on August 18, 1993. It seeks a declaration to that effect, a judgment compelling arbitration or, in the alternative, specific performance, and an injunction enjoining defendant from pursuing any further claims arising from the incident with Smith. After a trial to the court, the court found that defendant had accepted the settlement through Kaplan, and that the terms were sufficiently definite to be enforceable. Nevertheless, it ruled that the agreement was unenforceable because defendant had not signed a written agreement.[2]

Plaintiff first assigns error to the court's ruling that a settlement agreement arising out of mediation must be in writing. As plaintiff points out, the court did not cite any authority in support of its holding. Defendant argues that, as a matter of law, agreements reached during mediation should be in writing, because that is "in accord with the expectations of the legal community," due to the confidential nature of mediation, and because most of the negotiation that takes place in mediation occurs between the lawyers and the mediator, without the parties being present. Furthermore, she argues that "it is clear that [these] parties did not intend to be bound" until they signed a written agreement. We can find no authority that supports the proposition that settlements reached during mediation should receive special treatment or be analyzed differently from settlements reached in other settings. Therefore, we disagree with the trial court's holding in that respect.

Moreover, the issues raised by defendant are initially questions of fact about when the parties intended their agreement to become binding. In *Britt v. Thorsen*, the court faced a similar question of whether the parties intended an agreement to be effective immediately or only after the execution of a written agreement. The court explained:

> " 'Where parties agree to reduce their agreement to writing, the question arises as to whether their negotiations constitute a contract. * * * [W]here all the substantial terms of a contract have been agreed on and there is nothing left for future settlement, the fact alone that it was the understanding that the contract should be formally drawn up and put in writing does not leave the transaction incomplete and without binding force, in the absence of a positive agreement that it should not be binding until so reduced to writing and formally executed. Where, however, the writing is regarded as a prerequisite to the closing of a contract, the agreement does not become binding if there has been a failure to reduce it to writing.' "

481 P.2d 352, 354.

The objective manifestations of the parties as evidenced by their communications and acts control the resolution of this issue. The evidence indicates

---

[2] The trial court explained:

"The court holds in mediation only, an acceptance becomes irrevocable only after a party personally and physically agrees to and signs a written document.

"The process of mediation is bottomed on the premise of voluntariness. The interested parties are present volitionally. A settlement, if one is ever reached, is completely voluntary. No party should be able to back the other into accepting an agreement.

"Given this novel concept surrounding mediation, the [c]ourt does not believe that a standard contract law analysis is appropriate. Specifically, in the context of mediation, an acceptance of an offer does not occur and does not become binding until the offeree personally and physically signs or executes a written document."

that the parties intended that the settlement become binding on the evening of August 18. Plaintiffs attorneys made it clear to Kaplan that defendant was required either to accept or to reject the proposed settlement that night even though she had requested several days within which to consider it. Defendant authorized Kaplan to accept the offer before she went to dinner, and Kaplan notified the mediator thereafter that they "had settled the case." Furthermore, Kitchel testified that the purpose of having the attorneys sign the written memorandum was to meet any Statute of Frauds requirements. Defendant's argument that her intent was not to be bound until she had signed a written settlement agreement is not supported by the evidence. Her actions objectively manifested an intent to be bound that night.

Nevertheless, defendant argues that she did not give Kaplan authority to enter into a final settlement with plaintiff on August 18, and that she was not even aware of some of the terms listed in the agreement. She argues:

> "The mere fact of the attorney client relationship does not provide actual or apparent authority to settle. * * * [A]n attorney's authority to represent a person in negotiation does not provide actual or apparent authority for the attorney to settle. [Kaplan] had no actual authority to enter into a final settlement agreement, his only authority was to tell Kaiser to draft a written agreement."

A principal is bound by the acts of its agent when the acts are within the scope of the agent's real or apparent authority. In this case, there is ample evidence from defendant's objective manifestations to indicate that she gave Kaplan actual authority to accept the settlement offer, not just to tell plaintiff to draft a proposed agreement. . . . Defendant told Kaplan to accept the offer, but to make plaintiff wait awhile.

Furthermore, even if she was unaware of some of the terms in the offer, defendant had vested Kaplan with apparent authority to bind her. Apparent authority is created by conduct of the principal, which when reasonably interpreted causes a third party to believe that the principal has authorized the agent to act on the principal's behalf in the matter. In this case, the record shows that from the time Drake first contacted Kaplan, and especially during mediation, defendant permitted Kaplan to do all the negotiating regarding the case on her behalf, and in turn, he kept her apprised of his negotiations and made counteroffers on her behalf. . . . In sum, defendant's conduct was reasonably interpreted by plaintiff as having given Kaplan authorization to accept the entire offer.

Defendant next argues that the parties never reached a meeting of the minds on some of the essential terms, in particular, the arbitration, confidentiality, and release provisions. Defendant first argues that she was not personally aware of the arbitration provision and, therefore, could not have agreed to it. The short answer to that argument is again that, at the very least, Kaplan had apparent authority to settle defendant's claim on her behalf, and Kaplan accepted the arbitration provision as part of the settlement. "It is well settled that the conduct of an attorney who acts within the scope of his or her authority will be imputed to the client."

As to the arbitration provision, defendant argues that they never agreed to the form or the scope of arbitration, nor did they agree whether the arbitration result would be binding or nonbinding. However, Kitchel testified:

"[T]he discussion arose actually following the discussion about confidentiality and we were talking about the fact that obviously confidentiality was an important aspect to everybody, to [defendant], to [Smith], to [plaintiffs local affiliate], [plaintiff], so this was kind of a — confidentiality was a concept that everybody was interested in.

"And I said that — I a suggested an arbitration provision, especially given the confidentiality, because we didn't want to end up in court litigating these issues when all the parties had agreed to keep them confidential, and I suggested an arbitration provision.

"I suggested arbitration at that point, and [Kaplan], we chatted about it briefly. And [Kaplan] said, what do you have in mind.

"And I said, well, you know, we can make arbitration whatever way we want, and I said — I suggested we could use the Triple A process [rules of the American Arbitration Association] and I mentioned to him that I had heard about an employment arbitration process that Triple A had implemented.

"And [Kaplan] had not heard about it so we just said Triple A, kind of left it at that."

Kaplan testified that he did not remember discussing the AAA process with Kitchel, but he understood that the arbitration provision would cover only the confidentiality issue because everything else would be "self-executing * * *. There would be nothing left to arbitrate other than monitoring the confidentiality restriction." Kaplan's testimony is not necessarily inconsistent with Kitchel's understanding that the parties had agreed on an arbitration process and its scope.

Furthermore, there is ample evidence that both attorneys understood that the arbitration provision would be binding. Kitchel testified that she suggested arbitration "in lieu of litigation," and that the rules of AAA should apply. When considered in that context, we are convinced that the parties recognized that the confidentiality of their agreement would be preserved only through arbitration that was binding on both parties. In the light of that evidence and this state's policy to construe arbitration agreements broadly to enhance arbitrability of disputes, we conclude that the parties agreed to incorporate by reference the rules of the American Arbitration Association into their agreement and that that reference is sufficient and definite enough to make their agreement enforceable.

In summary, plaintiff is entitled to a declaration that the oral agreement of August 18, 1993, is a valid and enforceable agreement. The settlement agreement is specifically enforceable according to the terms agreed upon in the oral discussion and memorialized in the written document entitled "Essential Terms of the Agreement." Because we find that the parties agreed to arbitrate according to the rules of the American Arbitration Association, and those rules provide a method for plaintiff to proceed unilaterally with arbitration, the judgment should provide an arbitration provision that incorporates those rules. We decline to grant plaintiffs request for a preliminary injunction, because that would be premature on this record.

Reversed and remanded for entry of judgment consistent with this opinion.

NOTES

1. Why would the employer Kaiser have sought to mediate this dispute? What would have motivated the employee nurse who alleged sexual harassment to employ the mediation alternative? Were there practical reasons for the employee nurse to avoid mediation of this matter?

2. The *Kaiser Foundation Health Plan* decision, like many cases on the enforcement of mediated "agreements," applies traditional contract-law rules. Is the outcome of that analysis consistent with the mediation principle of self-determination? Shouldn't the client be required to sign an "agreement" in order to make it binding? Is the court's agency analysis persuasive? Some mediators feel that the essence of mediation is voluntary action. Isn't the result reached by the court of appeals coercive?

3. Some states do impose a writing requirement on settlement agreements reached in mediation. This creates tension with black letter contract rules, which usually recognize oral agreements. (*See, e.g.,* Tex. Civ. Prac. & Rem. Code Ann. § 154.071(a) (providing that an agreement reached in ADR that settles a dispute is enforceable as any other agreement if it is written and executed); Minn. Stat. Ann. § 572.35 (requiring that a mediated settlement agreement contain a provision stating it is binding and that the mediator cautioned the parties that signing it could affect their legal rights).) Court rules may be another source of writing requirements. In a case alleging trademark infringement, one competitor alleged that the other had breached an oral agreement reached in mediation that the parties would not copy each other's designs. The federal court held that under North Carolina law the agreement did not have to be written to be enforceable. It remanded, however, for the district court to consider whether enforcement would be inconsistent with its mediation rules, which require that "[u]pon reaching a settlement agreement at a mediated settlement conference, the parties shall forthwith reduce the agreement to writing." (*Ashley Furniture Industries, Inc. v. Saniacomo N.A. Ltd.*, 187 F.3d 363 (4th Cir. 1999).) Do rules like these impose an unreasonable burden on the parties, who usually are able to assume that an oral agreement will be enforceable? What are the advantages of rules requiring mediated agreements to be written and signed?

4. Are there practices concerning the form of mediated settlement agreements that could reduce subsequent litigation? If an agreement is reached in mediation, is it a good idea to leave without a document signed by the parties? Why do you think this frequently happens? What additional considerations come into play if the parties' attorneys are not present at the mediation? As a mediator, would you be willing to draft a settlement agreement or memorandum of understanding?

5. Consider the manner in which the issue of mediation confidentiality is handled in the *Kaiser Foundation Health Plan* decision. Doesn't the fact that the dispute resulted in litigation and, indeed, a published opinion, destroy a measure of confidentiality? How helpful is it that the nurse is here revealed as "Doe" and the alleged sexual harasser as "Dr. Smith"? Note that the putative settlement agreement contained a specific "mutual confidentiality clause." In addition, this mediation was conducted in Oregon, which has legislation making confidential documents and "communications made in or in connection with" mediation. When the declaratory judgment case went to trial the court admitted attorney testimony that appeared to be significant. Should this testimony have been considered "confidential" and excluded under the Oregon mediation confidentiality legislation? If "confidential," why is the testimony admissible?

6. Although the court did not apply them in this case, confidentiality rules can affect a party's ability to prove that the parties reached a mediated agreement and to demonstrate the content of that agreement. Under the Uniform Mediation Act, the "agreement" in *Kaiser Foundation Health Plan* would be considered a "mediation communication" and thus inadmissible absent a waiver by the holders or an exception to the mediation privilege. The UMA provides an exception for "an agreement evidenced by a record signed by all parties to the agreement," (§ 6(a)(1)), but the exception does not cover oral agreements. What is the rationale for limiting the exception in this way? What might be the consequences for protecting mediation communications if the exception encompassed oral agreements? If the UMA were in effect, would the agreement in *Kaiser Foundation Health Plan*, which was written but unsigned by the parties, have been admissible?

7. Notice that the mediator skipped the usual opening session at which all parties and lawyers were present. Instead the mediator used an "all caucus" mediation during which the disputants were never face to face. Why would the mediator use this approach? Are there reasons you might object to the "all caucus" style of mediation if you represented one of these parties? Could this approach have contributed to the unraveling of the "agreement?"

8. Notice that the mediator also chose to try to get the respective attorneys to first agree to settle and then, once agreement between attorneys was reached, assigned to counsel the task of obtaining the approval of their clients. Why would the mediator select this strategy? Did this strategy contribute to the subsequent failure to reach agreement? Is there anything that the mediator could have done to help solidify the agreement after the warring attorneys accepted the settlement terms? Is there any request of the mediator that the attorneys could have made that might have helped get the clients to sign the settlement agreement?

For a thorough discussion of the consent process in mediation, see Jacqueline M. Nolan-Haley, *Informed Consent in Mediation: A Guiding Principle for Truly Educated Decision Making*, 74 NOTRE DAME L. REV. 775 (1999) (advocating disclosure and consent safeguards to ensure that mediation participants truly understand the process and to safeguard mediation values of party autonomy and self-determination).

Another major category of disputes about mediated agreements involve cases in which a party acknowledges that he entered into an agreement, but claims that nonetheless he should not be required to comply. The party resisting enforcement usually seeks to invalidate or rescind the agreement based on contract a defense such as fraud, duress, undue influence, or mistake. These types of claims raise particularly thorny issues about fairness in mediation and about maintaining the confidentiality of mediation communications. The following cases illustrate two different approaches to these problems.

VICK v. WAITS
2002 Tex. App. LEXIS 3982

Before Justices KINKEADE, WRIGHT, and FITZGERALD.

Opinion by Justice WRIGHT.

Background

Appellants [Gary C. Vick and Carolyn Vick] contracted with Bantam [Properties, Inc.] for the construction of an office building for appellants. After the building was completed, a dispute arose between appellants and Bantam. After mediation, appellants and Bantam entered into a settlement agreement, in which Bantam assigned "all claims to perform repairs, corrective work, and warranty work" and agreed to use "its best efforts, without recourse or legal obligations, to cause all said subcontractors and engineers, . . . to cooperate with [appellants] on said construction project corrections." The settlement agreement did not identify any particular claims or warranties which existed on the building. Waits, individually, is not a party to the settlement agreement.

Several months later, appellants sued Bantam and Waits for breach of the settlement agreement and fraud. According to appellants, Bantam and Waits breached the settlement agreement because they did not "in good faith cooperate [ ] with [appellants] regarding the construction project warranties and corrections." Appellants also alleged that appellees fraudulently induced appellants into signing the settlement agreement because, during mediation, appellees represented (1) that the settlement agreement would be enforceable against the subcontractors and engineers, (2) they would use their best efforts to cooperate in the corrections, and (3) the warranties and other claims for corrective work would be assigned to appellants.

* * *

Fraud

Appellants also alleged appellees fraudulently induced appellants to sign the settlement agreement. Appellees sought summary judgment on the fraud cause of action because, among other things, appellants could not offer any evidence of false representations made to appellants. In response, appellees filed Gary Vick's affidavit listing numerous false representations Waites made to appellants during mediation. According to appellees, these false representations form the basis of their fraud claim.

Appellees objected to paragraphs two, three, four, five, six, seven, eight, ten, twelve, thirteen, twenty, and twenty-two of Gary Vick's affidavit because all of the alleged misrepresentations were made during mediation and under the Texas Alternative Dispute Resolution Procedures Act (Texas ADR Act) the complained-of statements are confidential. In its order granting summary judgment, the trial court sustained appellees' objections to appellants' summary judgment evidence.

* * *

Section 154.073 of the Texas ADR Act provides that, subject to certain narrow exceptions not applicable in this case, "a communication relating to the subject matter of any civil or criminal dispute made by a participant in an alternative dispute resolution procedure, whether before or after the institution of formal judicial proceedings, is confidential, is not subject to disclosure, and may not be used as evidence against the participant in any judicial or administrative proceeding." Here, all of the alleged misrepresentations forming the basis of appellants' fraudulent inducement claim were made during mediation. * * *

We agree with appellants that they may bring suit for fraudulent inducement. However, appellant's ability to bring suit for fraudulent inducement does not answer the question of whether appellees' statements made during mediation are admissible. Section 154.073 expressly prohibits the use of any statements made during the mediation and appellants do not attempt to explain why that section does not apply to its summary judgment evidence. The Texas ADR Act does not include an exception for claims of fraud, and this Court will not create an exception to the confidentiality provisions of the Texas ADR Act. Because all of the alleged misrepresentations were made during mediation, these statements are confidential and the trial court properly sustained appellees' objections to paragraphs two, three, four, five, six, seven, eight, ten, twelve, thirteen, twenty, and twenty-two of Gary Vick's affidavit. * * *

Because none of the evidence offered to show a false representation was admissible, appellees failed to meet their burden to present enough evidence to raise a genuine fact issue. Thus, the trial court did not err in granting appellees' motion for summary judgment on the fraud claim.

OLAM v. CONGRESS MORTGAGE COMPANY
68 F. SUPP. 2D 1110 (N.D. Cal. 1999)

BRAZIL, United States Magistrate Judge.

* * *

[T]he parties participated in a lengthy mediation that was hosted by this court's ADR Program Counsel-an employee of the court who is both a lawyer and an ADR professional. At the end of the mediation (after midnight), the parties signed a "Memorandum of Understanding" (MOU) that states that it is "intended as a binding document itself. . . ." Contending that the consent she apparently gave was not legally valid, plaintiff has taken the position that the MOU is not enforceable. She has not complied with its terms. Defendants have filed a motion to enforce the MOU as a binding contract.

One of the principal issues with which the court wrestles, below, is whether evidence about what occurred during the mediation proceedings, including testimony from the mediator, may be used to help resolve this dispute. * * *

THE PERTINENT FACTUAL AND PROCEDURAL BACKGROUND

The events in the real world out of which the current dispute arises began unfolding in 1992, when Ms. Olam applied for and received a loan from Congress Mortgage in the amount of $187,000. The 1992 loan is secured by two single-family homes located in San Francisco and owned by Ms. Olam. These properties are referred to as the "Athens Property" and the "Naples Property" because they are located on Athens Street and Naples Street, respectively.

* * *

Ms. Olam contends that she could not afford the monthly payments on the 1992 loan. Eventually she defaulted. Thereafter, Congress Mortgage initiated foreclosure proceedings on both the Athens and Naples Properties.

[The parties entered into a workout agreement. Later, Mrs. Olam claimed she had been coerced into signing it and again defaulted on her loan payments. After a second foreclosure notice, the parties entered into another agreement, which Mrs. Olam similarly claims is unenforceable. In 1995 Mrs. Olam filed suit in state court against Congress Mortgage, its president Robert Gaddis, and Equity Holders Servicing Company. The case was removed and proceeded in federal court on state and federal claims, including a claim under the federal Truth in Lending Act and claims for fraud and breach of fiduciary duty. One mediation was scheduled under the court-sponsored ADR program, but was cancelled at the last minute by Mrs. Olam's counsel, who cited problems communicating with her client. Later, with the court's encouragement, the parties again agreed to mediate.]

* * *

At approximately 10:00 a.m. on September 9, 1998, Ms. Olam, her attorney, Ms. Voisenat, Mr. Gaddis, Russel Hulme (a representative of Congress Mortgage), and Mr. Stea (defendants' lawyer) met with Mr. Herman [the mediator] to commence the mediation. The mediation continued throughout the day and well into the evening.

Sometime around 10:00 p.m. Mr. Herman, Ms. Voisenat, and Mr. Stea retired to Mr. Herman's office to type up what they believed were the essential terms of a binding settlement agreement [the MOU]. * * * It contemplated the subsequent preparation of a formal settlement contract but expressly declared that it was "intended as a binding document itself." The essential terms of the purported settlement are clearly set forth in the typed MOU. At approximately 1:00 a.m., when the mediation concluded, Ms. Olam and her lawyer, and Messrs. Gaddis and Hulme and their lawyer, signed the MOU.

Following the conclusion of the mediation, Mr. Herman drove Ms. Voisenat and Ms. Olam to their homes.

Later on September 10, 1998, [counsel for both parties and Mr. Herman informed the court that the case had settled.]

* * *

On April 21, 1999, more than seven months after the mediation, defendants filed a Motion to Enforce the Original Settlement . . . and to Enter Judgment Thereon (hereafter "Motion to Enforce").

* * *

On May 14, 1999, Ms. Olam, through [a] new attorney, filed her "Opposition" to the defendants' motion to enforce. Two separate grounds for the opposition were set forth. The first was that the MOU was unconscionable. We considered and rejected that contention in a separate order. The second ground for opposition was that at the time she affixed her name to the MOU (at the end of the mediation) the plaintiff was incapable (intellectually, emotionally, and physically) of giving legally viable consent. Specifically, Ms. Olam contended that at the time she gave her apparent consent she was subjected to "undue influence" as that term is defined by California law.

[P]laintiff alleges that at the time she signed the MOU she was suffering from physical pain and emotional distress that rendered her incapable of exercising her own free will. She alleges that after the mediation began during the morning of September 9, 1998, she was left *alone* in a room *all* day and into the early hours of September 10, 1998, while all the other mediation participants conversed in a nearby room. She claims that she did not understand the mediation process. In addition, she asserts that she felt pressured to sign the MOU-and that her physical and emotional distress rendered her unduly susceptible to this pressure. As a result, she says, she signed the MOU against her will and without reading and/or understanding its terms.

* * *

WAIVERS BY THE PARTIES (BUT NOT THE MEDIATOR) OF THEIR MEDIATION PRIVILEGE

[T]he plaintiff and the defendants have expressly waived confidentiality protections conferred by the California statutes * * *. Both the plaintiff and the defendants have indicated, clearly and on advice of counsel, that they want the court to consider evidence about what occurred during the mediation, including testimony directly from the mediator, as the court resolves the issues raised by defendants' motion to enforce the settlement agreement.

* * *

THE MEDIATOR'S PRIVILEGE

California law confers on mediators a privilege that is independent of the privilege conferred on parties to a mediation. By declaring that, subject to exceptions not applicable here, mediators are incompetent to testify "as to any statement, conduct, decision, or ruling, occurring at or in conjunction with [the mediation]," section 703.5 of the Evidence Code has the effect of making a mediator the holder of an independent privilege. Section 1119 of the Evidence Code appears to have the same effect — as it prohibits courts from compelling disclosure of evidence about mediation communications and directs that all such communications "shall remain confidential." As the California Court of Appeal recently pointed out, "the Legislature intended that the confidentiality provision of section 1119 may be asserted by the mediator as well as by the participants in the mediation." It follows that, under California law, a waiver of the mediation privilege by the parties is not a sufficient basis for a court to permit or order a mediator to testify. Rather, an independent determination must be made before testimony from a mediator should be permitted or ordered.

In the case at bar, the mediator (Mr. Herman) was and is an employee of the federal court (a "staff neutral"). He hosted the mediation at the behest of the court and under this court's ADR rules. These facts are not sufficient to justify ordering him to testify about what occurred during the mediation — even when the parties have waived their mediation privilege and want the mediator to testify. Mr. Herman is a member of the California bar — and no doubt feels bound to honor the directives of California law. He also is a professional in mediation — and feels a moral obligation to preserve the essential integrity of the mediation process — an integrity to which he believes the promise of confidentiality is fundamental.

Out of respect for these feelings, the court chose not to put Mr. Herman in an awkward position where he might have felt he had to choose between being a loyal employee of the court, on the one hand, and, on the other, asserting the mediator's privilege under California law. Instead, the court announced that it would proceed on the assumption that Mr. Herman was respectfully and appropriately asserting the mediator's privilege and was formally objecting to being called to testify about anything said or done during the mediation.

Regardless of whether Mr. Herman invoked the mediator's privilege, the wording of section 703.5 can be understood as imposing an independent duty on the courts to determine whether testimony from a mediator should be accepted. Unlike some other privilege statutes, which expressly confer a right on the holder of the privilege to refuse to disclose protected communications, as well as the power to prevent others from disclosing such communications, section 703.5 is framed in terms of competence to testify. In its pertinent part, it declares that (subject to exceptions not applicable here) a mediator is not competent to testify "in any subsequent civil proceeding" about words uttered or conduct occurring during a mediation. This wording appears to have two consequences: it would not empower a mediator to prevent others from disclosing mediation communications, but it would require courts, on their own initiative, to determine whether it would be lawful to compel or permit a mediator to testify about matters occurring within a mediation.

So the issue of whether it was appropriate under California law in these circumstances to compel the mediator to testify was squarely raised both by the court's assuming that Mr. Herman invoked the applicable statutes and by the court's understanding of its independent duty to address this question.

* * *

We turn to the issue of whether, under California law, we should compel the mediator to testify-despite the statutory prohibitions set forth in sections 703.5 and 1119 of the Evidence Code. The most important opinion by a California court in this arena is *Rinaker v. Superior Court*, 62 Cal.App.4th 155, 74 Cal.Rptr.2d 464 (3d Dist.1998). In that case the Court of Appeal held that there may be circumstances in which a trial court, over vigorous objection by a party and by the mediator, could compel testimony from the mediator in a juvenile delinquency proceeding (deemed a "civil" matter under California law). * * *

In essence, the *Rinaker* court instructs California trial judges to conduct a two-stage balancing analysis. The goal of the first stage balancing is to determine whether to compel the mediator to appear at an *in camera* proceeding to determine precisely what her testimony would be. In this first stage, the judge considers all the circumstances and weighs all the competing rights and interests, including the values that would be threatened not by public disclosure of mediation communications, but by ordering the mediator to appear at an *in camera* proceeding to disclose only to the court and counsel, out of public view, what she would say the parties said during the mediation. At this juncture the goal is to determine whether the harm that would be done to the values that underlie the mediation privileges simply by ordering the mediator to participate in the *in camera* proceedings can be justified — by the prospect that her testimony might well make a singular and substantial contribution to protecting or advancing competing interests of comparable or greater magnitude.

The trial judge reaches the second stage of balancing analysis only if the product of the first stage is a decision to order the mediator to detail, *in camera,* what her testimony would be. A court that orders the *in camera* disclosure gains precise and reliable knowledge of what the mediator's testimony would be-and only with that knowledge is the court positioned to launch its second balancing analysis. In this second stage the court is to weigh and comparatively assess (1) the importance of the values and interests that would be harmed if the mediator was compelled to testify (perhaps subject to a sealing or protective order, if appropriate), (2) the magnitude of the harm that compelling the testimony would cause to those values and interests, (3) the importance of the rights or interests that would be jeopardized if the mediator's testimony was not accessible in the specific proceedings in question, and (4) how much the testimony would contribute toward protecting those rights or advancing those interests-an inquiry that includes, among other things, an assessment of whether there are alternative sources of evidence of comparable probative value.

* * *

[T]he product of the first stage of the analysis was my decision that it was necessary to determine (through sealed proceedings) what Mr. Herman's testimony would be. Reaching that determination involved the following considerations. First, I acknowledge squarely that a decision to require a mediator to give evidence, even *in camera* or under seal, about what occurred during a mediation threatens values underlying the mediation privileges. As the *Rinaker* court suggested, the California legislature adopted these privileges in the belief that without the promise of confidentiality it would be appreciably more difficult to achieve the goals of mediation programs. Construing an earlier version of the mediation privilege statute, the same court of appeal had opined a few years before that without assurances of confidentiality "some litigants [would be deterred] from participating freely and openly in mediation." That court also quoted approvingly the suggestion from a practice guide that "[c]onfidentiality is absolutely essential to mediation," in part because without it "parties would be reluctant to make the kinds of concessions and admission that pave the way to settlement."

While this court has no occasion or power to quarrel with these generally applicable pronouncements of state policy, we observe that they appear to have appreciably less force when, as here, the parties to the mediation have waived confidentiality protections, indeed have asked the court to compel the mediator to testify — so that justice can be done.

If a party to the mediation were objecting to compelling the mediator to testify we would be faced with a substantially more difficult analysis. But the absence of such an objection does not mean that ordering the mediator to disclose, even *in camera,* matters that occurred within the mediation does not pose some threat to values underlying the mediation privileges. As the *Rinaker* court pointed out, ordering mediators to participate in proceedings arising out of mediations imposes economic and psychic burdens that could make some people reluctant to agree to serve as a mediator, especially in programs where that service is pro bono or poorly compensated.

This is not a matter of time and money only. Good mediators are likely to feel violated by being compelled to give evidence that could be used against a party with whom they tried to establish a relationship of trust during a mediation. Good mediators are deeply committed to being and remaining neutral and non-judgmental, and to building and preserving relationships with parties. To force them to give evidence that hurts someone from whom they actively solicited trust (during the mediation) rips the fabric of their work and can threaten their sense of the center of their professional integrity. These are not inconsequential matters.

Like many other variables in this kind of analysis, however, the magnitude of these risks can vary with the circumstances. Here, for instance, all parties to the mediation want the mediator to testify about things that occurred during the mediation — so ordering the testimony would do less harm to the actual relationships developed than it would in a case where one of the parties to the mediation objected to the use of evidence from the mediator.

We acknowledge, however, that the possibility that a mediator might be forced to testify over objection could harm the capacity of mediators in general to create the environment of trust that they feel maximizes the likelihood that constructive communication will occur during the mediation session. But the level of harm to that interest likely varies, at least in some measure, with the perception within the community of mediators and litigants about how likely it is that any given mediation will be followed at some point by an order compelling the neutral to offer evidence about what occurred during the session. I know of no studies or statistics that purport to reflect how often courts or parties seek evidence from mediators — and I suspect that the incidence of this issue arising would not be identical across the broad spectrum of mediation programs and settings. What I can report is that this case represents the first time that I have been called upon to address these kinds of questions in the more than fifteen years that I have been responsible for ADR programs in this court. Nor am I aware of the issue arising before other judges here. Based on that experience, my partially educated guess is that the likelihood that a mediator or the parties in any given case need fear that the mediator would later be constrained to testify is extraordinarily small.

That conviction is reinforced by another consideration. As we pointed out above, under California law, and this court's view of sound public policy, there should be no occasion to consider whether to seek testimony from a mediator for purpose of determining whether the parties entered an enforceable settlement contract unless the mediation produced a writing (or competent record) that appears on its face to constitute an enforceable contract, signed or formally assented to by all the parties. Thus, it is only when there is such a writing or record, and when a party nonetheless seeks to escape its apparent effect, that courts applying California law would even consider calling for evidence from a mediator for purposes of determining whether the parties settled the case. Surely these circumstances will arise after only a tiny fraction of mediations.

*   *   *

* * * [T]he kind of testimony sought from the mediator in this case poses less of a threat to fairness and reliability values than the kind of testimony that was sought from the mediator in *Rinaker*. During the first stage balancing analysis in the case at bar, the parties and I assumed that the testimony from the mediator that would be most consequential would focus not primarily on what Ms. Olam said during the mediation, but on how she acted and the mediator's perceptions of her physical, emotional, and mental condition. The purpose would not be to nail down and dissect her specific words, but to assess at a more general and impressionistic level her condition and capacities. That purpose might be achieved with relatively little disclosure of the content of her confidential communications. As conceded above, that does not mean that compelling the testimony by the mediator would pose no threat to values underlying the privileges — but that the degree of harm to those values would not be as great as it would be if the testimony was for the kinds of impeachment purposes that were proffered in *Rinaker*. And in a balancing analysis, probable degree of harm is an important consideration.

What we have been doing in the preceding paragraphs is attempting, as the first component of the first stage balancing analysis, to identify the interests that might be threatened by ordering the mediator, in the specific circumstances presented here, to testify under seal — and to assess the magnitude of the harm that ordering the testimony would likely do to those interests. Having assayed these matters, we turn to the other side of the balance. We will identify the interests that ordering the testimony (under seal, at least initially) might advance, assess the relative importance of those interests, and try to predict the magnitude of the contribution to achieving those interests that ordering the testimony would likely make (or the extent of the harm that we likely would do to those interests if we did not compel the testimony).

The interests that are likely to be advanced by compelling the mediator to testify in this case are of considerable importance. Moreover, as we shall see, some of those interests parallel and reinforce the objectives the legislature sought to advance by providing for confidentiality in mediation.

The first interest we identify is the interest in doing justice. Here is what we mean. For reasons described below, the mediator is positioned in this case to offer what could be crucial, certainly very probative, evidence about the central factual issues in this matter. There is a strong possibility that his testimony will greatly improve the court's ability to determine reliably what the pertinent historical facts actually were. Establishing reliably what the facts were is critical to doing justice (here, justice means this: applying the law correctly to the real historical facts). It is the fundamental duty of a public court in our society to do justice — to resolve disputes in accordance with the law when the parties don't. Confidence in our system of justice as a whole, in our government as a whole, turns in no small measure on confidence in the courts' ability to do justice in individual cases. So doing justice in individual cases is an interest of considerable magnitude.

When we put case-specific flesh on these abstract bones, we see that "doing justice" implicates interests of considerable importance to the parties-all of whom want the mediator to testify. From the plaintiff's perspective, the interests that the defendants' motion threatens could hardly be more funda-mental. According to Ms. Olam, the mediation process was fundamentally unfair to her-and resulted in an apparent agreement whose terms are literally unconscionable and whose enforcement would render her homeless and virtually destitute. To her, doing justice in this setting means protecting her from these fundamental wrongs.

From the defendants' perspective, doing justice in this case means, among other things, bringing to a lawful close disputes with Ms. Olam that have been on-going for about seven years — disputes that the defendants' believe have cost them, without justification, at least scores of thousands of dollars. The defendants believe that Ms. Olam has breached no fewer than three separate contractual commitments with them (not counting the agreement reached at the end of the mediation) — and that those breaches are the product of a calculated effort not only to avoid meeting legitimate obligations, but also to make unfair use, for years, of the defendants' money.

Defendants also believe that Ms. Olam has abused over the years several of her own counsel — as well as the judicial process and this court's ADR program (for which she has been charged nothing). Through their motion, the defendants ask the court to affirm that they acquired legal rights through the settlement agreement that the mediation produced. They also ask the court to enforce those rights, and thus to enable the defendants to avoid the burdens, expense, delay, and risks of going to trial in this matter. These also are matters of consequence.

And they are not the only interests that could be advanced by compelling the mediator to testify. According to the defendants' pre-hearing proffers, the mediator's testimony would establish clearly that the mediation process was fair and that the plaintiff's consent to the settlement agreement was legally viable. Thus the mediator's testimony, according to the defendants, would re-assure the community and the court about the integrity of the mediation process that the court sponsored.

That testimony also would provide the court with the evidentiary confidence it needs to enforce the agreement. A publicly announced decision to enforce the settlement would, in turn, encourage parties who want to try to settle their cases to use the court's mediation program for that purpose. An order appropriately enforcing an agreement reached through the mediation also would encourage parties in the future to take mediations seriously, to understand that they represent real opportunities to reach closure and avoid trial, and to attend carefully to terms of agreements proposed in mediations. In these important ways, taking testimony from the mediator could strengthen the mediation program.

In sharp contrast, refusing to compel the mediator to testify might well deprive the court of the evidence it needs to rule reliably on the plaintiff's contentions — and thus might either cause the court to impose an unjust outcome on the plaintiff or disable the court from enforcing the settlement. In this setting, refusing to compel testimony from the mediator might end up being tantamount to denying the motion to enforce the agreement — because a crucial source of evidence about the plaintiff's condition and capacities would be missing. Following that course, defendants suggest, would do considerable harm not only to the court's mediation program but also to fundamental fairness. If parties believed that courts routinely would refuse to compel mediators to testify, and that the absence of evidence from mediators would enhance the viability of a contention that apparent consent to a settlement contract was not legally viable, cynical parties would be encouraged either to try to escape commitments they made during mediations or to use threats of such escapes to try to re-negotiate, after the mediation, more favorable terms-terms that they never would have been able to secure without this artificial and unfair leverage.

In sum, it is clear that refusing even to determine what the mediator's testimony would be, in the circumstances here presented, threatens values of great significance. But we would miss the main analytical chance if all we did was identify those values and proclaim their importance. In fact, when the values implicated are obviously of great moment, there is a danger that the process of identifying them will generate unjustified momentum toward a conclusion that exaggerates the weight on this side of the scale. Thus we emphasize that the central question is not which values are implicated, but how much they would be advanced by compelling the testimony or how much they would be harmed by not compelling it.

We concluded, after analysis and before the hearing, that the mediator's testimony was sufficiently likely to make substantial contributions toward achieving the ends described above to justify compelling an exploration, under seal, of what his testimony would be. While we did not assume that there were no pressures or motivations that might affect the reliability of the mediator's testimony, it was obvious that the mediator was the only source of presumptively disinterested, neutral evidence. The only other witnesses with personal knowledge of the plaintiff's condition at the mediation were the parties and their lawyers-none of whom were disinterested. And given the foreseeable testimony about the way the mediation was structured (with lots of caucusing by the mediator with one side at a time), it was likely that the mediator would have had much more exposure to the plaintiff over the course of the lengthy mediation than any other witness save her lawyer.

But it also was foreseeable that substantial questions would be raised about the reliability of the testimony that Ms. Olam's former lawyer, Phyllis Voisenat, would give. We knew, when we conducted this first stage balancing, that Ms. Voisenat no longer represented Ms. Olam. We also knew that strains had developed in that relationship before it had ended, and that lawyer and client had felt that their ability to communicate with one another left a great deal to be desired. Moreover, Ms. Olam had suggested through her new lawyer (the fifth attorney to work with her in connection with her disputes with the defendants) that she might contend during the hearing that Ms. Voisenat, her former lawyer, had been one of the sources of unlawful pressure on her to sign the settlement agreement at the end of the mediation. And there were at least rumblings from the plaintiff's camp about a malpractice suit by Ms. Olam against Ms. Voisenat, who, understandably, expressed concerns about the possible use against her in such litigation of testimony she would give in these proceedings. For all these reasons, there was a substantial likelihood that plaintiff would raise serious questions about the accuracy of Ms. Voisenat's testimony and that, given all the circumstances, the court would not be sure how much it should rely on the evidence Ms. Voisenat would give.

* * *

In short, there was a substantial likelihood that testimony from the mediator would be the most reliable and probative on the central issues raised by the plaintiff in response to the defendants' motion. And there was no likely alternative source of evidence on these issues that would be of comparable probative utility. So it appeared that testimony from the mediator would be crucial to the court's capacity to do its job — and that refusing to compel that testimony posed a serious threat to every value identified above. In this setting, California courts clearly would conclude the first stage balancing analysis by ordering the mediator to testify *in camera* or under seal — so that the court, aided by inputs from the parties, could make a refined and reliable judgment about whether to use that testimony to help resolve the substantive issues raised by the pending motion.

[W]e called the mediator to testify (under seal) after all other participants in the mediation had been examined and cross-examined — so that the lawyers (and the court) would be able to identify all the subjects and questions that they should cover with the mediator. With the record thus fully developed, we were well situated to determine whether using (and publicly disclosing) the mediator's testimony would make a contribution of sufficient magnitude to justify the level of harm that using and disclosing the testimony would likely cause, in the circumstances of this case, to the interests that inform the mediation privilege law in California. As our detailed account, later in this opinion, of the evidence from all sources demonstrates, it became clear that the mediator's testimony was essential to doing justice here — so we decided to use it and unseal it.

THE EVIDENTIARY HEARING

[The court held an evidentiary hearing, taking Mr. Herman's testimony under seal.]

PLAINTIFF'S CONSENT TO THE SEPTEMBER 9-10, 1998 SETTLEMENT AGREEMENT MEMORIALIZED BY THE MEMORANDUM OF UNDERSTANDING WAS NOT THE RESULT OF "UNDUE INFLUENCE"

* * *

II. *The Legal Basis for Plaintiff's Claim of Undue Influence*

* * *

[W]e conclude that under California law a party cannot successfully invoke the doctrine of "undue influence" to escape an apparent contract unless that party proves two things: (1) that she had a lessened capacity to make a free contract and (2) that the other party applied its excessive strength to her to secure her agreement. "In combination, the elements of undue susceptibility in the servient person and excessive pressure by the dominating person make the latter's influence undue."

There is no precise formula of factors that, when applied, will identify for the court whether undue influence has occurred. The court should consider whether-in light of the entire context-there is a "supremacy of one mind over another by which that other is prevented from acting according to his own wish or judgment, and whereby the will of the person is over-borne and he is induced to do or forbear to do an act which he would not do, or would do, if left to act freely."

Although the court must make its determination based on its assessment of all the circumstances, California courts have identified various indicia of undue weakness and of undue pressure.

Undue susceptibility

According to California authorities, courts should consider the following factors, among others, when determining whether plaintiff was in an unduly weakened condition at the time she agreed to the terms of the MOU: lack of full vigor due to age, physical condition, physical exhaustion, and emotional anguish.

The presence of any one or more of these factors may support-but does not necessitate-a finding of undue susceptibility. Moreover, "[a]s a general rule, age, physical condition, and suffering of pain furnish no basis for setting aside a conveyance if the [party seeking rescission] exercised a free and untrammeled mind."

Undue pressure

Excessive pressure need not involve misrepresentation or the threat of force. The following factors may indicate that plaintiff was subjected to excessive persuasion: (1) discussion of the transaction at an unusual or inappropriate time, (2) consummation of the transaction in an unusual place, (3) insistent demand that the business be finished at once, (4) extreme emphasis on the untoward consequences of delay, (5) use of multiple persuaders by the dominant side against a servient party, (6) absence of third-party advisors to the servient party, and (7) statements that there is no time to consult financial advisers or attorneys.

As previously stated, the court considers the presence or absence of each of the above factors in light of all the circumstances.

III. *Ms. Olam's Testimony About September 9-10, 1998*

[Ms. Olam testified that she had no understanding of how the mediation would proceed, that she was left alone in a room alone while all the other mediation participants conversed in a nearby room, that she was in considerable pain, and that she signed the MOU without reading it or having it explained to her.]

* * *

IV. *Did Ms. Olam Prove That Her Consent to the MOU Was Obtained As A Result of Undue Influence?*

A. *Was Ms. Olam rendered unduly susceptible by physical and emotional distress?*

It is undisputed that Ms. Olam was 65 years old at the time the mediation took place. It also is undisputed that the mediation lasted for more than 12 hours and that all participants were tired (and, presumably, hungry) when the process finally came to a close sometime between midnight and 1:00 a.m. on September 10, 1998. Nor do defendants contend that Ms. Olam did not suffer, at least at some times in the summer and fall of 1998, from high blood pressure, headaches, and abdominal pains. And no one quarrels with the notion that the interests of Ms. Olam's that were at stake in the litigation and the negotiations were of considerable importance to her. So, in some measure, the situation was inherently stressful-and would have been so experienced by almost anyone. But these facts fall far short, as a matter of law, of establishing the "undue susceptibility" that plaintiff must prove to satisfy the first element of the two part test for undue influence. That element would be satisfied only if she proved that she was in fact suffering the acute distress that she described on the stand. When we consider all of the evidence, and the accompanying indicia of credibility, we find that Ms. Olam's testimony about the severity of her condition was implausible and inaccurate — leaving no factual basis for a finding that she was unduly susceptible at any point during the mediation or at the time she signed the MOU.

* * *

[The other participants and the mediator testified that Mrs. Olam did not seem to be in physical distress, did not complain, was repeatedly told she could end the mediation, and expressed relief that the litigation was over during the car ride to her home.]

The evidence indicates that Ms. Olam fully participated in the mediation

[Mr. Herman and Ms. Voisenat testified that the mediation session began with all participants together in a joint session and that Ms. Voisenat remained with Ms. Olam virtually the day while Mr. Herman caucused with each side in turn.]

Mr. Herman also testified that at some point during the mediation he began to suspect that the relationship between plaintiff and her counsel may have been less than perfect. As a result, he "made [his] very best effort to review more closely with the client herself, with Mrs. Olam herself, all of the terms that [they] were discussing and took on a more active role in working directly with her than [he] might otherwise have done had [he] perceived her lawyer filling this role."

According to Mr. Herman, plaintiff was actively involved in negotiating the terms that eventually became paragraphs 1, 3, 4, 5, 6a, and 6b of the MOU. In addition, Mr. Herman specifically recalls discussing what became terms number 7 and 8, with plaintiff.

* * *

"She did affirm to [him] that she understood the idea that if this agreement were signed her case would be dismissed, and this would be over." Mr. Herman also discussed with plaintiff the idea that any agreement signed that evening would be intended to be a binding contract-even though the lawyers would later draft a more formal agreement.

Ms. Voisenat believed that the parties actually had an understanding by early or mid-afternoon that a settlement would be reached-but that determining how to structure it turned out to be a substantial challenge. It wasn't until sometime between 10:00 and 11:00 p.m. that Mr. Herman was confident that the parties had agreed to all the essential terms. At that juncture he, Mr. Stea, and Ms. Voisenat adjourned to his office (in the courthouse) to type the MOU. As counsel had some difficulty agreeing on specific wording, the process of memorializing the agreement took longer than expected. Mr. Herman testified unequivocally, however, that the substantive terms in the MOU as he finally typed it "absolutely" were the same as the substantive terms that he had explained to plaintiff and to which she had agreed before he began the typing process.

Mr. Herman testified that after the typing was completed he gave a copy of the MOU to defendants and he and Ms. Voisenat presented a copy to plaintiff. Plaintiff appeared to read the document. Mr. Herman stated, "[i]n the context of the entire day, it was inconceivable to me that she could be doing anything but reading the document closely. This had been a mediation in which Mrs. Olam was engaged in active conversation with me throughout the process-where we went over point by point, term by term, repeatedly."

* * *

* * * Given all the circumstances and evidence, as well as Mr. Herman's considerable experience as a mediator and a mediation teacher, the court finds patently implausible Ms. Olam's testimony that she was left alone all day, that she did not participate in any negotiations, that she was told virtually nothing, and that after 20 hours she was asked to sign a document that she neither read nor understood. Instead, I find that she participated actively throughout the process — with a "free and untrammeled mind" — and that she understood fully the terms of the MOU that she signed.

B. Was Ms. Olam unduly pressured to sign the MOU?

There is an additional, independently sufficient basis for the court's decision to grant defendants' Motion to Enforce the Settlement.

Plaintiff has failed completely to satisfy the second, essential element of the test for undue influence: she has not proved that she was subjected by anyone to "undue pressure." In the factual setting before us, there are three *theoretically* possible sources of undue pressure: defendants and/or their counsel, the mediator, and plaintiff's attorney — Phyllis Voisenat.

1. Mr. Herman

Plaintiff has never contended that Mr. Herman was the source of undue pressure. Nor is it clear that relief under California Civil Code §§ 1689(b)(1) and 1575 would be appropriate even if a party proved that a mediator had subjected her to undue pressure.

2. Ms. Voisenat

Plaintiff vaguely intimated at some point that her own lawyer at the time, Ms. Voisenat, somehow pushed or "urged" her to settle. The court rejects any attempt to expand California Civil Code §§ 1689(b)(1) and 1575 to include as a source of "undue influence" the complaining party's own lawyer. Plaintiff has set forth no law that would support extension of the doctrine of undue influence in this respect. Expanding the doctrine in this way would encourage clients and counsel to manufacture bases for trying to avoid commitments otherwise fully enforceable. The law offers alternative avenues of recourse to clients who are in fact abused by their own lawyers.

We hasten to add that the evidence in the record falls woefully short of supporting a finding that Ms. Voisenat pressured Ms. Olam to do anything. According to Ms. Olam, she had very little contact with Ms. Voisenat all day. Surely a half nod from a lawyer (as Ms. Olam says she saw from Ms. Voisenat just before signing the MOU) cannot constitute undue pressure. From all the evidence, we find that Ms. Voisenat was the secondary player in these negotiations, which were in fact dominated by her client. There is absolutely no basis for a finding that any action by Ms. Voisenat remotely overbore plaintiff's will.

3. *Defendants and Their Counsel*

Similarly, there is no evidence that could support a finding that the defendants or their lawyer put any pressure on Ms. Olam during the mediation. As the plaintiff herself testified, there was essentially no interaction and no communication between her and defendants (or their lawyer) during the mediation.

* * *

In sum, there is no evidence that plaintiff was subjected to anything remotely close to undue pressure.

CONCLUSION

Because plaintiff has failed to prove either of the necessary elements of undue influence, and because she has established no other grounds to escape the contract, she signed on September 10, 1998, the court GRANTS defendants' Motion to Enforce the settlement contract that is memorialized in the MOU.

Mr. Herman's August 23, 1999 testimony is UNSEALED.

NOTES

1. Do you think the bright line rule applied in *Vick v. Waits* is the appropriate policy for maintaining the confidentiality of mediation communications in the context of enforcing agreements? What was the effect of this rule on the Vicks' attempt to prove fraudulent inducement? Other jurisdictions have made the opposite policy choice regarding confidentiality in this setting, creating bright line rules that allow disclosure for the purpose of enforcing settlements. For example, in Wyoming, the state mediation privilege does not apply when "[o]ne of the parties seeks judicial enforcement of the mediated agreement." (WYO. STAT. § 1-43-103(c)(v).) A somewhat narrower variation does not permit parties to make disclosures merely to demonstrate an agreement or its contents. North Carolina, for example, permits evidence of mediation communications in enforcement actions, but only for written and executed agreements. (N.C. GEN. STAT. § 7A-38.1(*l*) (court mediation program).) Is one of these options preferable to the strict exclusionary rule enforced in *Vick v. Waits*?

2. In contrast to a bright line rule, the court in *Olam* applied a balancing test, weighing the need for the evidence against the importance of maintaining confidentiality. Is this approach preferable? Consider the following argument:

> A more complex solution than a bright-line rule is needed when a party challenges the validity of a mediated settlement. Absent eliminating such challenges entirely, there is no simple threshold requirement that can protect the mediation communications that led up to the challenged agreement. The formality of a writing can provide some assurance that the parties reached an agreement, but does not in itself ensure that the agreement was obtained free of duress, fraud or the other infirmities that are the subjects of contract defenses. . . .
>
> A blanket rule — either permitting parties to raise contract defenses without restriction or prohibiting them from ever raising them — is an inadequate response to these circumstances. Both types of rules create incentives that are inconsistent with the goals of mediation. In jurisdiction with a rule that mediation confidentiality must always give way when settlement enforcement is at issue, the incentives are similar to those likely to arise in jurisdictions that do not protect confidentiality adequately as an initial matter. Parties will know that any claim of duress, no matter how weak, can throw the mediation open to scrutiny. Once they see this happen a few times, it is likely to undermine parties' confidence in confidentiality and diminish their willingness to be forthcoming in mediation.
>
> There are equally serious problems with the opposite approach favoring absolute confidentiality. A party who actually is a rare victim of duress may have no means to prove this if all testimony concerning the mediation is precluded. Unless the fraud or coercion occurred outside the mediation process, a strict rule of confidentiality would thwart any attempt to challenge the validity of the agreement. In this context, other mediation values compete with confidentiality. Mediation would no longer be a consensual process if a party could be tricked or forced into an agreement and have no recourse. In light of the potential consequences for the mediation process, precluding all exceptions to confidentiality is an untenable, as well as an impractical, solution. [llen E. Deason, *Enforcing Mediated Settlement Agreements: Contract Law Collides with Confidentiality*, 35 DAVIS L. REV. 33, 89–90 (2001).]

Do you agree? Should this decision be placed in the hands of the courts on a case-by-case basis or should legislatures make a blanket determination? As a party, would you value the flexibility of the balancing approach or the security of a bright line rule?

3. The Uniform Mediation Act adopts a balancing framework similar to that used by the court in *Olam*. Mediation communications may be introduced to avoid liability on a mediated agreement despite the privilege if a court holds an *in camera* hearing and decides that the evidence is not otherwise available and that the need for the evidence "substantially outweighs" the interest in protecting confidentiality. (UMA § 6(b)(2).) The Act stipulates, however, that a mediator may not be compelled to provide this evidence. (§ 6(c).) Is it wise to rule out mediator testimony?

4. In a portion of the *Olam* opinion omitted here, the federal court concluded that it must apply state law to the issue of contract enforcement. Under a provision called the "state law proviso" of Federal Rule of Evidence 501, state privileges also apply in federal courts "in civil actions and proceedings with respect to an element of a claim or defense as to which State law supplies the rule of decision." Thus, in a case based on diversity jurisdiction with state law claims, a federal court would typically apply state law privileges. (*See, e.g., Haghighi v. Russian-American Broadcasting Co.*, 945 F. Supp. 1233, 1235 (D. Minn. 1996), *rev'd on other grounds*, 173 F.3d 1086 (8th Cir. 1999).)

The application of Rule 501 is complicated, however, when state law claims are joined with federal claims. In *Folb v. Motion Picture Industry Pension and Health Plans*, reprinted in Part A of this chapter, the court decided it must apply the *federal* common law of privilege because Folb's state-law claims were joined with federal ERISA claims. (16 F. Supp. 2d at 1169–80.) In contrast, the *Olam* court determined that a state law mediation privilege applied, even though the case included a mixture of state and federal claims, because the privilege was relevant only to the issue of contract enforcement — a state-law claim. (*See* 68 F. Supp. 2d at 1119–25.) For a more complete discussion of how choice-of-law issues affect mediation privileges in federal court, see Ellen E. Deason, *Predictable Mediation Confidentiality in the U.S. Federal System*, 17 OHIO STATE J. ON DISP. RESOL. 239 (2002).

5. The *Olam* court's reading of California law has been controversial. One of the California confidentiality provisions makes mediators incompetent to testify: "No person presiding at any judicial or quasi-judicial proceedings, and no arbitrator or mediator shall be competent to testify, in any subsequent civil proceeding, as to any statement, conduct, decision, or ruling, occurring at or in conjunction with the prior proceeding, except as to a statement or conduct that could [give rise to contempt, constitute a crime, trigger investigation by the State Bar or the commission of Judicial Performance, or give rise to disqualification proceedings]." (California Evidence Code § 703.5.) The federal court interpreted this as requiring it to determine whether the mediator's testimony would be lawful. Do you agree that this was the intent of the statute?

6. The court believed that when the parties have waived their privilege, as in the *Olam* case, the reasons to protect the confidentiality of the mediation by preventing mediator testimony "have less force." Do you agree? What about the independent justifications for a mediator's privilege? Should the policy of protecting mediator neutrality be "trumped" by the parties' decision to disclose?

7. The *Olam* court speculated that cases in which mediators are asked or compelled to testify are rare. Yet it also provided a convincing account of why a neutral is a reliable source of testimony about events that occur in mediation. A recent study of case law found 568 court opinions in disputes over the enforcement of mediated agreements over a four-year period. The authors concluded that "[o]utside of California, and perhaps Texas, relevant mediation communications appear to be used regularly in court to establish or refute contractual defenses such as fraud, mistake, or duress." (Coben & Thompson, 2006 at 69.) Even if those cases represent a small fraction of all the mediations held across the country in four years, and even if mediators testified in only some of them, what is the likely effect of compelling mediator testimony in a high profile case like *Olam*?

The court was influenced in its thinking that enforcement cases would be rare by the fact that, under California evidence law, only written and signed agreements (or under some circumstances, assent recorded in a court proceeding) are admissible. (68 F. Supp. 2d at 1134.) Do you think requiring a writing as a prerequisite for admission of an agreement changes the concerns about admitting a mediator's testimony?

8. The *Olam* court also thought that mediator testimony about a party's actions in order to indicate her condition and capacities would be a less harmful breach of confidentiality than mediator testimony about a party's statements and admissions. (68 F. Supp. 2d at 1134–36.) Do you agree? When the issue is a party's capacity to enter an agreement, is the mediator's testimony about his impressions on that topic any less harmful to mediator neutrality than testimony about admissions on the merits of the underlying claims?

9. Did the court really need the mediator's testimony? Could it have resolved the dispute solely on the basis of the inadequacy of plaintiff's evidence to support a finding of undue pressure, the second element required to show undue influence under California law? Were there nonetheless advantages to the more complete record? Might the court have felt it was necessary to refute Mrs. Olam's claims about the way the mediation was conducted?

10. Note the difficulty of proving undue influence and the limited applicability of the doctrine. The common law action of duress similarly is restricted to threats by the adverse party, not the mediator or the party's own counsel. Mutual mistake and fraud are also difficult to prove, even when mediation communications are admissible. The study of mediation litigation found that in most enforcement cases the court enforced the mediated agreement in whole or in part. (Coben & Thompson, 2006). Does this support a conclusion that mediation is largely free of coerced agreements and should be given a clean bill of health? Do you think that raising contract-law defenses in court provides adequate protection for mediation values? Consider the following commentary:

> In general, the courts have demonstrated an understanding of the mediation process, a sensitivity to the core values and principles of mediation, and a clear desire to further the general policy favoring settlement in deciding cases involving mediation process issues. * * *

On the other hand, the general policy favoring settlement, while advancing the goal of judicial economy, may not always be consistent with mediation principles and values. In particular, allegations of settlement coercion raise troubling issues relating to mediation's core values of party self-determination, voluntariness, and mediator impartiality that may not be easily discerned or correctable through the judicial process. Allegations of coercion by a party or the mediator in the context of a party's attempt to rescind a mediated agreement and a subsequent enforcement action have sometimes led to troubling results. [Alfini & McCabe at 205, 2001.]

11. Commentators who conclude that traditional contract defenses are inadequate to ensure a fair process and an agreement consistent with the principle of self-determination have suggested a cooling-off period in which either party could cancel the agreement. Even if Mrs. Olam was not under undue influence when she signed the settlement agreement, what if she later decided it was not in her best interest? What if the employee nurse in *Kaiser Foundation Health Plan* had signed the agreement, but decided the next day that it was unacceptable? Should she have been able to rescind the settlement? What would be the advantages of this procedure? Would it be practical to implement? What time limits should apply to "self-determination"? For a discussion of proposals for a rescission period and an expanded coercion defense, see Nancy A. Welsh, *The Thinning Vision of Self-Determination in Court-Connected Mediation: The Inevitable Price of Institutionalization?* 6 HARV. NEGOT. L. REV. 1, 87–92 (2000).

12. Others have proposed that it should be easier, not harder, to enforce a mediated agreement than an ordinary contract. Does it seem fair that Kaiser Foundation Health Plan and Congress Mortgage Company had to go to court to get their settlement agreements enforced? They entered into those agreements anticipating finality and instead had to return to litigation. Is an attempt to avoid complying with an agreement that the parties freely entered into consistent with the principle of self-determination? Does litigation to enforce agreements contribute to mediation's attractiveness as a speedy, reliable, and relatively low-cost process? The drafters of the UMA considered several approaches for expediting enforcement, such as treating a mediated agreement as an arbitral award or providing a mechanism for the parties to stipulate to a court judgment in accordance with their agreement. The final Act, however, does not include an enforcement provision. Would such a provision be a good idea? Do you think that *mediated* agreements should be treated any differently for enforcement purposes than settlement agreements negotiated without the help of a mediator? Does it make any difference if the mediation is ordered by the court? (*See* Ellen E. Deason, *Procedural Rules for Complementary Systems of Litigation and Mediation — Worldwide,* 80 NOTRE DAME L. REV. 553 (2005).)

C. ETHICAL AND PROFESSIONALISM ISSUES IN MEDIATION

The mediation process raises numerous ethical and professionalism issues for the attorney mediator and for counsel representing parties to the dispute.

Some of the ethical issues presented are unique to divorce mediation. Others are presented in other types of mediation, but are particularly symptomatic of divorce mediation.

1. PROFESSIONALISM IN MEDIATION: GENERAL CONSIDERATIONS

For many years, the conduct of most private mediators was virtually unregulated. Attorney-mediators were minimally affected by the Code of Professional Responsibility or the more recent Model Rules of Professional Conduct (Morgan & Rotunda, 2000; Folberg & Taylor, 1984, at 252–55). Neutral intervenors from other disciplines were governed by their own ethical codes (Folberg & Taylor, 1984, at 250–51). Judicial mediators were subject to minimal due process constraints. It was generally acknowledged that while mediators might emphasize different aspects of proposed settlements to each side to focus on the terms most beneficial to each, overt deception would never be appropriate (Cooley, 1997; Benjamin, 1995). Deliberate deception would destroy the integrity mediators require to function effectively as neutral facilitators, and it would undermine party respect for the mediation process.

States did not prescribe detailed standards that had to be satisfied by individuals who wished to function as neutral intervenors. So long as particular persons were acceptable to disputants, they could act as mediators. Even states with minimal prerequisites only required a limited amount of training. Although public and private appointing agencies generally listed only persons with neutral experience, it was not difficult for most applicants to qualify.

By the early 1990s, the laissez faire approach to mediator regulation had begun to change. ADR neutrals increasingly considered themselves part of a distinct profession, and they began to appreciate the need for separate professional standards. The first step was taken in 1994, when the American Arbitration Association (AAA), the American Bar Association (ABA), and the Society of Professionals in Dispute Resolution (SPIDR) adopted "The Standards of Conduct for Mediators."The standards had three stated functions: to guide the conduct of mediators, to inform participants in mediation, and to promote public confidence in mediation as a process for resolving disputes. A number of states adopted the standards to govern their court-annexed programs. A decade later, the standards were revisited to consider changes that might be needed to reflect the vast increase in the use of mediation in many varying contexts. In 1995, the AAA, the ABA Section on Dispute Resolution, and the Association for Conflict Resolution adopted "Model Standards of Conduct for Mediators," which are reprinted in Appendix D.

The Standards are designed to provide basic, fundamental ethical guidelines applicable to mediation in all practice settings, with the recognition that additional standards may be appropriate to maintain integrity in particular settings. In keeping with the importance of the parties' decisionmaking role in the process, the standards do not endorse any particular style of mediation. (*See* R. Wayne Thorpe & Susan M. Yates, *An Overview of the Revised Model Standards of Conduct for Mediators*, DISP. RESOL. MAG., Winter 2006, at 30.)

What purposes should ethical standards serve in the context of mediation? Consider this question as you read the following point and counterpoint.

MICHAEL L. MOFFITT, THE WRONG MODEL, AGAIN: WHY THE DEVIL IS NOT IN THE DETAILS OF THE NEW MODEL STANDARDS OF CONDUCT FOR MEDIATORS, Dispute Resol. Mag., Spring 2006, at 31–33 *

The Model Standards of Conduct for Mediators have been revived. To be certain, all of us who care about mediation should be interested in finding ways to promote high-quality, ethical practices. The current version of the Model Standards, however, is more harmful than helpful.

* * *

It would be easy to pick at some of the details of the Model Standards because they form a complex document, drafted by a committee of talented but disparate members. * * *

But this is a case in which the devil is not in the details. Instead, the problem with the Model Standards is the very framework they adopt as their basis. The template for the Model Standards is so fundamentally flawed that no matter how the drafters filled it in, the final product was bound to be problematic.

* * * After careful consideration, I reluctantly conclude that it would be better for mediation to be a practice with no articulation of ethical principles than to have this document be perceived as our shared statement of ethical parameters.

Problem #1: *The Model Standards ignore ethical tensions.*

Ironically, for a document that purports to provide ethical guidelines for practitioners, the Model Standards ignore the very prospect of any ethical tensions in the practice of mediation. Instead, they merely set out a series of absolute, hortative prescriptions, such as the following: "Mediators shall conduct a mediation based on the principle of party self-determination." "A mediator shall conduct a mediation in an impartial manner and avoid conduct that gives the appearance of partiality." "A mediator shall conduct a mediation in a manner that promotes diligence, timeliness, safety, presence of the appropriate participants, party participation, procedural fairness, party competency and mutual respect among all participants." And the list goes on.

Most mediators would agree that an ideal mediation would include each of the values articulated above. An ideal mediation would be one in which a mediator protected participants' ability to decide for themselves, did so in a way that appeared impartial and promoted the appropriate participation of every interested party.

But the reality of mediation practice makes these ideals just that — ideals. Complex cases and the reality of human interaction produce instances in which ethical tensions arise, circumstances in which two or more competing values are pitted against one another. It is no ethical tension for a mediator to sit and wonder, "Should I protect party self-determination?" The answer is clearly yes. We need no standards of practice to tell us that.

We need ethical guidelines precisely when ethical challenges arise. And a case produces an ethical tension when a mediator's action to support one value may risk some other value. In other words, ethical dilemmas arise when there is some acknowledged tension between competing values. If I value self-determination and informed consent, I should be concerned that the plaintiff appears to be settling this claim in complete ignorance of the relief the law would afford. And yet if I value the appearance of impartiality, I cannot intervene in any way that would appear to have me favoring the plaintiff's interests over those of the defendant. It is no answer to say that I should advise the plaintiff to seek an attorney's help, because the very act of doing so, particularly if it comes precisely at the moment just before settlement, will reasonably be perceived by the defendant as conduct favoring the plaintiff. That is an ethical tension — a real world occurrence in which two or more of the important values may not be perfectly preserved simultaneously. And the practice of mediation is filled with such moments.

The first failing of the Model Standards is that their structure suggests that such tensions do not arise. Within the entirety of the Model Standards, in only one instance do they acknowledge even the possibility of a tension-between "informed consent" and "quality of the process." Instead, the standards tell us, in absolute terms, that we who mediate are simply to uphold every one of these standards at an absolute level. According to the Model Standards, mediators shall maintain impartiality and self-determination and procedural fairness and mutual respect, to name a few. "Just do it" is the unarticulated guidance the standards offer mediators. As sources of insight into the ethical realities of mediation, therefore, the standards fall woefully short.

*   *   *

Problem #2: *The Model Standards create no hierarchy of ethical concerns, providing no guidance to practitioners.*

I am not suggesting that idealized principles have no possible role in ethical standards. I could imagine a very helpful document laying out a handful of aspirational standards — but only on one of two conditions. Either the document must explicitly name the standards as aspirational or it must set out a hierarchy among the standards it articulates. The Model Standards do neither.

In lawyers' ethics, we see a model of hierarchical values. Lawyers have a duty to protect a client's interests and confidences. They owe a duty of candor to the court. They have a duty to provide pro bono legal services to those who cannot afford to pay. In an idealized setting, an attorney can accomplish each of these to an absolute level. But when push comes to shove, in the moment of greatest ethical tension, attorneys' ethical codes provide guidance about which of these ideals trumps. An attorney's duty to provide competent service to existing clients trumps the duty to provide pro bono services. And an attorney's duty of candor to the court trumps even the duty of client loyalty.

Perhaps the Model Standards could maintain their current structure if the sponsoring organizations were willing to articulate an overarching ethical norm — a single value that would trump others. But that's not what the Model

Standards include — probably because there is nothing close to a consensus among mediation practitioners about which values should be seen as highest. Is impartiality more important than party self-determination? More important than informed consent? More important than "procedural fairness"? Lawyers may be able to say that they are foremost officers of the court. Doctors may be able to say that they first ought to do no harm. Mediators, at the moment at least, have yet to articulate such an overarching ethic.

The Model Standards structure themselves in a way that demands some sort of hierarchy, but they provide none. * * *

Problem #3: *Despite these shortcomings, the Model Standards purport to establish a standard of practice.*

The most significant addition to the latest version of the Model Standards is probably also its most troublesome feature. Buried at the bottom of a new section inconspicuously labeled "Note on Construction" sits this paragraph:

> *These Standards, unless and until adopted by a court or other regulatory authority, do not have the force of law. Nonetheless, the fact that these Standards have been adopted by the respective sponsoring entities should alert mediators to the fact that the Standards might be viewed as establishing a standard of care for mediators.*

What a casual reader may miss in the standards is that they are no longer simply a collection of aspirations. The very terms of the standards seem to invite others to view them as establishing a standard of care — or at the very least do not discourage others from reading them that way.

Why does this matter? In short, it matters because it signals the prospect that these flawed standards may be used as the basis of a malpractice action against a mediator.

* * *

As I have articulated in other articles, I think malpractice liability may be an important and underused vehicle for curtailing truly awful mediator misbehavior. But exposing mediators to liability for breaching unattainable standards makes no sense. In short, the Model Standards set up a fictitious standard of care — one that I would expect responsible practicing mediators to oppose.

I wonder how practicing mediators would feel if the Model Standards were articulated differently (but to the same effect). As a mental exercise, when you reread the Model Standards, in lieu of the phrase "A mediator shall," substitute the phrase, "It shall be professional misconduct tantamount to negligence for a mediator not to. . . ." Mediators are negligent if they conduct a mediation in which the basis is not self-determination, if they fail to avoid the appearance of a conflict of interest, if they fail to conduct themselves in an impartial manner, if they fail to promote procedural fairness, and party competency, and diligence, and mutual respect among all participants.

It could be that part of the problem is that the Model Standards provide very little interpretive guidance. Perhaps I would be less nervous if I knew what the drafters intended each provision to mean-and knew that others would interpret it similarly. But unlike the attorneys' ethical rules, the Model Standards provide neither extensive notes nor illustrative examples to give flesh to the broad pronouncements. Furthermore, no Bar committee or other interpretive body exists to provide official clarification. Each of us is left to make meaning of phrases like "conduct[ing] a mediation based on the principle of self-determination." That would be appropriate if these were aspirational goals, but not if the prospect of liability hangs in the balance.

Because the Model Standards seem to welcome the prospect of being treated as a standard of care, they go from being descriptively inaccurate and ethically unhelpful to being actually dangerous to practicing mediators. What if I find myself in a genuine ethical dilemma? Should I disclose this information that I have learned in order to preserve informed consent, but potentially at the expense of perceived impartiality? Should I suggest that we include a currently absent party, even though doing so will disrupt the explicit choices of one or more of the parties? Should I make a suggestion I genuinely believe will move the discussions forward, even though I think that one side may be offended at my suggestion? In these situations, mediators will find no guidance from the Model Standards. Instead, what they will find is that whatever they decide, they may face the prospect of liability for having failed to live up to one of the multiple, absolute, unattainable ideals articulated as ethical baselines. * * *

JOSEPH B. STULBERG, THE MODEL STANDARDS OF CONDUCT: A REPLY TO PROFESSOR MOFFITT, Disp. Resol. Mag. 2006, at 35–36[*]

The adoption of the Model Standards of Conduct for Mediators (September 2005) signals an important development in the dispute resolution field. Promoting their broad-based understanding is a significant, continuing responsibility of their sponsoring organizations and those involved in their development. In that spirit, I welcome the opportunity to respond to Professor Michael Moffitt's provocative critique and rejection of the Model Standards.

* * * [Professor Moffitt's claims] are both descriptively inaccurate and conceptually unpersuasive; I hope that by showing why that is so, we gain an enriched understanding of the Model Standards.

Interplay among the standards

Professor Moffitt believes that for the Model Standards to provide guidance *in their current structure,* they need two features that he claims are absent: (1) They must acknowledge that ethical tensions for mediators arise when two or more values of the mediation process conflict, and (2) Unless merely aspirational in purpose, the Model Standards must evidence a hierarchy among them, thereby crystallizing "an overarching ethical norm-a single value that would trump others."

Professor Moffitt's first claim is wrong descriptively. As for his second claim, the Model Standards do identify a hierarchy among some standards, but do

---

not embrace his suggestion that there is one single value (or standard) that trumps all others. By not embracing Professor Moffitt's call for a "single value that trumps all others," the Model Standards take the more desirable conceptual approach.

The Model Standards recognize the possibility of conflict among standards in multiple areas and suggest how those conflicts should be handled. Professor Moffitt claims that the drafters view each standard as "an absolute, inviolate, co-equal principle-providing no guidance to those who feel they are forced to choose." That claim is importantly wrong — the drafters were much more nuanced — and the following provisions are illustrative. After each example I explain how a practicing mediator might interpret the language.

Standard III: Conflicts of Interest

(E) If a mediator's conflict of interest might reasonably be viewed as undermining the integrity of the mediation, a mediator shall withdraw from or decline to proceed with the mediation regardless of the expressed desire or agreement of the parties to the contrary.

Mediator's Response: "My obligation to be impartial, set out in Standard II, and my obligation to conduct a quality mediation process, set out in Standard VI, trump my duty to promote party self-determination (Standard I(A)) as to mediator selection."

Standard IV. Competence

(A) A mediator shall mediate only when the mediator has the necessary competence to satisfy the reasonable expectation of the parties.

(B) If a mediator, during the course of a mediation, determines that the mediator cannot conduct the mediation competently, the mediator shall discuss that determination with the parties as soon as is practicable and take appropriate steps to address the situation, including but not limited to, withdrawing or requesting appropriate assistance.

Mediator's Response: "My obligation is to mediate only if I have the competence to do so. Even if the parties believe I am competent (Standard IV(A)) I may realize that I am not (Standard IV(B)). In that instance, (B) takes priority over (A), and I must take some action — bring in a co-mediator or withdraw — to address the matter."

Standard VI. Quality of the Process

(A)(5) [A] mediator may provide information that the mediator is qualified by training or experience to provide, only if the mediator can do so consistent with these Standards.

Mediator's Response: "If a party or counsel ask me for my assessment of the law governing a contested matter, I can respect that exercise of party self-determination (Standard I(A)) and, if qualified, provide that information (Standard VI(A)(5)), but I can do so only if I can remain impartial (Standard II(B)), so Standard II takes priority."

Standard VIII. Fees and Other Charges

VIII(B)(2): While a mediator may accept unequal fee payments from the parties, a mediator should not allow such a fee arrangement to adversely impact the mediators ability to conduct a mediation in an impartial manner.

Mediators Response: "If the plaintiff contributes nothing to the payment of my fee and the defendant pays the entire fee, that is acceptable (Standard VIII(B)(2)) as long as it does not undermine my ability to conduct the mediation impartially (Standard II(B)). In assessing the appropriate balance, Standard II(B) trumps."

The possibility of multiple answers

Professor Moffitt lauds documents such as the lawyers' Model Rules of Professional Responsibility because he claims that they provide clear, unequivocal answers. * * * He criticizes the Model Standards for not providing similar certainty, given that the standards are designed to guide mediator conduct. While there is much to commend the approach Professor Moffitt endorses, and it is one that lawyers particularly might find appealing, it strikes me there is ample room for differences of opinion regarding the degree of guidance a governing document ought to provide.

In my judgment, an approach that embraces a desire for certainty, even if conceptually plausible (which I do not believe it is), is purchased at the cost of underestimating and disregarding the richness and unpredictability of the human experience, including mediation sessions. In his earlier work criticizing the original Model Standards, Professor Moffitt offers a framework for analyzing mediator ethical dilemmas and walks through an example where considerations of self-determination, impartiality and informed consent clash. That is a wonderful exercise — for a classroom or practitioner discussion. Such an approach does not translate into a viable "Code;" more importantly, it does not negate the value of articulating standards of practice.

Yes, one consequence of providing guidance at a more general level than the exhaustive, answer-book approach that Professor Moffitt appears to endorse is that it leaves open the possibility that there might be two or more compelling interpretations that generate different results when deciding how best to resolve a given dilemma. It does not follow from that, however, that "any rationalization" is compelling. I think that this general mode of guidance and interpretation is more desirable and appropriate — and akin to how we use and interpret the U.S. Constitution, for example — than is the call for a mechanical application of one supreme value. Does that mean that the Model Standards might be "ambiguous" on various questions? Yes. But that certainly does not entail that the standards, because of ambiguity in the hard case, are "structurally deficient."

Performance standards

The Model Standards reflect important, considerable changes in format from the 1994 version. One significant structural change is to target the statement and application of the standards to mediators. Another change is the addition of a statement in the introductory paragraphs that explicitly indicates that a practicing mediator should be aware that some court or regulatory authority might look to these standards as establishing a standard of care for mediators. Professor Moffitt criticizes the latter language because he asserts that the Model Standards lack sufficient clarity to guide mediator conduct.

* * * Professor Moffitt's criticism is misdirected, for the question this introductory language addresses is how other people or agencies, not mediators, might view the Model Standards. During Committee deliberations, there was evidence that a substantial number of court systems in various states had adopted, either verbatim or in substantial measure, the 1994 version as governing norms for their programs. So, as a matter of alerting colleagues to potential developments, this new paragraph is important empirically.

I applaud Professor Moffitt for constructively suggesting alternative ways to approach the challenges that confronted the drafters. However, I personally find each of his proposed options unhelpful for guiding mediator conduct and unpersuasive conceptually. Professor Moffitt reluctantly concludes that mediation practice is better off without an articulation of principles than it is having the Model Standards perceived as a shared statement of ethical parameters. I could not disagree more.

NOTES

1. *Applying the Model Standards.* What do the model standards say about the situations in the following scenarios? Do the standards provide adequate guidance in your view? The scenarios are selected from Michael Moffitt, *Ten Ways to Get Sued: A Guide for Mediators*, 8 HARV. NEG. L. REV. 81 (2003).

a. Melissa Mediator is a member of a small consulting firm specializing in corporate dispute resolution. One of the firm's clients is a large, multi-national conglomerate. Unlike most of her colleagues, Melissa has never done work for the conglomerate. A dispute arises between one of the subsidiaries of the conglomerate and a local business. Melissa agrees to mediate the dispute and discloses nothing about the relationship between the conglomerate and her firm.

b. Mortimer Mediator facilitates an agreement between disputing former business partners. The agreement includes a voluntary dismissal of certain pieces of litigation, a new licensing agreement on the partnership's intellectual property, and a division of the partnership's assets. Based on Mortimer's advice about a "tax smart" way to craft the deal, the parties agree to a novel agreement structure proposed and drafted by Mortimer. Later, a dispute arises over the interpretation of a poorly drafted clause in the agreement, and both parties find themselves stuck with substantial tax burdens that could have been avoided with a more standard agreement.

c. To the surprise of the disputants, Marcus Mediator calls a press conference during a break in the mediation. At the press conference, Marcus reveals that the plaintiffs have indicated an intention not to pursue at least certain parts of their original lawsuit against the City. Marcus further says to the press, "Now, with a little flexibility from the City, we should be able to get the whole thing settled."

d. Plaintiffs brought suit seeking injunctive relief to force a change in a particular policy at the defendant corporation and seeking modest monetary damages. During a private caucus, Marsha Mediator learns that the defendant has already decided to change the policies in question, in a way the plaintiffs will embrace. When Marsha asks defense counsel why they have not told the plaintiffs about the corporation's plans, they indicate that they hope to use the change in policies as a "trade-off concession" in order to minimize or eliminate any financial payment. In a subsequent private meeting with the plaintiffs, without the consent of the defendant, Marsha says, "Look, the defendants have already told me that they're going to make the policy change. The only issue is money."

e. Maurice Mediator learns during a conversation with a divorcing couple that the children are regularly subjected to living arrangements tantamount to abuse or neglect. Maurice mentions his concern, but both of the parents swear that the circumstances will change once they can finalize the divorce. Maurice says nothing to anyone outside of the mediation and proceeds to assist the parties in finalizing the terms of the divorce.

f. Mitchell Mediator's website touts his mediation services as "expert." In part, it says, "Over 1,000 cases of experience. Certified and sanctioned by the State and by prominent national mediation organizations." Mitchell is a former judge who presided over more than a thousand civil cases during his years on the bench. He has formally mediated, however, only a few dozen cases. Furthermore, neither the state nor the national mediation organizations to which Mitchell belongs certifies or sanctions mediators. Mitchell is simply a member of the mediation rosters each body maintains.

g. During the mediation, Muriel Mediator adopts an aggressive approach to creating settlement. As always, she had told the parties, a divorcing couple, "Bring your toothbrushes when you show up to my mediation." The divorcing wife, unrepresented by counsel, is visibly worn down by Muriel's relentless efforts at "persuasion." When the wife protests and indicates a desire to leave, Muriel threatens to report to the judge that the wife did not participate in the mediation in good faith. Muriel further indicates that such a report would "all but guarantee that you'll lose your claim for custody of the children."

h. In a private caucus, the plaintiffs tell Manuel Mediator that they would be able to break this case wide open if only they could get some cooperation from a few important executives in the defendant corporation. They admit, however, that they have had no luck so far in their efforts. Manuel then sits down privately with the general counsel for the defendant and says, "Look, I spoke with the plaintiffs. They have just lined up some key insider witnesses, including a couple members of your management team. It's time for you to end this." The general counsel looks surprised but increases the defendant's offer considerably. The mediator takes the new offer to the plaintiffs, who quickly agree to it.

2. Other legal provisions also contain professional obligations for mediators. The UMA, for example, establishes specific obligations with regard to confidentiality and reporting. In addition, it requires mediators to make disclosures about conflicts of interests. Before accepting a mediation, a mediator must:

(1) make an inquiry that is reasonable under the circumstances to determine whether there are any known facts that a reasonable individual would consider likely to affect the impartiality of the mediator, including a financial or personal interest in the outcome of the mediation and an existing or past relationship with a mediation party or foreseeable participant in the mediation; and

(2) disclose any such known fact to the mediation parties as soon as is practical before accepting a mediation. [UMA § 9(a).]

This disclosure obligation is ongoing if a mediator later learns a relevant fact. In addition, if a party requests, a mediator must disclose her qualifications to mediate a dispute.

3. The ABA Model Rules of Professional Conduct that set professional standards for lawyers have been criticized for failing to take account of their roles as a neutrals. (*See* Carrie Menkel-Meadow, *Ethics in Alternative Dispute Resolution: New Issues, No Answers from the Adversary Conception of Lawyers' Responsibilities*, 38 S. TEXAS L. REV. 407 (1997).) With the aim of providing specific standards for attorney-neutrals, the CPR-Georgetown Commission on Standards and Ethics in ADR prepared a Model Rule for the Lawyer as Third-Party Neutral, available at http://www.cpradr.org/pdfs/CPRGeorge-ModelRule.pdf

4. In 2002, the ABA Model Rules were amended to delete Rule 2.2, the provision that governed a lawyer acting as an "intermediary." The Model Rules now contain a new provision specifically applicable to lawyers in the role of a third party neutral.

RULE 2.4 LAWYER SERVING AS THIRD-PARTY NEUTRAL

(a) A lawyer serves as a third-party neutral when the lawyer assists two or more persons who are not clients of the lawyer to reach a resolution of a dispute or other matter that has arisen between them. Service as a third-party neutral may include service as an arbitrator, a mediator or in such other capacity as will enable the lawyer to assist the parties to resolve the matter.

(b) A lawyer serving as a third-party neutral shall inform unrepresented parties that the lawyer is not representing them. When the lawyer knows or reasonably should know that a party does not understand the lawyer's role in the matter, the lawyer shall explain the difference between the lawyer's role as a third-party neutral and a lawyer's role as one who represents a client.

The comments to the rule recognize the lawyers serving as mediators face unique problems because of the differences between the role of a neutral and the role of a lawyer as a client representative. Confusion between these roles is a special danger when parties participate in mediation without a representative. The explanation required by subsection (b) should be tailored to the parties' experience with mediation.

5. A lawyer who serves as a third-party neutral subsequently may be asked to serve as a lawyer representing a client in the same matter. The amended version of the ABA Model Rules recognizes that these conflicts of interest arise for mediators as well as for judges and arbitrators. The conflicts affect both the individual lawyer and the lawyer's law firm.

RULE 1.12 FORMER JUDGE, ARBITRATOR, MEDIATOR OR OTHER THIRD-PARTY NEUTRAL

(a) Except as stated in paragraph (d), a lawyer shall not represent anyone in connection with a matter in which the lawyer participated personally and substantially as a judge or other adjudicative officer or law clerk to such a person or as an arbitrator, mediator or other third-party neutral, unless all parties to the proceeding give informed consent, confirmed in writing.

(b) A lawyer shall not negotiate for employment with any person who is involved as a party or as lawyer for a party in a matter in which the lawyer is participating personally and substantially as a judge or other adjudicative officer or as an arbitrator, mediator or other third-party neutral. * * *

(c) If a lawyer is disqualified by paragraph (a), no lawyer in a firm with which that lawyer is associated may knowingly undertake or continue representation in the matter unless:

(1) the disqualified lawyer is screened from any participation in the matter and is apportioned no part of the fee therefrom; and

(2) written notice is promptly given to the parties and any appropriate tribunal to enable them to ascertain compliance with the provisions of this rule.

(d) An arbitrator selected as a partisan of a party in a multimember arbitration panel is not prohibited from subsequently representing that party.

Compare the Model Standards of Conduct for Mediators, which provide as follows in Standard III. Conflicts of Interest:

F. Subsequent to a mediation, a mediator shall not establish another relationship with any of the participants in any matter that would raise questions about the integrity of the mediation. When a mediator develops personal or professional relationships with parties, other individuals or organizations following a mediation in which they were involved, the mediator should consider factors such as time elapsed following the mediation, the nature of the relationships established, and services offered when determining whether the relationships might create a perceived or actual conflict of interest.

Does the ABA Model Rule give a lawyer-mediator this degree of discretion?

2. Mediation and the Practice of Law

Bruce Meyerson, Lawyers Who Mediate are Not Practicing Law, 14 Alternatives to the High Cost of Ligigation 74 (CPR Institute for Dispute Resolution 1996) *

Carrie Menkel-Meadow, a professor at Georgetown and UCLA Law Schools, has initiated an important discussion concerning a core issue confronting dispute resolvers: what exactly are we doing? (*Alternatives,* May 1996 at p. 57.) Ms. Menkel-Meadow believes that mediation is the practice of law because mediators often evaluate the respective legal positions of the parties and sometimes predict the outcomes of disputes. I respectfully disagree.

Generally speaking, to practice law, one must have a client. Assuming that mediators clarify with parties that no attorney-client relationship exists, engaging in a legal discussion would not be the practice of law. Specifically, in order for a mediator's conduct in advising parties about the legal aspects of a particular dispute to be considered the practice of law, the party to the mediation must view the mediator as her lawyer and assume that she is receiving legal advice for her personal benefit. If the parties are represented by counsel, or if the mediator has carefully clarified that the unrepresented parties do not view the mediator as their lawyer, I cannot imagine a situation where parties to the mediation will be confused about the mediator's role and mistakenly assume that the mediator is functioning as a lawyer.

To be sure, a lawyer acting in another professional capacity can sometimes inadvertently create an attorney-client relationship. For example, when a person reasonably believes that a lawyer is acting as his attorney, relies on that belief and relationship and the lawyer does not refute that belief, an attorney-client relationship is created. *In re Neville*, 147 Ariz. 106, 708 P.2d 1297 (1985).

For this reason, the American Bar Association House of Delegates recently promulgated Model Rule 5.7 concerning ancillary services. This rule covers cases in which the attorney is not practicing law, but is engaged in activities so closely related to the practice of law that a third party might believe the attorney is representing him or her. In such cases, the rule requires that attorneys follow the Rules of Professional Conduct. The rule expressly identifies mediation as an ancillary service.

If, as Ms. Menkel-Meadow argues, mediators are practicing law anytime they give evaluations or predict outcomes, a number of undesirable consequences will follow. First, lawyer-mediators would be subject to all of the duties and obligations under the Model Rules, and presumably would owe these duties to the parties in the mediation. Although it is possible that a lawyer can function as a neutral mediator on behalf of clients in certain limited circumstances, Ethics Rule 2.2, in most instances the role of a mediator is fundamentally incompatible with an attorney's role in representing a client. For example, a mediator is supposed to be impartial and evenhanded during the mediation. On the other hand, a lawyer representing a client owes that

---

client a duty of undivided loyalty. Most certainly, this obligation is inconsistent with the neutral duties a mediator owes to all parties in a mediation. In this respect, Model Rule 5.7 should not be applied to attorney-mediators.

Second, a conclusion that mediation is the practice of law would raise the specter that thousands of professionals in other disciplines are engaged in the unauthorized practice of law. Surely, this is casting the "practice of law" net too widely.

Third, if mediation is the practice of law, judges presiding over settlement conferences would be breaking ethical rules in many jurisdictions. That could happen in states that prohibit judges from practicing law while they serve on the bench. Under these rules, judges would be practicing law when, in an attempt to settle a case, they discuss the legal merits of a case with disputing parties. A judge engaged in this common settlement technique would be engaged in unethical conduct. Therefore, although the function judges perform in settlement efforts is the same as that performed by a lawyer-mediator, it's impractical to label the judge's actions as the practice of law.

At the heart of Ms. Menkel-Meadow's analysis is an effort to find appropriate standards of accountability for mediators who undertake responsibilities which we have associated historically with the practice of law. We can achieve this laudable goal without denominating mediation as the practice of law.

A number of professional organizations have adopted ethical standards that are useful reference points. . . .

Some states have placed specific affirmative duties upon lawyer-mediators. In these states, lawyers are required to inform parties that they specifically do not represent them and that they may not represent them in subsequent proceedings. Other states require that lawyers explain the proceedings and the advantages of obtaining independent counsel.

In a leading article on this subject, one author has suggested that a lawyer-mediator should have the duty to be sure that mediation: (1) meets the parties' own sense of fairness; (2) does not violate minimal societal notions of fairness between parties to a contract; (3) and does not violate minimal standards of fairness toward unrepresented third parties. L. Riskin, "Toward New Standards for the Neutral Lawyer in Mediation," 26 *Ariz. L. Rev.* 329 (1984).

Another scholar has argued that the Rules of Professional Conduct should be amended to add a new rule dealing with lawyer mediation. J. Maute, "Public Values and Private Justice: A Case for Mediator Accountability," 4 *Geo. J. L. Ethics* 503 (1991). This author proposes that lawyers be permitted to act as mediators when the parties are reasonably informed about the mediation process and the lawyer reasonably believes that: (1) the mediation can be undertaken impartially; and (2) the dispute is suitable for mediation and the parties are able to participate effectively and to make adequately informed decisions. She also proposes additional guidelines for mediations in which the parties are not separately represented.

Although these articles concern regulation of lawyer mediators, the principles can extend to nonlawyer mediators. These principles can be part of credentialing by a state professional association, or standards imposed by a state regulatory body. In addition, maybe it's time to reexamine proposals to make mediators immune from malpractice liability. Because mediators do not adjudicate disputes, the need for immunity is far less in mediation than in other ADR contexts, like court-annexed arbitration.

Clearly, we need a framework for regulating mediation. But we can develop that framework without labeling mediation as the practice of law.

NOTES

1. The Myerson article is a response to an earlier article contending that mediation can constitute the practice of law. (*See* Menkel-Meadow, 1996). Professor Menkel-Meadow focuses on the evaluation process in which the mediator evaluates the strengths and weaknesses of the disputants' positions and concludes this process necessarily is the practice of law. She argues that the practice of law "entails applying legal principles to concrete facts" and cites authority holding that case evaluation by insurance adjusters constitutes legal advice. (*Id.* at 61, citing *Dauphin County Bar Association v. Mazzacaro*, 465 Pa. 545, 351 A.2d 229 (1976).)

2. The Meyerson article contends that the adoption of separate ethical standards for mediators should achieve the degree of accountability and impartiality needed for mediation to be fair and to thrive. Is Meyerson's practical position reasonable or is it overly optimistic? Are the Standards of Conduct jointly adopted by the ABA, the AAA, and ACR an adequate answer to the problem?

3. Should it make a difference if the mediator is a lawyer or non-lawyer when deciding if mediation is the practice of law? According to one commentator, the answer is a resounding yes. (*See* Morrison, 1987 (concluding that divorce mediation by lawyers should be analyzed as the practice of law but divorce mediation by non-lawyer mediators should not be considered the practice of law).)

4. Mediation statutory confidentiality has limits because of statutory exceptions. How should the mediator handle the process of informing the disputants of these limits? Existing professional standards for mediators mandate disclosure of the limits of confidentiality. A mediator who fails to disclose the limits of confidentiality to the parties may be guilty of serious breach of ethics. (*See* Brown, 1991, at 307, 311.) Will mediation participants be less candid after learning that some comments made will not be confidential?

5. The debate continues regarding whether mediation is the practice of law. For the position that mediators who "evaluate" a disputant's case practice law while those who merely "facilitate" do not practice law, see Joshua R. Schwartz, *Laymen Cannot Lawyer, But is Mediation the Practice of Law?*, 20 Cardozo L. Rev. 1715 (1999).

3. THE LAWYER'S OBLIGATION TO COUNSEL CLIENTS ABOUT MEDIATION

A growing number of mediators (and arbitrators) feel that the attorney who files a lawsuit without discussing the possibility of mediation or arbitration is acting unethically. The theory supporting this position is simple: because a lawsuit will probably generate greater attorneys fees than either mediation or arbitration, the attorney who files without presenting the merits of alternatives to litigation has a conflict of interest with the client.

While this position has some intrinsic appeal (this is information valuable to the client), it has not fully embedded in ethics rules. Only a few states require a broad attorney ethical duty to counsel about ADR before filing suit. Virginia ethical norms, effective in 2000, create a client right to consult with the lawyer about "the objectives of representation," the "means" of attorney representation and now directly require the lawyer to "advise the client about the advantages, disadvantages and availability of dispute resolution processes that might be appropriate." (Comment to Model Rule 1.2.)

The ABA's Model Rule 1.2 is far more tepid. It requires the lawyer to "consult with the client" regarding the means of representation but still avoids directly mandating that the lawyer explain and discuss alternatives such as mediation. Under the ABA rules the attorney is not required to give advice until requested to do so by the client. Some feel that the current rule, while vague, is specific enough in the general duty to consult, to mention forms of dispute resolution such as mediation whenever alternatives to litigation are reasonable.

D. MEDIATOR IMMUNITY AND QUALIFICATIONS

1. MEDIATOR IMMUNITY

The question of whether mediators should hold immunity from suit has been hotly debated. If minimal mediator qualifications are not required by the state, then some liability exposure is arguably needed to assure mediator quality. Several states have passed legislation granting a degree of immunity to mediators. Consider Oregon's legislation:

> Mediators, mediation programs and dispute resolution programs . . . are not civilly liable for any act or omission done or made while engaged in efforts to assist or facilitate a mediation, unless the act or omission was made or done in bad faith, with malicious intent or in a manner exhibiting a willful, wanton disregard of the rights, safety or property of another. [ORS 36.210 (1999).]

(*See also* COLO. REV. STAT. § 13-22-305 (2000) (granting mediator immunity except for "willful and wanton misconduct"); IOWA CODE § 13.16 (making farm foreclosure mediators immune unless they act in bad faith, with malice, or in willful and wanton disregard of human rights, safety or property); *Postma v. First Federal Savings & Loan of Sioux City*, 74 F.3d 160 (8th Cir. 1996) (court affirms grant of immunity in action against Iowa farm mediators).) Note that such legislation does not provide complete immunity from suit. The exceptions, while narrow, afford plaintiffs the ability to try to fit into a range of potential liability. Not surprisingly, many in the mediation community oppose such exceptions and seek even stronger protection in the form of total immunity.

Note also that the above statutes cover both private mediation and mediation done under court programs.

The policy argument supporting mediator immunity contends that "the importance of encouraging people to act as mediators exceeds the significance of permitting mediator liability as a means to compensate injured parties or ensure quality in mediation." (Cole, Rogers & McEwen, 2d ed. 1994 (Supp. 2006), at § 11.3.) The states that have considered and rejected enacting positive law creating mediator immunity have feared that immunity can expose the public to potential injury and that immunity may be premature at the present developmental stage of integrating mediation in the disputing norms. (*See generally,* New Jersey Supreme Court Task Force on Community Dispute Resolution 1990; Richardson, 1990 (disapproving of new Florida legislation providing mediator immunity); Chaykin, 1986.)

It is useful to compare the notion of judicial immunity to that of mediator immunity. Judges and others in law enforcement (arbitrators, witnesses, prosecutors, court reporters and administrative agency officials), have received a degree of common law immunity. The theory behind this grant of immunity is that courts need immunity to preserve their complete independence when deciding cases and to provide repose or an end to a dispute. (*See Bradley v. Fisher,* 80 U.S. (13 Wall.) 335 (1871) (granting immunity to judges).) Judge Learned Hand premised immunity by reasoning that it is "better to leave unredressed the wrongs done by dishonest officers than to subject those who try to do their duty to the constant dread of retaliation." (*Gregoire v. Biddle,* 177 F.2d 579, 581 (2d Cir. 1949), *cert. denied,* 339 U.S. 949 (1950).)

While a legislative grant of immunity to mediators clarifies matters, the question of some form of common law mediator immunity is troublesome. Is the work of a mediator of a judicial character and deserving of immunity?

In *Wagshal v. Foster,* 28 F.3d 1249 (D.C. Cir. 1994), the court of appeals affirmed a district court grant of a motion for summary judgment dismissing a § 1983 Civil Rights Act claim against a court appointed mediator. The defendant lawyer was appointed as a mediator in a mandatory District of Columbia court annexed program and assigned the role of settlement "case evaluator." The district court struck a first mediator assigned to the case after the plaintiff Wagshal complained of a conflict of interest. After the plaintiff accused the defendant mediator Foster of not being neutral and also having a conflict of interest, Foster requested that the court recuse him as a case evaluator. The court rules prevented the case evaluator from testifying for either party and required that the evaluator be "neutral." Foster's letter to the court characterized the plaintiffs conflict of interest claims as "attenuated," stated that the case should settle, and suggested that the court "remonstrate with [plaintiff] Mr. Wagshal as to his obligations under the court's rules concerning mediation." (*Wagshal v. Foster,* 1993 WL 86499 (D.D.C. 1993).) The court recused Foster and observed, in a telephone conference call, that the conflict of interest claim was attenuated.

The underlying case settled and Wagshal sued the mediator case evaluator Foster, claiming that his comments to the court reflected unfavorably on plaintiffs case and forced an unsatisfactory settlement.

The trial court's grant of immunity reasoned that Foster was discharging a court duty and acting with the knowledge and approval of the trial judge. It observed that "traditional agents of the judicial process have . . . been held to possess . . . immunity when they act in their official capacities." (*Id.* at 2.) The Court of Appeals agreed with this absolute immunity analysis, reasoning that the defendant had performed a judicial function by identifying issues and coordinating settlement efforts. It also concluded that Foster had acted within the scope of his defined official duties. (28 F.3d at 1252–53.) The trial court invited the defendant and his law partners, who were also named as defendants, to apply for Rule 11 sanctions.

Is the *Wagshal* decision as simple as it appears? Should sanctions as a "frivolous" case have been requested and granted? Did the plaintiff have a valid claim that the evaluator breached a confidence by his letter to the court? (*See* English, 1995).

Could the reasoning of *Wagshal* support a claim of immunity against a private mediator who is not part of a court mandated program of court annexed mediation? In *Howard v. Drapkin*, 222 Cal. App. 3d 843 (1990), the court conferred immunity on a psychologist working on a domestic relations case and, in dicta, observed that similar immunity would be awarded to mediators related to the judicial process. Despite the *Howard* case, Cole, Rogers and McEwen take the position that "[i]f not protected by an existing statutory or common law immunity, it seems unlikely that the courts will recognize a new common law immunity for mediators." (Cole, Rogers & McEwen, 2d ed. 1994 (Supp. 2006), at § 11.3.) Should the issue of mediator immunity be tied to whether a state sets entry qualifications for mediators? If a state will allow virtually anyone to mediate, shouldn't an injured party have a right to sue an allegedly negligent mediator?

2. MEDIATOR QUALIFICATIONS

Up until recent years there was little or no "entry" regulation of mediators. Anyone who wanted to mediate would advertise for work and begin to mediate without any formal certification or licensing by the state. In law and economics terms entry was easy and a competitive market of many providers existed. The role of the state was nonexistent.

With the increasing popularity of mediation and the growing need for mediators there has been an increased call for some minimal governmental credentialing of mediators to ensure that only qualified individuals mediate. Numerous jurisdictions now set minimal qualifications for mediators in court-connected programs. There is little agreement on the extent and nature of qualifications that should be required to mediate. Several states have educational or training requirements (e.g., 60 hours of training needed to mediate a child custody dispute). A few jurisdictions mandate that a mediator have a professional degree in counseling or psychology or social work in order to mediate certain family law disputes.

Meaningful measurement of mediator competency is difficult. The following excerpt describes what the Chief Mediator in one of the federal courts of appeals looks for when he hires a new mediator.

> Our [mediator] position announcements call for "proven exceptional ability to manage collaborative problem solving and consensus building processes . . . in highly competitive situations." What this office seeks first and foremost in a candidate is an inclination and an ability to see value and similarity of interests in apparently conflicting points of view, and to seek integration or synthesis of valid perspectives rather than dominance by any one of them. We look for life and work experience that demonstrates intelligence and skill in working with people in conflict in a way that brings about the kind of integration or synthesis just mentioned. While court mediation offices undoubtedly tend to look first at candidates with litigation backgrounds, a background in business or politics might be just as useful. These qualities are almost impossible to quantify or apply as objective qualifications. They are found between the lines in resumes, in candidates' interviews, and in probing reference checks. Our experience is that a person so oriented, who also has demonstrated initiative, emotional maturity, good judgment, exceptional interpersonal communications and social skills, integrity, and success with previous endeavors, is likely to become an excellent mediator. * * * Litigation and federal court experience, prior mediation training, and prior mediation experience are all valuable, but are considered less critical than the personal qualifications just described. To the best of my knowledge, there still are no specific objective education, training, experience, or subject matter expertise criteria that have been shown to predict high quality or success in mediators. Thus, rigid application of qualifications based on such criteria probably only creates a false sense of security and makes the selection process easier and faster; it will not assure high quality mediation and might, in fact, cause a court to exclude its best candidate. [Robert W. Rack, Jr., *Thoughts of a Chief Circuit Mediator on Federal Court-Annexed Mediation*, 17 Ohio St. J. on Disp. Resol. 609, 615 (2002).]

The new Model Standards for Conduct for Mediators also avoids requirements for specific levels of education or experience. The touchstone is instead the reasonable expectation of the parties:

Standard IV. Competence

> A. A mediator shall mediate only when the mediator has the necessary competence to satisfy the reasonable expectations of the parties.

> 1. Any person may be selected as a mediator, provided that the parties are satisfied with the mediator's competence and qualifications. Training, experience in mediation, skills, cultural understandings and other qualities are often necessary for mediator competence. A person who offers to serve as a mediator creates the expectation that the person is competent to mediate effectively.

2. A mediator should attend educational programs and related activities to maintain and enhance the mediator's knowledge and skills related to mediation.

3. A mediator should have available for the parties' information relevant to the mediator's training, education, experience and approach to conducting a mediation.

B. If a mediator, during the course of a mediation determines that the mediator cannot conduct the mediation competently, the mediator shall discuss that determination with the parties as soon as is practicable and take appropriate steps to address the situation, including, but not limited to, withdrawing or requesting appropriate assistance.

C. If a mediator's ability to conduct a mediation is impaired by drugs, alcohol, medication or otherwise, the mediator shall not conduct the mediation.

Under the Model Standards, the mediator is responsible for self-regulation, in consultation with the parties. Are the parties capable of evaluating mediator qualifications? Has that capability changed as mediator has become more prevalent in court programs? Is a "Standard of Conduct" a sufficient mechanism to ensure competent mediation?

In recent years, three has been increased interest in certification programs for mediators. The Association for Conflict Resolution (ACR) authorized a Task Force on Mediator Certification, which recommended a voluntary mediator certification program. An applicant would submit a portfolio of experience, training, and education to ACR, which would evaluate the portfolio. If the review is favorable, an applicant would be required to take a written test to become eligible for placement on the ACR roster. Applicants must document both training and mediation experience.

First, a minimum of 100 hours of training or academic coursework in conflict resolution would be required for ACR certification, of which 80 hours must be training in mediation process skills. A mediator may satisfy up to 20 of the 100 hours as a trainer or teacher. Second, an applicant would need to demonstrate 100 hours of mediation or co-mediation experience within the last five years or 500 hours over a lifetime. Applicants must obtain professional liability insurance, disclose criminal convictions, and provide letters of reference in order to gain and maintain placement on the roster. Successful applicants would be subject to periodic recertification and decertification for ethical and professional standards violations. Unsuccessful applicants would be entitled to appeal the decision. (*See* ACR Task Force on Mediator Certification, Report and Recommendations to the Board of Directors (March 31, 2004), available at www.acrnet.org.)

In the State of Florida, mediators who wish to referrals from Florida courts must be certified by the Supreme Court of Florida. Certification standards vary with the type of court and mediation, but applicants must complete training courses and meet requirements for academic qualifications. Florida's

Supreme Court Committee on Alternative Dispute Resolution Rules and Policy has recommended an amendment to the existing mediator certification requirements that would change the state's approach to credentialing. The goal is to create a more flexible system that will also promote diversity in mediators' training and background.

The proposed plan would de-emphasize paper credentials and use a point system that would credit experience as well as education. For example, to be certified for circuit court mediations, an applicant would need 100 points. A minimum of 30 points must be earned by completing training approved by the Florida Supreme Court, education and experience must contribute at least 25 points, and 30 points must be earned working with a mentor to observe mediations and mediate under supervision. Whereas currently mediators must have a law degree to qualify for this category of certification, the proposal would change the minimum educational requirement to a bachelor's degree. (*See* Florida Dispute Resolution Center, The Resolution Report (October 2004) at www.flcourts.org/gen_public/adr/bin/oct04news.pdf.)

Some commentators believe that widespread certification programs are premature. Consider the following arguments:

Sarah Rudolph Cole, Mediator Certification: Has the Time Come?, Disp. Resol. Mag., Spring 2005, at 7–10 *

To assess whether [the] movement toward certification is cause for commendation or for concern, we must first consider the stated goals of certification, along with the related questions of whether, and to whom, those goals are important. Second, if the goals are worthwhile, we should consider the efficacy of the various certification approaches in achieving the goals. This article explores both of these topics, and suggests potential areas of concern regarding each. It ultimately concludes that the organizations should make greater efforts to ensure that there is buy-in regarding the appropriate goals. It further concludes that the certification proposals now on the table may, in fact, be counterproductive, even for achieving the currently stated goals.

Goals of certification The goals of mediator certification include: (1) protecting consumers from the effect of "bad" mediators, (2) reducing court congestion (assuming that more cases will settle if high quality mediators handle them), and (3) promoting mediation by, among other things, improving mediator credibility through an external indication of quality. The ACR Task Force on Mediator Certification stated that a voluntary certification process would also: (1) provide uniform verification of a basic level of training, (2) create among mediators a "more solid foundation of competency and professionalism," (3) assist consumers in selecting a mediator, and (4) enable certified mediators to influence the development of the mediation field.

Assessing the goals As a general matter, these goals all seem directed at three interrelated and symbiotic objectives: protecting and assisting consumers, improving overall mediator quality, and enhancing the credibility of "good" mediators in the marketplace. The first question, then, is whether these

---

are necessary, or even worthwhile, goals to pursue. Do consumers need greater protection from bad mediators or more help in selecting qualified mediators? Do "good" mediators need or want to enhance their market credibility through certification? In the mediation circles, anecdotal tales of bad mediators are common. But is there a consensus on what constitutes a bad mediator, or, conversely, on what characteristics "good" mediators share?

Defining a quality mediator The last question is perhaps the most elusive. For some time, the mediation community has believed that a key component of a good mediation is a quality mediator. But the necessary attributes of a quality mediator are often described in subjective terms that may not easily lend themselves to paper-file-based certification programs. For example, some have suggested that quality mediators must listen actively; identify issues; frame issues so that mediation parties understand them; use clear, neutral language; deal ably with complex factual scenarios; show respect for parties; earn the trust of parties; and separate their own values from the issues before them. Magistrate Judge Wayne Brazil has offered additional characteristics: moral integrity, honesty, sensitivity, sustainable energy and positive spirit, commitment to procedural fairness, and the ability to refrain from forming premature opinions.

All of these characteristics sound good — it is hard to argue against moral integrity and honesty — yet sources for concern remain as we consider certification designed to achieve or promote "quality" mediators. First, notwithstanding the various attributes listed above, it is not wholly clear that there is as yet a widely shared consensus on exactly which attributes, and in what proportions, lead to mediator quality. Is "sensitivity" really necessary, and if so, what exactly does it mean, and how much of it is required? Of course a mediator should "earn the trust of parties," but how is that accomplished, and which mediator attributes facilitate it?

In short, if the goal of certification programs is "separating the wheat from the chaff," more work should be done to determine how to differentiate the two. Until there is a shared consensus on which attributes we should be looking for, it is difficult at best to discuss the specifics of certification programs for assessing whether those attributes are present.

Considering consumers Nor is it clear that consensus within the mediation community as to what constitutes mediator quality is the final answer on that issue. If a goal of mediator certification is to enhance the market credibility (and thus, perhaps, the market value) of "good" mediators, perhaps we should be looking to mediation consumers to ascertain what they think constitutes mediator quality. * * *

* * *

Current certification system design Even if we assume that the characteristics listed above reflect some shared notion of "quality" that we can use without further investigation, issues still arise with regard to current certification system design. If certification is intended to be a mark of quality, then a certification program should design its standards to assess whether a given applicant possesses the attributes that have been identified as important to quality. Because the attributes themselves are subjective, however, the certification proposals to date have largely relied on proxies for demonstrating quality. That is, rather than attempting to assess the presence of desirable characteristics in a given applicant directly, the proposals look to things like experience, education, and training — things that may suggest that the applicant has the necessary skill set.

But, if the certification programs are going to rely on these indirect metrics, the burden is on the organizations backing the programs to demonstrate the positive correlation between the presence of the indirect attributes and the desired attributes. That is, no one cares (or should care), in the abstract, that a mediator has been trained. It is only if mediator training, at least as a general matter, leads to a higher quality mediation experience, that questions regarding an applicant's training are relevant. The same is true of education or experience. It is not the existence of those factors per se, but their correlation to mediator quality that makes them relevant.

Linking training and quality To date, however, remarkably little empirical work has been done that demonstrates a strong link between training or education, on the one hand, and mediator quality on the other. I am aware of only one study that has looked at the issue, and that study concluded that the only relevant variable for predicting mediator quality was experience. If that study is correct (and more studies would certainly be welcome), certification programs that impose training or educational requirements seem ill-suited to the task of improving mediator quality, identifying high-quality mediators, or protecting the consumers of mediation services.

* * *

Ensuring diversity The hour-and-point requirements identified in the [ACR and Florida] proposals may undermine the goal of ensuring high quality mediation. ACR, for example, claims that its proposed voluntary certification process is "designed with heightened attention and respect for all manner of diversity in the broadest sense." While ACR's intent to ensure diversity in the mediation pool is laudable, the goal of ensuring a diverse mediator pool will not be achieved through point systems and testing. Unfortunately, such systems tend to reward those who have sufficient funds to pay for mediation training and advanced degrees.

Moreover, members of historically disadvantaged groups are unlikely to be able to satisfy experiential requirements necessary to obtain certification if they do not have the same ability to network as do members of the majority. While Florida's proposal moves in the right direction (currently, certification relies almost exclusively on the mediator obtaining academic degrees), its proposal could go further to protect diversity within the mediator pool.

In addition, the hours-and-point-centered plans might exclude a number of mediators who would otherwise satisfy the existing view of what constitutes a quality mediator. For example, imagine a man who began his mediation career 20 years ago when there was little formal mediation training available. He mediated frequently for 15 years and then became a professional mediator trainer. He would not qualify for the certification ACR proposed because he has insufficient training and cannot satisfy the experience requirement. While he could satisfy the 500-hour lifetime experience requirement, he failed to document his mediations.

Or imagine an attorney who graduated from law school five years ago. She took mediation during law school (Does a law school course satisfy the training requirement?) and is now affiliated with a local law firm. In an effort to put herself in a position to become a professional mediator, she volunteers once a month at small claims court and as a federal and state settlement-week mediator. Like the hypothetical older male mediator, she may not satisfy the training requirement and does not satisfy the experience requirement. We could imagine a variety of mediators who could not qualify under ACR's proposed rules but who would certainly satisfy the definition of a "quality mediator."

Adding holistic review One way of ensuring (at least during the period where the mediation community moves toward certification) that quality mediators are capable of obtaining certification would be to maintain existing hour-or-point requirements, but to allow a committee at ACR or another organization to engage in an additional holistic review of an applicant's portfolio. Holistic review, where a committee could deviate from the rigid standards in appropriate cases, might be more successful in protecting a diverse mediator pool and ensuring that mediators who have considerable experience but lack formal training, or those who have considerable training but lack experience, may nevertheless receive certification. While certification programs may be inevitable, they should not undermine diversity nor preclude qualified mediators from continuing to practice their chosen profession.

Evaluating the written test In addition, ACR and the ABA should carefully consider the effectiveness of ACR's proposed written test. According to ACR, the proposed test is designed to test 11 areas of knowledge including communication; conflict theory; content management and resources; cultural diversity; ethics; history of mediation; models, strategies and styles; negotiation; process structure; role of third party; and systems and group dynamics. While ACR contemplates that the written test would have to be carefully written and evaluated before it would be promulgated, and that a mediator could engage in self-study to pass the test, there may be little correlation between a mediator's score on the test and whether she is a quality mediator.

Although I hesitate to supply an anecdote to support a point, I recall attending an ABA Section on Dispute Resolution meeting where the question of developing a written certification test for mediators was discussed. After a sample question was put on an overhead, the audience debated the correct answer to the question for more than 30 minutes. While one anecdote does not prove the difficulty of creating an effective testing instrument, it does suggest that the varying backgrounds of mediators, together with their varied approaches to different types of mediation, would make it quite difficult to draft a meaningful test that would also be fair to potential test takers.

Certifying the trainers Finally, it may be that the current certification movement is focusing on the wrong audience. To ensure quality mediators, it would seem sensible to focus on those entities training the mediators rather than on the mediators alone. Because training appears to be a major component of all certification proposals, if training can be correlated with quality mediation, evaluation of existing training programs, with a focus on ensuring quality in those programs, makes sense. Moreover, because the target audience is much smaller, it might be considerably less expensive to put a trainer certification into place.

The ABA Section on Dispute Resolution clearly contemplated this possibility when it created a task force to address this issue. This task force completed a draft report in October 2002. [http://www.abanet.org/dispute/taksforce_report_2003.pdf] Among other things, the report recommended that the task force develop "model standards for mediator preparation programs [and] outline one or more model systems of mediator credentialing to recommend to states or to the field, focusing initially on the accreditation of mediator preparation programs." Since ACR's proposal on mediator certification came out, however, the ABA appears to have abandoned the effort to credential training entities. Because quality mediators are more likely to come out of reputable training institutions, adding trainer certification to the focus of current certification plans would be an excellent idea.

Recommendations While certification, correctly structured, could provide benefits to the mediation field by protecting the public, promoting mediation, increasing the likelihood that some mediators may have more productive careers and reducing court congestion, providing certification through points accumulation and written testing is problematic. Moreover, even though the current certification plans are voluntary, the ACR-ABA plan is to explore creation of a national mediator certification program. If certification becomes widespread, it seems likely that certification will be viewed as an essential characteristic of a mediator and that mediators who choose not to pursue certification or who do not meet the proposed standards will not be able to maintain a viable practice.

In an effort to preserve diversity within the mediation field and to avoid precluding qualified mediators from obtaining certification, the national mediator certification effort should add a holistic review to the certification process for mediator applicants whose background strongly suggests that they could be quality mediators. Advocates of national mediator certification should also consider certifying mediator preparation programs. These efforts would be more consistent with the various articulated organizational goals and would be more equitable to existing and future mediators. At the same time, this refocusing might provide a more useful credential for mediators as well as helpful information to consumers that they might utilize when selecting a mediator.

———

At this time, there seem to be no easy answers to the questions regarding mediator immunity or minimal mediator qualifications. At present, wide variations exist among jurisdictions. Future changes are highly likely. Some critics of immunity desire some assurance of mediator quality (and formal qualifications) in return for a degree of mediator immunity. Is this a desirable tradeoff?

Chapter 8

COMMON USES OF MEDIATION

A. DIVORCE MEDIATION

1. THE NATURE OF DIVORCE MEDIATION

A variety of disputes relating to divorce are increasingly resolved not by litigation but, instead, by mediation. It is now common to mediate matters regarding child custody, property division, alimony, and other disputes arising from divorce. The use of divorce mediation is growing and raises numerous questions about its supply and quality.

In many jurisdictions divorce mediation is voluntary and requires the agreement of both spouses. Alternatively, divorce mediation can be offered as part of a required, court mandated process. (*See, e.g.*, CAL. FAM. CODE § 3170 (Supp. 2001) (requiring the court to order mediation where custody or visitation issues are contested).) Numerous states have legislation that authorizes courts to order divorcing parties to mediate. (*See, e.g.*, LA. REV. STAT. ANN. § 9:332 (Supp. 2000) (allowing court ordered mediation to address custody issues); OR. REV. STAT. § 107.765 (1999) (permitting court to mandate mediation in disputes regarding child custody or visitation).) California has had considerable experience with mandatory family mediation. (*See, e.g.*, Deis, 1985.)

Divorce mediation is increasingly popular without mandatory court order. "Spouses whose marriages have fallen into a state of irreparable disrepair seek increasingly to dissolve them in a nonadversarial setting." (*Barbour v. Barbour*, 505 A.2d 1217, 1220 (Vt. 1986).) Divorcing parties frequently seek the services of a mediator to attempt to avoid the perceived acrimony, delay and expense of a drawn-out judicial resolution of their differences. While there are those who contend that divorce mediation is less successful than advertised, (*see Divorce Mediation Critics, infra*), there is little doubt that the use of mediation to resolve a variety of issues common to divorce is on the rise.

The provision of divorce mediation comes in various forms. First, the mediator may be a lawyer who supplies mediation services as well as being licensed to practice law. Alternatively, the mediator may be a non-lawyer professional such as a social worker, psychologist, or marriage counselor. Another model of divorce mediation can involve a team approach with both a lawyer and a non-lawyer professional acting as co-mediators for the parties. As would be expected, the non-lawyers often stress the personal and emotional aspects of the conflict, and the lawyer-mediator may focus on more pragmatic factual and legal issues. While it is difficult to generalize, the mediation process requires multiple conferences with the mediator. The routine case calls for weekly sessions that may last up to two hours each. (Blades, 1985, at 37, 39, 63.)

H. Jay Folberg, Divorce Mediation: A Workable Alternative, *from* ABA, Alternative Means of Family Dispute Resolution 12, 13–17, 41 (Howard Davidson et al. eds., 1982) *

Divorce mediation is defined here as a non-therapeutic process by which the parties together, with the assistance of a neutral resource person or persons, attempt to systematically isolate points of agreement and disagreement, explore alternatives and consider compromises for the purpose of reaching a consensual settlement of issues relating to their divorce or separation. Mediation is a process of conflict resolution and management that gives back to the parties the responsibility for making their own decisions about their own lives. It is usually conducted in private without the presence of the parties' attorneys. It has identifiable stages and divisible tasks, but no universal pattern.

In order to better distinguish and isolate mediation from other interventions, we might look at what it is not. It is not . . . a therapeutic process. . . . It is not focused on insight to personal conflict or in changing historically set personality patterns. It is much more an interactive process than an interpsychic one. Mediation is task-directed and goal-oriented. It looks at resolution and results between the parties rather than the internalized causes of conflict behavior. It discourages dependence on the professional provider rather than promoting it. Though some approaches to therapy can make similar claims, therapy in any mode is a form of treatment, which mediation is not.

Mediation is not arbitration. In arbitration, the parties authorize a neutral third person or persons to *decide* upon a binding resolution of the issues. The process used in arbitration is adjudicatory, but is typically less formal than that utilized in court and is usually conducted in private. Other than its informality and privacy, arbitration is much like the judicial process, except the "judge" is chosen or agreed upon by the parties and derives his or her authority from the agreement to arbitrate. In mediation the parties may choose the mediator, but do not authorize the mediator to make the decisions for them. . . .

Mediation is not the same as traditional negotiation of divorce disputes. Negotiation is generally a "sounding out" process to aid dispute resolutions but is not accomplished through any established framework and may be pursued through representatives, most often attorneys. Negotiation does not normally utilize a neutral resource person and is premised on an adversary model. Private negotiation may, however, precede mediation, follow unsuccessful mediation, or in some settings go on simultaneously.

Mediation is not conciliation, though the two terms are often used interchangeably. The two can be distinguished by looking at their historical development and application to the field of family law. California first offered court-connected conciliation services in 1939. The initial focus of these services was on providing marriage counseling aimed at effecting a reconciliation of spouses. With the adoption of no-fault divorce and the increase in the divorce rate, the focus of conciliation has shifted from marriage counseling aimed at reconciling parties to separation counseling and evaluation services for

---

purposes of assisting the domestic relations judges in making child custody and visitation orders. Indeed, in California, where mandatory custody mediation is usually performed by conciliation personnel, the distinction between conciliation and mediation has become somewhat obfuscated. . . . Conciliation is by practice and tradition limited to personal issues of custody and parental relationships among family members. . . .

Divorce is both a legal event and part of a family process. It is a matter of the heart and of the law. The strong emotional forces accompanying the dissolution of an existing family relationship argue for more delicately wrought measures than could be provided in a court imposed solution. Mediation can educate the parties about each other's needs and provide a personalized model for dispute resolution, both now and in the future should circumstances change or differences arise. It can help them learn to work together, isolate the issues to be decided and see that through cooperation all can make positive gains.

*   *   *

Family mediation furthers the policy of minimum state intervention. . . . Parents should be presumed to have the capacity, authority and responsibility to determine and do what is best for their children as well as what is best for their entire family constellation, regardless of how it may be rearranged following divorce. Psychological theory, as well as constitutional considerations, argue for parental autonomy and family privacy when there is no direct evidence that the interests of children are jeopardized in the process. Parents should have the first opportunity to meet the needs of their children and continue the maintenance of family ties without state interference.

A policy that provides parents with the option of mediation to facilitate their own decision-making and encourages self-determination should enhance continuing family ties and reassert the dignity and importance of the family as a self-governing unit. One of the most noble functions of law is to serve as a model of what is expected. Family law and procedure, instead of providing a model, is too often used coercively to supplant family self-determination upon inadequate evidence that the personal and societal cost of such interventions are absolutely required.

*   *   *

Divorce mediation has been touted as a replacement for the adversary system and a way of making divorce less painful. Though it may serve as an alternative for those that choose to use it, it is neither a panacea that will create love where there is hate, nor will it totally eliminate the role of the adversary system in divorce. It may, however, reduce acrimony by promoting cooperation and it may lessen the burden of the courts in deciding many cases that can be diverted to less hostile and costly procedures. Divorce mediation does appear to be a rational alternative attracting considerable interest. It is still in its infancy in the United States and, therefore, along with its promises, it has raised substantial issues. The resolution of these issues will require additional empirical research, experience and dialogue.

NOTES

1. Notice the policy of privatization that underlies Professor Folberg's position. He contends that mediation of family disputes is essentially a private matter. Is this true? Aren't there major public policy issues concerning property division, child custody, visitation and other divorce matters? Should we leave all such matters exclusively to a privatized mediation process? In the so-called "legal model" of divorce mediation, completed mediated agreements must be approved by the court. Does this requirement provide enough in the way of state involvement to avoid public policy objections to privatized dispute resolution?

2. Divorce conciliation, often the process of trying to reconcile the parties to their marriage, differs from mediation, the process of achieving a divorce agreement with minimal hostility and cost. Non-lawyer professionals usually supply divorce conciliation services.

3. Much of the interest in divorce mediation is based upon the supposed abuses of using litigation to process divorce disputes. The stereotypical divorce litigator has suffered numerous insults in comparison to those involved in the supply of mediation. Yet, are the prevailing attitudes toward the divorce lawyer fair? Consider the comments of Professor Clark:

> [W]riting on mediation take[s] as [a] starting point the familiar cliches about the iniquities of the "adversary process" and of lawyers, who are assumed to devote their energies to stirring up hostility in their clients and to provoking litigation when their clients would be better served by compromising their claims. The continued currency of these cliches is puzzling in view of the well established fact that even before the advent of mediation a very large proportion of divorce cases were uncontested, the function of the courts in such cases being merely to approve arrangements already worked out by the parties and their lawyers. The stereotype of the rashly aggressive divorce lawyer who litigates every case in disregard of the . . . interests of his clients . . . bears little resemblance to one's experience with the practicing divorce bar. [Clark, 1988, at 580.]

4. Divorce mediation, like divorce litigation, can cover a number of different issues such as property division and child custody. It is possible that the parties to divorce may negotiate solutions of some issues and then need to mediate only one or two remaining issues. Child custody issues are thought to be especially appropriate for mediation. (*See* Folberg, 1985 (stressing advantages of divorce mediation as a tool to educate parties and a means to create a self-governing family unit).)

5. With the increase of interest in and use of family mediation, standards of conduct were needed. The American Bar Association Section on Family Law and the Association of Family and Conciliation Courts led a drafting effort that resulted in the 1984 *Standards of Practice for Lawyer Mediators in Family Law Disputes*. At the time, some thought that the role of mediator was inconsistent with lawyers' professional responsibilities, and the 1984 Standards helped define how lawyers could be family mediators while staying within the professional guidelines for attorneys. In the following decade, family mediation grew rapidly. Beginning in the mid-1990s, the standards were revisited in a multi-year collaborative effort to redefine the role of family mediation. Representatives of family mediation organizations convened as the "Model Standards Symposium." In 2000, they issued the *Model Standards of Practice for Family and Divorce Mediation.* The Standards cover such issues as domestic violence and child abuse, the mediator's role in ensuring that the agreement serves the best interest of the child, and the special training and experience that is appropriate for family mediation. The Standards are available at http://www.afccnet.org/resources/resources_model_mediation.asp, and are reprinted in Appendix F.

6. The ABA Divorce Mediation Standards of Practice contemplate that a successful mediation will end with a mutually acceptable agreement following largely cooperative negotiations. The mediator will urge each party to use his or her own advisory attorney to evaluate the fairness of any contemplated agreements. This type of process usually ends with a court approving the mediated agreement and, accordingly, has been labeled a "legal model" of divorce mediation. (*See, e.g.,* Schwebel et al., 1994.)

7. Other models of divorce mediation exist. One model focuses on providing therapy to the mediating parties in order to allow them to participate effectively in the divorce mediation process. This type of approach, sometimes called a "therapeutic model," requires an active mediator role to alleviate the causes of impasse. (*See* Schwebel et al., 1993.) This type of mediation requires a mediator trained in mental health and de-emphasizes the role of attorneys. Children may be involved in the mediation sessions. This model usually focuses on issues relating to children and is seldom used for monetary disputes such as property division.

8. Parties without an attorney to represent them or review the provisions of their agreement pose ethical challenges in mediation. Standard VI of the *Model Standards of Practice for Family and Divorce Mediation* makes clear that mediators are not to provide legal advice and that they should recommend that each party obtain independent legal advice:

> Standard VI. A family mediator shall structure the mediation process so that the participants make decisions based on sufficient information and knowledge.
>
> A. The mediator should facilitate full and accurate disclosure and the acquisition and development of information during mediation so that the participants can make informed decisions. This may be accomplished by encouraging participants to consult appropriate experts.
>
> B. Consistent with standards of impartiality and preserving participant self-determination, a mediator may provide the participants with information that the mediator is qualified by training or experience to provide. The mediator shall not provide therapy or legal advice.
>
> C. The mediator should recommend that the participants obtain independent legal representation before concluding an agreement.

D. If the participants so desire, the mediator should allow attorneys, counsel or advocates for the participants to be present at the mediation sessions.

E. With the agreement of the participants, the mediator may document the participants' resolution of their dispute. The mediator should inform the participants that any agreement should be reviewed by an independent attorney before it is signed.

Do you think the mediator's recommendations will ensure attorney participation? Does the fact that the mediator may "document" the parties' agreement encourage them to view the mediator as providing legal services? Does the standard appropriately limit the mediator's role? What should a mediator do if a party fails to obtain independent review by an attorney?

MEDIATION CASE STUDY NO. 1: THE NORTON MEDIATION

A lawyer-mediator is assigned to mediate the pending divorce dispute between Andrew and Sarah Norton. At the session Sarah shows up with an attorney and Andrew arrives without counsel. The mediator specifically sets a rule that there be no interruptions and requests each side to acknowledge that the mediation sessions be confidential. Sarah's attorney and Andrew respond affirmatively. After a 20-minute summary of the mediation process and a statement that each party can use or consult an attorney, the mediator asks that Andrew and Sarah summarize their own positions in the dispute. The mediator requests that Andrew begin.

Andrew: It's too bad but our 11-year marriage is over. We simply have nothing in common any longer except our children, Becky, age 11, and Ben, age 9. I would like to reach some kind of a fair split on our property. Our assets consist of a home (assessed value of $300,000; $200,000 owed on a 30-year mortgage with 23 years remaining), $5,500 in Nike stock, $7,500 in savings, $10,000 in personal property, and a $500,000 whole life insurance policy. I've already moved out, leaving Sarah and the kids in the house. I really miss the house for entertaining. It's not fair that the man always loses the house in a divorce.

My annual income is $70,000 as an engineer with Index, Inc., a maker of engineering work stations. I've had the same job assignment for seven years and, at my present age of 41, am unlikely to get an appreciable raise or new major responsibilities. I'm a high paid grunt.

I really miss the kids. I don't see why I shouldn't have custody over at least Ben. Ben is a potential major league baseball player — a natural — and I played second base for Stanford in college. I can teach Ben a great deal about baseball. I already have helped his fielding.

Sarah: Andrew, you sound like a saint. We'd never know that Sally has moved into your apartment. Sally is Andrew's 24-year-old live-in lover. She is also a very bad influence on the kids. She spends hours designing clothes for Becky whenever Becky visits Andrew and it is affecting the way Becky relates to me. Last weekend the kids stayed with Andrew who had, as usual, Sally "visiting." The next night Becky asked "why I couldn't design her clothes" and refused when I tried to read her a bedtime story. Sally has caused a rift between Sarah and me. I don't want the kids to stay with Andrew if Sally is around. Andrew has a right to see them but Sally does not.

Sarah's Attorney: Sarah, I'll take it from here.

Mediator: Please proceed.

Sarah's Attorney: Sarah deserves the house because it is in the best interests of the children to continue a stable home environment while their parents divorce. The court will give Sarah the house. The court will keep Sally away from the kids. It is in the best interests of the kids that their father not be given the house and that they not spend time with their father's lover.

Andrew: That's bull_____.

Mediator: Please, we've agreed not to interrupt.

Andrew: I'm sorry but it's hard to keep quiet when there are lies being told about me and about my fiancée Sally.

Sarah: Oh come off it Andrew. Why would you want to marry someone half your age?

Andrew: At least she's still alive.

Mediator: All right. I think we've had a productive opening with each side having an opportunity to state their case. Now let's caucus. Andrew, would you mind going to the room down the hall while I meet with Sarah and her attorney?

[*Exit Andrew*]

Caucus #1: Sarah: Andrew lied about his assets. We also own Andrew's retirement plan. He's got about $210,000 worth of Nike stock in the plan.

Mediator: Is that right? Are there any other marital assets that have not been disclosed?

Sarah's Attorney: Under our state's law, Sarah is entitled to one-half of her spouse's pension. Right now, that would be about $105,000.

Mediator: Let's discuss custody. Would Andrew be a good custodial parent?

Sarah: No way. I would not stand for Andrew getting custody of either of our children. That would just be turning the kids over to Sally. Andrew's a workaholic who is never home before seven or eight in the evening.

Mediator: He has a right to see his kids. What do you want to get out of this dispute?

Sarah: I want the house, custody of the kids, and half of our assets. I also want to continue my education. I've four semesters left on my B.A. degree at State U. I dropped out to raise our children and need $5,500 per year for tuition and books to continue the progress I've made this term.

Sarah's Attorney: The school expenses are non-negotiable.

Mediator: Thanks. What can I take to offer Andrew?

Sarah's Attorney: Child custody to Sarah, $11,000 for two more years of school, a $100,000 share in the retirement plan, full title to the family home, and one-half interest in their life insurance and personal property. I also want Andrew to agree not to let Sally interact with Becky when he has visitation rights.

Mediator: I'll pass this on to Andrew.

Caucus #2: [mediator details Sarah's offer]

Andrew: I can't believe it. What else could she possibly want?

Mediator: Have you thought about joint custody of the kids?

Andrew: Well, maybe.

Mediator: Would you be interested? That would be a win-win way to avoid either of you having sole custody.

Andrew: Let's go for it. I love my kids and could spend quality time with them.

Mediator: Would your job permit the degree of time it would take in those periods in which you would have the children?

Andrew: Yes. I could change that.

Mediator: What about Sally? Sarah seems concerned about Sally's influence on Becky and Becky's affection for Sally.

Andrew: I want to seal a deal here and am willing to give ground on this issue. I can talk to Sally and have her stay at her place on those nights I have the kids.

Mediator: That's helpful. What about after you and Sally are married? How will Sarah's demand be met then?

Andrew: Well, we haven't set a date yet. I think that's two or three years down the road and by then Becky will be 14 years old and much less impressionable.

Mediator: Good point. What about Sarah's monetary demands? You should consult an attorney regarding the legal issues relevant to them.

Andrew: I talked to our house counsel before today's session and have a handle on the issues here. I am willing to give Sarah one-half of everything except our house. My uncle left me that house during our first year of marriage. It's my house. Sarah can live in it with the kids until they grow up but then it reverts to me. She should pay a reasonable rent while she's there, also, at least $800 per month.

Mediator: But these are your kids living with her in the house. Shouldn't you pay for some of their living expenses, including rent?

Andrew: Yeah, I guess. Please pass all this on to Sarah.

Mediator: O.K., I'll be back.

Caucus #3: [mediator relates Andrew's demands to Sarah]

Sarah's Attorney: Sarah, the house is essentially one-half yours. Don't give it away without getting something in return.

Sarah: I want sole custody. That's the only way I can keep Sally from stealing Becky's affection from me.

Mediator: Will you have the time for sole custody if you are in school?

Sarah's Attorney: Sure she will. We will give Andrew all he wants except Sarah gets sole custody. Andrew's visitation rights are to be one full weekend per month. He may use the house in any way but must leave it clean at the end of the weekend. Sally is not to visit the house during this period.

Sarah: This sounds good.

Mediator: All right. I will pass this on to Andrew.

Caucus #4: [mediator restates Sarah's offer]

Andrew: I'll take it. I accept.

Mediator: Are you sure the visitation scheme is realistic? What about Sally? Won't she want to stay with you?

Andrew: Sally's job takes her away at least one full week a month. We will schedule my visits to my house to coincide with Sally's business travel.

Mediator: Anything else?

Andrew: I like this. I'm willing to forego my interest in the house to strike this deal.

Mediator: Are you sure?

Andrew: Let's do it.

Mediator: You and Sarah will need to sign an agreement on each of these points of agreement. Have you considered retaining counsel to help draft and review your agreement?

Andrew: Yes, good idea. I'll talk to our house counsel before I sign.

Mediator: [The mediator meets with both parties again. He lists the points of agreement, asks if these items are agreeable and urges each party to sign an agreement.]

NOTES

1. This is obviously not the model for a perfect mediation. Critique this mediation. First, analyze the performance of the mediator. List the positive moves made by the mediator during the session. Explain why you feel these developments constituted good mediation practice. List the mediator's negative actions and be prepared to describe why such conduct was counter-productive.

2. Analyze the quality of representation of Sarah's attorney. If this were a negotiation without a mediator, would this have been an acceptable job by counsel? Should the attorney act any differently with the mediator present? Should the attorney always follow the mediator's lead?

3. Focus on Andrew and his lack of attorney representation. Has the mediator handled this aspect of the mediation well? Was it appropriate to let Andrew begin and to caucus first with Sarah and her attorney? Was the mediator protective of Andrew? Too protective? Less protective than adequate? Does the mediation end appropriately from an attorney representation perspective?

4. What would you have done as mediator to deal with the problem of Sally's influence on Becky? Is it an option to let Sarah and Andrew work this issue out between themselves? Is the mediator responsible for initiating resolution of all the rough issues? What about the house? Is the agreement relating to the house likely to work well and last? What would you have done, as mediator, to deal with this question?

5. Focus on the stages of this mediation. Did the opening segment achieve the results necessary to get the mediation off to a proper start? Did the mediator handle the end of the mediation well?

Did the mediator's actions comply with the mediator's obligations under Standard VIII of the *Model Standards of Practice for Family and Divorce Mediation*?

> Standard VIII. A family mediator shall assist participants in determining how to promote the best interests of children.
>
> A. The mediator should encourage the participants to explore the range of options available for separation or post divorce parenting arrangements and their respective costs and benefits. Referral to a specialist in child development may be appropriate for these purposes. The topics for discussion may include, among others:
>
> 1. information about community resources and programs that can help the participants and their children cope with the consequences of family reorganization and family violence;
>
> 2. problems that continuing conflict creates for children's development and what steps might be taken to ameliorate the effects of conflict on the children;
>
> 3. development of a parenting plan that covers the children's physical residence and decision-making responsibilities for the children, with appropriate levels of detail as agreed to by the participants;
>
> 4. the possible need to revise parenting plans as the developmental needs of the children evolve over time; and
>
> 5. encouragement to the participants to develop appropriate dispute resolution mechanisms to facilitate future revisions of the parenting plan.

* * *

BENNETT v. BENNETT
587 A.2d 463 (Me. 1991)

[Lloyd and Colleen Bennett participated in a court ordered mediation following the filing of an action for divorce. The parties reached agreement at the mediation but Colleen refused to sign the mediated agreement. The trial court denied Lloyd's motion to require Colleen to sign the mediation agreement and submit it to the court for approval. Lloyd appealed.]

Lloyd first contends that the provisions of 19 M.R.S.A. § 665 (Supp. 1990) required the trial court to grant his motion to compel Colleen to sign and submit to the court the alleged agreement of the parties. We disagree. Section 665 provides:

> [t]he court may, in any case under this subchapter, at any time refer the parties to mediation on any issues. *Any agreement reached by the parties through mediation on any issues shall be reduced to writing, signed by the parties and presented to the court for approval as a court order.* When agreement through mediation is not reached on any issue the court must determine that the parties made a good faith effort to mediate the issue before proceeding with a hearing. If the court finds that either party failed to make a good faith effort to mediate, the court may order the parties to submit to mediation, may dismiss the action or any part of the action, may render a decision or judgment by default, may assess attorney's fees and costs or may impose any other sanction that is appropriate in the circumstances. [Emphasis added].

Section 665 allows the parties to a divorce action to attempt through mediation to reach an agreement on any of the issues presented by that action without the involvement of the court in the mediation process. The provisions in section 665 governing the requirements of an agreement reached through mediation explicitly assure the court of the parties' consent to and willingness to be bound by the terms of their agreement. Absent such a signed, written agreement being submitted to it, the court makes a determination of the issues presented by an action for divorce based on the evidence adduced by the parties at the time of the trial of that action.

Lloyd did not contend before the trial court, nor does he here, that Colleen failed to make a good faith effort to mediate, thereby engaging the authority provided in section 665 for the court to impose such sanctions as the court in its discretion deems appropriate in the circumstances. His contention is that because Colleen did not sign the alleged mediated agreement between the parties, section 665 mandates that the court order Colleen to sign the document and submit it to the court for its approval. To read such a mandate into the language of section 665 would of necessity require the trial court to engage in the time-consuming process of exploring what transpired between the parties during the course of the mediation in order to determine if they had reached any agreement and, if so, the actual terms of that agreement. Clearly, this is contrary to and would undermine the basic policy of the mediation process that parties be encouraged to arrive at a settlement of disputed issues without the intervention of the court. Accordingly, the trial court properly denied Lloyd's motion requesting that the court order Colleen to sign and submit to the court for its approval the alleged agreement of the parties.

* * *

Judgment affirmed.

NOTES

1. Should a court ever force a party to a mediation to agree to terms? How would such coercive action by a judicial figure fit into the theory of mediation? For a similar case, see *Rivkin v. Rivkin*, 449 N.W.2d 685 (Mich. Ct. App. 1989) (reversing trial court order that had based property settlement on an unsigned mediation "agreement").

2. Note that in *Bennett* the parties reached agreement at the mediation but one side failed to sign the written agreement. Why would such an event happen? What should a mediator do when one side orally agrees to terms but later refuses to sign? Should the mediator urge the parties to renew discussions? Should the mediator hold a joint session to learn why the agreement was not signed? Or should the mediator meet privately with the nonsigning party to find out why the mediation agreement is not agreeable?

3. One way to explain the *Bennett* case is to accept the uncertainty of unsigned "agreements." Mediation, like negotiation, is a process of give and take that, if successful, leads to a signed contract. A successful mediation requires a final contract. It is always possible that a party will tentatively "agree" and then have second thoughts and refuse to sign. In divorce mediation, a dispute process in which emotions are typically hot, the possibility of doubts about "agreement" is especially acute. What should a court do if, unlike the *Bennett* case, the parties *sign* a fully mediated agreement and then later urge the trial court to not approve the mediated settlement? In *Matter of Marriage of Ames*, 860 S.W.2d 590 (Tex. Ct. App. 1993), the parties were ordered to mediation. They reached and signed an agreement on property division. Five days after signing the mediated property division the husband wrote to his attorney seeking to withdraw his consent from the agreement. The trial court entered a divorce and property settlement decree that followed the terms of the mediated agreement and the court of appeals affirmed:

> [Husband] contends that the trial court erred in entering its decree of divorce on the basis of the settlement agreement because he had repudiated the agreement. We disagree. In its order of mediation, the trial court stated that "[t]his case is appropriate for mediation pursuant to Tex. Civ. Prac. & Rem. Code §§ 154.001 *et seq.*" Chapter 154 of the Texas Civil Practice and Remedies Code is entitled "Alternative Dispute Resolution Procedures." Section 154.071(a) states: "If the parties reach a settlement and execute a written agreement disposing of the dispute, the agreement is enforceable in the same manner as any other written contract." We interpret this statute to mean, *inter alia*, that a party who has reached a settlement agreement disposing of a dispute through alternative dispute resolution procedures may not unilaterally repudiate the agreement.
>
> While parties may be compelled by a court to participate in mediation, "[a] mediator may not impose his own judgment on the issues for that of the parties." Put another way, a court can compel disputants to sit down with each other but it cannot force them to peaceably resolve their differences. *Decker v. Lindsay*, 824 S.W.2d 247, 250 (Tex. App. 1992). The job of a mediator is simply to facilitate communication

between parties and thereby encourage reconciliation, settlement and understanding among them. Hopefully, mediation will assist the parties in reaching a voluntary agreement that will serve to resolve their dispute and avoid the need for traditional litigation.

If voluntary agreements reached through mediation were non-binding, many positive efforts to amicably settle differences would be for naught. If parties were free to repudiate their agreements, disputes would not be finally resolved and traditional litigation would recur. In order to effect the purposes of mediation and other alternative dispute resolution mechanisms, settlement agreements must be treated with the same dignity and respect accorded other contracts reached after arm's length negotiations. Again, no party to a dispute can be forced to settle the conflict outside of court; but if a voluntary agreement that disposes of the dispute is reached, the parties should be required to honor the agreement. [860 S.W.2d at 591-92.]

4. The *Ames* decision arguably reflects a pro-mediation attitude by forcing the parties to live up to their mediated bargain. Yet, does it promote mediation to force parties to honor agreements they oppose? In *Cary v. Cary*, 894 S.W.2d 111 (Tex. App. 1995), the court of appeals rejected the *Ames* reasoning. The court reasoned that although a mediated agreement was a contract, a trial court should not enter "a valid consent judgment unless at the time of rendition, all parties consent to the agreement underlying the judgment" and cited Texas legislation allowing divorcing parties to repudiate written agreements regarding property prior to the divorce decree:

Were we to hold otherwise, we would transform mediation into binding arbitration. The Legislature has crafted a distinction between the two procedures and their effects, which we are not authorized to alter. We reject husband's argument that our holding will make mediation meaningless. Mediation will continue to provide an efficient method of dispute resolution, and agreements reached thereby will continue to be enforceable *between* the parties. We merely decline to elevate mediation to something other than the Legislature declared by statute.

Husband is not totally bereft. He retains a cause of action for breach of contract, which may be tried contemporaneously with his divorce suit. His remedies may include both contract damages and specific performance, where applicable. [894 S.W.2d at 113.]

Which approach is preferable, *Ames* (mediated result is final and should be accepted by the court) or *Cary* (parties may repudiate their mediated contracts)? Will the possibility of damages for breach of the mediation contract deter parties from breach? In hotly contested divorce proceedings, any agreements between the disputants are inherently fragile. Does this fragility support *Ames* or *Cary*? Consider *Wyskowski v. Wyskowski*, 536 N.W.2d 603 (Mich. Ct. App. 1995) (court approves judgment of divorce based upon signed mediation agreement and rejects argument of wife who opposed entry of judgment because mediation signatures had not been notarized).

5. Divorce mediation in California has been both controversial and plentiful. California mandates mediation if child custody or visitation is contested by divorcing parties. (CAL. FAM. CODE § 3170 (1994).) Each county is mandated to make a mediator available. Mediators must meet minimum qualifications. Lawyers may not mediate unless they have a master's degree in social work, psychology or counseling. While the mediation sessions are confidential and held in private, the mediator is required to make a visitation or custody evaluation recommendation to the court if the disputants are unable to reach agreement. Counties may choose not to require the report. Some criticize the report as compromising the mediation process and preventing confidential treatment of statements made during mediation.

In *McLaughlin v. Superior Court for San Mateo County*, 140 Cal. App. 3d 473 (1983), the court held that a county violated due process if it required a mediation report but disallowed cross-examination of the mediator. The plaintiff sought to restrain the trial court from ordering a mandatory mediation without a court order either excluding the mediator's report or permitting the right to cross-examine the mediator at trial if a report was issued. The county had required the submission of the mediator's report to the judge if agreement on child custody was not reached. A subsequent case took the position that *McLaughlin* should only apply if the mediator is directly employed by the court. (*Ohmer v. Superior Court of California, Co. of Los Angeles*, 148 Cal. App. 3d 661 (1983).)

6. *Financing Institutionalized Divorce Mediation*: There are various ways to finance divorce mediation. One way is to order the parties to pay the mediator's fee. Where the parties cannot afford the mediation fee, some provision can be made to offer free mediation services. Other very different approaches are to use court staff to provide mediation services to some couples without a fee or to use a volunteer cohort of mediators who charge below market fees. Other courts invest taxpayer funds in mediation by educating parties about the mediation process or having court personnel screen cases for diversion to mediation. For a thorough description of the serious problems associated with inadequate funding of institutionalized mediation programs, see Carol J. King, *Burdening Access to Justice: The Cost of Divorce Mediation on the Cheap*, 73 ST. JOHNS L. REV. 375 (1999) (recommending publicly funded divorce mediation to guarantee access to equal justice).

2. DIVORCE MEDIATION CRITICS

Despite the popularity of divorce mediation, numerous critics have voiced objections to both mandatory divorce mediation and voluntary, privately supplied divorce mediation. The criticisms attack divorce mediation in a variety of ways. Many of these critics are leaders of the women's movement who contend that women will achieve worse results in mediation than in court. They argue that women lack the power to fare as well in the contentious negotiating atmosphere of divorce mediation. In addition, they assert that formal legal rights, which are often very beneficial to divorcing women, are sacrificed in mediation but protected in court. Furthermore, they prefer the certainty and publicity that the legal system offers in contrast to the secret and sometimes inconsistent outcomes that can occur in mediation. These arguments raise legitimate concerns that merit consideration as you read the following materials.

LAURIE WOODS, MEDIATION: A BACKLASH TO WOMEN'S PROGRESS ON FAMILY LAW ISSUES, 19 Clearinghouse Rev. 431, 431–33, 435–36 (1985) [*]

Women have made significant advances in the past few years in their efforts to secure legal recognition of their work and their rights in the family. These advances have occurred on both the state and the federal level, in both the courts and the legislatures.

* * *

Women's advocates have made many gains over the years, but they feel that, with the advent of the growing trend in this country to use mediation in family law disputes, their gains may be dissipated. Mediation seeks to privatize family law problems once again, denying women the opportunity to enforce and consolidate their victories and to empower themselves further through the development of new rights in the legislatures and the courts.

* * *

Because of increased arrests and pro se access to civil courts, prosecutors, judges and courts are faced with the large number of domestic violence cases that formerly were diverted from the courts. Prosecutors, judges and court administrators seek to use mediation both because of their belief that domestic violence is a private matter and not a crime, and because they seek to reduce their caseloads. Rather than responding to such cases, which would ultimately reduce the number of cases by reducing recidivism, the courts look to mediation to divert the cases from their calendars. However, mediation is both inappropriate and ineffective. Mediation not only fails to protect battered women, but it is dangerous because it functions to perpetuate the violence. This diversion to mediation signals to the victim and the batterer that this type of violence is not a crime. The batterer is not required to admit his guilt, and he escapes the stigma of being a criminal. Furthermore, mediation offers no incentive for the abuser to cease his violence. Diversion to mediation thus permits and encourages further violence, encourages privatization of the violence, and ignores the fact that battery is permitted to exist because the legal system condones it.

* * *

Mediation can be effective if and only if (1) the issue is capable of resolution through modification of perceptions, attitudes and/or behavior; (2) relative parity of power exists between the parties; (3) there is no need for punishment, deterrence or redress; and (4) the parties are capable of entering into and carrying out an agreement.

---

* * *

In divorce or family law mediation there is no process by which the dependent spouse can verify the extent of the assets or attempt to discover hidden assets of the propertied spouse. A full, honest and forthright accounting of marital assets by a self-interested spouse is unlikely. The legal system offers various means of obtaining this disclosure, including depositions, subpoenaing of records and coercive sanctions for noncompliance or false representations. Similarly, dissipation of assets may go unnoticed and unaccounted for in the mediation process, while the legal system offers various safeguards. In mediation, the parties are not informed of their legal rights and have no rules or precedents to guide them as to what is equitable or reasonable under the circumstances. The parties deal directly with each other, without an independent advocate who can address the issues without the emotional involvement burdening the parties. Thus, the parties are susceptible to forfeiting rights out of guilt, domination, intimidation, lack of resources or coercion. Settlements may be agreed upon, but they may not be equitable or enforceable. Only those issues that both parties wish to discuss are settled. Not all issues are foreseen by the parties. There is no guarantee of confidentiality of communications made either to the mediator or in the mediation sessions. Accordingly, the parties may use statements made in mediation as admissions in a later court proceeding. In many jurisdictions, mediators make recommendations to the court but cannot be cross-examined with respect to their recommendations.

Mediation trivializes family law issues by relegating them to a lesser forum. It diminishes the public perception of the relative importance of laws addressing women's and children's rights in the family by placing these rights outside society's key institutional system of dispute resolution — the legal system — while continuing to allow corporate and other "important" matters to have unfettered access to that system. Loss of one's children and protection of one's physical safety should be considered too important to entrust to any other but the legal system.

Mediation is problematic regardless of whether the mediator is a lawyer or a nonlawyer. Lawyer mediators cannot represent either side, cannot exercise professional judgment, and, at best, can only offer "impartial legal advice." The dangers of lawyer mediation are that each party may assume that the lawyer-mediator is looking out for the individual party's interest and that every statement made by the lawyer-mediator is based on legal expertise. The American Bar Association Standards of Practice for Divorce Mediators would require the mediator, whether or not he or she is a lawyer, to recommend that each party seek independent legal representation during the process. This recognition of the need for independent counsel is implicit recognition of the fact that mediation is not and cannot be an alternative to legal representation.

A nonlawyer mediator may be able to define the points of agreement that are consuming the parties' attention at the moment, but it is unlikely that a nonlawyer could knowledgeably deal with all foreseeable contingencies such as the moving of the custodial spouse or the future unemployment of the paying spouse. A nonlawyer may not understand the legal, tax or public assistance effects and consequences of alternative compromises such as the form of custody agreed upon; how to valuate different forms of property, such as pension benefits, closed corporations and loss of inheritance; what constitutes marital and separate property; how to valuate appreciation of separate property through active or passive contributions of the nontitled spouse; and how to valuate nonmonetary contributions of the homemaker spouse. Lay mediation is, in the words of one commentator, "[a] self-determination process between two uninformed spouses guided by a neutral person unfamiliar with the legal rights of the parties, operating without standards or rules which may produce an unenforceable agreement."

NOTES

1. Most participants in divorce mediation are happy with the process. (*See generally* Pearson & Thoennes, 1989, at 19, 27; Pearson & Thoennes, 1984, at 505.)

The above studies are based upon questions put to mediation participants. Are there reasons to distrust such studies? Are parties in the best position to assess the success or failure of the process? Should the studies have asked others (e.g., lawyers who took part representing mediation parties, the mediators) their opinions?

2. How did mediation of spousal abuse or wife battering disputes develop? According to Lisa Lerman, such cases were regarded as "too trivial to deserve court attention" and placed in the dockets of community mediation programs for economic reasons. (Lerman, 1984, at 68–69.) The growth of spousal abuse mediation reflects the cost of criminal prosecutions and the backlogs of both domestic relations and criminal courts. (*Id.*) Professor Lerman has articulated several criticisms of mediation of spousal abuse:

Mediation as a remedy for wife abuse is criticized for several different reasons. First, many critics disagree with mediators' assumptions about the nature and seriousness of family violence, about the role of the state in family life, and about the usefulness of formal legal action in stopping violence. Second, relying largely on experience with their own clients and on a limited amount of research, the critics believe that mediation is an ineffective remedy for abuse. Third, the goals of mediation — reaching an agreement, reconciling the parties, recognizing mutual responsibility for the problem, and removing abuse cases from the court system — are arguably incompatible with the law enforcement model's primary goal of stopping violence.

Fourth, many structural aspects of mediation are criticized as ill-suited to the problems presented by a wife abuser and his victim. These problems revolve around the summary nature of mediation, the lack of accountability, the failure to account for the parties' vastly unequal bargaining power, and the use of mediation to bar abused women from access to courts for enforceable protection from future violence or punishment of the abuser for past violence. Although mediation of wife abuse cases aids the justice system by disposing of a group of troublesome cases, this remedy may not be useful to protect victims.

Finally, critics of mediation point out that the agreements reached in abuse cases are woefully inadequate, not only because they have no legal force, but also because they fail to address the issue of violence, or treat the violence as caused at least in part by the victim. [*Id.* at 72.]

(*See also* Bethal & Singer, 1982; Gagnon, 1992 on the topic of mediating spousal abuse disputes.)

3. Assume that the criticisms of mediation of spousal abuse are valid. Does that mean that mediation should not be used to resolve such disputes? Will we curb spousal abuse if we leave disposition of such matters exclusively to the criminal courts, the civil tort system, and the injunctive powers of divorce court judges?

4. Professor Lerman suggests ways that mediators of spousal abuse may help to improve the process. These include focusing the hearing goals to stop violence and screening cases to refer the most violent matters immediately to criminal court. (Lerman, *supra*, at 100–101.) Lerman also advocates that the mediator use the following procedures at domestic violence mediation: begin the session by meeting privately with each party, thoroughly discuss past instances of violence, urge the disputants to use advocates, require the alleged abuser to take part in counseling prior to mediation, and keep open an option that no agreement be reached. Some of these suggestions run counter to the typical mediation. (*Id.* at 102-06.) Try to explain why each suggestion could be useful to improve domestic violence mediation.

TRINA GRILLO, THE MEDIATION ALTERNATIVE: PROCESS DANGERS FOR WOMEN, 100 Yale L.J. 1545 (1991)*

[P]eople vary greatly in the extent to which their sense of self is "relational" — that is, defined in terms of connection to others. If two parties are forced to engage with one another, and one has a more relational sense of self than the other, that party may feel compelled to maintain her connection with the other, even to her own detriment. For this reason, the party with the more relational sense of self will be at a disadvantage in a mediated negotiation. Several prominent researchers have suggested that, as a general rule, women have a more relational sense of self than do men, although there is little agreement on what the origin of this difference might be. Thus, rather than being a feminist alternative to the adversary system, mediation has the potential actively to harm women.

*   *   *

The introduction of mediation into family court processes was another part of the effort to make the adversary system fit the realities of divorce more closely. Mediators stepped into the increasingly uncertain legal world of

---

dissolution with a new process which minimized the role of principles and fault. Mediation appeared to provide the opportunity to bring the lessons of context and subjective experience to dissolution proceedings. In mediation, the parties' legal rights would not be central. Instead of relying solely on abstract principles and rules, parties and mediators could attend to the reality of complex relationships. Precedent, legal rules and a legalized formulation of the facts might be seen as irrelevant to the mediation process and an unnecessary constraint on the mediator. Individuals could be seen in relation to one another, and morality treated as "a question of responsibilities to particular people in particular contexts."

The informal law of the mediation setting requires that discussion of principles, blame, and rights, as these terms are used in the adversarial context, be deemphasized or avoided. Mediators use informal sanctions to encourage the parties to replace the rhetoric of fault, principles, and values with the rhetoric of compromise and relationship. For example, mediators typically suggest that the parties "eschew the language of individual rights in favor of the language of interdependent relationships." They orient the parties toward reasonableness and compromise, rather than moral vindication. The conflict may be styled as a personal quarrel, in which there is no right and wrong, but simply two different, and equally true or untrue, views of the world.

The reason for the lack of focus on values and principles in many models of mediation is, in part, simply practical. If the essence of mediation entails trading off interests and compromising, each person's interests are important, but which person violated societal values and why he did so, is not. To the extent that principles and faultfinding based on those principles enter into the discussion, reaching an agreement might be delayed or disrupted. Deemphasizing principles also might appear to be the sensible approach in a society that is increasingly pluralistic in terms of cultures, religions, and varieties of family structures. Where there are conflicting moral codes, as there often are when couples divorce, making the only standard for agreement be that it is accepted by both parties means that it will not be necessary for a third party to decide which moral code is superior.

Sometimes, however, all agreements are not equal. It may be important, from both a societal and an individual standpoint, to have an agreement that reflects cultural notions of justice and not merely one to which there has been mutual assent. Many see the courts as a place where they can obtain vindication and a ruling by a higher authority. It is also important in some situations for society to send a clear message as to how children are to be treated, what the obligations of ex-spouses are to each other and to their children, and what sort of behavior will not be tolerated. Because the mediation movement tends to regard negotiated settlements as morally superior to adjudication, these functions of adjudication may easily be overlooked.

*   *   *

Another criticism of the traditional adversary method of dispute resolution is that it does not provide a role for emotion. Decisions by adversarial parties are posited as rational, devoid of emotion, self-interested, and instrumental (result-oriented). Some proponents of mediation and other methods of alternative dispute resolution believe these characteristics should be retained in mediation to the extent they permit parties to serve their self-interests efficiently. Others have argued that mediation and other forms of alternative dispute resolution provide an opportunity to bring intuition and emotion into the legal process. This latter group of proponents points out that family conflicts in particular often involve a combination of emotional and legal complaints, so that the "real" issues are often obscured in the adversarial setting. Thus, "there may be a great need for an open-ended, unstructured process that permits the disputants to air their true sentiments."

Although mediation is claimed to be a setting in which feelings can be expressed, certain sentiments are often simply not welcome. In particular, expressions of anger are frequently overtly discouraged. This discouragement of anger sends a message that anger is unacceptable, terrifying and dangerous. For a person who has only recently found her anger, this can be a perilous message indeed. This suppression of anger poses a stark contrast to the image of mediation as a process which allows participants to express their emotions.

Women undergoing a divorce, especially ones from nondominant cultural groups, are particularly likely to be harmed by having their anger actively discouraged during the dissolution process. Women have been socialized not to express anger, and have often had their anger labelled "bad." A woman in the throes of divorce may for the first time in her life have found a voice for her anger. As her early, undifferentiated, and sometimes inchoate expressions of anger emerge, the anger may seem as overwhelming to her as to persons outside of it. And yet this anger may turn out to be the source of her energy, strength, and growth in the months and years ahead. An injunction from a person in power to suppress that anger because it is not sufficiently modulated may amount to nothing less than an act of violence.

* * *

In California, lawyers typically are excluded from mediation sessions, and the parties are required to speak for themselves, whether or not they wish to do so.[246] Some argue that exclusion of lawyers contributes to client empowerment. In evaluating whether their exclusion actually furthers client empowerment, it is useful to consider the reasons why a person engaged in a divorce might want the services of a lawyer. First, and most obviously, lawyers are hired for their expertise, particularly their expertise in protecting their clients' rights. Of equal importance, however, is the fact that lawyers

---

[246] CAL. CIV. CODE § 4607(d) (West 1983) provides in relevant part:

"The mediator shall have the authority to exclude counsel from participation in the mediation proceedings where, in the discretion of the mediator, exclusion of counsel is deemed by the mediator to be appropriate or necessary." . . .

Attorneys are normally excluded from mediation sessions in California. It is not until an agreement is reached by the parties that counsel become involved:

"Any agreement reached by the parties as a result of mediation shall be reported to counsel for the parties by the mediator on the day set for mediation or as soon thereafter as practical, but prior to its being reported to the court. . . ."

CAL. CIV. CODE § 4807(e) (West Supp. 1990).

are hired to provide a buffer, a layer of insulation, between the client and her spouse. Neither of these rationales for the presence of an attorney disappears in the context of mediation.

[Editor's note: These provisions have been repealed. A mediator's authority to exclude counsel is now codified at CAL. FAM. CODE § 3182.]

A lawyer who is excluded from the mediation sessions may be hampered in protecting her client's rights, particularly if custody is ultimately to be litigated in court. For example, privileged or irrelevant material, which the lawyer does not believe should be disclosed, may mistakenly be revealed in mediation. Once such privileged information is disclosed, it is often impossible to keep it out of a later court proceeding.

In states with an evidentiary privilege protecting mediation, a party would not be able to use in court any documents obtained in mediation. In many instances, however, he could obtain the documents in some other manner, once he knows of their existence. Moreover, even if the information is not introduced formally, it may nonetheless subtly influence the proceedings at a later date.

* * *

As discussed earlier, several feminist scholars have suggested that women have a more "relational" sense of self than do men. The most influential of these researchers, Carol Gilligan, describes two different, gendered modes of thought. The female mode is characterized by an "ethic of care" which emphasizes nurturance, connection with others, and contextual thinking. The male mode is characterized by an "ethic of justice" which emphasizes individualism, the use of rules to resolve moral dilemmas, and equality. Under Gilligan's view, the male mode leads one to strive for individualism and autonomy, while the female mode leads one to strive for connection with and caring for others. Some writers, seeing a positive virtue in the ethic of care, have applied Gilligan's work to the legal system. But her work has been criticized by others for its methodology, its conflation of biological sex with gender, and its failure to include race and class differences in its analysis.

* * *

Some commentators have identified mediation as a way to incorporate the ethic of care into the legal system and thereby modify the harshness of the adversary process. And, indeed, at first glance, mediation in the context of divorce might be seen as a way of bringing the woman-identified values of intimacy, nurturance, and care into a legal system that is concerned with the most fundamental aspects of women's and men's lives.

If mediation does not successfully introduce an ethic of care, however, but instead merely sells itself on that promise while delivering something coercive in its place, the consequences will be disastrous for a woman who embraces a relational sense of self. If she is easily persuaded to be cooperative, but her partner is not, she can only lose. If it is indeed her disposition to be caring and focused on relationships, and she has been rewarded for that focus and characterized as "unfeminine" when she departs from it, the language of relationship, caring, and cooperation will be appealing to her and make her vulnerable. Moreover, the intimation that she is not being cooperative and caring or that she is thinking of herself instead of thinking selflessly of the children can shatter her self-esteem and make her lose faith in herself. In short, in mediation, such a woman may be encouraged to repeat exactly those behaviors that have proven hazardous to her in the past.

* * *

It has been said that "[d]isputes are cultural events, evolving within a framework of rules about what is worth fighting for, what is the normal or moral way to fight, what kinds of wrongs warrant action, and what kinds of remedies are acceptable." The process by which a society resolves conflict is closely related to its social structure. Implicit in this choice is a message about what is respectable to do or want or say, what the obligations are of being a member of the society or of a particular group within it, and what it takes to be thought of as a good person leading a virtuous life. In the adversary system, it is acceptable to want to win. It is not only acceptable, but expected, that one will rely on a lawyer and advocate for oneself without looking out for the adversary. The judge, a third party obligated to be neutral and bound by certain formalities, bears the ultimate responsibility for deciding the outcome. To the extent that women are more likely than men to believe in communication as a mode of conflict resolution and to appreciate the importance of an adversary's interests, this system does not always suit their needs.

On the other hand, under a scheme of mediation, the standards of acceptable behavior and desires change fundamentally. Parties are to meet with each other, generally without their lawyers. They are encouraged to look at each other's needs and to reach a cooperative resolution based on compromise. Although there are few restrictions on her role in the process, the mediator bears no ultimate, formal responsibility for the outcome of the mediation. In sum, when mediation is the prototype for dispute resolution, the societal message is that a good person — a person following the rules — cooperates, communicates, and compromises.

The glories of cooperation, however, are easily exaggerated. If one party appreciates cooperation more than the other, the parties might compromise unequally. Moreover, the self-disclosure that cooperation requires, when imposed and not sought by the parties, may feel and be invasive. Thus, rather than representing a change in the system to accommodate the "feminine voice," in actuality, mandatory mediation overrides real women's voices saying that cooperation might, at least for the time being, be detrimental to their lives and the lives of their children. Under a system of forced mediation, women are made to feel selfish for wanting to assert their own interests based on their need to survive.

* * *

NOTES

1. *Divorce Mediation and Relational Contract Theory.* Conventional mediation theory supports mediation of disputes between parties with long-term relationships. The need to preserve the relationship is deemed bilateral and transcends the instant dispute. The mediator will likely stress each party's self-interest in preserving the relationship. In divorce mediation this reasoning may still hold even if the disputants' marital relationship has ended or is not reparable, because the continuing needs of children force a parenting relationship to continue. The Grillo excerpt theorizes that differences between men and women may produce a structural obstacle to women in divorce mediation — a woman's instincts to preserve "relationships" or be "caring" may be inconsistent with a man's instincts and, for that reason, women are disadvantaged in mediation. Is this thesis valid? If men are less "relational" or "caring," won't mediated agreements be difficult to achieve? Or does Grillo's "relational" thesis merely suggest that men engaged in divorce mediation will be more willing to exploit the natural female instincts to be relational? Assuming the validity of Grillo's position, is there anything a mediator can do to, in Grillo's terms, mitigate a woman's natural "vulnerability"? Shouldn't a mediator be able to prevent a woman from harming herself? Or is such a suggestion of greater mediator concern really inappropriate activism by the mediator who needs to be slavishly neutral?

2. *The Role of Lawyers and Law in Mediation.* What should be made of Grillo's argument that legal rights and lawyers should have a greater role in divorce mediation? One answer is to exclude attorneys during mediation but have the mediator urge the parties to meet with their own attorneys before signing any final agreement. This commonly used approach allows "legal" input into the mediation process and may provide that no party to mediation will unknowingly give up "legal rights." However, does this approach permit legal input too late in the process? If a party to a mediation has reached a tentative agreement, how effective is the lawyer, a late comer, who may counsel that signing a mutually acceptable property division agreement is against the client's legal interests?

Grillo's points are especially appropriate when mediation is made mandatory in divorce proceedings. Others criticize mandatory mediation programs for failing to use lawyers to protect their client's legal rights, and thereby creating an inherently unfair process. (*See, e.g.,* Bryan, 1992.) While some jurisdictions do mandate divorce mediation and prevent or minimize lawyer participation, not all states prohibit attorney participation. A recent article urges adoption of a "lawyer-participant" approach to divorce mediation in which the attorneys participate actively in court mandated divorce mediation. (*See* McEwen et al., 1995.) The authors point to the mandatory mediation system in Maine, ME. REV. STAT. ANN. tit. 19, § 752(4) (Supp. 1994). Although Maine's legislation is mandatory, courts review the mediator's agreement before it is incorporated as a formal court order. (ME. REV. STAT. ANN. tit. 19, § 752(4) (Supp. 1994).) The authors' questionnaire concluded that Maine lawyers "believed that their primary role in mediation is to provide a check on unfairness" and that the widely held belief that lawyers were "spoilers" (*i.e.,* that lawyers' adversarial zeal would harm settlement and prevent clients from meaningful participation in mediation) was inaccurate. (McEwen, et al. at 1360, 1364–73.)

3. *Participation of Party Representative or Advocate.* Under Standard VI of the *Model Standards of Practice for Family and Divorce Mediation,* a mediator should allow a party's attorney or advocate to be present at the mediation session if the party so desires. The Uniform Mediation Act, which applies to family mediations in the states where it is adopted, is even stronger. It provides that an attorney or "other individual" who is designated by a party may accompany the party and participate in the mediation process. Furthermore, if a party waives this right before the mediation, the waiver may be rescinded. (UMA § 10.) Why do you think the UMA, which primarily concerns confidentiality, includes this provision? If parties can bring any person they designate, what will prevent a soon-to-be-former spouse from bringing his or her new partner to the mediation? What effect might this have on the process? Is there anything a mediator can do if this issue arises?

4. *Power Imbalances.* Inherent in the Grillo argument is the notion that women are at a disadvantage in divorce mediation because of an imbalance of power with their male adversaries. (*Accord* Delgado et al. (1985) (questioning fairness of ADR to selected minority groups and individuals and stressing power imbalances between adversaries).) Is this position valid? Is a party who lacks power necessarily vulnerable in mediation? Should the mediator take steps to aid a party perceived as lacking power? Won't adding lawyers to the mediation help reduce the severity of this problem? Power imbalances undoubtedly occur in litigation. Will they be any worse in mediation?

5. For discussion of using Navajo "Peacemaking" to deal with domestic violence among members of the Navajo Native Americans, see Donna Coker, *Enhancing Autonomy For Battered Women: Lessons from Navajo Peacemaking,* 47 UCLA L. REV. 1 (1999) (stressing the preservation of relationships that is advanced in Navajo Peacemaking, a type of informal adjudication that may be compared to mediation).

B. COMMERCIAL MEDIATION

Interest in and use of mediation to resolve commercial disputes is increasing. There are numerous reasons explaining the growth of commercial mediation. First, there is a perception among businesses, whether or not true, that litigation is expensive and protracted and that the expense of litigation compares unfavorably with the cost of mediation. Second, some business disputants who have used arbitration are less than pleased with the results. Arbitration is the form of alternative dispute resolution that most closely resembles trial. As such, it can be slow and expensive. Indeed, recent reforms in arbitration have called for enhanced discovery and pretrial processes and have caused disputants to complain that arbitration is becoming little different than going to court. Third, many disputants prefer mediation because it permits a degree of party control unavailable in either litigation or arbitration. Rather than let a third party such as an arbitrator or judge "decide" their dispute, parties increasingly feel better about retaining control over their own dispute through mediation. Fourth, there exists enhanced awareness of an "order" to disputing alternatives. Many firms are quite prepared to litigate or arbitrate but first want to try negotiation to resolve their disputes and, if negotiation does not succeed, attempt mediation. This line of reasoning suggests that a comparatively inexpensive round of mediation should be routinely sought prior to the more formal, expensive disputing options such as litigation or arbitration. (This reasoning supports the "two step ADR clause" that requires the parties to first mediate and, if unsuccessful, to arbitrate.)

Perhaps more than any other factors the comparative inexpense and nonadjudicative nature of mediation are its present selling points. One sometimes hears corporate counsel say, "We might as well take a chance at resolving this dispute through mediation. In mediation we won't spend much money and will not be stuck with an undesirable result we dislike. The only 'results' in mediation will be negotiated agreements that each party desires. It's worth a shot. Plus, even if we cannot agree, each side can learn a great deal about their own case and the other side's position from mediation. You can win even without agreement by participating in mediation. If I mediate, I will obtain some important discovery from my opponent. My opponent and I have tried negotiation but it's not working to resolve this dispute. We each need someone to help us listen to one another more effectively. A good mediator can do that."

Commercial disputes are often between parties who have had long-term relationships. Examples are disputes between bank lenders and borrowers, franchisors and franchisees, product suppliers and buyers, builders and building customers, and licensee-licensor. A dispute has the potential to destroy a business relationship. Disputing procedures that are "hot" such as litigation and arbitration have the potential to be adversarial and acrimonious. In contrast, disputing procedures that are "cool," such as mediation and negotiation, may be perceived as more cooperative and less contentious means of resolving a dispute. Mediation, then, can be thought of as more "acceptable" than litigation in the corporate culture. Indeed, the Center for Public Resources, an organization created and designed by big business to foster alternatives to litigation, actively recruits corporate members and requires each to take a "pledge" not to litigate without first seeking a "cool" alterative. Mediation is culturally "in" as a tool to resolve business disputes between firms who share a relationship.

Mediation of "relational" disputes can, if successful, avoid the termination of the relationship and allow it to continue. Mediation of a relational business dispute can also reform or change the relationship to take into account the problem that caused the dispute. In this way commercial mediation can go beyond the instant dispute and transform the relationship of the disputants. This ability to recreate and redirect a business relationship has such strong possibilities that many firms (e.g., banks, franchisors) now include pre-dispute mediation clauses in their relational contracts.

Some commercial mediation occurs outside the relational context. Professor Ian Macneil has theorized two basic types of contracts, "relational contracts" between two persons or entities that have a long-term, ongoing relationship and "transactional contracts" between individuals or entities that lack a long-term relationship and share only a unique or random contractual partnership.

(*See generally,* Macneil, 1978, at 10–16, 210–13 (discussing transactional and relational contract structure).) In theory, the advantage to mediation of commercial relations should not exist in purely transactional settings. Why, then, does non-relational or transactional commercial mediation occur? One answer is that the parties may still think mediation to be preferable to the alternatives despite their lack of a long-term relationship as a special driving force underlying the mediation.

Construction Mediation. Construction mediation is one example of an area of recent growth. The construction industry is and has been a long-term user of arbitration. Many of the firms that are party to complex construction contracts are engaged in long-term relations that extend beyond the disputed building project. For example, an electrical supply company that has contracted to supply services and equipment to a general contractor for one building may also have contracted with the same general contractor on other building projects. These two firms have a business relationship that is worth nurturing. Mediation could be the answer and is increasingly being sought in the construction industry. (*See* Fisher, 1994, at 8 (emphasizing high cost of conventional litigation because of factual detail inherent in construction disputes); Hinchey, 1992, at 38 (stressing increased popularity of construction mediation to resolve building industry disputes)).

Securities Mediation. In July 1995, the Securities and Exchange Commission approved amendments to the National Association of Securities Dealers ("NASD") Code of Arbitration to provide rules that govern mediation. The NASD is the sponsor of arbitrations between investors and their brokers. Until 1995, arbitration was the sole mode of ADR used by the NASD. The theory of the 1995 amendments is that many of the over 6,000 securities arbitrations disposed of annually could be resolved more speedily and in a less adversary manner through mediation instead of using the judicial like hearings that characterize securities arbitration. Under these rules, mediation could be used in any case eligible for securities arbitration. Parties pay for their own mediator and could either select one from a list supplied by NASD staff or, alternatively, find their own from the many neutrals available. The arbitration hearing date would not be stayed pending mediation. No person serving as a mediator would be allowed to participate later as an arbitrator or a lawyer on the same or a related dispute.

What are the policy reasons for not staying the arbitration? Will this program be likely to attract parties to mediation? These mediations usually involve claims by customers against their brokers. The typical claim is a violation of the federal securities laws or state common law theories such as fraud or negligence. Investors usually seek damages for losses because the broker placed the customer in an unsuitable investment, churned an account, or failed to explain the risk inherent in a particular type of investment. Do these disputes involve "relational" contracts that might be especially appropriate for mediation? Or do these customer-broker disputes involve relationships that are over, with nothing or little left to preserve? The remedy sought in the vast majority of these claims is purely monetary relief. If you represented an investor who has accused his former broker of illegally churning an account, would you be attracted to this mediation program or would you want to bypass mediation and proceed directly to arbitration?

Farm Foreclosure Mediation. Numerous states now mandate the mediation of farm loan foreclosures. The parties to these mediations are farmers (borrowers) and lenders. Often the lending institution will be a local bank or savings and loan facing numerous farm loan defaults. The theory of mediating such disputes is to force the disputants into a structural negotiation which may result in something short of an actual foreclosure and forced sale of what is often the proverbial family farm. Will this happen? Will lenders be likely to give ground when they possess a clear legal ability to drive the defaulting farmer off the land? What tactics can and should the mediator use where one party holds all or almost all the legal chips?

GRAHAM v. BAKER
447 N.W.2d 397 (Iowa 1989)

SNELL, JUSTICE.

In 1979, the Henrys purchased a parcel of agricultural land from the Grahams under a real estate contract requiring annual payments. During the course of the next several years, as commodity prices fell and the farm economy worsened, it became increasingly more difficult for the Henrys to make those annual payments. As a result, the parties agreed to some minor adjustments to the contract that allowed the Henrys to maintain their end of the bargain until December 1, 1987, when they were unable to make their annual payment.

The Grahams enlisted the services of attorney George Flagg, granting him a power of attorney in relation to the contract. On December 29, 1987 Flagg served the Henrys with notice of forfeiture. IOWA CODE section 654A.6 (1987) requires a creditor to request mediation and obtain a mediation release before undertaking forfeiture proceedings. For this reason the notice of forfeiture was withdrawn and a mediation session eventually was held on February 19, 1988.

At that session, Flagg refused to cooperate with the mediator, denying the Henrys any opportunity to put forward their proposals for resolving the situation, and demanding that he be given a mediation release. It was clear that Flagg was hostile to the Henrys, the mediator, and the mediation process. He issued an ultimatum that the Henrys either sell the land within thirty days and remit the balance due on the contract to the Grahams or acquiesce in its forfeiture. As the meeting went on, Flagg became increasingly more agitated and belligerent, seizing upon statements made by the Henrys' attorney to accuse them of bad faith in failing to pay and continuing to demand that his client be given a mediation release.

Basing its decision on Flagg's behavior, the mediation service refused to issue the Grahams a release, granting instead an extra thirty days to attempt mediation. In spite of the fact that no release had been issued, Flagg filed and served a second notice of forfeiture on the Grahams' behalf shortly after the February 19 mediation session. The Henrys brought suit to enjoin the Grahams from continuing forfeiture proceedings, based upon the Grahams' failure to obtain a mediation release. The district court granted the Henrys an injunction, and the Grahams went to court seeking what they characterized as a writ of mandamus to force the mediation service to issue the release. After a hearing, the court ordered that a release be granted and the Henrys appealed.

* * *

The scope of authority granted to the mediation service is minimal. . . . The procedural requirements imposed by the statute mandate only that a creditor request mediation and participate therein. IOWA CODE § 654A.6 (1987). The statute grants no coercive authority to the mediation service to impose a solution on the parties. It mandates, instead, that a release not be granted until the creditor has participated in at least one mediation meeting. IOWA CODE § 654A.11(3) (1987).

* * *

The core of the Henrys' appeal presents us with the question of whether Flagg's behavior at the mediation proceeding constitutes "participation" as that term is intended by the statute. IOWA CODE § 654A.11(3). Our review is de novo. *Osborn*, 324 N.W.2d at 474. Section 654A.11 provides for three types of mediation release. If the parties agree to a resolution of their difficulties short of forfeiture or foreclosure, they sign an agreement drafted by the mediator which becomes a binding contract and is characterized as a mediation release. IOWA CODE § 654A.11(1), (2). If the borrower waives mediation or an agreement is not reached, the parties may sign a statement prepared by the mediator stating that there is no agreement. IOWA CODE § 654A.11(3) (1987). If one of the parties refuses to sign the statement, the statute requires the mediator to sign it. The statement is characterized as a mediation release. The single requirement is that the creditor "participate" in one mediation session. IOWA CODE § 654A.11(3) (1987).

The word "participate" means "to take part in something (as an enterprise or activity) usu[ally] in common with others." *Webster's Third International Dictionary*. Participation "means to take part in, to receive or have a part in an activity." *Burrell v. Ford Motor Co.*, 386 Mich. 486, 192 N.W.2d 207, 211 (1971).

> The word 'participating' has no clear and unmistakable meaning. In its primary sense, it means simply a sharing or taking part with others but when it is applied to a particular situation, it takes on secondary implications that render it ambiguous. Under some circumstances it may denote a mere passive sharing while under other circumstances an implication of active engagement may accompany its use. *Fireman's Fund Indem. Co. v. Hudson Associates, Inc.*, 91 A.2d 454, 455, 97 N.H. 434 (1952).

Given Flagg's attitude during the session, the mediator urged his supervisors not to issue a release, basing his recommendation upon standards for gauging participation formulated by the mediation service itself. His supervisors concurred and no release was issued. By so doing, however, the mediation service arrogated to itself a discretionary function not granted by the statute. In the first instance, the service's standards are in fact rules of good conduct for the participants in mediation sessions. Nowhere in chapter 654A is the mediation service authorized to formulate or adopt such guidelines. Flagg attended the mediation session as required, and participated to the extent of stating that his position was not negotiable.

The statute does not give the mediation service the power to compel either creditor or debtor to negotiate. It merely attempts to set up conditions in which the parties might find a solution to their problems short of forfeiture or foreclosure. In this regard, the mediator's duties are to *listen* to both creditor and borrower, *attempt* to mediate the situation, *advise* the parties as to the existence of assistance programs, *encourage* adjustment or refinancing of the debt, and to *advise*, *counsel*, and *assist* the parties in agreeing as to future financial relations. IOWA CODE § 654A.9 (1995). The choice of such words is a clear indication that the role of the mediation service is advisory only. In this case, the mediator did all that is contemplated by section 654A.9.

Flagg's behavior which ranged between acrimony and truculency precluded any beneficial result to the parties from the mediation process. It has cost his clients considerable time and expense. Nevertheless, his inappropriate behavior is not determinative. We find that Flagg's presence at the mediation meeting satisfied the minimal participation required by the statute.

The statute commands that the mediator shall sign the release if one of the parties refuses to attach his or her signature to it. IOWA CODE § 654A.11(3) (1987). Given Flagg's participation, it was incumbent upon the mediator promptly to draw up the required document, to secure Flagg's signature, and to sign the document himself. In short, the mediator's duty in this instance was ministerial — to sign and issue the release — and allowed him no discretion to refuse. Thus, mandamus should be issued to compel the mediator to prepare the proper statement, affix his signature if the Henrys or the Grahams refuse to sign, and issue the release.

* * *

The judgment of the district court is affirmed.

NOTES

1. After *Graham*, is the Iowa foreclosure mediation program mandatory in nature? Can the Iowa program be described as mandatory if showing up at the session is required but cooperation is not necessary?

2. The Iowa legislation involved in *Graham* lacked a requirement that participation in the foreclosure mediation be "in good faith." Some other state enactments mandating mediation of agricultural loan disputes contain a "good faith" participation feature. (*See, e.g.*, Minn. Stat. § 583.27.) Assume that attorney Flagg toned down his behavior a notch and (a) sat through the mediation orientation session silently and (b) "presented" his side of the case at the opening session by saying "my client has a clear legal right to foreclose and there are no defenses." At that point Flagg refuses to negotiate and requests the mediator to sign the mediation release. Has Flagg participated in "good faith"?

3. Several commentators have discussed state farm foreclosure mediation. (*See* Cooper, 1993; Comment, 1991; Comment, 1988, at 1050-59.) Certain federal programs use mediation to resolve agricultural disputes. The Farmers Home Administration supports state programs to mediate loan disputes between creditors and farmers. (*See* Riskin, 1993; Bailey, 1994.)

4. *Transformative Commercial Mediation.* It is sometimes said that commercial mediation is never transformative and always problem solving in nature. In a typical commercial mediation the mediator feels that resolution of the dispute is the goal and may be indifferent to "empowerment" and "recognition," especially because each party is represented by counsel. Is the above generalization that commercial mediation cannot be transformative a bit of an overstatement? Won't it be possible for a careful mediator to ask questions to each party showing the value of their opponent, often former business partners? Won't "recognition" of the business worth of the opponent facilitate their empowerment? Commercial mediation is often successful in repairing relationships between a manufacturer and a distributor or a franchisor and a franchisee. Can't the successful mediation of such relationships sometimes be labeled as transformative?

C. ENVIRONMENTAL MEDIATION

Mediation of public policy disputes involving the environment is also increasing. Environmental disputes are often (but not always) "complex" because of the presence of complicated scientific issues and multiple parties. Environmental disputes are also complicated because of the potential presence of state, federal and local governments as parties or interested regulators of the dispute. The monetary and political stakes are often very high in environmental disputes. Not surprisingly, then, environmental litigation is often labeled as costly, drawn-out and inevitably complicated.

These factors have led a wide variety of entities and commentators to suggest that environmental disputes be mediated. A number of environmental groups such as the National Wildlife Federation and the Conservation Foundation have actively promoted environmental mediation. Federal agencies under President Reagan began to mediate environmental disputes. The Environmental Protection Agency has begun to use mediation as well as other forms of ADR in enforcement actions. (*See* Grad, 1989, at 173-77; Peterson, 1992.) "Corporations have . . . donated large sums to promote mediation efforts." (Amy, 1987, at 98–99 (offering example of Atlantic-Richfield giving seed money to help found RESOLVE, a provider of mediation services, and emphasizing that other oil companies with "very poor environmental records" have "invested money in promoting environmental mediation").) General commentary has been largely favorable toward using mediation to resolve environmental conflicts. (*See, e.g.,* Susskind, 1981; Patton, 1984; Bacow & Wheeler, 1984, at 156-58; Bingham, 1985; Mays, 1988.) Some, however, have questioned the propriety of agencies using environmental mediation to reduce backlogs. (*See* Brunet, 1988.)

MEDIATION CASE STUDY NO. 2: BRAYTON POINT CONVERSION

[In the aftermath of the first oil embargo (1973), Congress passed legislation authorizing the Department of Energy (DOE) to prohibit the burning of oil to generate electricity and to substitute conversion to coal burning energy production facilities. Energy Supply and Environmental Coordination Act of 1974, § 2, 15 U.S.C. § 792 (1994). Under this legislation DOE was promoting coal use. Investor owned utilities feared the huge cost of installing scrubbers, pollution control devices used to remove sulphur dioxide. Public interest groups were concerned that pollution would increase unless scrubbers were installed.

In the late 1970's DOE became interested in converting the Brayton Point Station, a large oil burning power station near Fall River, Massachusetts, to a coal burning facility. Initially the state and DOE sought the installation of scrubbers to mitigate the sulfur dioxide emissions. The utility owners of Brayton Point, the New England Power Co. (NEPCO), contended that conversion to coal would be impossible because of the high cost of pollution control.]

LAWRENCE SUSSKIND, ENVIRONMENTAL MEDIATION AND THE ACCOUNTABILITY PROBLEM, 6 Vt. L. Rev. 1, 24–30 (1981)*

Brayton Point Station is the largest fossil fuel-powered electric generating plant in New England. The plant is located in Somerset, Massachusetts; nearby are the city of Fall River and Narraganset Bay. In June 1977, New England Power Company (NEPCO), which operates the plant, received notice from the U.S. Department of Energy (DOE) that it intended to prohibit the burning of oil in three of the units at Brayton Point and would require NEPCO to burn coal instead. DOE was acting under authority granted by the Energy Supply and Environmental Coordination Act of 1974 (ESECA) which Congress had passed in response to the oil embargo of 1973-74.

DOE estimated that conversion of Brayton Point to coal would lead to an annual increase of more than six million dollars in NEPCO's net cost for producing electricity. The additional cost would largely be due to the expense involved in meeting the necessary standards for compliance with air pollution controls. To comply with the emission limits of the State Implementation Plan (SIP) under the Clean Air Act, NEPCO would have to burn expensive low sulfur coal and would likely have to install flue gas desulfurization equipment ("scrubbers").

NEPCO challenged the DOE estimates. It estimated that the cost of conversion would be much greater. NEPCO was particularly opposed to any conversion plan that would require the use of scrubbers and announced that it was prepared to contest the DOE Prohibition Order in court. For NEPCO, the Prohibition Order created a serious problem. To comply, it would have to burn coal at the plant and ensure that emissions would not violate either state or federal air quality standards. It would also have to avoid a significant increase in the cost of electricity and thus, a reduction in efficiency.

The Prohibition Order is quite complex. The Environmental Protection Agency (EPA) must certify that a converting plant can meet applicable emission limits and protect both primary and secondary air quality standards while burning coal. DOE must prepare a comprehensive Environmental

---

* Copyright © 1981. Reprinted with permission.

Impact Statement (EIS) and also certify that conversion is economically practicable. The governor of the state must give his prior written concurrence which is then included in the Notice of Effectiveness issued by DOE. Thus, the ESECA program divides regulatory responsibilities among a number of state and federal agencies and offers no mechanism for resolving whatever conflicts might exist among them.

At the outset, it appeared that the prospects for conversion of Brayton Point in a manner that would satisfy all concerned parties (i.e., NEPCO, the regulatory agencies, and energy consumers) were very poor. The ESECA program was new and unclear, and its relationship to other regulatory programs, particularly those concerned with air pollution, appeared contradictory. Further, the principal parties were uncertain of one another's motives for opposing or promoting conversion and were apparently so mired in the legal and technical complexities of the process that they were unable to consider the possibility of conversion in a manner that would encourage progress rather than stalemate.

At this point, the Center for Energy Policy, a nonprofit organization concerned with the resolution of energy and environmental disputes, suggested to the principal parties that they enlist the services of a mediator. In April 1977, the Center for Energy Policy organized a meeting attended by officials of NEPCO, DOE, EPA, and the Massachusetts Department of Environmental Quality Engineering (DEQE) to examine the prospects for conversion. The meeting was pivotal, producing a number of crucial agreements on how best to proceed. NEPCO agreed that the addition of some new equipment (electrostatic precipitators) to control particulate emissions might be required to make conversion environmentally practical. Regulatory agency officials agreed that economic considerations might preclude the use of scrubbers or low sulfur coal.

DOE agreed to participate in a mediation process, but also made clear that it would continue to pursue conversion through the ESECA process. While continuing with the formal conversion process — issuance of a Prohibition Order, preparation of an EIS, and cooperation with EPA in obtaining certification under the State Implementation Plan — DOE indicated that it would participate in and cooperate with a mediation effort that might achieve an agreement regarding voluntary conversion. Eleven months of long and arduous negotiation followed. By March 1978, an agreement had been reached on all issues. Under the terms of the settlement, NEPCO agreed to install additional pollution control equipment to reduce the emission of particulate matter. The Massachusetts DEQE agreed to promulgate a new regulation for the control of air pollution from Brayton Point that would set sulfur and particulate emission limits for at least ten years. The essence of the plan was to achieve certainty regarding both the emissions from the plant and the economic effect of the regulations under which conversion would take place. The mediation process consisted of three phases.

First, the parties agreed to an agenda which dictated the order of issues to be discussed and the groups to participate in each phase of the discussion. Second, for several months, the group focused on technical and quantitative analysis. EPA performed a study of violations of the air pollution standard for particulates in the Fall River area and found that most violations were attributable to wind-blown dust, rather than to power plant emissions. This finding led EPA and the DEQE to consider relaxing some emission limits for the plant.

The negotiation process culminated with bilateral negotiation between NEPCO and DEQE during early 1978 which established the form, level, and duration of new particulate and sulfur emissions standards for the plant. These standards and their schedule of application, in turn, dictated the timing of the coal conversion process.

The final agreement indicated limits on the sulfur content of the coal to be burned and special particulate standards for the plant. Providing that EPA approval of the DEQE compromise was not delayed, NEPCO agreed to begin burning coal at unit one in 1981, unit two in 1982, and unit three of the plant in 1983. Unit four could continue to burn oil.

DOE, in addition to preparing an EIS which examined conversion under the plans generated by the formal process, prepared a second EIS that examined the probable impacts of conversion under the terms of the revised plan prepared through mediation. DOE encouraged EPA to analyze the prospects for certification under each of the plans being considered. Thus, both agencies were able to fulfill their statutory responsibilities while still cooperating with and supporting a mediation effort seeking voluntary conversion.

DOE felt that there were clear advantages to be gained by a voluntary conversion and was eager to participate in a mediation process that could achieve them. At the same time, both DOE and EPA officials were concerned about fulfilling their regulatory responsibilities under the ESECA process. DOE decided that there was nothing inherently contradictory about pursuing both paths simultaneously. Both DOE and EPA took the necessary actions — preparation of an alternative EIS and SIP certification — to assure that they could promptly fulfill their regulatory responsibility if the mediation effort were not successful. This model for agency participation in environmental mediation insulated the public agencies from the charge that they were shirking their duty, yet permitted participation in less formal processes that produced a voluntary agreement.

David O'Connor, the mediator from the Center for Energy Policy, performed several activities. At the outset, he operated primarily as a facilitator/ organizer. His first task was to obtain group approval of a set of informal procedural groundrules for setting agenda, raising issues, making proposals, dealing with the press, documenting discussion, and formalizing agreements. Responsibility for convening meetings, keeping written records of the meetings, and documenting areas of agreement was given to the mediator. He also moderated discussions, ensuring that each party had an opportunity to be heard. The mediator thoroughly explained all technical and legal matters to ensure the complete understanding of all parties. O'Connor regularly pointed out areas of group progress or agreement in an effort to prevent frustration and to keep the group moving toward a settlement. O'Connor spent a considerable amount of time meeting privately with individual parties. In these meetings, O'Connor sought to discover the most important concerns and to understand the technical details that influenced each party's position. He tried to help each party develop a clear understanding of its own position by diplomatically challenging positions and underlying assumptions. In these private meetings O'Connor served as a sounding board for new positions or proposals, allowing parties some feedback on ideas without the risks inherent in presenting them to the group as a whole. On occasion, he presented ideas and options of his own in an effort to broaden the spectrum of possibilities under consideration.

The working group that did the negotiating decided to involve only those parties most directly concerned with the conversion in the final negotiations. This decision facilitated the drafting of an agreement, but required additional procedures (i.e., public hearings) for gaining the approval of interested but unrepresented parties. The ongoing formal regulatory reviews ensured that these opportunities would be available. Several features of this case have been singled out as the key factors accounting for successful mediation: (1) All the parties agreed on the basic policy issues when mediation began. They all agreed that coal conversion was inevitable, that air pollution emissions must be controlled, and that expensive pollution control equipment could not be installed since such installation would have forced NEPCO to shut down the three older units at Brayton Point. (2) Mediation was begun when the parties were completely aware of the issues and of each other's basic objectives. (3) The mediator maintained his flexibility. Overall policy sessions were open to the entire group and smaller, bilateral sessions addressed more specific, technical issues. (4) Since the parties generally had agreed on basic policy issues at the outset of mediation and since the FEA Notice of Intent imposed some urgency none of the parties attempted delay tactics. (5) Parallel hearings and public meetings also were held to solidify public acceptance of the agreement.

*   *   *

NOTES

1. Notice how the Brayton Point mediator orchestrated multilateral (many parties) and bilateral (two party) negotiations. This effort to break down a large complicated dispute into parts may be essential. The strategy of subdividing (i.e., divide and conquer) is used regularly by judges who must manage complex cases. Will the exclusion of some parties from negotiations be routinely desirable on certain issues? Why was the DOE not party to the bilateral 1978 negotiation between the state DEQE and NEPCO? Can you think of a good reason for this omission?

2. Were all parties allowed to participate fully in the Brayton Point mediation? What about public interest groups? Is it fair to delay the participation of public interest groups until at or near the end of the process? Won't it be difficult for such groups to criticize a plan already deemed acceptable to other groups that participated earlier in the mediation? Can the public interest be adequately represented by either the DOE or the state?

3. Did the DOE and the State do their job to enforce existing environmental statutes when agreeing to the type of conversion allowed in Brayton Point? Should an agency be permitted to not enforce pollution prevention laws? Some would argue that the agency's task is to enforce substantive laws and that an agency seeking compromise is inconsistent with its basic mission. (*See* Brunet, 1988.) Did mediation of the Brayton Point dispute produce a good solution for the utility? Is it too good of a deal (i.e., a "sweetheart deal") from a public interest perspective?

MEDIATION CASE STUDY NO. 3: THE FOOTHILLS DAM PROJECT

[This mediation grew out of a plan of the Denver Water Board (DWB) to build a dam and water treatment facility on the South Platte River 25 miles southwest of Denver. The plan included building a dam at Strontia Springs in Waterton Canyon, a popular steep walled canyon with great recreational and wildlife opportunities. The DWB was under pressure to increase water supply because of projected population growth and demand for new water resources. In 1972 Denver voters rejected a bond measure to fund the foothills project. Just one year later the voters approved the project's funding in an election in which under 14% of the electorate voted. The United States had interests because the project affected federal lands and rights of way and required dredge and fill permits under the Clean Water Act. The project also needed an environmental impact statement. Public interest groups (Water Users Alliance, Trout Unlimited and the National Wildlife Federation) were opposed to Foothills because of the projected harm to wildlife and recreational sites and because of the increased pollution and growth that would be caused. The EPA Regional Director strongly opposed the project. He was quoted by the *Denver Post* saying "Strontia Springs is not going to be built . . . I think the Denver Water Board should realize that and modify their proposal." The *Denver Post* supported the foothills project in a series of hotly worded editorials, some with an anti-Washington tone. Numerous suits were brought regarding the legality of the foothills project.]

LAWRENCE SUSSKIND, ENVIRONMENTAL MEDIATION AND THE ACCOUNTABILITY PROBLEM, 6 Vt. L. Rev. 1, 30–37 (1981)[*]

The Foothills project is a raw water treatment facility that will be owned and operated by the Denver Water Department, an independent government agency. In addition to the treatment plant itself, the project consists of a dam and reservoir on the South Platte River approximately twenty-five miles southwest of Denver, Colorado. The first phase of the project is designed to treat 125 millions gallons of water a day, although the dam, reservoir, and conduit system will allow ultimate expansion to a 500 million gallons per day capacity.

The Foothills project is funded by the Denver Water Department which will finance construction with municipal bonds. No federal money is involved. The federal government became embroiled in the Foothills controversy, however, because the dam and reservoir were to be sited on sixty acres of national forest land and fifty-one acres of land administered by the Bureau of Land Management (BLM). For this reason, the Denver Water Board was required to obtain right-of-way permits from these two agencies.

---

[*] Copyright © 1981. Reprinted with permission.

The Water Department also had to obtain a "404" dredge-and-fill permit from the Corps of Engineers since a dam is considered to be fill material. Since the construction process is expected to dump additional fill material into the South Platte River, a navigable stream, a 404 permit was a prerequisite to construction. Although the Corps of Engineers is the primary agency responsible for reviewing 404 permits, the Corps is required to consult with the EPA to assure that the project will not excessively damage the environment.

There were numerous reasons that a locally supported, and locally funded project could create a controversy. First, there was some question about the need for additional water treatment. The Denver Water Board, in its application and throughout the controversy, contended that the water treatment capacity of the Denver Water Department would be inadequate by 1980 because of increasing population growth and increasing per capita water use. To ensure a margin for error, the Water Board wanted to bring Foothills into the system by 1977, ensuring continued "unlimited" treated water supplies to the Denver metropolitan area.

The Denver Water Board's analysis was disputed by many environmentalists, the EPA, and to a lesser extent, by the BLM and the Corps of Engineers. The environmentalists and the EPA made the strongest case, contending that the additional treatment capacity was needed only "to allow unlimited lawn watering through the year 1988." According to the analyses of EPA and environmentalists the project could be made unnecessary by conservation or a water rationing program. The environmentalists contended that either of these alternatives would have significantly fewer harmful effects and would be substantially less expensive than the proposed Foothills project.

A second major facet in the fight over Foothills concerned the control of urban sprawl and air pollution. The pattern of growth in Denver has been characterized by low density urban sprawl. This sprawl necessitates high per capita use of the automobile — the source of most of Denver's air pollution. Many observers have suggested that the best way to control air pollution in Denver is to control and direct growth — slowing the absolute rate of growth, if possible, and directing the growth that does occur into existing urban centers. Since there is a strong link between the availability of public services and the pattern of settlement in many cities, control over the distribution of water (i.e., preventing Foothills from being built) was seen by some as a means of controlling population growth and air pollution. Proponents of Foothills disagreed. They argued that growth would occur regardless of the construction of Foothills. Citing the experiences of several other rapidly growing cities in arid areas, proponents, including the BLM, contended that Foothills would neither suppress nor encourage migration into the Denver area. Whether or not the absolute rate of growth could be altered by the availability (or lack) of water, all parties agreed that the provision of water would influence the pattern of whatever development did occur. Since the Water Board was required by law to respond to all requests for service within the city limits, growth would be channeled into the city rather than into outlying areas if water taps were limited.

According to EPA, "construction of the Foothills project would make the attainment and maintenance of national ambient air quality standards in

Denver more difficult and perhaps impossible." It was on this basis (as well as others) that EPA declared the project to be "unsatisfactory from the standpoint of public health, welfare and environmental quality."

A third concern was that the Foothills project would probably have direct and detrimental impacts on Waterton Canyon, a unique and valuable recreation and wildlife area. According to project opponents, the permanent loss of such a unique area clearly outweighed the temporary benefits that Foothills might bring.

A fourth issue concerned the future development of additional raw water supplies for the Denver area. If no new additional supplies are developed, Denver will probably face raw water shortages beginning in 1988, regardless of whether the Foothills project is built. One likely source of water is the construction of an additional large dam and reservoir upstream from the Foothills treatment plant on the South Platte River. This project, called Two Forks Dam and Reservoir, has been planned by the Water Board for many years. Two Forks is highly controversial because of its likely environmental impacts. Furthermore, Foothills was seen by many as the first step toward implementation of the Two Forks project.

When the idea of mediation was first suggested by Congressional Representative Pat Schroeder in May 1977, the Denver Water Board refused to participate. The Board had the same response to Schroeder's renewed efforts to bring in the University of Washington's Office of Environmental Mediation in the winter and spring of 1978.* Even with costs increasing daily, the Board was absolutely steadfast in its insistence that the project had to be built as designed. Given EPA's opposition and the resistance of many local environmentalists to the proposed dam site, the Water Board saw no benefit to be gained from mediation. Only when another mediator, Congressman Tim Wirth, was suggested, did the prospect of mediation emerge.

Contrary to theory — and contrary to reason — Tim Wirth's success was based largely on the fact that he was widely perceived to be in favor of the Foothills project. Indeed, Wirth had written to the BLM in 1977 supporting the construction of Foothills at the 125 million gallons per day level. When the notion of mediation was suggested by Wirth, the Water Board assumed it would work to their benefit. Naturally, they were more interested than they had been previously, and discussions went well.

Wirth started the process privately and carefully. He talked with the Regional Administrator of EPA, with whom he was friendly. Although the Regional Administrator had previously been under heavy political pressure and had dropped his opposition to the project as a whole, he still objected to the issuance of the 404 permit because he felt that alternatives to the proposed dam site had not been considered adequately. Since the proposed dam was likely to be damaging to the environment, he felt that the alternatives should be studied carefully. Wirth concluded that if he could arrange such a study of alternatives, the Regional Administrator would have to agree to the [mediation] process. Since the Corps was already involved in the dispute, and

---

* [Eds. Representative Schroeder held a press conference at the mouth of Waterton Canyon where she urged the parties to mediate and accused all sides of ignoring the value of compromise.]

had widely acknowledged expertise in dam design, a Corps' study of the alternatives seemed logical.

Negotiations among Wirth, the Corps, EPA and the Water Board continued in Washington, Omaha, and Denver until finally on June 16, 1978, the parties agreed to a procedure. The Denver Water Board, EPA, and the Corps reached agreement on a proposal for a "final, full and complete consideration of the most significant outstanding controversy still surrounding Foothills, the Strontia Springs Dam in Waterton Canyon." The Corps agreed "to go beyond its normal review procedures to conduct a major study of the Strontia Springs Dam and alternatives to it." "Both the Water Board and the EPA have agreed that they would have no problem with the Corps' decision — as long as the procedure established and carried out is fair and thorough."

Although the publicly released description of the proposed process was not referred to as mediation, some of the participants in fact hoped the review would result in a negotiated settlement. Although they did not agree in advance that the Corps' findings would be binding, Wirth's press release and the follow-up stories in the *Denver Post* gave strong indications that the parties had agreed to allow the Corps to act as data mediators and, if its study was fair and thorough, to abide by the results.

The Corps' study was eventually expanded beyond the simple review of alternatives proposed by the Water Board to encompass all the major outstanding issues. As listed in the first Foothills Newsletter (which became a forum for formal announcements concerning the progress of the Corps' study), three major topics were identified as key: the "need for additional water treatment; the existence of superior alternatives to either the project as a whole or just the Strontia Springs dam; and the severity of environmental, social, and economic impacts, whether direct or indirect." The end result was a study which, although not perfect, was far more complete than the Corps had originally planned.

With the study in hand, the parties closed in on a final agreement. Wirth convened an evening meeting with the Corps, EPA, and the Water Board. The meeting was preceded by drinks and dinner which relaxed the participants and strengthened the growing mood of friendliness (and to some extent trust) that had developed. Negotiations began at 10:00 p.m. and continued — at Wirth's insistence — until agreement was reached.* The strain increased the sense of common purpose. Though some of the participants disapproved of these tactics, all stayed until a settlement was reached.

Wirth's political position gave him clout even when he chose not to use it. This clout was apparently respected by all the participants. Almost all the participants felt that Wirth's clout was a key ingredient in achieving the settlement that was obtained. Although a mediator without clout might have been able to succeed in a less polarized dispute, in this case political pressure was necessary to force concessions from parties who had insisted on winning it all.

Wirth negotiated the basic settlement among the Corps, EPA, and the Water Board before he brought in other parties. Although risky, this tactic was

---

* [Eds. The all night mediation session ended at 5:00 a.m.]

essential since negotiating with the first three parties was so difficult. Wirth and his assistants assumed that the most visible environmentalist, John Birmingham, could speak for all the members of the environmental coalition. When he could not, they had further problems. A sense of momentum, common purpose, and cooperation prevailed, however, and a settlement was indeed negotiated. Birmingham presented the agreement to other environmentalists who insisted on a few minor changes. The basic structure of the agreement was maintained, however. The final settlement contained some victories for all sides and some major concessions — even from the Water Board. More importantly, it gave all the parties a better result than they thought they were likely to get either in court or through a federally-imposed decision. The Water Board got its 404 permit for the plant and the dam at the site it wanted. Although the dam was a blow to EPA and the environmentalists, they did get promises of a stream improvement program and minimum streamflow guarantees that would actually increase the flow in the river beyond what it was prior to construction. In addition, EPA got a mandatory water conservation program stricter than the Water Board had planned. The environmentalists also got a citizen's advisory committee to watch over, if not to advise, the Water Board's planning process. Finally, the Water Board agreed to pay the attorneys' fees that the environmentalists had accumulated during years of litigation. Many charged that this award was extortion, but it was a small price to pay for obtaining a settlement. Further, according to most of the parties, the court costs were a key to obtaining the settlement.

The judge presiding over the various court suits that had been held in abeyance during the mediation effort refused to sign the consent decree. He prepared a three page statement explaining the shortcomings of the agreement. He was extremely critical of the provision forcing the Water Board to pay the environmental attorneys' fees, citing "serious doubts as to both the legality and ethical propriety" of such payments. He also questioned the legal status of a mediated settlement and whether it was judicially enforceable. Although the judge did not try to block the agreement, the parties were all disturbed by his conclusions. Nonetheless, they expressed their continued support for the agreement. The attorneys' fees were paid, a conservation plan initiated, a citizen's advisory committee established, and law suits dismissed. A year later the agreement held; the threat of adverse publicity helped to keep it in place. Problems may arise in the next drought year when some fear the Water Board will violate the minimum streamflow requirements to meet peak summer demands. If that occurs, Wirth has threatened to denounce publicly the action as both illegal and unethical.

*   *   *

NOTES

1. Can Congressman Wirth be considered an ordinary mediator in the Foothills controversy? Doesn't he have a stake in the outcome? Even if he did not have a stake, didn't he announce a position on the matter that would preclude his neutrality? Was he too active in promoting this settlement? Was Representative Wirth successful in his efforts *because* of his lack of neutrality?

Notice the untraditional start of his effort to mediate. Can you come up with a good reason for Congressman Wirth's decision not to hold the traditional opening session?

2. The controversy was resolved following negotiations that began at 10:00 p.m. and ended only after agreement was reached at 5:00 a.m. Should such mediator tactics be routinized? Judge Jack B. Weinstein was successful in holding a tiring yet productive weekend of round the clock mediation when settling the Agent Orange class action. As a practical matter, if agreement is reached do the means become largely irrelevant?

3. How important to the solution of Foothills was the Corps of Engineers study? How did the mediator manage to get the study produced and shared? How useful was the newsletter that publicized the Corps study over its long period of gestation?

4. Notice how Congressman Wirth bifurcated the Foothills mediation and first helped to negotiate an agreement between the EPA, Corps of Engineers and the Water Board before he started negotiating with other parties, including public interest groups. Why did the mediator employ this strategy? Should such a procedure be used often?

5. Was every "party" allowed to participate in the Foothills controversy? Was anyone left out? Notice that the mediator attempted to let one environmental group representative be a broker to obtain approval by other groups. How well did this work here? Will such a procedure work well generally?

6. *Environmental Convening.* One significant function played by then-Congressman Wirth was to begin or convene the process of settlement negotiation. This process is sometimes called environmental convening. The "convener" may be a mediator and may subsequently be hired by the parties to mediate their dispute. The "convener's" primary role, however, is to jump start a settlement process in a multiparty dispute by getting the disputants together and begin a procedure which can lead to face to face negotiation and, perhaps, to mediation. The convener is generally well versed in mediation techniques. The convener will aid the parties to identify issues and try to help the parties to remove any obstacles to negotiation or mediation. The first session of a convener can resemble the opening phase of a mediation. Yet, the convener may not be paid by the parties for this attempt and some clear agreement to mediate is, of course, needed to formalize the mediation process.

Environmental convening plays a significant role in hazardous waste Superfund litigation. In the past EPA has invested in ADR by paying for a convener to participate in selected disputes. Superfund cases brought under CERCLA, 42 U.S.C. § 9604 *et seq.*, are good candidates for using a convener. In these suits the EPA will sue multiple parties for illegally releasing hazardous wastes. The cases usually raise numerous complex legal and factual issues. Under CERCLA the defendants — past and present owners of facilities on which hazardous wastes have been released, together with numerous parties who have transported and dumped waste on the site — are jointly and severally liable for cleanup costs. There are strong incentives to settle and to take seriously negotiating opportunities. It is not atypical to have more than 25 defendants in such actions. In addition, some or all of the alleged damages may be within a defendant's insurance coverage. The net result is that multiple alleged polluters and their insurers are involved in deciding CERCLA liability. Is it in any firm's interest to try such actions, particularly when CERCLA uses a liability scheme that makes firms jointly and severally liable? It is common to seek negotiation and mediation of proportionate liability shares in CERCLA suits. Mediation of these Superfund disputes is not necessarily a pretty sight — the initial positions of the different defendants are often diametrically opposed and the multiple parties and insurers can mean high transaction costs. Nonetheless, mediation of CERCLA matters is increasingly common. In these circumstances the use of a convener to begin the important settlement process makes great sense and has the potential to save EPA enforcement costs by encouraging early settlement.

7. Mediation of environmental citizen suits presents interesting problems for the parties and the mediator. These suits are brought by private citizens, often represented by public interest groups, who sue to collect money penalties for environmental harm. *See, e.g., Middlesex County Sewerage Auth. v. National Sea Clammers Ass'n*, 453 U.S. 1, 14 (1981) (recognizing the availability of civil penalties in suits brought under 33 U.S.C. § 1365(a), the citizen suit provision of the Federal Water Pollution Control Amendments of 1972). If these suits end with a litigated judgment in court, any monetary penalties awarded to the plaintiff go directly to the United States Treasury. Plaintiffs who seek some monetary pay-out for environmental projects have a greater chance obtaining it from negotiation or mediation than from a litigated judgment. Under the governing legislative scheme, they may get nothing in court but may obtain project money if the terms of any settlement so provide. Under such circumstances, the urge to go to trial may not be very great for plaintiffs who are fully or partially driven by a monetary goal. While we like to think that all those who initiate such suits are only driven to protect the environment, some plaintiffs may want to direct the expenditure of settlement funds into directions of their own interest, such as an environmental clean-up fund that a court may not approve in a final litigated decree. The plaintiffs will have more to say about the terms of a settlement than a final decree of a judge. In addition, some plaintiff's attorneys may be working on a contingent fee basis for their clients and also share the goal of obtaining a monetary settlement.

Given these factors, it may appear that such cases are easy to settle for a mediator because the defendant probably does not want the publicity and expense of trial and the plaintiffs and their attorney may want a more certain monetary payoff, available only from a pre-trial settlement. What should the mediator do with this set of dynamics? To some defendants it may appear that a plaintiff who is driven by money may be willing to accept a small pay-out instead of risking obtaining nothing in court. This point causes some to say that there are likely to be low settlement offers in such cases. Of course, a litigated judgment may be much more costly for the defendant and the mediator may try to make this very clear. Yet, the defendant who perceives the plaintiff as primarily wanting money or wanting to control money in a pre-trial settlement may be hard to budge from a very low offer. Of course, some truly "principled" plaintiffs are willing to get zero in court in return for obtaining valuable environmental enforcement. How should the mediator calculate such principles in handling the mediation? Who should bring up this problem?

The joint and several liability principle of the environmental Superfund program seems to create incentives to settle. For a discussion of these incentives and the impact of potential change in liability for polluters, see Howard Chang and Hilary Sigman, *Incentives to Settle Under Joint and Several Liability: An Empirical Analysis of Superfund Litigation*, 29 J. LEGAL STUD. 205 (2000).

8. Water allocation decisions are often hotly contested, complicated, protracted, and have multiple disputants. Ranchers, farmers, states, developers, Native American resource users, public interest groups, and federal agencies each have a stake in allocation of water decisions. With these characteristics such decisions pose great potential for mediation. For treatment of the recent mediation of a water resources dispute involving the Umatilla River in Oregon, *see* Neuman, 1996. The Umatilla conflict involved a long standing dispute between farmers, Native Americans, the U.S. Bureau of Reclamation, the Oregon Water Resources Department, and several public interest groups.

9. *Regulatory Negotiation.* Many administrative agencies are now using negotiation to resolve environmental disputes at the rulemaking stage. Regulatory negotiation, as the process is termed, involves convening interested and divergent parties to participate in the drafting of an agency regulation. Consensus is the goal of regulatory negotiation, a mediative process that replaces the typical notice and comment rulemaking process. The regulatory negotiation process is arguably speedier and more effective than the normal rulemaking processes and is growing in popularity. For more detailed treatment of regulatory negotiation, see Chapter 14, *infra.*

D. MEDIATION OF EMPLOYMENT DISPUTES

In the very recent past, the popularity of arbitration of employment disputes greatly eclipsed mediation of disputes between employers and employees. After all, arbitration of employee grieva nces was the norm under collective bargaining agreements. Two developments have contributed to an emerging trend of increasing use of mediation to resolve employment disputes. First, as fewer employees are covered by collective bargaining agreements — now close to only 10% of private sector American workers are members of a labor union — most employers select the arbitration option in a less routine way. Presently a non-union employer thinking about dispute resolution options might prefer to use mediation because of its prompt, relatively inexpensive, and consensual nature. Second, even employers with a union contract have found mediation useful. Mediation of collective bargaining issues has a long, honored tradition. If labor problems and strife are severe it is common for unions and employers to contact a private mediator or turn to the Federal Mediation Service. Moreover, numerous collective bargaining agreements make provision for mediation of individual employee grievances. The chief reason behind the interest in mediation is that grievance arbitration is expensive, slow and formal when compared to the mediation option. Grievance mediation may forge creative options that are more satisfactory to employees and employers. Moreover, selection of the mediation option does not preclude a subsequent arbitration. Accordingly, employers frequently contract for a two-step ADR grievance process: first mediation and, if needed, arbitration. For full treatment of grievance mediation, see Goldberg, 1982.

Predispute employment mediation clauses come in numerous varieties and are capable of being custom crafted to achieve different goals. Consider the American Arbitration's recommended clause for employment mediation:

> If a dispute arises out of or relates to this [employment application; employment ADR program; employment contract] or the breach thereof, and if the dispute cannot be settled through negotiation, the parties agree first to try in good faith to settle the dispute by mediation administered by the American Arbitration Association under its National Rules for the Resolution of Employment Disputes, before resorting to arbitration, litigation or some other dispute resolution procedure. [AAA, *Resolving Employment Disputes — A Practical Guide* (2003).]

The above clause is one calling for mediation of any future disputes. Even without such a clause the parties may agree to mediate an existing dispute. Note that the above clause calls for negotiation to precede mediation. Try to articulate a logical reason for this requirement. In addition, the above clause requires a standard of a "good faith" effort to settle in mediation. How will this standard be measured? Will the standard be breached by a party who shows up at a mediation session, listens to the mediator and other side, and then leaves?

The nature of employment mediation calls for informal mediation. There is no record of the mediation process. (*See* AAA, *National Rules for the Resolution of Employment Disputes*, Employment Mediation Rule 13 (1996).) The mediator may wish to consult with an expert regarding technical issues. This can happen if the parties agree and are willing to pay the expert's fee. (*See* Galton, 1995.)

Are there any policy reasons to fear or oppose mediation of employment disputes? From the employer's perspective mediation is especially attractive — low cost, no imposition of result by a third party, quick, and private. Most of these attributes are equally attractive to employees. Privacy, however, is a two-edged sword. There may be times when the public may have an interest in a private employment dispute. For example, should mediation of repeat sexual harassment claims brought by multiple female employees against a repeat harassing supervisor be hidden from public view? Doesn't the process enable the repeat offender to keep his job and cause yet another dispute? Will the voluntary actions of the "market" (e.g., the employer) take care of this problem? Is there any way to reap the obvious advantages of mediation but to prevent "repeat offenders" from keeping their transgressions private?

E. VICTIM-OFFENDER MEDIATION

Mediation in the criminal law area between victims and offenders is growing rapidly in popularity. As of April, 2000, close to 300 programs supplying victim-offender mediation ("VOM") existed throughout the United States. U.S. Dept. Justice, *National Survey of Victim-Offender Mediation Programs in the United States* (April 2000). During the 1970s and 1980s, several factors coalesced to create widespread interest in mediation as a means of resolving criminal as well as civil cases. Courts were congested with criminal cases, and correctional facilities became overcrowded as well. A growing "Victims' Rights" movement demanded that the criminal justice system involve crime victims and attend to their needs — including both emotional healing and financial restitution — as well as the punishment of convicted offenders. Critics of the formal justice system called for community-based alternatives; many localities instituted their own dispute resolution programs, and the United States Department of Justice created model Neighborhood Justice Centers in several cities. Theorists proposed that all parties to a criminal offense — victim, offender, and society — would benefit if each participated in the criminal adjudication process, rather than relying exclusively on the state to make things right. Religious leaders sought ways of dealing with criminal behavior that relied more on restoration of the offender to society than on retribution.

In 1974 the city of Kitchener, Ontario instituted a Victim-Offender Rehabilitation Program (VORP), the first of its kind in North America. The program, which was administered jointly by the local probation department and the Mennonite Central Committee, began by bringing two young men, who had vandalized the property of twenty-two people, together with each of their victims. Its goal was both to develop a satisfactory plan for restitution and to impress upon the offenders the fact that each had a responsibility to compensate their victims for the damage they had suffered. The sponsors deemed the experiment a success when the young men met their mediated restitution obligations within six months.

In 1978, a citizens' group in Elkhart, Indiana instituted a VORP. Soon communities and states throughout the United States adopted programs based at least partly on the same principles. While they vary widely, these programs include what is known generically as "victim-offender mediation" or VOM. By 1991, more than half the cases mediated in New York State's Community Dispute Resolution Centers involved crime and delinquency. In 1994 more than one hundred VOM programs were operating in the United States; in 1993, they disposed of 16,500 cases involving more than 14,000 offenders. (*See PACT Institute of Justice*, 1993, at 1.) As of April, 2000, 289 VOM programs were conducting mediation of criminal cases. The most common offenses of mediation are vandalism, minor assaults, theft and burglary.

Proponents of VOM base their thinking on an alternative paradigm of criminal conduct and correction — another "lens" through which these phenomena may be viewed. (*See* Zehr, 1990). They point out that the traditional retributive paradigm relies on proxies rather than directly involving either party to a criminal offense.

> The competing restorative justice paradigm is outcome-oriented, emphasizing collective problem-solving through direct negotiations between the offender and the victim. The mediation of restitution is a means to an end, namely, the reconciliation of victim and offender and the restoration of interpersonal relationships damaged by criminal conflict. The direct involvement of victim, offender, and community are integral to the process of justice, not tangential. Crime is personal and social. Justice includes restoring victims and the community. The idea of crime as rule-violation, the adversary nature of the process, the peripheral roles of victim and offender, and the fixation on punishment are held counter-productive and antithetical to justice. [Mika, 1993, at 2195.]

According to this view, mediation of the dispute between offender and victim constitutes an integral part of the corrections process. While fashioning a restitution agreement is a core objective, the sometimes dramatic face-to-face encounter between victim and offender also aims for positive emotional and behavioral results. In 1992, the federal Office of Juvenile Justice and Delinquency funded a youth-oriented project based on this model, with programs in several cities nationwide. (*See* Bazemore & Umbreit, 1994.)

Advocates of VOM claim that these programs have been successful. They point to the high rate of satisfaction among participants. In one study, nearly all face-to-face encounters between offender and victim resulted in written contracts, which generally include either monetary restitution or service to the victim. Most of these contracts were eventually completed. (*See* Coates & Gehm, 1989, at 25.) The samples are small for rigorous statistical analysis, however, and they comprise program participants — selected according to screening criteria — rather than a cross-section of criminal offenders. Anecdotal accounts of particular mediations provide much of what we know about the effectiveness of VOM. (*See, e.g.,* Umbreit, 1989, at 99, 102–09.)

JENNIFER GERARDA BROWN, THE USE OF MEDIATION TO RESOLVE CRIMINAL CASES: A PROCEDURAL CRITIQUE, 43 Emory L.J. 1247, 1262–66 (1994) *

Most VOM programs involve face-to-face meetings between crime victims and offenders in the presence of trained mediators. Beyond this basic description, VOM programs defy generalization. The programs vary in two important ways: They aspire to different goals and they exploit different degrees of state coercion. The differences are significant because they affect the extent to which VOM serves the interests of victims, offenders, and the state.

VOM programs aspire to various ends. Sometimes their goals are not articulated explicitly, but are reflected in operational details of the programs, such as the criteria used to select cases for mediation. Some VOM programs focus on cases involving misdemeanors — mostly nonviolent property crimes. Some programs limit their cases to felonies. Most programs mediate some combination of misdemeanors and felonies. Some proponents of VOM even encourage its use in select cases of violent felonies, including homicide, armed

---

robbery, and rape. Selection criteria reflect the different program goals. The more serious the crimes a program is willing to mediate, the more that program probably aspires to serve as an alternative to incarceration. In addition, programs that mediate more serious crimes reflect a willingness to displace some of the state's authority, since states presumably take a greater interest in resolving more serious cases.

The diverse goals of programs involving victim-offender mediation are also reflected in their relative entanglement in the criminal justice system. Most VOM programs are distinguishable from standard community mediation programs (even though community mediation programs may also handle cases involving technically criminal conduct) because the VOM programs mediate cases in which the participants' roles as victim and wrongdoer are more clearly determined. Indeed, community mediation programs receive referrals primarily from civil, rather than criminal, courts. Community mediation programs provide an alternative to the adversary system altogether, diverting cases before they even enter the criminal justice system. Referrals to VOM, in contrast, are usually made by law enforcement or criminal court personnel after an offender has entered the criminal justice system; often the adversary system takes the case to the point of conviction (following adjudication or a plea).

A final way in which the goals of VOM programs differ is the degree of importance placed on "reconciliation of the conflict (*i.e.*, the expression of feelings; greater understanding of the event and each other; closure)." While many programs concern themselves primarily with hammering out restitution agreements, others also seek to address emotional issues surrounding the crime. This difference can have an especially strong effect on victims. While the potential benefits of "reconciliation" may be great, a program's strong emphasis on this goal could harm victims who are not ready or willing to forgive their offenders.

In addition to different goals, VOM programs display a varying willingness to exploit state coercion. The timing of the mediation can have a tremendous effect on the level of coercion experienced by an offender. VOM programs conduct mediation at various points in the criminal justice process: on the early side, some mediations occur after arrest and before any charges are filed; on the late side, some mediations follow an offender's conviction and sentencing. As an offender's case progresses through the system, the offender may gather information about the evidence, the severity of the charges, and the likelihood of conviction. The fear of state punishment may lead offenders to agree both to mediation generally and to a victim's demands specifically.

Programs that conduct mediation early in the criminal process, when the offender still lacks information about the likely outcome of the case, can more effectively exploit the offender's fear of state punishment in order to secure the offender's cooperation. A VOM program appears to lack some of the state's coercive power, because the offender can refuse to mediate. But the offender's freedom to reject mediation can be constrained if the offender fears indirect punishment for the refusal to mediate (this could occur if the offender's failure to cooperate in mediation is taken into account at the time of sentencing). Even if the VOM program does not actively exercise coercive power, it can exploit the offender's fear of state coercion by scheduling mediation at a time when the offender's uncertainty is greatest.

The differences among VOM programs, outlined above, make it difficult to formulate a "typical" model for VOM. For the sake of discussion . . . let us assume a VOM program that exclusively takes adult offenders. The program receives most of its case referrals from courts and probation officers before the offenders enter a formal guilty plea or receive their sentence. Once referred, each case is assigned to a mediator — in most programs, a volunteer from the community — who contacts the victim and offender individually. If the parties agree to mediate, the mediator sets a time and place for the mediation to be held and conducts the mediation. If the parties reach agreement, they enter into a written contract outlining the provisions of their agreement, both monetary and nonmonetary. The mediator returns a written report of the mediation and a copy of the contract to the VOM program office, and the administrator of the program forwards the contract (often with a copy of the report as well) to the referring agency. In most programs, VOM program staff monitor performance of the contract; in some systems, the probation office will also check to insure that the restitution is paid if it is a condition of probation. If, on the other hand, one of the parties refuses to mediate or the parties cannot resolve the case in mediation, the case is returned to the referring agency — the prosecutor's office, the court, or the probation office. There, the offender will be subject to state prosecution and sentencing. Sometimes the mediator will report back to the referring agency about the case. If the offender was somehow responsible for the failure to resolve the case (by refusing to mediate or agree to the victim's demands), the case will return to the system with the mediator's report and "the judge will have to decide whether to order restitution or alter the sentence in some way." Similarly, if the victim's uncooperative attitude prevented the parties from mediating or reaching agreement, a judge subsequently setting a restitution amount could also be made aware of the victim's actions.

NOTES

1. As Professor Brown suggests, some advocates of VOM promote it as an alternative to the traditional criminal justice system in the United States; others consider it a supplement to the existing system. At one extreme, some observers "have argued for what would effectively be the end of criminal law, replacing it with the civil law of torts." (Van Ness, 1993, at 262.) Van Ness argues instead for a restorative justice approach alongside the conventional system. "[M]aintaining the criminal law is desirable inasmuch as it provides an effective method of vindicating the rights of secondary victims, it restrains and channels in acceptable ways retributive emotions in society, and it offers procedural efficiencies in enforcing public values." (*Id.* at 265.)

Would it be possible to fashion an all-inclusive restorative justice system that includes victim-offender mediation and performs the basic functions of the criminal justice system? If so, how would such a system deal with "victimless" or consensual crimes such as illicit drug use and prostitution? How would "society" or "the community," as a party to the conflict, have its interests represented in such a system? (*See* Ashworth, 1993.)

2. Professor Brown and other critics of VOM point out that it necessarily contains an element of coercion, since the alternative to mediation for the alleged offender may be a return to the mainstream justice system — a criminal trial and the possibility of incarceration. Victims may also feel pressured to forgive their offenders as part of the healing process. How does this influence your thinking about mediation of criminal disputes? Can mediation truly be voluntary if it includes this element? If it is not voluntary, is it truly mediation?

3. Both critics and advocates discuss the "net-widening" effect of these programs. VOM reaches many minor offenders whose cases may never come to trial because of the limited resources of the judicial and law-enforcement systems. Thus it effectively broadens the state's exercise of its coercive powers. This phenomenon renders suspect statistical comparisons between VOM and "traditional" ways of dealing with criminal offenders, and it indicates that the programs may reach people who do not need them. (*See, e.g.,* Van Ness, *supra,* at 272.) If it is true that VOM programs widen the net cast to haul in criminal offenders, is this a valid criticism? Might it be that the additional "catch" includes persons who can be and should be influenced appropriately through means other than criminal proceedings? If so, does this strengthen the argument for VOM as a supplement to the existing criminal justice system?

4. Victims and offenders are screened before they participate in VOM programs, since practitioners find that certain parties are unlikely to participate constructively. (*See, e.g.,* Gerencser, 1995, at 47: "Abusers must know that domestic abuse is criminal, with no potential for any conciliatory process.") Does this fact indicate that VOM may result in a two-track justice system, with certain offenders destined for trial and incarceration and others for more "genteel" proceedings and outcomes? Consider that persons with certain cultural or socioeconomic backgrounds may find it more difficult to participate in a highly verbal, conciliatory process and others may find it difficult to express remorse, which is commonly required of offenders in VOM. Assume VOM does discriminate against less articulate offenders. Is that a reason to discontinue the process?

5. Would widespread use of VOM undermine the general deterrence goal of punishment? Consider a "rational criminal" who calculates the expected value of a contemplated criminal act — i.e., the probability of success times the value of a favorable outcome — and disregards any social implications of crime or punishment. To take a simplified example, a person might consider embezzling $60,000 from an employer and reason that chances are two in three that she will succeed in obtaining the money and avoiding punitive consequences; the act has a favorable expectation value of $40,000. To make a rational decision, though, she must also consider the probability and (negative) value of an *unfavorable* outcome. Under a retributive justice system, she will multiply the one-third probability of incurring punitive consequences by the (negative) value of the consequences — say, three years in jail. In deciding whether to commit the theft, the criminal will weigh the $40,000 positive value against one year in jail.

A system of restorative justice alone would radically alter the potential thief's calculations. The major consequence of being apprehended and processed through VOM would be the loss of any money gained by the act (assuming relatively insignificant transaction and opportunity costs). The money was not the offender's, however, so its loss would not be a cost. No matter how large the probability that the offender will have to "pay the price," in other words, the price would not come out of her pocket. Since no significant negative value attaches to an unfavorable outcome, there is no reason not to embezzle the funds.

Such a "rational criminal" may present difficulties for a program of restorative justice. On the other hand, a rational criminal who is apprehended and brought into a VOM program may benefit from the program and find that her "rational behavior" has social consequences that are unacceptable to her. If she continues this pattern of decision making, though, the program — even if it results in a successfully completed restitution contract — will have failed in its goal of rehabilitating the offender. Would this be simply an individual failure, or is it an endemic feature of the restorative justice model? Note that the same rational criminal might go through the conventional criminal justice process, including a sentence of imprisonment, and still choose to engage in similar conduct as a result of rational deliberation. Should VOM programs screen out repeat offenders who appear to rely on antisocial but "rational" decision-making processes? If so, does this invite the problems of a two-track justice system?

6. Many raised in the Euro-American tradition have difficulty seeing VOM as an alternative to the mainstream criminal justice system, with its reliance on prosecution by the state and on punishment as a means of dealing with criminal behavior. Yet many other cultures rely on restorative or mediative techniques as means of resolving criminal offenses. (*See, e.g.*, Benham & Barton, 1996; Melton, 1995; Wall & Callister, 1995, at 45.)

7. *Recent Trends.* An April, 2000, survey of U.S. VOM programs reveals interesting features. First, it is common to use co-mediation in these cases. Can you speculate why co-mediation is popular in VOM cases? Second, a larger number of programs have managed to routinely attract the parents of juvenile offenders to attend. Attempts are also made to invite and involve the family and friends of the victim; the label "family group conferencing" describes this VOM procedure. Why is this desirable? Third, these sponsoring programs often train unpaid "community volunteers" as mediators. Fourth, the nature of VOM sessions is becoming more clear. Issues of guilt or innocence are not mediated. The focus in VOM is on accountability of the offender, the empowerment of the victim and the restoration of the victim's loss. Pre-session caucusing with the victim and the offender are often conducted to ensure a productive joint session. (*See generally*, U.S. Dept. Justice, *National Survey of Victim-Offender Mediation Programs in the United States* (April 2000).)

Part THREE

ARBITRATION

Chapter 9

INTRODUCTION: THE MANY FACES OF ARBITRATION

While arbitration has settled characteristics, its rapid development and rising popularity have created numerous types or subspecies of arbitration. Arbitration of employment grievances has long been a popular feature of collective bargaining agreements. Business partners to international joint ventures use arbitration to resolve disputes. Various industries — banking, securities sellers, textiles — use the arbitration mechanism to resolve significant numbers of disputes. Most of these arbitrations occur pursuant to settled, contractual relationships. Arbitration has recently been integrated into a much different context, that of negligent torts, to resolve disputes between patients and their physicians, patients and hospitals, and insurers and insureds, and it has been used to resolve intentional claims of alleged discrimination. This chapter details how arbitration works in each of these areas. It will necessarily focus on some of the areas of arbitration's greatest successes. It is important to ask whether the growth of arbitration into new subject matter areas will be as successful as arbitration has been in the fields in which it has worked well historically.

A. THE ESSENTIAL CHARACTERISTICS OF ARBITRATION

The many different types of arbitration each have their own unique features. Indeed, one of the main selling points of arbitration is its ability to incorporate the precise dispute resolution characteristics desired by the parties. Commercial arbitrations held under the Rules of the American Arbitration Association differ greatly from grievance arbitrations held pursuant to collective bargaining agreements. Yet, there are certain characteristics common to most, if not all, contracts to arbitrate. These characteristics make up a "folklore" model of arbitration that most lawyers associate with the term "arbitration."

1. ADJUDICATION: REASONED PRESENTATIONS OF PROOF TO A DECIDER

An arbitration represents an adjudicatory trial. While arbitrations are normally more informal than court trials, they nonetheless constitute reasoned presentations of proof by the disputants to the decisionmaker, a single arbitrator or multiple arbitrators. Arbitration is, essentially, a trial like device. At the arbitration hearing the disputants make presentations of their proof to the arbitrators who must resolve the relevant issues.

2. PRIVACY (SECRECY)

Arbitration hearings take place entirely in private, removed from the public eye. For many parties to arbitral contracts, privacy is the single most important feature. Some disputants desire strongly that the subject matter of their dispute be kept private. Arbitration satisfies this demand. (*See* Soia Mentschikoff, *Commercial Arbitration*, 61 COLUM. L. REV. 846, 849 (1961) (describing "desire for privacy" as one of "chief motivating factors" underlying commercial arbitration).) Parties who may want privacy include sellers of allegedly defective products, banks, securities brokers, and suppliers of medical services. "In addition to the private location of hearings, the results of arbitration are also private; published opinions are rare." (Edward Brunet, *Arbitration and Constitutional Rights*, 71 NORTH CAROLINA L. REV. 81, 85 (1992).) Only in a few, specialized types of arbitrations do arbitrators routinely craft written decisions — labor arbitrations, international commercial arbitrations, and maritime arbitrations. The privacy concept associated with arbitration guarantees that the results of most arbitrations are kept secret. The normal arbitration ends silently with a cryptic written "award" that is not disclosed to the public.

3. INFORMAL PROCEDURAL RULES

Arbitration is an informal, flexible process. When compared with trial judges, arbitrators have relatively few procedural rules to curb their discretion in administering a hearing. Formal rules of evidence do not prevail. (American Arbitration Association, Commercial Arbitration rules, Rule 31 ("conformity to legal rules of evidence shall not be necessary").) Formal pleading rules do not apply in arbitration. While rights to minimal discovery are increasingly available in arbitration, arbitrators have discretion to control the timing and nature of discovery. Broad litigation style discovery is usually avoided in arbitration. Arbitration trial procedures are highly informal. To be sure, some arbitrational organizations now have rules mandating a record, usually of a relatively inexpensive tape-recorded variety. The parties are also free to craft their own rules of procedure and can agree to particular features of litigation procedure if they desire. Yet, parties to an arbitration rarely opt for "extra" formalities because their choice of arbitration demonstrates a preference for speedy, comparatively inexpensive procedures of an informal nature.

4. SUBORDINATION OF SUBSTANTIVE LAW

Arbitrators need not apply principles of substantive law. "[A]rbitrators are not bound by precedent." (*Shearson/American Express, Inc. v. McMahon*, 482 U.S. 220, 259 (1987) (Blackmun, J., concurring in part and dissenting in part).) The very nature of arbitration amounts to signatories to a written contract agreeing to opt out of a legal system characterized by substantive rules. It is, accordingly, not surprising that courts have long permitted arbitrators to "disregard strict rules of law or evidence and decide according to their sense of equity." (*Fudickar v. Guardian Mut. Life Ins. Co.*, 62 N.Y. 392, 400 (1875).) The arbitrator will tend to "do justice as he sees it" and to custom craft an arbitral award based upon the facts presented. The award may reflect a compromise. Neither party may prevail and the award may make no one happy.

Arbitrators are, of course, free to apply legal rules if they desire. They are certainly influenced by rules of law that are not strictly binding upon them.

Many arbitrators use substantive legal rules when they make decisions. (Mentschikoff, *supra*, at 861.) Nonetheless, it is fair to say that substantive legal rules play a subordinate role in arbitration. The fact that arbitrators generally do not provide findings of fact or written explanations for their awards contributes to the subordination of legal rules. In effect, arbitration privatizes substantive law. (*See* Stephen Ware, *Default Rules from Mandatory Rules: Privatizing Law Through Arbitration*, 83 MINN. L. REV. 703 (1999).)

The parties may depart from the "folklore" model of arbitration and choose to select a more judicialized type of arbitration. They may customize their arbitration by requiring the arbitrator to apply legal principles. This can be done by drafting the arbitration clause to require findings of fact and conclusions of law.

5. FINALITY

Arbitration awards are said to be "final." "Arbitrators are not bound by rules of law and their decisions are essentially final." (*In Re Aimcee Wholesale Corp. (Tomor Products, Inc.)*, 21 N.Y.2d 621, 626, 237 N.E.2d 223, 225, 289 N.Y.S.2d 968, 971 (1968).) There is no true appeal from an arbitral award, and instead, the ability to "set aside" an arbitration result is so severely limited that it would be incorrect to label it an "appeal." "The whole point of arbitration is that the merits of the disputes will not be reviewed in the courts." (*International Standard Elec. Corp. v. Bridas Sociedad Anonima Petrolera, Industrial y Comercial*, 745 F. Supp. 172, 178 (S.D.N.Y. 1990).) According to Professor Richard Speidel, finality is a "core ingredient" of arbitration that "supposedly gives arbitration an advantage over litigation." (Richard Speidel, *Arbitration of Statutory Rights Under the Federal Arbitration Act: The Case for Reform*, 4 OHIO ST. J. ON DISP. RESOL. 157, 191 (1989).) The theory of arbitral finality posits that the signatories to an arbitration contract seek a result that is informal, prompt and fair and one not associated with the delays or formalities of appellate justice; the parties have a preference for a final decision instead of an appellate court's second-guess. (*See* Wharton Poor, *Arbitration Under the Federal Statute*, 36 YALE L.J. 667, 676 (1927).)

Under existing arbitration statutes and rules, parties unhappy with the results of an arbitration may attempt to have the result modified or vacated on narrow grounds. Clear fraud by the arbitrator can be a reason for vacating an award. (*See* 9 U.S.C. § 10(a) (permitting arbitral awards to be set aside or vacated because of "fraud, corruption or undue means").) In addition, a losing party to an arbitration may seek to have the award vacated as inconsistent with "public policy." (*See generally* Stewart Sterk, *Enforceability of Agreements to Arbitrate: An Examination of the Public Policy Defense*, 2 CARDOZO L. REV. 481, 492–93 (1981) (asserting that public policy defense should apply "only . . . where legal rules are designed to protect the interests of third parties or the public at large, and thus foster ends other than fairly resolving the dispute between the parties").)

Yet, those avenues available for vacating arbitral awards are restricted. Courts construe these methods narrowly and, in so doing, facilitate the concept of arbitral finality. (*See, e.g., A.G. Edwards & Sons, Inc. v. McCollough*, 967

F.2d 1401, 1403 (9th Cir. 1992) (asserting that "federal court review of arbitration awards is extremely limited"), *cert. denied*, 506 U.S. 1050 (1993); *Antwine v. Prudential Bache Sec., Inc.*, 899 F.2d 410, 413 (5th Cir. 1990) ("judicial review of an arbitration award is extraordinarily narrow"); *Northrop Corp. v. Triad-Int'l Mktg., S.A.*, 811 F.2d 1265, 1271 (9th Cir.) (reversing trial court's refusal to enforce arbitral award because result contrary to public policy), *cert. denied*, 484 U.S. 914 (1987).) Courts also refuse to overturn awards because of mere "errors of law." (*See, e.g., Merrill Lynch Pierce, Fenner & Smith, Inc. v. Bobker*, 808 F.2d 930, 933 (2d Cir. 1986) (rejecting vacation of arbitral awards because of "error of law" and refusing to overturn awards under notion that result "in manifest disregard of law").)

There are parties who may want a judicialized type of arbitration with some ability to obtain review of an arbitrator's mistaken award. This can be achieved by two alternative departures from the "folklore" arbitration model. The arbitration clause can set up an appellate arbitration panel or it may specify that the award can be reviewed for "errors of law" by the courts.

6. EXPERTISE AND LACK OF JURY

Arbitrators are often selected because of their impartial expertise. Historically, expertise of the arbitrator ranks as one of the essential characteristics of arbitration. (*See generally* Thomas J. Stipanowich, *Rethinking American Arbitration*, 63 IND. L.J. 425 (1988) *passim* (stressing advantages of using expert arbitrators to resolve commercial disputes).) When textile arbitration became common in the garment district of New York, it was common to hear that the arbitration option was chosen in order to "get an expert knowledgeable in the field." One hears similar comments about the expertise of construction and labor arbitrators.

It is interesting that the expertise of the arbitrator is nowhere legally mandated. No laws condition arbitrator expertise as a requisite for the job. Qualifications, however, are often set by arbitral organizations who supply arbitrators.

It is useful to consider the relationship between arbitral expertise and the civil jury. Many parties to arbitration proceedings are clearly opting for a system of adjudication other than a civil jury trial. For these parties, often businesses, the expert arbitrator represents a greatly preferred alternative to the civil jury.

B. COMMON SUBTYPES OF ARBITRATION

1. LABOR ARBITRATION

Over 95 percent of collective bargaining agreements between unions and employers contain provisions for arbitration of job related grievances between employees and employers. Arbitration of workplace grievances has been an immensely successful way to resolve such disputes and compares favorably to litigation. The cost of litigating workplace disputes in court would be prohibitive. The adversary nature of litigation would also sour the continuing relationship between the employee and the employer. Grievance arbitration affords an opportunity to let a neutral listen to the employee and employer, treat each party with dignity in a fair manner, and rule by taking into account the nature of the workplace (sometimes called the "law of the shop"). Expert labor arbitrators, many of whom are not lawyers, can hear the grievance and input their own labor experience into the matter.

The presence of non-lawyers as labor arbitrators understandably affects the nature of the process. The resolution of labor arbitrations tends to be quite fact sensitive. Workplace or shop traditions matter greatly in labor arbitration. At the same time, legal rules play a relatively minor rule in these disputes. The labor arbitrator is "bound, not by decisions of courts or other arbitrators in somewhat comparable matters, but by [the arbitrator's] judgment as to how the cases should be decided on the facts in the record and the arguments advanced." (Peter Seitz, *The Citation of Authority and Precedent in Arbitration (Its Use and Abuse)*, ARB. J., Dec. 1983, at 58–59. *See also* Carlton J. Snow, *An Arbitrator's Use of Precedent*, 94 DICK. L. REV. 665, 666–70 (1990) (asserting that arbitrators, not reviewing courts, should decide precedential value of earlier awards).) The labor arbitrator is considered to be an expert at fairly deciding disputes between employers and employees.

Unlike most arbitrations, labor arbitrators often prepare written opinions to accompany and explain their awards. Private publishers, Commerce Clearing House (CCH) and the Bureau of National Affairs (BNA), routinely publish and market these opinions. These opinions seldom express binding legal rules. Rather, they recite the evidence considered and the rationale offered. The written opinion usually sets forth that the award resulted from a process that was fundamentally fair. This attention to fairness, sometimes labeled the "due process of arbitration" or "industrial due process" is characteristic of labor arbitration. Labor arbitrators use this concept to ensure a fair hearing and guarantee that the disputants receive notice, are not unfairly surprised and have the chance to confront accusers. Robben Fleming, *Some Problems of Due Process and Fair Procedure in Labor Arbitration*, 13 STAN. L. REV. 235, 235–48 (1961). Under the due process of arbitration, arbitrators offer a measure of civil liberty protection during arbitrations but do so voluntarily and out of respect for the parties' intent rather than because of the formalities of constitutional compulsion. *See* Edward Brunet, *Arbitration and Constitutional Rights*, 71 N.C. L. REV. 81, 90–93 (1992); *United Steelworkers v. Enterprise Wheel & Car Corp.*, 363 U.S. 593, 597 (1960) (an arbitration award "is legitimate only so long as it draws its essence from the collective bargaining agreement").

GODDARD SPACE FLIGHT CENTER, NASA
89-1 Lab. Arb. Awards (CCH) ¶ 8038 (1988)

BERKELEY, ARBITRATOR

[An electrician employed at NASA was discharged following a guilty plea of possessing cocaine with the intent to sell. He received a three-year suspended sentence and a $5000 fine. When a supervisor, ["B,"], recommended that the employee ["A"] should be discharged, the employee's union representative argued that the off-duty offense was unrelated to A's job. When assessing the appropriate sanction, ["C"], the Director of Management, considered an Office of Inspector General ("OIG") report on the criminal action. The report detailed that a convicted felon ("F") had set up A's arrest and had previously sold cocaine to A. The OIG report also stated that A was actively involved in drug use and dealing and that a fellow employee was also involved in drug use.]

*   *   *   *   *   *

The two barest rudiments of due process are to be informed, in writing, of the specific charges against you, and be afforded an opportunity to present a defense on those charges to an unbiased party or tribunal.

It is beyond dispute that Mr. [A] did not enjoy these rudimentary features of due process in this case. As to the specification of charges contained in the letter of proposed adverse action from Mr. [B], no nexus whatsoever was alleged — or even known at the time — between Mr. [A]'s off-duty misconduct and the efficiency of the service.

As the Union argued, these lapses of due process were of such a serious and fundamental nature that there was "harmful error." Under the guidance of *Cornelius v. Nutt* [472 U.S. 648 (1985)], this standard means that the employee's interest was compromised by the Agency's error, specifically, that the error must be found to have affected the Agency's decision to take the adverse action under review.

While the Agency argues that Mr. [A] "was not prejudiced in the least by the fact that the notice of proposed removal was silent with regard to nexus," this is unpersuasive. Indeed, there would have been no adverse action but for the nexus and the nexus was neither alleged or known at the time the letter of proposed adverse action was issued. To omit mention — or investigation — of the heart of the case against the Grievant is clearly to prejudice his interest and clearly constitutes harmful error.

This harmful error cannot be cured by evidence which later surfaces, just as in criminal law, a search cannot be legally justified by the contraband it reveals. Put another way, the Agency cannot "bootstrap" its case by producing evidence neither available nor cited at the time of the letter of proposed adverse action.

It therefore follows that the second element of rudimentary due process was likewise not met. Ms. [C], the deciding official, was perforce, not a properly unbiased party because she had access to — and extensively used — the information in the OIG report not available to or used by the proposing official. That the Union had the opportunity to controvert the OIG report is of no consequence here because the OIG report was not properly used by the deciding official. In a criminal case, the due process defect of an unlawful search which turns up contraband is not cured simply when the defendant's counsel has the opportunity to controvert the quality and probative value of the evidence if the evidence is constitutionally inadmissible in the first place. Similarly, the defect is not cured when the judge in a criminal case is capable of objectively examining the probative value of unconstitutionally obtained evidence, evidence not properly before him.

The conclusion thus is inescapable that Mr. [A] was denied substantive and procedural due process, that this constituted harmful error as the failure of the Agency to allege nexus or to present evidence at the time of the letter of proposed adverse action of nexus directly affected the Agency's decision to take the adverse action under review here.

Therefore, the appropriate remedy is to direct that Mr. [A] be put back on the job he formerly encumbered and that he receive full back pay and benefits due him.

*   *   *   *   *   *

The Union vehemently objected to admission of testimony by one of Mr. [A]'s co-workers, [I]. After Mr. [A]'s employment had been terminated, Mr. [I] told Supervisor Hansen that the Grievant had introduced him to cocaine use and together they had used the drug frequently. * * * As the information provided by Mr. [I] to the Agency about Mr. [A]'s drug use and involvement came to light well after the decision to terminate the Grievant was made, and could not have therefore possibly affected the decision, the testimony is inadmissible against Mr. [A] and may not be considered by the undersigned.

Admission of the testimony of Mr. [I] does not seem at all consistent with any concept of due process. For the arbitrator to consider this testimony while at the time the decision was taken to initiate or propose the adverse action, no one in management knew anything about Mr. [I]'s alleged drug involvement with Mr. [A] would be wrong. One cannot seek to bulwark a decision by subsequent events or matters which come to light after the decision has been made. To use an analogy from criminal law previously cited, a search is not justified by what contraband it reveals; a search must be justified constitutionally before it is undertaken. The decision both to propose and to effectuate Mr. [A]'s removal was made before this information came to light. Even if credible, Mr. [I]'s testimony is inadmissible in this proceeding.

*   *   *   *   *   *

NOTES

1. Is the arbitrator overturning the discharge because the employer used unfair procedures in the discharge process or because fundamental principles of fairness dictate reinstatement? Does "due process of arbitration" apply during the arbitral process or in the workplace itself? After reinstating the grievant, could the agency discharge him based upon subsequently discovered information provided by [I]?

2. In *City of Detroit*, 79-2 LAB. ARB. AWARDS (CCH) ¶ 8533 (1979) (Roumell, Arb.), the arbitrator set aside the suspension of a prison guard after his employer disciplined him without permitting him to offer his own version of the facts. The employer had relied upon information that the guard had allowed prisoners to consume alcohol and engage in sexual activities. The arbitrator's opinion found that "industrial due process" mandated "that the employee be advised promptly of the charges against him, in detail, and be given an opportunity to explain his version of the story before discipline is administered." (*Id.* at 5358.)

3. What is the source of industrial due process in matters, like *Goddard* and *City of Detroit*? Is it the constitution? Can the constitution play any role in arbitration, a process in which the parties have explicitly used a private contract to opt out of the court system? Or is the source the contract or the collective bargaining agreement? Many collective bargaining agreements require "just cause" to discipline an employee. Are arbitrators merely relying on the contractual need for "just cause" when they use industrial due process to overturn the improper discipline of employees? Professor St. Antoine has described the arbitrator as a "contract reader" whose assignment is to follow the instructions of the contract signatories. (Theodore J. St. Antoine, *Judicial Review of Labor Arbitration Awards: A Second Look at* Enterprise Wheel *and Its Progeny*, 75 MICH. L. REV. 1137, 1138–44 (1977).) He views the arbitrator as the disputants' "joint *alter ego* for the purpose of striking whatever supplementary bargain is necessary to handle the anticipated omissions of the initial agreement." (*Id.* at 1140.) Under this theory the source of the due process of arbitration may be the parties themselves. However, some labor arbitration decisions articulate a vision of "industrial due process" without any need for "just cause" under a collective bargaining agreement. When this happens there is no express contract rationale. Is it proper to imply a term in a contract calling for arbitrations that use due process concepts? Or is the source of due process in labor arbitration merely the arbitrator's freedom to decide disputes without being hemmed-in by legal rules? Labor arbitrators believe that their work helps to facilitate productive and peaceful labor-management relations and that mandating due process principles aids this process. The use of constitutional rules within labor arbitration helps to prolong "relational contracts" — contracts based on long-term relationships in which each contract party has a great amount of past investment in their continued bilateral association. (*See* IAN R. MACNEILL, CONTRACTS: EXCHANGE TRANSACTIONS AND RELATIONS 10–16, 210–13 (2d ed. 1978) (describing "relational contracts" and contrasting "transactional" contracts which involve short term one-shot interactions rather than long term relations), Ian R. Macneil, *Relational Contract: What We Do and Do Not Know*, 1985 WIS. L. REV. 483.) The use of constitutional rules in labor arbitration also creates a positive environment for labor-management governance — it permits parties to a long term relationship to independently resolve their own problems rather than have an external set of doctrinal rules dictate a result. (*See* St. Antoine, *supra* at 1138 ("The key to the special status of labor arbitration is that it is an integral component of union and management's autonomous regulation of their ongoing relationship").) It is thought that such positive labor-management governance furthers productivity and serves to avoid future problems. (*See* Charles Craver, *Labor Arbitration as a Continuation of the Collective Bargaining Process*, 66 CHI. KENT L. REV. 571 (1990).)

4. Labor arbitrations occur pursuant to collective bargaining agreements between unions and employers. Many labor arbitrations involve public employees who work for government bodies, 40 percent of whom are unionized. However, what will be the future role of labor arbitration now that less than

11% of private sector workers are covered by collective bargaining agreements? Is there a role for labor arbitrations held pursuant to individual employment contracts entered into at the time non-union employees are hired?

For the view issued by a Blue Ribbon Committee that such employment arbitration should be generally encouraged, see the Report and Recommendations of the Commission on the Future of Labor Management Relations ("Dunlop Commission Report"), issued January 9, 1995. The Dunlop Commission Report endorsed the use of voluntary alternative dispute resolution processes for employment disputes. At the time the Report was issued John Dunlop, former Secretary of Labor and a Harvard professor, said that he foresaw a future with "a less litigious workplace with more ADR." The Dunlop Commission Report recommends that employment ADR meet high quality standards. It opposes unilateral imposition of ADR by employers as a condition of employment.

The National Academy of Arbitrators Board of Governors has now formally approved of using ADR, including arbitration, in the nonunion context. (104 Daily Labor Rep. A-4-5 (May 31, 1995).) The Board, like the Dunlop Commission, recommended that grievance arbitration involving nonunion employees be fair, credible and compatible with due process.

The following chapters on arbitration, however, will present materials questioning whether arbitration should be used to resolve non-union employee claims against their employers or former employers. Numerous commentators have recently raised significant concerns regarding the arbitration of non-union employment disputes. (*See, e.g.*, Note, *Arbitration of State-Law Claims By Employees: An Argument for Containing Federal Arbitration Law*, 80 CORNELL L. REV. 1695 (1995) (concluding that arbitration of state law claims is outside FAA and that FAA should be interpreted to exempt "contracts of employment" from its coverage); Stephen E. Ware, *Employment Arbitration and Voluntary Consent*, 25 HOFSTRA L. REV. 83 (1996) (critiquing whether non-union employees validly consent to arbitrate).) In addition, some arbitration providers have indicated their opposition to routine arbitration of all non-union employee contracts to resolve disputes with their employers. The American Arbitration Association has announced that it will refuse to hear "mandatory" employment arbitrations that restrict employee rights, such as the right to an attorney or the right to bring claims for damages.

5. *Interest Arbitration.* The *Goddard Space Flight Center* arbitration was a dispute involving employee grievances. Such disputes involving employees' contractual "rights" are routinely arbitrated. Grievance arbitrations focus on disputes between individual employees and their employers. Arbitration is also used to resolve disputes between unions and management. Often these disputes concern issues or "interests" of major significance. The arbitrator focuses on matters of "interest" of each party and may seek a solution that advances the respective interests. This brand of arbitration is sometimes called "interest arbitration."

Interest arbitration typically decides a significant feature of a relationship between two disputants, such as wages or hours of employment, but excludes a decision on their rights. Frequently interest arbitration will focus on the basic terms of a relationship. It is used often to determine terms of collective bargaining relationships in the public sector where a public sector union is at an impasse with a governmental employer and public employee strikes are prohibited.

6. Occasionally a type of arbitration is used to resolve labor disputes that is called "non-binding arbitration." The arbitrator's decision is announced but is really not binding. Is this really arbitration? Don't arbitral awards have to be binding? Is non-binding arbitration really more a type of mediation?

7. Although the "folklore" model of arbitration calls for a quick and low cost process, the reality is sometimes less successful. After complaints of delays in the employee grievance arbitration process, the American Arbitration Association designed an "Excelleration Program" to provide a simple hearing within 15 days of the filing of the grievance and a quick award within 24 hours of the close of evidence. (14 BNA EMP. REL. WEEKLY 345 (1996).) If the parties agree, the decision could be rendered without hearing live evidence and using only documents.

2. COMMERCIAL ARBITRATION

Arbitration between two businesses is perceived as one of the most successful types of dispute resolution and is prospering. Commercial arbitration has a long and established history. It was "firmly established in England by the 14th Century as the preferred method of dispute resolution for members of the merchant and craft guilds." (C. EDWARD FLETCHER, at 12. *See also*, Earl Wolaver, *The Historical Background of Commercial Arbitration*, 83 U. PA. L. REV. 132 (1934).) One of the earliest and most popular forms of commercial arbitration in the United States involved the resolution of disputes in the New York garment industry. The theory of the contracts to arbitrate New York textile disputes was simple — rather than go to court, let a trusted, expert third party who was knowledgeable in the trade and industry customs decide the dispute. Arbitrator expertise was primarily responsible for the success of these textile arbitrations and led the way as other specialized areas of commerce (e.g., construction arbitration) turned toward arbitration and away from litigation.

Today the term "commercial arbitration" has a broad meaning and encompasses many types of disputes. The most common types of commercial arbitration include intra-industry disputes (e.g., two energy companies), disputes between product buyers and suppliers, franchisees and franchisors, or lenders and business borrowers. In addition to a desire to avoid the cost and delay associated with conventional trials, these forms of commercial arbitration usually involve disputants who themselves are known to one another. In a sense, commercial arbitration often involves "relational contracts," contracts between business parties who have a long-term relationship rather than a one-shot "transaction" between strangers. In theory, arbitration is a "friendly" way to preserve an established relationship and avoid the hassles and animosities that folklore suggests will occur if the more adversary process of litigation is used to resolve the dispute. Individuals or businesses involved in long-term relationships have more incentive to resolve their differences than do disputants who know one another less well. (Frank

Sander, *Varieties of Dispute Processing*, 70 F.R.D. 111, 120–122 (1976).) Such business signatories to arbitration clauses also are often of relatively equal bargaining power and capable of understandably contracting to arbitrate. For discussion of the theoretical distinction between relational and transactional contracts, see Ian MacNeil, *Contracts: Exchange Transactions and Relations* 10–16, 210–13 (2d ed. 1978); Ian Macneil, *Contracts: Adjustments of Long-Term Economic Relations Under Classical, Neoclassical and Relational Contract Law*, 72 Nw. U. L. Rev. 854 (1978); Ian Macneil, *The Many Futures of Contracts*, 47 S. Cal. L. Rev. 691 (1974); Ian Macneil, *Relational Contract: What We Do and Do Not Know*, 1985 Wis. L. Rev. 483.

Parties involved in commercial arbitration are generally familiar with the arbitration process. They often select the largest provider of arbitration services, the American Arbitration Association ("AAA") to sponsor the arbitration. AAA procedures permit the parties to select an arbitrator who has experience in the particular type of dispute involved.

Commercial arbitration can be a dominant mode of dispute resolution in certain industries. Certainly this is the case in the construction industry where most major construction contracts have arbitration clauses. Many parties to construction contracts have long-term relationships, may have additional business beyond the contract at issue, and, accordingly, need a way to resolve disputes quickly, efficiently and, if possible, amicably. Construction arbitration is universally acclaimed as a success. (*See, e.g.*, Thomas J. Stipanowich, *Beyond Arbitration: Innovation and Evolution in the United States Construction Industry*, 31 Wake Forest L. Rev. 65 (1996) (discussing history of use of arbitration in construction industry and growing pains and experimentation in dispute resolution within industry).) Nonetheless, even the construction industry is concerned with the cost of arbitration and its potential for adjudicatory excess and, accordingly, is presently turning to mediation as a complement to its historic use of arbitration.

The definition of "commercial" arbitration is itself not uncontroversial. As treated here the term commercial arbitration focuses upon arbitration between two businesses, each knowledgeable about the arbitration process and each with bargaining abilities and power. The term, however, is often used loosely. One sometimes hears the term commercial arbitration used to cover factual contexts in which one party is a business and the other a private individual with little or no business acumen and no prior experience in the arbitration process. For example, a contract calling for the arbitration of a medical malpractice claim or a bank's use of an arbitration clause to resolve disputes with account customers might be termed "commercial arbitration" because *tone* party to the contract is in commerce. Yet, these transactions are unbalanced and the individuals in these two examples may lack experience and understanding regarding arbitration.

3. International Commercial Arbitration

Arbitration between businesses involved in an international commercial dispute is increasingly popular. While the reasons for the growth of international commercial arbitration mirror those that have caused domestic businesses to turn to commercial arbitration, there are special circumstances that lie behind the move to international arbitration. The opportunity costs of international litigation are very high. Where two businesses, each based in different countries, sign a contract, each may fear the uncertainties of litigating in a distant and potentially hostile forum. The risk of costly and unsuccessful litigation encourages the parties to avoid contracting without an arbitration option.

Two business parties to an international joint venture frequently agree to arbitrate before one of the growing number of centers for international arbitration. Leading providers or sponsors of international arbitration include the American Arbitration Association, the International Chamber of Commerce ("ICC") (based in Paris), the Stockholm Chamber of Commerce, and the Hong Kong Centre for Dispute Resolution. New international arbitration providers have emerged recently, largely due to the growth of world trade, the popularity of international arbitration of commercial disputes and the ease of entry into a growing and largely unregulated market of arbitration providers.

The success of international arbitration raises a number of interesting questions about the arbitral process itself and the arbitrators' use of substantive law. Of course, parties to an international contract may choose to be bound by a particular state's law. Choice of law clauses are common in international business transactions. Choice of law clauses increase the certainty that businesses seek in potentially risky international transactions. On the other hand, contractual partners may fear a specific choice of law. Parties to a contract that calls for international arbitration intentionally may seek to avoid the court system of their contractual partner. For example, a Japanese or Taiwanese business involved in a joint venture relationship with an American company may want nothing to do with U.S. courts and their potentially high jury verdicts, risk of punitive damages, and broad, costly discovery processes. It is indeed possible that these same businesses would not fear litigation in their own countries.

The arbitration option permits these foreign firms to avoid principles of U.S. substantive law that would be applicable in court. Among the most significant attractions of international commercial arbitration is avoidance of domestic substantive law. Demand exists for a "de-localized" type of arbitration. One of the tenets of international arbitration is *amiable compositeur*, the power to ignore the law. Instead, international arbitrators usually emphasize the normal brand of fact-based "justice" that typically characterizes arbitration.

International arbitrators may also apply an "international blend" of increasingly similar domestic substantive commercial law principles to their cases — a common law of international arbitration exists that is based on international custom and usage. (*See, e.g.*, W.L. CRAIG, W. PARK, & J. PAULSSON, INTERNATIONAL CHAMBER OF COMMERCE ARBITRATION, § 35.01 (3d ed. Oceana 2000).) The rules of sponsor organizations of international commercial arbitration typically provide that trade customs and usage norms should apply. For example, the Arbitration Rules of the ICC specify that "[i]n all cases the Arbitral Tribunal shall take account of the provisions of the contract and the relevant trade usages." (Rules of the ICC art. 17(2) (1998). *Accord*, International Rules of the AAA, cert. 28(2) (1997) (requiring the tribunal to "take into account usages of the trade applicable to the contract").) Arbitrator use of such common business customs and usages may be attractive to arbitration adversaries because it permits the parties to use customs to guide their pre-dispute behavior in a preventative law manner and avoids a potentially arbitrary arbitral result that can occur when arbitrators ignore business reality in crafting an award. The use of a common law of international arbitration is generally familiar to the disputants and comes as no surprise. This means that from the disputant's perspective, the type of substantive law chosen by international arbitrators may be preferable to ordinary domestic substantive norms.

The processes of international arbitration more closely resemble conventional litigation than most other forms of arbitration. Some would say that many international arbitrations employ a judicialized model of arbitration. A common reference of the parties is to the Commercial Arbitration Rules of the American Arbitration Association. The arbitrators usually sit in panels of three. The rules of the international arbitration providers often permit some modest discovery. The hearings themselves are not necessarily any more speedy than conventional trials. Indeed, several American companies have been parties to international arbitrations in London that have lasted over a year and consumed large sums in attorneys fees — hardly the type of quick, inexpensive and informal "alternative" that one normally associates with alternative dispute resolution. Informality and speed are not the biggest reasons that disputants select international commercial arbitration. Businesses are typically drawn to the process out of fear of foreign litigation processes and the application of foreign legal rules.

A significant difference between international commercial arbitration and its typical domestic equivalent is that international arbitrators normally write opinions explaining their awards. The parties want these opinions which operate as a check against arbitrariness — the arbitrators explain the reasons for their result and cite the substantial authority that forms the common law of international arbitration. These written opinions, in turn, are valuable to the development of the growing common law of international arbitration. They are available to attorneys and others both in the free market — they can be purchased — and in the files of international providers of arbitration.

The success and increasing popularity of international commercial arbitration forces one to ask why arbitrators do not write explanatory opinions or decisions in all arbitrations. A quick explanation may be that the demand for privacy (or secrecy) is so great that it outweighs the benefits of written arbitral awards. Nonetheless, parties to international arbitration appear to prefer written opinions to privacy. This trade-off remains to be fully fleshed out. Some parties to domestic arbitrations do require a written arbitral award. Arbitration critics have called for routinized opinion writing as part of the normal conclusion of an arbitration. (*See* Edward Brunet, *Questioning the Quality of Alternative Dispute Resolution*, 62 TULANE L. REV. 1 (1987); Laura Macklin, *Promoting Settlement, Foregoing the Facts*, 14 N.Y.U. REV. L. & SOC. CHANGE 575 (1986); Lynn Katzler, *Should Mandatory Written Opinions Be Required in All Securities Arbitrations?: The Practical and Legal Implications to the Securities Industry*, 45 AM. U. L. REV. 151 (1995).) It may be that international arbitration can serve as a useful model for future growth and refinement of the domestic arbitration equivalent.

International arbitration has been enthusiastically supported by the United States Supreme Court. In *Scherk v. Alberto-Culver*, 417 U.S. 506 (1975), the Court required the parties to arbitrate a fraud claim brought under the federal securities laws because the underlying contract between the parties, which included an arbitration clause, was "truly international." More recently in *Mitsubishi Motors Corp. v. Soler Chrysler-Plymouth, Inc.*, 473 U.S. 614 (1985), the Supreme Court required the arbitration of an international antitrust dispute despite the fact that most U.S. courts had found domestic antitrust claims to be not arbitrable. Together, the *Scherk* and *Mitsubishi* opinions combine to emphasize the positive attributes of international arbitration and demonstrate a hospitable reception toward international arbitration by the Supreme Court.

4. MARITIME ARBITRATION

Maritime Arbitration, the arbitration of ocean shipping claims, is closely related to international commercial arbitration. The contract to arbitrate has a long and respected history in the shipping industry, one in which ocean carriers and shippers often are businesses from different nations. The maritime industry has chosen arbitration for some of the same reasons as other users of commercial arbitration — low cost, speedier, informal dispute resolution and the use of expert arbitrators who are familiar with the industry. (*See* Wilfred Feinberg, *Maritime Arbitration and the Federal Courts*, 5 FORDHAM INT'L L.J. 245, 246 (1982) (describing the benefit of technical and sophisticated maritime arbitrators).) Numerous providers, including the Society of Maritime Arbitrators and the American Arbitration Association, supply maritime arbitration services.

Maritime arbitration often employs a more judicialized type of arbitration. The Society of Maritime Arbitrators generally publishes its maritime arbitration awards. The practice is helpful to the arbitrators and, if needed, to courts asked to review arbitral awards. (*See* Feinberg, *supra* at 249.) Maritime arbitrators are not bound by previously published maritime arbitration awards. Nonetheless, they "invariably do take heed of prior awards" and sometimes refer to previously published awards. (Robert Force & Anthony Mavronicolas, *Two Models of Maritime Dispute Resolution: Litigation and Arbitration*, 65 TUL. L. REV. 1461, 1503 (1991).) In this way, maritime awards possess a "recognized precedential value" that advances fairness and consistency policies. (*See* Thomas E. Carbonneau, *Rendering Arbitral Awards With Reasons: The Elaboration of a Common Law of International Transactions*, 23 COLUM. J. TRANSNAT'L L. 579, 587 (1985).)

The combined impact of maritime awards is said to have created a sort of general maritime law or a *lex maritima*. (*See generally* William Tetley, *The General Maritime Law — The Lex Maritima*, 20 SYRACUSE J. INT'L L. & COM. 105 (1994).) Much of the content of the *lex maritima* represents a sort of international trade usage and practice in the industry. It is a particular type of the common law of merchants based upon trade usage, sometimes termed the *lex mercatoria*. The *lex maritima* exists, as a formal matter, outside the confines of the formal domestic law of any specific motion. As the *lex maritima* develops, it holds the attraction of providing arbitrators and disputants with a neutral, industry specific set of norms. For further discussion of the *lex mercatoria* see Thomas E. Carbonneau (ed.), LEX MERCATORIA AND ARBITRATION (1990).

5. SECURITIES ARBITRATION

The typical dispute between an investor and her stockbroker never sees the inside of the courthouse. Since the 1970's the vast percentage of brokerages have included arbitration clauses in their new account agreements for customers with margin or option accounts. In addition, numerous firms have an arbitration clause in their ordinary cash accounts. The typical clause calls for the parties to use the arbitral services of the National Association of Securities Dealers ("NASD"), a joint venture of securities sellers that possesses an experienced and professional arbitration department. The following is a typical clause:

> Unless unenforceable due to federal or state law, any controversy arising out of or relating to my accounts, the transactions with you for me, or to this agreement or the breach thereof, shall be settled by arbitration in accordance with the rules then in effect of the National Association of Securities Dealers, Inc. or the Boards of Directors of the New York Stock Exchange, Inc. and/or the American Stock Exchange, Inc. as I may elect. If I do not make such election by registered mail addressed to you at your main office within five (5) days after demand by you that I make such election then you may make such election. Judgment upon any award ordered by the arbitrators may be entered in any court hearing jurisdiction thereof. [*Rodriguez de Quijas v. Shearson/Lehman Bros., Inc.*, 845 F.2d 1296, 1297 n.2 (5th Cir. 1988), *aff'd sub nom., Rodriguez de Quijas v. Shearson/American Express, Inc.*, 490 U.S. 477 (1989).]

The volume of disputes disposed of by the NASD is considerable. In 2003, investors filed over 7,000 disputes with the NASD. The mean time to disposition of these claims is over one year, more than the mean time to trial in federal courts. The Securities and Exchange Commission oversees securities arbitration as part of its overall regulation of the sale of securities and its regulation of self regulatory organizations such as the stock exchanges. In addition to securities arbitrations sponsored by the NASD, other organizations sponsor securities arbitration, including the New York Stock Exchange, the American Stock Exchange, the Chicago Board Options Exchange and the American Arbitration Association. When arbitration sponsored by these other organizations is taken into account, the volume of securities disputes increases considerably.

The NASD, by far the largest provider of securities arbitration, uses three-person arbitration panels to hear most of its disputes. Under NASD rules, two of the three arbitrators must be so-called "public arbitrators" — individuals with no ties to the industry. The third arbitrator is normally a non-lawyer former broker who brings industry expertise to the panel.

In recent years, complaints of pro-industry bias have been made against the NASD. Some contend that the structural presence of the former broker on the panel needlessly prejudices results in favor of the respondents who are usually individual stockbrokers and their employers. Critics have urged the NASD to take steps to remove any appearance of bias from its procedures by discontinuing the use of an industry arbitrator. To date, however, all NASD arbitrator panels still have a former broker member. Some attorneys who represent claimants against brokers opt for arbitration before a competitor provider organization with different rules on the composition of arbitration panels. Indeed, the AAA hears a significant volume of securities arbitration (it received 495 cases in 1988) and uses its own panels of neutral arbitrators on these matters.

The available statistics do not fully resolve claims that customers fare more poorly in arbitration than in litigation. Data from 1980–88 demonstrated that customers recover in about one-half of the arbitrations in which they take part. (*See* C. EDWARD FLETCHER, ARBITRATING SECURITIES DISPUTES 98–99 (1990).) A Securities and Exchange Commission review of a study comparing results in securities litigation and arbitration by the accounting firm Deloitte, Haskins & Sells concluded that there were no statistically significant differences between arbitration and litigation. Professor Fletcher concluded that the Deloitte study "is ambiguous in its results" but did show that "customers are not obviously more likely to recover more in one forum than the other." (FLETCHER, *supra* at 102.) A 1992 report of the General Accounting Office ("GAO") suggested that arbitrations conducted by securities industry forums "show no indication of a pro-industry bias." (GAO, *How Investors Fare* 7 (GAO/GGD-92-74) (1992).) A recent blue ribbon task force appointed by the NASD to study and recommend changes in NASD arbitration found that from 1991–1995, securities arbitrators "awarded damages to customer claimants in 50 percent of all cases they decided." (Report of the Arbitration Policy Task Force, SECURITIES ARBITRATION REFORM 18 (1996) (hereinafter "Task Force Report").) A survey of securities arbitration results demonstrated that the "win" rate for investors increases as the damage claim increases. The survey also found that in claims of over $1 million, 7% of claimants were awarded punitive damages. (Michael Siconolfi, *For Brokerage Awards, Bigger is Better*, WALL ST. J., June 21, 1996, p. B7.) An internal NASD study shows that customers were awarded damages in 53% of all cases in 2000 and 61% of all cases in 1999.

Securities arbitration is at a crossroads. Its supporters refer to its success in processing a considerable volume of arbitration and the cost savings passed on to investors and industry. (*See, e.g.,* Deborah Masucci, *Securities Arbitration — A Success Story: What Does the Future Hold?*, 31 WAKE FOREST L. REV. 183 (1996).) Critics, however, continually point to the appearance of impropriety in using industry arbitrators as panelists. The 1996 Task Force Report recommended major changes in securities arbitration, some of which would increase the cost of the process by adopting judicialized procedures. Task Force recommendations for securities arbitration reform included using pretrial motions to deal with limitations issues, permitting but capping (at $750,000) punitive damages, allowing written opinions explaining punitive damage awards, and appointing arbitrators earlier in the case in order to help manage the judicial-like arbitration process. As of 2001 only the last recommendation has been approved but others are pending action.

6. CONSUMER ARBITRATION: ARBITRATION OUTSIDE THE RELATIONAL CONTRACT

The arbitration of claims arising outside a close business relationship is a fairly recent development. Disputants who end up in a tort dispute usually lack the preexisting contractual relationship that may result in a contract to arbitrate. Nonetheless, some tort arbitration and other non-relational contract arbitration now occurs. For example, some health care providers such as hospitals and physicians, have forms calling for arbitration of disputes between patients and hospitals or doctors. Auto insurers commonly call for arbitration of disputes with insureds regarding uninsured motorist coverage. Banks routinely present loan documents containing arbitration clauses to new customers. Banks have also recently begun to send old account customers notice of intent to arbitrate disputes. Many securities arbitrations may also be considered outside the relational contract. Although some brokers and customers have long term relationships, numerous customers and brokers have short term dealings and find their relationship severed by a dispute.

Arbitration under these types of short-term transactions presents a challenge. Huge power imbalances typically exist between the contractual partners. Boilerplate contracts with fine print arbitration clauses may be used. The consumer may know little about dispute resolution and nothing regarding arbitration.

These uses of arbitration present obstacles to the process and have come under some criticism. Banks, doctors, hospitals and insurance companies each desire to avoid juries and potentially high monetary liability associated with conventional trials. Their "partners" in such arbitration (bank customers, computer purchasers, patients and insureds) are private individuals who are comparatively unsophisticated in the arbitration process. Is it fair to subject these parties to arbitration? Do such parties have the capacity to knowingly consent to arbitration? The following arbitration chapters will explore this problem in detail.

Arbitration in a box. Product sellers are drawn to arbitratioin increasingly. For a detailed examination of arbitration between consumers and sellers, see Katherine Van Wetzel Stone, *Rustic Justice: Community and Coercion Under the Federal Arbitration Act*, 77 N.C. L. REV. 931 (1999) [hereinafter Katherine Stone, *Rustic Justice*]. Professor Stone analyzes the problem of "arbitration in a box," our term for the buyer who opens a box and reads that disputes with the seller are to be arbitrated. (*See, e.g., Hill v. Gateway 2000, Inc.*, 105 F.3d 1147 (7th Cir. 1997) (upholding arbitration set forth in a product information book in a Gateway computer box).) Banks and credit card issuers now routinely insert arbitration features in amendments to their Credit Card agreements. For example, MBNA America Bank, N.A., recently sent its credit card holders a notice stating that "As provided in your Credit Card Agreement and under Delaware law, we are amending the Credit Card Agreement to include an Arbitration Section."

Lemon Law Arbitration. Arbitration of so-called "lemon law" claims brought by automobile buyers against automobile manufacturers represents a grand experiment in the use of alternative dispute resolution outside the relational contract context. It is almost axiomatic that every year numerous automobile "lemons" are sold to American consumers. In the Magnuson-Moss Warranty Act, 15 U.S.C. §§ 2301–12, Congress encouraged manufacturers to settle consumer warranty claims through informal settlement mechanisms. (15 U.S.C. § 2310(a).) Under this legislation numerous automobile manufacturers have created arbitration tribunals to resolve consumer warranty claims. The decision is not binding on either party, but the warrantor (manufacturer) must "act in good faith in determining whether . . . [to] abide by a . . . decision." (16 C.F.R. § 703.2(g)(2005).) Most automobile manufacturers evidence their "good faith" by agreeing in advance of arbitration to be bound by the award. These arbitration programs are designed to be speedy and operate at a low cost. The consumer claimant pays no fee and, under Federal Trade Commission regulations, is to receive a decision within 40 days of a claim. (16 C.F.R. § 703.5(d)(2005).) Most consumers do not bother using an attorney to represent them. Initiation of these arbitration programs are voluntary for manufacturers; several foreign manufacturers of cars sold in the U.S. do not operate arbitration settlement facilities.

The settlement programs offered by automobile manufacturers differ in significant ways. The programs of some manufacturers operate entirely on the basis of written submissions. Other manufacturers use the Better Business Bureau to administer their arbitration systems under the Autoline program. Arbitrators need not be lawyers and, as one would suspect, hold highly informal hearings.

The lemon law arbitration programs can be influenced significantly by state lemon law legislation. The vast percentage of states have lemon laws and some of these schemes regulate the automobile warranty arbitration programs. The state lemon law arbitration procedures vary greatly. Some states make available quasi-judicial arbitration to their consumers; others do not. New York, for example, permits the consumer to select binding arbitration by the an arbitration administrator of her own choosing rather than use the more standard "mechanism" provided by the auto manufacturer. (*See* N.Y. GEN. BUS. LAW § 198-a(k) (2001).) Massachusetts has also mandated the use of independent, professional arbitrators to hear automobile warranty lemon law disputes. (MASS. GEN. ANN. LAWS, Ch. 90, § 7N 1/2(6) (2005); Paula Gold, *Massachusetts Lemon Law Arbitration Program: 1987 Report*, ARB. J., Sept. 1988, at 48 (Mass. arbitrators decide in favor of consumers in 2/3 of claims and these results lead others to settle prior to hearings).) Oregon requires a consumer to use the typical informal warranty dispute resolution system set up by the automobile manufacturers but makes arbitration decisions binding on the manufacturer. (OR. REV. STAT. § 646.355 (2005).) For a comparison of differing state lemon law arbitration legislation, see Note, *Alternative Dispute Resolution Under Ohio's Lemon Laws: A Critical Analysis*, 6 OHIO ST. J. ON DISP. RES. 333 (1991).

C. LEGISLATION

1. THE FAA

The United States Arbitration Act, 9 U.S.C. § 1, *et seq.* [sometimes called the Federal Arbitration Act ("FAA"), reprinted in Appendix A], was passed in 1925. It was patterned after 1920 New York legislation and designed to reverse the prevailing judicial attitude that had been antagonistic to contracts "ousting" or depriving courts of jurisdiction to hear disputes. The New York law made predispute agreements to arbitrate valid and enforceable and created court authority to stay suits pending completion of arbitration. (New York Arbitration Act, N.Y. Sess. Laws 1920, Ch. 275.) At common law, private contracts to arbitrate future disputes that might arise were perceived as unenforceable efforts to oust courts of jurisdiction. (*See, e.g., Home Ins. Co. v. Morse,* 87 U.S. 445, 451 (1874) ("agreements in advance to oust the courts of the jurisdiction conferred by law are illegal and void"); *Meacham v. Jamestown, F & C R.R. Co.,* 211 N.Y. 346, 354, 105 N.E. 653, 656 (1914) ("The jurisdiction of our courts is established by law, and it is not to be diminished, any more than it is to be increased, by the convention of the parties") (Cardozo, J. concurring); *Pepin v. Societe St. Jean Baptiste,* 49 A. 387, 388 (R.I. 1901) (waiver of a judicial forum by an adverse agreement to arbitrate violates public policy).)

The goal of FAA was to change the existing thinking that courts were superior to arbitration and, instead, enlist judges as facilitators of the disputants' contractual agreements to decide their differences through private arbitral efforts. For extended discussion of the FAA's legislative history co-authored by one of the drafters of the FAA, see Julius Cohen & Kenneth Dayton, *The New Federal Arbitration Law*, 12 VA. L. REV. 265 (1926). For full treatment of the passage of the FAA, see IAN MACNEIL, AMERICAN ARBITRATION LAW (1992).

A few selected features regarding the legislative history of the FAA should be stressed:

(1) An American Bar Association committee drafted the first version of the bill that eventually became the FAA. (*See* Report of the Committee on Commerce, Trade and Commercial Law, 47 A.B.A. Rep. 288, 293–94 (1922).) This bill was patterned after New York arbitration legislation passed in 1920.

(2) The goal of the ABA was to make the resolution of commercial disputes more efficient. (*Id.* at 293–295.) Indeed, the legislative hearings include testimony indicating that the lawmakers sought only to pass legislation permitting binding arbitration between businesses. "Contracts between merchants or between others in the business world are . . . those contracts primarily which the legislature in passing the Arbitration Law wished to cover." (Lional S. Popkin, *Judicial Construction of the New York Arbitration Law of 1920*, 11 CORNELL L.Q. 329 (1926).) Many of the business groups supporting passage of the FAA were trade or industrial associations that had successfully used arbitration to resolve disputes among their members; "expert" arbitrators would be selected who were fellow merchants. (*See*

Katherine Von Wetzel Stone, Rustic Justice, supra, at 976–94 (stressing role of trade groups in the early 20th century history of arbitration).)

(3) The legislation was designed to affect federal courts by forcing federal judges to enforce contracts to arbitrate.

(4) While the terms of the FAA have broad application to all contracts to arbitrate involving interstate commerce there is no indication in the legislative history that Congress envisioned that the FAA could apply under a specific line of commerce (e.g., the entire brokerage or securities industry's use of a standard form contract containing an arbitration clause when contracting with individual customers). (*See* Rita M. Cain, *Preemption of State Arbitration Statutes: The Exaggerated Federal Policy Favoring Arbitration*, 19 J. CONTEMP. L. 1, 12 (1993).)

The full text of the FAA is set out in Appendix A, *infra*. You should refer to the text throughout this part of the book. The major provisions of the FAA accomplish the following:

FAA § 2: A written agreement to arbitrate "shall be valid, irrevocable and enforceable, save upon such grounds as exist at law or in equity for the revocation of any contract."

FAA § 3: If a suit is brought in federal court that is referable to arbitration the court, "upon being satisfied that the issue in such suit . . . is referable to arbitration . . . shall on application of one of the parties stay the trial of the action until such arbitration has been had in accordance with the terms of the agreement . . ."

FAA § 4: A party who is "aggrieved" by the failure or refusal to arbitrate under a written agreement to arbitrate "may petition any United States district court . . . for an order directing that such arbitration proceed in the manner provided for in such agreement * * * The court shall hear the parties, and upon being satisfied that the making of the agreement for arbitration or the failure to comply therewith is not in issue, the court shall make an order directing the parties to proceed to arbitration." Jury trial may be demanded.

FAA § 5: If the arbitration agreement provides for a method of naming the arbitrator(s), it "shall be followed; but if no method" is provided, or if there is a "lapse" in the selection "the court shall designate and appoint an arbitrator."

FAA § 7: Arbitrators "may summon in writing any person to attend before them" as a witness and bring documents. If the witness refuses to obey the summons, the parties may petition the U.S. court in the district of the arbitration to compel attendance.

FAA § 9: If the parties have agreed that a judgment of the court shall be entered upon the arbitration award, the court may, within one year of the award, confirm the award.

FAA § 10: This section sets forth limited power for courts to vacate arbitration awards, including:

§ 10(a)(1) "corruption, fraud or undue means";

§ 10(a)(2) "evident partiality or corruption in the arbitrators";

§ 10(a)(3) misconduct in refusing to postpone the hearing or refusing to hear material evidence or misbehavior of the arbitrator "by which the rights of any party have been prejudiced"; and

§ 10(a)(4) "where the arbitrators exceeded their powers, or so imperfectly" acted "that a mutual, final, and definite award . . . was not made."

FAA § 11: The court has the power to "modify" or "correct" an award if there was "an evident material miscalculation of figures . . . or an evident material mistake in the description of any person, thing or property referred to in the award" or where the arbitrators' award covers a "matter not submitted to them."

2. THE MODEL STATE ARBITRATION ACT

Versions of the Model State Arbitration Act (Uniform Arbitration Act), reprinted in Appendix C, have been adopted, in whole or part, by 34 states. The remainder of the states also have either arbitration legislation or common law decisions regarding arbitration. (*See* Joseph T. McLoughlin: *Arbitrability: Current Trends in the United States*, 59 ALB. L. REV. 905, 933 (1996).) The Uniform Act was approved by the Commissioners for Uniform State Laws in 1956. Its mechanics work much like the FAA in that the MSAA makes arbitration awards the equivalent of court judgments, allows courts to stay court cases pending arbitration, grants courts the power to compel written arbitration agreements, and sets forth very narrow grounds for judicial review. The Uniform Act was recently revised thoroughly in 2000. (*See Uniform Act, Appendix C.) The revision was a major undertaking and a considerable achievement. It is much more detailed than the FAA and includes coverage on the important subjects of arbitration immunity, provisional remedies, discovery, jurisdiction, venue and arbitrator disclosures.*

The primary reason that state arbitration legislation is needed relates to the interstate commerce requirement of the FAA. To the degree that purely intrastate matters are affected, the FAA is inapplicable.

Under both the FAA and the MSAA a party seeking to force a contractual partner to arbitrate can file suit seeking an order compelling arbitration. Because of the broad, general subject matter jurisdiction of the state courts, a state court is a hospitable forum for such a suit. The federal courts also routinely hear suits to compel arbitration. Nonetheless, federal courts need an independent subject matter jurisdiction basis to hear such suits. Consider this language from *Mose H. Cone Memorial Hosp. v. Mercury Constr. Corp.*, 460 U.S. 1, 25 (1983):

> [t]he Arbitration Act is something of an anomaly in the field of federal-court jurisdiction. It creates a body of federal-court substantive law establishing and regulating the duty to honor an agreement to arbitrate, yet it does not create any independent federal-question jurisdiction under 28 U.S.C. § 1331 . . . or otherwise. Section 4 provides for an order compelling arbitration only when the federal district court would have jurisdiction over a suit on the underlying dispute; hence, there must be diversity of citizenship or some other independent basis for federal jurisdiction before the order can issue.

Accordingly, state courts may be the appropriate forum for suits to compel arbitration that lack federal jurisdictional basis. The FAA, of course, is broader in nature than state arbitration legislation which is typically intrastate in effect. Can a suit to compel arbitration predicated on the federal FAA be brought in a state court? This question, along with others dealing with the relationship of state and federal arbitration law, is addressed in the next chapter.

Chapter 10

ARBITRATION PREEMPTION AND THE RELEVANCE OF STATE ARBITRATION LAW

Numerous states have laws that affect the arbitration process directly or indirectly. For example, some states require that arbitration clauses that are part of form contracts be printed in large, boldface type to help the signer notice and question the arbitration agreement. These legal requirements may be viewed as part of contract law, a field traditionally regulated by state law and one in which the federal government has historically deferred to state regulation. The potential for conflict with the FAA exists and questions of constitutional preemption of state law are often presented.

SOUTHLAND CORP. v. KEATING
465 U.S. 1 (1984)

CHIEF JUSTICE BURGER delivered the opinion of the Court.

We noted probable jurisdiction to consider (a) whether the California Franchise Investment Law, which invalidates certain arbitration agreements covered by the Federal Arbitration Act, violates the Supremacy Clause and (b) whether arbitration under the Federal Act is impaired when a class action structure is imposed on the process by the state courts.

I

Appellant The Southland Corporation is the owner and franchisor of 7-Eleven convenience stores. Southland's standard franchise agreement provides each franchisee with a license to use certain registered trademarks, a lease or sublease of a convenience store owned or leased by Southland, inventory financing, and assistance in advertising and merchandising. The franchisees operate the stores, supply bookkeeping data, and pay Southland a fixed percentage of gross profits. The franchise agreement also contains the following provision requiring arbitration: "Any controversy or claim arising out of or relating to this Agreement or the breach thereof shall be settled by arbitration in accordance with the Rules of the American Arbitration Association . . . and judgment upon any award rendered by the arbitrator may be entered in any court having jurisdiction thereof."

Appellees are 7-Eleven franchisees. Between September 1975 and January 1977, several appellees filed individual actions against Southland in California Superior Court alleging, among other things, fraud, oral misrepresentation, breach of contract, breach of fiduciary duty, and violation of the disclosure requirements of the California Franchise Investment Law, Cal. Corp. Code § 31000 *et seq.* (1977). Southland's answer, in all but one of the individual actions, included the affirmative defense of failure to arbitrate.

451

In May 1977, appellee Keating filed a class action against Southland on behalf of a class that assertedly includes approximately 800 California franchisees. Keating's principal claims were substantially the same as those asserted by the other franchisees. After the various actions were consolidated, Southland petitioned to compel arbitration of the claims in all cases, and appellees moved for class certification.

The Superior Court granted Southland's motion to compel arbitration of all claims except those claims based on the Franchise Investment Law. The court did not pass on appellees' request for class certification. Southland appealed from the order insofar as it excluded from arbitration the claims based on the California statute. Appellees filed a petition for a writ of mandamus or prohibition in the California Court of Appeal arguing that the arbitration should proceed as a class action.

The California Court of Appeal reversed the trial court's refusal to compel arbitration of appellees' claims under the Franchise Investment Law. 109 Cal. App. 3d 784, 167 Cal. Rptr. 481 (1980). That court interpreted the arbitration clause to require arbitration of all claims asserted under the Franchise Investment Law, and construed the Franchise Investment Law not to invalidate such agreements to arbitrate. Alternatively, the court concluded that if the Franchise Investment Law rendered arbitration agreements involving commerce unenforceable, it would conflict with § 2 of the Federal Arbitration Act, 9 U.S.C. § 2 (1976), and therefore be invalid under the Supremacy Clause. 167 Cal. Rptr. at 493–494. The Court of Appeal also determined that there was no "insurmountable obstacle" to conducting an arbitration on a classwide basis, and issued a writ of mandate directing the trial court to conduct class certification proceedings.

The California Supreme Court, by a vote of 4-2, reversed the ruling that claims asserted under the Franchise Investment Law are arbitrable. 31 Cal.3d 584, 183 Cal. Rptr. 360, 645 P.2d 1192 (1982). The California Supreme Court interpreted the Franchise Investment Law to require judicial consideration of claims brought under that statute and concluded that the California statute did not contravene the federal Act. *Id.*, at 604, 183 Cal. Rptr., at 371–372, 645 P.2d, at 1203–1204. The court also remanded the case to the trial court for consideration of appellees' request for classwide arbitration.

We postponed consideration of the question of jurisdiction pending argument on the merits. We reverse in part and dismiss in part.

* * *

III

. . . [T]he California Franchise Investment Law provides: "Any condition, stipulation or provision purporting to bind any person acquiring any franchise to waive compliance with any provision of this law or any rule or order hereunder is void." Cal. Corp. Code § 31512 (1977). The California Supreme Court interpreted this statute to require judicial consideration of claims brought under the State statute and accordingly refused to enforce the parties' contract to arbitrate such claims. So interpreted the California Franchise

Investment Law directly conflicts with § 2 of the Federal Arbitration Act and violates the Supremacy Clause.

In enacting § 2 of the federal Act, Congress declared a national policy favoring arbitration and withdrew the power of the states to require a judicial forum for the resolution of claims which the contracting parties agreed to resolve by arbitration. . . .

The Federal Arbitration Act rests on the authority of Congress to enact substantive rules under the Commerce Clause. In *Prima Paint Corp. v. Flood & Conklin Manufacturing Corp.*, 388 U.S. 395 (1967), the Court examined the legislative history of the Act and concluded that the statute "is based upon . . . the incontestable federal foundations of 'control over interstate commerce and over admiralty.'" The contract in *Prima Paint*, as here, contained an arbitration clause. One party in that case alleged that the other had committed fraud in the inducement of the contract, although not of arbitration clause in particular, and sought to have the claim of fraud adjudicated in federal court. The Court held that, notwithstanding a contrary state rule, consideration of a claim of fraud in the inducement of a contract "is for the arbitrators and not for the courts," *id.*, at 400. The Court relied for this holding on Congress' broad power to fashion substantive rules under the Commerce Clause.

At least since 1824 Congress' authority under the Commerce Clause has been held plenary. *Gibbons v. Ogden*, 22 U.S. 1, 196 (1824). In the words of Chief Justice Marshall, the authority of Congress is "the power to regulate; that is, to prescribe the rule by which commerce is to be governed." *Ibid.* The statements of the Court in *Prima Paint* that the Arbitration Act was an exercise of the Commerce Clause power clearly implied that the substantive rules of the Act were to apply in state as well as federal courts. As Justice Black observed in his dissent, when Congress exercises its authority to enact substantive federal law under the Commerce Clause, it normally creates rules that are enforceable in state as well as federal courts. *Prima Paint*, 388 U.S., at 420 (Black, J., dissenting).

In *Moses H. Cone Memorial Hospital v. Mercury Construction Corp.*, we reaffirmed our view that the Arbitration Act "creates a body of federal substantive law" and expressly stated what was implicit in *Prima Paint*, *i.e.*, the substantive law the Act created was applicable in state and federal court. *Moses H. Cone* began with a petition for an order to compel arbitration. The District Court stayed the action pending resolution of a concurrent state court suit. In holding that the District Court had abused its discretion, we found no showing of exceptional circumstances justifying the stay and recognized "the presence of federal-law issues" under the federal Act as "a major consideration weighing against surrender [of federal jurisdiction]." We thus read the underlying issue of arbitrability to be a question of substantive federal law: "Federal law in the terms of the Arbitration Act governs that issue in either state or federal court."

Although the legislative history is not without ambiguities, there are strong indications that Congress had in mind something more than making arbitration agreements enforceable only in the federal courts. The House Report plainly suggests the more comprehensive objectives: "The purpose of this bill is to make valid and enforceable agreements for arbitration contained in *contracts involving interstate commerce* or within the jurisdiction or [*sic*] admiralty, or which may be the subject of litigation in the Federal courts." H.R. Rep. No. 96, 68th Cong., 1st Sess. 1 (1924) (Emphasis added.)

This broader purpose can also be inferred from the reality that Congress would be less likely to address a problem whose impact was confined to federal courts than a problem of large significance in the field of commerce. * * *

[T]he House Report contemplated a broad reach of the Act, unencumbered by state law constraints. As was stated in *Metro Industrial Painting Corp. v. Terminal Construction Corp.*, 287 F.2d 382, 387 (2d Cir. 1961) (Lumbard, Chief Judge, concurring), "the purpose of the act was to assure those who desired arbitration and whose contracts related to interstate commerce that their expectations would not be undermined by federal judges, or . . . by state courts or legislatures." Congress also showed its awareness of the widespread unwillingness of state courts to enforce arbitration agreements, and that such courts were bound by state laws inadequately providing for "technical arbitration by which, if you agree to arbitrate under the method provided by the statute, you have an arbitration by statute[;] but [the statutes] ha[d] nothing to do with validating the contract to arbitrate." . . .

Justice O'Connor argues that Congress viewed the Arbitration Act "as a procedural statute, applicable only in federal courts." If it is correct that Congress sought only to create a procedural remedy in the federal courts, there can be no explanation for the express limitation in the Arbitration Act to contracts "involving commerce." 9 U.S.C. § 2. For example, when Congress has authorized this Court to prescribe the rules of procedure in the federal Courts of Appeals, District Courts, and bankruptcy courts, it has not limited the power of the Court to prescribe rules applicable only to causes of action involving commerce. *See, e.g.*, 28 U.S.C. §§ 2072, 2075, 2076 (1976). We would expect that if Congress, in enacting the Arbitration Act, was creating what it thought to be a procedural rule applicable only in federal courts, it would not so limit the Act to transactions involving commerce. On the other hand, Congress would need to call on the Commerce Clause if it intended the Act to apply in state courts. Yet at the same time, its reach would be limited to transactions involving interstate commerce. We therefore view the "involving commerce" requirement in § 2, not as an inexplicable limitation on the power of the federal courts, but as a necessary qualification on a statute intended to apply in state and federal courts.

Under the interpretation of the Arbitration Act urged by JUSTICE O'CONNOR, claims brought under the California Franchise Investment Law are not arbitrable when they are raised in state court. Yet it is clear beyond question that if this suit had been brought as a diversity action in a federal district court, the arbitration clause would have been enforceable. *Prima Paint, supra*. The interpretation given to the Arbitration Act by the California Supreme Court would therefore encourage and reward forum shopping. We are unwilling to attribute to Congress the intent, in drawing on the comprehensive powers of the Commerce Clause, to create a right to enforce an arbitration contract and yet make the right dependent for its enforcement on the particular forum in which it is asserted. And since the overwhelming proportion of all civil litigation in this country is in the state courts, we cannot believe

Congress intended to limit the Arbitration Act to disputes subject only to *federal*-court jurisdiction.[9] Such an interpretation would frustrate Congressional intent to place "[a]n arbitration agreement . . . upon the same footing as other contracts, where it belongs." H.R. Rep. No. 96, *supra*, 1.

* * *

In creating a substantive rule applicable in state as well as federal courts, Congress intended to foreclose state legislative attempts to undercut the enforceability of arbitration agreements. We hold that § 31512 of the California Franchise Investment Law violates the Supremacy Clause.

IV

The judgment of the California Supreme Court denying enforcement of the arbitration agreement is reversed; as to the question whether the Federal Arbitration Act precludes a class action arbitration and any other issues not raised in the California courts, no decision by this Court would be appropriate at this time. As to the latter issues, the case is remanded for further proceedings not inconsistent with this opinion.

It is so ordered.

JUSTICE STEVENS, concurring in part and dissenting in part.

The Court holds that an arbitration clause that is enforceable in an action in a federal court is equally enforceable if the action is brought in a state court. I agree with that conclusion. Although JUSTICE O'CONNOR'S review of the legislative history of the Federal Arbitration Act demonstrates that the 1925 Congress that enacted the statute viewed the statute as essentially procedural in nature, I am persuaded that the intervening developments in the law compel the conclusion that the Court has reached. I am nevertheless troubled by one aspect of the case that seems to trouble none of my colleagues.

For me it is not "clear beyond question that if this suit had been brought as a diversity action in a Federal District Court, the arbitration clause would have been enforceable." The general rule prescribed by § 2 of the Federal Arbitration Act is that arbitration clauses in contracts involving interstate transactions are enforceable as a matter of federal law. That general rule, however, is subject to an exception based on "such grounds as exist at law or in equity for the revocation of any contract." I believe that exception leaves room for the implementation of certain substantive state policies that would be undermined by enforcing certain categories of arbitration clauses.

The exercise of State authority in a field traditionally occupied by State law will not be deemed preempted by a federal statute unless that was the clear and manifest purpose of Congress. *Ray v. Atlantic Richfield Co.*, 435 U.S. 151, 157 (1978); *see generally*, Hamilton, *The Federalist*, No. 32, 300 (Van Doren Ed.1945). Moreover, even where a federal statute does displace State

---

[9] While the Federal Arbitration Act creates federal substantive law requiring the parties to honor arbitration agreements, it does not create any independent Federal-question jurisdiction under 28 U.S.C. § 1331 or otherwise. * * *

authority, it "rarely occupies a legal field completely, totally excluding all participation by the legal systems of the states. . . . Federal legislation, on the whole, has been conceived and drafted on an ad hoc basis to accomplish limited objectives. It builds upon legal relationships established by the states, altering or supplanting them only so far as necessary for the special purpose." P. BATOR, P. MISHKIN, D. SHAPIRO, & H. WECHSLER, HART AND WECHSLER'S THE FEDERAL COURTS AND THE FEDERAL SYSTEM 470–471 (2d ed. 1973).

The limited objective of the Federal Arbitration Act was to abrogate the general common-law rule against specific enforcement of arbitration agreements, S. Rep. No. 536, 68th Cong., 1st Sess., 2–3 (1924), and a state statute which merely codified the general common-law rule — either directly by employing the prior doctrine of revocability or indirectly by declaring all such agreements void — would be preempted by the Act. However, beyond this conclusion, which seems compelled by the language of § 2 and case law concerning the Act, it is by no means clear that Congress intended entirely to displace State authority in this field. Indeed, while it is an understatement to say that "the legislative history of the . . . Act . . . reveals little awareness on the part of Congress that state law might be affected," it must surely be true that given the lack of a "clear mandate from Congress as to the extent to which state statutes and decisions are to be superseded, we must be cautious in construing the act lest we excessively encroach on the powers which Congressional policy, if not the Constitution, would reserve to the states."

The textual basis in the Act for avoiding such encroachment is the provision of § 2 which provides that arbitration agreements are subject to revocation on such grounds as exist at law or in equity for the revocation of any contract. The Act, however, does not define what grounds for revocation may be permissible, and hence it would appear that the judiciary must fashion the limitations as a matter of federal common law. In doing so, we must first recognize that as the " 'saving clause' in § 2 indicates, the purpose of Congress in 1925 was to make arbitration agreements as enforceable as other contracts, but not more so." The existence of a federal statute enunciating a substantive federal policy does not necessarily require the inexorable application of a uniform federal rule of decision notwithstanding the differing conditions which may exist in the several States and regardless of the decisions of the States to exert police powers as they deem best for the welfare of their citizens. Indeed, the lower courts generally look to State law regarding questions of formation of the arbitration agreement under § 2, which is entirely appropriate so long as the state rule does not conflict with the policy of § 2.

A contract which is deemed void is surely revocable at law or in equity, and the California legislature has declared all conditions purporting to waive compliance with the protections of the Franchise Disclosure Act, including but not limited to arbitration provisions, void as a matter of public policy. Given the importance to the State of franchise relationships, the relative disparity in the bargaining positions between the franchisor and the franchisee, and the remedial purposes of the California Act, I believe this declaration of State policy is entitled to respect. * * *

We should not refuse to exercise independent judgment concerning the conditions under which an arbitration agreement, generally enforceable under the Act, can be held invalid as contrary to public policy simply because the source of the substantive law to which the arbitration agreement attaches is a State rather than the Federal Government. I find no evidence that Congress intended such a double standard to apply, and I would not lightly impute such an intent to the 1925 Congress which enacted the Arbitration Act.

A state policy excluding wage claims from arbitration, or a state policy of providing special protection for franchisees, such as that expressed in California's Franchise Investment Law, can be recognized without impairing the basic purposes of the federal statute. Like the majority of the California Supreme Court, I am not persuaded that Congress intended the pre-emptive effect of this statute to be "so unyielding as to require enforcement of an agreement to arbitrate a dispute over the application of a regulatory statute which a state legislature, in conformity with analogous federal policy, has decided should be left to judicial enforcement."

Thus, although I agree with most of the Court's reasoning and specifically with its jurisdictional holdings, I respectfully dissent from its conclusion concerning the enforceability of the arbitration agreement. On that issue, I would affirm the judgment of the California Supreme Court.

JUSTICE O'CONNOR, with whom JUSTICE REHNQUIST joins, dissenting.

* * *

II

The majority opinion decides three issues. First, it holds that § 2 creates federal substantive rights that must be enforced by the state courts. Second, though the issue is not raised in this case, the Court states, *ante*, at 861, n. 9, that § 2 substantive rights may not be the basis for invoking federal court jurisdiction under 28 U.S.C. § 1331. Third, the Court reads § 2 to require state courts to enforce § 2 rights using procedures that mimic those specified for federal courts by FAA §§ 3 and 4. The first of these conclusions is unquestionably wrong as a matter of statutory construction; the second appears to be an attempt to limit the damage done by the first; the third is unnecessary and unwise.

A

One rarely finds a legislative history as unambiguous as the FAA's. That history establishes conclusively that the 1925 Congress viewed the FAA as a procedural statute, applicable only in federal courts, derived, Congress believed, largely from the federal power to control the jurisdiction of the federal courts.

In 1925 Congress emphatically believed arbitration to be a matter of "procedure." At hearings on the Act congressional subcommittees were told: "The theory on which you do this is that you have the right to tell the Federal courts how to proceed." The House Report on the FAA stated: "Whether an agreement for arbitration shall be enforced or not is a question of procedure. . . ." On the floor of the House Congressman Graham assured his fellow members that the FAA

> "does not involve any new principle of law except to provide a simple method . . . in order to give enforcement. . . . It creates no new legislation, grants no new rights, except a remedy to enforce an agreement in commercial contracts and in admiralty contracts."

* * *

If characterizing the FAA as procedural was not enough, the draftsmen of the Act, the House Report, and the early commentators all flatly stated that the Act was intended to affect only federal court proceedings. Mr. Cohen, the American Bar Association member who drafted the bill, assured two congressional subcommittees in joint hearings: "Nor can it be said that the Congress of the United States, directing its own courts . . . , would infringe upon the provinces or prerogatives of the States. . . . [T]he question of the enforcement relates to the law of remedies and not to substantive law. The rule must be changed for the jurisdiction in which the agreement is sought to be enforced. . . . There is no disposition therefore by means of the Federal bludgeon to force an individual State into an unwilling submission to arbitration enforcement."

* * *

Yet another indication that Congress did not intend the FAA to govern state court proceedings is found in the powers Congress relied on in passing the Act. The FAA might have been grounded on Congress's powers to regulate interstate and maritime affairs, since the Act extends only to contracts in those areas. There are, indeed, references in the legislative history to the corresponding federal powers. More numerous, however, are the references to Congress's pre-*Erie* power to prescribe "general law" applicable in all federal courts. At the congressional hearings, for example: "Congress rests solely upon its power to prescribe the jurisdiction and duties of the Federal courts."

* * *

Plainly, a power derived from Congress's Article III control over federal court jurisdiction would not by any flight of fancy permit Congress to control proceedings in state courts.

* * *

III

Section 2, like the rest of the FAA, should have no application whatsoever in state courts. Assuming, to the contrary, that § 2 does create a federal right that the state courts must enforce, state courts should nonetheless be allowed, at least in the first instance, to fashion their own procedures for enforcing the right. Unfortunately, the Court seems to direct that the arbitration clause at issue here must be specifically enforced; apparently no other means of enforcement is permissible.[20]

It is settled that a state court must honor federally created rights and that it may not unreasonably undermine them by invoking contrary local procedure. * * * But absent specific direction from Congress the state courts have always been permitted to apply their own reasonable procedures when enforcing federal rights. Before we undertake to read a set of complex and mandatory procedures into § 2's brief and general language, we should at a minimum allow state courts and legislatures a chance to develop their own methods for enforcing the new federal rights. Some might choose to award compensatory or punitive damages for the violation of an arbitration agreement; some might award litigation costs to the party who remained willing to arbitrate; some might affirm the "validity and enforceability" of arbitration agreements in other ways. Any of these approaches could vindicate § 2 rights in a manner fully consonant with the language and background of that provision.

The unelaborated terms of § 2 certainly invite flexible enforcement. At common law many jurisdictions were hostile to arbitration agreements. That hostility was reflected in two different doctrines: "revocability," which allowed parties to repudiate arbitration agreements at any time before the arbitrator's award was made, and "invalidity" or "unenforceability," equivalent rules that flatly denied any remedy for the failure to honor an arbitration agreement. In contrast, common-law jurisdictions that enforced arbitration agreements did so in at least three different ways — through actions for damages, actions for specific enforcement, or by enforcing sanctions imposed by trade and commercial associations on members who violated arbitration agreements. In 1925 a forum allowing *any one* of these remedies would have been thought to recognize the "validity" and "enforceability" of arbitration clauses.

This Court has previously rejected the view that state courts can adequately protect federal rights only if "such courts in enforcing the Federal right are to be treated as Federal courts and subjected pro hac vice to [federal] limitations. . . ." *Minneapolis & St. Louis R. v. Bombolis*, 241 U.S. 211, 221 (1916). As explained by Professor Hart, "The general rule, bottomed deeply in belief in the importance of state control of state judicial procedure, is that federal law takes the state courts as it finds them. . . . Some differences in remedy and procedure are inescapable if the different governments are to retain a measure of independence in deciding how justice should be administered. If the differences become so conspicuous as to affect advance calculations of outcome, and so to induce an undesirable shopping between forums, the remedy does not lie in the sacrifice of the independence of either government. It lies rather in provision by the federal government, confident of the

---

[20] If my understanding of the Court's opinion is correct, the Court has made § 3 of the FAA binding on the state courts. But as we have noted, . . . § 3 by its own terms governs only *federal court* proceedings. Moreover, if § 2, standing alone, creates a federal right to specific enforcement of arbitration agreements §§ 3 and 4 are, of course, largely superfluous. And if § 2 implicitly incorporates §§ 3 and 4 procedures for making arbitration agreements enforceable before arbitration begins, why not also § 9 procedures concerning venue, personal jurisdiction, and notice for enforcing an arbitrator's award after arbitration ends? One set of procedures is of little use without the other.

justice of its own procedure, of a federal forum equally accessible to both litigants."

In summary, even were I to accept the majority's reading of § 2, I would disagree with the Court's disposition of this case. After articulating the nature and scope of the federal right it discerns in § 2, the Court should remand to the state court, which has acted, heretofore, under a misapprehension of federal law. The state court should determine, at least in the first instance, what procedures it will follow to vindicate the newly articulated federal rights.

IV

The Court . . . rejects the idea of requiring the FAA to be applied only in federal courts partly out of concern with the problem of forum shopping. The concern is unfounded. Because the FAA makes the federal courts equally accessible to both parties to a dispute, no forum shopping would be possible even if we gave the FAA a construction faithful to the congressional intent. In controversies involving incomplete diversity of citizenship there is simply no access to federal court and therefore no possibility of forum shopping. In controversies with complete diversity of citizenship the FAA grants federal court access equally to both parties; no party can gain any advantage by forum shopping. Even when the party resisting arbitration initiates an action in state court, the opposing party can invoke FAA § 4 and promptly secure a federal court order to compel arbitration.

* * *

In summary, forum shopping concerns in connection with the FAA are a distraction that do not withstand scrutiny. The Court ignores the drafters' carefully devised plan for dealing with those problems.

V

Today's decision adds yet another chapter to the FAA's already colorful history. In 1842 this Court's ruling in *Swift v. Tyson* [41 U.S. 1 (1842)] set up a major obstacle to the enforcement of state arbitration laws in federal diversity courts. In 1925 Congress sought to rectify the problem by enacting the FAA; the intent was to create uniform law binding only in the federal courts. In *Erie* [304 U.S. 64] (1938), and then in *Bernhardt* [350 U.S. 198] (1956), this Court significantly curtailed federal power. In 1967 our decision in *Prima Paint* upheld the application of the FAA in a federal court proceeding as a valid exercise of Congress's Commerce Clause and Admiralty powers. Today the Court discovers a federal right in FAA § 2 that the state courts must enforce. Apparently confident that state courts are not competent to devise their own procedures for protecting the newly discovered federal right, the Court summarily prescribes a specific procedure, found nowhere in § 2 or its common-law origins, that the state courts are to follow.

Today's decision is unfaithful to congressional intent, unnecessary, and, in light of the FAA's antecedents and the intervening contraction of federal power, inexplicable. Although arbitration is a worthy alternative to litigation, today's exercise in judicial revisionism goes too far. I respectfully dissent.

NOTES

1. Who has the better of the argument regarding whether the FAA was meant to apply outside the federal courts? Are Justices O'Connor and Stevens correct in their reading of the FAA's legislative history? Assuming they are correct, can the majority be excused for seeking a result that will encourage arbitration and undercut forum shopping? For an attack on the *Keating* majority as inconsistent with the legislative history of the FAA, see Barbara Atwood, *Issues in Federal State Relations Under the Federal Arbitration Acts*, 37 FLORIDA L. REV. 61 (1985). Professor Atwood reads the legislative history of the 1925 federal legislation to predicate passage based upon Congress' power over federal court procedure. Of course, the FAA makes reference to "interstate commerce" and could rest comfortably upon that base of federal authority. Nonetheless, the FAA's prime drafter, Julius Cohen, testified in 1924 that Congress "[h]ad the right to tell the Federal Courts how to proceed" and submitted written testimony that the FAA was not based upon either the interstate or the admiralty powers of Congress. (*Joint Hearings on S. 1005 and H.R. 646 Before the Subcomm. of the Committees on the Judiciary*, 68th Cong., 1st Sess. 21 (1924).) Professor Atwood points out that "proponents of the arbitration bill stressed the procedural characterization to counter fears that the legislation might nullify substantive rights governed by state law." (Atwood, *supra*, at 77.) For a thorough exploration of the FAA's legislative history, see Ian Macneil, *American Arbitration Law* (1992). Professor Macneil's detailed examination also concludes that the original intent of the drafters of the FAA was to limit its application to the federal courts and attacks *Keating* as "History be Damned!" (*See id.* at 111–14, 117–19, 139.)

2. In *Perry v. Thomas*, 482 U.S. 483 (1987), the Supreme Court held that California legislation that allowed employees to litigate to collect wages without regard to arbitration agreements was preempted by the FAA. While the *Perry* decision followed the preemption analysis of *Southland*, it directed lower courts to look to the contract law of the states when interpreting the validity of the arbitration law:

> [When interpreting defenses such as unconscionability] the text of § 2 provides the touchstone for choosing between state-law principles and the principles of federal common law envisioned by the passage of that statute: An agreement to arbitrate is valid, irrevocable and enforceable, *as a matter of federal law* . . . save upon such grounds as exist at law or in equity for the revocation of *any* contract. 9 U.S.C. § 2 (emphasis added).

Thus state law, whether of legislative or judicial origin, is applicable if that law arose to govern issues concerning the validity, revocability, and enforceability of contracts generally. A state-law principle that takes its meaning precisely from the fact that a contract to arbitrate is at issue does not comport with this requirement of § 2 . . . A court may not, then, in assessing the rights of litigants to enforce an arbitration agreement, construe that agreement in a manner different from that on which it otherwise construes non-arbitration agreements under state law. Nor may a court rely on the uniqueness of an agreement to arbitrate as a basis for a state law holding that enforcement would be unconscionable, for this would enable the court to effect what we hold today the state legislature cannot. [482 U.S. at 492 n.9.]

Was the *Perry* decision directing courts to look generally to contract law principles or the specific contract law of a particular state? For analysis supporting the latter position, see IAN MACNEIL, RICHARD SPEIDEL & THOMAS STIPANOWICH, I FEDERAL ARBITRATION LAW § 10.6.2 (1995). (*Accord, Eassa Properties v. Shearson Lehman Bros., Inc.*, 851 F.2d 1301, 1304 (11th Cir. 1988) ("while federal law may govern the interpretation and enforcement of a valid arbitration agreement, state law governs the question of whether such an agreement exists in the first instance").)

3. In *Barker v. Golf U.S.A., Inc.*, 154 F.3d 788 (8th Cir. 1998), the court of appeals faced the issue of whether the parties had validly contracted to arbitrate. A franchisee contended that the making of its arbitraton agreement with its franchiser was fraudulent. Citing *Perry v. Thomas*, the court concluded that "[T]o decide whether the parties' agreement to arbitrate is valid, we look to state contract law." (*Id.* at 791.) The court went on to assert that it "may apply state law to arbitration agreements only to the extent that it applies to contracts in general," a subject matter defined by the court as "only a state's general contract defenses." (*Id.*) Does this reasoning seem valid? Is there reason to limit the application of state law to state defenses?

4. *Is Arbitration Law Substantive or Procedural?* In *Bernhardt v. Polygraphic Co.*, 350 U.S. 198 (1956), the Supreme Court upheld a decision of the trial court requiring a federal judge sitting in diversity to apply Vermont arbitration law that made an arbitration agreement revocable at any time prior to the award. The plaintiff had sued alleging that his discharge breached an employment contract and, after removal to federal court, the defendant had moved to stay pending arbitration. The Supreme Court used the "outcome" test of *Guaranty Trust Co. of New York v. York*, 326 U.S. 99 (1945), to require the application of Vermont's arbitration law. The *Bernhardt* decision treated arbitration legislation as substantive in nature. Is *Bernhardt* inconsistent with *Southland* or does its federal diversity setting make it inapposite?

VOLT INFORMATION SCIENCES, INC. v. BOARD OF TRUSTEES OF LELAND STANFORD JUNIOR UNIVERSITY
489 U.S. 468 (1989)

[Stanford University ("Stanford") contracted with Volt for the construction of electrical conduits as part of a campus building project. The parties signed a form contract used by the American Institute of Architects. It contained an arbitration clause and a choice-of-law clause that provided that "[t]he Contract shall be governed by the law of the place where the Project is located." Volt demanded arbitration when a dispute about payment occurred. Stanford filed suit in a California state court alleging breach of contract and fraud and named as defendants Volt and two other firms that had worked on the same construction project. The contracts with the additional defendants lacked arbitration clauses. When Volt moved to compel arbitration Stanford moved to stay arbitration under California legislation that authorized a state court to "stay arbitration pending resolution of related litigation between a party to the arbitration agreement and third parties not bound by it, where there is a possibility of conflicting rulings on a common issue of law or fact." The trial court granted Stanford's motion. On appeal, the California Court of Appeal affirmed. It found that the FAA governed and that the FAA did not provide for stays in such a context, observed that the parties had injected the California stay procedure into their bargain by selecting California law, and rejected Volt's argument that the FAA preempted California procedural law.

[The majority opinion of Chief Justice Rehnquist stressed that the parties' choice of California law included incorporation of state arbitration procedures. He rejected Volt's contention that the courts below had ignored the federal rule of construction requiring that questions of arbitrability must be resolved with a healthy regard for the federal policy favoring arbitration.]

*   *   *

There is no federal policy favoring arbitration under a certain set of procedural rules; the federal policy is simply to ensure the enforceability, according to their terms of private agreements to arbitrate. Interpreting a choice-of-law clause to make applicable state rules governing the conduct of arbitration — rules which are manifestly designed to encourage resort to the arbitral process — simply does not offend the rule of liberal construction set forth in *Moses H. Cone*, nor does it offend any other policy embodied in the FAA.

The question remains whether, assuming the choice-of-law clause meant what the Court of Appeal found it to mean, application of Cal. Civ. Proc. Code § 1281.2(c) is nonetheless pre-empted by the FAA to the extent it is used to stay arbitration under this contract involving interstate commerce. * * *

The FAA contains no express pre-emptive provision, nor does it reflect a congressional intent to occupy the entire field of arbitration. * * * But even when Congress has not completely displaced state regulation in an area, state law may nonetheless be pre-empted to the extent that it actually conflicts with federal law — that is, to the extent that it "stands as an obstacle to the accomplishment and execution of the full purposes and objectives of Congress." *Hines v. Davidowitz*, 312 U.S. 52, 67. The question before us, therefore, is whether application of Cal. Civ. Proc. Code § 1281.2(c) to stay arbitration under this contract in interstate commerce, in accordance with the terms of the arbitration agreement itself, would undermine the goals and policies of the FAA. We conclude that it would not.

The FAA was designed "to overrule the judiciary's long-standing refusal to enforce agreements to arbitrate," and to place such agreements " 'upon the same footing as other contracts.' " While Congress was no doubt aware that the Act would encourage the expeditious resolution of disputes, its passage "was motivated, first and foremost, by a congressional desire to enforce agreements into which parties had entered." Accordingly, we have recognized that the FAA does not require parties to arbitrate when they have not agreed to do so, *see id.*, at 219 (the Act "does not mandate the arbitration of all claims"), nor does it prevent parties who do agree to arbitrate from excluding certain claims from the scope of their arbitration agreement. It simply requires courts to enforce privately negotiated agreements to arbitrate, like other contracts, in accordance with their terms. *See Prima Paint, supra*, at 404, n. 12 (the Act was designed "to make arbitration agreements as enforceable as other contracts, but not more so").

In recognition of Congress' principal purpose of ensuring that private arbitration agreements are enforced according to their terms, we have held that the FAA pre-empts state laws which "require a judicial forum for the resolution of claims which the contracting parties agreed to resolve by arbitration." *Southland Corp. v. Keating*, 465 U.S. 1, 10 (1984) (finding pre-empted a state statute which rendered agreements to arbitrate certain franchise claims unenforceable); *Perry v. Thomas*, 482 U.S., at 490 (finding pre-empted a state statute which rendered unenforceable private agreements to arbitrate certain wage collection claims). But it does not follow that the FAA prevents the enforcement of agreements to arbitrate under different rules than those set forth in the Act itself. Indeed, such a result would be quite inimical to the FAA's primary purpose of ensuring that private agreements to arbitrate are enforced according to their terms. Arbitration under the Act is a matter of consent, not coercion, and parties are generally free to structure their arbitration agreements as they see fit. Just as they may limit by contract the issues which they will arbitrate, so too may they specify by contract the rules under which that arbitration will be conducted. Where, as here, the parties have agreed to abide by state rules of arbitration, enforcing those rules according to the terms of the agreement is fully consistent with the goals of the FAA, even if the result is that arbitration is stayed where the Act would otherwise permit it to go forward. By permitting the courts to "rigorously enforce" such agreements according to their terms, we give effect to the contractual rights and expectations of the parties, without doing violence to the policies behind by the FAA.

The judgment of the Court of Appeals is

Affirmed.

[The dissent of Mr. Justice Brennan, joined by Mr. Justice Marshall, argued that the majority's ruling frustrated the policy favoring arbitration over litigation and contended that the parties' choice of California law had a "substantive" intent to select California substantive rules and failed to incorporate any reference to California procedures.]

ALLIED-BRUCE TERMINIX CO. v. DOBSON
513 U.S. 265 (1995)

Justice BREYER delivered the opinion of the Court.

This case concerns the reach of § 2 of the Federal Arbitration Act. That section makes enforceable a written arbitration provision in "a contract *evidencing* a transaction *involving* commerce." 9 U.S.C. § 2 (emphasis added). Should we read this phrase broadly, extending the Act's reach to the limits of Congress' Commerce Clause power? Or, do the two underscored words — "involving" and "evidencing" — significantly restrict the Act's application? We conclude that the broader reading of the Act is the correct one; and we reverse a State Supreme Court judgment to the contrary.

I

In August 1987 Steven Gwin, a respondent, who owned a house in Birmingham, Alabama, bought a lifetime "Termite Protection Plan" (Plan) from the local office of Allied-Bruce Terminix Companies, a franchise of Terminix International Company. In the Plan, Allied-Bruce promised "to protect" Gwin's house "against the attack of subterranean termites," to reinspect periodically, to provide any "further treatment found necessary," and to repair, up to $100,000, damage caused by new termite infestations. App. 69. Terminix International "guarantee[d] the fulfillment of the terms" of the Plan. *Ibid.* The Plan's contract document provided in writing that "*any controversy or claim . . .* arising out of or relating to the interpretation, performance or breach of any provision of this agreement *shall be settled exclusively by arbitration.*" *Id.*, at 70 (emphasis added).

In the Spring of 1991 Mr. and Mrs. Gwin, wishing to sell their house to Mr. and Mrs. Dobson, had Allied-Bruce reinspect the house. They obtained a clean bill of health. But, no sooner had they sold the house and transferred the Termite Protection Plan to Mr. and Mrs. Dobson than the Dobsons found the house swarming with termites. Allied-Bruce attempted to treat and repair the house, but the Dobsons found Allied-Bruce's efforts inadequate. They therefore sued the Gwins, and (along with the Gwins, who cross-claimed) also sued Allied-Bruce and Terminix in Alabama state court. Allied-Bruce and Terminix, pointing to the Plan's arbitration clause and § 2 of the Federal Arbitration Act, immediately asked the court for a stay, to allow arbitration to proceed. The court denied the stay. Allied-Bruce and Terminix appealed.

The Supreme Court of Alabama upheld the denial of the stay on the basis of a state statute, Ala.Code § 8-1-41(3) (1993), making written, predispute arbitration agreements invalid and "unenforceable." 628 So.2d 354, 355 (Ala.1993). To reach this conclusion, the court had to find that the Federal Arbitration Act, which pre-empts conflicting state law, did not apply to the termite contract. It made just that finding. The court considered the federal Act inapplicable because the connection between the termite contract and interstate commerce was too slight. In the court's view, the Act applies to a contract only if " 'at the time [the parties entered into the contract] and accepted the arbitration clause, they *contemplated* substantial interstate activity.' " *Ibid.* (emphasis in original) (quoting *Metro Industrial Painting*

Corp. v. Terminal Constr. Co., 287 F.2d 382, 387 (2d Cir.) (Lumbard, C.J., concurring), *cert. denied*, 368 U.S. 817 (1961)). Despite some interstate activities (e.g., Allied-Bruce, like Terminix, is a multistate firm and shipped treatment and repair material from out of state), the court found that the parties "contemplated" a transaction that was primarily local and not "substantially" interstate.

Several state courts and federal district courts, like the Supreme Court of Alabama, have interpreted the Act's language as requiring the parties to a contract to have "contemplated" an interstate commerce connection. Several federal appellate courts, however, have interpreted the same language differently, as reaching to the limits of Congress' Commerce Clause power. We granted certiorari to resolve this conflict, and, as we said, we conclude that the broader reading of the statute is the right one.

* * *

II

[S]ome initially assumed that the Federal Arbitration Act represented an exercise of Congress' Article III power to "ordain and establish" federal courts, U.S. Const., Art. III, § 1. In 1967, however, this Court held that the Act "is based upon and confined to the incontestable federal foundations of 'control over interstate commerce and over admiralty.'" *Prima Paint Corp. v. Flood & Conklin Mfg. Co.*, 388 U.S. 395, 405 (1967). The Court considered the following complicated argument: (1) The Act's provisions (about contract remedies) are important and often outcome-determinative, and thus amount to "substantive" not "procedural" provisions of law; (2) *Erie R. Co. v. Tompkins*, 304 U.S. 64 (1938), made clear that federal courts must apply state substantive law in diversity cases, therefore; (3) federal courts must not apply the Federal Arbitration Act in diversity cases. This Court responded by agreeing that the Act set forth substantive law, but concluding that, nonetheless, the Act applied in diversity cases because Congress had so intended. The Court wrote: "Congress may prescribe how federal courts are to conduct themselves with respect to subject matter over which Congress plainly has power to legislate." *Prima Paint, supra.*

Third, the holding in *Prima Paint* led to a further question. Did Congress intend the Act also to apply in state courts? Did the Federal Arbitration Act pre-empt conflicting state antiarbitration law, or could state courts apply their antiarbitration rules in cases before them, thereby reaching results different from those reached in otherwise similar federal diversity cases? In *Southland Corp. v. Keating*, [465 U.S. 1 (1984)], this Court decided that Congress would not have wanted state and federal courts to reach different outcomes about the validity of arbitration in similar cases. The Court concluded that the Federal Arbitration Act pre-empts state law; and it held that state courts cannot apply state statutes that invalidate arbitration agreements.

We have set forth this background because respondents, supported by 20 state attorneys general, now ask us to overrule *Southland* and thereby to permit Alabama to apply its antiarbitration statute in this case irrespective of the proper interpretation of § 2. The *Southland* Court, however, recognized that the pre-emption issue was a difficult one, and it considered the basic arguments that respondents and amici now raise (even though those issues were not thoroughly briefed at the time). Nothing significant has changed in the 10 years subsequent to *Southland*; no later cases have eroded *Southland*'s authority; and, no unforeseen practical problems have arisen. Moreover, in the interim, private parties have likely written contracts relying upon *Southland* as authority. Further, Congress, both before and after *Southland*, has enacted legislation extending, not retracting, the scope of arbitration. *See, e.g.,* 9 U.S.C. § 15 (eliminating the Act of State doctrine as a bar to arbitration); 9 U.S.C. §§ 201–208 (international arbitration). For these reasons, we find it inappropriate to reconsider what is by now well-established law.

We therefore proceed to the basic interpretive questions aware that we are interpreting an Act that seeks broadly to overcome judicial hostility to arbitration agreements and that applies in both federal and state courts. We must decide in this case whether that Act used language about interstate commerce that nonetheless limits the Act's application, thereby carving out an important statutory niche in which a State remains free to apply its antiarbitration law or policy. We conclude that it does not.

III

The Federal Arbitration Act, § 2, provides that a "written provision in any maritime transaction or a contract *evidencing a transaction involving commerce* to settle by arbitration a controversy thereafter arising out of such contract or transaction . . . shall be valid, irrevocable, and enforceable, save upon such grounds as exist at law or in equity for the revocation of any contract." 9 U.S.C. § 2 (emphasis added).

The initial interpretive question focuses upon the words "involving commerce." These words are broader than the often-found words of art "in commerce." They therefore cover more than " 'only persons or activities *within the flow of* interstate commerce.' " But, how far beyond the flow of commerce does the word "involving" reach? Is "involving" the functional equivalent of the word "affecting?" That phrase — "affecting commerce" — normally signals a congressional intent to exercise its Commerce Clause powers to the full. We cannot look to other statutes for guidance for the parties tell us that this is the only federal statute that uses the word "involving" to describe an interstate commerce relation.

After examining the statute's language, background, and structure, we conclude that the word "involving" is broad and is indeed the functional equivalent of "affecting." For one thing, such an interpretation, linguistically speaking, is permissible. The dictionary finds instances in which "involve" and "affect" sometimes can mean about the same thing. V Oxford English Dictionary 466 (1st ed. 1933) (providing examples dating back to the mid-nineteenth century, where "involve" means to "include or affect in . . . operation"). For another, the Act's legislative history, to the extent that it is informative, indicates an expansive congressional intent. *See, e.g.,* H.R. Rep. No. 96, 68th Cong., 1st Sess., 1 (1924) (the Act's "control over interstate commerce reaches not only the actual physical interstate shipment of goods but also contracts relating to interstate commerce"); 65 Cong. Rec. 1931 (1924) (the Act "affects contracts relating to interstate subjects and contracts in admiralty") (remarks of Rep. Graham). * * *

Further, this Court has previously described the Act's reach expansively as coinciding with that of the Commerce Clause. *See, e.g., Perry v. Thomas*, [482 U.S. 483 (1987)], (the Act "embodies Congress' intent to provide for the enforcement of arbitration agreements within the full reach of the Commerce Clause"); *Southland Corp. v. Keating* (the " 'involving commerce' " requirement is a constitutionally "necessary qualification" on the Act's reach, marking its permissible outer limit); *see also Prima Paint Corp. v. Flood & Conklin Mfg. Co.* (Harlan, J., concurring) (endorsing *Robert Lawrence Co. v. Devonshire Fabrics, Inc.*, 271 F.2d 402, 407 (2d Cir. 1959) (Congress, in enacting the FAA, "took pains to utilize as much of its power as it could . . .")).

Finally, a broad interpretation of this language is consistent with the Act's basic purpose, to put arbitration provisions on "the same footing" as a contract's other terms. Conversely, a narrower interpretation is not consistent with the Act's purpose, for (unless unreasonably narrowed to the flow of commerce) such an interpretation would create a new, unfamiliar, test lying somewhere in a no-man's land between "in commerce" and "affecting commerce," thereby unnecessarily complicating the law and breeding litigation from a statute that seeks to avoid it.

We recognize arguments to the contrary: The pre-New Deal Congress that passed the Act in 1925 might well have thought the Commerce Clause did not stretch as far as has turned out to be so. But, it is not unusual for this Court in similar circumstances to ask whether the scope of a statute should expand along with the expansion of the Commerce Clause power itself, and to answer the question affirmatively — as, for the reasons set forth above, we do here.

* * *

Thus, the Court interpreted the words "involving commerce" as broadly as the words "affecting commerce"; and, as we have said, these latter words normally mean a full exercise of constitutional power. * * * And, we conclude that the word "involving," like "affecting," signals an intent to exercise Congress's commerce power to the full.

IV

Section 2 applies where there is "a contract *evidencing a transaction involving commerce.*" 9 U.S.C. § 2 (emphasis added). The second interpretive question focuses on the underscored words. Does "evidencing a transaction" mean only that the transaction (that the contract "evidences") must turn out, in fact, to have involved interstate commerce? Or, does it mean more?

Many years ago, Second Circuit Chief Judge Lumbard said that the phrase meant considerably more. He wrote: "The significant question . . . is not whether, in carrying out the terms of the contract, the parties *did* cross state lines, but whether, *at the time they entered into it* and accepted the arbitration clause, they *contemplated* substantial interstate activity. Cogent evidence regarding their state of mind at the time would be the terms of the contract, and if it, on its face, evidences interstate traffic . . . , the contract should come within § 2. In addition, evidence as to how the parties expected the contract to be performed and how it was performed is relevant to whether substantial interstate activity was contemplated."

The Supreme Court of Alabama, and several other courts, have followed this view, known as the "contemplation of the parties" test.

We find the interpretive choice difficult, but for several reasons we conclude that the first interpretation ("commerce in fact") is more faithful to the statute than the second ("contemplation of the parties"). First, the "contemplation of the parties" interpretation, when viewed in terms of the statute's basic purpose, seems anomalous. That interpretation invites litigation about what was, or was not, "contemplated." Why would Congress intend a test that risks the very kind of costs and delay through litigation (about the circumstances of contract formation) that Congress wrote the Act to help the parties avoid?
* * *

* * *

Section 2 gives States a method for protecting consumers against unfair pressure to agree to a contract with an unwanted arbitration provision. States may regulate contracts, including arbitration clauses, under general contract law principles and they may invalidate an arbitration clause "upon such grounds as exist at law or in equity for the revocation of *any* contract." 9 U.S.C. § 2 (emphasis added). What States may not do is decide that a contract is fair enough to enforce all its basic terms (price, service, credit), but not fair enough to enforce its arbitration clause. The Act makes any such state policy unlawful, for that kind of policy would place arbitration clauses on an unequal "footing," directly contrary to the Act's language and Congress's intent. *See Volt Information Sciences, Inc.*, 489 U.S., 468 (1989), at 474.

For these reasons, we accept the "commerce in fact" interpretation, reading the Act's language as insisting that the "transaction" in fact "involve" interstate commerce, even if the parties did not contemplate an interstate commerce connection.

V

The parties do not contest that the transaction in this case, in fact, involved interstate commerce. In addition to the multistate nature of Terminix and Allied-Bruce, the termite-treating and house-repairing material used by Allied-Bruce in its (allegedly inadequate) efforts to carry out the terms of the Plan, came from outside Alabama.

Consequently, the judgment of the Supreme Court of Alabama is reversed and the case is remanded for further proceedings consistent with this opinion.

It is so ordered.

JUSTICE O'CONNOR, concurring.

I agree with the Court's construction of § 2 of the Federal Arbitration Act. As applied in federal courts, the Court's interpretation comports fully with my understanding of congressional intent. A more restrictive definition of "evidencing" and "involving" would doubtless foster prearbitration litigation that would frustrate the very purpose of the statute. As applied in state courts, however, the effect of a broad formulation of § 2 is more troublesome. The reading of § 2 adopted today will displace many state statutes carefully calibrated to protect consumers, *see, e.g.*, Mont. Code Ann. § 27-5-114(2)(b) (1993) (refusing to enforce arbitration clauses in consumer contracts where the consideration is $5,000 or less), and state procedural requirements aimed at ensuring knowing and voluntary consent, *see, e.g.*, S.C. Code Ann. § 15-48-10(a) (Supp. 1993) (requiring that notice of arbitration provision be prominently placed on first page of contract). I have long adhered to the view, discussed below, that Congress designed the Federal Arbitration Act to apply only in federal courts. But if we are to apply the Act in state courts, it makes little sense to read § 2 differently in that context. In the end, my agreement with the Court's construction of § 2 rests largely on the wisdom of maintaining a uniform standard.

I continue to believe that Congress never intended the Federal Arbitration Act to apply in state courts, and that this Court has strayed far afield in giving the Act so broad a compass. *See Southland Corp. v. Keating.* We have often said that the pre-emptive effect of a federal statute is fundamentally a question of congressional intent. * * * Yet, over the past decade, the Court has abandoned all pretense of ascertaining congressional intent with respect to the Federal Arbitration Act, building instead, case by case, an edifice of its own creation. I have no doubt that Congress could enact, in the first instance, a federal arbitration statute that displaces most state arbitration laws. But I also have no doubt that, in 1925, Congress enacted no such statute.

Were we writing on a clean slate, I would adhere to that view and affirm the Alabama court's decision. But, as the Court points out, more than 10 years have passed since *Southland*, several subsequent cases have built upon its reasoning, and parties have undoubtedly made contracts in reliance on the Court's interpretation of the Act in the interim. After reflection, I am persuaded by considerations of *stare decisis*, which we have said "have special force in the area of statutory interpretation," to acquiesce in today's judgment. Though wrong, *Southland* has not proved unworkable, and, as always, "Congress remains free to alter what we have done." *Ibid.*

Today's decision caps this Court's effort to expand the Federal Arbitration Act. Although each decision has built logically upon the decisions preceding it, the initial building block in *Southland* laid a faulty foundation. I acquiesce in today's judgment because there is no "special justification" to overrule *Southland*. It remains now for Congress to correct this interpretation if it wishes to preserve state autonomy in state courts.

JUSTICE THOMAS, with whom JUSTICE SCALIA joins, dissenting.

I disagree with the majority at the threshold of this case, and so I do not reach the question that it decides. In my view, the Federal Arbitration Act (FAA) does not apply in state courts. I respectfully dissent.

I

In *Southland Corp. v. Keating*, this Court concluded that § 2 of the FAA "appl[ies] in state as well as federal courts," and "withdr[aws] the power of the states to require a judicial forum for the resolution of claims which the contracting parties agreed to resolve by arbitration." In my view, both aspects of *Southland* are wrong.

A

Section 2 of the FAA declares that an arbitration clause contained in "a contract evidencing a transaction involving commerce" shall be "valid, irrevocable, and enforceable, save upon such grounds as exist at law or in equity for the revocation of any contract." 9 U.S.C. § 2; *see also* § 1 (defining "commerce," as relevant here, to mean "commerce among the several States or with foreign nations"). On its face, and considered out of context, § 2 draws no apparent distinction between federal courts and state courts. But not until 1959 — nearly 35 years after Congress enacted the FAA — did any court suggest that § 2 applied in state courts. This Court waited until 1984 to conclude, over a strong dissent by Justice O'CONNOR, that § 2 extends to the States. *See Southland, supra.*

The explanation for this delay is simple: the statute that Congress enacted actually applies only in federal courts. At the time of the FAA's passage in 1925, laws governing the enforceability of arbitration agreements were generally thought to deal purely with matters of procedure rather than substance, because they were directed solely to the mechanisms for resolving the underlying disputes.[1] * * * It would have been extraordinary for Congress to attempt to prescribe procedural rules for state courts. And because the FAA was enacted against this general background, no one read it as such an attempt.

Indeed, to judge from the reported cases, it appears that no state court was even asked to enforce the statute for many years after the passage of the FAA. Federal courts, for their part, refused to apply state arbitration statutes in cases to which the FAA was inapplicable. Their refusal was not the outgrowth of this Court's decision in *Swift v. Tyson* [41 U.S. 1 (1842)], which held that certain categories of state judicial decisions were not "laws" for purposes of the Rules of Decision Act and hence were not binding in federal courts; even under *Swift*, state statutes unambiguously constituted "laws." Rather, federal courts did not apply the state arbitration statutes because the statutes were not considered *substantive* laws. In short, state arbitration statutes prescribed rules for the state courts, and the FAA prescribed rules for the federal courts.

It is easy to understand why lawyers in 1925 classified arbitration statutes as procedural. An arbitration agreement is a species of forum-selection clause: without laying down any rules of decision, it identifies the adjudicator of disputes. A strong argument can be made that such forum-selection clauses

---

[1] ". . . That the enforcement of arbitration contracts is within the law of procedure as distinguished from substantive law is well settled by the decisions of our courts" . . . As discussed below, moreover, the FAA's text clearly reflects Congress' view that the statute it enacted was purely procedural.

concern procedure rather than substance. And if a contractual provision deals purely with matters of judicial procedure, one might well conclude that questions about whether and how it will be enforced also relate to procedure.

The context of § 2 confirms this understanding of the FAA's original meaning. Most sections of the statute plainly have no application in state courts, but rather prescribe rules either for federal courts or for arbitration proceedings themselves. Thus, § 3 provides: "If any suit or proceeding be brought in *any of the courts of the United States* upon any issue referable to arbitration under an agreement in writing for such arbitration, the court in which such suit is pending, upon being satisfied that the issue involved in such suit or proceeding is referable to arbitration under such an agreement, shall on application of one of the parties stay the trial of the action until such arbitration has been had in accordance with the terms of the agreement, providing the applicant for the stay is not in default in proceeding with such arbitration." 9 U.S.C. § 3 (emphasis added). Section 4 addresses the converse situation, in which a party breaches an arbitration agreement not by filing a lawsuit but rather by refusing to submit to arbitration: "A party aggrieved by the alleged failure, neglect, or refusal of another to arbitrate under a written agreement for arbitration may petition *any United States district court which, save for such agreement, would have jurisdiction under title 28, in a civil action or in admiralty of the subject matter of a suit arising out of the controversy between the parties*, for an order directing that such arbitration proceed in the manner provided for in such agreement. . . . The court shall hear the parties, and upon being satisfied that the making of the agreement for arbitration or the failure to comply therewith is not in issue, the court shall make an order directing the parties to proceed to arbitration in accordance with the terms of the agreement." (Emphasis added.) The Act then turns its attention to the covered arbitration proceedings themselves, treating the arbitration forum as an extension of the federal courts. Section 7, for instance, provides that the fees for witnesses "shall be the same as the fees of witnesses before masters of the United States courts"; it adds that if a witness neglects a summons to appear at an arbitration hearing, "upon petition the United States district court for the district in which such arbitrators . . . are sitting may compel the attendance of such person . . . or punish said person . . . for contempt in the same manner provided by law for securing the attendance of witnesses or their punishment for neglect or refusal to attend in the courts of the United States." Likewise, when the arbitrator eventually issues an award, either party (absent contrary directions in the agreement) may apply to "the United States court in and for the district within which such award was made" for an order confirming the award. § 9. The District Court may also vacate or modify the award in a few specified circumstances, §§ 10–11, but generally it will simply enter a confirmatory judgment, § 9, which is then docketed and given the same effect as a judgment in an ordinary civil case, § 13.

Despite the FAA's general focus on the federal courts, of course, § 2 itself contains no such explicit limitation. But the text of the statute nonetheless makes clear that § 2 was not meant as a statement of substantive law binding on the States. After all, if § 2 really was understood to "creat[e] federal substantive law requiring the parties to honor arbitration agreements,"

Southland, then the breach of an arbitration agreement covered by § 2 would give rise to a federal question within the subject-matter jurisdiction of the federal district courts. *See* 28 U.S.C. § 1331. Yet the ensuing provisions of the Act, without expressly taking away this jurisdiction, clearly rest on the assumption that federal courts have jurisdiction to enforce arbitration agreements only when they would have had jurisdiction over the underlying dispute. *See* 9 U.S.C. §§ 3, 4, 8. In other words, the FAA treats arbitration simply as one means of resolving disputes that lie within the jurisdiction of the federal courts; it makes clear that the breach of a covered arbitration agreement does not itself provide any independent basis for such jurisdiction. Even the *Southland* majority was forced to acknowledge this point, conceding that § 2 "does not create any independent federal-question jurisdiction under 28 U.S.C. § 1331 or otherwise." But the *reason* that § 2 does not give rise to federal-question jurisdiction is that it was enacted as a purely procedural provision. For the same reason, it applies only in the federal courts.

* * *

Even if the interstate commerce requirement raises uncertainty about the original meaning of the statute, we should resolve the uncertainty in light of core principles of federalism. While "Congress may legislate in areas traditionally regulated by the States" as long as it "is acting within the powers granted it under the Constitution," we assume that "Congress does not exercise [this power] lightly." To the extent that federal statutes are ambiguous, we do not read them to displace state law. Rather, we must be "absolutely certain" that Congress intended such displacement before we give preemptive effect to a federal statute. In 1925, the enactment of a "substantive" arbitration statute along the lines envisioned by *Southland* would have displaced an enormous body of state law: outside of a few States, predispute arbitration agreements either were wholly unenforceable or at least were not subject to specific performance. Far from being "absolutely certain" that Congress swept aside these state rules, I am quite sure that it did not.

B

Suppose, however, that the first aspect of *Southland* was correct: § 2 requires States to enforce the covered arbitration agreements and pre-empts all contrary state law. There still would be no textual basis for *Southland*'s suggestion that § 2 requires the States to enforce those agreements through the remedy of specific performance — that is, by forcing the parties to submit to arbitration. A contract surely can be "valid, irrevocable and enforceable" even though it can be enforced only through actions for damages. Thus, on the eve of the FAA's enactment, this Court described executory arbitration agreements as being "valid" and as creating "a perfect obligation" under federal law even though federal courts refused to order their specific performance.

To be sure, §§ 3 and 4 of the FAA require that federal courts specifically enforce arbitration agreements. These provisions deal, respectively, with the potential plaintiffs and the potential defendants in the underlying dispute:

§ 3 holds the plaintiffs to their promise not to take their claims straight to court, while § 4 holds the defendants to their promise to submit to arbitration rather than making the other party sue them. Had this case arisen in one of the "courts of the United States," it is § 3 that would have been relevant. Upon proper motion, the court would have been obliged to grant a stay pending arbitration, unless the contract between the parties did not "evidenc[e] a transaction involving [interstate] commerce." Because this case arose in the courts of Alabama, however, petitioners are forced to contend that § 2 imposes precisely the same obligation on all courts (both federal and state) that § 3 imposes solely on federal courts. Though *Southland* supports this argument, it simply cannot be correct, or § 3 would be superfluous.

*   *   *

NOTES

1. Does Justice Breyer's *Allied-Bruce* majority opinion, one of his first written as a member of the Supreme Court, cover the preemption arguments that form the basis of Justice O'Connor's and Justice Thomas' opinions? Is Justice Breyer's statutory construction contention convincing? Is statutory construction a satisfactory way to deal with a question of preemption?

2. Justice O'Connor seems to think that *Southland* should be overruled. How, then, can she concur? Is her *stare decisis* rationale persuasive?

3. The amicus brief of twenty state attorney generals argued that "this case is ultimately more about federalism than about arbitration." Has the majority run roughshod over state interests in the arbitration arena? Arbitration law is a form of contract law and, traditionally, contract law has been left to the states. Numerous states regulate the procedures used to draft arbitration clauses. Is such state legislation on shaky ground after *Allied-Bruce*?

4. When will a transaction be so local in nature that the FAA will not be activated? In *Sisters of the Visitation v. Cochran Plastering Co.*, 775 So. 2d 759 (Ala. 2000), the Alabama Supreme Court refused to apply the FAA to a local construction contract to repair and restore a Catholic chapel. The court held that Alabama Code 1975 § 8-1-41(3), which blocks the specific enforcement of predispute arbitration clauses, was not preempted by the *Terminix* decision.

DOCTOR'S ASSOCIATES, INC. v. CASAROTTO
116 S. Ct. 1652 (1996)

JUSTICE GINSBURG delivered the opinion of the Court.

This case concerns a standard form franchise agreement for the operation of a Subway sandwich shop in Montana. When a dispute arose between parties to the agreement, franchisee Paul Casarotto sued franchisor Doctor's Associates, Inc. (DAI) and DAI's Montana development agent, Nick Lombardi, in a Montana state court. DAI and Lombardi sought to stop the litigation pending arbitration pursuant to the arbitration clause set out on page nine of the franchise agreement.

The Federal Arbitration Act declares written provisions for arbitration "valid, irrevocable, and enforceable, save upon such grounds as exist at law or in equity for the revocation of any contract." Montana law, however, declares an arbitration clause unenforceable unless "[n]otice that [the] contract is subject to arbitration" is "typed in underlined capital letters on the first page of the contract." Mont. Code Ann. § 27-5-114(4) (1995). The question here presented is whether Montana's law is compatible with the federal Act. We hold that Montana's first-page notice requirement, which governs not "any contract," but specifically and solely contracts "subject to arbitration," conflicts with the FAA and is therefore displaced by the federal measure.

I

Petitioner DAI is the national franchisor of Subway sandwich shops. In April 1988, DAI entered a franchise agreement with respondent Paul Casarotto, which permitted Casarotto to open a Subway shop in Great Falls, Montana. The franchise agreement stated, on page nine and in ordinary type:

"Any controversy or claim arising out of or relating to this contract or the breach thereof shall be settled by Arbitration. . . ."

In October 1992, Casarotto sued DAI and its agent, Nick Lombardi, in Montana state court, alleging state-law contract and tort claims relating to the franchise agreement. DAI demanded arbitration of those claims, and successfully moved in the Montana trial court to stay the lawsuit pending arbitration.

The Montana Supreme Court reversed. *Casarotto v. Lombardi*, 268 Mont. 369, 886 P.2d 931 (1994). That court left undisturbed the trial court's findings that the franchise agreement fell within the scope of the FAA and covered the claims Casarotto stated against DAI and Lombardi. The Montana Supreme Court held, however, that Mont. Code Ann. § 27-5-114(4) rendered the agreement's arbitration clause unenforceable. The Montana statute provides:

Notice that a contract is subject to arbitration . . . shall be typed in underlined capital letters on the first page of the contract; and unless such notice is displayed thereon, the contract may not be subject to arbitration.

Notice of the arbitration clause in the franchise agreement did not appear on the first page of the contract. Nor was anything relating to the clause typed in underlined capital letters. Because the State's statutory notice requirement had not been met, the Montana Supreme Court declared the parties' dispute "not subject to arbitration."

DAI and Lombardi unsuccessfully argued before the Montana Supreme Court that § 27-5-114(4) was preempted by § 2 of the FAA.[1] DAI and Lombardi dominantly relied on our decisions in *Southland Corp. v. Keating*, 465 U.S.

---

[1] Section 2 provides, in relevant part: "A written provision in . . . a contract evidencing a transaction involving commerce to settle by arbitration a controversy thereafter arising out of such contract or transaction, or the refusal to perform the whole or any part thereof, . . . shall be valid, irrevocable, and enforceable, save upon such grounds as exist at law or in equity for the revocation of any contract." 9 U.S.C. § 2.

1 (1984), and *Perry v. Thomas*, 482 U.S. 483 (1987). In *Southland*, we held that § 2 of the FAA applies in state as well as federal courts, and "withdr[aws] the power of the states to require a judicial forum for the resolution of claims which the contracting parties agreed to resolve by arbitration." We noted in the pathmarking *Southland* decision that the FAA established a "broad principle of enforceability," and that § 2 of the federal Act provided for revocation of arbitration agreements only upon "grounds as exist at law or in equity for the revocation of any contract." In *Perry*, we reiterated: "[S]tate law, whether of legislative or judicial origin, is applicable if that law arose to govern issues concerning the validity, revocability, and enforceability of contracts generally. A state-law principle that takes its meaning precisely from the fact that a contract to arbitrate is at issue does not comport with [the text of § 2]."

The Montana Supreme Court, however, read our decision in *Volt Information Sciences, Inc. v. Board of Trustees of Leland Stanford Junior Univ.*, 489 U.S. 468 (1989), as limiting the preemptive force of § 2 and correspondingly qualifying *Southland* and *Perry*. As the Montana Supreme Court comprehended *Volt*, the proper inquiry here should focus not on the bare words of § 2, but on this question: Would the application of Montana's notice requirement, contained in § 27-5-114(4), "undermine the goals and policies of the FAA."

Section 27-5-114(4), in the Montana court's judgment, did not undermine the goals and policies of the FAA, for the notice requirement did not preclude arbitration agreements altogether; it simply prescribed "that before arbitration agreements are enforceable, they be entered knowingly."

DAI and Lombardi petitioned for certiorari. Last Term, we granted their petition, vacated the judgment of the Montana Supreme Court, and remanded for further consideration in light of *Allied-Bruce Terminix Cos. v. Dobson*, 115 S.Ct. 834 (1995). In *Allied-Bruce*, we restated what our decisions in *Southland* and *Perry* had established:

> States may regulate contracts, including arbitration clauses, under general contract law principles and they may invalidate an arbitration clause "upon such grounds as exist at law or in equity for the revocation of any contract." 9 U.S.C. § 2 (emphasis added).

What States may not do is decide that a contract is fair enough to enforce all its basic terms (price, service, credit), but not fair enough to enforce its arbitration clause. The Act makes any such state policy unlawful, for that kind of policy would place arbitration clauses on an unequal 'footing,' directly contrary to the Act's language and Congress's intent.

On remand, without inviting or permitting further briefing or oral argument, the Montana Supreme Court adhered to its original ruling. The court stated: "After careful review, we can find nothing in the [*Allied-Bruce*] decision which relates to the issues presented to this Court in this case." *Casarotto v. Lombardi*, 901 P.2d 596, 598 (1995). Elaborating, the Montana court said it found "no suggestion in [*Allied-Bruce*] that the principles from *Volt* on which we relied [to uphold § 27-5-114(4)] have been modified in any way." We again granted certiorari, and now reverse.

II

Section 2 of the FAA provides that written arbitration agreements "shall be valid, irrevocable, and enforceable, save upon such grounds as exist at law or in equity for the revocation of *any* contract." 9 U.S.C. § 2 (emphasis added). Repeating our observation in *Perry*, the text of § 2 declares that state law may be applied "if that law arose to govern issues concerning the validity, revocability, and enforceability of contracts generally." Thus, generally applicable contract defenses, such as fraud, duress or unconscionability, may be applied to invalidate arbitration agreements without contravening § 2 (citations omitted).

Courts may not, however, invalidate arbitration agreements under state laws applicable only to arbitration provisions. By enacting § 2, we have several times said, Congress precluded States from singling out arbitration provisions for suspect status, requiring instead that such provisions be placed "upon the same footing as other contracts."

Montana's § 27-5-114(4) directly conflicts with § 2 of the FAA because the State's law conditions the enforceability of arbitration agreements on compliance with a special notice requirement not applicable to contracts generally. The FAA thus displaces the Montana statute with respect to arbitration agreements covered by the Act. *See* 2 I. Macneil, R. Speidel, T. Stipanowich, & G. Shell, *Federal Arbitration Law* § 19.1.1, pp. 19:4–19:5 (1995) (under *Southland* and *Perry*, "state legislation requiring greater information or choice in the making of agreements to arbitrate than in other contracts is preempted").[3]

The Montana Supreme Court misread our *Volt* decision and therefore reached a conclusion in this case at odds with our rulings. *Volt* involved an arbitration agreement that incorporated state procedural rules, one of which, on the facts of that case, called for arbitration to be stayed pending the resolution of a related judicial proceeding. The state rule examined in *Volt* determined only the efficient order of proceedings; it did not affect the enforceability of the arbitration agreement itself. We held that applying the state rule would not "undermine the goals and policies of the FAA," because the very purpose of the Act was to "ensur[e] that private agreements to arbitrate are enforced according to their terms." Applying § 27-5-114(4) here, in contrast, would not enforce the arbitration clause in the contract between DAI and Casarotto;

---

[3] At oral argument, counsel for Casarotto urged a broader view, under which § 27-5-114(4) might be regarded as harmless surplus. Montana could have invalidated the arbitration clause in the franchise agreement under general, informed consent principles, counsel suggested. She asked us to regard § 27-5-114(4) as but one illustration of a cross-the-board rule: unexpected provisions in adhesion contracts must be conspicuous. But the Montana Supreme Court announced no such sweeping rule. The court did not assert as a basis for its decision a generally applicable principle of "reasonable expectations" governing any standard form contract term. *Cf. Transamerica Ins. Co. v. Royle*, 202 Mont. 173, 180, 656 P.2d 820, 824 (1983) (invalidating provision in auto insurance policy that did not "honor the reasonable expectations" of the insured). Montana's decision trains on and upholds a particular statute, one setting out a precise, arbitration-specific limitation. We review that disposition, and no other. It bears reiteration, however, that a court may not "rely on the uniqueness of an agreement to arbitrate as a basis for a state-law holding that enforcement would be unconscionable, for this would enable the court to effect what . . . the state legislature cannot." *Perry v. Thomas*, 482 U.S. 483, 492 (1987).

instead, Montana's first-page notice requirement would invalidate the clause. The "goals and policies" of the FAA, this Court's precedent indicates, are antithetical to threshold limitations placed specifically and solely on arbitration provisions. Section 2 "mandate[s] the enforcement of arbitration agreements," "save upon such grounds as exist at law or in equity for the revocation of any contract." Section 27-5-114(4) of Montana's law places arbitration agreements in a class apart from "any contract," and singularly limits their validity. The State's prescription is thus inconsonant with, and is therefore preempted by, the federal law.

For the reasons stated, the judgment of the Supreme Court of Montana is reversed, and the case is remanded for further proceedings not inconsistent with this opinion.

JUSTICE THOMAS, dissenting.

For the reasons given in my dissent last term in *Allied-Bruce Terminix Cos. v. Dobson*, I remain of the view that § 2 of the Federal Arbitration Act, does not apply to proceedings in state courts. Accordingly, I respectfully dissent.

NOTES

1. The *Casarotto* case had a lengthy and tumultuous history. After the Supreme Court's 1995 remand in light of *Allied-Bruce*, the Montana Supreme Court stuck to its guns and held that *Allied-Bruce* did not modify *Volt* and, accordingly, upheld the Montana legislation designed to alert the consumer to an arbitration clause by using underlined capital letters. Even after the 1996 Supreme Court holding striking down the Montana law, two members of the Montana Supreme Court defiantly refused to sign the usual Supreme Court remand order. While this action has no specific legal impact, the two judges used sharp language. They called the *Casarotto* decision "legally unfounded, socially detrimental and philosophically misguided." One of those who refused to sign was Justice Trieweiler, who specially concurred in the first *Casarotto* decision of the Montana Supreme Court. His opinion refers to the "arrogance" of "federal judges who consider forced arbitration as the panacea for their 'heavy case loads' and who consider the reluctance of state courts to buy into the arbitration program as a sign of intellectual inadequacy." (*Casarotto v. Lombardi*, 886 P.2d 931, 939–40 (1994).)

2. The second Montana opinion in this case, *Casarotto v. Lombardi*, 901 P.2d 596 (Mont. 1995), reasoned that Montana's notice requirement "would not 'undermine the goals and policies of the FAA.'" (901 P.2d at 597 (citing and quoting *Volt*).) Was the Montana Supreme Court correct? Is consent to arbitrate a feature of the FAA? If consent is embedded in the FAA, how can a Montana statute aiding a knowing and intelligent consent to arbitrate be held to be preempted by the FAA? Aren't the two renegade judges correct? According to Justice Ginsburg, the act of singling out arbitration clauses for special state treatment is the reason for the preemption holding. How is the "singling out" feature related to the basic idea of preemption? Is arbitration in Montana discouraged by use of the Montana notice law? *Volt* held that state arbitration law is preempted only where it "stands as an obstacle to the accomplishment and execution of the full purposes and objectives of Congress."

(489 U.S. 468, 477 (1989).) On balance, does Montana's law frustrate the FAA as an "obstacle" under *Volt*? Or have new wave "liberals" on the Supreme Court (e.g., Justices Breyer and Ginsburg) mothballed the *Volt* opinion?

3. California legislation still requires 10-point bold red type be used in arbitration clauses in contracts for medical services. (CAL. CIV. PROC. CODE § 1295.) The bold print notice must warn parties that "you are giving up your right to a jury or court trial." (*Id.*) California also mandates that arbitration clauses contained in real property conveyances must be printed in at least eight-point bold type. (CAL. CIV. PROC. CODE § 1298 (1999).) New York requires that an HMO contract that contains an arbitration clause be printed in at least twelve point boldface type above the signature line. (N.Y. PUB. HEALTH LAW § 4406-a (McKinney 1996).) Texas requires that arbitration clauses in specific types of contracts be signed by the attorneys of the respective parties. (TEX. REV. CIV. PRAC. & REM. § 171.001 (Supp. 1996).) For the argument that such clauses are now preempted after *Casarotto*, see Stephen J. Ware, *Arbitration and Unconscionability After Doctor's Associates, Inc. v. Casarotto*, 31 WAKE FOREST L. REV. 1001 (1996). Can any special state efforts to notify parties of an arbitration clause now stand?

4. *State Arbitration Legislation Limiting Time to Move to Vacate.* Recall that "the FAA contains no express preemptive provision, nor does it reflect a congressional intent to occupy the entire field of arbitration." (*Volt*, 489 U.S. at 468 (1989).) In that light, should provisions of state arbitration law that place restricted time limits on motions to vacate awards be preempted by the FAA? (*See Ekstrom v. Value Health, Inc.*, 68 F.3d 1391, 1395–96 (D.C. Cir. 1995) (holding that Connecticut statute requiring motions to vacate arbitral awards be filed within 30 days of the award "surely does not conflict with the FAA's primary purpose"); *New England Utilities v. Hydro-Quebec*, 10 F. Supp. 2d 53 (D. Mass. 1998) (dictating that Mass. Legislation requiring a motion to vacate to be filed within 30 days of delivery of the award would, if applicable, not be preempted by the FAA).) Are these decisions properly decided after the *Casarotto* case? Does applying these provisions of state arbitration procedure conflict with the basic policy of the FAA?

MASTROBUONO v. SHEARSON LEHMAN HUTTON, INC.
514 U.S. 52 (1995)

JUSTICE STEVENS delivered the opinion of the Court.

New York law allows courts, but not arbitrators, to award punitive damages. In a dispute arising out of a standard-form contract that expressly provides that it "shall be governed by the laws of the State of New York," a panel of arbitrators awarded punitive damages. The District Court and Court of Appeals disallowed that award. The question presented is whether the arbitrators' award is consistent with the central purpose of the Federal Arbitration Act to ensure "that private agreements to arbitrate are enforced according to their terms." *Volt Information Sciences, Inc. v. Board of Trustees of Leland Stanford Junior Univ.*, 489 U.S. 468 (1989).

I

In 1985 petitioners, Antonio Mastrobuono, then an assistant professor of medieval literature, and his wife Diana Mastrobuono, an artist, opened a securities trading account with respondent Shearson Lehman Hutton, Inc. (Shearson), by executing Shearson's standard-form Client's Agreement. Respondent Nick DiMinico, a vice president of Shearson, managed the Mastrobuonos' account until they closed it in 1987.[1] In 1989, petitioners filed this action in the United States District Court for the Northern District of Illinois, alleging that respondents had mishandled their account and claiming damages on a variety of state and federal law theories.

Paragraph 13 of the parties' agreement contains an arbitration provision and a choice-of-law provision. Relying on the * * * Federal Arbitration Act (FAA), respondents filed a motion to stay the court proceedings and to compel arbitration pursuant to the rules of the National Association of Securities Dealers. The District Court granted that motion, and a panel of three arbitrators was convened. After conducting hearings in Illinois, the panel ruled in favor of petitioners.

In the arbitration proceedings, respondents argued that the arbitrators had no authority to award punitive damages. Nevertheless, the panel's award included punitive damages of $400,000, in addition to compensatory damages of $159,327. Respondents paid the compensatory portion of the award but filed a motion in the District Court to vacate the award of punitive damages. The District Court granted the motion, 812 F.Supp. 845 (ND Ill.1993), and the Court of Appeals for the Seventh Circuit affirmed. 20 F.3d 713 (1994). Both courts relied on the choice-of-law provision in Paragraph 13 of the parties' agreement, which specifies that the contract shall be governed by New York law. Because the New York Court of Appeals has decided that in New York the power to award punitive damages is limited to judicial tribunals and may not be exercised by arbitrators, *Garrity v. Lyle Stuart, Inc.*, 353 N.E.2d 793 (1976), the District Court and the Seventh Circuit held that the panel of arbitrators had no power to award punitive damages in this case.

We granted certiorari because the Courts of Appeals have expressed differing views on whether a contractual choice-of-law provision may preclude an arbitral award of punitive damages that otherwise would be proper. * * * We now reverse.

II

Earlier this Term, we upheld the enforceability of a predispute arbitration agreement governed by Alabama law, even though an Alabama statute provides that arbitration agreements are unenforceable. *Allied-Bruce Terminix Cos. v. Dobson*, 115 S. Ct. 834 (1995). Writing for the Court, JUSTICE BREYER observed that Congress passed the FAA "to overcome courts' refusals to enforce agreements to arbitrate." *See also Volt Information Sciences, Inc. v. Board of Trustees of Leland Stanford Junior Univ., supra; Dean Witter Reynolds Inc. v. Byrd*, 470 U.S. 213 (1985). After determining that the FAA

---

[1] [Ed. Note: DiMinico was a former college student of his customer, Mastrobuono.]

applied to the parties' arbitration agreement, we readily concluded that the federal statute pre-empted Alabama's statutory prohibition.

Petitioners seek a similar disposition of the case before us today. Here, the Seventh Circuit interpreted the contract to incorporate New York law, including the *Garrity* rule that arbitrators may not award punitive damages. Petitioners ask us to hold that the FAA pre-empts New York's prohibition against arbitral awards of punitive damages because this state law is a vestige of the "ancient" judicial hostility to arbitration. * * *

Respondents answer that the choice-of-law provision in their contract evidences the parties' express agreement that punitive damages should not be awarded in the arbitration of any dispute arising under their contract. Thus, they claim, this case is distinguishable from *Southland* and *Perry*, in which the parties presumably desired unlimited arbitration but state law stood in their way. Regardless of whether the FAA pre-empts the *Garrity* decision in contracts not expressly incorporating New York law, respondents argue that the parties may themselves agree to be bound by *Garrity*, just as they may agree to forgo arbitration altogether. In other words, if the contract says "no punitive damages," that is the end of the matter, for courts are bound to interpret contracts in accordance with the expressed intentions of the parties — even if the effect of those intentions is to limit arbitration.

* * *

Relying on our reasoning in *Volt*, respondents thus argue that the parties to a contract may lawfully agree to limit the issues to be arbitrated by waiving any claim for punitive damages. On the other hand, we think our decisions in *Allied-Bruce*, *Southland*, and *Perry* make clear that if contracting parties agree to include claims for punitive damages within the issues to be arbitrated, the FAA ensures that their agreement will be enforced according to its terms even if a rule of state law would otherwise exclude such claims from arbitration. Thus, the case before us comes down to what the contract has to say about the arbitrability of petitioners' claim for punitive damages.

III

Shearson's standard-form "Client Agreement," which petitioners executed, contains 18 paragraphs. The two relevant provisions of the agreement are found in Paragraph 13. The first sentence of that paragraph provides, in part, that the entire agreement "shall be governed by the laws of the State of New York." The second sentence provides that "any controversy" arising out of the transactions between the parties "shall be settled by arbitration" in accordance with the rules of the National Association of Securities Dealers (NASD), or the Boards of Directors of the New York Stock Exchange and/or the American Stock Exchange. The agreement contains no express reference to claims for punitive damages. To ascertain whether Paragraph 13 expresses an intent to include or exclude such claims, we first address the impact of each of the two relevant provisions, considered separately. We then move on to the more important inquiry: the meaning of the two provisions taken together. *See*

Restatement (Second) of Contracts § 202(2) (1979) ("A writing is interpreted as a whole").

The choice-of-law provision, when viewed in isolation, may reasonably be read as merely a substitute for the conflict-of-laws analysis that otherwise would determine what law to apply to disputes arising out of the contractual relationship. Thus, if a similar contract, without a choice-of-law provision, had been signed in New York and was to be performed in New York, presumably "the laws of the State of New York" would apply, even though the contract did not expressly so state. In such event, there would be nothing in the contract that could possibly constitute evidence of an intent to exclude punitive damages claims. Accordingly, punitive damages would be allowed because, in the absence of contractual intent to the contrary, the FAA would pre-empt the Garrity rule. *See supra*, at 4.

Even if the reference to "the laws of the State of New York" is more than a substitute for ordinary conflict-of-laws analysis and, as respondents urge, includes the caveat, "detached from otherwise-applicable federal law," the provision might not preclude the award of punitive damages because New York allows its courts, though not its arbitrators, to enter such awards. *See Garrity*. In other words, the provision might include only New York's substantive rights and obligations, and not the State's allocation of power between alternative tribunals. Respondents' argument is persuasive only if "New York law" means "New York decisional law, including that State's allocation of power between courts and arbitrators, notwithstanding otherwise-applicable federal law." But, as we have demonstrated, the provision need not be read so broadly. It is not, in itself, an unequivocal exclusion of punitive damages claims.

The arbitration provision * * * does not improve respondents' argument. On the contrary, when read separately this clause strongly implies that an arbitral award of punitive damages is appropriate. It explicitly authorizes arbitration in accordance with NASD rules;[5] the panel of arbitrators in fact proceeded under that set of rules. The NASD's Code of Arbitration Procedure indicates that arbitrators may award "damages and other relief." NASD Code of Arbitration Procedure § 3741(e) (1993). While not a clear authorization of punitive damages, this provision appears broad enough at least to contemplate such a remedy. Moreover, as the Seventh Circuit noted, a manual provided to NASD arbitrators contains this provision:

> "B. Punitive Damages "The issue of punitive damages may arise with great frequency in arbitrations. Parties to arbitration are informed that arbitrators can consider punitive damages as a remedy."

20 F.3d, at 717. Thus, the text of the arbitration clause itself surely does not support — indeed, it contradicts — the conclusion that the parties agreed to foreclose claims for punitive damages.

---

[5] The contract also authorizes (at petitioners' election) that the arbitration be governed by the rules of the New York Stock Exchange or the American Stock Exchange, instead of those of the NASD. App. to Pet. for Cert. 44. Neither set of alternative rules purports to limit an arbitrator's discretion to award punitive damages. Moreover, even if there were any doubt as to the ability of an arbitrator to award punitive damages under the Exchanges' rules, the contract expressly allows petitioners, the claimants in this case, to choose NASD rules; and the panel of arbitrators in this case in fact proceeded under NASD rules.

Although neither the choice-of-law clause nor the arbitration clause, separately considered, expresses an intent to preclude an award of punitive damages, respondents argue that a fair reading of the entire Paragraph 13 leads to that conclusion. On this theory, even if "New York law" is ambiguous, and even if "arbitration in accordance with NASD rules" indicates that punitive damages are permissible, the juxtaposition of the two clauses suggests that the contract incorporates "New York law relating to arbitration." We disagree. At most, the choice-of-law clause introduces an ambiguity into an arbitration agreement that would otherwise allow punitive damages awards. As we pointed out in *Volt*, when a court interprets such provisions in an agreement covered by the FAA, "due regard must be given to the federal policy favoring arbitration, and ambiguities as to the scope of the arbitration clause itself resolved in favor of arbitration."

Moreover, respondents cannot overcome the common-law rule of contract interpretation that a court should construe ambiguous language against the interest of the party that drafted it. Respondents drafted an ambiguous document, and they cannot now claim the benefit of the doubt. The reason for this rule is to protect the party who did not choose the language from an unintended or unfair result. That rationale is well-suited to the facts of this case. As a practical matter, it seems unlikely that petitioners were actually aware of New York's bifurcated approach to punitive damages, or that they had any idea that by signing a standard-form agreement to arbitrate disputes they might be giving up an important substantive right. In the face of such doubt, we are unwilling to impute this intent to petitioners.

Finally the respondents' reading of the two clauses violates another cardinal principle of contract construction: that a document should be read to give effect to all its provisions and to render them consistent with each other. *See, e.g., In re Halas*, 104 Ill. 2d 83, 92, 83 Ill. Dec. 540, 546, 470 N.E.2d 960, 964 (1984); *Crimmins Contracting Co. v. City of New York*, 74 N.Y.2d 166, 172–173, 544 N.Y.S.2d 580, 583–84, 542 N.E.2d 1097, 1100 (1989); *Trump-Equitable Fifth Avenue Co. v. H.R.H. Constr. Corp.*, 106 App. Div. 2d 242, 244, 485 N.Y.S.2d 65, 67 (1985); Restatement (Second) of Contracts § 203(a) and Comment b (1979); *id.* § 202(5). We think the best way to harmonize the choice-of-law provision with the arbitration provision is to read "the laws of the State of New York" to encompass substantive principles that New York courts would apply, but not to include special rules limiting the authority of arbitrators. Thus, the choice-of-law provision covers the rights and duties of the parties, while the arbitration clause covers arbitration; neither sentence intrudes upon the other. In contrast, respondents' reading sets up the two clauses in conflict with one another: one foreclosing punitive damages, the other allowing them. This interpretation is untenable.

We hold that the Court of Appeals misinterpreted the parties' agreement. The arbitral award should have been enforced as within the scope of the contract. The judgment of the Court of Appeals is, therefore, reversed.

It is so ordered.

[The dissenting opinion of Justice Thomas argued that *Volt* required courts to enforce choice-of-law provisions that incorporated state procedural rules relating to arbitration. Justice Thomas asserted that the choice of New York law was no different than the choice of California law in *Volt*. He also observed that the majority's view that the choice of New York law need not include both substantive and procedural law was a position rejected in *Volt*. His dissenting opinion continues:]

The majority relies upon two assertions to defend its departure from *Volt*. First, it contends that "[a]t most, the choice-of-law clause introduces an ambiguity into an arbitration agreement." We are told that the agreement "would otherwise allow punitive damages awards," because of Paragraph 13's statement that arbitration would be conducted "in accordance with the rules then in effect, of the National Association of Securities Dealers, Inc." It is unclear which NASD "rules" the parties mean, although I am willing to agree with the majority that the phrase refers to the NASD Code of Arbitration Procedure. But the provision of the NASD Code offered by the majority simply does not speak to the availability of punitive damages. It only states: "The award shall contain the names of the parties, the name of counsel, if any, a summary of the issues, including the type(s) of any security or product, in controversy, the damages and other relief requested, the damages and other relief awarded, a statement of any other issues resolved, the names of the arbitrators, the dates the claim was filed and the award rendered, the number and dates of hearing sessions, the location of the hearings, and the signatures of the arbitrators concurring in the award." NASD Code of Arbitration Procedure § 41(e) (1985).

It is clear that § 41(e) does not define or limit the powers of the arbitrators; it merely describes the form in which the arbitrators must announce their decision. The other provisions of § 41 confirm this point. *See, e.g.*, § 41(a) ("All awards shall be in writing and signed by a majority of the arbitrators. . ."); § 41(c) ("Director of Arbitration shall endeavor to serve a copy of the award" to the parties); § 41(d) (arbitrators should render an award within 30 days); § 41(f) (awards shall be "publicly available"). The majority cannot find a provision of the NASD Code that specifically addresses punitive damages, or that speaks more generally to the types of damages arbitrators may or may not allow. Such a rule simply does not exist. The Code certainly does not require that arbitrators be empowered to award punitive damages; it leaves to the parties to define the arbitrators' remedial powers.

The majority also purports to find a clear expression of the parties' agreement on the availability of punitive damages in "a manual provided to NASD arbitrators." But Paragraph 13 of the Client Agreement nowhere mentions this manual; it mentions only "the rules then in effect of the [NASD]." The manual does not fit either part of this description: it is neither "of the [NASD]," nor a set of "rules."

First, the manual apparently is not an official NASD document. The manual was not promulgated or adopted by the NASD. Instead, it apparently was compiled by members of the Securities Industry Conference on Arbitration (SICA) as a supplement to the Uniform Code of Arbitration, which the parties clearly did not adopt in Paragraph 13. Petitioners present no evidence that the NASD has a policy of giving this specific manual to its arbitrators. Nor do petitioners assert that this manual was even used in the arbitration that gave rise to this case. More importantly, there is no indication in the text of the Client's Agreement that the parties *intended* this manual to be used by the arbitrators.

Second, the manual does not provide any "rules" in the sense contemplated by Paragraph 13; instead, it provides general information and advice to the arbitrator, such as "Hints for the Chair." SICA, Arbitrator's Manual 21 (1992). The manual is nothing more than a sort of "how to" guide for the arbitrator. One bit of advice, for example, states: "Care should be exercised, particularly when questioning a witness, so that the arbitrator does not indicate disbelief. Grimaces, frowns, or hand signals should all be avoided. A 'poker' face is the goal." *Id.*, at 19.

Even if the parties had intended to adopt the manual, it cannot be read to resolve the issue of punitive damages. When read in context, the portion of the SICA manual upon which the majority relies seems only to explain what punitive damages are, not to establish whether arbitrators have the authority to award them: "The issue of punitive damages may arise with great frequency in arbitrations. Parties to arbitration are informed that arbitrators can consider punitive damages as a remedy. Generally, in court proceedings, punitive damages consist of compensation in excess of actual damages and are awarded as a form of punishment against the wrongdoer. If punitive damages are awarded, the decision of the arbitrators should clearly specify what portion of the award is intended as punitive damages, and the arbitrators should consider referring to the authority on which they relied." *Id.*, at 26. A glance at neighboring passages, which explain the purpose of "compensatory/actual damages," "injunctive relief," "interest," "attorneys' fees," and "forum fees," *see id.*, at 26–29, confirms that the SICA manual does not even attempt to provide a standardized set of procedural rules.

Even if one made the stretch of reading the passage on punitive damages to relate to an NASD arbitrator's authority, the SICA manual limits its own applicability in the situation presented by this case. According to the manual's Code of Ethics for Arbitrators, "[w]hen an arbitrator's authority is derived from an agreement of the parties, the arbitrator should neither exceed that authority nor do less than is required to exercise that authority completely." *Id.*, at 38. Regarding procedural rules, the Code states that "[w]here the agreement of the parties sets forth procedures to be followed in conducting the arbitration or refers to rules to be followed, it is the obligation of the arbitrator to comply with such procedures or rules." *Id.*, at 38–39. The manual clearly contemplates that the parties' agreement will define the powers and authorities of the arbitrator. Thus, we are directed back to the rest of Paragraph 13 and the intent of the parties, whose only expression on the issue is their decision to incorporate the laws of New York.

My examination of the Client Agreement, the choice-of-law provision, the NASD Code of Procedure, and the SICA manual demonstrates that the parties made their intent clear, but not in the way divined by the majority. New York law specifically precludes arbitrators from awarding punitive damages, and it should be clear that there is no "conflict," as the majority puts it, between the New York law and the NASD rules. The choice-of-law provision speaks directly to the issue, while the NASD Code is silent. Giving effect to every provision of the contract requires us to honor the parties' intent, as indicated in the text of the agreement, to preclude the award of punitive damages by arbitrators.

Thankfully, the import of the majority's decision is limited and narrow. This case amounts to nothing more than a federal court applying Illinois and New York contract law to an agreement between parties in Illinois. Much like a federal court applying a state rule of decision to a case when sitting in diversity, the majority's interpretation of the contract represents only the understanding of a single federal court regarding the requirements imposed by state law. As such, the majority's opinion has applicability only to this specific contract and to no other. But because the majority reaches an erroneous result on even this narrow question, I respectfully dissent.

NOTES

1. The majority focuses on the need to uphold the intent of the signers of the arbitration clause. Does the majority really uphold the intent of the parties? Why did the brokerage firm, Shearson Lehman Hutton, Inc., select New York law? Isn't it likely this choice of law was motivated by the *Garrity* decision? Isn't there a way, however, in which the majority is, in fact, upholding the intent of the parties?

2. Assume the same facts as presented by the *Mastrobuono* decision, but assume that the arbitration clause reads as follows: "The parties select arbitration by the NASD using NASD procedures. The parties agree that the arbitrators lack authority to grant punitive damages." After *Mastrobuono,* how should such a clause be interpreted?

3. At present, the New York Stock Exchange has rules that prevent arbitration agreements from placing conditions on the arbitrators' awards. The SEC interprets this rule as forbidding the parties from agreeing to waive punitive damages.

4. Read together, *Volt* and *Mastrobuono* forge a theory that the parties to a contract to arbitrate have broad power to control the course of their future dispute resolution procedures. These are cases that rest on a belief in freedom of contract and the freedom to custom craft arbitration procedures. Does the existing text of the FAA support this "contract" model of arbitration? This theory of arbitration amounts to privatization of law-making on a grand scale. Simply by agreeing to arbitrate the parties are opting out of the court system and avoiding its procedures. Under *Volt* and *Mastrobuono,* parties to arbitration may create their own universe of procedural and, if desired, substantive norms to guide their future relationship. Is such a broad delegation of law-making power to private parties wholly desirable? What should a court do if the parties' arbitration clause asserts that "the courts will review for errors of law"? Should a court uphold the intent of the parties (the contract model of arbitration)? For full discussion of this issue, see *Gateway Technologies, Inc. v. MCI Telecommunications Corp.*, 64 F.3d 993 (5th Cir. 1995) (upholding clause and vacating award), *infra*. Does it matter that while arbitration clauses have historically been between parties with equal bargaining power and entrenched relationships, we now see more arbitration agreements involving short-term "transactions" and even arbitration clauses for tort cases?

Chapter 11

THE DISTINCTIVE ROLES OF THE ARBITRATOR AND THE COURT

This chapter deals with the role of the court and, in great contrast, the task of the arbitrator. Under the "folklore" model of arbitration, when parties contract to arbitrate they essentially opt out of the court system and agree to a binding adjudication before an expert arbitrator. The parties to an arbitration agreement have chosen intentionally to eschew courts and, instead, to use a private mode of dispute resolution. They want their dispute privatized. On one hand, then, there is no role whatsoever for a court to participate in any fashion in arbitration, a privatized, external system of justice.

Yet, historically the state has had a role in dispute resolution and even the arbitration system is not without connections to government. The Federal Arbitration Act sets forth numerous grounds for setting aside arbitral awards. It also creates a major role for courts to facilitate arbitration by issuing injunctive orders compelling arbitration and staying litigation pending the completion of arbitration. At present, courts have an equivocal rule relating to arbitration. They encourage arbitration in various ways but discourage arbitration by occasionally setting aside arbitral awards under the narrow statutory standards of the Federal Arbitration Act. As you begin this chapter try to identify the optimal role that courts can play in the arbitration system.

A. THE *PRIMA PAINT* DOCTRINE AND THE CONCEPT OF SEVERABILITY

PRIMA PAINT CORP. v. FLOOD & CONKLIN MFG. CO.
388 U.S. 395 (1967)

MR. JUSTICE FORTAS delivered the opinion of the Court.

This case presents the question whether the federal court or an arbitrator is to resolve a claim of "fraud in the inducement," under a contract governed by the United States Arbitration Act of 1925, where there is no evidence that the contracting parties intended to withhold that issue from arbitration.

[Flood & Conklin entered into two contracts with Prima Paint. A "consulting agreement" called for F&C to provide advice regarding the formulae, manufacturing process and sales of Prima accounts. Services were to be performed by F&C's chairman. The consulting contract appended a customer list and provided that F&C would make no "trade sales" of paint in its existing territory or to current customers. A second contract called for the purchase by Prima of F&C's paint business. An arbitration clause provided that "any controversy or claim arising out of or relating to this Agreement, or the breach thereof, shall be settled by arbitration in the City of New York, in accordance with the rules . . . of the American Arbitration Association."

[Soon thereafter F&C filed for bankruptcy protection. Prima then refused to pay F&C arguing that F&C "had fraudulently represented that it was in fact solvent and able to perform its contractual obligations, whereas it was in fact insolvent" and intended to file for bankruptcy protection. F&C served an intent to arbitrate. Prima filed suit, seeking rescission of the consulting agreement on the basis of alleged fraud and seeking an order enjoining F&C from arbitration. F&C sought an order staying the litigation pending arbitration and contended that the fraud issue was for the arbitrators. The trial court ruled that the fraud issue should be decided by the arbitrators. 212 F. Supp. 605. The Court of Appeals affirmed, 360 F.2d 315.

[The Supreme Court found that the contract was in "commerce" because F&C had 175 wholesale clients in numerous states and called for a change in the place of manufacturing from New Jersey to Maryland.]

* * *

Having determined that the contract in question is within the coverage of the Arbitration Act, we turn to the central issue in this case: whether a claim of fraud in the inducement of the entire contract is to be resolved by the federal court, or whether the matter is to be referred to the arbitrators. The courts of appeals have differed in their approach to this question. The view of the Court of Appeals for the Second Circuit, as expressed in this case and in others, is that — *except where the parties otherwise intend* — arbitration clauses as a matter of federal law are "separable" from the contracts in which they are embedded, and that where no claim is made that fraud was directed to the arbitration clause itself, a broad arbitration clause will be held to encompass arbitration of the claim that the contract itself was induced by fraud.[9] The Court of Appeals for the First Circuit, on the other hand, has taken the view that the question of "severability" is one of state law, and that where a State regards such a clause as inseparable a claim of fraud in the inducement must be decided by the court. *Lummus Co. v. Commonwealth Oil Ref. Co.*, 280 F.2d 915, 923–924 (1st Cir.), *cert. denied*, 364 U.S. 911 (1960).

With respect to cases brought in federal court involving maritime contracts or those evidencing transactions in "commerce," we think that Congress has provided an explicit answer. That answer is to be found in § 4 of the Act, which provides a remedy to a party seeking to compel compliance with an arbitration agreement. Under § 4, with respect to a matter within the jurisdiction of the federal courts save for the existence of an arbitration clause, the federal court is instructed to order arbitration to proceed once it is satisfied that "the making of the agreement for arbitration or the failure to comply (with the arbitration agreement) is not in issue." Accordingly, if the claim is fraud in

---

[9] The Court of Appeals has been careful to honor evidence that the parties intended to withhold such issues from the arbitrators and to reserve them for judicial resolution. *See El Hoss Engineer. & Transport Co. v. American Ind. Oil Co., supra.* We note that categories of contracts otherwise within the Arbitration Act but in which one of the parties characteristically has little bargaining power are expressly excluded from the reach of the Act. *See* § 1.

the inducement of the arbitration clause itself — an issue which goes to the "making" of the agreement to arbitrate — the federal court may proceed to adjudicate it. [12] But the statutory language does not permit the federal court to consider claims of fraud in the inducement of the contract generally. Section 4 does not expressly relate to situations like the present in which a stay is sought of a federal action in order that arbitration may proceed. But it is inconceivable that Congress intended the rule to differ depending upon which party to the arbitration agreement first invokes the assistance of a federal court. We hold, therefore, that in passing upon a § 3 application for a stay while the parties arbitrate, a federal court may consider only issues relating to the making and performance of the agreement to arbitrate. In so concluding, we not only honor the plain meaning of the statute but also the unmistakably clear congressional purpose that the arbitration procedure, when selected by the parties to a contract, be speedy and not subject to delay and obstruction in the courts.

* * *

In the present case no claim has been advanced by Prima Paint that F & C fraudulently induced it to enter into the agreement to arbitrate "[a]ny controversy or claim arising out of or relating to this Agreement, or the breach thereof." This contractual language is easily broad enough to encompass Prima Paint's claim that both execution and acceleration of the consulting agreement itself were procured by fraud. Indeed, no claim is made that Prima Paint ever intended that "legal" issues relating to the contract be excluded from arbitration, or that it was not entirely free so to contract. Federal courts are bound to apply rules enacted by Congress with respect to matters — here, a contract involving commerce — over which it has legislative power. The question which Prima Paint requested the District Court to adjudicate preliminarily to allowing arbitration to proceed is one not intended by Congress to delay the granting of a § 3 stay. Accordingly, the decision below dismissing Prima Paint's appeal is affirmed.

Affirmed.

[The concurring opinion of MR. JUSTICE HARLAN is omitted.]

MR. JUSTICE BLACK, with whom MR. JUSTICE DOUGLAS and MR. JUSTICE STEWART join, dissenting.

The Court here holds that the United States Arbitration Act, . . . as a matter of federal substantive law, compels a party to a contract containing a written arbitration provision to carry out his "arbitration agreement" even though a court might, after a fair trial, hold the entire contract — including the arbitration agreement — void because of fraud in the inducement. The

---

[12] This position is consistent both with the decision in *Moseley v. Electronic & Missile Facilities*, 374 U.S. 167, 171 (1963), and with the statutory scheme. As the "saving clause" in § 2 indicates, the purpose of Congress in 1925 was to make arbitration agreements as enforceable as other contracts, but not more so. To immunize an arbitration agreement from judicial challenge on the ground of fraud in the inducement would be to elevate it over other forms of contract — a situation inconsistent with the "saving clause."

Court holds, what is to me fantastic, that the legal issue of a contract's voidness because of fraud is to be decided by persons designated to arbitrate factual controversies arising out of a valid contract between the parties. And the arbitrators who the Court holds are to adjudicate the legal validity of the contract need not even be lawyers, and in all probability will be nonlawyers, wholly unqualified to decide legal issues, and even if qualified to apply the law, not bound to do so. I am by no means sure that thus forcing a person to forgo his opportunity to try his legal issues in the courts where, unlike the situation in arbitration, he may have a jury trial and right to appeal, is not a denial of due process of law. I am satisfied, however, that Congress did not impose any such procedures in the Arbitration Act. And I am fully satisfied that a reasonable and fair reading of that Act's language and history shows that both Congress and the framers of the Act were at great pains to emphasize that nonlawyers designated to adjust and arbitrate factual controversies arising out of valid contracts would not trespass upon the courts' prerogative to decide the legal question of whether any legal contract exists upon which to base an arbitration.

* * *

The Court today affirms this holding for three reasons, none of which is supported by the language or history of the Arbitration Act. First, the Court holds that because the consulting agreement was intended to supplement a separate contract for the interstate transfer of assets, it is itself a "contract evidencing a transaction involving commerce," the language used by Congress to describe contracts the Act was designed to cover. But in light of the legislative history which indicates that the Act was to have a limited application to contracts between merchants for the interstate shipment of goods, and in light of the express failure of Congress to use language making the Act applicable to all contracts which "affect commerce," the statutory language Congress normally uses when it wishes to exercise its full powers over commerce, I am not at all certain that the Act was intended to apply to this consulting agreement. Second, the Court holds that the language of § 4 of the Act provides an "explicit answer" to the question of whether the arbitration clause is "separable" from the rest of the contract in which it is contained. Section 4 merely provides that the court must order arbitration if it is "satisfied that the making of the agreement for arbitration * * * is not in issue." That language, considered alone, far from providing an "explicit answer," merely poses the further question of what kind of allegations put the making of the arbitration agreement in issue. Since both the lower courts assumed that but for the federal Act, New York law might apply and that under New York law a general allegation of fraud in the inducement puts into issue the making of the agreement to arbitrate (considered inseparable under New York law from the rest of the contract), the Court necessarily holds that federal law determines whether certain allegations put the making of the arbitration agreement in issue. And the Court approves the Second Circuit's fashioning of a federal separability rule which overrides state law to the contrary. The Court thus holds that the Arbitration Act, designed to provide merely a procedural remedy which would not interfere with state substantive law, authorizes federal courts to fashion a federal rule to make arbitration clauses "separable" and valid. And the Court approves a rule which is not only contrary to state law, but contrary to the intention of the parties and to accepted principles of contract law — a rule which indeed elevates arbitration provisions above all other contractual provisions. As the Court recognizes, that result was clearly not intended by Congress. * * *

Let us look briefly at the language of the Arbitration Act itself as Congress passed it. Section 2, the key provision of the Act, provides that "[a] written provision in * * * a contract * * * involving commerce to settle by arbitration a controversy thereafter arising out of such contract * * * shall be valid, irrevocable, and enforceable, *save upon such grounds as exist at law or in equity for the revocation of any contract.*" (Emphasis added.) Section 3 provides that "[i]f any suit * * * be brought * * * *upon any issue referable to arbitration* under an agreement in writing for such arbitration, the court * * * *upon being satisfied that the issue involved in such suit * * * is referable to arbitration under such an agreement,* shall * * * stay the trial of the action until such arbitration has been had * * *." (Emphasis added.) The language of these sections could not, I think, raise doubts about their meaning except to someone anxious to find doubts. They simply mean this: an arbitration agreement is to be enforced by a federal court unless the court, not the arbitrator, finds grounds "at law or in equity for the revocation of any contract." Fraud, of course, is one of the most common grounds for revoking a contract. If the contract was procured by fraud, then, unless the defrauded party elects to affirm it, there is absolutely no contract, nothing to be arbitrated. Sections 2 and 3 of the Act assume the existence of a valid contract. They merely provide for enforcement where such a valid contract exists. These provisions were plainly designed to protect a person against whom arbitration is sought to be enforced from having to submit his legal issues as to validity of the contract to the arbitrator. The legislative history of the Act makes this clear. Senator Walsh of Montana, in hearings on the bill in 1923, observed, "The court has got to hear and determine whether there is an agreement of arbitration, undoubtedly, and it is open to all defenses, equitable and legal, that would have existed at law * * *." Mr. Piatt, who represented the American Bar Association which drafted and supported the Act, was even more explicit: "I think this will operate something like an injunction process, except where he would attack it on the ground of fraud." And then Senator Walsh replied: "If he should attack it on the ground of fraud, to rescind the whole thing. * * * I presume that it merely [is] a question of whether he did make the arbitration agreement or not, * * * and then he would possibly set up that he was misled about the contract and entered into it by mistake* * * ."

Finally, it is clear to me from the bill's sponsors' understanding of the function of arbitration that they never intended that the issue of fraud in the inducement be resolved by arbitration. They recognized two special values of arbitration: (1) the expertise of an arbitrator to decide factual questions in regard to the day-to-day performance of contractual obligations,[13] and (2) the

---

[13] "Not all questions arising out of contracts ought to be arbitrated. It is a remedy peculiarly suited to the disposition of the ordinary disputes between merchants as to questions of fact — quantity, quality, time of delivery, compliance with terms of payment, excuses for non-performance, and the like. It has a place also in the determination of the simpler questions of law — the questions of law which arise out of these daily relations between merchants as to the

speed with which arbitration, as contrasted to litigation, could resolve disputes over performance of contracts and thus mitigate the damages and allow the parties to continue performance under the contracts. Arbitration serves neither of these functions where a contract is sought to be rescinded on the ground of fraud. On the one hand, courts have far more expertise in resolving legal issues which go to the validity of a contract than do arbitrators.[15] On the other hand, where a party seeks to rescind a contract and his allegation of fraud in the inducement is true, an arbitrator's speedy remedy of this wrong should never result in resumption of performance under the contract. And if the contract were not procured by fraud, the court, under the summary trial procedures provided by the Act, may determine with little delay that arbitration must proceed. The only advantage of submitting the issue of fraud to arbitration is for the arbitrators. Their compensation corresponds to the volume of arbitration they perform. If they determine that a contract is void because of fraud, there is nothing further for them to arbitrate. I think it raises serious questions of due process to submit to an arbitrator an issue which will determine his compensation. *Tumey v. State of Ohio*, 273 U.S. 510.

*   *   *

The avowed purpose of the Act was to place arbitration agreements "upon the same footing as other contracts."[30] The separability rule which the Court applies to an arbitration clause does not result in equality between it and other clauses in the contract. I had always thought that a person who attacks a contract on the ground of fraud and seeks to rescind it has to seek rescission of the whole, not tidbits, and is not given the option of denying the existence of some clauses and affirming the existence of others. Here F & C agreed both to perform consulting services for Prima and not to compete with Prima. Would any court hold that those two agreements were separable, even though Prima in agreeing to pay F & C not to compete did not directly rely on F & C's representations of being solvent? The simple fact is that Prima would not have agreed to the covenant not to compete or to the arbitration clause but for F & C's fraudulent promise that it would be financially able to perform consulting services. As this Court held in *United States v. Bethlehem Steel Corp.*, 315 U.S. 289, 298: "Whether a number of promises constitute one contract (and are non-separable) or more than one is to be determined by inquiring "whether the parties assented to all the promises as a single whole, so that there would have been no bargain whatever, if any promise or set of promises were struck out." Under this test, all of Prima's promises were part of one, inseparable contract.

---

passage of title, the existence of warranties, or the questions of law which are complementary to the questions of fact which we have just mentioned." Cohen & Dayton, *The New Federal Arbitration Law*, 12 Va. L. Rev. 265, 281 (1926).

[15] "It [arbitration] is not a proper remedy for * * * questions with which the arbitrators have no particular experience and which are better left to the determination of skilled judges with a background of legal experience and established systems of law." Cohen & Dayton, supra, at 281.

[30] H.R. Rep. No. 96, 68th Cong., 1st Sess. (1924).

* * *

* * * The plain purpose of the Act as written by Congress was this and no more: Congress wanted federal courts to enforce contracts to arbitrate and plainly said so in the Act. But Congress also plainly said that whether a contract containing an arbitration clause can be rescinded on the ground of fraud is to be decided by the courts and not by the arbitrators. Prima here challenged in the courts the validity of its alleged contract with F & C as a whole, not in fragments. If there has never been any valid contract, then there is not now and never has been anything to arbitrate. If Prima's allegations are true, the sum total of what the Court does here is to force Prima to arbitrate a contract which is void and unenforceable before arbitrators who are given the power to make final legal determinations of their own jurisdiction, not even subject to effective review by the highest court in the land. That is not what Congress said Prima must do. * * *

FIRST OPTIONS OF CHICAGO, INC. v. KAPLAN
514 U.S. 938 (1995)

[First Options, a business that clears stock trades, requested arbitration of a dispute with a debtor by a panel of the Philadelphia Stock Exchange. The dispute focused upon a "workout agreement" between First Options and three parties, Manuel Kaplan, his wife Carol Kaplan and his wholly owned company MKI. Only MKI had signed an arbitration clause. Mr. and Mrs. Kaplan contended they had not signed an agreement to arbitrate. While MKI had unquestionably agreed to arbitrate, the Kaplans denied their own dispute with First Options was arbitrable because they had not covenanted to arbitrate. The arbitrators decided they had the power to rule on the merits and found against the Kaplans. The trial court refused to set aside the award. The Court of Appeals, however, reversed, viewing that the dispute was not arbitrable. 19 F.3d 1503 (3d Cir. 1994). Justice Breyer's opinion focused on "who should have the primary power to decide" the question of whether the Kaplans had agreed to arbitrate.]

Although the question is a narrow one, it has a certain practical importance. That is because a party who has not agreed to arbitrate will normally have a right to a court's decision about the merits of its dispute (say, as here, its obligation under a contract). But, where the party has agreed to arbitrate, he or she, in effect, has relinquished much of that right's practical value. The party still can ask a court to review the arbitrator's decision, but the court will set that decision aside only in very unusual circumstances. *See, e.g.*, 9 U.S.C. § 10 (award procured by corruption, fraud, or undue means; arbitrator exceeded his powers); *Wilko v. Swan*, 346 U.S. 427, 436–437 (1953) (parties bound by arbitrator's decision not in "manifest disregard" of the law), over-ruled on other grounds; *Rodriguez de Quijas v. Shearson/American Express, Inc.*, 490 U.S. 477 (1989). Hence, who — court or arbitrator — has the primary authority to decide whether a party has agreed to arbitrate can make a critical difference to a party resisting arbitration.

We believe the answer to the "who" question (*i.e.*, the standard-of-review question) is fairly simple. Just as the arbitrability of the merits of a dispute depends upon whether the parties agreed to arbitrate that dispute, so the question "who has the primary power to decide arbitrability" turns upon what the parties agreed about *that* matter. Did the parties agree to submit the arbitrability question itself to arbitration? If so, then the court's standard for reviewing the arbitrator's decision about *that* matter should not differ from the standard courts apply when they review any other matter that parties have agreed to arbitrate. That is to say, the court should give considerable leeway to the arbitrator, setting aside his or her decision only in certain narrow circumstances. *See, e.g.*, 9 U.S.C. § 10. If, on the other hand, the parties did *not* agree to submit the arbitrability question itself to arbitration, then the court should decide that question just as it would decide any other question that the parties did not submit to arbitration, namely independently. These two answers flow inexorably from the fact that arbitration is simply a matter of contract between the parties; it is a way to resolve those disputes — but only those disputes — that the parties have agreed to submit to arbitration.

We agree with First Options, therefore, that a court must defer to an arbitrator's arbitrability decision when the parties submitted that matter to arbitration. Nevertheless, that conclusion does not help First Options win this case. That is because a fair and complete answer to the standard-of-review question requires a word about how a court should decide whether the parties have agreed to submit the arbitrability issue to arbitration. And, that word makes clear that the Kaplans did not agree to arbitrate arbitrability here.

When deciding whether the parties agreed to arbitrate a certain matter (including arbitrability), courts generally (though with a qualification we discuss below) should apply ordinary state-law principles that govern the formation of contracts. The relevant state law here, for example, would require the court to see whether the parties objectively revealed an intent to submit the arbitrability issue to arbitration.

This Court, however, has (as we just said) added an important qualification, applicable when courts decide whether a party has agreed that arbitrators should decide arbitrability: Courts should not assume that the parties agreed to arbitrate arbitrability unless there is "clea[r] and unmistakabl[e]" evidence that they did so. In this manner the law treats silence or ambiguity about the question "*who* (primarily) should decide arbitrability" differently from the way it treats silence or ambiguity about the question "*whether* a particular merits-related dispute is arbitrable because it is within the scope of a valid arbitration agreement" — for in respect to this latter question the law reverses the presumption.

But, this difference in treatment is understandable. The latter question arises when the parties have a contract that provides for arbitration of some issues. In such circumstances, the parties likely gave at lest some thought to the scope of arbitration. And, given the law's permissive policies in respect to arbitration, one can understand why the law would insist upon clarity before concluding that the parties did *not* want to arbitrate a related matter. On the other hand, the former question — the "who (primarily) should decide arbitrability" question — is rather arcane. A party often might not focus upon that question or upon the significance of having arbitrators decide the scope of their own powers. And, given the principle that a party can be forced to arbitrate only those issues it specifically has agreed to submit to arbitration, one can understand why courts might hesitate to interpret silence or ambiguity on the "who should decide arbitrability" point as giving the arbitrators that power, for doing so might too often force unwilling parties to arbitrate a matter they reasonably would have thought a judge, not an arbitrator, would decide.

On the record before us, First Options cannot show that the Kaplans clearly agreed to have the arbitrators decide (*i.e.*, to arbitrate) the question of arbitrability. First Options relies on the Kaplans' filing with the arbitrators a written memorandum objecting to the arbitrators' jurisdiction. But merely arguing the arbitrability issue to an arbitrator does not indicate a clear willingness to arbitrate that issue, *i.e.*, a willingness to be effectively bound by the arbitrator's decision on that point. To the contrary, insofar as the Kaplans were forcefully objecting to the arbitrators deciding their dispute with First Options, one naturally would think that they did *not* want the arbitrators to have binding authority over them. This conclusion draws added support from (1) an obvious explanation for the Kaplans' presence before the arbitrators (*i.e.*, that MKI, Mr. Kaplan's wholly owned firm, was arbitrating workout agreement matters); and (2) Third Circuit law that suggested that the Kaplans might argue arbitrability to the arbitrators without losing their right to independent court review.

*   *   *

We conclude that, because the Kaplans did not clearly agree to submit the question of arbitrability to arbitration, the Court of Appeals was correct in finding that the arbitrability of the Kaplan/First Options dispute was subject to independent review by the courts.

NOTES

1. Notice Justice Breyer's assertion that "arbitration is simply a matter of contract between the parties." If this were literally true could there be any role whatsoever for the courts? Doesn't *First Options of Chicago* leave the court with a routine role to decide arbitrability — whether the issue is referable to arbitration? Doesn't this mean that in the typical arbitration situation the court will have at least one major function?

2. Under *Prima Paint* and *First Options of Chicago*, who should decide questions about whether a written arbitration agreement is an adhesion contract? Doesn't the text of the FAA suggest that such questions be left to the court? Under *First Chicago Options*, however, can't the parties take away this judicial power simply by contracting that the arbitrators should decide such questions? If you answer this question in the affirmative, aren't you allocating responsibility to decide legal issues to the arbitrators? Is this an appropriate division of labor between court and arbitrators? Is such an allocation of function consistent with the FAA?

3. The context in which most trial courts participate in the arbitration process is in hearing the defendant's dual motions to stay litigation and to compel arbitration. In a sense, these motions could be said to require minimal judicial interference in the arbitration process. A judge hearing the motion to compel is essentially advancing arbitration by stopping a case that had sought to ignore a contract to arbitrate. Yet, the court hearing these motions performs a number of tasks:

> [F]irst, it must determine whether the parties agreed to arbitrate; second, it must determine the scope of the agreement; third, if federal statutory claims are asserted, it must consider whether Congress intended these claims to be nonarbitrable; and fourth, if the court concludes that some, but not all, of the claims in the action are subject to arbitration, it must determine whether to stay the remainder of the proceedings pending arbitration. [*Creative Sec. Corp. v. Bear Stearns & Co.*, 671 F. Supp. 961, 965 (S.D.N.Y. 1987), *aff'd*, 847 F.2d 834 (2d Cir. 1988).]

Are these tasks so significant as to render inaccurate the slogan that parties to an arbitration have opted out of the court system? Or, alternatively, are these four tasks relatively narrow in nature, leaving the core of the dispute with the arbitrator?

4. In *AT & T Technologies v. CWA*, 475 U.S. 643 (1986), the Court held that district courts, and not arbitrators, are generally to determine whether parties to a collective-bargaining agreement have agreed to submit particular disputes to arbitration. "[T]he question of arbitrability — whether a collective-bargaining agreement creates a duty for the parties to arbitrate the particular grievance — is undeniably an issue for judicial determination. Unless the parties clearly and unmistakably provide otherwise, the question of whether the parties agreed to arbitrate is to be decided by the court, not the arbitrator." (475 U.S. at 649.) Nonetheless, the *AT & T Technologies* Court emphasized the limited function to be performed by courts when deciding arbitrability questions.

> [I]n deciding whether the parties have agreed to submit a particular grievance to arbitration, a court is not to rule on the potential merits of the underlying claims. * * * [T]here is a presumption of arbitrability in the sense that "[a]n order to arbitrate the particular grievance should not be denied unless it may be said with positive assurance that the arbitration clause is not susceptible of an interpretation that covers the asserted dispute. Doubts should be resolved in favor of coverage. [475 U.S. at 649–50, quoting *United Steelworkers v. Warrior & Gulf Navigation Co.*, 363 U.S. 574, 582–83 (1960).]

If a court initially determines that a dispute is arbitrable, may the arbitrator thereafter decide that the grievance is actually beyond the scope of the contractual arbitration provision? Has the court held that the underlying controversy is "actually arbitrable" or only "arguably arbitrable"?

In *Pennzoil Explorations v. Ramco Energy Ltd.*, 139 F.3d 1061 (5th Cir. 1998), the court relied on the *AT&T Technologies* case in holding that a judge should decide whether a dispute falls within the four corners of an arbitration agreement. Unlike *AT&T Technologies*, the *Pennzoil Exploration* decision did not involve an interpretation of a collective bargaining agreement. Should the presence of an agreement to arbitrate between a union and an employer be treated any differently than other agreements to arbitrate? Aren't all agreements to arbitrate really contracts? The *Pennzoil Exploration* court asserted that "the question of whether a party can be compelled to arbitrate, as well as the question of what issues a party can be compelled to arbitrate, is an issue for the court rather than the arbitrator to decide." (*Id.* at 1066.)

6. Reconsider *Prima Paint*. If a plaintiff files suit and in count I seeks a declaration that a signed arbitration clause is invalid on the grounds of fraud in the inducement, should the court apply the *Prima Paint* doctrine and deny relief on the grounds that the question is for the arbitrator? Doesn't the *Prima Paint* case suggest that the court should keep this question for itself? For an affirmative answer, see *Letizia v. Prudential-Bache Securities, Inc.*, 802 F.2d 1185, 1188 (9th Cir. 1986) (question for court where attack is purely on the arbitration clause itself). What if, however, the plaintiff's federal court action contends that the defendant's alleged fraud infected the entire contract? How would *Prima Paint* answer this question? (*See Three Valleys Mun. Water Dist. v. E.F. Hutton & Co., Inc.*, 925 F.2d 1136, 1140 (9th Cir. 1991).)

7. Who should decide whether a prior arbitration is res judicata, thereby barring a later suit between the parties In *Chiron Corp. v. Ortho Diagnostic Systems, Inc.*, 207 F.3d 1126 (9th Cir. 2000), the court of appeals affirmed a trial court order compelling an arbitrator's determination of the issue. The court reasoned that the issue of whether a previous arbitration constitutes res judicata goes to the merits of the case and, accordingly, falls under a broadly worded arbitration clause calling for the disputants to arbitrate "any dispute, controversy or claim arising out of or relating to" the agreement between the parties.

8. *Enforcement of Arbitration Clauses Against Non-Signatories. In First Options of Chicago, supra*, the Supreme Court upheld a court of appeals finding that a dispute was not arbitrable because the Kaplans did not sign a contract to arbitrate. Can a court ever force arbitration of a dispute when one has not signed a contract to arbitrate? In *International Paper Co. v. Schwabedissen Maschinen & Anlagen GMBH*, 206 F.3d 411 (4th Cir. 2000), the court of appeals required a buyer of an industrial saw to arbitrate despite the fact that the buyer was not a signatory party to a contract containing an arbitration clause between the defendant German manufacturer and its distributor. The court reasoned that the plaintiff buyer was bound to arbitrate because it sought remedies under the contract containing the arbitration clause and had received a direct benefit under this contract.

HOWSAM v. DEAN WITTER REYNOLDS, INC.
537 U.S. 79 (2002)

Justice BREYER delivered the opinion of the Court.

This case focuses upon an arbitration rule of the National Association of Securities Dealers (NASD). The rule states that no dispute "shall be eligible for submission to arbitration . . . where six (6) years have elapsed from the occurrence or event giving rise to the . . . dispute." NASD Code of Arbitration Procedure § 10304 (1984). We must decide whether a court or an NASD arbitrator should apply the rule to the underlying controversy. We conclude that the matter is for the arbitrator.

I.

The underlying controversy arises out of investment advice that Dean Witter Reynolds, Inc. (Dean Witter), provided its client, Karen Howsam, when, some time between 1986 and 1994, it recommended that she buy and hold interests in four limited partnerships. Howsam says that Dean Witter misrepresented the virtues of the partnerships. The resulting controversy falls within their standard Client Service Agreement's arbitration clause, which provides:

> "[A]ll controversies . . . concerning or arising from . . . any account . . ., any transaction . . ., or . . . the construction, performance or breach of . . . any . . . agreement between us . . . shall be determined by arbitration before any self-regulatory organization or exchange of which Dean Witter is a member."

The agreement also provides that Howsam can select the arbitration forum. And Howsam chose arbitration before the NASD.

To obtain NASD arbitration, Howsam signed the NASD's Uniform Submission Agreement. That agreement specified that the "present matter in controversy" was submitted for arbitration "in accordance with" the NASD's "Code of Arbitration Procedure." And that Code contains the provision at issue here, a provision stating that no dispute "shall be eligible for submission . . . where six (6) years have elapsed from the occurrence or event giving rise to the . . . dispute." NASD Code § 10304.

After the Uniform Submission Agreement was executed, Dean Witter filed this lawsuit in Federal District Court. It asked the court to declare that the dispute was "ineligible for arbitration" because it was more than six years old. App. 45. And it sought an injunction that would prohibit Howsam from proceeding in arbitration. The District Court dismissed the action on the ground that the NASD arbitrator, not the court, should interpret and apply the NASD rule. The Court of Appeals for the Tenth Circuit, however, reversed. 261 F.3d 956 (2001). In its view, application of the NASD rule presented a question of the underlying dispute's "arbitrability"; and the presumption is that a court, not an arbitrator, will ordinarily decide an "arbitrability" question. *See, e.g., First Options of Chicago, Inc. v. Kaplan,* 514 U.S. 938 (1995).

The Courts of Appeals have reached different conclusions about whether a court or an arbitrator primarily should interpret and apply this particular NASD rule. *Compare, e.g.,* 261 F.3d 956 (10th Cir. 1001) (case below) (holding that the question is for the court); *J.E. Liss & Co. v. Levin,* 201 F.3d 848, 851 (7th Cir. 2000) (same), *with PaineWebber Inc. v. Elahi,* 87 F.3d 589 (1st Cir. 1996) (holding that NASD § 15, currently § 10304, is presumptively for the arbitrator); *Smith Barney Shearson, Inc. v. Boone,* 47 F.3d 750 (5th Cir. 1995) (same). We granted Howsam's petition for certiorari to resolve this disagreement. And we now hold that the matter is for the arbitrator.

II.

This Court has determined that "arbitration is a matter of contract and a party cannot be required to submit to arbitration any dispute which he has not agreed so to submit." *Steelworkers v. Warrior & Gulf Nav. Co.*, 363 U.S. 574, 582 (1960); *see also First Options, supra.* Although the Court has also long recognized and enforced a "liberal federal policy favoring arbitration agreements," *Moses H. Cone Memorial Hospital v. Mercury Constr. Corp.*, 460 U.S. 1, 24–25, (1983), it has made clear that there is an exception to this policy: The question whether the parties have submitted a particular dispute to arbitration, *i.e.*, the *"question of arbitrability,"* is "an issue for judicial determination [u]nless the parties clearly and unmistakably provide otherwise." *AT & T Technologies, Inc. v. Communications Workers*, 475 U.S. 643, 649 (1986) (emphasis added); *First Options, supra,* at 944. We must decide here whether application of the NASD time limit provision falls into the scope of this last-mentioned interpretive rule.

Linguistically speaking, one might call any potentially dispositive gateway question a "question of arbitrability," for its answer will determine whether the underlying controversy will proceed to arbitration on the merits. The Court's case law, however, makes clear that, for purposes of applying the interpretive rule, the phrase "question of arbitrability" has a far more limited scope. The Court has found the phrase applicable in the kind of narrow circumstance where contracting parties would likely have expected a court to have decided the gateway matter, where they are not likely to have thought that they had agreed that an arbitrator would do so, and, consequently, where reference of the gateway dispute to the court avoids the risk of forcing parties to arbitrate a matter that they may well not have agreed to arbitrate.

Thus, a gateway dispute about whether the parties are bound by a given arbitration clause raises a "question of arbitrability" for a court to decide. *See id.,* at 943–946 (holding that a court should decide whether the arbitration contract bound parties who did not sign the agreement); *John Wiley & Sons, Inc. v. Livingston*, 376 U.S. 543 (1964) (holding that a court should decide whether an arbitration agreement survived a corporate merger and bound the resulting corporation). Similarly, a disagreement about whether an arbitration clause in a concededly binding contract applies to a particular type of controversy is for the court. *See, e.g., AT & T Technologies, supra* (holding that a court should decide whether a labor-management layoff controversy falls within the arbitration clause of a collective-bargaining agreement); *Atkinson v. Sinclair Refining Co.*, 370 U.S. 238 (1962) (holding that a court should decide whether a clause providing for arbitration of various "grievances" covers claims for damages for breach of a no-strike agreement).

At the same time the Court has found the phrase "question of arbitrability" *not* applicable in other kinds of general circumstance where parties would likely expect that an arbitrator would decide the gateway matter. Thus " 'procedural' questions which grow out of the dispute and bear on its final disposition" are presumptively *not* for the judge, but for an arbitrator, to decide. *John Wiley, supra,* at 557 (holding that an arbitrator should decide whether the first two steps of a grievance procedure were completed, where these steps are prerequisites to arbitration). So, too, the presumption is that the arbitrator should decide "allegation[s] of waiver, delay, or a like defense to arbitrability." *Moses H. Cone Memorial Hospital, supra.* Indeed, the Revised Uniform Arbitration Act of 2000 (RUAA), seeking to "incorporate the holdings of the vast majority of state courts and the law that has developed under the [Federal Arbitration Act]," states that an "arbitrator shall decide whether a condition precedent to arbitrability has been fulfilled." RUAA § 6(c), and comment 2, 7 U.L.A. 12-13 (Supp.2002). And the comments add that "in the absence of an agreement to the contrary, issues of substantive arbitrability . . . are for a court to decide and issues of procedural arbitrability, *i.e.,* whether prerequisites such as *time limits,* notice, laches, estoppel, and other conditions precedent to an obligation to arbitrate have been met, are for the arbitrators to decide." *Id.,* § 6, comment 2, 7 U.L.A., at 13 (emphasis added).

Following this precedent, we find that the applicability of the NASD time limit rule is a matter presumptively for the arbitrator, not for the judge. The time limit rule closely resembles the gateway questions that this Court has found not to be "questions of arbitrability." *E.g., Moses H. Cone Memorial Hospital, supra,* at 24–25 (referring to "waiver, delay, or a like defense"). Such a dispute seems an "aspec[t] of the [controversy] which called the grievance procedures into play." *John Wiley, supra.*

Moreover, the NASD arbitrators, comparatively more expert about the meaning of their own rule, are comparatively better able to interpret and to apply it. In the absence of any statement to the contrary in the arbitration agreement, it is reasonable to infer that the parties intended the agreement to reflect that understanding. *Cf. First Options,* 514 U.S., at 944-945. And for the law to assume an expectation that aligns (1) decisionmaker with (2) comparative expertise will help better to secure a fair and expeditious resolution of the underlying controversy — a goal of arbitration systems and judicial systems alike.

We consequently conclude that the NASD's time limit rule falls within the class of gateway procedural disputes that do not present what our cases have called "questions of arbitrability." And the strong pro-court presumption as to the parties' likely intent does not apply.

* * *

For these reasons, the judgment of the Tenth Circuit is

Reversed.

Justice O'CONNOR took no part in the consideration or decision of this case. The dissent of Justice THOMAS is omitted.

NOTES

1. Recall the presumption in favor of arbitrability. Did it affect the result in the *Howsam* case?

2. Consider the "gateway" label. Is it a rule or a concept of general use that might not apply?

3. Is there a right to appeal allegedly erroneous evidentiary rulings by an arbitrator to a federal court? In *Odjfell SA v. Celanese AG,* 380 F. Supp. 2d

297 (S.D.N.Y. 2005), the district court overturned and remanded an order of an arbitration panel regarding attorney-client objections to a document production order. Is this the proper procedure for the court to use? When a court provides review of a pre-trial order of an arbitrator isn't it taking the matter out of the arbitrator's decisional authority? Is this proper under the teachings of *Howsam*?

B. JUDGING CONSENT TO ARBITRATE

Arbitration is the creature of contract. In order for arbitration to occur the parties must agree to arbitrate. Consent to arbitrate is one of the main characteristics of arbitration. (*See* IAN MACNEIL, RICHARD SPEIDEL & THOMAS STIPANOWICH, I. FED. ARBITRATION LAW § 2.1.3 (1994).) This section examines the degree of care used by courts to regulate the consent process. This section also incorporates attacks on arbitration on the grounds that arbitration clauses can be contracts of adhesion or unconscionable contracts.

AMERICAN ITALIAN PASTA CO. v. AUSTIN CO.
914 F.2d 1103 (8th Cir. 1990)

WOLLMAN, CIRCUIT JUDGE.

The Austin Company appeals from the district court's order denying its motion to compel arbitration. We reverse.

I.

American Italian Pasta Company (American Pasta) entered into a contract with Austin under which Austin agreed to design and build a pasta factory. Article 16 of the contract provides: "In the event of any dispute or disagreement arising under this contract, it is mutually agreed, that upon written notice of either to the other party, both Owner and Austin will use their best efforts to settle such disputes or disagreement in a manner that is fair and equitable to both parties before either party can exercise the right of any legal action. If both parties agree that a dispute or disagreement is of such nature that it cannot be settled as provided for above, then such dispute or disagreement may be submitted to arbitration in accordance with the Rules of The American Arbitration Association in which event, the decision of the arbitrators shall be final and binding upon the parties."

A dispute arose between the parties, and settlement negotiations were unsuccessful. Austin notified the American Arbitration Association to proceed with arbitration. American Pasta filed an application for stay of arbitration in state court. Austin removed the case to federal court. The district court concluded that the contract between the parties permits, but does not compel, participation in arbitration.

II.

The Federal Arbitration Act, 9 U.S.C. § 1 et seq., which the parties agree governs this contract, expresses Congress' "declaration of a liberal policy favoring arbitration agreements." *Moses H. Cone Memorial Hosp. v. Mercury Constr.*, 460 U.S. 1, 24 (1983); *I.S. Joseph Co., Inc. v. Michigan Sugar Co.*, 803 F.2d 396, 399 (8th Cir. 1986). Notwithstanding this liberal policy in favor of arbitration agreements, the Arbitration Act does not require parties to arbitrate when they have not agreed to do so. *Volt Info. Sciences v. Board of Trustees*, 489 U.S. 468 (1989); *Recold, S.A. De C.V. v. Monfort of Colorado, Inc.*, 893 F.2d 195, 197 (8th Cir. 1990). Our task, then, is to determine whether the language the parties used in Article 16 reflects the parties' intention to consent to mandatory arbitration. *I.S. Joseph Co., Inc.*, 803 F.2d at 399.

The Fifth Circuit found arbitration mandatory under a contract that stated: "If the Union and the Company fail to agree, the dispute may be submitted to the arbitration and the decision of the arbitrator shall be final." *Deaton Truck Line, Inc. v. Local Union 612*, 314 F.2d 418, 421 (5th Cir. 1962). The court held that "may" should be construed to give either party the option to require arbitration. *Id.* at 422.

In *Bonnot v. Congress of Indep. Unions Local # 14*, 331 F.2d 355 (8th Cir. 1964), we construed a contract that provided: "In the event the two parties do not agree after the steps outlined . . . above, then either party may request arbitration and follow the following procedure." *Id.* at 356. We adopted the interpretation in *Deaton* and held that the purpose of "may" was to give an aggrieved party the choice between arbitration or the abandonment of its claim. *Id.* at 359.

We construe a contract to give effect to all of its provisions and to avoid rendering any provisions meaningless. *Johnson Controls, Inc. v. City of Cedar Rapids*, 713 F.2d 370, 374 (8th Cir. 1983). When viewed in the light of this rule of construction and the holdings in *Deaton* and *Bonnot*, we conclude that the structure and language of the contract reflect that Austin and American Pasta intended arbitration to be mandatory. The phrase "[i]f both parties agree" in the second paragraph of Article 16 refers to the inability of the parties to reach a settlement rather than to the submission of the dispute to arbitration. There would be no reason for the arbitration language in Article 16 if the parties intended it to be permissive, for the parties could voluntarily have agreed to submit a dispute to arbitration in the absence of such a provision.

The judgment is reversed, and the case is remanded with directions to enter judgment compelling arbitration.

FLOYD R. GIBSON, SENIOR CIRCUIT JUDGE, dissenting.

I respectfully dissent. The majority too easily gives an adhesion contract authority in the allegedly good name of arbitration. While the reasoning of the majority soundly follows the congressional declaration that generously prefers arbitration, I believe its citation and analysis of authority from this court is too thin a foundation to support the claim that arbitration is compelled by the ambiguous contract sub judice.

The contract which Austin presented to American Pasta says only that "[if] both parties agree that a dispute or disagreement . . . cannot be settled . . . then such dispute or disagreement may be submitted to arbitration [as per the rules of the American Arbitration Association]." The majority has found compulsory arbitration in that language on two grounds. The first is that in *Bonnot v. Congress of Indep. Unions Local # 14*, 331 F.2d 355, 359 (8th Cir. 1964) we held that a particular dispute was compulsorily arbitrable where the contract of the parties used only the phrase "may request arbitration." The second is that courts must construe contracts to give meaning to their provisions; that is, without giving "may" a compulsory meaning in the contract in this case, arguably the arbitration clause is rendered meaningless because with or without it the parties *may* consent to arbitration of a dispute. This is one avenue of analyzing this issue and not unsound reasoning, however more salient reasons support the contrary result.

The first, each contract must be interpreted in light of the facts surrounding it. The second, Austin wrote this contract, and we should construe it against its drafter. With regard to the first point, I suggest that because "may" was found to be compulsory language in a contract (a collective bargaining agreement) between two parties of relatively equal bargaining power (a union and an employer) with respect to one particular dispute, *see Bonnot*, 331 F.2d at 359, does not mean that "may" has a compulsory meaning in this case.[2] And, *Bonnot* expressly held "the contract unambiguously expresses the agreement of the parties that arbitration was to be resorted to for this dispute's settlement." *Id.* But, here, on the contrary "may" seems only to mean "may," and probably misled the appellee in its view of the contract terms. The least Austin should have done to clarify the adhesion contract was to state, as was in the contract in *Bonnot*, "*either* party may request arbitration." *Id.* at 356 (emphasis added).

Which brings me to my second point — Austin was the drafter. Though Congress has directed that arbitration be given a favorable nod where possible, the Supreme Court has reminded us that each case is controlled by its own contract and the parties cannot be made to do what they have not agreed to do. *See Volt Info. Sciences v. Board of Trustees*, 489 U.S. 468 (1989). Though Austin obviously wants to compel arbitration, its own contract says only that arbitration may occur "*[if] both parties agree that a dispute or disagreement is of such a nature that it cannot be settled as provided for. . . .*" American Pasta apparently does not agree to arbitration. While mindful of the liberal interpretation we are to give arbitration clauses, I am unwavering in the view that adhesion contracts still must be construed against their makers.

That rule of contract construction is paramount to the rule cited by the majority with respect to rendering provisions meaningless, particularly in this case. I render nothing meaningless by denying Austin compulsory arbitration. It is Austin who has made its bed. If the arbitration clause is meaningless, it is no less so than the preceding paragraph of Article 16 which amounts to

---

[2] "In *Bonnot* we held that *in certain circumstances* the term 'may' merely allows that an employee may choose not to pursue his grievance but that if he does pursue it, he must seek arbitration." *Anderson v. Alpha Portland Industries, Inc.*, 752 F.2d 1293, 1300 (8th Cir.) (*en banc*) (emphasis added), *cert. denied*, 471 U.S. 1102 (1985) (further subsequent history omitted). *Bonnot* is a labor case that does not necessarily translate into every case with an arbitration clause. Similarly, *Deaton Truck Line, Inc. v. Local Union 612*, 314 F.2d 418 (5th Cir. 1962), is distinguishable as a case involving a labor union, an employer, and a collective bargaining agreement. Each case should be decided on its own contract.

little more than an empty promise to make best efforts. Has not Austin rendered that provision meaningless by seeking arbitration? When disputes arise between parties, best efforts often fail and legal action becomes inevitable. If one party's rights thereto are going to be restricted by the other party, it should be spelled out to the "t." I think that Austin failed to cross the t's in arbitration, and I am unwilling to cross them for it.

While parties are still free to contract, there should be a clear meeting of the minds before arbitration is made mandatory. For all the foregoing reasons, I cannot conclude that American Pasta consented to *compulsory* arbitration by signing Austin's preprinted adhesion contract. I respectfully dissent and would affirm the district court.

C.H.I. INC. v. MARCUS BROTHERS TEXTILE, INC.
930 F.2d 762 (9th Cir. 1991)

BOOCHEVER, CIRCUIT JUDGE:

C.H.I. appeals the district court's dismissal for failure to arbitrate its breach of contract claim against Marcus Brothers. C.H.I. argues that the arbitration clause in the Marcus Brothers' confirmation form is unenforceable because: 1) it is an adhesion contract; 2) C.H.I. did not knowingly consent to arbitration; [and] 3) C.H.I. signed it under economic duress; * * *

BACKGROUND

During the fall of 1989, C.H.I., a California corporation, submitted several fabric purchase orders to Marcus Brothers, a New York corporation. The orders stated, "[p]urchaser and supplier agree that any disputes arising between them shall be subject to the jurisdiction of the courts of the State of California and further agree that the laws of the State of California shall be applied to resolve any such disputes." Marcus Brothers responded to each order with a contract confirmation form which C.H.I.'s president signed. The Marcus Brothers' form stated, "[t]his confirmation is subject to all of the terms and conditions on the face and reverse side hereof, including the provision for arbitration. . . , all of which are accepted by buyer, supersede buyer's order form if any, and constitute the entire contract between buyer and seller. . . ." On the back of the Marcus Brothers' form was a standard arbitration clause designating New York as the place of arbitration.

In March, 1990, C.H.I. filed a complaint for breach of contract and declaratory relief in California Superior Court. In April, 1990, the Marcus Brothers' petition to remove the case to the United States District Court for the Central District of California was granted on the basis of diversity of citizenship. In June, 1990, the court granted Marcus Brothers' motion to dismiss for failure to arbitrate.

DISCUSSION

* * *

C.H.I. argues that it did not knowingly agree to arbitrate and that even if it did, the Marcus Brothers' form should be rejected as an adhesion contract.

It claims that during oral negotiations neither party mentioned arbitration. Moreover, its own purchase form, which made no mention of arbitration, clearly provides that any disputes be resolved in California courts pursuant to California law. C.H.I. alleges that it signed the Marcus Brothers' confirmation form under duress as it had made commitments to third parties which depended upon receipt of the fabric.

Federal case law supports the district court's dismissal for failure to arbitrate. As in this case, *N & D Fashions, Inc. v. DHJ Industries, Inc.*, 548 F.2d 722 (8th Cir. 1977), involved a fabric manufacturer and purchaser who orally agreed to the purchase of fabric. N & D, as purchaser, subsequently sent DHJ a purchase order which did not contain an arbitration clause. DHJ returned four confirmation forms which N & D's agent officer signed. Each form stated, "this contract is subject to all the terms and conditions printed on the reverse side." *Id.* at 724. The reverse side contained sixteen terms, including a standard arbitration agreement. N & D subsequently brought suit for misrepresentation and fraud. The Eighth Circuit reversed the district court's ruling that the arbitration clause was void as a material alteration of the initial contract. It found that, by signing the confirmation forms, N & D expressly agreed to its provisions: ". . . While a party may not be subjected to a provision which materially alters the contract by failing to object to it, he cannot avoid the effect of his written acceptance of a contract which expressly, above his signature on the face of the contract, incorporates the provisions on the reverse side of the document." *Id.* at 727. As Marcus Brothers points out, its case against C.H.I. is even more compelling than *N & D Fashions* because its arbitration provision was specifically mentioned on the face of the confirmation form, directly above the signature line.

C.H.I. provides no evidence to establish that this was an adhesion contract entered into under fraud and economic duress. It instead gives only conclusory statements referring to the initial oral agreement, unequal bargaining power and a "last minute" refusal to ship. C.H.I. does not deny that its president actually read and signed the confirmation forms. Indeed, the fact that C.H.I. alleges Marcus Brothers would not ship an order until C.H.I. signed the corresponding confirmation form indicates C.H.I.'s knowledge of provisions it was hesitant to adopt as part of the bargain.

Due to the lack of evidence substantiating C.H.I.'s claims, and since C.H.I.'s president knowingly signed the confirmation forms, we do not find that this was an adhesion contract nor that C.H.I. was coerced into signing it under economic duress.

*   *   *

CONCLUSION

The arbitration agreement was not part of an adhesion contract which C.H.I. unknowingly entered into under economic duress. * * * We AFFIRM.

NOTES

1. Did the American Pasta Co. understand the consequences of signing a printed contract to arbitrate? Did the majority opinion in *American Italian Pasta* carefully examine the factual process leading to the signature of the contract? Should a court do so? Is Judge Gibson, the dissenting judge, correct that there was not a meeting of the minds?

2. In the *CHI* decision, the Ninth Circuit ignored the direction contained in the purchase order form that California courts were to hear any dispute. Was this appropriate in the factual context? To what extent should it matter that both the *American Italian Pasta* and *CHI* decisions involved contracts to arbitrate entered into among businesses in arms length transactions?

3. For a full discussion of contracts of adhesion, see generally Todd D. Rakoff, *Contracts of Adhesion: An Essay in Reconstruction*, 96 HARV. L. REV. 1173, 1173–84 (1983) (suggesting that form terms in an adhesion contract should be presumptively unenforceable); Friedrich Kessler, *Contracts of Adhesion — Some Thoughts About Freedom of Contract*, 43 COLUM. L. REV. 629, 631 (1943) (growing use of standardized "form" or "mass" contract is an "inevitable" efficiency device used by informed bargainers to avoid future risks); Stanley D. Henderson, *Contractual Problems in the Enforcement of Agreements to Arbitrate Medical Malpractice*, 58 VA. L. REV. 947, 991–93 (1972) (suggesting that courts will uphold arbitration clauses when confronted with attacks based upon adhesion contracts).

4. In *Madden v. Kaiser Foundation Hospitals*, 17 Cal. 3d 699, 552 P.2d 1178 (1976), the California Supreme Court upheld a contract to arbitrate a medical malpractice claim and rejected the argument that the agreement to arbitrate was a contract of adhesion. In *Madden* the plaintiff employee had not personally contracted to arbitrate. Instead, her employer, the state of California, had an employee health plan calling for arbitration of medical malpractice claims. The court observed that the agreement to arbitrate had been negotiated between the health care provider, an HMO, and an employee "representative":

> In many cases of adhesion contracts, the weaker party lacks not only the opportunity to bargain but also any realistic opportunity to look elsewhere for a more favorable contract; he must either adhere to the standardized agreement or forego the needed service . . . [And] in all prior contract of adhesion cases, the courts have concerned themselves with weighted contractual provisions which served to limit the obligation, or liability of the stronger party. The arbitration [clause], by way of contrast, bears equally on Kaiser and the members. It does not detract from Kaiser's duty to use reasonable care in treating patients, nor limit its liability for breach of this duty, but merely substitutes one forum for another. [17 Cal. 3d at 711.]

5. Is *Madden* correct that the employee has the capacity to consent to arbitrate through the bargaining, purportedly in the employee's interest, of an institutional surrogate such as the employee pension fund? Is it relevant that damages awarded to the plaintiff may be considerably lower in arbitration than in litigation? Was there any evidence in *Madden* that the agreement to arbitrate was forced on insured employees in a "take it or leave it" context?

6. Can a party to a contract containing an arbitration clause argue successfully that she never read or understood the clause? Is there a duty to read and try to understand each term of a contract, regardless of how long or detailed the contract? (*See Southern Tile v. Commercial Const. Co.*, 548 So. 2d 2047, 48–49 (La. Ct. App. 1989) (upholding validity of signed acknowledgment of goods containing an arbitration clause because of the plaintiff's duty to read); *Federico v. Frick*, 3 Cal. App. 3d 872, 876 (1970) (failing to understand arbitration and its potential non-neutral nature is not a ground for vacating arbitral result); *Avila Group, Inc. v. Norma J.*, 426 F. Supp. 537, 540 (S.D.N.Y. 1977) (mandating arbitration and rejecting argument that a failure to read or assent particularly to arbitration clauses in a contract can avoid operation of the arbitration clause).) The position of Judge Learned Hand was unequivocal: "[A] man must indeed read what he signs and he is charged, if he does not." (*Gaunt v. John Hancock Mut. Life Ins. Co.*, 160 F.2d 599, 602 (2d Cir.), *cert. denied*, 331 U.S. 849 (1947).)

7. Consider *Prudential Insurance Co. of America v. Lai*, 42 F.3d 1299 (9th Cir. 1994), *cert. denied*, 116 S. Ct. 61 (1995). Lai was employed as a registered representative stockbroker. As a condition of employment she was required to sign a form containing an arbitration clause. According to Lai, her employer told her the form was an application to take a test needed for employment. Arbitration was never mentioned. Lai filed suit alleging sex discrimination. The Court of Appeals reversed a district court order compelling arbitration. According to the *Lai* decision, "Congress intended there to be at least a knowing agreement to arbitrate employment disputes before an employee may be deemed to have waived the comprehensive statutory rights, remedies and procedural protections proscribed in Title VII and related state statutes." (*Id.* at 1304.)

The *Lai* decision was criticized in *Maye v. Smith Barney, Inc.*, 897 F. Supp. 100 (S.D.N.Y. 1995). *Maye* compelled the arbitration of a claim by two African-American men who sued alleging that their discharges were the result of sexual harassment and racial discrimination in violation of Title VII. The plaintiffs, who had only secondary school education and who worked in the defendant's purchasing departments, signed an arbitration clause contained in Smith Barney's "Principles of Employment." This contract contained an arbitration clause and the words "Understood and Agreed" above the signature line. The court reasoned that most arbitration agreements would be vulnerable if it upheld the plaintiffs' attack on the arbitration clause.

Lai relied on the legislative history of Title VII of the Civil Rights Act to reverse the order compelling arbitration. What result would the court have reached if this were a commercial dispute between businesses? If this were a breach of contract dispute brought by a former blue collar employee against his former employer?

8. The requirement that parties must consent to arbitrate has become almost a cliche. It is useful to ponder the meaning of consent to arbitrate. Consent is the fundamental premise of contract doctrine. (*See* Randy Barnett,

A Consent Theory of Contract, 86 COLUM. L. REV. 269 (1986).) Parties to an agreement must show their assent to the terms in order for the contract to be valid. (E. ALLAN FARNSWORTH, CONTRACTS § 3.1 (2d ed. 1990).) Because "arbitration is a creature of contract," agreements to arbitrate require the "valid mutual consent of the parties." (MACNEIL, SPEIDEL & STIPANOWICH, FEDERAL ARBITRATION LAW § 17.1.1 (1994).) Typical consent principles merely require some objective manifestation of assent in order to form a contract. Farnsworth at § 3.6. Professor Stephen Ware has challenged routine valida-tion of signed, standard form arbitration clauses by reasoning that "when a non-drafting party signs a standardized agreement, a reasonable drafting party understands that the non-drafting party is not necessarily consenting to all the terms of that agreement." (Stephen J. Ware, *Employment Arbitration and Voluntary Assent*, 25 HOFSTRA L. REV. 83 (1996).) He relies upon a Restatement of Contracts comment. (*See* Restatement (Second) of Contracts § 211, comment *f* (non-drafting party "does not assent to a term if the other party has reason to believe that the [non-drafting] party would not have accepted the agreement if he had known that the agreement contained the particular term").) Professor Ware theorizes that this Restatement rule is consistent with behavior — many people sign forms that they have read only superficially on the theory that a court will not force them to the terms of an oppressive contract. Would this application of the Restatement of Contracts prevent validation of most signed arbitration clauses? Of only a few? Could an employee who is presented an offer of employment together with an employment contract containing an arbitration clause make use of this argument?

RAMIREZ v. SUPERIOR COURT
103 Cal. App. 3d 746, 163 Cal. Rptr. 223 (1980)

[At the age of nine months, plaintiff's mother brought her to the defendant hospital after an extended fever and elevated pulse and respiration rate. Prior to a physical examination, a nurse gave plaintiff's mother a Spanish language version of an agreement to arbitrate. The mother's complaint stated that she was "handed a piece of paper and told to sign it" without any explanation of the contract's meaning and that she signed the agreement without ever reading it because she believed her signature was necessary to her child's examination. The plaintiff and mother were sent home after an examination by an emergency room physician failed to diagnose meningitis. The plaintiff's suit sought damages for blindness and paralysis due to an alleged failure to properly diagnose her injuries. The agreement given plaintiff was a Spanish language version of a contract to arbitrate specified by California Code of Procedure § 1295. This legislation requires that contracts calling for arbitra-tion of medical malpractice clauses state that the parties are giving up their rights to trial by jury and do so in "at least 10 point bold red type," permits rescission within 30 days of signing and states that it is "not a contract of adhesion, nor unconscionable nor otherwise improper" if the contract meets the statutory requirements.

[The trial court granted the hospital's motion to compel arbitration and the plaintiff sought a writ of mandamus to vacate the trial court order.]

* * *

The powers of the superior court to pass upon a motion to compel arbitration are delineated in section 1281.2 which provides: "On petition of a party to an arbitration agreement alleging the existence of a written agreement to arbitrate a controversy and that a party thereto refuses to arbitrate such controversy, the court shall order the petitioner and the respondent to arbitrate the controversy if it determines that an agreement to arbitrate the controversy exists, unless it determines that: (a) The right to compel arbitration has been waived by the petitioner; or (b) Grounds exist for the revocation of the agreement." Section 1281.2 requires the court to determine whether an agreement to arbitrate actually exists since a party cannot be compelled to arbitrate a matter she has not agreed to arbitrate. (*Freeman v. State Farm Mut. Auto Ins. Co.*, 14 Cal.3d 473 (1975), at p. 480, 121 Cal. Rptr. 477, 535 P.2d 341; *Wheeler v. St. Joseph Hospital* (1976) 63 Cal. App. 3d 345, 355, 133 Cal. Rptr. 775.) If the trial court erred in its determination that there was an agreement to arbitrate, an essential jurisdictional fact was missing and hence the order compelling arbitration constituted an abuse of discretion. (*Wheeler*, *supra*, at p. 355, 133 Cal. Rptr. 775.)

Prior to the passage of section 1295, it was settled that an arbitration agreement contained in a negotiated group health care contract, because it was negotiated between parties possessing parity of bargaining strength, could not be voided as to individual health plan members on adhesion contract principles. (*See Madden v. Kaiser Foundation Hospitals, supra*, 17 Cal.3d 699, 131 Cal. Rptr. 882, 552 P.2d 1178.) The same was not true, however, of agreements signed by individual patients in connection with admission to hospitals. In *Wheeler v. St. Joseph Hospital, supra*, 63 Cal. App. 3d 345, 133 Cal. Rptr. 775, the Fourth District refused to enforce an "Arbitration Option" provision contained in a hospital admission form. To signify nonagreement with the arbitration provision, a patient could either place his initials in the space provided or notify the hospital within 30 days of discharge. The plaintiff-wife stated that her husband had signed the admission form without reading it, no one at the hospital called their attention to the arbitration provision, and the plaintiffs were never provided with a copy of the agreement. The trial court ordered arbitration when Mr. Wheeler and his wife brought a medical malpractice suit. After arbitration on the merits resulted in an award for the defendants, the plaintiffs sought to vacate the award *inter alia* on the trial court's alleged abuse of discretion in ordering arbitration.

On appeal, the court recognized that while arbitration is favored as a method for settling disputes, it is consensual in nature. When there is no agreement to arbitrate, an essential jurisdictional fact is missing and a court abuses its discretion if it compels arbitration. To compel arbitration there must be a voluntary agreement to arbitrate which is openly and fairly entered into. (*Id.*, at p. 356, 133 Cal. Rptr. 775.)

The court found that the hospital's "Conditions of Admission" was a contract of adhesion since it was a standardized form drafted by the hospital on a take-it-or-leave-it basis, negating any realistic choice by the plaintiffs. The enforceability of such a contract then depends upon whether the terms are beyond the reasonable expectations of an ordinary person or are oppressive or unconscionable. This is a particular problem in the medical services context which presents distinct problems of the patients' awareness. Normally in a contract of adhesion, conspicuousness and clarity may not be enough. If the provision would defeat the strong expectations of the weaker party, it may be necessary to point out the provision and explain its meaning. This is especially important during admission to a hospital which is an "anxious, stressful, and frequently a traumatic experience." (*Id.*, at pp. 359–360, 133 Cal. Rptr., at 786.) In its analysis the court noted that an emergency room patient cannot be expected to read, much less understand, a broad arbitration clause. Unless advised otherwise a patient will think she has no choice but to enter her physician's hospital and sign all the forms. (*Id.*, at p. 360, 133 Cal. Rptr. 775.) While *Madden* held that an express waiver of a jury trial is not required, it is still a valuable right which should not be deemed to be waived lightly. (*Id.*, at p. 361, 133 Cal. Rptr. 775.) The patient should be made aware of the arbitration provision and its implications. Otherwise the patient does not have an opportunity to exercise a real choice. The court felt that: "These procedural requirements will not impose an unreasonable burden on the hospital. The hospital's admission clerk need only direct the patient's attention to the arbitration provision, request him to read it, and give him a simple explanation of its purpose and effect, including the available options. Compliance will not require the presence of the hospital's house counsel in the admission office." (*Id.*)

*   *   *

The required language and warning make clear to anyone who reads them that the signing of the agreement waives the right to jury trial. The statute prescribes that the warning be made in at least 10-point bold red type and be placed immediately before the signature line, making every effort to insure that the patient will read the warning. The question we must answer is whether, in light of the warnings, there is any basis for a signing party's claim that she did not read the form or understand that she was agreeing to arbitrate medical malpractice disputes. Has the Legislature, by making the warnings clear, providing for later rescission of the contract, and decreeing that the contract is not a contract of adhesion, unconscionable nor otherwise improper, removed all bases for attacking the agreement?

"Ordinarily when a person with capacity of reading and understanding an instrument signs it, he may not, in the absence of fraud, imposition or excusable neglect, avoid its terms on the ground he failed to read it before signing it." (*Bauer v. Jackson* (1971) 15 Cal. App. 3d 358, 370, 93 Cal. Rptr. 43, 50; *Madden v. Kaiser Foundation Hospitals*, supra, 17 Cal.3d 699, 710, 131 Cal. Rptr. 882, 552 P.2d 1178; *Wheeler v. St. Joseph Hospital*, *supra*, 63 Cal. App. 3d 345, 359, 133 Cal. Rptr. 775; 1 Witkin, Summary of Cal. Law (8th ed. 1973) Contracts, § 89, p. 93.) This rule does not apply, however, where the contract may be properly characterized as a contract of adhesion. (*See Bauer v. Jackson, supra*, 15 Cal. App. 3d at p. 370, 93 Cal. Rptr. 43.) Thus, if the Legislature's declaration that a medical services arbitration agreement in proper form is not a contract of adhesion has effectively removed that exception, petitioners could avoid arbitration only by showing "fraud, imposition or excusable neglect" and proving that Ms. Ramirez did not read the contract for one of those reasons. Absent such a showing, they would be bound by the terms of the agreement she signed.

Petitioners argue that the Legislature cannot establish a conclusive presumption that a signed arbitration agreement in proper form is not a contract of adhesion. They contend that such a presumption would clash with their rights to jury trial, which may be waived only in a "knowing, intelligent and voluntary" manner. They rely as well upon decisions which acknowledge that permanent irrebuttable presumptions have long been disfavored under the due process clauses of the Fifth and Fourteenth Amendments. (*Vlandis v. Kline*, 412 U.S. 441 (1973).)

[Defendant] responds to these arguments by asserting that section 1295 was a legislative response to a health care crisis in California, that arbitration was viewed as a partial solution to the crisis, that public policy favors arbitration over litigation, that arbitration agreements have been upheld against due process arguments, and that such contracts are not contracts of adhesion because section 1295, subdivision (e) has so decreed. As far as [defendant's] argument goes, it is accurate and persuasive. However, in all its particulars it assumes that the patient has knowingly and voluntarily signed the agreement or that the agreement was entered by an agent of the patient who was aware of the arbitration provision. [Defendant] does not address the question of whether section 1295 can properly bind one who has signed the agreement under coercion or without knowledge or understanding of its provisions.

We conclude that in order to avoid constitutional infirmity section 1295 must be read as permitting a very limited species of attack by one who has signed an agreement in proper form. Our conclusion is drawn from our reading of the constitutional right to trial by jury in civil cases.

Under the federal Constitution, "In Suits at common law, where the value in controversy shall exceed twenty dollars, the right of trial by jury shall be preserved, . . ." (U.S. Const., 7th Amend.) Under the California Constitution, "Trial by jury is an inviolate right and shall be secured to all, but in a civil cause three-fourths of the jury may render a verdict. . . . In a civil cause a jury may be waived by the consent of the parties expressed as prescribed by statute." (Cal. Const., art. 1, § 16.) The importance of the right to jury trial has been expressed in the following terms: "The right to jury trial is immemorial; it was brought from England to this country by the colonists, and it has become a part of the birthright of every free man. The right to have a trial by a jury is a fundamental right in our democratic judicial system, including our federal jurisprudence. It is a right which is justly dear to the American people, and, whether guaranteed by the Constitution or provided by statute, should be jealously guarded by the courts. Any seeming curtailment of this right should be scrutinized with the utmost care."

* * *

In light of the constitutional protection for the right to jury trial in civil cases, we conclude that the Legislature may not establish a conclusive presumption that one signing an agreement meeting the requirements of section 1295 has in fact consented to arbitration. We therefore read section 1295 as permitting a party to seek to show that he or she was coerced into signing or did not read the many waiver notices provided and did not realize that the agreement was an agreement to arbitrate. Because of the nature of the warnings on the form, a party attacking the arbitration agreement will doubtless have a difficult time: she will have to explain how her eyes avoided the 10-point red type above the signature line; she will have to explain why she did not ask questions about what she was signing; she will have to show that no one explained the document to her or asked her to read it before signing it; and she will have to explain why she did not rescind the agreement within 30 days after it was signed. The trial court will then make a factual ruling on the questions of coercion and of whether the person signing the document actually knew or reasonably should have known that he or she was waiving jury trial rights and agreeing to arbitrate any medical malpractice controversy. We do not believe the trial courts will be unduly burdened by the requirement that they make such a factual determination when ruling on a petition to compel arbitration. To the extent a burden is imposed, the Constitution requires it.

We note that in some respects, the trial court's inquiry may compare to an inquiry into whether a signature was obtained through "fraud, imposition or excusable neglect," which caused a failure to read the instrument. (*See Bauer v. Jackson, supra*, 15 Cal. App. 3d 358, 370, 93 Cal. Rptr. 43.) However, where the arbitration agreement is signed as part of the admission procedure in an emergency room, something less than fraud or imposition would surely suffice for explaining failure to read the instrument.

As we read the trial court's order compelling arbitration, it rests upon the fact that the mother signed a document with proper warnings printed thereon. The court's language suggests that it did not resolve the conflict between the hospital's evidence and Ms. Ramirez' statements that she was told to sign the document, that she did so without reading it, that no one told her treatment could take place without her signature, and that she never read the document after leaving the hospital. If all her evidence were found to be true, she would make a strong case for an unknowing, involuntary signature on the arbitration agreement. Her greatest hurdle would be explaining why she did not read the agreement during the 30-day "cooling off" period provided by the statute.

Since the trial court did not resolve the factual issues of coercion and of whether Ms. Ramirez knew or reasonably should have known what she was agreeing to (or within 30 days reasonably should have known what she had agreed to and that she had a right to rescind), we must annul the prior ruling and return the matter for redetermination.

NOTES

1. *Compare Wheeler v. St. Joseph Hospital*, 63 Cal. App. 3d 345 (1976). In *Wheeler* the court refused to enforce an arbitration clause contained in a printed form contract presented to hospital admittees. Plaintiff was having chest pains at the time he signed the contract containing an arbitration clause while in the hospital admitting room and claimed he had not read the contract. No procedures specifically alerted the patient to the arbitration clause. Could unconscionability have been used to attack the use of arbitration in the *Wheeler* factual context? Contrast *Sosa v. Paulos*, 924 P.2d 357 (Utah 1996). In *Sosa*, a patient about to have knee surgery was presented with three contracts containing malpractice arbitration clauses less than one hour before her surgery and after she was already in surgical clothing. She sued and alleged that she had not read the contracts. The Utah Supreme court found that presenting the contracts just before surgery was procedurally unconscionable but that a revocation clause in the contracts — a patient had 14 days to review and revoke the agreement unilaterally — cured the taint of unconscionability. Should the "cure" feature of this contract force the patient to arbitration? Was there really a knowing, intentional choice to arbitrate made by this patient?

2. Should unconscionability be available as a weapon to attack the identity of the arbitrator? In *Graham v. Scissor-Tail, Inc.*, 28 Cal. 3d 807, 623 P.2d 165 (1981), the California Supreme Court reversed a trial court order confirming an arbitral award and compelling arbitration and reasoned that enforcement should be denied because of unconscionability. The court found the arbitration clause unconscionable because it appointed the musician's union to be the arbitrator and one of the disputants, Leon Russell, was a member of the union. The Arizona Supreme Court found a similar arbitrator appointment to be unconscionable in *Broemmer v. Abortion Services of Phoenix, Ltd.*, 840 P.2d 1013 (Ariz. 1992). There the arbitration clause used by a physician's clinic that performed abortions called for arbitration before licensed physicians who specialized in obstetrics or gynecology. Do the *Broemmer* and *Graham* decisions ignore the expertise that the selected arbitrators would lend to the process? Are these wise decisions or ambiguous extensions of unconscionability doctrine?

Can unconscionability be used to void arbitration clauses in employment contracts? In *Armendariz v. Foundation Health Psychcare Services, Inc.*, 24 Cal. 4th 83, 6 P.3d 669 (2000), the California Supreme Court concluded that an employment contract that limited the employee's damage to an amount equal to earnings from the date of initial employment was unconscionable. The court noted that the agreement effectively limited employee damages, while it did not restrict the amounts owed the employer. It concluded that the arbitration agreement lacked "a modicum of bilaterality."

3. Could unconscionability be used in *Ramirez*? Are there reasons to use unconscionability instead of other means to deny enforcement of an arbitral award or to refuse to compel arbitration? Unconscionability is "incapable of precise definition." (E. ALLEN FARNSWORTH, CONTRACTS, § 4.28 (2d ed. 1990).) Should unconscionability be avoided because of its inherently ambiguous nature? For a thorough discussion of the use of unconscionability in the arbitration context, see Stephen E. Ware, *Arbitration and Unconscionability After* Doctor's Associates, Inc. v. Casarotto, 31 WAKE FOREST L. REV. 1001 (1996).

4. *Ramirez* assumes that the court, not the arbitrators, should decide whether the arbitration clause was agreed to by the parties. Is this a correct interpretation of the *Prima Paint* separability question?

5. Do cases like *Wheeler* and *Ramirez* make you want to rethink the validity of the Supreme Court's *Casarotto* decision preempting state efforts to make the selection of arbitration more legitimately consensual? Should the FAA be amended to force more information into the consent process?

6. *Securities Arbitration and Consent*: Over 7,000 new arbitrations are filed annually by investors against their brokers alleging a variety of claims. These arbitrations are based upon signed contracts to arbitrate presented to customers. Almost the entire brokerage industry uses arbitration clauses for margin accounts and most firms employ arbitration clauses in their ordinary cash accounts. Investors frequent arguments that such contracts are adhesive generally fall on the deaf ears of courts. There is no question, however, that these arbitrations are based upon the strong desire to arbitrate by one party — the industry, which wants to avoid a risky jury trial at all costs. The other party, the investor, will often know little about arbitration and may not even read the fine print of the contract to arbitrate. Professor Speidel has termed contracts of adhesion "the dark side of arbitration." (*See* Richard Speidel, *Contract Theory and Securities Arbitration: Whither Consent*, 62 BROOK. L. REV. 1335 (1996).) He asserts that "most contracts to arbitrate in the securities industry have the characteristics of adhesion contracts." These adhesive features are (1) the use of standard form contracts with general terms, that are (2) designed to aid the drafting party, (3) these terms are likely not to be analyzed or easily grasped at the time of signing and (4) the drafting party has the economic power to not bargain over the "take it or leave it" clause. (*See* 2 MACNEIL, SPEIDEL & STIPANOWICH, *supra*, § 19.3.3.) Professor Speidel analyzes the tension between arbitration clauses and adhesion contracts and concludes that "the adhesion contract to arbitrate, particularly in the securities industry, is enforceable under § 2 of the FAA." Speidel, *supra*. Is this a desirable state of affairs? The blue ribbon NASD Task Force endorsed the present "adhesion" model of arbitration contracting but did recommend that "predispute arbitration agreements should provide clear notice that the customer is entering into an arbitration agreement and the consequences." (ARBITRATION POLICY TASK FORCE REPORT, NASD, INC., SECURITIES ARBITRATION REFORM 19 (1996).) Is this a workable solution? Should the investor have a right to opt out of the securities arbitration model? Some have argued that expanded judicial review is the answer. The next section of this chapter addresses this topic.

7. *Employee Handbooks and Consent to Arbitrate*. Employers of non-union workers increasingly prefer to arbitrate wrongful dismissal and other disputes with former and even current employees. The question of obtaining employee consent to arbitrate presents interesting questions. In *Kummetz v. Tech Mold, Inc.*, 152 F.3d 1153 (9th Cir. 1998), the employee was presented a handbook detailing an arbitration procedure for disputes, together with a form "acknowledgment" that he had read the handbook. The court of appeals refused to compel arbitration of an age discrimination claim, reasoning that the signed form acknowledgment was silent regarding the arbitration clause. The thrust of *Kummetz* is that the employer needs to notify the employee of its arbitration program in order to trigger consent.

What if, at the time of the job interview the employer hands the new prospective employee a contract containing an arbitration clause and offers the job on the condition that arbitration is agreed upon. Is consent present?

HILL v. GATEWAY, 2000
105 F.3d 1147 (7th Cir. 1997)

EASTERBROOK, Circuit Judge.

A customer picks up the phone, orders a computer, and gives a credit card number. Presently a box arrives, containing the computer and a list of terms, said to govern unless the customer returns the computer within 30 days. Are these terms effective as the parties' contract, or is the contract term-free because the order-taker did not read any terms over the phone and elicit the customer's assent?

One of the terms in the box containing a Gateway 2000 system was an arbitration clause. Rich and Enza Hill, the customers, kept the computer more than 30 days before complaining about its components and performance. They filed suit in federal court arguing, among other things, that the product's shortcomings make Gateway a racketeer (mail and wire fraud are said to be the predicate offenses), leading to treble damages under RICO for the Hills and a class of all other purchasers. Gateway asked the district court to enforce the arbitration clause; the judge refused, writing that "[t]he present record is insufficient to support a finding of a valid arbitration agreement between the parties or that the plaintiffs were given adequate notice of the arbitration clause." Gateway took an immediate appeal, as is its right.

The Hills say that the arbitration clause did not stand out: they concede noticing the statement of terms but deny reading it closely enough to discover the agreement to arbitrate, and they ask us to conclude that they therefore may go to court. Yet an agreement to arbitrate must be enforced "save upon such grounds as exist at law or in equity for the revocation of any contract." 9 U.S.C. § 2. *Doctor's Associates, Inc. v. Casarotto*, 517 U.S. 681 (1996), holds that this provision of the Federal Arbitration Act is inconsistent with any requirement that an arbitration clause be prominent. A contract need not be read to be effective; people who accept take the risk that the unread terms may in retrospect prove unwelcome. *Carr v. CIGNA Securities, Inc.*, 95 F.3d 544, 547 (7th Cir. 1996); *Chicago Pacific Corp. v. Canada Life Assurance Co.*, 850 F.2d 334 (7th Cir. 1988). Terms inside Gateway's box stand or fall together. If they constitute the parties' contract because the Hills had an opportunity to return the computer after reading them, then all must be enforced.

ProCD, Inc. v. Zeidenberg, 86 F.3d 1447 (7th Cir. 1996), holds that terms inside a box of software bind consumers who use the software after an opportunity to read the terms and to reject them by returning the product. Likewise, *Carnival Cruise Lines, Inc. v. Shute*, 499 U.S. 585 (1991), enforces a forum-selection clause that was included among three pages of terms attached to a cruise ship ticket. *ProCD* and *Carnival Cruise Lines* exemplify the many commercial transactions in which people pay for products with terms to follow; *ProCD* discusses others. The district court concluded in *ProCD* that the contract is formed when the consumer pays for the software; as a result, the court held, only terms known to the consumer at that moment are part of the contract, and provisos inside the box do not count. Although this is one way a contract could be formed, it is not the only way: "A vendor, as master of the offer, may invite acceptance by conduct, and may propose limitations on the kind of conduct that constitutes acceptance. A buyer may accept by performing the acts the vendor proposes to treat as acceptance." *Id.* at 1452. Gateway shipped computers with the same sort of accept-or-return offer ProCD made to users of its software. *ProCD* relied on the Uniform Commercial Code rather than any peculiarities of Wisconsin law; both Illinois and South Dakota, the two states whose law might govern relations between Gateway and the Hills, have adopted the UCC; neither side has pointed us to any atypical doctrines in those states that might be pertinent; *ProCD* therefore applies to this dispute.

Plaintiffs ask us to limit *ProCD* to software, but where's the sense in that? *ProCD* is about the law of contract, not the law of software. Payment preceding the revelation of full terms is common for air transportation, insurance, and many other endeavors. Practical considerations support allowing vendors to enclose the full legal terms with their products. Cashiers cannot be expected to read legal documents to customers before ringing up sales. If the staff at the other end of the phone for direct-sales operations such as Gateway's had to read the four-page statement of terms before taking the buyer's credit card number, the droning voice would anesthetize rather than enlighten many potential buyers. Others would hang up in a rage over the waste of their time. And oral recitation would not avoid customers' assertions (whether true or feigned) that the clerk did not read term X to them, or that they did not remember or understand it. Writing provides benefits for both sides of commercial transactions. Customers as a group are better off when vendors skip costly and ineffectual steps such as telephonic recitation, and use instead a simple approve-or-return device. Competent adults are bound by such documents, read or unread. For what little it is worth, we add that the box from Gateway was crammed with software. The computer came with an operating system, without which it was useful only as a boat anchor. Gateway also included many application programs. So the Hills' effort to limit *ProCD* to software would not avail them factually, even if it were sound legally — which it is not.For their second sally, the Hills contend that ProCD should be limited to executory contracts (to licenses in particular), and therefore does not apply because both parties' performance of this contract was complete when the box arrived at their home. This is legally and factually wrong: legally because the question at hand concerns the *formation* of the contract rather than its *performance*, and factually because both contracts were incompletely performed. *ProCD* did not depend on the fact that the seller characterized the transaction as a license rather than as a contract; we treated it as a contract for the sale of goods and reserved the question whether for other purposes a "license" characterization might be preferable. All debates about characterization to one side, the transaction in *ProCD* was no more executory than the one here: Zeidenberg paid for the software and walked out of the store with a box under his arm, so if arrival of the box with the product ends the time for revelation of contractual terms, then the time ended in *ProCD* before Zeidenberg opened the box. But of course ProCD had not completed performance with delivery of the box, and neither had Gateway. One element of the transaction was the warranty, which obliges sellers to fix defects in their products. The Hills have invoked Gateway's warranty and are not satisfied with its response, so they are not well positioned to say that Gateway's obligations were fulfilled when the motor carrier unloaded the box. What is more, both ProCD and Gateway promised to help customers to use their products. Long-term service and information obligations are common in the computer business, on both hardware and software sides. Gateway offers "lifetime service" and has a round-the-clock telephone hotline to fulfil this promise. Some vendors spend more money helping customers use their products than on developing and manufacturing them. The document in Gateway's box includes promises of future performance that some consumers value highly; these promises bind Gateway just as the arbitration clause binds the Hills.

Next the Hills insist that *ProCD* is irrelevant because Zeidenberg was a "merchant" and they are not. Section 2-207(2) of the UCC, the infamous battle-of-the-forms section, states that "additional terms [following acceptance of an offer] are to be construed as proposals for addition to a contract. Between merchants such terms become part of the contract unless. . . ." Plaintiffs tell us that *ProCD* came out as it did only because Zeidenberg was a "merchant" and the terms inside ProCD's box were not excluded by the "unless" clause. This argument pays scant attention to the opinion in *ProCD,* which concluded that, when there is only one form, "sec. 2-207 is irrelevant." The question in *ProCD* was not whether terms were added to a contract after its formation, but how and when the contract was formed — in particular, whether a vendor may propose that a contract of sale be formed, not in the store (or over the phone) with the payment of money or a general "send me the product," but after the customer has had a chance to inspect both the item and the terms. *ProCD* answers "yes," for merchants and consumers alike. Yet again, for what little it is worth we observe that the Hills misunderstand the setting of *ProCD.* A "merchant" under the UCC "means a person who deals in goods of the kind or otherwise by his occupation holds himself out as having knowledge or skill peculiar to the practices or goods involved in the transaction", § 2-104(1). Zeidenberg bought the product at a retail store, an uncommon place for merchants to acquire inventory. His corporation put *ProCD*'s database on the Internet for anyone to browse, which led to the litigation but did not make Zeidenberg a software merchant.

At oral argument the Hills propounded still another distinction: the box containing ProCD's software displayed a notice that additional terms were within, while the box containing Gateway's computer did not. The difference is functional, not legal. Consumers browsing the aisles of a store can look at the box, and if they are unwilling to deal with the prospect of additional terms can leave the box alone, avoiding the transactions costs of returning the package after reviewing its contents. Gateway's box, by contrast, is just a shipping carton; it is not on display anywhere. Its function is to protect the product during transit, and the information on its sides is for the use of handlers rather than would-be purchasers.

Perhaps the Hills would have had a better argument if they were first alerted to the bundling of hardware and legal-ware after opening the box and wanted to return the computer in order to avoid disagreeable terms, but were dissuaded by the expense of shipping. What the remedy would be in such a case — could it exceed the shipping charges? — is an interesting question, but one that need not detain us because the Hills knew before they ordered the computer that the carton would include *some* important terms, and they did not seek to discover these in advance. Gateway's ads state that their products come with limited warranties and lifetime support. How limited was the warranty — 30 days, with service contingent on shipping the computer back, or five years, with free onsite service? What sort of support was offered? Shoppers have three principal ways to discover these things. First, they can ask the vendor to send a copy before deciding whether to buy. The Magnuson-Moss Warranty Act requires firms to distribute their warranty terms on request, 15 U.S.C. § 2302(b)(1)(A); the Hills do not contend that Gateway would have refused to enclose the remaining terms too. Concealment would be bad for business, scaring some customers away and leading to excess returns from others. Second, shoppers can consult public sources (computer magazines, the Web sites of vendors) that may contain this information. Third, they may inspect the documents after the product's delivery. Like Zeidenberg, the Hills took the third option. By keeping the computer beyond 30 days, the Hills accepted Gateway's offer, including the arbitration clause.

*   *   *

NOTES

1. What did Mr. and Mrs. Hill do to consent to arbitrate?

2. Is the consent requirement taken seriously enough by Judge Easterbrook?

3. A different court has concluded that Gateway's arbitration clause in a box is substantively unconscionable. (*See Brower v. Gateway, 2000, Inc.*, 246 A.D.2d 246, 676 N.Y.S.2d 569 (1998).) The court reasoned that the agreement to arbitrate in Chicago under the ICC rules was unreasonably costly because of an advance payment of $4,000 in forum fees.

4. Consent to Credit Card terms. Not all courts will analyze this issue similarly. In *Badie v. Bank of America*, 67 Cal. App. 4th 779 (1998), the court of appeals held that a bank's new customer agreement empowering the bank to change terms or conditions of a customer account would not be a sufficient basis to justify consumer consent to the banks later and unilateral imposition of an arbitration program for customer disputes. The *Bodie* decision refused to give the bank carte blanche to modify any provision of the initial customer agreement. To give the bank such broad powers would make the contract illusory and would be inconsistent with the initial contract.

INGLE v. CIRCUIT CITY STORES
328 F.3d 1165 (9th Cir. 2003)

Pregerson, Circuit Judge.

This appeal arises from the district court's denial of defendant-appellant Circuit City Stores, Inc.'s (Circuit City) motion to compel arbitration. Circuit City moved to compel arbitration in response to the action plaintiff-appellee Catherine Ingle filed in the Southern District of California, in which she alleged employment discrimination in violation of state and federal civil rights statutes. Circuit City argues on appeal that the district court erred in declining to enforce an arbitration agreement requiring Ingle and Circuit City to arbitrate employment-related legal claims. We have jurisdiction under 9 U.S.C. § 16(a), and we affirm.

FACTS and PROCEDURAL BACKGROUND

In September 1996, Catherine Ingle applied to become an Associate at a Circuit City electronics retail store in San Diego County, California. Ingle was required to sign an arbitration agreement for Circuit City to consider her employment application. By signing the arbitration agreement, Ingle agreed to resolve all employment-related legal claims through arbitration.

On June 21, 1999, Ingle filed this action against Circuit City in the Southern District of California. In her complaint, Ingle alleged claims of sexual harassment, sex discrimination, and disability discrimination under the California Fair Employment and Housing Act, Cal. Gov't Code § 12940, *et seq.* (FEHA). She also alleged claims of sex discrimination and retaliation under Title VII of the Civil Rights Act of 1964, 42 U.S.C. § 2000e, *et seq.*

On July 16, 1999, Circuit City moved to compel arbitration. On September 22, 1999, the district court entered an order denying the motion on the ground that the arbitration agreement was unenforceable under *Duffield v. Robertson*, Stephens & Co., 144 F.3d 1182 (9th Cir. 1998). The district court held that Circuit City's form application for employment unlawfully conditioned Ingle's employment on her agreement to forego statutory rights and remedies. Circuit City now appeals, arguing primarily that its arbitration agreement is enforceable under *Duffield* and California contract law.

STANDARD OF REVIEW

We review de novo a district court's denial of a motion to compel arbitration. *Ticknor v. Choice Hotels Int'l, Inc.*, 265 F.3d 931, 936 (9th Cir. 1001), *cert. denied*, 534 U.S. 1133 (2002); *United Food & Commercial Workers Union, Local 770 v. Geldin Meat Co.*, 13 F.3d 1365, 1368 (9th Cir. 1994).

DISCUSSION

I. Circuit City's Arbitration Agreement

Circuit City compels all of its employees and job applicants to sign an arbitration agreement requiring arbitration of all employment-related legal claims. The "Circuit City Dispute Resolution Rules and Procedures" (Rules and Procedures) determine the substance and procedures of the arbitration agreement. Ingle and Circuit City agree that the arbitration agreement Ingle signed provided that the Rules and Procedures governing an arbitration would be those in effect at the time the claim arose. Because the 1998 Rules and Procedures were in effect at the time Ingle's civil rights claims arose, we examine these rules in analyzing whether this arbitration agreement is enforceable. However, our holdings as to substantive unconscionability reside with the discrete provisions we examine, and therefore would likely extend beyond this particular version of the Rules and Procedures.

II. The Doctrine of Unconscionability

The Federal Arbitration Act (FAA) provides that arbitration agreements generally "shall be valid, irrevocable, and enforceable." 9 U.S.C. § 2 (2002). But when grounds "exist at law or in equity for the revocation of any contract," courts may decline to enforce such agreements. *Id.*

It is a settled principle of law that "arbitration is a matter of contract." Federal law "directs courts to place arbitration agreements on equal footing with other contracts." *EEOC v. Waffle House, Inc.*, 534 U.S. 279, 293 (2002). Arbitration agreements, accordingly, are subject to all defenses to enforcement that apply to contracts generally. *See* 9 U.S.C. § 2 (2002). To evaluate the validity of an arbitration agreement, federal courts "should apply ordinary state-law principles that govern the formation of contracts." *First Options of Chicago, Inc. v. Kaplan*, 514 U.S. 938, 944 (1995). Ingle was employed in California; we therefore evaluate Circuit City's arbitration agreement under the contract law of that state. *Circuit City Stores, Inc. v. Adams*, 279 F.3d 889, 892 (9th Cir. 1002) ("*Adams III*"); *see also Ticknor*, 265 F.3d at 937 (applying Montana law to determine whether arbitration clause was valid).

Because unconscionability is a generally applicable defense to contracts, California courts may refuse to enforce an unconscionable arbitration agreement. *See Ferguson*, 298 F.3d at 782. Unconscionability refers to "an absence of meaningful choice on the part of one of the parties together with contract terms which are unreasonably favorable to the other party." *A & M Produce Co. v. FMC Corp.*, 135 Cal. App. 3d 473, 486 (1982); *see also* U.C.C. § 2-302; Cal. Civ. Code § 1670.5; Restatement (Second) of Contracts § 208 (1981). Thus, a contract to arbitrate is unenforceable under the doctrine of unconscionability when there is "both a procedural and substantive element of unconscionability." *Ferguson*, 298 F.3d at 783; *accord Armendariz v. Found. Health Psychcare Servs., Inc.*, 24 Cal. 4th 83, 114 (2000). Significantly, the California Supreme Court has noted that procedural and substantive unconscionability "need not be present in the same degree." *Id.* In *Armendariz,* the court held that: "[e]ssentially a sliding scale is invoked which disregards the regularity of the procedural process of the contract formation, that creates the terms, in proportion to the greater harshness or unreasonableness of the substantive terms themselves." In other words, the more substantively oppressive the contract term, the less evidence of procedural unconscionability is required to come to the conclusion that the term is unenforceable, and vice versa. *Id.* at 114 (quoting 15 Williston on Contracts § 1763A, at 226–27 (3d ed. 1972)) (other citations omitted).

A. Procedural Unconscionability

To determine whether the arbitration agreement is procedurally unconscionable the court must examine "the manner in which the contract was negotiated and the circumstances of the parties at that time." *Kinney v. United Healthcare Servs., Inc.*, 70 Cal. App. 4th 1322, 1329 (1999). An inquiry into whether Circuit City's arbitration agreement involves oppression or surprise is central to that analysis. A contract is oppressive if an inequality of bargaining power between the parties precludes the weaker party from enjoying a meaningful opportunity to negotiate and choose the terms of the contract. *Stirlen v. Supercuts, Inc.*, 51 Cal. App. 4th 1519, 1532 (1997) (citation omitted). "Surprise involves the extent to which the supposedly agreed-upon terms of the bargain are hidden in the prolix printed form drafted by the party seeking to enforce the disputed terms." *Id.*

There is no doubt that Circuit City's arbitration agreement is oppressive. In *Adams III*, we held that the arbitration agreement at issue in that case was procedurally unconscionable under California law because:

> Circuit City, which possesses considerably more bargaining power than nearly all of its employees or applicants, drafted the contract and uses it as its standard arbitration agreement for all of its new employees. The agreement is a prerequisite to employment, and job applicants are not permitted to modify the agreement's terms — they must take the contract or leave it.

Procedurally, there is absolutely no difference between the version of the arbitration agreement we evaluated in *Adams III* and the version we review in this case. Because of the stark inequality of bargaining power between Ingle and Circuit City, we conclude that Circuit City's 1998 arbitration agreement is also procedurally oppressive. *See id.; Ferguson*, 298 F.3d at 783–84; *Armendariz*, 24 Cal. 4th at 114–15; *see also Stirlen*, 51 Cal. App. 4th at 1533–34 (finding procedural unconscionability when an arbitration clause was part of a contract of adhesion in which the employee was presented with an employment contract on a "take it or leave it" basis).

Circuit City argues that because Ingle had sufficient time — three days — to consider the terms of the arbitration agreement, the court should not find this agreement procedurally unconscionable. We disagree. The amount of time Ingle had to consider the contract is irrelevant. We follow the reasoning in *Szetela v. Discover Bank*, 97 Cal. App. 4th 1094 (2002), in which the California Court of Appeal held that the availability of other options does not bear on whether a contract is procedurally unconscionable. *Id.* at 1100. Rather, when a party who enjoys greater bargaining power than another party presents the weaker party with a contract without a meaningful opportunity to negotiate, "oppression and, therefore, procedural unconscionability, are present." *Ferguson*, 298 F.3d at 784; *Szetela*, 97 Cal. App. 4th at 1100.

Circuit City contended at oral argument that our recent decisions in *Circuit City Stores, Inc. v. Najd*, 294 F.3d 1104 (9th Cir. 1002), and *Circuit City Stores, Inc. v. Ahmed*, 283 F.3d 1198 (9th Cir. 1002), should bear on our analysis regarding procedural unconscionability. However, we clearly stated that the arbitration agreements in those cases were not procedurally unconscionable *only* because Najd and Ahmed each had a meaningful opportunity to opt out of the arbitration program. To invoke the holdings in *Ahmed* and *Najd*, Circuit City must show that it provided Ingle a meaningful opportunity to decline to enter into the arbitration agreement.[4] Ingle had no such opportunity, and therefore our holding in *Adams III* controls in this decision.

The California Supreme Court's decision in *Armendariz* is also instructive in this case. The *Armendariz* court held that it is procedurally unconscionable to require employees, as a condition of employment, to waive their right to seek redress of grievances in a judicial forum. *See Armendariz,* 24 Cal. 4th at 114–15. Circuit City's arbitration agreement similarly requires, as a condition of employment, that employees waive their right to bring future claims in court. *See Ferguson,* 298 F.3d at 784. Ingle had no meaningful opportunity to opt out of the arbitration agreement, nor did she have any power to negotiate the terms of the agreement. Therefore, because Circuit City presented the arbitration agreement to Ingle on an adhere-or-reject basis, we conclude that the agreement is procedurally unconscionable.

B. Substantive Unconscionability

Substantive unconscionability centers on the "terms of the agreement and whether those terms are so one-sided as to shock the conscience." *Kinney,* 70 Cal. App. 4th at 1330. In evaluating the substance of a contract, courts must analyze the contract "as of the time [it] was made." *A & M Produce,* 135 Cal. App. 3d at 487.

Several substantive terms of Circuit City's arbitration agreement are one-sided. The provisions concerning coverage of claims, the statute of limitations, the prohibition of class actions, the filing fee, cost-splitting, remedies, and Circuit City's unilateral power to modify or terminate the arbitration agreement all operate to benefit the employer inordinately at the employee's expense. Because these one-sided provisions grossly favor Circuit City, we conclude that, under California law, these terms are substantively unconscionable, and address each term in turn.

1. Claims Subject to Arbitration

The one-sided coverage we found objectionable in *Adams III* remains in the version of the arbitration agreement we evaluate in this case.[5] *See Adams*

---

[4] Circuit City does not even consider the applications from job applicants who elect not to enter into the arbitration agreement. Ingle had no meaningful option; she either had to walk away from the employer altogether or sign the arbitration agreement for fear of automatic rejection or termination at the outset of her employment. *See Adams III,* 279 F.3d at 893.

[5] Rule 2 of the arbitration agreement provides:

> Except as otherwise limited herein, any and all employment-related legal disputes, controversies or claims *of an Associate* arising out of, or relating to, an Associate's application or candidacy for employment, employment or cessation of employment with Circuit City or one of its affiliates shall be settled exclusively by final and binding arbitration before a neutral, third-party Arbitrator selected in accordance with these Dispute Resolution Rules and Procedures. Arbitration shall apply to any and all such disputes, controversies or claims whether asserted against the Company and/or against any employee, officer, alleged agent, director or affiliate company.

> All previously unasserted *Associate* claims arising under federal, state or local statutory or common law shall be subject to arbitration. Merely by way of example, these claims include, but are not limited to, claims arising under the Age Discrimination in

III, 279 F.3d at 893–94. Circuit City's arbitration agreement applies only to "any and all employment-related legal disputes, controversies or claims of an Associate," thereby limiting its coverage to claims brought by employees. By the terms of this agreement, Circuit City does not agree to submit to arbitration claims it might hypothetically bring against employees. Without a reasonable justification for such a glaring disparity based on "business realities," "it is unfairly one-sided for an employer with superior bargaining power to impose arbitration on the employee as plaintiff but not to accept such limitations when it seeks to prosecute a claim against the employee." *Armendariz,* 24 Cal. 4th at 117. Therefore, as we held in *Adams III,* this "unjustified one-sidedness deprives the [arbitration agreement] of the 'modicum of bilaterality' that the California Supreme Court requires for contracts to be enforceable under California law." *Adams III,* 279 F.3d at 894; *Armendariz,* 24 Cal. 4th at 117.

> This case presents a broad concern with respect to arbitration agreements between employers and employees. Circuit City argues that the arbitration agreement subjects Circuit City to the same terms that apply to its employees. But this argument is "exceedingly disingenuous," because the agreement is one-sided anyway. Because the possibility that Circuit City would initiate an action against one of its employees is so remote, the lucre of the arbitration agreement flows one way: the employee relinquishes rights while the employer generally reaps the benefits of arbitrating its employment disputes.[7]

The only claims realistically affected by an arbitration agreement between an employer and an employee are those claims employees bring against their employers. By essentially covering only claims that employees would likely bring against Circuit City, this arbitration agreement's coverage would be substantively one-sided even without the express limitation to claims brought by employees.

> Employment Act (ADEA), Title VII of the Civil Rights Act of 1964, as amended, including the amendments of the Civil Rights Act of 1991, the Americans with Disabilities Act (ADA), the Fair Labor Standards Act (FLSA), 42 U.S.C. § 1981, as amended, including the amendments of the Civil Rights Act of 1991, the Employee Polygraph Protection Act, the Employee Retirement Income Security Act (ERISA), state discrimination statutes, state statutes and/or common law regulating employment termination, the law of contract or the law of tort; including, but not limited to, claims for malicious prosecution, wrongful discharge, wrongful arrest/wrongful imprisonment, intentional/negligent infliction of emotional distress or defamation.

> Claims by Associates for state employment insurance (e.g., unemployment compensation, workers' compensation, worker disability compensation) or under the National Labor Relations Act shall not be subject to arbitration. Statutory or common law claims alleging that Circuit City retaliated or discriminated against an Associate for filing a state employment insurance claim, however, shall be subject to arbitration. (emphasis added).

[7] *See Armendariz,* 24 Cal. 4th at 115; *see also Ting,* 319 F.3d at 1150 (citing *Mercuro v. Superior Court,* 96 Cal. App. 4th 167, for the proposition that the "arbitration forum, though equally applicable to both parties . . . [is] relevant to finding of unconscionability because 'repeat player effect' rendered provision disadvantageous to weaker party"). *See generally* Jean R. Sternlight, *Mandatory Binding Arbitration and the Demise of the Seventh Amendment Right to a Jury Trial,* 16 Ohio St. J. on Disp. Resol. 669 (2001).

Thus, we conclude that, under California law, a contract to arbitrate between an employer and an employee, such as the one we evaluate in this case, raises a rebuttable presumption of substantive unconscionability. Unless the employer can demonstrate that the effect of a contract to arbitrate is bilateral — as is required under California law — with respect to a particular employee, courts should presume such contracts substantively unconsciona-ble.[10] See Ferguson, 298 F.3d at 784–85; Adams III, 279 F.3d at 893–94; Armendariz, 24 Cal. 4th at 115–17; Stirlen, 51 Cal. App. 4th at 1536–39.

Circuit City's arbitration agreement expressly limits its scope to claims brought by employees, which alone renders it substantively unconscionable. Even if the limitation to claims brought by employees were not explicit, an arbitration agreement between an employer and an employee ostensibly binds to arbitration only employee-initiated actions. Circuit City does not furnish any evidence that would indicate that the coverage of the arbitration agree-ment is mutual. Therefore, we conclude that the coverage of the arbitration agreement is substantively unconscionable.[11]

2. Statute of Limitations

The Circuit City arbitration agreement states that the form by which an employee requests arbitration:

> shall be submitted not later than one year after the date on which the Associate knew, or through reasonable diligence should have known, of the facts giving rise to the Associate's claim(s). The failure of an Associate to initiate an arbitration within the one-year time limit shall constitute a waiver with respect to that dispute relative to that Associate.

We have already expressly criticized Circuit City's statute of limitations provision, Adams III, 279 F.3d at 894–95, finding that Circuit City's "strict one year statute of limitations on arbitrating claims . . . would deprive [Associates] of the benefit of the continuing violation doctrine available in FEHA suits." Id. This rule is identical to the one we held unconscionable in Adams III. Id. While Circuit City insulates itself from potential damages, an employee foregoes the possibility of relief under the continuing violations

---

[10] We note that our conclusion is consistent with the federal policy favoring arbitration agree-ments. The FAA does express Congress's intention to give effect to arbitration agreements generally, but it does not supplant state law governing the unconscionability of adhesive contracts. Adams III, 279 F.3d at 895; Ticknor, 265 F.3d at 935. We do not here utter a blanket rule outlawing arbitration agreements in the employment context. Rather, consistent with California law, we find the coverage of such arbitration agreements typically and grossly one-sided, and therefore, presumptively substantively unconscionable. An employer may rebut this presumption if it can demonstrate that its contract to arbitrate maintains the "modicum of bilaterality" required under California contract law. See Armendariz, 24 Cal. 4th at 117–18. Moreover, under California contract law, a court may only refuse to enforce a contract or contract provision if it is both substantively and procedurally unconscionable. See Ahmed, 283 F.3d at 1199–1200 (enforcing an arbitration agreement that was substantively unconscionable but lacked procedural uncons-cionability).

[11] This holding — assuming procedural unconscionability — would suffice to render this agreement unconscionable, but we elect to address other substantive terms of Circuit City's arbitration agreement.

doctrine. Therefore, because the benefit of this provision flows only to Circuit City, we conclude that the statute of limitations provision is substantively unconscionable.

3. Prohibition of Class Actions

Circuit City's arbitration agreement directs arbitrators not to consolidate claims of different employees into one proceeding and generally prohibits the arbitrator from hearing an arbitration as a class action. We find that this bar on class-wide arbitration is patently one-sided, and conclude that it is substantively unconscionable.

The ability to pursue legal claims in a class proceeding has firm roots in both the federal and California legal systems. The United States Supreme Court has held that the "class suit was an invention of equity to enable it to proceed to a decree in suits where the number of those interested in the subject of the litigation is so great that their joinder as parties in conformity to the usual rules of procedure is impracticable." *Hansberry v. Lee*, 311 U.S. 32, 41 (1940). The California class action statute "rests upon considerations of necessity and paramount convenience, and was adopted to prevent a failure of justice." *Weaver v. Pasadena Tournament of Roses Ass'n*, 32 Cal.2d 833, 837 (1948); *see* Cal. Civ. Proc. § 382 (2003); Fed. R. Civ. P. 23.

In *Szetela*, the California Court of Appeal severed a provision barring class-wide arbitration from a credit card company's arbitration agreement. *Szetela*, 97 Cal. App. 4th at 1100–02. In the court's view, by barring class arbitration in a contract of its own drafting, the defendant "sought to create for itself virtual immunity from class or representative actions despite their potential merit, while suffering no similar detriment to its own rights." *Id.* at 1101. The *Szetela* court found the bar on class arbitration "harsh and unfair" to those who could benefit from proceeding as a class and offensive to the policies underlying class actions, such as promoting "judicial economy and streamlin[-ing] the litigation process in appropriate cases." *Id.* at 1101–02. The court reasoned that the manifest one-sidedness of the no class action provision at issue here is blindingly obvious.

> Although styled as a mutual prohibition on representative or class actions, it is difficult to envision the circumstances under which the provision might negatively impact Discover, because credit card companies typically do not sue their customers in class action lawsuits.

Szetela, 97 Cal. App. 4th at 1100–01.

The *Szetela* court rejected Discover Bank's bar on class-wide proceedings as substantively unconscionable because the actual effect of the provision was to deny a procedural benefit only its customers would employ. In the context of an arbitration agreement between an employer and an employee, Circuit City adopts just such a provision. We cannot conceive of any circumstances under which an employer would bring a class proceeding against an employee. Circuit City, through its bar on class-wide arbitration, seeks to insulate itself from class proceedings while conferring no corresponding benefit to its employees in return. This one-sided provision proscribing an employee's ability to initiate class-wide arbitration operates solely to the advantage of Circuit

City. Therefore, because Circuit City's prohibition of class action proceedings in its arbitral forum is manifestly and shockingly one-sided, it is substantively unconscionable.

4. Filing Fee

Under the terms of the arbitration agreement, to initiate a complaint against Circuit City, an employee must submit an "Arbitration Request Form with a required filing fee of $75 (made payable with a cashier's check or money order to Circuit City Stores, Inc.)." Under California law, "when an employer imposes mandatory arbitration as a condition of employment, the arbitration agreement or arbitration process cannot generally require the employee to bear any *type* of expense that the employee would not be required to bear if he or she were free to bring the action in court." *Armendariz,* 24 Cal. 4th at 110–11 (emphasis in original).

Though denominated a "filing fee," the employee-claimant must pay the required seventy-five dollars here directly to Circuit City, rather than to the arbitration service Circuit City identifies in the arbitration agreement. It thus appears that the employee is required to pay Circuit City for the privilege of bringing a complaint. While a true filing fee might be appropriate under *Armendariz,* the fee required by Circuit City is not the "*type* of expense that the employee would be required to bear" in federal court, and is therefore inappropriate under *Armendariz.* Moreover, by requiring employees to pay the fee to the very entity against which they seek redress, Circuit City may very well deter employees from initiating complaints.

The seventy-five dollar fee poses an additional problem. In federal court, plaintiffs in all types of cases may be exempt from paying court fees upon a showing of indigence. *See* 28 U.S.C. § 1915(a)(1). Circuit City's arbitration agreement, however, makes no similar provision for waiver of the filing fee (or other fees and costs of arbitration). Without such a provision for waiver in cases of indigence, employees in that category might well find it prohibitively expensive to pay seventy-five dollars to file a complaint. For these reasons, the arbitration agreement's fee provision is manifestly one-sided.

We therefore find the fee provision substantively unconscionable.

5. Cost-splitting

We have previously rejected the Circuit City arbitration agreement's cost-splitting provision. *Adams III,* 279 F.3d at 894. In *Adams III,* we held that Circuit City's "fee allocation scheme alone would render an arbitration agreement unenforceable." *Id.* Although in that case we evaluated an older version of the arbitration agreement, the version we review here contains the same provision that "each party shall pay one-half of the costs of arbitration following the issuance of the arbitration award." [16] Moreover, the arbitration

---

[16] The costs of arbitration, as defined by the arbitration agreement, include:

the daily or hourly fees and expenses (including travel) of the Arbitrator who decides the case, filing or administrative fees charged by the Arbitration Service, the cost of a reporter who transcribes the proceeding, and expenses of renting a room in which the arbitration is held. Incidental costs include such items as photocopying or the costs of producing witnesses or proof.

agreement provides that "the Arbitrator may require the Associate to pay Circuit City's share of the costs of arbitration and incidental costs" should Circuit City prevail at arbitration. Under Circuit City's arbitration agreement, even an employee who has succeeded on her claim against Circuit City could be held liable for her share of the costs of the arbitration, because the arbitrator's authority to require Circuit City to pay in such circumstances is discretionary. Furthermore, the Circuit City arbitration agreement provides that if an employee does not succeed on her claim, the arbitrator has the discretion to charge the employee for Circuit City's share of the arbitrator's services.

By itself, the fact that an employee could be held liable for Circuit City's share of the arbitration costs should she fail to vindicate employment-related claims renders this provision substantively unconscionable. Combined with the fact that Circuit City's fee-splitting scheme would sanction charging even a successful litigant for her share of arbitration costs, this scheme blatantly offends basic principles of fairness. *See Ting,* 319 F.3d at 1151; *Armendariz,* 24 Cal. 4th at 110–11. Because Circuit City's cost-splitting provision is harsh and unfair to employees seeking to arbitrate legal claims we conclude that it is substantively unconscionable.[18]

6. Remedies

In *Adams III,* we criticized the limitations on available remedies in Circuit City's arbitration agreement. The arbitration agreement we evaluate in this case, as in *Adams III,* similarly "fails to provide for all the types of relief that would otherwise be available in court." *Adams III,* 279 F.3d at 895; *see also Paladino v. Avnet Computer Techs., Inc.,* 134 F.3d 1054, 1059 (11th Cir. 1998) (holding unenforceable an arbitration agreement that limited remedies otherwise available in court).

The Circuit City arbitration agreement delimits what relief is available to employees who succeed in arbitration claims against Circuit City. The agreement grants the arbitrator the discretion to award (1) injunctive relief, including reinstatement; (2) one year of full or partial back pay, subject to reductions by interim earnings or public or private benefits received; (3) two years of front pay; (4) compensatory damages in accordance with applicable law; and (5) punitive damages up to $5000 or the equivalent of a claimant's monetary award (back pay plus front pay), whichever is greater. This provision is identical to the one we held substantively unconscionable in *Adams III. See Adams III,* 279 F.3d at 895; *accord Morrison,* 317 F.3d at 670–74. Because the remedies limitation improperly proscribes available statutory remedies,[20] we again conclude that it is substantively unconscionable.

---

[18] Although Circuit City has included provisions in the arbitration agreement limiting an employee's liability for fees, we again reject the provisions because "the default rule is that employees will share equally in the cost of arbitration. As a result, we cannot interpret the agreement to prohibit sharing costs, as the court did in *Cole,* 105 F.3d at 1485, or find the issue of fees too speculative, as in *Green Tree [Fin. Corp.-Alabama v. Randolph,* 531 U.S. 79, 91 (2000)]." *Adams III,* 279 F.3d at 895 n. 5.

[20] The provision places limits on an employee's total damages, while federal law limits only

7. Unilateral termination/modification

Circuit City's arbitration agreement provides that "Circuit City may alter or terminate the Agreement and these Dispute Resolution Rules and Procedures on December 31st of any year upon giving 30 calendar days written notice to Associates." Circuit City, then, may modify or terminate any and all dispute resolution agreements with its employees unilaterally. Notably, the arbitration agreement affords no such power to employees. The United States Supreme Court has held that "arbitration is a matter of contract and a party cannot be required to submit to arbitration any dispute which he has not agreed so to submit." *United Steelworkers of America v. Warrior & Gulf Nav. Co.*, 363 U.S. 574, 582 (1960); *see also Mastrobuono v. Shearson Lehman Hutton, Inc.*, 514 U.S. 52, 57 (1995) (confirming that arbitration under the FAA is a matter of "consent, not coercion"). Although the agreement requires Circuit City to provide exiguous notice to its employees of termination or any modification, such notice is trivial when there is no meaningful opportunity to negotiate the terms of the agreement. By granting itself the sole authority to amend or terminate the arbitration agreement, Circuit City proscribes an employee's ability to consider and negotiate the terms of her contract. Compounded by the fact that this contract is adhesive in the first instance, this provision embeds its adhesiveness by allowing only Circuit City to modify or terminate the terms of the agreement. Therefore, we conclude that the provision affording Circuit City the unilateral power to terminate or modify the contract is substantively unconscionable.

C. Severance

* * *

While it is within this court's discretion to sever unconscionable provisions, because an "insidious pattern" exists in Circuit City's arbitration agreement "that functions as a thumb on Circuit City's side of the scale should an employment dispute ever arise between the company and one of its employees," we conclude that the agreement is wholly unenforceable. *Adams III, 279* F.3d at 892. The adhesive nature of the contract and the provisions with respect to coverage of claims, the statute of limitations, class claims, the filing fee, cost-splitting, remedies, and Circuit City's unilateral power to terminate or modify the agreement combine to stack the deck unconscionably in favor of Circuit City. Any earnest attempt to ameliorate the unconscionable aspects of Circuit City's arbitration agreement would require this court to assume the role of contract author rather than interpreter. Because that would extend far beyond the province of this court we are compelled to find the entire contract unenforceable. *See Ferguson,* 298 F.3d at 787–88; *Adams III,* 279 F.3d at 895–96; *Armendariz,* 24 Cal. 4th at 124–27.

---

the sum of punitive and certain compensatory damages, *see* 42 U.S.C. § 1981a; 42 U.S.C. § 2000e-5(g)(1), and contravenes federal law by limiting an employee's front-pay award to two years' salary. *See Pollard v. E.I. du Pont de Nemours & Co.*, 532 U.S. 843, 848–54 (2001). The provision also improperly limits punitive damages awards. *See Morrison,* 317 F.3d at 672–73.

*   *   *

CONCLUSION

Because the Circuit City arbitration agreement is unconscionable under California contract law, we affirm the district court's denial of Circuit City's motion to compel arbitration.

AFFIRMED.

NOTES

1. Although California appears the most willing jurisdiction to use the unconscionability approach, decisions from other jurisdictions are sometimes willing to use this vague concept to invalidate alleged agreements to arbitrate. Consider these not necessarily consistent examples.

In *Engalla v. Permanente Medical Group*, 64 Cal. Rptr. 2d 843 (Cal. 1997), the California Supreme Court held, in a case of first impression, that a large HMO may have fraudulently induced its members to agree to arbitration of disputes with it. The court remanded the case back to the trial court to resolve factual issues and overturned a lower appellate decision that had reversed the trial court's refusal to compel arbitration. The facts of this complex dispute are particularly striking and appear to condemn the manner in which the large HMO administered its arbitration program. Believing that he was forced to arbitrate a malpractice claim, the fatally ill plaintiff requested, but was unable to receive a prompt arbitration hearing from his HMO. Mostly due to the respondent's delays in obtaining medical information from its own expert physicians, the parties were unable to agree on the selection of a neutral arbitrator prior to the death of the plaintiff, which occurred almost six months after filing his arbitration claim. When a hearing could not then be scheduled, the plaintiff's representative filed suit and the HMO moved to compel arbitration. During the litigation's discovery phase the plaintiffs learned that on average it took almost 2 ½ years to reach a hearing in an arbitration against the respondent HMO.

The California Supreme Court's opinion concluded that the normally strong policy in favor of sending matters to arbitration was outweighed by the facts supporting the plaintiffs' claim of fraud. The opinion points out that the arbitration agreement called for the appointment of party arbitrators within 30 days and of a neutral arbitrator within 60 days and for the hearing to be held within a "reasonable time," 64 Cal. Rptr. 2d at 857, and concluded that the HMO had a duty to exercise good faith and reasonable diligence in the appointment of arbitrators. The court was greatly troubled that the HMO knew of the delays in reaching arbitration hearings speedily but continued to contractually promise expeditious treatment to its insureds. While the court was unwilling to conclude that the arbitration agreement was unconscionable, the tone of Engalla and the remand to the trial court are clear indications of frustration with the arbitration program run by one of the largest HMOs in California.

The *Engalla* case stands as one set of cases willing to criticize a corporate arbitration scheme. The concurring opinion of Justice Kennard stresses the "essential role of the courts in ensuring that the arbitration system delivers not only speed and economy but also fundamental fairness." (64 Cal. Rptr. 2d at 866.)

Is it fair for an HMO to administer its own arbitration program that will hear cases against the HMO? Should a neutral third party always administer such cases? The American Arbitration Association is considering changing its policy and refusing to administer mandatory arbitration programs regarding patients' health-care claims against HMOs. In 1997 the AAA administered almost 200 such programs. Why should an organization like the AAA be worried about such programs?

See also *Washington Mutual Finance Group, LLC v. Bailey*, 364 F.3d, 268 (5th Cir. 2004), where the court of appeals upheld an arbitration agreement entered into by illiterate plaintiffs and found that the inability of the plaintiffs to read did not make the arbitration agreement unconscionable.

2. In *Hooters of America, Inc. v. Phillips*, 173 F.3d 933 (4th Cir. 1999), the court of appeals affirmed a trial court refusal to compel a signed contract to arbitrate. The plaintiff restaurant chain sought to implement a company-wide dispute resolution program. It conditioned raises, transfers and promotions on an employee signing an arbitration agreement. While the employee Phillips, who sought to litigate a sexual harassment charge, clearly signed the contract to arbitrate, the court of appeals concluded that the agreement to arbitrate was unenforceable because the arbitration program and rules breached a duty of good faith by being "so one sided that their only possible purpose is to undermine the neutrality of the proceeding." (173 F.3d at 937.) The rules required the employee to give specific written notice to Hooters of her claim but failed to require respondent Hooters "to file any responsive pleadings or to notice its defenses." *Id.* Similarly, while the employee seeking arbitration had to provide Hooters with a list of all witnesses and a brief summary of facts each knew, Hooters was not compelled to provide corresponding information. Also, the selection of the arbitration panel appeared to favor Hooters. While Hooters and its complaining employee each appointed an arbitrator, the neutral third arbitrator had to be selected by the other two arbitrators from a list of arbitrators formulated by Hooters. Hooters alone could cancel the agreement to arbitrate on 30 days notice and could move for summary judgment within the arbitration process. These procedures were so favorable to Hooters that a Senior Vice-President of the AAA testified that the rules deviated from the minimum due process safeguards and a member of the AAA Board of Directors testified that "this is without a doubt the most unfair arbitration programs I have ever encountered." (*Id.*, at 939.)

3. Is it unconscionable to bar consumer class actions?

In *Szetela v. Discover Bank*, 118 Cal. Rptr. 2d 862,868 (Ct. App. 2002), *cert. denied*, 537 U.S. 1226 (2003), the court concluded that the arbitration clause barring class actions was unconscionable because it granted "Discover a get out of jail card free while compromising important consumer rights"and "served as a disincentive for Discover to avoid the type of conduct that might lead to class action litigation in the first place." (*Contra, Iberia Credit Bureau v. Cingular*, 379 F.3d 159, 174–75 (5th Cir. 2004) (relying on potential enforcement by state attorney general to reject use of unconscionability where contracts of telephone company banned class action arbitrations).)

4. Can choice of forum be unconscionable? (*See Swain v. Auto Services, Inc.*, 128 S.W.3d 103(Mo. App. 2003).) The Missouri Court of Appeals affirmed a lower court finding that a choice of arbitration venue was unconscionable. A Missouri resident purchased an automobile from a local dealer and a service plan from the defendant, an Arkansas corporation. The latter contract called for arbitration to be conducted in Arkansas. While the appellate court upheld the agreement to arbitrate, reasoning that an agreement to arbitrate is not one that "no man in his senses" would make, it severed and refused to enforce the choice of Arkansas venue. The court concluded that the average Missouri purchaser of a car would not reasonably anticipate that arbitration would occur in another state and that, accordingly, the agreement's choice of forum was unconscionably unfair.

Arbitration in a Box. Professor Katherine Stone has described the fascinating subject of arbitration in a box. A new Gateway computer box contains a surprise inside. One of the enclosed forms contains an arbitration clause. (*See* Katherine Van Wetzel Stone, *Rustic Justice: Community and Coercion Under the Federal Arbitration Act*, 77 N.C. L. REV. 931 (1999).)

Has the computer buyer consented to the arbitration option? In *Hill v. Gateway 2000, Inc.*, 105 F.3d 1147 (7th Cir. 1997), and *Brown v. Gateway 2000, Inc.*, 676 N.Y.S.2d 569 (App. Div. 1998), courts found the arbitration clause binding. Contract law allows conduct to evidence agreement to terms and the party who opens the box and uses the computer without objecting to the terms of the deal has shown an intent to be bound by the arbitration option.

C. JUDICIAL REVIEW AND ARBITRATION

1. THE FAA AND FINALITY: THE ROLE OF JUDICIAL REVIEW IN ARBITRATION

According to Professor Speidel, finality "is one of the core ingredients of arbitration." (Richard E. Speidel, *Arbitration of Statutory Rights Under the Federal Arbitration Act: The Case for Reform*, 4 OHIO ST. DISP. RES. J. 157 (1989).) When the parties knowingly opt to arbitrate, they want a binding, final decision that avoids time consuming and expensive appeals. What, then, is left for the courts but to aid the parties in the enforcement of their arbitration bargain? Should there be any room for appeal to the courts under this view of arbitration?

The prevailing view is that courts should be very reluctant to interfere with arbitral awards. In the words of one court "more often than not — and certainly that is so here — [seeking to judicially attack an arbitrator's award] is a poor mask for a desire to have the court redetermine the facts — even just a tiny bit — or reach a legal conclusion on them as found or hoped for which differs from that of the consensually annointed judge." (*Gulf States Tel. Co. v. Local 1692, Int. Bro. of Elec. Wkrs.*, 416 F.2d 198, 201 (5th Cir. 1969).)

Courts normally take an extremely narrow role in the arbitration process. If the parties have agreed "for resolution by an arbitrator whose decision is likely to be final and binding, there is every likelihood that that chosen umpire may well make errors both of fact and of law — that is errors in the eyes of Judges now having a narrowly circumscribed function." (*Dallas Typographical Union No. 173 v. A.H. Belo Corp.*, 372 F.2d 577, 581 (5th Cir. 1967).)

REVERE COPPER & BRASS, INC. v. OVERSEAS PRIVATE INVESTMENT CORP.
628 F.2d 81 (D.C. Cir. 1980), *cert. denied*, 446 U.S. 983 (1980)

PER CURIAM:

Appellant, Revere Copper and Brass Incorporated (Revere), seeks reversal of the district court's denial of Revere's motion to correct or vacate in part an arbitration award. The origin of the arbitration award in question is an insurance contract under which the appellee, Overseas Private Investment Corporation (OPIC), an agency of the United States, insured Revere against losses incurred by expropriation of Revere's investment in its wholly-owned subsidiary's aluminum mining and refinery complex in Jamaica. Section 10.01 of the contract provides that any disputes thereon "shall be settled by arbitration . . . [and] . . . [t]he award rendered by the arbitrator shall be final and binding upon the parties. . . ."

Following a change in administration of the Jamaican government, Revere made claim upon OPIC for compensation, alleging that actions by the new government constituted an expropriation of Revere's property. When OPIC denied the claim, Revere submitted the dispute to arbitration. The arbitrators determined that there was expropriatory action but awarded Revere $1,131,144, instead of the $64,131,000 that Revere had claimed.

Revere then filed its motion in the district court, seeking to correct or vacate the portions of the arbitrators' award in which the amount of the award was determined. Judge Charles R. Richey concluded that "Revere's claims amount to no more than the contention that the arbitrators misconstrued the contract. . . . [which] 'is not open to judicial review.' *Bernhardt v. Polygraphic Co. of America, Inc.*, 350 U.S. 198, 203 n. 4 (1956)." Judge Richey rejected Revere's claim that the award must be set aside for public policy reasons because it violates the rule of *contra proferentum*. *Contra proferentum* is "the rule of construction that ambiguities in insurance contracts are resolved favorably to the insured." *Continental Casualty Co. v. Beelar*, 405 F.2d 377, 378 (D.C. Cir. 1968). The rule developed in recognition that insurance policies are usually written by the insurer, and the insurer ought not be allowed to benefit from any ambiguities in the language which it chose. 13 J. Appleman, Insurance Law & Practice § 7401 (rev. ed. 1976). After questioning whether any ambiguity in the Revere-OPIC insurance contract had been shown, Judge Richey declared that "[p]ublic policy is involved in this case, but not in the manner the petitioner [Revere] contends. There is a strong public policy behind judicial enforcement of binding arbitration clauses." From this ruling Revere appeals. We affirm.

Revere's motion in the district court was made pursuant to sections 10 and 11 of the Federal Arbitration Act, 9 U.S.C. §§ 10–11 (1976). The Act was originally passed in 1925. Pub.L. No. 68-401, 43 Stat. 883. As stated in the Act's preamble, Congress intended it to be "An Act To make valid and enforceable written provisions or agreements for arbitration of disputes arising out of contracts, maritime transactions, or commerce among the States or Territories or with foreign nations." *Id.* In the ensuing years, "[t]he federal courts have recognized a strong federal policy in favor of voluntary commercial arbitration, as embodied in the [Act] . . . ." *Hanes Corp. v. Millard*, 174 U.S.App.D.C. 253, 265, 531 F.2d 585, 597 (1976). The goal of Congress in passing the Act was to establish an alternative to the complications of litigation. * * * As a result, judicial review of an arbitration award has been narrowly limited.

We see no reason for holding that the failure of arbitrators to apply the rule of *contra proferentum* is sufficient cause for upsetting the award. In *Amicizia Societa Navegazione v. Chilean Nitrate & Iodine Sales Corp.*, 274 F.2d 805 (2d Cir. 1960), the court was faced with a challenge to "arbitrators' reliance upon the principle that ambiguous language is to be construed against the author." *Id.* at 808. The court resolved the issue in declaring that "the misapplication . . . of such rules of contract interpretation does not rise to the stature of a 'manifest disregard' of law." *Id.*

Our disposition makes it clear that we do not find credence in Revere's claim that it was compelled to accept the arbitration provision in its contract with OPIC. This allegation appears to have surfaced after the arbitration award was announced. Revere is willing, on the other hand, to let stand the arbitrators' majority decision in Revere's favor that the Jamaican government expropriated Revere's property. Such an after-the-fact, pick-and-choose approach to an arbitration award is hardly consonant with the underlying concept of arbitration or with Revere's claim that it was forced to agree to arbitration in the first place.

* * *

We are satisfied that the arbitration award should be sustained. The judgment of the district court, therefore, is

Affirmed.

NOTES

1. The thrust of *Revere Copper & Brass* is that courts will not readily review findings of arbitrators. Note, however, that the decision did provide a degree of judicial review. Is this appropriate? Should courts hold to an "opt out" model of arbitration theory in which they provide no review whatsoever following an arbitration award? Under an "opt out" theory parties who sign a contract to arbitrate are opting out of the court system and, instead, are choosing an expert arbitrator for a final decision.

2. *Revere Copper & Brass* represents a typical judicial attitude regarding efforts to set aside arbitral awards. (*See generally* Note, *Judicial Review of Arbitration Awards on the Merits*, 63 HARV. L. REV. 681 (1950).)

3. What should be the scope of review when a court of appeals reviews a trial court decision confirming an award? One circuit took the position that the federal policy favoring arbitration required it to apply a lenient "abuse of discretion" standard on all issues, even on legal issues, when reviewing district court orders confirming arbitral awards. (*See Robbins v. Day*, 954 F.2d 679, 681–82 (11th Cir.), *cert. denied*, 506 U.S. 870 (1992).) In *First Options of Chicago, Inc. v. Kaplan*, 115 S. Ct. 1920 (1995), the Supreme Court rejected this position:

> We believe, however, that the majority of Circuits is right in saying that courts of appeals should apply ordinary, not special, standards when reviewing district court decisions upholding arbitration awards. For one thing, it is undesirable to make the law more complicated by proliferating review standards without good reasons. More importantly, the reviewing attitude that a court of appeals takes toward a district court decision should depend upon "the respective institutional advantages of trial and appellate courts," not upon what standard of review will more likely produce a particular substantive result. *Salve Regina College v. Russell*, 499 U.S. 225, 231–233 (1991). The law, for example, tells all courts (trial and appellate) to give administrative agencies a degree of legal leeway when they review certain interpretations of the law that those agencies have made. *See, e.g., Chevron U.S.A. Inc. v. Natural Resources Defense Council, Inc.*, 467 U.S. 837, 843–844 (1984). But, no one, to our knowledge, has suggested that this policy of giving leeway to agencies means that a court of appeals should give *extra* leeway to a district court decision that upholds an agency. Similarly, courts grant arbitrators considerable leeway when reviewing most arbitration decisions; but that fact does not mean that appellate courts should give *extra* leeway to district courts that uphold arbitrators. First Options argues that the Arbitration Act is special because the Act, in one section, allows courts of appeals to conduct interlocutory review of certain anti-arbitration district court rulings (*e.g.*, orders enjoining arbitrations), but not those upholding arbitration (*e.g.*, orders refusing to enjoin arbitrations). 9 U.S.C. § 16 (1988 ed., Supp. V). But that portion of the Act governs the timing of review; it is therefore too weak a support for the distinct claim that the court of appeals should use a different *standard* when reviewing certain district court decisions. The Act says nothing about standards of review.

4. Section 10 of the FAA specifies particular grounds for vacating or setting aside arbitral awards. Section 10(a)(1) of the FAA authorizes judicial power to vacate an award "procured by corruption, fraud, or undue means." (9 U.S.C. § 10(a)(1).) Most interpretations of this section focus on "corruption" or "fraud." (*See, e.g., Bonar v. Dean Witter Reynolds, Inc.*, 835 F.2d 1378, 1383 (11th Cir. 1988) ("perjury constitutes fraud" under § 10(a)); *Newark v. Stereotypers' Union No. 18 v. Newark Morning Ledger Co.*, 397 F.2d 594, 600 (3d Cir.) (proof of perjury constituting fraud will not result in court vacating award unless fraud central to actual core of dispute), *cert. denied*, 393 U.S. 954 (1968).)

5. Section 10(a)(3) of the FAA permits an arbitral award to be vacated under these terms:

> Where the arbitrators were guilty of misconduct in refusing to postpone the hearing, upon sufficient cause shown, or is refusing to hear evidence pertinent and material to the controversy; or of any other misbehavior by which the rights of any party have been prejudiced.

This subsection has been interpreted to allow an award to be set aside when the arbitrators fail to offer a party a "fundamentally fair hearing." *Apex Fountain Sales, Inc. v. Kleinfeld*, 818 F.2d 1089, 1094 (3d Cir. 1987). While courts have the power to set aside awards for erroneously admitting or failing to admit evidence, in actuality the only decisions that result in awards being vacated because of arbitral evidentiary error are where an arbitrator's rulings result in one party being "totally blocked." (C. EDWARD FLETCHER, ARBITRATING SECURITIES DISPUTES 384 (1990).)

The use of the word "rights" in § 10(a)(3) is intriguing. One might think this word misplaced in arbitration because the parties have opted out of formal judicial rights and, instead, chosen an informal system of adjudication. If neither rules of evidence nor substantive rules apply in arbitration, "how can Congress have chosen denials of 'rights' as a ground for setting aside arbitral awards?" (Edward Brunet, *Arbitration and Constitutional Rights*, 71 N.C. L. REV. 81, 116 (1992).) The presence of this word in the FAA, however, must mean that the drafters intended that courts should have some ability to set aside awards because of denials of "rights." The legislative history of the FAA supports this view. The drafter of the FAA, Julius Cohen, observed that "[I]f arbitrators awards are subject to mistakes and other human frailties, as necessarily they must be, it is obvious that review solely by a judge sitting at a motion term will not suffice to safeguard the party whose rights will have been substantially violated by the arbitrators." (Julius Cohen & Kenneth Dayton, *The New Federal Arbitration Law*, 12 VA. L. REV. 265, 274 (1926).) Cohen urged that there be serious judicial review under the FAA: "to deny any *right* of appeal at all would be to take away a most important privilege and safeguard without a compensating gain." (*Id.*) Accordingly, some type of judicial review of "rights" denied in arbitration was contemplated by the drafters of the FAA. Is judicial review of rights compatible with the idea of "finality" that we associate with arbitration?

Remember the low threshold needed for consent under the FAA. Remember also that consumers are now being forced to arbitrate claims earlier heard in courts. Consider the concerns of Cliff Palefsky, a San Francisco employment lawyer:

> Mandatory arbitration is one of the great scandals of our time. . . . And it has been perpetrated by the courts . . . millions of people are being denied constitutionally guaranteed access to the courthouse, all because arbitration is being misrepresented and foisted on an unsuspecting public. [*See* Michael Wagner, *Fine Print is Forcing More Consumer Disputes Into Hands of Private Judges, Critics Say It Favors the Powerful*, L.A. TIMES, March 8, 1998, A1.]

6. The attitude of recent decisions toward judicial review of arbitration awards continues to be generally grudging in nature. In *Marshed & Co. v. Duke*, 941 F. Supp. 12107, 1210 (N.D. Ga. 1995), *aff'd* 114 F.3d 188 (11th Cir. 1997) (per curiam), the court construed the FAA to not allow courts to "roam unbridled" when reviewing arbitration actions. In *Scott v. Prudential Securities, Inc.*, 141 F.3d 1007 (11th Cir. 1998), the court of appeals affirmed a decision refusing to vacate an arbitration award against a commodities trader. The court noted that "a mere error in the [arbitrator's] application of the law will not support the reversal of an arbitration award." (*Id.*, at 1018.) While the court would permit a challenge to an award that was "arbitrary and capricious," it interpreted this mode of attack restrictively, saying that the arbitration awards would be set aside only under "narrow circumstances" and that the arbitrator was to be given "considerable leeway." (*Id.*, at 1014, 1017, *citing First Options of Chicago*, 514 U.S. 938, 943 (1995).)

ADVANCED MICRO DEVICES, INC. v. INTEL CORP.
9 Cal. 4th 362, 885 P.2d 994 (1994)

WERDEGAR, JUSTICE.

California law allows a court to correct or vacate a contractual arbitration award if the arbitrators "exceeded their powers." (Code Civ. Proc., §§ 1286.2, subd. (d), 1286.6, subd. (b).) In *Moncharsh v. Heily & Blase*, 3 Cal. 4th 1, 28, 10 Cal. Rptr. 2d 183, 832 P.2d 899 (1992), we held arbitrators do not exceed their powers merely by erroneously deciding a contested issue of law or fact; we did not, however, have occasion there to further delineate the standard for measuring the scope of arbitrators' authority. This case requires us to decide the standard by which courts are to determine whether a contractual arbitrator has exceeded his or her powers in awarding relief for a breach of contract.

An arbitrator determined the Intel Corporation (Intel) had breached portions of its 1982 technology exchange agreement with Advanced Micro Devices, Inc. (AMD), including the implied covenant of good faith and fair dealing. The superior court confirmed the award, but the Court of Appeal, holding the arbitrator had exceeded his authority in awarding AMD the right to use certain Intel intellectual property, ordered the award corrected by eliminating the disputed relief.

We conclude that, in the absence of more specific restrictions in the arbitration agreement, the submission or the rules of arbitration, the remedy an arbitrator fashions does not exceed his or her powers if it bears a rational relationship to the underlying contract as interpreted, expressly or impliedly, by the arbitrator and to the breach of contract found, expressly or impliedly, by the arbitrator. The remedy fashioned by the arbitrator here was within the scope of his authority as measured by that standard. We therefore reverse the contrary judgment of the Court of Appeal.

FACTS AND PROCEEDINGS[1]

[From 1978–1981 two rival computer microprocessor procedures, Intel and AMD, entered into a "second source" agreement regarding the 8086 microprocessor. Such agreements call for the licensing by a chip maker of a new technology to a rival firm to allow customers the virtues of reliable supply and a degree of competition. AMD sought a long-term arrangement and to make sure it would have access to second sourcing the second generation of the 8086 family of chips.

The parties signed a 1982 contract, calling for a 10 year term, terminable after 5 years or 1 year's notice. Either firm could be a second source for the other's products; royalties were required. An arbitration clause called for "final and binding resolution of . . . disagreement."

Each side had different views of the contract. AMD thought it was a true joint venture that would avoid duplicitive research and provide each firm a full produce line. Intel saw the contract as "an armed truce with no continuing obligations."

When a dispute arose AMD sought a 1987 order compelling arbitration and Intel served a notice of termination. The parties agreed to arbitration rules allowing the arbitrator to "grant any remedy or relief [demand] just or equitable and within the scope of the agreement, including, but not limited to, specific performance of a contract."

The arbitration lasted 4 1/2 years with 355 days of hearings. The arbitrator found for AMD because Intel had breached its obligation to act in good faith and deal fairly. Intel, which felt the contract was not to its advantage, took no more than two AMD products. AMD thought its Intel agreement "had a future." Intel internal memos set out a strategy to "keep AMD in the Intel camp . . . keep talking . . . and prevent AMD from entering a similar contract with Intel rivals. The arbitrator also found that AMD had delayed improvement chips and delayed starting arbitration.

The arbitrator awarded AMD a permanent, nonexclusive and royalty-free license to any Intel intellectual property embodied in the Am386 (paragraph 5 of the award). He also awarded AMD a further two-year extension of certain patent and copyright licenses, insofar as they related to the Am386, that originated in a 1976 agreement between the parties, which had been extended under the 1982 contract to 1995 (paragraph 6 of the award).The arbitrator designated these items as remedies for breach of the covenant of good faith and fair dealing, as well as for failure to negotiate in good faith over the QPDM specifications and for other breaches.]

AMD petitioned the superior court to confirm the award (Code Civ. Proc., § 1286); Intel petitioned for the award to be corrected (Code Civ. Proc., § 1286.6) by vacating paragraphs 5 and 6, on the ground they exceeded the

---

[1] The facts stated are taken primarily from the arbitrator's award and memoranda of decision. As the parties recognize, courts may not review for sufficiency the evidence supporting an arbitrator's award. (*Moncharsh v. Heily & Blase, supra*, 3 Cal. 4th at p. 11, 10 Cal. Rptr. 2d 183, 832 P.2d 899.) We therefore take the arbitrator's findings as correct without examining a record of the arbitration hearings themselves; indeed, the appellate record contains neither a reporter's transcript of the hearings nor the exhibits introduced therein.

arbitrator's powers. The superior court confirmed the award, but the Court of Appeal reversed. Although it recognized the scope of judicial review did not extend to redeciding the merits of the controversy, the court believed the extent of the arbitrator's remedial powers was reviewable "de novo." The Court of Appeal found itself unable to locate a "rational nexus" between paragraphs 5 and 6 of the award and the contract itself. Therefore, the court concluded, the arbitrator had improperly "rewr[itten] the parties' agreement" in paragraphs 5 and 6 of the award. Determining those paragraphs could be treated as surplusage without affecting the merits of the decision, the court ordered the award corrected and confirmed rather than vacated. We granted review.

DISCUSSION

I. Standard of Review of the Remedies Fashioned by a Private Arbitrator

*   *   *

B. Review of Remedies

Intel contends that even if California precedents require deference to an arbitrator's assessment of arbitrability, a different, less deferential rule applies to an arbitrator's choice of remedies. Intel's position is neither logically persuasive nor supported by precedent.

In providing for judicial vacation or correction of an award, our statutes (§§ 1286.2, subd. (d), 1286.6, subd. (b)) do not distinguish between arbitrators' power to decide an issue and their authority to choose an appropriate remedy; in either instance the test is whether arbitrators have "exceeded their powers." Because determination of appropriate relief also constitutes decision on an issue, these two aspects of the arbitrators' authority are not always neatly separable.

*   *   *

Deference to the arbitrator is also required by the character of the remedy decision itself. Fashioning remedies for a breach of contract or other injury is not always a simple matter of applying contractually specified relief to an easily measured injury. It may involve, as in the present case, providing relief for breach of implied covenants, as to which the parties have not specified contractual damages. It may require, also as in this case, finding a way of approximating the impact of a breach that cannot with any certainty be reduced to monetary terms. Passage of time and changed circumstances may have rendered any remedies suggested by the contract insufficient or excessive. As the United States Supreme Court explained in the leading case on review of arbitral remedies in the collective bargaining context, the arbitrator is required "to bring his informed judgment to bear to reach a fair solution of a problem. . . . There the need is for flexibility in meeting a wide variety of situations. The draftsmen may never have thought of what specific remedy should be awarded to meet a particular contingency."

The choice of remedy, then, may at times call on any decision maker's flexibility, creativity and sense of fairness. In private arbitrations, the parties have bargained for the relatively free exercise of those faculties. Arbitrators, unless specifically restricted by the agreement to following legal rules, " 'may base their decision upon broad principles of justice and equity. . . .' [Citations.] As early as 1852, this court recognized that, 'The arbitrators are not bound to award on principles of dry law, but may decide on principles of equity and good conscience, and make their award *ex aequo et bono* [according to what is just and good].' [Citation.]" (*Moncharsh, supra*, 3 Cal. 4th at pp. 10–11, 10 Cal. Rptr. 2d 183, 832 P.2d 899.) Were courts to reevaluate independently the merits of a particular remedy, the parties' contractual expectation of a decision according to the arbitrators' best judgment would be defeated.

Independent reevaluation by a court, moreover, is unlikely to be either expeditious or accurate. Arbitrations may, as this case demonstrates, be lengthy and complicated. The proceedings may be informal and a complete stenographic record may not be prepared. A reviewing court is thus not in a favorable position to substitute its judgment for that of the arbitrators as to what relief is most just and equitable under all the circumstances. Further, independent review of remedies, no less than of other arbitrated questions, would tend to increase the cost and delay involved. "If the courts were free to intervene on these grounds [disagreement with the arbitrators' 'honest judgment' as to remedy] the speedy resolution of grievances by private mechanisms would be greatly undermined."

We do not, by the above, intend to suggest an arbitrator's exercise of discretion in ordering relief is unrestricted or unreviewable. Such an extreme position enjoys no support in our statutes or cases. The powers of an arbitrator derive from, and are limited by, the agreement to arbitrate. Awards in excess of those powers may, under sections 1286.2 and 1286.6, be corrected or vacated by the court. Unless the parties "have conferred upon the arbiter the unusual power of determining his own jurisdiction," the courts retain the ultimate authority to overturn awards as beyond the arbitrator's powers, whether for an unauthorized remedy or decision on an unsubmitted issue.

What does follow from the considerations discussed above is that review of remedies cannot be, as the Court of Appeal characterized it in this case, "de novo." Nor are Intel and allied amici curiae correct in describing judicial review of remedies as "independent." To the contrary, an appropriately deferential review starts not from the beginning, but from the arbitrator's own rational assessment of his or her contractual powers and is dependent on (that is, rests on acceptance of) this and any other factual or legal determination made by the arbitrator. The principle of arbitral finality, the practical demands of deciding on an appropriate remedy for breach, and the prior holdings of this court all dictate that arbitrators, unless expressly restricted by the agreement or the submission to arbitration, have substantial discretion to determine the scope of their contractual authority to fashion remedies, and that judicial review of their awards must be correspondingly narrow and deferential.

C. Standard of Review

Having rejected the extremes of "de novo" review on the one hand, and complete unreviewability on the other, we must attempt to articulate a standard capturing the middle ground of deferential yet meaningful review.

* * *

[S]tatements of the standard tend to focus the inquiry on the arbitrator's construction of the contract. Useful as such an examination may sometimes be, it is incomplete as a test of whether arbitrators have exceeded their powers in awarding a particular item of damages or other relief. The critical question with regard to remedies is not whether the arbitrator has rationally interpreted the parties' agreement, but whether the remedy chosen is rationally drawn from the contract as so interpreted. This case illustrates the distinction; Intel argues not that the arbitrator misconstrued the contract, but that the remedy he fashioned bore an insufficient relationship to the agreement as he interpreted it.

* * * Decisions from the federal courts applying the "essence" test announced in *Steelworkers v. Enterprise Corp.*, [363 U.S. 593 (1960)], properly focus on the source of the arbitrators' chosen remedy.

In *Enterprise*, a labor arbitrator ordered several workers reinstated with backpay upon finding their dismissal improper. The collective bargaining agreement authorizing the arbitration, however, had expired after the workers' dismissal but before the award. The company argued the award of reinstatement, and of backpay after expiration of the agreement, was therefore unenforceable. The high court held the award could not be refused enforcement on this ground. If the arbitrator was relying solely on statutory requirements extraneous to the contract, he exceeded his powers under the submission. But if the award derived from the arbitrator's construction of the agreement, even an erroneous construction, it was within his authority. Ambiguity on this point, which the court found to exist, was insufficient grounds to refuse enforcement.

In reaching its holding the high court explained the limits on an arbitrator's authority to fashion remedies as follows: "[A]n arbitrator is confined to interpretation and application of the collective bargaining agreement; he does not sit to dispense his own brand of industrial justice. He may of course look for guidance from many sources, yet *his award is legitimate only so long as it draws its essence from the collective bargaining agreement.* When the arbitrator's words manifest an infidelity to this obligation, courts have no choice but to refuse enforcement of the award."

Judicial review of remedies as outlined in the *Enterprise* decision thus looks not to whether the arbitrator correctly *interpreted* the agreement, but to whether the award is drawn from the agreement *as the arbitrator interpreted it* or derives from some extrinsic source. As the court explained in a later labor case, where an arbitrator is authorized to determine remedies for contract violations, "courts have no authority to disagree with his honest judgment in that respect. . . . [A]s long as the arbitrator is even arguably construing or applying the contract and acting within the scope of his authority, that a court is convinced he committed serious error does not suffice to overturn his decision." (*United Paperworkers v. Misco*, 484 U.S. 29, 389 (1987).)

* * *

We distill from these cases what we believe is a meaningful, workable and properly deferential framework for reviewing an arbitrator's choice of remedies. Arbitrators are not obliged to read contracts literally, and an award may not be vacated merely because the court is unable to find the relief granted was authorized by a specific term of the contract. The remedy awarded, however, must bear some rational relationship to the contract and the breach. The required link may be to the contractual terms as actually interpreted by the arbitrator (if the arbitrator has made that interpretation known), to an interpretation implied in the award itself, or to a plausible theory of the contract's general subject matter, framework or intent. The award must be related in a rational manner to the breach (as expressly or impliedly found by the arbitrator). Where the damage is difficult to determine or measure, the arbitrator enjoys correspondingly broader discretion to fashion a remedy.

The award will be upheld so long as it was even arguably based on the contract; it may be vacated only if the reviewing court is compelled to infer the award was based on an extrinsic source.

* * *

II. Application to this Case

As mentioned, section 42 of the rules of arbitration agreed upon by the parties authorized the arbitrator to grant "any remedy or relief which the Arbitrator deems just and equitable and within the scope of the agreement. . . ." The order of reference similarly empowered him to "fashion such remedy as he may in his discretion determine to be fair and reasonable but not in excess of his jurisdiction." The arbitration clause itself contained no special limitations.

Section 42 is identical to a provision of the Commercial Arbitration Rules of the American Arbitration Association (AAA). (AAA, Commercial Arbitration Rules (1993) rule 43, p. 17.) The AAA rule has been described as "a broad grant of authority to fashion remedies" (*Marine Tug & Barge v. North Am. Towing, supra*, 607 F.2d 649 at p. 651), and as giving the arbitrator "broad scope" in choice of relief (*Malekzadeh v. Wyshock, supra*, 611 A.2d at p. 22; *see also De Laurentiis v. Cinematografica De Las Americas, S.A.* (1961) 9 N.Y.2d 503, 215 N.Y.S.2d 60, 64, 174 N.E.2d 736, 738–739 [AAA rule was grant of authority so broad no particular items of damages claimed could be eliminated in advance of arbitration]). Nothing in the contract's arbitration clause, section 42 of the rules adopted here, or the order of reference indicates an intent to place any special restrictions on the arbitrator's discretion to fashion remedies.

Intel emphasizes that the question of what remedies could be awarded was discussed prior to arbitration by the parties and the arbitrator (sitting as a temporary judge of the superior court), and that all concerned agreed the arbitrator's choice of remedies would be subject to later judicial review. A review of the cited portions of the record, however, reveals the parties and the arbitrator agreed only that any relief awarded could be judicially reviewed for excess of jurisdiction. The record does not reflect an agreement for any heightened review beyond that already available by statute, namely, review to determine if the award "exceeded [the arbitrator's] powers." (§§ 1286.2, subd. (d), 1286.6, subd. (b).)

Paragraphs 5 and 6 of the award did not exceed the arbitrator's power under the standard previously stated. The contested items of relief were rationally drawn from the arbitrator's conception of the contract's subject matter and the effects on AMD of Intel's breach. The available facts do not compel the conclusion the arbitrator fashioned a remedy by reaching outside the contract to some extrinsic source; we are not constrained, in other words, to find he attempted "to dispense his own brand of industrial justice."

* * *

As already explained, the arbitrator found the framework of the contract required good-faith negotiation over technology exchanges, for the purpose of allowing both parties to expand their product lines. In particular, AMD, having foregone other alliances that might have gained it entry into the 32-bit chip market in order to help Intel establish the iAPX architecture as the industry leader, required a mechanism by which it could reasonably hope to become a second source for the successors of the 8086, as well as for the 8086 itself. If a party could or would not negotiate in good faith, it should terminate the agreement pursuant to the cancellation clause.

Intel breached this implied covenant, as well as the implied covenant of good faith and fair dealing, by secretly deciding not to accept any more AMD products, while maintaining the public posture that AMD would be a second source for the 80386. One example of this breach was its summary rejection of the QPDM, as to which it was obliged to negotiate specifications in good faith. Intel's strategy succeeded, in that for about two years AMD continued to believe the contract offered it future rewards. Although AMD also delayed unnecessarily in turning to alternative strategies (e.g., reverse engineering the 80386 or forming an alliance with a different chip maker) after concluding it would not be able to obtain the 80386 under the contract, the arbitrator found AMD had indeed lost some "immeasurable" amount of profits and goodwill as a result of Intel's bad faith conduct.

Paragraph 6 of the award, which extends for two years (insofar as they related to the Am386) certain licenses to Intel patents and copyrights originally granted AMD in 1976 and extended to 1995 under the 1982 agreement, bears a clear and rational relationship to the contract and the effects of Intel's breach. Having found Intel succeeded in keeping AMD in the Intel camp for about two years through its bad-faith conduct, the arbitrator extended for that same period rights that AMD had enjoyed under the contract and that could be useful to it in recovering from the breach's effects.

Paragraph 5 awards AMD a nonexclusive, royalty-free license to any Intel copyrights, patents, trade secrets or maskwork rights contained in the Am386.

Because the question whether AMD had appropriated any Intel intellectual property in creating the Am386 was apparently one of the issues between the parties in federal litigation at the time this award was made, Intel contends the arbitrator went outside the scope of the arbitration in fashioning paragraph 5 of the award. Intel points to language the arbitrator used that suggests extrinsic concerns. In the award itself the arbitrator stated he intended paragraph 5 to provide AMD a defense in the pending federal litigation. In the accompanying opinion he explained paragraphs 5 and 6 were intended to end "the incessant warfare" between the parties, and in his final summary he added his "hope[ ]" the additional competition "will be beneficial to the parties . . . and to the consumer world wide through lower prices."

Whatever optimism the arbitrator expressed about the effects of his award, the record demonstrates paragraph 5 derived rationally from his interpretation of the contract and the breach he found Intel to have committed. As already discussed, the arbitrator found AMD had been damaged by Intel's breach: the breach "to some extent contributed to AMD's delay in reverse engineering the 80386." Finding the amount of actual damages indeterminable and nominal damages alone inequitable, the arbitrator determined the "proper remedy" was to block Intel's interference with AMD's own attempts to mitigate its damage by marketing its reverse-engineered 32-bit chip. The award was thus rationally related to the arbitrator's plausible findings as to the subject matter of the contract and the effects of the breach. We repeat that in doubtful cases the arbitrator's choice of remedies must stand. (*Local 120 v. Brooks Foundry, Inc., supra*, 892 F.2d at p. 1289.)

Intel emphasizes paragraph 5 gave AMD rights it had not earned in performance of the contract. As we have explained, however . . . , a valid award for breach of contract does not require exact correspondence with the particular benefits the injured party would have received had the contract been fully performed. The arbitrator acted within his powers by fashioning a remedy rationally designed to alleviate the unfair results of Intel's breach, a breach that was not specifically anticipated in the parties' agreement. The parties' general restriction on the arbitrator's powers — that he fashion relief he deemed "just and equitable and within the scope of the agreement" — did not preclude him from choosing a remedy consonant with his construction of the contract's implied covenants and rationally related to the effects of a breach he found to have occurred.

* * *

This principle applies fully to arbitral awards of nonmonetary relief. "Arbitrators have broad discretion in fashioning a remedy for the injustice which is found to have occurred." Because the parties to an arbitration have the freedom to determine the rules by which their dispute will be resolved, including the scope of available relief, "courts will uphold awards of specific performance by arbitrators in instances in which the equitable remedy would not have been available if the dispute had originally been litigated in court." (1 Domke on Commercial Arbitration (rev. ed. 1994) § 30.01, p. 441.) As one federal court succinctly stated, "[a]n arbitration panel may grant equitable relief that a Court could not." (*Sperry International Trade, Inc. v. Government of Israel* (S.D.N.Y.1982) 532 F. Supp. 901, 905, *aff'd* 689 F.2d 301 (2d Cir. 1982).)

* * *

Equitable relief is by its nature flexible, and the maxim allowing a remedy for every wrong (Civ. Code, § 3523) has been invoked to justify the invention of new methods of relief for new types of wrongs. In actions founded on contract, courts have available for use in appropriate cases, in addition to specific performance, equitable remedies based on reformation, excuse of conditions and rescission as well as quasi-specific performance by constructive trust and indirect enforcement of a covenant by negative decree.

In light of the inherently flexible nature of equitable remedies, the principle of arbitral finality which forbids judicial inquiry into the legal correctness of the arbitrator's decisions on submitted issues, and the related principle that remedies available to a court are only the minimum available to an arbitrator (unless restricted by agreement), we cannot agree with the dissent the relief in this case was beyond the arbitrator's powers simply because the license awarded did not correspond in all its terms with a license that could have been earned through performance of the agreement.

CONCLUSION

We conclude the challenged portions of the arbitrator's award were within his authority to fashion remedies for a breach of contract. The superior court correctly confirmed the award under section 1286. The judgment of the Court of Appeal, reversing that of the superior court, is reversed.

LUCAS, C.J., and ARABIAN and GEORGE, JJ., concur.

[The dissent of Justice KENNARD is omitted.]

NOTES

1. Note that the California Supreme Court acknowledged the difficulty of reviewing the arbitration because of the lack of a formal record. The *Advanced Micro Devices* court had no access to a transcript or exhibits. Does it seem fair or even possible for the losing arbitration party, Intel, to try to set aside an award when a record is lacking? If you believe in a broader scope of review of arbitrators' awards how can appellate courts effectively review without a record? If you allow greater court review of arbitration awards, haven't you undercut the notion that awards are "final"? Is this consistent with the intent of the parties?

2. Arbitration is supposedly a speedy and comparatively inexpensive form of dispute resolution. While Intel's battle with Advanced Micro Devices was admittedly the paradigmatic "complex case," can an arbitration with 355 days of hearings over a four-year period really represent an "alternative" form of dispute resolution? Few civil court cases have had hearings the length of this arbitration. While arbitration can be "speedy and inexpensive," such a generalization is often inaccurate. Arbitrations involving disputes between natural gas pipelines and gas producers and international arbitrations between disputing businesses are exceedingly complicated, expensive, and can take every bit as much trial time as a conventional court case.

3. *Contrasting Refusal to Review for Error of Law with Manifest Disregard of the Law*: In *Moncharsh v. Heily & Blase*, 3 Cal. 4th 1, 832 P.2d 899 (1992), the California Supreme Court held that courts could not set aside an arbitration award merely because of erroneous applications of law or erroneous factfinding by the arbitrator. *Moncharsh*, then, means that error of law or fact will not be a ground for vacatur. In *Merrill, Lynch, Pierce, Fenner & Smith, Inc. v. Bobker*, 808 F.2d 930 (2d Cir. 1986), the trial court vacated what appeared to be a "compromise award" — the claimant sought $23,000 and received $12,500 — using the reasoning that the award was in "manifest disregard of the law." This widely interpreted concept was acknowledged by the Supreme Court's dictum in *Wilko v. Swan*, 346 U.S. 427, 436–37 (1953):

> [the] power to vacate an award is limited. . . . In restricted submission, such as the present margin agreements envisage, the interpretations of the law by the arbitrators *in contrast to manifest disregard* are not subject, in the federal courts, to judicial review for error in interpretation (emphasis added).

The manifest disregard of the law concept is one of the few ways that arbitration losing parties have, to seek to set aside awards outside the specific terms of the FAA. The *Bobker* Court of Appeals decision reversed the trial court and narrowed the scope of the *Wilko* dictum: to set aside an award there must be more than a showing that the award is clearly erroneous; error must be obvious and capable of being understood as error by an average person qualified to be an arbitrator. *Bobker* has been cited approvingly by other circuits. (*See, e.g., Kanuth v. Prescott, Ball & Turben, Inc.*, 949 F.2d 1175, 1182 (D.C. Cir. 1991) ("[M]anifest disregard means much more than a failure to apply the correct law")). One reason for adopting *Bobker's* deferential standard toward the arbitrator is the difficulty of determining the exact meaning of "manifest disregard of the law." Judge Oakes has remarked "How courts are to distinguish in the Supreme Court's phrase between 'erroneous interpretation' of a statute, or, for that matter, a clause in a contract, and 'manifest disregard' of it, we do not know: one man's 'interpretation' may be another's 'disregard.' Is an 'irrational' misinterpretation a 'manifest disregard'?" (*I/S Stauborg v. National Metal Converters, Inc.*, 500 F.2d 424, 430 (2d Cir. 1974). *Accord, Dawahare v. Spencer*, 210 F.3d 666, 669 (6th Cir. 2000) (to find manifest disregard of the law a court must find two things: the relevant law must be clearly defined and the arbitrator must have consciously chosen not to apply it).) For a general discussion of the "manifest disregard" concept, see Note, *Vacatur of Commercial Arbitration Awards in Federal Court: Contemplating the Use and Utility of the "Manifest Disregard of the Law" Standard*, 27 IND. L. REV. 241 (1993) (noting that no appellate court has ever used manifest disregard to uphold the vacating of an award).

The position of the Fifth Circuit regarding manifest disregard of the law is typical: the doctrine is an "extremely narrow, judicially-created rule with limited applicability." (*Prestige Ford v. Ford Dealer Computer Services, Inc.*, 324 F.3d 391, 396 (5th Cir. 2003).) Similarly, the Second Circuit now takes the position that it will confirm an arbitration award "if we are able to discern any colorable justification for the arbitrator's judgment, even if that reasoning would be based on an error of fact or law." (*Westerbeke Corp. v. Daihatsu Motor Co.*, 304 F.3d 200, 212 (2d Cir. 2002).)

4. The FAA permits vacatur of an award if "the arbitrators exceeded their powers." (9 U.S.C. § 10(a)(4).) "[E]fforts to secure vacatur of commercial arbitration awards on the ground that the arbitrator exceeded his powers seldom succeed." (Stephen Hayford, *Law in Disarray: Judicial Standards for Vacatur of Commercial Arbitration Awards*, 30 Ga. L. Rev. 731, 751 (1996). *See, e.g., Davis v. Chevy Chase Fin. Ltd.*, 667 F.2d 160, 165 (D.C. Cir. 1981) (court reasons that "it is particularly necessary to accord the 'narrowest of readings'" to the excess-of-authority provision of section 10(a)(4)).) How should courts decide if the arbitrator has exceeded his powers? One plain meaning answer is to look to the parties and their contract as a source of possible limitations on arbitrator powers. (*See, e.g., Eljer Mfg., Inc. v. Kowin Dev. Corp.*, 14 F.3d 1250, 1255–56 (7th Cir.), *cert. denied*, 114 S. Ct. 2675 (1994).) Arguably this ground for attacking an award is where the losing arbitration party can use the "manifest disregard" standard. Yet, the FAA says nothing specifically about vacating awards because of legal error. Does this mean that an attack upon "manifest disregard" grounds should be rejected as wholly outside the statutory scope of review of an arbitrator's award? (*Compare Chameleon Central Products, Inc. v. Jackson*, 925 F.2d 223, 226 (7th Cir. 1991) (court of appeals refuses to apply manifest disregard standard and asserts that "we have consistently held that the exclusive grounds for vacating or modifying a commercial arbitration award are found in § 10 and § 11 of the Arbitration Act"); *Federated Dep't. Stores, Inc. v. J.V.B. Indus., Inc.*, 894 F.2d 862, 866 (6th Cir. 1990) ("[a]rbitrators do not exceed their authority unless they display a manifest disregard of the law"); *Barbier v. Shearson Lehman Hutton, Inc.*, 948 F.2d 117, 1120 (2d Cir. 1991) (an arbitration award may be vacated only if one of the grounds specified in the FAA is found to exist); *Brown v. Rauscher Pierce Refsnes, Inc.*, 796 F. Supp. 496, 505–06 (M.D. Fla. 1992) (courts restricted to FAA statutory grounds when asked to vacate arbitral awards).)

Professors Macneil, Speidel and Stipanowich take the position that manifest disregard of the law (and other nonstatutory grounds for vacating arbitral awards) can be considered within the § 10(a)(4) "exceeded powers" legislation. (*See* Macneil, Speidel & Stipanowich, *supra*, § 40.5.1.3.) They reason that without some judicial gloss there would be little within § 10(a)(4) in the way of grounds to set aside an award. (*Id.*) Professor Hayford attacks this position as inconsistent with the intent of the FAA and the basic notion that only the parties can determine the powers of the arbitrator. (Hayford, *supra*, 30 Ga. L. Rev. at 824–827.)

5. *Mastrobuono* relied on the parties' selection of the arbitral forum and on the arbitration rules of the arbitral organization (the NASD). NASD norms state that the "arbitrators are not strictly bound by case precedence or statutory law" but then state that "if an arbitrator manifestly disregards the law, an award may be vacated." (NASD, The Arbitrators Manual 26 (1992).) Should courts bootstrap this standard into use through the parties choice of it, citing *Mastrobuono*?

6. *The Application of Law Clause.* Assume that two large corporations agree to arbitrate any disputes between them but want substantive legal rules to govern the arbitration. Is this a good idea? A poor one? A growing number of companies want their arbitrators to "apply the law" to reward the company's effort to follow the law strictly in its business interactions. These firms seek to reduce the risk of an arbitrator deciding the case "equitably" or arbitrarily. When drafting an arbitration clause to advance this goal, is it enough to merely draft a choice of law clause? (e.g., California law will be applied by the arbitrators). Alternatively, should the clause be written to provide that "the arbitrators shall be governed by California law when deciding this dispute and shall enter findings of fact and conclusions of law to reflect their application of California law"? The latter option is sometimes called an application of law clause, as contrasted with a "choice of law" clause.

7. What is the appropriate role of rules of preclusion (*res judicata* and collateral estoppel) in judicial review of arbitral awards? Assume that awards are "final" and that the parties had a full and fair opportunity to litigate during the arbitration hearing. There is substantial authority that the party who requests that a court set aside the award is really starting a second suit and should be subject to rules of preclusion and prevented from attacking the award. *See Schattner v. Girard, Inc.*, 668 F.2d 1366, 1371 (D.C. Cir. 1981) ("the rules of res judicata and collateral estoppel must govern our review of such proceedings if we are to advance the goal of promoting arbitration as an alternative to the complication and costs of litigation"). (*See also* Shell, *Res Judicata and Collateral Estoppel Effects of Commercial Arbitration*, 35 U.C.L.A. L. Rev. 623 (1988); Motomura, *Arbitration and Collateral Estoppel: Using Preclusion to Shape Procedural Choices*, 63 Tulane L. Rev. 29 (1988).)

8. In *McDonald v. City of West Branch*, 466 U.S. 284 (1984), the Supreme Court declined to give *res judicata* or collateral estoppel impact to an unappealed arbitration award. The *McDonald* decision involved an alleged federal civil rights violation brought under 42 U.S.C. § 1983. The Court asserted that "arbitration . . . cannot provide an adequate substitute for a judicial proceeding in protecting the federal statutory and constitution rights that Section 1983 is designed to safeguard." (466 U.S. at 290.) The *McDonald* case expressed concerns about the lack of arbitrator expertise *or* regarding the relevant law: "an arbitrator's expertise 'pertains primarily to the law of the shop, not the law of the land.'" (*Id.*) Is *McDonald* an exception to the idea that all disputes are arbitrable or is it a more particular holding that courts won't prevent § 1983 claims that were earlier heard in an arbitration?

9. *Punitive Damages.* The *Advanced Micro Devices* decision reaffirms the powers of arbitrators to craft a broad range of remedies. Presumably these general powers include the ability to award punitive damages. (*See generally* Stephen Ware, *Punitive Damages in Arbitration: Contracting Out of Government's Role in Punishment and Federal Preemption of State Law*, 63 Fordham L. Rev. 529 (1994) (suggesting that the parties have the power to allow or disallow punitive damages in their arbitral reference and that courts may award punitive damages if the parties "default" and fail to clearly specify whether punitive damages are allowable).) While arbitrators are less likely than juries to include punitive damages in their awards, it is not uncommon to learn of arbitrators incorporating a punitive damages remedy. Such arbitral awards are more frequent, particularly where the respondent's conduct is outrageous — a recent multimillion dollar punitive damage award in an arbitration sexual harassment case is illustrative.

The parties clearly possess the power to expressly permit or, alternatively, to prohibit, punitive damages in the award. "If the arbitration clause plainly states that the arbitrators have no power to award punitive damages, that ends the matter." (E. Allan Farnsworth, *Punitive Damages in Arbitration*, 20 STETSON L. REV. 395, 408 (1991).) The *Mastrobuono* decision, *supra*, teaches that efforts to forbid punitive damages must be explicit in order to be binding on arbitrators. There the Supreme Court upheld the arbitrators' award of $400,000 in punitive damages in a claim involving the alleged mishandling of a brokerage account. The *Mastrobuono* contract to arbitrate included a choice of New York law. New York law holds that arbitrators lack the general power to award punitive damages. (*Garrity v. Lyle Stewart, Inc.*, 40 N.Y.2d 354, 353 N.E.2d 793 (1976).) Nonetheless, the Supreme Court referred to the parties' selection of the National Association of Securities Dealers as the arbitral sponsor and the fact that the NASD rules expressly provided for broad arbitrator discretion to award appropriate remedies.

At present, the ability of a seller of securities to contractually prohibit punitive damages has been circumscribed. The rules of the New York Stock Exchange forbid agreements conditioning arbitrators in their fixing an award. (NYSE Rule 636(4).) The SEC reads this rule as forbidding the parties to waive punitive damages.

10. *Injunctive Powers and Arbitration.* In the *Advanced Micro Devices* arbitration the arbitrator crafted an award that ordered Intel to give competitor AMD a royalty-free technology license. This feature of the award was essentially a type of injunctive relief. While injunctions are classified as equitable and exclusively within the province of judges, arbitrators may also possess similar powers. If arbitration is designed to be creative and custom crafted to the facts presented, is there a reason to limit the powers of arbitrators to do justice as they see it?

In *Advanced Micro Devices*, the California Supreme Court had to construe legislation permitting a court to vacate an award if the arbitrators "exceeded their powers." (CAL. CODE CIV. PRO. §§ 1286.2(d), 1286.6(b)). Does the *Advanced Micro Devices* decision limit the arbitrators' remedial powers in any way? Can a court ever set aside a remedy if the parties have not restricted arbitrator equitable powers?

For discussion of the scope of an arbitrator's remedial powers and a recommendation that judicial review require an adequate record including arbitrator findings, see Jessica Martin, *Advanced Micro Devices v. Intel Corp. and Judicial Review of Commercial Arbitration Awards: When Does a Remedy "Exceed" Arbitral Powers?* 46 HASTINGS L.J. 1907 (1995).

11. *Arbitration Rules and Injunctive Relief.* The rules of various organizations that administer arbitration often grant specific powers to the arbitrator. For example, the AAA Employment Dispute Rules provide that "[t]he arbitrator may grant any remedies or relief that the arbitrator deems just and equitable, including any remedy or relief that would have been available to the parties had the matter been heard in court." (AAA Employment Disputes, Rule 34(d).) This rule was used to uphold an amount of $2,322,325 in stock options to a corporate executive terminated from his position of division president. (*See Brown v. Coleman, Inc.*, 220 F.3d 1180, 1183–84 (10th Cir. 2000).)

In contrast, AAA rules for commercial arbitration grant the arbitrators broad equitable powers *"within the scope of the agreement of the parties."* AAA Commercial Arbitration Rule 45(a) (emphasis added). Why is this rule different than the above rule used in employment disputes?

GATEWAY TECHNOLOGIES, INC. v. MCI TELECOMMUNICATIONS CORP.
64 F.3d 993 (5th Cir. 1995)

EDITH H. JONES, Circuit Judge.

MCI Telecommunications Corp. ("MCI") appeals a district court order affirming the judgment of an arbitrator who found that MCI breached its contract with Gateway Technologies, Inc., ("Gateway") and awarded attorneys' fees as actual damages as well as $2,000,000 in punitive damages. MCI contends that its contract with Gateway provides for de novo review by this court of the errors of law in the arbitration award and urges vacation of the entire award, claiming that the arbitrator improperly assessed both attorneys' fees and punitive damages as well as excluded critical evidence. While we agree that the contract provides for de novo judicial review of "errors of law" in the arbitration award, this court vacates only the punitive damages and otherwise affirms the arbitration award.

I. FACTUAL BACKGROUND

During 1990, the Virginia Department of Corrections ("VADOC") solicited bids to design and implement a telephone system that would enable inmates to place collect calls to authorized individuals without operator assistance. After successfully bidding for the project, MCI subcontracted with Gateway. Under their contract, MCI, as a telephone service carrier, agreed to secure the local access lines over which inmate calls would be made, while Gateway promised to furnish, install, and maintain all the equipment and technology necessary to provide the automated collect calls. The contract expressly provided that the parties were independent contractors and neither partners, joint venturers, nor agents.

Further, it imposed on the parties a duty to negotiate in good faith any disputes arising from the contract. In the event that such good faith negotiations proved fruitless, the parties agreed to binding arbitration, "except that errors of law shall be subject to appeal."

After installment of the VADOC phone system, MCI complained to Gateway that the automated system it had designed was improperly completing many collect calls. Ostensibly, because of the problems with Gateway's system, MCI integrated its own automated system to bypass the defective one. During the arbitration, however, the arbitrator found that MCI's decision to migrate from the Gateway system was motivated primarily by the significant profits promised by integration.[2] Once MCI had integrated its own system, it sent a default notice to Gateway. Although Gateway proposed to cure the defects with updated software, MCI refused to sign a confidentiality agreement for this software, thus leaving the problems with the original system unsolved. In January 1993, MCI formally terminated its contract with Gateway.

On July 30, 1993, the arbitrator found that MCI had breached its contractual duty to negotiate in good faith and awarded actual as well as punitive damages to Gateway. MCI filed a motion in the United States District Court for the Northern District of Texas to vacate the award; Gateway simultaneously moved to confirm it. Although the district court purported to review the award according to the standard agreed upon in the contract, it did not interpret "errors of law" as requiring "a scrutiny as strict as would be applied by an appellate court reviewing the actions of a trial court." Rather, it chose to "review the [a]ward under the harmless error standard, but with due regard for the federal policy favoring arbitration." Applying this standard, the district court confirmed the award in its entirety.

II. DISCUSSION

A. Standard of Review

This court reviews the district court's confirmation of an arbitration award under a de novo standard. As the Supreme Court recently explained, this is not a special standard, but reflects the application of typical appellate principles. *First Options of Chicago, Inc. v. Kaplan*, 115 S. Ct. 1920, 1925 (1995).

Usually, however, the district court's "review of an arbitration award is extraordinarily narrow." *Antwine v. Prudential Bache Securities, Inc.*, 899 F.2d 410, 413 (5th Cir. 1990). In a proceeding to confirm or vacate an arbitration award, the Federal Arbitration Act ("FAA") circumscribes the review of the court, providing that an award shall not be vacated unless: (1) the award was procured by corruption, fraud, or undue means; (2) there is evidence of partiality or corruption among the arbitrators; (3) the arbitrators were guilty of misconduct which prejudiced the rights of one of the parties; or (4) the arbitrators exceeded their powers. 9 U.S.C. § 10(a)(1)–(4) (Supp.1995).

In this case, however, the parties contractually agreed to permit expanded review of the arbitration award by the federal courts. Specifically, their contract details that "[t]he arbitration decision shall be final and binding on both parties, except that errors of law shall be subject to appeal." Such a contractual modification is acceptable because, as the Supreme Court has emphasized, arbitration is a creature of contract and the FAA's pro-arbitration policy does not operate without regard to the wishes of the contracting parties. . . . "[I]t does not follow that the FAA prevents the enforcement of agreements to arbitrate under different rules than those set forth in the Act

---

[2] During the arbitration, Gateway presented internal MCI memoranda that supported this conclusion. One estimate suggested that MCI would earn a net revenue from savings of nearly $84,000 per month if it migrated from the Gateway system.

itself. *Indeed, such a result would be quite inimical to the FAA's purpose of ensuring that private agreements to arbitrate are enforced according to their terms.* Arbitration under the Act is a matter of consent, not coercion, and parties are generally free to structure their arbitration agreements as they see fit. Just as they may limit by contract the issues which they will arbitrate, so too may they specify by contract the rules under which that arbitration will be conducted." *Mastrobuono v. Shearson Lehman Hutton, Inc.*, 115 S.Ct. 1212, 1216, (1995) (quoting *Volt Information Sciences, Inc. v. Board of Trustees of Leland Stanford Junior Univ.*, 489 U.S. 468, 479 (1989)) (emphasis added). *See also Vimar Seguros y Reaseguros, S.A., v. M/V Sky Reefer*, 115 S.Ct. 2322 (1995) (enforcing a contractual provision mandating arbitration in Tokyo, Japan); *First Options of Chicago v. Kaplan*, 115 S.Ct. 1920, 1925 (1995) (observing that "the basic objective in this area is not to resolve disputes in the quickest manner possible, no matter what the parties' wishes, but to ensure that commercial arbitration agreements, like other contracts are enforced according to their terms.") (citations omitted); *Allied-Bruce Terminix Companies, Inc., v. Dobson*, 115 S. Ct. 834 (1995) (the FAA "intended courts to enforce arbitration agreements into which parties had entered and to place such agreements upon the same footing as other contracts.") (citations omitted); *Shearson/American Express, Inc. v. McMahon*, 482 U.S. 220, 226 (1987) (stressing that courts should "rigorously enforce agreements to arbitrate."). Because these parties contractually agreed to expand judicial review, their contractual provision supplements the FAA's default standard of review and allows for de novo review of issues of law embodied in the arbitration award.[3]

The district court accordingly erred when it refused to review the "errors of law" de novo, opting instead to apply its specially crafted "harmless error standard." This choice apparently reflected the district court's unwillingness to enforce the parties' contract because "the parties have sacrificed the simplicity, informality, and expedition of arbitration on the altar of appellate review." Prudent or not, the contract expressly and unambiguously provides for review of "errors of law"; to interpret this phrase short of de novo review would render the language meaningless and would frustrate the mutual intent of the parties. When, as here, the parties agree contractually to subject an arbitration award to expanded judicial review, federal arbitration policy demands that the court conduct its review according to the terms of the arbitration contract.

Because the district court erroneously employed "harmless error" review of the award, both the actual and punitive damages awarded to Gateway were scrutinized and confirmed less rigorously than the parties had intended. As a result, this court will review the award de novo for "errors of law."[4]

---

[3] Of course, the FAA would govern review of the arbitration had the contract been silent. However, the FAA does not prohibit parties who voluntarily agree to arbitration from providing contractually for more expansive judicial review of the award. "There is no federal policy favoring arbitration under a certain set of procedural rules; the federal policy is simply to ensure the enforceability, according to their terms, of private agreements to arbitrate." *Volt Info. Sciences, Inc.*, 489 U.S. at 469.

[4] MCI also contends that it was an "error of law" for the arbitrator to exclude from evidence an audio tape and a video tape purporting to demonstrate the failures of the Gateway system. We disagree. MCI makes no headway on this point because arbitrators' evidentiary decisions

* * *

C. Punitive Damages

The award of actual damages was coupled with a $2,000,000 award of punitive damages. In an extremely confusing passage, the arbitrator found that the punitive damages were justified "in part for an *additional reason perhaps not assigned by Claimant, but found by the Arbitrator*: that Respondent's attempt to terminate Claimant for default was part of a deceptive scheme in wanton disregard of Respondent's obligations to Claimant."[7]

Beyond this lone, opaque statement, the arbitration award is silent about its rationale for imposing punitive damages against MCI.

Notwithstanding the district court's reference to "federal law" as the rule of decision, any punitive damage award must be consistent with the substantive state law governing the arbitration. The arbitrator, hearing the dispute in Richmond, Virginia, avowedly applied the substantive law of Virginia to this dispute.[8] For instance, during the arbitration proceeding the arbitrator "announced, of course, earlier that I was going to apply Virginia law, if there was no choice of law in the [arbitration] clause. . . ."[9]

Additionally, the arbitrator speculated that Virginia courts might have jurisdiction to review the award, suggesting strongly that Virginia law governed the arbitrator's resolution of the dispute.

If Virginia law allowed the arbitrator to impose punitive damages and if the arbitration contract did not expressly prevent the arbitrator from doing so, then such an award would have fallen under the arbitrator's broad discretion to decide damages and fashion remedial relief. Other federal courts addressing the issue generally concur. *See, e.g., Baravati v. Josephthal, Lyon & Ross, Inc.*, 28 F.3d 704 (7th Cir. 1994) (award of punitive damages for defamation did not exceed arbitrator's authority); *Lee v. Chica*, 983 F.2d 883 (8th Cir. 1993) (arbitrator could award punitive damages for fraud and breach of fiduciary duty), *cert. denied*, 510 U.S. 906 (1993); *Todd Shipyards Corp. v. Cunard Line, Ltd.*, 943 F.2d 1056 (9th Cir. 1991) (upholding an award of punitive damages and attorneys' fees for bad faith); *Raytheon Co. v. Automated Business Sys., Inc.*, 882 F.2d 6 (1st Cir. 1989) (tort claims allowed for punitive damages); *Bonar v. Dean Witter Reynolds, Inc.*, 835 F.2d 1378, 1386–87 (11th Cir. 1988) (language of arbitration contract did not prevent arbitrator from awarding punitive damages). Moreover, the Supreme Court has just confirmed that arbitrators presumptively enjoy the power to award punitive damages unless, unlike this case, the arbitration contract unequivocally excludes punitive damages claims. *Mastrobuono*, 115 S. Ct. at 1216–17.

---

should be reviewed with unusual deference. Because the arbitrator could have easily found that the tapes were merely cumulative of testimony already before him, it was not an abuse of his discretion to exclude them from evidence.

[7] Award of Arbitrator, July 30, 1993 (emphasis added). . . .

[8] Gateway admits that the arbitrator announced that he would apply Virginia law. Although Gateway suggests that Virginia law did not govern every issue before the arbitrator, it finds no support in the record for this suggestion.

[9] The arbitration clause did not contain a choice of law provisions.

Although the arbitrator in this case wielded the power to impose punitive damages, his rationale for doing so must be consistent with Virginia law. Under Virginia law, punitive damages cannot be imposed merely for breach of contract. In different terms, punitive damages must be predicated on tort liability. . . . Quite simply, if MCI is not liable to Gateway for tort damages, then the arbitrator cannot impose punitive damages.

*   *   *

. . . [T]he punitive damage award issued by the arbitrator must be vacated because, as a matter of law, the facts do not sustain a claim for breach of fiduciary duty.[13] Initially, there is no formal relationship between MCI and Gateway that would impose fiduciary duties on MCI since their contract expressly provides that "[e]ach party shall act as an independent contractor and not as agent for, partner of, or joint venturer with the other party. The parties create no other relationship outside of that contemplated by the terms of this Subcontract."

Also, Gateway did not share in either profits or losses under the contract, but received instead a fixed percentage of gross collected revenues. *Id.* The Agreement did not create a partnership capital account and provided for no joint ownership of property or for the filing of partnership tax returns. The language of the contract is unambiguous and establishes that the parties intended no formal relationship which would impose fiduciary duties on MCI.

Because there is no formal fiduciary relationship between the parties, Gateway attempts to establish an "informal" fiduciary relationship. Under Virginia law, the existence of such a fiduciary relationship is a question of fact. A fiduciary relationship may arise " 'when special confidence has been reposed in one who in equity and good conscience is bound to act in good faith and with due regard for the interests of the one reposing the confidence.' "

But no genuine issue of material fact demonstrates that the relationship between MCI and Gateway was one of special confidence. Instead, Gateway admits that it was "nominally the subcontractor in the ensuing contract with VADOC," and that it understood that MCI was "a competitor of Gateway even before the [contract] was signed. . . ." Given their history as competitors as well as the language of the contract disclaiming any present fiduciary relationship, the argument that Gateway and MCI had a special, informal relationship of repose and trust that imposed fiduciary duties on MCI is untenable.

Further, neither Gateway's observation that MCI enjoyed "vastly superior financial resources" nor that "Gateway was entirely dependent upon MCI to represent Gateway fairly and honestly in MCI's communications with VA-DOC" transforms the relationship from contractual to fiduciary. Of course, financial disparity between parties is not sufficient to make them fiduciaries. Also, the record belies Gateway's complete dependence on MCI and establishes that, although MCI was the prime contractor with VADOC, Gateway operated

---

[13] While this court applies the substantive law of Virginia to the claims before the arbitrator, Gateway concedes that there are no material differences between Texas and Virginia law on fiduciary duty.

as an independent subcontractor. For example, Gateway had access to the Virginia prisons to operate and maintain its equipment and software. Additionally, if necessary, Gateway could communicate directly with VADOC. Properly understood, Gateway's agreement with MCI was nothing more than a standard subcontract that imposed contractual obligations on both parties but which did not create either a formal or an informal fiduciary relationship.

There is no support under Virginia law for holding that MCI and Gateway were fiduciaries. As a result, the arbitrator's award of punitive damages is not supported by an independent tort and is contrary to Virginia law.

III. CONCLUSION

For the reasons provided, this court VACATES the award of punitive damages and otherwise AFFIRMS the arbitration award.

NOTES

1. *Gateway* is the leading case representing the contract model of arbitration. Note how far arbitration is here transformed to a contract model from the simple "folklore" model of arbitration in which a brief, informal hearing leads to a "final" award with no rights to judicial review. In *Gateway* the court appears to permit the parties full control over the procedures relating to the arbitration.

2. The *Gateway* appellate court provides a full, *de novo* review of the arbitral award. How difficult was this process for the court of appeals? Is the court's overturning of the punitive damage award evidence that courts can review awards effectively or, alternatively, does the second (punitive damage) part of *Gateway* illustrate why courts should steer clear of reviewing arbitral awards?

3. How far should courts go in defending the rights of the parties to provide procedural safeguards in arbitration? Several other federal decisions take the position that a court should honor the desires of the parties to judicialize arbitration. For example, in *Western Employers, Ins. Co. v. Jefferies & Co., Inc.*, 958 F.2d 258 (9th Cir. 1992), the Ninth Circuit overturned a trial court's denial of petition to vacate a NASD arbitral award in which the panel ignored the parties' agreement that they enter findings of fact and conclusions of law. The investor, an insurance company, authorized its broker to invest up to $20,000,000. At the investor's request, the broker agreed to alter the standard form arbitration agreement to require the arbitrators to supplement the award with findings of fact and conclusions of law. The award failed to include findings and conclusions. The Court of Appeals based its decision on the panel's failure to arbitrate consistent with the conditions set by the arbitral parties and concluded that the panel's refusal to follow the parties' instructions amounted to action exceeding the panel's authority under § 10(a)(4) of the FAA. The *Western Employers* opinion was not entirely positive regarding the ability of the parties to contract freely for judicialized arbitration. In dictum, Judge Nelson observed that the use of findings of fact and conclusions of law would not change the nature of court review of arbitral awards. Citing *Local Joint Executive Bd. v. Riverboat Casino, Inc.*, 817 F.2d 524 (9th Cir.

1987), the *Western Employers* decision reasoned that it would not alter the otherwise deferential standard of review of awards even where findings reveal that the arbitrator had misapplied the law. (958 F.2d at 261.) This reasoning is hardly startling. Findings of fact and conclusions of law are routine in labor grievance arbitration. Systematic and enhanced judicial review of such findings has long been rejected. (*See, e.g., American Postal Workers v. U.S. Postal Service*, 682 F.2d 1280, 1285 (9th Cir. 1982) ("award will not be vacated because of erroneous findings of fact or misinterpretations of law").) Similarly in *Fils et Cables d'Acier de Lens v. Midland Metals Corp.*, 584 F. Supp. 240 (S.D.N.Y. 1984), the trial court upheld the parties' desires that the arbitrator "shall make findings of fact and shall render an award based thereon" and that the trial court, when determining whether to confirm the award, "shall have the power to review (1) whether the findings of fact rendered by the arbitrator are . . . supported by substantial evidence, and (2) whether as a matter of law" the award should be affirmed, modified or vacated." (*Id.* at 242.) *Fils* analyzed the issue as one controlled by contract principles — the court viewed the arbitration as "wholly dependent upon agreement." (*Id.* at 244.) The *Fils* decision also reasoned that the arbitral parties possessed the contractual power to bind the court "absent a jurisdictional or public policy barrier." (*Id.*) The court found no violation of public policy because the task of reviewing the arbitrator's findings is "clearly a far less searching and time consuming inquiry than full trial." (*Id.*)

4. Not every decision is hospitable to the parties' desires to judicialize arbitration. In *Chicago Typographical Union No. 16 v. Chicago Sun Times, Inc.*, 935 F.2d 1501 (7th Cir. 1991), Judge Posner refused to give enhanced judicial review to a written opinion accompanying a labor arbitration award. Judge Posner's reasoning focused on federal jurisdiction, a subject that he viewed as beyond the parties' powers to create by contract. In his terms the arbitral parties "cannot contract for *judicial* review of that [arbitral] award; federal jurisdiction cannot be created by contract." (*Id.* at 1505.) Such reasoning appears questionable. It is undoubtedly true that the FAA does not itself create federal subject matter jurisdiction. (*See, e.g., General Automic Co. v. United Nuclear Corp.*, 655 F.2d 968, 969 (9th Cir. 1981) (independent subject matter jurisdiction needed for federal court to hear case brought under FAA to confirm arbitral award).) Yet, the *Chicago Typographical Union* decision seems predicated upon federal subject matter jurisdiction which was clearly present in a case based upon a federal question. Judge Posner also based his refusal to provide more than the customary deferential review standard upon a second point. He asserted that : "it would be a serious practical mistake . . . to subject the reasoning in arbitrators' opinions to beady-eyed scrutiny [because] it might discourage them from writing opinions at all." (935 F.2d at 1506.) Judge Posner reasoned that the process of writing arbitral opinions is desirable "because writing disciplines thought" and review of such opinions would create disincentives to their production. (*Id.*) This analysis is supportive of arbitral judicialization at least in the sense that Judge Posner appears to support arbitration opinion writing. It is only enhanced judicial review that Judge Posner opposes in the *Chicago Typographical Union*. Such advanced review would probably be sought following most labor grievance arbitrations if it were available. Did the labor grievance factual context make a difference in this case?

In *Kyocera Corp. v. Prudential-Bache Trade Services*, 341 F.3d 976 (9th Cir. 2003), *cert. dismissed,* 540 U.S. 1098 (2004) (*en banc*), the Ninth Circuit held that the parties lack the authority to expand the scope of judicial review by agreement. The *en banc* opinion of the court of appeals overturned an earlier panel decision that had upheld the parties' agreement to expand review and had reversed a district court refusal to provide the broad review agreed to by the parties. (130 F.3d 884 (9th Cir. 1997).) The arbitration before the International Court of Arbitration of the International Chamber of Commerce took four years to run its course and contained a lengthy record. The panel decisionsheld that the trial court must honor the terms of the parties' arbitration clause; the agreement called for the trial court to vacate the award if the conclusions of law were not supported by substantial evidence or were clearly erroneous. The court reasoned that the Supreme Court's arbitration decisions (*Volt, Mastrobuono, First Options of Chicago*) "make it clear that the primary purpose of the FAA is to ensure enforcement of private agreements to arbitrate in accordance with the agreements' terms." (*Id.*, at 889.) andconsidered the trial court's refusal to follow the parties' wishes as a position that "would turn the FAA on its head" because federal arbitration legislation "was enacted to ensure enforcement of arbitration in accordance with the parties' agreements." (*Id.* at 889–90.) For another decision upholding an agreement that any party may petition a court of competent jurisdiction for review of [arbitrator] errors of law and dicta that the court would ignore the parties' agreement if it "provided that the district court would review the award by flipping a coin or studying the entrails of a dead fowl," see *New England Utilities v. Hydro-Quebec*, 10 F. Supp. 2d 53, 57, 64 (D. Mass. 1998).

The court of appeals for the Eighth Circuit has taken a contrary position in *UHC Management Co. v. Computer Sciences Corp.*, 148 F.3d 992 (8th Cir. 1998). While the precise holding of *UHC Management Co.* reserved ruling on whether the parties could mandate judicial review for errors of law, the decision casts doubt on the *LaPine Technology and Gateway Technology* decisions. The court asserted that "[i]t is not clear . . . that parties have a say in how a federal court will review an arbitration award when Congress has ordained a specific, self-limiting procedure for how such review is to occur." (*Id.*, at 997.) The court reasoned that the FAA set forth the exclusive means to set aside arbitration awards. For a full discussion of the extent to which the parties can control the nature of their arbitrations, see Edward Brunet, *Replacing Folklore Arbitration with a Contract Model of Arbitration*, 74 Tulane L. Rev. 39 (1999) (arguing that arbitration providers and courts now use a "contract model" which upholds the choice of the parties and advances disputant autonomy). (*Accord*, Alan Scott Rau, *Contracting Out of the Arbitration Act*, 8 Am. Rev. Int'l. Arb. 225 (1997) (characterizing the FAA as a set of default rules). *Contra*, Amy J. Schmitz, *Ending a Mud Bowl: Defining Arbitration's Finality Through Functional Analysis*, 37 Ga. L. Rev. 123 (2002); Hans Smit, *Contractual Modification of the Scope of Judicial Review of Arbitration Awards*, 6 Am. Rev. Int'l. Arb. 147, 149 (1997) (contending that *LaPine Technology* is "wholly incompatible with the essence of arbitration as we know it").)

2. The Public Policy Exception

The high stakes often involved in arbitration create a context in which the losing party is desperate for any means to set aside an award. The attack that an award is contrary to public policy, another so-called non-statutory ground of vacatur, is often relied upon as a grounds to seek judicial review.

UNITED PAPERWORKERS INTERNATIONAL UNION, AFL-CIO v. MISCO, INC.
484 U.S. 29 (1987)

[Under the terms of a collective bargaining agreement, Misco, a paper converting business, agreed to arbitrate disputes with employee members of the paperworkers union. The agreement reserved to management the establishment and enforcement of employee discipline and discharge. Among the listed causes for discharge was consuming or possessing alcohol or drugs on company property (Rule II.1). Employee Cooper, who worked on a hazardous paper cutting machine, was arrested and pleaded guilty to marijuana possession after police observed Cooper seated in a car parked in the company lot. The car was filled with marijuana smoke and a lighted marijuana cigarette was in the ashtray. Misco fired Cooper. Cooper filed an employee grievance. Misco did not learn of the marijuana being found in Cooper's car until the arbitration hearing itself.

[The arbitrator upheld the grievance and ordered Cooper reinstated with back pay because there was not just cause for discharge at the time of Cooper's firing. The arbitrator refused to accept into evidence facts relating to finding marijuana in the car on company property because Misco was unaware of this fact at the time of Cooper's discharge.

[The company sued in federal court to set aside the arbitration award. The trial court set aside the award and the court of appeals affirmed, reasoning that reinstatement would violate public policy "against the operation of dangerous machinery by persons under the influence of drugs or alcohol." 768 F.2d 739, 743 (5th Cir. 1985).]

* * *

II

The Union asserts that an arbitral award may not be set aside on public policy grounds unless the award orders conduct that violates the positive law, which is not the case here. But in the alternative, it submits that even if it is wrong in this regard, the Court of Appeals otherwise exceeded the limited authority that it had to review an arbitrator's award entered pursuant to a collective-bargaining agreement. Respondent, on the other hand, defends the public policy decision of the Court of Appeals but alternatively argues that the judgment below should be affirmed because of erroneous findings by the arbitrator. We deal first with the opposing alternative arguments.

A

Collective-bargaining agreements commonly provide grievance procedures to settle disputes between union and employer with respect to the interpretation and application of the agreement and require binding arbitration for unsettled grievances. In such cases, and this is such a case, the Court made clear almost 30 years ago that the courts play only a limited role when asked to review the decision of an arbitrator. The courts are not authorized to reconsider the merits of an award even though the parties may allege that the award rests on errors of fact or on misinterpretation of the contract. "The refusal of courts to review the merits of an arbitration award is the proper approach to arbitration under collective bargaining agreements. The federal policy of settling labor disputes by arbitration would be undermined if courts had the final say on the merits of the awards." *Steelworkers v. Enterprise Wheel & Car Corp.*, 363 U.S. 593, 596 (1960). As long as the arbitrator's award "draws its essence from the collective bargaining agreement," and is not merely "his own brand of industrial justice," the award is legitimate. *Id.*, at 597. "The function of the court is very limited when the parties have agreed to submit all questions of contract interpretation to the arbitrator. It is confined to ascertaining whether the party seeking arbitration is making a claim which on its face is governed by the contract. Whether the moving party is right or wrong is a question of contract interpretation for the arbitrator. In these circumstances the moving party should not be deprived of the arbitrator's judgment, when it was his judgment and all that it connotes that was bargained for. "The courts, therefore, have no business weighing the merits of the grievance, considering whether there is equity in a particular claim, or determining whether there is particular language in the written instrument which will support the claim." *Steelworkers v. American Mfg. Co.*, 363 U.S. 564, 567–568 (1960). *See also AT & T Technologies, Inc. v. Communications Workers*, 475 U.S. 643, 649–650 (1986).

The reasons for insulating arbitral decisions from judicial review are grounded in the federal statutes regulating labor-management relations. These statutes reflect a decided preference for private settlement of labor disputes without the intervention of government: The Labor Management Relations Act of 1947, 61 Stat. 154, 29 U.S.C. § 173(d), provides that "[f]inal adjustment by a method agreed upon by the parties is hereby declared to be the desirable method for settlement of grievance disputes arising over the application or interpretation of an existing collective-bargaining agreement." *See also AT & T Technologies, supra*, at 650. The courts have jurisdiction to enforce collective-bargaining contracts; but where the contract provides grievance and arbitration procedures, those procedures must first be exhausted and courts must order resort to the private settlement mechanisms without dealing with the merits of the dispute. Because the parties have contracted to have disputes settled by an arbitrator chosen by them rather than by a judge, it is the arbitrator's view of the facts and of the meaning of the contract that they have agreed to accept. Courts thus do not sit to hear claims of factual or legal error by an arbitrator as an appellate court does in reviewing decisions of lower courts. To resolve disputes about the application of a collective-bargaining agreement, an arbitrator must find facts and a court may not reject those findings simply because it disagrees with them. The same is true of the arbitrator's interpretation of the contract. The arbitrator may not ignore the plain language of the contract; but the parties having authorized the arbitrator to give meaning to the language of the agreement, a court should not reject an award on the ground that the arbitrator misread the contract. *Enterprise Wheel, supra,* 363 U.S., at 599. So, too, where it is contemplated that the arbitrator will determine remedies for contract violations that he finds, courts have no authority to disagree with his honest judgment in that respect. If the courts were free to intervene on these grounds, the speedy resolution of grievances by private mechanisms would be greatly undermined. Furthermore, it must be remembered that grievance and arbitration procedures are part and parcel of the ongoing process of collective bargaining. It is through these processes that the supplementary rules of the plant are established. As the Court has said, the arbitrator's award settling a dispute with respect to the interpretation or application of a labor agreement must draw its essence from the contract and cannot simply reflect the arbitrator's own notions of industrial justice. But as long as the arbitrator is even arguably construing or applying the contract and acting within the scope of his authority, that a court is convinced he committed serious error does not suffice to overturn his decision. Of course, decisions procured by the parties through fraud or through the arbitrator's dishonesty need not be enforced. But there is nothing of that sort involved in this case.

B

The Company's position, simply put, is that the arbitrator committed grievous error in finding that the evidence was insufficient to prove that Cooper had possessed or used marijuana on company property. But the Court of Appeals, although it took a distinctly jaundiced view of the arbitrator's decision in this regard, was not free to refuse enforcement because it considered Cooper's presence in the white Cutlass, in the circumstances, to be ample proof that Rule II.1 was violated. No dishonesty is alleged; only improvident, even silly, factfinding is claimed. This is hardly a sufficient basis for disregarding what the agent appointed by the parties determined to be the historical facts.

Nor was it open to the Court of Appeals to refuse to enforce the award because the arbitrator, in deciding whether there was just cause to discharge, refused to consider evidence unknown to the Company at the time Cooper was fired. The parties bargained for arbitration to settle disputes and were free to set the procedural rules for arbitrators to follow if they chose. Article VI of the agreement, entitled "Arbitration Procedure," did set some ground rules for the arbitration process. It forbade the arbitrator to consider hearsay evidence, for example, but evidentiary matters were otherwise left to the arbitrator. App. 19. Here the arbitrator ruled that in determining whether Cooper had violated Rule II.1, he should not consider evidence not relied on by the employer in ordering the discharge, particularly in a case like this where there was no notice to the employee or the Union prior to the hearing that the Company would attempt to rely on after-discovered evidence. This, in effect, was a construction of what the contract required when deciding discharge cases: an arbitrator was to look only at the evidence before the employer at the time of discharge. As the arbitrator noted, this approach was consistent with the practice followed by other arbitrators. And it was consistent with our observation in *John Wiley & Sons, Inc. v. Livingston*, 376 U.S. 543, 557 (1964), that when the subject matter of a dispute is arbitrable, "procedural" questions which grow out of the dispute and bear on its final disposition are to be left to the arbitrator.

Under the Arbitration Act, the federal courts are empowered to set aside arbitration awards on such grounds only when "the arbitrators were guilty of misconduct . . . in refusing to hear evidence pertinent and material to the controversy." 9 U.S.C. § 10(a)(3). *See Commonwealth Coatings Corp. v. Continental Casualty Co.*, 393 U.S. 145 (1968). If we apply that same standard here and assume that the arbitrator erred in refusing to consider the disputed evidence, his error was not in bad faith or so gross as to amount to affirmative misconduct. Finally, it is worth noting that putting aside the evidence about the marijuana found in Cooper's car during this arbitration did not forever foreclose the Company from using that evidence as the basis for a discharge.

Even if it were open to the Court of Appeals to have found a violation of Rule II.1 because of the marijuana found in Cooper's car, the question remains whether the court could properly set aside the award because in its view discharge was the correct remedy. Normally, an arbitrator is authorized to disagree with the sanction imposed for employee misconduct. In *Enterprise Wheel*, for example, the arbitrator reduced the discipline from discharge to a 10-day suspension. The Court of Appeals refused to enforce the award, but we reversed, explaining that though the arbitrator's decision must draw its essence from the agreement, he "is to bring his informed judgment to bear in order to reach a fair solution of a problem. *This is especially true when it comes to formulating remedies*." 363 U.S., at 597 (emphasis added). The parties, of course, may limit the discretion of the arbitrator in this respect; and it may be, as the Company argues, that under the contract involved here, it was within the unreviewable discretion of management to discharge an employee once a violation of Rule II.1 was found. But the parties stipulated that the issue before the arbitrator was whether there was "just" cause for the discharge, and the arbitrator, in the course of his opinion, cryptically observed that Rule II.1 merely listed causes for discharge and did not expressly provide for immediate discharge. Before disposing of the case on the ground that Rule II.1 had been violated and discharge was therefore proper, the proper course would have been remand to the arbitrator for a definitive construction of the contract in this respect.

C

The Court of Appeals did not purport to take this course in any event. Rather, it held that the evidence of marijuana in Cooper's car required that the award be set aside because to reinstate a person who had brought drugs onto the property was contrary to the public policy "against the operation of dangerous machinery by persons under the influence of drugs or alcohol." 768 F.2d, at 743. We cannot affirm that judgment.

A court's refusal to enforce an arbitrator's award under a collective-bargaining agreement because it is contrary to public policy is a specific application of the more general doctrine, rooted in the common law, that a court may refuse to enforce contracts that violate law or public policy. *W.R. Grace & Co. v. Rubber Workers*, 461 U.S. 757, 766 (1983); *Hurd v. Hodge*, 334 U.S. 24, 34–35 (1948). That doctrine derives from the basic notion that no court will lend its aid to one who founds a cause of action upon an immoral or illegal act, and is further justified by the observation that the public's interests in confining the scope of private agreements to which it is not a party will go unrepresented unless the judiciary takes account of those interests when it considers whether to enforce such agreements. *E.g., McMullen v. Hoffman*, 174 U.S. 639, 654–655 (1899); *Twin City Pipe Line Co. v. Harding Glass Co.*, 283 U.S. 353, 356– 358 (1931). In the common law of contracts, this doctrine has served as the foundation for occasional exercises of judicial power to abrogate private agreements.

In *W.R. Grace*, we recognized that "a court may not enforce a collective-bargaining agreement that is contrary to public policy," and stated that "the question of public policy is ultimately one for resolution by the courts." 461 U.S., at 766. We cautioned, however, that a court's refusal to enforce an arbitrator's *interpretation* of such contracts is limited to situations where the contract as interpreted would violate "some explicit public policy" that is "well defined and dominant, and is to be ascertained 'by reference to the laws and legal precedents and not from general considerations of supposed public interests.'" *Ibid.* (quoting *Muschany v. United States*, 324 U.S. 49, 66 (1945)). In *W.R. Grace*, we identified two important public policies that were potentially jeopardized by the arbitrator's interpretation of the contract: obedience to judicial orders and voluntary compliance with Title VII of the Civil Rights Act of 1964. We went on to hold that enforcement of the arbitration award in that case did not compromise either of the two public policies allegedly threatened by the award. Two points follow from our decision in *W.R. Grace*. First, a court may refuse to enforce a collective-bargaining agreement when the specific terms contained in that agreement violate public policy. Second, it is apparent that our decision in that case does not otherwise sanction a broad judicial power to set aside arbitration awards as against public policy. Although we discussed the effect of that award on two broad areas of public policy, our decision turned on our examination of whether the award created any explicit conflict with other "laws and legal precedents" rather than an assessment of "general considerations of supposed public interests." 461 U.S., at 766. At the very least, an alleged public policy must be properly framed under the approach set out in *W.R. Grace*, and the violation of such a policy must be clearly shown if an award is not to be enforced.

As we see it, the formulation of public policy set out by the Court of Appeals did not comply with the statement that such a policy must be "ascertained 'by reference to the laws and legal precedents and not from general considerations of supposed public interests.'" *Ibid.* (quoting *Muschany v. United States, supra*, 324 U.S., at 66.) The Court of Appeals made no attempt to review existing laws and legal precedents in order to demonstrate that they establish a "well-defined and dominant" policy against the operation of dangerous machinery while under the influence of drugs. Although certainly such a judgment is firmly rooted in common sense, we explicitly held in *W.R. Grace* that a formulation of public policy based only on "general considerations of supposed public interests" is not the sort that permits a court to set aside an arbitration award that was entered in accordance with a valid collective-bargaining agreement.

Even if the Court of Appeals' formulation of public policy is to be accepted, no violation of that policy was clearly shown in this case. In pursuing its public policy inquiry, the Court of Appeals quite properly considered the established fact that traces of marijuana had been found in Cooper's car. Yet the assumed connection between the marijuana gleanings found in Cooper's car and Cooper's actual use of drugs in the workplace is tenuous at best and provides an insufficient basis for holding that his reinstatement would actually violate the public policy identified by the Court of Appeals "against the operation of dangerous machinery by persons under the influence of drugs or alcohol." 768 F.2d, at 743. A refusal to enforce an award must rest on more than speculation or assumption.

In any event, it was inappropriate for the Court of Appeals itself to draw the necessary inference. To conclude from the fact that marijuana had been found in Cooper's car that Cooper had ever been or would be under the influence of marijuana while he was on the job and operating dangerous machinery is an exercise in factfinding about Cooper's use of drugs and his amenability to discipline, a task that exceeds the authority of a court asked to overturn an arbitration award. The parties did not bargain for the facts to be found by a court, but by an arbitrator chosen by them who had more opportunity to observe Cooper and to be familiar with the plant and its problems. Nor does the fact that it is inquiring into a possible violation of public policy excuse a court for doing the arbitrator's task. If additional facts were to be found, the arbitrator should find them in the course of any further effort the Company might have made to discharge Cooper for having had marijuana in his car on company premises. Had the arbitrator found that Cooper had possessed drugs on the property, yet imposed discipline short of discharge because he found as a factual matter that Cooper could be trusted not to use them on the job, the Court of Appeals could not upset the award because of its own view that public policy about plant safety was threatened. In this connection it should also be noted that the award ordered Cooper to be reinstated in his old job or in an equivalent one for which he was qualified. It is by no means clear from the record that Cooper would pose a serious threat to the asserted public policy in every job for which he was qualified.

The judgment of the Court of Appeals is reversed.

So ordered.

JUSTICE BLACKMUN, with whom JUSTICE BRENNAN joins, concurring.

I join the Court's opinion, but write separately to underscore the narrow grounds on which its decision rests and to emphasize what it is not holding today. In particular, the Court does not reach the issue upon which certiorari was granted: whether a court may refuse to enforce an arbitration award rendered under a collective-bargaining agreement on public policy grounds only when the award itself violates positive law or requires unlawful conduct by the employer. The opinion takes no position on this issue. Nor do I understand the Court to decide, more generally, in what way, if any, a court's authority to set aside an arbitration award on public policy grounds differs from its authority, outside the collective-bargaining context, to refuse to enforce a contract on public policy grounds. Those issues are left for another day.

I agree with the Court that the judgment of the Court of Appeals must be reversed, and I summarize what I understand to be the three alternative rationales for the Court's decision:

1. The Court of Appeals exceeded its authority in concluding that the company's discharge of Cooper was proper under the collective-bargaining agreement. The Court of Appeals erred in considering evidence that the arbitrator legitimately had excluded from the grievance process, in second-guessing the arbitrator's factual finding that Cooper had not violated Rule II.1, and in assessing the appropriate sanction under the agreement. Absent its overreaching, the Court of Appeals lacked any basis for disagreeing with the arbitrator's conclusion that there was not "just cause" for discharging Cooper.

2. Even if the Court of Appeals properly considered evidence of marijuana found in Cooper's car and legitimately found a Rule II.1 violation, the public policy advanced by the Court of Appeals does not support its decision to set aside the award. The reinstatement of Cooper would not contravene the alleged public policy "against the operation of dangerous machinery by persons under the influence of drugs or alcohol." 768 F.2d 739, 743 (5th Cir. 1985). The fact that an employee's car contains marijuana gleanings does not indicate that the employee uses marijuana on the job or that he operates his machine while under the influence of drugs, let alone that he will report to work in an impaired state in the future. Moreover, nothing in the record suggests that the arbitrator's award, which gives the company the option of placing Cooper in a job equivalent to his old one, would require Cooper to operate hazardous machinery.

3. The public policy formulated by the Court of Appeals may not properly support a court's refusal to enforce an otherwise valid arbitration award. In *W.R. Grace & Co. v. Rubber Workers*, 461 U.S. 757, we stated that the public policy must be founded on " 'laws and legal precedents.' " *Id.*, at 766. The Court of Appeals identified no law or legal precedent that demonstrated an "explicit public policy," 461 U.S., at 766, against the operation of dangerous machinery by persons under the influence of drugs. Far from being "well defined and dominant," as *W.R. Grace* prescribed, the Court of Appeals' public policy was ascertained merely "from general considerations of supposed public interests." I do not understand the Court, by criticizing the company's public policy formulation, to suggest that proper framing of an alleged public policy under the approach set out in *W.R. Grace* would be sufficient to justify a court's refusal to enforce an arbitration award on public policy grounds. Rather, I understand the Court to hold that such compliance is merely a necessary step if an award is not to be enforced.

It is on this understanding that I join the opinion of the Court.

NOTES

1. Does the text of the FAA permit courts to refuse enforcement of arbitral awards on grounds that the award is against public policy? Most commentators refer to the public policy exception as a nonstatutory ground of vacatur. Should a court prefer the statute (FAA) to using common law grounds such as the public policy exception? The public policy exception is, however, a historic part of contract law under which courts can refuse to enforce contracts (e.g., gambling contracts) that undermine established public policies. If courts have such a common law power, shouldn't the FAA be interpreted to permit some type of judicial review of public policy? It is clear that the popularity of arbitration has increased substantially since the 1953 *Wilko* decision. Should this enhanced popularity work its way into a more narrow judicial interpretation of the public policy exception?

2. Can an attack based upon public policy be linked to the specific FAA grounds for setting aside awards? Recall that § 10(a)(4) permits an award to be set aside when the arbitrator has exceeded his powers. Can the public policy concept be placed in this statutory pigeonhole? Does it matter? It may matter to those judges who seek to premise their actions upon legislative guidance. For the position that the public policy standard should be placed within § 10(a)(4), see MACNEIL, SPEIDEL & STIPANOWICH, *supra*, § 40.5.1.3.

3. *National R.R. Passenger Corp. v. Consolidated Rail Corp.*, 892 F.2d 1066 (D.C. Cir. 1990), narrowly construed the public policy exception. The case involved Amtrak's efforts to use the public policy exception to avoid an arbitration involving indemnification by Amtrak of suits filed following a disastrous 1987 collision of Amtrak passenger train in Maryland. Amtrak raised the public policy exception as a defense to a suit by Conrail to compel arbitration. The trial court entered a declaratory judgment that Amtrak need not indemnify Conrail and decided that the public policy exception should apply. It reasoned that "public policy will not allow enforcement of indemnification provisions that appear to cover such extreme misconduct because serious and significant disincentives to railroad safety would ensue." (698 F. Supp. 951, 972 (D.D.C. 1988).) The D.C. Circuit reversed. Judge Ginsburg's opinion took a restrictive view regarding judicial use of the public policy exception prior to arbitration. In his view the FAA authorized the courts to compel arbitration and "courts are simply not authorized to 'expand' a statutory provision beyond its intended reach. . . . A court cannot . . . bypass the arbitration process simply because a public policy issue might arise." (892 F.2d at 1070–71.)

4. Is the question of whether the award violates public policy an arbitral one for the arbitrator or for the court? Doesn't the approach of Judge Ginsburg in the Amtrak case, *supra*, suggest that the arbitrators should at least consider whether an award would violate public policy? By divesting the trial court of the ability to decide in advance that an arbitration would violate public policy, the Amtrak case seems to signal arbitrators that they should tackle the public policy question. Does the *Misco* decision take a position on this question? For authority that the issue of whether an arbitration award violates public policy is a question for the court, see, e.g., *Bd. of County Comm'rs v. L. Robert Kimball & Assoc.*, 860 F.2d 683, 686 (6th Cir. 1988), *cert. denied*, 494 U.S. 1030 (1990). For the suggestion that the parties should draft an arbitration clause to direct the arbitrator to consider public policy, see, e.g., Deanna Mouser, *Analysis of the Public Policy Exception After Paperworkers v. Misco: A Proposal to Limit the Public Policy Exception and to Allow the Parties to Submit the Public Policy Question to the Arbitrator*, 12 IND. REL. L.J. 89 (1990).

5. The public policy exception remains a way in which some courts permit attack on arbitration awards that frustrate important public safety policies. Consider *Delta Air Lines, Inc. v. Airlines Pilots Ass'n*, 861 F.2d 665, 671 (11th Cir. 1988), *cert. denied*, 493 U.S. 871 (1989), where the court invoked the public policy exception and affirmed the trial courts vacatur of an award reinstating a pilot who had been discharged following his piloting of an aircraft while intoxicated. Similarly, in *Iowa Elec. Light and Power Co. v. Local Union 204 of the Int'l Bhd. of Elec. Workers*, 834 F.2d 1424, 1428 (8th Cir. 1987), the court of appeals found that an award violated public policy because the arbitrators reinstated a nuclear power plant machinist who had deliberately violated Nuclear Regulatory Commission rules when he knowingly pulled a fuse on a containment area door. (*Accord, Exxon Shipping Co. v. Exxon Seamen's Union*, 993 F.2d 357 (3d Cir. 1993) (affirming trial court's vacatur of arbitration award that had reinstated a helmsman who had been fired after testing positively for marijuana use after a 635 foot oil tanker ran aground in the Mississippi River).) For a decision upholding the use of the public policy exception to vacate an arbitration award reinstating a male newspaper employee who was discharged for sexually harassing female employees, see *Newsday v. Long Island Typographical Union*, 915 F.2d 840 (2d Cir. 1990) (finding a well documented judicial policy against work place sexual harassment and a well-recognized public policy in Title VII of the Civil Right Act and EEOC regulations), *cert. denied*, 499 U.S. 922 (1991). Some commentators support active use of the public policy exception whenever on the job employee drug use is involved. (*See, e.g.*, Jesse Schaudies & Christopher Miller, *The Critical Role of a Judicially Recognized Public Policy Against Illegal Drug Use in the Workplace*, 12 IND. RELATIONS L.J. 153 (1990).) Others have criticized the extent of judicial intervention under the public policy exception. (*See, e.g.*, Charles Craver, *Labor Arbitration as a Continuation of the Collective Bargaining Process*, 66 CHI-KENT L. REV. 571 (1992).)

6. In *Eastern Associated Coal Corp. v. United Mine Workers*, 121 S. Ct. 462 (2000), the Supreme Court reconfirmed the test set forth in the *Misco* decision and declined to expand the *Misco* test to restrict arbitrator discretion in cases involving employee drug use. The Court characterized the public policy exception set forth in *Misco* as "narrow" (121 S. Ct. at 467) and rejected the employer's argument that the arbitrator's three month suspension and reinstatement of an employee truck driver who had twice tested positive for marijuana use violated public policy. Justice Breyer's opinion acknowledged that Federal drug transportation testing legislation sought to eliminate the use of illegal drugs but concluded that the federal legislation also contained "remedial" provisions designed to rehabilitate workers who, like the employee in question, had tested positively for drug use. The Supreme Court concluded that the arbitrators reinstatement award was not contrary to a "dominant" or "explicit" public policy set out in "well-defined" legislation.

SEYMOUR v. BLUE CROSS/BLUE SHIELD
988 F.2d 1020 (10th Cir. 1993)

[Seymour was insured by Blue Cross through his employer. At the beginning of Seymour's employment, Blue Cross covered liver transplants. Later Blue Cross amended coverage to exclude liver transplants and notified employers and employees. Seymour claimed he never received his copy. Neither his employer nor Seymour agreed in writing to the amendment as required by Utah law; however, the original policy stated that Blue Cross could unilaterally amend at any time. Seymour's son was born, diagnosed with congenital liver disease, needed a liver transplant, and was denied coverage. The arbitration panel found that Blue Cross was not obligated to pay. Seymour moved to vacate; Blue Cross moved to confirm. The District Court confirmed the award and rejected Seymour's argument that the court should refuse to enforce the award because Blue Cross' unilateral modification of the original policy was against public policy.]

SEYMOUR, CIRCUIT JUDGE.

* * *

II.

So long as an arbitrator draws his decision from the parties' agreements, a reviewing court is generally precluded from disturbing the award. *United Paperworkers Int'l Union v. Misco, Inc.*, 484 U.S. 29, 36 (1987) (citing *Steelworkers v. Enterprise Wheel & Car Corp.*, 363 U.S. 593, 597 (1960)). "[A] federal court may not overrule an arbitrator's decision simply because the court believes its own interpretation of the contract would be a better one." *W.R. Grace and Co. v. Local Union No. 759*, 461 U.S. 757, 764 (1983); *see Enterprise Wheel*, 363 U.S. at 596. "[A]s long as the arbitrator is even arguably construing or applying the contract and acting within the scope of his authority, that a court is convinced he committed serious error does not suffice to overturn his decision." *Misco*, 484 U.S. at 38. * * *

If a court is to disturb an award, it can only do so under strict statutory or judicially-created standards. The Federal Arbitration Act, 9 U.S.C. § 10 (1990), provides the statutory grounds upon which a court may vacate an arbitrator's award. In addition, the Supreme Court has recognized a public policy exception that permits a court to decline to enforce an arbitrator's award. *See Misco*, 484 U.S. at 42; *W.R. Grace*, 461 U.S. at 766. It is this judicially-created ground for vacating an arbitration award upon which the Seymours rely.

The public policy exception is rooted in the common law doctrine of a court's power to refuse to enforce a contract that violates public policy or law. It derives legitimacy from the public's interest in having its views represented in matters to which it is not a party but which could harm the public interest. *Misco*, 484 U.S. at 42. This judicially-created exception was explained in *Misco*, drawing upon *W.R. Grace*:

Two points follow from our decision in *W.R. Grace*. First, a court may refuse to enforce a collective-bargaining agreement when the specific terms contained in that agreement violate public policy. Second, it is apparent that our decision in that case does not otherwise sanction a broad judicial power to set aside arbitration awards as against public policy. Although we discussed the effect of that award on two broad areas of public policy, our decision turned on our examination of whether the award created any explicit conflict with other "laws and legal precedents" rather than an assessment of "general considerations of supposed public interests." At the very least, an alleged public policy must be properly framed under the approach set out in *W.R. Grace*, and the violation of such a policy must be clearly shown if an award is not to be enforced.

Id. at 43 (citations omitted).

The circuit courts, as well as both parties here, disagree on whether a "broad" or "narrow" view of the public policy exception should be applied to assess arbitration awards. *Compare, e.g., Stead Motors v. Automotive Machinists Lodge 1173*, 886 F.2d 1200 (9th Cir. 1989) (*en banc*) (narrow view), *cert. denied*, 495 U.S. 946 (1990), *with Stroehmann Bakeries v. Local No. 776, Int'l Bhd. of Teamsters*, 969 F.2d 1436 (3d Cir.) (broad view), *cert. denied*, 506 U.S. 1022 (1992); *Delta Air Lines v. Air Line Pilots Ass'n Int'l*, 861 F.2d 665 (11th Cir. 1988) (same), *cert. denied*, 493 U.S. 871 (1989). Significantly, however, the Court in *Misco* granted certiorari because of a prior split in the circuits, noting that "[t]he decision below accords with the broader view of the court's power taken by the First and Seventh Circuits. A narrower view has been taken by the Ninth and District of Columbia Circuits." *Misco*, 484 U.S. at 35 n. 7. The Court reversed the broader view that permitted a court to overturn an arbitrator's decision based only on a general view of supposed public interests without a review of the relevant laws and legal precedents to determine whether they established a " 'well-defined and dominant' policy against the [described conduct]."

Given the Supreme Court's clear guidance in *Misco* that we have quoted above, we believe it unhelpful to describe the public policy test as either broad or narrow as some of the courts are continuing to do. Rather, in determining whether an arbitration award violates public policy, a court must assess whether "the specific terms contained in [the contract] violate public policy," *id.* at 43, by creating an "explicit conflict with other 'laws and legal precedents,' " *id.*, keeping in mind the admonition that an arbitration award is not to be lightly overturned, *see United Food & Commercial Workers, Local No. 7R v. Safeway Stores, Inc.*, 889 F.2d 940, 948 (10th Cir. 1989); *Communication Workers v. Southeastern Elec. Co-op.*, 882 F.2d 467, 468 (10th Cir. 1989).

III.

We turn now to the award in this case and the alleged violation of public policy. The Seymours assert that the arbitrator's award violates Utah's clearly expressed public policy that an insurance policy may not be modified to reduce benefits unless the parties agree in writing. *See* Utah Code Ann. § 31-19-26 (*repealed* in 1985). BCBSU responds that the Utah insurance laws are preempted by ERISA. However, we recently held in *Winchester v. Prudential Life Ins. Co.*, 975 F.2d 1479, 1484–85 (10th Cir. 1992), that while ERISA preempts state insurance laws as applied to self-funded ERISA plans, it does not preempt state insurance laws insofar as they regulate purchased insurance policies. Because the insurance contract in this case was purchased, it remains regulated by the Utah insurance statutes.

BCBSU alternatively points out that section 31-19-26 was replaced in 1985 by Utah Code Ann. § 31A-21-106, which provides:

> (1) No insurance policy may contain any agreement or incorporate any provision not fully set forth in the policy or in an application or other document attached to and made a part of the policy at the time of its delivery. . . .

> (2) or as otherwise mandated by law, no purported modification of a contract during the term of the policy affects the obligations of a party to the contract unless the modification is in writing and agreed to by the party against whose interest the modification operates.

> (3) Subsection (2) does not prevent a change in coverage under group contracts resulting from provisions of an employer eligibility rule, the terms of a collective bargaining agreement, or provisions in Federal Employee Retirement Income Security Act plan documents.

While recognizing that subsection (2) of this statute requires the modification of an insurance contract during the term of the policy to be in writing and agreed to by the parties against whose interest the modification operates, BCBSU contends that subsection (3) of the statute exempts ERISA plans from this requirement. The Seymours, on the other hand, assert that subsection (3) is intended to apply only to modifications that result from action taken by the employer and employees. Under their interpretation, therefore, the requirements of subsection (2) are eliminated only where the employer and the employees agree to modify a group contract, collective bargaining agreement, or ERISA plan. The Seymours claim that no such employer-employee action is involved here and therefore subsection (3) is not applicable.

We need not resolve the parties' dispute as to the applicability of section 31A-21-106(3) because even if the Seymours are correct that subsection (2) governs, we hold that they have not established a public policy violation sufficient to overturn the arbitrator's award. Under the public policy standard we have articulated above, the arbitrator's decision in favor of BCBSU does not violate a clearly expressed law. The arbitrators could have reasonably construed the facts of this case to meet the requirement of subsection (2) that a modification be "in writing and agreed to by the party against whose interest the modification operates." BCBSU reissued the Seymours' policy in March 1987, shortly after Brayden was born. The new policy contained the organ transplant exclusion. The Seymours acknowledge that they received the new policy, and both the Seymours and Bookcraft paid the insurance premiums without protest. An arbitrator could have reasonably concluded that acceptance and payment of premiums meets the "agreed to" requirement. We cannot say subsection (2) *clearly* provides that these facts would not constitute an agreement by the company and the Seymours to the modification. We therefore conclude there was no clear violation of Utah public policy.

WE AFFIRM the district court order confirming the arbitration award.

NOTES

1. How well does the *Seymour* decision grapple with the test set forth by *Misco*? Is the *Misco* test easy to apply? Is it understandable? Isn't every law, whether legislative or common law in nature, premised upon public policy?

2. The public policy exception has been used typically by employers who seek to avoid what they think are arbitrary and unfair arbitral awards following employee grievances. Rarely are courts willing to vacate arbitration awards on public policy grounds where the award did not arise in an employment context. (*See* Jeffrey Stempel, *Pitfalls of Public Policy: The Case of Arbitration Agreements*, 22 ST. MARY'S L.J. 259 (1990).) Is this surprising? What is it about employment disputes that makes public policy particularly relevant? Is the *Misco* approach limited to use in employment disputes? Should it be? For discussion of the public policy exception in a commercial law dispute, see *Arizona Electric Power Co-op., Inc. v. Berkeley*, 59 F.3d 988 (9th Cir. 1995) (upholding award and refusing to apply the public policy exception in a dispute involving a grant of $7,000,000 in attorneys' fees despite allegations of unethical attorney behavior involving a breach of fiduciary duty). In the *Arizona Electric Power* decision, the Ninth Circuit expressed a clear preference for a narrow public policy exception:

> [C]ourts should be reluctant to vacate arbitral awards on public policy grounds. The primary reason that parties resort to arbitration is to gain the benefit of a quicker, easier dispute resolution process. These benefits would be radically diminished if courts readily entertained public policy challenges to arbitral awards. The finality of arbitral awards must be preserved if arbitration is to remain a desirable alternative to courtroom litigation. [59 F.3d at 992.]

Is the above narrow vision of the public policy exception consistent with the *Misco* decision?

3. In *PainWebber, Inc. v. Argon*, 49 F.3d 347 (8th Cir. 1995), the court of appeals interpreted the public policy grounds for vacatur in this way:

> We are not entitled to merely substitute our judgment for that of the arbitration panel, no matter how wrong we may believe the panel's decision to be. In this limited review we accept the facts found by the arbitration panel, but review its conclusions *de novo* to determine if they violate public policy. [49 F.3d at 350.]

Is the Eighth Circuit's vision of the public policy exception overly restrictive? Does *Misco* call for such a narrow public policy exception?

4. In *Prudential-Bache Securities, Inc. v. Tanner*, 72 F.3d 234 (1st Cir. 1995), the court of appeals affirmed a trial court refusal to set aside an award of close to $3,000,000 in favor of four former employees who brought wrongful termination arbitration claims. The court of appeals rejected Prudential-Bache's attempt to use the public policy as a grounds for vacating the award.

Prudential-Bache argued that the employees were terminated for their failure to record securities transactions and pointed out that there is a well-defined public policy that securities firms should maintain accurate records, citing the reporting requirements set forth in Section 17(a) of the Securities Exchange Act of 1934, 15 U.S.C. § 789(a) (1994) and various Securities Exchange Commission rules promulgated under the Act. (*See* 72 F.3d at 241.) The First Circuit, however, failed to address whether these laws constituted a conflict with the award and, instead, asserted that the appellant Prudential-Bache had not shown, under *Misco*, that a violation of the public policy had been "clearly shown." The court reasoned that because the arbitrators had failed to write an opinion, it could not safely conclude that the arbitrators had "necessarily found that there was a recording violation and we refuse to do so in their stead." (*Id.* at 242.) Is this a correct interpretation of the *Misco* reading of public policy?

Chapter 12

UNIVERSAL ARBITRATION OF ALL TYPES OF DISPUTES

Partners often argue that a dispute is not subject to arbitration. If arbitration were merely a matter of contract, courts would automatically and unquestionably enforce all covenants to arbitrate. However, resolution of disputes has a long history in the public domain. As the following cases show, past decisions have demonstrated considerable reluctance to approve arbitration of every type of dispute. Julius Cohen, the primary drafter of the FAA, stated that "not all questions arising out of contracts ought to be arbitrated." (Julius Cohen & Kenneth Dayton, *The New Federal Arbitration Law*, 12 Va. L. Rev. 265, 281 (1926).) The modern Supreme Court, however, has displayed a hospitable attitude toward broad arbitrability of a broad range of disputes.

A. SECURITIES ARBITRATION

SHEARSON/AMERICAN EXPRESS, INC. v. McMAHON
482 U.S. 220 (1987)

Justice O'CONNOR delivered the opinion of the Court.

This case presents two questions regarding the enforceability of predispute arbitration agreements between brokerage firms and their customers. The first is whether a claim brought under § 10(b) of the Securities Exchange Act of 1934 (Exchange Act), 48 Stat. 891, 15 U.S.C. § 78j(b), must be sent to arbitration in accordance with the terms of an arbitration agreement. The second is whether a claim brought under the Racketeer Influenced and Corrupt Organizations Act (RICO), 18 U.S.C. § 1961 et seq., must be arbitrated in accordance with the terms of such an agreement.

* * *

[Plaintiffs, customers of defendant Shearson, a brokerage firm, signed a customer agreement containing an arbitration clause. After a dispute arose plaintiff filed suit alleging (1) violation of § 10(b) of the Securities Exchange Act and SEC Rule 10b-5 by engaging in fraudulent and excessive trading in plaintiffs' accounts and making false statements and omitting material facts. They also pleaded violations of RICO and state common law fraud and breach of duty. The trial court granted Shearson's motion to compel arbitration in part, finding only the RICO claim not arbitrable. The Court of Appeals affirmed on the state law and RICO claims but reversed on the Exchange Act claims. 788 F.2d 94 (2d Cir. 1986). It reasoned that "public policy" factors prevented arbitration of RICO claims and that *Wilko v. Swan*, 346 U.S. 427 (1953), should be extended to prevent arbitration of Exchange Act claims.]

II

The Federal Arbitration Act provides the starting point for answering the questions raised in this case. The Act was intended to "revers[e] centuries of judicial hostility to arbitration agreements," *Scherk v. Alberto-Culver Co.* [417 U.S. 506 (1974)], by "plac[ing] arbitration agreements 'upon the same footing as other contracts.' "The Arbitration Act accomplishes this purpose by providing that arbitration agreements "shall be valid, irrevocable, and enforceable, save upon such grounds as exist at law or in equity for the revocation of any contract." 9 U.S.C. § 2. The Act also provides that a court must stay its proceedings if it is satisfied that an issue before it is arbitrable under the agreement, § 3; and it authorizes a federal district court to issue an order compelling arbitration if there has been a "failure, neglect, or refusal" to comply with the arbitration agreement, § 4.

The Arbitration Act thus establishes a "federal policy favoring arbitration," *Moses H. Cone Memorial Hospital v. Mercury Construction Corp.*, 460 U.S. 1, 24 (1983), requiring that "we rigorously enforce agreements to arbitrate." This duty to enforce arbitration agreements is not diminished when a party bound by an agreement raises a claim founded on statutory rights. As we observed in *Mitsubishi Motors Corp. v. Soler Chrysler-Plymouth, Inc.*, [473 U.S. 614 (1985)], "we are well past the time when judicial suspicion of the desirability of arbitration and of the competence of arbitral tribunals" should inhibit enforcement of the Act " 'in controversies based on statutes.' " Absent a well-founded claim that an arbitration agreement resulted from the sort of fraud or excessive economic power that "would provide grounds 'for the revocation of any contract,' " the Arbitration Act "provides no basis for disfavoring agreements to arbitrate statutory claims by skewing the otherwise hospitable inquiry into arbitrability."

The Arbitration Act, standing alone, therefore mandates enforcement of agreements to arbitrate statutory claims. Like any statutory directive, the Arbitration Act's mandate may be overridden by a contrary congressional command. The burden is on the party opposing arbitration, however, to show that Congress intended to preclude a waiver of judicial remedies for the statutory rights at issue. If Congress did intend to limit or prohibit waiver of a judicial forum for a particular claim, such an intent "will be deducible from [the statute's] text or legislative history," *ibid.*, or from an inherent conflict between arbitration and the statute's underlying purposes.

To defeat application of the Arbitration Act in this case, therefore, the McMahons must demonstrate that Congress intended to make an exception to the Arbitration Act for claims arising under RICO and the Exchange Act, an intention discernible from the text, history, or purposes of the statute. We examine the McMahons' arguments regarding the Exchange Act and RICO in turn.

III

When Congress enacted the Exchange Act in 1934, it did not specifically address the question of the arbitrability of § 10(b) claims. The McMahons contend, however, that congressional intent to require a judicial forum for the resolution of § 10(b) claims can be deduced from § 29(a) of the Exchange Act, which declares void "[a]ny condition, stipulation, or provision binding any person to waive compliance with any provision of [the Act]."

First, we reject the McMahons' argument that § 29(a) forbids waiver of § 27 of the Exchange Act. Section 27 provides in relevant part: "The district courts of the United States . . . shall have exclusive jurisdiction of violations of this title or the rules and regulations thereunder, and of all suits in equity and actions at law brought to enforce any liability or duty created by this title or the rules and regulations thereunder."

The McMahons contend that an agreement to waive this jurisdictional provision is unenforceable because § 29(a) voids the waiver of "any provision" of the Exchange Act. The language of § 29(a), however, does not reach so far. What the antiwaiver provision of § 29(a) forbids is enforcement of agreements to waive "compliance" with the provisions of the statute. But § 27 itself does not impose any duty with which persons trading in securities must "comply." By its terms, § 29(a) only prohibits waiver of the substantive obligations imposed by the Exchange Act. Because § 27 does not impose any statutory duties, its waiver does not constitute a waiver of "compliance with any provision" of the Exchange Act under § 29(a).

We do not read *Wilko v. Swan*, as compelling a different result. In *Wilko*, the Court held that a predispute agreement could not be enforced to compel arbitration of a claim arising under § 12(2) of the Securities Act. The basis for the ruling was § 14 of the Securities Act, which, like § 29(a) of the Exchange Act, declares void any stipulation "to waive compliance with any provision" of the statute. At the beginning of its analysis, the *Wilko* Court stated that the Securities Act's jurisdictional provision was "the kind of 'provision' that cannot be waived under § 14 of the Securities Act." This statement, however, can only be understood in the context of the Court's ensuing discussion explaining why arbitration was inadequate as a means of enforcing "the provisions of the Securities Act, advantageous to the buyer." The conclusion in *Wilko* was expressly based on the Court's belief that a judicial forum was needed to protect the substantive rights created by the Securities Act: "As the protective provisions of the Securities Act require the exercise of judicial direction to fairly assure their effectiveness, it seems to us that Congress must have intended § 14 . . . to apply to waiver of judicial trial and review." *Wilko* must be understood, therefore, as holding that the plaintiff's waiver of the "right to select the judicial forum," arbitration was judged inadequate to enforce the statutory rights created by § 12(2).

Indeed, any different reading of *Wilko* would be inconsistent with this Court's decision in *Scherk v. Alberto-Culver Co.* In *Scherk*, the Court upheld enforcement of a predispute agreement to arbitrate Exchange Act claims by parties to an international contract. The *Scherk* Court assumed for purposes of its opinion that *Wilko* applied to the Exchange Act, but it determined that an international contract "involve[d] considerations and policies significantly different from those found controlling in *Wilko*." The Court reasoned that arbitration reduced the uncertainty of international contracts and obviated the danger that a dispute might be submitted to a hostile or unfamiliar forum. At the same time, the Court noted that the advantages of judicial resolution were diminished by the possibility that the opposing party would make "speedy resort to a foreign court." The decision in *Scherk* thus turned on the Court's judgment that under the circumstances of that case, arbitration was an adequate substitute for adjudication as a means of enforcing the parties' statutory rights. *Scherk* supports our understanding that *Wilko* must be read as barring waiver of a judicial forum only where arbitration is inadequate to protect the substantive rights at issue. At the same time, it confirms that where arbitration does provide an adequate means of enforcing the provisions of the Exchange Act, § 29(a) does not void a predispute waiver of § 27 — *Scherk* upheld enforcement of just such a waiver.

The second argument offered by the McMahons is that the arbitration agreement effects an impermissible waiver of the substantive protections of the Exchange Act. Ordinarily, "[b]y agreeing to arbitrate a statutory claim, a party does not forgo the substantive rights afforded by the statute; it only submits to their resolution in an arbitral, rather than a judicial, forum." The McMahons argue, however, that § 29(a) compels a different conclusion. Initially, they contend that predispute agreements are void under § 29(a) because they tend to result from broker overreaching. They reason, as do some commentators, that *Wilko* is premised on the belief "that arbitration clauses in securities sales agreements generally are not freely negotiated." *See, e.g., Sterk, Enforceability of Agreements to Arbitrate: An Examination of the Public Policy Defense*, 2 Cardozo L. Rev. 481, 519 (1981). According to this view, *Wilko* barred enforcement of predispute agreements because of this frequent inequality of bargaining power, reasoning that Congress intended for § 14 generally to ensure that sellers did not "maneuver buyers into a position that might weaken their ability to recover under the Securities Act." 346 U.S., at 432. The McMahons urge that we should interpret § 29(a) in the same fashion.

We decline to give *Wilko* a reading so far at odds with the plain language of § 14, or to adopt such an unlikely interpretation of § 29(a). The concern that § 29(a) is directed against is evident from the statute's plain language: it is a concern with whether an agreement "waive[s] compliance with [a] provision" of the Exchange Act. The voluntariness of the agreement is irrelevant to this inquiry: if a stipulation waives compliance with a statutory duty, it is void under § 29(a), whether voluntary or not. Thus, a customer cannot negotiate a reduction in commissions in exchange for a waiver of compliance with the requirements of the Exchange Act, even if the customer knowingly and voluntarily agreed to the bargain. Section 29(a) is concerned, not with whether brokers "maneuver[ed customers] into" an agreement, but with whether the agreement "weaken[s] their ability to recover under the [Exchange] Act." The former is grounds for revoking the contract under ordinary principles of contract law; the latter is grounds for voiding the agreement under § 29(a).

The other reason advanced by the McMahons for finding a waiver of their § 10(b) rights is that arbitration does "weaken their ability to recover under the [Exchange] Act." That is the heart of the Court's decision in *Wilko*, and respondents urge that we should follow its reasoning. *Wilko* listed several grounds why, in the Court's view, the "effectiveness [of the Act's provisions] in application is lessened in arbitration." First, the *Wilko* Court believed that arbitration proceedings were not suited to cases requiring "subjective findings on the purpose and knowledge of an alleged violator." *Wilko* also was concerned that arbitrators must make legal determinations "without judicial instruction on the law," and that an arbitration award "may be made without explanation of [the arbitrator's] reasons and without a complete record of their proceedings." Finally, *Wilko* noted that the "[p]ower to vacate an award is limited," and that "interpretations of the law by the arbitrators in contrast to manifest disregard are not subject, in the federal courts, to judicial review for error in interpretation." *Wilko* concluded that in view of these drawbacks to arbitration, § 12(2) claims "require[d] the exercise of judicial direction to fairly assure their effectiveness."

As Justice Frankfurter noted in his dissent in *Wilko*, the Court's opinion did not rest on any evidence, either "in the record . . . [or] in the facts of which [it could] take judicial notice," that "the arbitral system . . . would not afford the plaintiff the rights to which he is entitled." Instead, the reasons given in *Wilko* reflect a general suspicion of the desirability of arbitration and the competence of arbitral tribunals — most apply with no greater force to the arbitration of securities disputes than to the arbitration of legal disputes generally. It is difficult to reconcile *Wilko*'s mistrust of the arbitral process with this Court's subsequent decisions involving the Arbitration Act. *See, e.g., Mitsubishi Motors Corp. v. Soler Chrysler-Plymouth, Inc., supra; Dean Witter Reynolds Inc. v. Byrd*, 470 U.S. 213 (1985); *Southland Corp. v. Keating*, 465 U.S. 1 (1984); *Moses H. Cone Memorial Hospital v. Mercury Construction Corp., supra; Scherk v. Alberto-Culver Co., supra.*

Indeed, most of the reasons given in *Wilko* have been rejected subsequently by the Court as a basis for holding claims to be nonarbitrable. In *Mitsubishi*, for example, we recognized that arbitral tribunals are readily capable of handling the factual and legal complexities of antitrust claims, notwithstanding the absence of judicial instruction and supervision. Likewise, we have concluded that the streamlined procedures of arbitration do not entail any consequential restriction on substantive rights. Finally, we have indicated that there is no reason to assume at the outset that arbitrators will not follow the law; although judicial scrutiny of arbitration awards necessarily is limited, such review is sufficient to ensure that arbitrators comply with the requirements of the statute. * * *

The suitability of arbitration as a means of enforcing Exchange Act rights is evident from our decision in *Scherk*. Although the holding in that case was limited to international agreements, the competence of arbitral tribunals to resolve § 10(b) claims is the same in both settings. Courts likewise have routinely enforced agreements to arbitrate § 10(b) claims where both parties are members of a securities exchange or the National Association of Securities Dealers (NASD), suggesting that arbitral tribunals are fully capable of handling such matters. And courts uniformly have concluded that *Wilko* does not apply to the submission to arbitration of existing disputes, even though the inherent suitability of arbitration as a means of resolving § 10(b) claims remains unchanged.

Thus, the mistrust of arbitration that formed the basis for the *Wilko* opinion in 1953 is difficult to square with the assessment of arbitration that has prevailed since that time. This is especially so in light of the intervening changes in the regulatory structure of the securities laws. Even if *Wilko*'s assumptions regarding arbitration were valid at the time *Wilko* was decided, most certainly they do not hold true today for arbitration procedures subject to the SEC's oversight authority.

In 1953, when *Wilko* was decided, the Commission had only limited authority over the rules governing self-regulatory organizations (SROs) — the national securities exchanges and registered securities associations — and this authority appears not to have included any authority at all over their arbitration rules. Since the 1975 amendments to § 19 of the Exchange Act, however, the Commission has had expansive power to ensure the adequacy of the arbitration procedures employed by the SROs. No proposed rule change may take effect unless the SEC finds that the proposed rule is consistent with the requirements of the Exchange Act, 15 U.S.C. § 78s(b)(2); and the Commission has the power, on its own initiative, to "abrogate, add to, and delete from" any SRO rule if it finds such changes necessary or appropriate to further the objectives of the Act, 15 U.S.C. § 78s(c). In short, the Commission has broad authority to oversee and to regulate the rules adopted by the SROs relating to customer disputes, including the power to mandate the adoption of any rules it deems necessary to ensure that arbitration procedures adequately protect statutory rights.

In the exercise of its regulatory authority, the SEC has specifically approved the arbitration procedures of the New York Stock Exchange, the American Stock Exchange, and the NASD, the organizations mentioned in the arbitration agreement at issue in this case. We conclude that where, as in this case, the prescribed procedures are subject to the Commission's § 19 authority, an arbitration agreement does not effect a waiver of the protections of the Act. While *stare decisis* concerns may counsel against upsetting *Wilko*'s contrary conclusion under the Securities Act, we refuse to extend *Wilko*'s reasoning to the Exchange Act in light of these intervening regulatory developments. The McMahons' agreement to submit to arbitration therefore is not tantamount to an impermissible waiver of the McMahons' rights under § 10(b), and the agreement is not void on that basis under § 29(a).

* * *

IV

Unlike the Exchange Act, there is nothing in the text of the RICO statute that even arguably evinces congressional intent to exclude civil RICO claims from the dictates of the Arbitration Act. This silence in the text is matched by silence in the statute's legislative history. The private treble-damages provision codified as 18 U.S.C. § 1964(c) was added to the House version of the bill after the bill had been passed by the Senate, and it received only abbreviated discussion in either House. There is no hint in these legislative debates that Congress intended for RICO treble-damages claims to be excluded from the ambit of the Arbitration Act.

Because RICO's text and legislative history fail to reveal any intent to override the provisions of the Arbitration Act, the McMahons must argue that there is an irreconcilable conflict between arbitration and RICO's underlying purposes. Our decision in *Mitsubishi Motors Corp. v. Soler Chrysler-Plymouth, Inc.*, however, already has addressed many of the grounds given by the McMahons to support this claim. In *Mitsubishi*, we held that nothing in the nature of the federal antitrust laws prohibits parties from agreeing to arbitrate antitrust claims arising out of international commercial transactions. Although the holding in *Mitsubishi* was limited to the international context, much of its reasoning is equally applicable here. Thus, for example, the McMahons have argued that RICO claims are too complex to be subject to arbitration. We determined in *Mitsubishi*, however, that "potential complexity should not suffice to ward off arbitration." Antitrust matters are every bit as complex as RICO claims, but we found that the "adaptability and access to expertise" characteristic of arbitration rebutted the view "that an arbitral tribunal could not properly handle an antitrust matter."

Likewise, the McMahons contend that the "overlap" between RICO's civil and criminal provisions renders § 1964(c) claims nonarbitrable. Yet § 1964(c) is no different in this respect from the federal antitrust laws. In *Sedima, S.P.R.L. v. Imrex Co.* [473 U.S. 479 (1985)], we rejected the view that § 1964(c) "provide[s] civil remedies for offenses criminal in nature." In doing so, this Court observed: "[T]he fact that conduct can result in both criminal liability and treble damages does not mean that there is not a bona fide civil action. The familiar provisions for both criminal liability and treble damages under the antitrust laws indicate as much." *Ibid. Mitsubishi* recognized that treble-damages suits for claims arising under § 1 of the Sherman Act may be subject to arbitration, even though such conduct may also give rise to claims of criminal liability. We similarly find that the criminal provisions of RICO do not preclude arbitration of bona fide civil actions brought under § 1964(c).

The McMahons' final argument is that the public interest in the enforcement of RICO precludes its submission to arbitration. *Mitsubishi* again is relevant to the question. In that case we thoroughly examined the legislative intent behind § 4 of the Clayton Act in assaying whether the importance of the private treble-damages remedy in enforcing the antitrust laws precluded arbitration of § 4 claims. We found that "[n]otwithstanding its important incidental policing function, the treble-damages cause of action . . . seeks primarily to enable an injured competitor to gain compensation for that injury." Emphasizing the priority of the compensatory function of § 4 over its deterrent function, *Mitsubishi* concluded that "so long as the prospective litigant effectively may vindicate its statutory cause of action in the arbitral forum, the statute will continue to serve both its remedial and deterrent function."

*   *   *

Not only does *Mitsubishi* support the arbitrability of RICO claims, but there is even more reason to suppose that arbitration will adequately serve the purposes of RICO than that it will adequately protect private enforcement of the antitrust laws. Antitrust violations generally have a widespread impact on national markets as a whole, and the antitrust treble-damages provision gives private parties an incentive to bring civil suits that serve to advance the national interest in a competitive economy. RICO's drafters likewise sought to provide vigorous incentives for plaintiffs to pursue RICO claims that would advance society's fight against organized crime. But in fact RICO actions are seldom asserted "against the archetypal, intimidating mobster." The special incentives necessary to encourage civil enforcement actions against organized crime do not support nonarbitrability of run-of-the-mill civil RICO claims brought against legitimate enterprises. The private attorney general role for the typical RICO plaintiff is simply less plausible than it is for the typical antitrust plaintiff, and does not support a finding that there is an irreconcilable conflict between arbitration and enforcement of the RICO statute.

In sum, we find no basis for concluding that Congress intended to prevent enforcement of agreements to arbitrate RICO claims. The McMahons may effectively vindicate their RICO claim in an arbitral forum, and therefore there is no inherent conflict between arbitration and the purposes underlying § 1964(c). Moreover, nothing in RICO's text or legislative history otherwise demonstrates congressional intent to make an exception to the Arbitration Act for RICO claims. Accordingly, the McMahons, "having made the bargain to arbitrate," will be held to their bargain. Their RICO claim is arbitrable under the terms of the Arbitration Act.

V

Accordingly, the judgment of the Court of Appeals for the Second Circuit is reversed, and the case is remanded for further proceedings consistent with this opinion.

It is so ordered.

Justice BLACKMUN, with whom Justice BRENNAN and Justice MARSHALL join, concurring in part and dissenting in part.

I concur in the Court's decision to enforce the arbitration agreement with respect to respondents' RICO claims and thus join Parts I, II, and IV of the Court's opinion. I disagree, however, with the Court's conclusion that respondents' § 10(b) claims also are subject to arbitration.

* * *

II

The Court today appears to argue that the *Wilko* Court's assessment of arbitration's inadequacy is outdated, first, because arbitration has improved since 1953, and, second, because the Court no longer considers the criticisms of arbitration made in *Wilko* to be valid reasons why statutory claims, such as those under § 10(b), should not be sent to arbitration. It is true that arbitration procedures in the securities industry have improved since *Wilko's* day. Of particular importance has been the development of a code of arbitration by the Commission with the assistance of representatives of the securities industry and the public.

Even those who favor the arbitration of securities claims do not contend, however, that arbitration has changed so significantly as to eliminate the essential characteristics noted by the *Wilko* Court. Indeed, proponents of arbitration would not see these characteristics as "problems," because, in their view, the characteristics permit the unique "streamlined" nature of the arbitral process. As at the time of *Wilko*, preparation of a record of arbitration proceedings is not invariably required today. Moreover, arbitrators are not bound by precedent and are actually discouraged by their associations from giving reasons for a decision. *See* R. Coulson, Business Arbitration — What You Need to Know 29 (3d ed. 1986) ("Written opinions can be dangerous because they identify targets for the losing party to attack"). Judicial review is still substantially limited to the four grounds listed in § 10 of the Arbitration Act and to the concept of "manifest disregard" of the law.

The Court's "mistrust" of arbitration may have given way recently to an acceptance of this process, not only because of the improvements in arbitration, but also because of the Court's present assumption that the distinctive features of arbitration, its more quick and economical resolution of claims, do not render it inherently inadequate for the resolution of statutory claims. Such reasoning, however, should prevail only in the absence of the congressional policy that places the statutory claimant in a special position with respect to possible violators of his statutory rights. As even the most ardent supporter of arbitration would recognize, the arbitral process at best places the investor on an equal footing with the securities-industry personnel against whom the claims are brought.

Furthermore, there remains the danger that, at worst, compelling an investor to arbitrate securities claims puts him in a forum controlled by the securities industry. This result directly contradicts the goal of both securities Acts to free the investor from the control of the market professional. The Uniform Code provides some safeguards but despite them, and indeed because of the background of the arbitrators, the investor has the impression, frequently justified, that his claims are being judged by a forum composed of individuals sympathetic to the securities industry and not drawn from the public. It is generally recognized that the codes do not define who falls into the category "not from the securities industry." Accordingly, it is often possible for the "public" arbitrators to be attorneys or consultants whose clients have been exchange members or SROs. *See* Panel of Arbitrators 1987-1988, CCH American Stock Exchange Guide 158-160 (1987) (71 out of 116 "public" arbitrators are lawyers). The uniform opposition of investors to compelled arbitration and the overwhelming support of the securities industry for the process suggest that there must be some truth to the investors' belief that the securities industry has an advantage in a forum under its own control. *See* N.Y. Times, Mar. 29, 1987, section 3, p. 8, col. 1 (statement of Sheldon H. Elsen, Chairman, American Bar Association Task Force on Securities Arbitration: "The houses basically like the present system because they own the stacked deck").[20]

---

[20] Commentators have argued that more public participation in the SRO arbitration procedures is needed to give investors the impression that they are not in a forum biased in favor of the securities industry. The amici in support of petitioners and some commentators argue that the statistics concerning the results of arbitration show that the process is not weighted in favor of the securities industry. Such statistics, however, do not indicate the damages received by customers in relation to the damages to which they believed they were entitled. It is possible for an investor to "prevail" in arbitration while recovering a sum considerably less than the damages he actually incurred.

More surprising than the Court's acceptance of the present adequacy of arbitration for the resolution of securities claims is its confidence in the Commission's oversight of the arbitration procedures of the SROs to ensure this adequacy. Such confidence amounts to a wholesale acceptance of the Commission's present position that this oversight undermines the force of *Wilko* and that arbitration therefore should be compelled because the Commission has supervisory authority over the SROs' arbitration procedures. The Court, however, fails to acknowledge that, until it filed an amicus brief in this case, the Commission consistently took the position that § 10(b) claims, like those under § 12(2), should not be sent to arbitration, that predispute arbitration agreements, where the investor was not advised of his right to a judicial forum, were misleading, and that the very regulatory oversight upon which the Commission now relies could not alone make securities-industry arbitration adequate. It is most questionable, then, whether the Commission's recently adopted position is entitled to the deference that the Court accords it.

The Court is swayed by the power given to the Commission by the 1975 amendments to the Exchange Act in order to permit the Commission to oversee the rules and procedures of the SROs, including those dealing with arbitration. Subsequent to the passage of these amendments, however, the Commission has taken the consistent position that predispute arbitration agreements, which did not disclose to an investor that he has a right to a judicial forum, were misleading and possibly actionable under the securities laws. The Commission remained dissatisfied with the continued use of these arbitration agreements and eventually it proposed a rule to prohibit them, explaining that such a prohibition was not inconsistent with its support of arbitration for resolving securities disputes, particularly existing ones. *See* Disclosure Regarding Recourse to the Federal Courts Notwithstanding Arbitration Clauses in Broker-Dealer Customer Agreements, SEC Exchange Act Rel. No. 19813 (May 26, 1983), [1982-1983 Transfer Binder] CCH Fed.Sec.L.Rep. ¶ 83,356, p. 85,967. While emphasizing the Court's *Wilko* decision as a basis for its proposed rule, the Commission noted that its proposal also was in line with its own understanding of the problems with such agreements and with the "[c]ongressional determination that public investors should also have available the special protection of the federal courts for resolution of disputes arising under the federal securities laws." *Id.*, at p. 85,968. Although the rule met with some opposition, it was adopted and *remains in force today*.

Moreover, the Commission's own description of its enforcement capabilities contradicts its position that its general overview of SRO rules and procedures can make arbitration adequate for resolving securities claims. The Commission does not pretend that its oversight consists of anything other than a general review of SRO rules and the ability to require that an SRO adopt or delete a particular rule. It does not contend that its "sweeping authority," includes a review of specific arbitration proceedings. It thus neither polices nor monitors the results of these arbitrations for possible misapplications of securities laws or for indications of how investors fare in these proceedings. Given, in fact, the present constraints on the Commission's resources in this time of market expansion, it is doubtful whether the Commission could undertake to conduct any such review.

Finally, the Court's complacent acceptance of the Commission's oversight is alarming when almost every day brings another example of illegality on Wall Street. *See, e.g.*, N.Y. Times, Jan. 2, 1987, p. B6, col. 3. Many of the abuses recently brought to light, it is true, do not deal with the question of the adequacy of SRO arbitration. They, however, do suggest that the industry's self-regulation, of which the SRO arbitration is a part, is not functioning acceptably. Moreover, these abuses have highlighted the difficulty experienced by the Commission, at a time of growth in the securities market and a decrease in the Commission's staff, to carry out its oversight task. Such inadequacies on the part of the Commission strike at the very heart of the reasoning of the Court, which is content to accept the soothing assurances of the Commission without examining the reality behind them. Indeed, while the amici cite the number of arbitrations of securities disputes as a sign of the success of this process in the industry, these statistics have a more portentous meaning. In this era of deregulation, the growth in complaints about the securities industry, many of which find their way to arbitration, parallels the increase in securities violations and suggests a market not adequately controlled by the SROs. In such a time, one would expect more, not less, judicial involvement in resolution of securities disputes.

III

*   *   *

[The opinion of Justice STEVENS, concurring in part and dissenting in part, is omitted.]

NOTES

1. *Wilko v. Swan*, 346 U.S. 427 (1953), held that a predispute agreement could not be enforced to compel arbitration of a claim arising under § 12(2) of the Securities Act of 1933. *Wilko*'s rationale appeared to be partially predicated on skepticism toward arbitration of alleged violations of the securities laws. Does any of *Wilko*'s fear of arbitration survive *McMahon*? Was *Wilko* impliedly overruled by *McMahon*?

2. Two years after *McMahon* the Supreme Court made the overruling of *Wilko* official. In *Rodriguez de Quijas v. Shearson/American Express, Inc.*, 490 U.S. 477 (1989), the Court ruled 5-4 that courts could compel predispute arbitration of alleged violations of the Securities Act of 1933, and, in so doing, expressly overruled *Wilko v. Swan*. According to the *Rodriguez de Quijas* majority, *Wilko* was incorrectly decided because the 1933 and 1934 securities statutes need to be construed harmoniously to discourage litigants from manipulating legal proceedings. The Court also reasoned that the substantive rights of the investor would not be undermined by resorting to arbitration. *Wilko* was said to be pervaded by an outmoded hostility toward arbitration that had been rejected in *McMahon*, *Mitsubishi* and other post-*Wilko* Supreme Court arbitration decisions. "To the extent that *Wilko* rested on suspicion of arbitration as a method of weakening the protections afforded in the substantive law to would-be complainants, it has fallen far out of step with our current strong endorsement of the federal statutes favoring this method of resolving disputes." (490 U.S. at 481.) The majority also asserted that *Wilko* had ignored the strong policy in favor of arbitration established by the FAA. The dissenters argued vehemently that the court should respect *Wilko*, itself a statutory construction premised decision, because Congress had elected not to amend the settled *Wilko* result for over 35 years.

3. Whether or not one agrees with *Rodriguez*, that decision simplifies matters. It is now clear that all claims brought under the federal securities laws are arbitrable. This means that a claimant who raises various legal theories against a broker knows that each must go to arbitration and that a "dual-track" attack, one in court and the other in arbitration, is no longer warranted. The rhetoric of *McMahon* and *Rodriguez*, together with the almost universal coverage of the FAA force one to ask a broader question, namely, whether there is any variety of a civil claim that is not arbitrable? The subsequent sections of this chapter deal with this question.

4. *McMahon* surely represents the high-watermark of securities arbitration. Since 1987, the year of the *McMahon* decision, the quantity of disputes between broker and investor decided by arbitration has risen dramatically. Yet, what should we make of the opaque statement by the *McMahon* majority that the degree of judicial review of arbitral awards "is sufficient to ensure that arbitrators comply with the requirements of the statute"? Was the Supreme Court suggesting that federal courts review awards for error of law? This sentence has, this far, been largely ignored by courts in the post-*McMahon* years.

5. The *McMahon* decision relied on *Moses H. Cone Memorial Hospital v. Mercury Construction Corp.*, 460 U.S. 1 (1983). The *Moses H. Cone* case involved a construction dispute. The contractor filed a federal lawsuit seeking to compel arbitration. Before this suit the hospital sought declaratory relief in a state court that the matter was not arbitrable. Both suits involved the same issue; whether the dispute should be arbitrable. The Supreme Court affirmed a court of appeals decision compelling arbitration. The decision referred to a "federal policy favoring arbitration" and pronounced boldly that "we vigorously enforce agreements to arbitrate."

6. Recall the discussion of Securities Arbitration at Chapter 8, *supra*. In terms of numbers of cases filed, Securities Arbitration is a success. Over 6,000 claims were filed in 1995, 5,500 in 2000 and 7,000 in 2003. Yet, criticisms of securities arbitration persist, mainly directed at the lack of legitimate consent — the industry uses a standard form contract to impose arbitration on an investor. The recent report of a blue ribbon task force appointed by the NASD urged numerous changes in existing securities arbitration procedure, ranging from earlier appointment of arbitrators, sanctions for discovery abuse, the option for the losing party in a punitive damage award to seek a written opinion with reasons, some pretrial motions, and limited application of law on matters relating to the timeliness of the claim. Some have praised these changes as a step in the right direction. (*See, e.g.*, Joel Seligman, *The Quiet Revolution: Securities Arbitration Confronts the Hard Questions*, 33 HOUS. L. REV. 327 (1996); Edward Brunet, *Toward Changing Models of Securities Arbitration*, 62 BROOK. L. REV. 1459 (1996).) Others have been strongly critical of these "reforms" because of their tendency to shift the arbitration model to one more closely resembling litigation. (*See, e.g.,* Bruce Selya, *Arbitration Unbound: The Legacy of McMahon,* 62 BROOK. L. REV. 1433 (1996).) Some of these suggested reforms are still awaiting action.

B.   EMPLOYMENT ARBITRATION

ALEXANDER v. GARDNER-DENVER COMPANY
415 U.S. 36 (1974)

Mr. Justice POWELL delivered the opinion of the Court.

This case concerns the proper relationship between federal courts and the grievance-arbitration machinery of collective-bargaining agreements in the resolution and enforcement of an individual's rights to equal employment opportunities under Title VII of the Civil Rights Act of 1964, 78 Stat. 253, 42 U.S.C. § 2000e *et seq.* Specifically, we must decide under what circumstances, if any, an employee's statutory right to a trial *de novo* under Title VII may be foreclosed by prior submission of his claim to final arbitration under the nondiscrimination clause of a collective-bargaining agreement.

I

In May 1966, petitioner Harrell Alexander, Sr., a black, was hired by respondent Gardner-Denver Co. (the company) to perform maintenance work at the company's plant in Denver, Colorado. In June 1968, petitioner was awarded a trainee position as a drill operator. He remained at that job until his discharge from employment on September 29, 1969. The company informed petitioner that he was being discharged for producing too many defective or unusable parts that had to be scrapped.

On October 1, 1969, petitioner filed a grievance under the collective-bargaining agreement in force between the company and petitioner's union, Local No. 3029 of the United Steelworkers of America (the union). The grievance stated: "I feel I have been unjustly discharged and ask that I be reinstated with full seniority and pay." No explicit claim of racial discrimination was made.

Under Art. 4 of the collective-bargaining agreement, the company retained "the right to hire, suspend or discharge [employees] for proper cause." Article 5, § 2, provided, however, that "there shall be no discrimination against any employee on account of race, color, religion, sex, national origin, or ancestry," and Art. 23, § 6(a), stated that "[n]o employee will be discharged, suspended or given a written warning notice except for just cause." The agreement also contained a broad arbitration clause covering "differences aris[ing] between the Company and the Union as to the meaning and application of the provisions of this Agreement" and "any trouble aris[ing] in the plant." Disputes were to be submitted to a multistep grievance procedure, the first four steps of which involved negotiations between the company and the union. If the dispute remained unresolved, it was to be remitted to compulsory arbitration. The company and the union were to select and pay the arbitrator, and his decision was to be "final and binding upon the Company, the Union, and any employee or employees involved." The agreement further provided that "[t]he arbitrator shall not amend, take away, add to, or change any of the provisions of this Agreement, and the arbitrator's decision must be based solely upon an interpretation of the provisions of this Agreement." The parties also agreed that there "shall be no suspension of work" over disputes covered by the grievance arbitration clause.

The union processed petitioner's grievance through the above machinery. In the final pre-arbitration step, petitioner raised, apparently for the first time, the claim that his discharge resulted from racial discrimination. The company rejected all of petitioner's claims, and the grievance proceeded to arbitration. Prior to the arbitration hearing, however, petitioner filed a charge of racial discrimination with the Colorado Civil Rights Commission, which referred the complaint to the Equal Employment Opportunity Commission on November 5, 1969.

At the arbitration hearing on November 20, 1969, petitioner testified that his discharge was the result of racial discrimination and informed the arbitrator that he had filed a charge with the Colorado Commission because he "could not rely on the union." The union introduced a letter in which petitioner stated that he was "knowledgeable that in the same plant others have scrapped an equal amount and sometimes in excess, but by all logical reasoning I . . . have been the target of preferential discriminatory treatment." The union representative also testified that the company's usual practice was to transfer unsatisfactory trainee drill operators back to their former positions.

On December 30, 1969, the arbitrator ruled that petitioner had been "discharged for just cause." He made no reference to petitioner's claim of racial discrimination. The arbitrator stated that the union had failed to produce evidence of a practice of transferring rather than discharging trainee drill operators who accumulated excessive scrap, but he suggested that the company and the union confer on whether such an arrangement was feasible in the present case.

On July 25, 1970, the Equal Employment Opportunity Commission determined that there was not reasonable cause to believe that a violation of Title VII of the Civil Rights Act of 1964, 42 U.S.C. § 2000e *et seq.*, had occurred. The Commission later notified petitioner of his right to institute a civil action in federal court within 30 days. Petitioner then filed the present action in the United States District Court for the District of Colorado, alleging that his discharge resulted from a racially discriminatory employment practice in violation of § 703(a)(1) of the Act, 42 U.S.C. § 2000e — 2(a)(1).

The District Court granted respondent's motion for summary judgment and dismissed the action. 346 F.Supp. 1012 (1971). The court found that the claim of racial discrimination had been submitted to the arbitrator and resolved adversely to petitioner. It then held that petitioner, having voluntarily elected to pursue his grievance to final arbitration under the nondiscrimination clause of the collective-bargaining agreement, was bound by the arbitral decision and thereby precluded from suing his employer under Title VII. The Court of

Appeals for the Tenth Circuit affirmed *per curiam* on the basis of the District Court's opinion. 466 F.2d 1209 (1972).

We granted petitioner's application for certiorari. We reverse.

II

Congress enacted Title VII of the Civil Rights Act of 1964, 42 U.S.C. § 2000e *et seq.*, to assure equality of employment opportunities by eliminating those practices and devices that discriminate on the basis of race, color, religion, sex, or national origin. Cooperation and voluntary compliance were selected as the preferred means for achieving this goal. To this end, Congress created the Equal Employment Opportunity Commission and established a procedure whereby existing state and local equal employment opportunity agencies, as well as the Commission, would have an opportunity to settle disputes through conference, conciliation, and persuasion before the aggrieved party was permitted to file a lawsuit. In the Equal Employment Opportunity Act of 1972, Pub. L. 92 — 261,86 Stat. 103, Congress amended Title VII to provide the Commission with further authority to investigate individual charges of discrimination, to promote voluntary compliance with the requirements of Title VII, and to institute civil actions against employers or unions named in a discrimination charge.

Even in its amended form, however, Title VII does not provide the Commission with direct powers of enforcement. The Commission cannot adjudicate claims or impose administrative sanctions. Rather, final responsibility for enforcement of Title VII is vested with federal courts. The Act authorizes courts to issue injunctive relief and to order such affirmative action as may be appropriate to remedy the effects of unlawful employment practices. 42 U.S.C. §§ 2000e — 5(f) and (g) (1970 ed., Supp. II). Courts retain these broad remedial powers despite a Commission finding of no reasonable cause to believe that the Act has been violated. *McDonnell Douglas Corp. v. Green* [411 U.S. 792 (1973)]. Taken together, these provisions make plain that federal courts have been assigned plenary powers to secure compliance with Title VII.

In addition to reposing ultimate authority in federal courts, Congress gave private individuals a significant role in the enforcement process of Title VII. Individual grievants usually initiate the Commission's investigatory and conciliatory procedures. And although the 1972 amendment to Title VII empowers the Commission to bring its own actions, the private right of action remains an essential means of obtaining judicial enforcement of Title VII. 42 U.S.C. § 2000e — 5(f)(1) (1970 ed., Supp. II). In such cases, the private litigant not only redresses his own injury but also vindicates the important congressional policy against discriminatory employment practices.

Pursuant to this statutory scheme, petitioner initiated the present action for judicial consideration of his rights under Title VII. The District Court and the Court of Appeals held, however, that petitioner was bound by the prior arbitral decision and had no right to sue under Title VII. Both courts evidently thought that this result was dictated by notions of election of remedies and waiver and by the federal policy favoring arbitration of labor disputes, as enunciated by this Court in *Textile Workers Union v. Lincoln Mills*, 353 U.S. 448 (1957). We disagree.

III

Title VII does not speak expressly to the relationship between federal courts and the grievance-arbitration machinery of collective-bargaining agreements. It does, however, vest federal courts with plenary powers to enforce the statutory requirements; and it specifies with precision the jurisdictional prerequisites that an individual must satisfy before he is entitled to institute a lawsuit. In the present case, these prerequisites were met when petitioner (1) filed timely a charge of employment discrimination with the Commission, and (2) received and acted upon the Commission's statutory notice of the right to sue. 42 U.S.C. § 2000e — 5(b), (e), and (f). There is no suggestion in the statutory scheme that a prior arbitral decision either forecloses an individual's right to sue or divests federal courts of jurisdiction.

In addition, legislative enactments in this area have long evinced a general intent to accord parallel or overlapping remedies against discrimination. In the Civil Rights Act of 1964, 42 U.S.C. § 2000a *et seq.*, Congress indicated that it considered the policy against discrimination to be of the 'highest priority.' Consistent with this view, Title VII provides for consideration of employment-discrimination claims in several forums. *See* 42 U.S.C. § 2000e — 5(b) (1970 ed., Supp. II) (EEOC); 42 U.S.C. § 2000e — 5(c) (1970 ed., Supp. II) (state and local agencies); 42 U.S.C. § 2000e — 5(f) (1970 ed., Supp. II) (federal courts). And, in general, submission of a claim to one forum does not preclude a later submission to another. Moreover, the legislative history of Title VII manifests a congressional intent to allow an individual to pursue independently his rights under both Title VII and other applicable state and federal statutes. The clear inference is that Title VII was designed to supplement rather than supplant, existing laws and institutions relating to employment discrimination. In sum, Title VII's purpose and procedures strongly suggest that an individual does not forfeit his private cause of action if he first pursues his grievance to final arbitration under the nondiscrimination clause of a collective-bargaining agreement.

In reaching the opposite conclusion, the District Court relied in part on the doctrine of election of remedies. That doctrine, which refers to situations where an individual pursues remedies that are legally or factually inconsistent, has no application in the present context. In submitting his grievance to arbitration, an employee seeks to vindicate his contractual right under a collective-bargaining agreement. By contrast, in filing a lawsuit under Title VII, an employee asserts independent statutory rights accorded by Congress. The distinctly separate nature of these contractual and statutory rights is not vitiated merely because both were violated as a result of the same factual occurrence. And certainly no inconsistency results from permitting both rights to be enforced in their respectively appropriate forums. The resulting scheme is somewhat analogous to the procedure under the National Labor Relations Act, as amended, where disputed transactions may implicate both contractual and statutory rights. Where the statutory right underlying a particular claim may not be abridged by contractual agreement, the Court has recognized that consideration of the claim by the arbitrator as a contractual dispute under the collective-bargaining agreement does not preclude subsequent consideration of the claim by the National Labor Relations Board as an unfair labor practice charge or as a petition for clarification of the union's representation certificate under the Act. *Carey v. Westinghouse Electric Corp.*, 375 U.S. 261 (1964). There, as here, the relationship between the forums is complementary since consideration of the claim by both forums may promote the policies underlying each. Thus, the rationale behind the election-of-remedies doctrine cannot support the decision below.

We are also unable to accept the proposition that petitioner waived his cause of action under Title VII. To begin, we think it clear that there can be no prospective waiver of an employee's rights under Title VII. It is true, of course, that a union may waive certain statutory rights related to collective activity, such as the right to strike. These rights are conferred on employees collectively to foster the processes of bargaining and properly may be exercised or relinquished by the union as collective-bargaining agent to obtain economic benefits for union members. Title VII, on the other hand, stands on plainly different ground; it concerns not majoritarian processes, but an individual's right to equal employment opportunities. Title VII's strictures are absolute and represent a congressional command that each employee be free from discriminatory practices. Of necessity, the rights conferred can form no part of the collective-bargaining process since waiver of these rights would defeat the paramount congressional purpose behind Title VII. In these circumstances, an employee's rights under Title VII are not susceptible of prospective waiver. *See Wilko v. Swan*, 346 U.S. 427 (1953).

The actual submission of petitioner's grievance to arbitration in the present case does not alter the situation. Although presumably an employee may waive his cause of action under Title VII as part of a voluntary settlement, mere resort to the arbitral forum to enforce contractual rights constitutes no such waiver. Since an employee's rights under Title VII may not be waived prospectively, existing contractual rights and remedies against discrimination must result from other concessions already made by the union as part of the economic bargain struck with the employer. It is settled law that no additional concession may be exacted from any employee as the price for enforcing those rights.

Moreover, a contractual right to submit a claim to arbitration is not displaced simply because Congress also has provided a statutory right against discrimination. Both rights have legally independent origins and are equally available to the aggrieved employee. This point becomes apparent through consideration of the role of the arbitrator in the system of industrial self-government. As the proctor of the bargain, the arbitrator's task is to effectuate the intent of the parties. His source of authority is the collective-bargaining agreement, and he must interpret and apply that agreement in accordance with the "industrial common law of the shop" and the various needs and desires of the parties. The arbitrator, however, has no general authority to invoke public laws that conflict with the bargain between the parties:

"[A]n arbitrator is confined to interpretation and application of the collective bargaining agreement; he does not sit to dispense his own brand of industrial justice. He may of course look for guidance from many sources, yet his award is legitimate only so long as it draws its essence from the collective bargaining agreement. When the arbitrator's words manifest an infidelity to this obligation, courts have no choice but to refuse enforcement of the award." . . .

If an arbitral decision is based "solely upon the arbitrator's view of the requirements of enacted legislation," rather than on an interpretation of the collective-bargaining agreement, the arbitrator has "exceeded the scope of the submission," and the award will not be enforced. *Ibid.* Thus the arbitrator has authority to resolve only questions of contractual rights, and this authority remains regardless of whether certain contractual rights are similar to, or duplicative of, the substantive rights secured by Title VII.

IV

The District Court and the Court of Appeals reasoned that to permit an employee to have his claim considered in both the arbitral and judicial forums would be unfair since this would mean that the employer, but not the employee, was bound by the arbitral award. In the District Court's words, it could not "accept a philosophy which gives the employee two strings to his bow when the employer has only one." This argument mistakes the effect of Title VII. Under the Steelworkers trilogy, an arbitral decision is final and binding on the employer and employee, and judicial review is limited as to both. But in instituting an action under Title VII, the employee is not seeking review of the arbitrator's decision. Rather, he is asserting a statutory right independent of the arbitration process. An employer does not have "two strings to his bow" with respect to an arbitral decision for the simple reason that Title VII does not provide employers with a cause of action against employees. An employer cannot be the victim of discriminatory employment practices.

The District Court and the Court of Appeals also thought that to permit a later resort to the judicial forum would undermine substantially the employer's incentive to arbitrate and would "sound the death knell for arbitration clauses in labor contracts." 346 F.Supp., at 1019. Again, we disagree. The primary incentive for an employer to enter into an arbitration agreement is the union's reciprocal promise not to strike. As the Court stated in *Boys Markets, Inc. v. Retail Clerk's Union*, 398 U.S. 235, 248 (1970), "a no-strike obligation, express or implied, is the quid pro quo for an undertaking by the employer to submit grievance disputes to the process of arbitration." It is not unreasonable to assume that most employers will regard the benefits derived from a no-strike pledge as outweighing whatever costs may result from according employees an arbitral remedy against discrimination in addition to their judicial remedy under Title VII. Indeed, the severe consequences of a strike may make an arbitration clause almost essential from both the employees' and the employer's perspective. Moreover, the grievance-arbitration machinery of the collective-bargaining agreement remains a relatively inexpensive and expeditious means for resolving a wide range of disputes, including claims of discriminatory employment practices. Where the collective-bargaining agreement contains a nondiscrimination clause similar to Title VII, and where arbitral procedures are fair and regular, arbitration may well produce a settlement satisfactory to both employer and employee. An employer thus has an incentive to make available the conciliatory and therapeutic processes of arbitration which may satisfy an employee's perceived need to resort to the judicial forum, thus saving the employer the expense and aggravation associated with a lawsuit. For similar reasons, the employee also has a strong incentive to arbitrate grievances, and arbitration may often eliminate those misunderstandings or discriminatory practices that might otherwise precipitate resort to the judicial forum.

V

Respondent contends that even if a preclusion rule is not adopted, federal courts should defer to arbitral decisions on discrimination claims where: (i) the claim was before the arbitrator; (ii) the collective-bargaining agreement prohibited the form of discrimination charged in the suit under Title VII; and (iii) the arbitrator has authority to rule on the claim and to fashion a remedy. Under respondent's proposed rule, a court would grant summary judgment and dismiss the employee's action if the above conditions were met. The rule's obvious consequence in the present case would be to deprive the petitioner of his statutory right to attempt to establish his claim in a federal court.

At the outset, it is apparent that a deferral rule would be subject to many of the objections applicable to a preclusion rule. The purpose and procedures of Title VII indicate that Congress intended federal courts to exercise final responsibility for enforcement of Title VII; deferral to arbitral decisions would be inconsistent with that goal. Furthermore, we have long recognized that "the choice of forums inevitably affects the scope of the substantive right to be vindicated." *U.S. Bulk Carriers v. Arguelles*, 400 U.S. 351, 359-60 (1971) (Harlan, J., concurring). Respondent's deferral rule is necessarily premised on the assumption that arbitral processes are commensurate with judicial processes and that Congress impliedly intended federal courts to defer to arbitral decisions on Title VII issues. We deem this supposition unlikely.

Arbitral procedures, while well suited to the resolution of contractual disputes, make arbitration a comparatively inappropriate forum for the final resolution of rights created by Title VII. This conclusion rests first on the special role of the arbitrator, whose task is to effectuate the intent of the parties rather than the requirements of enacted legislation. Where the collective-bargaining agreement conflicts with Title VII, the arbitrator must follow the agreement. To be sure, the tension between contractual and statutory objectives may be mitigated where a collective-bargaining agreement contains provisions facially similar to those of Title VII. But other facts may still render arbitral processes comparatively inferior to judicial processes in the protection of Title VII rights. Among these is the fact that the specialized competence of arbitrators pertains primarily to the law of the shop, not the law of the land. *United Steelworkers of America v. Warrior & Gulf Navigation Co.*, 363 U.S. 574 (1960). Parties usually choose an arbitrator because they trust his knowledge and judgment concerning the demands and norms of industrial relations. On the other hand, the resolution of statutory or constitutional issues is a primary responsibility of courts, and judicial construction has proved especially necessary with respect to Title VII, whose broad language frequently can be given meaning only by reference to public law concepts.

Moreover, the factfinding process in arbitration usually is not equivalent to judicial factfinding. The record of the arbitration proceedings is not as complete; the usual rules of evidence do not apply; and rights and procedures common to civil trials, such as discovery, compulsory process, cross-examination, and testimony under oath, are often severely limited or unavailable. And as this Court has recognized, "[a]rbitrators have no obligation to the court to give their reasons for an award." *United Steelworkers of America v. Enterprise Wheel & Car Corp.*, 363 U.S. [593 (1960)], at 598. Indeed, it is the informality of arbitral procedure that enables it to function as an efficient, inexpensive, and expeditious means for dispute resolution. This same characteristic, however, makes arbitration a less appropriate forum for final resolution of Title VII issues than the federal courts.

It is evident that respondent's proposed rule would not allay these concerns. Nor are we convinced that the solution lies in applying a more demanding deferral standard, such as that adopted by the Fifth Circuit in *Rios v. Reynolds Metals Co.*, 467 F.2d 54 (5th Cir. 1972). As respondent points out, a standard that adequately insured effectuation of Title VII rights in the arbitral forum would tend to make arbitration a procedurally complex, expensive, and time-consuming process. And judicial enforcement of such a standard would almost require courts to make *de novo* determinations of the employees' claims. It is uncertain whether any minimal savings in judicial time and expense would justify the risk to vindication of Title VII rights.

A deferral rule also might adversely affect the arbitration system as well as the enforcement scheme of Title VII. Fearing that the arbitral forum cannot adequately protect their rights under Title VII, some employees may elect to bypass arbitration and institute a lawsuit. The possibility of voluntary compliance or settlement of Title VII claims would thus be reduced, and the result could well be more litigation, not less.

We think, therefore, that the federal policy favoring arbitration of labor disputes and the federal policy against discriminatory employment practices can best be accommodated by permitting an employee to pursue fully both his remedy under the grievance-arbitration clause of a collective-bargaining agreement and his cause of action under Title VII. the federal court should consider the employee's claim de novo. The arbitral decision may be admitted as evidence and accorded such weight as the court deems appropriate.[21]

The judgment of the Court of Appeals is reversed.

---

[21] We adopt no standards as to the weight to be accorded an arbitral decision, since this must be determined in the court's discretion with regard to the facts and circumstances of each case. Relevant factors include the existence of provisions in the collective bargaining agreement that conform substantially with Title VII, the degree of procedural fairness in the arbitral forum, adequacy of the record with respect to the issue of discrimination, and the special competence of particular arbitrators. Where an arbitral determination gives full consideration to an employee's Title VII rights, a court may properly accord it great weight. This is especially true where the issue is solely one of fact, specifically addressed by the parties and decided by the arbitrator on the basis of an adequate record. But courts should ever be mindful that Congress, in enacting Title VII, thought it necessary to provide a judicial forum for the ultimate resolution of discriminatory employment claims. It is the duty of courts to assure the full availability of this forum.

GILMER v. INTERSTATE/JOHNSON LANE CORPORATION
500 U.S. 20 (1991)

Justice WHITE delivered the opinion of the Court.

The question presented in this case is whether a claim under the Age Discrimination in Employment Act of 1967 (ADEA) can be subjected to compulsory arbitration pursuant to an arbitration agreement in a securities registration application. The Court of Appeals held that it could, 895 F.2d 195 (4th Cir. 1990), and we affirm.

I

Respondent Interstate/Johnson Lane Corporation (Interstate) hired petitioner Robert Gilmer as a Manager of Financial Services in May 1981. As required by his employment, Gilmer registered as a securities representative with several stock exchanges, including the New York Stock Exchange (NYSE). His registration application, entitled "Uniform Application for Securities Industry Registration or Transfer," provided, among other things, that Gilmer "agree[d] to arbitrate any dispute, claim or controversy" arising between him and Interstate "that is required to be arbitrated under the rules, constitutions or by-laws of the organizations with which I register." Of relevance to this case, NYSE Rule 347 provides for arbitration of "[a]ny controversy between a registered representative and any member or member organization arising out of the employment or termination of employment of such registered representative."

Interstate terminated Gilmer's employment in 1987, at which time Gilmer was 62 years of age. After first filing an age discrimination charge with the Equal Employment Opportunity Commission (EEOC), Gilmer subsequently brought suit in the United States District Court for the Western District of North Carolina, alleging that Interstate had discharged him because of his age, in violation of the ADEA. In response to Gilmer's complaint, Interstate filed in the District Court a motion to compel arbitration of the ADEA claim. In its motion, Interstate relied upon the arbitration agreement in Gilmer's registration application, as well as the Federal Arbitration Act (FAA), 9 U.S.C. § 1 *et seq.* The District Court denied Interstate's motion, based on this Court's decision in *Alexander v. Gardner-Denver Co.*, 415 U.S. 36 (1974), and because it concluded that "Congress intended to protect ADEA claimants from the waiver of a judicial forum." The United States Court of Appeals for the Fourth Circuit reversed, finding "nothing in the text, legislative history, or underlying purposes of the ADEA indicating a congressional intent to preclude enforcement of arbitration agreements." We granted certiorari, to resolve a conflict among the Courts of Appeals regarding the arbitrability of ADEA claims.

II

The FAA was originally enacted in 1925, 43 Stat. 883, and then reenacted and codified in 1947 as Title 9 of the United States Code. Its purpose was to reverse the longstanding judicial hostility to arbitration agreements that had existed at English common law and had been adopted by American courts, and to place arbitration agreements upon the same footing as other contracts. Its primary substantive provision states that "[a] written provision in any maritime transaction or a contract evidencing a transaction involving commerce to settle by arbitration a controversy thereafter arising out of such contract or transaction . . . shall be valid, irrevocable, and enforceable, save upon such grounds as exist at law or in equity for the revocation of any contract." 9 U.S.C. § 2. The FAA also provides for stays of proceedings in federal district courts when an issue in the proceeding is referable to arbitration, § 3, and for orders compelling arbitration when one party has failed, neglected, or refused to comply with an arbitration agreement, § 4. These provisions manifest a "liberal federal policy favoring arbitration agreements." *Moses H. Cone Memorial Hospital v. Mercury Construction Corp.*, 460 U.S. 1, 24 (1983).[2]

It is by now clear that statutory claims may be the subject of an arbitration agreement, enforceable pursuant to the FAA. Indeed, in recent years we have held enforceable arbitration agreements relating to claims arising under the Sherman Act, of the Securities Exchange Act of 1934; the civil provisions of the Racketeer Influenced and Corrupt Organizations Act (RICO), and § 12(2) of the Securities Act of 1933. In these cases we recognized that "[b]y agreeing to arbitrate a statutory claim, a party does not forgo the substantive rights afforded by the statute; it only submits to their resolution in an arbitral, rather than a judicial, forum."

Although all statutory claims may not be appropriate for arbitration, "[h]aving made the bargain to arbitrate, the party should be held to it unless Congress itself has evinced an intention to preclude a waiver of judicial remedies for the statutory rights at issue." In this regard, we note that the burden is on Gilmer to show that Congress intended to preclude a waiver of a judicial forum for ADEA claims. If such an intention exists, it will be discoverable in the text of the ADEA, its legislative history, or an "inherent conflict" between arbitration and the ADEA's underlying purposes. Throughout such an inquiry, it should be kept in mind that "questions of arbitrability

---

[2] Section 1 of the FAA provides that "nothing herein contained shall apply to contracts of employment of seamen, railroad employees, or any other class of workers engaged in foreign or interstate commerce." 9 U.S.C. § 1. Several amici curiae in support of Gilmer argue that that section excludes from the coverage of the FAA all "contracts of employment." Gilmer, however, did not raise the issue in the courts below; it was not addressed there; and it was not among the questions presented in the petition for certiorari. In any event, it would be inappropriate to address the scope of the § 1 exclusion because the arbitration clause being enforced here is not contained in a contract of employment. The FAA requires that the arbitration clause being enforced be in writing. *See* 9 U.S.C. §§ 2, 3. The record before us does not show, and the parties do not contend, that Gilmer's employment agreement with Interstate contained a written arbitration clause. Rather, the arbitration clause at issue is in Gilmer's securities registration application, which is a contract with the securities exchanges, not with Interstate. The lower courts addressing the issue uniformly have concluded that the exclusionary clause in § 1 of the FAA is inapplicable to arbitration clauses contained in such registration applications. [Citing cases.] We implicitly assumed as much in *Perry v. Thomas*, 482 U.S. 483 (1987), where we held that the FAA required a former employee of a securities firm to arbitrate his statutory wage claim against his former employer, pursuant to an arbitration clause in his registration application. Unlike the dissent, we choose to follow the plain language of the FAA and the weight of authority, and we therefore hold that § 1's exclusionary clause does not apply to Gilmer's arbitration agreement. Consequently, we leave for another day the issue raised by *amici curiae*.

must be addressed with a healthy regard for the federal policy favoring arbitration."

III

Gilmer concedes that nothing in the text of the ADEA or its legislative history explicitly precludes arbitration. He argues, however, that compulsory arbitration of ADEA claims pursuant to arbitration agreements would be inconsistent with the statutory framework and purposes of the ADEA. Like the Court of Appeals, we disagree.

A

Congress enacted the ADEA in 1967 "to promote employment of older persons based on their ability rather than age; to prohibit arbitrary age discrimination in employment; [and] to help employers and workers find ways of meeting problems arising from the impact of age on employment." To achieve those goals, the ADEA, among other things, makes it unlawful for an employer "to fail or refuse to hire or to discharge any individual or otherwise discriminate against any individual with respect to his compensation, terms, conditions, or privileges of employment, because of such individual's age." This proscription is enforced both by private suits and by the EEOC. In order for an aggrieved individual to bring suit under the ADEA, he or she must first file a charge with the EEOC and then wait at least 60 days. An individual's right to sue is extinguished, however, if the EEOC institutes an action against the employer. § 626(c)(1). Before the EEOC can bring such an action, though, it must "attempt to eliminate the discriminatory practice or practices alleged, and to effect voluntary compliance with the requirements of this chapter through informal methods of conciliation, conference, and persuasion."

As Gilmer contends, the ADEA is designed not only to address individual grievances, but also to further important social policies. We do not perceive any inherent inconsistency between those policies, however, and enforcing agreements to arbitrate age discrimination claims. It is true that arbitration focuses on specific disputes between the parties involved. The same can be said, however, of judicial resolution of claims. Both of these dispute resolution mechanisms nevertheless also can further broader social purposes. The Sherman Act, the Securities Exchange Act of 1934, RICO, and the Securities Act of 1933 all are designed to advance important public policies, but, as noted above, claims under those statutes are appropriate for arbitration. "[S]o long as the prospective litigant effectively may vindicate [his or her] statutory cause of action in the arbitral forum, the statute will continue to serve both its remedial and deterrent function."

We also are unpersuaded by the argument that arbitration will undermine the role of the EEOC in enforcing the ADEA. An individual ADEA claimant subject to an arbitration agreement will still be free to file a charge with the EEOC, even though the claimant is not able to institute a private judicial action. Indeed, Gilmer filed a charge with the EEOC in this case. In any event, the EEOC's role in combating age discrimination is not dependent on the filing of a charge; the agency may receive information concerning alleged violations of the ADEA "from any source," and it has independent authority to investigate age discrimination. Moreover, nothing in the ADEA indicates that Congress intended that the EEOC be involved in all employment disputes. Such disputes can be settled, for example, without any EEOC involvement. Finally, the mere involvement of an administrative agency in the enforcement of a statute is not sufficient to preclude arbitration. For example, the Securities Exchange Commission is heavily involved in the enforcement of the Securities Exchange Act of 1934 and the Securities Act of 1933, but we have held that claims under both of those statutes may be subject to compulsory arbitration. *See Shearson/American Express, Inc. v. McMahon*, 482 U.S. 220 (1987). *Rodriguez de Quijas v. Shearson/American Express, Inc.*, 490 U.S. 477 (1989).

Gilmer also argues that compulsory arbitration is improper because it deprives claimants of the judicial forum provided for by the ADEA. Congress, however, did not explicitly preclude arbitration or other nonjudicial resolution of claims, even in its recent amendments to the ADEA. "[I]f Congress intended the substantive protection afforded [by the ADEA] to include protection against waiver of the right to a judicial forum, that intention will be deducible from text or legislative history." Moreover, Gilmer's argument ignores the ADEA's flexible approach to resolution of claims. The EEOC, for example, is directed to pursue "informal methods of conciliation, conference, and persuasion," 29 U.S.C. § 626(b), which suggests that out-of-court dispute resolution, such as arbitration, is consistent with the statutory scheme established by Congress. In addition, arbitration is consistent with Congress' grant of concurrent jurisdiction over ADEA claims to state and federal courts, (allowing suits to be brought "in any court of competent jurisdiction"), because arbitration agreements, "like the provision for concurrent jurisdiction, serve to advance the objective of allowing [claimants] a broader right to select the forum for resolving disputes, whether it be judicial or otherwise."

B

In arguing that arbitration is inconsistent with the ADEA, Gilmer also raises a host of challenges to the adequacy of arbitration procedures. Initially, we note that in our recent arbitration cases we have already rejected most of these arguments as insufficient to preclude arbitration of statutory claims. Such generalized attacks on arbitration "res[t] on suspicion of arbitration as a method of weakening the protections afforded in the substantive law to would-be complainants," and as such, they are "far out of step with our current strong endorsement of the federal statutes favoring this method of resolving disputes." Consequently, we address these arguments only briefly.

Gilmer first speculates that arbitration panels will be biased. However, "[w]e decline to indulge the presumption that the parties and arbitral body conducting a proceeding will be unable or unwilling to retain competent, conscientious and impartial arbitrators." In any event, we note that the NYSE arbitration rules, which are applicable to the dispute in this case, provide protections against biased panels. The rules require, for example, that the parties be informed of the employment histories of the arbitrators, and that they be allowed to make further inquiries into the arbitrators' backgrounds. In addition, each party is allowed one peremptory challenge and unlimited challenges for cause. Moreover, the arbitrators are required to disclose "any circumstances which might preclude [them] from rendering an objective and impartial determination." The FAA also protects against bias, by providing that courts may overturn arbitration decisions "[w]here there was evident partiality or corruption in the arbitrators." 9 U.S.C. § 10(b). There has been no showing in this case that those provisions are inadequate to guard against potential bias.

Gilmer also complains that the discovery allowed in arbitration is more limited than in the federal courts, which he contends will make it difficult to prove discrimination. It is unlikely, however, that age discrimination claims require more extensive discovery than other claims that we have found to be arbitrable, such as RICO and antitrust claims. Moreover, there has been no showing in this case that the NYSE discovery provisions, which allow for document production, information requests, depositions, and subpoenas, will prove insufficient to allow ADEA claimants such as Gilmer a fair opportunity to present their claims. Although those procedures might not be as extensive as in the federal courts, by agreeing to arbitrate, a party "trades the procedures and opportunity for review of the courtroom for the simplicity, informality, and expedition of arbitration." Indeed, an important counterweight to the reduced discovery in NYSE arbitration is that arbitrators are not bound by the rules of evidence.

A further alleged deficiency of arbitration is that arbitrators often will not issue written opinions, resulting, Gilmer contends, in a lack of public knowledge of employers' discriminatory policies, an inability to obtain effective appellate review, and a stifling of the development of the law. The NYSE rules, however, do require that all arbitration awards be in writing, and that the awards contain the names of the parties, a summary of the issues in controversy, and a description of the award issued. In addition, the award decisions are made available to the public. Furthermore, judicial decisions addressing ADEA claims will continue to be issued because it is unlikely that all or even most ADEA claimants will be subject to arbitration agreements. Finally, Gilmer's concerns apply equally to settlements of ADEA claims, which, as noted above, are clearly allowed.[4]

It is also argued that arbitration procedures cannot adequately further the purposes of the ADEA because they do not provide for broad equitable relief and class actions. As the court below noted, however, arbitrators do have the power to fashion equitable relief. Indeed, the NYSE rules applicable here do not restrict the types of relief an arbitrator may award, but merely refer to "damages and/or other relief." The NYSE rules also provide for collective proceedings. But "even if the arbitration could not go forward as a class action or class relief could not be granted by the arbitrator, the fact that the [ADEA] provides for the possibility of bringing a collective action does not mean that

---

[4] Gilmer also contends that judicial review of arbitration decisions is too limited. We have stated, however, that "although judicial scrutiny of arbitration awards necessarily is limited, such review is sufficient to ensure that arbitrators comply with the requirements of the statute" at issue. *Shearson/American Express Inc. v. McMahon*, 482 U.S. 220, 232 (1987).

individual attempts at conciliation were intended to be barred." Finally, it should be remembered that arbitration agreements will not preclude the EEOC from bringing actions seeking class-wide and equitable relief.

C

An additional reason advanced by Gilmer for refusing to enforce arbitration agreements relating to ADEA claims is his contention that there often will be unequal bargaining power between employers and employees. Mere inequality in bargaining power, however, is not a sufficient reason to hold that arbitration agreements are never enforceable in the employment context. Relationships between securities dealers and investors, for example, may involve unequal bargaining power, but we nevertheless held in *Rodriguez de Quijas* and *McMahon* that agreements to arbitrate in that context are enforceable. As discussed above, the FAA's purpose was to place arbitration agreements on the same footing as other contracts. Thus, arbitration agreements are enforceable "save upon such grounds as exist at law or in equity for the revocation of any contract." 9 U.S.C. § 2. "Of course, courts should remain attuned to well-supported claims that the agreement to arbitrate resulted from the sort of fraud or overwhelming economic power that would provide grounds 'for the revocation of any contract.' "There is no indication in this case, however, that Gilmer, an experienced businessman, was coerced or defrauded into agreeing to the arbitration clause in his registration application. As with the claimed procedural inadequacies discussed above, this claim of unequal bargaining power is best left for resolution in specific cases.

IV

In addition to the arguments discussed above, Gilmer vigorously asserts that our decision in *Alexander v. Gardner-Denver Co.*, 415 U.S. 36 (1974), and its progeny — *Barrentine v. Arkansas-Best Freight System, Inc.*, 450 U.S. 728 (1981), and *McDonald v. West Branch*, 466 U.S. 284 (1984) — preclude arbitration of employment discrimination claims. Gilmer's reliance on these cases, however, is misplaced.

In *Gardner-Denver*, the issue was whether a discharged employee whose grievance had been arbitrated pursuant to an arbitration clause in a collective-bargaining agreement was precluded from subsequently bringing a Title VII action based upon the conduct that was the subject of the grievance. In holding that the employee was not foreclosed from bringing the Title VII claim, we stressed that an employee's contractual rights under a collective-bargaining agreement are distinct from the employee's statutory Title VII rights: "In submitting his grievance to arbitration, an employee seeks to vindicate his contractual right under a collective-bargaining agreement. By contrast, in filing a lawsuit under Title VII, an employee asserts independent statutory rights accorded by Congress. The distinctly separate nature of these contractual and statutory rights is not vitiated merely because both were violated as a result of the same factual occurrence."

We also noted that a labor arbitrator has authority only to resolve questions of contractual rights. The arbitrator's "task is to effectuate the intent of the parties" and he or she does not have the "general authority to invoke public laws that conflict with the bargain between the parties." By contrast, "in instituting an action under Title VII, the employee is not seeking review of the arbitrator's decision. Rather, he is asserting a statutory right independent of the arbitration process." We further expressed concern that in collective-bargaining arbitration "the interests of the individual employee may be subordinated to the collective interests of all employees in the bargaining unit."[5]

Barrentine and *McDonald* similarly involved the issue whether arbitration under a collective-bargaining agreement precluded a subsequent statutory claim. In holding that the statutory claims there were not precluded, we noted, as in *Gardner-Denver*, the difference between contractual rights under a collective-bargaining agreement and individual statutory rights, the potential disparity in interests between a union and an employee, and the limited authority and power of labor arbitrators.

There are several important distinctions between the *Gardner-Denver* line of cases and the case before us. First, those cases did not involve the issue of the enforceability of an agreement to arbitrate statutory claims. Rather, they involved the quite different issue whether arbitration of contract-based claims precluded subsequent judicial resolution of statutory claims. Since the employees there had not agreed to arbitrate their statutory claims, and the labor arbitrators were not authorized to resolve such claims, the arbitration in those cases understandably was held not to preclude subsequent statutory actions. Second, because the arbitration in those cases occurred in the context of a collective-bargaining agreement, the claimants there were represented by their unions in the arbitration proceedings. An important concern therefore was the tension between collective representation and individual statutory rights, a concern not applicable to the present case. Finally, those cases were not decided under the FAA, which, as discussed above, reflects a "liberal federal policy favoring arbitration agreements." *Mitsubishi*, 473 U.S., at 625. Therefore, those cases provide no basis for refusing to enforce Gilmer's agreement to arbitrate his ADEA claim.

V

We conclude that Gilmer has not met his burden of showing that Congress, in enacting the ADEA, intended to preclude arbitration of claims under that Act. Accordingly, the judgment of the Court of Appeals is

Affirmed.

Justice STEVENS, with whom Justice MARSHALL joins, dissenting.

[The dissent argued that the FAA was intended to exclude arbitration agreements between employees and employers and that Gilmer was forced to agree to arbitrate as a condition of employment.]

---

[5] The Court in *Alexander v. Gardner-Denver Co.*, also expressed the view that arbitration was inferior to the judicial process for resolving statutory claims. That "mistrust of the arbitral process," however, has been undermined by our recent arbitration decisions. *McMahon.* "[W]e are well past the time when judicial suspicion of the desirability of arbitration and of the competence of arbitral tribunals inhibited the development of arbitration as an alternative means of dispute resolution." *Mitsubishi Motors Corp. v. Soler Chrysler-Plymouth, Inc.,* 473 U.S. 614, 626-27 (1985).

* * *

III

Not only would I find that the FAA does not apply to employment-related disputes between employers and employees in general, but also I would hold that compulsory arbitration conflicts with the congressional purpose animating the ADEA, in particular. As this Court previously has noted, authorizing the courts to issue broad injunctive relief is the cornerstone to eliminating discrimination in society. The ADEA, like Title VII of the Civil Rights Act of 1964, authorizes courts to award broad, class-based injunctive relief to achieve the purposes of the Act. Because commercial arbitration is typically limited to a specific dispute between the particular parties and because the available remedies in arbitral forums generally do not provide for class-wide injunctive relief, I would conclude that an essential purpose of the ADEA is frustrated by compulsory arbitration of employment discrimination claims. Moreover, as Chief Justice Burger explained: "Plainly, it would not comport with the congressional objectives behind a statute seeking to enforce civil rights protected by Title VII to allow the very forces that had practiced discrimination to contract away the right to enforce civil rights in the courts. For federal courts to defer to arbitral decisions reached by the same combination of forces that had long perpetuated invidious discrimination would have made the foxes guardians of the chickens." * * * The Court's holding today clearly eviscerates the important role played by an independent judiciary in eradicating employment discrimination.

IV

When the FAA was passed in 1925, I doubt that any legislator who voted for it expected it to apply to statutory claims, to form contracts between parties of unequal bargaining power, or to the arbitration of disputes arising out of the employment relationship. In recent years, however, the Court "has effectively rewritten the statute", and abandoned its earlier view that statutory claims were not appropriate subjects for arbitration. *See Mitsubishi Motors v. Soler Chrysler-Plymouth, Inc.*, 473 U.S. 614, 646-651 (1985) (Stevens, J., dissenting). Although I remain persuaded that it erred in doing so, the Court has also put to one side any concern about the inequality of bargaining power between an entire industry, on the one hand, and an individual customer or employee, on the other. Until today, however, the Court has not read § 2 of the FAA as broadly encompassing disputes arising out of the employment relationship. I believe this additional extension of the FAA is erroneous. Accordingly, I respectfully dissent.

NOTES

1. How broad is *Gilmer*? Does the *Gilmer* decision mean that courts should enforce all employment arbitration agreements, even those raising claims under state or federal statutes? Is the *Gardner-Denver* decision still good law after *Gilmer*? For the view that not all state employee claims should be arbitrable, see Note, *Arbitration of State Law Claims By Employees: An*

Argument for Containing Federal Arbitration Law, 80 CORNELL L. REV. 1695 (1995).

2. What should be made of footnote #4 of *Gilmer*? It seems to suggest that courts should review arbitral awards to ensure their consistency with applicable statutes. The critical language of the note was first set forth in the 1987 *McMahon* decision and was here reasserted in *Gilmer*. Because this footnote is asserted in two major cases one might assume it is both important and correct. Is such a broad judicial review function consistent with the "finality" theory of arbitration? Do courts really require arbitrators to apply the law? Isn't the footnote both impractical and inconsistent with the FAA?

3. Does *Gilmer* open the door for arbitration of employment disputes generally? Even if courts can hear claims brought under Title VII (*Gardner*), § 1983 (*McDonald v. City of West Branch*, 466 U.S. 284 (1984)), and the Fair Labor Standards Act (*Barrentine*), won't employers now try to arbitrate all other claims? Will any employers try to force employees to arbitrate even these claims as a prerequisite to subsequent judicial consideration of them? (*See Kuehner v. Dickinson & Co.*, 84 F.3d 316 (9th Cir. 1996) (requiring securities firm employee to exhaust NASD arbitral procedures before seeking judicial redress under Fair Labor Standards Act).) How closely should the courts regulate the contract to arbitrate disputes between employers and nonunionized employees? If the employee is offered a job and handed a form contract containing an arbitration clause, is the employee in any position to freely refuse to sign? Won't almost all employees sign the contract when offered a valuable job without even trying to understand the meaning of the arbitration "option"? Would you feel similarly if the non-unionized employee was given an arbitration agreement later, after employment?

4. *Austin v. Owens-Brockway Glass Container, Inc.*, 78 F.3d 875 (4th Cir. 1996), *cert. denied*, 65 U.S.L.W. 1873 (1996), represents a case that demonstrates the apparent inconsistencies between the *Gilmer* and *Gardner-Denver* decisions. In *Austin*, a discharged former employee sued her employer alleging a violation of the ADA and Title VII of the Civil Rights Act by terminating her when she was on medical leave and then not offering her light-duty work upon her return following medical leave. Relying on *Gilmer*, the Fourth Circuit affirmed the trial court's view that the employee was required to use the arbitration framework that had been set forth in the collective bargaining agreement. The court of appeals reasoned "*Gilmer* . . . made clear that agreements to arbitrate statutory claims are enforceable." (78 F.3d at 880.) It also noted that judicial review of arbitration awards will be adequate to permit compliance with existing legislative requirements. (*Id.*) The court found that the employee failed to meet her burden to show that "Congress intended to preclude arbitration of statutory claims." (*Id.* at 882.) The dissent viewed *Gardner-Denver* as holding that the employees' individual rights could not be waived by her union. Several other courts have used the reasoning employed by the *Austin* majority. (*See, e.g., Bender v. A.G. Edwards & Sons, Inc.*, 971 F.2d 698 (11th Cir. 1992) (requiring arbitration of Title VII claim brought by stockbroker who had signed an agreement to arbitrate disputes with her employer); *Mago v. Shearson Lehman Hutton, Inc.*, 956 F.2d 932 (9th Cir. 1992) (court finds that employee who filed sexual harassment suit did not meet her *Gilmer* burden).) A minority of other decisions have reached seemingly conflicting results, however. (*See, e.g., Tran v. Tran*, 54 F.3d 115 (2d Cir. 1995) (allowing employee wage and hour suit despite arbitration agreement).)

Courts continue to struggle with the question of whether Title VII claims are arbitrable.

In *EEOC v. Franks Nursery & Crafts, Inc.*, 177 F.3d 448 (6th Cir. 1999), the Sixth Circuit distinguished *Gilmer* and allowed the EEOC to bring a claim for monetary Title VII relief on behalf of an individual who had signed an arbitration clause. Although *Gilmer* had asserted that "arbitration agreements will not preclude the EEOC from bringing actions seeking class-wide or equitable relief," (500 U.S. at 32), the court of appeals did not "read the Court's language as excluding other kinds of relief." (177 F.3d at 461.)

In *Duffield v. Robertson Stephens*, 144 F.3d 1182 (9th Cir. 1998), the Ninth Circuit refused to force arbitration of claims under the Civil Rights Act of 1991 and Title VII. Other circuits have held to the contrary. (*See, e.g., Koveleskie v. SBC Capital Markets*, 167 F.3d 361 (7th Cir. 1999) ("We respectfully disagree with the Ninth Circuit on this issue"); *Sues v. John Nuveen*, 146 F.3d 165 (3d Cir. 1998).)

5. In *Wright v. Universal Maritime Service*, 525 U.S. 70 (1998), the Supreme Court ducked a chance to decide whether *Gilmer* had overruled *Gardner-Denver*. Wright brought an Americans with Disabilities Act claim against his employer who contended that such claims must be arbitrated under the terms of a collective bargaining agreement. The Supreme Court held that the normal presumption of arbitrability of claims does not apply to statutory claims but decided that a clear and unmistakable agreement to arbitrate would prevent litigation. On the record presented Wright was not forced to arbitrate because a clear and unmistakable waiver of statutory rights was not presented.

Following the *Wright* decision, management attorneys desiring to avoid litigating statutory claims have begun expressly listing statutory grounds in the collective bargaining contracts. Courts have responded favorably to this tactic. (*See, e.g., Rogers v. N.Y.U.*, 220 F.3d 73 (2d Cir. 2000) (court refuses to compel arbitration of ADA claim where, under *Wright* test, generalized clause too vague to be "clear and unmistakable" but, in dictum, suggests that explicit references to statutory claims will require arbitration); *Carson v. Giant Foods, Inc.*, 175 F.3d 325, 331-32 (4th Cir. 1999) (court will uphold arbitration of expressly listed statutes).)

6. What should be made of footnote 2 from *Gilmer*? There the *Gilmer* decision left "for another day" the argument that all employment contracts are outside the scope of the FAA under the broad language of § 1 ("nothing herein contained shall apply to contracts of employment of seamen, railroad employees or any other class of workers engaged in foreign or interstate commerce"). A sharply divided Supreme Court decided the issue in March, 2001, in *Circuit City Stores, Inc. v. Adams*, 121 S. Ct. 1302 (2001). Justice Kennedy, writing for a 5 person majority, narrowly construed the § 1 FAA exemption to be limited to transportation workers. The majority opinion rejected a broader interpretation of § 1 and purported to rely on the text of the FAA.

The 4 person dissent of Justice Stevens focused on the legislative history of the FAA which clearly seemed directed at issues of commercial arbitration and was unrelated to matters of employment disputes. Justice Stevens stressed that organized labor dropped its opposition to the FAA in exchange for the exclusionary language added to § 1 to exempt labor disputes from the FAA.

The impact of *Circuit City* is significant. Now employment contracts are clearly within the FAA and its policy favoring arbitration. Presumably, *Circuit City* should cause even broader use of arbitration to resolve employment disputes, one of the few growth areas of litigation in recent years.

7. *Rape Arbitration?* Gilmer, as an employee of a securities broker-dealer, was obligated to sign an arbitration agreement as a condition of employment. In *Hill v. J.J.B.Hilliard*, 945 S.W.2d 948 (Ky. 1996), a vice-president of a securities firm sued her employer and an executive of the firm, alleging that she was raped while on a business trip. She alleged assault and battery, retaliation and sexual harassment. The trial court dismissed the claims against the employer and mandated arbitration. The State Supreme Court's arbitration denial left standing the Kentucky Court of Appeals affirmance. Should tort claims involving an alleged rape be the subject of mandatory arbitration? Does it matter that under the terms of the arbitration agreement the employee agrees to arbitrate "any dispute with my employer"?

8. *Due Process Protocol.* Responding to claims by groups of workers critical of mandatory employment arbitration outside of the collective bargaining context, in 1995 the ABA developed a "due process protocol." The protocol endorsed requirements for a neutral arbitrator, an employee role in arbitrator selection, reasonable discovery, court-like remedies, right to counsel and a written opinion. These procedural protections have been incorporated into American Arbitration Association and JAMS employment arbitration rules. Yet, many systems of employer-required arbitration do not meet the minimal standards of the due process protocol. For discussion of National Academy of Arbitrators condemnation of mandatory employment arbitration and opposition to arbitration sponsoring organizations that fail to implement the due process protocol, see Michael Green, *Debunking the Myth of Employer Advantage From Using Mandatory Arbitration for Discrimination Claims*, 31 RUTGERS L.J. 399, 424-27 (2000). The EEOC maintained a longstanding policy against mandatory employment arbitration as a condition of employment throughout the Clinton Administration.

COLE v. BURNS INTERNATIONAL SECURITY SERVICES
105 F.3d 1465 (D.C. Cir. 1997)

EDWARDS, J.

This case raises important issues regarding whether and to what extent a person can be required, *as a condition of employment,* to (1) waive all rights to a trial by jury in a court of competent jurisdiction with respect to any dispute relating to recruitment, employment, or termination, including claims involving laws against discrimination, and (2) sign an agreement providing that, at the employer's option, any such employment disputes must be arbitrated. At its core, this appeal challenges the enforceability of conditions of employment requiring individuals to arbitrate claims resting on statutory rights. The issues at hand bring into focus the seminal decision of Gilmer v. Interstate/Johnson Lane Corp., and call into question the limits of the Supreme Court's holdings in that case. . . .

Clinton Cole used to work as a security guard at Union Station in Washington, D.C. for a company called LaSalle and Partners ("LaSalle"). In 1991, Burns Security took over LaSalle's contract to provide security at Union Station and required all LaSalle employees to sign a "Pre-Dispute Resolution Agreement" in order to obtain employment with Burns.

In October 1993, Burns Security fired Cole. After filing charges with the Equal Employment Opportunity Commission, Cole filed the instant complaint in the United States District Court for the District of Columbia, alleging racial discrimination, harassment based on race, retaliation for his writing a letter of complaint regarding sexual harassment of a subordinate employee by another supervisor at Burns, and intentional infliction of emotional distress. Burns moved to compel arbitration of the dispute and to dismiss Cole's complaint pursuant to the terms of the contract.

The District Court found that the arbitration agreement clearly covered Cole's claims. The court also rejected Cole's suggestions (1) that the Pre-Dispute Resolution Agreement was excluded from coverage under the Federal Arbitration Act under 9 U.S.C. § 1, and (2) that the agreement was an unenforceable and unconscionable contract of adhesion. As a result, the trial court granted Burns Security's motion to compel arbitration and dismissed Cole's complaint. . . .

In order to properly consider the validity of the arbitration agreement in this case, it is crucial to emphasize the distinction between arbitration in the context of collective bargaining and mandatory arbitration of *statutory claims* outside of the context of a union contract. These are vastly different situations, involving very different considerations. Arbitration in collective bargaining has a rich tradition in the United States, and a plethora of case law to support it. Arbitration of statutory claims, however, is the proverbial "new kid on the block," mostly an attempt to reduce the burdens and expenses of formal litigation. And arbitration of statutory claims is hardly legendary, for it is not only a new idea, but it comes in no clear form, and it has many detractors. Not surprisingly, because traditional labor arbitration is so celebrated in the United States, it is easy for the uninitiated to fall prey to the suggestion that the legal precepts governing the enforcement and review of arbitration emanating from collective bargaining should be equally applicable to arbitration of *all* employment disputes. This is a mischievous idea, one that we categorically reject. . . .

> [A] private agreement to arbitrate statutory claims cannot be viewed entirely in terms of a calculus of private gain and loss that presumably is best left to the parties themselves. . . . If the award purports to resolve a claim under external law (and hence preclude relitigation of that claim in any other forum), there is a public interest in the manner in which the external-law norms are articulated and applied in the arbitral forum. Thus, . . . when arbitrators sit to adjudicate

a dispute governed by external law, there is a tension between the tradition of limited judicial review of arbitration awards and the presence of an independent public interest in ensuring that the law is correctly and consistently being applied, and that substantive policies reflected in the law are neither under-enforced nor over-enforced.

Estreicher, 66 CHI.-KENT L. REV. at 777; *see also* Lamont E. Stallworth & Martin H. Malin, *Conflicts Arising Out of Work Force Diversity*, PROC. OF THE 46TH ANN. MEETING OF THE NAT'L ACAD. OF ARB. 104, 119 (1994) ("Many issues of public law require a choice between conflicting public values, which should be resolved by judges and other officials charged with lawmaking in the public interest, rather than by private dispute resolvers."). Yet, unlike a judge, an arbitrator is neither publicly chosen nor publicly accountable.

Arbitration of public law issues is also troubling, on a less abstract level, because the structural protections inherent in the collective bargaining context are not duplicated in cases involving mandatory arbitration of individual statutory claims. Unlike the labor case, in which both union and employer are regular participants in the arbitration process, only the employer is a repeat player in cases involving individual statutory claims. As a result, the employer gains some advantage in having superior knowledge with respect to selection of an arbitrator. *See, e.g.,* Lewis Maltby, *Paradise Lost — How the* Gilmer *Court Lost the Opportunity for Alternative Dispute Resolution to Improve Civil Rights,* 12 N.Y.L. SCH. J. HUM. RTS. 1, 4–5 (1994) (arguing that individual employees are disadvantaged vis-a-vis employers in determining whether given arbitrator is truly neutral because employees lack financial resources to research arbitrator's past decisions); Sternlight, 74 WASH. U. L.Q. at 685 (arguing that "one-shot players" such as employees and consumers are less able to make informed selections of arbitrators than "repeat-player" companies); Getman, 88 YALE L.J. at 936 (same); Gorman, 1995 U. ILL. L. REV. at 656 (same); Reginald Alleyne, *Statutory Discrimination Claims: Rights "Waived" and Lost In the Arbitration Forum,* 13 HOFSTRA LAB. L.J. 381, 403, 426 (1996) (same).

Additionally, while a lack of public disclosure of arbitration awards is acceptable in the collective bargaining context, because both employers and unions monitor such decisions and the awards rarely involve issues of concern to persons other than the parties, in the context of individual statutory claims, a lack of public disclosure may systematically favor companies over individuals. Judicial decisions create binding precedent that prevents a recurrence of statutory violations; it is not clear that arbitral decisions have any such preventive effect. The unavailability of arbitral decisions also may prevent potential plaintiffs from locating the information necessary to build a case of intentional misconduct or to establish a pattern or practice of discrimination by particular companies. *See* Sternlight, 74 WASH. U. L.Q. at 686.

Furthermore, as in the instant case, mandatory arbitration agreements in individual employees' contracts often are presented on a take-it-or-leave-it basis; there is no union to negotiate the terms of the arbitration arrangement. Thus, employers are free to structure arbitration in ways that may systematically disadvantage employees. *See* Alfred W. Blumrosen, *Exploring Voluntary*

Arbitration of Individual Employment Disputes, 16 U. MICH. J.L. REFORM 249, 254–55 (1983) ("In non-unionized private sector employment, there is no organization analogous to the union to represent employee interests in developing arbitration procedures. Therefore, the employer and its lawyers have a comparatively free hand in drafting the details of an arbitration clause. . . . Under these circumstances, some employers may seek to unfairly narrow the legal rights of employees in the arbitration clause." (footnote omitted)); L.M. Sixel, *Case Leads Employers to Rethink Arbitration Rules,* HOUSTON CHRON., Jan. 29, 1996 ("Starting about three years ago, employers trying to avoid big, expensive lawsuits began forcing their employees to agree to binding arbitration in order to keep their jobs or get new ones. And many employers adopted stiff, self-serving arbitration rules that, for example, prohibit punitive damages or put severe limits on evidence-gathering by employees.").

For example, a company might impose a requirement that the employee pay the fees for an arbitrator's time in order to discourage or prevent employees from bringing a claim. *See* Blumrosen, 16 U. MICH. J.L. REFORM at 262 (proposing model arbitration clause that requires employer to pay arbitrator's fees because "to tax the employee with the burden of paying for a private judge might seem overreaching" when the employer is already "avoiding the risk of a jury trial"); Sternlight, 74 WASH. U. L.Q. at 682–83 (suggesting ways employers might structure arbitration to discourage claims, including requiring employees to pay arbitrators' fees, and noting that "at least when one goes to court the judge is free"); Ellie Winninghoff, *In Arbitration, Pitfalls For Consumers,* N.Y. TIMES, Oct. 22, 1994, at 37 (An attorney with arbitration experience says it is a myth "that [arbitration is] cheaper — that's definitely not true. If you go to trial, you get the judge for free.").

Finally, the competence of arbitrators to analyze and decide purely legal issues in connection with statutory claims has been questioned. Many arbitrators are not lawyers, and they have not traditionally engaged in the same kind of legal analysis performed by judges.

For instance, arbitrators often cite to and rely extensively on treatises. . . . A court is unlikely to rely on a treatise — even . . . a widely respected one. Similarly, arbitrators frequently rely on leading cases on the subject of employment discrimination, such as *Texas Department of Community Affairs v. Burdine (Burdine)*, and *McDonnell Douglas Corp. v. Green (McDonnell Douglas)*, without citing to subsequent lower courts or less publicized cases. This means that an arbitrator's decision may be based on broad stroke principles to the exclusion of cases more analogous to the claim being decided. . . .

Nonetheless, the Supreme Court now has made clear that, as a general rule, statutory claims are fully subject to binding arbitration, at least outside of the context of collective bargaining. *See Gilmer,* 500 U.S. at 26, 34–35, 111 S.Ct. at 1652, 1656–57 (collecting cases and distinguishing *Gardner-Denver*). Rejecting "generalized attacks on arbitration" of statutory claims as based " 'on suspicion of arbitration as a method of weakening the protections afforded in the substantive law to would-be complainants' " and " 'far out of step with [the] current strong endorsement' " of arbitration, *id.* at 30 (*quoting Rodriguez de Quijas v. Shearson / American Express, Inc.,* 490 U.S. 477, 481 (1989)), the

Court has emphasized that " '[b]y agreeing to arbitrate a statutory claim, a party does not forego the substantive rights afforded by the statute; it only submits to their resolution in an arbitral, rather than a judicial, forum.' " *Id.* at 26 (*quoting Mitsubishi Motors Corp. v. Soler Chrysler-Plymouth, Inc.*, 473 U.S. 614, 628 (1985)). The Court has stressed that " '[s]o long as the prospective litigant effectively may vindicate [his or her] statutory cause of action in the arbitral forum, the statute will continue to serve both its remedial and deterrent function.' " *Id.* at 28.

It is plain that the Supreme Court saw a critical distinction in the situations raised by *Gardner-Denver* and *Gilmer: Gardner-Denver* involved arbitration in the context of collective bargaining, which almost invariably means that the union controls the presentation of the statutory issue to the arbitrator. Thus, the *Gardner-Denver* Court knew that arbitration might not be fair to the individual employee, because an arbitrator would of necessity be required to deal with the union's interests vis-a-vis the employer, and the union's interests are not necessarily the same as the employee's interests, especially with respect to a claim of employment discrimination. *Gilmer*, on the other hand, raised an individual employee claim outside the collective bargaining context, so the pitfalls seen in *Gardner-Denver* did not present themselves in *Gilmer.*

Despite the Supreme Court's recent endorsement of arbitration of statutory claims, however, concerns remain regarding arbitration's ability to live up to the Court's expectations, particularly in cases involving mandatory arbitration of statutory claims which is imposed as a condition of employment. In fact, the Equal Employment Opportunity Commission has taken the position that such agreements are unenforceable in a number of cases being litigated around the country. *See, e.g.,Duffield v. Robertson Stephens & Co.*, No. C-95-0109-EFL (N.D. Cal.) (amicus brief filed by EEOC); *Cosgrove v. Shearson Lehman Bros.*, No. 95-3432 (6th Cir. 1997) (amicus brief filed by EEOC); *EEOC v. River Oaks Imaging & Diagnostic*, Civ. A. H-95-75 (S.D. Tex.); *EEOC v. Midland Food Services, LLC*, No. 1:96-MC-107 (N.D. Ohio); *Johnson v. Hubbard Broadcasting, Inc.*, No. 4-96-cv-107 (D. Minn.) (amicus brief filed by EEOC). In *Duffield,* the agency's position was stated as follows:

> The Commission strongly favors the voluntary use of arbitration and other forms of alternative dispute resolution ("ADR"), and believes that properly used it can speed and simplify the process of adjudicating discrimination claims. However, arbitration that is not knowing and voluntary deprives individuals of substantial rights provided by Congress, especially where — as alleged here — the procedures are unfair and specifically designed *not* to safeguard statutory rights.

Pierre Levy, Gilmer *Revisited: The Judicial Erosion of Employee Statutory Rights,* 26 N.M. L. Rev. 455, 478 n.193 (1996) (quoting Memorandum of Points and Authorities of the EEOC as Amicus Curiae, *Duffield v. Robertson Stephens & Co.*, No. C-95-0109-EFL at 1 (N.D. Cal. filed Aug. 4, 1995) ("EEOC Memorandum")). The EEOC's objections to the procedures at issue were described as follows:

[Arbitration] (1) is not governed by the statutory requirements and standards of Title VII; (2) is conducted by arbitrators given no training and possessing no expertise in employment law; (3) routinely does not permit plaintiffs to receive punitive damages and attorneys' fees to which they would otherwise be entitled under the statute; and (4) forces them to pay exorbitant "forum fees" in the tens of thousands of dollars, greatly discouraging aggrieved employees from seeking relief. *Id.* at 478 (quoting EEOC Memorandum at 3).

The National Labor Relations Board also has expressed some concerns. At one point, officials with the Board took the position that it is an unfair labor practice to require an employee to agree to mandatory arbitration of all claims. *See* Margaret A. Jacobs, *Firms With Policies Requiring Arbitration Are Facing Obstacles*, WALL ST. J., Oct. 16, 1995, at B5 (quoting Rochelle Kentov, regional director of the NLRB in Tampa, Florida as saying, "The requirement that an employee or job applicant sign a mandatory arbitration policy is an unfair labor practice, as is their discharge for not signing.").

With this background in mind, we turn to the arbitration agreement before us in this case.

2. *The Validity of the Agreement to Arbitrate in This Case*

We start with the assumption that, under *Gilmer,* a person may agree to arbitrate statutory claims. We do not assume, however, that an employer has a free hand in requiring arbitration as a condition of employment.

Fortunately, in the instant case, the parties largely agree on the meaning of their arbitration agreement. Each side concurs in the following propositions:

(1) The agreement allows the employer the option of forcing statutory claims into arbitration for the resolution of public law issues;

(2) The agreement's waiver of a jury trial is absolute, *i.e.,* it operates even if the employer does not seek arbitration;

(3) The agreement does not affect an employee's ability to seek relief from the Equal Employment Opportunity Commission;

(4) The arbitrator is fully bound to apply Title VII and other applicable public law, both as to substance and remedy, in accordance with statutory requirements and prevailing judicial interpretation; and

(5) The agreement provides for appointment of a neutral arbitrator through the American Arbitration Association ("AAA") and for the conduct of the arbitration proceeding in accordance with AAA rules.

*   *   *

The parties stipulated that arbitrators' fees are commonly $500 to $1,000 *or more* per day. Significantly, however, the AAA Rules do not prescribe any particular allocation of responsibility for the payment of the arbitrators' fees.

Our dissenting colleague has it completely wrong in suggesting that the applicable AAA Rules determine the allocation of the Neutral Arbitrator's Compensation. They do not. Rule 32 says, in relevant part, that "the arbitrator shall . . . assess arbitration fees, expenses, and compensation *as provided in Sections 35, 36, and 37. . . .*" Rule 37 (entitled "Neutral Arbitrator's Compensation"), in turn, says that "[a]n appropriate daily rate and other arrangements will be discussed by the administrator with the parties and the arbitrator. If the parties fail to agree to the terms of compensation, an appropriate rate shall be established by the AAA and communicated in writing to the parties." Nothing in these rules indicates how an arbitrator's compensation is to be allocated. Instead, it is quite clear that AAA hedged on this question in the *National Rules for the Resolution of Employment Disputes* (effective June 1, 1996) (probably because the issue was seen to be so controversial). In contrast, in the AAA *Labor Arbitration Rules,* at 16 (as amended and effective January 1, 1996), it is clearly provided that, "[u]nless mutually agreed otherwise, the arbitrator's compensation shall be borne equally by the parties, in accordance with the fee structure disclosed in the arbitrator's biographical profile submitted to the parties." There is no such provision in the *National Rules for the Resolution of Employment Disputes.* It is therefore unclear in the instant case whether an arbitrator's fees (as distinguished from "administrative fees") are to be paid by the employee alone, the employer alone, or by the parties together. For the reasons that follow, we hold that an arbitrator's compensation and expenses must be paid by the employer alone.

The starting point of our analysis is the Supreme Court's decision in *Gilmer.* In that case, the Court held that an employee's agreement to arbitrate employment-related disputes may require him to arbitrate statutory claims under the ADEA because "[b]y agreeing to arbitrate a statutory claim, [an employee] does not forgo the substantive rights afforded by the statute; [he] only submits to their resolution in an arbitral, rather than a judicial, forum." *Gilmer,* 500 U.S. at 26 (quoting *Mitsubishi,* 473 U.S. at 628, 105 S.Ct. at 3354) (first alteration in original). As noted above, the Court emphasized that "so long as the prospective litigant effectively may vindicate [his or her] statutory cause of action in the arbitral forum, the statute will continue to serve both its remedial and deterrent function." *Id.* at 28 (quoting *Mitsubishi,* 473 U.S. at 637) (alteration in original).

In *Gilmer,* the employee raised four challenges to arbitration under the New York Stock Exchange Rules, claiming that arbitration impermissibly diminished his ability to effectively vindicate his statutory rights. First, Gilmer challenged the impartiality of the arbitrators. *See id.* at 30, 111 S.Ct. at 1654. The Court rejected this challenge, finding that the NYSE Rules themselves provide protection against biased arbitrators and that judicial review under the FAA would allow the courts to set aside any decision in which there "was evident partiality or corruption in the arbitrators." *Id.* at 30–31(quoting 9 U.S.C. § 10(b)). Second, Gilmer objected that the limited discovery allowed in arbitration would unfairly hamper his ability to prove discrimination. *Id.* at 31. Again, the Court rejected this claim, pointing out that the NYSE Rules provided for discovery and that agreements to arbitrate are desirable precisely because they trade the procedures of the federal courts for the simplicity, informality, and expedition of arbitration. *Id.* (quotation omitted). Third, Gilmer objected that, because arbitrators do not always issue written awards, public knowledge of discrimination, appellate review, and the development of the law would be undermined by arbitration of his statutory claims. *Id.* This claim too was rejected because, in fact, the NYSE Rules require that arbitration awards be in writing and allow public access to awards. *Id.* at 31–32.

Finally, Gilmer's objection that arbitration did not provide for equitable relief was rejected because the NYSE Rules did not restrict the types of relief available. *Id.* at 32.

Obviously, *Gilmer* cannot be read as holding that an arbitration agreement is enforceable no matter what rights it waives or what burdens it imposes. *See* Gorman, 1995 U. ILL. L. REV. at 644 ("The Supreme Court in the *Gilmer* case did not hold that *any* sort of arbitration procedure before *any* manner of arbitrator would be satisfactory in the adjudication of public rights."). Such a holding would be fundamentally at odds with our understanding of the rights accorded to persons protected by public statutes like the ADEA and Title VII. The beneficiaries of public statutes are entitled to the rights and protections provided by the law. Clearly, it would be unlawful for an employer to condition employment on an employee's agreement to give up the right to be free from racial or gender discrimination. *See Gardner-Denver* ("[T]here can be no prospective waiver of an employee's rights under Title VII. . . . Title VII's strictures are absolute and represent a congressional command that each employee be free from discriminatory practices. . . . [W]aiver of these rights would defeat the paramount congressional purpose behind Title VII."). Any such condition of employment would violate Title VII, regardless of whether or not the agreement was viewed as a contract of adhesion. Thus, in a subsequent suit by the employee raising a viable claim of racial discrimination or sexual harassment, it would be no defense that the employee had signed a contract giving up her right to be free from discrimination.

Similarly, an employee cannot be required as a condition of employment to waive access to a neutral forum in which statutory employment discrimination claims may be heard. For example, an employee could not be required to sign an agreement waiving the right to bring Title VII claims in any forum. Although the employer could argue that such an agreement does not waive the substantive protections of the statute, surely such an agreement would nonetheless violate the law by leaving the employee's substantive rights at the mercy of the employer's good faith in adhering to the law. At a minimum, statutory rights include both a substantive protection *and* access to a neutral forum in which to enforce those protections. *See Graham Oil Co. v. ARCO Products Co.*, 43 F.3d 1244, 1246–48 (9th Cir. 1994) (arbitration clause that purported to waive remedies provided by federal statute and to shorten statute of limitations for filing such claims violated statute and was unenforceable); Jerold S. Auerbach, JUSTICE WITHOUT LAW? 144–45 (1983) (preservation of "individual rights requires an accessible legal system for their protection" and enforcement).

We believe that all of the factors addressed in *Gilmer* are satisfied here. In particular, we note that the arbitration arrangement (1) provides for neutral arbitrators, (2) provides for more than minimal discovery, (3) requires a written award, (4) provides for all of the types of relief that would otherwise be available in court, and (5) does not require employees to pay either unreasonable costs *or* any arbitrators' fees or expenses as a condition of access to the arbitration forum. Thus, an employee who is made to use arbitration as a condition of employment "effectively may vindicate [his or her] statutory cause of action in the arbitral forum." *Gilmer,* 500 U.S. at 28, 111 S.Ct. at

1653); *see* Gorman, 1995 U. ILL. L. REV. at 645 ("[D]espite the strong FAA policy of ordering arbitration hearings and implementing arbitration awards, minimal standards of procedural fairness must be satisfied before a civil action may be stayed and arbitration ordered. . . . [A] federal court, before enforcing an employer's demand for arbitration under an employment contract, may — indeed must — scrutinize the agreed-upon or contemplated arbitration system.").

3. *The Obligation to Pay Arbitrators' Fees*

Although we find that the disputed arbitration agreement is legally valid, there is one point that requires amplification. The arbitration agreement in this case presents an issue not raised by the agreement in *Gilmer:* can an employer condition employment on acceptance of an arbitration agreement that requires the employee to submit his or her statutory claims to arbitration and then requires the employee to pay all or part of the arbitrators' fees? This was not an issue in *Gilmer* (and other like cases), because, under NYSE Rules and NASD Rules, it is standard practice in the securities industry for employers to pay all of the arbitrators' fees. Employees may be required to pay a filing fee, expenses, or an administrative fee, but these expenses are routinely waived in the event of financial hardship.

Thus, in *Gilmer,* the Supreme Court endorsed a system of arbitration in which employees are not required to pay for the arbitrator assigned to hear their statutory claims. There is no reason to think that the Court would have approved arbitration in the absence of this arrangement. Indeed, we are unaware of any situation in American jurisprudence in which a beneficiary of a federal statute has been required to pay for the services of the judge assigned to hear her or his case. Under *Gilmer,* arbitration is supposed to be a reasonable substitute for a judicial forum. Therefore, it would undermine Congress's intent to prevent employees who are seeking to vindicate statutory rights from gaining access to a judicial forum and then require them to pay for the services of an arbitrator when they would never be required to pay for a judge in court.

There is no doubt that parties appearing in federal court may be required to assume the cost of filing fees and other administrative expenses, so any reasonable costs of this sort that accompany arbitration are not problematic. However, if an employee like Cole is required to pay arbitrators' fees ranging from $500 to $1,000 per day *or more,* in addition to administrative and attorney's fees, is it likely that he will be able to pursue his statutory claims? We think not. *See* David W. Ewing, JUSTICE ON THE JOB: RESOLVING GRIEVANCES IN THE NONUNION WORKPLACE (Harvard Business School Press 1989) at 291 (quoting corporate director of industrial relations at Northrop explaining why Northrop pays arbitrators' fees: "[W]e bear the cost of the arbitration for the very practical reason that most of the employees who seek arbitration of their grievances simply couldn't afford it if we did not."). There is no indication in AAA's rules that an arbitrator's fees may be reduced or waived in cases of financial hardship. These fees would be prohibitively expensive for an employee like Cole, especially after being fired from his job, and it is unacceptable to require Cole to pay arbitrators' fees, because such fees are unlike anything that he would have to pay to pursue his statutory claims in court.

Arbitration will occur in this case only because it has been mandated by the employer as a condition of employment. Absent this requirement, the employee would be free to pursue his claims in court without having to pay for the services of a judge. In such a circumstance — where arbitration has been imposed by the employer and occurs only at the option of the employer — arbitrators' fees should be borne solely by the employer.

Some commentators have suggested that it would be a perversion of the arbitration process to have the arbitrator paid by only one party to the dispute. We fail to appreciate the basis for this concern. If an arbitrator is likely to "lean" in favor of an employer — something we have no reason to suspect — it would be because the employer is a source of future arbitration business, and not because the employer alone pays the arbitrator. It is doubtful that arbitrators care about who pays them, so long as they are paid for their services.

One empirical study that found that employees recover less on their claims against repeat-player companies, defined as companies that use arbitration more than once in a year, than they do against non-repeat players. *See* Sternlight, 74 WASH. U. L.Q. at 685 (citing unpublished study by Prof. Lisa Bingham); David Segal, *Short-Circuiting the Courts; An Overburdened Legal System Has Turned Mediation Into Big Business,* WASH. POST, Oct. 7, 1996, at F12 (Bingham study shows that repeat-player employers win in arbitration twice as often as non-repeat players). It is hard to know what to make of these studies without assessing the relative *merits* of the cases in the surveys.

Furthermore, there are several protections against the possibility of arbitrators systematically favoring employers because employers are the source of future business. For one thing, it is unlikely that such corruption would escape the scrutiny of plaintiffs' lawyers or appointing agencies like AAA. Corrupt arbitrators will not survive long in the business. . . . Finally, if the arbitrators who are assigned to hear and decide statutory claims adhere to the professional and ethical standards set by arbitrators in the context of collective bargaining, there is little reason for concern. In this sense, the rich tradition of arbitration in collective bargaining *does* serve as a valuable model.

In sum, we hold that Cole could not be required to agree to arbitrate his public law claims as a condition of employment if the arbitration agreement required him to pay all or part of the arbitrator's fees and expenses. In light of this holding, we find that the arbitration agreement in this case is valid and enforceable. We do so because we interpret the agreement as requiring Burns Security to pay all of the arbitrator's fees necessary for a full and fair resolution of Cole's statutory claims.

As we noted earlier, the disputed agreement does not explicitly address this issue; it merely incorporates the provisions of the AAA Rules. However, the AAA Rules are also silent on this point, so there is no clear allocation of responsibility for payment of arbitrator's fees. It is well understood that, where a contract is unclear on a point, an interpretation that makes the contract lawful is preferred to one that renders it unlawful. *See 1010 Potomac Assoc.*

v. Grocery Mfrs. of Am., Inc., 485 A.2d 199, 205 (D.C.1984) (a contract "must be interpreted as a whole, giving a reasonable, *lawful,* and effective meaning to all its terms." It is also accepted that ambiguous provisions are construed against the drafter of the contract, in this case, Burns. [W]e interpret the arbitration agreement between Cole and Burns as requiring Burns to pay all arbitrators' fees in connection with the resolution of Cole's claims.

4. *Judicial Review*

The final issue in this case concerns the scope of judicial review of arbitral awards in cases of this sort, where an employee is compelled as a condition of employment to arbitrate statutory claims. Cole has argued that the arbitration agreement is unconscionable, because any arbitrator's rulings, even as to the meaning of public law under Title VII, will not be subject to judicial review. Cole is wrong on this point.

Judicial review of arbitration awards covering statutory claims is necessarily focused, but that does not mean that meaningful review is unavailable. The FAA itself recognizes a number of grounds on which arbitration awards may be vacated . . .

* * *

The grounds listed in the FAA, however, are not exclusive. Indeed, even in the context of arbitration in collective bargaining — where judicial review of arbitral awards is extremely limited — awards may be set aside if they are contrary to "some explicit public policy" that is "well defined and dominant" and ascertained "by reference to the laws and legal precedents." *See United Paperworkers Int'l Union v. Misco, Inc.,* 484 U.S. 29, 43 (1987) There is no doubt that the scope of review of arbitration in cases involving mandatory arbitration of statutory claims is *at least* as great as the judicial review available in the context of collective bargaining.

The Supreme Court has also indicated that arbitration awards can be vacated if they are in "manifest disregard of the law." *See First Options of Chicago, Inc. v. Kaplan,* 514 U.S. 938 (1995) (citing *Wilko v. Swan,* 346 U.S. 427, 436–37 (1953), overruled on other grounds in *Rodriguez de Quijas v. Shearson/American Express, Inc.,* 490 U.S. 477 (1989)). Although this term has not been defined by the Court, and the circuits have adopted various formulations, we believe that this type of review must be defined by reference to the assumptions underlying the Court's endorsement of arbitration. As discussed above, the strict deference accorded to arbitration decisions in the collective bargaining arena may not be appropriate in statutory cases in which an employee has been forced to resort to arbitration as a condition of employment. Rather, in this statutory context, the "manifest disregard of law" standard must be defined in light of the bases underlying the Court's decisions in *Gilmer*-type cases.

Two assumptions have been central to the Court's decisions in this area. First, the Court has insisted that, " '[b]y agreeing to arbitrate a statutory claim, a party does not forego the substantive rights afforded by the statute; it only submits to their resolution in an arbitral, rather than a judicial, forum.'" *Gilmer,* 500 U.S. at 26, 111 S.Ct. at 1652 (quoting *Mitsubishi,* 473 U.S. at 628); *see also McMahon,* 482 U.S. at 229–30. Second, the Court has stated repeatedly that, "'although judicial scrutiny of arbitration awards necessarily is limited, such review is sufficient to ensure that arbitrators comply with the requirements of the statute' at issue." *Gilmer,* 500 U.S. at 32 n. 4 (quoting *McMahon,* 482 U.S. at 232, 107 S.Ct. at 2340). These twin assumptions regarding the arbitration of statutory claims are valid only if judicial review under the "manifest disregard of the law" standard is sufficiently rigorous to ensure that arbitrators have properly interpreted and applied statutory law.

The value and finality of an employer's arbitration system will not be undermined by focused review of arbitral legal determinations. Most employment discrimination claims are entirely factual in nature and involve well-settled legal principles. In fact, one study done in the 1980s found that discrimination cases involve factual claims approximately 84 % of the time. *See* Michele Hoyman & Lamont E. Stallworth, *The Arbitration of Discrimination Grievances in the Aftermath of* Gardner-Denver, 39 ARB. J. 49, 53 (Sept.1984). As a result, in the vast majority of cases, judicial review of legal determinations to ensure compliance with public law should have no adverse impact on the arbitration process. Nonetheless, there will be some cases in which novel or difficult legal issues are presented demanding judicial judgment. In such cases, the courts are empowered to review an arbitrator's award to ensure that its resolution of public law issues is correct. Indeed, at oral argument, Burns conceded the courts' authority to engage in such review. Because meaningful judicial review of public law issues is available, Cole's agreement to arbitrate is not unconscionable or otherwise unenforceable.

* * *

For the foregoing reasons, we affirm the District Court's order dismissing the complaint and compelling arbitration.

NOTES

1. Does Judge Edwards' opinion in the *Cole* decision give appropriate weight to the intent of the parties? Is consent an issue in this dispute?

2. Other decisions have dealt with agreements to bear arbitration costs. Who should pay for arbitration? Some courts have invalidated mandatory arbitration agreements that impose significant costs on employees. The Eleventh Circuit invalidated a mandatory arbitration agreement that required the employee to pay a $2,000 filing fee and half of the arbitrator's fee in *Paladino v. Avnet Computer Technologies,* 134 F.3d 1054 (11th Cir. 1998). Similarly, in *Shankle v. B-G Maintenance Management of Colorado,* 163 F.3d 1230 (10th Cir. 1999), the Tenth Circuit invalidated an arbitration agreement that forced the employee to pay one-half of the $250 hourly arbitrator's fee. What is the rationale for these decisions?

C. ANTITRUST ARBITRATION

Antitrust cases are often complex disputes that bristle with public policy questions and are characterized by heavy pretrial practice and substantial discovery. In the past, these themes led courts to barantitrust arbitration. Consider these points as you read the following case.

MITSUBISHI MOTORS CORP. v. SOLER CHRYSLER-PLYMOUTH, INC.
473 U.S. 614 (1985)

Justice BLACKMUN delivered the opinion of the Court.

The principal question presented by these cases is the arbitrability, pursuant to the Federal Arbitration Act, and the Convention on the Recognition and Enforcement of Foreign Arbitral Awards (Convention), of claims arising under the Sherman Act, and encompassed within a valid arbitration clause in an agreement embodying an international commercial transaction.

*   *   *

[A dispute arose between Soler, a Puerto Rican auto dealer and Mitsubishi, a joint venture of Chrysler International, a Swiss corporation, and Mitsubishi Heavy Industries, Inc., a Japanese corporation. The auto distribution agreement between Chrysler and Soler did not contain an arbitration clause. A separate contract between Soler and the joint venture called for purchase of cars from Mitsubishi. A specific contract relating to Soler's purchase of autos from Mitsubishi called for "arbitration in Japan in accordance with the rules and regulations of the Japanese Arbitration Act" and contained a choice of law clause providing for the application of Swiss law. Soler sought to delay or cancel orders and to divert some automobiles to Central America. Mitsubishi rejected Soler's diversion effort, because the autos lacked equipment and service needed in Central America. Mitsubishi sued to compel arbitration and sought arbitration in Japan. Soler counterclaimed under the federal Automobile Dealers Day in Court Act, Puerto Rican contract and competition laws and the federal Sherman Act. The antitrust court alleged a conspiracy between Mitsubishi and Chrysler International to divide territories. The trial court compelled arbitration and rejected *American Safety Equipment Corp. v. J.P. MacGuire & Co.*, 391 F.2d 821 (2d Cir. 1968), a leading decision holding that antitrust claims were inappropriate for arbitration. The Court of Appeals reversed, 723 F.2d 155 (1st Cir. 1983), reasoning that the *American Safety* doctrine prevented arbitration of the antitrust allegations.]

We granted certiorari primarily to consider whether an American court should enforce an agreement to resolve antitrust claims by arbitration when that agreement arises from an international transaction.

II

At the outset, we address the contention raised in Soler's cross-petition that the arbitration clause at issue may not be read to encompass the statutory counterclaims stated in its answer to the complaint. In making this argument,

Soler does not question the Court of Appeals' application of * * * the Sales Agreement to the disputes involved here as a matter of standard contract interpretation. Instead, it argues that as a matter of law a court may not construe an arbitration agreement to encompass claims arising out of statutes designed to protect a class to which the party resisting arbitration belongs "unless [that party] has expressly agreed" to arbitrate those claims, by which Soler presumably means that the arbitration clause must specifically mention the statute giving rise to the claims that a party to the clause seeks to arbitrate. Soler reasons that, because it falls within the class for whose benefit the federal and local antitrust laws and dealers' Acts were passed, but the arbitration clause at issue does not mention these statutes or statutes in general, the clause cannot be read to contemplate arbitration of these statutory claims.

* * *

There is no reason to depart from these guidelines where a party bound by an arbitration agreement raises claims founded on statutory rights. Some time ago this Court expressed "hope for [the Act's] usefulness both in controversies based on statutes or on standards otherwise created," *Wilko v. Swan*, 346 U.S. 427, 432 (1953) (footnote omitted); *see Merrill Lynch, Pierce, Fenner & Smith, Inc. v. Ware*, 414 U.S. 117, 135, n. 15 (1973), and we are well past the time when judicial suspicion of the desirability of arbitration and of the competence of arbitral tribunals inhibited the development of arbitration as an alternative means of dispute resolution. Just last Term in *Southland Corp.* [*v. Keating*, 465 U.S. 1 (1984)], where we held that § 2 of the Act declared a national policy applicable equally in state as well as federal courts, we construed an arbitration clause to encompass the disputes at issue without pausing at the source in a state statute of the rights asserted by the parties resisting arbitration. 465 U.S., at 15, and n. 7.[15] Of course, courts should remain attuned to well-supported claims that the agreement to arbitrate resulted from the sort of fraud or overwhelming economic power that would provide grounds "for the revocation of any contract." 9 U.S.C. § 2; *see Southland Corp.*, 465 U.S., at 16, n. 11; *The Bremen v. Zapata Off-Shore Co.*, 407 U.S. 1, 15. But, absent such compelling considerations, the Act itself provides no basis for disfavoring agreements to arbitrate statutory claims by skewing the otherwise hospitable inquiry into arbitrability.

That is not to say that all controversies implicating statutory rights are suitable for arbitration. There is no reason to distort the process of contract interpretation, however, in order to ferret out the inappropriate. Just as it is the congressional policy manifested in the Federal Arbitration Act that requires courts liberally to construe the scope of arbitration agreements covered by that Act, it is the congressional intention expressed in some other statute on which the courts must rely to identify any category of claims as

---

[15] The claims whose arbitrability was at issue in *Southland Corp.* arose under the disclosure requirements of the California Franchise Investment Law, Cal.Corp.Code Ann. § 31000 et seq. (1977). While the dissent in *Southland Corp.* disputed the applicability of the Act to proceedings in the state courts, it did not object to the Court's reading of the arbitration clause under examination.

to which agreements to arbitrate will be held unenforceable. For that reason, Soler's concern for statutorily protected classes provides no reason to color the lens through which the arbitration clause is read. By agreeing to arbitrate a statutory claim, a party does not forgo the substantive rights afforded by the statute; it only submits to their resolution in an arbitral, rather than a judicial, forum. It trades the procedures and opportunity for review of the courtroom for the simplicity, informality, and expedition of arbitration. We must assume that if Congress intended the substantive protection afforded by a given statute to include protection against waiver of the right to a judicial forum, that intention will be deducible from text or legislative history. *See Wilko v. Swan, supra.* Having made the bargain to arbitrate, the party should be held to it unless Congress itself has evinced an intention to preclude a waiver of judicial remedies for the statutory rights at issue. Nothing, in the meantime, prevents a party from excluding statutory claims from the scope of an agreement to arbitrate. *See Prima Paint Corp.*, 388 U.S. 395, 406 (1967).

In sum, the Court of Appeals correctly conducted a two-step inquiry, first determining whether the parties' agreement to arbitrate reached the statutory issues, and then, upon finding it did, considering whether legal constraints external to the parties' agreement foreclosed the arbitration of those claims. We endorse its rejection of Soler's proposed rule of arbitration-clause construction.

III

We now turn to consider whether Soler's antitrust claims are nonarbitrable even though it has agreed to arbitrate them. In holding that they are not, the Court of Appeals followed the decision of the Second Circuit in *American Safety Equipment Corp. v. J.P. Maguire & Co.* Notwithstanding the absence of any explicit support for such an exception in either the Sherman Act or the Federal Arbitration Act, the Second Circuit there reasoned that "the pervasive public interest in enforcement of the antitrust laws, and the nature of the claims that arise in such cases, combine to make . . . antitrust claims . . . inappropriate for arbitration." We find it unnecessary to assess the legitimacy of the *American Safety* doctrine as applied to agreements to arbitrate arising from domestic transactions. As in *Scherk v. Alberto-Culver Co.*, 417 U.S. 506 (1974), we conclude that concerns of international comity, respect for the capacities of foreign and transnational tribunals, and sensitivity to the need of the international commercial system for predictability in the resolution of disputes require that we enforce the parties' agreement, even assuming that a contrary result would be forthcoming in a domestic context.

Even before *Scherk*, this Court had recognized the utility of forum-selection clauses in international transactions. In *The Bremen, supra*, an American oil company, seeking to evade a contractual choice of an English forum and, by implication, English law, filed a suit in admiralty in a United States District Court against the German corporation which had contracted to tow its rig to a location in the Adriatic Sea. Notwithstanding the possibility that the English court would enforce provisions in the towage contract exculpating the German party which an American court would refuse to enforce, this Court gave effect to the choice-of-forum clause. It observed: "The expansion of American business and industry will hardly be encouraged if, notwithstanding solemn contracts, we insist on a parochial concept that all disputes must be resolved under our laws and in our courts. . . . We cannot have trade and commerce in world markets and international waters exclusively on our terms, governed by our laws, and resolved in our courts." Recognizing that "agreeing in advance on a forum acceptable to both parties is an indispensable element in international trade, commerce, and contracting," the decision in *The Bremen* clearly eschewed a provincial solicitude for the jurisdiction of domestic forums.

Identical considerations governed the Court's decision in *Scherk*, which categorized "[a]n agreement to arbitrate before a specified tribunal [as], in effect, a specialized kind of forum-selection clause that posits not only the situs of suit but also the procedure to be used in resolving the dispute." * * *

At the outset, we confess to some skepticism of certain aspects of the *American Safety* doctrine. As distilled by the First Circuit, the doctrine comprises four ingredients. First, private parties play a pivotal role in aiding governmental enforcement of the antitrust laws by means of the private action for treble damages. Second, "the strong possibility that contracts which generate antitrust disputes may be contracts of adhesion militates against automatic forum determination by contract." Third, antitrust issues, prone to complication, require sophisticated legal and economic analysis, and thus are "ill-adapted to strengths of the arbitral process, i.e., expedition, minimal requirements of written rationale, simplicity, resort to basic concepts of common sense and simple equity." Finally, just as "issues of war and peace are too important to be vested in the generals, . . . decisions as to antitrust regulation of business are too important to be lodged in arbitrators chosen from the business community — particularly those from a foreign community that has had no experience with or exposure to our law and values." *See American Safety*.

Initially, we find the second concern unjustified. The mere appearance of an antitrust dispute does not alone warrant invalidation of the selected forum on the undemonstrated assumption that the arbitration clause is tainted. A party resisting arbitration of course may attack directly the validity of the agreement to arbitrate. Moreover, the party may attempt to make a showing that would warrant setting aside the forum-selection clause — that the agreement was "[a]ffected by fraud, undue influence, or overweening bargaining power"; that "enforcement would be unreasonable and unjust"; or that proceedings "in the contractual forum will be so gravely difficult and inconvenient that [the resisting party] will for all practical purposes be deprived of his day in court." But absent such a showing — and none was attempted here — there is no basis for assuming the forum inadequate or its selection unfair.

Next, potential complexity should not suffice to ward off arbitration. We might well have some doubt that even the courts following *American Safety* subscribe fully to the view that antitrust matters are inherently insusceptible to resolution by arbitration, as these same courts have agreed that an undertaking to arbitrate antitrust claims entered into after the dispute arises is acceptable. And the vertical restraints which most frequently give birth to antitrust claims covered by an arbitration agreement will not often occasion the monstrous proceedings that have given antitrust litigation an image of intractability. In any event, adaptability and access to expertise are hallmarks of arbitration. The anticipated subject matter of the dispute may be taken into account when the arbitrators are appointed, and arbitral rules typically provide for the participation of experts either employed by the parties or appointed by the tribunal. Moreover, it is often a judgment that streamlined proceedings and expeditious results will best serve their needs that causes parties to agree to arbitrate their disputes; it is typically a desire to keep the effort and expense required to resolve a dispute within manageable bounds that prompts them mutually to forgo access to judicial remedies. In sum, the factor of potential complexity alone does not persuade us that an arbitral tribunal could not properly handle an antitrust matter.

For similar reasons, we also reject the proposition that an arbitration panel will pose too great a danger of innate hostility to the constraints on business conduct that antitrust law imposes. International arbitrators frequently are drawn from the legal as well as the business community; where the dispute has an important legal component, the parties and the arbitral body with whose assistance they have agreed to settle their dispute can be expected to select arbitrators accordingly. We decline to indulge the presumption that the parties and arbitral body conducting a proceeding will be unable or unwilling to retain competent, conscientious, and impartial arbitrators.

We are left, then, with the core of the *American Safety* doctrine — the fundamental importance to American democratic capitalism of the regime of the antitrust laws. Without doubt, the private cause of action plays a central role in enforcing this regime. As the Court of Appeals pointed out: " 'A claim under the antitrust laws is not merely a private matter. The Sherman Act is designed to promote the national interest in a competitive economy; thus, the plaintiff asserting his rights under the Act has been likened to a private attorney-general who protects the public's interest.' " The treble-damages provision wielded by the private litigant is a chief tool in the antitrust enforcement scheme, posing a crucial deterrent to potential violators.

The importance of the private damages remedy, however, does not compel the conclusion that it may not be sought outside an American court. Notwithstanding its important incidental policing function, the treble-damages cause of action conferred on private parties by § 4 of the Clayton Act, 15 U.S.C. § 15, and pursued by Soler here by way of its third counterclaim, seeks primarily to enable an injured competitor to gain compensation for that injury. "Section 4 . . . is in essence a remedial provision. It provides treble damages to [a]ny person who shall be injured in his business or property by reason of anything forbidden in the antitrust laws. . . .' Of course, treble damages also play an important role in penalizing wrongdoers and deterring wrongdoing, as we also have frequently observed. . . . It nevertheless is true that the treble-damages provision, which makes awards available only to injured parties, and measures the awards by a multiple of the injury actually proved, is designed primarily as a remedy." * * *

There is no reason to assume at the outset of the dispute that international arbitration will not provide an adequate mechanism. To be sure, the international arbitral tribunal owes no prior allegiance to the legal norms of particular states; hence, it has no direct obligation to vindicate their statutory dictates. The tribunal, however, is bound to effectuate the intentions of the parties. Where the parties have agreed that the arbitral body is to decide a defined set of claims which includes, as in these cases, those arising from the application of American antitrust law, the tribunal therefore should be bound to decide that dispute in accord with the national law giving rise to the claim.[19] And so long as the prospective litigant effectively may vindicate its statutory cause of action in the arbitral forum, the statute will continue to serve both its remedial and deterrent function.

Having permitted the arbitration to go forward, the national courts of the United States will have the opportunity at the award-enforcement stage to ensure that the legitimate interest in the enforcement of the antitrust laws has been addressed. The Convention reserves to each signatory country the right to refuse enforcement of an award where the "recognition or enforcement of the award would be contrary to the public policy of that country." Art. V(2)(b), 21 U.S.T., at 2520. While the efficacy of the arbitral process requires that substantive review at the award-enforcement stage remain minimal, it would not require intrusive inquiry to ascertain that the tribunal took cognizance of the antitrust claims and actually decided them.[20]

As international trade has expanded in recent decades, so too has the use of international arbitration to resolve disputes arising in the course of that trade. The controversies that international arbitral institutions are called upon to resolve have increased in diversity as well as in complexity. Yet the potential of these tribunals for efficient disposition of legal disagreements arising from commercial relations has not yet been tested. If they are to take a central place in the international legal order, national courts will need to "shake off the old judicial hostility to arbitration," and also their customary

---

[19] In addition to the clause providing for arbitration before the Japan Commercial Arbitration Association, the Sales Agreement includes a choice-of-law clause which reads: "This Agreement is made in, and will be governed by and construed in all respects according to the laws of the Swiss Confederation as if entirely performed therein." The United States raises the possibility that the arbitral panel will read this provision not simply to govern interpretation of the contract terms, but wholly to displace American law even where it otherwise would apply. Brief for United States. The International Chamber of Commerce opines that it is "[c]onceivabl[e], although we believe it unlikely, [that] the arbitrators could consider Soler's affirmative claim of anticompetitive conduct by CISA and Mitsubishi to fall within the purview of this choice-of-law provision, with the result that it would be decided under Swiss law rather than the U.S. Sherman Act." At oral argument, however, counsel for Mitsubishi conceded that American law applied to the antitrust claims and represented that the claims had been submitted to the arbitration panel in Japan on that basis. The record confirms that before the decision of the Court of Appeals the arbitral panel had taken these claims under submission. We therefore have no occasion to speculate on this matter at this stage in the proceedings, when Mitsubishi seeks to enforce the agreement to arbitrate, not to enforce an award. Nor need we consider now the effect of an arbitral tribunal's failure to take cognizance of the statutory cause of action on the claimant's capacity to reinitiate suit in federal court. We merely note that in the event the choice-of-forum and choice-of-law clauses operated in tandem as a prospective waiver of a party's right to pursue statutory remedies for antitrust violations, we would have little hesitation in condemning the agreement as against public policy.

[20] * * * We note, for example, that the rules of the Japan Commercial Arbitration Association provide for the taking of a "summary record" of each hearing, Rule 28.1; for the stenographic recording of the proceedings where the tribunal so orders or a party requests one, Rule 28.2; and for a statement of reasons for the award unless the parties agree otherwise, Rule 36.1(4). Needless to say, we intimate no views on the merits of Soler's antitrust claims.

and understandable unwillingness to cede jurisdiction of a claim arising under domestic law to a foreign or transnational tribunal. To this extent, at least, it will be necessary for national courts to subordinate domestic notions of arbitrability to the international policy favoring commercial arbitration.

Accordingly, we "require this representative of the American business community to honor its bargain," by holding this agreement to arbitrate "enforce[-able] . . . in accord with the explicit provisions of the Arbitration Act."

The judgment of the Court of Appeals is affirmed in part and reversed in part, and the cases are remanded for further proceedings consistent with this opinion.

It is so ordered.

Justice POWELL took no part in the decision of these cases.

Justice STEVENS, with whom Justice BRENNAN joins, and with whom Justice MARSHALL joins except as to Part II, dissenting.

One element of this rather complex litigation is a claim asserted by an American dealer in Plymouth automobiles that two major automobile companies are parties to an international cartel that has restrained competition in the American market. Pursuant to an agreement that is alleged to have violated § 1 of the Sherman Act, 15 U.S.C. § 1, those companies allegedly prevented the dealer from transshipping some 966 surplus vehicles from Puerto Rico to other dealers in the American market.

*   *   *

On several occasions we have drawn a distinction between statutory rights and contractual rights and refused to hold that an arbitration barred the assertion of a statutory right. Thus, in *Alexander v. Gardner-Denver Co.*, 415 U.S. 36 (1974), we held that the arbitration of a claim of employment discrimination would not bar an employee's statutory right to damages under Title VII of the Civil Rights Act of 1964, 42 U.S.C. §§ 2000e — 2000e-17, notwithstanding the strong federal policy favoring the arbitration of labor disputes. In that case the Court explained at some length why it would be unreasonable to assume that Congress intended to give arbitrators the final authority to implement the federal statutory policy:

> [W]e have long recognized that 'the choice of forums inevitably affects the scope of the substantive right to be vindicated.' Respondent's deferral rule is necessarily premised on the assumption that arbitral processes are commensurate with judicial processes and that Congress impliedly intended federal courts to defer to arbitral decisions on Title VII issues. We deem this supposition unlikely.
>
> Arbitral procedures, while well suited to the resolution of contractual disputes, make arbitration a comparatively inappropriate forum for the final resolution of rights created by Title VII. This conclusion rests first on the special role of the arbitrator, whose task is to effectuate the intent of the parties rather than the requirements of enacted legislation. . . . But other facts may still render arbitral processes comparatively inferior to judicial processes in the protection of Title

VII rights. Among these is the fact that the specialized competence of arbitrators pertains primarily to the law of the shop, not the law of the land. Parties usually choose an arbitrator because they trust his knowledge and judgment concerning the demands and norms of industrial relations. On the other hand, the resolution of statutory or constitutional issues is a primary responsibility of courts, and judicial construction has proved especially necessary with respect to Title VII, whose broad language frequently can be given meaning only by reference to public law concepts.

415 U.S., at 56–57.

In addition, the Court noted that the informal procedures which make arbitration so desirable in the context of contractual disputes are inadequate to develop a record for appellate review of statutory questions.[14] Such review is essential on matters of statutory interpretation in order to assure consistent application of important public rights.

In *Barrentine v. Arkansas-Best Freight System, Inc.*, 450 U.S. 728 (1981), we reached a similar conclusion with respect to the arbitrability of an employee's claim based on the Fair Labor Standards Act, 29 U.S.C. §§ 201-219. We again noted that an arbitrator, unlike a federal judge, has no institutional obligation to enforce federal legislative policy:

Because the arbitrator is required to effectuate the intent of the parties, rather than to enforce the statute, he may issue a ruling that is inimical to the public policies underlying the FLSA, thus depriving an employee of protected statutory rights.

Finally, not only are arbitral procedures less protective of individual statutory rights than are judicial procedures, but arbitrators very often are powerless to grant the aggrieved employees as broad a range of relief. Under the FLSA, courts can award actual and liquidated damages, reasonable attorney's fees, and costs. 29 U.S.C. § 216(b). An arbitrator, by contrast, can award only that compensation authorized by the wage provision of the collective-bargaining agreement. . . . It is most unlikely that he will be authorized to award liquidated damages, costs, or attorney's fees.

450 U.S., at 744–45.

The Court has applied the same logic in holding that federal claims asserted under the Ku Klux Act of 1871, 42 U.S.C. § 1983, and claims arising under § 12(2) of the Securities Act of 1933, 15 U.S.C. § 77l (2), may not be finally resolved by an arbitrator. *McDonald v. City of West Branch*, 466 U.S. 284 (1984); *Wilko v. Swan*, 346 U.S. 427 (1953).

---

[14] "Moreover, the factfinding process in arbitration usually is not equivalent to judicial factfinding. The record of the arbitration proceedings is not as complete; the usual rules of evidence do not apply; and rights and procedures common to civil trials, such as discovery, compulsory process, cross-examination, and testimony under oath, are often severely limited or unavailable. And as this Court has recognized, § [a]rbitrators have no obligation to the court to give their reasons for an award.' Indeed, it is the informality of arbitral procedure that enables it to function as an efficient, inexpensive, and expeditious means for dispute resolution. This same characteristic, however, makes arbitration a less appropriate forum for final resolution of Title VII issues than the federal courts."

The Court's opinions in *Alexander*, *Barrentine*, *McDonald*, and *Wilko* all explain why it makes good sense to draw a distinction between statutory claims and contract claims. In view of the Court's repeated recognition of the distinction between federal statutory rights and contractual rights, together with the undisputed historical fact that arbitration has functioned almost entirely in either the area of labor disputes or in "ordinary disputes between merchants as to questions of fact," it is reasonable to assume that most lawyers and executives would not expect the language in the standard arbitration clause to cover federal statutory claims. Thus, in my opinion, both a fair respect for the importance of the interests that Congress has identified as worthy of federal statutory protection, and a fair appraisal of the most likely understanding of the parties who sign agreements containing standard arbitration clauses, support a presumption that such clauses do not apply to federal statutory claims.

III

The Court has repeatedly held that a decision by Congress to create a special statutory remedy renders a private agreement to arbitrate a federal statutory claim unenforceable. * * * The reasons that motivated those decisions apply with special force to the federal policy that is protected by the antitrust laws.

* * *

The unique public interest in the enforcement of the antitrust laws is repeatedly reflected in the special remedial scheme enacted by Congress. Since its enactment in 1890, the Sherman Act has provided for public enforcement through criminal as well as civil sanctions. * * *

In view of the history of antitrust enforcement in the United States, it is not surprising that all of the federal courts that have considered the question have uniformly and unhesitatingly concluded that agreements to arbitrate federal antitrust issues are not enforceable. In a landmark opinion for the Court of Appeals for the Second Circuit, Judge Feinberg wrote:

> A claim under the antitrust laws is not merely a private matter. The Sherman Act is designed to promote the national interest in a competitive economy; thus, the plaintiff asserting his rights under the Act has been likened to a private attorney-general who protects the public's interest. . . . Antitrust violations can affect hundreds of thousands — perhaps millions — of people and inflict staggering economic damage. . . . We do not believe that Congress intended such claims to be resolved elsewhere than in the courts. We do not suggest that all antitrust litigations attain these swollen proportions; the courts, no less than the public, are thankful that they do not. But in fashioning a rule to govern the arbitrability of antitrust claims, we must consider the rule's potential effect. For the same reason, it is also proper to ask whether contracts of adhesion between alleged monopolists and their customers should determine the forum for trying antitrust violations."

American Safety Equipment Corp. v. J.P. Maguire & Co., 391 F.2d 821, 826-827 (1968) (footnote omitted). This view has been followed in later cases from that Circuit and by the First, Fifth, Seventh, Eighth, and Ninth Circuits. It is clearly a correct statement of the law.

This Court would be well advised to endorse the collective wisdom of the distinguished judges of the Courts of Appeals who have unanimously concluded that the statutory remedies fashioned by Congress for the enforcement of the antitrust laws render an agreement to arbitrate antitrust disputes unenforceable. Arbitration awards are only reviewable for manifest disregard of the law, 9 U.S.C. §§ 10, 207, and the rudimentary procedures which make arbitration so desirable in the context of a private dispute often mean that the record is so inadequate that the arbitrator's decision is virtually unreviewable. Despotic decisionmaking of this kind is fine for parties who are willing to agree in advance to settle for a best approximation of the correct result in order to resolve quickly and inexpensively any contractual dispute that may arise in an ongoing commercial relationship. Such informality, however, is simply unacceptable when every error may have devastating consequences for important businesses in our national economy and may undermine their ability to compete in world markets. Instead of "muffling a grievance in the cloakroom of arbitration," the public interest in free competitive markets would be better served by having the issues resolved "in the light of impartial public court adjudication."

* * *

In my opinion, the elected representatives of the American people would not have us dispatch an American citizen to a foreign land in search of an uncertain remedy for the violation of a public right that is protected by the Sherman Act. This is especially so when there has been no genuine bargaining over the terms of the submission, and the arbitration remedy provided has not even the most elementary guarantees of fair process. Consideration of a fully developed record by a jury, instructed in the law by a federal judge, and subject to appellate review, is a surer guide to the competitive character of a commercial practice than the practically unreviewable judgment of a private arbitrator.

Unlike the Congress that enacted the Sherman Act in 1890, the Court today does not seem to appreciate the value of economic freedom. I respectfully dissent.

NOTES

1. Is it significant that Soler, a firm that could be characterized as a small business, had no arbitration clause in its basic distribution agreement with Chrysler? Soler, of course, did sign an independent agreement to arbitrate disputes with the Chrysler International and Mitsubishi joint venture that supplied the automobiles related to the dispute.

2. Is there any room for the *American Safety* doctrine under the Federal Arbitration Act? Is the *American Safety* doctrine a judge made, common law exception to the FAA or, alternatively, is it a construction of the Sherman Act?

If you are not comfortable with either of the above options can we place *American Safety* within the public policy exception to the norm of arbitrability?

3. What influence should the choice of Swiss law be in this case? Doesn't the choice of law clause effectively prevent the arbitrators from applying U.S. arbitral law? Is it fair for a U.S. court to send the matter to an international arbitration that will apply Swiss law and dismiss the case?

4. Doesn't the *Mitsubishi* decision undercut the theoretical foundation of *American Safety*? Wouldn't you expect the Supreme court to rebuke *American Safety* if it has the chance? The opportunity may arise given the present conflict of circuits on the question of whether the federal courts should compel arbitration of domestic antitrust disputes. The Ninth Circuit has relied on the reasoning of *Mitsubishi* to overrule an earlier decision that barred arbitration of antitrust claims. (*Nghien v. NEC Electronic, Inc.*, 25 F.3d 1437 (9th Cir.) *cert. denied*, 115 S. Ct. 638 (1994). *Accord, Sanjuan v. American Bd. of Psychiatry and Neurology, Inc.*, 40 F.3d 247, 250 (7th Cir. 1994), *cert. denied*, 116 S. Ct. 1044 (1996).) The Ninth Circuit's *Nghien* decision reasoned that *Mitsubishi* "specifically refuted the analysis of *American Safety*," that *Gilmer* had cited *Mitsubishi* "for the general proposition that antitrust claims can be arbitrated" and that *McMahon* had clarified that statutory claims were subject to arbitration. (25 F.3d at 1441-42.) In contrast, the Eleventh Circuit held that *Mitsubishi* does not mandate its reversal of earlier decisions that domestic antitrust claims are not arbitrable. (*Kotam Elect., Inc. v. JBL Consumer Prod., Inc.*, 59 F.3d 1155 (11th Cir. 1995).) Although a dissent in the *Kotam* decision reasoned that *Mitsubishi* "dealt a death blow to" cases adhering to *American Safety*, 59 F.3d at 1159, the majority emphasized the qualification in the *Mitsubishi* decision that certiorari was granted in a factual context when an arbitration "agreement arises from an international transaction." (59 F.3d at 1157, *citing* 473 U.S. at 624.) Is this too fine a distinction?

Antitrust Arbitration Revisited: On rehearing *en banc,* the Eleventh Circuit reversed the panel decision in *Kotam Electronics, Inc. v. JBL Consumer Products, Inc.,* 93 F.3d 724 (11th Cir. 1996), holding that courts must enforce valid domestic antitrust claims. The Court of Appeals relied upon the reasoning of the Supreme Court's *Mitsubishi* decision, language in *McMahon* that the reasoning of *Mitsubishi* would apply to domestic cases, and the assertion in *Gilmer* that "claims under the Sherman Act are appropriate for arbitration." Similarly, the Second Circuit affirmed without opinion a trial court's holding applying *Mitsubishi* reasoning to a domestic antitrust case. (*Hough v. Merrill Lynch*, 757 F. Supp. 283 (S.D.N.Y.), *aff'd without op.*, 946 F. 2d 883 (2d Cir. 1991).) Given this reasoning, is there much doubt how the Supreme Court will eventually rule when it finally decides an antitrust arbitrability claim in a domestic context?

5. There is little question that the *Mitsubishi* majority rejected the reasoning of *American Safety*. Are the four concerns listed by the Supreme Court the only reasons to oppose antitrust arbitration? What about the privacy aspect of arbitration? Should "public" type issues, such as antitrust, be adjudicated in secret? Doesn't the public have a significant interest in whether antitrust disputes should be effectively walled-off from public scrutiny? The published opinions of litigated cases help to guide third parties in their behavior. This guidance or "public good" function of conventional litigation is normally lost when arbitration takes place. *See, e.g.*, John O'Hara, *The New Jersey Alternative Procedure for Dispute Resolution Act: Vanguard of a "Better Way"?*, 136 U. PA. L. REV. 1723, 1750-51 (1988) (critical of rising arbitration to resolve important high technology software dispute of first impression between IBM and Fujitsu because of failure to develop a new guiding principle of intellectual property law).

6. *Patent and Copyright Arbitration.* The arbitration of copyright and patent validity and infringement issues provides a useful analogy to concerns about antitrust arbitration. In 1982 Congress amended the Patent Act to expressly permit the voluntary arbitration of patent infringement and validity issues. (35 U.S.C. § 294 (1988).) Prior to this legislation numerous decisions prevented the arbitration of patent issues. Some courts were concerned that issues of patent infringement and validity were of public interest and should not be hidden from public view. (*See, e.g., Diematic Mfg. Corp. v. Packaging Indus., Inc.*, 381 F. Supp. 1057, 1061 (S.D.N.Y. 1974) ("questions of patent law are not mere private matters"), *appeal dismissed*, 516 F.2d 975 (2d Cir.), *cert. denied*, 423 U.S. 913 (1975); *Beckman Instruments v. Technical Dev. Corp.*, 433 F.2d 55, 63 (7th Cir. 1970) (validity questions inappropriate for arbitration "given the public interest in challenging invalid patents"), *cert. denied*, 401 U.S. 976 (1971).) While the 1982 legislation makes patent arbitration possible, it requires the patent arbitrator to consider certain substantive defenses and provides that the arbitration award is to affect only those parties to the arbitration. (35 U.S.C. § 294(b) & (c) (1988).) A unique feature of this legislation provides that the award can be modified if a court later invalidates a patent found to be valid in the arbitration. 35 U.S.C. § 294(c). What is the theory that supports this provision?

While available, many firms elect to not use patent arbitration. (*See, e.g.*, Gregg A. Paradise, *Arbitration of Patent Infringement Disputes: Encouraging the Use of Arbitration Through Evidence Rules Reform*, 64 FORDHAM L. REV. 247, 248 (1995) ("most patent attorneys and their clients still avoid arbitration").) Businesses fear the lack of full discovery, the tendency of arbitrators to issue "compromise" awards, and the lack of evidence rules in the arbitration itself. (*Id.* at 265-73.) Firms could cure these potential shortcomings by customizing their arbitration clauses to increase the judicialization of the process.

Unlike the Patent Act, copyright legislation does not expressly authorize arbitration of copyright infringement or validity. These are issues with considerable public interest impact and ones that some would prefer to be in the public domain. Nonetheless, the Seventh Circuit has asserted "that federal law does not forbid arbitration of the validity of a copyright, at least where that validity becomes an issue in the arbitration of a contract dispute." (*Saturday Evening Post Co. v. Rumble-Seat Press Inc.*, 816 F.2d 1191, 1199 (7th Cir. 1987) (court holds that parties to a suit involving copyright infringement may agree to arbitrate the dispute).) For the position that the Copyright Act should be amended to expressly permit arbitration, see Rupak Nag, *It's Time to Write Voluntary Arbitration Into the Copyright Act*, 51 DISP. RES. J. 8 (No. 4 1996).

Following an award in a patent arbitration, the patentee or licensee must give written notice to the Director of the Patent Office. The Director, in turn, enters the award in the prosecution record of the patent. (35 U.S.C. § 294(c).) Thus, the results of the private arbitration are available to the public.

However, the nature of arbitration keeps the decision process involving patent validity and infringement private. Essentially the adjudicatory procedure used in patent arbitration is a secret. Critics of patent arbitration argue that such secrecy is inconsistent with the transparent public policies that should envelop the patent system. A recent article argues that the "secrecy of ADR patent proceedings is antithetical to the patent bargain" and lauds the typical published decision which can "draw attention to inadequacies or signal defects in the law." (*See*, Marion Lim, *ADR of Patent Disputes: A Customized Prescription, Not an Over-the-Counter Remedy*, 6 CARDOZO J. OF CONFLICT RES. 155, 183 (2004).) Another recent article points out that arbitration lacks the ability to "signal defects in the laws" and emphasizes the harm caused by the inability to assess carefully the process and results of patent validity disputes resolved by arbitration. (Paul Janicke, *Maybe We Shouldn't Arbitrate": Some Aspects of the Risk/Benefit Calculus of Agreeing to Binding Arbitration of Patent Disputes*, 39 HOUST. L. REV. 693, 726–27 (2002).)

Patent litigators appear considerably more comfortable with mediation than with arbitration. An empirical survey of patent litigators revealed substantially greater satisfaction with mediation. (*See* Eugene R. Quinn, Jr., *Using Alternative Dispute Resolution to Resolve Patent Litigation: A Survey of Patent Litigators*, 3 MARQ. INTELL. PROP. L. REV. 77 (1999).) The reasons for preferring mediation include the retention of party control over the result, the possibility for mutually beneficial bargains, and lower comparative cost. Keep in mind that patent litigation probably has the greatest cost and greatest potential for delay than any other type of American litigation.

7. The *Mitsubishi* majority seems to treat arbitration agreements as a variety of forum selection clause. Is this linkage appropriate? Arbitration, like forum selection, surely involves selection of where to adjudicate. Arbitration, however, represents an entire system of disputing and thereby constitutes a much more dramatic and systematic choice than that of a mere selection of a forum in a forum selection clause.

8. Assume that in 2009, the Supreme Court ultimately holds that domestic antitrust disputes are freely arbitrable. Antitrust arbitrations become routine. Should the arbitrators be expected to apply established antitrust principles? Given the present state of arbitration law, there are substantial arguments to the contrary. A number of scholars, however, argue that antitrust arbitrators should and will follow the substantive law. Professor Lee reasons that applying substantive antitrust law "might be less costly than developing an alternative set of principles . . . and then applying them to the claim at hand." (Mark R. Lee, *Antitrust and Commercial Arbitration: An Economic Analysis*, 62 ST. JOHN'S L. REV. 1, 26 (1987).) Professor Allison asserts that the incentives will cause the arbitrators to apply antitrust law because the parties will expect arbitrators to act responsibly. (John R. Allison, *Arbitration Agreements and Antitrust Claims: The Need for Enhanced Accommodation of*

Conflicting Public Policies, 64 N.C. L. REV. 219, 242-43 (1986).) Is applying the law without the direction of the parties appropriate or responsible? If arbitration is the creature of contract, the parties could have directed the arbitrator to use substantive law by inserting an application of law clause or by requiring findings of fact and conclusions of law in the award.

VERTICAL ARBITRATION CLAUSES AND THE ARBITRABILITY OF ANTITRUST CLAIMS

It is increasingly common to see arbitration clauses in contracts that set forth the basic structure of vertical relationships between firms up and down a product distribution chain. Such clauses are typical in franchise contracts between franchisee and franchisor, supplier and purchaser, and distribution contracts generally. One reason for the enhanced popularity of such clauses is increasing realization of the need to preserve the long term business investments that exist in vertical relationships. Such vertical interactions are inherently "relational contracts," agreements that last over a long period and ones in which each party is well known to the other and in which a bilateral sense of dependency may exist.

Antitrust disputes present a challenge to the contract drafter desirous of sweeping all antitrust disputes into arbitration and might not be within the typical arbitration agreement. The standard arbitration clause calls for "arbitration of any dispute relating to or arising under this contract." To be sure, some types of antitrust claims are certainly related to the vertical contract signed by the parties. Other types of antitrust claims, however, are arguably outside the specific scope of the standard form arbitration clause used in vertical relational contracts. This was the problem in a 1985 joint venture between Coors Brewing Co. and Molson Breweries, a Canadian brewer. The parties agreed that Molson was to license and distribute Coors products in Canada. The above standard arbitration clause was used. In 1993 Molson entered into a "partnership" arrangement with Miller Brewing, a major competitor of Coors, in which each company made one another the exclusive distributor of the other's products in the U.S. and Canada. In addition, Miller was given one seat on the Molson Board of Directors and purchased 20% of Molson. Coors filed an antitrust suit against Molson and Miller, alleging, *inter alia*, that the Miller-Molson partnership "controlled" the marketing of Coors in Canada and that the two restrained trade. The Tenth Circuit found that some of the antitrust claims could be litigated. (*Coors Brewing Co. v. Molson Breweries*, 51 F.3d 1511 (10th Cir. 1995).) It reasoned that antitrust claims "that do not implicate the contract are litigable. Because Miller was not a party to the contract to arbitrate, a market division strategy between Molson and Miller would presumably not be within the four corners of the contract between Coors and Molson." Antitrust claims that Miller and Molson dominated the market would also, according to the court of appeals, not be related to the contract. For elaboration on this problem, see Donald I. Baker & Mark R. Stabile, *Arbitration of Antitrust Claims: Opportunities and Hazards for Corporate Counsel*, 48 BUS. LAW 395 (1993) (contending that some types of antitrust claims — dispute between competitors and disputes relating to injury to the market — "are not suited to arbitration because they do not normally involve contract relationships"). The result of this problem, of course, is that resolution of Coors' claims will take place in two forums, arbitration *and* litigation. Is this a practical result? Is there any way that an arbitration clause could be drafted to cover these types of claims? Coors recently received a major victory in the arbitration phase of its dispute with Molson.

In October, 1996, an arbitration panel ruled that Molson must pay an unspecified amount of "lost profits" to Coors and set a second hearing to determine the amount of damages for 1997. Molson, faced with the looming certainty of a significant damage loss and the risk of an extremely large damage award from the arbitrators, negotiated a settlement with Coors. Coors received $72,000,000 and signed a joint venture contract with Molson and Foster Brewing to form a partnership to manage Coors brands of beer in Canada. (Wall St. J., April 18, 1997.)

Chapter 13

ARBITRATION PROCEDURE

A. ARBITRATOR ETHICS: THE IMPARTIAL AND EXPERT ARBITRATOR

Just as unbiased judges form the cornerstone of our judiciary, impartial arbitrators are essential to the integrity of the arbitration process. As the following materials make clear, arbitration procedures mandate arbitrator impartiality. At the same time, arbitrators are often selected because of their expertise. Arbitrator expertise is often gained through prior experience that may involve interaction with parties to a future arbitration or issues to be later heard as an arbitrator. As you read the following materials, be careful to reconcile the need for arbitrator expertise *and* neutrality and try to sort out the tension between this tradeoff.

COMMONWEALTH COATINGS CORP. v. CONTINENTAL CASUALTY CO.
393 U.S. 145 (1968)

Mr. Justice BLACK delivered the opinion of the Court.

At issue in this case is the question whether elementary requirements of impartiality taken for granted in every judicial proceeding are suspended when the parties agree to resolve a dispute through arbitration.

* * *

[The trial court refused to set aside an award in a construction arbitration held before three arbitrators and the court of appeals affirmed. The losing party contended the award should be set aside because of the failure of a neutral arbitrator who was an engineering consultant to disclose that one of the disputants was a regular customer who, from time to time, hired him. There had been no dealings between this arbitrator and the disputant for about one year prior to the arbitration. The arbitrator had received over $12,000 in fees from this party over a five-year period and had worked as a consultant on the project at issue. None of these facts were revealed during the arbitration.]

* * *

In 1925 Congress enacted the United States Arbitration Act, which sets out a comprehensive plan for arbitration of controversies coming under its terms, and both sides here assume that this Federal Act governs this case. Section 10, quoted below, sets out the conditions upon which awards can be vacated. The two courts below held, however, that § 10 could not be construed in such a way as to justify vacating the award in this case. We disagree and reverse.

Section 10 does authorize vacation of an award where it was "procured by corruption, fraud, or undue means" or "[w]here there was evident partiality * * * in the arbitrators." These provisions show a desire of Congress to provide not merely for any arbitration but for an impartial one. It is true that petitioner does not charge before us that the third arbitrator was actually guilty of fraud or bias in deciding this case, and we have no reason, apart from the undisclosed business relationship, to suspect him of any improper motives. But neither this arbitrator nor the prime contractor gave to petitioner even an intimation of the close financial relations that had existed between them for a period of years. We have no doubt that if a litigant could show that a foreman of a jury or a judge in a court of justice had, unknown to the litigant, any such relationship, the judgment would be subject to challenge. This is shown beyond doubt by *Tumey v. State of Ohio*, 273 U.S. 510 (1927), where this Court held that a conviction could not stand because a small part of the judge's income consisted of court fees collected from convicted defendants. Although in *Tumey* it appeared the amount of the judge's compensation actually depended on whether he decided for one side or the other, that is too small a distinction to allow this manifest violation of the strict morality and fairness Congress would have expected on the part of the arbitrator and the other party in this case. Nor should it be at all relevant, as the Court of Appeals apparently thought it was here, that "[t]he payments received were a very small part of [the arbitrator's] income * * *." For in *Tumey* the Court held that a decision should be set aside where there is "the slightest pecuniary interest" on the part of the judge, and specifically rejected the State's contention that the compensation involved there was "so small that it is not to be regarded as likely to influence improperly a judicial officer in the discharge of his duty * * *." Since in the case of courts this is a *constitutional* principle, we can see no basis for refusing to find the same concept in the broad statutory language that governs arbitration proceedings and provides that an award can be set aside on the basis of "evident partiality" or the use of "undue means." It is true that arbitrators cannot sever all their ties with the business world, since they are not expected to get all their income from their work deciding cases, but we should, if anything, be even more scrupulous to safeguard the impartiality of arbitrators than judges, since the former have completely free rein to decide the law as well as the facts and are not subject to appellate review. We can perceive no way in which the effectiveness of the arbitration process will be hampered by the simple requirement that arbitrators disclose to the parties any dealings that might create an impression of possible bias.

While not controlling in this case, § 18 of the Rules of the American Arbitration Association, in effect at the time of this arbitration, is highly significant. It provided as follows: "Section 18. Disclosure by Arbitrator of Disqualification — At the time of receiving his notice of appointment, the prospective Arbitrator is requested to disclose any circumstances likely to create a presumption of bias or which he believes might disqualify him as an impartial Arbitrator. Upon receipt of such information, the Tribunal Clerk shall immediately disclose it to the parties, who if willing to proceed under the circumstances disclosed, shall, in writing, so advise the Tribunal Clerk. If either party declines to waive the presumptive disqualification, the vacancy thus created shall be filled in accordance with the applicable provisions of this Rule." And based on the same principle as this Arbitration Association rule is that part of the 33d Canon of Judicial Ethics which provides: "33. Social Relations. * * * [A judge] should, however, in pending or prospective litigation before him be particularly careful to avoid such action as may reasonably tend to awaken the suspicion that his social or business relations or friendships, constitute an element in influencing his judicial conduct."

This rule of arbitration and this canon of judicial ethics rest on the premise that any tribunal permitted by law to try cases and controversies not only must be unbiased but also must avoid even the appearance of bias. We cannot believe that it was the purpose of Congress to authorize litigants to submit their cases and controversies to arbitration boards that might reasonably be thought biased against one litigant and favorable to another.

Reversed.

Mr. Justice WHITE, with whom Mr. Justice MARSHALL joins, concurring.

While I am glad to join my Brother BLACK's opinion in this case, I desire to make these additional remarks. The Court does not decide today that arbitrators are to be held to the standards of judicial decorum of Article III judges, or indeed of any judges. It is often because they are men of affairs, not apart from but of the marketplace, that they are effective in their adjudicatory function. This does not mean the judiciary must overlook outright chicanery in giving effect to their awards; that would be an abdication of our responsibility. But it does mean that arbitrators are not automatically disqualified by a business relationship with the parties before them if both parties are informed of the relationship in advance, or if they are unaware of the facts but the relationship is trivial. I see no reason automatically to disqualify the best informed and most capable potential arbitrators.

The arbitration process functions best when an amicable and trusting atmosphere is preserved and there is voluntary compliance with the decree, without need for judicial enforcement. This end is best served by establishing an atmosphere of frankness at the outset, through disclosure by the arbitrator of any financial transactions which he has had or is negotiating with either of the parties. In many cases the arbitrator might believe the business relationship to be so insubstantial that to make a point of revealing it would suggest he is indeed easily swayed, and perhaps a partisan of that party.[*] But if the law requires the disclosure, no such imputation can arise. And it is far better that the relationship be disclosed at the outset, when the parties are free to reject the arbitrator or accept him with knowledge of the relationship and continuing faith in his objectivity, than to have the relationship come to light after the arbitration, when a suspicious or disgruntled party can seize on it as a pretext for invalidating the award. The judiciary should minimize its role in arbitration as judge of the arbitrator's impartiality. That role is best consigned to the parties, who are the architects of their own arbitration process, and are far better informed of the prevailing ethical standards and reputations within their business.

---

[*] In fact, the District Court found — on the basis of the record and petitioner's admissions — that the arbitrator in this case was entirely fair and impartial. I do not read the majority opinion as questioning this finding in any way.

Of course, an arbitrator's business relationships may be diverse indeed, involving more or less remote commercial connections with great numbers of people. He cannot be expected to provide the parties with his complete and unexpurgated business biography. But it is enough for present purposes to hold, as the Court does, that where the arbitrator has a substantial interest in a firm which has done more than trivial business with a party, that fact must be disclosed. If arbitrators err on the side of disclosure, as they should, it will not be difficult for courts to identify those undisclosed relationships which are too insubstantial to warrant vacating an award.

Mr. Justice FORTAS, with whom Mr. Justice HARLAN and Mr. Justice STEWART join, dissenting.

I dissent and would affirm the judgment.

The facts in this case do not lend themselves to the Court's ruling. The Court sets aside the arbitration award despite the fact that the award is unanimous and no claim is made of actual partiality, unfairness, bias, or fraud.

The arbitration was held pursuant to provisions in the contracts between the parties. It is not subject to the rules of the American Arbitration Association. It is governed by the United States Arbitration Act.

Each party appointed an arbitrator and the third arbitrator was chosen by those two. The controversy relates to the third arbitrator.

The third arbitrator was not asked about business connections with either party. Petitioner's complaint is that he failed to volunteer information about professional services rendered by him to the other party to the contract, the most recent of which were performed over a year before the arbitration. Both courts below held, and petitioner concedes, that the third arbitrator was innocent of any actual partiality, or bias, or improper motive. There is no suggestion of concealment as distinguished from the innocent failure to volunteer information.

The third arbitrator is a leading and respected consulting engineer who has performed services for "most of the contractors in Puerto Rico." He was well known to petitioner's counsel and they were personal friends. Petitioner's counsel candidly admitted that if he had been told about the arbitrator's prior relationship "I don't think I would have objected because I know Mr. Capacete [the arbitrator]."

Clearly, the District Judge's conclusion, affirmed by the Court of Appeals for the First Circuit, was correct, that "the arbitrators conducted fair, impartial hearings; that they reached a proper determination of the issues before them, and that plaintiff's objections represent a 'situation where the losing party to an arbitration is now clutching at straws in an attempt to avoid the results of the arbitration to which it became a party.'"

The Court nevertheless orders that the arbitration award be set aside. It uses this singularly inappropriate case to announce a per se rule that in my judgment has no basis in the applicable statute or jurisprudential principles: that, regardless of the agreement between the parties, if an arbitrator has any prior business relationship with one of the parties of which he fails to inform the other party, however innocently, the arbitration award is always subject to being set aside. This is so even where the award is unanimous; where there is no suggestion that the nondisclosure indicates partiality or bias; and where it is conceded that there was in fact no irregularity, unfairness, bias, or partiality. Until the decision today, it has not been the law that an arbitrator's failure to disclose a prior business relationship with one of the parties will compel the setting aside of an arbitration award regardless of the circumstances.

I agree that failure of an arbitrator to volunteer information about business dealings with one party will, prima facie, support a claim of partiality or bias. But where there is no suggestion that the nondisclosure was calculated, and where the complaining party disclaims any imputation of partiality, bias, or misconduct, the presumption clearly is overcome.

I do not believe that it is either necessary, appropriate, or permissible to rule, as the Court does, that, regardless of the facts, innocent failure to volunteer information constitutes the "evident partiality" necessary under § 10(b) of the Arbitration Act to set aside an award. "Evident partiality" means what it says: conduct — or at least an attitude or disposition — by the arbitrator favoring one party rather than the other. This case demonstrates that to rule otherwise may be a palpable injustice, since all agree that the arbitrator was innocent of either "evident partiality" or anything approaching it.

Arbitration is essentially consensual and practical. The United States Arbitration Act is obviously designed to protect the integrity of the process with a minimum of insistence upon set formulae and rules. The Court applies to this process rules applicable to judges and not to a system characterized by dealing on faith and reputation for reliability. Such formalism is not contemplated by the Act nor is it warranted in a case where no claim is made of partiality, of unfairness, or of misconduct in any degree.

NOTES

1. Does *Commonwealth Coatings* rely upon due process in its holding? Does that mean that there is a constitutional right to an unbiased arbitrator? If that proposition is true, do other constitutional rights apply in arbitration hearings? Or, alternatively, is *Commonwealth Coatings* purely a construction of the FAA? Justice Black relied on *Tumey v. Ohio*, 273 U.S. 510 (1927), which held that due process requires a court decision to be set aside if it is shown that the judge had the "slightest pecuniary interest" in the result. (*Id.* at 524.) In *Tumey* the trial judge was paid a percentage of the traffic fines imposed. Does the text of the FAA support Justice Black's vacating of the award? If not, isn't Black resting his holding on the Constitution?

2. Was the arbitrator in *Commonwealth Coatings* merely a victim of his own expertise? How important is it that counsel for the losing arbitration party conceded that he would not have rejected the arbitrator even if a full disclosure had been made?

3. The Second Circuit has concluded that "much of Justice Black's [*Commonwealth Coatings*] opinion must be read as dicta, and we are left in the dark as to whether an 'appearance of bias' will suffice to meet the seemingly more stringent 'evident partiality' standard of the FAA." (*See Morelite Constn. Corp. v. New York City Dist. Council Carpenters Benefit Funds*, 748 F.2d 79, 83 (2d Cir. 1984). *See also* Note, *The Standard of Impartiality Applied to Arbitrators by the Federal Courts and Codes of Ethics*, 3 GEO. J. LEGAL ETHICS 821, 824 (1990) (criticizing the "less than clear standard" of *Commonwealth Coatings*).) Some decisions refuse to hold arbitrators to the same "appearances of bias" standard as judges. (*See, e.g., Toyota of Berkeley v. Auto Salesmen's Union, Local 1095*, 834 F.2d 751, 755-56 (9th Cir. 1987), *cert. denied*, 486 U.S. 1043 (1988).) Other cases apply a watered down version of the constitutionality premised "appearance of bias" test. (*See, e.g., Tamani v. Backe Helsey Stuart, Inc.*, 619 F.2d 1196, 1199, 1200 (7th Cir.) (applying an "appearance of bias" test and suggesting test is "objective" and "less exacting" than that applied to judges), *cert. denied*, 449 U.S. 873 (1980); *United States Wrestling Fed'n v. Wrestling Div. of AAU, Inc.*, 605 F.2d 313, 317-19 (7th Cir. 1979).) In *University Commons-Urbana Ltd. v. Universal Constructors, Inc.*, 304 F.3d 1331 (11th Cir. 2002), the appellate court vacated a district court order confirming an award and remanded for consideration of evident partiality. The arbitrator had failed to disclose that he was co-counsel with one of the parties in a different dispute. The evident partiality standard was met where the arbitrator fails to disclose "information that would lead a reasonable person to believe that a potential conflict exists" and requires proof that "must be direct, definite and capable of demonstration."

4. As a practical matter, the organizations that sponsor arbitration such as the American Arbitration Association and JAMS monitor and facilitate the concept of arbitrator impartiality. The very existence of these organizations depends upon the success of arbitration as a form of dispute resolution and causes them to maintain procedures to help assure arbitrator impartiality. Arbitrators who serve on panels organized by the AAA and NASD submit biographical data to these sponsoring organizations which is sent to the parties and used by the staff in selecting arbitrators for individual cases. Following the parties' tentative selection of an arbitrator a staff member will inform the prospective arbitrator of the names of the parties, the attorneys and potential witnesses. Staff will learn if the arbitrator has a conflict. Sponsor organization rules require the arbitrator to disclose an association with any of the parties, witnesses or attorneys and, in turn, notify the disputants of any facts disclosed by the arbitrator. Canon II of the Code of Ethics for Arbitrators in Commercial Disputes reads that "an arbitrator should disclose any interest or relationship likely to affect impartiality or that might create an appearance of partiality or bias."

5. Numerous arbitration organizations have rules that permit a party to challenge an arbitrator peremptorily and for cause. As in court, an arbitral party may exercise a peremptory challenge without any explanation. Does the normal strategy of peremptory challenges apply when used to remove prospective arbitrators?

6. Recall that one of the FAA's grounds for vacating arbitral awards is "evident partiality or corruption in the arbitrators, or either of them." (9 U.S.C. § 10(a)(2).) Does this subsection call for a broader scope of judicial review than other provisions of the FAA? Consider *Olson v. Merrill Lynch Pierce Fenner*

& *Smith, Inc.*, 51 F.3d 157 (8th Cir. 1995). One of the arbitrators failed to disclose that he was a vice-president of a firm that did a significant amount of municipal bond underwriting business with the party Merrill Lynch. The arbitrator was not personally involved in bond work, nor did he select securities firms to participate in underwriting. Nonetheless, the court of appeals reversed the trial court's refusal to set aside the award. It reasoned that the arbitrator's relationship with Merrill Lynch created an impression of bias. The court also cited § 23 of the NASD rules which requires arbitrator disclosure of financial, business or professional relationships that "might reasonably create an appearance of partiality or bias." (*Accord, Schmitz v. Zilveti*, 20 F.3d 1043, 1046 (9th Cir. 1994) (" '[E]vident partiality' is present when undisclosed facts show 'a reasonable impression of partiality' "); *Woods v. Saturn Distribution Corp.*, 78 F.3d 424, 427 (9th Cir. 1996) ("adoption of a standard of impartiality for arbitrators is reviewed *de novo*).) However, contrary cases call for a stronger showing of bias and seem to reject the idea that a mere appearance of impropriety is sufficient to prove bias. (*See, e.g., Arizona Elec. Power Corp. v. Berkeley*, 59 F.3d 988, 993 (9th Cir. 1995); *Peoples Sec. Life Ins. v. Monumental Life Ins.*, 991 F.2d 141, 146 (4th Cir. 1993) ("a mere appearance of bias is insufficient to demonstrate evident partiality").)

7. Should it make a difference whether the "evident partiality" claim is made in a case of nondisclosure or, alternatively, in actual bias cases? Should an appearance of bias be enough to set aside a claim of actual bias? Recall that *Commonwealth Coatings* was a nondisclosure case. For the position that greater proof than an appearance of bias is essential to set aside an award challenging the arbitrators' award for actual bias, see *Wood v. Saturn Distribution Corp.*, 78 F.3d 424, 427 (9th Cir. 1996) (upholding award terminating Saturn automobile dealer franchise where four arbitrators included two Saturn dealers, a Saturn marketing representative and a Saturn consultant); *Schmitz v. Zilveti*, 20 F.3d 1043, 1047 (9th Cir. 1994) ("in an actual bias case, a court must find actual bias").

8. *"Structural Bias"*: Is a panel biased when it is comprised of an "industry panel" drawn from the business of one of the arbitration parties? In *Harter v. Iowa Grain Co.*, 220 F.3d 544 (7th Cir. 2000), the court of appeals rejected a structural bias agreement where a farmer signed an arbitration agreement calling for a panel that would include owners of grain elevators. (*Accord, Rosenberg v. Merrill, Lynch, et al.*, 170 F.3d 1, 14-15 (1st Cir. 1999) (affirming the impartiality of a panel comprised of financial industry employers in same business as the respondent).)

9. *Party Appointed Arbitrators.* Parties to arbitration clauses sometimes agree to each appoint their own arbitrators, and, in turn, have these *"party-appointed arbitrators"* select a third, neutral arbitrator. Can a party-appointed arbitrator meet with counsel for one side and report on actual arbitrator deliberations? (*See Delta Mine Holding Co. v. AFC Coal Properties, Inc.*, 280 F.3d 815 (8th Cir. 2001) (citing AAA Commercial Arbitration Rules for the proposition that party-appointed arbitrators are presumed to be non-neutral and holding that *ex parte* communications between party-appointed arbitrator and his appointing party regarding the nature of panel deliberations are not a grounds for vacatur).) Rule 4.5.2(a)(1) of the Model Rules for the Lawyer as Third Party Neutral requires a party appointed arbitrator to both discuss and obtain party consent concerning *ex parte* communications. The 2004 Revision of the AAA Code of Ethics for Arbitrators in Commercial Disputes now limits the circumstances in which the part appointed arbitrator may engage in *ex parte* discussions to the subject of the appointment of the neutral arbitrator and prohibits discussion of the merits of the case. (Canon III.B(1), AAA Code of Ethics for Arbitrators in Commercial Disputes.) In *Lozano v. Maryland Casualty Company*, 850 F.2d 1470, 1472 (11th Cir. 1988), the court acknowledged that the party arbitrator "is a partisan only one step removed from the controversy and need not be impartial." Can the party-appointed arbitrator meet with the party prior to the hearing? (*See Sunkist Soft Drinks v. Sunkist Growers*, 10 F.3d 753, 759 (11th Cir. 1993) (evident partiality not shown by party-appointed arbitrator attending prehearing meetings with party, suggesting testimony and advising expert witness).)

10. *Stringent State Standards.* In 2002 California legislation expanded the disclosure requirements for arbitrators and made some failures to disclose grounds for vacatur of an award. (CAL. CODE CIV. PROC. § 1286.2.) These comprehensive requirements, termed the Ethics Standards for Neutral Arbitrators in Contractual Arbitration, set forth a general standard that the appointed arbitrator make early disclosure of "all matters that could cause a person aware of the facts to reasonably entertain a doubt that the proposed arbitrator would be able to be impartial." The requirements then list multiple examples of facts that would have to be disclosed, including family or personal or business relationships with an arbitration party, family relationships with a lawyer participating in the arbitration, cases in which the arbitrator has served in the past 5 years involving a party or a lawyer participating in the present arbitration, service by the arbitrator as a non-arbitrator neutral in a case involving the lawyer or party participating in the current case and financial interests in a party or the subject of the arbitration. Are these specific subjects for disclosure consistent with the FAA? Are they preempted by the FAA?

SELECTING THE ARBITRATOR

Parties sometimes include the subject of arbitrator selection in their arbitration clause. While they are allowed to identify a single arbitrator or panel of arbitrators, it is far more common to, instead, select a sponsoring organization (e.g., "the parties agree to arbitrate before a panel of National Association of Securities Dealers Arbitrators"). Although selection of a particular arbitrator is far easier before a dispute arises, the potential unavailability of the chosen arbitrator causes most drafters to eschew this option. Instead, they will usually agree to arbitrate before an arbitrator approved by a particular sponsor, such as the NASD or the American Arbitration Association.

Once a dispute arises, one of the parties will contract the sponsoring organization. It, in turn, will typically provide the disputants and their attorneys with a list of approved arbitrators. Ideally, the parties will be capable of jointly selecting an arbitrator or a panel. If this is not possible, the court will appoint an arbitrator as a last resort. Different sponsoring organizations employ different procedures regarding arbitrator selection. For example, the AAA provides lists of arbitrators and data regarding arbitrator experience and specialty. The disputants cross out any arbitrators they do not want and rank their preferences. The Center for Public Responsibility (CPR) leaves arbitrator selection entirely to the parties and offers "to assist only if the parties cannot agree." (EDWARD DAUER, A MANUAL OF DISPUTE RESOLUTION §§ 11.05, 11.12 (1994).)

B.   THE INFORMAL NATURE OF ARBITRATION HEARINGS

1.   DISCOVERY

One of the characteristics of arbitration is informal procedure. Parties are attracted to arbitration by the lack of the formal, rigid rules that characterize conventional litigation. Therefore, the broad discovery rules that one associates with court proceedings are absent in arbitration. In the common "folklore" of arbitration, there is little or no discovery.

This is not to say that discovery does not occur in arbitration. The Federal Arbitration Act permits the arbitrator to issue subpoenas. (9 U.S.C. § 7.) The Uniform Arbitration Act awards arbitrators the discretionary power to issue subpoenas for "the attendance of a witness and for the production of records and other evidence" and allows the deposition of a witness who cannot be subpoenaed or is unable to attend a hearing. (Uniform Arbitration Act §§ 17(a), 17(b).) The Commercial Arbitration rules of the AAA allow parties or the Association to request a preliminary hearing "to discuss the future conduct of the case, including clarification of the issues and the claims." (Rule 22, AAA Commercial Arbitration Rules.) Similarly, AAA rules require the parties to "produce such evidence as the arbitrator may deem necessary to an understanding and determination of the dispute." (Rule 33, AAA Commercial Arbitration Rules.) A rule of the International Chamber of Commerce dictates that in international arbitration an arbitrator is to establish the facts "by all appropriate means." (ICC Arbitration Rules, Article 14(1), reprinted in International Chamber of Commerce, Guide to ICC Arbitration (1994).) While the ability to obtain discovery in arbitration is usually discretionary with the arbitrator, securities arbitrators routinely grant discovery requests involving documents. (C. Edward Fletcher, *Privatizing Securities Disputes Through the Enforcement of Arbitration Agreements*, 71 MINN. L. REV. 393, 453 (1987).) Depositions, however, are somewhat rare in arbitration generally and in securities arbitration in particular.

There is, of course, a significant difference in tone between litigation discovery and arbitration discovery. The right to discovery in litigation is close to absolute; in arbitration the parties often must seek arbitrator approval to engage in discovery. In litigation severe sanctions propel the parties to voluntarily comply with discovery; in arbitration, the arbitrator is typically reluctant to impose sanctions because of the inability to find parties in contempt and the common sense that awards of sanctions may make it difficult for the arbitrator to find further work. While arbitral discovery subpoenas are enforceable in court, judges are a distant and expensive step removed from the arbitral process. Moreover, the spirit of arbitration is inconsistent with full discovery. Arbitration is designed to work speedily but detailed discovery takes time and hands-on management by a judge. These factors tend to make arbitration discovery modest and, in some cases non-existent.

It bears mention that the parties are the masters of their own disputing destiny and have the power to agree to greater discovery. In complex business disputes the arbitration clause could specify that discovery under the Federal Rules of Civil Procedure is available. While such clauses are possible, they are rare. Arbitration parties usually want to avoid the cost and abuse of full discovery and, if experienced at arbitration, know that they will have to pay for any arbitrator participation in the discovery process.

Some parties to arbitration criticize the availability of discovery in arbitration. They feel that arbitration needs to be different than litigation, where some argue that discovery abuse is a serious problem. These complaints often criticize the discretionary power of the arbitrator to grant litigation-like discovery requests. Arbitrators also have criticized the extent of their discovery powers, reasoning that they would prefer to browbeat lawyers into discovery compliance and, in so doing, lose some of their neutrality.

2. EVIDENCE RULES

Formal rules of evidence do not apply at arbitration hearings. (Rule 33 AAA Commercial Arbitration Rules ("[c]onformity to legal rules of evidence shall not be necessary"); NASD, Code of Arbitration Procedure, section 10323 ("The arbitrators shall determine the materiality and relevance of any evidence proffered and shall not be bound by rules governing the admissibility of evidence").) While the adversaries may object to the admission of tenuous evidence, the typical attitude of most arbitrators is to receive evidence. One of the only ways that a party can seek to have an arbitration award set aside is unfair failure of an arbitrator to accept evidence. Recall that one of the grounds for vacating awards is that the arbitrator has refused "to hear evidence pertinent and material to the controversy." (9 U.S.C. § 10(a)(3).) Accordingly, the usual tendency of the arbitrator is to permit evidence to be presented. The position of the AAA on the policy of evidentiary admission is striking: "everything that could further an understanding of the case should be heard." (AAA, *Guide for Commercial Arbitrators* 19 (1993).) The net result is that arbitrators tend to let in the bulk of the evidence offered.

The attitude of the courts is that of predictable reluctance to set aside awards because of evidentiary error. This passage from an appellate opinion affirming a trial court's refusal to set aside an award in favor of a law firm and against a former partner is typical:

> [Appellant's] contention — that the arbitrator did not permit him to offer material evidence — could be made in virtually every case where the arbitrator has excluded some evidence or placed limitations on discovery. . . . Plainly, this type of attack on the arbitrator's decision, if not properly limited, could swallow the rule that arbitration awards are generally not reviewable on the merits. [*Schlessinger v. Rosenfeld,*

Meyer & Susman, 40 Cal. App. 4th 1096, 1110, 47 Cal. Rptr. 2d 650, 659 (1995).]

Note how the *Schlessinger* reasoning emphasizes the workload consequences of judicial review. Courts are understandably concerned about their limited resources.

The Federal Arbitration Act's only provision on evidence allows courts to vacate arbitral awards "[w]here the arbitrators were guilty of misconduct . . . in refusing to hear evidence pertinent and material to the controversy. . . ." (9 U.S.C. § 10(a)(3).) As a literal matter this provision would appear to encourage efforts to set aside awards for exclusion of evidence. In reality, however, courts are reluctant to use this provision as a basis to set aside an award. Judges realize that arbitrators themselves decide the "materiality and relevance of any evidence that is proffered, and are not bound by any formal rules governing the admissibility of evidence." (*Swink & Co. v. Norris & Hirshberg, Inc.*, 845 F.2d 789, 790 (8th Cir. 1988).) Generally, when courts are faced with the contention that the exclusion of evidence necessitates that an award be vacated, they look for evidence that supports the award and refuse to set aside an award as long as a "fundamentally fair hearing" has been held. (*See, e.g., Bell Aerospace Co. Division of Textron v. Local 516*, 500 F.2d 921, 923 (2d Cir. 1974) (arbitrator must "grant the parties a fundamentally fair hearing"); *Moseley, Hallgarten, Estabrook & Weeden, Inc. v. Ellis*, 849 F.2d 264, 268 (7th Cir. 1988) (rejecting claim that an arbitrator's refusal to consider evidence violated due process and upholding award because hearing procedures used were fair); *Pompano-Windy City Partners, Ltd. v. Bear Stearns & Co.*, 794 F. Supp. 1265, 1278 (S.D.N.Y. 1992) (in upholding award because of "wealth of evidence in the record to support" it, court asserts that arbitrator "need not follow all the niceties observed by the federal courts and . . . need only grant the parties a fundamentally fair hearing").)

3. AWARDS AND (THE LACK OF) FINDINGS

Arbitrations usually end silently, without any findings of fact or conclusions of law. "It is well established that arbitrators are not required to either make formal findings of fact or state reasons for the awards they issue." (*Prudential-Bache Securities, Inc. v. Tanner*, 72 F.3d 234, 240 (1st Cir. 1995).) Written opinions are a rarity, except in labor arbitration, maritime and international arbitration. Indeed, the AAA urges arbitrators to avoid writing opinions as a means to keep the arbitral participants from challenging awards. Arbitrations typically end silently and tersely with the parties receiving a short "award" that merely states the result of the case without reasoning or factfinding. The typical arbitration award is inscrutable.

Several commentators have criticized the lack of arbitral factfinding. (*See, e.g.*, Laura Macklin, *Promoting Settlement, Foregoing the Facts*, 14 N.Y.U. REV. L. & SOC. CHANGE 575 (1986); Edward Brunet, *Questioning the Quality of Alternative Dispute Resolution*, 62 TULANE L. REV. 1 (1987). *Cf., McDonald v. City of West Branch*, 466 U.S. 284, 291 (1984) (rejecting preclusive effect of arbitration award because "arbitral factfinding is generally not equivalent to judicial factfinding").) They argue that a written explanation of an arbitrator's result tends to lend legitimacy and reasonableness to the process.

According to this reasoning, a cryptic award can seem arbitrary but a fully explained award lends rationality and dignity to the process. These arguments are bolstered by the prevailing process in labor grievance arbitrations in which attorneys usually give the written arbitration opinions to their clients to permit the client to see for themselves that the arbitrator listened to the evidence and acted rationally based upon the evidence in the record.

The increased use of a more judicialized model of arbitration illustrates that the parties themselves may desire to mandate findings and reasons in arbitral awards. The *Gateway Technologies* decision, *supra*, evidences that some companies seek a more expensive but less arbitrary model of arbitration in which arbitral finality and award inscrutability is not desired. Under *Volt* and *Mastrobuono*, the parties may have the legal power to tinker with arbitration procedures and we may see more of awards that contain judicialized features such as findings of fact and conclusions of law. These, in turn, could lead to a greater ability of courts to review arbitration awards.

Whether or not courts review arbitrator findings or reasons, there is much to be said for the process of drafting an award with reasons or findings. A reasoned arbitration opinion "tends to engender confidence in the integrity of the process and aids in clarifying the underlying agreement." (*United Steelworkers v. Enterprise Wheel & Car Corp.*, 363 U.S. 593, 598 (1960).) Judge Posner has praised the process of writing arbitration opinions "because writing disciplines thought." (*Chicago Typographical Union No. 16 v. Chicago Sun Times*, 935 F.2d 1501, 1506 (7th Cir. 1991).)

Critics of reasoned awards list several reasons for preferring a nonexplanatory award. Such awards are said to be more difficult to attack in court, are cheaper (arbitrators will bill for reasons and findings — these take time), and provide a more informal style of arbitration approximating the "folklore" model.

4. RECORD

It is difficult to generalize regarding the use of an arbitration record. If the parties agree, the arbitrator will generally arrange for a record. The arbitral sponsor may have rules that provide for a record. For example, NASD Securities arbitrations are on the record; a tape recorded transcript is usually taken during the hearing. (NASD Code of Arbitration Procedure § 10326(a) ("A verbatim record by stenographic reporter or tape recording of all arbitration hearings shall be kept").) Other sponsoring organizations may choose not to use a record to keep the hearing informal and as inexpensive as possible.

5. CLASS ACTION ARBITRATIONS

In the not too distant past, the thought of adjudicating class action claims in arbitration seemed fanciful. Class actions were thought to be within the exclusive province of the courts and, in contrast, arbitration proceedings were deemed too speedy and informal to embrace the complex formalities of class action procedure.

In the past few years, however, arbitration agreements between corporations and similarly situated consumers occur with increasing frequency. For example, bank, credit card issuers, insurance companies, health care providers, consumer goods sellers, and communications providers have all sought to arbitrate claims brought against them by consumers and drafted a variety of purported agreements to arbitrate. If you apply for a new credit card or cell phone or buy a computer on the web you may potentially be part of a class of consumers with a legal claim. In response to this development, classes of consumers have either initiated conventional class action suits or brought class actions in an arbitral forum.

The specter of class action arbitration raises a host of questions. Does an agreement to arbitrate effectively waive any right to the class action remedy? Should state or federal law govern the legal issues presented? Who, arbitrator or court, should decide questions of arbitrability raised by class actions that must be arbitrated? Should arbitrations of class actions be allowed or should such legalistic procedures be left to the courts?

These questions will be addressed in the following segment of materials.

GREEN TREE FINANCIAL CORP. v. BAZZLE
539 U.S. 444 (2003)

Justice BREYER announced the judgment of the Court and delivered an opinion, in which Justice SCALIA, Justice SOUTER, and Justice GINSBURG join.

This case concerns contracts between a commercial lender and its customers, each of which contains a clause providing for arbitration of all contract-related disputes. The Supreme Court of South Carolina held (1) that the arbitration clauses are silent as to whether arbitration might take the form of class arbitration, and (2) that, in that circumstance, South Carolina law interprets the contracts as permitting class arbitration. 351 S.C. 244 (2002). We granted certiorari to determine whether this holding is consistent with the Federal Arbitration Act.

We are faced at the outset with a problem concerning the contracts' silence. Are the contracts in fact silent, or do they forbid class arbitration as petitioner Green Tree Financial Corp. contends? Given the South Carolina Supreme Court's holding, it is important to resolve that question. But we cannot do so, not simply because it is a matter of state law, but also because it is a matter for the arbitrator to decide. Because the record suggests that the parties have not yet received an arbitrator's decision on that question of contract interpretation, we vacate the judgment of the South Carolina Supreme Court and remand the case so that this question may be resolved in arbitration.

I.

In 1995, respondents Lynn and Burt Bazzle secured a home improvement loan from petitioner Green Tree. The Bazzles and Green Tree entered into a contract, governed by South Carolina law, which included the following arbitration clause:

> "ARBITRATION — All disputes, claims, or controversies arising from or relating to this contract or the relationships which result from this contract . . . *shall be resolved by binding arbitration by one*

arbitrator selected by us with consent of you. This arbitration contract is made pursuant to a transaction in interstate commerce, and shall be governed by the Federal Arbitration Act. THE PARTIES VOLUNTARILY AND KNOWINGLY WAIVE ANY RIGHT THEY HAVE TO A JURY TRIAL, EITHER PURSUANT TO ARBITRATION UNDER THIS CLAUSE OR PURSUANT TO A COURT ACTION BY U.S. (AS PROVIDED HEREIN) . . . . The parties agree and understand that the arbitrator shall have all powers provided by the law and the contract. These powers shall include all legal and equitable remedies, including, but not limited to, money damages, declaratory relief, and injunctive relief." App. 34.

Respondents Daniel Lackey and George and Florine Buggs entered into loan contracts and security agreements for the purchase of mobile homes with Green Tree. These agreements contained arbitration clauses that were, in all relevant respects, identical to the Bazzles' arbitration clause. (Their contracts substitute the word "you" with the word "Buyer[s]" in the italicized phrase.)

At the time of the loan transactions, Green Tree apparently failed to provide these customers with a legally required form that would have told them that they had a right to name their own lawyers and insurance agents and would have provided space for them to write in those names. The two sets of customers before us now as respondents each filed separate actions in South Carolina state courts, complaining that this failure violated South Carolina law and seeking damages.

In April 1997, the Bazzles asked the court to certify their claims as a class action. Green Tree sought to stay the court proceedings and compel arbitration. On January 5, 1998, the court both (1) certified a class action and (2) entered an order compelling arbitration. App. 7. Green Tree then selected an arbitrator with the Bazzles' consent. And the arbitrator, administering the proceeding as a class arbitration, eventually awarded the class $10,935,000 in statutory damages, along with attorney's fees. The trial court confirmed the award, App. to Pet. for Cert. 27a-35a, and Green Tree appealed to the South Carolina Court of Appeals claiming, among other things, that class arbitration was legally impermissible.

Lackey and the Buggses had earlier begun a similar court proceeding in which they, too, sought class certification. Green Tree moved to compel arbitration. The trial court initially denied the motion, finding the arbitration agreement unenforceable, but Green Tree pursued an interlocutory appeal and the State Court of Appeals reversed. *Lackey v. Green Tree Financial Corp.,* 330 S.C. 388 (1998). The parties then chose an arbitrator, indeed the same arbitrator who was subsequently selected to arbitrate the Bazzles' dispute.

In December 1998, the arbitrator certified a class in arbitration. App. 18. The arbitrator proceeded to hear the matter, ultimately ruled in favor of the class, and awarded the class $9,200,000 in statutory damages in addition to attorney's fees. The trial court confirmed the award. App. to Pet. for Cert. 36a-54a. Green Tree appealed to the South Carolina Court of Appeals claiming, among other things, that class arbitration was legally impermissible.

The South Carolina Supreme Court withdrew both cases from the Court of Appeals, assumed jurisdiction, and consolidated the proceedings. 351 S.C., at 249. That court then held that the contracts were silent in respect to class arbitration, that they consequently authorized class arbitration, and that arbitration had properly taken that form. We granted certiorari to consider whether that holding is consistent with the Federal Arbitration Act.

II.

The South Carolina Supreme Court's determination that the contracts are silent in respect to class arbitration raises a preliminary question. Green Tree argued there, as it argues here, that the contracts are not silent — that they forbid class arbitration. And we must deal with that argument at the outset, for if it is right, then the South Carolina court's holding is flawed on its own terms; that court neither said nor implied that it would have authorized class arbitration had the parties' arbitration agreement forbidden it.

Whether Green Tree is right about the contracts themselves presents a disputed issue of contract interpretation. THE CHIEF JUSTICE believes that Green Tree is right; indeed, that Green Tree is so clearly right that we should ignore the fact that state law, not federal law, normally governs such matters, (STEVENS, J., concurring in judgment and dissenting in part), and reverse the South Carolina Supreme Court outright, (REHNQUIST, C.J., dissenting). THE CHIEF JUSTICE points out that the contracts say that disputes "shall be resolved . . . by one arbitrator selected by us [Green Tree] with consent of you [Green Tree's customer]." And it finds that class arbitration is clearly inconsistent with this requirement. After all, class arbitration involves an arbitration, not simply between Green Tree and a *named customer,* but also between Green Tree and *other* (represented) customers, all taking place before the arbitrator chosen to arbitrate the initial, *named customer's* dispute.

We do not believe, however, that the contracts' language is as clear as THE CHIEF JUSTICE believes. The class arbitrator *was* "selected by" Green Tree "with consent of" Green Tree's customers, the named plaintiffs. And insofar as the other class members agreed to proceed in class arbitration, they consented as well.

Of course, Green Tree did *not* independently select *this* arbitrator to arbitrate its disputes with the *other* class members. But whether the contracts contain this additional requirement is a question that the literal terms of the contracts do not decide. The contracts simply say (I) "selected by us [Green Tree]." And that is literally what occurred. The contracts do not say (II) "selected by us [Green Tree] to arbitrate this dispute and no other (even identical) dispute with another customer." The question whether (I) in fact implicitly means (II) is the question at issue: Do the contracts forbid class arbitration? Given the broad authority the contracts elsewhere bestow upon the arbitrator, (the contracts grant to the arbitrator "all powers," including certain equitable powers "provided by the law and the contract"), the answer to this question is not completely obvious.

At the same time, we cannot automatically accept the South Carolina Supreme Court's resolution of this contract-interpretation question. Under the terms of the parties' contracts, the question — whether the agreement forbids class arbitration — is for the arbitrator to decide. The parties agreed to submit to the arbitrator "*[a]ll* disputes, claims, or controversies arising from or relating to this contract or the relationships which result from this contract." *Ibid.* (emphasis added). And the dispute about what the arbitration contract in each case means (*i.e.,* whether it forbids the use of class arbitration procedures) is a dispute "relating to this contract" and the resulting "relationships." Hence the parties seem to have agreed that an arbitrator, not a judge, would answer the relevant question. *See First Options of Chicago, Inc. v. Kaplan,* 514 U.S. 938, 943 (1995) (arbitration is a "matter of contract"). And if there is doubt about that matter — about the " 'scope of arbitrable issues' " — we should resolve that doubt " 'in favor of arbitration.' " *Mitsubishi Motors Corp. v. Soler Chrysler-Plymouth, Inc.,* 473 U.S. 614, 626 (1985).

In certain limited circumstances, courts assume that the parties intended courts, not arbitrators, to decide a particular arbitration-related matter (in the absence of "clea[r] and unmistakabl[e]" evidence to the contrary). *AT & T Technologies, Inc. v. Communications Workers,* 475 U.S. 643, 649 (1986). These limited instances typically involve matters of a kind that "contracting parties would likely have expected a court" to decide. *Howsam v. Dean Witter Reynolds, Inc.,* 537 U.S. 79, 83 (2002). They include certain gateway matters, such as whether the parties have a valid arbitration agreement at all or whether a concededly binding arbitration clause applies to a certain type of controversy. *See generally Howsam, supra. See also John Wiley & Sons, Inc. v. Livingston, 376 U.S. 543, 546–547 (1964) (whether an arbitration agreement survives a corporate merger); AT & T, supra, at 651–652 (whether a labor-management layoff controversy falls within the scope of an arbitration clause).*

The question here — whether the contracts forbid class arbitration — does not fall into this narrow exception. It concerns neither the validity of the arbitration clause nor its applicability to the underlying dispute between the parties. Unlike *First Options,* the question is not whether the parties wanted a judge or an arbitrator to decide *whether they agreed to arbitrate a matter.* 514 U.S., at 942–945. Rather the relevant question here is what *kind of arbitration proceeding* the parties agreed to. That question does not concern a state statute or judicial procedures, *cf. Volt Information Sciences, Inc. v. Board of Trustees of Leland Stanford Junior Univ.,* 489 U.S. 468, 474–476 (1989). It concerns contract interpretation and arbitration procedures. Arbitrators are well situated to answer that question. Given these considerations, along with the arbitration contracts' sweeping language concerning the scope of the questions committed to arbitration, this matter of contract interpretation should be for the arbitrator, not the courts, to decide. *Cf. Howsam, supra,* at 83, 123 (finding for roughly similar reasons that the arbitrator should determine a certain procedural "gateway matter").

III.

With respect to this underlying question — whether the arbitration contracts forbid class arbitration — the parties have not yet obtained the arbitration decision that their contracts foresee. As far as concerns the *Bazzle* plaintiffs, the South Carolina Supreme Court wrote that the "trial court" issued "an order granting class certification" and the arbitrator subsequently "administered" class arbitration proceedings "without further involvement of the trial court." 351 S.C., at 250–251, 569 S.E.2d, at 352. Green Tree adds that "the class arbitration was imposed on the parties and the arbitrator by the South Carolina trial court." Brief for Petitioner 30. Respondents now deny that this was so, but we can find no convincing record support for that denial.

As far as concerns the *Lackey* plaintiffs, what happened in arbitration is less clear. On the one hand, the *Lackey* arbitrator (the same individual who later arbitrated the *Bazzle* dispute) wrote: "*I* determined that a class action should proceed in arbitration based upon *my* careful review of the broadly drafted arbitration clause prepared by Green Tree." App. to Pet. for Cert. 84a (emphasis added). And respondents suggested at oral argument that the arbitrator's decision was independently made.

On the other hand, the *Lackey* arbitrator decided this question after the South Carolina trial court had determined that the identical contract in the *Bazzle* case authorized class arbitration procedures. And there is no question that the arbitrator was aware of the *Bazzle* decision, since the *Lackey* plaintiffs had argued to the arbitrator that it should impose class arbitration procedures in part because the state trial court in *Bazzle* had done so. In the court proceedings below (where Green Tree took the opposite position), the *Lackey* plaintiffs maintained that "to the extent" the arbitrator decided that the contracts permitted class procedures (in the *Lackey* case or the *Bazzle* case), "it was a reaffirmation and/or adoption of [the *Bazzle* c]ourt's prior determination."

On balance, there is at least a strong likelihood in *Lackey* as well as in *Bazzle* that the arbitrator's decision reflected a court's interpretation of the contracts rather than an arbitrator's interpretation. That being so, we remand the case so that the arbitrator may decide the question of contract interpretation — thereby enforcing the parties' arbitration agreements according to their terms. 9 U.S.C. § 2; *Volt, supra,* at 478–479.

The judgment of the South Carolina Supreme Court is vacated, and the case is remanded for further proceedings.

So ordered.

Justice STEVENS, concurring in the judgment and dissenting in part.

The parties agreed that South Carolina law would govern their arbitration agreement. The Supreme Court of South Carolina has held as a matter of state law that class-action arbitrations are permissible if not prohibited by the applicable arbitration agreement, and that the agreement between these parties is silent on the issue. 351 S.C. 244, 262–266 (2002). There is nothing in the Federal Arbitration Act that precludes either of these determinations by the Supreme Court of South Carolina. *See Volt Information Sciences, Inc. v. Board of Trustees of Leland Stanford Junior Univ.,* 489 U.S. 468, 475–476 (1989).

Arguably the interpretation of the parties' agreement should have been made in the first instance by the arbitrator, rather than the court. *See Howsam v. Dean Witter Reynolds, Inc.,* 537 U.S. 79 (2002). Because the decision to conduct a class-action arbitration was correct as a matter of law, and because petitioner has merely challenged the merits of that decision without claiming that it was made by the wrong decisionmaker, there is no need to remand the case to correct that possible error.

Accordingly, I would simply affirm the judgment of the Supreme Court of South Carolina. Were I to adhere to my preferred disposition of the case, however, there would be no controlling judgment of the Court. In order to avoid that outcome, and because Justice BREYER's opinion expresses a view of the case close to my own, I concur in the judgment.

Chief Justice REHNQUIST, with whom Justice O'CONNOR and Justice KENNEDY join, dissenting.

The parties entered into contract, with an arbitration clause that is governed by the Federal Arbitration Act (FAA), 9 U.S.C. § 1 *et seq.* The Supreme Court of South Carolina held that arbitration under the contract, could proceed as a class action even though the contract do not by their terms permit class-action arbitration. The plurality now vacates that judgment and remands the case for the arbitrator to make this determination. I would reverse because this determination is one for the courts, not for the arbitrator, and the holding of the Supreme Court of South Carolina contravenes the terms of the contract, and is therefore pre-empted by the FAA.

The agreement to arbitrate involved here, like many such agreements, is terse. Its operative language is contained in one sentence:

> "All disputes, claims, or controversies arising from or relating to this contract or the relationships which result from this contract . . . shall be resolved by binding arbitration by one arbitrator selected by us with consent of you."

The decision of the arbitrator on matters agreed to be submitted to him is given considerable deference by the courts. *See Major League Baseball Players Assn. v. Garvey*, 532 U.S. 504, 509–510 (2001) *(per curiam).* The Supreme Court of South Carolina relied on this principle in deciding that the arbitrator in this case did not abuse his discretion in allowing a class action. 351 S.C. 244, 266–268 (2002). But the decision of *what* to submit to the arbitrator is a matter of contractual agreement by the parties, and the interpretation of that contract is for the court, not for the arbitrator. As we stated in *First Options of Chicago, Inc. v. Kaplan*, 514 U.S. 938, 945 (1995):

> "[G]iven the principle that a party can be forced to arbitrate only those issues it specifically has agreed to submit to arbitration, one can understand why courts might hesitate to interpret silence or ambiguity on the 'who should decide arbitrability' point as giving the arbitrators that power, for doing so might too often force unwilling parties to arbitrate a matter they reasonably would have thought a judge, not an arbitrator would decide."

Just as fundamental to the agreement of the parties as *what* is submitted to the arbitrator is to *whom* it is submitted. Those are the two provisions in the sentence quoted above, and it is difficult to say that one is more important than the other. I have no hesitation in saying that the choice of arbitrator is as important a component of the agreement to arbitrate as is the choice of what is to be submitted to him.

Thus, this case is controlled by *First Options,* and not by our more recent decision in *Howsam v. Dean Witter Reynolds, Inc.,* 537 U.S. 79 (2002). There, the agreement provided that any dispute "shall be determined by arbitration before any self-regulatory organization or exchange of which Dean Witter is a member." *Id.,* at 81. Howsam chose the National Association of Securities Dealers (NASD), and agreed to that organization's "Uniform Submission Agreement" which provided that the arbitration would be governed by NASD's "Code of Arbitration Procedure." *Id.,* at 82. That code, in turn, contained a limitation. This Court held that it was for the arbitrator to interpret that limitation provision: " '[P]rocedural' questions which grow out of the dispute and bear on its final disposition' are presumptively *not* for the judge, but for an arbitrator, to decide. *John Wiley* [*& Sons, Inc. v. Livingston,* 376 U.S. 543 (1964)] (holding that an arbitrator should decide whether the first two steps of a grievance procedure were completed, where these steps are prerequisites to arbitration). So, too, the presumption is that the arbitrator should decide 'allegation[s] of waiver, delay, or a like defense to arbitrability.' " *Id.,* at 84.

I think that the parties' agreement as to how the arbitrator should be selected is much more akin to the agreement as to what shall be arbitrated, a question for the courts under *First Options,* than it is to "allegations of waiver, delay, or like defenses to arbitrability," which are questions for the arbitrator under *Howsam.*

"States may regulate contracts, including arbitration clauses, under general contract law principles," *Allied-Bruce Terminix Cos. v. Dobson,* 513 U.S. 265, 281 (1995). "[T]he interpretation of private contracts is ordinarily a question of state law, which this Court does not sit to review." *Volt Information Sciences, Inc. v. Board of Trustees of Leland Stanford Junior Univ.,* 489 U.S. 468, 474 (1989). But "state law may nonetheless be pre-empted to the extent that it actually conflicts with federal law — that is, to the extent that it 'stands as an obstacle to the accomplishment and execution of the full purposes and objectives of Congress.' " *Id.,* at 477, 109 S. Ct. 1248 (quoting *Hines v. Davidowitz,* 312 U.S. 52, 67 (1941)).

The parties do not dispute that these contracts fall within the coverage of the FAA. 351 S.C., at 257. The "central purpose" of the FAA is "to ensure that private agreements to arbitrate are enforced according to their terms." *Mastrobuono v. Shearson Lehman Hutton, Inc.,* 514 U.S. 52, 53–54 (1995) (quoting *Volt, supra,* at 479, 109 S. Ct. 1248 (internal quotation marks omitted)). *See also Doctor's Associates, Inc. v. Casarotto,* 517 U.S. 681, 688 (1996); *First Options, supra,* at 947. In other words, Congress sought simply to "place such agreements upon the same footing as other contracts." *Volt, supra,* at 474 (quoting *Scherk v. Alberto-Culver Co.,* 417 U.S. 506, 511 (1974) (internal quotation marks omitted)). This aim "requires that we rigorously enforce agreements to arbitrate," *Mitsubishi Motors Corp. v. Soler Chrysler-Plymouth, Inc.,* 473 U.S. 614, 626 (1985), in order to "give effect to the contractual rights and expectations of the parties," *Volt, supra,* at 479. *See also Mitsubishi Motors, supra,* at 626 ("[A]s with any other contract, the parties' intentions control").

Under the FAA, "parties are generally free to structure their arbitration agreements as they see fit." *Volt, supra,* at 479. Here, the parties saw fit to agree that any disputes arising out of the contracts "shall be resolved by binding arbitration by one arbitrator selected by us with consent of you." Each contract expressly defines "us" as petitioner, and "you" as the respondent or respondents named in that specific contract. (" 'We' and 'us' means the Seller *above,* its successors and assigns"; " 'You' and 'your' means each Buyer *above* and guarantor, jointly and severally" (emphasis added)). Each contract also specifies that it governs all "disputes . . . arising from . . . *this* contract or the relationships which result from *this* contract." *Id.,* at 34 (emphasis added). These provisions, which the plurality simply ignores make quite clear that petitioner must select, and each buyer must agree to, a particular arbitrator for disputes between petitioner and that specific buyer.

While the observation of the Supreme Court of South Carolina that the agreement of the parties was silent as to the availability of class-wide arbitration is literally true, the imposition of class-wide arbitration contravenes the just-quoted provision about the selection of an arbitrator. To be sure, the arbitrator that administered the proceedings was "selected by [petitioner] with consent of" the Bazzles, Lackey, and the Buggses. But petitioner had the contractual right to choose an arbitrator for each dispute with the other 3,734 individual class members, and this right was denied when the same arbitrator was foisted upon petitioner to resolve those claims as well. Petitioner may well have chosen different arbitrators for some or all of these other disputes; indeed, it would have been reasonable for petitioner to do so, in order to avoid concentrating all of the risk of substantial damages awards in the hands of a single arbitrator. As petitioner correctly concedes, the FAA does not prohibit parties from choosing to proceed on a class-wide basis. Here, however, the parties simply did not so choose.

"Arbitration under the Act is a matter of consent, not coercion." *Volt, supra,* at 479. Here, the Supreme Court of South Carolina imposed a regime that was contrary to the express agreement of the parties as to how the arbitrator would be chosen. It did not enforce the "agreemen[t] to arbitrate . . . according to [its] terms." *Mastrobuono, supra,* at 54. I would therefore reverse the judgment of the Supreme Court of South Carolina.

Justice THOMAS, dissenting.

I continue to believe that the Federal Arbitration Act (FAA), 9 U.S.C. § 1 *et seq.,* does not apply to proceedings in state courts. *Allied-Bruce Terminix Cos. v. Dobson,* 513 U.S. 265, 285–297 (1995) (THOMAS, J., dissenting). *See also Doctor's Associates, Inc. v. Casarotto,* 517 U.S. 681, 689 (1996) (THOMAS, J., dissenting). For that reason, the FAA cannot be a ground for pre-empting a state court's interpretation of a private arbitration agreement. Accordingly, I would leave undisturbed the judgment of the Supreme Court of South Carolina.

NOTES

1. What exactly was decided by the *Bazzle* case? Was anything decided?

2. After *Bazzle,* what decisions are for the arbitrator and what decisions are left for the court?

3. How does *Bazzle* allocate power between the states and the federal government?

4. Judge Frank Easterbrook has reasoned that "a contract to arbitrate the dispute removes the [signing] person from those eligible to represent a class of litigants." (*Caudle v. AAA*, 230 F.3d 920 (7th Cir. 2000).) After *Bazzle* is this reasoning valid? Could an arbitrator appropriately borrow such reasoning?

5. For a thorough examination of arbitration clauses seeking to ban consumers from initiating class actions and discussion of possible arbitration of class actions, see generally, Jean Sternlight, *As Mandatory Binding Arbitration Meets the Class Action, Will the Class Action Survive?* 42 Wm. & Mary L. Rev. 1 (2000).

AAA Rules Regarding Class Action Arbitration

In the wake of *Bazzle,* the AAA passed Supplemental Rules for Class Action Arbitration. www.adr.org. Under these rules, the arbitrator decides whether the class action is arbitrable ("The arbitrator shall determine as a threshold matter, in a reasoned partial award . . . whether the applicable clause permits the arbitration to proceed on behalf or against a class"). The rules appear to permit reconsideration of this ruling by a court. If no party seeks review, then the arbitrator determines the class certification issue. AAA will not administer class action arbitration claims if the arbitration agreement prohibits claims, unless a court order mandates the parties to arbitrate their claims on a class basis.

The standards for deciding whether the class claims are certifiable are similar to Rule 23 of the Federal Rules of Civil Procedure. In brief, the class claims must be common to class members, typical and must be advanced by representative parties and competent counsel. Class issues must "predominate" over individual issues. The AAA rules require a written and "reasoned" award certifying (or refusing to certify) the class. Following the decision, the award is stayed for thirty days to permit the losing party to seek judicial review. The arbitrator then proceeds to administer notice to the class members and the hearing itself.

Any decision on the merits must be reasoned and in writing. Like FRCP 23, any settlement of the claims must be approved by the arbitrator who must also notify the class members and hold a hearing to assure that the terms of settlement are "fair, reasonable, and adequate."

The AAA rules regarding confidentiality call for a degree of transparency. The presumption of privacy and confidentiality does not apply to class action arbitrations. "All class action arbitration hearings . . . may be made public." The rules also mandate that AAA maintain a web site docket of class action arbitrations that includes a copy of the demand for arbitration and discloses the parties' identities.

Why do the AAA rules opt for transparency over privacy? Why do they call for a degree of participation by courts in the class action arbitration process?

In what has been labeled a "hybrid" procedure, California caselaw calls for courts to rule on matters of law in class action arbitrations. In *Keating v.*

Superior Court, 645 P.2d 1192 (Cal. 1982), the court observed that "Without doubt a judicially ordered classwide arbitration would entail a greater degree of judicial involvement than is normally associated with arbitration." *Keating* also called for the court to protect the due process rights of absent class members. (*See* Kristen M. Blankley, *Class Actions Behind Closed Doors? How Consumer Claims Can (and Should) Be Resolved by Class Action Arbitration*, 20 OHIO ST. J. DISPUTE RES. 451 (2005).)

C. WAIVER OF THE RIGHT TO ARBITRATE

Parties sometimes hesitate before commencing arbitration. They, instead, first appear and participate in litigation and then belatedly try to arbitrate. Some decisions find that agreements to arbitrate are waived and, consequently, of no effect if the party seeking arbitration first participated in litigation.

CABINETREE OF WIS. v. KRAFTMAID CABINETRY, INC.
50 F.3d 388 (7th Cir. 1995)

Before POSNER, Chief Judge, and CUMMINGS and ROVNER, Circuit Judges.

POSNER, Chief Judge.

This appeal in a diversity breach of contract suit requires us to consider the circumstances in which a procedural choice operates as a waiver of a contractual right to arbitrate. The plaintiff, Cabinetree, had made a contract with the defendant, Kraftmaid, in 1989 whereby Cabinetree became a franchised distributor in Wisconsin of kitchen and bath cabinets made by Kraftmaid. In September 1993, Cabinetree filed suit in a Wisconsin state court against Kraftmaid, charging that Kraftmaid had terminated the franchise in violation of the Wisconsin Fair Dealership Law, Wis.Stat. §§ 135.01 et seq., and of Wisconsin common law as well. The case was removable to federal district court, and within the thirty-day limit specified by law Kraftmaid removed the case to a federal district court in Wisconsin. 28 U.S.C. §§ 1441(a), 1446(b). Discovery began. In January 1994, a trial date of December 6, 1994, was set. In response to Kraftmaid's discovery demands, Cabinetree produced almost two thousand documents. Kraftmaid dragged its heels in responding to Cabinetree's discovery demands.

On July 11 Kraftmaid dropped a bombshell into the proceedings. It moved the district court under 9 U.S.C. § 3 to stay further proceedings pending arbitration of the parties' dispute. (A plaintiff who wants arbitration moves for an order to arbitrate. 9 U.S.C. § 4. A defendant who wants arbitration is often content with a stay, since that will stymie the plaintiff's effort to obtain relief unless he agrees to arbitrate.) The franchise agreement, which had been drafted by Kraftmaid, provides that "any controversy, claim, dispute, credit, or other matter in question should be decided by arbitration in Cleveland, Ohio in accordance with the rules of the American Arbitration Association." Cleveland is Kraftmaid's headquarters.

The district court denied the motion, and Kraftmaid appeals, as it is entitled to do, even though the denial of its motion to stay was an interlocutory ruling. 9 U.S.C. § 16(a)(1)(A).

Our decision in *St. Mary's Medical Center of Evansville, Inc. v. Disco Aluminum Products Co.*, 969 F.2d 585 (7th Cir. 1992), establishes four principles that frame our analysis in this case: 1. Review of a finding that a party has waived its contractual right to invoke arbitration is for clear error only; it is not plenary. 2. Such a waiver can be implied as well as express. 3. In determining whether a waiver has occurred, the court is not to place its thumb on the scales; the federal policy favoring arbitration is, at least so far as concerns the interpretation of an arbitration clause, merely a policy of treating such clauses no less hospitably than other contractual provisions. 4. To establish a waiver of the contractual right to arbitrate, a party need not show that it would be prejudiced if the stay were granted and arbitration ensued.

Today we take the next step in the evolution of doctrine, and hold that an election to proceed before a nonarbitral tribunal for the resolution of a contractual dispute is a presumptive waiver of the right to arbitrate. Although not compelled by our previous cases, this presumption is consistent with them; for we have deemed an election to proceed in court a waiver of a contractual right to arbitrate, without insisting on evidence of prejudice beyond what is inherent in an effort to change forums in the middle (and it needn't be the exact middle) of a litigation. *Ohio-Sealy Mattress Mfg. Co. v. Kaplan*, 712 F.2d 270, 273-74 (7th Cir. 1983); *Midwest Window Systems, Inc. v. Amcor Industries, Inc.*, 630 F.2d 535, 537 (7th Cir. 1980). And the District of Columbia Circuit likewise. *National Foundation for Cancer Research v. A.G. Edwards & Sons, Inc.*, 821 F.2d 772 (D.C. Cir. 1987), esp. p. 777. Other courts require evidence of prejudice — but not much. *E.g., Kramer v. Hammond*, 943 F.2d 176, 179-80 (2d Cir. 1991); *Miller Brewing Co. v. Fort Worth Distributing Co.*, 781 F.2d 494, 497-98 (5th Cir. 1986); *S & H Contractors, Inc. v. A.J. Taft Coal Co.*, 906 F.2d 1507, 1514 (11th Cir. 1990). Ours may be the minority position but it is supported by the principal treatise on arbitration. 2 IAN R. MACNEIL, RICHARD E. SPEIDEL & THOMAS J. STIPANOWICH, FEDERAL ARBITRATION LAW: AGREEMENTS, AWARDS, AND REMEDIES UNDER THE FEDERAL ARBITRATION ACT § 21.3.3 (1994). It is not a revival of the doctrine of election of remedies, which survives only as a bar to double recovery. *Olympia Hotels Corp. v. Johnson Wax Development Corp.*, 908 F.2d 1363, 1371 (7th Cir. 1990); UCC § 2-703, Official Comment 1. For what is in question here is not a choice between remedies in the usual sense (rescission versus damages, damages versus an injunction, and so forth) but the selection of the forum. *Cf.* 1 DAN DOBBS, LAW OF REMEDIES: DAMAGES-EQUITY-RESTITUTION § 1.1 (2d ed. 1993). We add that in ordinary contract law, a waiver normally is effective without proof of consideration or detrimental reliance. E. ALLAN FARNSWORTH, CONTRACTS § 8.5 (2d ed. 1990); 3A Arthur Linton Corbin, CORBIN ON CONTRACTS § 753 (1960); and see the majority and dissenting opinions in *Wisconsin Knife Works v. National Metal Crafters*, 781 F.2d 1280 (7th Cir. 1986).

An arbitration clause gives either party the choice of an alternative, nonjudicial forum in which to seek a resolution of a dispute arising out of the contract. But the intention behind such clauses, and the reason for judicial enforcement of them, are not to allow or encourage the parties to proceed, either simultaneously or sequentially, in multiple forums. Cabinetree, which initiated this litigation, could, instead of filing suit in a Wisconsin state court, have demanded arbitration under the contract. It did not, thus signifying its election not to submit its dispute with Kraftmaid to arbitration. Kraftmaid if it wanted arbitration could have moved for a stay of Cabinetree's suit in the Wisconsin state court. It did not. Instead it removed the case to federal district court. By doing so without at the same time asking the district court for an order to arbitrate, it manifested an intention to resolve the dispute through the processes of the federal court. To resolve the dispute thus is not to resolve it through the processes of the American Arbitration Association.

We have said that invoking judicial process is *presumptive* waiver. For it is easy to imagine situations — they have arisen in previous cases — in which such invocation does not signify an intention to proceed in a court to the exclusion of arbitration. *Miller v. Drexel Burnham Lambert, Inc.*, 791 F.2d 850, 854 (11th Cir. 1986) (per curiam); *Dickinson v. Heinold Securities, Inc.*, 661 F.2d 638, 641-42 (7th Cir. 1981). There might be doubts about arbitrability, and fear that should the doubts be resolved adversely the statute of limitations might have run. Some issues might be arbitrable, and others not. The shape of the case might so alter as a result of unexpected developments during discovery or otherwise that it might become obvious that the party should be relieved from its waiver and arbitration allowed to proceed. We need not try to be exhaustive. It is enough to hold that while normally the decision to proceed in a judicial forum is a waiver of arbitration, a variety of circumstances may make the case abnormal, and then the district court should find no waiver or should permit a previous waiver to be rescinded. *Envirex, Inc. v. K.H. Schussler* fur Umwelttechnik GmbH, 832 F. Supp. 1293, 1296 (E.D.Wis.1993); *see also Gilmore v. Shearson/American Express, Inc.*, 811 F.2d 108, 113 (2d Cir. 1987). In such a case prejudice to the other party, the party resisting arbitration, should weigh heavily in the decision whether to send the case to arbitration, as should the diligence or lack thereof of the party seeking arbitration — did that party do all it could reasonably have been expected to do to make the earliest feasible determination of whether to proceed judicially or by arbitration?

In this case, despite the one-sided character of the compliance to date with the demands for discovery, there would have been no demonstrable prejudice to Cabinetree from ordering arbitration in July 1994, even though that was nine months after the filing of the lawsuit and eight months after the removal of the suit to federal district court. Although the discovery provisions of the Federal Rules of Civil Procedure are more generous than those of the American Arbitration Association, Kraftmaid has agreed to match all disclosures that Cabinetree has made to it in compliance with its demands for discovery; breach of that agreement would surely warrant the dissolution of the stay, if one were granted, though we cannot find any case on the point. Given this agreement, it is not even clear that the delay in filing the motion for a stay has prolonged Cabinetree's suit, since the delay was taken up productively by the making of and complying with requests for discovery. Nor is delay automatically a source of prejudice.

Still we think the judge was right to find a waiver. The presumption that an election to proceed judicially constitutes a waiver of the right to arbitrate has not been rebutted. There is no plausible interpretation of the reason for the delay except that Kraftmaid initially decided to litigate its dispute with Cabinetree in the federal district court, and that later, for reasons unknown and with no shadow of justification, Kraftmaid changed its mind and decided it would be better off in arbitration. Neither in its briefs nor at oral argument did Kraftmaid give any reason for its delay in filing the stay besides needing time "to weigh its options." That is the worst possible reason for delay. It amounts to saying that Kraftmaid wanted to see how the case was going in federal district court before deciding whether it would be better off there or in arbitration. It wanted to play heads I win, tails you lose.

Selection of a forum in which to resolve a legal dispute should be made at the earliest possible opportunity in order to economize on the resources, both public and private, consumed in dispute resolution. This policy is reflected not only in the thirty-day deadline for removing a suit from state to federal court but also in the provision waiving objections to venue if not raised at the earliest opportunity. Fed. R. Civ. P. 12(h)(1). Parties know how important it is to settle on a forum at the earliest possible opportunity, and the failure of either of them to move promptly for arbitration is powerful evidence that they made their election — against arbitration. Except in extraordinary circumstances not here presented, they should be bound by their election.

AFFIRMED.

NOTES

1. Judge Posner clearly opts for a robust rule of waiver and predicates it upon policies of litigation efficiency, requiring a party to raise arbitration early in litigation or risk losing the right to arbitrate. Is Fed. R. Civ. P. 8(c) also relevant? This rule lists arbitration as an affirmative defense and mandates that a party with an affirmative defense raise it affirmatively. Is this rule consistent with Judge Posner's *Cabinetree* result?

2. Waiver is not mentioned by the FAA and appears to be a judge-made doctrine. Waiver is also inconsistent with the parties' intent to arbitrate as is evidenced by their written agreement to arbitrate. Is the broad doctrine of wavier articulated by the *Cabinetree* decision questionable because of its antagonism with the intent of the parties and the silence of the FAA?

3. Some courts have sought to confine the judge-made waiver doctrine. For example, the Ninth Circuit has asserted that the party who is advancing waiver of arbitration bears a heavy burden of proof. (*Fisher v. A.G. Becker, Paribas, Inc.*, 791 F.2d 691 (9th Cir. 1986).) The Eighth Circuit employs a different procedural twist. It has stated that "in view of the strong federal policy in favor of arbitration, 'any doubt concerning . . . waiver, delay or a like defense to arbitrability' should be resolved in favor of arbitration." (*Nesslage v. York Securities, Inc.*, 823 F.2d 231, 234 (8th Cir. 1987).) Would use of either of these positions have changed the result in *Cabinetree*?

4. Assume that A and B sign a contract containing an arbitration clause. A sues B ignoring the clause. B requests and receives from the court two months additional time to answer. B then moves to stay the litigation and requests an order compelling arbitration. Has B waived its right to arbitrate? (*See Peterson v. Shearson/American Express, Inc.*, 849 F.2d 464 (10th Cir.

1988) (court considers multiple factors in evaluating waiver including time and effort expended on litigation prior to arbitration request and whether opponent to arbitration has been prejudiced by the delay in seeking arbitral forum).)

5. To what extent are economic costs relevant to the waiver of arbitration doctrine? Some parties arguing that their opponent has waived the ability to arbitrate may be able to contend that they have suffered economic harm because of a delayed arbitration request. In *Leadertex, Inc. v. Morganton Dyeing & Finishing Corp.*, 67 F.3d 20 (2d Cir. 1995), the Court of Appeals held that a belated attempt to seek arbitration resulted in a waiver where the delay has in fact caused economic harm to the client. In *Leadertex*, the plaintiff brought breach of contract, warranty, negligence, replevin and conversion claims against the defendant in a New York state court. The defendant removed and filed a collection counterclaim. Defendant's subsequently filed answer raised numerous affirmative defenses. When the plaintiff moved for partial summary judgment the defendant finally moved to compel arbitration. The trial court deemed the prior arbitration agreement to be waived and the Second Circuit affirmed. The court focused on the practical business harm caused by the failure to promptly move for arbitration. The many months of uncertainty in legal rights caused a significant decrease in sales and orders — a practical form of "prejudice" to the business of the party opposing a belated motion to compel arbitration.

6. Under the *Prima Paint* doctrine, who should decide whether a party to an existing court proceeding has waived a right to arbitrate, the court or the arbitrator? Doesn't this decision seem naturally one for the court? For the position that such a decision is for the arbitrators in suits to compel arbitration brought under § 4 of the FAA, see *World Brilliance Corp. v. Bethlehem Steel Co.*, 342 F.2d 362, 364-65 (2d Cir. 1965); *Prudential Lines, Inc. v. Exxon Corp.*, 704 F.2d 59, 67 (2d Cir. 1983) (defense of waiver an arbitrable issue). For the contrary position, within the very same circuit, see *Doctors Associates v. Distajo*, 66 F.3d 438, 454-457 (2d Cir. 1995) (issue of waiver of arbitration by having related company sue to evict franchisee is one for court where the party's waiver actions were based upon conduct in the instant suit as opposed to conduct in previous litigation).

D. PROCEDURAL CONSIDERATIONS RELEVANT TO DRAFTING AND REVIEWING THE CONTRACT TO ARBITRATE

The task of drafting or reviewing the contract to arbitrate is often executed under extreme time pressure. An attorney may be given thirty minutes to review a proposed agreement containing an arbitration clause. In contrast, counsel may be asked to spend considerable thought on the optimal disputing conditions and procedures that should apply to future disputes. Numerous considerations are relevant to the task of drafting the arbitration clause. Consider the following article.

Edward Brunet & Walter Stern, Controlling Dispute Resolution: Drafting the Effective ADR Clause for Natural Resources and Energy Contracts, 10 Nat. R. & Env. 7 (1996) *

Environmental, energy and natural resources attorneys understand the value of using alternatives to conventional litigation for dispute resolution. Disputes arising in the commercial setting in these practice areas frequently lend themselves to resolution through mediation or arbitration. Historically, natural gas transportation contracts often provide for arbitration. And, long-term power sales agreements often include agreements to arbitrate. More recently, mediation and arbitration of Superfund allocation disputes has become increasingly popular. While the use of Alternative Dispute Resolution ("ADR") is becoming common in these fields, the task of drafting the ADR clause, however, is far from routine and requires careful consideration of a number of factors. Without a carefully crafted ADR clause, alternative dispute resolution may not serve the desired goals of expeditious and cost-effective resolution. This article seeks to outline some of the key components every ADR clause should contain.

Policies at both federal and state levels promote use of arbitration or other forms of ADR. Federal and state statutes provide specifically for arbitration of disputes. These laws, if applicable, should be consulted during the process of developing an ADR clause.

Form vs. Customized ADR Clauses

Perhaps the very first question to consider is whether to use one of the standard form or boilerplate ADR clauses provided by a sponsoring organization such as the American Arbitration Association or JAMS/Endispute. Standard clauses have the advantage of prior use and some judicial interpretation. Counsel who employ a boilerplate AAA clause may be able to avoid novel and potentially expensive litigation interpreting the arbitration clause. Boilerplate clauses are more predictable and make counseling easier. If a dispute arises there may be case law to answer inevitable questions. But, that is not always the case, and the answers may vary from jurisdiction to jurisdiction. Further, many form clauses may not include all the provisions necessary to achieve effective dispute resolution.

Boilerplate forms provide a useful starting point in drafting a sound ADR clause. Counsel may decide to add specific additions to the AAA boilerplate form. Use of a "mix and match" combination of particular innovations and a boilerplate clause is an attractive option. If this "mix and match" approach is considered, be sure that there are no inconsistencies between the boilerplate clause and any customized additions to it.

Customizing the ADR clause is increasingly attractive. Mediation and arbitration are the creatures of contract. Mediators and arbitrators must follow the written directives of the disputants and courts tend to rely on the written intent of the parties when interpreting the meaning of ADR clauses.

The recent decision in *Mastrobuono v. Shearson Lehman Hutton, Inc.*, 115 S. Ct. 1212 (1995), confirmed that courts must follow the parties' intent when interpreting the arbitration clause. If, for example, the parties want arbitration but fear a potentially expensive long, drawn-out arbitration hearing, there is much to be said for inserting a clause requiring the arbitration hearing itself to conclude within a maximum time frame. Such an efficiency device is not included in the AAA form. Similarly, standard forms tend not to address discovery issues. The custom clause can describe whether any discovery is permissible, and if so, the extent of discovery available.

The Scope of the ADR Clause

Questions of whether to mandate ADR and, if so, how broad or narrow to make the selection of ADR confront all contract drafters. In a number of cases, courts have had to decipher the meaning of so-called "discretionary" ADR clauses, which provide that the parties "may arbitrate." Such clauses are fraught with peril because they are subject to conflicting interpretations. Some decisions read discretionary language merely to give either party the option to require arbitration. *See, e.g., Bonnot v. Congress of Ind. Unions Local #14*, 331 F.2d 355 (8th Cir. 1964). However, if the ADR clause combines both the "may" language and a mandate that "decisions of arbitrators shall be final and binding," a court can read the entire clause to require arbitration. *American Italian Pasta Co. v. Austin Co.*, 914 F.2d 1103 (8th Cir. 1990). Parties who want to bind one another to use ADR should avoid the discretionary "may" and provide that "the parties *shall* arbitrate."

Many parties are so desirous to avoid litigation that they select the broadest possible clause. An example is: "the parties agree to arbitrate any dispute arising out of, in connection with, or relating in any way to this agreement or the relationship of the parties." This language should cover any future dispute between the parties whether or not the dispute relates to contract interpretation or performance. In contrast, some contracting parties may prefer to narrow the scope of ADR to selected issues or to disputes arising under the contract itself. For example, "the parties agree to arbitrate all disputes concerning interpretation or performance under this contract;" "all disputes regarding the sales price of natural gas"; "all disputes arising under the federal environmental laws"; or "all disputes regarding questions of fact." With the exception of the last quoted provision, each approach may be appropriate depending on the parties' goals. The "questions of fact" approach is not recommended. While that provision might have legal issues for judicial resolution, it invites a separate dispute — and higher legal costs — in resolving the difficult question of whether the dispute is one of fact, law or both.

Attorneys should be precise when seeking to narrow the scope of arbitration. Courts have read clauses that provide for arbitration of disputes "arising under" a contract to incorporate only the interpretation and performance of the contract's terms. *See, e.g., Mediterranean Enterprises, Inc. v. Ssangyong Corp.*, 708 F.2d 1458 (9th Cir. 1983). In contrast, a covenant to arbitrate disputes "relating to" the contract reflects a broad intent to arbitrate all disputes relating to the relationship between the signatories. Generally speaking, given policies promoting arbitration, ambiguities may be construed in favor of arbitration.

Counsel should consider whether the future might bring claims of fraud, illegality or repudiation against their contractual partner. Each of these claims could arguably cover the formation of the original contract itself, including the arbitration clause. Under certain clauses, courts have found that claims of illegality cannot avoid arbitration. *See, e.g., National R.R. Passenger Corp. v. Consolidated Rail Corp.*, 892 F.2d 1066, 1070-71 (D.C. Cir. 1990). Decisions also hold that contract repudiation claims must be arbitrated where the disputants earlier contracted to arbitrate "all disputes." *See, e.g., Mewbourne Oil Co. v. Blackburn*, 793 S.W.2d 735, 737 (Tex. App. Amarillo 1990). However, courts may assert jurisdiction over claims that the arbitration clause itself has been specifically repudiated or is tainted with fraud. *See, e.g., Prima Paint Corp. v. Flood & Conklin Mfg. Co.*, 388 U.S. 395 (1967); *Shearson Lehman Hutton, Inc. v. McKay*, 763 S.W.2d 934, 938 (Tex. App. San Antonio 1989, no writ). While such authority may provide comfort to the contract drafter, one should consider express treatment of these matters. Courts are likely to follow the contract and parties' desires to either arbitrate or, in contrast, litigate these issues relating to fraud, illegality or repudiation.

The drafter should consider mediation and arbitration alternatives when outlining the scope and structure of the ADR clause. Mediation, of course, permits the parties themselves to fashion the remedy rather than putting the authority to decide in a third party — the court or arbitration. This has obvious benefits.

Parties may want a two-step ADR clause, one that first sends any dispute to mediation and, if the dispute remains unresolved, to arbitration. Consider also the possibility that selected issues may be better suited for resolution by mediation than by arbitration. While the parties certainly possess the power to draft a clause requiring any future disputes to be mediated, it may be preferable to choose to mediate only particular issues. Then, one can decide whether those matters should proceed to arbitration or to court if the mediation does not work. For example, in a long-term power sales contract parties sometimes avoid specific price terms and, instead, contract to purchase power at "market prices." Mediation of a dispute relating to the correct price may be especially desirable. If mediation of one type of dispute seems desirable but mediation of other matters less appropriate, there is nothing to stop the parties from adopting a narrow selection of mediation on one issue. The parties have tremendous flexibility here; the drafter should raise the various options, and reflect the choices in the ADR clause.

Choice of Procedures

The parties also have great power to select the procedures they desire in future ADR. For example, they may specifically bootstrap the rules of mediation or arbitration providers into their contracts (*e.g.*, the parties agree to mediate under the commercial mediation rules of the American Arbitration Association). The notion of agreeing to use the rules of a major ADR supplier holds real appeal for parties less experienced with ADR — these rules are relatively uncontroversial and are broadly available. In contrast, the parties may decide to be creative and customize their ADR process. For example, the facts of Superfund allocation disputes are sometimes hotly contested and some attorneys want substantial discovery even when mediating or arbitrating such disputes. On the other hand, attorneys may not want to contract for the wide open, free discovery associated with conventional litigation. One option is to provide for some exchange of documents and a limited number of depositions and a short deadline to complete any discovery. Or, consider depositions only of witnesses the opposing party will call and exchange only exhibits to be used. This type of clause permits informed negotiation and eliminates trial by ambush, but prevents the abuses of open discovery that may occur in litigation. If you decide to provide for discovery, consider what authority the arbitrators will have to control discovery. State arbitration acts may or may not grant an arbitration panel subpoena power. In some states, courts may have the power to issue subpoenas for use in arbitration discovery disputes. Alternatively, parties who feel the facts of any dispute are likely to be easily identifiable may want little or no discovery. Of course, parties are free to covenant to permit no discovery whatsoever in any future mediation or arbitration.

Another procedural restraint sometimes included in ADR clauses concerns measures to avoid delay and expense. Arbitration of complex energy and environmental disputes often takes a long time if completely unregulated. The parties can choose to limit the time of the arbitration hearing itself or to provide that an arbitration hearing begin within a specified time following the demand for arbitration. Another potential concern associated with arbitration can be a long wait for the arbitrator's award (a problem not unique to ADR). The parties can mitigate this problem by providing that the award be rendered with a set and appropriate length of time (*e.g.*, 20 or 30 days) following the arbitration hearing.

Regulation of timing issues can save the parties time and money. Much of the potential cost advantage of arbitration is lost if the arbitrator receives every bit of evidence and prolongs an arbitration hearing. To be sure, fairness dictates that arbitrators normally receive evidence at the hearing. Yet, if the parties foresee the chance of a complex dispute, tying themselves to a hearing of short duration and a rushed award can backfire. Attorneys who contemplate such a clause should be careful to make the time for hearing long enough to provide for a fair, thorough, hearing. A number of arbitrations have been cut short unnecessarily and arbitrarily by the selection of too short a hearing period. While procedural innovation in arbitration holds great promise, the parties should be prudent when creating procedures that will guide future hearings.

Some drafters of ADR clauses have provided for a sanction or penalty should one of the parties fail to comply with the agreement to use ADR. *See* Whitmore Gray, *Dispute Resolution Clauses: Some Thoughts on Ends and Means*, 2 Alternatives to the High Cost of Litigation 12 (No. 8 1984). For example, the parties could provide that there was no right to arbitrate their dispute unless they first completed a mediation in good faith. Alternatively, a monetary sanction could be used to penalize a party who refused to follow the disputing procedure set forth.

Application and Choice of Law

Arbitration doctrine holds that courts will not set aside arbitration awards for mere mistakes of law. Legal error in an arbitration will not be a grounds for reversal of an award in the courts. Because arbitration is designed to achieve finality, a broad standard of judicial review would undermine the important finality concept that separates arbitration from a rights-based system such as litigation. Accordingly, arbitrators need not apply substantive legal principles when deciding a case. *Moncharsh v. Heily & Blase*, 3 Cal. 4th 1, 10 Cal. Rptr. 2d 183, 832 P.2d 899 (1992). While the arbitrator is free to follow the law, he may choose to be guided more by factual equity or a sense of justice.

Parties troubled by the lack of substantive legal rules in arbitration may fear the arbitrator who is more guided by the rough justice of a dispute. In those circumstances, the contracting party has the power to force the arbitrator to apply the law. The arbitration clause can include a requirement that the arbitrator apply substantive legal rules. In order to be sure that the arbitrator does use the law, parties desiring application of law sometimes mandate that the arbitrator include conclusions of law in the arbitration award itself. As with other provisions, this language serves to define the arbitrators' authority or power.

Like most choices, there are advantages and disadvantages associated with a so-called "application of law" clause. Such provisions tend to avoid arbitrariness. An arbitrator who must apply the law will generally be forced to decide for one party and against another. Chances of a "compromise award," where each side wins and loses, are much lower when the parties contract for the application of law. A client who has just adjusted its business to conform with a lengthy opinion letter may want the application of law clause. Firms that pay significant sums to counsel in order to comply with the law tend to like such clauses. A number of Fortune 500 firms now routinely employ "application of law" clauses in order to reach a result that they feel will vindicate their efforts to comply with legal rules. Businesses that follow the equities rather than the law may be worse off with such a clause. They may be better off with a fact sensitive arbitrator.

If the "application of law" clause is used the chances of the award being set aside by a court increase exponentially. Courts will review an award that is to be based on law. Judicial review is available to determine if an arbitrator exceeded his or her authority or power. Although the scope of review following an arbitration is usually extremely narrow, courts are willing to examine whether the arbitrator has been a proper "contract reader." If the contract requires that the arbitrator follow the law, a court will review to see if this contractual direction has been followed.

The Supreme Court's 1995 decision in *Mastrobuono, supra*, requires courts to enforce the intent of the parties in their selection of arbitration procedure. A use of the application of law clause may delay the resolution of the dispute and correspondingly increase the costs of dispute resolution. If such a clause is used the parties may decide to provide for dispositive motions to be heard by the arbitrator in order to avoid a potentially unnecessary arbitration hearing. (Of course, providing for dispositive motions may be a desirable addition to every arbitration clause.) Parties unfamiliar with the concept of arbitration motions should be aware that motions are increasingly common in arbitration. They have particular utility where there may be a statute of limitations defense to the claimant's demand. Be advised, however, that some courts consider application of a statute of limitation, in contrast to a contractual limitation period, not to be arbitrable. *See Smith Barney Harris & Upham & Co. v. Luckie*, 647 N.E.2d 1308 (N.Y. 1995).

The application of law clause is not the same thing as a choice of law. The latter clause selects the law to be applied and usually chooses the law of a particular state or nation. If selected in the clause the arbitrator and any reviewing court must follow the parties' selection. The application of law clause requires the parties to apply substantive rules when deciding an arbitration; the choice of law clause goes a step further and mandates that a particular jurisdiction's law should guide the result.

The result in *Mastrobuono, supra*, should not discourage the use of choice of law in arbitration. There the Supreme Court seemingly ignored the parties' selection of New York law in a securities arbitration clause. Under New York law punitive damages were unavailable in arbitration. *Garrity v. Lyle Stuart, Inc.*, 40 N.Y.2d 354, 386 N.Y.S.2d 831, 353 N.E.2d 793 (1976). Undoubtedly the brokerage respondent sought New York law in order to avoid punitive damages. The *Mastrobuono* decision, however, found the selection of New York law to be ambiguous because the contract had also provided for arbitration under the rules of the National Association of Securities Dealers. These rules granted full remedial powers to the arbitrators. The Supreme Court found that the specific selection of rules was more particular than the more general application of New York law, and, accordingly, upheld an award of punitive damages by the arbitrators. The lesson of *Mastrobuono* is that counsel who choose to use the rules of an ADR sponsoring organization should consider carefully any potential inconsistency with a choice of law clause. The latter may give way when the former is more specific. Parties who wish to draft a clause prohibiting arbitrator use of punitive damages have little to fear from the *Mastrobuono* decision. Such a clause is enforceable and should stand unless it is somehow inconsistent with a more particular reference in the parties' contract. Such a likelihood is difficult to imagine; the specificity of the parties' desire to avoid punitive damages should control.

Selection of the ADR "Neutral"

The ADR clause can contain numerous features regarding arbitrator selection. It may select a firm that supplies ADR services (*e.g.*, JAMS/Endispute or the American Arbitration Association). It can go a step further and identify a specific person as a mediator or arbitrator. In arbitration, the parties can also agree that each party can select one arbitrator and that the two arbitrators themselves will pick a third member of the panel.

Expertise is one of the chief selling points of mediation and arbitration. Undoubtedly the reputation of the ADR "neutral" selected will and should be a significant factor in drafting the arbitration clause. The parties will save time and effort later if they agree at the time of contracting on an expert mediator or arbitrator to chair any future disputes. If specific individuals are named in the ADR clause, the contract should always specify for their selection "if available." If the parties are unable to name an individual, they should consider naming a sponsoring organization. It is far easier to agree on such matters before a dispute arises when the parties are on good terms than later, once the parties have changed roles and become disputants. As noted above, the parties may wish to opt affirmatively into the rules of a provider or organization (*e.g.*, "the parties agree to arbitrate using the 1994 edition of the AAA COMMERCIAL ARBITRATION RULES"). This election may include supplying the "neutral."

Consideration should be awarded to how many arbitrators or mediators are needed and when they should be chosen. Should there be a three-arbitrator panel or is one expert arbitrator all that is needed? Is co-mediation by two mediators, one an expert nonlawyer and the other a mediator-lawyer, desirable? One mediator or arbitrator is normally enough, especially if the parties can agree before a dispute on the identity of this individual. Once selected and named in the contract, however, the parties lose flexibility and are stuck with their choice unless they subsequently amend their agreement.

It may be more desirable to wait until a dispute arises and the parties can compare the expertise and likely leanings of a potential arbitrator or mediator with the type of dispute. Of course, waiting to select an arbitrator or mediator until the dispute arises can make the selection more difficult. One way to avoid this problem is to insert some initial parameters for selection in the ADR clause. The parties might be able to develop a list of potential mediators or arbitrators for subsequent use. Another possibility is to arrive at a method for later selection in the ADR clause. In addition, the parties may require certain educational or professional experience for the arbitration. Some clauses provide that in the event the parties cannot agree upon selection, they delegate selection power to a specific judge such as the Chief Judge of the United States District in the district where the parties are resident. Before doing this, make sure that cooperation by the court will be forthcoming.

Use of two mediators is increasingly popular. In a hazardous waste allocation dispute one could profitably combine the expertise of an expert scientist or engineer with the lawyer mediator. While this may be more expensive than a single mediator, there may be benefits that outweigh those costs.

Similarly, the three-person arbitrator panel can potentially bring even greater expertise to the arbitration process. Some three-person panels are selected as part of so-called "party-appointed" arbitration. Each party selects their "own" arbitrator and they meet and select a third "neutral" arbitrator. If this arbitration is used the neutral has great power and may end up with the deciding vote. There is some thought, however, that arbitrator integrity (and the desire for further work) make party-appointed arbitrators independent. *See* Andreas Lowenfeld, *The Party-Appointed Arbitrator in International Controversies: Some Reflections*, 30 TEXAS INT'L L.J. 59 (1995). Expense may be an issue here also; the parties pay for their own arbitrator and split the cost of the "neutral," unless provision is made for the losing party to pay certain costs and fees. One option to consider is to provide that the only role of the party-appointed arbitrator is to select the neutral.

The Award

The arbitration clause can effect the award itself. Many parties shape the award by excluding punitive damages or providing for attorneys fees for the prevailing party. Similarly, it is not uncommon to set a maximum limit for monetary damages in the arbitration clause. A variation calls for use of "high-low," or "baseball," arbitration — the arbitrator must set damages at one of the parties' suggested damage amounts and is divested of discretion to select any other damage level. Such clauses avoid so-called compromise awards.

The arbitration award typically is a short, cryptic announcement of result without underlying reasoning or explanation. ADR sponsoring organizations have defended the succinct award because it helps to achieve finality by preventing efforts to set aside the award. However, some parties may want written reasons or findings of fact explaining the arbitration award. These can help the parties to accept the award as rational and reasoned. In labor and international commercial arbitration written reasons routinely accompany arbitration awards and help the parties understand the arbitration process.

An arbitration clause typically provides that the award will be binding on the parties. While federal and state arbitration legislation makes arbitration results binding, a statement in the clause calling for finality demonstrates party intent that all results be final, subject to a narrow standard of judicial review.

Limitations upon certain remedies should also be considered. Some ADR clauses dealing with arbitration restrict remedies to damages in order to prevent broad injunctive style remedies. Unless restricted in some way by the arbitral parties, arbitrators possess judicial-like powers to fashion non-damage relief in ways similar to judges. Intel Corporation knows this all too well. In a much publicized lengthy arbitration that dragged on for four years, an arbitrator ordered Intel to provide AMD, a competitor, a royalty-free license to Intel intellectual property. Although Intel achieved temporary relief in the lower appellate court, the California Supreme Court ultimately upheld the arbitrator's power to include injunctive type orders in his award. *Advanced Micro Devices, Inc. v. Intel Corp*, 9 Cal. 4th 362, 36 Cal. Rptr. 2d 581 (1994). The parties have the power, if they desire, to prevent such a result by prohibiting non-damage remedies in the ADR clause.

Attorneys fees present a similar problem. If left unregulated the arbitrator may or may not possess the power to include attorneys fees in the award. Parties who fear attorney fee shifting by an arbitrator may want to prevent this practice in the ADR clause. Alternatively, parties who hope to deter arbitration can provide that the arbitrator award fees and costs to the prevailing party.

Other Drafting Considerations

Confidentiality should also be addressed in ADR clauses. Almost all parties to alternatives to conventional trial have strong desires to keep their dispute private. The ADR clause can help to achieve privacy. It can provide for a "confidential" mediation or arbitration. It can require the arbitrator or mediator to keep all results confidential. The clause can also call for any agreements or awards to remain confidential.

In some types of arbitration it is common to have the arbitrator write an opinion — labor arbitrations, international commercial arbitrations and maritime arbitrations. There is enough demand for such opinions that some publishers routinely select among the most interesting and sell them by publishing arbitration reports in these areas. The particular disputant who wants to avoid its dispute from going public has the power to prevent the arbitrator from publishing the opinion and accompanying award.

Conclusion

Drafting today's ADR clause has increased in complexity. While attorneys may incorporate a boilerplate arbitration clause without thinking of mediation or innovative mechanisms such as mini-trial or mediation-arbitration, developments make it clear that counsel should devote careful thought to developing a precise dispute resolution mechanism or clause. Creativity in ADR clauses is on the increase and requires attorneys to consider multiple factors when drafting a contract.

NOTES

1. The above article deals with arbitration clauses used in contracts regarding the sale of energy and natural resources. Is there any reason that the tenets of the article are not relevant to arbitration clauses generally? The natural resources and energy contracts often involve (a) relational agreements between long-time contractual partners and (b) significant amounts of money and risk. Do these facts mean that the teachings of the article are limited to these factual contexts?

2. One of the themes of the article is that attorneys should give careful consideration to customizing their arbitration clauses. Is this a safe course of action? Aren't there reasons to use the form, AAA boilerplate clause? There will be cases construing the AAA boilerplate clause and these will tend to provide a desirable degree of predictability to the client. Yet, a customized clause is likely to be enforced by a court and also achieve predictable results.

3. *Boilerplate Clauses.* The following arbitration clause is a form recommended by United States Arbitration and Mediation, Inc.:

> In the event a dispute shall arise between the parties to this _____ (contract, lease, etc.) It is hereby agreed that the dispute shall be referred to UA&M, Inc., for arbitration in accordance with its Rules of Arbitration. The arbitrator's decision shall be final and binding and judgment may be entered thereon.
>
> In the event a party fails to proceed with arbitration, unsuccessfully challenges the arbitrator's award, or fails to comply with the arbitrator's award, the other party is entitled to costs of suit including a reasonable attorney's fee for having to compel arbitration or enforce the award.

This arbitration agreement substantially affects your legal rights. By agreeing to arbitrate, parties give up their legal right to bring a court action and have a jury trial. Contact an attorney if you have any questions concerning the use of this arbitration clause."

The similar clause of the American Arbitration Association calls for arbitration of "[a]ny controversy or claim arising out of or relating to this contract." Note the different wording of these boilerplate forms. Which is broader? Which is preferable?

4. *Narrow Arbitration Clauses.* One sometimes sees narrow arbitration clauses intended to cover only a particular type of foreseeable dispute rather than the broad agreement "to arbitrate any dispute between the parties." For example, a law firm partnership agreement called for arbitration of "any ambiguities or questions of interpretation of this contract." (*See Coady v. Ashcroft & Gerel*, 223 F.3d 1, 6 (1st Cir. 2000) (arbitrators exceeded the scope of their authority by entering findings calling for bonus).) Such a focused agreement is intentionally narrowly drawn. Why would the drafters seek arbitration only on contract interpretation questions?

5. *Who Pays for Arbitration?* The question of who should pay for arbitration is deceptively simple. As arbitration is the creature of contract, one would expect that courts will enforce agreements regarding payment. With the rapid growth of arbitration between large businesses and consumers, however, questions of fairness and potential unconscionability complicate the issue.

In *Cole v. Burns Int'l Sec. Serv.*, 105 F.3d 1465 (D.C. Cir. 1997), the court of appeals held that an employer cannot mandate an employee to arbitrate all disputes and to pay all or even part of the cost of arbitration. (*Accord, Armendariz v. Foundation Health Psychiatric Service*, Inc., 6 P.3d 669 (Cal. 2000) (mandatory employment arbitration clause cannot force employee to pay for expense of arbitration).) In contrast, the First Circuit has upheld an agreement to arbitrate that would charge an employee a forum fee of up to $3000. (*Rosenberg v. Merril Lynch, Pierce, Fenner & Smith*, 170 F.3d 1 (1999).)

Some arbitration providers have rules regarding payment. AAA Consumer Arbitration Rules provide that consumers do not pay a filing fee and pay a maximum of $125 in arbitration fees. The National Arbitration Forum restricts small claims consumer fees to a maximum of $175.

Many arbitration contracts between consumers and big businesses are silent regarding fees. In *Green Tree Financial Corp-Alabama v. Randolph*, 121 S. Ct. 513 (2000), the Supreme Court reversed a court of appeals decision that found unenforceable an agreement to arbitrate a consumer-lender dispute that was silent regarding arbitration costs and fees. The Eleventh Circuit reasoned that the claimants' Truth in Lending Act claims were at risk because of the possibility of steep arbitration costs. Chief Justice Rehnquist reinforced the court's willingness to allow arbitration of statutory claims and found the risk of deterrence of statutory claims "too speculative to justify the invalidation of an arbitration agreement." (121 S. Ct. at 522.)

E.   INTERNATIONAL ARBITRATION: ENFORCING THE DOMESTIC AND INTERNATIONAL ARBITRATION AWARD

A civil judgment is of little value if it cannot be enforced effectively by the prevailing party. Likewise, an arbitral award has minimal impact if it lacks a means of easy enforcement.

The drafters of the FAA gave enforcement of the arbitration award a high priority. They provided that courts "must grant . . . an order" confirming an arbitral award "if the parties in their agreement have agreed that a judgment of the court shall be entered upon the award." (9 U.S.C. § 9.) Application for court enforcement of arbitral awards must be made "within one year after the award is made." (*Id.*) Arbitration clauses routinely provide that the parties agree that arbitration awards shall be entered as civil judgments. The combined impact of the FAA and standard arbitration practice is that U.S. arbitration awards become the equivalent of fully enforceable court judgments.

The issue of enforcement of arbitral awards is of particular importance in international arbitration. Perhaps because of the fear of the unknown, many nations had historic reservations about routinely adopting and enforcing foreign judgments. The modern needs of international trade demand a smoothly functioning dispute resolution system and have caused arbitration of international commercial disputes to flourish. This development led to the adoption of the so-called New York Convention or the United Nations Convention on the Recognition and Enforcement of Foreign Arbitral Awards in 1957. (9 U.S.C. §§ 201-08 (*see* Appendix B).) The Convention provides that a party to an international arbitration apply to a U.S. court for an order confirming the award. Under the New York Convention there are noteworthy exceptions to the prevailing norm of enforcement of the international awards. Parties can try to oppose enforcement on the ground that the award is "contrary to the public policy" of the United States. (New York Convention. Art. V(2)(b).) Parties can also try to show that they were not given notice or were "otherwise unable to present [their] . . . case." (New York Convention, art. V(1)(b).)

NATIONAL OIL CORP. v. LIBYAN SUN OIL COMPANY
733 F. Supp. 800 (D. Del. 1990)

LATCHUM, Senior District Judge.

In this case the Court has been called upon to examine and evaluate, among other things, the legal significance of the current state of relations between Libya and the United States. The facts and arguments presented by the parties have put this Court in the unenviable and precarious position of having to place legal labels on the foreign policy maneuvers of the Bush administration. Unfortunately, the Court has no choice but to proceed.

Petitioner, National Oil Corporation ("NOC"), seeks to have this Court enter an order confirming a foreign arbitral award rendered in NOC's favor against respondent, Libyan Sun Oil Company ("Sun Oil"). NOC brings this action pursuant to the Convention on the Recognition and Enforcement of Foreign Arbitral Awards ("the Convention"), a treaty ratified by the United States and implemented through Congressional legislation. *See* 9 U.S.C. §§ 201-208 (1970). Sun Oil has moved to dismiss the petition or, in the alternative, to deny recognition of the award. This Court has jurisdiction pursuant to 28 U.S.C. § 1331 as this case arises under federal law.

FACTUAL BACKGROUND

NOC is a corporation organized under the laws of the Socialist People's Libyan Arab Jamahiriya ("Libya"), and wholly owned by the Libyan Government. Sun Oil is a Delaware corporation and a subsidiary of Sun Company, Inc. The dispute currently before the Court stems from an Exploration and Production Sharing Agreement ("EPSA") entered into by the parties on November 20, 1980. The EPSA provided, *inter alia,* that Sun Oil was to carry out and fund an oil exploration program in Libya.

Sun Oil began exploration activities in the first half of 1981. On December 18, 1981, Sun Oil invoked the *force majeure* provision contained in the EPSA and suspended performance. Sun Oil claimed that a State Department order prohibiting the use of United States passports for travel to Libya prevented its personnel, all of whom were U.S. citizens, from going to Libya. Thus, Sun Oil believed it could not carry out the EPSA "in accordance with the intentions of the parties to the contract." NOC disputed Sun Oil's claim of *force majeure* and called for continued performance.)

In March of 1982, the U.S. Government banned the importation into the United States of any oil from Libya and severely restricted exports from the United States to Libya. Export regulations issued by the U.S. Department of Commerce required a license for the export of most goods, including all technical information. Because it "had planned to export substantial quantities of technical data and oil technology to Libya in connection with the exploration program," Sun Oil claims that it filed for such an export license "so as to be prepared to resume operations in Libya promptly in the event the U.S. Government lifted the passport prohibition." The application for a license was denied. Thereafter, in late June of 1982, Sun Oil notified NOC that it was claiming the export regulations as an additional event of *force majeure.*

On July 19, 1982, NOC filed a request for arbitration with the Court of Arbitration of the International Chamber of Commerce ("the ICC") in Paris, France, pursuant to the arbitration provision contained in the EPSA. The members of the arbitration panel ("the Arbitral Tribunal") were chosen in accordance with the arbitration clause. Each party picked one arbitrator; the third was chosen by the International Chamber of Commerce. Sun Oil selected Edmund Muskie, a former United States Senator and Secretary of State. NOC selected Professor Hein Kotz, Director of the Max Planck Institut in West Germany. Robert Schmelck, a former chief justice of France's supreme court (*la Cour de Cassation*), was selected as the third arbitrator by the ICC Court of Arbitration.

The arbitration proceedings were held in Paris, France. In May and June of 1984, the Arbitral Tribunal held hearings on the issue of *force majeure.* It issued an initial award on May 31, 1985, that stated there had been no *force majeure* within the meaning of the EPSA. The Arbitral Tribunal later held further hearings, and on February 23, 1987, it rendered a second and final award in favor of NOC and against Sun Oil in the amount of twenty million U.S. dollars. NOC has since been unable to collect payment from Sun Oil.

NOC filed this petition for confirmation of the Tribunal's award on July 24, 1989. On September 15, 1989, Sun Oil moved to dismiss the petition. The Court heard oral argument on November 29, 1989 and January 26, 1990.

*　　*　　*

THE MOTION TO ENFORCE THE ARBITRAL AWARD

The Convention on the Recognition and Enforcement of Foreign Arbitral Awards attempts "to *encourage* the recognition and enforcement of commercial arbitration agreements in international contracts and to unify the standards by which agreements to arbitrate are observed and arbitral awards are enforced in the signatory countries." *Scherk v. Alberto-Culver Co.*, 417 U.S. 506, 520 n. 15 (1974) (citations omitted) (emphasis added). This Court must recognize the award rendered by the ICC Arbitral Tribunal in NOC's favor unless Sun Oil can successfully assert one of the seven defenses enumerated in Article V of the Convention. *Cf. Parsons & Whittemore Overseas Co., Inc. v. Societe Generale de l'Industrie du Papier (RAKTA)*, 508 F.2d 969, 973 (2d Cir. 1974). Sun Oil has invoked three of the seven defenses against recognition. (D.I. 12 at 23–24.) It bears the burden of proving that any of these defenses is applicable.

After considering the evidence and arguments of the parties, this Court, for the reasons outlined below, rejects Sun Oil's defenses and concludes that the arbitral award is entitled to recognition and enforcement under the Convention.

I. *Use of "False and Misleading" Testimony*

Sun Oil's first ground for asserting that the arbitral award should not be recognized revolves around the Arbitral Tribunal's reliance on the testimony of a Mr. C. James Blom, a witness for NOC. Essentially, Sun Oil claims that Mr. Blom's testimony was false and misleading, that this testimony was critical to the Arbitral Tribunal's decision, and, therefore, that recognition of the award would violate Sun Oil's due process rights. Mr. Blom's testimony was misleading, according to Sun Oil, because the Arbitral Tribunal was given the incorrect impression that Mr. Blom, a former vice president of Occidental Petroleum Corporation ("Occidental"), was in charge of Occidental's Libyan operations during the time period at issue. Sun Oil also charges that Mr. Blom's testimony, "on the central issue of the case" was false. Specifically, Sun Oil challenges Mr. Blom's assertion before the Tribunal that Occidental replaced its 230 American employees in Libya primarily with Canadians from its Canadian subsidiary. According to Sun Oil, this assertion was critical because one of NOC's main contentions during the arbitration was Sun Oil's alleged ability to perform under the EPSA by drawing on its Canadian subsidiary for personnel, as Occidental had allegedly done.

Intentionally giving false testimony in an arbitration proceeding would constitute fraud. But "in order to protect the finality of arbitration decisions, courts must be slow to vacate an arbitral award on the ground of fraud." *Id.* (citation omitted). Accordingly, "[t]he fraud must not have been discoverable upon the exercise of due diligence prior to the arbitration." *Id.* (citation omitted). The alleged fraud must also relate to a material issue. *See Newark Stereotypers' Union No. 18 v. Newark Morning Ledger Co.*, 397 F.2d 594, 600 (3d Cir.) (perjury does not justify vacation of an arbitral award if it relates to "an issue remote from the question to be decided"), *cert. denied,* 393 U.S. 954 (1968).

a. Mr. Blom's Credentials

Sun Oil's first challenge, regarding the alleged misrepresentation of Mr. Blom's credentials, borders on the frivolous. It is true that the Tribunal appears to have misunderstood the extent of Mr. Blom's actual duties. But there is no reason to conclude that NOC was at fault for this misapprehension.

Mr. Blom's testimony was completely accurate. During the 1984 hearings, he stated, on direct examination by counsel for NOC, that he lived and worked in Libya from 1967 to 1969, when he was transferred to Bakersfield. He also stated that after his transfer he was eventually promoted to vice president of Eastern Hemisphere Exploration, although he continued to reside in Bakersfield. If the Tribunal got the wrong impression about Mr. Blom's relationship with Occidental's Libyan operations or the meaning of his area of responsibility (the "Eastern Hemisphere"), it is Sun Oil's own fault.

Counsel for Sun Oil had ample opportunity to cross-examine Mr. Blom regarding the extent of his duties. Counsel simply chose not to do so. Moreover, Mr. Blom's appearance as a witness was not a surprise. NOC had provided Sun Oil with its list of witnesses over six months before Mr. Blom testified. That list not only identified Mr. Blom as an NOC witness, but also noted his credentials and relationship to Occidental, and stated as to which matters he would testify.[21]

Sun Oil emphasizes Mr. Blom's *second* appearance before the Tribunal, after the First Award had already been entered.[22] Sun Oil argues that at this point,

---

[21] *Bonar v. Dean Witter Reynolds, Inc.*, 835 F.2d 1378 (11th Cir. 1988), on which Sun Oil relies, presents very different facts. First, as NOC emphasizes, the appellants in *Bonar* were not given advance notice that the expert in question was going to testify, while Sun Oil received information about Mr. Blom over half a year in advance. Secondly, the misperception as to the *Bonar* expert's credentials was caused *by the expert,* who deliberately perjured himself on the stand. Even more importantly, however, the "expert" in *Bonar* turned out to be an actual fake. That is, he lied about *all* of his credentials — where he went to school, what degrees he had, and what jobs he had held.

Mr. Blom, on the other hand, was completely truthful about his credentials. It was the Tribunal itself that drew the wrong conclusion. Moreover, this "error" was not material. Even though Mr. Blom was not in Libya or in charge of Occidental's Libyan operations during the period when the EPSA was negotiated and in effect, Sun Oil has not argued that he was not qualified to give an expert opinion as to the meaning of the EPSA or market conditions for qualified personnel for oil exploration activities in Libya. Unlike the *Bonar* "expert," Mr. Blom did have legitimate credentials: he had previously lived and worked in Libya, and during the relevant period was still working as a vice president for Occidental.

[22] As already explained, *see supra* p. 805, the first set of hearings were held in 1984 and resulted

since the Tribunal's misapprehension of Mr. Blom's credentials was apparent from its statements in the First Award, NOC should have informed the Tribunal of the "error" if it was going to rely on Mr. Blom's testimony again. Although perhaps NOC should have corrected the Tribunal's misperception,[23] it did not present any false testimony, even at Mr. Blom's second appearance. Thus, there was no "knowing use of false testimony," as Sun Oil defines the alleged fraud.

b. Alleged Use of Canadian Personnel

Sun Oil's second challenge to Mr. Blom's testimony has more force, but is nonetheless not sufficient to warrant nonrecognition of the Tribunal's award. Mr. Blom's statement that Occidental replaced its American personnel with Canadians does in fact appear to have been inaccurate But, as with its first challenge, Sun Oil has not produced any evidence to show that this inaccuracy was anything other than unintentional.

Mr. Blom testified that about half of Occidental's 230 American employees in Libya were replaced primarily by Canadians from its Canadian subsidiary and British citizens from Occidental's London office. Mr. Blom now states that those 230 American employees were replaced with "non-Americans," half of whom came from within the Occidental organization. Therefore, the essential point of Mr. Blom's testimony is reaffirmed in his affidavit: Sun Oil could have replaced its personnel in Libya with non-Americans, as Occidental did.[24] The affidavits offered by Sun Oil to counter Mr. Blom's testimony do not controvert this critical point.

The most important consideration of all, however, is that Sun Oil was able to present all of these arguments to the Arbitral Tribunal Mr. Blom's affidavit, which recounts what transpired during his second appearance before the

---

in the issuance of the Tribunal's "First Award," which determined that Sun Oil had not properly invoked the EPSA's *force majeure* provisions. Subsequently, more hearings were held in December of 1985 and June of 1986. In February of 1987, the Tribunal issued its "Final Award," which dealt with the issues of liability and damages.

Mr. Blom testified initially during the pre-First Award hearings. A transcript is available of this testimony. Mr. Blom testified a second time in June of 1986. Apparently, no transcript of this testimony is available.

[23] Even if this were viewed as an impropriety on NOC's part, such misconduct would not be sufficient grounds for refusing to recognize the Tribunal's award. In light of all of the facts, the Court finds that NOC's failure to act affirmatively to correct the Tribunal's misunderstanding regarding Mr. Blom's credentials is hardly the type of misconduct that would deprive Sun Oil of a fair hearing. *Cf.Apex Fountain Sales, Inc. v. Kleinfeld*, 818 F.2d 1089, 1094 (3d Cir. 1987) ("[M]isconduct apart from corruption, fraud, or partiality in the arbitrators justifies reversal only if it so prejudices the rights of a party that it denies the party a fundamentally fair hearing.").

[24] Contrary to Sun Oil's assertions, the Court concludes that Mr. Blom's inaccurate statement that Occidental had used some Canadian employees of its Canadian subsidiary was not material to the Arbitral Tribunal's decision. The Tribunal's own characterization of Mr. Blom's testimony illustrates the fact that the critical issue was whether *any* non-Americans, not necessarily Canadians, were available to replace Sun Oil's American personnel in Libya:

Mr. Blom has testified that Occidental Oil Corporation was able to continue its Libyan production and exploration operations despite the Passport Order by replacing, within a few months, no less than 230 American nationals by an equal number of non-U.S. personnel partly from within the Occidental group of companies, partly from outside sources.

Tribunal in June of 1986, attests to the fact that all of Sun Oil's current arguments were made to, and hence implicitly rejected by, the Tribunal:

> 5. At those [June 1986] hearings, although no prior notice had been provided to me or counsel for NOC, counsel for Sun Oil raised issues concerning my credibility and the accuracy of the testimony which I had given at the *force majeure* hearings two years earlier. In particular, counsel for Sun Oil, purporting to establish that I had misrepresented my credentials to the Tribunal, read to the Tribunal from a statement of Dudley Miller pointing out that I was not in charge of Occidental's Libyan operations in 1981 and 1982. In addition, counsel for Sun Oil asserted that my testimony concerning Occidental's replacement of its U.S. personnel with Canadian personnel from its subsidiary CanOxy was erroneous and read from a statement of Ian Cumming that no CanOxy personnel were used in Occidental's Libyan operations. These statements which were offered to the Arbitral Tribunal in 1986 are identical in all material respects to the statements presented to this Court in the affidavits of Mr. Miller and Mr. Cumming.

The Court therefore accepts Mr. Blom's description of the second hearing, and concludes that Sun Oil was not prevented from presenting its case. *See* Convention, art. V., sec. 1(b). In addition, Sun Oil has not proven fraud. Alternatively, even assuming the alleged fraud did occur, it did not relate to a material issue in the arbitration, and Sun Oil could have discovered it during the proceedings.

II. *Damage Award Not Supported by the Evidence*

Sun Oil's second challenge to confirmation of the award focuses on the $20 million the Tribunal granted in damages. According to Sun Oil, confirmation of the award should be denied based on article V, section 1(c),[27] because the arbitrators exceeded their authority, and based on article V, section 2(b), the Convention's public policy defense, because confirmation would violate due process. Sun Oil argues that the Tribunal exceeded its authority because it did not base its damage award on the evidence presented and instead acted as an *amiable compositeur,* which tries to reach merely an equitable, and not necessarily legal, result.[28] Sun Oil also argues that the Tribunal did not have jurisdiction to consider NOC's claims based on Article 8.2 of the EPSA because such claims were outside the scope of the Terms of Reference to which the parties agreed before submitting their dispute to arbitration.

Article V, section (1)(c) of the Convention, on which Sun Oil relies, "tracks in more detailed form § 10(d) of the Federal Arbitration Act, 9 U.S.C. § 10(d),

---

[27] Recognition may be denied if "[t]he award deals with a difference not contemplated by or not falling within the terms of the submission to arbitration, or it contains decisions on matters beyond the scope of the submission to arbitration. . . ." Convention, art. V, sec. 1(c).

[28] When submitting a dispute to arbitration, the parties can request that the arbitrators act as *amiable compositeurs,* which means that the arbitrators can "tak[e] into consideration not only legal rules, but also what they believe justice, fairness, and equity direct[ ]." Lecuyer-Thieffry & Thieffry, *Negotiating Settlement of Disputes Provisions in International Business Contracts: Recent Developments in Arbitration and Other Processes,* 45 Bus. Law. 577, 591 (1990).

which authorizes vacating an award '[w]here the arbitrators exceeded their powers.' " *Parsons & Whittemore Overseas Co.,* 508 F.2d at 976. Like other Convention defenses to enforcement of a foreign arbitral award, this defense "should be construed narrowly." *Id.* Its counterpart, section 10(d) of the Federal Arbitration Act, has also been given a narrow reading.

The Third Circuit recently addressed a claim that an arbitral award should be vacated because the arbitrators exceeded their powers in violation of section 10(d) of the Federal Arbitration Act. That case, *Mutual Fire, Marine & Inland Insurance Co. v. Norad Reinsurance Co.,* 868 F.2d 52 (3d Cir. 1989), describes the inquiry a court should undertake as follows:

> It is . . . well established that the "court's function in confirming or vacating a commercial [arbitration] award is severely limited." In conducting our review we must examine both the form of relief awarded by the arbitrator as well as the terms of that relief. We must determine if the form of the arbitrators' award can be *rationally derived* either from the agreement between the parties or from the parties submissions [sic] to the arbitrators. In addition, the terms of the arbitral award will not be subject to judicial revision unless they are *"completely irrational."*

Norad Reinsurance Company, 868 F.2d at 56 (citations omitted) (emphasis added). For the reasons stated below, the Court finds that the Tribunal's award of damages was "rationally derived" from the parties' agreement and that the terms of the award are not "completely irrational."

a. Jurisdiction of the Tribunal

The arbitration clause contained in the EPSA is very broad. It provides, *inter alia,* that *"[a]ny controversy or claim* arising out of or relating to this Agreement, or breach thereof, shall, in the absence of an amicable arrangement between the Parties, be settled by arbitration. . . ." (D.I. 3, Exhibit A, Annex 1, EPSA ¶ 23.2, 47 [emphasis added].) The Terms of Reference, pursuant to which the dispute underlying this case was submitted to arbitration, specifically state that one of the "issues to be determined" at arbitration was "[t]o what relief, if any, is each party entitled?" (D.I. 3, Exhibit A, Annex 2, Terms of Reference ¶ IV(E), at 5.) In addition, as stated in the Terms of Reference, NOC's claims included the allegation that Sun Oil was "liable to NOC for all remedies and amounts available under the EPSA and the applicable law. . . ." (*Id.* ¶ III(A)(2), at 2–3.) Thus, the issue of damages, under Article 8.2 or any other provision of the EPSA, was properly before the arbitrators.

*   *   *

c. Sun Oil's Due Process Rights

Sun Oil argues that its due process rights would be violated by confirmation of this damages award. Hence, it asks that the award not be recognized based on the Convention's public policy defense. Because the Court has already concluded that the Tribunal's award is rationally derived from the language contained in the EPSA and Libyan law, Sun Oil's due process argument does not have any merit. [32]

III. *Violation of U.S. Public Policy*

Sun Oil's final challenge to confirmation of the award rests solely on the public policy exception contained in article V, section 2(b), of the Convention. Both parties in this case agree that the public policy defense "should be construed narrowly," and that confirmation of a foreign award should be denied on the basis of public policy "only where enforcement would violate the forum state's most basic notions of morality and justice." *Parsons & Whittemore Overseas Co.,* 508 F.2d at 974 (citations omitted); *see also Waterside Ocean Navigation Co., Inc. v. International Navigation Ltd.,* 737 F.2d 150, 152 (2d Cir. 1984). Not too surprisingly, however, the parties do not agree as to whether this particular case fits within such a definition of the public policy defense.

Sun Oil argues that confirmation of the award in this case would violate the public policy of the United States for three reasons. First, Sun Oil contends that because confirmation would "penalize Sun for obeying and supporting the directives and foreign policy objectives of its government," other companies and individuals would be less likely to support U.S. sanctions programs, thereby diminishing "[t]he ability of the U.S. government to make and enforce policies with economic costs to U.S. citizens and corporations. . . ." (D.I. 12 at 51.) Secondly, Sun Oil contends that confirming the award would simply be "inconsistent with the substance of United States antiterrorism policy" (*id.*), and thirdly, that it would also "undermine the internationally-supported antiterrorism policy . . . by sending a contradictory signal concerning U.S. commitment to this policy and by making possible the transfer to . . . Libya . . . funds which could be employed to finance its continuing terrorist activities." (*Id.* at 54.) Sun Oil also presents much statistical and historical information designed to demonstrate the character of the Qadhafi Government. (*See, e.g.,* D.I. 16 at 24 [asserting that Libyan activities "threaten the most basic standards of human behavior"].)

The problem with Sun Oil's arguments is that "public policy" and "foreign policy" are not synonymous. For example, in *Parsons & Whittemore Overseas Company,* 508 F.2d at 974, the Second Circuit addressed this very issue, saying: "To read the public policy defense as a parochial device protective of national political interests would seriously undermine the Convention's utility. This provision was not meant to enshrine the vagaries of international politics under the rubric of 'public policy.'"

In *Parsons,* the court faced a situation similar to the one in this case. There, a U.S. corporation claimed *force majeure* when, following the outbreak of the

---

[32] To some extent, Sun Oil's due process argument is really a claim that the Tribunal erred in its interpretation of Libyan law. A mere error of law would not, however, be sufficient grounds to refuse recognition of the award. Restatement (Third) of the Foreign Relations Law of the United States § 488 comment a (1987); *see Northrop Corp. v. Triad Int'l Mktg. S.A.,* 811 F.2d 1265, 1269 (9th Cir.), *cert. denied,* 484 U.S. 914 (1987); *cf. Brandeis Intsel Limited v. Calabrian Chemicals Corp.,* 656 F. Supp. 160, 165 (S.D.N.Y.1987) (not even "manifest disregard of the law" would be sufficient to deny recognition of a foreign arbitral award based on the Convention's public policy exception). Moreover, here there is no reason to believe the Tribunal made any error whatsoever.

Arab-Israeli Six Day War, the Egyptian government severed diplomatic ties with the U.S. and ordered most Americans out of Egypt. The U.S. corporation contended that "various actions by United States officials subsequent to the severance of American-Egyptian relations . . . required Overseas [the U.S. corporation], as a loyal American citizen, to abandon the project." *Id.* Sun Oil argues that this case is different because Libya's terrorist activities, which have been condemned internationally, are hardly just a parochial interest of the U.S. On the other hand, the U.S. Government's policy towards Egypt in the 1960's, the foreign policy at issue in *Parsons,* was just "an outgrowth of an important but nonetheless conventional regional conflict."

Despite Sun Oil's attempts to distinguish *Parsons,* it is clear that the policy objectives at issue here and the ones at issue in *Parsons* differ, at most, in degree and not in kind. This Court does not doubt that the ugly picture of the Qadhafi Government painted by Sun Oil's papers is accurate. The Court is similarly cognizant of the fact that Libya itself is not a signatory to the Convention; and hence, "if the tables were turned," as Sun Oil points out, a U.S. company would not necessarily be able to enforce an arbitral award against NOC in the Libyan courts. (D.I. 16 at 26 n. 37.) But Libya's terrorist tactics and opportunistic attitude towards international commercial arbitration are simply *beside the point.*

The United States has not declared war on Libya, and President Bush has not derecognized the Qadhafi Government. In fact, the current Administration has specifically given Libya *permission* to bring this action in this Court. Given these facts and actions by our Executive Branch, this Court simply cannot conclude that to confirm a validly obtained, foreign arbitral award in favor of the Libyan Government would violate the United States' "most basic notions of morality and justice."[34]

Although Sun Oil argues that confirmation of this award would mean that U.S. dollars would end up financing Qadhafi's terrorist exploits, the Court has already pointed out that the President is empowered to prevent any such transfer through the Libyan Sanctions Regulations. Furthermore, Sun Oil's argument that U.S. companies will be less likely to support sanctions if this award is confirmed *assumes* that Sun Oil is correct on the central issue in the arbitration underlying this petition for confirmation: that is, that Sun Oil was justified in suspending performance under the EPSA. The Arbitral Tribunal, however, concluded that Sun Oil was *not* justified in suspending performance because of U.S. actions at that time. Because Sun Oil was able to present all of these arguments, regarding *force majeure* and Sun's attempts to support U.S. policy, before the Arbitral Tribunal, this Court will not reexamine that issue here.

---

[34] In light of the circumstances presented here, the Court need not express any opinion as to whether, when, or to what extent a foreign policy objective or dispute might ever be sufficiently compelling to warrant invocation of the Convention's public policy defense against confirmation of a foreign arbitral award.

* * *

CONCLUSION

The Court will recognize and enforce the Tribunal's award in favor of NOC and against Sun Oil in the amount of 20 million U.S. dollars, with prejudgment and postjudgment interest as described above.

A final judgment will be entered in accordance with this opinion; but execution on the judgment will be stayed, and the judgment may not be registered and transferred in accordance with 28 U.S.C. § 1963 unless the Libyan Sanctions Regulations are complied with, particularly 31 C.F.R. §§ 550.210, 550.413, and 550.511.

NOTES

1. What should be the scope of judicial review when courts are asked to enforce awards under the New York Convention? Is the role of a court any different when a judge reviews an award under the FAA?

2. What is the scope of judicial review used in the *National Oil Corporation* decision? Is the court deferring to the arbitrator, or, alternatively, are the arguments used to set aside the award qualitatively weak?

3. The *National Oil Corporation* case typifies arbitral award enforcement. The prevailing party in arbitration needs help enforcing an award, mere words on a piece of paper. Both the FAA and the New York Convention provide efficient procedures used to make the award the equivalent of a court judgment. The typical award winner is a plaintiff seeking to enforce the award. In the recurring pattern of enforcement litigation, the typical defendant, the losing party in arbitration, musters up various attempts to oppose the arbitration award. The pro-award attitude of the trial judge in *National Oil Corporation* represents the majority view.

4. The New York Convention was passed in 1958. The United States did not ratify it until 1970. Europe initially embraced the treaty, with France ratifying in 1959, Germany in 1961 and Italy in 1969. One hundred thirty-six nations have now adopted the New York Convention.

IRAN AIRCRAFT INDUS. v. AVCO CORP.
980 F.2d 141 (2d Cir. 1992)

LUMBARD, Circuit Judge:

* * *

Beginning in 1976, Avco entered into a series of contracts whereby it agreed to repair and replace helicopter engines and related parts for the Iranian parties. After the Iranian Revolution of 1978-79, disputes arose as to Avco's performance of, and the Iranian parties' payments under, those contracts. On January 14, 1982, the parties' disputes were submitted to the Tribunal for binding arbitration.

The Tribunal was created by the Algiers Accords (the "Accords"), an agreement between the United States and Iran, through the mediation of Algeria, which provided for the release of the 52 hostages seized at the American Embassy in Tehran on November 4, 1979. In addition to providing conditions for the release of the hostages, the Accords established the Tribunal to serve as a forum for the binding arbitration of all existing disputes between the governments of each country and the nationals of the other. Accordingly, the Tribunal was vested with exclusive jurisdiction over claims by nationals of the United States against Iran, claims by nationals of Iran against the United States, and counterclaims arising from the same transactions. *See* Claims Settlement Declaration, Art. II(1).

On May 17, 1985, the Tribunal held a pre-hearing conference to consider, *inter alia*, "whether voluminous and complicated data should be presented through summaries, tabulations, charts, graphs or extracts in order to save time and costs." *See Avco Corp. v. Iran Aircraft Indus.*, Case No. 261, 19 Iran-U.S.Cl.Trib.Rep. 200, 235 (1988) (Brower, J., concurring and dissenting). At the conference, Avco's counsel, Dean Cordiano, requested guidance from the Tribunal as to the appropriate method for proving certain of its claims which were based on voluminous invoices, stating:

> In the interest of keeping down some of the documentation for the Tribunal we have not placed in evidence as of yet the actual supporting invoices. But we have those invoices and they are available and if the Tribunal would be interested in seeing them we can obviously place them in evidence or we can use a procedure whereby an outside auditing agency, uh, certifies to the amounts of the, uh, summaries vis-a-vis the underlying invoices. Both of those approaches can be taken. But I want to assure the Tribunal that all of the invoices reflected in our exhibits to the memorial . . . exist and are available.

Id. at 235-36. After noting that the Iranian parties "obviously have had those invoices all along," Cordiano stated that he would:

> like the Tribunal's guidance as to whether, uh, you would like this outside certifying agency to go through the underlying invoices and certify as to the summary amounts or that the Tribunal feels at this point that the, uh — that you would rather have the, uh, raw data, so to speak — the underlying invoices. Uh, we're prepared to do it either way.

Id. at 236.

The Chairman of Chamber Three,[5] Judge Nils Mangard of Sweden, then engaged in the following colloquy with Cordiano:

> Mangard: I don't think we will be very, very much enthusiastic getting kilos and kilos of invoices.
>
> Cordiano: That, that's what I thought so . . .

---

[5] Pursuant to the procedure mandated by the Accords, the claim was heard by a "Chamber" or panel of three arbitrators: one from Iran, one from the United States, and one from a group of arbitrators from other countries selected by mutual agreement of Iran and the United States. *See* Claims Settlement Declaration, Art. III(1).

Mangard: So I think it will help us . . .

Cordiano: We'll use . . .

Mangard: To use the alternative rather.

Cordiano: Alright . . .

Mangard: On the other hand, I don't know if, if any, if there are any objections to any specific invoices so far made by the Respondents. But anyhow as a precaution maybe you could . . .

Cordiano: Yes sir.

Mangard: Get an account made.

Id. at 236. Neither counsel for the Iranian parties nor the Iranian Judge attended the pre-hearing conference.

On July 22, 1985, Avco submitted to the Tribunal a Supplemental Memorial, which stated in part:

In response to the Tribunal's suggestion at the Prehearing Conference, Avco's counsel has retained Arthur Young & Co., an internationally recognized public accounting firm, to verify that the accounts receivable ledgers submitted to the Tribunal accurately reflect the actual invoices in Avco's records.

Attached to the Supplemental Memorial was an affidavit of a partner at Arthur Young & Co. which verified that the accounts receivable ledgers submitted by Avco tallied with Avco's original invoices, with the exception of one invoice for $240.14. *Id.* at 237.

The Tribunal held its hearing on the merits on September 16-17, 1986. By that time, Judge Mangard had resigned as Chairman of Chamber Three and had been replaced by Judge Michel Virally of France. At the hearing, Judge Parviz Ansari of Iran engaged in the following colloquy with Cordiano:

Ansari: May I ask a question? It is about the evidence. It was one of the first or one of the few cases that I have seen that the invoices have not been submitted. So what is your position on this point about the substantiation of the claim?

Cordiano: Your Honor, this point was raised at the pre-hearing conference in May of last year.

Ansari: I was not there.

Cordiano: I remember that you weren't there. I think we were kind of lonely that day. We were on one side of the table, the other side was not there . . . We could have produced at some point the thousands of pages of invoices, but we chose to substantiate our invoices through . . . the Arthur Young audit performed specifically for this tribunal proceeding.

Id. at 237.

The Tribunal issued the Award on July 18, 1988. Of particular relevance here, the Tribunal disallowed Avco's claims which were documented by its audited accounts receivable ledgers, stating, "[T]he Tribunal cannot grant Avco's claim solely on the basis of an affidavit and a list of invoices, even if the existence of the invoices was certified by an independent audit." *Id.* at 211 (majority opinion).

Judge Brower, the American judge and the only judge of the panel who was present at the pre-hearing conference, filed a separate Concurring and Dissenting Opinion in which he stated:

> I believe the Tribunal has misled the Claimant, however, unwittingly, regarding the evidence it was required to submit, thereby depriving Claimant, to that extent, of the ability to present its case . . . Since Claimant did exactly what it previously was told to do by the Tribunal the denial in the present Award of any of those invoice claims on the ground that more evidence should have been submitted constitutes a denial to Claimant of the ability to present its case to the Tribunal.

* * *

The Iranian parties contend that the district court erred in refusing to enforce the Award because the Tribunal's awards are "directly" enforceable in United States courts, irrespective of the defenses to the enforcement of foreign arbitral awards provided for in the New York Convention. The Iranian parties do not, and cannot, point to any mechanism in the Accords for direct enforcement of Tribunal awards issued against United States nationals. Nevertheless, the Iranian parties argue that Tribunal awards must be "directly" enforced because the Accords state that "All decisions and awards of the Tribunal shall be final and binding." *See* Claims Settlement Declaration, Art. IV(1).

The Tribunal's own interpretation of the Accords reveals the lack of merit in the Iranian parties' position. In *Islamic Republic of Iran v. United States*, Case No. A/21, 14 Iran-U.S.Cl.Trib.Rep. 324 (1987), the Tribunal considered whether the Accords obligated the United States to satisfy awards issued in favor of Iran or its nationals upon the default of United States nationals. The Tribunal ruled that while the United States had no such obligation under the Accords, it had assumed a treaty obligation to provide an enforcement mechanism for the Tribunal's awards, stating:

> It is therefore incumbent on each State Party to provide some proce-dure or mechanism whereby enforcement may be obtained within its national jurisdiction, and to ensure that the successful Party has access thereto. If procedures did not already exist as part of the State's legal system they would have to be established, by means of legislation or other appropriate measures. Such procedures must be available on a basis *at least as favorable* as that allowed to parties who seek recognition or enforcement of foreign arbitral awards.

Id. at 331 (emphasis added). Accordingly, the Accords require only that we grant the Award "at least as favorable" treatment as we grant other "final and binding" foreign arbitral awards.

The Iranian parties argue that where parties agree to "final" or "binding" arbitration, the resulting arbitral award must be treated as a final, res judicata judgment against the non-prevailing party. We disagree. The terms "final" and "binding" merely reflect a contractual intent that the issues joined and resolved in the arbitration may not be tried de novo in any court. *See I/S Stavborg v. National Metal Converters, Inc.*, 500 F.2d 424, 427 (2d Cir. 1974). Furthermore, we have held that even a "final" and "binding" arbitral award is subject to the defenses to enforcement provided for in the New York Convention. *See Fotochrome, Inc. v. Copal Co., Ltd.*, 517 F.2d 512, 519 (2d Cir. 1975).[7] Accordingly, the "final and binding" language in the Accords does not bar consideration of the defenses to enforcement provided for in the New York Convention.

B. *The New York Convention*

Avco argues that the district court properly denied enforcement of the Award pursuant to Article V(1)(b) of the New York Convention because it was unable to present its case to the Tribunal. The New York Convention provides for nonenforcement where:

> The party against whom the award is invoked was not given proper notice of the appointment of the arbitrator or of the arbitration proceedings or was *otherwise unable to present his case* . . .

New York Convention, Art. V(1)(b) (emphasis added).

We have recognized that the defense provided for in Article V(1)(b) "essentially sanctions the application of the forum state's standards of due process," and that due process rights are "entitled to full force under the Convention as defenses to enforcement." *Parsons & Whittemore Overseas Co., Inc. v. Societe Generale de L'Industrie du Papier (RAKTA)*, 508 F.2d 969, 975-76 (2d Cir. 1974). Under our law, "[t]he fundamental requirement of due process is the opportunity to be heard 'at a meaningful time and in a meaningful manner.'"*Mathews v. Eldridge*, 424 U.S. 319, 333, 96 S. Ct. 893, 902, 47 L. Ed. 2d 18 (1976) (quoting *Armstrong v. Manzo*, 380 U.S. 545, 552, 85 S. Ct. 1187, 1191, 14 L. Ed. 2d 62 (1965)). Accordingly, if Avco was denied the opportunity to be heard in a meaningful time or in a meaningful manner, enforcement of the Award should be refused pursuant to Article V(1)(b).

At the pre-hearing conference, Judge Mangard specifically advised Avco not to burden the Tribunal by submitting "kilos and kilos of invoices." Instead, Judge Mangard approved the method of proof proposed by Avco, namely the submission of Avco's audited accounts receivable ledgers. Later, when Judge Ansari questioned Avco's method of proof, he never responded to Avco's explanation that it was proceeding according to an earlier understanding. Thus, Avco was not made aware that the Tribunal now required the actual

---

[7] *Accord* International Standard Electric Corp. v. Bridas Sociedad Anonima Petrolera, Industrial y Comercial, 745 F. Supp. 172 (S.D.N.Y.1990) (New York Convention defenses considered with regard to "final[ ]" arbitral award); Sesotris, S.A.E. v. Transportes Navales, S.A., 727 F. Supp. 737, 741 (D. Mass. 1989) (declining to enforce "final" arbitral award pursuant to Article V(1)(b) of the New York Convention); Al Haddad Bros. Enterprises, Inc. v. M/S AGAPI, 635 F. Supp. 205 (D.Del.1986) (considering New York Convention defenses with regard to "final and binding" arbitral award), *aff'd*, 813 F.2d 396 (3d Cir. 1987); Biotronik Mess-und Therapiegeraete GmbH & Co. v. Medford Medical Instrument Co., 415 F. Supp. 133 (D.N.J.1976) (same).

invoices to substantiate Avco's claim. Having thus led Avco to believe it had used a proper method to substantiate its claim, the Tribunal then rejected Avco's claim for lack of proof.

We believe that by so misleading Avco, however unwittingly, the Tribunal denied Avco the opportunity to present its claim in a meaningful manner. Accordingly, Avco was "unable to present [its] case" within the meaning of Article V(1)(b), and enforcement of the Award was properly denied.

Affirmed.

CARDAMONE, Circuit Judge, dissenting:

The issue before us is whether Avco was denied an opportunity to present its case before the Iran-United States Claims Tribunal at the Hague. To rule, as the majority does, that it was denied such an opportunity renders the Tribunal's award unenforceable under article V(1)(b) of the United Nations Convention on the Recognition and Enforcement of Foreign Arbitral Awards, June 10, 1958, 21 U.S.T. 2517 (the New York Convention). I respectfully dissent because it seems to me that a fair reading of this record reveals that Avco was not denied such an opportunity. Thus, in my view the arbitral award is enforceable under the New York Convention.

*   *   *

The New York Convention obligates U.S. courts to enforce foreign arbitral awards unless certain defenses provided in article V(1) of the Convention are established. The specific defense with which we deal in the case at hand appears in article V(1)(b). That section states that enforcement of an arbitral award may be denied if the court is satisfied that the party against whom the award is sought to be enforced was unable to present its case before the arbitration panel.

Based on the facts before us, Avco fails to meet the legal standard of being unable to present its case before the arbitral Tribunal so as to render the award unenforceable under the New York Convention. That standard, as the majority points out, essentially involves a due process inquiry to see whether the party against whom enforcement is sought has been put on notice and has had an opportunity to respond. *See Parsons & Whittemore Overseas Co. v. Societe Generale de l'Industrie* du Papier (RAKTA), 508 F.2d 969, 975-76 (2d Cir. 1974). Unfortunately, only limited case law exists on this issue, and those cases that can be found merely note, in applying article V(1)(b), that due process serves as an interpretive guide.

One of the reasons for this dissent is because until today no federal or foreign case appears to have used article V(1)(b)'s narrow exception as a reason to refuse to enforce an arbitral award due to the arbitration panel's failure to consider certain evidence. Moreover, some decisions have rejected the article V(1)(b) defense under other, somewhat analogous circumstances. For example, in *Parsons & Whittemore Overseas Co.*, 508 F.2d at 975-76, we refused to use the defense to bar enforcement based on an arbitral Tribunal's refusal to accommodate a key witness' schedule, stating that the inability to present one's witness was "a risk inherent in an agreement to submit to arbitration." Similarly, another court has held that a party was not denied the opportunity to present its defenses under article V(1)(b) when it had notice of an arbitration, but chose not to respond. *See Goetech Lizenz AG v. Evergreen Systems*, 697 F. Supp. 1248, 1253 (E.D.N.Y.1988). The court in *Evergreen Systems* ruled that the defendant's "failure to participate was a decision that was reached only after the Company had full knowledge of the peril at which it acted." *Id.* In the face of Judge Ansari's repeated questioning of Avco's counsel, Avco was plainly placed on similar notice of the possible risk that the panel would choose not to rely on invoice summaries in determining whether to grant it an award.

Further support for finding that Avco was not denied due process arises from a like exception to enforceability that appears in the Federal Arbitration Act, 9 U.S.C. § 10 (1988). That Act also provides an exception to enforcement for the inability to present one's case at arbitration. The more extensive case law available under § 10 supports the conclusion that Avco was not denied due process before the Iran-U.S. Claims Tribunal. Avco's protests that the events in this case were more "egregious" than in other cases involving the inability to present one's case at arbitration are unpersuasive. The ruling by the Hague Tribunal in the instant matter was not high-handed or arbitrary as are those cases, upon which Avco relies, arising under the Federal Arbitration Act. A reading of those cases reveals that they either involve arbitration hearings actually cut short and not completed before an award was rendered, *see Confinco, Inc. v. Bakrie & Bros, N.V.*, 395 F. Supp. 613, 615 (S.D.N.Y.1975); *Teamsters, Local Union No. 506 v. E.D. Clapp Corp.*, 551 F. Supp. 570, 577-78 (N.D.N.Y.1982), *aff'd*, 742 F.2d 1441 (2d Cir. 1983), or a panel's outright refusal to hear certain relevant evidence at all, *see Harvey Aluminum Inc. v. United Steelworkers*, 263 F. Supp. 488, 493 (C.D. Cal. 1967).

The present picture is vastly different. Avco had a full opportunity to present its claims, and was on notice that there might be a problem with its proof, especially given Judge Ansari's concerns voiced at trial. The earlier panel surely had never said that the invoices themselves would not be accepted or considered as evidence at trial. Nor did the pre-trial colloquy clearly indicate that the earlier panel had issued a definitive ruling that account summaries would be sufficient substitute proof for the invoices. Avco did not declare, after hearing Judge Ansari's comments, that it had been precluded by the pre-trial colloquy from producing the invoices, nor did it then attempt to introduce them before the panel. Rather than address Judge Ansari's concerns through producing the invoices themselves, Avco reiterated its "choice" to produce only a summary of the invoices. In so doing it took a calculated risk. Under these circumstances, Avco can scarcely credibly maintain that it was prevented from presenting its case before the Tribunal.

III

When reviewing the grant of summary judgment which dismissed the action to enforce the award, we must view the facts in the light most favorable to the Iranian parties. When so viewed those facts fail to demonstrate that Avco was denied the opportunity to present its claims to the Tribunal. For the reasons stated I think the district court erred in reaching the opposite conclusion. Accordingly, I dissent and vote to enforce the award.

NOTES

1. Does the majority opinion reach a conclusion that properly promotes arbitration? Is it appropriate to equate a party's inability "to present his case" with due process?

2. The dissent of Judge Cardamone refuses to find due process violated and reasons that Avco had an opportunity to present its claims. Is this true? Did counsel for Avco do everything possible to submit proper evidence after Judge Ansari questioned the need for substantiation of the invoices? Did Judge Ansari's concerns constitute a form of notice?

3. The New York Convention is now widely accepted. Over one-hundred countries are now parties to the Convention. Do its exceptions promote international arbitration adequately?

4. *Arbitration in China.* Arbitration of international joint venture disputes between Chinese companies and their foreign partners has been both plentiful and controversial. Use of arbitration to resolve such disputes is understandingly common. Typically, the parties arbitrate before CIETAC, the Chinese International Economic and Trade Arbitration Commission. Chinese companies seek a local form of dispute resolution and foreign partners distrust Chinese courts. After criticism of CIETAC arbitrator impartiality, CIETAC amended its rules in 2005. Commentators had called for improvement of CIETAC procedures to provide for greater party autonomy, improved impartiality, and more transparency. (*See* Jerome Cohen, *Time to Fix China's Arbitration,* Far Eastern Economic Review, Jan. 2005, at 31.) The new rules, while not meeting all the criticisms leveled at CIETAC, are a step in the right direction. They increase arbitrator disclosure requirements, allow parties to select arbitrators independently without using pre-approved CIETAC listed neutrals, provide that the parties may draft their own procedural rules, create more specialist panels, and allow flexibility regarding the location of an arbitration. Efforts by the Chinese Supreme People's Court have raised hopes for a more even-handed enforcement, especially in the commercial centers, of both international awards and domestic awards with a foreign "nexus." But deeper institutional issues remain, such as the independence of the judiciary and state-sponsored arbitration bodies from domestic Chinese influence.

CHROMALLOY AEROSERVICES v. ARAB REPUBLIC OF EGYPT
939 F. Supp. 907 (D.D.C. 1996)

June L. Green, District Judge.

I. Introduction

This matter is before the Court on the Petition of Chromalloy Aeroservices, Inc., ("CAS") to Confirm an Arbitral Award, and a Motion to Dismiss that Petition filed by the Arab Republic of Egypt ("Egypt"), the defendant in the arbitration. This is a case of first impression. The Court GRANTS Chromalloy Aeroservices' Petition to Recognize and Enforce the Arbitral Award, and DENIES Egypt's Motion to Dismiss, because the arbitral award in question is valid, and because Egypt's arguments against enforcement are insufficient to allow this Court to disturb the award.

II. Background

This case involves a military procurement contract between a U.S. corporation, Chromalloy Aeroservices, Inc., and the Air Force of the Arab Republic of Egypt.

On June 16, 1988, Egypt and CAS entered into a contract under which CAS agreed to provide parts, maintenance, and repair for helicopters belonging to the Egyptian Air Force. On December 2, 1991, Egypt terminated the contract by notifying CAS representatives in Egypt. . . . On December 15, 1991, CAS notified Egypt that it rejected the cancellation of the contract "and commenced arbitration proceedings on the basis of the arbitration clause contained in Article XII and Appendix E of the Contract."

. . .

On February 23, 1992, the parties began appointing arbitrators, and shortly thereafter, commenced a lengthy arbitration. On August 24, 1994, the arbitral panel ordered Egypt to pay to CAS the sums of $272,900 plus 5 percent interest from July 15, 1991, . . . and $16,940,958 plus 5 percent interest from December 15, 1991, (interest accruing until the date of payment). The panel also ordered CAS to pay to Egypt the sum of 606,920 pounds sterling, plus 5 percent interest from December 15, 1991.

On October 28, 1994, CAS applied to this Court for enforcement of the award. On November 13, 1994, Egypt filed an appeal with the Egyptian Court of Appeal, seeking nullification of the award. On March 1, 1995, Egypt filed a motion with this Court to adjourn CAS's Petition to enforce the award. On April 4, 1995, the Egyptian Court of Appeal suspended the award, and on May 5, 1995, Egypt filed a Motion in this Court to Dismiss CAS's petition to enforce the award. On December 5, 1995, Egypt's Court of Appeal at Cairo issued an order nullifying the award. This Court held a hearing in the matter on December 12, 1995.

Egypt argues that this Court should deny CAS' Petition to Recognize and Enforce the Arbitral Award out of deference to its court. CAS argues that this Court should confirm the award because Egypt "does not present any serious argument that its court's nullification decision is consistent with the New York Convention or United States arbitration law."

III. Discussion

* * *

1. The Standard under the Convention

This Court must grant CAS's Petition to Recognize and Enforce the arbitral "award unless it finds one of the grounds for refusal . . . of recognition or enforcement of the award specified in the . . . Convention." 9 U.S.C. § 207. Under the Convention, "Recognition and enforcement of the award may be refused" if Egypt furnishes to this Court "proof that . . . [t]he award has . . . been set aside . . . by a competent authority of the country in which, or under the law of which, that award was made." Convention, Article V(1) & V(1)(e) (emphasis added), 9 U.S.C. § 201. In the present case, the award was made in Egypt, under the laws of Egypt, and has been nullified by the court designated by Egypt to review arbitral awards. Thus, the Court may, at its discretion, decline to enforce the award.

While Article V provides a discretionary standard, Article VII of the Convention requires that, "The provisions of the present Convention shall not . . . deprive any interested party of any right he may have to avail himself of an arbitral award in the manner and to the extent allowed by the law . . . of the count[r]y where such award is sought to be relied upon." 9 U.S.C. § 201 note (emphasis added). In other words, under the Convention, CAS maintains all rights to the enforcement of this Arbitral Award that it would have in the absence of the Convention. Accordingly, the Court finds that, if the Convention did not exist, the Federal Arbitration Act ("FAA") would provide CAS with a legitimate claim to enforcement of this arbitral award. See 9 U.S.C. §§ 1-14. . . .

2. Examination of the Award under 9 U.S.C. § 10

* * *

An arbitral award will . . . be set aside if the award was made in " 'manifest disregard' of the law." *First Options of Chicago v. Kaplan*, 115 S. Ct. 1920, 1923 (1995). "Manifest disregard of the law may be found if [the] arbitrator[s] understood and correctly stated the law but proceeded to ignore it." *Kanuth v. Prescott, Ball, & Turben, Inc.*, 949 F.2d 1175, 1179 (D.C. Cir. 1991).

> Plainly, this non-statutory theory of vacatur cannot empower a District Court to conduct the same *de novo* review of questions of law that an appellate court exercises over lower court decisions. Indeed, we have in the past held that it is clear that [manifest disregard] means more than error or misunderstanding with respect to the law.

Al-Harbi v. Citibank, 85 F.3d 680, 683 (D.C. Cir. 1996).

In *Al-Harbi*, "The submission agreement under which the arbitrator decided the controversy mandated that the arbitrator apply 'the procedural and substantive laws of the Southern District of New York, U.S.A.' "*Id.* at 684. The arbitrator in *Al-Harbi* ruled that a court applying the laws of New York would dismiss the case on forum non conveniens grounds. *Id.* Appellant argued on appeal that the arbitrator had manifestly disregarded the substantive laws of New York by disposing of the case on procedural grounds. *Id.* The D.C. Circuit emphatically rejected this argument, stating that:

> Appellant's argument then depends upon the proposition that where a tribunal is to render [a] decision based on procedural and substantive law that tribunal has not only erred, but acted in manifest disregard of the law if it finds that procedural factors are dispositive of the case without then going on to consider substantive law rendered apparently moot by that procedural decision. To state that proposition is to reject it. We find no basis for vacatur.

Id.

In the present case, the language of the arbitral award that Egypt complains of reads:

> The Arbitral tribunal considers that it does not need to decide the legal nature of the contract. It appears that the Parties rely principally for their claims and defences, on the interpretation of the contract itself and on the facts presented. Furthermore, the Arbitral tribunal holds that the legal issues in dispute are not affected by the characterization of the contract.

(Award at 30.)

Like the arbitrator in *Al-Harbi*, the arbitrators in the present case made a procedural decision that allegedly led to a misapplication of substantive law. After considering Egypt's arguments that Egyptian administrative law should govern the contract, the majority of the arbitral panel held that it did not matter which substantive law they applied — civil or administrative. Id. At worst, this decision constitutes a mistake of law, and thus is not subject to review by this Court. See *Al-Harbi*, 85 F.3d at 684.

In the United States, "[W]e are well past the time when judicial suspicion of the desirability of arbitration and of the competence of arbitral tribunals inhibited the development of arbitration as an alternative means of dispute resolution." *Mitsubishi Motors Corp. v. Soler Chrysler-Plymouth, Inc.*, 473 U.S. 614, 626-27 (1985). In Egypt, however, "[I]t is established that arbitration is an exceptional means for resolving disputes, requiring departure from the normal means of litigation before the courts, and the guarantees they afford." (Nullification Decision at 8.) Egypt's complaint that, "[T]he Arbitral Award is null under Arbitration Law, . . . because it is not properly 'grounded' under Egyptian law," reflects this suspicious view of arbitration, and is precisely the type of technical argument that U.S. courts are not to entertain when reviewing an arbitral award.

The Court's analysis thus far has addressed the arbitral award, and, as a matter of U.S. law, the award is proper. . . . The Court now considers the question of whether the decision of the Egyptian court should be recognized as a valid foreign judgment.

* * *

C. The Decision of Egypt's Court of Appeal

1. The Contract

"The arbitration agreement is a contract and the court will not rewrite it for the parties." *Williams v. E.F. Hutton & Co., Inc.*, 753 F.2d 117, 119 (D.C. Cir. 1985) The Court "begin[s] with the 'cardinal principle of contract construction: that a document should be read to give effect to all its provisions and to render them consistent with each other.'" *United States v. Insurance Co. of North America*, 83 F.3d 1507, 1511 (D.C. Cir. 1996) (quoting *Mastrobuono v. Shearson Lehman Hutton, Inc.*, 115 S. Ct. 1212, 1219, (1995)). Article XII of the contract requires that the parties arbitrate all disputes that arise between them under the contract. Appendix E, which defines the terms of any arbitration, forms an integral part of the contract. The contract is unitary.

Appendix E to the contract defines the "Applicable Law Court of Arbitration." The clause reads, in relevant part:

> It is . . . understood that both parties have irrevocably agreed to apply Egypt (sic) Laws and to choose Cairo as seat of the court of arbitration. . . . The decision of the said court shall be final and binding and cannot be made subject to any appeal or other recourse.

This Court may not assume that the parties intended these two sentences to contradict one another, and must preserve the meaning of both if possible. Egypt argues that the first quoted sentence supersedes the second, and allows an appeal to an Egyptian court. Such an interpretation, however, would vitiate the second sentence, and would ignore the plain language on the face of the contract. The Court concludes that the first sentence defines choice of law and choice of forum for the hearings of the arbitral panel. The Court further concludes that the second quoted sentence indicates the clear intent of the parties that any arbitration of a dispute arising under the contract is not to be appealed to any court. This interpretation, unlike that offered by Egypt, preserves the meaning of both sentences in a manner that is consistent with the plain language of the contract. The position of the latter sentence as the seventh and final paragraph, just before the signatures, lends credence to the view that this sentence is the final word on the arbitration question. In other words, the parties agreed to apply Egyptian Law to the arbitration, but, more important, they agreed that the arbitration ends with the decision of the arbitral panel.

2. The Decision of the Egyptian Court of Appeal

The Court has already found that the arbitral award is proper as a matter of U.S. law, and that the arbitration agreement between Egypt and CAS precluded an appeal in Egyptian courts. The Egyptian court has acted, however, and Egypt asks this Court to grant res judicata effect to that action.

The "requirements for enforcement of a foreign judgment . . . are that there be 'due citation' [i.e., proper service of process] and that the original claim not violate U.S. public policy." *Tahan v. Hodgson*, 662 F.2d 862, 864 (D.C. Cir. 1981) (citing *Hilton v. Guyot*, 159 U.S. 113, 202, (1895)). . . . Correctly understood, "[P]ublic policy emanates [only] from clear statutory or case law, 'not from general considerations of supposed public interest.' "*Id.* (quoting *American Postal Workers Union v. United States Postal Service*, 789 F.2d 1 (D.C. Cir. 1986)).

The U.S. public policy in favor of final and binding arbitration of commercial disputes is unmistakable, and supported by treaty, by statute, and by case law. The Federal Arbitration Act "and the implementation of the Convention in the same year by amendment of the Federal Arbitration Act," demonstrate that there is an "emphatic federal policy in favor of arbitral dispute resolution," particularly "in the field of international commerce." *Mitsubishi v. Soler Chrysler-Plymouth*, 473 U.S. 614, 631 (1985) (internal citation omitted). A decision by this Court to recognize the decision of the Egyptian court would violate this clear U.S. public policy.

3. International Comity

"No nation is under an unremitting obligation to enforce foreign interests which are fundamentally prejudicial to those of the domestic forum." *Laker Airways Ltd. v. Sabena, Belgian World Airlines*, 731 F.2d 909, 937 (D.C. Cir. 1984). "[C]omity never obligates a national forum to ignore the rights of its own citizens or of other persons who are under the protection of its laws.' *Id.* at 942. Egypt alleges that, "Comity is the chief doctrine of international law requiring U.S. courts to respect the decisions of competent foreign tribunals." However, comity does not and may not have the preclusive effect upon U.S. law that Egypt wishes this Court to create for it.

* * *

[I]n the present case, the question is whether this Court should give res judicata effect to the decision of the Egyptian Court of Appeal, not whether that court properly decided the matter under Egyptian law. Since the "act of state doctrine," as a whole, does not require U.S. courts to defer to a foreign sovereign on these facts, comity, which is but one of several "policies" that underlie the act of state "doctrine" . . . does not require such deference either.

5. Conflict between the Convention & the FAA

As a final matter, Egypt argues that, "Chromalloy's use of [A]rticle VII [to invoke the Federal Arbitration Act] contradicts the clear language of the Convention and would create an impermissible conflict under 9 U.S.C. § 208," by eliminating all consideration of Article V of the Convention. *See Vimar Seguros y Reaseguros, S.A. v. M/V Sky Reefer*, 115 S. Ct. 2322, 2325, (1995) (holding that, "[W]hen two statutes are capable of coexistence . . . it is the duty of the courts, absent a clearly expressed congressional intention to the contrary, to regard each as effective"). As the Court has explained, however, Article V provides a permissive standard, under which this Court may refuse to enforce an award. Article VII, on the other hand, mandates that this Court must consider CAS' claims under applicable U.S. law.

Article VII of the Convention provides that:

> The provisions of the present Convention shall not . . . deprive any interested party of any right he may have to avail himself of an arbitral award in the manner and to the extent allowed by the law . . . of the count[r]y where such award is sought to be relied upon.

9 U.S.C. § 201. Article VII does not eliminate all consideration of Article V; it merely requires that this Court protect any rights that CAS has under the domestic laws of the United States. There is no conflict between CAS' use of Article VII to invoke the FAA and the language of the Convention.

IV. Conclusion

The Court concludes that the award of the arbitral panel is valid as a matter of U.S. law. The Court further concludes that it need not grant res judicata effect to the decision of the Egyptian Court of Appeal at Cairo. Accordingly, the Court GRANTS Chromalloy Aeroservices' Petition to Recognize and Enforce the Arbitral Award, and DENIES Egypt's Motion to Dismiss that Petition.

NOTES

1. Under Article V of the New York Convention, now codified as United States legislation, the trial court has seeming discretion to refuse to enforce the award if it is shown that a court of the country where the award was made has set aside the award. Was the *Chromalloy* decision too quick to exercise that discretion? Shouldn't U.S. courts honor valid foreign judgments?

2. Assume the *Chromalloy* case is appealed. What will be the scope of review on appeal? It would appear that the trial court was merely exercising its discretion under the New York Convention and that a narrow, abuse of discretion standard should apply. But what should be made of *First Options of Chicago* and its *de novo* scope of review?

3. Does the *Chromalloy* opinion give enough deference to the parties' choice of law? The parties did agree to be bound by Egyptian law. Doesn't this agreement include law permitting an Egyptian court to set aside the award for errors of law? Yet, didn't the very next sentence of the CAS-Egypt air force contract say that the arbitration result was "final" and not "subject to appeal"? Is it possible to interpret the choice of law clause to give it some effect? The *Chromalloy* case is criticized in Georgios Petrochilos, *Enforcing Awards Annulled in Their State of Origin Under the New York Convention*, 48 INTL. & COMP. L.Q. 856 (1999), and in Ray Chan, *The Enforceability of Annulled Foreign Arbitral Awards in the United States: A Critique of Chromalloy*, 17 B.U. INT. L.J. 141 (1999).

4. Judge Green's *Chromalloy* opinion linked the FAA and the New York Convention. Is this an appropriate way to read these two statutes? One might criticize the linkage on the grounds that the case involved an international arbitration and, therefore, the more specific statute, the New York Convention, should apply.

5. For a helpful general discussion of the mechanics of the New York Convention, see John P. McMahon, *Implementation of the United Nations Convention on Foreign Arbitral Awards in the United States*, 2 J. MARIT. L. & COMM. 735 (1971).

6. How does the FAA relate to the New York Convention? Does the FAA have any applicability in the international context? In *Yusuf Ahmed Alghanim & Sons v. Toys "R" Us, Inc.*, 126 F.2d 15 (2d Cir. 1997), the Second Circuit Court of Appeals considered (and rejected) grounds to vacate under the FAA in an enforcement suit brought under the New York Convention. For criticism of this result, see William W. Park, *The Specificity of International Arbitration: The Case for Reform*, 36 VAND. J. TRANS'L. L. 1241, 1245–48 (2003).

7. *The UNCITRAL Model Law on Commercial Arbitration.* In 1985 the Model Law on Commercial Arbitration was passed by the United Nations Commission on International Trade Law. The provisions of this arbitration code, unlike the New York Convention, largely apply to the procedures used in international arbitration such as the constitution of the arbitration tribunal. Like the New York Convention, the UNCITRAL Model Law, seeks to support decisions of the arbitration panel and set out a minimal role for courts in arbitration.

The Model law has served as just that, a model for domestic legislation needed to more fully administer the international arbitration process. American states and other countries have used language derived from the UNCITRAL Model Law when legislating regarding international arbitration. Commentators have criticized the Model Law as setting forth only minimal and very general standards. (*See, e.g.,* Alan S. Reid, *The UNCITRAL Model Law on International Commercial Arbitration and the English Arbitration Act: Are the Two Systems Poles Apart?* 21 J. INT'L ARB. 227, 237 (2004).)

F. HYBRID PROCESSES

1. MED-ARB

In med-arb the same person serves first as a mediator and, if the dispute has not been resolved through mediation, as an arbitrator. The theory of this hybrid device is that the threat of a looming arbitration will drive the parties to settle within the mediation process. Arbitration serves as an incentive to successfully mediate.

Critics of med-arb contend that the mediation phase is conceptually flawed by the fact that the same person will be the mediator and the arbitrator. They argue that the parties will be less likely to be candid when caucusing before a mediator who may later judge them. This criticism could be cured by use of a different person to arbitrate. Supporters counter that it is highly efficient to hire the same person for the two roles and that the scheduling of the sessions back-to-back facilitates low transactions costs.

2. ARB-MED

Arb-Med is almost the flip side of med-arb. The disputants first hold an arbitration hearing before the arbitrator. At the conclusion of the arbitration the arbitrator does not announce an award. Instead, the arbitrator then mediates the dispute. In theory, the mediator will be "educated" by the presentation of proof during the arbitration phase. In fact, the mediator may have already made up his or her mind on the arbitration outcome. This point, of course, is known to the parties who listen intently to signals sent by the mediator and, hopefully, reach agreement.

Proponents of arb-med point to the effectiveness of mediation by a person who really knows the dispute well. Critics contend that the cost of this method may not justify the mediation phase. The parties may spend additional time and money on a mediation that reaches results quite similar to an already completed arbitration phase.

3. FINAL OFFER OR "BASEBALL" ARBITRATION

Final offer arbitration is an effort to avoid the all-to-common "compromise award" which "splits the difference" among the disputants and tends to satisfy no one. Under final offer arbitration each side submits a proposed award to the arbitrator at the start of the arbitration. The parties then engage in the typical arbitration. At the conclusion of the arbitration, however, the arbitrator must select one of the two awards proposed by the disputants at the beginning of the arbitration. This device greatly restricts the creativity and freedom of the arbitrator but does prevent the "compromise award" that is disliked by some (but certainly not all) disputants. Parties who win a baseball arbitration "win big" in this "winner take all" device.

Final offer arbitration has been used to set salaries of major league baseball players since 1974. The team proposes its salary and the player counters with his own suggested salary. At the hearing each side submits salaries of "comparable" players and the arbitrator sides with the disputant with the better position. The proof at these hearings is not unlike real estate tax valuation hearings where the value of a parcel of property is established by examining the value of comparable properties. Presentations of evidence are short; they are limited to one hour of initial presentation and a thirty-minute rebuttal. the arbitrator considers only salaries of comparable players, the player's last year's performance, and team attendance and success. Explanation of the salary selected by the arbitrator is forbidden. (*See* John Fizel, *Baseball Arbitration After 20 Years*, 49 DISP. RESOL. J. 42 (June 1994).)

Some believe that baseball owners have suffered from the results of salary arbitration. Manager Whitey Herzog, for example, has said that arbitration is the worst thing to have happened to baseball owners. (THE SPORTING NEWS, February 24, 1996, p.8.) New York Yankee owner George Steinbreuner has said that "arbitration will be the cancer of baseball." (WALL ST. J., April 2, 1993, p.A1.) Individual owners have called for a new contract with the players union that would eliminate baseball arbitration. Few complaints about baseball arbitration are heard from players or their agents.

The winner-take-all nature of baseball arbitration or final offer arbitration is a feature that will appeal to only some disputants. Many fear this mechanism. Even those who agree to final offer arbitration can be deterred from the arbitration hearing because of the inherent risk of a mandatory win-lose result. This feature serves as an incentive to reactivate settlement negotiations on the eve of the arbitration hearings. Many baseball arbitration hearings that are set for 1:00 p.m. on a future date are negotiated to a successful resolution by that time. A very high percentage of player arbitration filings result in negotiated settlements. This "settlement impact" of baseball arbitration is one of the most positive features of final offer arbitration. Nonetheless, some baseball team owners argue that settlements prior to baseball arbitrations occur under conditions close to duress.

Baseball arbitration is based upon the arbitrator's use of a player's comparable worth. In this sense baseball arbitration is just a procedure to determine "fair value." Final offer arbitration represents a potentially attractive way to decide disputes of fair value which occur in a range of areas in our economy, ranging from property tax assessments to the value of minority shares. (*See* Paul Gordon, *Submitting "Fair Value" to Final Offer Arbitration*, 63 U. COLO. L. REV. 751 (1992).) Fair value or comparable worth decisions are based upon how others value comparable property or, in the case of baseball, how well other owners pay comparable players. Jerry Reinsdorf, chairman of the Chicago White Sox, has criticized this characteristic of baseball arbitration, which he terms a process in which teams "pay players what our dumbest competitors pay players." (WALL ST. J., April 12, 1993, p.A1.)

Final offer arbitration is frequently employed in the collective bargaining area. Some states require their public sector unions and public employers to use final offer arbitration to resolve "interest arbitrations." In this context the arbitrator will consider the salary and benefit packages of "comparable" employees and employers. Some final offer arbitration provisions require arbitrators to resolve disputes on a "package" basis (i.e., they must accept the entire final offer of the union or the employer), or, alternatively, on an "issue by issue" basis. The latter type provision allows arbitrators to structure compromise awards.

The most well-known recent matter regarding baseball arbitration is the 2005 salary of future Hall of Fame pitcher Roger Clemens. Clemens retired from the New York Yankees in 2003 but signed a one-year $5 million contract with his home town Houston Astros for 2004. Following a strong performance in 2004, Clemens opted to arbitrate his salary for the following season, 2005. Clemens demanded $22 million, the highest baseball arbitration demand in history. His team countered with $13.5 million.

Shortly before the matter was set to be arbitrated, Clemens signed a one-year contract for $18 million. What caused this matter to settle and not be arbitrated? Although many players opt for salary arbitration, baseball's sole arbitrator gets little business. Is it relevant that the negotiated deal for $18 million is about the midpoint of the proposed figures advanced by the parties(the midpoint is $17.75 million)? Clemens' contract is the highest one-year contract in baseball history, topping Greg Maddux's $14.75 million deal with the Atlanta Braves in 2003.

G. ARBITRATION VS. MEDIATION: A POSTSCRIPT

At this point in the study of ADR, the student should have a thorough grounding in negotiation, mediation and arbitration. You should begin thinking, however, about the comparative worth of these methods in relation to one another.

One often hears today that "mediation is the preferred ADR method of choice — negotiation sometimes doesn't work, arbitration has too many troublesome features and is too expensive but mediation is usually worth a shot." The general thinking among corporate counsel is that "mediation is the hottest ADR tool at the moment." They reason that the parties' ability to control their own destiny is a feature of mediation lacking in more risky third party controlled dispute resolution mechanisms such as arbitration.

A recent survey of litigators and house counsel illustrates the general popularity of mediation. The survey, conducted by the National Law Journal and the American Arbitration Association, compared arbitration and mediation. Survey questionnaires were sent to leading litigators and Fortune 500 house-counsel. 69% of litigators and 88% of house-counsel preferred mediation. 80% of the litigators and 88% of house-counsel surveyed liked mediation because it saves time and money. (*See* Lisa Brennan, *What Lawyers Like: Mediation*, NATIONAL LAW J., Nov. 9, 1999.)

Are such generalizations valid? Will they fit all cases? Won't arbitration be the method of choice where the "right to be heard" is essential? Some might argue that these generalizations give too little preference to simple negotiation: if two cooperative parties are trained to negotiate effectively, they may be able to arrive at an acceptable resolution of their controversy at a comparatively low cost without use of any third party. Is this thinking an appropriate response to today's slogan that "mediation is the preferred ADR method of choice"?

Part FOUR

GOVERNMENT SPONSORED ADR: COURT- AND AGENCY-ANNEXED ALTERNATIVES TO TRIAL

Chapter 14

COURT-ANNEXED ALTERNATIVES

This chapter focuses upon the ADR procedures used by courts to help process pending litigation. To say that judicially sponsored alternatives to conventional trial are on the increase would be an understatement. ADR is now as prevalent in the courts as it is in the free market outside the courts. Some of ADR's staunchest supporters are judges. Court-annexed procedures — use of ADR through court sponsored programs — have mushroomed in popularity and initiation since the early 1990's. Many considered the initial efforts in the late 1970's and 1980's, to begin court mandated ADR, to be an experiment. Most commentators would now declare the experiment over. The Alternative Dispute Resolution Act of 1998 mandates that every U.S. District Court is required to adopt and implement an ADR program. 28 U.S.C.A. § 651(b). Many now consider the resulting court mandated ADR procedures a success. Yet, how is "success" measured? Are the cases that have been removed from the docket by ADR ones that would have settled through little or no court involvement? If so, adding mandatory court-annexed ADR may be little more than requiring an extra layer of procedure. Some members of the bar, particularly those representing plaintiffs, are less than happy with court mandated ADR, which they see as preventing their clients from easily getting before juries. As you read the following materials, ask yourself whether these devices should be mandated or be voluntary and try to assess whether the benefits are worth the costs.

A. ESSENTIAL TYPES AND CHARACTERISTICS OF COURT-ANNEXED ADR

1. COURT-ANNEXED ARBITRATION (CAA)

Following the filing of a civil suit the case is diverted to an arbitrator for hearing. Generally the case must come within a prescribed category to qualify for diversion. Monetary limits (e.g., all civil suits seeking under $100,000 in damages) are typical. Many court systems exclude cases seeking injunctive relief.

The court-annexed arbitration hearing is adjudicatory — the parties submit evidence and the arbitrator's ruling is based on the proof submitted. Although not required to do so, the court-annexed arbitrator tends to apply substantive legal doctrine. The parties may "appeal" the result and receive a conventional trial, sometimes called a trial *de novo*. However, most jurisdictions penalize a party that "appeals" from an arbitration but fails to improve the arbitration result. While court-annexed arbitrations are not binding, their "penalty" feature and their expense give substance to the result reached and cause some attorneys not to request a trial *de novo*.

2. EARLY NEUTRAL EVALUATION (ENE)

Early Neutral Evaluation involves assigning the case to a neutral for some initial "evaluation" and subsequent communication by the neutral to the parties of the likelihood of success or failure of the various claims and defenses presented. ENE may also involve an attempt by the neutral to settle the case. The neutral permits each party to present its case in an abbreviated time period. The neutral asks questions, prepares a case evaluation, including a range of damages, and discloses his or her evaluation following a possible attempt at settlement. If the case does not settle, the neutral aids the disputants in preparing a case management plan. (*See* Wayne D. Brazil, et al., *Early Neutral Evaluation: An Experimental Effort to Expedite Dispute Resolution*, 69 JUDICATURE 279, 282 (1986); David I. Levine, *Early Neutral Evaluation: The Second Phase*, 1989 J. DISP. RES. 1, 48.)

3. SUMMARY JURY TRIAL

A summary jury trial is an abbreviated (e.g., 3 hours) trial to a jury which renders a non-binding verdict. The verdict serves to predict the likely jury verdict if a conventional trial is needed. There are a variety of types of summary jury trial. In one model, the jurors are not told that their verdict is non-binding. In another model, the court tells the jury that their summary jury trial is non-binding and predictive. Some courts use more than one jury. Most courts require all "proof" to be in the form of attorney summations and limit the trial time severely (e.g., three hours).

In numerous jurisdictions summary jury trials are required for all civil jury cases seeking less than a certain amount in damages (e.g., less than $100,000). Some theorize that this device works best in cases involving small or moderate damage amounts.

4. COURT-ANNEXED MEDIATION

The formal use of mediation in the United States developed during the twentieth century first as a means to resolve disputes between labor unions and management. During the 1960s and 1970s innovators used mediation as an approach to resolve racial and community conflicts and a few courts began experimental programs for neighborhood disputes. The use of mediation in the courts was stimulated by the 1976 Pound Conference — formally known as the National Conference on the Sources of Popular Dissatisfaction with the Administration of Justice. Chief Justice Warren Burger urged increased use of informal dispute resolution processes and Harvard Law Professor Frank Sander gave a presentation entitled "Varieties of Dispute Processing," which is credited as the source of the idea of a "multi-door courthouse" that offers multiple processes for resolving disputes. Recognizing a need for a less-adversarial process in divorce, many state courts developed programs for those cases during the 1980s. Court programs then expanded to civil cases. Florida took the lead in 1988 with legislation authorizing courts to refer any civil case to mediation, and mediation is now an accepted part of the litigation process in many states.

The use of mediation in the federal courts was stimulated by the Civil Justice Reform Act of 1990, which required district courts to create plans to reduce cost and delay. Along with case management techniques, many districts embraced mediation as a means of reducing court dockets. Federal encouragement continued with the Alternative Dispute Resolution Act of 1998's requirement that every district court to offer an ADR program. Mediation is the ADR process most commonly available in the federal courts; as of 2005, 61 of 94 district courts had local rules authorizing mediation. Mediation is also available in many state and federal appellate courts. In the federal courts of appeals, Rule 33 of the Federal Rules of Appellate Procedure authorizes "judicial settlement conferences," which are mediation programs in most of the circuits. Backlogs of appeals are, at present, crowding appellate dockets even more than trial dockets. Use of mediation, even at this stage, can help alleviate the problem by removing cases from an appellate calendar.

The process by which mediation has become associated with courts as a case settlement procedure is often referred to as the "institutionalization" of mediation. The design of court-annexed mediation programs varies greatly among the states, and often within a state, so it is difficult to generalize about these programs. But all face the challenge of merging a process that values party autonomy, self-determination, and empowerment into an institution designed for an adversarial process grounded in legal rights.

The merger has led to increased use and understanding of mediation, although critics charge that both mediation and the courts have been changed for the worse. One controversial product of institutionalization is mandatory mediation, in which a court requires parties to mediate as a prerequisite for continuing the adjudicatory process. Mandatory mediation has further led, in some courts, to the need for standards that define an acceptable level of participation in mediation for parties who have been ordered to mediate against their wishes. The issues associated with these developments are considered in Part C of this chapter.

5. JUDICIAL SETTLEMENT CONFERENCES AND MEDIATION

Perhaps the oldest form of court provided settlement is the Rule 16 pre-trial conference held by the judge assigned to the case. (*See* Fed. R. Civ. P. 16.) From the earliest version of the federal rules, settlement has been one of the chief goals of the pre-trial conference. Succeeding revisions of Rule 16 have pushed settlement even more into the limelight and with the ascendancy of so-called "managerial judging," use of settlement techniques at pre-trial conferences is quite common. (Resnik, 1982.)

Judicial techniques at pre-trial conferences range along a continuum from facilitative mediation to more active intervention in "settlement conferences." The labels are not always indicative of the actual process, but mediation conducted by judges tends to include the parties as well as their attorneys, while settlement conferences are usually conducted by a judge with the participation of attorneys only. Judges conducting settlement conferences tend to be more evaluative than facilitative. They will typically stress the weak points of a party's case and emphasize the strengths of the opponent's case in an effort to prime the attorneys, and through them their clients, for compromise.

6. THE MINI-TRIAL

A mini-trial is an adversary presentation of evidence to a neutral expert hired by the parties. The neutral listens to the evidence and prepares a ruling. The neutral's ruling is non-binding. It is customary for the neutral to explore the possibility of settlement before announcing a ruling. Settlement chances are helped by another distinctive feature of the mini-trial: clients with full settlement authority are expected to attend, to consider the evidence and to personally participate in the settlement discussions with the neutral expert. While the mini-trial is here listed as a court-annexed device, it could be initiated by disputants prior to the filing of a lawsuit and, accordingly, is not purely a court-annexed mechanism. The mini-trial has had much heralded results in settling protracted civil business disputes with the full participation of CEOs.

7. PRIVATE JUDGING

Once a case is filed, a number of jurisdictions permit the parties to hire a private jurist to decide the dispute. This device resembles arbitration but has unique features that are distinctive. A private judge, sometimes called a "rent-a-judge," is typically a retired jurist. In California, the state in which this device has had the greatest use, early retirement possibilities have led many judges to leave the bench to work for private ADR providers, such as JAMS. Because many California counties have lengthy (four to five years) backlogs of civil cases awaiting trial, parties frequently hire a private judge and effectively jump the queue of cases. In theory, the California legislation permits the decision of the private judge to be appealed and the case can be tried before a jury. In practice, these latter two options are seldom sought — the parties seek finality before a skilled, expert judge and usually do not want the greater uncertainty of a jury trial or an appeal. While most private judging occurs as a court-annexed alternative for pending cases, it is possible to hire judges as arbitrators (essentially private judges) before a case is even filed. Private judges command hefty rates; a rate of $400–500 per hour, split by the parties, is not atypical.

8. PREDICTION

Each of the above forms of court-annexed ADR provides the parties and their attorneys with a prediction as to how the case will be later decided. In theory, this impartial prediction is helpful to the attorneys in evaluating the case and in assessing prior settlement offers. The attorneys may be too close to a case to evaluate it properly and their clients too influenced by their attorneys' biased enthusiasm. The predictions will aid settlement and, ideally, will occur early enough in the case to avoid unnecessary expenditures on expensive discovery and pre-trial motions.

9. DISCOVERY

Each of these court-annexed ADR devices can be a form of discovery. At the time most of these devices were first used by courts, the cases involved were "trial-ready." Today the court-annexed procedures are used early in a case and often before the completion of discovery. The attorneys who participate in a summary jury trial or an ENE will learn a great deal about their opponent's case. This discovery can have valuable or harmful strategic consequences. Of course, the opponents are also learning about your case. While there will be times when the information gained from these devices is asymmetrical, often the information exchanged is equally beneficial. The quantum of discovery is helpful in assessing uncertainty and thus facilitates settlement.

10. ADR AS PART OF THE CASE MANAGEMENT PROCESS

ADR mechanisms are part of a comprehensive scheme of case management. Each judge is increasingly a case manager, and the individual ADR processes are an integral part of this system. The pre-trial conference plays a significant role in relating ADR to an efficient administration of each case. Rule 16(c)(9) authorizes the court, at a pretrial conference, to act regarding "settlement and the use of special procedures to assist in resolving the dispute when authorized by statute or court rule." (Fed. R. Civ. P. 16(c)(9).)

B. JUDICIAL SETTLEMENT CONFERENCES AND MEDIATION

Judicial settlement conferences are explicitly authorized by Rule 16 of the Federal Rules of Civil Procedure. As originally adopted, Rule 16 contemplated pretrial conferences as an important step in trial preparation, but did not mention any role for the court in encouraging settlement. It has evolved over the years to provide authority for settlement activities.

When Rule 16 was amended in 1983, it recognized the increasingly common practice of using pretrial conferences as judicial settlement conferences or as a forum to discuss other settlement procedures for use in a case. The new Rule 16(c)(7) stated: "the parties at any conference under this rule may consider and take action with respect to * * * the possibility of settlement or the use of extrajudicial procedures to resolve the dispute."

After further amendment in 1993, Rule 16 now contains language authorizing courts to use pretrial conferences to consider and to "take appropriate action, with respect to * * * (9) settlement and the use of special procedures to assist in resolving the dispute when authorized by statute or local rule." (Fed. R. Civ. P. 16(c)(9).) According to the advisory committee that recommended the change, its primary purpose was to "eliminate questions that have occasionally been raised regarding the authority of the court to make appropriate orders designed either to facilitate settlement or to provide for an efficient and economical trial. The prefatory language * * * is revised to clarify the court's power to enter appropriate orders at a conference notwithstanding the objection of a party." (Fed. R. Civ. P. 16(c) advisory committee's notes.)

The Alternative Dispute Resolution Act of 1998 specifies settlement conferences as one of the forms of ADR that satisfy a federal district court's obligation to offer alternative procedures. Any claim that they are "alternative" is questionable in that they have been associated with litigation for a long time. While there is little empirical work on what happens during settlement conferences, most commentators regard them as distinct from mediation. The judges who lead them are not usually trained in facilitative techniques and a typical settlement conference is likely to involve only the attorneys, to be limited to legal issues, and to draw on the judge's skills in evaluating cases.

The identity of the judge who conducts the settlement conference is a matter of some controversy, especially when the judge is purporting to mediate. In many courts, the process is conducted by a judge other than the one assigned to hear the case, or by a magistrate judge. In some small state courts, judges have established a "buddy system" with a judge in a neighboring county so that each provides settlement services for the other's cases. By separating settlement and adjudicative functions, courts avoid the perception that a judge who engages in settlement with the parties may not approach a later trial with an open mind. If the processes are separate, a judicial officer who asks pointed questions that might expose latent case weaknesses or offers forthright assessments concerning the persuasiveness of particular arguments can do so without the parties fearing prejudice if their dispute ultimately has to be tried. The parties know that if the case does not settle, their candid settlement disclosures will be inadmissible in the succeeding judicial proceedings and cannot influence the decisionmaker because a different individual will preside at adjudications.

Nonetheless, not all jurisdictions are able or willing to guarantee that settlement conference judges will not be assigned to try the cases they are unable to mediate successfully. In many courts, judges routinely hold settlement conferences or mediate in cases they are assigned to try. Some find nothing objectionable about this practice, pointing out that the information that a judge acquires about a case while deciding pretrial motions can be used to advantage in a mediation or settlement conference. Proponents of this view feel that courts can later try a case impartially if the dispute fails to settle. They feel the parties are likely to value the opinions of the judge on the likelihood of subsequent success, because they have already seen the judge in the dispute and have confidence in the court's knowledge about the dispute. Moreover, the participation of the eventual adjudicator in settlement discussions may encourage the participants to be more conciliatory; neither wants to appear obstinate in front of the individual who will preside at any resulting adjudication. They may also be more hesitant to unduly exaggerate the strength of their claims or to engage in outright mendacity because they recognize that either approach would become apparent at trial. They also do not wish to develop reputations for uncooperative behavior that could adversely affect their representational efforts in future cases.

Occasionally, a court may appoint an individual from outside the court system as a "settlement master." This practice tends to be limited to complex cases or series of cases. For example, Judge Jack Weinstein appointed widely respected attorney Kenneth Feinberg to be the special settlement master in the Agent Orange cases involving a class of Vietnam veterans who alleged that their exposure to Agent Orange had harmed them. (*See* PETER SCHUCK, AGENT ORANGE ON TRIAL: MASS TOXIC DISASTERS IN THE COURTS (1986).) In Michigan, Judge Enslen appointed a special master in a complex dispute over the allocation of fishing rights in waters of the Great Lakes. The dispute was complex because of the number of competing interests: the United States, three Indian tribes, and the State of Michigan were the named parties and sport fisherman and commercial fisherman participated as "litigating amici." It was also challenging because of the complexity of the scientific questions involved in predicting fish stocks and developing management plans. The master supervised the pre-trial process with an expedited discovery schedule and simultaneously mediated a multi-stage settlement process. (*See* Francis McGovern, *Toward a Functional Approach for Managing Complex Litigation*, 53 U. CHI. L. REV. 440 (1986).) A special master appointment can avoid appearance of partiality that can arise from judicial involvement in settlement and also the opportunity costs associated with judges spending time mediating or convening settlement conferences. However a special master is an expensive proposition that is probably justified only in cases that are expensive to litigate.

Another important issue is the extent to which a court should mandate participation of parties in settlement conferences. Some jurisdictions have held that a judge has the power to compel parties with settlement authority to attend a pretrial settlement conference. (*See G. Heileman Brewing Co. v. Joseph Oat Corp.*, 871 F.2d 648 (7th Cir. 1989) (en banc) (holding that courts have inherent power to require party attendance).) Consider the following arguments for allowing courts to order attendance:

> There are several reasons for requiring the presence of authorized representatives as a settlement conference. During the conference, counsel for both sides are given an opportunity to argue their clients' respective positions to the court, including pointing out strengths and weaknesses of each party's case. In this discussion, it is often true that client representatives and insurers learn, for the first time, the difficulties they may have in prevailing at a trial. They must, during the conference, weigh their own positions in light of the statements and arguments made by counsel for the opposing parties. It is often true that as a result of such presentations, the clients' positions soften to the extent that meaningful negotiation, previously not seriously entertained, becomes possible. This dynamic is not possible if the only person with authority to negotiate is located away from the courthouse and can be reached only by telephone, if at all. The absent decision-maker learns only what his or her attorney conveys by phone, which can be expected to be largely a recitation of what has been conveyed in previous discussions. At best, even if the attorney attempts to convey the weaknesses of that client's position as they have been presented by opposing counsel at the settlement conference, the message, not unlike those in the children's game of "telephone," loses its impact through repetition, and it is simply too easy for that person to reject, out of hand, even a sincere desire on the part of counsel to

negotiate further. At worst, a refusal to have an authorized representative in attendance may become a weapon by which parties with comparatively greater financial flexibility may feign a good faith settlement posture by those in attendance at the conference, relying on the absent decision-maker to refuse to agree, thereby unfairly raising the stakes in the case, to the unfair disadvantage of a less wealthy opponent. In either case, the whole purpose of the settlement conference is lost, and the result is an even greater expenditure of the parties' resources, both time and money, for naught. [*Dvorak v. Shibata*, 123 F.R.D. 608, 609-10 (D. Neb. 1988).]

The *G. Heileman Brewing Co.* case, which held that judges have inherent power to compel parties to attend settlement conferences, resulted in several opinions. The following express the thoughts of some of the judges who concluded that courts may not order parties with settlement authority to attend settlement conferences. Judge Posner considered arguments on both sides of the question but came down against inherent power:

The only possible reason for wanting a represented party to be present is to enable the judge or magistrate to explore settlement with the principals rather than with just their agents. Some district judges and magistrates distrust the willingness or ability of attorneys to convey to their clients adequate information bearing on the desirability and terms of settling a case in lieu of pressing forward to trial. * * *

The question of the district court's power to summon a represented party to a settlement conference is a difficult one. . . . [T]here are obvious dangers in too broad an interpretation of the federal courts' inherent power to regulate their procedure. One danger is that it encourages judicial high-handedness ("power corrupts"); several years ago one of the district judges in this circuit ordered Acting Secretary of Labor Brock to appear before him for settlement discussions on the very day Brock was scheduled to appear before the Senate for his confirmation hearing. The broader concern illustrated by the Brock episode is that in their zeal to settle cases judges may ignore the value of other people's time. One reason people hire lawyers is to economize on their own investment of time in resolving disputes. It is pertinent to note in this connection that Oat is a defendant in this case; it didn't want its executives' time occupied with this litigation.

On the other hand, die Not bricht Eisen ["necessity breaks iron"]. Attorneys often are imperfect agents of their clients, and the workload of our district courts is so heavy that we should hesitate to deprive them of a potentially useful tool for effecting settlement, even if there is some difficulty in finding a legal basis for the tool. Although few attorneys will defy a district court's request to produce the client, those few cases may be the very ones where the client's presence would be most conducive to settlement. [*G. Heileman Brewing Co.*, F.2d at 657 (Posner, J., dissenting).]

Judge Coffey stressed the linkage between problems that arise from compelling a party to attend a settlement conference and those that arise when the judge who is assigned to try the case also attempts to settle it:

I believe we are all aware of the fact that the appearance of fairness, impartiality and justice is all imperative, and based upon logic I fail to understand how a litigant sitting at a command appearance before a judge who injects himself into an adversarial role for either of the parties' positions during settlement negotiations can feel that he or she (the litigant) will have a fair trial before the judge if he or she fails to agree with the judge's reasoning or direction regarding a recommended settlement. We may express in grandiose terms all sorts of theory and postulation about being careful not to influence, intimidate and/or coerce a settlement, but under the pressure that our trial judges experience today from their ever-burgeoning caseloads, we would be foolhardy not to anticipate an undesirable and unnecessary psychological impact upon the litigant in circumstances of this nature. The difficulties associated with active judicial participation in settlement negotiations is expressly exacerbated when the trial is scheduled before the court rather than a jury of one's peers. The appearance of partiality and impropriety must be avoided at all lengths if our nation is to continue to show respect for its judicial judgments. Since litigants are neither trained in the law nor have the basic understanding of the nuances of legal proceedings that we as lawyers have gained through years of education, professional training and experience, they could well be confused and dismayed with judicial participation in settlement negotiations. [*G. Heileman Brewing Co.*, 71 F.2d at 662 (Coffey, J., dissenting).]

The current Rule 16 is ambiguous regarding requirements for a party to attend a conference in person. It states:

At least one of the attorneys for each party participating in any conference before trial shall have authority to enter into stipulations and to make admissions regarding all matters that the participants may reasonably anticipate may be discussed. If appropriate, the court may require that a party or its representatives be present or reasonably available by telephone in order to consider possible settlement of the dispute. [Fed. R. Civ. P. 16(c).]

While the advisory committee notes state that "[t]he explicit authorization in the rule to require personal participation in the manner stated is not intended to limit the reasonable exercise of the court's inherent powers [citing *Joseph Oat Corp.*]," they also admonish:

The selection of the appropriate representative should ordinarily be left to the party and its counsel. . . . [I]t should be noted that the unwillingness of a party to be available, even by telephone, for a settlement conference may be a clear signal that the time and expense involved in pursuing settlement is likely to be unproductive and that personal participation by the parties should not be required. [Fed. R. Civ. P. 16(c) advisory committee notes.]

Underlying the debate on compelling attendance at settlement conferences are more fundamental questions about the efficacy of mandatory settlement conferences. Consider the views of Professor Menkel-Meadow:

Note . . . the persistence of the view that such mandatory settlement techniques do affect court caseloads, despite the empirical evidence to the contrary. The empirical evidence on the effectiveness of mandatory settlement conferences in reducing court dockets does not support a claim that settlement conferences should be used for efficiency purposes. As a judge and scholar, Judge Posner raises the efficiency issue by suggesting that if judges spend their time at mandatory settlement conferences, they may actually reduce court efficiency by being less available to try cases. [Carrie Menkel-Meadow, *Pursuing Settlement in an Adversary Culture: A Tale of Innovation Co-opted or "The Law of ADR"*, 19 FLA. ST. L. REV. 1, 21 (1991) (citations omitted).]

Any claim that judicial participation in settlement is efficient must be able to deal with the opportunity cost of judicial mediation and settlement conferences — the output of the court had the judges been doing something other than engaging in settlement.

C. COURT-ANNEXED MEDIATION

1. INSTITUTIONALIZATION OF MEDIATION IN THE COURTS

LOUISE PHIPPS SENFT & CYNTHIA A. SAVAGE, ADR IN THE COURTS: PROGRESS, PROBLEMS, AND POSSIBILITIES, 108 Penn St. L. Rev. 327, 327-33 (2003) *

ADR has come a long way. . . . The institutionalization of ADR in the courts has led to far greater use of ADR throughout the country. . . . Other benefits of institutionalization include increased public awareness of alternatives to litigation and growing sophistication regarding appropriate alternative processes among lawyers and judges. Parties can choose the dispute resolution process that best meets their interests. Research and evaluation of court-connected ADR programs have enriched our knowledge of ADR as well. There is evidence that ADR options can lead to more efficient use of resources by the courts, savings of time and money by litigants, and reduced levels of subsequent litigation. Mediation in particular enjoys consistently high satisfaction rates by participants. There is also evidence that ADR options have increased the public's trust and confidence in the courts.

But along with this progress have come problems, in particular with regard to the courts' use of mediation. The definition of what process is being provided is unclear. While what is being called "mediation" in the courts may encompass the interest-based, problem-solving, or relational approaches, which mediation advocates envisioned fifteen or twenty years ago, the combination of increased participation by lawyers and the close connection with litigation of court-referred mediation cases is leading to the increased "legalization" of mediation. Court-referred clients often believe the desired outcome that propelled them to court initially will be met. Their misplaced assumptions

---

about the type of process being ordered and the degree of court oversight can lead to disappointment with the process, the outcome, and the courts in general. Similar disappointment can result if promises that mediation is "faster, cheaper, and better" are not met. Perhaps most dangerous, the blurring of boundaries in the court's roles can lead to confusion and leave room for the possibility of coercion.

* * *

II. Progress

A. More Extensive Use of ADR

The use of ADR in cases that are in litigation or are potential lawsuits has exploded over the last twenty-seven years. When Frank Sander first proposed the multi-door courthouse in 1976, there were no state offices of dispute resolution, no ethical requirements that lawyers advise their clients of alternatives to litigation, and no explicit authorizations for courts to refer cases to ADR. As of June 30, 2003, there are now thirty-five state offices of dispute resolution, a number of states have ethical requirements that lawyers advise their clients of alternatives to litigation, and many states have explicitly authorized their judges to refer cases to ADR. . . . The federal district courts are required to offer at least one ADR process, and all of the federal appellate courts have in-house ADR programs.

Historically, voluntary mediation programs have not been well attended. Theories as to why this is so include: parties do not know about or do not understand the possible benefits of mediation; parties (and their lawyers) prefer to choose familiar processes (i.e., litigation); when angry, people tend to choose adversarial rather than cooperative processes; American culture has created a litigious society; barriers remain related to many attorneys' negative assumptions about the quality of volunteer mediators and doubts about the neutrality of mediators associated with a court program; and parties (and their lawyers) do not want to look weak by being the first to suggest mediation — or any other settlement process. Although still controversial, it has taken the mandate of the courts for many citizens to engage in mediation or other ADR processes, which has greatly increased participation in those processes.

B. Increased Public Awareness

Through mandatory referrals to ADR by the courts, the public has become more aware of alternatives to litigation. Each and every party and lawyer involved in the increasing number of cases referred to mediation by the courts now knows of at least one alternative to trial, and many of them have first-hand knowledge through participation in that ADR process. Florida's experience, though to a lesser degree, can be multiplied by the fifty states and added to by the federal court-annexed programs to estimate that millions of people participate in ADR processes, primarily mediation, every year. Even the media is beginning to reflect, as well as add to, this greater public awareness, for example by incorporating references to and scenes involving mediations (or processes called mediations) in law-related television shows.

C. Greater Sophistication Among Lawyers and Judges

Lawyers and judges are becoming increasingly sophisticated about ADR. They are less apt to use the words "mediation" and "arbitration" interchangeably. They will sometimes engage in discussions with potential mediators about whether or not the mediator will provide an "evaluative" approach to their case. In some parts of the country, lawyers are involved as volunteers in providing mediation services. . . .

D. More Matching of Cases and Dispute Resolution Process

Court referrals to ADR have increasingly been based on attempting to match cases with appropriate dispute resolution processes, which is the essence of the multi-door courthouse approach, whether or not the programs have been explicitly labeled "multi-door courthouse." . . . More varieties of ADR are being invented or designed to fit particular needs of disputes and of parties. . . . There are half day and one day programs for attorneys that instruct on how to prepare and empower clients in mediation; and for litigants, there are orientation to mediation workshops, how to communicate and negotiate so that both parties get what they need. . . .

E. Increased Choice and Expertise of Providers

As the need for mediators has grown, so have the numbers and types of providers. There is increased choice and varying types of expertise of ADR providers, including public, private, and court-annexed ADR professionals who are lawyers, former judges, and non-lawyers; and the fees for services range from no charge to parties by some community mediation centers, up to hundreds of dollars per hour by some former judges and experienced family and commercial litigators. Many states have begun modest efforts to regulate mediators by requiring training, experience, and adherence to ethical codes.

F. Increased Research and Evaluation

Use of ADR by the courts has led to increased research and evaluation as to the effects of such use. Studies of mediation offered both by the courts and court-annexed programs have consistently shown high satisfaction rates by the participants when measured against the prospects of going to trial. Some studies have shown time and cost savings for parties and the courts through the use of ADR. Research is beginning to look more closely at best practices in implementing ADR programs, including the most beneficial timing of court referral to ADR.

G. Beginnings of a Culture Shift

The growth of ADR has contributed to the beginnings of a revolutionary change in the court's conception of its role, from that of a passive provider of trials to an active, problem solving case manager, or, as in some courts, to a catalyst in community change and conflict transformation. Some of the principles of mediation (empowerment, problem solving) are being explicitly incorporated into the courthouse in Colorado, through case management conferences conducted early in domestic relations and juvenile cases by court facilitators, magistrates, or judges. Courts are beginning to embrace the concept of litigation as a last resort, rather than a first resort, at least for some types of cases.

NOTES

1. In Florida, a state recognized as a leader in developing court-connected dispute resolution programs, there are 111 mediation programs in place offering services in family, civil, county and dependency cases. (Dorothy J. Della Noce et al., *Assimilative, Autonomous, or Synergistic Visions: How Mediation Programs in Florida Address the Dilemma of Court Connection*, 3 PEPP. DISP. RESOL. L.J. 11 (2002).) Over 76,000 court-connected cases were mediated in 2002, although these official statistics are probably a significant underestimate; a large private mediation sector accompanies the court-connected programs, so that many cases never enter the court system. (Sharon Press, *Institutionalization of Mediation in Florida: At the Crossroads*, 108 PENN. ST. L. REV. 43, 55 (2003).)

2. Court-connected mediation programs employ many different structures to provide mediation and some courts combine multiple models, either using more than one at once or creating a hybrid model. First, some courts employ full-time in-house neutrals and provide mediation services to parties free of charge. This is the model used in most of the federal appellate courts. Second, courts contract directly with mediators for neutral services, but they are not court employees.

Third, courts use a structure in which they contract with a nonprofit organization that provides neutrals and administers the program. This form of organization evolved in some states as neighborhood justice centers which offered mediation to the community became associated with courts, who could refer them a steady stream of disputes. This association usually takes one of two forms. Under one, parties are charged very little (or nothing) for services from volunteer mediators or mediators paid at below-market rates through a contract with the court. Alternatively, the nonprofit organization charges parties substantial fees, which are used to pay the neutrals.

Fourth, some courts administer a program in which services are provided free to the parties by volunteer mediators who are trained and supervised by the court. And finally, there are courts that maintain a list of mediators to whom they refer parties, who are then responsible for making their own financial arrangements. A court might establish minimum requirements for mediators to be listed on its "roster," but typically these courts play little role in ensuring the quality of mediation services.

3. Many courts instituted mediation programs for the purpose of increasing the court's efficiency. It was thought that encouraging settlement through mediation would reduce court dockets, speed up the termination of cases, and save both the courts and litigants money. Is court-annexed mediation having the effects that courts hoped it would? Certainly cases are settling in mediation. Most studies of court-annexed mediation for small claims cases report settlement rates between 47 and 87 percent. Settlement rates tend to be slightly lower for general jurisdiction civil cases, ranging between 37 and 63 percent. The difficulty is in determining, against a backdrop of high settlement rates generally, whether mediation increases settlement and reduces trial rates or has no effect because these cases would settle in any event. The studies of court-annexed mediation programs are split on this point. Half of the studies found that cases referred to mediation had a higher settlement rate, or a lower rate of trial or summary judgment, than cases not referred. The other half, however, found no differences between the two groups of cases. (*See* Roselle L. Wissler, *The Effectiveness of Court-Connected Dispute Resolution in Civil Cases*, 22 CONFLICT RESOL. Q. 55, 58, 65 (2004).)

Efficiency gains have generally not been demonstrated. Although there are varied outcomes, the majority of studies of mediation in general civil jurisdiction cases conclude that there are no differences between mediation cases and non-mediation cases in terms of transaction costs, the amount of discovery, or the number of motions filed. Some studies report reduced time to disposition or greater compliance with the outcome for mediated cases. But other studies find no differences in these measures. (*Id.* at 81.)

4. Court-annexed mediation is generally evaluated favorably in terms of both process and outcomes in surveys of participants. In studies of mediation programs for civil cases,

> [m]ost litigants said the mediation process was fair and gave them sufficient opportunity to present their case. A majority of litigants felt they had control over the process or had input in determining the outcome. Most litigants thought the mediator was neutral, did not pressure them to settle, understood their views and the issues in dispute, and treated them with respect. A majority of litigants felt the mediated settlement was fair or were satisfied with it.
>
> The twenty studies that examined attorneys' assessments consistently reported high ratings of the mediation process and the mediator. . . . Most said they would recommend mediation to others or would use mediation again. . . . Most attorneys felt that the mediated settlement was fair or were satisfied with it. [Roselle L. Wissler, *The Effectiveness of Court-Connected Dispute Resolution in Civil Cases*, 22 CONFLICT RESOL. Q. 55, 65-66 (2004) (citations omitted).]

5. What do Senft and Savage mean when they refer to the "increased 'legalization' of mediation" in court-annexed programs? The following excerpt describes the picture of mediator styles that emerged from interviews with mediators and attorneys who participate in court-annexed mediation in Florida.

JAMES J. ALFINI, TRASHING, BASHING, AND HASHING IT OUT: IS THIS THE END OF "GOOD MEDIATION"? 19 Fla. St. U. L. Rev. 47, 66-73 (1991) *

Does circuit court mediation — because it is mandatory and conducted by legal professionals — anticipate a deviation from traditional mediation styles and strategies? Our interviews with the circuit mediators and lawyers revealed three distinct styles. These three approaches to the mediation process are characterized as (1) trashing, (2) bashing, and (3) hashing it out.

---

1. Trashing

The mediators who employ a trashing methodology spend much of the time "tearing apart" the cases of the parties. . . . "I try to get them to a point where they will put realistic settlement figures on the table." To facilitate uninhibited trashing of the parties' cases, the overall strategy employed by these mediators discourages direct party communication. Following the mediator's orientation and short (five to ten minutes) opening statements by each party's attorney, the mediator puts the parties in different rooms. The mediator then normally caucuses with the plaintiff's attorney and her client in an effort to get them to take a hard look at the strengths and weaknesses of their case. One plaintiff's lawyer described the initial caucus:

> The mediator will tell you how bad your case is . . . try to point out the shortcomings of the case to the parties and try to get the plaintiff to be realistic. They point out that juries aren't coming back with a lot of money anymore on these types of cases. They ask you tough questions to get you to see where you might have a liability problem or the doctor says you don't have a permanent injury so you may get nothing. They will try to get you to take a hard look at the deficiencies in your case that obviously I already know, but sometimes it enlightens the plaintiff to hear it from a impartial mediator.

Having torn down the case in this manner, the mediator will try to get the plaintiff and plaintiff's attorney to consider more "realistic" settlement options. The mediator then gives the plaintiff's lawyer and her client an opportunity to confer, while the mediator shuttles off to caucus with the defense.

* * *

> During the defense caucus, the mediator will usually say, "Well you know they've asked for this figure and they think they have a strong case in this regard. Their figure is 'x.' They're willing to negotiate. They have told me that they'll take this amount which is obviously lower than the original demand" — if he has authority from the plaintiff to reveal that to you. If he doesn't, he won't say anything about that. He asks, "What do you think the case is worth? Why?" . . . He'll then work through the case with us, pointing out outstanding medicals, lost wages and other special damages, then tallying them up and a certain percentage of pain and suffering and come up with a figure. And then they may discuss the strength of the case. I've had mediators say things to me in the caucus such as, "I was impressed by the plaintiff; I think they're going to be believable. Have you factored that into your evaluation of the case?"

* * *

Once the trasher has achieved the goal of getting both sides to put what she believes to be more realistic settlement figures on the table, she will shuttle back and forth trying to forge an agreement. If this is accomplished, the mediator may or may not bring the parties back together to work out the details of the agreement. One trasher explained that, once separated, he never brings the parties back together even at the final agreement stage. On the whole, the attorneys appeared to accept, if not appreciate, the extreme caucusing methodology of the trasher. * * *

Mediators who employ a trashing methodology tend to draw on their own experiences with the litigation process to get the parties to take a hard look at their cases. Indeed, all of the trashers that were interviewed are experienced trial lawyers. They call upon their own experiences not only to expose procedural and substantive weaknesses on both sides, but also to get the parties to consider the costs of litigation. * * *

2. Bashing

Unlike the trashers, the mediators who use a bashing technique tend to spend little or no time engaging in the kind of case evaluation that is aimed at getting the parties to put "realistic" settlement figures on the table. Rather, they tend to focus initially on the settlement offers that the parties bring to mediation and spend most of the session bashing away at those initial offers in an attempt to get the parties to agree to a figure somewhere in between. Their mediation sessions thus tend to be shorter than those of the trashers, and they tend to prefer a longer initial joint session, permitting direct communication between the parties.

Most of the bashers interviewed were retired judges who draw on their judicial experience and use the prestige of their past judicial service to bash out an agreement. * * *

> The judge has to be very careful. Because if he expresses an opinion, the next thing he knows he's going to be asked to excuse himself because one side or the other will think he's taking sides. In mediation, you don't have to worry about that. You can say to the plaintiff, "there's no way the defendant is going to pay you that kind of money." You can say things as a mediator that you can't say as a judge.

As soon as the basher has gotten the parties to place settlement offers on the table, as one attorney explained, "there is a mad dash for the middle." One of the retired judges described a case he had mediated that morning:

> [T]he plaintiff wanted $75,000. The defendant told me he would pay $40,000. I went to the plaintiff and said to him, "They're not going to pay $75,000. What will you take?" He said, "I'll take $60,000." I told him I wasn't sure I could get $60,000 and asked if he would take $50,000 if I could get it. He agreed. I then went back to the defendant and told him I couldn't settle for $40,000, but "you might get the plaintiff to take $50,000" and asked if he would pay it. The answer was yes. Neither of them were bidding against themselves. I was the guy who was doing it, and that's the role of the mediator.

                              *   *   *

Although the basher style is the most directive of the three circuit mediation styles, it apparently is preferred by some attorneys in circuits where it is the predominant style. A mediation program director in one of these circuits explained that she has received complaints from attorneys who felt that the mediator assigned to their case was "not pushy enough." They said that the attorneys had come to expect mediators who would "hammer some sense" into the other side.

3. Hashing It Out

The third circuit mediation style can best be described as one involving a hashing out of a settlement agreement because it places greater reliance on direct communication between the opposing attorneys and their clients. The hashers tend to take a much more flexible approach to the mediation process, varying their styles and using techniques such as caucusing selectively, depending on their assessment of the individual case and the needs and interests of the parties. When asked to describe the mediator's role in one sentence, a hasher responded, "Facilitator, orchestrator, referee, sounding board, scapegoat."

The hasher generally adopts a much less directive posture than the trashers and bashers, preferring that the parties speak directly with one another and hash out an agreement. However, if direct communication appears counterproductive, the hasher acts as a communication link.

* * *

In addition to this more flexible orchestration of the process, the hasher is also unwilling to keep the parties at the mediation session if they express a desire to leave, unlike the trashers and bashers. * * *

* * *

Flexibility apparently is the hallmark of the hasher style of mediation. Although hashers prefer to adopt a style that encourages direct party communication to hash out an agreement, they are willing to employ trasher or basher methodologies if they believe it to be appropriate in a particular case.

NOTES

1. What is your answer to Professor Alfini's question? Do these styles signal the end of "good mediation"? Is there consensus on what constitutes "good mediation"?

2. Professor Alfini concludes that the literature describes a wide range of mediator behavior, including styles similar to the three he reports for Florida court-annexed mediation. Do you see any similarities between the approaches of trashers and bashers and a directive version of evaluative mediation? Between hashers and facilitative mediation?

2. CRITIQUES OF THE INSTITUTIONALIZATION OF MEDIATION IN THE COURTS

The institutionalization of mediation in the courts is not without its critiques. Commentators such as Owen Fiss and Judge Harry T. Edwards, whose work you read in Chapter 1(E), point out the limitations of using informal methods to resolve disputes. Others express concern that weaker parties may be disadvantaged in mediation as compared to litigation. (*See, e.g.,* Delgado, et al. 1985; Grillo 1991 in Chapter 8(A).)

In terms of the principles that guide dispute resolution institutions, there are scholars who are critical of what the trend toward mediation has done to the courts and scholars who are critical of what association with the courts has done to mediation. The former argue that the growing emphasis on mediation in the courts undermines values of the judicial system. The latter object to the association of mediation with the courts from the opposite perspective, maintaining that the use of mediation as a means to settle litigation has detracted from some of the core values associated with the process.

DEBORAH R. HENSLER, OUR COURTS, OURSELVES: HOW THE ALTERNATIVE DISPUTE RESOLUTION MOVEMENT IS RE-SHAPING OUR LEGAL SYSTEM, 108 Penn St. L. Rev. 165, 194-198 (2003) *

* * * There is little evidence that alternative dispute resolution procedures within courts have reduced the average time to dispose of civil lawsuits, or the average public or private expense to litigate cases in a system that has long relied on settlement rather than adjudication to resolve most cases. There is also little evidence that alternative dispute resolution procedures outside of courts have reduced the transaction costs of resolving conflicts that would never have gone to trial anyway, although they may be contributing to a drop in civil case filings. * * * Whether alternative dispute resolution processes outside or within courts have significantly increased the preexisting imbalance of power between the "haves" and "have nots" is unclear. While there are reasons to believe that ADR sometimes disadvantages the less powerful, the traditional litigation process may not do much better in creating a level playing field.

If lawyers succeed in shaping alternative dispute resolution procedures to comport with traditional notions of settlement, the immediate outcomes of the dispute resolution movement may simply be to increase the costs of litigation by substituting paid lawyer-settlers for publicly subsidized judge-settlers. The story of the alternative dispute resolution movement might then appear to be just a very old tale, retold.

But I find it hard to believe that the myriad new statutes and court rules promoting or mandating private dispute resolution, the thousands of mediator training sessions, promotional videotapes, and educational programs, and the public rhetoric that has accompanied all of these will have so little long-term consequence. To encourage people to consider alternatives to litigation, in federal and state courts nationwide, judges and mediators are telling claimants that legal norms are antithetical to their interests, that vindicating their legal rights is antithetical to social harmony, that juries are capricious, that judges cannot be relied upon to apply the law properly, and that it is better to seek inner peace than social change. To drive these messages home, courts and legislatures mandate mediation [and] preclude dissemination of information about what transpires during mediation sessions * * * . Moreover, both

---

legislatures and courts display a breezy indifference to the qualifications of those who act as third-party neutrals and to the costs imposed on litigants by alternative dispute resolution mandates — all apparently based on the belief that any alternative to adversarial conflict must be beneficial.

Looking backwards, we may well come to view the dispute resolution movement as contributing to — if not creating — a profound change in our view of the justice system. With increasing barriers to litigating, fewer citizens will find their own way into court (although they may be brought there to answer criminal charges). Those who are not barred from using the courts by contractual agreement will increasingly find themselves shepherded outside the courthouse to confidential conferences presided over by private neutrals in private venues. With little experience of public adjudication and little information available about the process or outcomes of dispute resolution, citizens' abilities to use the justice system effectively to achieve social change will diminish markedly. Surrounded by a culture that celebrates social harmony and self-realization and disparages social conflict — whatever its causes or aims — citizens' tendencies to turn to the court as a vehicle for social transformation will diminish as well. Over the long run, all of the doors of the multi-door courthouse may swing outward.

Why should we care? If disputes are resolved efficiently in private by private individuals and organizations, if conflict is avoided and citizens learn to seek compromise when disputes do arise, won't society be better off? Leaving aside the still unanswered question about whether private dispute resolution is, in fact, more efficient than public dispute resolution, and the considerable evidence that in most circumstances people already avoid conflict by compromising or "learning to live with" life's misfortunes and unfairness, I think the answer is "no." Owen Fiss, Judith Resnik, and others have written about the importance of public adjudication for the articulation of legal norms. I think there are also important political values that derive from widespread access to, and use of, the public justice system.

The public spectacle of civil litigation gives life to the "rule of law." To demonstrate that the law's authority can be mobilized by the least powerful as well as the most powerful in society, we need to observe employees and consumers successfully suing large corporations and government agencies, minority group members successfully suing majority group members, and persons engaged in unpopular activities establishing their legal rights to continue those activities. Dispute resolution behind closed doors precludes such observation. In a democracy where many people are shut out of legislative power either because they are too few in number, or too dispersed to elect representatives, or because they do not have the financial resources to influence legislators, collective litigation in class or other mass form provides an alternative strategy for group action. Private individualized dispute resolution extinguishes the possibility of such collective litigation. Conciliation has much to recommend it. But the visible presence of institutionalized and legitimized conflict, channeled productively, teaches citizens that it is not always better to compromise and accept the status quo because, sometimes, great gains are to be had by peaceful contest.

NANCY A. WELSH, THE THINNING VISION OF SELF-DETERMINATION IN COURT-CONNECTED MEDIATION: THE INEVITABLE PRICE OF INSTITUTIONALIZATION? 6 Harv. Negot. L. Rev. 1, 3-5, 25-27 (2001)*

[T]his Article will demonstrate that the originally dominant vision of self-determination, which borrowed heavily from concepts of party empowerment, is yielding to a different vision in the court-connected context. Perhaps not surprisingly, this vision is more consistent with the culture of the courts.

Believers in the originally dominant vision of self-determination assumed that the disputing parties would be the principal actors and creators within the mediation process. The parties would: 1) actively and directly participate in the communication and negotiation that occurs during mediation, 2) choose and control the substantive norms to guide their decision-making, 3) create the options for settlement, and 4) control the final decision regarding whether or not to settle. The mediator's role was to enable the parties' will to emerge and thus support their exercise of self-determination. Many mediation advocates continue to adhere to this vision.

However, as mediation has been institutionalized in the courts and as evaluation has become an acknowledged and accepted part of the mediator's function, the original vision of self-determination is giving way to a vision in which the disputing parties play a less central role. The parties are still responsible for making the final decision regarding settlement, but they are cast in the role of consumers, largely limited to selecting from among the settlement options developed by their attorneys. Indeed, it is the parties' attorneys, often aided by mediators who are also attorneys, who assume responsibility for actively and directly participating in the mediation process, invoking the substantive (i.e., legal) norms to be applied and creating settlement options. Thus, even as most mediators and many courts continue to name party self-determination as the "fundamental principle" underlying court-connected mediation, the party-centered empowerment concepts that anchored the original vision of self-determination are being replaced with concepts that are more reflective of the norms and traditional practices of lawyers and judges, as well as the courts' strong orientation to efficiency and closure of cases through settlement.

* * *

Perhaps inevitably, current evidence strongly suggests that the "legitimacy handed to [the ADR movement] by its assimilation into the court system" has come at a price. Court-connected mediation of non-family civil cases is developing an uncanny resemblance to the judicially-hosted settlement conference. In certain types of cases, such as personal injury and medical malpractice, the defendants regularly fail to attend mediation sessions. Even when all of the clients do attend, their attorneys are likely to do much, if not all, of the talking, particularly in joint sessions. An increasing number of mediators are abandoning or greatly minimizing the joint session, preferring to move quickly to caucuses. The attorneys are choosing mediators who, like judges, are expected to have the knowledge and experience which would permit them to comment on the parties' legal arguments. Indeed, mediators now often focus on the legal issues and opine regarding the strengths and weaknesses of each party's case and appropriate settlement ranges. Finally, it appears that few mediators now actively promote the search in mediation for creative, non-monetary settlements.

To a large extent, the presence of lawyers, as advocates and as mediators, explains why court-connected mediation now looks like a judicial settlement conference. First, attorneys have long operated within an "adversary culture." As they were ordered to participate with their clients in the mysterious process called "mediation," they brought with them a "standard philosophical map," assumptions regarding their relationship with their clients, and expectations and tactics that they had honed in their prior experience with traditional judicial settlement conferences. Second, as more and more attorneys and retired judges were attracted to mediation as a remunerative activity, they brought to the role of mediator the skills and knowledge that had served them well in their careers, as well as certain assumptions about "the role of the [quasi-]judicial host." Parties and their attorneys began to select mediators who could and would provide reasoned evaluation. Increasingly, mediators were willing to provide it.

NOTES

1. The incorporation of mediation into court operations and shifting views concerning the purpose and functions of courts raise questions about the appropriate structure of the court as an institution and the role of judges. Professor Hensler contends:

> * * * Recent court decisions suggest that at least some jurists have embraced a new vision of the objectives of the justice system, a vision in which the purpose of legal dispute resolution is to achieve social harmony, rather than to assess factual and legal claims and articulate public norms. * * * There is little evidence that jurists who have embraced these new visions of the courts have carefully considered their institutional implications. Should generalist judges lead courts dedicated to social harmony, problem solving and self-understanding? Or would such courts be better led by communication experts, risk management specialists, and counseling psychologists? What role should the public play in selecting the experts who will shape the new dispute resolution process? Can a justice system dedicated to conciliation rather than adjudication of facts and law maintain its status as a third branch of government, equal to the legislature and executive? Whatever their failures in achieving efficient and fair justice for citizens, the core competence of today's courts is adjudication. Re-imagining the purpose of courts requires re-thinking their institutional structure as well. [Deborah R. Hensler, *Our Courts, Ourselves: How the Alternative Dispute Resolution Movement Is Re-shaping Our Legal System*, 108 PENN ST. L. REV. 165, 193-94 (2003).]

2. Some critics maintain that the task of a judge is to try cases rather than to seek settlement. Federal Judge G. Thomas Eisele takes this view:

> Simply put, I believe I was appointed to serve as a trial judge in a trial court. I find great satisfaction in that role. I do not understand those trial judges who appear to believe that every trial represents a failure of the system. I believe and accept that some cases should be tried. Principle should be vindicated, truth ascertained and determined, rights established and declared, extortion resisted, and justice — pure justice — done, at least occasionally. [G. Thomas Eisele, *Differing Visions-Differing Values: A Comment on Judge Parker's Reformation Model for Federal District Courts*, 46 SMU L. REV. 1935, 1965 (1993).]

There is much to be said in support of Judge Eisele's position. Is it fair, however, to suggest that judicial participation in settlement will not produce a form of justice? While the nature of "justice" achieved from a trial will differ from that resulting from a settlement, won't each achieve a level of justice?

3. Much of the criticism of court-annexed mediation is aimed at its primary focus on settlement and the evaluative techniques that many mediators are using to reach settlements. Consider the following analysis by two administrators of state court ADR programs:

> [T]he courts have relied primarily on attorneys to judge the relative values of settlement processes and outcomes. In part because of this hands-off approach, in part because of the elevation of settlement as the primary desired outcome, in part because of differences in values between mediators and lawyers and judges, and perhaps due to a lack of sufficient resources, mediation in a significant number of court-annexed programs has begun to look more like the traditional pretrial settlement conference, and less like the alternative process originally intended by its proponents.
>
> Getting one or both sides to compromise on their perceived positions or on their perceived amounts of damages is what mediation has come to mean and the way that mediation has come to be practiced in many court settings. Instead of providing litigants the originally intended alternative process of mediation, the courts' mediations have capitulated to a watered down version of the alternative — a process that is merely not a trial. This process that is merely not a trial is at best a settlement conference focused on a compromise, and at worst a non-productive posturing session for the attorneys without a genuine interest in attempting to settle the case. Either way, it is what mediation has often come to mean in the court context and the way that it has come to be practiced in many court settings. It is this assumption that mediation is simply a settlement conference that is at the heart of the concerns being raised around many courts' use of mediation. [Louise Phipps Senft & Cynthia A. Savage, *ADR in the Courts: Progress, Problems, and Possibilities*, 108 PENN ST. L. REV. 327, 335-36 (2003).]

What are the "core values" of the court system and mediation? Are they necessarily incompatible or can they co-exist in court-mediation programs?

Senft and Savage suggest that the traditions of adjudication and mediation both share interests in creating confidence in the dispute resolution process, fostering long-term efficiency, encouraging parties to resolve their own disputes, and providing parties with notice as to what is expected of them. While a single-minded focus on short-term efficiency can lead to coercive tactics and poor quality mediation, long-term efficiency requires high quality dispute resolution that reduces the incidence of disputes that parties will bring back to court. They maintain that this depends on long lasting, satisfactory outcomes reached through a process that responds to the human dimension of the conflict with an emphasis on the traditional values associated with mediation. (*Id.* at 338-39.)

4. Are parties in court-annexed mediation getting the advantage of mediation's potential for flexibility and creative outcomes? Studies of court-connected programs suggest that this depends to some extent on the type of case being mediated. Settlements in personal injury cases mostly involve only monetary terms. But settlements in a majority of contract cases included some non-monetary provisions. (*See* Roselle L. Wissler, *Court-Connected Mediation in General Civil Cases: What We Know from Empirical Research*, 17 Ohio St. J. on Disp. Resol. 641 (2002).)

5. To what extent does the institutionalization of mediation in the courts undermine values associated with mediation as an alternative to litigation: party self-determination, opportunity for voice, and relationship building? The answer appears to be: "it depends." The design and structure of court-connected programs affect the way in which the values of mediation and adjudication are combined. Three different approaches to program design have been identified: assimilative, autonomous, and synergistic. (Della Noce et al., 2002.)

Programs that take an assimilative approach adapt mediation to the norms of the court system. These programs tend to adopt practices that cloak mediation with the formality and authority of the court, such as a location in the courthouse, official court mailings, and the presence of mediators in the courtroom. They often also use the language associated with litigation, calling the schedule a "docket" and the mediation session a "hearing." These programs treat case processing as a major goal, framing disputes as "cases" and emphasizing moving cases through the system toward settlement.

The goal of mediation programs with an autonomous approach is to maintain an identity separate from the court. These programs are often located outside the courthouse or occupy a distinct area within the court building. They take a flexible approach to defining the scope of the conflict to be mediated and in many programs may convene a mediation before a case is filed. Mediation sessions tend to be free of time limitations and capable of accommodating multiple parties. Another characteristic is an emphasis on the conflict interaction, with quality control measures focused on what happens during the mediation session.

A synergistic approach maintains the values of party voice and choice that underlie the mediation process while also adapting to the needs of case processing within the courts. Often these programs are led by individuals who act as a bridge between mediators and court officials and communicate well with both. Many such programs have a formalized mechanism for community input through advisory boards or social agencies. There is an emphasis on preserving party choice while balancing that value with the constraints of the judicial system.

The authors conclude that these three models demonstrate different reconciliations of the values of the judicial system and mediation. They characterize the assimilative approach as elevating the values of the judicial system over those of mediation; the autonomous approach as emphasizing the traditional values of mediation over those of the judicial system; and the synergistic approach as trying to integrate the values of both traditions. (*See* Dorothy J. Della Noce et al., *Assimilative, Autonomous, or Synergistic Visions: How Mediation Programs in Florida Address the Dilemma of Court Connection*, 3 PEPP. DISP. RESOL. L.J. 11 (2002).)

6. As mediation has become more institutionalized in courts, emphasis has shifted from establishing programs to ensuring their quality. "Best practices" are being developed for designing, implementing, and monitoring programs. Do you think that some of the aspects of court-annexed mediation that have raised concerns among critics could be avoided with better mediator training and supervision? Supervision of a confidential process is challenging, not the least because of the difficulties in establishing measurable evaluation criteria. Some of the means available are evaluative surveys of participants, complaint mechanisms, direct observations, and co-mediation. Do you think the quality of mediators should be a court responsibility? Consider the following view:

> Courts that require parties to mediate and provide lists of mediators to choose from may feel some responsibility to assure the competence of the mediators on those lists — especially if the parties are paying the mediators. In the case of court-employed mediators, there are additional considerations. One, of course, is the need to account for the efficacy of spending tax dollars on mediation offices. Another is the need to assure that court mediators are behaving in accordance with the high standards of skill, integrity, and sensitivity to the reputation and image of the judiciary that our society rightfully expects. Court mediators interact with a large number of lawyers and litigants in private, sensitive settings. Even with the promise of confidentiality, court mediators still present themselves as court officials, a role that carries authority at least over the mediation process and the conduct of the participants. [Robert W. Rack, Jr., *Thoughts of a Chief Circuit Mediator on Federal Court-Annexed Mediation*, 17 OHIO ST. J. ON DISP. RESOL. 609, 619-20 (2002).]

Do you think the importance of providing quality mediation is any less when mediators are not court employees? How might members of the public view mediators whose names are on a list provided by a court? What are the practical difficulties a court faces if it assumes responsibility for the quality of mediation?

7. One open question is how to determine the best timing for mediation in the life of a case. Earlier mediation, in theory, can produce to greatest cost savings because if the case settles more pretrial expenses are avoided. There is some evidence that settlement is more likely when mediation is held earlier in the process. In addition, it appears that if a case that is mediated early does not settle, fewer motions are filed and time to disposition is shorter. The extent of discovery prior to mediation can be important, both in determining potential cost savings and because some parties may be unwilling to settle until they have gained a better picture of their case through discovery. The status of dispositive motions is also important. Would you advise your client to settle a case in mediation if you had filed a summary judgment motion and were still awaiting a decision that could terminate the case in your favor?

8. What "best practices" might be relevant for attorneys who represent clients in court-annexed mediation? One seems to be good preparation of parties for mediation. There are indications that when parties are more prepared by their attorneys the case is more likely to settle, the parties feel less pressure to settle, and the parties and their attorneys view the process as more fair than when parties are less prepared for mediation. (*See* Roselle L. Wissler, *Court-Connected Mediation in General Civil Cases: What We Know from Empirical Research*, 17 Ohio St. J. on Disp. Resol. 641 (2002).)

3.   Mandatory Court-Annexed Mediation

The extent to which mediation is "mandatory" or parties have a choice to mediate also varies greatly among jurisdictions. In some courts, mediation is offered as an option for parties who agree to use the process. In others, judges informally "suggest" that the parties attempt to settle using mediation. True voluntariness in this situation is likely to depend on the strength of the suggestion. In order to increase the use of mediation, many courts have created procedures to formalize its use. Some jurisdictions require that attorneys discuss mediation or other dispute resolution processes with their clients. This can be called a "mandatory consideration" rule. In others, courts order parties to mediate disputes selected on a case-by-case basis. And finally, in some courts mediation is a standard step in the litigation process that the court mandates for whole categories of cases.

There are also procedural variations when courts order mediation, either for particular cases or by blanket referrals of cases. A jurisdiction may screen out cases with certain characteristics. For example, in some jurisdictions that require mediation of child custody issues, mediation is not permitted if there has been domestic violence. Another common approach is to provide a procedure by which parties can "opt-out" of the process, often by providing reasons to a judge. Or, courts introduce an element of choice by requiring parties to use ADR, but offering a menu of processes.

Mandatory structures for mediation have been criticized by those who fear that "coercion into the mediation process translates into coercion in the mediation process, creating undue settlement pressures that produce unfair outcomes." (Wissler, 1997, at 565.)

ROSELLE L. WISSLER, THE EFFECTS OF MANDATORY MEDIATION: EMPIRICAL RESEARCH ON THE EXPERIENCE OF SMALL CLAIMS AND COMMON PLEAS COURTS, 33 Willamette L. Rev. 565, 570-71, 581, 583-84, 588, 593, 596, 601-04 (1997)*

Despite parties' typically high levels of satisfaction with mediation, mediation programs that depend on parties' willingness to participate attract relatively few cases, even when offered at low or no cost. One reason for the low rate of utilization is thought to be the parties' lack of familiarity with mediation. A second reason is the lack of familiarity among attorneys whose recommendations and encouragement are key factors in their clients' choice of process. A third reason is some parties' and attorneys' reluctance to express an interest in mediation out of fear that the other side might regard it as a sign of weakness. In addition, some parties are not interested in the type of discussion and amicable resolution afforded by mediation, preferring instead a right-wrong determination of a factual issue or a ruling on a legal issue.

In order to increase the use of mediation, many states have mandated mediation for a variety of disputes. Mandatory mediation programs have been established for: small claims and domestic relations matters; misdemeanors and other criminal matters between related people; truancy and delinquency problems; farmer-creditor disputes; specific categories of civil litigation, such as consumer disputes and medical malpractice; and community-wide civil rights and environmental or public resource disputes.

* * *

[In a study of small claims divisions of four courts in the metropolitan Boston area, m]andatory mediation cases were marginally less likely to settle (46%) than were voluntary mediation cases (62%). The fact that the settlement rate was not substantially lower in cases that were required to mediate suggests that successful settlement in mediation is not solely due to the self-selection of cases into the process. * * * Finding the settlement rate was not higher in mandatory mediation suggests that parties required to try mediation did not feel compelled to accept a settlement. * * *

* * *

Parties who were required to mediate did not describe the mediation process differently than did those who chose to mediate. Most importantly, they did not differ in their ratings regarding how much opportunity they had to tell their side of the story; the level of control they had over their presentation; and, for those who reached an agreement, the level of control they had over the final settlement. Thus, although some parties had no control over whether they entered mediation, once in the process they did not feel they lacked control over the process or its outcome.

* * *

For parties who reached an agreement in mediation, the mandatory or voluntary nature of the process did not affect the size or nature of the outcome or parties' evaluations of and compliance with their agreement. Agreements reached in mandatory versus voluntary mediation did not differ in the percentage of the plaintiff's claim they comprised, whether they involved nonmonetary conditions instead of or in addition to monetary terms, or whether they included provisions for immediate or installment payments. Parties who were required to mediate did not differ from those who chose to mediate in terms of how fair they thought the agreement was, how satisfied they were with the agreement, how the agreement compared to the outcome they expected, or how close the agreement came to what they wanted relative to what the other side wanted. Mandatory mediation did not affect compliance with the agreement or the extent to which defendants felt obligated to fulfill the agreement. Nor did parties in mandatory mediation differ from those in voluntary mediation regarding whether they felt the dispute truly was resolved.

* * *

[A second] study examined mandatory and voluntary mediation during "Settlement Week" in the general division of three common pleas courts in Ohio. * * *

Cases could enter Settlement Week mediation at the court's nomination or at the nomination of either side; thus, both sides did not have to nominate the case in order to have it referred to mediation. This process produced three groups of cases corresponding to the three different types of case nomination: (1) voluntary cases, nominated by both sides; (2) mandatory cases, nominated by the court with neither side requesting mediation; and (3) partially voluntary/partially mandatory cases, in which one side nominated the case for mediation and the court compelled the other side to attend.

* * *

The manner in which the case entered mediation had a marginally significant effect on the likelihood of settlement. * * * [M]ediation was more likely to result in settlement when both sides had requested mediation than when neither side had. The fact that the settlement rate was not higher in court-nominated cases suggests that mandatory mediation does not compel settlement. In cases that did not settle, the manner in which the case entered mediation did not affect the degree of progress made toward settlement (i.e., settlement of some issues, narrowing of discovery, sharpening of trial issues, or no progress).

[Findings in the common pleas settlement week study were generally similar to those in small claims study for cases that settled.] For parties who reached an agreement in mediation, the manner in which the case entered mediation did not affect the dollar amount of the agreement, whether the agreement involved nonmonetary provisions, or the parties' satisfaction with the agreement.

* * *

[The studies did differ somewhat in parties' evaluations of the process, the mediator, and the court. For parties in the general civil common pleas cases and parties in small claims court whose cases did not settle,] [t]he manner in which the case entered mediation did not affect parties' evaluations of the mediation process or the mediator. * * * Nor did the manner in which the case entered mediation affect whether parties would recommend mediation to a friend or colleague with a similar problem. * * * [Parties in small claims mandatory mediation with cases that settled, however, viewed the process as less fair, were less satisfied with it, and were less likely to report they would use mediation again in a future dispute than were those who chose to mediate.]

* * *

Consistent with prior research, [both] studies found no general pattern of differences between women and men, or between nonwhite parties and white parties, in their responses to mandatory mediation. Most notably, no differences appeared on the following critical assessments: pressure by the mediator to settle, opportunity to present one's views, control over the process and outcome, neutrality of the mediator, fairness of the process, and satisfaction with the outcome. * * *

* * *

* * * As implemented in these courts, * * * mandatory mediation entailed relatively few costs compared to voluntary mediation. The somewhat lower settlement rate in mandatory cases, the small number of dimensions on which participants' assessments of mandatory versus voluntary mediation differed, and the limited gender and racial differences in evaluations suggest little support for concerns about pressures to accept unfair settlements. * * *

NOTES

1. In addition to the mandatory mediation programs listed by Professor Wissler in which categories of cases are sent to mediation, many jurisdictions authorize judges to order mediation in specific cases. In the federal courts, courts may order parties to mediate under both Rule 16 of the Federal Rules of Civil Procedure and the Alternative Dispute Resolution Act of 1998 when there is an authorizing local rule. The First Circuit has held that, even without a local rule, courts have inherent power to order mediation "so long as the case is an appropriate one and the order contains adequate safeguards." (*In re Atlantic Pipe Corp.*, 304 F.3d 135, 138 (1st Cir. 2002).)

2. "Mandatory consideration" rules do not require mediation, but instead require parties to consider its use. Such requirements avoid mandatory programs' explicit compulsion to use mediation, but in practice the effects can be similar depending on the other court rules that accompany mandatory consideration. In Minnesota, courts have had a "mandatory consideration" rule since 1994: attorneys are required to consider the use of ADR in every civil case, discuss ADR with their clients and opposing counsel, and advise the court about their plans to use (or not use) ADR. In addition, judges can order parties to use an ADR process on a case-by-case basis. After the mandatory consideration rule became effective, judges in the Twin Cities often ordered ADR, sometimes even when the parties and counsel had advised the court that it was not appropriate. Against the backdrop of judges' routine orders to engage in ADR, attorneys began to select mediation "voluntarily"and within a few years its use became "institutionalized." (*See* Bobbi McAdoo & Nancy A. Welsh, *Look Before You Leap and Keep on Looking: Lessons from the Institutionalization of Court-Connected Mediation*, 5 Nev. L.J. 339 (2004-2005).)

3. Does mandatory mediation have ripple effects that increase the use of mediation beyond those cases in which it is required? Attorney's recommendations have a large effect on litigants' decisions to use ADR. A study of the factors that are related to attorney's advice to use mediation and other forms of ADR found that experience with the mediation process as counsel in a mediated case had by far the strongest relationship with attorney recommendations that clients use mediation for a dispute or include a mediation clause in a contract. Experience as a mediator also had a relationship to positive advice about using mediation, but it was not nearly as strong as experience representing clients in mediation. Interestingly, continuing legal education was only weakly related to offering advice to use mediation and taking a law school class in ADR had no relationship to recommending ADR to clients. The author of the study concluded that "policies that bring more cases, and therefore more attorneys, into ADR programs, such as by mandating ADR use in certain types of cases or by increasing the use of judicial referral, are likely to increase attorneys' ADR recommendations to clients." (Roselle Wissler, *When Does Familiarity Breed Content? A Study of the Role of Different Forms of ADR Education and Experience in Attorneys' ADR Recommendations*, 2 Pepp. Disp. Resol. L.J. 199, 238 (2002).)

4. Mandatory mediation is subject to the same criticisms made of court-annexed mediation in general — that it reduces scrutiny of important issues and opportunities to establish precedent. There are also, however, objections that stem directly from the fact that the mediation is mandatory. One fundamental concern is that requiring an extra step in the litigation process burdens parties' access to adjudication and infringes on their due process rights. The simple answer is that mediation is non-binding and the parties have the choice to proceed with litigation. But the process could create practical obstacles if it increased costs substantially, created significant delay, or triggered financial penalties for failing to settle. Undue pressure to settle also has the potential to interfere with a litigant's choice to resolve a dispute through adjudication.

5. Does the use of trashing or bashing styles of mediation concern you when the parties are required to mediate? Are those styles inconsistent with the consensual nature of reaching an agreement in mediation? James Alfini observes that, "the parties are not only forced to the table by the mandatory character of the program, but, * * * many mediators believe that it is the mediator's prerogative to decide when the session is over." (Alfini, 1991, at

74.) Is it inevitable that the pressures of the adversarial litigation system will introduce a coercive element to mediation?

6. Maintaining the consensual nature of mediation when participation is mandatory is a particular worry if there is a power imbalance between parties that might translate into coercion within the mediation process. Litigants who are uninformed about mediation may tend to think that if a court has ordered the process, their rights will be protected. Unrepresented parties in particular may look to the mediator for support and protection; they might be unduly influenced if the mediator assesses the strengths and weaknesses of the case or recommends options. Some courts attempt to minimize these concerns by exempting from mandatory mediation those cases that are most likely to be characterized by power imbalances, such as cases where the parties have a history of domestic violence and cases involving pro se parties. Is this enough to address the potential problem?

4. GOOD FAITH PARTICIPATION IN COURT-ANNEXED MEDIATION

The growth of court-connected mediation has led to a debate over the nature of lawyers' and parties' participation in the process. When parties are required to mediate, there will inevitably be some who are not interested in settling and who try to use mediation as an adversarial tool. The following excerpts present opposing views on whether courts should, and realistically can, regulate the quality of participation in mediation.

KIMBERLEE K. KOVACH, GOOD FAITH IN MEDIATION — REQUESTED, RECOMMENDED, OR REQUIRED? A NEW ETHIC, 38 S. Tex. L. Rev. 575, 591, 593-96, 620 (1997)[*]

[M]ediation has often been treated as nothing more than another step in the litigation path to the courthouse. This view of mediation is coincidental with, and likely caused by the assimilation of mediation within the legal system. Yet if good faith participation was required, mediation would likely be a different process, one more consistent with earlier definitions, such as assisting parties in reaching a mutually satisfactory or acceptable resolution and assisting individuals in achieving a new perception of their relationship and attitudes.

* * *

One specific example of process abuse is the request of mediation for the sole purpose of discovery, which has been alleged on occasions. Similarly, mediation has been used only to assess the other side in terms of their potential effectiveness at trial. Another objective is to wear down a litigant where one party is more financially able than the other. By scheduling a mediation or urging a court to order the process where there is no intent to settle, but where the parties share the expense equally, the process can drain

---

the other's resources so that the financially challenged party must choose between paying for the mediation or the attorney.

Another troublesome situation is where fraud or misrepresentation occurs within the content of the mediation which leads one side to make an agreement they likely otherwise would not have. Some parties may later discover it, while others will not. While a remedy exists, that is to set aside any agreement reached, time and money would have to be spent. And in the case where no agreement is reached in the mediation, the process will often be seen as a waste of time, money, and other resources.

Even more deplorable is the presence of actual deception during and as part of the mediation. In a Texas case, which may not be cited due to confidentiality, when one side inquired as to who a stranger present at the mediation was, the reply was that he was a business associate of the other party who was present to work on other matters during the "down time" of the mediation. A few hours later the inquiring attorneys looked in a local telephone directory, and found that the individual was a jury consultant. When directly confronted, it was admitted that he was present to size up the party for the trial which was set to begin within the next couple weeks. Clearly that party was present with no intention to settle and, in fact only, to use the mediation process to gain advantage in the trial process. This type of conduct is not what mediation was designed for, nor should it be used for such purposes. Other mechanisms exist within pretrial procedure through which such tactics and strategies can be employed.

* * * Some will argue that misrepresentation and fraud are part of legal negotiation and accepted as such; therefore carry over to mediation is not surprising. Yet this lack of good faith cannot be good for the process [or] for most of the participants. When a party hears that mediation can be used to deceive, his perception of this alternative is damaged. If mediation is going to thrive as an alternative means to solving disputes, as it should, based upon the parties' satisfaction and the options for problem solving it affords, then measures must be taken to assure that the process is not manipulated to do harm.

*   *   *

If good faith is not present, all we will be left with is a pro forma mediation, one more procedural task to be checked off of the long list of items to be covered in order to get to the trial. In fact, now, the term "pro forma mediation" is one that is heard when the parties, or more often their lawyers, arrive at mediation only because the court mandated them to do so. They unequivocally state that they have no intention of resolving the matter and really do not participate. These mediations are usually a waste of time for the mediator, a waste of time for the attorneys, unless it is used for free discovery or as trial preparation, and a waste of expense for the parties. * * * [T]o allow parties to show up without authority, without preparation, and without a desire or an ability to even discuss options and alternatives makes a mockery of mediation. Furthermore, to permit participants to use mediation to deceive or gain strategic advantage over another is to undermine its very purpose.

* * *

Whether called good faith, "meaningful participation," or another similar term, some action to require a specific conduct conducive to the mediation process must be required. Whether by court rule, legislation, or a code of ethics, such an obligation should be constructed and implemented immediately. * * *

JOHN LANDE, USING DISPUTE SYSTEM DESIGN METHODS TO PROMOTE GOOD-FAITH PARTICIPATION IN COURT-CONNECTED MEDIATION PROGRAMS, 50 UCLA L. Rev. 69, 74–77, 86, 98-99, 102, 139–40 (2002)*

The controversy over good-faith requirements is part of a larger debate over the purpose and nature of court-connected mediation programs. This debate focuses on competing program goals and ideas about what is needed to ensure the programs' integrity. On one side of the debate, people view mediation programs as mechanisms to dispose of a portion of court dockets. Courts order parties to spend time and money for mediation and want to be sure that the time and money are well-spent. Courts also want to ensure that parties and attorneys comply with their orders and cooperate with the courts' case management systems. From this perspective, a good-faith requirement seems to be the logical way to ensure the integrity of court-connected mediation programs.

On the other side of the debate, people focus on the integrity of the mediation process, defined as an adherence to mediation practice norms. Many mediators are especially concerned that people participate in mediation without coercion, take advantage of opportunities for open discussion and problem-solving, and receive assurance that courts will honor confidentiality protections. From this perspective, good-faith requirements seem to violate mediation norms and thus undermine the integrity of court-connected mediation programs. Although this brief summary oversimplifies the debate, it captures a real tension in the debates about the future of court-connected mediation programs.

[G]ood-faith requirements are likely to be ineffective and counterproductive in ensuring the integrity of court-connected mediation programs. * * * [They] should be adopted only as a last resort, after a court * * * seriously tries other policy options, and finds that those options do not resolve significant problems of bad faith in mediation.

* * *

* * * These options include collaborative education about good mediation practice, use of pre-mediation consultations and document submissions, a narrow requirement of attendance for a limited and specified time, and protections against misrepresentation.

---

* Copyright © 2002. Reprinted with permission.

* * *

The definition of good faith in mediation is one of the most controversial issues about good-faith requirements. Legal authorities establishing good-faith requirements and commentators' proposals do not give clear guidance about what conduct is prohibited. As a result, mediation participants may feel uncertain about what actions mediators and judges would consider bad faith. This uncertainty could result in inappropriate bad-faith charges as well as a chilling of legitimate mediation conduct.

* * *

Although a good-faith requirement presumably would deter and punish some inappropriate conduct, it might also encourage surface bargaining, as well as frivolous claims of bad faith or threats to make such claims. Proponents seem to assume that participants who might act in bad faith but for the requirement would behave properly in fear of legal sanctions. It seems at least as likely that savvy participants who want to take inappropriate advantage of mediation would use surface bargaining techniques so that they can pursue their strategies with little risk of sanction. This would be fairly easy given the vagueness of a good-faith requirement. * * *

Similarly, tough mediation participants could use good-faith requirements offensively to intimidate opposing parties and interfere with lawyers' abilities to represent their clients' legitimate interests. Given the vagueness and overbreadth of the concept of bad faith, innocent participants may have legitimate fears about risking sanctions when they face an aggressive opponent and do not know what a mediator would say if called to testify. * * *

* * *

Establishing a good-faith requirement undermines the confidentiality of mediation. The mere prospect of adjudicating bad-faith claims by using mediator testimony can distort the mediation process by damaging participants' faith in the confidentiality of mediation communications and the mediators' impartiality.

* * *

Kovach argues that a good-faith requirement would include "some restrictions on the behavior of a few so that the majority of participants will have positive, meaningful experiences and outcomes." This Article suggests that it would produce precisely the opposite result. Actively enforcing a good-faith requirement would subject all participants to uncertainty about the impartiality and confidentiality of the process and could heighten adversarial tensions and inappropriate pressures to settle cases. Although such a requirement could deter and punish truly egregious behavior in what Kovach describes as a few cases, it would do so at the expense of overall confidence in the system of mediation. Barring evidence of a substantial number of problems of real bad faith (as opposed to loose litigation talk), the large cost of a bad-faith sanctions regime is not worth the likely small amount of benefit, especially considering the alternative policy options available.

WAYNE D. BRAZIL, CONTINUING THE CONVERSATION ABOUT THE CURRENT STATUS AND THE FUTURE OF ADR: A VIEW FROM THE COURTS, 2000 J. Disp. Resol. 11, 31–33 (2000) *

[There are] considerations that counsel against formally imposing a requirement that parties participate in court ordered mediation "in good faith." The first such consideration (not necessarily in order of importance) is the difficulty of defining "good faith" in this setting. As case law suggests, a refusal to settle, by itself, does not constitute "bad faith." Would it be "bad faith" for a party to decline to expose, during a mediation, all the private reasoning that supported the decisions the party was making about settlement, or to decline to disclose how the party intended to develop and present its case at trial? Or are at least some such declinations supportable on the ground that the information sought is protected by the work product doctrine and/or the attorney client privilege? Given these legal issues, and the elusiveness of the concept of "good faith" itself, courts are likely to feel confident that a party has violated a requirement to proceed in "good faith" only when the offender's conduct is extreme, e.g., when she fails to show up at all or walks out after five minutes. But when the offending conduct is extreme, courts are likely to be able to impose an appropriate sanction without resort to any "good faith" requirement.

Moreover, the indeterminacy of the concept increases the threat it poses to other important values. One such value is fundamental fairness — which requires that parties be able to understand, pretty clearly, what they must do to comply with a norm whose violation could expose them to punishment. It would be unseemly, at best, for courts to impose a requirement whose contours they could not clearly define.

As important, uncertainty about what "good faith" is would increase the harm that such a requirement could do to the mediation process itself. A vague or expansive "good faith" requirement could distort both the role of the neutral and the way the parties participate in the mediation.

A mediator who knows that the parties have a legal duty (whether imposed by court order, rule, or legislation) to participate in "good faith" might well feel obligated to pass judgment on the quality or character of each player's participation. A mediator who accepts that duty converts herself, in part, to a judge. Yet to many mediators there is a fundamental incompatibility between being a judge and being a facilitator. To these mediators, there would be a deep and irreconcilable tension between a duty to pass judgment and the need they feel, as mediators, to build relationships with the parties that are grounded fundamentally in trust, confidence, and confidentiality. A duty to pass judgment also would threaten a core component of their sense of professional self — a sense at the center of which is a version of "neutrality" built around the notion that a facilitative mediator is never to form or express normative or analytical critiques.

Mediators who know that the law requires the parties to participate in "good faith" are more likely to worry about whether they have a duty to report, on their own initiative, perceived violations of that duty. They also are more likely to fear that they will be pressed by a court or a party to divulge their private views on these matters, or to give testimony in a proceeding to determine whether sanctions should be imposed. Apprehension about such duties or pressures could create counter-productive distractions for mediators who are trying to build relationships and to help the parties during a mediation, and even could discourage some good mediators from agreeing to serve.

Imposing a requirement of "good faith" participation also is likely to distort, in some measure, the ways the parties and their counsel interact with the mediator. Parties who feel that the mediator is passing judgment on the character of their participation may well fear the mediator — and fear that she might feel constrained to report them to the court. They also will be tempted to "perform" for her. To the extent that they feel fear and a compulsion to perform, they are less likely to let down their litigation hair — less likely to be open, less likely to feel comfortable, less likely to trust the process and the person at its center. Moreover, if they worry that their mediator is forming judgments about how they participate, they also might worry that she is forming judgments about other matters, e.g., the viability of their positions on the merits, or the moral force of their arguments about proposed terms of settlement. And if they worry that she is being evaluative, they will be tempted to try to manipulate her, or the flow of information to her — as part of an understandable desire to convert her into an ally in settlement negotiations with their opponents. Most mediators are likely to believe that all such impulses damage prospects for constructive mediation.

Imposing a requirement of "good faith" participation also could distort the dynamic between the parties during or after the mediation. Knowing that his opponent might be tempted to report him, or seek to have him sanctioned, for an alleged violation of a "good faith" requirement could intensify a party's or a lawyer's distrust and fear of his opponent. Increasing fear and distrust across party lines is not likely to enhance mediations. Moreover, the existence of an explicit, highly visible "good faith" requirement likely would increase some litigants' temptation to file tactically driven motions for sanctions — i.e., motions whose primary purpose is not to protect the integrity of mediation, but to gain some litigation advantage or to turn the judge against an opponent.

As the preceding paragraphs suggest, formalizing a requirement of "good faith" participation might well have the ironic effect of intensifying the temptations to "litigize" mediation — and thus to corrupt its spirit and frustrate achievement of its potential. Realizing this, we should proceed with considerable caution. * * * In sum, while there are arguments in favor of adopting a requirement that parties participate in mediation in "good faith," I believe that policy makers and courts should decline to impose such a duty at least until its proponents have made a stronger showing of need.

NOTES

1. Do you think the abuses of the mediation process cited by Professor Kovach are inherent in the involvement of lawyers in mediation, a result of mediation's connection to courts, a side-effect of making mediation a mandatory process, or due to other causes? What might make abuses more likely to occur in mediation that takes place in a litigation setting?

2. In order to stimulate discussion, Professor Kovach set forth a suggested statutory basis for a good faith participation requirement in the mediation process:

MEDIATION CODE 001. All parties and their counsel shall participate in mediation in good faith. "Good Faith" includes the following:

a. Compliance with the terms and provisions of [cite to state statute or other rule setting forth mediation * * *];

b. Compliance with any specific court order referring the matter to mediation;

c. Compliance with the terms and provisions of all standing orders of the court and any local rules of the court;

d. Personal attendance at the mediation by all parties who are fully authorized to settle the dispute, which shall not be construed to include anyone present by telephone;

e. Preparation for the mediation by the parties and their representatives, which includes the exchange of any documents requested or as set forth in a rule, order, or request of the mediator;

f. Participation in meaningful discussions with the mediator and all other participants during the mediation;

g. Compliance with all contractual terms regarding mediation which the parties may have previously agreed to;

h. Following the rules set out by the mediator during the introductory phase of the process;

i. Remaining at the mediation until the mediator determines that the process is at an end or excuses the parties;

j. Engaging in direct communication and discussion between the parties to the dispute, as facilitated by the mediator;

k. Making no affirmative misrepresentations or misleading statements to the other parties or the mediator during the mediation; and

l. In pending lawsuits, refraining from filing any new motions until the conclusion of the mediation.

002. "Good Faith" does not require the parties to settle the dispute. The proposals made at mediation, monetary or otherwise, in and of themselves do not constitute the presence or absence of good faith.

003. Determination of Good Faith

a. In court-annexed cases, the court shall make the final determination of whether good faith was present in the mediation.

b. Where a lawsuit has not been filed, the responsibility for finding a violation of the good faith duty rests upon the mediator, who shall use the elements of this statute and context of any contract between the parties as a basis for deliberation and decision-making.

004. Consequences for the Failure to Mediate in Good Faith If it is determined that a party or a representative of a party has failed the mediate in good faith, the following actions can be instituted at the discretion of the court or mediator:

a. The individual shall pay all fees, costs, and reasonable expenses incurred by the other participants.

b. The individual will pay the costs of another mediation.

c. The individual will be fined in an amount no greater than $5,000.00.

d. The individual, at their own cost, will attend a seminar or other educational program on mediation, for a minimum or eight (8) hours. [Kimberlee K. Kovach, *Good Faith in Mediation-Requested, Recommended, or Required? A New Ethic*, 38 S. Tex. L. Rev. 575, 622-23 (1997).]

Do you favor Kovach's provision? Specifically, do you think that good-faith participation should necessarily entail attendance, in person, by all parties, (001)(d)? Even though Rule 16 is not this stringent for settlement conferences? Is the provision that participants must remain until the mediator excuses them, (001)(i), consistent with your ideas of party autonomy and self-determination within mediation? What is the effect of making the mediator responsible for a determination that the parties mediated in good-faith, (003)(b)? What is the effect of the mediator making a determination that will trigger monetary sanctions, (004)? How will a court obtain the information necessary to make a determination of good-faith participation, (003)(a)? After a "bad-faith" mediation, should the parties be required to try again, (004)(b)?

3. Professor Lande sees court-imposed requirements as a last resort to ensure good-faith participation. Do you think that any other measures will be effective in eliminating the type of behaviors that have been documented?

4. Professor Lande observes that "[i]n practice, the courts have limited their interpretation of good faith in mediation to attendance, submission of pre-mediation memoranda, and, in some cases, attendance of organizational representatives with adequate settlement authority." (John Lande, *Using Dispute System Design Methods to Promote Good-Faith Participation In Court-connected Mediation Programs*, 50 UCLA L. Rev. 69, 86 (2002).) In contrast, the language in most proposals and some rules is much more expansive. If the application of "good-faith participation" requirements were limited to the elements listed above, would you object to such requirements? Would any of Professor Lande's and Magistrate Judge Brazil's objections still apply?

5. Enforcing a good faith standard of participation can be inconsistent with confidentiality protections for mediation communications. In *Foxgate Home-owners' Association v. Bramalea*, 25 P.3d 1117 (Cal. 2001), the principle of confidentiality of court-ordered mediation came into tension with "the power of a court to control proceedings before it and other persons 'in any manner connected with a judicial proceeding before it,' by imposing sanctions on a party or the party's attorney for statements or conduct during mediation." (*Id.*) The mediator reported that the defendant's attorney had refused to bring defendant's experts to a mediation session called for the purpose of having the party's experts interact on the question of construction defects. The mediator recommended that the trial court order the defendant and its attorney to reimburse the other parties for their expenses resulting from the failed mediation. While the California Court of Appeal reasoned that the legislature could not have intended California's confidentiality provisions to shield parties from sanctions if they disobey orders requiring their participation in mediation, the Supreme Court refused to read an exception into the plain language of the statute. It held that communications could not be disclosed absent an express statutory exception without undermining the legislature's purpose of encouraging mediation by ensuring confidentiality. Do you agree with the California Supreme Court's decision? With the California legislature's policy decision? Will the outcome encourage parties to mediate?

6. In states that have adopted the Uniform Mediation Act, there is a strict limitation on the information mediators may report to the court. (*See* UMA § 7(a)(1).) This limit does not permit mediators to report a participant's level of preparation or participation. The Act does permit mediators to disclose particular facts, including attendance and whether a settlement was reached, but good faith participation requirements that go beyond requiring attendance at mediation sessions are inconsistent with the UMA's reporting limitations.

7. Consider the following situation: Plaintiff has sued her employer for sexual harassment and retaliation. The parties agreed to mediate pursuant to local rule, and the court issued a standard order of referral. Among other things, the order stated "each party will provide the neutral with a memorandum" prior to the ADR conference and required a representative "having authority to settle claims" to attend each conference and "participate in good faith." Defendant's counsel told plaintiff's counsel that he did not think mediation would be fruitful, but did not ask the court to cancel the session. The plaintiff provided a memorandum to the neutral and attended the conference, accompanied by her court-appointed attorney. The defendant did not provide a memorandum. Its counsel and a local regional manager attended the mediation. The local regional manager did not have independent knowledge of plaintiff's claim; she did not have authority to reconsider defendant's position regarding settlement; and the limit of her settlement authority was $500. At the mediation, the plaintiff made two settlement offers. Both were rejected by the defendant without a counter-offer. In response to an order to show cause why it should not be sanctioned, the defendant maintained that the requirement for a memorandum is only a guideline and that preparing one would have wasted time and money. It further commented that the order to show cause was a result of "understandable frustration that cases like the one plaintiff foists upon the Court clog the Court's docket." If you were the judge, would you order sanctions? (*See Nick v. Morgan's Foods, Inc.*, 99 F. Supp. 2d 1056 (E.D. Mo. 2000).)

8. Some courts have been willing to sanction participants for their lack of adequate participation in court-ordered mediation. Often the sanction consists of an award of the other party's costs to prepare for and attend the mediation. But sometimes the sanctions are more severe. (*See, e.g., Triad Mack Sales & Serv. v. Clement Bros. Co.*, 438 S.E.2d 485 (N.C. Ct. App. 1994) (default judgment granted because of defendant's failure to attend mediation without good cause); *Schulz v. Nienhuis*, 448 N.W.2d 655 (Wis. 1989) (case dismissed due to plaintiff's lack of good faith in failing to attend mediation).)

5. APPELLATE MEDIATION

Mediation also exists at the appeals level. All but one of the federal courts of appeals and many state appellate courts have adopted appellate mediation programs. Appellate mediation is both similar to and different from than trial level mediation. The techniques used by the mediators are very similar — the typical search for common ground and interests. Most jurisdictions use professional mediators who try to settle cases that have already taken up considerable court system resources at the trial level. What is quite different about appellate mediation is, of course, the advanced stage of the litigation at the time the appellate mediator seeks to facilitate settlement. At this stage, it is an understatement to say that some parties have entrenched positions and may resist typical efforts to settle. Nonetheless, the considerable pressure on the appellate docket drives appellate mediation and most appellate courts have declared their own programs a success.

Appellate mediation is typically not global — there is no effort to mediate every case. In the federal courts of appeals, although the First and Second Circuits refer virtually all civil cases to mediation, most circuits screen cases for likely candidates. Screening occurs soon after the docketing of a notice of appeal. Criminal cases are usually excluded.

The nature of the screening process used to select cases for appellate mediation varies. Several federal circuits do not refer cases involving governmental agencies, pro se litigation, and prisoner petitions. (Can you guess why?) Several circuits select civil cases at random from a pool that meets basis eligibility criteria. Other circuits select cases that appear most likely to settle. These factors are used to screen cases for possible mediation:

- Number of parties
- Interest of the parties in mediation
- Complexity of use and monetary relief sought
- Nature of dispute and issues on appeal
- Presence of incentives to settle or simplify case

(*See generally* Robert J. Niemic, MEDIATION AND CONFERENCE PROGRAMS IN THE FEDERAL COURTS OF APPEALS: A SOURCEBOOK FOR JUDGES AND LAWYERS (1997).)

In appellate mediation, a third party mediator, not a judge, serves as the conciliator. In some courts, the mediator is a full time administrative member of the appellate court staff. A few courts, including the United States Court of Appeals for the District of Columbia Circuit, rely exclusively upon a pool of voluntary mediators and maintain no full-time staff mediators. The D.C. Circuit's panel contains heavyweight litigators with sterling reputations who volunteer their services. Most programs offer appellate mediation at no cost to the parties.

The nature of the appellate mediation process is not that different than ordinary mediation. In the Ninth Circuit, the process begins with an "assessment conference" conducted on the telephone. The mediation staff and counsel discuss the litigation history and possibility of settlement. About 50% of these conferences lead to actual appellate mediation. In most programs, appellate mediation will not delay case progress. Time for oral argument and brief filings are unaffected.

Programs at courts that cover a large geographical area often hold mediation sessions primarily by telephone in order to keep costs down, but other programs tend to hold sessions in person. Mediators often follow up with the attorneys after the mediation session and hold additional caucuses or joint sessions as the negotiations progress.

In the appellate programs that have been studied, most had settlement rates between 29 and 47 percent. In studies that compared appeals assigned to mediation with those that were not, the cases sent to mediation were 10 to 20 percent more likely to settle before briefing or argument. (*See* Roselle L.Wissler, *The Effectiveness of Court-Connected Dispute Resolution in Civil Cases*, 22 CONFLICT RESOL. Q. 55, 73-74 (2004).) While these settlement rates are considerably lower than those reached in trial court-annexed mediations, remember that appellate civil backlogs are substantial (e.g., 15.2 months median disposition time in 9th Circuit from filing of appeal to final disposition). (*See* LEONIDAS MECHAM, 1999 ANNUAL REPORT, JUDICIAL BUSINESS OF THE UNITED STATES COURTS.) A study of the Sixth Circuit mediation program determined, after accounting for cases that would have settled without the program, that it was highly cost effective compared to the cost of the additional appellate judges (and their staffs) it would have taken to decide the cases that settled in mediation. (*See* Robert W. Rack, Jr., *Thoughts of a Chief Circuit Mediator on Federal Court-Annexed Mediation*, 17 OHIO ST. J. ON DISP. RESOL. 609, 611 (2002).)

D. EARLY NEUTRAL EVALUATION AND THE MINI-TRIAL

Early neutral evaluation and the mini-trial are each based upon a theory that the adversary attorney may lack the ability to evaluate his case clearly and may be overly optimistic and unable to point out the negative features of a case to his client. The introduction of the neutral affords a reality check — the lawyer and client receive the opinion of an impartial third party regarding the case. (*See generally*, Wayne D. Brazil *et al.*, *Early Neutral Evaluation: An Experimental Effort to Expedite Dispute Resolution*, 69 JUDICATURE 279 (1986).) Each side is given the opportunity to summarize and support its current positions. When this process is finished, the neutral indicates which side she believes has the better claim with respect to each issue in dispute. When litigants are involved, the neutral states how she thinks a court would be likely to resolve the dispute. If the evaluator is an experienced and respected neutral, the parties would probably find that person's assessment persuasive. By carefully pointing out the strengths and weaknesses in each party's case, the neutral may be able to generate searching party reappraisals and renewed bargaining efforts.

When transactional negotiations are involved, the neutral can still provide an independent evaluation of the strengths and weaknesses of each proposal. Whether the participants are attempting to structure a domestic or international business deal, resolve a collective bargaining dispute, or agree upon a rezoning arrangement, the perspective of a neutral professional can be beneficial. The neutral can suggest the way in which she thinks each item should be allocated and hope that this device induces the interested parties to reconsider their existing bargaining positions.

Litigants who have been unable to achieve a negotiated resolution of their controversy may be ignoring the real consequences of nonsettlement. One or both sides may be entertaining delusions of grandeur regarding the likely outcome of the adjudication process. So long as these unrealistic expectations continue, it would be virtually impossible for a conciliator to generate a mutual accord. The neutral intervenor may attempt to educate the recalcitrant participants concerning the realities of the situation through the use of mini-trial procedure.

1. EARLY NEUTRAL EVALUATION (ENE)

To some extent full-fledged ENE is a substitute for the Rule 16 pre-trial conference in which the judge provides the function of a reality check. Judges routinely "signal" their likes and dislikes about a case at a pre-trial. They may initiate *sua sponte* motions (e.g., *sua sponte* summary judgment) or suggest to a party with a favorable case that they make a dispositive motion. With an ENE program some of this evaluative function is effectively transferred to the neutral. This frees up the court for other trials and, in a sense, makes it possible for the court to be more neutral by removing some (but certainly not all) of the need for case signaling from the bench.

DAVID I. LEVINE, NORTHERN DISTRICT OF CALIFORNIA Adopts EARLY NEUTRAL EVALUATION TO EXPEDITE DISPUTE RESOLUTION, 72 Judicature 235 (1989) *

Since 1985, the federal court for the Northern District of California has operated an experimental program in expedited dispute resolution, called Early Neutral Evaluation (ENE). After a lengthy period of analysis and revision, the court has permanently adopted ENE based on considerable evidence that it is an effective way to improve the resolution of civil disputes. * * *

The developers of ENE were motivated by the desire of the judges of the Northern District to make litigation less expensive and burdensome for clients. They thought that this could best be accomplished by getting a neutral party to intervene in the early stages of the litigation process and to inject

---

a dose of "intellectual discipline, common sense, and more direct communication."

The heart of ENE was to be an early, frank and thoughtful assessment of the parties' relative positions and the overall value of the case. Each evaluation was to be given by a neutral, very experienced and highly respected private attorney, called the evaluator. The confidential evaluation, based on the evaluator's reaction to the parties' written evaluation statements and oral presentations, was to be presented orally to the parties and their attorneys. The developers of ENE hoped to accomplish a variety of specific goals: (1) to force the parties to confront the merits of their own case and their opponents'; (2) to identify which matters of law and fact actually were in dispute as early as possible; (3) to develop an efficient approach to discovery; and (4) to provide a frank assessment of the case. Later, fostering early settlements was added as an explicit goal.

The court decided to assign a limited number of cases to a small pilot study before committing itself to a larger experimental program. * * *

It appeared that many of the goals of ENE were being met, largely because the evaluators were providing helpful assessments of the cases to the litigants. The program needed some improvement, especially in the areas of clearly communicating the evaluation to the clients, incorporating follow-up into the standard ENE process and, where appropriate, taking advantage of opportunities to settle the case. On the basis of the information obtained by studying the pilot cases, the court concluded that ENE was sufficiently promising to warrant making the recommended modifications and expanding the program to a second phase of experimentation with a larger number of cases.

* * *

Analysis of an extensive body of empirical data indicates that ENE works. The procedure makes counsel and parties confront their cases systematically; it enables the parties to exchange detailed information about their cases and can help identify the areas in need of additional discovery; it contributes greatly to the parties' understanding of the issues in their cases; it provides a vehicle for communication between the parties that can be more efficient than formal discovery and more productive than most scheduling or status conferences; it gives parties a fresh perspective on their case and a frank assessment of the relative strengths of their competing positions from a neutral and experienced evaluator; and it creates opportunities to conduct settlement negotiations before the parties have wasted resources on ritual pretrial skirmishes.

The parties and attorneys have shown considerable confidence in the integrity of ENE. By overwhelming margins, they report that ENE is fair and the evaluators are unbiased. Those who have experienced ENE strongly endorse its expansion to more cases, even where the session did not lead to the direct settlement of the action. As a final indication that the participants believe that ENE is valuable, they are willing to be charged a substantial fee (approximately $500, split between the parties) for the services of the evaluators.

Although, in general, ENE is working very well, it could be improved. The materials sent to litigants must be as clear as possible. Evaluators need to be especially careful that they are doing all that they can to help the litigants focus on case development planning, where that is necessary. Evaluators must also take great pains to improve the likelihood that the clients who attend the evaluation sessions really hear and understand what they are told about their cases. The program ought to strive to meet its goal of having evaluation sessions within approximately 100 days of filing the case.

*   *   *

The ENE program will be presumptively mandatory for the assigned cases, in order to ensure that there will be a program that is substantial enough to justify the commitments of the evaluators and the court. The cases are "presumptively mandatory" because the judge to whom the case is assigned originally will have the power to remove the case from ENE on his or her own initiative (such as at the initial status conference) or upon a showing of good cause by counsel. * * *

Because of the limitations on the number of available evaluators, the court designated only certain categories of cases as being eligible for ENE. The first criterion is the subject matter category. The categories include many contract and personal injury matters, employment civil rights cases, wrongful termination matters and certain types of commercial litigation, such as actions under the securities and antitrust laws and civil RICO. These categories were selected because of their frequency on the Northern District docket and because of the court's confidence that it could develop and maintain a pool of well-qualified neutrals for these matters without severe problems of conflicts of interest. (Such conflicts proved to arise frequently in those subjects where the bar is comparatively small and highly specialized.)

The second set of criteria for identifying cases was based on the experiences suggesting that certain cases would be less appropriate for ENE. These are where: (1) at least one party is proceeding *in pro per*; (2) the principal relief sought is equitable, not monetary; (3) the case raises an important issue of public policy on which a judicial pronouncement is sought; or (4) the legal standards on which the disposition will turn are not clear and the parties will need judicial pronouncement on the law to resolve the matter. The first two can be applied administratively; the last two can be considered by the trial judge or upon motion as a basis for removing a case from the ENE program. * * *

NOTES

1. Early neutral evaluation, while very popular in selected court systems, is not yet in broad use throughout the United States. The Federal Judicial Center reports that 14 of the 94 federal district courts have an ENE program. Almost all of these courts, however, have adopted ENE within the past six years. (*See* Elizabeth Plapinger & Donna Stienstra, *Federal Court ADR: A Practitioner's Update*, 14 ALTERNATIVES TO HIGH COST LITIGATION 7, 9 (1996).)

2. What sort of attorneys should be assigned the role of an ENE neutral? A number of jurisdictions require a minimum (e.g., five years) experience for assignment to a list of neutrals performing ENE services. Is this an adequate screening? Should judges pick and choose among litigators to find the best neutrals? The heralded ENE Program of the Northern District of California mandates that its ENE neutrals have at least 15 years of law practice, experience in the substantive area of the assigned case, and ENE training conducted by the court.

3. To some extent, courts choose among the various types of court-annexed procedures when deciding to start a new ADR program. Why would a court select ENE instead of a program of mandatory mediation? Which is more coercive? Aren't there real similarities between these devices, especially if the court approved mediator uses, a substance-oriented style?

4. A statistical study of both court-annexed mediation and ENE in six U.S. Federal District Courts concluded that there was no strong evidence that use of these two procedures "significantly affected time to disposition, litigation costs, or attorney views of fairness or satisfaction with case management." The study did find that the use of these ADR programs appeared to increase the likelihood of a monetary settlement. The study also found evidence that some participants want to be more fully informed about their opponent's case prior to the ADR session. (*See, generally,* James. S. Kakalik, et. al., *An Evaluation of Mediation and Early Neutral Evaluation Under the Civil Justice Reform Act,* 3 DISP. RES. MAG. 4 (1997).) Should we be surprised at these conclusions? Because the timing of an ENE session is often very early in a case, before motions seeking summary judgment or much discovery, it may be understandable that some parties and their counsel feel the need for additional information.

5. *Attendance at ENE Sessions:* Some jurisdictions mandate that the client attend the ENE session and that the client's representative possess settlement authority. Can you explain the justification for the attendance requirement?

2. THE MINI-TRIAL

Like ENE, the mini-trial serves a predictive function and uses the services of an expert neutral. Unlike ENE, however, the mini-trial usually involves more formal presentations of proof to the neutral expert who renders a non-binding "result" and may explore the possibility of settlement. It is critical that the mini-trial be attended by the opposing clients with authority to settle the case. Consider the comments of Eric Green, one of the originators of the mini-trial:

> The typical mini-trial contains only one of the two features of a trial: after a short period of pretrial preparation, the lawyers (and their experts, if desired) make informal, abbreviated, and confidential presentations of each side's best case. The mini-trial drops the second main feature of a trial: no third party pronounces judgment. The most distinctive characteristic of the mini-trial is that the lawyers present their cases not to a judge, an arbitrator, a jury, or any other third party

with the power to make a binding decision, but rather to the principals themselves.

In the classic mini-trial with corporations involved, the principals are business executives with settlement authority. The lawyers design their presentations to give the parties a clear and balanced conception of the strengths and weaknesses of the positions on both sides. In other words, the principals receive a crash course on the subject of the dispute conducted in an informal setting but through the adversary process. The purpose of the presentation phase is to exchange information. The principals enter confidential settlement negotiations immediately afterwards.

In the classic format, mini-trials have been presided over by a jointly selected "neutral adviser." The adviser moderates the proceedings, poses questions, and highlights crucial facts and issues. But during the presentation phase, he does not preside like a judge, an arbitrator, or even a mediator. If the principals do not reach settlement quickly after the information exchange, they may ask the neutral adviser to give a nonbinding opinion about how a judge or a jury would decide the case and why. With these views in hand, the parties then resume direct negotiations. [Eric Green, *Growth of the Mini-Trial*, 9 LITIGATION 12 (Fall 1982).]

The neutral adviser who presides at the mini-trial holds a flexible position. He may be requested to mediate following the presentation of evidence. If the parties seem willing to attempt serious negotiation themselves, the neutral may do nothing more than offer his mediation services if needed. Mini-trials have been particularly useful in complex cases involving high technology issues such as patent infringement. Is there any reason that the mini-trial should be confined to such cases?

Judge Hubert Will has developed a modified mini-trial approach that he describes as his "Lloyds of London" technique. (*See* Hubert L. Will et al., *The Role of the Judge is the Settlement Process*, 75 F.R.D. 203, 206–07 (1977).) He asks the disputants themselves to analyze their controversy from the perspective of an insurance company representative. After both sides have summarized their respective positions, each is instructed to objectively assess the likely trial result if the case were adjudicated. What is the probability the plaintiff would prevail? If the plaintiff were to obtain a favorable determination, what would be the anticipated monetary judgment? The presiding neutral then multiplies each side's probability estimate, times that side's predicted award if the plaintiff were to win.

In most cases, plaintiff attorneys predict a greater likelihood of success than defendant lawyers, and plaintiff advocates generally forecast higher verdicts than defense counsel. For example, the plaintiff-attorney may predict an 80 percent probability of trial success and a $200,000 judgment if he/she were to prevail, while the defendant-lawyer may anticipate a 50 percent probability of plaintiff success with a likely $150,000 result. From the plaintiff's perspective the case appears to be worth $160,000 (0.8 × $200,000), while the defense would seem to value the case at $75,000 (0.5 × $150,000). Each party is then asked how much it believes it would cost to try the case. The plaintiff might suggest an overall cost of $30,000, with the defendant projecting a $50,000 cost.

The difference between the parties' projected $160,000 and $75,000 valuations may seem insurmountable. Nonetheless, once the transaction costs are factored in, the picture dramatically changes. The plaintiff must *subtract* the expected $30,000 cost from its anticipated $160,000 verdict, because it would have to expend that time and resources, while the defendant must *add* the anticipated $50,000 cost to its predicted $75,000 award for the same reason. With a plaintiff value of $130,000 ($160,000 − $30,000) and a defendant value of $125,000 ($75,000 + $50,000), a more manageable $5,000 gap remains. A proficient neutral should be able to convince the litigants that a settlement in the $125,000 to $130,000 range would be preferable to the risks and emotional costs associated with trial.

E. SUMMARY JURY TRIAL

Like CAA and ENE, the summary jury trial affords the attorney and client a prediction of likelihood of success at a later, conventional trial. This device is designed to reduce uncertainty and ease the probability assessments that underlie settlement. The theory of the summary jury trial is that a short presentation of trial proof to an impartial jury will render a "verdict" that attorneys and clients can use to accurately assess their respective cases. The summary jury trial is usually held in private, without public access. As you read the following materials, ask yourself whether the critical reduction in uncertainty that fosters settlement will be achieved and whether the trial features of this device necessitate rethinking the holding of these trials behind locked doors.

THOMAS D. LAMBROS, THE SUMMARY JURY TRIAL — AN ALTERNATIVE METHOD OF RESOLVING DISPUTES, 69 Judicature 286 (1986)[*]

* * * One shortcoming of nearly every settlement alternative, however, is the absence of a jury in the decisionmaking process.

A jury is important for two reasons central to the American tradition of justice. First, jurors bring a fresh viewpoint to the analysis of human affairs, free from the biases of the professional lawyer and judge. Second, the jury system involves the citizens of this country in the process of deciding issues of importance to their community.

Settlement discussions invariably become difficult at the point where the judge and the lawyers attempt to view the case through the eyes of the prospective jury. Traditionally, judges and lawyers have relied on their past experiences to evaluate cases. Although this method is somewhat effective, its limitations are manifested in the many cases that go to trial despite their great settlement potential.

Settlement discussions also become difficult when the parties themselves have an unrealistic view of the facts or the law surrounding their case, either because they have been poorly advised by their counsel or have refused to consider the facts from their opponent's standpoint. Many times, parties like this do not "awaken" to the true merits of their case until they hear their opponent's trial presentation. No amount of theorizing or abstract discussion between attorney and client can solve this problem; the client must be *shown* the way his or her case will appear at trial.

The summary jury trial was born from these concerns. While the rules and the limits of the procedure are very flexible, the summary jury trial usually involves a summarized presentation of a civil case to an advisory jury for the purpose of showing the parties (as well as the lawyers and the judge) how a jury reacts to the dispute. The procedure is non-binding (unless agreed to by all parties) and, therefore, does not impair the constitutional right of any party to proceed to jury trial. However, a full jury trial after a summary jury trial is almost always unnecessary because the procedure fosters settlement of the dispute.

The evidentiary and procedural rules governing summary jury trial are few and flexible. Nevertheless, to achieve the goal of facilitating settlement, the summary jury trial is conducted in open court with appropriate formalities, and clients and other key decisionmakers with settlement authority are required to attend. The lawyers are expected to have their case in a state of trial readiness, and to present to the jury the best possible summation of their claims. The procedure is normally concluded in a half-day and rarely lasts longer than a full day.

* * *

The summary jury trial is intended primarily for cases that will not settle using more traditional methods. This should be most obvious to the judge in the matter when he or she has conducted one or more pre-trial conferences and finds that the parties are failing to reach a settlement of the case for any of the following reasons:

• There is a substantial difference of opinion among the lawyers as to the jury's evaluation of unliquidated damages such as "pain and suffering;"

• There is an irreconcilable difference of opinion over the jury's expected perception of the application of the facts to such hard-to-define legal concepts as "reasonableness" and "ordinary care;"

• One or more of the parties (or their counsel) appears to have an unrealistic view of the merits of the case when confronted with a reasonable presentation of the argument being made by their opponent;

• One or more of the parties is reluctant to reach any settlement agreement because of the desire to have their "day in court" and to have the case evaluated by an impartial jury.

The decision to use summary jury trial rarely turns on the substantive legal aspects of a case, but rather depends upon the dynamics of the controversy. Summary jury trial has been used in a wide range of cases from relatively simple negligence and contract actions to complex mass tort and antitrust cases. Many lawyers and some judges might shy away from assigning a complex case to summary jury trial; it is, however, the complex case that is most suitable for this alternative method of dispute resolution.

Obviously, if a case is only expected to require a day or two to try, there is little advantage in conducting a summary jury trial — the litigants and the court might as well simply try the case. While there may be some grounds to suggest that a highly technical case is difficult for a jury to resolve, those factors apply as much to a standard trial as they do to the summary jury process. At least in the summary jury process, the jurors will have the entire fact situation presented to them in a period of time during which they can focus their full attention on the case, rather than spread out over weeks or months when key facts can be forgotten. This advantage has been borne out in actual summary jury trial situations where complex antitrust cases have been effectively presented (and resolved) through the summary jury trial process. Thus, the court should generally assume that the longer the trial, the greater the potential value of the summary jury proceeding.

The psychological effect of "courtroom combat" is important with regard to litigants who are either too stubborn to see their opponent's point of view, or who feel that settlement would be an admission of weakness and would prefer to have their "day in court." Any trial, however long or short, exacts some sacrifice or penalty from the litigants in the form of financial costs and emotional stress. Some litigants have the ability to handle that stress, others do not. The summary jury trial provides a forum in which the litigant can get a taste of the trial ahead and thereby more logically evaluate his or her position.

Effective pre-trial conferencing is the best method for determining the suitability of a case for summary jury trial. The give and take between the parties at such a conference provides the judge with the soundest basis for assessing whether summary jury trial is in order. Ideally, after discussing the possibility of a summary jury trial during the pre-trial conference, the parties will decide that use of summary jury trial is in their beset interest. Such acceptance is desirable because it heightens the chances that the parties will accept the result of the summary jury trial and settle their case.

It is to be anticipated that certain parties will not readily consent to the use of summary jury trial. Whenever a judge initiates a procedure with which attorneys are unfamiliar, objections from counsel are to be expected. When proposing the use of summary jury trial, a judge should, of course, be receptive to any objections counsel may raise and should determine whether the objections are well taken in light of the circumstances of the case. However, if these objections are without merit the judge should not hesitate to direct the parties to proceed to summary jury trial.

*   *   *

The format of a summary jury trial is very similar to that of a traditional civil jury trial. A judge or magistrate presides over the court, which is formally brought to order. Attendance of the parties with complete settlement authority is required.

It is best if the judge who will try the case conducts the summary jury trial because, through presiding over the summary jury trial, the judge will obtain a thorough understanding of the issues presented by the case and the strengths and weaknesses of each parties' position. The judge's participation in the summary jury trial will also facilitate an open and frank discussion of the evidence during post-summary jury trial settlement negotiations. Because the jury remains the ultimate trier of fact, the outcome of a subsequent trial probably will not be affected by the participation of the judge who presided over the summary jury trial. Indeed, the quality of the actual jury may be improved because the jury will have become intimately acquainted with the legal issues posed by the case.

* * *

The judge opens the summary jury trial with a few introductory remarks in which he or she introduces the trial participants and explains briefly what the case is about. The judge then explains the summary jury trial procedure to the jury. The judge normally states that the lawyers have reviewed all of the relevant materials and interviewed all of the witnesses and now have been asked to condense all of the evidence and present it to the jury in a narrative form. They are also told that the attorneys will be permitted to summarize both the evidence and legal arguments in support of their respective positions.

The prospective jurors are advised that at the conclusion of the case they will be instructed on the applicable law and the use of the verdict form. They are further advised they are expected to consider the case just as seriously as they would if the case was presented to them in the conventional manner and that their verdict must be a true verdict based on the evidence. They are further told that the proceeding will be completed in a single day and that their verdict will aid and assist the parties in resolving their dispute. Nothing more is said about the non-binding nature of the summary jury trial; nothing more need be said. Although the jurors are not misled to believe that the proceeding is equivalent to a binding jury trial, the non-binding character of the proceeding is not emphasized. By adopting this balance the judge may candidly explain the procedure without minimizing the jurors' responsibilities.

Following the judge's introduction of the case to the prospective jurors, the judge conducts a brief voir dire generally posing questions to the jury collectively. This process is expedited through the use of the completed juror profile forms. The judge may make additional inquiries of the jury based on voir dire questions proposed by the attorneys. Counsel are normally permitted to exercise challenges for cause as well as peremptory challenges, although the number of challenges should be limited, and counsel should be encouraged to accept the jurors as they find them, since prolonged voir dire will defeat the goal of conducting the summary jury trial efficiently.

Jury selection is followed by the presentations of counsel. Although the goal of expedited presentation is always kept in mind, the length and format of the proceeding may be adjusted to accommodate the particular needs of the case. Counsel are usually given one hour each for the presentations. This period is usually broken down so that the plaintiff devotes approximately 45 minutes to its case in chief, followed by defendant being given a similar period for its main presentation. A 15 minute period may then be given to the parties for their respective rebuttal and surrebuttal. The total time of the proceeding may be extended if the case involves particularly complex issues or more than two parties. It is recommended that each side give the jury a three-to-five minute overview of its case before the formal presentations. This will give the jury a "fix" on the whole case, obviating the need to wait a full hour before learning about the defense.

* * *

In making their presentations to the jury, counsel are limited to presentations based on evidence that would be admissible at trial. Although counsel are permitted to mingle representations of fact with legal arguments, considerations of responsibility and restraint must be observed. Counsel may only make factual representations supportable by reference to discovery materials. These materials include depositions, stipulations, signed statements of witnesses, and answers to interrogatories or requests for admissions. Additionally, an attorney may make representations based on the assurance that he or she has personally spoken with a witness and is repeating what that witness stated. Discovery materials may be read aloud but not at undue length. Counsel may submit these materials in full to the jury for their consideration during deliberations. Each juror is provided a note pad and is permitted to take notes.

Physical evidence, including documents, may be exhibited during a presentation and submitted for the jury's examination during deliberations. These exhibits may be marked for identification, but are returned to the appropriate party at the end of the proceeding.

By virtue of the nature of the summary jury trial, objections during the proceeding are not encouraged. However, in the event counsel overstep the bounds of propriety as to a material aspect of the case, an objection will be received and, if well taken, will be sustained and the jury instructed appropriately.

At the conclusion of the summary jury trial presentations, the jury is given an abbreviated charge dealing primarily with the applicable substantive law and, to a lesser extent, with such boilerplate concepts as burden of proof and credibility. The jury is normally given a verdict form containing specific interrogatories, a general inquiry as to liability, and an inquiry as to the plaintiff's damages. The jurors are encouraged to return a unanimous verdict and are given ample time to reach such a consensus. However, if, after diligent efforts, they are unable to return a unanimous verdict, each juror should be given a verdict form and should be instructed to return a separate verdict. These separate views will be of value to the lawyers in exploring settlement.

Once the jury has been excused to deliberate, the court may engage the parties in settlement negotiations. These negotiations have a special sense of urgency in that they are conducted in the shadow of an imminent verdict. The negotiations are informed by the perspectives gained through observation of the summary jury trial.

When the jurors complete their deliberations, the court receives their unanimous verdict or individual verdicts. At this time, the judge, the attorneys, the parties, and the jurors engage in a dialogue unique to summary jury trial.

The judge may ask the jurors a broad variety of questions ranging from the general reason for the decision to their perceptions of each party's presentation. Counsel may also inquire of the jurors both as to their perspectives on the merits of the case and their responses to the style of the attorney's presentations. This dialogue affords an opportunity to gain an in-depth understanding of the strengths and weaknesses of the parties' respective positions. The dialogue may serve as a springboard for meaningful settlement negotiations.

*   *   *

CINCINNATI GAS AND ELECTRIC CO. v. GENERAL ELECTRIC CO.
854 F.2d 900 (6th Cir. 1988)

KEITH, Circuit Judge.

Appellants, The Cincinnati Post, et al., appeal . . . from orders issued by the district court. . . , which appellants contend denied them their first amendment right of access to the summary jury trial conducted in the underlying action. For the reasons set forth below, we AFFIRM the district court.

I.

This appeal arises out of a lawsuit involving the design and construction of the William H. Zimmer Nuclear Power Plant ("Plant"). The plaintiffs below, The Cincinnati Gas and Electric Company, The Dayton Power and Light Company and Columbus and Southern Ohio Electric Company (plaintiffs-appellees), were three Ohio electric utility companies that undertook jointly to build the Plant. In July of 1984, plaintiffs filed a lawsuit against the General Electric Company and Sargent & Lundy Engineers (defendants-appellees), an architectural and engineering firm, alleging breach of contractual duties and common law concerning the modification of the Plant. Plaintiffs later amended their complaint against the General Electric Company to add fraud and RICO claims.

From the outset of this litigation, the parties recognized the need for confidential treatment of much of the material that would be produced in discovery. As a result, the parties negotiated a comprehensive protective order, which the magistrate approved on December 6, 1984. This order provided varying degrees of protection for documents classified as "Confidential" or "Highly Confidential" by the party producing them. The order restricted the use by nonproducing parties of documents accorded either level of confidentiality to "the prosecution or defense of this action," or to other proceedings arising in connection with the Plant. In addition, the order provided that any reference to "Highly Confidential" documents in motions, briefs, or other court papers or filings had to be accompanied by appropriate markings and separately filed under seal.

On June 26, 1987, the district court issued an order requiring the parties to participate in a summary jury trial scheduled to commence on September

8, 1987. The order included a provision closing the proceeding to the press and public. That provision stated that "[t]he proceedings, and all results thereof, shall be confidential, and shall not be disclosed other than to the parties, their attorneys, consultants and insurers. The jurors shall be appropriately instructed as to such confidential treatments."

On September 4, 1987, appellants moved to intervene in the underlying action for the limited purpose of challenging the order closing the summary trial. On September 14, 1987 [117 F.R.D. 597], the district court denied appellants' motion to intervene, holding that they had no right to attend the summary jury trial. The court observed that "[t]he summary jury trial, for all it may appear like a trial, is a settlement technique." Accordingly, the court held that the press had no first amendment right of access because: (1) there is no tradition of access to summary jury trials or to other recognized settlement devices, and (2) public access "does not play a particularly significant positive role" in the functioning of the summary jury trial because "the proceeding is non-binding and has no effect on the merits of the case, other than settlement."

On October 5, 1987, the district court amended its September 14, 1987, order: (1) to incorporate an oral order issued on September 21, 1987, restricting communications between the mock jurors and the press and public until the case had ended; and (2) to add a provision requiring that "the list identifying prospective jurors on the panel for the summary jury trial, as well as those who actually served on the summary jury trial, shall remain sealed until the conclusion of this litigation." The court explained that "[t]o disclose [the mock jurors'] identity at this time may defeat the confidentiality of the jury's decision and would be inconsistent with our Order closing the proceedings to the public."

Less than two months after the conclusion of the summary jury trial, the parties reached a settlement. On November 20, 1987, the district court issued an order approving the terms of the settlement and dismissing the action with prejudice. The court continued the gag orders and the sealing of the transcript and jury list, ruling that "all other Orders in this case concerning the confidentiality of documents and the summary jury trial remain in effect."

II.

The precise issue before us is whether the first amendment right of access attaches to the summary jury proceeding in this case. Appellants argue that the district court erred in refusing to allow them to intervene for the purpose of attending the summary jury trial proceeding. Appellants specifically argue that: (1) the summary jury proceeding is analogous in form and function to a civil or criminal trial on the merits, and therefore, the first amendment right of access which encompasses civil and criminal trial and pre-trial proceedings also encompasses the summary jury proceedings; and (2) public access would play a significant positive role in the functioning of the judicial system and summary jury trials.

Appellees contend that the first amendment right of access does not apply to summary jury proceedings. Appellees argue that settlement proceedings are totally lacking in any tradition of public access, and that appellants exalt form over function in arguing that a summary jury trial is no different from a trial on the merits. *See, e.g., Palmieri v. New York*, 779 F.2d 861, 865 (2d Cir. 1985) (citation omitted) ("[s]ecrecy of settlement terms . . . is a well-established American litigation practice . . ."). Appellees further argue that public access would not play a significant positive role in the functioning of summary jury trials. We agree with appellees' arguments and hold that the first amendment right of access does not attach to summary jury trial proceedings.

*   *   *

In *Press Enterprise II* [478 U.S. 1 (1986)] the Court held that a qualified right of access applied in criminal proceedings to a preliminary hearing which was conducted before a magistrate in the absence of a jury. The Court held that the analysis of a first amendment claim of access involves two "complimentary considerations." First, the proceeding must be one for which there has been a "tradition of accessibility." This inquiry requires a court to determine "whether the place and process [to which access is sought] has historically been open to the press and general public." Second, public access must play a "significant positive role in the functioning of the particular process in question." Moreover, even if these elements are satisfied, the right of access is a qualified one and must be outweighed by a strong countervailing interest in maintaining the confidentiality of the proceedings.

With regard to the first part of the test, we concur with the district court that "there is no historically recognized right of access to summary jury trials in that this mechanism has been in existence for less than a decade." The summary jury trial is a device that is designed to settle disputes.[4] [Lambros, *The Summary Jury Trial, A Report to the Judicial Conference of the United States*, 103 F.R.D. 461, 465 (1984).] Settlement techniques have historically been closed to the press and public. Thus, we find that "while the history of the summary jury trial is limited, there is general agreement that historically settlement techniques are closed procedures rather than open."

Appellants argue that summary jury trials are structurally similar to ordinary civil jury trials, which have historically been open to the public. However, it is clear that while the summary jury trial is a highly reliable predictor of the likely trial outcome, there are manifold differences between it and a real trial. In a summary jury proceeding, attorneys present abbreviated arguments to jurors who render an informal verdict that guides the settlement of the case. Normally, six mock jurors are chosen after a brief voir dire conducted by the court. Following short opening statements, all evidence is presented in the form of a descriptive summary to the mock jury through the parties' attorneys. Live witnesses do not testify, and evidentiary objections are discouraged. Thus, some of the evidence disclosed to the mock jury might

---

[4] Courts have the power to conduct summary jury trials under either Fed. R. Civ. P. 16, or as a matter of the court's inherent power to manage its cases. *See Link v. Wabash Railroad Co.,* 370 U.S. 626, 82 S. Ct. 1386, 8 L. Ed. 2d 734 (1962); *see also* Lambros, The Summary Jury Trial, A Report to the Judicial Conference of the United States, 103 F.R.D. at 469.

be inadmissible at a real trial. *See* Spiegel, *Summary Jury Trials*, 54 U. CIN. L. REV. 829, 830–31 (1986).

Following counsels' presentations, the jury is given an abbreviated charge and then retires to deliberate. The jury then returns a "verdict." To emphasize the purely settlement function of the exercise, the mock jury is often asked to assess damages even if it finds no liability. Also, the court and jurors join the attorneys and parties after the "verdict" is returned in an informal discussion of the strengths and weaknesses of each side's case. [Lambros, *The Summary Jury Trial — An Alternative Method of Resolving Disputes*, 69 JUDI-CATURE 286, 289 (Feb.-Mar. 1986).]

At every turn the summary jury trial is designed to facilitate pretrial settlement of the litigation, much like a settlement conference. It is important to note that the summary jury trial does not present any matter for adjudication by the court.[5] Thus, we find appellants' argument to be unpersuasive and therefore hold that the "tradition of accessibility" element has not been met.

* * *

Appellants' claim of a public "right to know" has no validity with regard to summary jury trials. As the lower court correctly noted, the public would have no entitlement to observe any negotiations leading to a traditional settlement of the case, and the parties would be under no constitutional obligation to reveal the content of the negotiations. Thus, the public has no first amendment right to access to the summary jury trial.

Appellants also argue that the summary jury trial should be open to the public because the facilitation of a settlement between the parties has a final and decisive effect on the outcome of the litigation. To support their argument, appellants rely on the Court's language in *Press-Enterprise II* that preliminary criminal hearings must be open to the public because of their decisive effect on criminal cases. We disagree.

In contrast to the summary proceedings in this case, the proceeding at issue in *Press-Enterprise II* resulted in a binding judicial determination which directly affected the rights of the parties. Summary jury trials do not present any matters for adjudication by the court.[7] Thus, it is the presence of the exercise of a court's coercive powers that is the touchstone of the recognized right to access, not the presence of a procedure that might lead the parties to voluntarily terminate the litigation. Therefore, we find appellant's argument to be meritless.

Accordingly, for the reasons set forth above, we AFFIRM the judgment of Judge Arthur Spiegel, United States District Court, Southern District of Ohio.

---

[5] Appellants' assertion that the summary jury trial is like an adjudication because the parties are compelled to participate is incorrect. The district court expressly stated that the proceeding was undertaken with the cooperation of the parties. * * *

[7] Summary jury trials do not affect the parties' right to a full trial de novo on the merits. "If one or both parties feel the result of the jurors' deliberations is grossly inequitable, the right to proceed to a full trial is in no way prejudiced." [Lambros, *The Summary Jury Trial*, 103 F.R.D. at 482.]

GEORGE CLIFTON EDWARDS, Jr., Senior Circuit Judge, concurring in part and dissenting in part.

The proceeding conducted in this case resulted in a settlement and a court decree. It resembled both settlement negotiations and a bench trial. While I join the majority in holding that the negotiations which led to the settlement of this case could properly be conducted in camera, I do not agree that the record can appropriately continue to be sealed after a settlement has been effected. I recognize that the view expressed above might impede some settlements, but I cannot reconcile complete suppression of this record with the First Amendment which our forefathers placed as the first condition for the founding of our nation.

STRANDELL v. JACKSON COUNTY, ILLINOIS
838 F.2d 884 (7th Cir. 1988)

Before WOOD and RIPPLE, Circuit Judges, and GORDON, Senior District Judge.

RIPPLE, Circuit Judge.

In this appeal, we must decide whether a federal district court can *require* litigants to participate in a nonbinding summary jury trial. In a nonbinding summary jury trial, attorneys summarize their case before a jury, which then renders a nonbinding verdict. The purpose of this device is to motivate litigants toward settlement by allowing them to estimate how an actual jury may respond to their evidence. Thomas Tobin, Esquire, appeals from a judgment of criminal contempt for refusing to participate in such a procedure.

* * *

I

FACTS

Mr. Tobin represents the parents of Michael Strandell in a civil rights action against Jackson County, Illinois. The case involves the arrest, strip search, imprisonment, and suicidal death of Michael Strandell. In anticipation of a pretrial conference on September 3, 1986, the plaintiffs filed a written report concerning settlement prospects. The plaintiffs reported that they were requesting $500,000, but that the defendants refused to discuss the issue. At the pretrial conference, the district court suggested that the parties consent to a summary jury trial. A summary jury trial generally lasts one day, and consists of the selection of six jurors to hear approximations by counsel of the expected evidence. After receiving an abbreviated charge, the jury retires with directions to render a consensus verdict. After a verdict is reached, the jury is informed that its verdict is advisory in nature and nonbinding. The objective of this procedure is to induce the parties to negotiate a settlement. Mr. Tobin informed the district court that the plaintiffs would not consent to a summary jury trial, and filed a motion to advance the case for trial. The district court ordered that discovery be closed on January 15, 1987, and set the case for trial.

During discovery, the plaintiffs had obtained statements from 21 witnesses. The plaintiffs learned the identity of many of these witnesses from information provided by the defendants. After discovery closed, the defendants filed a motion to compel production of the witnesses' statements. The plaintiffs responded that these statements constituted privileged work-product; they argued that the defendants could have obtained the information contained in them through ordinary discovery. The district court denied the motion to compel production; it concluded that the defendants had failed to establish "substantial need" and "undue hardship," as required by Rule 26(b)(3) of the Federal Rules of Civil Procedure.

On March 23, 1987, the district court again discussed settlement prospects with counsel. The court expressed its view that a trial could not be accommodated easily on its crowded docket and again suggested that the parties consent to a summary jury trial. On March 26, 1987, Mr. Tobin advised the district court that he would not be willing to submit his client's case to a summary jury trial, but that he was ready to proceed to trial immediately. He claimed that a summary jury trial would require disclosure of the privileged statements. The district court rejected this argument, and ordered the parties to participate in a summary jury trial.

On March 31, 1987, the parties and counsel appeared, as ordered, for selection of a jury for the summary jury trial. Mr. Tobin again objected to the district court's order compelling the summary jury trial. The district court denied this motion. Mr. Tobin then respectfully declined to proceed with the selection of the jury. The district court informed Mr. Tobin that it did not have time available to try this case, nor would it have time for a trial "in the foreseeable months ahead." The court then held Mr. Tobin in criminal contempt for refusing to proceed with the summary jury trial.

The district court postponed disposition of the criminal contempt judgment until April 6, 1987. On that date, the district court asked Mr. Tobin to reconsider his position on proceeding with the summary jury trial. Mr. Tobin reiterated his view that the court lacked the power to compel a summary jury trial, and maintained that such a proceeding would violate his client's rights. The district court entered a criminal contempt judgment of $500 against Mr. Tobin. Mr. Tobin filed a notice of appeal that same day.

II

The District Court Opinion

The district court filed a memorandum opinion setting forth its reasons for ordering a summary jury trial. *Strandell v. Jackson County*, 115 F.R.D. 333 (S.D. Ill. 1987). The district court noted that trial in this case was expected to last five to six weeks, and that the parties were "poles apart in terms of settlement." It further noted that summary jury trials had been used with great success in such situations.

In determining that it had the power to compel a summary jury trial, the court relied on a resolution adopted in 1984 by the Judicial Conference of the United States. The original draft of the resolution endorsed summary jury trials "with the voluntary consent of the parties." *Id.* at 335 (quoting *Report of the Judicial Conference Committee on the Operation of the Jury System Agenda* G-13, at 4 (Sept. 1984)). The final draft of the resolution, however, omitted this phrase. *Id.* (quoting *Report of the Proceedings of the Judicial Conference of the United States*, at 88 (Sept.1984)).

The court then determined that Rule 16 of the Federal Rules of Civil Procedure permits a mandatory summary jury trial. The court pointed out that Rule 16(a) authorizes a court in its discretion to require attorneys "to appear before it for a conference or conferences before trial for such purposes as (1) expediting the disposition of the action . . . and . . . (5) facilitating the settlement of the case." Furthermore, Rule 16(c) provides that "[t]he participants at any conference under this rule may consider and take action with respect to . . . (7) the possibility of settlement or the use of extrajudicial procedures to resolve the dispute . . . and . . . (11) such other matters as may aid in the disposition of the action." The court admitted that "its discretion in this context is not unbridled." However, the court held that Rule 16 grants district courts "the power to order the litigants to engage in a process which will enhance the possibility of fruitful negotiations."

* * *

III

Analysis

We begin by noting that we are presented with a narrow question: Whether a trial judge may *require* a litigant to participate in a summary jury trial to promote settlement of the case. We are *not* asked to determine the manner in which summary jury trials may be used with the consent of the parties. Nor are we asked to express a view on the effectiveness of this technique in settlement negotiations.

A.

In turning to the narrow question before us — the legality of *compelled* participation in a summary jury trial — we must also acknowledge, at the very onset, that a district court no doubt has substantial inherent power to control and to manage its docket. That power must, of course, be exercised in a manner that is in harmony with the Federal Rules of Civil Procedure. Those rules are the product of a careful process of study and reflection designed to take "due cognizance both of the need for expedition of cases and the protection of individual rights." * * *

In this case, the district court quite properly acknowledged, at least as a theoretical matter, this limitation on its power to devise a new method to encourage settlement. Consequently, the court turned to Rule 16 of the Federal Rules of Civil Procedure in search of authority for the use of a mandatory summary jury trial. In the district court's view, two subsections of Rule 16(c) authorized such a procedure. As amended in 1983, those subsections read:

The participants at any conference under this rule may consider and take action with respect to

. . . .

(7) the possibility of settlement or the use of extrajudicial procedures to resolve the dispute;

. . . .

(11) such other matters as may aid in the disposition of the action.

Fed. R. Civ. P. 16(c)(7), (11).

Here, we must respectfully disagree with the district court. We do not believe that these provisions can be read as authorizing a *mandatory* summary jury trial. In our view, while the pretrial conference of Rule 16 was intended to foster settlement through the use of extrajudicial procedures, it was not intended to require that an unwilling litigant be sidetracked from the normal course of litigation. The drafters of Rule 16 certainly intended to provide, in the pretrial conference, "a neutral forum" for discussing the matter of settlement. Fed. R. Civ. P. 16 advisory committee's note. However, it is also clear that they did not foresee that the conference would be used "to impose settlement negotiations on unwilling litigants&hellip ." *Id.*; *see also* 6 C. WRIGHT, A. MILLER & M. KANE, FEDERAL PRACTICE AND PROCEDURE § 1525 (Supp.1987) ("As the Advisory Committee Note indicates, this new subdivision does not force unwilling parties into settlement negotiations."). While the drafters intended that the trial judge "*explor[e]* the use of procedures other than litigation to resolve the dispute," — including "*urging* the litigants to employ adjudicatory techniques outside the courthouse,"they clearly did not intend to *require* the parties to take part in such activities. Fed. R. Civ. P. 16 advisory committee's note (emphasis supplied). As the Second Circuit, commenting on the 1983 version of Rule 16, wrote: "Rule 16 . . . was not designed as a means for clubbing the parties — or one of them — into an involuntary compromise." *Kothe v. Smith*, 771 F.2d 667, 669 (2d Cir. 1985).

* * *

The use of a mandatory summary jury trial as a pretrial settlement device would also affect seriously the well-established rules concerning discovery and work-product privilege. *See* Fed. R. Civ. P. 26(b)(3); *see also Hickman v. Taylor*, 329 U.S. 495, 67 S. Ct. 385, 91 L. Ed. 451 (1947). These rules reflect a carefully-crafted balance between the needs for pretrial disclosure and party confidentiality. Yet, a compelled summary jury trial could easily upset that balance by requiring disclosure of information obtainable, if at all, through the mandated discovery process. We do not believe it is reasonable to assume that the Supreme Court and the Congress would undertake, in such an oblique fashion, such a radical alteration of the considered judgments contained in Rule 26 and in the case law. If such radical surgery is to be performed, we can expect that the national rule-making process outlined in the Rules Enabling Act will undertake it in quite an explicit fashion.

B.

The district court, in explaining its decision to compel the use of the summary jury trial, noted that the Southern District of Illinois faces crushing caseloads. The court suggested that handling that caseload, including compliance with the Speedy Trial Act, required resort to such devices as compulsory summary jury trials. We certainly cannot take issue with the district court's conclusion that its caseload places great stress on its capacity to fulfill its responsibilities. However, a crowded docket does not permit the court to avoid the adjudication of cases properly within its congressionally-mandated jurisdiction. * * * As this court said in *Taylor v. Oxford*, 575 F.2d 152 (7th Cir. 1978): "Innovative experiments may be admirable, and considering the heavy case loads in the district courts, understandable, but experiments must stay within the limitations of the statute."

* * *

JUDGMENT OF CONTEMPT VACATED.

NOTES

1. Are you comfortable with the closed trial analysis of the *Cincinnati Gas & Elec. Co.* decision? Is it possible to consider the summary jury trial as something more than a settlement device? Does the participation by an Article III judge make a difference? Does the fact that juries, themselves constitutional bodies, participate in summary trial mean that the results of summary jury trial go beyond mere settlement? The claims in the *Cincinnati Gas & Elec. Co.* decision were settled for a significant amount — close to $80,000,000. Does that fact make the substance of the summary jury trial newsworthy and increase the need for an "open" process?

2. Courts possess the power to mandate that the parties participate in a pretrial conference settlement discussion. (*See, e.g., G. Heileman Brewing Co. v. Joseph Oat Corp.*, 871 F.2d 648 (7th Cir. 1989) (finding judicial power to require party attendance at a Rule 16 conference and affirming sanctions against corporate party that failed to send a principal to the conference).) From what source do courts derive such a coercive power? The *G. Heileman Brewing Co.* decision premised the court's authority upon the inherent powers of judges outside the text of specific procedural rules. In *Link v. Wabash R.R. Co.*, 370 U.S. 626 (1962), the Supreme Court found an " 'inherent power' governed not by rule or statute but by the control necessarily vested in courts to manage their own affairs so as to achieve the orderly and expeditious disposition of cases." (*Id.* at 630–631.) Why wasn't this inherent power present in *Strandell*? If the court has power to compel attendance to a pre-trial settlement conference, why can't it compel attendance at a summary jury trial? Is the answer in the potentially differing levels of participation and work involved in the two procedures? Consider the position of Professor Sherman, who contends that the *Strandell* plaintiffs' attorney "would certainly have been entitled . . . to hold back the work-product evidence for sole use at trial. Of course, that could mean that he would not do as well with the summary jury as he hoped he would do at trial. Since the summary jury trial is non-binding, all he risked was an adverse summary jury trial verdict that might conceivably weaken his bargaining position for settlement before trial." (Edward Sherman, *Court-Mandated Alternative Dispute Resolution: What Form of Participation Should Be Required?* 46 SMU L. REV. 2079, 2101–02 (1993).) For a case rejecting the *Strandell* position, see, for example, *Arabian American Oil Co. v. Scarfone*, 119 F.R.D. 448 (M.D. Fla. 1988). Under the Civil Justice Reform Act of 1990, the civil justice and delay reduction plans promulgated by the local district courts may now mandate that client representatives "with authority to bind them in settlement discussions" be available during a settlement conference. (*See* 28 U.S.C. § 473(b)(5).)

3. *Accuracy and Summary Jury Trials.* How well will the summary jury trial predict the outcome of the real jury trial? Is Judge Lambros convincing in his confidence that the SJT will generate a high level of prediction? Assume that a court limits summary jury trials to three hours in length and requires evidence to be in the form of attorney summations. Live presentations of proof by witnesses are prohibited. Is there an accuracy problem significant enough to inhibit the prediction yielded by the summary jury trial verdict? Consider these comments:

> The attorney summations of evidence . . . add an additional layer of distance from the actual events that are the object of factfinding. Moreover, attorney witness summations cannot resolve factual questions of veracity and credibility. . . . [T]he trier of fact has expertise in discerning witness credibility and veracity. A full trial achieves careful consideration of witness believability. These advantages of trial are absent from summary jury trial. [Edward Brunet, *Questioning the Quality of Alternative Dispute Resolution*, 62 TULANE L. REV. 1, 40 (1987).]

Is this view overly skeptical of the abilities of attorneys to accurately portray evidence? For a contrary view, see Edward F. Sherman, *Reshaping the Lawyers' Skills for Court-Supervised ADR*, 51 TEX. B.J. 47, 48–49 (1988) (attorneys are skilled in the "art of summarization [which] is the centerpiece of court-supervised ADR" and are constantly asked to summarize in closing argument, written narratives and many other phases of litigation).

Courts can and do employ procedures to improve the accuracy of attorney summations. Some judges enter orders refusing to admit into evidence at a trial following a summary jury trial any testimony inconsistent with that offered at a summary jury proceeding. Such a measure deters attorneys from "stretching" evidence in their summary jury trial presentations. A second measure used by some judges is to limit the use of summary jury trial to selected cases in which the court is familiar with and trusts the attorneys involved. In theory, attorneys who can be trusted will be accurate in their evidence summations. Is such an approach unfairly prejudiced in favor of local counsel and unfairly prejudiced against newer attorneys who have yet to make an impression on the court? Does the imposition of these measures demonstrate that judges themselves have concluded that summary jury trials need improvement to increase their reliability and accuracy? For discussion of the

predictive value of summary jury trial, see Lucille M. Ponte, *Putting Mandatory Summary Jury Trial Back on the Docket: Recommendations on the Exercise of Judicial Authority*, 63 FORDHAM L. REV. 1069, 1082–84 (1995).

Commentators have urged that summary jury trials would be more accurate
if multiple summary juries were empaneled, a summary jury trial of equal
size to the trial jury were used, and jurors were told of the non-binding nature
of their verdicts. (*See, e.g.,* Donna Shetowsky, *Improving Summary Jury
Trials: Insights From Psychology*, 18 OHIO ST. J. ON DISP. RES. 469 (2003).)

4. *Summary Jury Trial and Efficiency.* Advocates of summary jury trial
contend that use of the device saves the court trial time and saves the client
attorneys' fees. (*See* Thomas Lambros, *The Summary Jury Trial and Other
Alternative Methods of Dispute Resolution*, 103 F.R.D. 461 (1984); Thomas
Metzloff, *Reconfiguring the Summary Jury Trial*, 41 DUKE L.J. 806, 832–35
(1992) (study concludes that SJT cases resolved more quickly and with cost
savings).) Judge Posner has challenged this assumption. He contends that the
vaunted "80% settlement rate" (over 80% of cases put to summary trial are
not tried) may not be efficient. (*See* Richard Posner, *The Summary Jury Trial
and Other Methods of Alternative Dispute Resolution: Some Cautionary
Observations*, 53 U. CHI. L. REV. 366 (1986).) He observes that expenditures
spent on summary jury trial need to be compared to sums expended on
conventional case disposition. Because close to 95% of all cases settle without
trial, Posner questions if the money and time expended on summary jury trials
is efficient. The real question about the "80% success rate" is "compared to
what." We need more comparative data to be sure summary jury trials advance efficiency.

5. *Summary Jury Trial v. ENE and CAA.* Each of the above devices shares
the characteristic of providing a prediction as to how a case would be decided
after a trial. Are these devices duplicative? Should an ENE ever be conducted
on a case later slated for either summary jury trial or CAA? Try to compare
these devices and their strengths and weaknesses. Which works best to
provide an accurate prediction? Which costs the most to the court? Which costs
the most to the parties?

6. *Timing of the Summary Jury Trial.* When should the summary jury trial
be held? Should it be held at the end of the discovery process? Should the final
pre-trial conference precede or follow the summary jury trial? Judge Thomas
Lambros, a leading pioneer of the device, has asserted that the summary trial
should take place after "discovery has been substantially completed" and that
the decision to hold a summary trial "is normally made at the final pre-trial
conference." (Thomas Lambros, *The Summary Jury Trial — An Alternative
Method of Resolving Disputes*, 69 JUDICATURE 286, 287 (1986).) Judge Lambros believes that timing the pre-trial conference before the summary trial
affords the opportunity for planning "housekeeping details" relating to the
trial and setting restrictions on the presentation of evidence, including
motions *in limine.* (*Id. See* Lambros, 103 F.R.D. 461, *supra.*)

7. *Juror Management and the Summary Jury Trial.* Should jurors be told
that their verdict is non-binding and advisory only? As originally theorized,
the presiding trial judge keeps jurors partially in the dark on this question
in order to assure that jurors grapple equally hard with issues tried by

summary trials. Of course, some jurors may be offended by not learning that a particular verdict is non-binding. In addition, there is evidence that even mock juries "continue to take their advisory role quite seriously in rendering non-binding verdicts." (Ponte, *Putting Mandatory Summary Jury Trial Back on the Docket, supra,* at 1084.) Out of respect and reverence toward our jury system some courts now disclose fully to jurors the nonbinding nature of the summary jury process.

8. *Extent of Use.* A recent Federal Judicial Center study reports that over one-half of the federal districts have procedures allowing judges to conduct summary jury trials. While the summary trials are heavily used in selected cities, in most districts there may be only a few summary trials per year.

9. *Should Summary Jury Trial Use be Restricted to Big Cases?* Some think that the most efficient use of summary jury trial is in cases with large amounts in controversy, where the cost of trial is great and also where risks are similarly high. A carefully tried summary jury trial can be expensive, particularly the costs of integrating expert witnesses into the process. This expense is best made in high stakes cases, according to some commentators. (*See, e.g.,* Judge Harvey G. Brown, *Summary Jury Trial Part II: Perspectives of the Bench and Bar,* 38 HOUSTON LAWYER 16 (May/June 2001).)

F.   COURT-ANNEXED ARBITRATION: A CLOSER LOOK

The introduction of new programs mandating arbitration of civil cases has burgeoned in the last decade. These programs appear to be popular with both the parties and the courts in which court-annexed arbitration has been used. Yet, there has been only modest recent growth of courts adopting new arbitration programs. As you read the following excerpt, ask yourself whether use of court-annexed arbitration should increase, can be improved, or should be cut back.

LISA BERNSTEIN, UNDERSTANDING THE LIMITS OF COURT-CONNECTED ADR: A CRITIQUE OF FEDERAL COURT-ANNEXED ARBITRATION PROGRAMS, 141 U. Pa. L. Rev. 2169 (1993) *

The trend towards publicly sponsored or mandated ADR shows no signs of abating. One of the six "cornerstone principles" of the Civil Justice Reform Act of 1990 was "expanding and enhancing the use of alternative dispute resolution." The Act directed each federal district court to complete a cost and delay reduction plan and to specifically consider the possibility of instituting court-connected ADR programs. As of February 1992, thirty-two of the thirty-four federal courts that had completed these plans either endorsed or adopted some type of court-connected ADR. In addition, the Federal Courts Study Committee, which was created to "develop a long-range plan for . . . the Federal judiciary, including assessments involving . . . alternative methods of dispute resolution," recommended that Congress "broaden statutory authorization for local rules for alternative and supplementary procedures in civil litigation, including rules for cost and fee incentives."

Despite its widespread acceptance by lawmakers and most legal scholars, the effects of court-annexed arbitration programs on parties' litigation decisions have yet to be systematically examined. Furthermore, in their rush to adopt court-connected ADR programs, whose benefits were allegedly proven by the widespread use of private ADR, lawmakers have ignored a fundamental difference between the programs they laud and the legislation they have passed, namely that private ADR proceedings are conducted with the parties' consent, while participation in many public ADR processes is required by law.

*   *   *

I. THE BASIC FEATURES OF COURT-ANNEXED ARBITRATION PROGRAMS

The Judicial Improvements and Access to Justice Act[22] sets out the basic structure of federal CAA programs, but gives each district the authority to adopt local rules specifying important program features.

Suits for predominantly money damages that fall below a particular amount in controversy, which, depending on the district, ranges from $50,000 to $150,000 and do not involve federal constitutional claims or conspiracies to interfere with civil rights, must be submitted to non-binding arbitration before a trial can be requested. In some districts, the parties or the trial judge may make a motion to exempt the case from arbitration where "the objectives of arbitration would not be realized (1) because the case involves complex or novel legal issues, (2) because legal issues predominate over factual issues, or (3) for other good cause." In most districts the maximum amount in controversy is a jurisdictional limit, not a cap on the damages an arbitrator can award.

Hearings are conducted by either a single arbitrator or a panel of three arbitrators chosen from a volunteer pool of lawyers. Hearings take place 80 to 180 days after the filing of the answer and decisions are rendered shortly thereafter. In some districts, hearings are open to the public, in others, they are closed. The amount of pre-arbitration discovery permitted and the types of pre-trial motions decided prior to the hearing are governed by local rule, subject to certain constraints imposed by Congress.

At the arbitration hearing, the Federal Rules of Evidence do not apply. Arbitrators may permit the introduction of any credible non-privileged evidence, including hearsay. The arbitrators are not required to issue written or oral findings of fact or conclusions of law, and at least one district prohibits them from doing so. A few districts encourage live testimony, while others discourage it, providing by local rule that "the presentation of testimony shall be kept to a minimum, and that cases shall be presented to the arbitrators primarily through the statements and arguments of Counsel." One district bans live testimony altogether and requires that "[a]ll evidence shall be presented through counsel who may incorporate argument on such evidence in his or her presentation." Some programs limit the length of the hearing.

Good faith participation in the arbitration hearing is required of both the parties and their counsel. Most districts require parties to be present at the

---

[22] Pub. L. No. 100–702 . . . (codified as amended in scattered sections of 28 U.S.C.).

hearing, and some districts require the presence of a person with full settlement authority. Although the authority of the court to order a person with settlement authority to be present at an arbitration hearing has yet to be definitively established, an en banc panel of the Seventh Circuit has upheld a district judge's authority to order a person with full settlement authority to be present at a settlement conference.[44] In some districts, if either the nonattendance of a party or the preparation and presentation of counsel is deemed not to constitute "participation in a meaningful way" in the arbitration process, the court can impose monetary sanctions and/or strike a party's demand for a trial de novo ("trial"). The court's authority to strike a party's demand for a trial has been upheld by several district courts,[46] but has not yet been considered by any court of appeals.

After the arbitrator has rendered an award, which may, depending on the local rule, include costs, each party has thirty days to request a trial. When a party requests a trial, the case is restored to its original place on the docket and treated as if it had never been arbitrated; neither the record of the hearing, if made, nor the arbitrators' decision are admissible at trial. In the pilot districts, trial de novo request rates range from forty-six to seventy-four percent of arbitrated cases.

Some districts have disincentives to requesting a trial. Most districts require the party requesting a trial to post a bond with the court in the amount of the arbitrators' fees and costs which, depending on the district and the number of arbitrators, can range from $125 to $450 for the typical case. Although complex cases often cost substantially more to arbitrate, most districts put a cap on the amount of the bond a party can be required to post in order to obtain a trial. If the party requesting the trial improves his position at trial, this bond is returned to him; if he fails to do so, it is retained by the court.

In the past, some districts had a rule requiring the party requesting a trial to pay his opponent's post-arbitration attorneys' fees and/or costs if he failed to improve his position at trial. The authority of courts to enact such local rules absent congressional authorization was a question of some dispute. In 1988, Congress decided that pending further study by the Federal Courts Study Committee, such provisions should not be part of the pilot programs. However, in its 1990 report, the Committee recommended that Congress authorize the pilot districts to experiment with fee and cost-shifting provisions, common features of many state CAA programs.

If a trial is not requested within thirty days of the arbitration decision, the decision is entered as the judgment of the court and has the same force and effect as a trial judgment. It cannot, however, be appealed.

The pilot programs also permit litigants in any civil action or in any adversarial bankruptcy proceeding to voluntarily submit their case to arbitration. In some districts, when cases are submitted to the program with the parties' consent and a trial is requested, the court

---

[44] *See* G. Heileman Brewing Co. v. Joseph Oat Corp., 848 F.2d 1415 (7th Cir. 1988) (en banc); *see also* Lockhart v. Patel, 115 F.R.D. 44, 46, 47 (E.D. Ky. 1987). . . .

[46] *See, e.g.,* New England Merchants Nat'l Bank v. Hughes, 556 F. Supp. 712 (E.D. Pa. 1983). . . .

may assess costs . . . and reasonable attorney fees against the party demanding trial de novo if . . . such party fails to obtain a judgment, exclusive of interest and costs . . . which is substantially more favorable to such party than the arbitration award, and . . . the court determines that the party's conduct in seeking a trial de novo was in bad faith.[62]

Although all districts permit parties to voluntarily submit disputes to arbitration either for free or at a minimal cost, litigants rarely choose this option. In Michigan, where CAA has been available since 1978 and cases submitted to the program by consent are subject to a post-arbitration fee and cost-shifting rule, only two cases have been submitted to the program by consent. In the Northern District of California where voluntary CAA has also been available since 1978, but cases submitted to the program by consent are not subject to a post-arbitration fee and cost-shifting rule, voluntary participation in the CAA program is also rare.

*   *   *

A primary goal of CAA programs is to reduce the private and social cost of disputing. However, a review of the empirical literature on federal CAA programs . . . suggests that there is no conclusive evidence that CAA programs reduce either the private or social cost of disputing.

One measure of social cost is the per-case processing cost. A recent study of the North Carolina CAA program found that "the average cost to the court of each closed . . . [arbitration track] case was $1209 and the average cost to the court of each closed control group case was $1240," but cautioned that "[t]he difference in cost was not statistically significant." One district discontinued its program "due to disproportionately high administrative costs . . . 14% of the district's administrative resources were devoted to handling arbitration cases, which represented only 7.2% of its civil caseload."

Even if CAA programs had no effect on the per-case processing cost, they might produce aggregate social cost savings if they reduced the trial rate. There is no conclusive evidence, however, that the programs have reduced the trial rate, and because so few of the cases subject to the programs would have gone to trial in a trial-only jurisdiction, it would take many years of data to reliably detect changes in the trial rate.

There is some evidence that the programs may slightly reduce the private costs of disputing, but the reductions reported are small, the studies are inconclusive, and the results may be marred by serious response bias. Furthermore, studies that found some reduction in the private cost of disputing to the plaintiff did not observe any changes in the contingent fee percentages charged by plaintiff's lawyers. This suggests that in the tort context CAA programs may benefit plaintiff's lawyers, but not plaintiffs themselves.

*   *   *

Another goal of CAA programs is to reduce delay. A Federal Judicial Center study of the time from filing to disposition concluded that "speedier dispositions are not an automatic benefit of arbitration programs," and a RAND study

---

[62] [28 U.S.C.] § 655(e).

found no statistically significant difference in disposition times. Nevertheless, even if the programs did succeed in reducing average case processing times, as long as the arbitration award is non-binding, the party with the superior ability to bear the costs of delay can still threaten to request a trial. Delay is just another cost of litigation. Although CAA proponents would view any reduction in disposition time as evidence of a program's success, regardless of the average disposition time, the parties' relative ability to bear delay will continue to be reflected in the settlement range at each stage of the litigation process and delay will continue to affect access to justice. CAA programs that do not have strong disincentives to requesting a trial do not reduce either the potential litigation costs or the amount of delay that the parties can threaten to inflict on each other, and may well increase such costs particularly when a trial is demanded. Because it is the specter of these enormous potential costs (rather than whether or not they are actually incurred) that has the effect of limiting access to the justice system, innovations that leave potential costs either unchanged and/or add additional levels of costly procedure cannot increase access to justice-particularly for those of limited means.

*   *   *

Although a CAA hearing is likely to be less expensive than a trial on the merits, the hearing may nonetheless impose substantial costs on the parties. Because these costs do not, for the most part, vary greatly with claim size, they impose a greater burden on plaintiffs with small claims-the very litigants the programs are designed to help.

*   *   *

Reducing the cost of civil discovery is a central goal of all CAA programs. However, CAA programs, particularly those with post-arbitration fee and cost-shifting provisions, may increase the cost of discovery while reducing the amount of material information exchanged.

*   *   *

Most CAA programs attempt to reduce the cost of discovery by imposing strict time limits; some districts allow only ninety days for the completion of the discovery process. Discovery time limits create an incentive for lawyers to make broader initial discovery requests than they would in a TOJ.* Lawyers fear that if they later need additional information, they may not be able to obtain it since the discovery period will have elapsed. These broader requests are likely to increase response costs and may not reveal much material information. The shortened discovery period may result in fewer rounds of discovery requests, which will limit the opportunity for parties to use the information learned from earlier requests to shape subsequent requests. The programs may therefore increase the amount and cost of discovery, decrease the amount of material information revealed, and increase a party's ability to hide adverse information. In addition, the programs may

---

* [Eds. "TOJ" is the acronym for a trial only jurisdiction that does not offer CAA.]

increase the benefit of withholding information during pre-arbitration discovery since the information will never be revealed if the arbitration award is accepted.

Although there are no studies comparing the amount and cost of discovery in TOJ and CAA jurisdictions, a recent study of the North Carolina CAA program, which gives the parties ninety days to complete pre-arbitration discovery, rarely permits extensions, and does not permit any post-arbitration discovery, suggests that time limits may increase both the private and social costs of discovery. The study, which compared cases randomly assigned to either a CAA or a trial-only track, found that more discovery motions were filed in cases assigned to the arbitration track. Lawyers attributed the increase to the fact that the shortened discovery process gave them less time to reach an accommodation with opposing counsel.

* * *

The asymmetric benefits of delay are one of the main reasons that parties might not enter into an agreement to resolve their dispute through private ADR even when doing so would create private benefits. However, this does not provide a strong justification for mandatory non-binding CAA programs. As long as the arbitration award is non-binding, the party better able to bear the costs of delay can still exploit his advantage by requesting a trial. Post-arbitration fee and cost-shifting provisions do not strongly constrain a party's ability to inflict delay on his opponent relative to a TOJ. Although such provisions may, in fact, slightly improve the disadvantaged party's bargaining position, the party better able to bear the cost of delay can adjust his presentation at the arbitration hearing to minimize the probability that he will suffer a post-arbitration fee and cost-shifting sanction. A party's ability to manipulate the amount of the arbitration award in this manner is subject only to the weak constraints of the programs' "meaningful participation" requirement and the applicable state code of legal ethics. Thus, the programs will not only fail to prevent a party from taking advantage of his opponent's inability to bear the costs of delay, but will also create incentives for parties to present different information at the arbitration hearing than they would at trial.

The incentives for strategic behavior created by the programs suggest that, given the many reasons for the parties to manipulate the evidence presented at the arbitration hearing, the hearings are unlikely to give the parties reliable information that they would not have obtained through pre-trial discovery. Furthermore, the signal generated by the arbitration award, even assuming that it was a perfect reflection of the information presented at the hearing, may be a poor predictor of the trial outcome. Thus, CAA programs will not meaningfully prevent parties who enjoy strategic advantages in a TOJ from exploiting them in a CAA jurisdiction. As long as the arbitration award is non-binding, even programs with disincentives to requesting a trial will do little to remedy the problems created by parties' unequal bargaining power and the high litigation costs and long delays in the federal courts.

*   *   *

NOTES

1. Does Professor Bernstein make a persuasive case for questioning the implementation of court-annexed arbitration programs? How big a factor is her contention that court-annexed arbitration can harm plaintiffs with small stakes? Are there costs related to her point that discovery in court-annexed arbitration is likely to be intensive during the relatively short period for discovery? Will intensive and early discovery have a greater impact on small stakes cases? Does this effect harm plaintiffs with small stakes more than defendants? How does the contingent fee effect this analysis? In some states (e.g., Oregon, Washington) CAA is mandatory only in smaller cases (mandatory CAA for all cases under $50,000 in value). Does it make sense to go "small" when making CAA mandatory? Some plaintiff attorneys argue that they (or their clients in a non-contingent fee case) have only so much money they can spend on a trial and if CAA is mandatory the arbitration becomes the only "trial event" they can afford. Does this argument cut against CAA? Is CAA an adequate, quality substitute for a trial before a judge?

2. *Decisional Accuracy and CAA.* Should we be concerned about whether mandatory court-annexed arbitration achieves a comparable level of decisional accuracy when compared to litigation? In some CAA programs, attorneys face severe time limits for their case presentations. In addition, evidence is often truncated and attorney summaries of evidence may have to suffice instead of normal trial evidence. Some courts have local rules that restrict CAA proof to attorney summations and argument. Cross examination is sometimes disallowed in CAA. Are these features of CAA desirable? Why are they necessary? How can an arbitrator properly assess witness credibility issues if the evidence is submitted in summary form or through attorney summations? Won't the arbitration result be necessarily based upon potentially inaccurate evidentiary input and be flawed? Consider the comments of a respected Federal Judge about court-annexed arbitration:

> The evidence presented at a real trial is all-important. Any experienced judge will tell you that it is the proof and the evidence that determines the outcome of over 95 percent of the cases and not the eloquence or histrionic talents of the lawyers. And the procedures, rules, and the evidentiary safeguards incident to true trials ensure a high degree of reliability with respect to the results obtained. Not so with ADRs. They operate in a different atmosphere where fault, guilt or innocence, right or wrong are not central to the process; where one-tenth of a loaf is better than none; where the debating skills of attorneys — and not their real truth revealing, fact-establishing trial skills — are glorified; where the evidence is de-emphasized; where every claim is assumed to have some value; where true justice is considered too expensive or an unattainable abstraction. [G. Thomas Eisele, *The Case Against Mandatory Court-Annexed ADR Programs*, 75 JUDICATURE 34, 36 (June 1991).]

Should a system of CAA be fashioned using a conventional trial before the court-annexed arbitrator? Such a system is used in some state court CAA procedures.

3. *Litigant Satisfaction and CAA.* Most surveys of court-annexed arbitration indicate a high level of party satisfaction. (*See, e.g.,* Barbara Meierhoefer, *Federal Judicial Center, Court-Annexed Arbitration in Ten District Courts* (1990) (study polled lawyers, attorneys and judges and concluded that CAA not a form of second class justice).) A Rand survey found parties as happy with court-annexed arbitration as with conventional trials but concluded that the parties ranked these two trial type processes significantly higher than judicial settlement conferences. (*See* E. LIND, R. MACCOUN, P. EBENER, W. FELSTINER, D. HENSLER, J. RESNIK & T. TYLER, THE PERCEPTION OF JUSTICE: TORT LITIGANTS' VIEWS OF TRIAL, COURT-ANNEXED ARBITRATION, AND JUDICIAL SETTLEMENT CONFERENCES (1989).) Can you guess why? Litigants value their dignity in the form of being permitted a chance to be heard personally and to present their side of the case to an authoritative figure such as a judge or an arbitrator. In the court-annexed arbitrations held in Pittsburgh, courtrooms are sometimes used for the hearings and arbitrators wear black robes. Why are these measures taken? Should they become routine in the provision of CAA? Professor Bernstein has challenged the research methodology used to assess litigant satisfaction of CAA. She reasons that "Client satisfaction surveys . . . may be misleading, since the typical tort plaintiff is a one time player who has little or no ability to value a legal claim . . . [and] client satisfaction is generally surveyed soon after the award is made, which may simply reflect the average personal injury tort plaintiff's need for cash or exuberance at having 'won.'" (Lisa Bernstein, *supra*, 141 U. PA. L. REV. at 2196 n. 112.)

4. *Interchangeable "Judges."* To what extent are judges and arbitrators interchangeable? Does a litigant have a right to a trial before a federal Article III judge or a state elected or appointed judge? CAA is built upon a premise that the trial event is all that is owed a litigant and that the identity of the adjudicative figure (the judge or arbitrator) is immaterial. Is this premise desirable or valid? Should judges have a primary role of trying cases and a secondary role of "managing" disputes? Some contend that the adoption of widespread CAA programs puts judges more in the position of managing adjudication than trying cases. Consider the comments of Judge Eisele: "I view the Article III federal district court as something very special — the place where real trials are conducted, the truth determined, rights vindicated, and justice obtained." (Eisele, *supra*, at 35.) Will the arbitrator at a CAA be able to deliver these very desirable qualities to the parties?

5. Does CAA raise Seventh Amendment concerns? According to one federal judge, mandatory arbitration of cases in which a jury is demanded effectively amends the Seventh Amendment to add this language following the preservation of trial by jury: ". . . but for little folks, it [right to jury trial] shall be preserved only after they have incurred the cost of an administrative procedure." (William Wilson, *The Arguments for and Against Mandatory Arbitration*, 7 FED. JUD. CENTER DIRECTIONS 14, 15 (Dec. 1994). *Accord*, Eisele, *supra*, at 40 (CAA "may delay the trial and . . . may laden it down with extra, unnecessary costs . . . [and] put the right to jury trial "before a judge . . . at great risk").) There is no question that cases subjected to CAA are less likely to ever reach a civil jury. Judge Wilson sees CAA as part of a process in which "Article III judges become administrators rather than judges" and argues that because "trial by jury is the quintessential example of government reposed in the people . . . this venerable institution should not be cast away lightly." (Wilson, *supra*, at 15.) Judge Wilson's arguments raise significant concerns. Yet, isn't it true that numerous other procedures also make it more difficult to empanel a jury? Under Judge Wilson's analysis are settlement conferences conducted under Rule 16 a violation of the Seventh Amendment?

6. *"Michigan Mediation."* State and federal courts in Michigan use a process they call mediation that more closely resembles CAA. Three neutral lawyers are assigned to assess and evaluate the settlement value of cases ready for trial. They hear abbreviated evidence and try to get the parties to settle. If the parties are unable to reach a settlement, they may accept the panel's suggested settlement or, alternatively, select a full trial *de novo*. There is a trial disincentive feature to Michigan Mediation — the losing party who receives a trial *de novo* must improve its position by at least 10% or be liable for costs.

SILLIPHANT v. CITY OF BEVERLY HILLS
195 Cal. App. 3d 1229, 241 Cal. Rptr. 356 (1987)

BOREN, Associate Justice.

May a trial court effectively dismiss a lawsuit with prejudice for failure to participate in arbitration if the dismissal was preceded by repeated and unjustified attempts to delay and frustrate the judicial process? We conclude that the answer is yes and hold that the trial court's action in this case was proper. Because the trial court's decision was based upon appellant's failure to participate in the arbitration, as well as her continual dilatory tactics, it is clearly distinguishable from the Supreme Court's decision in *Lyons v. Wickhorst* (1986) 42 Cal. 3d 911, 231 Cal. Rptr. 738, 727 P.2d 1019. Accordingly, we uphold the trial court's exercise of its discretion and affirm.

FACTS

Appellant's case began with a parking ticket issued by Beverly Hills Police Officer Harold Moody on December 12, 1983. Appellant claims that what started as a simple misunderstanding escalated into a violent confrontation marked by excessive physical contact by Officer Moody, verbal harassment, and her unwarranted arrest. The incident culminated in an alleged strip search of appellant at the Beverly Hills jail. Appellant sued Officer Moody and the City of Beverly Hills for assault and battery, intentional infliction of emotional distress, false arrest and the violation of her civil rights.

* * *

[The plaintiff-appellant obtained an extension of time to answer interrogatories but failed to answer by the designated date. She was granted additional time to answer the interrogatories, and failed to answer by the new date. The court denied a motion to dismiss the case for failure to comply with discovery and set yet another date for plaintiff to answer defendants' interrogatories. Following a raucous attempt to depose plaintiff, the court assigned costs of $1,200 against plaintiff's counsel for "interrupting and interfering with . . . [her] deposition." Plaintiff's attorney then refused defendant's request to reschedule a court mandated arbitration hearing. Only defendants' counsel and a witness showed up at the arbitration hearing. The arbitrator delayed the start of the hearing and telephoned plaintiff's attorney, who "became rude and offensive and began cursing." The arbitrator then entered an award for the defendants. On the next day the plaintiff requested a trial *de novo*. The defense responded by moving to dismiss the case and to strike the trial *de novo* demand. The trial court granted the latter motion.]

DISCUSSION

We observe preliminarily that the trial court did not, strictly speaking, dismiss the case. Rather, it granted respondents' motion to strike appellant's request for trial de novo following the arbitrator's award in respondents' favor. The result was, however, the same as a dismissal because the court effectively ended appellant's lawsuit without a determination on the merits.

Appellant's underlying contentions, that she was misled by respondents and lulled into thinking the arbitration hearing would be continued and that she was entitled to a trial de novo as a matter of law, are without merit. After entry of an arbitration award, "[a]ny party may elect to have a de novo trial, by court or jury, both as to law and facts . . ." (Code Civ. Proc., § 1141.20, subd. (b)), provided the right is timely exercised. Nonetheless, "[i]t cannot be said that there is an absolute right to a de novo trial."

The principal case affecting our determination is *Lyons v. Wickhorst*, 42 Cal. 3d 911, 231 Cal. Rptr. 738, 727 P.2d 1019, and we conclude that it is factually distinguishable. In that case, the trial court dismissed the action solely on the basis of appellant's nonparticipation in the compulsory arbitration proceedings. The court in *Lyons* held that "An immediate and unconditional dismissal entered at the first suggestion of noncooperation [by a refusal to participate or present evidence at the arbitration hearing] is too drastic a remedy in light of the fact that arbitration was not intended to supplant traditional trial proceedings, but to expedite the resolution of small civil claims." The court noted that the "Legislature chose not to provide for dismissal as a sanction if a party refuses to participate [in the arbitration process]." Nonetheless, even without any express legislative authorization, "a trial court may, under certain circumstances, invoke its limited inherent discretionary power to dismiss claims with prejudice. [Citation.]" (*Id.* at p. 915.) Our state courts have upheld the imposition of the drastic sanction of dismissal for a party's evasive, obstructive or dilatory tactics in responding to civil discovery requirements.

The dismissal of the action in *Lyons* was also "without notice and without an opportunity to be heard." The lack of relevant statutes and case law at the time of the denial of the request for a trial de novo in Lyons also reflected a "lack of substantive guidelines . . . [by which the party's] conduct was to be judged."

In contrast to *Lyons*, the present case involves more than "the first suggestion of noncooperation" by the failure of appellant or her counsel to appear at the scheduled arbitration hearing. Regarding the taking of appellant's deposition, the court found "wilful conduct on the part of . . . [appellant's] counsel in interrupting and interfering with the deposition," such as to warrant a protective order, the supervision of the deposition by a referee and the imposition of costs, expenses and attorney's fees. Regarding respondents' difficulties in obtaining answers by appellant to interrogatories, the court found that appellant's failure to comply with a prior order was "wilful and without substantial justification" and required a further court order for compliance.

The day before the date scheduled for the arbitration hearing, appellant's counsel telephoned the arbitrator's receptionist but made no request for a continuance. Nor did appellant's counsel make such a request during his offensive telephone conversation with the arbitrator when he failed to appear for the hearing. His assertion that he believed the matter had been continued to some unspecified time at the end of November 1985 — because of an October 23 telephone communication between the secretaries for opposing counsel — is untenable because such a belief was never conveyed to respondents nor to the arbitrator. On the contrary, the only statement made to respondents regarding a continuance was that he was not willing to continue the arbitration matter.

Accordingly, the failure of appellant or her counsel to appear at the arbitration hearing was merely the culmination of a series of events demonstrating the dilatory or disobedient conduct of counsel. A "pattern of conduct . . . so 'severe [and] deliberate' as to constitute extreme circumstances" had been established, and "alternatives less severe than dismissal" had already been used and were thus not available to vindicate the court's authority.

Moreover, unlike the situation in *Lyons*, appellant had notice and an opportunity to be heard prior to the termination of her action and again when her motion to reconsider was heard and denied. Also unlike *Lyons*, appellant's counsel should have been aware of case law establishing dismissal as a proper sanction in appropriate circumstances for failure to comply with a court-ordered arbitration proceeding.

* * *

The judgment is affirmed.

NOTES

1. Assume that plaintiff Tiana Silliphant had selected a well-mannered attorney who answered the interrogatories in a timely fashion, behaved at her deposition, and was polite when talking to the arbitrator on the telephone. Assume, however, that her attorney attended the arbitration but did not present any evidence. Can the court refuse a trial *de novo*? Would your answer be different if the new counsel for Tiana Silliphant presented only an abbreviated case, say, with Tiana as the only witness?

2. Has the arbitration hearing itself become the primary trial event when a trial court refuses a trial *de novo* following a party's failure to participate in a court mandated arbitration hearing? Court-annexed arbitration was designed to "predict" outcome of trial. If *Silliphant* is the typical holding, haven't we shifted the purpose of court-annexed arbitration to one of a substitute for conventional trial?

G. PRIVATE JUDGING

Numerous states have legislation permitting disputants to have their case decided by a privately hired judge. (*See, e.g.*, CAL. CONST. ART. VI, § 21 (1952 & Supp. 1996); CAL. CIV. PROC. CODE §§ 638-645 (1976 & Supp. 1996); N.H. REV. STAT. ANN. § 519:9 (1974 & Supp. 1995); N.Y. CIV. PRC. L. & R. 4301–21 (1992); WASH. REV. CODE ANN. §§ 4.48.010 *et seq.* (1988).) Private judging represents a process imbued with free market characteristics. Adversaries can opt out of the wait for trial before a government supplied judge and, instead, contract with a retired judge for quick case resolution. Disputants can select among numerous potential private judges for the optimal choice. In a sense, private judges compete for work, primarily by the procedural and substantive manner in which they decide prior controversies.

The act of hiring a private judge will not necessarily mean that the trial itself will be brief. Indeed, a private judge may be willing to take lengthy testimony. A trial before a private judge can last weeks or months. It will normally begin, however, well before a court trial could be scheduled, because of the queue of cases awaiting trial in public forums.

In some jurisdictions trials to a private or "rent-a-judge" can have a jury and may even be appealed. Few parties choose to appeal privately judged cases. "Finality . . . is still a very important consideration . . . [and] the [private] judicial selection process . . . guarantees a high degree of confidence in the judge selected for the case." (Lester Olson, *Pick Your Own Judge: An Insider's Look at the California Rent-a-Judge System*, COMPLEAT LAWYER, 38, 40 (Winter 1987).) The strong drive for a certain and expert decision has also dissuaded the parties from selecting juries in most privately judged cases.

Private judging began as a reaction to the long queue of cases awaiting trial, particularly in California. The queue itself may reflect an attitude of a state reluctant to invest in additional judges or to increase court spending to eliminate the queue. As a philosophical matter, the growth of rent-a-judge mirrors a belief that the private provision of justice can be as or more effective than that supplied by the state. As you read the following, ask yourself if society would be well served by increasing the availability of private judging.

ANNE S. KIM, RENT-A-JUDGES AND THE COST OF SELLING JUSTICE, 44 Duke L.J. 166 (1994) *

In some ways, the rent-a-judge system seems to be an ideal hybrid of public and private justice. It offers the speed, efficiency, and convenience of arbitration and mediation along with an enforceable, appealable state court judgment. Although individual litigants have undoubtedly benefitted from rent-a-judges, the public interest has not. Unanswered are many troubling questions about the permissible scope of a rent-a-judge's authority and the role rent-a-judges should play in the state judicial system. Also troubling are the effects that rent-a-judges have on the public courts and their potential for eroding the courts' authority. Ultimately . . . the rent-a-judge system puts too much public power into private hands.

* * *

The primary purpose of a judicial system, whether public or private, is to settle disputes. The byproduct of that function is rulemaking. In private justice, rulemaking is of little concern; litigants pay arbitrators and mediators to resolve only the dispute at hand. Moreover, citizens do not look to arbitrators and mediators to formulate rules for society. In the public courts, however, rulemaking takes on far greater importance. Public courts play a pivotal role in society: "Their job is not to maximize the ends of private parties, nor simply to secure the peace, but to explicate and give force to the values embodied in authoritative texts such as the Constitution and statutes: to interpret those values and to bring reality into accord with them." The public courts, when they speak, speak not only for the government but for society. Thus, their decisions carry far greater social weight than the decisions of private tribunals.

The rent-a-judge system, however, blurs and devalues this distinction between public and private tribunals. Although they are nominally members of the state judiciary, rent-a-judges are chosen by the litigants, and they offer individualized, private justice, much like arbitrators and mediators. Consequently, their decisions carry less force and legitimacy in the eyes of the public than those of wholly public courts. * * *

Rent-a-judges, however, are chosen by private agreement, and the market is the only external check upon their behavior. The system itself imposes no quality control over the judges; consent of the litigants is the only requirement for the appointment of a rent-a-judge. California's general reference statutes state no qualifications that rent-a-judges must meet. Unlike their public court counterparts, rent-a-judges do not pass through the screening process of public election or governmental appointment. Moreover, there is no disciplining body for rent-a-judges, and unlike other public court judges, rent-a-judges apparently cannot be impeached or recalled. Thus, despite their public role, rent-a-judges are not publicly accountable. Although rent-a-judges nominally enjoy the authority of the state, this authority is undermined by the lack of a public mandate. Because rent-a-judges do not have the same institutional backing as their public court brethren, their judgments lack the public weight and authority of other state court rulings.

The element of choice also diminishes the authority of rent-a-judge judgments. The rent-a-judge system creates a buyer's market that the litigants control, and the judges must tailor their reputations and their decisionmaking to attract customers. * * * [S]ome California rent-a-judges have even toned down their personalities to make themselves more marketable. The rent-a-judge system upends the usual balance of power between judges and litigants. Moreover, the power of choice vested in litigants diminishes the threat of state authority, which is a chief source of power for the courts: "Among other things, government sanction implies the direct threat of compulsion by the state (and gives judgments) a degree of clarity and forcefulness." The ability to choose a judge, however, enables litigants to shape the ultimate judgment. And where the ultimate goal is customer satisfaction, rent-a-judges are also likely to de-emphasize their coercive powers as agents of the state. Thus by empowering litigants, the rent-a-judge system weakens the judiciary.

* * *

[R]ulemaking is a crucial function of the public courts. It is a function, however, that rent-a-judges cannot adequately perform. A rent-a-judge's public-private split personality is again the source of problems. As members of the public court system, rent-a-judges would best serve society by pronouncing broad rules of wide applicability. As privately hired dispute resolution experts, however, rent-a-judges are more likely to decide cases on very narrow grounds. As Judge Posner and Professor Landes note,

> [A] system of voluntary adjudication (such as rent-a-judge) is strongly biased against the creation of precise rules of any sort. Any rule that clearly indicates how a judge is likely to decide a case will assure that no disputes subject to the rule are submitted to that judge since one party will know that it will lose. Judges will tend to promulgate vague standards which give each party to a dispute a fighting chance.[181]

Thus, when shopping for a judge, litigants look for someone who is likely both to rule in their favor and to meet the approval of the opposing party. The ultimate choice will be a judge with a reputation for being impartial, though "impartial" is more likely to mean "accommodating." Rent-a-judges must avoid creating a coherent set of precedents; predictability could destroy a rent-a-judge's appeal to potential customers. In fact, the market provides great incentive for rent-a-judges to be deliberately inconsistent in their rulings. This behavior by rent-a-judges is destructive in several ways. The body of law thus created is nothing more than a confusing tangle of narrow and contradictory rules, many of which have little relevance to anyone beyond the immediate litigants. Even if the rules formulated by rent-a-judges are broad enough to be useful to society at large, they are not always likely to reflect the interests of the public. After all, the public is not a paying customer.

---

[181] Landes & Posner, *Adjudication as a Public Good*, 8 J. LEGAL STUD. 235, 239–40.

*   *   *

A rent-a-judge's dual, public-private nature also raises questions about the permissible depth and breadth of a rent-a-judge's decisionmaking authority. Rent-a-judges are chosen by private parties and are not accountable to the public. It is therefore troubling that they should have the authority to impose their rulings upon the whole of society. Rent-a-judges could conceivably address issues involving important civil liberties, such as gun control, school prayer, or abortion. California statutes allow rent-a-judges to hear any dispute if the parties consent. Moreover, rent-a-judge judgments are treated exactly the same as other state court judgments and thus presumably have the same effects of collateral estoppel and *res judicata*.

*   *   *

NOTES

1. Is the Kim excerpt too harsh on private judging or does it raise jurisprudential concerns that must be answered? Will the problems identified by Kim occur if only a modest number of cases are tried by private judges? It is clear that the greatest use of private judges exists not to try entire cases but, instead, to preside over discovery disputes. (Kim, *supra* at 178–179.) In 1989, private judges tried about 20,000 of the approximately 650,000 suits heard in California's state courts. (*A Taxonomy of Judicial ADR*, 9 ALTERNATIVES TO HIGH COSTS LITIG. 97, 110 (1991).) Most of these were either divorce or complex business disputes. (*See* Gail Cox, *The Best Judges Money Can Buy*, NAT'L L.J., Dec. 21, 1987 at 1.) Aren't the problems of erosion of the rule of law or the lack of public accountability of private judges, matters that could be significant social problems only if the popularity of rent-a-judge grows significantly?

2. *The Price of (Private) Justice.* The clients who use rent-a-judge seem to be satisfied customers. They receive a prompt rather than a delayed decision, an expert result, and often get the very judge they sought. Unlike mandatory CAA or ENE programs, private judging is not coercive and occurs purely at the option of the parties. These factors contribute to the positive reputation of rent-a-judge in the client community of users. Yet, what is the reaction of those unable to use the private judges? For those who cannot afford the rates, which are often $400–500 per hour, a long, multi-year wait for trial is the result. Some contend that their wait amounts to the creation of a two-track system of justice with "market cases" getting high priority and careful, prompt treatment and "public court" cases receiving second-class case administration. (*See generally*, Note, *The California Rent-a-Judge Experiment: Constitutional and Policy Considerations of Pay-As-You-Go Courts*, 94 HARV. L. REV. 1592 (1981).)

The $400–500 per hour rates changed by some private judges have, as expected, caused market forces to react. The *L.A. Times* reports that some ADR neutrals who are not former judges are now marketing their $250 per hour billing rates as below market rates. In turn, retired judges who work as private neutrals appear to be able to obtain more than enough work. JAMS, the largest provider of private judging by former judges, now has offices in over 20 cities and lists over 130 former judges as providers. (*See* Kenneth Reich, *An Equal Chance: Price of Success for Private Judging*, Los Angeles Times, Nov. 26, 1998, p. B8.) Many other retired judges market their ADR skills, which include traditional mediation and arbitration as well as private judging pursuant to a statutory reference to a retired judge, individually or in organizations with fewer providers.

JAMS now handles an average of about 10,000 cases per year. Theses cases are mediated and arbitrated, as well as adjudicated under private judging legislation. JAMS reports that the number of claims resolved recently rose to 30,000 due to the administration of class action suits. (*See* www.jamsadr.com/images/PDF/corporate_fact_sheet.pdf.)

3. *Public Access Issues.* Private adjudications are typically held in private. "At least one prominent lawyer has described private judging as 'secret judging for the privileged few.'" (Helen I. Bender & Richard Chernick, *Renting the Judge*, 21 LITIGATION 33 (Fall 1994).) Those desiring privacy focus on the similarity between private judging and arbitration. Critics argue that full public access is required in such cases because the dispute has been filed originally in court and is being processed pursuant to a statutory scheme. Some assert a First Amendment right to examine governmental institutions such as private judging first hand. (*See* Perry L. Glantz, *Analysis of a First Amendment Challenge to Rent-a-Judge Proceedings*, 14 PEPP. L. REV. 989 (1987).) In California, rent-a-judge trials were often held in public courthouses. However, public and judicial (competitor?) criticism of this practice has led to the routine scheduling of rent-a-judge trials outside the courthouse. Major private ADR providers such as JAMS/Endispute now have their own private courtrooms or rent office or hotel suites. Should the public have the right to attend these trials? The California Judicial Council has adopted rules designed to open up the private judging process. Presiding judges may order that rent-a-judge trials are to take place "at a site easily accessible to the public and appropriate for seating those who have made known their plan to attend hearings." (Cal. R. Ct. 244(e).) However, these orders for public trials are discretionary and far from automatic.

4. *Competition Among Private Judges.* The numerous providers of private judging compete vigorously for business and engage in market-style advertising. After former California Supreme Court Justice Armand Arabian left his judicial office he joined AAA and urged potential users of his services to obtain "justice in the southland of Los Angeles" by dialing 213-ARABIAN. (*See* Margaret Jacobs, *Retired Judges Seize Rising Role in Settling Disputes in California*, WALL ST. J., July 26, 1996, p.A-1, col. 6.) Over 400 retired California judges now serve as suppliers of private judging. (*Id.*) Some judges work for AAA, others sign with JAMS/Endispute and others form competing organizations to seek work. California legal newspapers now routinely print the market oriented advertisements of rival suppliers of private judging.

Chapter 15

AGENCY-ANNEXED ADR

The development and increased use of alternatives to conventional trials in administrative agencies should come as no surprise. Agencies, like courts, need to avoid unnecessary trials and to reduce backlogs of adjudications. Agencies have a variety of adjudications — some are potentially short and simple (e.g., social security claims, veterans claims) and others quite complex (e.g., requests for rate increases before the Federal Energy Regulatory Commission). Agency use of ADR has run the gamut from the simple to the complex case. Agencies also use ADR outside the adjudicatory context. Interest in regulatory negotiation — the process of having the "disputants" jointly draft an agency regulation — has grown greatly in recent years as a way to avoid the sometimes long, drawn out process of promulgating and litigating new agency regulations. The success of regulatory negotiation has led to increased interest in using ADR outside the conventional adjudicatory dispute and opened the door to using mediation and other ADR processes in the lawmaking processes so critical to the modern administrative agency.

The use of ADR by federal agencies was aided by the passage of the Administrative Dispute Resolution Act of 1990 ("ADRA"), 5 U.S.C. §§ 571–583 (1994). This was the first federal legislation that set forth how federal agencies were to use alternatives to litigation. The statute mandated that every federal agency "adopt a policy that addresses the use of [ADR] and case management." (Pub. L. 101-552, 104 Stat. 2736.) The legislation required agencies to consider using ADR in various stages of agency business, including enforcement suits, adjudication, contract administration and rulemaking. The ADRA contained findings that agency use of ADR may achieve "more creative, efficient, and sensible outcomes" than litigation. (*Id.*) These findings, when combined with the restrictions on agency budgets that characterized the 1990s, have created an atmosphere in which the modern administrative agency is looking to alternative procedures in carrying out its mandate. The original ADRA was reauthorized and modified in October 1996 by the Administrative Dispute Resolution Act of 1996, Pub. L. No. 104-320 (H.R. 4194), 110 Stat. 3870 (1996).

A. REGULATORY NEGOTIATION

It is useful to start with regulatory negotiation or "reg-neg" because of its unique use outside the traditional adjudicatory context and the relatively easy acceptance of its use.

During the 1970s numerous agencies began to use the regulation as their primary law enforcement tool. Legislative style regulations were seen as more efficient than rules created through adjudication because of the ability of an agency regulation to affect a large class of regulated parties. In contrast, agency case adjudication usually has an impact only upon the parties to the case and, accordingly, requires a comparatively large expenditure of scarce agency law enforcement resources. Agencies perceived that they got more enforcement bang for their regulation buck. This cost saving nature of the regulatory process has made regulations especially important in the budget conscious 1990s, a period when numerous agencies faced huge budget cuts and even shutdown.

The shift by agencies to heavy reliance upon regulations as a means to carry out their statutory mandates has not been ignored by the regulated groups themselves. As regulators diverted their resources to promulgating broader and more onerous regulations, regulatees began to rigorously fight the historic notice and comment rulemaking process with ever increasing vigor. The result was, for some agencies, a regulatory process characterized by escalating contentiousness between the regulators and the regulated.

Traditional notice and comment rulemaking can last many years and require a great deal of effort. When large federal, state, and municipal agencies regulate particular areas, the decision-making process may be protracted and expensive. Administrative procedure statutes require the publication of proposed regulations, the holding of public hearings, and documented agency deliberations. Once this process is finished and a new regulation is issued, adversely affected parties frequently request judicial intervention. The resulting court proceedings may continue for several years. If agency reconsideration is ultimately directed, five or more years may elapse before a rule becomes final. When highly contentious issues are involved, the regulatory process is usually protracted. This almost always happens when controversial environmental changes are involved or visible zoning modifications are being considered.

As the process of promulgating new regulations became more expensive and drawn out, agencies began to consider alternative ways to more effectively carry out their statutory mandates. The "traditional model for rulemaking provides for little 'buy-in' from outside the agency; encourages adversarial, uncooperative behavior on the part of private industry. . . ; and routinely results in decisions leading to dissatisfaction among private parties, which frequently leads to protracted litigation." (Philip Harter, *The Adolescence of Administrative ADR*, 21 AD. LAW & REG. L. NEWS 2 (No. 3 1996).)

This reasoning led to the passage of the Negotiated Rulemaking Act of 1990, 5 U.S.C. §§ 561–70 (1994).[*] The Act was designed to create an alternative to permit negotiation on the content of a rule between the parties who are the most affected, including the regulated businesses and those who benefit from regulation. The fruits of the negotiation may produce a proposed rule that will negate the need for "expensive and time-consuming litigation" regarding the legality of the rule. (*See* Negotiated Rulemaking Act of 1990 (Congressional Findings).) The experience with regulatory negotiation has been positive enough that Vice-President Gore's National Performance Review recommended an increase in the use of negotiated rulemaking. President Clinton's Executive Order regarding Regulatory Planning and Review urges agencies to use negotiated rulemaking specifically and also advocates the use

---

[*] This legislation was reauthorized by the Administrative Dispute Resolution Act of 1996, *supra*.

of consensus as a means to develop agency rules. (Exec. Order No. 12,866, 50 Fed. Reg. 51,735 (1993).) The Negotiated Rulemaking Act was reauthorized as part of the Administrative Dispute Resolution Act of 1996 (*see* 5 U.S.C. § 561 *et. seq*).

Regulatory negotiation involves the implementation of the negotiation process prior to the normal time a rule is proposed in an effort to avoid subsequent administrative and judicial proceedings. Instead of merely publishing proposed regulations, agencies initially determine the interest groups most likely to be affected by the contemplated rule. Representatives of these different groups are then asked to participate in what has become known as a "regulation-negotiation proceeding" — a "reg-neg proceeding" for short. The agency jump starts the process by initiating the negotiated rulemaking process.

Despite the reg-neg characterization, most regulation-negotiation proceedings are really "regulation-negotiation-mediation" proceedings, due to the participation of neutral facilitators. Respected neutral experts are asked to solicit the participation of the relevant interest groups, ranging from business organizations and administrative officials to public interest spokespersons. The process can only function effectively if all interest groups are adequately represented. It is thus better to err on the side of inclusion, rather than exclusion.

Once the diverse participant groups are selected, neutral facilitators attempt to elicit the information they need to determine and define the issues that must be addressed. When technical scientific, environmental, and/or economic issues are involved, respected experts may be asked to provide their insights. The individuals selected must be viewed as unbiased and enjoy general acceptability among the different groups if their opinions are to be persuasive.

When substantial questions must be overcome, it is often beneficial to appoint subcommittees, made up of representatives from each group, that will focus on specific issues or groups of issues. These subgroups can try to agree upon the precise problems that must be addressed and then look for alternatives that might prove mutually acceptable. It is especially important for the participants to explore options that will minimize the adverse impact on any group. Even if the final terms are not considered perfect by any constituency, the fact that these provisions are generally acceptable to everyone may prove to be more important to the overall success of the reg-neg process.

The neutral facilitators function as mediators. They must ensure that each group's interests receive thoughtful consideration. This helps to generate mutual respect among the different participants, which is conducive to the development of amicable solutions. If diverse participants can be induced to appreciate the concerns of opposing parties, this can significantly reduce distrust and enhance the dispute resolution process. Use of the single-text approach, in which the neutral focuses upon a single jointly authored text drafted by consensus, can be especially beneficial during reg-neg discussions. The single-text minimizes problems that might have resulted from considering multiple texts drafted by diverse participants regarding contentious issues.

After the participants have had the opportunity to define the relevant issues and evaluate the options available to them, they must begin to look for common ground. Whenever possible, decisions should be made by consensus, rather than by majority vote. Even if most participants support a particular proposal, if a group is unalterably opposed to that suggestion, it may be able to prevent the adoption of that provision or delay effectuation of that term through protracted litigation. It thus behooves the parties to respect the rights and interests of all representative groups.

When mutually acceptable regulations can be drafted, these should be recommended to the governing agency for final approval. Even when no overall agreement can be achieved, the reg-neg process may narrow the pertinent issues and induce the different groups to agree upon numerous factual matters. If these ideas are carefully considered by the agency during the formal rule-making process, it would decrease the likelihood of a subsequent legal challenge by a party dissatisfied with the promulgated regulations. Furthermore, even if litigation were to occur, a prior narrowing of the factual and legal issues should make the resulting legal proceedings more efficient. Nonetheless, an agency rule promulgated through negotiated rulemaking "shall not be accorded any greater deference by a court than a rule which is the product of other rulemaking procedures." (5 U.S.C. § 570 (2000).)

Philip J. Harter, Negotiating Regulations: A Cure for Malaise, 71 Geo. L.J. 1, 66–82 (1982) [*]

The agency representative, like his private sector counterparts, should be a relatively senior official. He should have the ability to assess and predict the ultimate position of his constituent, the agency. Further, the representative should be part of the substantive division of the agency that is responsible for the development of the regulation so that he can make the requisite decisions. Because the goal of the negotiations is to produce an agreement that will form the basis of a regulation issued by the agency, it is important to involve the agency's lawyers in the process. Moreover, it is critical that any legal concerns be addressed early because negotiations could be thrown off stride or discarded altogether if such questions arose late in the process. The agency negotiators should be able to tap the agency resources, including any data the agency may have collected, agency experts, and relevant staff. Thus, the negotiating team should have sufficient stature to permit it to draw on the agency's resources and coordinate its various concerns as it would if the regulation were being developed by the agency's own staff.

Summary of Agency Participation

Negotiations among the parties, with or without the agency, can expose the true interests of the respective parties. Negotiations thus narrow the range of disagreement, identify the research that needs to be conducted, and explore novel approaches to fulfilling the regulatory mandate. If the private parties themselves can reach agreements on all or even some of these topics, the agency's work will be greatly streamlined. Even if the agency does not participate, it can facilitate the negotiations process by providing guidance on the limits of available options and by supplying data and information available to the agency that may be unavailable to the private parties.

It seems clear from the foregoing analysis, however, that to achieve the full benefits of regulatory negotiation, the agency should participate as a full party. Although care must be taken to avoid the problems attendant to that role, doing so will not be difficult. If the agency does not participate in the negotiations, the fruits of the process may be bland recommendations akin to those proffered by traditional advisory committees. That result, in turn, would only add another layer and more delay to the rulemaking process.

The parties are likely to view the entire negotiation process with healthy skepticism. For years rules have been developed through a quasi-adversarial process in which each party views the other as an untrustworthy opponent. Negotiations could be viewed as naive, futile effort to induce the lamb to lie down with the lion. The lamb is likely to believe that by negotiating it may give up power provided by another process. Therefore, it may be far more comfortable with the traditional process, in which it is protected by a shepherd. If the parties are to be willing to participate, they must be shown that it is in their interest to negotiate. In addition, it is rarely clear from the outset which interests should be represented and who the representatives should be. Thus, considerable effort must be expended to establish the negotiations if the entire process is to be successful.

Neutral Judgment

The first question is who should be responsible for empanelling the group. The parties frequently can agree among themselves who the major players are. One way of assembling the group, therefore, would be to have the parties agree upon the participants in a negotiating group. Someone, however, would have to initiate and administer even this relatively simple process. Moreover, if a regulation is to be negotiated someone would have to determine whether the significant parties in interest were actually represented.

A second approach, and one likely to be more common, would require some individual to conduct a discrete preliminary inquiry to discover who the interested parties are and whether sufficient common ground for reaching an agreement through negotiation exists. For example, the individual might contact the line officer in an agency and ask what interests would be affected by the subject matter of the regulation and which groups would be likely to participate in the rulemaking proceeding. In addition, he would inquire about the issues likely to be involved in the proceeding. The person conducting the inquiry would then contact the individuals and organizations on that list and inquire about their views as to what the interests are, what issues are likely to be raised, and who the players should be. He also would ask what issues would be inappropriate for negotiation and whether the organization believed it could work with other parties in reaching an agreement. Thus, through such multiple iterations, the parties and the issues could be defined, both inclusively and exclusively.

The obvious organization to conduct this inquiry, or on whose behalf the inquiry would be conducted, is the agency that ultimately will issue the regulation. The agency must be comfortable with the process by which its own regulations are developed, and it might be hesitant to rely on a negotiating group assembled by someone outside its control. The agency thus appears to be a logical candidate.

There are, on the other hand, significant arguments for having someone other than the agency itself assemble the group. The point of the iterative process is to make discrete, confidential inquiries about a party's interests and the issues it believes reasonably can be discussed. A party may believe that its ultimate interests lie in the political or adversarial process, and it justifiably may be reluctant to talk candidly with the agency for fear of retribution if it does not agree to participate in the negotiation In addition, a party may believe that either proposing the negotiation process or agreeing to participate before other parties agree to do so would be an acknowledgement that it is unable to achieve its goal through the normal process; this in turn would diminish its power. Thus, the preliminary inquiry into whether negotiation is feasible, which requires touching base with the various interests while narrowing the issues, must be conducted in confidence and must permit a party to say "no." Otherwise, the very purpose of the discrete inquiry would not be fulfilled because the parties would not begin the negotiating process by trusting each other.

The political legitimacy of this process depends on the participation of representatives of the interested parties as negotiators. Thus, the parties and the world at large must have confidence that negotiators are indeed representatives of the significantly affected parties. Therefore, it would be inappropriate to permit any participant to be responsible for assembling the group because it might appear that one party selected interests and individuals to support its views.

The agency is particularly susceptible to charges of bias. For example, one allegation against intervenor funding is that agencies have a bias toward funding those interests that support its view. One regulatory agency, which wanted to draw on diverse views of experts in a particular field, asked the National Academy of Sciences to empanel a technical committee. An official of the agency believed that the panel's recommendations would be given far greater credence if the panel was not under the agency's own auspices because people would believe that the participants were selected on the merits, rather than because of bias in favor of the agency. The official indicated that he believed individuals with greater stature in their respective communities were willing to participate in the process precisely because they felt the neutral selection sustained the panel's legitimacy. Indeed, many statutes that require an agency to consult with an advisory panel before issuing a regulation also require the panel either to be appointed by or selected from nominees of the National Academy of Sciences. The obvious motivation for this trend is a desire to ensure the neutrality of the panels, and in particular, to remove the possibility that parties could allege that the agency stacked the committee to favor a point of view or to exclude some position.

To avoid the inevitable claims of bias and conflict, as well as the difficulty of securing the initial agreement of the parties to participate, an organization other than the agency that will ultimately issue the regulation should assemble the negotiating group, at least on a preliminary basis. The use of a neutral third party would enable the parties to express themselves with candor. In addition, a neutral third party is appropriate because many of the decisions made in the initial stage of negotiations will be of a judicial nature. Such preliminary decisions would include the identification of interests and their appropriate representation. Thus, an unbiased decisionmaker of the highest probity would be required. If an organization other than the agency assembles the negotiation group, the agency would have no stake in its composition. Thus, claims of agency bias or conflict in selection of the negotiating group would be avoided.

Convenor

Several existing Federal agencies could be used to perform the "convenor" function. The convenor would have responsibilities for the preliminary determination of the feasibility of negotiation, the interests to be represented, and the appropriate representatives of the interests.

The President's Task Force on Regulatory Relief is an interagency organization administered by the Office of Management and Budget (OMB) with the power to direct agencies to consider various regulatory alternatives and to coordinate agencies' approaches to regulatory questions. It has become the ultimate authority in the Executive Branch's management of the regulatory process. Although the Task Force could be extremely helpful in regulatory negotiations by assuring agencies of the legitimacy of the process, it is unlikely to serve as the convenor because it has no operational authority. Rather, the OMB provides staff to the Task Force.

The OMB, in addition to its general management authority and its duties under the Paperwork Reduction Act, has general authority to implement President Reagan's Executive Order 12,291. The Order requires the OMB to review regulations issued by the respective agencies and the regulatory impact analysis prepared by the agencies for major rules. The OMB attempts to ensure, at least in theory, that agencies have adequate support for the factual conclusions underlying regulations and that regulations are clearly within the agency's statutory mandate. It has become the central manager of the regulatory process. The OMB could make the preliminary determinations concerning regulatory negotiations as an adjunct to this regulatory management authority.

The significant drawback of this suggestion is that the White House — the Task Force and OMB — could be viewed as politically partisan and thus liable to select interests and representatives favorable to political views of the administration. Moreover, OMB's review function creates tension between the agencies and OMB that may frustrate the good working relationship necessary for such a system to work. This tension may cause the agency to use the traditional process to avoid dealing with the OMB, even if it otherwise believes negotiating would be appropriate.

Another alternative for the role of convenor would be the Federal Mediation and Conciliation Service (FMCS) which, among other things, develops "the art, science, and practice of dispute resolution." Until recently, the FMCS has been concerned almost exclusively with labor/management issues. Recently, however, it has undertaken a role in age discrimination cases and other nonlabor fields. Because FMCS has an expertise in conducting negotiations, it may be an appropriate convenor if it continues to expand its focus.

*   *   *

The convenor would be responsible for making the preliminary determinations of whether negotiation is a feasible way of establishing the rule, which interests should be represented, and who the representatives should be. The convenor should base these determinations primarily on agreement among the parties in interest. The process used to develop the regulation must also be acceptable to them. If the parties agree to develop a regulation through negotiation they could suggest a pre-formed group to the convenor. The group would then review the proposal to ensure that the proper interests are adequately represented and the issues involved are suitable for negotiation. If the convenor concurred with the participants and issue selection, it then would certify that decision to the responsible regulatory agency.

Preliminary Inquiries

As suggested above, an alternative way to initiate the regulatory negotiation process would be for a party — the agency, a private interest or conceivably even an interloper — to suggest to the convening organization that regulatory negotiation would be appropriate in certain situations. The request would briefly explain the reasons for favoring regulatory negotiation over alternative methods. The convenor then would inquire whether there is a substantial likelihood that the agency would consider issuing a rule on that particular subject matter developed by means of regulatory negotiation. If so, the convenor could make the discrete inquiries to determine (1) whether a limited number of interests would be substantially affected by the proposed rule; (2) whether individuals could be selected who could represent those interests; (3) whether those interests would be willing to make commitments to negotiate in good faith to reach a consensus on a proposed rule; (4) the issues raised by the subject matter in question; and (5) a tentative schedule for completing the work of the committee. Each of these inquiries is important and will be considered in turn.

Limited Number of Interests and Countervailing Power. The convenor first should assess the number and relative power of the affected interests. The negotiation process will not work if the participation of a large number of diverse interests is required. If any one of them, or a group of closely allied interests, has far more power than any other, the subject may be inappropriate for negotiation because the less powerful party may need the protections afforded by the traditional process. The threshold inquiry must be whether several parties have sufficient countervailing power such that no interest can achieve its will without incurring unacceptable sanctions from the others. If this situation exists, the outcome of the regulation will be uncertain, and the parties may be insecure and thus may view negotiation as the way to break the deadlock.

Individuals to Represent the Interests. Some of the interests may be so dispersed and unorganized that it would be impossible to select individuals to represent each respective interest. Simply because the impact of a regulation would be widely felt, however, does not mean that effective representation is impossible. For example, even though a regulation dealing with air pollution may affect all urban dwellers, at least one environmentally active group would likely represent those interests. A concern related to representation of such dispersed and unorganized interests is the need to identify precisely the interests that a party actually represents. For example, in one environmental negotiation, because the company involved was unsure of the interests the negotiators represented, it attempted to ascertain exactly which organizations would sign any agreement that was ultimately negotiated. The convenor may have to meet with several members of an interest to focus their attention on selecting a limited number of representatives because each member may believe that the representative selected as the negotiator should be its exclusive representative or that the member or it should be allowed to participate in addition to a closely aligned interest. If the interest cannot be persuaded to select representatives, the convenor should make the determinations described below.

Commitment to Negotiate in Good Faith. Even if the interests and their representatives are precisely identified, at least one major interest may refuse to participate. That interest may believe that it can secure its interests through the traditional rulemaking process, litigation, or legislation.

In regulatory negotiation, as in environmental negotiation, some parties may profit from delay or obstructionist tactics. If that organization is unwilling to participate, it would do little good to include the organization in negotiations. Such a party, however, may be necessary for the negotiations. Part of the preliminary inquiry with the interest groups should therefore involve a discussion of whether negotiations are the proper route. As part of this inquiry, the convenor could point out that the other interests have countervailing power and that *some* decision is inevitable. For example, an interest group, bent upon delay, might be convinced that the agency is likely to move ahead and that it cannot control the outcome. The convenor could convince the interest group that through participation in negotiations it might be able to exert some influence over the final decision.

If such an interest remained intransigent and refused to participate, the convenor then would have to decide whether negotiations could still be fruitful. Such a decision would involve several considerations. First, the convenor must decide whether other organizations whose interests are fairly close to those of the recalcitrant are willing to participate. Second, the convenor must determine whether the absent group's interests are significantly or only tangentially affected. Finally, the convenor must consider whether the group is such a major constituent that the agency would be reluctant to accept a negotiated agreement without its participation. Alternatively, the convenor could decide that the party ultimately would join in the discussions and participate in good faith in negotiations.

If the convenor ascertains that the appropriate interests are willing to participate in the negotiations, he should ask each party to pledge to negotiate in good faith to reach a consensus on a proposed rule. Of course, no party would be formally bound by such a pledge. The pledge, however, could prove to be a useful reminder to the parties of their commitment if negotiations and emotions become frayed, a circumstance that clearly should be anticipated.

Scope of Issues. The convenor should then facilitate the preliminary definition of the issues to be considered in the negotiation. One participant in an environmental negotiation commented that agreeing on the scope of the discussions was the most difficult part of the task of negotiation; once the issues were in place, negotiations proceeded in a straightforward manner. The convenor would facilitate definition of the issues through the iterative process of asking the parties what they believe should be involved in regulating a particular subject matter. The issues would not be defined in any concrete way at the preliminary stage; rather, the initial outlines would be set to make the parties aware of the scope of negotiations. Matters outside the scope of discussion, such as those irrelevant to the statute authorizing the regulation or those involving such fundamental values would be identified at this point.

Establishment of a Preliminary Schedule. A preliminary schedule for completing various stages of work should be established. Experienced negotiators have pointed out that deadlines have several beneficial effects; they provide an incentive to reach agreement and a sense of accomplishment once the deadline is met. The parties must realize that they may lose control of the regulatory process if they do not reach an agreement. A deadline, which may be required by that of a statute or court order, provides a reminder that some decision is inevitable and that the parties therefore need to reach a consensus. Further, a deadline enables the parties to measure the likelihood of success on the project; the inability to meet the deadline for agreement may indicate the futility of trying to negotiate the particular regulation.

Certification to the Agency

After making these preliminary assessments, the convenor may determine that negotiations among interested parties would be unlikely to result in an agreement on a proposed regulation. In such a situation, the convenor would issue a notice stating that negotiations were inappropriate, without blaming any party for sabotaging the result. Publicizing one party's refusal to participate would be counterproductive because it could cause communications to break down even further. If, however, negotiation would be inappropriate because the parties differ on fundamental issues, the convenor should acknowledge this reason so that the political process can attempt to resolve the conflict. The convenor might conclude that although successful negotiation of a proposed rule would be unlikely, bringing together the major parties in interest to discuss the subject matter is desirable. In such a situation, the agency should empanel an advisory committee. The advisory committee could aid in narrowing the differences, clarifying the issues and positions, and providing guidance to the agency on the data required to resolve important questions.

If the convenor determines that regulatory negotiation would be feasible and superior to traditional rulemaking for developing a proposed regulation, the convenor would recommend to the agency that the negotiations be initiated. The report would include recommendations on the interests to be included in the negotiations, representatives to lead the negotiating teams of those interests, the issues to be considered, and a schedule for completion of the work. These recommendations would comprise a "contract" among the parties that participated in the iterative preliminary process. Alternatively, if the parties did not reach an agreement informally, the convenor's own determination would form the recommendation.

In determining whether negotiations should be undertaken, the convenor should make a reasonable effort to ensure that the negotiating group is composed of individuals who are competent and qualified concerning the subject matter of the proposed rule or that knowledgeable individuals are available to them. The group also should be balanced so that no interest or group of allied interests dominates or constitutes more than a third of the members of the committee.

These criteria for determining the composition of the bargaining group are not binding on the convenor. Rather, they provide reasonable guidelines. For example, a rigorous analysis of the interests involved may reveal that a balance cannot be achieved because the number of interests is too great, or because an interest has no one who is technically competent in the subject matter of the regulation to represent the interest or to consult in the negotiations. Whether such situations would preclude successful negotiation thus would depend on whether the parties would be able to participate fully and on relatively equal footing. Consideration of these criteria is designed to aid in this determination.

If the convenor recommends that a regulatory negotiation process be established, the agency has several alternatives. The agency may decide, in its discretion, to adopt the recommendations. It may decide not to issue a rule at all or it may decide to follow more traditional procedures. If the agency decides to use regulatory negotiation, it should follow the recommendations of the convenor and use the proposed group of negotiators to ensure the effectiveness of the process. Alternatively, the agency and the convenor could agree to revise the recommendations.

The agency should take advantage of the convenor's recommendations because the agency can emphasize that the findings were made by a neutral third party and that the agency did not select the negotiating group. Further, following the convenor's recommendations would allow the agency to build on the preliminary work performed in bringing the group together. Although the agency could negotiate its differences concerning the recommendations with the convenor, it should be willing to commit itself to the preliminary findings of the convenor unless it has substantial cause for concern. The likelihood of success of the negotiation, and ultimately the legitimacy of the resulting rule, rests on the confidence of the parties in the integrity of the negotiation group. If the agency refuses to accept the convenor's recommendations and imposes its own recommendation, the other parties may lose confidence in the group's integrity. Finally, the agency's participation in the development of the group would minimize its tendency to reject the group's report as "not invented here."

Existing Organization

Voluntary standards have been used in many regulatory programs. In many ways, their development is a form of regulatory negotiation. The subject matter of a proposed regulation may be within the jurisdiction of an existing standards-writing organization. If such an organization exists and enjoys the support and confidence of the affected interests, it would be logical to conduct the negotiations under the auspices of that organization rather than to establish an entirely new framework for negotiations. The standards-writing organization may have developed procedures for ensuring fair representation of the respective interests and for ensuring that decisions actually reflect a consensus. In such situations, an existing committee within the standards-writing organization could be regarded as a regulatory negotiation group, or an agreement reached by such a committee could form the basis of a proposed regulation.

Mediator

The services of a mediator may benefit the regulatory negotiation process. If the issues are relatively well-defined or the participants have already established a good working relationship, a mediator may not be of significant help because the parties themselves could efficiently negotiate without outside intervention. In these instances, negotiations often take place within existing norms that govern their behavior. For example, in the labor context, the parties often have a well-established, ongoing relationship and the issues involved in the bargaining, such as wages, fringe benefits, seniority, and working conditions, are usually clear. Therefore, in labor negotiations the parties can confront the issues directly and neither side can afford to be preemptory [sic] with the other, lest it damage the ability to cooperate in the future. In the regulatory context, a number of interests may participate regularly in discussions on particular subjects. Despite the absence of a formal, ongoing relationship such as that of management and union, the interests may have established a working relationship that they have an interest in preserving. Thus, the negotiators may have developed sufficient trust and lines of communication to begin discussions and to confront relevant issues directly without the assistance of a mediator.

In most regulatory matters or environmental disputes, however, the issues are unclear and the parties may lack not only an established and ongoing relationship, but may be highly antagonistic to one another. Individuals assembled in an ad hoc manner for purposes of developing a regulation are likely to feel insecure about the process because it is novel and it requires the surrender of one form of power. A mediator or "facilitator" can help significantly in such situations. Indeed, such a person can help even when the parties do not begin the negotiation process with mutual distrust.

The first step in building the negotiating relationship among the parties occurs when the convenor establishes the initial working group of people willing to participate in the give and take of discussions. A mediator can continue that process through the negotiations. The mediator's function should be directed toward building trust and communication between the parties. Therefore, the parties must have faith and trust in the mediator. A mediator must be someone with whom each party can meet privately and discuss candidly its concerns about the positions taken by the other parties. In addition, the mediator must help each party separate its true concerns from its initial position, and define criteria by which it would measure an agreement. A mediator can focus the discussions in such private meetings and point out the extremes being taken by the parties. He can also offer creative solutions, both in private discussions and in face to face negotiations.

It is essential that the mediator preserve the trust of all parties. Therefore, he must justify his ideas and positions in terms of the parties' own interests. Unless the mediator gains the trust of the parties, they may try to capture his attention and use him as a bargaining tool. Alteratively, they may believe that he is not truly neutral and will not trust him with future communications.

As one experienced environmental mediator has observed, a mediator who has expertise in the subject matter of the regulation may interfere with this process. First, such a mediator is likely to rely too much on his own assumptions or values rather than on those of the parties. Second, he may filter information based on his own independent assessments and focus on technical differences rather than on underlying values Finally, he is more likely to lead the parties as opposed to facilitating communication among them. Thus, to avoid these difficulties, negotiations should not utilize a mediator with substantive expertise.

During the discussions an effective mediator can also resolve problems that could break down negotiations. For example, in one environmental negotiation, allegations indicating that one party was taking action inconsistent with its participation in the negotiations were published. If the allegations had been true talks would have broken down. After one party raised its concerns about the allegations with the mediator, the mediator investigated the stories and was able to assure the party that no problem existed. The mediator also informed nonparticipants of the progress of the negotiation and focused parties' efforts on reaching an agreement.

In short, the function of the mediator is to facilitate discussions between the interested parties without taking a position. This role must not be confused with that of an arbitrator or even a chairperson of a meeting. Although the mediator may explore issues, propose alternatives, help draft the agreement, and carry communications between the parties for their consideration, his function is to generate ideas and to aid the parties in focusing on issues. Thus, the mediator should not direct the course of discussions. Indeed, negotiations are likely to be most successful when the mediator is required to do very little.

The group should determine preliminarily whether a mediator would be useful. In most significant regulations, a mediator will be useful. The convenor who has worked with the parties in establishing the preliminary negotiating group would be the likely choice as a mediator. The convenor usually will have developed a trust relationship between himself and the parties. Indeed, if another person took over as the mediator he would have to rebuild such a relationship.

Federal Register Notice

After the agency decides to develop a regulation through the negotiation process, it would publish a notice in the *Federal Register*. The notice would include a description of the subject matter of the regulation; the representatives comprising the proposed regulatory negotiation committee, including a description of the interest represented by each member and the position held by each member; the name and position of the proposed agency representative; the name of the proposed mediator, if any; the issues the committee proposes to consider; and a proposed schedule for completing the work of the committee. The notice also would invite members of the public to comment on whether the use of regulatory negotiation in developing a rule is appropriate; whether the appropriate interests are represented; whether the members selected adequately represent their interests; whether the committee is considering the appropriate issues; whether the agency representative is appropriate; and any other matter of interest. Comments would be due thirty to sixty days after publication of the notice. The primary purpose of the notice would be to ensure that no organization with a substantial interest in the subject matter of the regulation was overlooked and that the selected representatives adequately represent the interests of members of nominal classes.

The Final Committee

The agency and the convenor would then consider all relevant materials submitted in response to the *Federal Register* notice. Two instances may arise in which the agency and the convenor would determine whether someone who is not in the preliminary group should be included on the final negotiations committee. Someone may argue that an appropriate interest is not represented. A nonparticipant might argue that it too should be allowed to participate directly with a representative at the table even though someone with a similar interest would be present.

Resolution of the inclusion question requires determination of three factors. The first question is whether the interest is sufficiently close to the issues under consideration that it has "standing" to participate. An interest may simply be too remote to be included. An interest, however, should be excluded only if its connection to the rule is so remote that its allegation to the contrary is frivolous. It seems unlikely that a group would want to participate unless it actually were interested in the outcome.

The second question is whether the proposed interest is different from the interests already represented. For example, a group that believes its representative should participate in the negotiation could argue that its position is different from that of another group that was selected to represent a certain interest. Although their initial positions may differ, their views may virtually coincide in the long run. The apparent differences might be manufactured to secure a representative at the negotiating table. The agency and the convenor, therefore, must determine whether the applicant's interests really are divergent from those interests proposed in the notice, and whether one of the interests already selected for the negotiations adequately represents its interests.

The final determination in the inclusion question is whether, even if the interest is already represented, the applicant nonetheless should have its own representative at the table. The negotiation committee is not composed of only one representative of each interest; rather, it includes representatives of groups that would be significantly affected. Those interests are likely to overlap to a significant degree. Thus, in determining whether to add another representative, the agency and convenor should consider the number of representatives already present, the diversity of their views, and the centrality of the new organization to the issues.

In determining whether additional organizations should participate, the agency and neutral convenor should seek the advice and consultation of the preliminary negotiation group. These interests and their representatives may be in the best position to determine whether a sufficient nexus exists between the applicant and the subject matter. The agency and the convenor, however, should not rely exclusively on the views of the preliminary negotiation group; rather, they should independently determine whether the new party should be represented. One of the main purposes of the *Federal Register* notice is to encourage interests that have not been identified by the consultative process to identify themselves and to seek admission to the negotiations. That the consultative process did not identify these interests may mean that the negotiation group, or at least some of its members, did not recognize or accept the legitimacy of the interests' positions. This possibility indicates the need for an independent assessment of the claim.

After reviewing the comment material, the agency and the convenor should agree on the final contours of the negotiating group, including its members, issues, and schedule. The agency would publish a notice in the *Federal Register* reflecting these determinations. The notice should provide the agency's reasons for the inclusion or exclusion of any interests. Because the issues, interests, and individuals engaged in the negotiations are likely to change over time, the *Federal Register* notice should not be regarded as limiting negotiations to the terms listed in the notice. Rather, its function is to provide notice of the negotiation, and like a notice of proposed rulemaking, it defines a sphere of possible actions. If, however, negotiations depart fundamentally from the terms of the original notice, another notice in the *Federal Register* should be published.

Assembling the final committee to negotiate the proposed rule undoubtedly will be a sensitive and important point in the regulatory negotiations. It is essential to the legitimacy of the process that each organization with a significant interest in the subject matter be offered representation in the group and that no interest should be turned away unless its connection to the regulation is remote. On the other hand, every interested individual person, firm, or organization cannot participate in negotiations because the process might become too unwieldy. If there are many potential participants, the major interests could be organized into caucuses to develop common positions and to use common representatives. The convenor may find it necessary to meet with the respective interests to convince them to coalesce. One advantage of such caucus formation in regulatory negotiations is that the espoused interest actually would be represented more effectively than it would be in the formal, adversarial process that could result if everyone insisted on being at the table.

At this stage the process could degenerate into a fight over who gets to sit at the table, unless the similar interests band together for purposes of representation. The convenor and the agency must take great care to ensure that their decision in assessing interests and putting together coalitions is of the highest integrity. Otherwise, the time consumed and acrimony generated by this wrangling could easily vitiate the benefits of the regulatory negotiation process.

The determination of the participants should not be subjected to judicial review independent of the review of the resulting negotiated rule. Judicial review at this stage would subject the entire process to delay and doubt and thus would interfere with the establishment of fruitful negotiations. Thus, a court decision could be deferred until the regulation is promulgated. The determination of the participants is not final agency action because the party seeking to participate would still be able to submit its views on the rule before it becomes final. Further, because the convenor, a neutral third party, makes the essentially judicial determination of the applicant's standing or adequate interests, subsequent judicial review would provide adequate protection for the interest against improper participation determinations.

NOTES

1. Harter presents a rosy picture of the way regulatory negotiation will be able to streamline the process of promulgating valid agency regulations. Consider, however, the position of the traditional prosecutorial administrative agency charged with prosecuting breaches of laws and regulations. Is there something unseemly about the agency (the regulators) cooperating with regulatees in the content of lawmaking affecting the regulated group? Should the Environmental Protection Agency, itself charged by statute to enforce anti-pollution laws, cooperate with polluters on the details of future regulations regarding the pollution laws?

2. A number of commentators have raised potentially valid criticisms of regulatory negotiation. (*See, e.g.,* William Funk, *When Smoke Gets in Your Eyes: Regulatory Negotiation and the Public Interest — EPA's Woodstove Standards*, 18 ENVTL. L. 55 (1987); Susan Rose-Ackerman, *Consensus Versus Incentives: A Skeptical Look at Regulatory Negotiation*, 43 DUKE L.J. 1206 (1994).) Professor Funk takes the position that the normal administrative agency has the task of determining the public interest and that regulatory negotiation can substitute the resolution of private rights for the public interest. He argues that regulatory negotiation "tends to subvert the principles and values of administrative rulemaking." Professor Funk's description of the reg-neg process used to develop a wood stove rule concludes that the rule adapted violated the Clean Air Act but went unchallenged in court because of agreement among the parties to the reg-neg. Why would the EPA and environmental groups agree to an "illegal" regulation?

Professor Funk has recently written that regulatory negotiation subverts the Rule of Law, subordinates the administrative agency as a critical "responsible actor," and frustrates application of the public interest. (*See* William Funk, *Bargaining Toward the New Millennium: Regulatory Negotiation and the Subversion of the Public Interest*, 46 DUKE L.J. 1351 (1997).)

Professor Rose-Ackerman contends that the positive aspects of reg-neg have been oversold, that benefits from the process have been highly speculative, and that the typical compliance for regulations adopted by standard methods is high. She asserts that traditional "incentive methods" that give the regulated group an incentive to meet a goal adopted by Congress and the agency are preferable to regulations adopted by the regulatory negotiation process.

3. Professor Coglianese's study of regulatory negotiation concludes that the length of time to conduct the rulemaking is not decreased and that the rate of litigation of negotiated rules is not any lower than that of conventional style "notice and comment" rulemaking. (*See* Cary Coglianese, *Assessing Consensus: The Promise and Performance of Negotiated Rulemaking*, 46 DUKE L.J. 1255 (1997).)

4. The Environmental Protection Agency has used regulatory negotiation with some success. In 1993 EPA concluded a regulatory negotiation that involved three regulations designed to improve the quality of drinking water. These regulations dealt with the potentially carcinogenous by-products of the necessary disinfectants used to purify water. EPA began the reg-neg process by having private mediators visit with interested parties to assess their interest in a reg-neg. Following positive feedback EPA commenced the process in September 1992. The seventeen parties involved federal agencies, public health officials, public interest groups, manufacturers and politicians who met over a ten-month period. The biggest challenges to the reg-neg were the significant differences of opinion regarding the degree of cancer risk and the scientific complexity of the topic. The procedures that facilitated the success included a technical working group, a collection of experts who focused on the complex scientific issues, drafting of "straw" option papers which helped focus the discussion and a bi-partisan drafting group.

5. After an agency has passed a regulation through the regulatory negotiation process, what should be the scope of judicial review? Is the normal deferential standard of review appropriate? Shouldn't courts dig more deeply when reviewing a regulation co-drafted by the regulated group, particularly when the reg-neg drafting group may have jointly agreed not to challenge the regulation in court? Or does the fact that an agency typically participates in the reg-neg process require a degree of deference? What is the impact of 5 U.S.C. § 570 (reg-neg regulations get no greater deference than any other rules)?

USA GROUP LOAN SERVICES, INC. v. RILEY
82 F.3d 708 (7th Cir. 1996)

POSNER, J.

[Following congressional inquiry, newly promulgated regulations adopted by the Secretary of Education in 1994 sought to curb fraud and mistakes in the servicing of federally insured student loans. Student loans are guaranteed by the federal government but made by banks. "Servicers" of student loans help to relieve banks, borrowers and universities of the administrative complexity perhaps inherent in the student loan programs. The loan servicers contended that an agency official had promised that the Department would agree to any consensus reached by the negotiating group unless there were compelling reasons to disagree. The Department rejected a provision of the negotiating group that placed a cap on the servicers' liability for student loan defaults. The new regulations were viewed as onerous by the servicers who brought suit to invalidate portions of the regulations.]

* * *

The remaining arguments are procedural and the main one is that the Secretary adopted the challenged regulation in violation of the conditions of "negotiated rulemaking," a novelty in the administrative process. The 1992 amendment to the Higher Education Act, under which the regulation was promulgated, required that the Secretary submit any draft regulation to a process of negotiated rulemaking, to be conducted in accordance with recommendations made by the Administrative Conference of the United States and codified in 1 C.F.R. §§ 305.82-4 and 305.85-5 and with "any successor recommendation, regulation, or law." 20 U.S.C. § 1098a(b). A "successor law" to the Administrative Conference's recommendations had in fact been enacted in 1990. It is the Negotiated Rulemaking Act, 5 U.S.C. §§ 561 *et seq.* It is to expire later this year but was applicable to the servicer rulemaking. * The Act and the Administrative Conference's recommendations authorize the agency, in advance of the notice and comment rulemaking proceeding, to submit draft regulations to the industry or other groups that are likely to be significantly affected by the regulations and to negotiate with them over the form and substance of the regulations. The hope is that these negotiations will produce a better draft as the basis for the notice and comment proceeding. The 1992 amendment to the Higher Education Act made negotiated rulemaking mandatory in proceedings implementing the amendment, as we have seen.

The servicers argue that the Department negotiated in bad faith with them. Neither the 1992 amendment nor the Negotiated Rulemaking Act specifies a remedy for such a case, and the latter act strongly implies there is none. 5 U.S.C. § 570. But even if a regulation could be invalidated because the agency had failed to negotiate in good faith, this would not carry the day for the servicers.

During the negotiations, an official of the Department of Education promised the servicers that the Department would abide by any consensus reached by them unless there were compelling reasons to depart. The propriety of such a promise may be questioned. It sounds like an abdication of regulatory authority to the regulated, the full burgeoning of the interest-group state, and the final confirmation of the "capture" theory of administrative regulation. At all events, although the servicers reached a firm consensus that they should not be liable for their mistakes the Department refused to abide by its official's promise. What is more, the draft regulations that the Department submitted to the negotiating process capped the servicers' liability at the amount of the fees they received from their customers, yet when it came time to propose a regulation as the basis for the notice and comment rulemaking the Department abandoned the cap. The breach of the promise to abide by consensus in the absence of compelling reasons not here suggested, and the unexplained withdrawal of the Department's proposal to cap the servicers' liability, form the basis for the claim that the Department negotiated in bad faith.

---

* [Eds. The Negotiated Rulemaking Act was reauthorized as part of the ADRA of 1996.]

We have doubts about the propriety of the official's promise to abide by a consensus of the regulated industry, but we have no doubt that the Negotiated Rulemaking Act did not make the promise enforceable. *Natural Resources Defense Council, Inc. v. EPA*, 859 F.2d 156, 194 (D.C. Cir. 1988) (per curiam). The practical effect of enforcing it would be to make the Act extinguish notice and comment rulemaking in all cases in which it was preceded by negotiated rulemaking; the comments would be irrelevant if the agency were already bound by promises that it had made to the industry. There is no textual or other clue that the Act meant to do this. Unlike collective bargaining negotiations, to which the servicers compare negotiated rulemaking, the Act does not envisage that the negotiations will end in a binding contract. The Act simply creates a consultative process in advance of the more formal arms' length procedure of notice and comment rulemaking. *See* 5 U.S.C. § 566(f).

The complaint about the Secretary's refusal to adhere to the proposal to cap the servicers' liability misconceives the nature of negotiation. The Secretary proposed the cap in an effort to be accommodating and deflect the industry's wrath. The industry, in retrospect improvidently, rejected the proposal, holding out for no liability. So, naturally, the Secretary withdrew the proposal. A rule that a rejected offer places a ceiling on the offeror's demands would destroy negotiation. Neither party would dare make an offer, as the other party would be certain to reject it in order to limit the future demands that his opponent could make. This concern lies behind the principle that settlement offers are not admissible in litigation if the settlement effort breaks down. Fed. R. Evid. 408. By the same token, the negotiating position of the parties in negotiated rulemaking ought not be admissible in a challenge to the rule eventually promulgated when the negotiation failed.

The servicers argue that they should be allowed to conduct discovery to uncover the full perfidy of the Department's conduct in the negotiations. Discovery is rarely proper in the judicial review of administrative action. The court is supposed to make its decision on the basis of the administrative record, not create its own record. There are exceptions . . . and the main one has some potential applicability here: discovery is proper when it is necessary to create a record without which the challenge to the agency's action cannot be evaluated. E.g., *Citizens to Preserve Overton Park, Inc. v. Volpe*, 401 U.S. 402, 420 (1971); *Edgewater Nursing Center, Inc. v. Miller*, 678 F.2d 716, 718–19 (7th Cir. 1982). Negotiated rulemaking does not usually produce a comprehensive administrative record, such as notice and comment rulemaking, or a cease and desist order proceeding, or a licensing proceeding would do, any more than a settlement conference will usually produce a full record. Some discovery was conducted in the district court in order to present a picture of what went on at the negotiations between the servicers and the Department. The servicers argue that if only they could get access to the notes of certain participants in the negotiating sessions they could demonstrate additional instances of bad faith on the part of the Department.

Their conception of "bad faith" reflects, as we have noted, a misconception of the negotiation process. It is not bad faith to withdraw an offer after the other side has rejected it. If as we doubt the Negotiated Rulemaking Act creates a remedy as well as a right, we suppose that a refusal to negotiate that *really* was in bad faith, because the agency was determined to stonewall, might invalidate the rule eventually adopted by the agency. But we do not think that the Act was intended to open the door wide to discovery in judicial proceedings challenging regulations issued after the notice and comment proceeding that followed the negotiations. If as in this case the public record discloses no evidence of bad faith on the part of the agency, that should be the end of the inquiry. Cf. *Citizens to Preserve Overton Park, Inc. v. Volpe*, *supra*, 401 U.S. at 420. A contrary conclusion would stretch out such judicial proceedings unconscionably. The Act's purpose — to reduce judicial challenges to regulations by encouraging the parties to narrow their differences in advance of the formal rulemaking proceeding — would be poorly served if the negotiations became a source and focus of litigation.

AFFIRMED.

NOTES

1. Judge Posner terms reg-neg a "novelty in the administrative process." Nonetheless, reg-neg has been around for some time. The Administrative Conference first recommended that agencies consider using reg-neg in 1982. The Reagan and Bush Administrations used the process to help resolve complex issues, particularly in environmental disputes. (*See generally* Philip J. Harter, *First Judicial Review of Reg Neg a Disappointment*, 22 ADMIN. & REG. L. NEWS 1 (no. 1 1996).)

2. Is it fair for Judge Posner to have said that reg-neg represents the "consensus of the regulated industry"? Under the reg-neg legislation, the agency is forced to decide if the reg-neg process is consistent with the public interest. (5 U.S.C. § 563(a).) Is Judge Posner fearing the "capture" of the agency by the regulated group?

3. Judge Posner is often associated with free market thinking and ideals. Isn't the reg-neg process consistent with a market philosophy of lawmaking? In a reg-neg the affected parties, together with the agency, custom craft a regulation which is then turned over to the agency for notice, comment and action. Rather than potentially heavy-handed direct regulation by government, reg-neg could be characterized as efficient, decentralized policymaking at an informed, grass-roots level. Why didn't Judge Posner's opinion resonate with these market themes?

4. Note that Congress mandated the reg-neg challenged in the *USA Group Loan Services* case. What conditions would lead Congress to "force" use of the reg-neg model and deny the agency the flexibility to use alternative forms of rulemaking?

5. What are the chances that a governmental agency official will abuse the reg-neg process by breaching a promise made during the negotiation process or even negotiating in bad faith? Won't the normal institutional pressures and bureaucratic hierarchies help to prevent abuse?

6. Should *Chevron* deference be accorded to rules that emerge from the reg-neg process? For a negative answer, see Robert Choo, *Judicial Review of Negotiated Rulemaking: Should Chevron Deference Apply?* 52 RUTGERS L.

REV. 1069 (2000). In *Central Arizona Water Conservation District v. EPA*, 990 F.2d 1531 (9th Cir. 1993), the court of appeals awarded an EPA negotiated rule deference and failed to attach particular significance to the negotiated feature of a controversial rule that halved the emissions reduction cost of a giant coal-fired power plant located in northern Arizona not far from the Grand Canyon.

B.   AGENCY MEDIATION

Agency interest and use of mediation is significantly greater than in arbitration. Both the non-binding nature of mediation and the ability of the disputants to retain control over the outcome of mediation is attractive to agencies. Agencies are less likely to fear losing control when considering mediation compared to arbitration.

Agency use of mediation, while still in the formative stages, is growing. The success of regulatory negotiation, a form of mediation, has helped agency acceptance of mediation techniques. Several agencies have begun programs providing for mediation of disputes involving complex issues or significant sums of money. For example, a series of pilot mediation programs at the Internal Revenue Service begun in 1995 permits taxpayers and the IRS Appeals Division to request mediation in cases pending in the Appeals process where previous attempts to settle the dispute have proved unsuccessful. The parties to these mediations are the taxpayer and the IRS Appeals staff. In summarizing this program, the IRS suggests that the mediation process is particularly useful for resolving factual issues "such as valuation, reasonable compensation and transfer price cases." (Announcement 95-86, 1995-44 I.R.B.) In the first years of this program mediation usually occurred in disputes involving a minimum of $10 million. (14 ALTERNATIVES 47 (Apr. 1996).) The program was amended in 1998 to permit broader use of mediation by lowering the minimum in dispute to one million dollars. The IRS Restructuring and Reform Act of 1998, 26 U.S.C. § 1, *et seq.* (2000), mandates that the Appeals Office establish procedures that allow taxpayers to request mediation. Expenses of the mediation are shared equally if the parties use a private mediator; the IRS will bear the expense of mediation if the taxpayer agrees to use an IRS employee as a mediator. IRS rules require that the parties sign a written agreement to mediate, that the parties submit a written summary of their position to the mediator, and that the mediator issue a short written report at the conclusion of the mediation process. Mediation may begin only when taxpayer negotiations with the IRS Appeals Division have failed.

There are pluses and minuses to the pilot IRS mediation program. Saving trial time achieves efficiency for the agency and taxpayer and greatly speeds up the dispute resolution process. The IRS also reaps considerable goodwill by using the mediation process and avoids the "scorched earth, take no prisoners" impression sometimes associated with the agency. Yet, some fear that mediating with the IRS will, in effect, grant the agency extra discovery that might be otherwise unavailable. Moreover, some IRS critics desire that the agency not compromise and use a profit maximization strategy that calls for the utmost "collections" possible. (*See* JOHN M. BEEHLER, *Mediating with the IRS*, THE TAX ADVISER 281 (May 1996).) Indeed, one reason that the IRS took so long to turn to mediation was that the Appeals Division has had significant success through its normal appeals process. Some attorneys are critical of the $1,000,000 mediation threshold. The IRS has now begun a new pilot mediation program in several states in tax deficiency cases of under $100,000.

Part of the recent efforts to create a "friendlier" IRS involves more reliance on alternative dispute resolution. The IRS has passed amended rules relating to mediation of civil tax disputes between taxpayers and the agency. "Mediation is no longer limited to issues involving an adjustment of $1 million or more." (IRS Rev. Proc. 2002-44 (2002).) Taxpayers may use mediation following unsuccessful negotiations to resolve internal appeals within the agency's dispute resolution procedures. Mediation is fully available for both legal and factual issues. Mediation is unavailable for an issue that is "designated for litigation or docketed in any court" (but note that the IRS has a different mediation program for docketed cases); for collection cases, for "issues for which mediation would not be consistent with sound tax administration" (e.g., res judicata or controlling Supreme Court precedent); or for cases where the taxpayer did not act in good faith during settlement discussions. (*Id.* at Sec. 4.03(1)-(5).)

Why would the agency try to avoid mediation on "controlling Supreme Court precedent"?

Is the IRS trying to avoid mediation on issues of law generally? Current IRS mediation rules appear to permit mediation of legal issues. Can't parties generally agree to not be bound or affected by specific cases? Why are Supreme Court cases any different?

Why would the agency not allow mediation of pending court cases? Cases settle every day and tax cases are not that different from other cases. Why limit the use of mediation in this respect? Is the IRS attempting to provide an incentive to mediate early, before a dispute gets to court? Why? It might be useful to know that most IRS administrative appeals are settled.

The taxpayer and the agency can select a mediator from a list of IRS-approved neutrals. The taxpayer may select a mediator not pre-approved by the agency but then must bear the cost of the mediator's fee.

Public utility regulatory commissions have also shown considerable interest in using mediation. The regulation of utility rates by these agencies typically involves long, drawn-out "rate cases" in which a utility's proposed rate increase is opposed in a complex case by both utility staff and numerous intervenors. As the following discussion shows, there is both considerable interest and some degree of skepticism associated with the introduction of mediation techniques into utility regulation.

CASE STUDY: OHIO ZIMMER RATE CASE MEDIATION

Numerous utility regulatory commissions have used mediation to help streamline protracted disputes regarding utility rates. These "rate cases" generally involve complex proceedings in which an investor owned utility seeks a rate increase from the regulatory commission. The law will generally permit an increase if the utility's costs are reasonable and "useful." The utility is typically opposed by the agency staff. Intervenors, large industrial customers or public interest groups, may also oppose the increase. These rate cases generally involve complex data and expert witnesses with complicated models, and they can consume months of testimony before a decision is reached.

These multi-party rate cases are generally divided into two phases. In the first phase, the utility regulators determine the total revenue that should reasonably be produced by the investor owned utility in a given time period. This stage focuses on particular types of utility costs and risks and tends to follow this simple equation:

utility revenue = RB (rate base) x R (rate of return) + ROC (reasonable operating costs)

The items in the rate base include the utility's plant — its transmission facilities and generating stations. In the case of a utility that owns a nuclear power plant the monetary amounts included as "useful" in the rate base can be staggering and present interesting and complex valuation questions. Their rate base is multiplied by the rate of return, the amount the utility needs to attract adequate capital and to pay shareholders a return on bonds and stock. The reasonable operating costs include short run costs such as labor expenditures. Phase two of the rulemaking process deals with a similarly complex set of issues. In phase two, the Commission allocates the total revenues due the utility among different classes of customers. Residential users are pitted against business users and peak loads receive substantial attention.

The following articles describe reactions to a mediation of the Public Utilities Commission of Ohio's three rate disputes involving the Zimmer plant, a former nuclear plant that was converted, at great cost and controversy, into a coal burning facility. The three investor owned utilities that co-owned the giant Zimmer plant sought rate increases that were mediated by Endispute. As the following excerpts show, there was real diversity of opinion regarding this use of mediation.

DONALD I. MARSHALL, ADR: NOT ABCs OF LITIGATION, 131 Pub. Util. Fort., Jan. 15, 1993, at 23. *

I have been involved in the regulatory arena for 20 years and have participated in fully litigated, partial settlement, and fully stipulated proceedings. Therefore, I was thoroughly excited about the prospects of the Public Utilities Commission of Ohio's announcement in September 1990 to solicit proposals to recommend methods to be used to resolve the most important rate case in my company's history. What was even more curious was the fact that our rate case filing, which initiated discovery and the traditional litigation posturing, would not be filed for at least six months. Further, the PUCO resolution technique was consistent with the company's settlement goal (which was initiated in the summer of 1990) with settlement discussions with our traditional intervenors. The primary reason for the rate case was to recover the cost of the Zimmer Generating Station, which began providing energy March 30, 1991. The used-and-useful case was resolved by a settlement agreement reached without an ADR process and approved by the PUCO in November 1985. The agreement ordered $861 million to be absorbed by the three owners' shareholders without any opportunity to either recover their investment or to earn a return on that investment, established a price cap for the converted facility of $3.6 billion, and set June 30, 1991 as the completion date for the conversion.

The importance of the last two points was that throughout the construction of the nuclear facility, a cloud of uncertainty hung over the cost and the completion date. Therefore, the settlement called for additional shareholder losses if the coal plant cost exceeded $3.6 billion or the completion date went beyond June 30, 1991.

There are several factors worth sharing before I discuss the ADR process. First, in July 1990, several months before the ADR process was initiated, the PUCO staff released an independent report that found the decision to convert prudent and that the project was managed efficiently and effectively. Second, the facility itself is operating beyond expectations to the extent that over 20 percent of customers' needs were being provided at Zimmer at an efficiency rate 7 percent greater than our other generating stations. The facility's used-and-useful nature was not an issue.

Additionally, Ohio ratemaking law uses a unique "date-certain" concept for determining rate base value. This "date certain" restricts rate case timing particularly whenever a major addition to rate base occurs like a new generating station. Once a rate case application is filed, the PUCO staff begins a detailed audit encompassing the useful nature of rate base at date certain and the fair and reasonableness of the level of operating expenses and revenues.

The PUCO's statutory responsibility is to render a decision 275 days after the date certain. If a decision is not rendered, the utility has the option to implement its noticed rates, subject to refund. While the Commission has a good track record in rendering timely decisions, in this particular instance, a decision was not rendered in the 275-day suspension period and one of the Zimmer owners did attempt to implement its noticed rates.

I believe ADR is a process that can and should be used in coping with changing regulation. An effective ADR process would establish goals such as a reduction in expenses and uncertainties associated with litigation. This would facilitate lower rates in the long run. It was estimated that the total rate case expense of the three Zimmer owners would be in excess of $3 million.

In my opinion, however, these goals can only be attainable when knowledgeable parties directly address the issue presented and change participants' mind-set. Regulatory culture needs to be changed and to be effective in the changing regulatory environment, some process other than litigation must be developed.

The vision of the PUCO in selecting a facilitator was consistent with the global change I believe is necessary in the regulatory process.

I remember vividly the initial meeting with the PUCO selected facilitator. That meeting was introductory in nature, but we did touch on some preliminary matters. When I mentioned the term "revenue requirements" and was subsequently asked to explain what I meant, I knew the PUCO's goal was in serious jeopardy.

However, to the facilitator's credit, a number of accomplishments were achieved. For example, all parties who had indicated an interest in the rate case outcome were informed during the entire process and were asked to participate.

While we started the more traditional negotiation process some six months earlier, we were unable to consistently attract all parties to the settlement discussions. Considerable time was spent on such issues as to whether to meet in Columbus or Cincinnati and participation and confidentiality, an issue that has never been a problem in traditional settlement discussions as far as I know. I was impressed with the level of confidentiality established in the ADR process simply because all parties were not represented by an attorney. To my knowledge, confidentiality was maintained throughout the process by all parties.

So why were the ADR consultants not successful in resolving our rate case? I am sure if you were to ask the intervenors, they could identify the company's shortcomings. In the same vein, however, I can assess the intervenors' role. I believe the intervenors' mind-set was not ready for change. The goal, either overt or covert, was to delay the ultimate rate increase. For every month of delay, the company lost $17 million. The final result was a rate decision five months after the traditional approval date.

The parties also pursued their litigation strategy, a process that resulted in approximately three months of additional time for discovery. There was clearly a reservation about the process even to the extent that a major industrial intervenor boycotted the meetings. Numerous settlement offers were made by the company and only one counteroffer was made by the intervenors. In addition, it was never clearly articulated whether that settlement offer was made on behalf of all the parties. Some argue that resources were strained. The company offered to fund a consultant to analyze the company's offer of settlement. Despite the allegation of strained resources, the parties actively participated in a two-month hearing, the longest in the company's history.

The company argued for Commission staff involvement, and the intervenors could not develop a consensus on this issue. Staff involvement is absolutely necessary due to its advisory role and its statutory responsibility to issue a general audit finding and recommendation. Beyond its statutory responsibility, staff could have been an additional resource to the intervenors. The ADR consultant did attempt to get staff involvement in one meeting, but some intervenors again boycotted the meeting while another left after finding the staff would be in attendance.

I thought, and continue to believe, that an ADR process would be a forum for conflict resolution, however, it never happened. There must have been numerous conflicts since a resolution was not accomplished, but those conflicts were not fully discussed nor resolved. A relatively easy issue, for example, which was not resolved among the parties was one dealing with the implementation of a rate increase, and whether the parties believed a phase-in or a one-time increase was appropriate. Early in the process, the company stated its position as one of indifference. The point here is that I believe conflict resolution should be the initial priority of the facilitator. Each party should be contacted, a list of conflicts should be obtained, and resolution should be developed.

One of the goals of the ADR process should be consistent results. In the Zimmer rate cases, the one case which was resolved was when the parties agreed to a rate increase which was 10 percent higher than the staff recommendation with no disallowance of the Zimmer investment. The two cases that were litigated ended with a rate increase 20 percent below the low end of the staff's recommendation and a 16 percent Zimmer investment disallowance. I believe these ranges of results are not within a range of reasonableness which would permit future settlements to be pursued. Added pressure will be to litigate cases in the future, because, if for no other reason, the litigated outcome here was so dramatically different than the ADR results. A footnote here is there is no consensus about whether or not the settled case was directly attributable to the process.

To advance the ADR process, a number of recommendations have been presented. In addition, however, parties must change their mind-set from one of litigation to one of resolution, including the realization that the outcome could be a rate increase. Intervenors need to be prepared to go forward and represent to their clients that a reasonable settlement is in everyone's best interest. The parties themselves should select the ADR facilitator. Most importantly, the facilitator should have experience in the ratemaking process and the regulatory agency must remain flexible. The political climate should dictate the participants in the process. The outcome should result in consistency and the goals of reducing litigation expenses and eliminating uncertainties associated with litigation should be pursued. Our future challenge is to define a workable process which is more productive and less costly than litigation.

DAVID C. BERGMANN, ADR: RESOLUTION OR COMPLICATION? 131 Pub. Uti. Fort., Jan. 15, 1993, at 20 *

Unfortunately, it may simply be that ADR is not appropriate for use in major rate cases. The particular pitfalls of ADR in the Zimmer rate cases may be grouped into the following categories:

- Voluntariness — As noted above, the intervenors had expressed grave doubts about the appropriateness of using ADR for the Zimmer rate cases. The ADR literature is virtually unanimous in noting that consent is a key to the success of any such process.

- Communication — Unfortunately, the Ohio Commission never took any formal action to address any of the concerns raised by the intervenors. Basically, the PUCO's ADR was a game without procedural rules; the parties made them up as they went along.

Both voluntariness and communication were rendered even more important by the other process concerns discussed here, which largely address the ability or capability of stakeholders to participate in an ADR effort.

• Timing — As Endispute noted in its final report to the PUCO, the timing of the ADR process placed additional strains on the stakeholders. Despite the fact that ADR was discussed initially prior to August 1990, the request for proposal was not issued until mid-September with responses arriving in October. Nevertheless, the mediator was not selected until mid-January 1991, a month and a half before the statutory ratemaking process began. Endispute was not able to hold initial meetings with stakeholders until a month later.

• Resources — This may be the single greatest obstacle to a successful ADR process. As noted in much of the literature, stakeholders in many regulatory processes have widely varying resources. Yet even the resources of a large utility can be strained by the need to follow more than one critical path at the same time. This double-tracking resource drain is an almost inevitable consequence of applying ADR during the investigative process of a rate case. No party can afford to neglect the litigative side because the negotiations may fail.

• Conflicts with statutory processes and requirements — The Zimmer ADR also presented a number of conflicts with certain statutory requirements such as commissioner involvement and commission staff involvement.

• Qualifications of the mediator — In the complex field of public utility law, it is vital if not mandatory for a mediator to have a firm grasp of the details of regulation. For instance, it does not help the negotiation of a multi-million-dollar rate case for a party to have to explain to a mediator what a revenue requirement is.

The Zimmer cases had no shortage of other baggage, which clearly had an influence on ADR. These included the rancorous history of Zimmer itself, the litigation by the city of Cincinnati as to the legality of the 1985 Zimmer settlement, the issuance of and bases for the "Staff Reconnaissance Report" which found the Zimmer conversion and construction to be prudent, the proposals in the Ohio General Assembly which would have deemed Zimmer prudent for ratemaking purposes, and the legislative rejection of OCC's proposals for consultants to review Zimmer prudence and excess capacity. Where major utility rate cases are concerned, it can easily be questioned whether ADR really leads to any result different from or superior to litigation.

Endispute made a series of recommendations for future ADR proceedings. These included: commission flexibility, explicit participation commitments, comprehensive search for participants, adherence to confidentiality agreements, involving senior participants, recognizing the importance of staff report timing, and staff review of settlements prior to their filing.

In DP&L, we saved the expense of going to hearing; however, in CG&E and CSP we expended resources on ADR which would have been better spent on preparing for litigation. Thus, although there were some benefits which arose from the ADR process, on the whole the Zimmer ADR process can be seen to have been less than a resounding success.

DAVID S. COHEN, MEDIATION: SANITY IN THE REGULATORY PROCESS, 131 Pub. Util. Fort., Jan. 15, 1993, at 18[*]

The regulatory process is in need of change. The adversarial model used by most regulatory agencies is an inefficient, expensive, and conflict-producing procedure. Ill-adapted to resolving issues of great public policy concern, regulation calls out for non-adversarial alternative processes to address the resolution of public policy disputes between the players in the regulatory process.

*   *   *

One likely scenario for use of mediation is the ratemaking process is where major issues of a rate case are a product of past repetitious litigation.

In the context of a rate moderation plan, the mediation process allows participants to put before the regulatory commission a plan incorporating broad areas of interest. It is a forum for expanding the typical rate proceeding into a negotiation in which many different long-term objectives can be achieved within the context of a single case. It allows the various parties to put issues on the table such as demand-side management, procurement policies, and other issues unrelated to the main point of the rate case. These issues otherwise would be unavailable for complete consideration within the pure context and confines of a normal rate proceeding.

The mediator's role is to reduce the amount of gamesmanship the parties will attempt to use in pushing their positions. A mediator with credibility can act as a "flack-catcher" and discard issues or claims meriting little or no respect.

Resolving territorial conflicts between utility companies is another area for the potential use of mediation. In such a scenario, participants to the dispute typically include two utilities and a potential customer of both. The issue is whether or not one utility can provide less expensive service to the customer than another. Not surprisingly, the customer seeks to avoid the more expensive utility and receive service from the cheaper utility.

In many instances, general rules of regulatory decisions are ignored by the adversaries, who marshall a number of different factual circumstances which allegedly would countervail prevailing utility principles. The advantages to the utilities of utilizing the mediation process are:

- It allows the utilities to avoid the public display of a conflict.
- It allows a mechanism to enable the utilities to overcome the emotions of the situation.
- It provides a mechanism for the customer to understand the limitations of the options available to it under public utility law.

- It is a process that does not require commission endorsement to start the process or to enable it to be successful.

- It is a means to reduce the costly litigation associated with a contested matter.

An area of significant potential for the mediation process is in transmission disputes between utilities or among utilities and third parties. As the utility industry moves toward integrated bulk power systems and the development and encouragement of open access on these systems, the use of mediation to resolve transmission questions becomes attractive.

The utility industry has not developed a particularly well defined process for resolving transmission disputes. In fact, transmission jurisdiction between various regulatory agencies itself is unclear. Interjecting the potential of open access rights onto the utility grid system and attempting to allocate entitlements and rights to the various potential users of the transmission system is a complex and technically difficult task.

Mediation is a far superior mechanism for resolving a transmission dispute between two parties or, for that matter, in creating a transmission policy for a statewide or regional system of allocating capacity. The mediation process allows the parties to talk to one another to resolve their dispute. The mediator is not the decision maker and is able to provide the parties with the objective and credible expertise to help resolve the dispute.

The benefit of mediation in the context of the transmissions dispute situation is its ability to avoid jurisdictional contests and issues that arise in any transmission dispute. It obviates the need to establish the regulatory agency's jurisdictional authority and speeds the process for resolving the issue. It provides the mechanism for the utility industry to resolve its traditionally unregulated relationships in a manner that preserves the freedom of action that the industry desires.

Mediation in the utility industry is extremely beneficial, although it has not been explored adequately as a general process for resolving disputes. It does not displace the function of the public service commission, but lends assistance to the efficient functioning of the system by removing the parties from the realm of the adversarial quasi-judicial setting and placing them in a setting of discourse and debate. It is a process that need not be dominated by lawyers, but rather by people of good business judgment and technical competence.

NOTES

1. Why did the ADR sponsoring organization not select an expert to be the mediator? Does the utility rate case seem like the type of case in which an expert would be useful? Or, alternatively, should an expert be avoided in such complex matters?

2. Was the Zimmer mediation necessarily a failure, as two of the writers suggest? Weren't some positive steps accomplished in the mediation? A full regulatory hearing was avoided in one of the three separate cases.

3. David Cohen suggests that mediation is particularly appropriate for disputes involving transmission, the process of transporting electricity over a distance. Cohen states that transmission disputes lack a well-defined process and the legal jurisdictional aspects are unclear. Does this sound like a subject matter particularly suited for mediation?

4. Donald Marshall blames delay for the mediation's failure to reach agreement. Can mediation avoid delay strategies? Marshall asserts that the intervenors sought and were benefitted by delay. Is this the mediation's fault? What step to avoid delay was taken in the Zimmer mediation?

5. Several other examples of administrative agency use of mediation should be mentioned.

(a) Several agencies make use of mediation to help achieve environmental protection. For example, EPA has used mediation to set conditions for new source permits issued under the Clean Air Act. In addition, the Coastal Zone Management Act provides that the Secretary of Commerce will seek to mediate any "serious disagreement between any federal agency and a coastal state" concerning development, implementation, or administration of the state's management program. (16 U.S.C. § 1456(h) (2001).) If a coastal state objects to a federally licensed activity, the agency's Office of Ocean and Coastal Resource Management is available to help resolve the dispute. (15 C.F.R. § 930.111 (2001).)

The Board of Contract Appeals of the Army Corps of Engineers has used mediation to resolve construction projects within its jurisdiction. (*See, e.g.*, Reba Page & Wesley Jockish, *The Corps of Engineers Board of Contract Appeals Use of Alternative Dispute Resolution*, 24 PUB. CONTRACT L.J. 453 (1995).) Use of mediation by the Corps of Engineers should not be surprising because ADR has long been popular in the engineering and construction fields, the Corps' area of specialization.

(b) Under § 252 of the Telecommunications Act of 1996, 47 U.S.C. § 252 (2001), state utility commissions must hear mediation requests of a party involved in an "interconnection" dispute in which one firm seeks to use the network services or equipment of an incumbent telecommunications firm. These can be complicated, multi-party disputes with high stakes. The mediations may be conducted by staff of the state utility commissions. Will this feature be attractive to industry? Are there reasons to avoid using staff as mediators?

(c) There is considerable interest in using mediation to resolve disputes under the Americans with Disabilities Act (ADA). The Administrative Conference of the United States issued a recommendation that mediation of ADA disputes be employed. (Use of Mediation under the Americans with Disabilities Act, 60 Fed. Reg. 43,115 (1995).) The EEOC conducted a 1994 pilot mediation program involving ADA cases regarding employee discipline, discharge or discrimination in terms and conditions of employment. While the pilot program has been viewed a success, fundamental questions remain regarding using mediation to resolve ADA claims. "Resolution of [ADA] disputes through mediation may result in a diminished ability to identify and resolve systematic discrimination problems." (Ann Hodges, *Mediation and the Americans with Disabilities Act*, 30 GEORGIA L. REV. 431, 461 (1996).) Mediation necessarily focuses on the claims of one alleged victim and the resolution of alleged abuse by a class of victims is difficult in the mediation format. Power imbalances also may exist in employee-employer disputes of ADA claims. On the other hand, the potential for reducing the expense and number of disputes definitely exists in this area.

(d) Perhaps the oldest and most successful federal agency use of mediation has been the work of the Federal Mediation and Conciliation Service ("FMCS"). The FMCS is a mediation agency formed in 1947 to mediate private sector labor relations disputes. The mediation expertise of the FMCS has caused it to expand into mediation of selected health care disputes and state and local public sector labor disputes.

(e) The Equal Employment Opportunity Commission has started a program to provide in-house mediation services to help resolve discrimination cases. This program, begun in 1991, offers mediation to help resolve discrimination claims brought against employers. A large volume of discrimination claims have been mediated under this program, over 52,000 from 1999 through 2003. Close to 70% of these mediations settled the charges of discrimination brought to the EEOC. The agency uses a combination of internal mediators who are employed by the EEOC, external mediators retained by contract, and pro bono mediators who volunteer to participate. The agency screens cases after they are filed to determine if the dispute is appropriate for mediation and attempts to complete this screening process efficiently to enable it to offer mediation early in the process. In theory, the EEOC program provides the parties the opportunity to request mediation at any stage. In practice, the agency mediates cases early in the process, prior to findings of discrimination.

The agency has sought to expand mediation of discrimination claims by encouraging employers to agree generally to mediate disputes by signing so-called "Universal Agreements to Mediate." As of 2003, hundreds of such agreements had been signed. These agreements shorten the time needed to consider the mediation process by getting employers to agree in advance to mediate discrimination claims. Why would an employer enter into such an agreement? From a public policy perspective, are there arguments against the wholesale mediation of employment discrimination claims?

(f) The US Postal Service maintains a high volume mediation program called REDRESS. The program, which originated out of the terms of the settlement of a Florida 1994 job discrimination class action, is designed to settle employment disputes using transformative mediation techniques. Mediations are conducted at the job site and during the time of employment. Mediators are external to the US Postal Service. The process has a high degree of party determination; the parties, typically the complaining employee and a supervisor, control the process itself and often make opening statements themselves. This process is available to all employees of the US Postal Service throughout the United States.

Most of the claims brought regard acts of alleged discrimination. Mediation sessions are usually conducted within 14-21 days from the filing of a claim. In the first 22 months of the program (1998-2000) mediators resolved about 80% of 17,645 disputes. Perhaps as important, the number of complaints brought decreased by 30% during the same period. Outside, independent evaluators have found a high degree of party satisfaction with the process.

What are the unique features of the REDRESS program? Couldn't any employer, including other governmental agencies, adopt a similar program of ADR? Is it realistic to theorize that transformative mediation can be interjected into a mass justice scheme? Note than the USPS has prevailed in about 90% of the discrimination cases it litigates. However, the outside mediators hired to engage in transformative mediation eschew any reference to this "shadow of the law" in order to not appear evaluative. Apologies are not uncommon in this process. For a positive review of the redress program, see *Addressing the "Redress": A Discussion of the Status of the United States Postal Service's Transformative Mediation Program*, CARDOZO ONLINE J. OF CONFLICT RES., www.cardozo.yu.edu/cojcr/final_site/symposia/ vol_2_symposia.

6. Assume that a published EPA regulation permits pollution up to 40 units per thousand of a particular substance. Much of the industry is in compliance with this regulation but the agency hears that numerous firms are violating the regulation by polluting at 60 units per thousand, 20 units over the maximum amount allowable. EPA initiates an administrative proceeding to sanction the polluter. EPA participates in a mediation of this dispute and agrees to drop its claim if the polluter decreases its pollution to 45 units per thousand. Should this mediation be considered a success? Consider the following critique of this problem:

> If ADR expands dramatically, then the resulting adverse effect upon third parties must be taken into account. In the worst case scenario, widespread ADR independent of substantive law could *increase* disputes since third parties would lack the incentive to perform in accordance with custom crafted legal norms. For example, a rational polluter would be foolish to comply with a published regulation permitting a low amount of emissions when it could probably pollute at a substantially greater amount through environmental mediation. This situation illustrates how disputes can be created by ADR; rather than comply with a paper law, our rational polluter will opt for the preferable result in mediation. In this situation the legal norms that ADR ignores regularly could atrophy and become inefficacious. Once a citizen loses the predictability of a probable law-constrained court outcome, the benefit of "law" as signal is lost. [Edward Brunet, *Questioning the Quality of Alternative Dispute Resolution*, 62 TUL. REV. 1, 19 (1987).]

Is this an overly skeptical view of the problem?

7. *Workshops.* Some utility commissions, in an effort to avoid protracted, multiparty rate cases, are now scheduling "workshops." These sessions are set early in a dispute, well before a hearing. They are informal efforts to brainstorm the parties' willingness to avoid a prolonged hearing and to examine alternatives to the traditional adjudicatory process. The utility staff typically tries to involve each interested party in a workshop. While a workshop is not necessarily a mediation, it can turn into one or trigger a later mediation. Utility staff can use professional "convenors" to lead a workshop. The theory of a workshop is similar to that used by judges when convening settlement conferences — it may be useful to just sponsor "an event" to bring disputants together where there is always a chance that disputant interaction can lead to settlement.

C. AGENCY ARBITRATION

While there is increased interest in agency arbitration generally, federal agency use of arbitration is in its infancy. Several reasons have slowed the growth of arbitration in agency adjudication.

First, many agencies have distrusted the idea of transferring decision making power on issues within their statutory jurisdiction to politically unaccountable private arbitrators. An executive order of the First Bush Administration prohibited agencies from seeking binding arbitration. (Executive Order 12778.) Agencies understandably want control over their own agendas and may regard the use of private arbitrators as potentially a delegation of decisional power that can permit the outside arbitrator to bind the agency. This thinking led Congress to include a provision in the original Administrative Dispute Resolution Act of 1990 ("ADRA") authorizing the head of any agency to vacate arbitration awards before they became final and to terminate arbitration proceedings. While the 1990 ADRA legislation facilitated the growth of administrative agency ADR, it did contain several other restrictions relating to arbitration. A decision to terminate or vacate an arbitration "shall be committed to the discretion of the agency and shall not be subject to judicial review." (5 U.S.C. § 591(b).) While the 1990 ADRA supported arbitration by permitting agencies to let disputants consent to arbitration, the feature that allowed withdrawal from arbitration indicated a degree of tension between arbitration and administrative policymaking.

The passage of the 1996 version of ADRA marks a shift in attitude concerning use of arbitration by federal agencies. The new legislation repealed the power of an agency head to terminate arbitration proceedings or to vacate arbitral awards. Instead, agency arbitration is now binding on the parties. (5 U.S.C. § 580(c) (2001).) This change symbolizes a degree of acceptance of agency arbitration. Nonetheless, the 1996 version of ADRA retains the section of the original 1990 legislation that requires the agency to consider not using ADR where "a definitive or authoritative resolution of the matter is required for precedential value" or "maintaining established policies is of special importance" or where "the agency must maintain continuing jurisdiction" over a dispute. (5 U.S.C. 572(b).) Such legislation illustrates fundamental tensions between an agency's missions and the mere resolution of a dispute.

Other factors have slowed the usage of arbitration by federal agencies. For some time it was thought that the Appointments Clause, art. II, § 2, cl. 2, prevented the United States from entering into agreements to participate in binding arbitration. (*See* CIVIL DIVISION, U.S. DEP'T OF JUSTICE, GUIDANCE ON THE USE OF ALTERNATIVE DISPUTE RESOLUTION FOR LITIGATION IN THE FEDERAL COURTS 4 n.8 (Aug. 1992).) The Appointments Clause delineates the means by which an officer of the United States can be validly appointed. The prevailing view of some agency personnel was that the appointment of private arbitrators to decide significant issues would be illegal under art. II, § 2, cl. 2. However, a recent opinion of the Department of Justice Office of Legal Counsel clarifies that the Appointments Clause does not prohibit the federal government from using binding arbitration. (Constitutional Limitations on Fed. Gov't Participation in Binding Arbitration, 19 Op. Off. Legal Counsel (Sept. 7, 1995).) This opinion is likely to force some federal agencies to rethink their opposition to arbitration. A February, 1996, Executive Order of the Clinton Administration revoked the earlier Bush Administration order that prohibited agencies from using binding arbitration. (Executive Order 12988.)

Other constitutional doctrines have also inhibited the use of arbitration by agencies. The general thrust of Article III probably limits the routine use of arbitration by agencies. Article III largely restricts the judicial power to judges. While Congress certainly has the power to allocate some adjudicatory responsibility to non-judicial actors (e.g., bankruptcy judges, administrative agency judges), Article III acts as a check that would seemingly prevent the establishment of arbitral tribunals to adjudicate routine business with finality. The test is to examine the practical impact of delegation of powers to arbitrators to determine if the "constitutionally assigned role of the federal judiciary" would be undermined. (*Commodity Futures Trading Commission v. Schor*, 478 U.S. 833, 851 (1986).)

THOMAS v. UNION CARBIDE AGRIC. PROD. CO.
473 U.S. 568 (1985)

Justice O'CONNOR delivered the opinion of the Court.

This case requires the Court to revisit the data-consideration provision of the Federal Insecticide, Fungicide, and Rodenticide Act (FIFRA), 61 Stat. 163, as amended, 7 U.S.C. § 136 *et seq.*, . . . In this case we address whether Article III of the Constitution prohibits Congress from selecting binding arbitration with only limited judicial review as the mechanism for resolving disputes among participants in FIFRA's pesticide registration scheme. We conclude it does not and reverse the judgment below.

* * *

[As part of the regulation of pesticides, federal law requires a manufacturer to transfer data to EPA regarding the product's safety impact on health and its environmental effects. The manufacturer or "registrant" who submits data is awarded one year of exclusive use of the information submitted. Later applicants, however, are permitted to access data in the EPA file if they agree to compensate the earlier registrant. Two "registrants," often competitors, must then negotiate the amount of compensation for the use of the data. Following a period of 90 days to reach agreement, either party can submit the question of the amount of compensation to binding arbitration. The arbitration program is administered by the American Arbitration Association.]

A

* * * The arbitrator's decision is subject to judicial review only for "fraud, misrepresentation, or other misconduct." *Ibid.* The statute contains its own sanctions. Should an applicant or data submitter fail to comply with the scheme, the Administrator is required to cancel the new registration or to consider the data without compensation to the original submitter. The Administrator may also issue orders regarding sale or use of existing pesticide stocks.

The concept of retaining statutory compensation but substituting binding arbitration for valuation of data by EPA emerged as a compromise. This approach was developed by representatives of the major chemical manufacturers, who sought to retain the controversial compensation provision, in discussions with industry groups representing follow-on registrants, whose attempts to register pesticides had been roadblocked by litigation since 1972. [Hearings on Extending and Amending FIFRA before the Subcommittee on Department Investigations, Oversight, and Research of the House Committee on Agriculture, 95th Cong., 1st Sess., 522–523 (1977) (testimony of Robert Alikonis, General Counsel to Pesticide Formulators Association).]

B

Appellees are 13 large firms engaged in the development and marketing of chemicals used to manufacture pesticides. Each has in the past submitted data to EPA in support of registrations of various pesticides. When the 1978 amendments went into effect, these firms were engaged in litigation in the Southern District of New York challenging the constitutionality under Article I and the Fifth Amendment of the provisions authorizing data-sharing and disclosure of data to the public. In response to this Court's decision in *Northern Pipeline Construction Co. v. Marathon Pipe Line Co.*, 458 U.S. 50 (1982), appellees amended their complaint to allege that the statutory mechanism of binding arbitration for determining the amount of compensation due them violates Article III of the Constitution. Article III, § 1, provides that "[t]he judicial Power of the United States, shall be vested" in courts whose judges enjoy tenure "during good Behaviour" and compensation that "shall not be diminished during their Continuance in Office." Appellees allege Congress in FIFRA transgressed this limitation by allocating to arbitrators the functions of judicial officers and severely limiting review by an Article III court.

The District Court granted appellees' motion for summary judgment on their Article III claims. It found the issues ripe because the "statutory compulsion to seek relief through arbitration" raised a constitutionally sufficient case or controversy. Although troubled by what appeared a "standardless delegation of powers," the District Court did not reach the Article I issue because it held that Article III barred FIFRA's "absolute assignment of [judicial] power" to arbitrators with only limited review by Article III judges. *Union Carbide Agricultural Products Co. v. Ruckelshaus*, 571 F.Supp. 117, 124 (1983). The District Court, rather than striking down the statutory limitation on judicial review, enjoined the entire FIFRA data use and compensation scheme.

[The Supreme Court remanded, finding the matter not ripe for decision.]

* * *

On remand in this case, appellees amended their complaint to reflect that EPA had, in fact, considered their data in support of other registration applications. The amended complaint also alleged that data submitted by appellee Stauffer Chemical Company (Stauffer), originator of the chemicals butylate and EPTC, had been used in connection with registrations by PPG Industries, Inc. (PPG), and Drexel Chemical Company of pesticides containing butylate and EPTC as active ingredients. The complaint further alleged Stauffer had invoked the arbitration provisions of § 3(c)(1)(D)(ii) against PPG, and appellees entered in evidence the award of the arbitration panel, handed down on June 28, 1983. Stauffer claimed the arbitrators' award fell far short of the compensation to which it was entitled.

In view of these developments, the District Court concluded that "[t]he claims presented by Stauffer challenging the constitutionality of FIFRA § 3(c)(1)(D) are ripe for resolution under the criteria established by the Supreme Court" in *Ruckelshaus v. Monsanto Co., supra*. The remaining plaintiffs, the District Court held, were aggrieved by the clear threat of compulsion to resort to unconstitutional arbitration. The District Court reinstated its prior judgment enjoining the operation of the data-consideration provisions as violative of Article III. EPA again took a direct appeal and we noted probable jurisdiction. This Court stayed the judgment pending disposition of the appeal.

* * *

III

Appellees contend that Article III bars Congress from requiring arbitration of disputes among registrants concerning compensation under FIFRA without also affording substantial review by tenured judges of the arbitrator's decision. Article III, § 1, establishes a broad policy that federal judicial power shall be vested in courts whose judges enjoy life tenure and fixed compensation. These requirements protect the role of the independent judiciary within the constitutional scheme of tripartite government and assure impartial adjudication in federal courts.

An absolute construction of Article III is not possible in this area of "frequently arcane distinctions and confusing precedents." *Northern Pipeline Construction Co. v. Marathon Pipe Line Co.*, 458 U.S., at 90. "[N]either this Court nor Congress has read the Constitution as requiring every federal question arising under the federal law . . . to be tried in an Art. III court before a judge enjoying life tenure and protection against salary reduction." Instead, the Court has long recognized that Congress is not barred from acting pursuant to its powers under Article I to vest decisionmaking authority in tribunals that lack the attributes of Article III courts. Many matters that involve the application of legal standards to facts and affect private interests are routinely decided by agency action with limited or no review by Article III courts.

*   *   *

A

Appellees contend that their claims to compensation under FIFRA are a matter of state law, and thus are encompassed by the holding of *Northern Pipeline*. We disagree. Any right to compensation from follow-on registrants under § 3(c)(1)(D)(ii) for EPA's use of data results from FIFRA and does not depend on or replace a right to such compensation under state law. *Cf. Northern Pipeline Construction Co., supra*, at 84 (contract claims at issue were matter of state law); *Crowell v. Benson* [285 U.S. 22, at 39–40 (1932)] (replacing traditional admiralty negligence action with administrative scheme of strict liability). As a matter of state law, property rights in a trade secret are extinguished when a company discloses its trade secret to persons not obligated to protect the confidentiality of the information. Therefore registrants who submit data with notice of the scheme established by the 1978 amendments, and its qualified protection of trade secrets as defined in § 10, can claim no property interest under state law in data subject to § 3(c)(1)(D)(ii). Nor do individuals who submitted data prior to 1978 have a right to compensation under FIFRA that depends on state law. To be sure, such users might have a claim that the new scheme results in a taking of property interests protected by state law. Compensation for any uncompensated taking is available under the Tucker Act. For purposes of compensation under FIFRA's regulatory scheme, however, it is the "mandatory licensing provision" that creates the relationship between the data submitter and the follow-on registrant, and federal law supplies the rule of decision.

Alternatively, appellees contend that FIFRA confers a "private right" to compensation, requiring either Article III adjudication or review by an Article III court sufficient to retain "the essential attributes of the judicial power." *Northern Pipeline Construction Co., supra*, at 77, 85–86. This "private right" argument rests on the distinction between public and private rights drawn by the plurality in *Northern Pipeline*. The *Northern Pipeline* plurality construed the Court's prior opinions to permit only three clearly defined exceptions to the rule of Article III adjudication: military tribunals, territorial courts, and decisions involving "public" as opposed to "private" rights. Drawing upon language in *Crowell v. Benson, supra*, at 50, the plurality defined "public rights" as "matters arising between the Government and persons subject to its authority in connection with the performance of the constitutional functions of the executive or legislative departments." 458 U.S., at 67–68. It identified "private rights" as " 'the liability of one individual to another under the law as defined.' " *Id.*, at 69–70.

This theory that the public rights/private rights dichotomy of *Crowell* and *Murray's Lessee v. Hoboken Land & Improvement Co.*, 18 How. 272 (1856), provides a bright-line test for determining the requirements of Article III did not command a majority of the Court in *Northern Pipeline*. Insofar as appellees interpret that case and *Crowell* as establishing that the right to an Article III forum is absolute unless the Federal Government is a party of record, we cannot agree. Nor did a majority of the Court endorse the implication of the private right/public right dichotomy that Article III has no force simply because a dispute is between the Government and an individual.

B

Chief Justice Hughes, writing for the Court in *Crowell*, expressly rejected a formalistic or abstract Article III inquiry, stating: "In deciding whether the Congress, in enacting the statute under review, has exceeded the limits of its authority to prescribe procedure . . . , *regard must be had, as in other cases where constitutional limits are invoked, not to mere matters of form but to the substance of what is required.*" 285 U.S. at 53 (emphasis added).

If the identity of the parties alone determined the requirements of Article III, under appellees' theory the constitutionality of many quasi-adjudicative activities carried on by administrative agencies involving claims between individuals would be thrown into doubt. *See* 5 K. DAVIS, ADMINISTRATIVE LAW § 29:23, p. 443 (2d ed. 1984) (concept described as "revolutionary"); Note, *A Literal Interpretation of Article III Ignores 150 Years of Article I Court History: Marathon Oil Pipeline Co. v. Northern Pipeline Construction Co.*, 19 NEW ENGLAND L. REV. 207, 231–232 (1983) ("public rights doctrine exalts form over substance"); Note, *The Supreme Court, 1981 Term*, 96 HARV. L. REV. 62, 262, n.39 (1982). For example, in *Switchmen v. National Mediation Board*, 320 U.S. 297 . . . the Court upheld as constitutional a provision of the Railway Labor Act that established a "right" of a majority of a craft or class to choose its bargaining representative and vested the resolution of disputes concerning representation solely in the National Mediation Board, without judicial review. The Court concluded: "The Act . . . writes into law the 'right' of the 'majority of any craft or class of employees' to 'determine who shall be the representative of the craft or class for purposes of this Act.' That 'right' is protected by [a provision] which gives the Mediation Board the power to resolve controversies concerning it. . . . A review by the federal district courts of the Board's determination is not necessary to preserve or protect that 'right.' Congress for reasons of its own decided upon the method for protection of the 'right' which it created." 320 U.S., at 300–301.

* * *

The Court has treated as a matter of "public right" an essentially adversary proceeding to invoke tariff protections against a competitor, as well as an administrative proceeding to determine the rights of landlords and tenants. *See Atlas Roofing Co. v. Occupational Safety and Health Review Comm'n*, 430 U.S. 442, 454–455 (1977), citing as an example of "public rights" the federal landlord/tenant law discussed in *Block v. Hirsh*, 256 U.S. 135 (1921); *Ex parte Bakelite Corp.*, 279 U.S. 438, 447 (1929) (tariff dispute). These proceedings surely determine liabilities of individuals. Such schemes would be beyond the power of Congress under appellees' interpretation of *Crowell*. In essence, the public rights doctrine reflects simply a pragmatic understanding that when Congress selects a quasi-judicial method of resolving matters that "could be conclusively determined by the Executive and Legislative Branches," the danger of encroaching on the judicial powers is reduced.

C

Looking beyond form to the substance of what FIFRA accomplishes, we note several aspects of FIFRA that persuade us the arbitration scheme adopted by Congress does not contravene Article III. First, the right created by FIFRA is not a purely "private" right, but bears many of the characteristics of a "public" right. Use of a registrant's data to support a follow-on registration serves a public purpose as an integral part of a program safeguarding the public health. Congress has the power, under Article I, to authorize an agency administering a complex regulatory scheme to allocate costs and benefits among voluntary participants in the program without providing an Article III adjudication. It also has the power to condition issuance of registrations or licenses on compliance with agency procedures. Article III is not so inflexible that it bars Congress from shifting the task of data valuation from the agency to the interested parties.

The 1978 amendments represent a pragmatic solution to the difficult problem of spreading the costs of generating adequate information regarding the safety, health, and environmental impact of a potentially dangerous product. Congress, without implicating Article III, could have authorized EPA to charge follow-on registrants fees to cover the cost of data and could have directly subsidized FIFRA data submitters for their contributions of needed data. *See St. Joseph Stockyards Co. v. United States*, 298 U.S. 38, 49–53 (1936) (ratemaking is an essentially legislative function). Instead, it selected a framework that collapses these two steps into one, and permits the parties to fix the amount of compensation, with binding arbitration to resolve intractable disputes. Removing the task of valuation from agency personnel to civilian arbitrators, selected by agreement of the parties or appointed on a case-by-case basis by an independent federal agency, surely does not diminish the likelihood of impartial decisionmaking, free from political influence. *See* 29 CFR § 1404.4, pt. 1440, App. § 7 (1984). Cf. *Northern Pipeline*, 458 U.S., at 58 (plurality opinion); *id.*, at 115–116 (WHITE, J., dissenting).

The near disaster of the FIFRA 1972 amendments and the danger to public health of further delay in pesticide registration led Congress to select arbitration as the appropriate method of dispute resolution. Given the nature of the right at issue and the concerns motivating the Legislature, we do not think this system threatens the independent role of the Judiciary in our constitutional scheme. "To hold otherwise would be to defeat the obvious purpose of the legislation to furnish a prompt, continuous, expert and inexpensive method for dealing with a class of questions of fact which are peculiarly suited to examination and determination by an administrative agency specially assigned to that task." *Crowell v. Benson*, supra, at 46. Cf. *Palmore v. United States*, 411 U.S. [389 (1973)], at 407–408 (the requirements of Art. III must in proper circumstances give way to accommodate plenary grants of power to Congress to legislate with respect to specialized areas); *Murray's Lessee v. Hoboken Land & Improvement Co.*, 18 How., at 282 (citing "[i]mperative necessity" to justify summary tax collection procedures).

We note as well that the FIFRA arbitration scheme incorporates its own system of internal sanctions and relies only tangentially, if at all, on the

Judicial Branch for enforcement. The danger of Congress or the Executive encroaching on the Article III judicial powers is at a minimum when no unwilling defendant is subjected to judicial enforcement power as a result of the agency "adjudication." *See, e.g.*, Hart, *The Power of Congress to Limit the Jurisdiction of Federal Courts: An Exercise in Dialectic*, 66 HARV. L. REV. 1362 (1953); Monaghan, *Marbury and the Administrative State*, 83 COLUM. L. REV. 1, 16 (1983); L. JAFFE, JUDICIAL CONTROL OF ADMINISTRATIVE ACTION 385 (1965) (historically judicial review of agency decisionmaking has been required only when it results in the use of judicial process to enforce an obligation upon an unwilling defendant).

We need not decide in this case whether a private party could initiate an action in court to enforce a FIFRA arbitration. *But cf.* 29 CFR pt. 1440, App. § 37(c) (1984) (under rules of American Arbitration Association, parties to arbitration are deemed to consent to entry of judgment). FIFRA contains no provision explicitly authorizing a party to invoke judicial process to compel arbitration or enforce an award. *Compare* § 3(c)(1)(D)(ii), 7 U.S.C. § 136a(c)(1)(D)(ii), *with* § 10(c), 7 U.S.C. § 136h(c) (authorizing applicant or registrant to institute action in district court to settle dispute with Administrator over trade secrets); 29 U.S.C. § 1401(b)(2) (Employee Retirement Income Security Act provision authorizing parties to arbitration to bring enforcement action in district court); *Union Pacific R. Co. v. Price*, 360 U.S. [601 (1959)], at 614, and n. 12 (statute authorized court enforcement of National Railroad Adjustment Board's money damages award); *and Crowell v. Benson*, 285 U.S., at 44 (providing for entry of judgment in federal court). *Cf. Utility Workers v. Edison Co.*, 309 U.S. 261 (1940) (as award to worker vindicates a "public right," agency alone has authority to institute enforcement proceeding). In any event, under FIFRA, the only potential object of judicial enforcement power is the follow-on registrant who explicitly consents to have his rights determined by arbitration. *See* 40 CFR § 162.9-5(b) (1984) (registration application must contain a written offer to pay compensation "to the extent required by FIFRA section 3(c)(1)(D)").

Finally, we note that FIFRA limits but does not preclude review of the arbitration proceeding by an Article III court. We conclude that, in the circumstances, the review afforded preserves the "appropriate exercise of the judicial function." *Crowell v. Benson, supra*, at 54. FIFRA at a minimum allows private parties to secure Article III review of the arbitrator's "findings and determination" for fraud, misconduct, or misrepresentation. § 3(c)(1)(D)(ii). This provision protects against arbitrators who abuse or exceed their powers or willfully misconstrue their mandate under the governing law. *Cf. Steelworkers v. Enterprise Wheel & Car Corp.*, 363 U.S. 593, 597 (arbitrator must be faithful to terms of mandate and does not sit to administer his "own brand of industrial justice"). Moreover, review of constitutional error is preserved, and FIFRA, therefore, does not obstruct whatever judicial review might be required by due process. We need not identify the extent to which due process may require review of determinations by the arbitrator because the parties stipulated below to abandon any due process claims. For purposes of our analysis, it is sufficient to note that FIFRA does provide for limited Article III review, including whatever review is independently required by due process considerations.

* * *

V

Our holding is limited to the proposition that Congress, acting for a valid legislative purpose pursuant to its constitutional powers under Article I, may create a seemingly "private" right that is so closely integrated into a public regulatory scheme as to be a matter appropriate for agency resolution with limited involvement by the Article III judiciary. To hold otherwise would be to erect a rigid and formalistic restraint on the ability of Congress to adopt innovative measures such as negotiation and arbitration with respect to rights created by a regulatory scheme. For the reasons stated in our opinion, we hold that arbitration of the limited right created by FIFRA § 3(c)(1)(D)(ii) does not contravene Article III. The judgment of the District Court is reversed, and the case is remanded for further proceedings consistent with this opinion.

So ordered.

[The concurring opinion of Justice BRENNAN, joined by Justices MARSHALL and BLACKMUN, is omitted.]

NOTES

1. In the FIFRA scheme arbitration is mandated without the consent of the parties. Does *Thomas* give any indication that the imposition of mandatory arbitration before a private arbitrator raises Article III concerns?

2. *Thomas* seems partially predicated upon the fact that FIFRA serves a public health purpose. Can't a "public purpose" be found in most administrative agency legislative histories? Does this affect the *Thomas* analysis, or does it mean that wholesale arbitration of adjudicatory claims within the jurisdiction of agencies is within the realm of constitutional reason?

3. *Due Process and Arbitration Revisited.* Does *Thomas* suggest that due process rights exist within arbitration hearings? Recall Justice Black's position in his dissent in *Prima Paint Corp. v. Float & Conklin Mfg. Co., supra.* Black worried that allocating to the arbitrator the task of deciding arbitrability "raises serious questions of due process" because the arbitrator would be deciding "an issue which will determine his compensation." (*Id.*) Does *Thomas* support Black's view that due process review of arbitral procedures is required?

4. Would *Thomas* support routine use of mandatory binding arbitration by the EPA to determine Superfund CERCLA cost allocation decisions? Such decisions are now negotiated and mediated and are often resolved without trial. Would a switch to mandatory arbitration of such decisions be particularized enough to satisfy Article III concerns? Would such a scheme be satisfied by a provision that "mandatory arbitration of CERCLA cost allocation disputes will be reviewable under the provisions of the Federal Arbitration Act"? If Congress can limit judicial review, why can't it provide for binding arbitration of matters within the regulatory authority of federal agencies?

5. The FIFRA legislation called for a small measure of judicial review for fraud, misconduct, or misrepresentation of the arbitrator's "findings and determination." What if Congress had merely said that the decision of a FIFRA arbitrator were "final" and had the effect of a court judgment? Could such legislation pass constitutional muster under the teachings of *Thomas*?

6. Numerous constitutional issues are raised when statutes or regulations dealing with public policy issues call for arbitration before private arbitrators. For a thorough discussion of these issues, see Harold Bruff, *Public Programs, Private Deciders: The Constitutionality of Arbitration in Federal Programs*, 67 TEX. L. REV. 441 (1989) (Congress has the power to order mandatory arbitration free of Article III concerns if it involves a specific topic in a federal program connected to the executive branch).

7. Does the FAA apply to FIFRA arbitration? FIFRA, of course, has its own statutory scheme and calls for a form of judicial review even more limited than the FAA. Under the FAA, the parties must consent to arbitrate. Under FIFRA, arbitration is mandatory regardless of consent. It would seem that the two arbitral schemes are very different and that the more specific FIFRA language would govern rather than the more general FAA provisions.

8. Congress has authorized several other specialized types of arbitration that resolve disputes and has incorporated the FAA rules into the agency arbitration process. For example, the Multi-Employer Pension Plan Amendments Act ("MPPAA"), legislation that is designed to protect the stability of a pension plan when one or more employers withdraw from a multi-employer plan holding unfunded pension benefits, calls for arbitration to determine the "withdrawal liability" of the withdrawing employer. (29 U.S.C. § 1381–1461.) Under the legislation the so-called Plan Sponsor must set the cost of "withdrawal liability" when an employer withdraws from the pension plan. Any disputes over the amount of liability set by the Plan Sponsor must be decided by arbitration. Unlike the FIFRA scheme, the MPPAA calls for arbitration to be decided "in the same manner" as under the FAA (29 U.S.C. § 1401(b)(3) (Lexis 2001)); the arbitration proceedings must be "fair and equitable." 29 U.S.C. § 1401(a)(2) (Lexis 2001). This scheme was attacked as a violation of the Seventh Amendment right to jury trial and of Article III in *Connors v. Ryan's Coal Co.*, 923 F.2d 1461 (11th Cir. 1991). The court upheld the arbitration system, reasoning that the MPPAA did not exist at common law and that the MPPAA was part of a "pervasive scheme for the regulation of multi-employer pension plans . . . [and] closely integrated into a public regulatory scheme." (*Id.* at 1465–66.) For discussion of the MPPAA arbitration procedures, see G. Richard Schell, *ERISA and Other Federal Employment Statutes: When Is Commercial Arbitration an "Adequate Substitute" for the Courts?* 68 TEX. L. REV. 509 (1990).

9. Other federal legislation and regulations call for arbitration. Superfund cost recovery claims not exceeding $500,000 may be arbitrated under regulations passed in 1989. (40 C.F.R. § 304.10 *et seq.* (Lexis 2001).) These arbitrations occur only if one or more of the disputants and the EPA Administrator desire arbitration. The award will be final only after a commentary period in which the EPA and the public may comment. Judicial review is not provided, except for review that the award was achieved by fraud, arbitrator misconduct, a violation of public policy, or that the arbitrator acted outside his or her authority. Are there any constitutional problems with this scheme? Are the problems cured by the voluntariness of these arbitrations?

10. *Telecommunications Arbitration.* Section 252 of the Telecommunications Act of 1996, 47 U.S.C. § 252 (Lexis 2001), calls for arbitration of disputes between incumbent telephone companies that control local service and newer competitors who wish to enter the market by using the network of the incumbent firm. (Telecommunications Act of 1996, Pub. L. No. 104-104, 10 Stat. 56 (1996).) The purpose of this legislation is to open up formerly protected local communications markets and to facilitate resale and interconnection among carriers. The statute permits parties to seek mediation and arbitration from state utility commissions of disputes involving interconnection. These disputes can involve powerful parties and complex issues regarding the cost of telecommunications services. The mediations could be complicated and, interestingly, may be mediated by the staff of the state commissions, the same staff that could act to later arbitrate these disputes. Are agency staff likely to be effective or neutral mediators? For a negative answer, see Scott Brown, *New Communications Law Encourages the Use of ADR*, 14 ALTERNATIVES TO HIGH COSTS LITIGATION 82 (1996). Agreements between the disputants must meet the intercommunication requirements set forth by the New Telecommunications Act of 1996 and applicable Federal Communications Commissions standards — parties who settle disputes must settle on terms consistent with the blueprint of the substantive law. If arbitration is requested the state commission must respond with a resolution within nine months of the initial petition for negotiation between the parties.

Judicial review of state commission decisions regarding interconnection arbitrations is available under this legislation in the federal trial courts. 47 U.S.C. § 252 (Lexis 2001) permits any aggrieved party to sue in the federal district court "to determine whether [an interconnection] agreement meets the requirements" of the Telecommunications Act. This review feature is unique because it places federal trial courts in the routine business of assessing the work of state agencies who themselves have been assigned a complicated task involving rates. Years ago, the Supreme Court effectively washed its hands of vigorous judicial review of complicated ratemaking orders of administrative agencies. (*See, e.g., FPC v. Hope Natural Gas Co.*, 320 U.S. 591 (1944).) The assignment of this review function is not likely to be viewed positively in the federal bench. The review process is further complicated by the idea that the courts will be evaluating state commission orders dealing with arbitration decisions, a function not normally carried out under the narrow grounds for setting aside awards under the FAA. The state commissions will review the interconnection arbitration decisions to determine if the results are consistent with the legal standards of the Telecommunications Act of 1996. Accordingly, courts should, in theory, employ a fairly broad scope of review for legal error; they are not technically reviewing private decisions of an arbitrator. Stay tuned for what are likely to be very interesting questions arising under this legislation.

11. *Final Offer Tax Shelter Arbitration Between the IRS and Taxpayers.* The IRS has instituted a form of baseball (final offer) arbitration for section 351 contingent liability investment programs. These disputes, which involve tax shelters, go to binding arbitration following the expiration of a 60 day period for negotiated agreement The sole issue to be submitted to the arbitrator is "Which of the two Final Offers presented by the parties" is preferable. (IRS

Rev. Proc. 2002-67 (2002).) IRS procedures prohibit the arbitrator from issuing an opinion or providing reasoning. Why? Can you form a rationale for the 60-day waiting period from the initiation of the request for arbitration to the date of the arbitration?

Pursuant to IRS procedures, neither the IRS nor the taxpayer has a right to offer witnesses in these final offer arbitrations. Only the arbitrator has the power to call and question witnesses or to order the parties to produce documents or exhibits. While the parties may submit written legal argument, there is no right to an oral hearing in a final offer arbitration. If the arbitrator desires a hearing, the time for the hearing is limited to 8 hours. There are millions at stake in these tax shelter disputes. Why put limits on the duration of the hearing?

12. *Arbitration of Taxpayer Appeals.* Recall the IRS mediation program for appeals pending before the agency. Where the taxpayer and the IRS fail to reach agreement on a mediated issue, the parties may seek arbitration. Prior law allowed arbitration only for docketed Tax Court cases. The IRS will pay the arbitrator's fee where the taxpayer selects an IRS approved arbitrator. Alternatively, the taxpayer can select an arbitrator not approved by the IRS but must then bear the cost of the arbitrator's fee. Do you see any problems with this selection of arbitrator process?

APPENDIX A

THE UNITED STATES ARBITRATION ACT ("FAA"), 9 U.S.C. §§ 1–16

9 U.S.C. § 1. "Maritime transactions" and "commerce" defined; exceptions to operation of title

"Maritime transactions", as herein defined, means charter parties, bills of lading of water carriers, agreements relating to wharfage, supplies furnished vessels or repairs to vessels, collisions, or any other matters in foreign commerce which, if the subject of controversy, would be embraced within admiralty jurisdiction; "commerce", as herein defined, means commerce among the several States or with foreign nations, or in any Territory of the United States or in the District of Columbia, or between any such Territory and another, or between any such Territory and any State or foreign nation, or between the District of Columbia and any State or Territory or foreign nation, but nothing herein contained shall apply to contracts of employment of seamen, railroad employees, or any other class of workers engaged in foreign or interstate commerce.

9 U.S.C. § 2. Validity, irrevocability and enforcement of agreements to arbitrate

A written provision in any maritime transaction or a contract evidencing a transaction involving commerce to settle by arbitration a controversy thereafter arising out of such contract or transaction, or the refusal to perform the whole or any part thereof, or an agreement in writing to submit to arbitration an existing controversy arising out of such a contract, transaction, or refusal, shall be valid, irrevocable, and enforceable, save upon such grounds as exist at law or in equity for the revocation of any contract.

9 U.S.C. § 3. Stay of proceedings where issue therein referable to arbitration

If any suit or proceeding be brought in any of the courts of the United States upon any issue referable to arbitration under an agreement in writing for such arbitration, the court in which such suit is pending, upon being satisfied that the issue involved in such suit or proceeding is referable to arbitration under such an agreement, shall on application of one of the parties stay the trial of the action until such arbitration has been had in accordance with the terms of the agreement, providing the applicant for the stay is not in default in proceeding with such arbitration.

9 U.S.C. § 4. Failure to arbitrate under agreement; petition to United States court having jurisdiction for order to compel arbitration; notice and service thereof; hearing and determination

A party aggrieved by the alleged failure, neglect, or refusal of another to arbitrate under a written agreement for arbitration may petition any United States district court which, save for such agreement, would have jurisdiction under Title 28, in a civil action or in admiralty of the subject matter of a suit arising out of the controversy between the parties, for an order directing that such arbitration proceed in the manner provided for in such agreement. Five days' notice in writing of such application shall be served upon the party in default. Service thereof shall be made in the manner provided by the Federal Rules of Civil Procedure. The court shall hear the parties, and upon being satisfied that the making of the agreement for arbitration or the failure to comply therewith is not in issue, the court shall make an order directing the parties to proceed to arbitration in accordance with the terms of the agreement. The hearing and proceedings, under such agreement, shall be within the district in which the petition for an order directing such arbitration is filed. If the making of the arbitration agreement or the failure, neglect, or refusal to perform the same be in issue, the court shall proceed summarily to the trial thereof. If no jury trial be demanded by the party alleged to be in default, or if the matter in dispute is within admiralty jurisdiction, the court shall hear and determine such issue. Where such an issue is raised, the party alleged to be in default may, except in cases of admiralty, on or before the return day of the notice of application, demand a jury trial of such issue, and upon such demand the court shall make an order referring the issue or issues to a jury in the manner provided by the Federal Rules of Civil Procedure, or may specially call a jury for that purpose. If the jury find that no agreement in writing for arbitration was made or that there is no default in proceeding thereunder, the proceeding shall be dismissed. If the jury find that an agreement for arbitration was made in writing and that there is a default in proceeding thereunder, the court shall make an order summarily directing the parties to proceed with the arbitration in accordance with the terms thereof.

9 U.S.C. § 5. Appointment of arbitrators or umpire

If in the agreement provision be made for a method of naming or appointing an arbitrator or arbitrators or an umpire, such method shall be followed; but if no method be provided therein, or if a method be provided and any party thereto shall fail to avail himself of such method, or if for any other reason there shall be a lapse in the naming of an arbitrator or arbitrators or umpire, or in filling a vacancy, then upon the application of either party to the controversy the court shall designate and appoint an arbitrator or arbitrators or umpire, as the case may require, who shall act under the said agreement with the same force and effect as if he or they had been specifically named therein; and unless otherwise provided in the agreement the arbitration shall be by a single arbitrator.

9 U.S.C. § 6. Application heard as motion

Any application to the court hereunder shall be made and heard in the manner provided by law for the making and hearing of motions, except as otherwise herein expressly provided.

9 U.S.C. § 7. Witnesses before arbitrators; fees; compelling attendance

The arbitrators selected either as prescribed in this title or otherwise, or a majority of them, may summon in writing any person to attend before them or any of them as a witness and in a proper case to bring with him or them any book, record, document, or paper which may be deemed material as evidence in the case. The fees for such attendance shall be the same as the fees of witnesses before masters of the United States courts. Said summons shall issue in the name of the arbitrator or arbitrators, or a majority of them, and shall be signed by the arbitrators, or a majority of them, and shall be directed to the said person and shall be served in the same manner as subpoenas to appear and testify before the court; if any person or persons so summoned to testify shall refuse or neglect to obey said summons, upon petition the United States district court for the district in which such arbitrators, or a majority of them, are sitting may compel the attendance of such person or persons before said arbitrator or arbitrators, or punish said person or persons for contempt in the same manner provided by law for securing the attendance of witnesses or their punishment for neglect or refusal to attend in the courts of the United States.

9 U.S.C. § 8. Proceedings begun by libel in admiralty and seizure of vessel or property

If the basis of jurisdiction be a cause of action otherwise justiciable in admiralty, then, notwithstanding anything herein to the contrary, the party claiming to be aggrieved may begin his proceeding hereunder by libel and seizure of the vessel or other property of the other party according to the usual course of admiralty proceedings, and the court shall then have jurisdiction to direct the parties to proceed with the arbitration and shall retain jurisdiction to enter its decree upon the award.

9 U.S.C. § 9. Award of arbitrators; confirmation; jurisdiction; procedure

If the parties in their agreement have agreed that a judgment of the court shall be entered upon the award made pursuant to the arbitration, and shall specify the court, then at any time within one year after the award is made any party to the arbitration may apply to the court so specified for an order confirming the award, and thereupon the court must grant such an order unless the award is vacated, modified, or corrected as prescribed in sections 10 and 11 of this title. If no court is specified in the agreement of the parties, then such application may be made to the United States court in and for the district within which such award was made. Notice of the application shall be served upon the adverse party, and thereupon the court shall have jurisdiction of such party as though he had appeared generally in the proceeding. If the adverse party is a resident of the district within which the award was made, such service shall be made upon the adverse party or his attorney as prescribed by law for service of notice of motion in an action in the same court. If the adverse party shall be a nonresident, then the notice of the application shall be served by the marshal of any district within which the adverse party may be found in like manner as other process of the court.

9 U.S.C. § 10.   Same; Vacation; Grounds; Rehearing

(a)   In any of the following cases the United States court in and for the district wherein the award was made may make an order vacating the award upon the application of any party to the arbitration —

(1)   Where the award was procured by corruption, fraud, or undue means.

(2)   Where there was evident partiality or corruption in the arbitrators, or either of them.

(3)   Where the arbitrators were guilty of misconduct in refusing to postpone the hearing, upon sufficient cause shown, or in refusing to hear evidence pertinent and material to the controversy; or of any other misbehavior by which the rights of any party have been prejudiced.

(4)   Where the arbitrators exceeded their powers, or so imperfectly executed them that a mutual, final, and definite award upon the subject matter submitted was not made.

(5)   Where an award is vacated and the time within which the agreement required the award to be made has not expired the court may, in its discretion, direct a rehearing by the arbitrators.

(b)   The United States district court for the district where an award was made that was issued pursuant to section 580 of title 5 may make an order vacating the award upon the application of a person, other than a party to the arbitration, who is adversely affected or aggrieved by the award, if the use of arbitration or the award is clearly inconsistent with the factors set forth in section 572 of title 5.

9 U.S.C. § 11.   Same; Modification or Correction; Grounds; Order

In either of the following cases the United States court in and for the district wherein the award was made may make an order modifying or correcting the award upon the application of any party to the arbitration —

(a)   Where there was an evident material miscalculation of figures or an evident material mistake in the description of any person, thing, or property referred to in the award.

(b)   Where the arbitrators have awarded upon a matter not submitted to them, unless it is a matter not affecting the merits of the decision upon the matter submitted.

(c)   Where the award is imperfect in matter of form not affecting the merits of the controversy.

The order may modify and correct the award, so as to effect the intent thereof and promote justice between the parties.

9 U.S.C. § 12. Notice of Motions to Vacate or Modify; Service; Stay of Proceedings

Notice of a motion to vacate, modify, or correct an award must be served upon the adverse party or his attorney within three months after the award is filed or delivered. If the adverse party is a resident of the district within which the award was made, such service shall be made upon the adverse party or his attorney as prescribed by law for service of notice of motion in an action in the same court. If the adverse party shall be a nonresident then the notice of the application shall be served by the marshal of any district within which the adverse party may be found in like manner as other process of the court. For the purposes of the motion any judge who might make an order to stay the proceedings in an action brought in the same court may make an order, to be served with the notice of motion, staying the proceedings of the adverse party to enforce the award.

9 U.S.C. § 13. Papers Filed with Order on Motions; Judgment; Docketing; Force and Effect; Enforcement

The party moving for an order confirming, modifying, or correcting an award shall, at the time such order is filed with the clerk for the entry of judgment thereon, also file the following

(a) The agreement: the selection or appointment, if any, of an additional arbitrator or umpire; and each written extension of the time, if any, within which to make the award.

(b) The award.

(c) Each notice, affidavit, or other paper used upon an application to confirm, modify, or correct the award, and a copy of each order of the court upon such an application.

The judgment shall be docketed as if it was rendered in an action.

The judgment so entered shall have the same force and effect, in all respects, as, and be subject to all the provisions of law relating to, a judgment in an action; and it may be enforced as if it had been rendered in an action in the court in which it is entered.

9 U.S.C. § 14. Contracts Not Affected

This title shall not apply to contracts made prior to January 1, 1926.

9 U.S.C. § 15. Inapplicability of the Act of State doctrine

Enforcement of arbitral agreements, confirmation of arbitral awards, and execution upon judgments based on orders confirming such awards shall not be refused on the basis of the Act of State doctrine.

9 U.S.C. § 16. Appeals

(a) An appeal may be taken from —

  (1) an order —

    (A) refusing a stay of any action under section 3 of this title,

    (B) denying a petition under section 4 of this title to order arbitration to proceed,

    (C) denying an application under section 206 of this title to compel arbitration,

    (D) confirming or denying confirmation of an award or partial award, or

    (E) modifying, correcting, or vacating an award;

  (2) an interlocutory order granting, continuing, or modifying an injunction against an arbitration that is subject to this title; or

  (3) a final decision with respect to an arbitration that is subject to this title.

(b) Except as otherwise provided in section 1292(b) of title 28, an appeal may not be taken from an interlocutory order

  (1) granting a stay of any action under section 3 of this title;

  (2) directing arbitration to proceed under section 4 of this title;

  (3) compelling arbitration under section 206 of this title; or

  (4) refusing to enjoin an arbitration that is subject to this title.

APPENDIX B

THE CONVENTION ON THE RECOGNITION AND ENFORCEMENT OF FOREIGN ARBITRAL AWARDS, 9 U.S.C. §§ 201–208

Chapter One

Article I

1. This Convention shall apply to the recognition and enforcement of arbitral awards made in the territory of a State other than the State where the recognition and enforcement of such awards are sought, and arising out of differences between persons, whether physical or legal. It shall also apply to arbitral awards not considered as domestic awards in the State where their recognition and enforcement are sought.

2. The term "arbitral awards" shall include not only awards made by arbitrators appointed for each case but also those made by permanent arbitral bodies to which the parties have submitted.

3. When signing, ratifying or acceding to this Convention, or notifying extension under article X hereof, any State may on the basis of reciprocity declare that it will apply the Convention to the recognition and enforcement of awards made only in the territory of another Contracting State. It may also declare that it will apply the Convention only to differences arising out of legal relationships, whether contractual or not, which are considered as commercial under the national law of the State making such declaration.

Article II

1. Each Contracting State shall recognize an agreement in writing under which the parties undertake to submit to arbitration all or any differences which have arisen or which may arise between them in respect of a defined legal relationship, whether contractual or not, concerning a subject matter capable of settlement by arbitration.

2. The term "agreement in writing" shall include an arbitral clause in a contract or an arbitration agreement, signed by the parties or contained in an exchange of letters or telegrams.

3. The court of a Contracting State, when seized of an action in a matter in respect of which the parties have made an agreement within the meaning of this article, at the request of one of the parties, refer the parties to

arbitration, unless it finds that the said agreement is null and void, inoperative or incapable of being performed.

Article III

Each Contracting State shall recognize arbitral awards as binding and enforce them in accordance with the rules of procedure of the territory where the award is relied upon, under the conditions laid down in the following articles. There shall not be imposed substantially more onerous conditions or higher fees or charges on the recognition or enforcement of arbitral awards to which this Convention applies than are imposed on the recognition or enforcement of domestic arbitral awards

Article IV

1. To obtain the recognition and enforcement mentioned in the preceding article, the party applying for recognition and enforcement shall, at the time of the application, supply:

(a) The duly authenticated original award or a duly certified copy thereof;

(b) The original agreement referred to in article II or a duly certified copy thereof.

2. If the said award or agreement is not made in an official language of the country in which the award is relied upon, the party applying for recognition and enforcement of the award shall produce a translation of these documents into such language. The translation shall be certified by an official or sworn translator or by a diplomatic or consular agent.

Article V

1. Recognition and enforcement of the award may be refused, at the request of the party against whom it is invoked, only if that party furnishes to the competent authority where the recognition and enforcement is sought, proof that:

(a) The parties to the agreement referred to in article II were, under the law applicable to them, under some incapacity, or the said agreement is not valid under the law to which the parties have subjected it or, failing any indication thereon, under the law of the country where the award was made; or

(b) The party against whom the award is invoked was not given proper notice of the appointment of the arbitrator or of the arbitration proceedings or was otherwise unable to present his case; or

(c) The award deals with a difference not contemplated by or not falling within the terms of the submission to arbitration, or it contains decisions on matters beyond the scope of the submission to arbitration, provided that, if the decisions on matters submitted to arbitration can be separated from those not so submitted, that part of the award which contains decisions on matters submitted to arbitration may be recognized and enforced; or

(d) The composition of the arbitral authority or the arbitral procedure was not in accordance with the agreement of the parties, or, failing such agreement, was not in accordance with the law of the country where the arbitration took place; or

(e) The award has not yet become binding on the parties or has been set aside or suspended by a competent authority of the country in which, or under the law of which, that award was made.

2. Recognition and enforcement of an arbitral award may also be refused if the competent authority in the country where recognition and enforcement is sought finds that:

(a) The subject matter of the difference is not capable of settlement by arbitration under the law of that country; or

(b) The recognition or enforcement of the award would be contrary to the public policy of that country.

Article VI

If an application for the setting aside or suspension of the award has been made to a competent authority referred to in article V (1) (e), the authority before which the award is sought to be relied upon may, if it considers it proper, adjourn the decision on the enforcement of the award and may also, on the application of the party claiming enforcement of the award, order the other party to give suitable security.

Article VII

1. The provisions of the present Convention shall not affect the validity of multilateral or bilateral agreements concerning the recognition and enforcement of arbitral awards entered into by the Contracting States nor deprive any interested party of any right he may have to avail himself of an arbitral award in the manner and to the extent allowed by the law or the treaties of the country where such award is sought to be relied upon.

2. The Geneva Protocol on Arbitration Clauses of 1923 and the Geneva Convention on the Execution of Foreign Arbitral Awards of 1927 shall cease to have effect between Contracting States on their becoming bound and to the extent that they become bound, by this Convention.

Article VIII

1. This Convention shall be open until 31 December 1958 for signature on behalf of any Member of the United Nations and also on behalf of any other State which is or hereafter becomes a member of any specialized agency of the United Nations, or which is or hereafter becomes a party to the Statute of the International Court of Justice, or any other State to which an invitation has been addressed by the General Assembly of the United Nations.

2. This Convention shall be ratified and the instrument of ratification shall be deposited with the Secretary-General of the United Nations.

Article IX

1. This Convention shall be open for accession to all States referred to in article VIII.

2. Accession shall be effected by the deposit of an instrument of accession with the Secretary-General of the United Nations.

Chapter Two

§ 201. Enforcement of Convention

The Convention on the Recognition and Enforcement of Foreign Arbitral Awards of June 10, 1958, shall be enforced in United States courts in accordance with this chapter.

§ 202. Agreement or Award Falling Under the Convention

An arbitration agreement or arbitral award arising out of a legal relationship, whether contractual or not, which is considered as commercial, including a transaction, contract, or agreement described in section 2 of this title, falls under the Convention. An agreement or award arising out of such a relationship which is entirely between citizens of the United States shall be deemed not to fall under the Convention unless that relationship involves property located abroad, envisages performance or enforcement abroad, or has some other reasonable relation with one or more foreign states. For the purpose of this section a corporation is a citizen of the United States if it is incorporated or has its principal place of business in the United States.

§ 203. Jurisdiction; Amount in Controversy

An action or proceeding falling under the Convention shall be deemed to arise under the laws and treaties of the United States. The district courts of the United States (including the courts enumerated in section 460 of title 28) shall have original jurisdiction over such an action or proceeding, regardless of the amount in controversy.

§ 204. Venue

An action or proceeding over which the district courts have jurisdiction pursuant to section 203 of this title may be brought in any such court in which save for the arbitration agreement an action or proceeding with respect to the controversy between the parties could be brought, or in such court for the district and division which embraces the place designated in the agreement as the place of arbitration if such place is within the United States.

§ 205. Removal of Cases From State Courts

Where the subject matter of an action or proceeding pending in a State court relates to an arbitration agreement or award falling under the Convention, the defendant or the defendants may, at any time before the trial thereof, remove such action or proceeding to the district court of the United States for the district and division embracing the place where the action or proceeding is pending. The procedure for removal of causes otherwise provided by law shall apply, except that the ground for removal provided in this section need not appear on the face of the complaint but may be shown in the petition for removal. For the purposes of Chapter 1 of this title any action or proceeding removed under this section shall be deemed to have been brought in the district court to which it is removed.

§ 206. Order to Compel Arbitration; Appointment of Arbitrators

A court having jurisdiction under this chapter may direct that arbitration be held in accordance with the agreement at any place therein provided for, whether that place is within or without the United States. Such court may also appoint arbitrators in accordance with the provisions of the agreement.

§ 207. Award of Arbitrators; Confirmation; Jurisdiction; Proceeding

Within three years after an arbitral award falling under the Convention is made, any party to the arbitration may apply to any court having jurisdiction under this chapter for an order confirming the award as against any other party to the arbitration. The court shall confirm the award unless it finds one of the grounds for refusal or deferral of recognition or enforcement of the award specified in the said Convention.

§ 208. Chapter 1; Residual Application

Chapter 1 applies to actions and proceedings brought under this chapter to the extent that that chapter is not in conflict with this chapter or the Convention as ratified by the United States.

APPENDIX C

UNIFORM ARBITRATION ACT

SECTION 1. DEFINITIONS. In this [Act]:

(1) "Arbitration organization" means a neutral association, agency, board, commission, or other entity that initiates, sponsors, or administers

(2) "Arbitrator" means an individual appointed to render an award in a controversy between persons who are parties to an agreement to arbitrate.

(3) "Authenticate" means:

(A) to sign; or

(B) to execute or adopt a record by attaching to or logically associating with the record, an electronic sound, symbol or process with the intent to sign the record.

(4) "Court" means [a court of competent jurisdiction in this State].

(5) "Knowledge" means actual knowledge.

(6) "Person" means an individual, corporation, business trust, estate, trust, partnership, limited liability company, association, joint venture, government; governmental subdivision, agency, or instrumentality; public corporation; or any other legal or commercial entity.

(7) "Record" means information that is inscribed on a tangible medium or that is stored in an electronic or other medium and is retrievable in perceivable form.

SECTION 2. NOTICE. Unless the parties to an agreement to arbitrate otherwise agree or except as otherwise provided in this [Act], a person gives notice to another person by taking action that is reasonably necessary to inform the other person in ordinary course, whether or not the other person acquires knowledge of the notice. A person has notice if the person has knowledge of the notice or has received notice. A person receives notice when it comes to the person's attention or the notice is delivered at the person's place of residence or place of business, or at another location held out by the person as a place of delivery of such communications.

SECTION 3. WHEN [ACT] APPLIES.

(a) Before [date], this [Act] governs agreements to arbitrate entered into:

(1) on or after [the effective date of this [Act]]; and

(2) before [the effective date of this [Act]], if all parties to the agreement to arbitrate or to arbitration proceedings agree in a record to be governed by this [Act].

829

(a)   On or after [date], this [Act] governs agreements to arbitrate even if the arbitration agreement was entered into prior to [the effective date of this [Act]].

SECTION 4.   EFFECT OF AGREEMENT TO ARBITRATE; NONWAIVABLE PROVISIONS.

(a)   Except as otherwise provided in subsection (b) and (c), the parties to an agreement to arbitrate or to an arbitration proceeding may waive or vary the requirements of this [Act] to the extent permitted by law.

(b)   Before a controversy arises that is subject to an agreement to arbitrate, the parties to the agreement may not:

(1)   waive or vary the requirements of Section 5(a), 6(a), 8, 17(a), 17(b), 26, or 28;

(2)   unreasonably restrict the right under Section 9 to notice of the initiation of an arbitration proceeding;

(3)   unreasonably restrict the right under Section 12 to disclosure of any facts by a neutral arbitrator; or

(4)   waive the right under Section 16 of a party to an agreement to arbitrate to be represented by a lawyer at any proceeding or hearing under this [Act], except that an employer and a labor organization may waive the right to representation by a lawyer in a labor arbitration.

(c)   The parties to an agreement to arbitrate may not waive or vary the requirements of this section or Section 3(a)(1), 3(b), 7, 14, 18, 20(c), 20(d), 22, 23, 24, 25(a), 25(b), 29, 30, 31, or 32.

SECTION 5.   [APPLICATION] TO COURT.

(a)   Except as otherwise provided in Section 28, an [application] for judicial relief under this [Act] must be made by [motion] to the court and heard in the manner and upon the notice provided by law or rule of court for making and hearing [motions].

(b)   Notice of an initial [motion] to the court under this [Act] must be served in the manner provided by law for the service of a summons in a civil action unless a civil action is already pending involving the agreement to arbitrate.

SECTION 6.   VALIDITY OF AGREEMENT TO ARBITRATE.

(a)   An agreement contained in a record to submit to arbitration any existing or subsequent controversy arising between the parties to the agreement is valid, enforceable, and irrevocable except upon a ground that exists at law or in equity for the revocation of contract.

(b)   The court shall decide whether an agreement to arbitrate exists or a controversy is subject to an agreement to arbitrate.

(c)   An arbitrator shall decide whether a condition precedent to arbitrability has been fulfilled and whether a contract containing a valid agreement to arbitrate is enforceable.

(d)   If a party to a judicial proceeding challenges the existence of, or claims that a controversy is not subject to, an agreement to arbitrate, the arbitration proceeding may continue pending final resolution of the issue by the court, unless the court otherwise orders.

SECTION 7.   [MOTION] TO COMPEL OR STAY ARBITRATION.

(a)   On [motion] of a person showing an agreement to arbitrate and alleging another person's refusal to arbitrate pursuant to the agreement, the court shall order the parties to arbitrate if the refusing party does not appear or does not oppose the [motion]. If the refusing party opposes the [motion], the court shall proceed summarily to decide the issue. Unless the court finds that there is no enforceable agreement to arbitrate, it shall order the parties to arbitrate. If the court finds that there is no enforceable agreement, it may not order the parties to arbitrate.

(b)   On [motion] of a person alleging that an arbitration proceeding has been initiated or threatened but that there is no agreement to arbitrate, the court shall proceed summarily to decide the issue. If the court finds that there is an enforceable agreement to arbitrate, it shall order the parties to arbitrate. If the court finds that there is no enforceable agreement, it may not order the parties to arbitrate.

(c)   The court may not refuse to order arbitration because the claim subject to arbitration lacks merit or grounds for the claim have not been established.

(d)   If a proceeding involving a claim referable to arbitration under an alleged agreement to arbitrate is pending in court, a [motion] under this section must be filed in that court. Otherwise a [motion] under this section may be filed in any court as required by Section 27.

(e)   If a party files a [motion] with the court to order arbitration under this section, the court shall on just terms stay any judicial proceeding that involves a claim alleged to be subject to the arbitration until the court renders a final decision under this section.

(f)   If the court orders arbitration, the court shall on just terms stay any judicial proceeding that involves a claim subject to the arbitration. If a claim subject to the arbitration is severable, the court may sever it and limit the stay to that claim.

SECTION 8.   PROVISIONAL REMEDIES.

(a)   Before an arbitrator is appointed and is authorized and able to act, the court, upon [motion] of a party to an arbitration proceeding and for good cause shown, may enter an order for provisional remedies to protect the effectiveness of the arbitration proceeding to the same extent and under the same conditions as if the controversy were the subject of a civil action.

(b)   After an arbitrator is appointed and is authorized and able to act, the arbitrator may issue such orders for provisional remedies, including interim awards, as the arbitrator finds necessary to protect the effectiveness of the arbitration proceeding and to promote the fair and expeditious resolution of the controversy, to the same extent and under the same conditions as if the controversy were the subject of a civil action. After an arbitrator is appointed and is authorized and able to act, a party to an arbitration proceeding may move the court for a provisional remedy only if the matter is urgent and the arbitrator is not able to act timely or if the arbitrator cannot provide an adequate remedy.

(c) A [motion] to a court for a provisional remedy under subsection (a) or (b) does not waive any right of arbitration.

SECTION 9. INITIATION OF ARBITRATION.

(a) A person initiates an arbitration proceeding by giving notice in a record to the other parties to the agreement to arbitrate in the agreed manner between the parties or, in the absence of agreement, by mail certified or registered, return receipt requested and obtained, or by service as authorized for the initiation of a civil action. The notice must describe the nature of the controversy and the remedy sought.

(b) Unless a person interposes an objection as to lack or insufficiency of notice under Section 15(c) not later than the commencement of the arbitration hearing, the person's appearance at the hearing waives any objection to lack of or insufficiency of notice.

SECTION 10. CONSOLIDATION OF SEPARATE ARBITRATION PROCEEDINGS.

(a) Except as otherwise provided in subsection (c), upon [motion] of a party to an agreement to arbitrate or to an arbitration proceeding, the court may order consolidation of separate arbitration proceedings as to all or some of the claims if:

(1) there are separate agreements to arbitrate or separate arbitration proceedings between the same persons or one of them is a party to a separate agreement to arbitrate or a separate arbitration proceeding with a third person;

(2) the claims subject to the agreements to arbitrate arise in substantial part from the same transaction or series of related transactions;

(3) the existence of a common issue of law or fact creates the possibility of conflicting decisions in the separate arbitration proceedings; and

(4) prejudice resulting from a failure to consolidate is not outweighed by the risk of undue delay or prejudice to the rights of or hardship to parties opposing consolidation.

(b) The court may order consolidation of separate arbitration proceedings as to certain claims and allow other claims to be resolved in separate arbitration proceedings.

(c) The court may not order consolidation of the claims of a party to an agreement to arbitrate which prohibits consolidation.

SECTION 11. APPOINTMENT OF ARBITRATOR; SERVICE AS A NEUTRAL ARBITRATOR.

(a) If the parties to an agreement to arbitrate agree on a method for appointing an arbitrator, that method must be followed, unless the method fails. If the parties have not agreed on a method, the agreed method fails, or an arbitrator appointed fails or is unable to act and a successor has not been appointed, the court, on [motion] of a party to the arbitration proceeding, shall appoint the arbitrator. The arbitrator so appointed has all the powers of an arbitrator designated in the agreement to arbitrate or appointed pursuant to the agreed method.

(b) An arbitrator who has a known, direct, and material interest in the outcome of the arbitration proceeding or a known, existing, and substantial relationship with a party may not serve as a

SECTION 12. DISCLOSURE BY ARBITRATOR.

(a) Before accepting appointment, an individual who is requested to serve as an arbitrator, after making a reasonable inquiry, shall disclose to all parties to the agreement to arbitrate and arbitration proceeding and to any other arbitrators any known facts that a reasonable person would consider likely to affect the impartiality of the arbitrator in the arbitration proceeding, including:

(1) a financial or personal interest in the outcome of the arbitration proceeding; and

(2) an existing or past relationship with any of the parties to the agreement to arbitrate or the arbitration proceeding, their counsel or representatives, witnesses, or the other arbitrators.

(b) An arbitrator has a continuing obligation to disclose to all parties to the agreement to arbitrate and arbitration proceedings and to any other arbitrators any facts that the arbitrator learns after accepting appointment which a reasonable person would consider likely to affect the impartiality of the arbitrator.

(c) If an arbitrator discloses a fact required by subsection (a) or (b) to be disclosed and a party timely objects to the appointment or continued service of the arbitrator based upon the disclosure, the objection may be a ground to vacate the award under Section 23(a)(2).

(d) If the arbitrator did not disclose a fact as required by subsection (a) or (b), upon timely objection of a party, an award may be vacated under Section 23(a)(2).

(e) An arbitrator appointed as a neutral who does not disclose a known, direct, and material interest in the outcome of the arbitration proceeding or a known, existing, and substantial relationship with a party is presumed to act with evident partiality under Section 23(a)(2).

(f) If the parties to an arbitration proceeding agree to the procedures of an arbitration organization or any other procedures for challenges to arbitrators before an award is made, substantial compliance with those procedures is a condition precedent to a [motion] to vacate an award on that ground under Section 23(a)(2).

SECTION 13. ACTION BY MAJORITY. If there is more than one arbitrator, the powers of the arbitrators must be exercised by a majority of them.

SECTION 14. IMMUNITY OF ARBITRATOR; COMPETENCY TO TESTIFY; ATTORNEY'S FEES AND COSTS.

(a) An arbitrator or an arbitration organization acting in such capacity is immune from civil liability to the same extent as a judge of a court of this State acting in a judicial capacity.

(b) The immunity afforded by this section supplements any other immunity.

(c) If an arbitrator does not make a disclosure required by Section 12, the nondisclosure does not cause a loss of immunity under this section.

(d) In any judicial, administrative, or similar proceeding, an arbitrator or representative of an arbitration organization is not competent to testify or required to produce records as to any statement, conduct, decision, or ruling occurring during the arbitration proceeding to the same extent as a judge of a court of this State acting in a judicial capacity. This subsection does not apply:

(1) to the extent necessary to determine the claim of an arbitrator or an arbitration organization or a representative of the arbitration organization against a party to the arbitration proceeding or

(2) if a party to the arbitration proceeding files a [motion] to vacate an award under Section 23(a)(1) or (2) and establishes prima facie that a ground for vacating the award exists.

(e) If a person commences a civil action against an arbitrator, an arbitration organization, or a representative of an arbitration organization arising from the services of the arbitrator, organization, or representative or if a person seeks to compel an arbitrator or a representative of an arbitration organization to testify in violation of subsection (d), and the court decides that the arbitrator, arbitration organization, or representative of an arbitration organization is immune from civil liability or that the arbitrator or representative of the organization is incompetent to testify, the court shall award to the arbitrator, organization, or representative reasonable attorney's fees and other reasonable expenses of litigation.

SECTION 15. ARBITRATION PROCESS.

(a) The arbitrator may conduct the arbitration in such manner as the arbitrator considers appropriate so as to aid in the fair and expeditious disposition of the proceeding. The authority conferred upon the arbitrator includes the power to hold conferences with the parties to the arbitration proceeding before the hearing and to determine the admissibility, relevance, materiality and weight of any evidence.

(b)   The arbitrator may decide a request for summary disposition of a claim or particular issue by agreement of all interested parties or upon request of one party to the arbitration proceeding if that party gives notice to all other parties to the arbitration proceeding and the other parties have a reasonable opportunity to respond.

(c)   The arbitrator shall set a time and place for a hearing and give notice of the hearing not less than five days before the hearing. Unless a party to the arbitration proceeding interposes an objection to lack of or insufficiency of notice not later than the commencement of the hearing, the party's appearance at the hearing waives the objection. Upon request of a party to the arbitration proceeding and for good cause shown, or upon the arbitrator's own initiative, the arbitrator may adjourn the hearing from time to time as necessary but may not postpone the hearing to a time later than that fixed by the agreement to arbitrate for making the award unless the parties to the arbitration proceeding consent to a later date. The arbitrator may hear and decide the controversy upon the evidence produced although a party who was duly notified of the arbitration proceeding did not appear. The court, on request, may direct the arbitrator to promptly conduct the hearing and render a timely decision.

(d)   If an arbitrator orders a hearing under subsection (c), the parties to the arbitration proceeding are entitled to be heard, to present evidence material to the controversy, and to cross-examine witnesses appearing at the hearing.

(e)   If there is more than one arbitrator, all of them shall conduct the hearing under subsection (c); however, a majority shall decide any issue and make a final award.

(f)   If an arbitrator ceases, or is unable, to act during the arbitration proceeding, a replacement arbitrator must be appointed in accordance with Section 11 to continue the hearing and to decide the controversy.

SECTION 16.   REPRESENTATION BY LAWYER. A party to an arbitration proceeding may be represented by a lawyer.

SECTION 17.   WITNESSES; SUBPOENAS; DEPOSITIONS; DISCOVERY.

(a)   An arbitrator may issue a subpoena for the attendance of a witness and for the production of records and other evidence at any hearing and may administer oaths. A subpoena must be served in the manner for service of subpoenas in a civil action and, upon [motion] to the court by a party to the arbitration proceeding or the arbitrator, enforced in the manner for enforcement of subpoenas in a civil action.

(b)   On request of a party to or a witness in an arbitration proceeding, an arbitrator may permit a deposition of any witness, including a witness who cannot be subpoenaed for or is unable to attend a hearing, to be taken under conditions determined by the arbitrator for use as evidence in order to make the proceeding fair, expeditious, and cost effective.

(c)   An arbitrator may permit such discovery as the arbitrator decides is appropriate in the circumstances, taking into account the needs of the parties to the arbitration proceeding and other affected persons and the desirability of making the proceeding fair, expeditious, and cost effective.

(d)   If an arbitrator permits discovery under subsection (c), the arbitrator may order a party to the arbitration proceeding to comply with the arbitrator's discovery-related orders, including the issuance of a subpoena for the attendance of a witness and for the production of records and other evidence at a discovery proceeding, and may take action against a party to the arbitration proceeding who does not comply to the extent permitted by law as if the controversy were the subject of a civil action in this State.

(e)   An arbitrator may issue a protective order to prevent the disclosure of privileged information, confidential information, trade secrets, and other information protected from disclosure as if the controversy were the subject of a civil action in this State.

(f)   All laws compelling a person under subpoena to testify and all fees for attending a judicial proceeding, a deposition, or a discovery proceeding as a witness apply to an arbitration proceeding as if the controversy were the subject of a civil action in this State.

(g)   The court may enforce a subpoena or discovery-related order for the attendance of a witness within this State and for the production of records and other evidence issued by an arbitrator in connection with an arbitration proceeding in another State upon conditions determined by the court in order to make the arbitration proceeding fair, expeditious, and cost effective. A subpoena or discovery-related order issued by an arbitrator must be served in the manner provided by law for service of subpoenas in a civil action in this State and, upon [motion] to the court by a party to the arbitration proceeding or the arbitrator, enforced in the manner provided by law for

SECTION 18.   COURT ENFORCEMENT OF PRE-AWARD RULING BY ARBITRATOR. If an arbitrator makes a pre-award ruling in favor of a party to the arbitration proceeding, the party may request the arbitrator to incorporate the ruling into an award under Section 19. The successful party may file a [motion] to the court for an expedited order to confirm the award under Section 22, in which case the court shall proceed summarily to decide the [motion]. The court shall issue an order to confirm the award unless the court vacates, modifies, or corrects the award of the arbitrator pursuant to Sections 23 and 24.

SECTION 19.   AWARD.

(a)   An arbitrator shall make a record of an award. The record must be authenticated by any arbitrator who concurs with the award. The arbitrator or the arbitration organization shall give notice of the award, including a copy of the award, to each party to the arbitration proceeding.

(b)   An award must be made within the time specified by the agreement to arbitrate or, if not specified therein, within the time ordered by the court. The court may extend or the parties to the arbitration proceeding may agree in a record to extend the time. The court or the parties may do so within or after the time specified or ordered. A party waives any objection that an award was not timely made unless the party gives notice of the objection to the arbitrator before receiving notice of the award.

SECTION 20. CHANGE OF AWARD BY ARBITRATOR.

(a) On [motion] to an arbitrator by a party to the arbitration proceeding, the arbitrator may modify or correct an award:

(1) upon the grounds stated in Section 24(a)(1) or (3);

(2) because the arbitrator has not made a final and definite award upon a claim submitted by the parties to the arbitration proceeding; or

(3) to clarify the award.

(b) A [motion] under subsection (a) must be made and served on all parties within 20 days after the movant receives notice of the award.

(c) A party to the arbitration proceeding must serve any objections to the [motion] within 10 days after receipt of the notice.

(d) If a [motion] to the court is pending under Section 22, 23, or 24, the court may submit the claim to the arbitrator to consider whether to modify or correct the award:

(1) upon the grounds stated in Section 24(a)(1) or (3);

(2) because the arbitrator has not made a final and definite award upon a claim submitted by the parties to the arbitration proceeding; or

(3) to clarify the award.

(e) An award modified or corrected pursuant to this section is subject to Sections 22, 23, and 24.

SECTION 21. REMEDIES; FEES AND EXPENSES OF ARBITRATION PROCEEDING.

(a) An arbitrator may award punitive damages or other exemplary relief if such an award is authorized by law in a civil action involving the same claim and the evidence produced at the hearing justifies the award under the legal standards otherwise applicable to the claim.

(b) An arbitrator may award attorney's fees and other reasonable expenses of arbitration if such an award is authorized by law in a civil action involving the same claim or by the agreement of the parties to the arbitration proceeding.

(c) As to all remedies other than those authorized by subsections (a) and (b), an arbitrator may order such remedies as the arbitrator considers just and appropriate under the circumstances of the arbitration proceeding. The fact that such a remedy could not or would not be granted by the court is not a ground for refusing to confirm an award under Section 22 or for vacating an award under Section 23.

(d) An arbitrator's expenses and fees, together with other expenses, must be paid as provided in the award.

(e) If an arbitrator awards punitive damages or other exemplary relief under subsection (a), the arbitrator shall specify in the award the basis in fact justifying and the basis in law authorizing the award and state separately the amount of the punitive damages or other exemplary relief.

SECTION 22. CONFIRMATION OF AWARD. After a party to the arbitration proceeding receives notice of an award, the party may file a [motion] with the court for an order confirming the award, at which time the court shall issue such an order unless the award is modified or corrected pursuant to Section 20 or 24 or is vacated pursuant to Section 23.

SECTION 23. VACATING AWARD.

(a) Upon [motion] of a party to the arbitration proceeding, the court shall vacate an award if:

(1) the award was procured by corruption, fraud, or other undue means;

(2) there was:

(A) evident partiality by an arbitrator appointed as a neutral;

(B) corruption by an arbitrator; or

(C) misconduct by an arbitrator prejudicing the rights of a party to the arbitration proceeding;

(3) an arbitrator refused to postpone the hearing upon showing of sufficient cause for postponement, refused to consider evidence material to the controversy, or otherwise conducted the hearing contrary to Section 15, so as to prejudice substantially the rights of a party to the arbitration proceeding;

(4) an arbitrator exceeded the arbitrator's powers;

(5) there was no agreement to arbitrate, unless the person participated in the arbitration proceeding without raising the objection under Section 15(c) not later than the commencement of the arbitration hearing; or

(6) the arbitration was conducted without proper notice of the initiation of an arbitration as required in Section 9 so as to prejudice substantially the rights of a party to the arbitration proceeding.

(b) A [motion] under this section must be filed within 90 days after the movant receives notice of the award in a record pursuant to Section 19 or within 90 days after the movant receives notice of an arbitrator's award in a record on a [motion] to modify or correct an award pursuant to Section 20, unless the [motion] is predicated upon the ground that the award was procured by corruption, fraud, or other undue means, in which case it must be filed within 90 days after such a ground is known or by the exercise of reasonable care should have been known by the movant.

(c) In vacating an award on a ground other than that set forth in subsection (a)(5), the court may order a rehearing before a new arbitrator. If the award is vacated on a ground stated in subsection (a)(3), (4), or (6), the court may order a rehearing before the arbitrator who made the award or the arbitrator's successor. The arbitrator must render the decision in the rehearing within the same time as that provided in Section 19(b) for an award.

(d) If a [motion] to vacate an award is denied and a [motion] to modify or correct the award is not pending, the court shall confirm the award.

SECTION 24. MODIFICATION OR CORRECTION OF AWARD.

(a) Upon [motion] filed within 90 days after the movant receives notice of the award in a record pursuant to Section 19 or within 90 days after the movant receives notice of an arbitrator's award in a record on a [motion] to modify or correct an award pursuant to Section 20, the court shall modify or correct the award if:

(1) there was an evident mathematical miscalculation or an evident mistake in the description of a person, thing, or property referred to in the award;

(2) the arbitrator has made an award on a claim not submitted to the arbitrator and the award may be corrected without affecting the merits of the decision upon the claims submitted; or

(3) the award is imperfect in a matter of form not affecting the merits of the decision on the claims submitted.

(b) If a [motion] filed under subsection (a) is granted, the court shall modify or correct and confirm the award as modified or corrected. Otherwise, the court shall confirm the award.

(c) A [motion] to modify or correct an award pursuant to this section may be joined with a [motion] to vacate the award.

SECTION 25. JUDGMENT ON AWARD; ATTORNEY'S FEES AND LITIGATION EXPENSES.

(a) Upon granting an order confirming, vacating without directing a rehearing, modifying, or correcting an award, the court shall enter a judgment in conformity therewith. The judgment may be recorded, docketed, and enforced as any other judgment in a civil action.

(b) A court may allow reasonable costs of the [motion] and subsequent judicial proceedings.

(c) On [application] of a prevailing party to a contested judicial proceeding under Section 22, 23, or 24, the court may add to a judgment confirming, vacating without directing a rehearing, modifying, or correcting an award, attorney's fees and other reasonable expenses of litigation incurred in a judicial proceeding after the award is made.

SECTION 26. JURISDICTION.

(a) A court of this State having jurisdiction over the dispute and the parties may enforce an agreement to arbitrate.

(b) An agreement to arbitrate providing for arbitration in this State confers exclusive jurisdiction on the court to enter judgment on an award under this [Act].

SECTION 27. VENUE. A [motion] pursuant to Section 5 must be filed in the court of the [county] in which the agreement to arbitrate specifies the arbitration hearing is to be held or, if the hearing has been held, in the court of the [county] in which it was held. Otherwise, the [motion] must be filed in any [county] in which an adverse party resides or has a place of business or, if no adverse party has a residence or place of business in this State, in the court of any [county] in this State. All subsequent [motions] must be filed in the court hearing the initial [motion] unless the court otherwise directs.

SECTION 28. APPEALS.

(a) An appeal may be taken from:

    (1) an order denying a [motion] to compel arbitration;

    (2) an order granting a [motion] to stay arbitration;

    (3) an order confirming or denying confirmation of an award;

    (4) an order modifying or correcting an award;

    (5) an order vacating an award without directing a rehearing; or

    (6) a final judgment entered pursuant to this [Act].

(b) An appeal under this section must be taken as from an order or a judgment in a civil action.

SECTION 29. UNIFORMITY OF APPLICATION AND CONSTRUCTION. In applying and construing this Uniform Act, consideration must be given to the need to promote uniformity of the law with respect to its subject matter among States that enact it.

SECTION 30. EFFECTIVE DATE. This [Act] takes effect on [effective date].

SECTION 31. REPEAL. Effective on [date], the [Uniform Arbitration Act] is repealed.

SECTION 32. SAVINGS CLAUSE. This [Act] does not affect an action or proceeding commenced or right accrued before this [Act] takes effect.

SECTION 33. RELATIONSHIP TO ELECTRONIC SIGNATURES IN GLOBAL AND NATIONAL COMMERCE ACT. The provisions of this Act governing the legal effect, validity, and enforceability of electronic records or electronic signatures, and of contracts performed with the use of such records or signatures conform to the requirements of section 102 of the Electronic Signatures in Global and National Commerce Act.

APPENDIX D

THE STANDARDS OF CONDUCT FOR MEDIATORS

The *Model Standards of Conduct for Mediators* was prepared in 1994 by the American Arbitration Association, the American Bar Association's Section of Dispute Resolution, and the Association for Conflict Resolution.[1] A joint committee consisting of representatives from the same successor organizations revised the Model Standards in 2005.[2] Both the original 1994 version and the 2005 revision have been approved by each participating organization.[3]

Preamble

Mediation is used to resolve a broad range of conflicts within a variety of settings. These Standards are designed to serve as fundamental ethical guidelines for persons mediating in all practice contexts. They serve three primary goals: to guide the conduct of mediators; to inform the mediating parties; and to promote public confidence in mediation as a process for resolving disputes.

Mediation is a process in which an impartial third party facilitates communication and negotiation and promotes voluntary decision making by the parties to the dispute.

Mediation serves various purposes, including providing the opportunity for parties to define and clarify issues, understand different perspectives, identify interests, explore and assess possible solutions, and reach mutually satisfactory agreements, when desired.

Note on Construction

These Standards are to be read and construed in their entirety. There is no priority significance attached to the sequence in which the Standards appear.

The use of the term "shall" in a Standard indicates that the mediator must follow the practice described. The use of the term "should" indicates that the practice described in the standard is highly desirable, but not required, and

---

[1] The Association for Conflict Resolution is a merged organization of the Academy of Family Mediators, the Conflict Resolution Education Network and the Society of Professionals in Dispute Resolution (SPIDR). SPIDR was the third participating organization in the development of the 1994 Standards.

[2] Reporter's Notes, which are not part of these Standards and therefore have not been specifically approved by any of the organizations, provide commentary regarding these revisions.

[3] The 2005 revisions to the Model Standards were approved by the American Bar Association's House of Delegates on August 9, 2005, the Board of the Association for Conflict Resolution on August 22, 2005 and the Executive Committee of the American Arbitration Association on September 8, 2005.

is to be departed from only for very strong reasons and requires careful use of judgment and discretion.

The use of the term "mediator" is understood to be inclusive so that it applies to co-mediator models.

These Standards do not include specific temporal parameters when referencing a mediation, and therefore, do not define the exact beginning or ending of a mediation.

Various aspects of a mediation, including some matters covered by these Standards, may also be affected by applicable law, court rules, regulations, other applicable professional rules, mediation rules to which the parties have agreed and other agreements of the parties. These sources may create conflicts with, and may take precedence over, these Standards. However, a mediator should make every effort to comply with the spirit and intent of these Standards in resolving such conflicts. This effort should include honoring all remaining Standards not in conflict with these other sources.

These Standards, unless and until adopted by a court or other regulatory authority do not have the force of law. Nonetheless, the fact that these Standards have been adopted by the respective sponsoring entities, should alert mediators to the fact that the Standards might be viewed as establishing a standard of care for mediators.

STANDARD I. SELF-DETERMINATION

A. A mediator shall conduct a mediation based on the principle of party self-determination. Self-determination is the act of coming to a voluntary, uncoerced decision in which each party makes free and informed choices as to process and outcome. Parties may exercise self-determination at any stage of a mediation, including mediator selection, process design, participation in or withdrawal from the process, and outcomes.

1. Although party self-determination for process design is a fundamental principle of mediation practice, a mediator may need to balance such party self-determination with a mediator's duty to conduct a quality process in accordance with these Standards.

2. A mediator cannot personally ensure that each party has made free and informed choices to reach particular decisions, but, where appropriate, a mediator should make the parties aware of the importance of consulting other professionals to help them make informed choices.

B. A mediator shall not undermine party self-determination by any party for reasons such as higher settlement rates, egos, increased fees, or outside pressures from court personnel, program administrators, provider organizations, the media or others.

STANDARD II. IMPARTIALITY

A. A mediator shall decline a mediation if the mediator cannot conduct it in an impartial manner. Impartiality means freedom from favoritism, bias or prejudice.

B. A mediator shall conduct a mediation in an impartial manner and avoid conduct that gives the appearance of partiality.

1. A mediator should not act with partiality or prejudice based on any participant's personal characteristics, background, values and beliefs, or performance at a mediation, or any other reason.

2. A mediator should neither give nor accept a gift, favor, loan or other item of value that raises a question as to the mediator's actual or perceived impartiality.

3. A mediator may accept or give de minimis gifts or incidental items or services that are provided to facilitate a mediation or respect cultural norms so long as such practices do not raise questions as to a mediator's actual or perceived impartiality.

C. If at any time a mediator is unable to conduct a mediation in an impartial manner, the mediator shall withdraw.

STANDARD III. CONFLICTS OF INTEREST

A. A mediator shall avoid a conflict of interest or the appearance of a conflict of interest during and after a mediation. A conflict of interest can arise from involvement by a mediator with the subject matter of the dispute or from any relationship between a mediator and any mediation participant, whether past or present, personal or professional, that reasonably raises a question of a mediator's impartiality.

B. A mediator shall make a reasonable inquiry to determine whether there are any facts that a reasonable individual would consider likely to create a potential or actual conflict of interest for a mediator. A mediator's actions necessary to accomplish a reasonable inquiry into potential conflicts of interest may vary based on practice context.

C. A mediator shall disclose, as soon as practicable, all actual and potential conflicts of interest that are reasonably known to the mediator and could reasonably be seen as raising a question about the mediator's impartiality. After disclosure, if all parties agree, the mediator may proceed with the mediation.

D. If a mediator learns any fact after accepting a mediation that raises a question with respect to that mediator's service creating a potential or actual conflict of interest, the mediator shall disclose it as quickly as practicable. After disclosure, if all parties agree, the mediator may proceed with the mediation.

E. If a mediator's conflict of interest might reasonably be viewed as undermining the integrity of the mediation, a mediator shall withdraw from or decline to proceed with the mediation regardless of the expressed desire or agreement of the parties to the contrary.

F. Subsequent to a mediation, a mediator shall not establish another relationship with any of the participants in any matter that would raise questions about the integrity of the mediation. When a mediator develops personal or professional relationships with parties, other individuals or organizations following a mediation in which they were involved, the mediator should consider factors such as time elapsed following the mediation, the nature of the relationships established, and services offered when determining whether the relationships might create a perceived or actual conflict of interest.

STANDARD IV. COMPETENCE

A. A mediator shall mediate only when the mediator has the necessary competence to satisfy the reasonable expectations of the parties.

1. Any person may be selected as a mediator, provided that the parties are satisfied with the mediator's competence and qualifications. Training, experience in mediation, skills, cultural understandings and other qualities are often necessary for mediator competence. A person who offers to serve as a mediator creates the expectation that the person is competent to mediate effectively.

2. A mediator should attend educational programs and related activities to maintain and enhance the mediator's knowledge and skills related to mediation.

3. A mediator should have available for the parties' information relevant to the mediator's training, education, experience and approach to conducting a mediation.

B. If a mediator, during the course of a mediation determines that the mediator cannot conduct the mediation competently, the mediator shall discuss that determination with the parties as soon as is practicable and take appropriate steps to address the situation, including, but not limited to, withdrawing or requesting appropriate assistance.

C. If a mediator's ability to conduct a mediation is impaired by drugs, alcohol, medication or otherwise, the mediator shall not conduct the mediation.

STANDARD V. CONFIDENTIALITY

A. A mediator shall maintain the confidentiality of all information obtained by the mediator in mediation, unless otherwise agreed to by the parties or required by applicable law.

1. If the parties to a mediation agree that the mediator may disclose information obtained during the mediation, the mediator may do so.

2. A mediator should not communicate to any non-participant information about how the parties acted in the mediation. A mediator may report, if required, whether parties appeared at a scheduled mediation and whether or not the parties reached a resolution.

3. If a mediator participates in teaching, research or evaluation of mediation, the mediator should protect the anonymity of the parties and abide by their reasonable expectations regarding confidentiality.

B. A mediator who meets with any persons in private session during a mediation shall not convey directly or indirectly to any other person, any information that was obtained during that private session without the consent of the disclosing person.

C. A mediator shall promote understanding among the parties of the extent to which the parties will maintain confidentiality of information they obtain in a mediation.

D. Depending on the circumstance of a mediation, the parties may have varying expectations regarding confidentiality that a mediator should address. The parties may make their own rules with respect to confidentiality, or the accepted practice of an individual mediator or institution may dictate a particular set of expectations.

STANDARD VI. QUALITY OF THE PROCESS

A. A mediator shall conduct a mediation in accordance with these Standards and in a manner that promotes diligence, timeliness, safety, presence of the appropriate participants, party participation, procedural fairness, party competency and mutual respect among all participants.

1. A mediator should agree to mediate only when the mediator is prepared to commit the attention essential to an effective mediation.

2. A mediator should only accept cases when the mediator can satisfy the reasonable expectation of the parties concerning the timing of a mediation.

3. The presence or absence of persons at a mediation depends on the agreement of the parties and the mediator. The parties and mediator may agree that others may be excluded from particular sessions or from all sessions.

4. A mediator should promote honesty and candor between and among all participants, and a mediator shall not knowingly misrepresent any material fact or circumstance in the course of a mediation.

5. The role of a mediator differs substantially from other professional roles. Mixing the role of a mediator and the role of another profession is problematic and thus, a mediator should distinguish between the roles. A mediator may provide information that the mediator is qualified by training or experience to provide, only if the mediator can do so consistent with these Standards.

6. A mediator shall not conduct a dispute resolution procedure other than mediation but label it mediation in an effort to gain the protection of rules, statutes, or other governing authorities pertaining to mediation.

7. A mediator may recommend, when appropriate, that parties consider resolving their dispute through arbitration, counseling, neutral evaluation or other processes.

8. A mediator shall not undertake an additional dispute resolution role in the same matter without the consent of the parties. Before providing such service, a mediator shall inform the parties of the implications of the change in process and obtain their consent to the change. A mediator who undertakes such role assumes different duties and responsibilities that may be governed by other standards.

9. If a mediation is being used to further criminal conduct, a mediator should take appropriate steps including, if necessary, postponing, withdrawing from or terminating the mediation.

10. If a party appears to have difficulty comprehending the process, issues, or settlement options, or difficulty participating in a mediation, the mediator should explore the circumstances and potential accommodations, modifications or adjustments that would make possible the party's capacity to comprehend, participate and exercise self-determination.

B. If a mediator is made aware of domestic abuse or violence among the parties, the mediator shall take appropriate steps including, if necessary, postponing, withdrawing from or terminating the mediation.

C. If a mediator believes that participant conduct, including that of the mediator, jeopardizes conducting a mediation consistent with these Standards, a mediator shall take appropriate steps including, if necessary, postponing, withdrawing from or terminating the mediation.

STANDARD VII. ADVERTISING AND SOLICITATION

A. A mediator shall be truthful and not misleading when advertising, soliciting or otherwise communicating the mediator's qualifications, experience, services and fees.

1. A mediator should not include any promises as to outcome in communications, including business cards, stationery, or computer-based communications.

2. A mediator should only claim to meet the mediator qualifications of a governmental entity or private organization if that entity or organization has a recognized procedure for qualifying mediators and it grants such status to the mediator.

B. A mediator shall not solicit in a manner that gives an appearance of partiality for or against a party or otherwise undermines the integrity of the process.

C. A mediator shall not communicate to others, in promotional materials or through other forms of communication, the names of persons served without their permission.

STANDARD VIII. FEES AND OTHER CHARGES

A. A mediator shall provide each party or each party's representative true and complete information about mediation fees, expenses and any other actual or potential charges that may be incurred in connection with a mediation.

1. If a mediator charges fees, the mediator should develop them in light of all relevant factors, including the type and complexity of the matter, the qualifications of the mediator, the time required and the rates customary for such mediation services.

2. A mediator's fee arrangement should be in writing unless the parties request otherwise.

B. A mediator shall not charge fees in a manner that impairs a mediator's impartiality.

1. A mediator should not enter into a fee agreement which is contingent upon the result of the mediation or amount of the settlement.

2. While a mediator may accept unequal fee payments from the parties, a mediator should not use fee arrangements that adversely impact the mediator's ability to conduct a mediation in an impartial manner.

STANDARD IX. ADVANCEMENT OF MEDIATION PRACTICE

A. A mediator should act in a manner that advances the practice of mediation. A mediator promotes this Standard by engaging in some or all of the following:

1. Fostering diversity within the field of mediation.

2. Striving to make mediation accessible to those who elect to use it, including providing services at a reduced rate or on a pro bono basis as appropriate.

3. Participating in research when given the opportunity, including obtaining participant feedback when appropriate.

4. Participating in outreach and education efforts to assist the public in developing an improved understanding of, and appreciation for, mediation.

5. Assisting newer mediators through training, mentoring and networking.

B. A mediator should demonstrate respect for differing points of view within the field, seek to learn from other mediators and work together with other mediators to improve the profession and better serve people in conflict.

APPENDIX E

UNIFORM MEDIATION ACT

SECTION 1. TITLE.

This [Act] may be cited as the Uniform Mediation Act.

SECTION 2. DEFINITIONS.

In this [Act]:

(1) "Mediation" means a process in which a mediator facilitates communication and negotiation between parties to assist them in reaching a voluntary agreement regarding their dispute.

(2) "Mediation communication" means a statement, whether oral or in a record or verbal or nonverbal, that occurs during a mediation or is made for purposes of considering, conducting, participating in, initiating, continuing, or reconvening a mediation or retaining a mediator.

(3) "Mediator" means an individual who conducts a mediation.

(4) "Nonparty participant" means a person, other than a party or mediator, that participates in a mediation.

(5) "Mediation party" means a person that participates in a mediation and whose agreement is necessary to resolve the dispute.

(6) "Person" means an individual, corporation, business trust, estate, trust, partnership, limited liability company, association, joint venture, government; governmental subdivision, agency, or instrumentality; public corporation, or any other legal or commercial entity.

(7) "Proceeding" means:

 (A) a judicial, administrative, arbitral, or other adjudicative process, including related pre-hearing and post-hearing motions, conferences, and discovery; or

 (B) a legislative hearing or similar process.

(8) "Record" means information that is inscribed on a tangible medium or that is stored in an electronic or other medium and is retrievable in perceivable form.

(9) "Sign" means:

 (A) to execute or adopt a tangible symbol with the present intent to authenticate a record; or

 (B) to attach or logically associate an electronic symbol, sound, or process to or with a record with the present intent to authenticate a record.

SECTION 3. SCOPE.

(a)   Except as otherwise provided in subsection (b) or (c), this [Act] applies to a mediation in which:

(1)   the mediation parties are required to mediate by statute or court or administrative agency rule or referred to mediation by a court, administrative agency, or arbitrator;

(2)   the mediation parties and the mediator agree to mediate in a record that demonstrates an expectation that mediation communications will be privileged against disclosure; or

(3)   the mediation parties use as a mediator an individual who holds himself or herself out as a mediator or the mediation is provided by a person that holds itself out as providing mediation.

(b)   The [Act] does not apply to a mediation:

(1)   relating to the establishment, negotiation, administration, or termination of a collective bargaining relationship;

(2)   relating to a dispute that is pending under or is part of the processes established by a collective bargaining agreement, except that the [Act] applies to a mediation arising out of a dispute that has been filed with an administrative agency or court;

(3)   conducted by a judge who might make a ruling on the case; or

(4)   conducted under the auspices of:

(A)   a primary or secondary school if all the parties are students or

(B)   a correctional institution for youths if all the parties are residents of that institution.

(c)   If the parties agree in advance in a signed record, or a record of proceeding reflects agreement by the parties, that all or part of a mediation is not privileged, the privileges under Sections 4 through 6 do not apply to the mediation or part agreed upon. However, Sections 4 through 6 apply to a mediation communication made by a person that has not received actual notice of the agreement before the communication is made.

SECTION 4. PRIVILEGE AGAINST DISCLOSURE; ADMISSIBILITY; DISCOVERY.

(a)   Except as otherwise provided in Section 6, a mediation communication is privileged as provided in subsection (b) and is not subject to discovery or admissible in evidence in a proceeding unless waived or precluded as provided by Section 5.

(b)   In a proceeding, the following privileges apply:

(1)   A mediation party may refuse to disclose, and may prevent any other person from disclosing, a mediation communication.

(2)   A mediator may refuse to disclose a mediation communication, and may prevent any other person from disclosing a mediation communication of the mediator.

(3) A nonparty participant may refuse to disclose, and may prevent any other person from disclosing, a mediation communication of the nonparty participant.

(c) Evidence or information that is otherwise admissible or subject to discovery does not become inadmissible or protected from discovery solely by reason of its disclosure or use in a mediation.

SECTION 5. WAIVER AND PRECLUSION OF PRIVILEGE.

(a) A privilege under Section 4 may be waived in a record or orally during a proceeding if it is expressly waived by all parties to the mediation and:

(1) in the case of the privilege of a mediator, it is expressly waived by the mediator; and

(2) in the case of the privilege of a nonparty participant, it is expressly waived by the nonparty participant.

(b) A person that discloses or makes a representation about a mediation communication which prejudices another person in a proceeding is precluded from asserting a privilege under Section 4, but only to the extent necessary for the person prejudiced to respond to the representation or disclosure.

(c) A person that intentionally uses a mediation to plan, attempt to commit or commit a crime, or to conceal an ongoing crime or ongoing criminal activity is precluded from asserting a privilege under Section 4.

SECTION 6. EXCEPTIONS TO PRIVILEGE.

(a) There is no privilege under Section 4 for a mediation communication that is:

(1) in an agreement evidenced by a record signed by all parties to the agreement;

(2) available to the public under [insert statutory reference to open records act] or made during a session of a mediation which is open, or is required by law to be open, to the public;

(3) a threat or statement of a plan to inflict bodily injury or commit a crime of violence;

(4) intentionally used to plan a crime, attempt to commit or commit a crime, or to conceal an ongoing crime or ongoing criminal activity;

(5) sought or offered to prove or disprove a claim or complaint of professional misconduct or malpractice filed against a mediator;

(6) except as otherwise provided in subsection (c), sought or offered to prove or disprove a claim or complaint of professional misconduct or malpractice filed against a mediation party, nonparty participant, or representative of a party based on conduct occurring during a mediation; or

(7) sought or offered to prove or disprove abuse, neglect, abandonment, or exploitation in a proceeding in which a child or adult protective services agency is a party, unless the

[Alternative A: [State to insert, for example, child or adult protection] case is referred by a court to mediation and a public agency participates.]

[Alternative B: public agency participates in the [State to insert, for example, child or adult protection] mediation].

(b)   There is no privilege under Section 4 if a court, administrative agency, or arbitrator finds, after a hearing in camera, that the party seeking discovery or the proponent of the evidence has shown that the evidence is not otherwise available, that there is a need for the evidence that substantially outweighs the interest in protecting confidentiality, and that the mediation communication is sought or offered in:

(1)   a court proceeding involving a felony [or misdemeanor]; or

(2)   except as otherwise provided in subsection (c), a proceeding to prove a claim to rescind or reform or a defense to avoid liability on a contract arising out of the mediation.

(c)   A mediator may not be compelled to provide evidence of a mediation communication referred to in subsection (a)(6) or (b)(2).

(d)   If a mediation communication is not privileged under subsection (a) or (b), only the portion of the communication necessary for the application of the exception from nondisclosure may be admitted. Admission of evidence under subsection (a) or (b) does not render the evidence, or any other mediation communication, discoverable or admissible for any other purpose.

SECTION 7.   PROHIBITED MEDIATOR REPORTS.

(a)   Except as required in subsection (b), a mediator may not make a report, assessment, evaluation, recommendation, finding, or other communication regarding a mediation to a court, administrative agency, or other authority that may make a ruling on the dispute that is the subject of the mediation.

(b)   A mediator may disclose:

(1)   whether the mediation occurred or has terminated, whether a settlement was reached, and attendance;

(2)   a mediation communication as permitted under Section 6; or

(3)   a mediation communication evidencing abuse, neglect, abandonment, or exploitation of an individual to a public agency responsible for protecting individuals against such mistreatment.

(c)   A communication made in violation of subsection (a) may not be considered by a court, administrative agency, or arbitrator.

SECTION 8.   CONFIDENTIALITY. Unless subject to the [insert statutory references to open meetings act and open records act], mediation communications are confidential to the extent agreed by the parties or provided by other law or rule of this State.

SECTION 9. MEDIATOR'S DISCLOSURE OF CONFLICTS OF INTEREST; BACKGROUND.

(a) Before accepting a mediation, an individual who is requested to serve as a mediator shall:

(1) make an inquiry that is reasonable under the circumstances to determine whether there are any known facts that a reasonable individual would consider likely to affect the impartiality of the mediator, including a financial or personal interest in the outcome of the mediation and an existing or past relationship with a mediation party or foreseeable participant in the mediation; and

(2) disclose any such known fact to the mediation parties as soon as is practical before accepting a mediation.

(b) If a mediator learns any fact described in subsection (a)(1) after accepting a mediation, the mediator shall disclose it as soon as is practicable.

(c) At the request of a mediation party, an individual who is requested to serve as a mediator shall disclose the mediator's qualifications to mediate a dispute.

(d) A person that violates subsection [(a) or (b)][(a), (b), or (g)] is precluded by the violation from asserting a privilege under Section 4.

(e) Subsections (a), (b), [and] (c), [and] [(g)] do not apply to an individual acting as a judge.

(f) This [Act] does not require that a mediator have a special qualification by background or profession.

[(g) A mediator must be impartial, unless after disclosure of the facts required in subsections (a) and (b) to be disclosed, the parties agree otherwise.]

SECTION 10. PARTICIPATION IN MEDIATION. An attorney or other individual designated by a party may accompany the party to and participate in a mediation. A waiver of participation given before the mediation may be rescinded.

SECTION 11. INTERNATIONAL COMMERCIAL CONCILIATION

(a) In this section, "Model Law" means the Model Law on International Commercial Conciliation adopted by the United Nations Commission on International Trade Law on 28 June 2002 and recommended by the United Nations General Assembly in a resolution (A/RES/57/18) dated 19 November 2002, and "international commercial mediation" means an international commercial conciliation as defined in Article 1 of the Model Law.

(b) Except as otherwise provided in subsections (c) and (d), if a mediation is an international commercial mediation, the mediation is governed by the Model Law.

(c) Unless the parties agree in accordance with Section 3(c) of this [Act] that all or part of an international commercial mediation is not privileged, Sections 4, 5, and 6 and any applicable definitions in Section 2 of this [Act] also apply to the mediation and nothing in Article 10 of the Model Law derogates from Sections 4, 5, and 6.

(d)   If the parties to an international commercial mediation have agreed under Article 1, subsection (7), of the Model Law that the Model Law shall not apply, this [Act] applies.

SECTION 12.   RELATION TO ELECTRONIC SIGNATURES IN GLOBAL AND NATIONAL COMMERCE ACT. This [Act] modifies, limits, or supersedes the federal Electronic Signatures in Global and National Commerce Act, 15 U.S.C. Section 7001 et seq., but this [Act] does not modify, limit, or supersede Section 101(c) of that Act or authorize electronic delivery of any of the notices described in Section 103(b) of that Act.

SECTION 13.   UNIFORMITY OF APPLICATION AND CONSTRUCTION. In applying and construing this [Act], consideration should be given to the need to promote uniformity of the law with respect to its subject matter among States that enact it.

SECTION 14.   SEVERABILITY CLAUSE. If any provision of this [Act] or its application to any person or circumstance is held invalid, the invalidity does not affect other provisions or applications of this [Act] which can be given effect without the invalid provision or application, and to this end the provisions of this [Act] are severable.

SECTION 15.   EFFECTIVE DATE. This [Act] takes effect . . . .

SECTION 16.   REPEALS. The following acts and parts of acts are hereby repealed:

(1)

(2)

(3)

SECTION 17.   APPLICATION TO EXISTING AGREEMENTS OR REFERRALS.

(a)   This [Act] governs a mediation pursuant to a referral or an agreement to mediate made on or after [the effective date of this [Act]].

(b)   On or after [a delayed date], this [Act] governs an agreement to mediate whenever made.

APPENDIX F

MODEL STANDARDS OF PRACTICE FOR FAMILY AND DIVORCE MEDIATION (2000)

Overview and Definitions

Family and divorce mediation ("family mediation" or "mediation") is a process in which a mediator, an impartial third party, facilitates the resolution of family disputes by promoting the participants' voluntary agreement. The family mediator assists communication, encourages understanding and focuses the participants on their individual and common interests. The family mediator works with the participants to explore options, make decisions and reach their own agreements.

Family mediation is not a substitute for the need for family members to obtain independent legal advice or counseling or therapy. Nor is it appropriate for all families. However, experience has established that family mediation is a valuable option for many families because it can:

- increase the self-determination of participants and their ability to communicate;

- promote the best interests of children; and

- reduce the economic and emotional costs associated with the resolution of family disputes.

Effective mediation requires that the family mediator be qualified by training, experience and temperament; that the mediator be impartial; that the participants reach their decisions voluntarily; that their decisions be based on sufficient factual data; that the mediator be aware of the impact of culture and diversity; and that the best interests of children be taken into account. Further, the mediator should also be prepared to identify families whose history includes domestic abuse or child abuse.

These *Model Standards of Practice for Family and Divorce Mediation ("Model Standards")* aim to perform three major functions:

1. to serve as a guide for the conduct of family mediators;

2. to inform the mediating participants of what they can expect; and

3. to promote public confidence in mediation as a process for resolving family disputes.

The *Model Standards* are aspirational in character. They describe good practices for family mediators. They are not intended to create legal rules or standards of liability.

The *Model Standards* include different levels of guidance:

- Use of the term "may" in a *Standard* is the lowest strength of guidance and indicates a practice that the family mediator should consider adopting but which can be deviated from in the exercise of good professional judgment.

- Most of the *Standards* employ the term "should" which indicates that the practice described in the *Standard* is highly desirable and should be departed from only with very strong reason.

- The rarer use of the term "shall" in a *Standard* is a higher level of guidance to the family mediator, indicating that the mediator should not have discretion to depart from the practice described.

Standard I

A family mediator shall recognize that mediation is based on the principle of self-determination by the participants.

A. Self-determination is the fundamental principle of family mediation. The mediation process relies upon the ability of participants to make their own voluntary and informed decisions.

B. The primary role of a family mediator is to assist the participants to gain a better understanding of their own needs and interests and the needs and interests of others and to facilitate agreement among the participants.

C. A family mediator should inform the participants that they may seek information and advice from a variety of sources during the mediation process.

D. A family mediator shall inform the participants that they may withdraw from family mediation at any time and are not required to reach an agreement in mediation.

E. The family mediator's commitment shall be to the participants and the process. Pressure from outside of the mediation process shall never influence the mediator to coerce participants to settle.

Standard II

A family mediator shall be qualified by education and training to undertake the mediation.

A. To perform the family mediator's role, a mediator should:

1. have knowledge of family law;

2. have knowledge of and training in the impact of family conflict on parents, children and other participants, including knowledge of child development, domestic abuse and child abuse and neglect;

3. have education and training specific to the process of mediation;

4. be able to recognize the impact of culture and diversity.

B. Family mediators should provide information to the participants about the mediator's relevant training, education and expertise.

Standard III

A family mediator shall facilitate the participants' understanding of what mediation is and assess their capacity to mediate before the participants reach an agreement to mediate.

A. Before family mediation begins a mediator should provide the participants with an overview of the process and its purposes, including:

1. informing the participants that reaching an agreement in family mediation is consensual in nature, that a mediator is an impartial facilitator, and that a mediator may not impose or force any settlement on the parties;

2. distinguishing family mediation from other processes designed to address family issues and disputes;

3. informing the participants that any agreements reached will be reviewed by the court when court approval is required;

4. informing the participants that they may obtain independent advice from attorneys, counsel, advocates, accountants, therapists or other professionals during the mediation process;

5. advising the participants, in appropriate cases, that they can seek the advice of religious figures, elders or other significant persons in their community whose opinions they value;

6. discussing, if applicable, the issue of separate sessions with the participants, a description of the circumstances in which the mediator may meet alone with any of the participants, or with any third party and the conditions of confidentiality concerning these separate sessions;

7. informing the participants that the presence or absence of other persons at a mediation, including attorneys, counselors or advocates, depends on the agreement of the participants and the mediator, unless a statute or regulation otherwise requires or the mediator believes that the presence of another person is required or may be beneficial because of a history or threat of violence or other serious coercive activity by a participant.

8. describing the obligations of the mediator to maintain the confidentiality of the mediation process and its results as well as any exceptions to confidentiality;

9. advising the participants of the circumstances under which the mediator may suspend or terminate the mediation process and that a participant has a right to suspend or terminate mediation at any time.

B. The participants should sign a written agreement to mediate their dispute and the terms and conditions thereof within a reasonable time after first consulting the family mediator.

C. The family mediator should be alert to the capacity and willingness of the participants to mediate before proceeding with the mediation and throughout the process. A mediator should not agree to conduct the mediation if the mediator reasonably believes one or more of the participants is unable or unwilling to participate.

D. Family mediators should not accept a dispute for mediation if they cannot satisfy the expectations of the participants concerning the timing of the process.

Standard IV

A family mediator shall conduct the mediation process in an impartial manner. A family mediator shall disclose all actual and potential grounds of bias and conflicts of interest reasonably known to the mediator. The participants shall be free to retain the mediator by an informed, written waiver of the conflict of interest. However, if a bias or conflict of interest clearly impairs a mediator's impartiality, the mediator shall withdraw regardless of the express agreement of the participants.

A. Impartiality means freedom from favoritism or bias in word, action or appearance, and includes a commitment to assist all participants as opposed to any one individual.

B. Conflict of interest means any relationship between the mediator, any participant or the subject matter of the dispute, that compromises or appears to compromise the mediator's impartiality.

C. A family mediator should not accept a dispute for mediation if the family mediator cannot be impartial.

D. A family mediator should identify and disclose potential grounds of bias or conflict of interest upon which a mediator's impartiality might reasonably be questioned. Such disclosure should be made prior to the start of a mediation and in time to allow the participants to select an alternate mediator.

E. A family mediator should resolve all doubts in favor of disclosure. All disclosures should be made as soon as practical after the mediator becomes aware of the bias or potential conflict of interest. The duty to disclose is a continuing duty.

F. A family mediator should guard against bias or partiality based on the participants' personal characteristics, background or performance at the mediation.

G. A family mediator should avoid conflicts of interest in recommending the services of other professionals.

H. A family mediator shall not use information about participants obtained in a mediation for personal gain or advantage

I. A family mediator should withdraw pursuant to *Standard IX* if the mediator believes the mediator's impartiality has been compromised or a conflict of interest has been identified and has not been waived by the participants.

Standard V

A family mediator shallfully disclose and explain the basis of any compensation, fees and charges to the participants.

A. The participants should be provided with sufficient information about fees at the outset of mediation to determine if they wish to retain the services of the mediator.

B. The participants' written agreement to mediate their dispute should include a description of their fee arrangement with the mediator.

C. A mediator should not enter into a fee agreement which is contingent upon the results of the mediation or the amount of the settlement.

D. A mediator should not accept a fee for referral of a matter to another mediator or to any other person.

E. Upon termination of mediation a mediator should return any unearned fee to the participants.

Standard VI

A family mediator shall structure the mediation process so that the participants make decisions based on sufficient information and knowledge.

A. The mediator should facilitate full and accurate disclosure and the acquisition and development of information during mediation so that the participants can make informed decisions. This may be accomplished by encouraging participants to consult appropriate experts.

B. Consistent with standards of impartiality and preserving participant self-determination, a mediator may provide the participants with information that the mediator is qualified by training or experience to provide. The mediator shall not provide therapy or legal advice.

C. The mediator should recommend that the participants obtain independent legal representation before concluding an agreement.

D. If the participants so desire, the mediator should allow attorneys, counsel or advocates for the participants to be present at the mediation sessions.

E. With the agreement of the participants, the mediator may document the participants' resolution of their dispute. The mediator should inform the participants that any agreement should be reviewed by an independent attorney before it is signed.

Standard VII

A family mediator shall maintain the confidentiality of all information acquired in the mediation process, unless the mediator is permitted or required to reveal the information by law or agreement of the participants.

A. The mediator should discuss the participants' expectations of confidentiality with them prior to undertaking the mediation. The written agreement to mediate should include provisions concerning confidentiality.

B. Prior to undertaking the mediation the mediator should inform the participants of the limitations of confidentiality such as statutory, judicially or ethically mandated reporting.

C. The mediator shall disclose a participant's threat of suicide or violence against any person to the threatened person and the appropriate authorities if the mediator believes such threat is likely to be acted upon as permitted by law.

D. If the mediator holds private sessions with a participant, the obligations of confidentiality concerning those sessions should be discussed and agreed upon prior to the sessions.

E. If subpoenaed or otherwise noticed to testify or to produce documents the mediator should inform the participants immediately. The mediator should not testify or provide documents in response to a subpoena without an order of the court if the mediator reasonably believes doing so would violate an obligation of confidentiality to the participants.

Standard VIII

A family mediator shall assist participants in determining how to promote the best interests of children.

A. The mediator should encourage the participants to explore the range of options available for separation or post divorce parenting arrangements and their respective costs and benefits. Referral to a specialist in child development may be appropriate for these purposes. The topics for discussion may include, among others:

  1. information about community resources and programs that can help the participants and their children cope with the consequences of family reorganization and family violence;

  2. problems that continuing conflict creates for children's development and what steps might be taken to ameliorate the effects of conflict on the children;

  3. development of a parenting plan that covers the children's physical residence and decision-making responsibilities for the children, with appropriate levels of detail as agreed to by the participants;

  4. the possible need to revise parenting plans as the developmental needs of the children evolve over time; and

  5. encouragement to the participants to develop appropriate dispute resolution mechanisms to facilitate future revisions of the parenting plan.

B. The mediator should be sensitive to the impact of culture and religion on parenting philosophy and other decisions.

C. The mediator shall inform any court-appointed representative for the children of the mediation. If a representative for the children participates, the mediator should, at the outset, discuss the effect of that participation on the mediation process and the confidentiality of the mediation with the participants. Whether the representative of the children participates or not, the mediator shall provide the representative with the resulting agreements insofar as they relate to the children.

D. Except in extraordinary circumstances, the children should not participate in the mediation process without the consent of both parents and the children's court-appointed representative.

E. Prior to including the children in the mediation process, the mediator should consult with the parents and the children's court-appointed representative about whether the children should participate in the mediation process and the form of that participation.

F. The mediator should inform all concerned about the available options for the children's participation (which may include personal participation, an interview with a mental health professional, or the mediator reporting to the parents, or a videotape statement) and discuss the costs and benefits of each with the participants.

Standard IX

A family mediator shall recognize a family situation involving child abuse or neglect and take appropriate steps to shape the mediation process accordingly.

A. As used in these Standards, child abuse or neglect is defined by applicable state law.

B. A mediator shall not undertake a mediation in which the family situation has been assessed to involve child abuse or neglect without appropriate and adequate training.

C. If the mediator has reasonable grounds to believe that a child of the participants is abused or neglected within the meaning of the jurisdiction's child abuse and neglect laws, the mediator shall comply with applicable child protection laws.

   1. The mediator should encourage the participants to explore appropriate services for the family.

   2. The mediator should consider the appropriateness of suspending or terminating the mediation process in light of the allegations.

Standard X

A family mediator shall recognize a family situation involving domestic abuse and take appropriate steps to shape the mediation process accordingly.

A. As used in these Standards, domestic abuse includes domestic violence as defined by applicable state law and issues of control and intimidation.

B. A mediator shall not undertake a mediation in which the family situation has been assessed to involve domestic abuse without appropriate and adequate training.

C. Some cases are not suitable for mediation because of safety, control or intimidation issues. A mediator should make a reasonable effort to screen for the existence of domestic abuse prior to entering into an agreement to mediate. The mediator should continue to assess for domestic abuse throughout the mediation process.

D. If domestic abuse appears to be present the mediator shall consider taking measures to insure the safety of participants and the mediator including, among others:

    1. establishing appropriate security arrangements;

    2. holding separate sessions with the participants even without the agreement of all participants;

    3. allowing a friend, representative, advocate, counsel or attorney to attend the mediation sessions;

    4. encouraging the participants to be represented by an attorney, counsel or an advocate throughout the mediation process;

    5. referring the participants to appropriate community resources;

    6. suspending or terminating the mediation sessions, with appropriate steps to protect the safety of the participants.

E. The mediator should facilitate the participants' formulation of parenting plans that protect the physical safety and psychological well-being of themselves and their children.

Standard XI

A family mediator shall suspend or terminate the mediation process when the mediator reasonably believes that a participant is unable to effectively participate or for other compelling reasons.

A. Circumstances under which a mediator should consider suspending or terminating the mediation, may include, among others:

    1. the safety of a participant or well-being of a child is threatened;

    2. a participant has or is threatening to abduct a child;

    3. a participant is unable to participate due to the influence of drugs, alcohol, or physical or mental condition;

    4. the participants are about to enter into an agreement that the mediator reasonably believes to be unconscionable;

5. a participant is using the mediation to further illegal conduct;

6. a participant is using the mediation process to gain an unfair advantage;

7. if the mediator believes the mediator's impartiality has been compromised in accordance with *Standard IV*.

B. If the mediator does suspend or terminate the mediation, the mediator should take all reasonable steps to minimize prejudice or inconvenience to the participants which may result.

Standard XII

A family mediator shall be truthful in the advertisement and solicitation for mediation.

A. Mediators should refrain from promises and guarantees of results. A mediator should not advertise statistical settlement data or settlement rates.

B. Mediators should accurately represent their qualifications. In an advertisement or other communication, a mediator may make reference to meeting state, national, or private organizational qualifications only if the entity referred to has a procedure for qualifying mediators and the mediator has been duly granted the requisite status.

Standard XIII

A family mediator shall acquire and maintain professional competence in mediation.

A. Mediators should continuously improve their professional skills and abilities by, among other activities, participating in relevant continuing education programs and should regularly engage in self-assessment.

B. Mediators should participate in programs of peer consultation and should help train and mentor the work of less experienced mediators.

C. Mediators should continuously strive to understand the impact of culture and diversity on the mediator's practice.

The *Model Standards* recognize the *National Standards for Court Connected Dispute Resolution Programs* (1992). There are also state and local regulations governing such programs and family mediators. The following principles of organization and practice, however, are especially important for regulation of mediators and court-connected family mediation programs. They are worthy of separate mention.

A. Individual states or local courts should set standards and qualifications for family mediators including procedures for evaluations and handling grievances against mediators. In developing these standards and qualifications, regulators should consult with appropriate professional groups, including professional associations of family mediators.

B. When family mediators are appointed by a court or other institution, the appointing agency should make reasonable efforts to insure that each mediator is qualified for the appointment. If a list of family mediators qualified for court appointment exists, the requirements for being included on the list should be made public and available to all interested persons.

C. Confidentiality should not be construed to limit or prohibit the effective monitoring, research, evaluation or monitoring of mediation programs by responsible individuals or academic institutions provided that no identifying information about any person involved in the mediation is disclosed without their prior written consent. Under appropriate circumstances, researchers may be permitted to obtain access to statistical data and, with the permission of the participants, to individual case files, observations of live mediations, and interviews with participants.

BIBLIOGRAPHY

NEGOTIATION & MEDIATION

Aarow, K., Mnookin, R., Ross, L., Tversky, A. & Wilson, R., Barriers To Conflict Resolution (W.W. Norton 1995).

Abramson, H., Mediation Representation (NITA 2004).

Abramson, H., *Problem-Solving Advocacy in Mediations: A Model of Client Representation*, 10 Harv. Negot. L. Rev. 103 (2005).

Ackerman, R., *Disputing Together: Conflict Resolution and the Search for Community*, 18 Ohio St. J. on Dis. Resol. 27 (2002).

Acuff, F., How to Negotiate Anything With Anyone Anywhere Around the World (American Management Assn. 1997).

Acuff & Villere, *Games Negotiators Play*, Bus. Horizons 70 (February 1976).

Adler, N., International Dimensions of Organizational Behavior (South-Western 4th ed. 2002).

Adler, R., *Flawed Thinking: Addressing Decision Biases in Negotiation*, 20 Ohio St. J. on Disp. Res. 683 (2005).

Adler, R. & Silverstein, E., *When David Meets Goliath: Dealing with Power Differentials in Negotiations*, 5 Harv. Negot. L. Rev. 1 (2000).

Alfini, J., *Settlement Ethics and Lawyering in ADR Proceedings: A Proposal to Revise Rule 4.1*, 19 N. Ill. U. L. Rev. 255 (1999).

Allred, K., *Distinguishing Best and Strategic Practices: A Framework for Managing the Dilemma Between Creating and Claiming*, Negot. J. 387 (Oct. 2000).

Allred, K., *Relationship Dynamics in Disputes, in* THE Handbook of Dispute Resolution 83 (M. Moffitt & R. Bardone, eds.) (Jossey-Bass 2005).

American Arbitration Association, Consumer Due Process Protocol (1998).

American Arbitration Association, National Rules for the Resolution of Employment Disputes (1996).

American Arbitration Association, Resolving Employment Disputes — A Practical Guide (2003).

Amy, D., The Politics of Environmental Mediation (Columbia U. Press 1987).

Anderson, D., Dispute Resolution: Bridging the Settlement Gap (JAI Press 1996).

Anderson, P., The Complete Idiot's Guide to Body Language (Alpha 2004).

Ashworth, A., *Some Doubts About Restorative Justice*, 4 Crim. L.F. 277 (1993).

Axelrod, R., The Evolution of Cooperation (Basic Books 1984).

Ayres, I., *Fair Driving: Gender and Race Discrimination in Retail Car Negotiations*, 104 Harv. L. Rev. 817 (1991).

Ayres, I., *Further Evidence of Discrimination in New Car Negotiations and Estimates of Its Cause*, 94 Mich. L. Rev. 109 (1995).

Ayres, I. & Nalebuff, B., *Common Knowledge as a Barrier to Negotiation*, 44 U.C.L.A. L. Rev. 1631 (1997).

Babcock, L. & Lascheve, S., Women Don't Ask (Princeton Univ. Press 2003).

Bacharach, S. & Lawler, E., Bargaining, Power, Tactics and Outcomes (Jossey-Bass 1981).

Bacow, L. & Wheeler, M., Environmental Dispute Resolution (Plenum Press 1984).

Baer, J., How to Be an Assertive (Not Aggressive) Woman in Life, Love, And on the Job (Signet 1976).

Bailey, C., *The Role of Mediation in the USDA*, 73 Neb. L. Rev. 142 (1994).

Balachandra, L. Bordone, R., Menkel-Meadow, C., Ringstrom, P. & Sarath, E., *Improvisation and Negotiation: Expecting the Unexpected*, 21 Negot. J. 415 (2005).

Barkai, J., *Teaching Negotiation and ADR: The Savvy Samurai Meets the Devil*, 75 Neb. L. Rev. 704 (1996).

Bartos, O., Process and Outcome of Negotiations (Columbia Univ. Press 1974).

Bartos, O., *Simple Model of Negotiation: A Sociological Point of View*, in The Negotiation Process: Theories and Applications 13 (I.W. Zartman, ed.) (Sage 1978).

Baruch Bush, R. & Folger, J., The Promise of Mediation (Jossey-Bass 1994).

Bastress, R. & Harbaugh, J., Interviewing, Counseling, and Negotiating (Little, Brown 1990).

Bazemore, G. & Umbreit, M., *Balanced and Restorative Justice: Program Summary* (United States Dept. of Justice, Office of Juvenile Justice and Delinquency Prevention 1994).

Bazerman, M., Curhan, J. & Moore, D., *The Death and Rebirth of the Social Psychology of Negotiation*, in Blackwell Handbook of Social Psychology: Interpersonal Processes 196 (G. Fletcher & M. Clark, eds. 2004).

Bazerman, M. & Neale, M., Negotiating Rationally (Free Press 1992).

Bazerman, M. & Shonk, K., *The Decision Perspective in Negotiation* in The Handbook of Dispute Resolution 52 (M. Moffitt & R. Bordone, eds.) (Jossey-Bass 2005).

Beier, E. & Valens, E., People Reading (Stein & Day 1975).

Bellow, G. & Moulton, B., The Lawyering Process: Negotiation (Foundation Press 1981).

Bendahmane, D., & McDonald, J., International Negotiation (Foreign Service Institute, U.S. Department of State 1984).

Bendahmane, D. & McDonald, J., Perspectives On Negotiation (Foreign Service Institute, U.S. Department of State 1986).

Benham, R. & Barton, A., *Alternative Dispute Resolution: Ancient Models Provide Modern Inspiration*, 12 Ga. St. U. L. Rev. 623 (1996).

Benjamin, R., *The Constructive Uses of Deception: Skills, Strategies, and Techniques of the Folkloric Trickster Figure and Their Application by Mediators*, 13 Mediation Quarterly 3 (1995).

Bernard, P. & Garth, B., Dispute Resolution Ethics (ABA Section on Disp. Res. 2002).

Berne, E., Games People Play (Grove Press 1964).

Bethel, C. & Singer, L. *Mediation: A New Remedy for Cases of Domestic Violence*, 7 Vt. L. Rev. 15 (1982).

Bickerman, J., *Evaluative Mediator Responds*, 14 Alternatives 70 (1996).

Bingham, G., Resolving Environmental Disputes: A Decade of Experience (Conservation Foundation 1986).

Bingham, L., *Why Suppose? Let's Find Out: A Public Policy Research Program on Dispute Resolution*, 2002 J. Disp. Resol. 101 (2002).

Binnendijk, H., National Negotiating Styles (Foreign Service Institute, U.S. Department of State 1987).

Birke, R. & Fox, C., *Psychological Principles in Negotiating Civil Settlements*, 4 Harv. Neg. L. Rev. 1 (1999).

Blades, J., Family Mediation: Cooperative Divorce Settlement (Prentice Hall 1985).

Bok, S., Lying: Moral Choice in Public and Private Life (Pantheon 1978).

Bordone, R., *Teaching Interpersonal Skills for Negotiation and For Life*, Negot. J. 377 (Oct. 2000).

Bordone, R., *Fitting the Ethics to the Forum: A Proposal for Process-Enabling Ethical Codes*, 21 Ohio St. J. on Disp. Res. 1 (2005).

Boskey, J., *The Proper Role of the Mediator: Rational Assessment, Not Pressure*, 10 Neg. J. 367 (1994).

Bowles, H., Babcock, L. & McGinn, K., *Constraints and Triggers: Situational Mechanics of Gender in Negotiation*, 89 J. Personality & Soc. Psych. 951 (2005).

Brand, N., How ADR Works (BNA Books 2002).

Brand, N., *Learning to Use the Mediation Process: A Guide for Lawyers*, 47 Arb. J. 6 (Dec. 1992).

Brazil, W., *Settling Civil Cases: What Lawyers Want From Judges*, JUDGES' J. 14 (Summer 1984).

BRETT, J., NEGOTIATING GLOBALLY (Jossey-Bass 2001).

Brett, J., Adair, W., Lempereur, A., Okumura, T., Skikhirev, P., Tinsley, C. & Lytle, A., *Culture and Joint Gains in Negotiation*, 14 NEGOT. J. 61 (1998).

BROCKNER, J. & RUBIN, J., ENTRAPMENT IN ESCALATING CONFLICTS: A SOCIAL PSYCHOLOGICAL ANALYSIS (Springer-Verlag 1985).

Brodt, S. & Thompson, L., *Negotiating Teams: A Levels of Analysis Approach*, 5 GROUP DYNAMICS: THEORY, RESEARCH, AND PRACTICE 208 (2001).

Brown, C., *Facilitative Mediation: The Classic Approach Retains Its Appeal*, 4 PEPP. DISP. RESOL. L.J. 279 (2004).

Brown, J., *Creativity and Problem-Solving*, 87 MARQUETTE L. REV. 697 (2004a).

Brown, J., *The Role of Apology in Negotiation*, 87 MARQUETTE L. REV. 665 (2004b).

Brown, J., *The Role of Hope in Negotiation*, 44 U.C.L.A. L. REV. 1661 (1997).

Brown, J., *The Use of Mediation to Resolve Criminal Cases: A Procedural Critique*, 43 EMORY L.J. 1247 (1994).

Brown, J. & Ayres, I., *Economic Rationales for Mediation*, 80 VA. L. REV. 323 (1994).

Brown, K., *Confidentiality in Mediation: Status and Implications*, 1991 J. DISP. RESOL. 307.

Brunet, E., *The Costs of Environmental Dispute Resolution*, 18 ENVTL. L. REP. 10,515 (1988).

Bryan, P., *Killing Us Softly: Divorce Mediation and the Politics of Power*, 40 BUFF. L. REV. 441 (1992).

BURGOON, J., BULLER, D. & WOODALL, W., NONVERBAL COMMUNICATION: THE UNSPOKEN DIALOGUE (McGraw-Hill 1996).

BURGOON, M., DILLARD, J.P. & Doran, N., *Friendly or Unfriendly Persuasion: The Effects of Violations of Expectations by Males and Females*, 10 HUMAN COMMUNICATION RES. 283 (1983).

Burrell, Donohue & Allen, *Gender-Based Perceptual Biases in Mediation*, 15 COMMUNICATION RES. 447 (1988).

Burton, Farmer, Gee, Johnson & Williams, *Feminist Theory, Professional Ethics, and Gender-Related Distinctions in Attorney Negotiation Styles*, 1991 J. DISP. RES. 199 (1991).

Bush, R. *"One Size Does Not Fit All": A Pluralistic Approach to Mediator Performance Testing and Quality Assurance*, 19 OHIO ST. J. ON DISP. RESOL. 965 (2004).

Bush, R., *Substituting Mediation For Arbitration: The Growing Market for Evaluative Mediation, and What it Means for the ADR Field*, 3 PEPP. DISP. RESOL. L.J. 111 (2002).

Bush, R. & Pope, S., *Changing the Quality of Conflict Interaction: The Principles and Practice of Transformative Mediation*, 3 PEPP. DISP. RESOL. L.J. 67 (2002).

CALERO, H., THE POWER OF NONVERBAL COMMUNICATION (Silver Lake Pub. 2005).

CAMERON, N., COLLABORATIVE PROCESS: DEEPENING THE DIALOGUE (Cont. Legal Educ. Soc. of British Columbia 2004).

CAMP, J., START WITH NO (Crown Bus. 2002).

Campbell, M. & Docherty, J., *What's in a Frame? (That Which We Call a Rose by Any Other Name Would Smell as Sweet)*, 87 MARQUETTE L. REV. 769 (2004).

Carli, L., *Gender and Social Influence*, 57 J. SOC. ISSUES 725 (2001).

Carter, R., *Oh, Ye of Little [Good] Faith: Questions, Concerns and Commentary on Efforts to Regulate Participant Conduct in Mediations*, 2002 J. DISP. RESOL. 367.

Cash, T. & Janda, L., *The Eye of the Beholder*, PSYCHOLOGY TODAY 46 (December 1984).

Chang, H. & Sigman, H., *Incentives to Settle Under Joint and Several Liability: An Empirical Analysis of Superfund Litigation*, 29 J. LEGAL STUD. 205 (2000).

Chantilis, P., *Mediation U.S.A.*, 26 U. MEMPHIS L. REV. 1031 (1996).

Chaykin, A., *The Liabilities and Immunities of Mediators: A Hostile Environment for Model Legislation*, 20 OHIO ST. J. ON DISP. RESOL. 47 (1986).

Chinkin, C., *Gender, Human Rights, and Peace Agreements*, 18 OHIO ST. J. ON DISP. RESOL. 867 (2003).

CLARK, H., THE LAW OF DOMESTIC RELATIONS IN THE UNITED STATES (2d ed. 1988).

Coates, R. & Gehm, J., *An Empirical Assessment*, in MEDIATION AND CRIMINAL JUSTICE: VICTIMS, OFFENDERS AND COMMUNITY (B. Galaway & M. Wright, eds.) (Sage 1989).

Coben, J., *Gollum, Meet Smeagol: A Schizophrenic Rumination on Mediator Values Beyond Self-Determination and Neutrality*, 5 CARDOZO J. CONFLICT RESOL. 65 (2004).

Coben, J. & Harley, P., *International Conversations About Restorative Justice, Mediation, and the Practice of Law*, 25 HAMLINE J.L. & POL'Y 235 (2004).

Coben, J. & Thompson, P., *Disputing Irony: A Systematic Look at Litigation About Mediation*, 11 Harv. Neg. L. Rev. 43 (2006).

Cochran, R., *Professional Rules and ADR: Control of Alternative Dispute Resolution Under the ABA Ethics 2000 Commission Proposal and Other Professional Responsibility Standards*, 29 FORDHAM URB. L.J. 895 (2001).

COHEN, H., NEGOTIATE THIS (Warner Bus. Books 2003).

COHEN, H., YOU CAN NEGOTIATE ANYTHING (Lyle Stuart 1980).

Cohen, J., *When People are the Means: Negotiating with Respect*, 14 GEO. J. LEGAL ETHICS 739 (2001).

COHEN, R., NEGOTIATING ACROSS CULTURES (U.S. Institute of Peace Press 1991).

Coker, D., *Enhancing Autonomy for Battered Women: Lessons from Navajo Peacemaking*, 47 U.C.L.A. L. REV. 1 (1999).

Cole, S., *Managerial Litigants? The Overlooked Problem of Party Autonomy in Dispute Resolution*, 51 HASTINGS L.J. 1199 (2000).

Cole, S., *Mediator Certification Has the Time Come?* DISP. RESOL. MAG., Spring 2005, at 7.

Cole, S., *Protecting Confidentiality in Mediation: A Promise Unfulfilled*, 54 Kan. L. Rev. _____ (2006).

COLE, S., ROGERS, N., & McEWEN, C., MEDIATION LAW, POLICY, PRACTICE (Thomson West 2d ed. 1994 & 2006 Supp.).

COLOSI, T., ON AND OFF THE RECORD: COLOSI ON NEGOTIATION (Amer. Arb. Assn. 2d ed. 2001).

Comment, *The Concern Over Confidentiality in Mediation — An In-Depth Look at the Protection Provided by the Proposed Uniform Mediation Act*, 2000 J. DISP. RESOL. 113 (2000).

Comment, *No Confidence: The Problem of Confidentiality by Local Rule in the ADR Act of 1998*, 78 TEX. L. REV. 1015 (2000).

Condlin, R., *Bargaining in the Dark: The Normative Incoherence of Lawyer Dispute Bargaining Role*, 51 MD. L. REV. 1 (1992).

Condlin, R., *"Cases on Both Side": Patterns of Argument in Legal Dispute-Negotiation*, 44 MD. L. REV. 65 (1985).

COOGLER, O., STRUCTURAL MEDIATION IN DIVORCE SETTLEMENTS: A HANDBOOK FOR MARITAL MEDIATORS (1978).

Cooley, J., *Mediation Magic: Its Use and Abuse*, 29 LOY. U. CHI. L.J. 1 (1997).

COOLEY, J., THE MEDIATOR'S HANDBOOK (NITA 2000).

Cooper, C., *The Role of Mediation in Farm Credit Disputes*, 29 TULSA L.J. 159 (1993).

CORMACK, M., WHAT THEY DON'T TEACH YOU AT HARVARD BUSINESS SCHOOL (Bantam 1984).

Craver, C., *Clinical Negotiating Achievement as a Function of Traditional Law School Success and as a Predictor of Future Negotiating Performance*, 1986 MO. J. DISP. RES. 63 (1986).

Craver, C., *Don't Forget Your Problem Solving Function*, 69 A.B.A. J. 254 (1983)

CRAVER, C., EFFECTIVE LEGAL NEGOTIATION AND SETTLEMENT (Lexis 2d ed. 2001).

Craver, C., *The Impact of Gender on Clinical Negotiating Achievement*, 6 OHIO ST. J. ON DISP. RESOL. 1 (1990).

Craver, C., *The Impact of a Pass/Fail Option on Negotiation Course Performance*, 48 J. LEGAL EDUC. 176 (1998).

Craver, C., *The Impact of Student GPAs and a Pass/Fail Option on Clinical Negotiation Course Performance*, 15 OHIO ST. J. ON DISP. RESOL. 373 (2000).

Craver, C., *Mediation: A Trial Lawyer's Guide*, 35 TRIAL 37 (June 1999).

Craver, C., *Negotiation as a Distinct Area of Specialization*, 9 AM. J. TRIAL ADVOC. 377 (1986).

Craver, C., *Negotiation Ethics: How to be Deceptive Without Being Dishonest/How to be Assertive Without Being Offensive*, 38 S. TEX. L. REV. 713 (1997).

Craver, C., *The Negotiation Process*, 27 AM. J. TRIAL ADVOC. 271 (2003).

Craver, C., *Negotiation Styles: The Impact on Bargaining Transactions*, DISP. RESOL. J. 48 (Feb.-Apr. 2003).

Craver, C., *Negotiation Techniques*, 24 TRIAL 65 (June 1988).

Craver, C., *Race and Negotiation Performance*, DISP. RESOL. MAG. 22 (Fall 2001).

Craver, C., *When Parties Can't Settle*, 26 JUDGES J. 4 (Winter 1987).

Craver, C. & Barnes, D., *Gender, Risk Taking and Negotiation Performance*, 5 MICH. J. GENDER & LAW 299 (1999).

CROSBY, P., THE ART OF GETTING YOUR OWN SWEET WAY (McGraw-Hill 1981).

Cross, J., *A Theory of the Bargaining Process*, in BARGAINING: FORMAL THEORIES OF NEGOTIATION 191 (O. Young, ed.) (Univ. of Illinois Press 1975).

CROWLEY, T., SETTLE IT OUT OF COURT (John Wiley & Sons 1994).

DAVIDSON, M. & GREENHALGH, L., *The Role of Emotion in Negotiation: The Impact of Anger and Race*, 7 RES. ON NEGOT. IN ORG. 3 (1999).

DAWSON, R., ROGER DAWSON'S SECRETS OF POWER NEGOTIATING (Career Press 1995) (2d ed. 2000).

DAWSON, R., YOU CAN GET ANYTHING YOU WANT (Simon & Schuster 1985).

DEAUX, K., THE BEHAVIOR OF WOMEN AND MEN (Brooks/Cole Publishing 1976).

Deason, E., *Competing and Complementary Rule Systems: Civil Procedures and ADR: Procedural Rules for Complementary Systems of Litigation and Mediation — Worldwide*, 80 NOTRE DAME L. REV. 553 (2005).

Deason, E., *Enforcing Mediated Settlement Agreements: Contract Law Collides with Confidentiality*, 35 U.C. DAVIS L. REV.33 (2001).

Deason, E., *Predictable Mediation in the U.S. Federal System*, 17 OHIO ST. J. ON DISP. RESOL. 239 (2002).

Deason, E., *The Quest for Uniformity in Mediation Confidentiality: Foolish Consistency or Crucial Predictability?* 85 MARQUETTE L. REV. 79 (2001).

Deis, M., *California's Answer: Mandatory Mediation of Child Custody and Visitation Disputes*, 1 OHIO ST. J. ON DISP. RESOL. 148 (1983).

Delgado, R., Dunn, C., Brown, P., Lee, H. & Hubbert, D., *Fairness and Formality: Minimizing the Risk of Prejudice in Alternative Dispute Resolution*, 1985 WIS. L. REV. 1359.

Della Noce, D., *From Practice to Theory to Practice: A Brief Retrospective on the Transformative Mediation Model*, 19 OHIO ST. J. ON DISP. RESOL. 925 (2004).

Della Noce, D., *Seeing Theory in Practice: An Analysis of Empathy in Mediation*, 15 NEGOT. J. 271 (1999).

Della Noce, D., Antes, J. & Saul, J., *Identifying Practice Competence in Transformative Mediators: An Interactive Rating Scale Assessment Model*, 19 OHIO ST. J. ON DISP. RESOL. 1005 (2004).

Della Noce, D. & Bush R., *Clarifying the Theoretical Underpinnings of Mediation: Implications for Practice and Policy*, 3 PEPP. DISP. RESOL. L.J. 39 (2002).

DePaulo, B. & Kashy, D., *Everyday Lies in Close and Casual Relationships*, 74 J. PERSONALITY & SOC. PSYCHOL. 63 (1998).

DePaulo, B., Kashy, D., Kirkendol, S., Wyer, M. & Epstein, J., *Lying in Everyday Life*, 70 J. PERSONALITY & SOC. PSYCHOL. 979 (1996).

DIETMEYER, B. & KAPLAN, R., STRATEGIC NEGOTIATION (Dearborn Trade Pub. 2004).

DIMITRIUS, J.-E. & MAZZARELLA, M., READING PEOPLE (Random House 1998).

Docherty, J., *Culture and Negotiation: Symmetrical Anthropology for Negotiators*, 87 MARQUETTE L. REV. 711 (2004).

Draft Principles for ADR Provider Organizations, 18 ALTERNATIVES 109 (2000).

Druckman, D., *Departures in Negotiation: Extensions and New Directions*, 20 NEGOT. J. 185 (2004).

DRUCKMAN, D., NEGOTIATIONS: SOCIAL PSYCHOLOGICAL PERSPECTIVES (Sage 1977).

DRUCKMAN, D., ROZELLE, R. & BAXTER, J., NONVERBAL COMMUNICATION (Sage 1982).

DUBLER, N. & LIEBMAN, C., BIOETHICS MEDIATION: A GUIDE TO SHAPING SHARED SOLUTIONS (United Hospital Fund 2004).

EDWARDS, H. & WHITE, J., THE LAWYER AS A NEGOTIATOR (West 1977).

Eisenberg, M., *Private Ordering Through Negotiation: Dispute-Settlement and Rulemaking*, 89 HARV. L. REV. 637 (1976).

EKMAN, P., TELLING LIES (Norton 1992).

EKMAN, P., TELLING LIES (Norton 1985).

EKMAN, P. & FRIESEN, W., UNMASKING THE FACE (Prentice-Hall 1975).

Ekman, P., O'Sullivan, M. & Frank, M., *A Few Can Catch a Liar*, 10 PSYCHOL. SCIENCE 263 (May 1999).

Ekman, P., O'Sullivan, M., Friesen, W. & Scherer, K., *Invited Article: Face, Voice, and Body in Detecting Deceit*, 15 J. NONVERBAL BEHAV. 125 (Summer 1991).

ELGIN, S., THE GENTLE ART OF VERBAL SELF-DEFENSE (Prentice-Hall 1980).

ENDERLIN, C., SHATTERED DREAMS (Other Press 2002).

English, C., *Mediator Immunity*, 63 GEO. WASH. L. REV. 759 (1995).

English, C., *Stretching the Doctrine of Absolute Quasi-Judicial Immunity: Wagshal v. Foster*, 63 GEO. WASH. L. REV. 759 (1995).

ERICKSON, S. & McKNIGHT, M., THE PRACTITIONER'S GUIDE TO MEDIATION (John Wiley & Sons 2001).

EVANS, G., PLAY LIKE A MAN, WIN LIKE A WOMAN (BROADWAY BOOKS 2000).

Evans, M. & Tyler-Evans, M., *Aspects of Grief in Conflict: Re-Visioning Response to Dispute*, 20 CONFLICT RESOL. Q. 83 (2002).

Fairman, C., *Ethics and Collaborative Lawyering: Why Put Old Hats on New Heads?* 18 OHIO ST. J. ON DISP. RESOL. 505 (2003).

Fairman, C., *A Proposed Model Rule for Collaborative Law*, 21 OHIO ST. J. ON DISP. RES. 73 (2005).

Fassina, N., *Constraining a Principal's Choice: Outcome Versus Behavior Contingent Agency Contracts in Representative Negotiations*, 20 NEGOT. J. 435 (2004).

FAST, J., BODY LANGUAGE (Pocket Books 1970).

Faure, G., *International Negotiation: The Cultural Dimension, in* INTERNATIONAL NEGOTIATION 392 (V. Kremenyuk, ed.) (Jossey-Bass 2d ed. 2002).

FAURE, G. & RUBIN, J., CULTURE AND NEGOTIATION (Sage Publications 1993).

Fay, *Settlement Approaches*, SEMINARS FOR NEWLY APPOINTED UNITED STATES DISTRICT JUDGES 67 (1973–1975).

Felder, R., *Bare-Knuckle Negotiation* (John Wiley & Sons 2004).

Feldman, R., Forrest, J. & Happ, B., *Self-Promotion and Verbal Deception: Do Self-Presenters Lie More?* 24 BASIC & APPLIED SOC. PSYCHOL. 163 (2002).

FIRTH, A., THE DISCOURSE OF NEGOTIATION (Pergamon 1995).

Fisher, R., *What About Negotiation as a Specialty?*, 69 A.B.A. J. 1221 (1983).

FISHER, R., KOPELMAN, E. & SCHNEIDER, A., BEYOND MACHIAVELLI (Harvard Univ. Press 1994).

FISHER, R. & SHAPIRO, D., BEYOND REASON: USING EMOTIONS AS YOU NEGOTIATE (Viking 2005).

FISHER, R., URY, W. & PATTTON, B., GETTING TO YES (Penguin 2d ed. 1991)

Fisher, T., *Construction Mediation*, DISP. RESOL. J. 8 (Mar. 1994).

Fiss, O., *Against Settlement*, 93 YALE L.J. 1073 (1984).

Folberg, J., *Divorce Mediation: A Workable Alternative*, reprinted in AMERICAN BAR ASSOCIATION, ALTERNATIVE MEANS OF FAMILY DISPUTE RESOLUTION (H. Davidson, L. Ray, R. Horowitz, eds.) (American Bar Association 1982).

Folberg, J., *Mediation of Child Custody Disputes*, 19 COLUM. J.L. & SOC. PROBS. 413 (1985).

FOLBERG, J. & GOLANN, D., LAWYER NEGOTIATION THEORY, PRACTICE, AND LAW (Aspen 2006).

FOLBERG, J. & TAYLOR, A., MEDIATION (Jossey-Bass 1984).

FORD, C., LIES! LIES!! LIES!!! THE PSYCHOLOGY OF DECEIT (Amer. Psychiatric Press 1996).

Forester, J., *Responding to Critical Moments with Humor, Recognition, and Hope*, 20 NEGOT. J. 221 (2004).

Forgas, J., *On Feeling Good and Getting Your Way: Mood Effects on Negotiator Cognition and Bargaining Strategies*, 74 J. PERSONALITY & SOC. PSYCHOL. 565 (1998).

Frank, M. & Ekman, P., *The Ability to Detect Deceit Generalizes Across Different Types of High-Stake Lies*, 72 J. PERSONALITY & SOC. PSYCHOL. 1429 (1997).

Freedman, L. & Prigoff, M., *Confidentiality in Mediation: The Need for Protection*, 2 OHIO ST. J. DISP. RESOL. 37 (1986).

Freshman, C., Hayes, A. & Feldman, G., *The Lawyer-Negotiator as Mood Scientist: What We Know and Don't Know About How Mood Relates to Successful Negotiation*, 2002 J. DISP. RESOL. 13.

Freshman, C., et al., *Mindfulness in the Law and ADR: Adapting Meditation to Promote Negotiation Success: A Guide to Varieties and Scientific Support*, 7 HARV. NEGOT. L. REV. 67 (2002).

FREUND, J., THE ACQUISITION MATING DANCE AND OTHER ESSAYS ON NEGOTIATING (Prentice Hall Law & Business 1987).

Freund, J., *Anatomy of a Split-Up: Mediating the Business Divorce*, 52 BUS. LAW. 479 (1997).

FREUND, J., THE NEUTRAL NEGOTIATOR: WHY AND HOW MEDIATION CAN WORK TO RESOLVE DOLLAR DISPUTES (Prentice Hall Law & Bus. 1994).

FREUND, J., SMART NEGOTIATING (Simon & Schuster 1992).

Freund, J., *Why and How Mediation Can Work to Resolve Dollar Disputes* (Prentice Hall Law & Bus. 1994).

Friedman, G. & Himmelstein, J., *Resolving Conflict Together: The Understanding-based Model of Mediation*, 4 J. AM. ARB. 225 (2005).

Friedman, R. & Shapiro, D., *Deception and Mutual Gains Bargaining: Are They Mutually Exclusive?* 11 NEGOT. J. 243 (1995).

Fry, P. & Coe, K., *Achievement Performance of Internally and Externally Oriented Black and White High School Students Under Conditions of*

Competition and Cooperation Expectancies, 50 BRIT. J. EDUC. PSYCHOL. 162 (1980).

Fuchs-Burnett, T., *Mass Public Corporate Apology*, 57 DISP. RESOL. J. 27 (May-June 2002).

Fuller, L., *Mediation: Its Forms and Functions*, 44 S. CAL. L. REV. 305 (1971).

Gagnon, A., *Ending Mandatory Divorce Mediation for Battered Women*, 15 HARV. WOMEN'S L.J. 272 (1992).

GALAWAY, B. & WRIGHT, M., MEDIATION AND CRIMINAL JUSTICE: VICTIMS, OFFENDERS, AND COMMUNITY (Sage 1989).

Galinsky, A. & Mussweiler, T., *First Offers as Anchors: The Role of Perspective-Taking and Negotiator Focus*, 81 J. PERSONALITY & SOC. PSYCHOL. 657 (2001).

Galton, E., *Experts Can Facilitate a Mediation*, DISP. RESOL. J. 64 (Oct.-Dec. 1995).

Gerencser, A., *Family Mediation: Screening for Domestic Abuse*, 23 FLA. ST. U. L. REV. 43 (1995).

GIFFORD, D., LEGAL NEG. THEORY AND APPLICATIONS (West 1989).

GELFAND, M. & BRETT, J., THE HANDBOOK OF NEGOTIATION AND CULTURE (Stanford Business Books 2004).

Getty, M., *The Process of Drafting the Uniform Mediation Act*, 22 N. ILL. U. L. REV. 157 (2002).

Gewurz, I., *(Re)Designing Mediation to Address the Nuances of Power Imbalance*, 19 CONFLICT RESOL. Q. 135 (2001).

Gibbons, L., Kennedy, R. & Gibbs, J., *Cyber-Mediation: Computer-Mediated Communications Medium Massaging the Message*, 32 N.M. L. REV. 27 (2002).

Gifford, D., *A Context-Based Theory of Strategy Selection in Legal Negotiation*, 46 OHIO ST. L.J. 141 (1985).

GIFFORD, D., LEGAL NEGOTIATION: THEORY AND APPLICATIONS (West 1989).

Gifford, D., *The Synthesis of Legal Counseling and Negotiation Models: Preserving Client-Centered Advocacy in the Negotiation Context*, 34 U.C.L.A. L. REV. 811 (1987).

Gillespie, J., Thompson, L., Loewenstein, J. & Gentner, D., *Lessons from Analogical Reasoning in the Teaching of Negotiation*, 15 NEGOT. J. 363 (1999).

GILLIGAN, C., IN A DIFFERENT VOICE (Harvard Univ. Press 1982).

Gilson, R. & Mnookin, R., *Disputing Through Agents: Cooperation and Conflict Between Lawyers in Litigation*, 94 COLUM. L. REV. 509 (1994).

Golann, D., *Death of a Claim: The Impact of Loss Reactions on Bargaining*, 20 NEGOT. J. 539 (2004).

Golann, D., *Is Legal Mediation a Process of Repair — or Separation? An Empirical Study, and Its Implications*, 7 HARV. NEGOT. L. REV. 301 (2002).

GOLANN, D., MEDIATING LEGAL DISPUTES (Aspen Law & Bus. 1996).

Golann, D., *Variations in Mediation: How — and Why — Legal Mediators Change Styles in the Course of a Case*, 2000 J. DISP. RESOL. 41 (2000).

Goldberg, S., *The Mediation of Grievances Under a Collective Bargaining Contract: An Alternative to Arbitration*, 77 NW. U. L. REV. 270 (1982).

Goldberg, S. & Brett, J., *An Experiment in the Mediation of Grievances*, 106 MONTHLY LAB. REV. 23 (March 1983).

GOLDMAN, A., SETTLING FOR MORE (B.N.A. 1991).

Goldstein, C. & Weber, S., *The Art of Negotiating*, 37 N.Y.L. SCH. L. REV. 325 (1992).

GOLEMAN, D., EMOTIONAL INTELLIGENCE (Bantham 1995).

GOLEMAN, D., WORKING WITH EMOTIONAL INTELLIGENCE (Bantam 1998).

GOODPASTER, G., A GUIDE TO NEGOTIATION AND MEDIATION (Transnational Publishers 1997).

Goodpaster, G., *A Primer on Competitive Bargaining*, 2 J. DISP. RESOL. 325 (1996).

Grad, F. *Alternative Dispute Resolution in Environmental Law*, 14 COLUM. J. ENVTL. L. 157 (1989).

GRAHAM, J. & SANO, Y., SMART BARGAINING: DOING BUSINESS WITH THE JAPANESE (Harper Business 1989).

Gray, B., *Negotiating with Your Nemesis*, 19 NEGOT. J. 299 (2003).

Grebe, S., *Building on Structured Mediation: An Integrated Model for Global Mediation of Separation and Divorce*, 12 MEDIATION Q. 15 (1994).

Green, E., *A Heretical View of a Mediation Privilege*, 2 OHIO ST. J. ON DISP. RESOL. 1 (1986).

Grillo, T., *The Mediation Alternative: Process Dangers for Women*, 100 YALE L.J. 1545 (1991).

Greenhalgh, L., *The Case Against Winning in Negotiations*, 3 NEGOT. J. 167 (1987).

Gross, S. & Syverud, K., *Getting to No: A Study of Settlement Negotiations and the Selection of Cases for Trial*, 90 MICH. L. REV. 319 (1991).

GUERNSEY, T., A PRACTICAL GUIDE TO NEGOTIATION (NITA 1996).

GUERNSEY, T. & ZWIER, P., ADVANCED NEGOTIATION AND MEDIATION THEORY AND PRACTICE: A REALISTIC INTEGRATED APPROACH (NITA 2005).

GULLIVER, P., DISPUTES AND NEGOTIATIONS: A CROSS-CULTURAL PERSPECTIVE (Academic Press 1979).

Gunning, I., *Diversity Issues in Mediation: Controlling Negative Cultural Myths*, 1995 J. DISP. RESOL. 55.

Gunning, I., *Know Justice, Know Peace: Further Reflections on Mediations*, 5 CARDOZO J. CONFLICT RESOL. 87 (2004).

Guthrie, C., *Better Settle than Sorry: The Regret Aversion Theory of Litigation Behavior*, 1999 U. ILL. L. REV. 43 (1999).

Guthrie, C., *Framing Frivolous Litigation: A Psychological Theory*, 67 U. CHI. L. REV. 163 (2000).

Guthrie, C., *Panacea or Pandora's Box? The Costs of Options in Negotiation*, 88 IOWA L. REV. 601 (2003).

Guthrie, C., *Principles of Influence in Negotiation*, 87 MARQUETTE L. REV. 829 (2004).

Guthrie, C., *Prospect Theory, Risk Preference, and the Law*, 97 NW. UNIV. L. REV. 1115 (2003).

Guthrie, C., Rachlinski, J. & Wistrich, A., *Inside the Judicial Mind*, 86 CORNELL L. REV. 777 (2001).

Guthrie, C. & Sally, D., *The Impcat of the Impact Bias on Negotiation*, 87 MARQUETTE L. REV. 817 (2004).

GUTTERMAN, S., COLLABORATIVE LAW: A NEW MODEL FOR DISPUTE RESOLUTION (Bradford Pub. 2004).

HAGBERG, J., REAL POWER (Winston Press 1984).

Hahn, *Negotiating with the Japanese*, CAL. LAW. 20 (March 1982).

HALL, E., THE HIDDEN DIMENSION (Doubleday 1966).

HALL, E., THE SILENT LANGUAGE (Doubleday 1973).

HALL, J., NONVERBAL SEX DIFFERENCES (Johns Hopkins Univ. Press 1984).

Halpern, R., *Negotiation Blunders: Allowing Yourself to be Double-Bracketed*, NEGOT. MAG. (Oct. 2003) (www.negotiatormagazine.com).

HAMMOND, J., KEENEY, R. & RAIFFA, H., SMART CHOICES (Harvard Business School Press 1999).

Hamner, W. & Yukl, G., *The Effectiveness of Different Offer Strategies in Bargaining*, in NEGOTIATIONS: SOCIAL PSYCHOLOGICAL PERSPECTIVES 137 (D. Druckman, ed.) (Sage 1977).

Hansen, M., *The New Model Rules*, A.B.A. J. 50 (Jan. 2001).

Hansen, T., *The Narrative Approach to Mediation*, 4 PEPP. DISP. RESOL. L.J. 297 (2004).

Harges, B., *Mediator Qualifications: The Trend Toward Professionalization*, 1997 B.Y.U. L. REV. 687 (1997).

HARPER, R., WEINS, A. & MATARAZZO, J., NONVERBAL COMMUNICATION: THE STATE OF THE ART (Wiley-Interscience 1978).

HARRAGAN, B., GAMES MOTHER NEVER TAUGHT YOU (Warner Books 1977).

Harrell, S., *Why Attorneys Attend Mediation Sessions*, 12 MEDIATION Q. 369 (1995).

Harsanyi, J., *Bargaining and Conflict Situations in Light of a New Approach to Game Theory*, in BARGAINING: FORMAL THEORIES OF NEGOTIATION 74 (O. Young, ed.) (Univ. of Illinois Press 1975).

Harter, P., *The Uniform Mediation Act: An Essential Framework for Self-Determination*, 22 N. ILL. U. L. REV. 251 (2002).

Hartje, *Lawyer's Skills in Negotiations: Justice in Unseen Hands*, 1984 MO J. DISP. RESOL. 119 (1984).

Hartwell, S., *Understanding and Dealing with Deception in Legal Negotiation*, 6 OHIO ST. J. DISP. ON RES. 171 (1991).

HARVARD BUSINESS ESSENTIALS, NEGOTIATION (Harvard Bus. School Press 2003).

Haussmann, B., *The ABA Ethical Guidelines for Settlement Negotiations: Exceeding the Limits of the Adversarial Ethic*, 89 CORNELL L. REV. 1218 (2004).

Haynes, J., *Mediation and Therapy: An Alternative View*, 10 MEDIATION Q. 21 (1992).

HENDEN, D., HENDEN, R. & HERBIG, P., CROSS-CULTURAL BUSINESS NEGOTIATIONS (Quorum 1996).

HENLEY, N., BODY POLITICS: POWER, SEX, AND NONVERBAL COMMUNICATION (Prentice-Hall 1977).

Hensler, D., *A Glass Half Full, a Glass Half Empty: The Use of Alternative Dispute in Mass Personal Injury Litigation*, 73 TEX. L. REV. 1587 (1995).

Hensler, D., *Suppose It's Not True: Challenging Mediation Ideology*, 2002 J. DISP. RESOL. 81.

HERMAN, G., CARY, J. & KENNEDY, J., LEGAL COUNSELING AND NEGOTIATING: A PRACTICAL APPROACH (LexisNexis 2001).

Hermann, M. & Kogan, N., *Effects of Negotiators' Personalities on Negotiating Behavior*, *in* NEGOTIATIONS: SOCIAL PSYCHOLOGICAL PERSPECTIVES 247 (D. Druckman, ed.) (Sage 1977).

HERMANN, P., BETTER SETTLEMENTS THROUGH LEVERAGE (Aqueduct 1965).

Hinchey, J., *Construction Industry: Building the Case for Mediation*, ARB. J. 38 (June 1992).

HOFFER, E., THE TRUE BELIEVER (Harper & Row 1951).

HODGSON, J., SANO, Y. & GRAHAM, J., DOING BUSINESS WITH THE NEW JAPAN (Rowman & Littlefield 2000).

HOFFER, E., THE TRUE BELIEVER (Harper & Row 1951).

HOGAN, K., THE PSYCHOLOGY OF PERSUASION (Pelican 1996).

Hopmann & Walcott, *The Impact of External Stresses and Tensions on Negotiations*, *in* NEGOTIATIONS: SOCIAL PSYCHOLOGICAL PERSPECTIVES 301 (D. Druckman, ed.) (Sage 1977).

HOUSTON & SUNSTEIN, *Risk Assessment, Resource Allocation, and Fairness: Evidence from Law Students*, 48 J. LEGAL EDUC. 496 (1998).

Hughes, S., *A Closer Look — The Case for a Mediation Confidentiality Privilege Still Has Not Been Made*, 5 DISP. RESOL. MAG. 14 (Winter 1998).

Hughes, S., *Mediator Immunity: The Misguided and Inequitable Shifting of Risk*, 83 OR. L. REV. 107 (2004).

Hughes, S., *The Uniform Mediation Act: To the Spoiled Go the Privileges*, 85 MARQUETTE L. REV. 9 (2001).

Hyman, J., *Trial Advocacy and Methods of Negotiation: Can Good Trial Advocates Be Wise Negotiators?* 34 U.C.L.A. L. REV. 863 (1987).

Hyman, J. & Love, L., *If Portia Were a Mediator: An Inquiry Into Justice in Mediation*, 9 CLINICAL L. REV. 157 (2002).

IKLE, F., HOW NATIONS NEGOTIATE (Harper & Row 1964).

ILICH, J., THE ART AND SKILL OF SUCCESSFUL NEGOTIATION (Prentice Hall 1973).

ILICH, J., DEALBREAKERS AND BREAKTHROUGHS (John Wiley & Sons 1992).

ILICH, J., POWER NEGOTIATING (Addison-Wesley 1980).

Izumi, C. & La Rue, H., *Prohibiting "Good Faith" Reports Under the Uniform Mediation Act: Keeping the Adjudication Camel Out of the Mediation Tent*, 2003 J. DISP. RESOL. 67 (2003).

JANDT, F., WIN-WIN NEGOTIATING: TURNING CONFLICT INTO AGREEMENT (Wiley 1985).

Johnston, J. & Waldfogel, J., *Does Repeat Play Elicit Cooperation? Evidence from Federal Civil Litigation*, 31 J. LEGAL STUD. 39 (2002).

Jones, E., *Evidentiary Concepts in Labor Arbitration: Some Modern Variations on Ancient Legal Themes*, 13 U.C.L.A. L. REV. 1241 (1966).

KAGEL, S. & KELLY, K., THE ANATOMY OF MEDIATION (B.N.A. 1989).

Kahane, D., *Dispute Resolution and the Politics of Cultural Generalization*, NEGOT. J. 5 (Jan. 2003).

Kahneman, Knetsch & Thaler, *Experimental Tests of the Endowment Effect and the Coase Theorem*, 98 J. POL. ECON. 1325 (1990).

Kahneman, D. & Tversky, A., *Conflict Resolution: A Cognitive Perpective*, in BARRIERS TO CONFLICT RESOLUTION 45 (K. Arrow, R. Mnookin, L. Ross, A. Tversky & R. Wilson eds.) (W.W. Norton 1995).

Kahneman, D. & Tversky, A., *Prospect Theory: An Analysis of Decision Under Risk*, 47 ECONOMETRICA 263 (1979).

KAPLOW, L. & SHAVELL, S., DECISION ANALYSIS, GAME THEORY, AND INFORMATION (Foundation Press 2004).

KARRASS, C., GIVE AND TAKE (Crowell 1974).

KARRASS, C., THE NEGOTIATING GAME (Crowell 1970).

KARRASS, G., NEGOTIATE TO CLOSE (Simon & Schuster 1985).

Kashy, D. & DePaulo, B., *Who Lies?*, 70 J. PERSONALITY & SOC. PSYCHOL. 1037 (1996).

Katsh, E., *Online Dispute Resolution, in* THE HANDBOOK OF DISPUTE RESOLUTION (M. Moffott & R. Bordone, eds.) (Jossey-Bass 2005).

KELLEY, T., THE ART OF INNOVATION (Doubleday 2001).

KENNEDY, G., KENNEDY ON NEGOTIATION (Gower 1998).

KHEEL, T., THE KEYS TO CONFLICT RESOLUTION (Four Walls Eight Windows 1999).

King, Carol J., *Burdening Access to Justice: The Cost of Divorce Mediation on the Cheap*, 73 ST. JOHNS L. REV. 375 (1999).

Kirtley, A., *The Mediation Privilege's Transition from Theory to Implementation: Designing a Mediation Privilege Standard to Protect Mediation Participants, the Process and the Public Interest*, 1995 J. DISP. RESOL. 1.

KOCHAN, T. & LIPSKY, D., NEGOTIATIONS AND CHANGE (ILR Press 2003).

KOHN, A., NO CONTEST (Houghton Mifflin 1986).

KOLB, D., THE MEDIATORS (MIT Press 1983).

Kolb, D., *More Than Just a Footnote: Constructing a Theoretical Framework for Teaching About Gender in Negotiation*, 16 NEGOT. J. 347 (Oct. 2000).

KOLB, D. & ASSOCIATES, WHEN TALK WORKS: PROFILES OF MEDIATORS (Jossey-Bass 1994).

Kolb, D. & Putnam, L., *Negotiation Through a Gender Lens, in* THE HANDBOOK OF DISPUTE RESOLUTION 135 (M. Moffitt & R. Bordone, eds.) (Jossey-Bass 2005).

KOLB, D. & WILLIAMS, J., EVERYDAY NEGOTIATION (Jossey-Bass 2003).

KOLB. D. & WILLIAMS, J., THE SHADOW NEGOTIATION (Simon & Schuster 2000).

KORDA, M., MALE CHAUVINISM: HOW IT WORKS (Random House 1973).

KORDA, M., POWER: HOW TO GET IT, HOW TO USE IT (Random House 1975).

Korobkin, R., *Aspirations and Settlement,* 88 CORNELL L. REV. 1 (2002).

Korobkin, R., *The Endowment Effect and Legal Analysis*, 97 NW. UNIV. L. REV. 1227 (2003).

KOROBKIN, R., NEGOTIATION THEORY AND STRATEGY (Aspen Law & Bus. 2002).

Korobkin, R., *A Positive Theory of Legal Negotiation*, 88 GEO. L.J. 1789 (2000).

Korobkin, R., *Psychological Impediments to Mediation Success: Theory and Practice*, 21 OHIO ST. J. ON DISP. RES. 281 (2006).

KOROBKIN, R., THE ROLE OF LAW IN SETTLEMENT IN THE HANDBOOK OF DISPUTE RESOLUTION 254 (M. Moffitt & R. Bordone, eds.) (Jossey-Bass 2005).

Korobkin, R. & Guthrie, C., *Heuristics and Biases at the Bargaining Table*, 87 MARQUETTE L. REV. 795 (2004).

Korobkin, R. & Guthrie, C., *Opening Offers and Out of Court Settlement: A Little Moderation Might Not Go a Long Way*, 10 OHIO ST. J. ON DISP. RESOL. 1 (1994).

Korobkin, R. & Guthrie, C., *Psychological Barriers to Litigation Settlement: An Experimental Approach*, 93 MICH. L. REV. 107 (1994).

KOVACH, K., MEDIATION: PRINCIPLES AND PRACTICE (West 2d ed. 2000).

KOVACH, K., MEDIATION: PRINCIPLES AND PRACTICE (West 1994).

Kovach, K., *New Wine Requires New Wineskins: Transforming Lawyer Ethics for Effective Representation in a Non-Adversarial Approach to Problem-Solving: Mediation*, 28 FORDHAM URB. L.J. 935 (2001).

Kovach, K. & Love, L., *"Evaluative" Mediation is an Oxymoron*, 14 ALTERNATIVES TO THE HIGH COST OF LITIG. 31 (1996).

Kramer, H., *Game, Set, Match: Winning the Negotiations Game* (ALM Pub. 2001).

Kray, L., Thompson, L. & Galinsky, A., *Battle of the Sexes: Gender, Stereotype Confirmation and Reactance in Negotiations*, 80 J. PERSONALITY & SOC. PSYCHOL. 942 (2001).

KREMENYUK, V., INTERNATIONAL NEGOTIATION (Jossey-Bass 2d ed. 2002).

KRIEGER, S., NEUMANN, R., McMANUS, K. & JAMAR, S., ESSENTIAL LAWYERING SKILLS (Aspen Law & Bus. 1999).

KRITEK, P., NEGOTIATING AT AN UNEVEN TABLE (Jossey-Bass 1994).

KRITZER, H., LET'S MAKE A DEAL (Univ. of Wisconsin Press 1991).

KRIVIS, J., IMPROVISATIONAL NEGOTIATION (Jossey-Bass 2006).

Krohnke, D., *ADR Ethic Rules to Be Added to Rules of Professional Conduct*, 18 ALTERNATIVES 108 (2000).

Kurtzberg & Medvec, *Can We Negotiate and Still be Friends?* 15 NEGOT. J. 355 (1999).

LADD, P., MEDIATION, CONCILIATION AND EMOTIONS (Univ. Press of America 2005).

Lande, J., *Possibilities for Collaborative Law: Ethics and Practice of Lawyer Disqualification and Process Control in a New Model of Lawyering*, 64 OHIO ST. L.J. 1315 (2003).

Lande, J. & Herman, G., *Fitting the Forum to the Family Fuss: Negotiating Divorce Cases*, 42 FAM. CT. REV. 280 (2004).

LANG, M. & TAYLOR, A., THE MAKING OF A MEDIATOR (Jossey-Bass 2000).

Latz, M., *Gain the Edge: Negotiating to Get What You Want* (St. Martin's Press 2004).

Lawless, R., Note, *The American Response to Farm Crises: Procedural Debtor Relief*, 1988 U. ILL. L. REV. 1037.

Lawrence, J., *Mediation Advocacy: Partnering with the Mediator*, 15 OHIO ST. J. ON DISP. RESOL. 425 (2000).

LAX, D. & SEBENIUS, J., THE MANAGER AS NEGOTIATOR: BARGAINING FOR COOPERATION AND COMPETITIVE GAIN (Free Press 1986).

Lax, D. & Sebenius, J., *Three Ethical Issues in Negotiation*, 2 NEGOT. J. 363 (1986).

LE BARON, M., BRIDGING CULTURAL CONFLICTS (Jossey-Bass 2003).

LEBOW, R., THE ART OF BARGAINING (Johns Hopkins University Press 1996).

Le Poole, S., NEVER TAKE NO FOR AN ANSWER (Kogan Page 1991).

Lerman, L., *Mediation of Wife Abuse Case: The Adverse Impact of Informal Dispute Resolution on Women*, 7 HARV. WOMEN'S L.J. 57 (1984).

Levi, D., *The Role of Apology in Mediation*, 72 NYU L. REV. 1165 (1997).

LEVIN, E., NEGOTIATING TACTICS (Fawcett 1980).

LEVINSON, J., SMITH, M. & WILSON, O., GUERRILLA NEGOTIATING (John Wiley & Sons 1999).

LEWICKI, R. & LITTERER, J., NEGOTIATION (Richard D. Irwin 1985).

LEWICKI, R., LITTERER, J., MINTON, J. & SAUNDERS, D., NEGOTIATION (Irwin 1994).

LEWICKI, R., SAUNDERS, D. & MINTON, J., NEGOTIATION: READINGS, EXERCISES AND CASES (Irwin McGraw-Hill 3d ed. 1999).

LEWICKI, R., LITTERER, J., SAUNDERS, D. & MINTON, J., NEGOTIATION: READINGS, EXERCISES AND CASES (Irwin 1993).

LEWIS, D., POWER NEGOTIATING TACTICS AND TECHNIQUES (Prentice-Hall 1981).

LIEBERMAN, D., NEVER BE LIED TO AGAIN (St. Martins Griffin 1998).

LISNEK, P., A LAWYER'S GUIDE TO EFFECTIVE NEGOTIATION AND MEDIATION (West 1993).

Lodder, A. & Zeleznikow, J., *Developing an Online Dispute Resolution Environment: Dialogue Tools and Negotiation Support Systems in a Three-Step Model*, 10 HARV. NEGOT. L. REV. 287 (2005).

Love, L., *The Top Ten Reasons Why Mediators Should Not Evaluate*, 24 FLA. ST. U.L. REV. 937 (1997).

Love, L. & Kovach, K., *ADR: An Eclectic Array of Processes, Rather than One Eclectic Process*, 2000 J. DISP. RESOL. 295.

Lowenthal, G., *A General Theory of Negotiation Process, Strategy, and Behavior*, 31 U. KAN. L. REV. 69 (1982).

MACCOBY, E. & JACKLIN, C., THE PSYCHOLOGY OF SEX DIFFERENCES (Stanford Univ. Press 1974).

Macduff, I., *Your Place or Mine? Culture, Time, and Negotiation*, 22 NEGOT. J. 31 (2006).

Macfarlane, J., *Experiences of Collaborative Law: Preliminary Results From the Collaborative Lawyering Research Project*, 2004 J. DISP. RESOL. 179 (2004).

MACNEIL, I., CONTRACTS: EXCHANGE TRANSACTIONS AND RELATIONS (Foundation Press 2d ed. 1978).

MADONIK, B., I HEAR WHAT YOU SAY, BUT WHAT ARE YOU TELLING ME? (Jossey-Bass 2001).

MAGGIOLO, W., TECHNIQUES OF MEDIATION IN LABOR DISPUTES (Oceana 1971).

Malter, D., Note, *Avoiding Farm Foreclosure Through Mediation of Agricultural Loan Disputes: An Overview of State and Federal Legislation*, 1991 J. DISP. RESOL. 335.

MARONE, N., WOMEN AND RISK (St. Martin's Press 1992).

Matz, D., *Ignorance and Interests*, 4 HARV. NEG. L. REV. 59 (1999).

Maxwell, D., *Gender Differences in Mediation Style and Their Impact on Mediator Effectiveness*, 9 MEDIATION Q. 353 (1992).

Mayer, B., BEYOND NEUTRALITY (Jossey-Bass 2004).

MAYER, B., THE DYNAMICS OF CONFLICT RESOLUTION (Jossey-Bass 2000).

MAYER, R., POWER PLAYS (Times Bus. 1996).

MAYNARD, D., INSIDE PLEA BARGAINING (Plenum 1984).

MAYO, C. & HENLEY, N. (Eds.), GENDER AND NONVERBAL BEHAVIOR (Spring-Verlag 1981).

Mays, R., *Alternative Dispute Resolution and Environmental Enforcement: A Noble Experiment or a Lost Cause*, 18 ENVTL. L. REP. 10,087 (1988).

Mazza, K., *Divorce Mediation*, 14 FAMILY ADVOCATE 40 (1992).

Mc Adoo, B., *A Report to the Minnesota Supreme Court: The Impact of Rule 114 on Civil Litigation Practice in Minnesota*, 25 HAMLINE L. REV. 401 (2002).

Mc Adoo, B. & Hinshaw, A., *The Challenge of Institutionalizing Alternative Dispute Resolution: Attorney Perspectives on the Effect of Rule 17 on Civil Litigation in Missouri*, 67 MO. L. REV. 473 (2002).

McCORMACK, M., ON NEGOTIATING (Dove Books 1995).

McCORMACK, M., WHAT THEY DON'T TEACH YOU AT HARVARD BUSINESS SCHOOL (Bantam 1984).

McDermott, E.P. & Obar, R., *"What's Going On" in Mediation: An Empirical Analysis of the Influence of a Mediator's Style on Party Satisfaction and Monetary Benefit*, 9 HARV. NEGOT. L. REV. 75 (2004).

McEwen, C., Rogers, N. & Maiman, R., *Bring in the Lawyers: Challenging the Dominant Approach to Ensuring Fairness in Divorce Mediation*, 79 MINN. L. REV. 1317 (1995).

McEwen, C. & Wissler, R., *Finding Out If It Is True: Comparing Mediation and Negotiation Through Research,* 2002 J. DISP. RESOL. 131 (2002).

McIntosh, P., *Feeling Like a Fraud*, (Wellesley College 1985) (Paper Published by Stone Center for Developmental Services and Studies Works in Progress Series).

McKay, R., *Ethical Considerations in Alternative Dispute Resolution*, 45 ARB. J. 15 (Mar. 1990).

Melton, A., *Indigenous Justice Systems and Tribal Society*, 79 JUDICATURE 126 (1995).

Mendelsohn, G., *Lawyers as Negotiators*, 1 HARV. NEGOT. L. REV. 139 (1996).

Menkel-Meadow, C., *Aha? Is Creativity in Legal Problem Solving and Teachable in Legal Education?* 6 HARV. NEGOT. L. REV. 97 (2001).

Menkel-Meadow, C., *The Art and Science of Problem-Solving Negotiation*, TRIAL 48 (June 1999).

Menkel-Meadow, C., *Ethics in ADR: The Many "Cs" of Professional Responsibility and Dispute Resolution*, 28 FORDHAM URB. L.J. 979 (2001).

Menkel-Meadow, C., *Ethics in Alternative Dispute Resolution: New Issues, No Answers from the Adversary Conception of Lawyers' Responsibilities*, 38 S. TEX. L. REV. 407 (1997).

Menkel-Meadow, C., *For and Against Settlement: Uses and Abuses of the Mandatory Settlement Conference*, 33 U.C.L.A. L. REV. 485 (1985).

Menkel-Meadow, C., *Is Mediation the Practice of Law?*, 14 ALTERNATIVES TO HIGH COST LITIG. 57 (1996).

Menkel-Meadow, C., *Pursuing Settlement in an Adversary Culture: A Tale of Innovation Co-Opted or "The Law of ADR"*, 19 FLA. ST. U. L. REV. 1.

Menkel-Meadow, C., *Remembrance of Things Past? The Relationship of Past to Future in Pursuing Justice in Mediation*, 5 CARDOZO J. CONFLICT RESOL. 97 (2004).

Menkel-Meadow, C., *The Silences of the Restatement of the Law Governing Lawyers: Lawyering as Only Adversary Practice*, 10 GEO. J. LEGAL ETHICS 631 (1997).

Menkel-Meadow, C., *Teaching About Gender and Negotiation: Sex, Truths, and Videotape*, 16 NEG. J. 357 (Oct. 2000).

Menkel-Meadow, C., *Toward Another View of Legal Negotiation: The Structure of Problem Solving*, 31 U.C.L.A. L. REV. 754 (1984).

MENKEL-MEADOW, C. & Wheeler, M., WHAT'S FAIR: ETHICS FOR NEGOTIATORS (Jossey-Bass (2004).

MERRILLS, J., INTERNATIONAL DISPUTE SETTLEMENT (Cambridge Univ. Press 1998).

Meyer, A., *Function of the Mediator in Collective Bargaining*, 13 INDUS. & LAB. REL. REV. 159 (1960).

Meyerson, B., *Lawyers Who Mediate are Not Practicing Law*, 14 ALTERNATIVES 74 (1996).

Mika, H., *The Practice and Prospect of Victim-Offender Programs*, 46 S.M.U. L. REV. 2191 (1993).

MILLER, L. & MILLER, J., A WOMAN'S GUIDE TO SUCCESSFUL NEGOTIATING (McGraw-Hill 2002).

Milner, N., *Mediation and Political Theory: A Critique of Bush and Folger*, 21 LAW & SOC. INQUIRY 737 (1996).

Mnookin, R., *Strategic Barriers to Dispute Resolution: A Comparison of Bilateral and Multilateral Negotiations*, 8 HARV. NEGOT. L. REV. 1 (2003).

Mnookin, R. & Kornhauser, L., *Bargaining in the Shadow of the Law: The Case of Divorce*, 88 YALE L.J. 950 (1979).

MNOOKIN, R., PEPPET, S. & TULUMELLO, A., BEYOND WINNING: NEGOTIATING TO CREATE VALUE IN DEALS AND DISPUTES (Harvard Univ. Press/ Belknap 2000).

Mnookin, R., Peppet, S. & Tulumello, A., *The Tension Between Empathy and Assertiveness*, 12 NEGOT. J. 217 (1996).

Mnookin, R. & Ross, L., *Introduction, in* BARRIERS TO CONFLICT RESOLUTION 2 (K. Arrow, R. Mnookin, L. Ross, A. Tversky & R. Wilson, eds., 1995).

Moffitt, M., *Contingent Agreements: Agreeing to Disagree About the Future*, 87 MARQUETTE L. REV. 691 (2004).

Moffitt, M., *Pleadings in the Age of Settlement*, 80 IND. L.J. 727 (2005).

Moffitt, M., *Suing Mediators*, 83 B.U. L. REV. 147 (2003a).

Moffitt, M., *Ten Ways to Get Sued: A Guide for Mediators*, 8 HARV. NEGOT. L. REV. 81 (2003b).

Moffitt, M., *The Wrong Model, Again: Why the Devil is not in the Details of the New Model Standards of Conduct for Mediators*, DISP. RESOL. MAG., Spring 2006, at 31.

MOFFITT, M. & BORDONE, R., THE HANDBOOK OF DISPUTE RESOLUTION (Jossey-Bass 2005).

Moore, C., *The Caucus: Private Meetings That Promote Settlement*, 16 MEDIATION Q. 87 (1987).

MOORE, C., THE MEDIATION PROCESS (2d ed. Jossey-Bass 1996).

MORAN, R., GETTING YOUR YEN'S WORTH: HOW TO NEGOTIATE WITH JAPAN, INC. (Gulf 1984).

MORGAN, T. & ROTUNDA, R., MODEL CODE OF PROFESSIONAL RESPONSIBILITY, MODEL RULES OF PROFESSIONAL CONDUCT, AND OTHER SELECTED STANDARDS ON PROFESSIONAL RESPONSIBILITY (Foundation Press 2000).

MORRIS, D., BODYTALK (Crown 1994).

Morris, M., Nadler, J., Kurtzberg, T. & Thompson, L., *Schmooze or Lose: Social Friction and Lubrication in E-Mail Negotiations*, 6 GROUP DYNAMICS: THEORY, RES. & PRAC. 89 (2002).

MURNIGHAN, J.K., BARGAINING GAMES (William Morrow 1992).

MUSASHI, M., THE BOOK OF FIVE RINGS (T. Cleary, ed.) (Shambhala 1993).

Nadler, J., *Distributing Adventitious Resources: The Effects of Relationship and Grouping*, 12 SOC. JUST. RES. 131 (1999).

Nadler, J., *Electronically-Mediated Dispute Resolution and E-Commerce*, NEGOT. J. 333 (Oct. 2001).

Nadler, J., *Rapport in Legal Negotiation: How Small Talk Can Facilitate E-Mail Dealmaking*, 9 HARV. NEGOT. L. REV. 223 (2004b).

Nadler, J., *Rapport in Negotiation and Conflict Resolution*, 87 MARQUETTE L. REV. 875 (2004a).

NELKEN, M., UNDERSTANDING NEGOTIATION (2001).

Neuman, J., *Run, River, Run: Mediation of Water Rights Dispute Keeps Fish and Farmers Happy, For a Time*, 67 U. COLO. L. REV. 259 (1996).

NEW JERSEY SUPREME COURT TASK FORCE ON COMMUNITY DISPUTE RESOLUTION, "TASK FORCE REPORT" (1990).

NIERENBERG, G., THE ART OF NEGOTIATING (Cornerstone 1968).

NIERENBERG, G., THE COMPLETE NEGOTIATOR (Barnes & Noble 1996).

NIERENBERG, G., FUNDAMENTALS OF NEGOTIATING (Hawthorne/Dutton 1973).

NIERENBERG, G. & CALERO, H., HOW TO READ A PERSON LIKE A BOOK (Cornerstone 1971).

NIERENBERG, G. & CALERO, H., META-TALK (Cornerstone 1981).

NIERENBERG, J. & ROSS, I., WOMEN AND THE ART OF NEGOTIATING (Simon & Schuster 1985).

NOLAN-HALEY, J., ALTERNATIVE DISPUTE RESOLUTION IN A NUTSHELL (West 1992).

Nolan-Haley, J., *Court Mediation and the Search for Justice Through Law*, 74 WASH. U. L.Q. 47 (1996).

Nolan-Haley, J., *Informed Consent in Mediation: A Guiding Principle for Truly Educated Decisionmaking*, 74 NOTRE DAME L. REV. 775 (1999).

Nolan-Haley, J., *Lawyers, Non-Lawyers, and Mediation: Rethinking the Professional Monopoly from a Problem-Solving Perspective*, 7 HARV. NEGOT. L. REV. 235 (2002).

Norton, E., *Bargaining and the Ethic of Process*, 64 N.Y.U. L. REV. 493 (1989).

Novey, P. & Novey, T., *Don't Make Daddy Mad or Teaching Women How to Negotiate with Men*, 13 TRANSACTIONAL ANALYSIS J. 97 (1983).

O'Brien, M., *At the Intersection of Public Policy and Private Process: Court-Ordered Mediation and the Remedial Process in School Funding Litigation*, 18 OHIO ST. J. ON DISP. RESOL. 391 (2003).

O'Hara, E. & Yarn, D., *On Apology and Conscience*, 77 WASH. L. REV. 1121 (2002).

O'Quin, K. & Aronoff, J., *Humor as a Technique of Social Influence*, 44 SOC. PSYCHOL. Q. 349 (1981).

ORDOVER, A. & DONEFF, A., ALTERNATIVES TO LITIGATION (NITA 2002).

Orr, D. & Guthrie, C., *Anchoring, Information, Expertise, and Negotiation: New Insights from Meta-Analysis*, 21 OHIO ST. J. ON DISP. RESOL. 597 (2006).

PACT Institute of Justice, Victim-Offender Reconciliation & Mediation Program Directory (1993).

Paplinger, E. & Menkel-Meadow, C., *ADR Ethics*, Disp. Resol. Mag. 20 (Summer 1999).

Patton, L., *Settling Environmental Disputes: The Experience With and Future of Environmental Mediation*, 14 Envtl. L. 547 (1984).

Pavlick, D., *Apology and Mediation: The Horse and Carriage of the Twenty-First Century*, 18 Ohio St. J. on Disp. Resol. 829 (2003).

Pearson, J. & Thoennes, N., *Divorce Mediation: Reflections on a Decade of Research*, *in* Mediation Research 9 (K. Kressel & D. Pruitt, eds.) (Jossey-Bass 1989).

Pearson, J., & Thoennes, N., *Mediating and Litigating Custody Disputes: A Longitudinal Evaluation*, 17 Fam. L.Q. 497 (1984).

Peck, C., Cases and Materials on Negotiation (B.N.A. 1980).

Peck, C. & Fletcher, R., *A Course on the Subject of Negotiation*, 21 J. Leg. Educ. 196 (1968).

Peppet, S., *Contractarian Economics and Meditation Ethics: The Case for Customizing Neutrality Through Contingent Fee Mediation*, 82 Tex. L. Rev. 227 (2003).

Peppet, S., *Contract Formation in Imperfect Markets: Should We Use Mediators in Deals?* 19 Ohio St. J. on Disp. Resol. 283 (2004).

Peppet, S., *Lawyers' Bargaining Ethics, Contract, and Collaboration: The End of the Legal Profession and the Beginning of Professional Pluralism*, 90 Iowa L. Rev. 475 (2005).

Perkins, A., *Negotiations: Are Two Heads Better than One?* 71 Harv. Bus. Rev. 13 (Nov.-Dec. 1993).

Perschbacher, R., *Regulating Lawyers' Negotiations*, 27 Ariz. L. Rev. 75 (1985).

Peters, G., *The Use of Lies in Negotiation*, 48 Ohio St. L.J. 1 (1987).

Peterson, L., *The Promise of Mediated Settlements of Environmental Disputes: The Experience of EPA Region V*, 17 Colum. J. Envtl. L. 327 (1992).

Phillips, B., Finding Common Ground: A Field Guide to Mediation (Hells Canyon Publishing 1994).

Phillips, B. & Piazza, A., *How to Use Mediation*, 10 Litigation 31 (Spr. 1984).

Phillips, J., *Mediation as One Step in Adversarial Litigation: One Country Lawyer's Experience*, 2002 J. Disp. Resol. 143.

Pines, A., Gat, H. & Tal, Y., *Gender Differences in Content and Style of Argument Between Couples During Divorce Mediation*, 20 Conflict Resol. Q. 23 (Fall 2002).

Pinkley, R. & Northcraft, G., Get Paid What You're Worth (St. Martin's Press 2000).

Pitulla, J., *The Ethics of Secretly Taping Phone Conversations*, ABA J. 102 (Feb. 1994).

Pitulla, J., *Using the Ultimate Threat Against an Opposing Party*, 78 A.B.A. J. 106 (Oct. 1992).

PRATKANIS, A. & ARONSON, E., AGE OF PROPAGANDA (W.H. Freeman 1992).

Prestia, P., *Decision Tree: Good Tool for Analysis*, LE NEUVELLES 60 (March 1994).

PRUITT, D., NEGOTIATION BEHAVIOR (Academic Press 1981).

PRUITT, D. & RUBIN, J., SOCIAL CONFLICT (Random House 1986).

Putnam, L., *Transformations and Critical Moments in Negotiations*, 20 NEGOT. J. 275 (2004).

Quilliam, S., BODY LANGUAGE (Firefly Books 2004).

Rachlinski, J., *Gains, Losses, and the Psychology of Litigation*, 70 S. CAL. L. REV. 113 (1996).

Rachlinski, J., *The Uncertain Psychological Case for Paternalism*, 97 NW. U. L. REV. 1165 (2003).

RAIFFA, H., THE ART AND SCIENCE OF NEGOTIATION (Belknap/Harvard 1982).

RAIFFA, H., NEGOTIATION ANALYSIS (Belknap/Harvard Univ. Press. 2003).

Rangaswomy, A. & Shell, G.R., *Using Computers to Realize Joint Gains in Negotiations: Towards an "Electronic Bargaining Table,"* MANAGEMENT SCIENCE, Vol. 43, No. 8 (Aug. 1997).

RAPOPORT, A., STRATEGY AND CONSCIENCE (Harper & Row 1964).

RAPOPORT, A., TWO-PERSON GAME THEORY (Univ. of Michigan Press 1966).

REARDON, K., THE SKILLED NEGOTIATOR (Jossey-Bass 2004).

Reich, J., *A Call for Intellectual Honesty: A Response to the Uniform Mediation Act's Privilege Against Disclosure*, 2001 J. DISP. RESOL. 197.

Reilly, P., *Teaching Law Students How to Feel: Using Negotiation Training to Increase Emotional Intelligence*, 21 NEGOT. J. 301 (2005).

Resnik, J., *Mediating Preferences: Litigant Preferences for Process and Judicial Preferences for Settlement*, 2002 J. DISP. RESOL. 155.

Reuben, R., *The Sound of Dust Settling: A Response to Criticisms of the UMA*, 2003 J. DISP. RESOL. 99.

Reubin, R. & Rogers, N., *Major Step Forward: Proposed Uniform Mediation Act Goes Public for Comments*, DISP. RESOL. MAG. 18 (Summer 1999).

RICH, A., INTERRACIAL COMMUNICATION (Harper & Row 1974).

Richardson, J., *Mediation: The Florida Legislature Grants Judicial Immunity to Court-Appointed Mediators*, 17 FLA. ST. U. L. REV. 623 (1990).

Ringer, R., *To Be or Not To Be Intimidated?* (M. Evans & Co. 2004).

RINGER, R., WINNING THROUGH INTIMIDATION (Fawcett 1974).

Riskin, L., *The Contemplative Lawyer: On the Potential Contributions of Mindfulness Meditation to Law Students, Lawyers, and Their Clients*, 7 HARV. NEGOT. L. REV. 601 (2002).

Risken, L., *Decisionmaking in Mediation: The New Old Grid and the New New Grid System*, 79 NOTRE DAME L. REV. 1 (2003).

Riskin, L., *Mediator Orientations, Strategies, and Techniques*, 12 ALTERNA-TIVES 111 (1994).

Riskin, L., *Two Concepts of Mediation in the FmHA's Farmer-Lender Mediation Program*, 45 ADMIN. L. REV. 21 (1993).

Riskin, L., *Who Decides What?* DISP. RESOL. MAG. 22 (Winter 2003).

Robinson, P., *Centuries of Contract Common Law Can't Be All Wrong: Proceedings Should Be Embraced and Broadened*, 2003 J. DISP. RESOL. 135.

ROGERS, N. & MCEWEN, C., MEDIATION: LAW, POLICY, PRACTICE (Clark Boardman Callaghan 1994).

Ross, L., *Reactive Devaluation in Negotiation and Conflict Resolution in* BARRIERS TO CONFLICT RESOLUTION 26 (K. Arrow, R. Mnookin, L. Ross, A. Tversky & R. Wilson, eds.) (Norton 1995).

ROTUNDA, R., PROFESSIONAL RESPONSIBILITY (West 1995).

Royce, T., *The Negotiator and the Bomber: Analyzing the Critical Role of Active Listening in Crisis Negotiations*, 21 NEGOT. J. 5 (2005).

Rubin, A., *A Causerie on Lawyers' Ethics in Negotiation*, 35 LA. L. REV. 577 (1975).

Rubin, A. & Will, H., *Some Suggestions Concerning the Judge's Role in Stimulating Settlement Negotiations*, 75 FED. RULES DECISIONS 227 (1977).

Rubin, J., *Psychological Traps*, PSYCHOLOGY TODAY 52 (March 1981).

RUBIN, J. & BROWN, B., THE SOCIAL PSYCHOLOGY OF BARGAINING AND NEGOTIATION (Academic Press 1975).

Rubin, M., *The Ethics of Negotiations: Are There Any?*, 56 LA. L. REV. 447 (1995).

Rubinstein, R., *Cross-Cultural Considerations in Complex Peace Operations*, NEGOT. J. 29 (Jan. 2003).

Ryan, E., *The Discourse Beneath: Emotional Epistemology in Legal Deliberation and Negotiation*, 10 HARV. NEGOT. L. REV. 231 (2005).

Sabatino, J., *ADR as "Litigation Lite": Procedural and Evidentiary Norms Embedded Within Alternative Dispute Resolution*, 47 EMORY L.J. 1289 (1998).

Said, I., *The Mediator's Dilemma: The Legal Requirements Exception to Confidentiality Under the Texas ADR Statute*, 36 S. TEX. L. REV. 579 (1995).

SALACUSE, J., THE GLOBAL NEGOTIATOR (Palgrave 2003).

SALACUSE, J., LESSONS FOR PRACTICE IN POWER AND NEGOTIATION 255 (I.W. Zartman & J. Rubin, eds.) (U. of Michigan Press 2002).

SALACUSE, J., MAKING GLOBAL DEALS (Houghton Mifflin 1991).

Samborn, H., *The Vanishing Trial*, ABA J. 24 (Oct. 2002).

Sammataro, J., *Business and Brotherhood, Can They Coincide? A Search Into Why Black Athletes Do Not Hire Black Agents*, 42 HOW. L.J. 535 (1999).

SAVIR, U., THE PROCESS (Random House 1998).

Sax, L., WHY GENDER MATTERS (Doubleday 2005).

SCANLON, K., MEDIATOR'S DESKBOOK (CPR Institute for Dispute Resolution 1999).

SCHATZKI, M., NEGOTIATION (Signet 1981).

SCHEFLEN, A., BODY LANGUAGE AND THE SOCIAL ORDER (Prentice-Hall 1972).

Schelling, T., *An Essay on Bargaining, in* BARGAINING: FORMAL THEORIES OF NEGOTIATION 319 (O. Young, ed.) (Univ. of Illinois Press 1975).

Schelling, T., *An Essay on Bargaining*, 46 AM. ECON. REV. 281 (1956).

SCHELLING, T., THE STRATEGY OF CONFLICT (Harvard Univ. Press 1960).

Schneider, A., *Aspirations in Negotiation*, 87 MARQUETTE L. REV. 675 (2004).

Schneider, A., *Building a Pedagogy of Problem-Solving: Learning to Choose Among ADR Processes*, 5 HARV. NEGOT. L. REV. 113 (2000).

Schneider, A., *Effective Responses to Offensive Comments*, NEGOT. J. 107 (April 1994).

Schneider, A., *Perception, Reputation and Reality*, DISP. RESOL. MAG. 24 (Summer 2000).

Schneider, A., *Shattering Negotiation Myths: Empirical Evidence on the Effectiveness of Negotiation Style*, 7 HARV. NEGOT. L. REV. 143 (2002).

Schoonmaker, A., NEGOTIATE TO WIN: GAINING THE PSYCHOLOGICAL EDGE (Prentice Hall 1989).

Schreier, L., *Emotional Intelligence and Mediation Training*, 20 CONFLICT RESOL. Q. 99 (2002).

SCHWARTZ, B., THE PARADOX OF CHOICE: WHY MORE IS LESS (Harper Collins 2004).

Schwartz, Joshua R., *Laymen Cannot Lawyer, But Is Mediation the Practice of Law?* 20 CARDOZO L. REV. 1715 (1999).

Schwebel, A., Gately, D.,Milburn, T. & Rennes, M., *Divorce Mediation: Four Models and Their Assumptions About Change in Parties' Positions*, 11 MED. Q. 211 (1994).

Schwebel, A., Gately, D., Milburn, T. & Rennes, M., *PMI-DM: A Divorce Mediation Approach that First Addresses Interpersonal Issues*, 4 J. FAM. PSYCHOTHERAPY 69 (No. 2 1993).

Schweitzer, M. & Croson, R., *Curtailing Deception: The Impact of Direct Questions on Lies and Omissions*, 10 INT'L J. CONFLICT MGMT. 225 (1999).

SCHWEITZER, S., WINNING WITH DECEPTION AND BLUFF (Prentice-Hall 1979).

SCOTT, B., NEGOTIATING (Paradigm 1988).

SCOTT, B., THE SKILLS OF NEGOTIATING (Wildwood House 1981).

Senger, J., *Decision Analysis in Negotiation*, 87 MARQUETTE L. REV. 723 (2004).

Shapiro, D., *Negotiating Emotions*, 20 CONFLICT RESOL. Q. 67 (2002).

SHAPIRO, R. & JANKOWSKI, M., THE POWER OF NICE (John Wiley & Sons 2001).

SHELL, G.R., BARGAINING FOR ADVANTAGE (Viking 1999).

SHER, B., WISHCRAFT: HOW TO GET WHAT YOU REALLY WANT (Ballantine 1979).

Shestowsky, D., *Procedural Preferences in Alternative Dispute Resolution: A Closer, Modern Look at an Old Idea*, 10 PSYCHOL. PUB. POL'Y & L. 211 (2004).

Shonholtz, R., *The Citizens' Role in Justice: Building a Primary Justice and Prevention System at the Neighborhood Level*, 494 ANNALS OF THE AM. ACAD. POLIT. & SOC. SCI. 42 (1987).

Sibley, S. & Merry, S., *Mediator Settlement Strategies*, 8 L. & POL'Y Q. 7 (1986).

SIEGEL, S. & FOURAKER, L., BARGAINING AND GROUP DECISION MAKING (McGraw-Hill 1960).

Silberman, L., *Professional Responsibility Problems of Divorce Mediation*, 16 FAM. L.Q. 107 (1982).

SINGER, L., SETTLING DISPUTES (Westview Press 2d ed. 1994).

SJÖSTEDT, G., PROFESSIONAL CULTURES IN INTERNATIONAL NEGOTIATION (Lexington Books 2003).

SKOPEC, E. & KIELY, L., EVERYTHING'S NEGOTIABLE WHEN YOU KNOW HOW TO PLAY THE GAME (Amacom 1994).

SLAIKEU, K., WHEN PUSH COMES TO SHOVE: A PRACTICAL GUIDE TO MEDIATING DISPUTES (Jossey-Bass 1996).

Smeltzer & Watson, *Gender Differences in Verbal Communication During Negotiations*, 3 COMMUNICATION RES. REP. 74 (1986).

SMITH, M., WHEN I SAY NO, I FEEL GUILTY (Bantam 1975).

SPIDR Commission on Qualifications, *Qualifying Neutrals: The Basic Principles*, DISP. RESOL. F., at 3 (May 1989).

Stamato, L., *Voice, Place, and Process: Research on Gender, Negotiation, and Conflict Resolution*, 9 MEDIATION Q. 375 (1992).

STARK, P. & FLAHERTY, J., THE ONLY NEGOTIATING GUIDE YOU'LL EVER NEED (Broadway Books 2003).

Steele, W., *Deceptive Negotiating and High-Toned Morality*, 39 VAND. L. REV. 1378 (1986).

STEINBERG, L., WINNING WITH INTEGRITY (Random House 1999).

Stempel, J., *Beyond Formalism and False Dichotomies: The Need for Institutionalizing a Flexible Concept of the Mediator's Role*, 24 FLA. ST. U. L. REV. 949 (1997).

Stempel, J., *The Inevitability of the Eclectic: Liberating ADR from Ideology*, 2000 J. DISP. RESOL. 247.

Sternlight, J., *Lawyers' Representation of Clients in Mediation: Using Economics and Psychology to Structure Advocacy in a Nonadversarial Setting*, 14 OHIO ST. J. ON DISP. RESOL. 269 (1999).

Stiver, *Work Inhibitions in Women* (Wellesley College 1983) (Paper Published by Stone Center for Developmental Services and Studies Works in Progress Series).

STRAUSS, A., NEGOTIATIONS: VARIETIES, CONTEXTS, PROCESSES, AND SOCIAL ORDER (Jossey-Bass 1978).

Student Project, *Recent Developments: The Uniform Arbitration Act*, 1999 J. DISP. RESOL. 219.

Stuhlmacher, A. & Walters, A., *Gender Differences in Negotiation Outcome: A Meta-Analysis*, 52 PERSONNEL PSYCHOL. 653 (1999).

Stulberg, J., *The Model Standards of Conduct: A Reply to Professor Moffitt*, DISP. RESOL. MAG., Spring 2006, at 35.

Stulberg, J., *The Theory and Practice of Mediation: A Reply to Professor Susskind*, 6 VT. L. REV. 85 (1981).

SUN TZU, THE ART OF WAR (J. Clavell, ed.) (Delacorte 1983).

Susskind, L., *Environmental Mediation and the Accountability Problem*, 6 VT. L. REV. 1 (1981).

Symposium, *Standards of Professional Conduct in Alternative Dispute Resolution*, 1995 J. DISP. RESOL. 95 (1995).

Taft, L., *Apology Subverted: The Commodification of Apology*, 109 YALE L.J. 1135 (2000).

TAN, J.S. & LIM, E., STRATEGIES FOR EFFECTIVE CROSS-CULTURAL NEGOTIATION (McGraw Hill 2004).

TANNEN, D., TALKING FROM 9 TO 5 (William Morrow 1994).

TANNEN, D., THAT'S NOT WHAT I MEANT (William Morrow 1986).

TANNEN, D., YOU JUST DON'T UNDERSTAND (William Morrow 1990).

TAYLOR, A., THE HANDBOOK OF FAMILY DISPUTE RESOLUTION (Jossey-Bass 2002).

Temkin, B., *Misrepresentation By Omission in Settlement Negotiations: Should There Be a Silent Safe Harbor?* 18 GEO. J. LEGAL ETHICS 179 (2004).

TEPLY, L., LEGAL NEGOTIATION IN A NUTSHELL (West 1992).

TESLER, P., COLLABORATIVE LAW: ACHIEVING EFFECTIVE RESOLUTION IN DIVORCE WITHOUT LITIGATION (ABA Section of Family Law 2001).

Thayer, N. & Weiss, S., *Japan: The Changing Logic of a Former Minor Power, in* NATIONAL NEGOTIATING STYLES 45 (H. Binnendijk, ed.) (Center for Study of Foreign Affairs, U.S. Department of State 1987).

THOMAS, J., NEGOTIATE TO WIN: THE 21 RULES FOR SUCCESSFUL NEGOTIATION (Collins 2005).

THOMPSON, L., THE MIND AND HEART OF THE NEGOTIATOR (Pearson Prentice Hall 3d ed. 2005).

THOMPSON, L., THE MIND AND HEART OF THE NEGOTIATOR (Prentice Hall 1998).

THOMPSON, L., LEVINE, J. & MESSICK, D., SHARED COGNITION IN ORGANIZATIONS (Lawrence Erlbaum Assoc. 1999).

Thompson, L. & Nadler, J., *Negotiating Via Information Technology: Theory and Application*, 58 J. SOC. ISSUES 109 (2002).

Thorpe, W., & Yates, S., *An Overview of the Revised Model Standards of Conduct for Mediators*, DISP. RESOL. MAG., Winter 2006, at 30.

Tinsley, C., O'Connor, K. & Sullivan, B., *Tough Guys Finish Last: The Perils of a Distributive Reputation*, 88 ORG. BEHAVIOR & HUMAN DEC. PROCESSES 621 (2002).

Tone, *The Role of the Judge in the Settlement Process*, SEMINARS FOR NEWLY APPOINTED UNITED STATES DISTRICT JUDGES 57 (1973–1975).

Tornquist, L., *The Active Judge in Pretrial Settlement: Inherent Authority Gone Awry*, 25 WILLAMETTE L. REV. 743 (1989).

TRACHTE-HUBER, E.W. & HUBER, S., MEDIATION AND NEGOTIATION (Anderson 1998).

Tversky, A. & Kahneman, D., *The Framing of Decisions and the Psychology of Choice*, 211 SCIENCE 453 (1981).

Umbreit, M., *Violent Offenders and Their Victims, in* MEDIATION AND CRIMINAL JUSTICE (B. Galaway & M. Wright, eds.) (Sage 1989).

The Uniform Mediation Act, 22 N. ILLINOIS U. L. REV. 165 (2002).

Uniform Mediation Act Symposium, 2003 J. DISP. RESOL. 1 (2003).

UNITED STATES DEPT. OF JUSTICE, NATIONAL SURVEY OF VICTIM-OFFENDER MEDIATION PROGRAMS IN THE UNITED STATES (April 2000).

URY, W., GETTING PAST NO (Bantam Books 1991).

URY, W., BRETT, J. & GOLDBERG, S., GETTING DISPUTES RESOLVED (Harvard Program on Negotiation 1993).

Van Boven, L., Gilovich, T. & Medvec, V., *The Illusion of Transparency in Negotiations*, 19 NEGOT. J. 117 (2003).

Van Ness, D., *New Wine and Old Wineskins: Four Challenges of Restorative Justice*, 4 CRIM. L.F. 251 (1993).

Van Zandt, H., *How to Negotiate in Japan*, HARV. BUS. REV. 45 (Nov.-Dec. 1970).

Volkema, R., Leverage: How to Get It and How to Keep It in Any Negotiation (Amacom 2006).

Volkema, R., The Negotiation Toolkit (Amacom 1999).

Von Neumann, J. & Morgenstern, O., Theory of Games and Economic Behavior (Princeton Univ. Press 1944, 1972).

Vrij, A., Detecting Lies and Deceit (John Wiley & Sons 2000).

Vuorela, T., *Laughing Matters: A Case Study of Humor in Multicultural Business Negotiations*, 21 Negot. J. 105 (2005).

Waldman, E., *Identifying the Role of Social Norms in Mediation: A Multiple Model Approach*, 48 Hastings L. Rev. 703 (1997).

Wall, J. & Callister, R., *Ho'oponopono: Some Lessons From Hawaiian Mediation*, 11 Negot. J. 45 (1995).

Wall, Rude & Schiller, *Judicial Participation in Settlement*, 1984 Mo. J. Disp. Resol. 25 (1984).

Walton, R. & McKersie, R., A Behavioral Theory of Labor Negotiations (McGraw-Hill 1965).

Warschaw, T., Winning By Negotiation (McGraw-Hill 1980).

Watkins, M., *Principles of Persuasion*, Negot. J. 115 (April 2001).

Watkins, M. & Rosegrant, S., Breakthrough in International Negotiation (Jossey-Bass 2001).

Watson, A., *Mediation and Negotiation: Learning to Deal with Psychological Responses*, 18 U. Mich. J. L. Reform 293 (1985).

Watson, L., *Effective Legal Representation in Mediation*, in Alternative Dispute Resolution in Florida (1995).

Watts, *Briefing the American Negotiator in Japan*, 16 Int'l Law. 597 (1982).

Weckstein, D., *Mediator Certification: Why and How*, 30 U.S.F. L. Rev. 757 (1996).

Welsh, N., *Disputants' Decision Control in Court-Connected Mediation: A Hollow Promise Without Procedural Justice*, 2002 J. Disp. Resol. 179.

Welsh, N., *Making Deals in Court-Connected Mediation: What's Justice Got to Do With It?* 79 Wash. U. L.Q. 787 (2001).

Welsh, N., *The Place of Court-Connected Mediation in a Democratic Justice System*, 5 Cardozo J. Conflict Resol. 117 (2004a).

Welsh, N., *Perceptions of Fairness in Negotiation*, 87 Marquette L. Rev. 753 (2004b).

Welsh, N., *Reconciling Self-Determination, Coercion, and Settlement in Court-Connected Mediation*, in Divorce and Family Mediation: Models, Techniques, and Applications 420 (Folberg, J., Milne, A. & Salem, P., eds., 2004c).

Welsh, N., *Stepping Back Through the Looking Glass: Real Conversations with Real Disputants About Institutionalized Mediation and Its Value*, 19 Ohio St. J. on Disp. Resol. 573 (2004d).

Welsh, N., *The Thinning Vision of Self-Determination in Court-Connected Mediation: The Inevitable Price of Institutionalization?*, 6 HARV. NEGOT. L. REV. (2001).

WENKE, R., THE ART OF NEGOTIATION FOR LAWYERS (Richter 1985).

Wetlaufer, G., *The Ethics of Lying in Negotiations*, 75 IOWA L. REV. 1219 (1990).

Wetlaufer, G., *The Limits of Integrative Bargaining*, 85 GEO. L.J. 369 (1996).

White, J., *The Lawyer as a Negotiator: An Adventure in Understanding and Teaching the Art of Negotiation*, 19 J. LEGAL EDUC. 337 (1967).

White, J., *Machiavelli and the Bar: Ethical Limitations on Lying in Negotiation*, 1980 AM. B. FOUND. RES. J. 926 (1980).

White, S. & Neale, M., *The Role of Negotiator Aspirations and Settlement Expectations in Bargaining Outcomes*, 57 ORGANIZATIONAL BEHAV. & HUM. DECISION PROCESSES 303 (1994).

WILL, H., MERHIGE, R. & RUBIN, A., THE ROLE OF THE JUDGE IN THE SETTLEMENT PROCESS (Fed. Judicial Center 1983).

Will, H., Merhige, R. & Rubin, A., *The Role of the Judge in the Settlement Process*, 75 FED. RULES DECISIONS 203 (1977).

WILLIAMS, G., A LAWYER'S HANDBOOK FOR EFFECTIVE NEGOTIATION AND SETTLEMENT (Professional Education Group 4th ed. 1992).

WILLIAMS, G., LEGAL NEGOTIATION AND SETTLEMENT (West 1983).

Williams, G., *Negotiation as a Healing Process*, 1996 J. DISP. RESOL. 1.

WINKLER, J., BARGAINING FOR RESULTS (Facts on File 1984).

Wiseman, V. & Poitras, J., *Mediation Within a Hierarchical Structure: How Can It Be Done Successfully?* 20 CONFLICT RESOL. Q. 51 (2002).

Wissler, R., *Barriers to Attorneys' Discussion and Use of ADR*, 19 OHIO ST. J. ON DISP. RESOL. 459 (2004).

Wissler, R. & Rack, Jr., R., *Assessing Mediator Performance: The Usefulness of Participant Questionnaires*, 2004 J. DISP. RESOL. 229.

Wistrich, A., Guthrie, C. & Rachlinski, J., *Can Judges Ignore Admissible Information? The Difficulty of Deliberately Disregarding*, 153 U. PA. L. REV. 1251 (2005).

Woods, L., *Mediation: A Backlash to Women's Progress in Family Law Issues*, 19 CLEARINGHOUSE REV. 431 (1985).

Woods, W., Note, *Model Rule 2.2 and Divorce Mediation: Ethics Guideline or Ethics Gap?*, 65 WASH. U. L.Q. 223 (1987).

WOOLF, B., FRIENDLY PERSUASION (G.P. Putnam's Sons 1990).

YOUNG, K., NEGOTIATING WITH THE CHINESE COMMUNISTS: THE UNITED STATES EXPERIENCE, 1953–1967 (McGraw-Hill 1968).

YOUNG, O. (ED.), BARGAINING: FORMAL THEORIES OF NEGOTIATION (Univ. of Illinois Press 1975).

Young, *Strategic Interaction and Bargaining, in* BARGAINING: FORMAL THEORIES OF NEGOTIATION 3 (O. Young, ed.) (Univ. of Illinois Press 1975).

ZARTMAN, I.W., THE FIFTY PERCENT SOLUTION (Doubleday 1976).

ZARTMAN. I.W., INTERNATIONAL MULTILATERAL NEGOTIATION (Jossey-Bass 1994).

ZARTMAN, I.W., THE NEGOTIATION PROCESS: THEORIES AND APPLICATIONS (Sage 1978).

ZARTMAN, I.W. & BERMAN, M., THE PRACTICAL NEGOTIATOR (Yale Univ. Press 1982).

ZARTMAN, I.W. & RUBIN, J., POWER AND NEGOTIATION (Univ. of Michigan Press 2002).

ZEHR, H., CHANGING LENSES (Herald Press 1990).

Zylstra, A., *Mediation and Domestic Violence: A Practical Screening Method for Mediators and Mediation Program Administrators*, 2001 J. DISP. RESOL. 253.

ARBITRATION

Allison, J., *Arbitration Agreements and Antitrust Claims: The Need for Enhanced Accommodation of Conflicting Public Policies*, 64 N.C. L. REV. 219 (1986).

Atwood, B., *Issues in Federal State Relations Under the Federal Arbitration Acts*, 37 FLA. L. REV. 61 (1985).

Brunet, E., *Arbitration and Constitutional Rights*, 71 N.C. L. REV. 1 (1992).

Brunet, E., *Questioning the Quality of Alternative Dispute Resolution*, 62 TUL. L. REV. 1 (1987).

Brunet, E., *Replacing Folklore Arbitration With A Contract Model of Arbitration,* 74 TUL. L. REV. 39 (1999).

Brunet, E., *Toward Changing Models of Securities Arbitration*, 62 BROOK. L. REV. 1459 (1997).

Brunet, E. & Stern, W., *Controlling Dispute Resolution: Drafting the Effective ADR Clause for Natural Resources and Energy Contracts*, 10 NAT. R. & ENV. 7 (1996).

Cain, R., *Preemption of State Arbitration Statutes: The Exaggerated Federal Policy Favoring Arbitration*, 19 J. CONTEMP. L. 1 (1993).

CARBONNEAU, T. (Ed.), LEX MERCATORIA AND ARBITRATION (1990).

Carbonneau, T., *Rendering Arbitral Awards With Reasons: The Elaboration of a Common Law of International Transactions*, 23 COLUM. J. TRANSNAT'L L. 579 (1985).

Chan, Ray, *The Enforceability of Annulled Foreign Arbitral Awards in the United States: A Critique of Chromalloy,* 17 B.U. INT'L L.J. 141 (1999).

Cohen, J. & Drayton, K., *The New Federal Arbitration Law*, 12 VA. L. REV. 265 (1926).

CRAIG, W., PARK, W. & PAULSON, J., INTERNATIONAL CHAMBER OF COMMERCE ARBITRATION (3d ed. Oceana 2000).

Craver, C., *Labor Arbitration as a Continuation of the Collective Bargaining Process*, 66 CHI. KENT L. REV. 571 (1990).

Farnsworth, A., *Punitive Damages in Arbitration*, 20 STETSON L. REV. 395 (1991).

Feinberg, W., *Maritime Arbitration and the Federal Courts*, 5 FORD INT'L L.J. 45 (1982).

Fleming, R., *Some Problems of Due Process and Fair Procedure in Labor Arbitration*, 13 STAN. L. REV. 235 (1961).

FLETCHER, C.E., ARBITRATING SECURITIES DISPUTES (1990).

Fletcher, C.E., *Privatizing Securities Disputes Through the Enforcement of Arbitration Agreements*, 71 MINN. L. REV. 393 (1987).

Force, R. & Mavronicolas, A., *Two Models of Maritime Dispute Resolution: Litigation and Arbitration*, 65 TUL. L. REV. 1461 (1991).

Gordon, P., *Submitting "Fair Value" to Final Offer Arbitration*, 63 U. COLO. L. REV. 751 (1992).

Green, Michael, *Debunking the Myth of Employer Advantage From Using Mandatory Arbitration for Discrimination Claims,* 31 RUTGERS L.J. 399 (2000).

Hayford, S., *Law in Disarray: Judicial Standards for Vacatur of Commercial Arbitration Awards*, 30 GA. L. REV. 731 (1996).

Henderson, S., *Contractual Problems in the Enforcement of Agreements to Arbitrate Medical Malpractice*, 58 VA. L. REV. 947 (1972).

Katzler, L., *Should Mandatory Written Opinions Be Required in All Securities Arbitrations?*, 45 AM. U. L. REV. 151 (1995).

Kolakowski, W., *The Federal Arbitration Act and Individual Employment Contracts: A Better Means to an Equally Just End*, 93 MICH. L. REV. 2171 (1995).

Lee, M., *Antitrust and Commercial Arbitration: An Economic Analysis*, 62 ST. JOHN'S L. REV. 1 (1987).

Macklin, L., *Promoting Settlement Foregoing the Facts*, 14 N.Y.U. REV. L. & SOC. CHANGE 575 (1986).

MACNEIL, I., AMERICAN ARBITRATION LAW (1992).

Macneil, I., *Contracts: Adjustments of Long-Term Economic Relations Under Classical, Neoclassical and Relational Contract Law*, 72 NW. U. L. REV. 854 (1978).

Macneil, I., *The Many Futures of Contracts*, 47 S. CAL. L. REV. 691 (1974).

Macneil, I., *Relational Contract: What We Do and Do Not Know*, 1985 WIS. L. REV. 483.

MACNEIL, I., SPEIDEL, R. & STIPANOWICH, T., FEDERAL ARBITRATION LAW (1995).

Martin, J., *Advanced Micro Devices v. Intel Corp. and Judicial Review of Commercial Arbitration Awards: When Does a Remedy "Exceed" Arbitral Powers?*, 46 HASTINGS L.J. 1907 (1995).

Masucci, D., *Securities Arbitration: A Success Story: What Does the Future Hold?*, 31 WAKE FOREST L. REV. 183 (1996).

McLoughlin, J., *Arbitrability: Current Trends in the United States*, 59 ALB. L. REV. 905 (1996).

McMahon, J., *Implementation of the United National Convention on Foreign Arbitral Awards in the United States*, 2 J. MARIT. L. & COMM. 735 (1971).

Mentschikoff, S., *Commercial Arbitration*, 61 COLUM. L. REV. 846 (1961).

Motomura, H., *Arbitration and Collateral Estoppel: Using Preclusion to Shape Procedural Choices*, 63 TUL. L. REV. 29 (1988).

Mouser, D., *Analysis of the Public Policy Exception After Paperworkers v. Misco: A Proposal to Limit the Public Policy Exception and to Allow the Parties to Submit the Public Policy Question to the Arbitrator*, 12 IND. REL. L.J. 89 (1990).

Nag, R., *Its Time to Write Voluntary Arbitration Into the Copyright Act*, 51 DISP. RESOL. J. 8 (No. 4 1996).

NATIONAL ASSOCIATION OF SECURITIES DEALERS REPORT OF THE ARBITRATION POLICY TASK FORCE, SECURITIES ARBITRATION REFORM (1996).

Paradise, G., *Arbitration of Patent Infringement Disputes: Encouraging the Use of Arbitration Through Evidence Rules Reform*, 64 FORD. L. REV. 247 (1995).

Petrochilos, Georgios, *Enforcing Awards Annulled in Their State of Origin under the New York Convention*, 48 INT'L. & COMP. L. Q. 856(1999).

Poor, W., *Arbitration Under the Federal Statute*, 36 YALE L.J. 667 (1927).

Popkin, L., *Judicial Construction of the New York Arbitration Law of 1920*, 11 CORNELL L.Q. 329 (1926).

Rau, Alan Scott, *Contracting Out of the Arbitration Act*, 8 AM. REV. INT'L. ARB. 225 (1997).

Sander, F., *Varieties of Dispute Processing*, 70 F.R.D. 111 (1976).

Seitz, P., *The Citation of Authority and Precedent in Arbitration (Its Use and Abuse)*, ARB. J., Dec. 1983, 58.

Seligman, *The Quiet Revolution: Securities Arbitration Confronts the Hard Questions*, 33 HOUS. L. REV. 327 (1996).

Shell, R., *Res Judicata and Collateral Estoppel Effects of Commercial Arbitration*, 35 U.C.L.A. L. REV. 623 (1988).

Smit, Hans, *Contractual Modification of the Scope of Judicial Review of Arbitration Awards,* 8 AM. REV. INT'L ARB. 147 (1997).

Snow, C., *An Arbitrator's Use of Precedent*, 94 DICK. L. REV. 665 (1990).

Speidel, R., *Arbitration of Statutory Rights Under the Federal Arbitration Act: The Case for Reform*, 4 OHIO ST. J. ON DISP. RESOL. 157 (1989).

Speidel, R., *Contract Theory and Securities Arbitration: Whither Consent*, 62 BROOK. L. REV. 1335 (1996).

St. Antoine, T., *Judicial Review of Labor Arbitration Awards: A Second Look at Enterprise Wheel and Its Progeny*, 75 MICH. L. REV. 1137 (1977).

Stempel, J., *Pitfalls of Public Policy: The Case of Arbitration Agreements*, 22 ST. MARY'S L.J. 259 (1990).

Sterk, S., *Enforceability of Agreements to Arbitrate: An Examination of the Public Policy Defense*, 2 CARDOZO L. REV. 481 (1981).

Stipanowich, T., *Beyond Arbitration: Innovation and Evolution in the United States Construction Industry*, 31 WAKE FOREST L. REV. 65 (1976).

Stipanowich, T., *Rethinking American Arbitration*, 63 IND. L.J. 425 (1988).

Stone, Katherine Van Wetzel, *Rustic Justice: Community and Coercion Under the Federal Arbitration Act*, 77 N. CAR. L. REV. 931 (1999).

Tetley, W., *The General Maritime Law: The Lex Maritime*, 20 SYRACUSE J. INT'L & COM. 105 (1994).

Ware, S., *Arbitration and Unconscionability After Doctor's Associate, Inc. v. Casarotto*, 31 WAKE FOREST L. REV. 1001 (1996).

Ware, S., *Default Rules from Mandatory Rules: Privatizing Law Through Arbitration*, 83 MINN. L. REV. 703 (1999).

Ware, S., *Employment Arbitration and Voluntary Consent*, 25 HOFSTRA L. REV. 83 (1996).

Ware, S., *Punitive Damages in Arbitration: Contracting Out of Government's Role in Punishment and Federal Preemption of State Law*, 63 FORD. L. REV. 529 (1994).

Wolaer, C., *The Historical Background of Commercial Arbitration*, 83 U. PA. L. REV. 132 (1934).

COURT– AND AGENCY–ANNEXED ADR

Alfini, J., *Trashing, Bashing, and Hashing it Out: Is This the End of "Good Mediation?"*, 19 FLA. ST. L. REV. 47 (1991).

Bergmann, D., *ADR: Resolution or Complication?*, 131 PUB. U. FORT. 20 (Jan. 15, 1993).

Bernstein, L., *Understanding the Limits of Court-Connected ADR: A Critique of Federal Court-Annexed Arbitration Programs*, 141 U. PA. L. REV. 2169 (1993).

Brazil, W., *Continuing the Conversation about the Current Status and the Future of ADR: A View from the Courts*, 2000 J. DISP. RESOL. 11.

Brazil, W., *Court ADR 25 Years After Pound: Have We Found a Better Way?*, 18 OHIO ST. J. ON DISP. RESOL. 93 (2002).

Brazil, W., *Early Neutral Evaluation: An Experimental Effort to Expedite Dispute Resolution*, 69 JUDICATURE 279 (1986).

Brazil, W., *Should Court-Sponsored ADR Survive?*, 21 OHIO ST. J. ON DISP. RESOL. 241 (2006).

Brown, S., *New Communication Law Encourages the Use of ADR*, 14 ALTERNATIVES TO THE HIGH COSTS LITIG. 82 (1996).

Bruff, H., *Public Programs, Private Deciders: The Constitutionality of Arbitration in Federal Programs*, 67 TEX. L. REV. 441 (1989).

Brunet, E., *Judicial Mediation and Signaling*, 3 NEV. L.J. 232 (2003-2004).

Bryden, P. & Black, W., *Mediation as a Tool for Resolving Human Rights Disputes: An Evaluation of the B.C. Human Rights Commission's Early Mediation Project*, 37 U.B.C. L. REV. 73 (2004).

Carrington, P., *ADR and Future Adjudication: A Primer on Dispute Resolution*, 15 REV. LIT. 485 (1996).

Choo, R., *Judicial Review of Negotiated Rulemaking: Should Chevron Deference Apply?*, 52 RUTGERS L. REV. 1069 (2000).

Coglianese, C., *Assessing Consensus: The Promise and Performance of Negotiated Rulemaking*, 46 DUKE L.J. 1255 (1997).

Coglianese, C., *Assessing the Performance of Negotiated Rulemaking: A Reply to Philip Harter*, 9 N.Y.U. ENVT'L L.J. 386 (2001).

Cohen, D., *Mediation: Sanity in the Regulatory Process*, 131 PUB. U. FORT. 18 (Jan. 15, 1993).

Comment, *No Confidence: The Problem of Confidentiality by Local Rule in the ADR Act of 1998*, 78 TEX. L. REV. 1015 (2000).

Deason, E., *Competing and Complementary Rule Systems: Civil Procedures and ADR: Procedural Rules for Complementary Systems of Litigation and Mediation — Worldwide*, 80 NOTRE DAME L. REV. 553 (2005).

Della Noce, D., *Mediation Theory and Policy: The Legacy of the Pound Conference*, 17 OHIO ST. J. ON DISP. RESOL. 545 (2002).

Della Noce, D., et al., *Assimilative, Autonomous, or Synergistic Visions: How Mediation Programs in Florida Address the Dilemma of Court Connection*, 3 PEPP. DIS. RESOL. L.J. 11 (2002).

Eisele, G.T., *Differing Visions, Differing Values: A Comment on Judge Parker's Reformation Model for Federal District Courts*, 46 SMU L. REV. 1935 (1993).

Freeman, J. & Langbein, L., *Regulatory Negotiation and the Legitimacy Benefit*, 9 N.Y.U. ENVT'L L.J. 60 (2000).

Funk, W., *Bargaining Toward the New Millennium: Regulatory Negotiation and the Subversion of the Public Interest*, 46 DUKE L.J. 1351 (1997).

Funk, W., *When Smoke Gets In Your Eyes: Regulatory Negotiation and the Public Interest: EPA's Woodstove Standards*, 18 ENVT'L L. 55 (1987).

Galanter, M., *The Vanishing Trial: An Examination of Trials and Related Matters in Federal and State Courts*, 1 J. EMPIRICAL L. STUD. 459 (2004).

Glantz, P., *Analysis of a First Amendment Challenge to Rent-a-Judge Proceedings*, 14 PEPP. L. REV. 989 (1987).

Green, E., *Growth of the Mini-Trial*, 9 LITIGATION 12 (Fall 1982).

Guthrie, C., *Procedural Justice Research and the Paucity of Trials*, 2002 J. DISP. RESOL. 127.

Hadfield, G., *Where Have All the Trials Gone? Settlements, Nontrial Adjudications, and Statistical Artifacts in the Changing Disposition of Federal Civil Cases*, 1 J. EMPIRICAL L. STUD. 705 (2004).

Harders, J., *Too Good to Last? Budget Cuts Force the EEOC to Terminate Contract Mediators From Its New, Highly Touted Program*, ABA J., April 2000, p. 30.

Harter, P. *Assessing the Assessors: The Actual Performance of Negotiated Rulemaking*, 9 N.Y.U. ENVT'L L.J. 32 (2000).

Harter, P., *Negotiating Regulations: A Cure for Malaise*, 71 GEO. L.J. 66 (1982).

Hensler, D., *Our Courts, Ourselves: How the Alternative Dispute Resolution Movement is Re-Shaping Our Legal System*, 108 PENN ST. L. REV. 165 (2003).

Hensler, D., *Suppose It's Not True: Challenging Mediation Ideology*, 2002 J. DISP. RESOL. 81.

Hodges, A., *Mediation and the Americans With Disabilities Act*, 30 GA. L. REV. 431 (1996).

KAKALIK, J., ET AL., EVALUATION OF MEDIATION AND EARLY NEUTRAL EVALUATION UNDER THE CIVIL JUSTICE REFORM ACT (Rand Corp. 1996).

Kim, A., *Rent-a-Judges and the Cost of Selling Justice*, 44 DUKE L.J. 166 (1994).

Kloppenberg, L., *Implementation of Court-Annexed Environmental Mediation: The District of Oregon Pilot Project*, 17 OHIO ST. J. ON DISP. RESOL. 559 (2002).

Kovach, K., *Good Faith in Mediation — Requested, Recommended, or Required? A New Ethic*, 38 S. TEX. L. REV. 575 (1997).

Lambros, *The Summary Jury Trial: An Alternative Method of Resolving Disputes*, 69 JUDICATURE 286 (1986).

Lambros, *The Summary Jury Trial and Other Alternative Methods of Dispute Resolution*, 103 F.R.D. 461 (1984).

Lande, J., *Using Dispute System Design Methods to Promote Good-Faith Participation in Court-Connected Mediation Programs*, 50 U.C.L.A. L. REV. 69 (2002).

Levine, D., *Early Neutral Evaluation: The Second Phase*, 1989 J. DISP. RESOL. 1.

Levine, D., *Northern District of California Adopts Early Neutral Evaluation to Expedite Discovery*, 72 JUDICATURE 235 (1989).

LIND, E., ET AL., THE PERCEPTION OF JUSTICE: TORT LITIGANTS VIEWS OF TRIAL, COURT-ANNEXED ARBITRATION, AND JUDICIAL SETTLEMENT CONFERENCES (Rand 1989).

Lynch, W., *Problems with Court-Annexed Mandatory Arbitration: Illustrations form the New Mexico Experience*, 32 N.M. L. Rev. 181 (2002).

Macfarlane, J., *Culture Change? A Tale of Two Cities and Mandatory Court-Connected Mediation*, 2002 J. Disp. Resol. 241.

Marshall, D., *ADR: Not ABC's of Litigation*, 131 Pub. U. Fort., Jan. 15, 1995, at 23.

McAdoo, B., *A Report to the Minnesota Supreme Court: The Impact of Rule 114 on Civil Litigation Practice in Minnesota*, 25 Hamline L. Rev. 401 (2002).

McAdoo, B. & Hinshaw, A., *The Challenge of Institutionalizing Alternative Dispute Resolution: Attorney Perspectives on the Effects of Rule 17 on Civil Litigation in Missouri*, 67 Mo. L. Rev. 473 (2002).

McAdoo, B. & Welsh, N., *Look Before You Leap and Keep on Looking: Lessons from the Institutionalization of Court-Connected Mediation*, 5 Nev. L.J. 339 (2004-05).

McGovern, F., *Toward A Functional Approach for Managing Complex Litigation*, 53 U. Chi. L. Rev. 440 (1986).

Meierhoefer, B., Court-Annexed Arbitration in Ten District Courts (Fed. Jud. Center 1990).

Meltzoff, *Reconfiguring the Summary Jury Trial*, 41 Duke L.J. 806 (1992).

Menkel-Meadow, C., *Pursuing Settlement in an Adversary Culture: A Tale of Innovation Co-opted or "The Law of ADR,"* 19 Fla. St. L. Rev. 1 (1991).

Niemic, Robert J., Mediation and Conference Programs in The Federal Courts of Appeals: A Sourcebook for Judges and Lawyers (1997).

Page, R. & Jockish, W., *The Corps of Engineers Board of Contract Appeals Use of Alternative Dispute Resolution*, 24 Pub. Contract L.J. 453 (1995).

Plapinger, E. & Stienstra, D., *Federal Court ADR: A Practitioner's Update*, 14 Alternatives to the High Cost Litig. 7 (1996).

Ponte, L., *Putting Mandatory Summary Jury Trial Back on the Docket: Recommendations on the Exercise of Judicial Authority*, 63 Fond. L. Rev. 1069 (1995).

Posner, R., *The Summary Jury Trial and Other Methods of Alternative Dispute Resolution: Some Cautionary Observations*, 53 U. Chi. L. Rev. 366 (1986).

Press, S., *Institutionalization of Mediation in Florida: At the Crossroads*, 108 Penn. St. L. Rev. 43 (2003).

Pugh, A. & Bales, R., *The Inherent Power of the Federal Courts to Compel Participation in Nonbinding Forms of Alternative Dispute Resolution*, 42 Duq. L. Rev. 1 (2003).

Rack, Jr., W., *Thoughts of a Chief Mediator on Federal Court-Annexed Mediation*, 17 Ohio St. J. on Disp. Resol. 609 (2002).

Rose-Ackerman, S., *Consensus Versus Incentives: A Skeptical Look at Regulatory Negotiation*, 43 DUKE L.J. 1206 (1994).

Sander, F., & Rozdeiczer, L., *Matching Cases and Dispute Resolution Procedures: Detailed Analysis Leading to a Mediation-Centered Approach*, 11 HARV. NEG. L.J. 1 (2006).

SCHUCK, P., AGENT ORANGE ON TRIAL: MASS TOXIC DISASTERS IN THE COURTS (1986).

Selmi, D., *The Promise and Limits of Negotiated Rulemaking: Evaluating the Negotiation of a Regional Air Quality Rule*, 35 ENVTL L. 415 (2005).

Senft, L. & Savage, C., *ADR in the Courts: Progress, Problems, and Possibilities*, 108 PENN ST. L. REV. 327 (2003).

Shack, J. & Yates, S., *Mediating Lanham Act Cases: The Role of Empirical Evaluation*, 22 N. ILL. U. L. REV. 287 (2002).

Shannon, B.D., *Confidentiality of Texas Mediations: Ruminations on Some Thorny Problems*, 32 TEX. TECH L. REV. 77 (2000).

Shell, G.R., *ERISA and Other Federal Employment Statutes: When Is Commercial Arbitration an "Adequate Substitute" for the Courts?*, 68 TEX. L. REV. 509 (1990).

Sherman, E., *Court-Mandated Alternative Dispute Resolution: What Form of Participation Should Be Required?*, 46 SMU L. REV. 2079 (1993).

Sherman, E., *Reshaping the Lawyers' Skills for Court-Supervised ADR*, 51 TEX. B.J. 47 (1988).

Shestowsky, D., *Improving Summary Jury Trials: Insights from Psychology*, 18 OHIO ST. J. ON DISP. RESOL. 469 (2003).

Stipanowich, T., *ADR and the "Vanishing Trial": The Growth and Impact of "Alternative Dispute Resolution,"* 1 J. EMPIRICAL L. STUD. 843 (2004).

STIENSTRA, D. & YATES, S. (EDS.), ADR HANDBOOK FOR JUDGES (2004).

Thompson, P., *Enforcing Rights Generated in Court-Connected Mediation — Tension Between the Aspiration of a Private Facilitative Process and the Reality of Public Adversarial Justice*, 19 OHIO ST. J. ON DISP. RESOL. 509 (2004).

Van Epps, D., *The Impact of Mediation on State Courts*, 17 OHIO ST. J. ON DISP. RESOL. 627 (2002).

Welsh, N., *The Place of Court-Connected Mediation in a Democratic Justice System*, 5 CARDOZO J. CONFLICT RESOL. 117 (2004).

Welsh, N., *Stepping Back Through the Looking Glass: Real Conversations With Real Disputants About Institutionalized Mediation and Its Value*, 19 OHIO ST. J. ON DISP. RESOL. 573 (2004).

Welsh, N., *The Thinning Vision of Self-Determination in Court-Connected Mediation: The Inevitable Price of Institutionalization?*, 6 HARV. NEG. L. REV. 1 (2001).

Weston, M., *Confidentiality's Constitutionality: The Incursion on Judicial Powers to Regulate Party Conduct in Court-Connected Mediation*, 8 HARV. NEGOT. L. REV. 29 (2003).

Will, H., et al., *The Rule of the Judge in the Settlement Process*, 75 F.R.D. 203 (1977).

Williams, G., *Negotiation as a Healing Process*, 1996 J. DISP. RESOL. 1 (1996).

Wissler, R., *Court-Connected Mediation in General Civil Cases: What We Know from Empirical Research*, 17 OHIO ST. J. ON DISP. RESOL. 641 (2002a).

Wissler, R., *The Effectiveness of Court-Connected Dispute Resolution in Civil Cases*, 22 CONFLICT RESOL. Q. 55 (2004).

Wissler, R., *The Effects of Mandatory Mediation: Empirical Research on the Experience of Small Claims and Common Pleas Courts*, 33 WILLAMETTE L. REV. 565 (1997).

Wissler, R., *When Does Familiarity Breed Content? A Study of the Role of Different Forms of ADR Education and Experience in Attorneys' ADR Recommendations*, 2 PEPP. DISP. RESOL. L.J. 199 (2002b).

TABLE OF CASES

[References are to pages. Principal cases are capitalized,
and the pages where they appear are in italics.]

[References are to pages. Principal cases are capitalized,
and the pages where they appear are in italics.]

[References are to pages. Principal cases are capitalized,
and the pages where they appear are in italics.]

[References are to pages. Principal cases are capitalized,
and the pages where they appear are in italics.]

[References are to pages. Principal cases are capitalized,
and the pages where they appear are in italics.]

[References are to pages. Principal cases are capitalized,
and the pages where they appear are in italics.]

[References are to pages. Principal cases are capitalized,
and the pages where they appear are in italics.]

W

INDEX

[References are to pages.]

[References are to pages.]

[References are to pages.]

[References are to pages.]

P

R

S

V